W9-BXV-710

CompTIA®
A+® Complete
Deluxe Study Guide
Second Edition

CompTIA®
A+® Complete
Deluxe Study Guide
Second Edition

Quentin Docter

Emmett Dulaney

Toby Skandier

WILEY

John Wiley & Sons, Inc.

Senior Acquisitions Editor: Jeff Kellum
Development Editor: Alexa Murphy
Technical Editors: Naomi Alpern and Ian Seaton
Production Editor: Dassi Zeidel
Copy Editor: Judy Flynn
Editorial Manager: Pete Gaughan
Production Manager: Tim Tate
Vice President and Executive Group Publisher: Richard Swadley
Vice President and Publisher: Neil Edde
Media Project Manager 1: Laura Moss-Hollister
Media Associate Producer: Shawn Patrick
Media Quality Assurance: Marilyn Hummel
Book Designers: Judy Fung and Bill Gibson
Compositor: Craig Woods, Happenstance Type-O-Rama
Proofreader: Josh Chase, Word One New York
Indexer: Ted Laux
Project Coordinator, Cover: Katherine Crocker
Cover Designer: Ryan Sneed
Cover Image: © Jeremy Woodhouse / Photodisc / Getty Images

Copyright © 2012 by John Wiley & Sons, Inc., Indianapolis, Indiana

Published simultaneously in Canada

ISBN: 978-1-118-32406-6

No part of this publication may be reproduced, stored in a retrieval system or transmitted in any form or by any means, electronic, mechanical, photocopying, recording, scanning or otherwise, except as permitted under Sections 107 or 108 of the 1976 United States Copyright Act, without either the prior written permission of the Publisher, or authorization through payment of the appropriate per-copy fee to the Copyright Clearance Center, 222 Rosewood Drive, Danvers, MA 01923, (978) 750-8400, fax (978) 646-8600. Requests to the Publisher for permission should be addressed to the Permissions Department, John Wiley & Sons, Inc., 111 River Street, Hoboken, NJ 07030, (201) 748-6011, fax (201) 748-6008, or online at http://www.wiley.com/go/permissions.

Limit of Liability/Disclaimer of Warranty: The publisher and the author make no representations or warranties with respect to the accuracy or completeness of the contents of this work and specifically disclaim all warranties, including without limitation warranties of fitness for a particular purpose. No warranty may be created or extended by sales or promotional materials. The advice and strategies contained herein may not be suitable for every situation. This work is sold with the understanding that the publisher is not engaged in rendering legal, accounting, or other professional services. If professional assistance is required, the services of a competent professional person should be sought. Neither the publisher nor the author shall be liable for damages arising herefrom. The fact that an organization or Web site is referred to in this work as a citation and/or a potential source of further information does not mean that the author or the publisher endorses the information the organization or Web site may provide or recommendations it may make. Further, readers should be aware that Internet Web sites listed in this work may have changed or disappeared between when this work was written and when it is read.

For general information on our other products and services or to obtain technical support, please contact our Customer Care Department within the U.S. at (877) 762-2974, outside the U.S. at (317) 572-3993 or fax (317) 572-4002.

Wiley publishes in a variety of print and electronic formats and by print-on-demand. Some material included with standard print versions of this book may not be included in e-books or in print-on-demand. If this book refers to media such as a CD or DVD that is not included in the version you purchased, you may download this material at http://booksupport.wiley.com. For more information about Wiley products, visit www.wiley.com.

Library of Congress Control Number: 2012944696

TRADEMARKS: Wiley, the Wiley logo, and the Sybex logo are trademarks or registered trademarks of John Wiley & Sons, Inc. and/or its affiliates, in the United States and other countries, and may not be used without written permission. CompTIA and A+ are registered trademarks of Computing Technology Industry Association, Inc. All other trademarks are the property of their respective owners. John Wiley & Sons, Inc. is not associated with any product or vendor mentioned in this book.

10 9 8 7 6 5 4 3

Dear Reader,

Thank you for choosing *CompTIA A+ Complete Deluxe Study Guide, Second Edition*. This book is part of a family of premium-quality Sybex books, all of which are written by outstanding authors who combine practical experience with a gift for teaching.

Sybex was founded in 1976. More than 30 years later, we're still committed to producing consistently exceptional books. With each of our titles, we're working hard to set a new standard for the industry. From the paper we print on, to the authors we work with, our goal is to bring you the best books available.

I hope you see all that reflected in these pages. I'd be very interested to hear your comments and get your feedback on how we're doing. Feel free to let me know what you think about this or any other Sybex book by sending me an email at nedde@wiley.com. If you think you've found a technical error in this book, please visit http://sybex.custhelp.com. Customer feedback is critical to our efforts at Sybex.

Best regards,

Neil Edde
Vice President and Publisher
Sybex, an Imprint of Wiley

For Kara, Abbie, Lauren, Reina, and Alina
—Quentin Docter

For Karen, Kristin, Evan, and Spencer
—Emmett Dulaney

For Karen, Toby, Tiffani, Trey, and Taylor
—Toby Skandier

Acknowledgments

As we were putting together this book, I was reminded of the proverb that begins, "It takes a small village…" That beginning definitely holds true to create a book of this scope and size. From beginning to end, there are scores of dedicated professionals focused on delivering the best book possible to you the readers.

First, I need to thank my coauthors, Emmett Dulaney and Toby Skandier. Their dedication to producing an excellent book that will best serve the needs of our readers is inspiring. Now, onto the rest of the team.

Jeff Kellum and Alexa Murphy kept us on track and moving forward, which was a challenge at times. Dassi Zeidel had the fun job of keeping us organized, which is akin to herding cats. Tech editors Naomi Alpern and Ian Seaton provided a great set of expert eyes and made excellent suggestions. Copyeditor Judy Flynn reminded me yet again that I am no master of the English language and saved me from butchering it (too badly). Many thanks also go out to proofreader Josh Chase at Word One, our indexer Ted Laux, and Craig Woods, our compositor at Happenstance. Without their great contributions this book would not have made it to your hands.

—Quentin Docter

I would like to thank Jeff Kellum—an acquisitions editor who knows how to do a difficult job extremely well. I would also like to thank my coauthors, Quentin Docter and Toby Skandier, without whom this text would have never happened.

—Emmett Dulaney

Quentin Docter and Emmett Dulaney are two of the most professional and expert coauthors anyone could request. I had the great fortune a few editions ago to be brought onboard this project without the need to request them. Truer serendipity is hard to find in this world. Thanks, guys.

I would like to thank our acquisitions editor, Jeff Kellum, and development editor, Alexa Murphy, for their expert guidance and project management. Without them, a work of this magnitude would surely be doomed.

Thanks to our technical editors, Naomi Alpern and Ian Seaton, for doing such a great job flagging any technical issues that existed during the writing process. I don't know how to possibly thank our production editor, Dassi Zeidel, and copyeditor, Judy Flynn, for the tireless work they put into parsing every word and image that was sent their way. This book is infinitely better as a result of their pains.

In addition, I'd like to thank our proofreader Josh Chase at Word One, indexer Ted Laux, typesetter Craig Woods, and the media developers, Laura Moss-Hollister, Shawn Patrick, and Marilyn Hummel.

Thank you to my associates at Global Knowledge and CenturyLink for the support and challenges you continue to offer.

—Toby Skandier

About the Authors

Quentin Docter A+, is an IT consultant who started in the industry in 1994. Since then he's worked as a tech and network support specialist, trainer, consultant, and webmaster. Throughout his career he's obtained A+, Network+, and several Microsoft, Cisco, Sun, and Novell certifications. He has written several books for Sybex, including books on A+, Server+, Windows, and Solaris 9 certifications as well as PC hardware and maintenance. Quentin can be reached at qdocter@yahoo.com.

Emmett Dulaney A+, Network+, Security+, is an associate professor at Anderson University. The former director of training for Mercury Technical Solutions, he holds or has held 18 vendor certifications and is the author of over 30 books, including the *CompTIA Security+ Study Guide*. He specializes in certification and cross-platform integration and is a columnist for *CertCities*. Emmett can be reached at eadulaney@comcast.net.

Toby Skandier A+, Network +, i-Net+, Server+, MCSE, CCNP, CCDP, and CCSI, began his career in 1985 and is founder of Talskan Technologies, LLC, a technical-education provider based in North Carolina. He has coauthored numerous books for Sybex, including *Network Administrator Street Smarts* and the best-selling *Network+ Study Guide*. Toby can be reached at tskandier@talskan.com.

Contents at a Glance

Contents

Appendix   B   Answers to Performance-Based Questions   1075

Table of Exercises

Exercises with a CD icon next to them include a video walk-through on the
companion CD.

CompTIA Certification

It Pays to Get Certified

CompTIA. In a digital world, digital literacy is an essential survival skill. Certification proves you have the knowledge and skills to solve business problems in virtually any business environment. Certifications are highly valued credentials that qualify you for jobs, increased compensation, and promotion.

LEARN		CERTIFY		WORK
IT is Everywhere	**IT Knowledge and Skills Get Jobs**	**Job Retention**	**New Opportunities**	**High Pay-High Growth Jobs**
IT is mission critical to almost all organizations and its importance is increasing.	Certifications verify your knowledge and skills that qualifies you for:	Competence is noticed and valued in organizations.	Certifications qualify you for new opportunities in your current job or when you want to change careers.	Hiring managers demand the strongest skill set.
• 79% of U.S. businesses report IT is either important or very important to the success of their company	• Jobs in the high growth IT career field • Increased compensation • Challenging assignments and promotions • 60% report that being certified is an employer or job requirement	• Increased knowledge of new or complex technologies • Enhanced productivity • More insightful problem solving • Better project management and communication skills • 47% report being certified helped improve their problem solving skills	• 31% report certification improved their career advancement opportunities	• There is a widening IT skills gap with over 300,000 jobs open • 88% report being certified enhanced their resume

Certification Advances Your Career

The CompTIA A+ credential provides foundation-level knowledge and skills necessary for a career in PC repair and support.

The starting salary for CompTIA A+ Certified individuals can be as much as $65,000 per year.

CompTIA A+ is a building block for other CompTIA certifications such as Network+, Security+, and vendor-specific technologies.

More than 850,000 individuals worldwide are CompTIA A+ certified.

Mandated/recommended by organizations worldwide such as Cisco, HP, and Ricoh, the US State Department, and US government contractors such as EDS, General Dynamics, and Northrop Grumman.

Here are some of the primary benefits individuals report from becoming A+ certified:

More efficient troubleshooting

Improved career advancement

More insightful problem solving

CompTIA Career Pathway

CompTIA offers a number of credentials that form a foundation for your career in technology and allow you to pursue specific areas of concentration. Depending on the path you choose to take, CompTIA certifications help you build upon your skills and knowledge, supporting learning throughout your entire career.

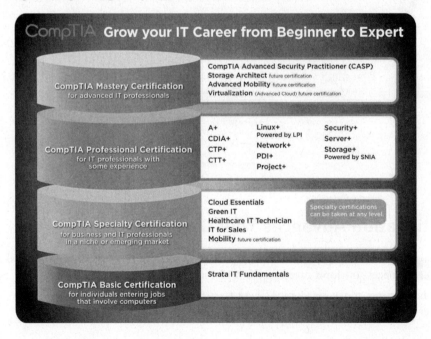

Steps to Certification

Steps to Getting Certified and Staying Certified

Review Exam Objectives	Review the certification objectives to make sure you know what is covered in the exam: http://certification.comptia.org/Training/testingcenters/examobjectives.aspx
Practice for the Exam	After you have studied for the certification, take a free assessment and sample test to get an idea what type of questions might be on the exam: http://certification.comptia.org/Training/testingcenters/samplequestions.aspx
Purchase an Exam Voucher	Purchase your exam voucher on the CompTIA Marketplace, which is located at www.comptiastore.com.
Take the Test!	Select a certification exam provider and schedule a time to take your exam. You can find exam providers at the following link: http://certification.comptia.org/Training/testingcenters.aspx

Join the Professional Community

Join the IT Pro Community at http://itpro.comptia.org. The free IT Pro online community provides valuable content to students and professionals.

Career IT job resources

> Where to start in IT

> Career assessments

> Salary trends

> US job board

Forums on networking, security, computing, and cutting-edge technologies

Access to blogs written by industry experts

Current information on cutting-edge technologies

Access to various industry resource links and articles related to IT and IT careers

Content Seal of Quality

This courseware bears the seal of **CompTIA Approved Quality Content.** This seal signifies that this content covers 100 percent of the exam objectives and implements important instructional design

principles. CompTIA recommends multiple learning tools to help increase coverage of the learning objectives.

Why CompTIA?

Global recognition: CompTIA is recognized globally as the leading IT nonprofit trade association and has enormous credibility. Plus, CompTIA's certifications are vendor neutral and offer proof of foundational knowledge that translates across technologies.

Valued by hiring managers: Hiring managers value CompTIA certification because it is vendor- and technology-independent validation of your technical skills.

Recommended or required by government and businesses: Many government organizations and corporations either recommend or require technical staff to be CompTIA certified (e.g., Dell, Sharp, Ricoh, the US Department of Defense, and many more).

Three CompTIA certifications ranked in the top 10: In a study by DICE of 17,000 technology professionals, certifications helped command higher salaries at all experience levels.

How to Obtain More Information

Visit CompTIA online: Visit www.comptia.org to learn more about getting CompTIA certified.

Contact CompTIA: Call (866) 835-8020 ext. 5 or email questions@comptia.org.

Introduction

Welcome to the *CompTIA A+ Complete Deluxe Study Guide*. This is the sixth version of our best-selling study guide for the A+ certification sponsored by CompTIA (Computing Technology Industry Association).

This book was written at an intermediate technical level; we assume that you already know how to *use* a personal computer and its basic peripherals, such as USB devices and printers, but we also recognize that you may be learning how to *service* some of that computer equipment for the first time. The exams cover basic computer service topics as well as some more advanced issues, and they cover some topics that anyone already working as a technician, whether with computers or not, should be familiar with. The exams are designed to test you on these topics in order to certify that you have enough knowledge to fix and upgrade some of the most widely used types of personal desktop computers.

We've included review questions at the end of each chapter to give you a taste of what it's like to take the exams. If you're already working as a technical service or support technician, we recommend that you check out these questions first to gauge your level of knowledge. (You can also take the assessment test at the end of this introduction, which is designed to see how much you already know.)

Don't just study the questions and answers—the questions on the actual exams will be different from the practice ones included in this book and on the CD. The exams are designed to test your knowledge of a concept or objective, so use this book to learn the objective *behind* the question.

You can use the book mainly to fill in the gaps in your current computer service knowledge. You may find, as many PC technicians have, that being well versed in all the technical aspects of the equipment is not enough to provide a satisfactory level of support—you must also have customer-relations skills. We include helpful hints to get the customers to help you help them.

What Is A+ Certification?

The A+ certification program was developed by the Computing Technology Industry Association (CompTIA) to provide an industry-wide means of certifying the competency of computer service technicians. The A+ certification is granted to those who have attained the level of knowledge and troubleshooting skills that are needed to provide capable support in the field of personal computers. It is similar to other certifications in the computer industry, such the Cisco Certified Network Associate (CCNA) program and the Microsoft certification programs. The theory behind these certifications is that if you need to have service performed on any of their products, you would sooner call a technician who has been certified in one of the appropriate certification programs than just call the first "expert" in the phone book.

The A+ certification program was created to offer a wide-ranging certification, in the sense that it is intended to certify competence with personal computers from many different makers/vendors. You must pass two tests to become A+ certified:

- The A+ 220-801 exam, which covers basic computer concepts, PC hardware, basic networking, soft skills (such as customer service), and safety
- The A+ 220-802 exam, which covers operating systems, security, mobile devices, and troubleshooting

You don't have to take the 220-801 and the 220-802 exams at the same time. The A+ certification is not awarded until you've passed both tests.

Why Become A+ Certified?

There are several good reasons to get your A+ certification. The CompTIA Candidate's Information packet lists five major benefits:

- It demonstrates proof of professional achievement.
- It increases your marketability.
- It provides greater opportunity for advancement in your field.
- It is increasingly a requirement for some types of advanced training.
- It raises customer confidence in you and your company's services.

Provides Proof of Professional Achievement

The A+ certification is quickly becoming a status symbol in the computer service industry. Organizations that include members of the computer service industry are recognizing the benefits of A+ certification and are pushing for their members to become certified. And more people every day are putting the "A+ Certified Technician" emblem on their business cards.

Increases Your Marketability

A+ certification makes individuals more marketable to potential employers. A+ certified employees also may receive a higher base salary because employers won't have to spend as much money on vendor-specific training.

What Is an ASC?

More service companies are becoming CompTIA A+ Authorized Service Centers (ASCs). This means that over 50 percent of the technicians employed by such service centers are A+ certified. Customers and vendors alike recognize that ASCs employ the most qualified service technicians. As a result, an ASC gets more business than a nonauthorized service center. And, because more service centers want to reach the ASC level, they will give preference in hiring to a candidate who is A+ certified over one who is not.

Provides Opportunity for Advancement

Most raises and advancements are based on performance. A+ certified employees work faster and more efficiently and are thus more productive. The more productive employees are, the more money they make for their company. And, of course, the more money they make for the company, the more valuable they are to the company. So if an employee is A+ certified, their chances of being promoted are greater.

Fulfills Training Requirements

A+ certification is recognized by most major computer hardware vendors. Some of these vendors apply A+ certification toward prerequisites in their own respective certification programs, which has the side benefit of reducing training costs for employers.

Raises Customer Confidence

As the A+ Certified Technician moniker becomes better known among computer owners, more of them will realize that the A+ technician is more qualified to work on their computer equipment than a noncertified technician is.

How to Become A+ Certified

A+ certification is available to anyone who passes the tests. You don't have to work for any particular company. It's not a secret society. It is, however, an elite group. To become A+ certified, you must do two things:

- Pass the A+ 220-801 exam
- Pass the A+ 220-802 exam

The exams can be taken at any Pearson VUE testing center. If you pass both exams, you will get a certificate in the mail from CompTIA saying that you have passed, and you will also receive a lapel pin and business card.

To register for the tests, call Pearson VUE at (877) 551-PLUS (7587) or go to www.vue.com. You'll be asked for your name, Social Security number (an optional number may be assigned if you don't wish to provide your Social Security number), mailing address, phone number, employer, when and where you want to take the test, and your credit card number (arrangement for payment must be made at the time of registration).

Although you can save money by arranging to take more than one test at the same seating, there are no other discounts. If you have to repeat a test in order to get a passing grade, you must pay for each retake.

Who Should Read This Book?

If you are one of the many people who want to pass the A+ exams, and pass them confidently, then you should buy this book and use it to study for the exams.

This book was written to prepare you for the challenges of the real IT world, not just to pass the A+ exams. This study guide will do that by describing in detail the concepts on which you'll be tested.

What Does This Book Cover?

This book covers everything you need to know to pass the A+ exam.

Part I of the book starts at Chapter 1 and concludes after Chapter 11. It will cover all the topics you will be tested on from exam 220-801:

Chapter 1, "Motherboards, Processors, and Memory"   Chapter 1 details the characteristics of motherboards, their slots, and built-in components. The CPU, RAM, and BIOS, which are attached to the motherboard, are also presented in Chapter 1.

Chapter 2, "Storage Devices and Power Supplies"   Chapter 2 presents the popular forms of storage devices in use today, including traditional hard drives, solid-state drives, floppy diskette drives, and flash drives and memory cards. Capacities, form factors, and makeup of these components is also discussed.

Chapter 3, "Peripherals and Expansion"   Chapter 3 covers installation and characteristics of expansion cards, the ports they and the motherboard present to the user, and the peripheral devices connected to these interfaces. Required cabling and its characteristics are also included.

Chapter 4, "Display Devices"   Chapter 4 runs the gamut of display devices and their characteristics. Everything from the classic CRT to the cutting-edge organic LED is covered in this chapter.

Chapter 5, "Custom Configurations"   Chapter 5 presents information based on a newer objective outlining the specialized systems we see more and more of in the field today. Examples include gaming PCs, graphic design and audio/video editing workstations, home theater PCs, and home servers.

Chapter 6, "Networking Fundamentals"   Chapter 6 covers characteristics of cable types and connectors, network devices, networking tools, and network topologies.

Chapter 7, "Introduction to TCP/IP"   Chapter 7 details the most common network protocol in use today. It covers TCP/IP structure, addressing (including IPv6), and common protocols in the suite.

Chapter 8, "Installing Wireless and SOHO Networks"   Chapter 8 contains two main sections. The first is on wireless networking standards and security, and the second discusses setting up a small office, home office (SOHO) network and choosing an Internet connection type.

Chapter 9, "Understanding Laptops"   Chapter 9 covers topics such as laptop-specific hardware, components within a laptop display, and laptop features.

Chapter 10, "Installing and Configuring Printers"   Chapter 10 starts by discussing different printing technologies, such as impact, inkjet, and laser printers. It then moves on to installing printers and performing printer maintenance.

Chapter 11, "Understanding Operational Procedures"   Chapter 11 covers the "softer" side of working with computers. Topics include following safety procedures, understanding environmental impacts, and practicing proper communication and professionalism.

Part II of the book, Chapter 12 through Chapter 20, looks at the topics from exam 220-802:

Chapter 12, "Operating System Basics"   Chapter 12 starts the examination of operating systems, and CompTIA expects you to know how to administer three of them, plus many of the various editions of each version: Microsoft's Windows XP, Windows Vista, and Windows 7.

Chapter 13, "Operating System Administration"   Chapter 13 continues the discussion begun in Chapter 12 and looks at utilities and features that exist in each of the three operating systems that you need to know for the exam.

Chapter 14, "Working with Windows 7"   Chapter 14 focuses only on Windows 7. It's newest of the three versions of operating systems that the 220-802 exam tests on, and this chapter looks at features unique to Windows 7 Starter, Windows 7 Home Premium, Windows 7 Professional, Windows 7 Ultimate, and Windows 7 Enterprise.

Chapter 15, "Working with Windows Vista"   Chapter 15 examines the often underappreciated Windows Vista and features unique to Windows Vista Home Basic, Windows Vista Home Premium, Windows Vista Business, Windows Vista Ultimate, and Windows Vista Enterprise.

Chapter 16, "Working with Windows XP"   Chapter 16 focuses only on Windows XP, the oldest of the three versions of operating systems that the 220-802 exam tests on. This chapter looks at features unique to Windows XP Home, Windows XP Professional, Windows XP Media Center, and Windows XP 64-bit Professional.

Chapter 17, "Security"   Just when you think this book couldn't get any better, we toss in a chapter devoted to security. This chapter looks at all the security topics on the exam and includes information on social engineering, best practices, and securing SOHO networks, both wired and wireless.

Chapter 18, "Mobile Devices"   Chapter 18 details the similarities and differences between Apple- and Android-based mobile devices. This chapter gives you extensive hands-on steps for configuring a variety of features and services on such devices.

Chapter 19, "Troubleshooting Theory, OSs, and Security"   If you collected a nickel every time someone requested a chapter on troubleshooting theory, you'd have enough to buy a decent pair of socks. Since CompTIA has an uncompromising view on the topic, you need to know the topic from the perspective of the objectives, and that is what you will find in Chapter 19.

Chapter 20, "Hardware and Network Troubleshooting"   The last chapter in the book covers a wide array of troubleshooting topics. Specific components include motherboards, RAM, CPUs, storage devices, display devices, printers, and laptops. Troubleshooting wired and wireless networks is also discussed.

What's Included in the Book

We've included several learning tools throughout the book:

Assessment test   At the end of this introduction is an assessment test that you can use to check your readiness for the exam. Take this test before you start reading the book; it will help you determine the areas you might need to brush up on. The answers to the assessment test questions appear on a separate page after the last question of the test. Each answer includes an explanation and a note telling you the chapter in which the material appears.

Objective map and opening list of objectives   At the beginning of the book, we have included a detailed exam objective map showing you where each of the exam objectives is covered. In addition, each chapter opens with a list of the exam objectives it covers. Use these to see exactly where each of the exam topics is covered.

Exam essentials   Each chapter, just before the summary, includes a number of exam essentials. These are the key topics you should take from the chapter in terms of areas to focus on when preparing for the exam.

Chapter review questions   To test your knowledge as you progress through the book, there are review questions at the end of each chapter. As you finish each chapter, answer the review questions and then check your answers—the correct answers and explanations are in Appendix A. You can go back to reread the section that deals with each question you got wrong to ensure that you answer correctly the next time you're tested on the material.

What's Included on the CD

We've included a number of additional study tools that can be found on the book's CD:

Sybex test engine   Using this custom software, you can identify up front the areas in which you are weak and then develop a solid studying strategy using the test engine for each of the robust testing features included with this book. In addition to the assessment test and the chapter review questions, you'll find a total of eight practice exams, four for exam 220-801 and four for exam 220-802. Take these practice exams just as if you were taking the actual exam (without any reference material). When you've finished the first exam, move on to the next one to solidify your test-taking skills. If you get more than 90 percent of the answers correct, you're ready to take the certification exam.

Electronic flashcards   Use these handy flashcards for quick and convenient review.

Instructional videos   We've included over an hour of instructional videos showing readers some of the more popular exam topics, including identifying the parts of a workstation and laptop and various storage devices, examining networking cables, and using the Windows operating systems.

E-book in all formats   Because we know many readers like to read on the go, we've included the study guide in various e-book formats, allowing you to read on most of the popular e-reader devices, tablets, and computers.

 Please see the appendix "About the Companion CD" for instructions on how to install the e-book files on your device.

PDF of key terms   We've included a searchable glossary so you can quickly find definitions for terms you're not familiar with.

How to Use This Book

If you want a solid foundation for preparing for the A+ exams, this is the book for you. We've spent countless hours putting together this book with the sole intention of helping you prepare for the exams.

This book is loaded with valuable information, and you will get the most out of your study time if you understand how we put the book together. Here's a list that describes how to approach studying:

1. Take the assessment test immediately following this introduction. It's okay if you don't know any of the answers—that's what this book is for. Carefully read over the explanations for any question you get wrong, and make note of the chapters where that material is covered.

2. Study each chapter carefully, making sure you fully understand the information and the exam objectives listed at the beginning of each one. Again, pay extra-close attention to any chapter that includes material covered in questions you missed on the assessment test.

3. Read over the summary and exam essentials. These will highlight the sections from the chapter you need to be familiar with before sitting for the exam.

4. Answer all the review questions at the end of each chapter. Specifically note any questions that confuse you, and study those sections of the book again. And don't just skim these questions—make sure you understand each answer completely.

5. Go over the electronic flashcards. These help you prepare for the latest A+ exams, and they're really great study tools.

6. Take the practice exams on the CD.

Minimum System Requirements

You should have a minimum of 45MB of disk space, as well as Windows 98 or higher, to use the Sybex test engine. You will also need Adobe Acrobat Reader (included).

Performance-Based Questions

With the latest A+ exams, CompTIA has introduced performance-based questions. These are not the traditional multiple-choice questions you're probably familiar with. These questions require the candidate to actually know how to perform a specific task or series of tasks. Although the A+ exams were not released at the time this book was written, we have a pretty good idea of how these questions will be laid out. The candidate will be presented with a scenario and will be asked to complete a task. They will be taken to a simulated environment where they will have to perform a series of steps and will be graded on how well they complete the task.

The Sybex test engine does not have the ability to include performance-based questions. However, we have included at the end of most chapters a section called "Performance-Based Questions" designed to measure how well you understood the chapter topics. Some simply ask you to complete a task for which there is only one correct response. Others are more subjective, with multiple ways to complete. We will provide the most logical or practical solution in Appendix B. Note that these may cover topic areas not covered in the actual A+ performance-based questions. However, we feel that being able to think logically is a great way to learn.

The A+ Exam Objectives

The A+ exams are made up of the 220-801 exam and the 220-802 exam. Following are the detailed exam objectives of each test.

 Exam objectives are subject to change at any time without prior notice and at CompTIA's sole discretion. Please visit the A+ Certification page of CompTIA's website (`http://certification.comptia.org/getCertified/certifications/a.aspx`) for the most current listing of exam objectives.

A+ Certification Exam Objectives: 220-801

The following table lists the domains measured by this examination and the extent to which they are represented on the exam:

Domain	Percentage of Exam
1.0 PC Hardware	40%
2.0 Networking	27%
3.0 Laptops	11%
4.0 Printers	11%
5.0 Operational Procedures	11%

1.0 PC Hardware

1.1 Configure and apply BIOS settings: Chapter 1

- Install firmware upgrades—flash BIOS
- BIOS component information: RAM; hard drive; optical drive; CPU
- BIOS configurations: Boot sequence; enabling and disabling devices; date/time; clock speeds; virtualization support; BIOS security (passwords; drive encryption: TPM; lo-jack)
- Use built-in diagnostics
- Monitoring: Temperature monitoring; fan speeds; intrusion detection/notification; voltage; clock; bus speed

1.2 Differentiate between motherboard components; their purposes; and properties: Chapter 1

- Sizes: ATX; Micro-ATX; ITX
- Expansion slots: PCI; PCI-X; PCIe; miniPCI; CNR; AGP2x, 4x, 8x
- RAM slots
- CPU sockets
- Chipsets: North Bridge; South Bridge; CMOS battery
- Jumpers
- Power connections and types
- Fan connectors
- Front panel connectors: USB; audio; power button; power light; drive activity lights; reset button
- Bus speeds

1.3 Compare and contrast RAM types and features: Chapter 1

- Types: DDR; DDR2; DDR3; SDRAM; SODIMM; RAMBUS; DIMM; parity vs. non-parity; ECC vs. non-ECC; RAM configurations (single channel vs. dual channel vs. triple channel); single sided vs. double sided
- RAM compatibility and speed

1.4 Install and configure expansion cards: Chapter 3

- Sound cards; video cards; network cards; serial and parallel cards; USB cards; FireWire cards; storage cards; modem cards; wireless/cellular cards; TV tuner cards; video capture cards; riser cards

1.5 Install and configure storage devices and use appropriate media: Chapter 2

- Optical drives: CD-ROM; DVD-ROM; Blu-ray
- Combo drives and burners: CD-RW; DVD-RW; dual layer DVD-RW; BD-R; BD-RE
- Connection types
  - External: USB; FireWire; eSATA; Ethernet
  - Internal SATA; IDE and SCSI: IDE configuration and setup (master; slave; cable select); SCSI IDs (0–15)
  - Hot-swappable drives
- Hard drives: magnetic; 5400 rpm; 7200 rpm; 10,000 rpm; 15,000 rpm
- Solid state/flash drives: CompactFlash; SD; Micro-SD; Mini-SD; xD; SSD
- RAID types: 0; 1; 5; 10
- Floppy drive
- Tape drive
- Media capacity: CD; CD-RW; DVD-RW; DVD; Blu-ray; tape; floppy; DL DVD

1.6 Differentiate among various CPU types and features and select the appropriate cooling method: Chapter 1

- Socket types
    - Intel: LGA, 775, 1155, 1156, 1366
    - AMD: 940, AM2, AM2+, AM3, AM3+, FM1, F
- Characteristics: speeds, cores, cache size/type, hyperthreading, virtualization support, architecture (32-bit vs. 64-bit), integrated GPU
- Cooling: heat sink, fans, thermal paste, liquid-based

1.7 Compare and contrast various connection interfaces and explain their purpose: Chapter 3

- Physical connections
    - USB 1.1 vs. 2.0 vs. 3.0 speed and distance characteristics. Connector types: A, B, mini, micro
    - FireWire 400 vs. FireWire 800 speed and distance characteristics
    - SATA1 vs. SATA2 vs. SATA3, eSATA, IDE speeds
    - Other connector types: serial, parallel, VGA, HDMI, DVI, Audio, RJ-45, RJ-11,
    - Analog vs. digital transmission: VGA vs. HDMI
- Speeds, distances and frequencies of wireless device connections: Bluetooth, IR, RF

1.8 Install an appropriate power supply based on a given scenario: Chapter 2

- Connector types and their voltages: SATA, Molex, 4/8-pin 12v, PCIe 6/8-pin, 20-pin, 24-pin, floppy
- Specifications: wattage, size, number of connectors, ATX, Micro-ATX; dual-voltage options

1.9 Evaluate and select appropriate components for a custom configuration, to meet customer specifications or needs: Chapter 5

- Graphic/CAD/CAM design workstation: powerful processor, high-end video, maximum RAM
- Audio/video editing workstation: specialized audio and video card, large fast hard drive, dual monitors
- Virtualization workstation: maximum RAM and CPU cores
- Gaming PC: powerful processor, high-end video/specialized GPU, better sound card, high-end cooling
- Home theater PC: surround sound audio, HDMI output, HTPC compact form factor, TV tuner
- Standard thick client: desktop applications, meets recommended requirements for running Windows

- Thin client: basic applications, meets minimum requirements for running Windows
- Home server PC: media streaming, file sharing, print sharing, Gigabit NIC, RAID array

1.10 Given a scenario, evaluate types and features of display devices: Chapter 4

- Types (CRT, LCD, LED, Plasma, Projector, OLED), refresh rates, resolution, native resolution, brightness/lumens, analog vs. digital, privacy/antiglare filters, multiple displays

1.11 Identify connector types and associated cables: Chapter 3

- Display connector types: DVI-D, DVI-I, DVI-A, DisplayPort, RCA, HD15 (i.e. DE15 or DB15), BNC, miniHDMI, RJ-45, miniDin-6
- Display cable types: HDMI, DVI, VGA, component, composite, S-video, RGB, coaxial, Ethernet
- Device connectors and pin arrangements: SATA, eSATA, PATA (IDE, EIDE), floppy, USB, IEEE1394 (SCSI), PS/2, parallel, serial, audio, RJ-45
- Device cable types: SATA, eSATA, IDE, EIDE, floppy, USB, IEEE1394, SCSI (68pin vs. 50pin vs. 25pin), parallel, serial, Ethernet, phone

1.12 Install and configure various peripheral devices: Chapter 3

- Input devices: mouse, keyboard, touch screen, scanner, barcode reader, KVM, microphone, biometric devices, game pads, joysticks, digitizer
- Multimedia devices: digital cameras, microphone, webcam, camcorder, MIDI enabled devices
- Output devices: printers, speakers, display devices

2.0 Networking

2.1 Identify types of network cables and connectors: Chapter 6

- Fiber. Connectors: SC, ST, and LC
- Twisted Pair. Connectors: RJ-11, RJ-45; wiring standards: T568A, T568B
- Coaxial. Connectors: BNC, F-connector

2.2 Categorize characteristics of connectors and cabling: Chapter 6

- Fiber. Types (single-mode vs. multi-mode); speed and transmission limitations
- Twisted pair. Types: STP, UTP, CAT3, CAT5, CAT5e, CAT6, plenum, PVC; speed and transmission limitations
- Coaxial. Types: RG-6, RG-59; speed and transmission limitations

2.3 Explain properties and characteristics of TCP/IP: Chapter 7

- IP class: Class A, Class B, Class C
- IPv4 vs. IPv6
- Public vs. private vs. APIPA
- Static vs. dynamic
- Client-side DNS
- DHCP
- Subnet mask
- Gateway

2.4 Explain common TCP and UDP ports, protocols, and their purpose: Chapter 7

- Ports: 21 - FTP, 23 - TELNET, 25 - SMTP, 53 - DNS, 80 - HTTP, 110 - POP3, 143 - IMAP, 443 - HTTPS, 3389 - RDP
- Protocols: DHCP, DNS, LDAP, SNMP, SMB, SSH, SFTP
- TCP vs. UDP

2.5 Compare and contrast wireless networking standards and encryption types: Chapter 8

- Standards: 802.11 a/b/g/n; speeds, distances, and frequencies
- Encryption types: WEP, WPA, WPA2, TKIP, AES

2.6 Install, configure, and deploy a SOHO wireless/wired router using appropriate settings: Chapter 8

- MAC filtering; channels (1–11); port forwarding, port triggering; SSID broadcast (on/off); wireless encryption; firewall; DHCP (on/off); DMZ; NAT; WPS; basic QoS

2.7 Compare and contrast Internet connection types and features: Chapter 8

- Cable, DSL, dial-up, fiber, satellite, ISDN, cellular (mobile hotspot), line of sight wireless Internet service, WiMAX

2.8 Identify various types of networks: Chapter 6

- LAN, WAN, PAN, MAN
- Topologies: mesh, ring, bus, star, hybrid

2.9 Compare and contrast network devices, their functions, and features: Chapter 6

- Hub, switch, router, access point, bridge, modem, NAS, firewall, VoIP phones, Internet appliance

2.10 Given a scenario, use appropriate networking tools: Chapter 6

- Crimper, multimeter, toner probe, cable tester, loopback plug, punchdown tool

3.0 Laptops

3.1 Install and configure laptop hardware and components: Chapter 9

- Expansion options: express card /34, express card /54, PCMCIA, SODIMM, flash
- Hardware/device replacement: keyboard, hard drive (2.5 vs. 3.5), memory, optical drive, wireless card, Mini-PCIe, screen, DC jack, battery, touchpad, plastics, speaker, system board, CPU

3.2 Compare and contrast the components within the display of a laptop: Chapter 9

- Types: LCD, LED, OLED, plasma
- Wi-Fi antenna connector/placement
- Inverter and its function
- Backlight

3.3 Compare and contrast laptop features: Chapter 9

- Special function keys: dual displays, wireless (on/off), volume settings, screen brightness, Bluetooth (on/off), keyboard backlight
- Docking station vs. port replicator
- Physical laptop lock and cable lock

4.0 Printers

4.1 Explain the differences between the various printer types and summarize the associated imaging process: Chapter 10

- Laser: imaging drum, fuser assembly, transfer belt, transfer roller, pickup rollers, separate pads, duplexing assembly. Imaging process: processing, charging, exposing, developing, transferring, fusing and cleaning.
- Inkjet: ink cartridge, print head, roller, feeder, duplexing assembly, carriage and belt. Calibration.
- Thermal: Feed assembly, heating element, special thermal paper
- Impact: Print head, ribbon, tractor feed, impact paper

4.2 Given a scenario, install, and configure printers: Chapter 10

- Use appropriate printer drivers for a given operating system
- Print device sharing: wired (USB, parallel, serial, Ethernet), wireless (Bluetooth, 802.11x, infrared [IR]). Printer hardware print server.
- Printer sharing: sharing local/networked printer via operating system settings

4.3 Given a scenario, perform printer maintenance: Chapter 10

- Laser: replacing toner, applying maintenance kit, calibration, cleaning
- Thermal: replace paper, clean heating element, remove debris
- Impact: replace ribbon, replace print head, replace paper

5.0 Operational Procedures

5.1 Given a scenario, use appropriate safety procedures: Chapter 11

- ESD straps
- ESD mats
- Self-grounding
- Equipment grounding
- Personal safety (disconnect power before repairing PC, remove jewelry, lifting techniques, weight limitations, electrical fire safety, CRT safety-proper disposal, cable management)
- Compliance with local government regulations

5.2 Explain environmental impacts and the purpose of environmental controls: Chapter 11

- MSDS documentation for handling and disposal
- Temperature, humidity level awareness and proper ventilation
- Power surges, brownouts, blackouts: battery backup, surge suppressor
- Protection from airborne particles: enclosures, air filters
- Dust and debris: compressed air, vacuums
- Component handling and protection: antistatic bags
- Compliance to local government regulations

5.3 Given a scenario, demonstrate proper communication and professionalism: Chapter 11

- Use proper language: avoid jargon, acronyms, slang when applicable
- Maintain a positive attitude

- Listen and do not interrupt the customer
- Be culturally sensitive
- Be on time (if late contact the customer)
- Avoid distractions: personal calls, talking to co-workers while interacting with customers, personal interruptions
- Dealing with difficult customer or situation
- Avoid arguing with customers and/or being defensive
- Do not minimize customer's problems
- Avoid being judgmental
- Clarify customer statements (ask open ended questions to narrow the scope of the problem, restate the issue or question to verify understanding)
- Set and meet expectations/timeline and communicate status with the customer
- Offer different repair/replacement options if applicable
- Provide proper documentation on the services provided
- Follow up with customer/user at a later date to verify satisfaction
- Deal appropriately with customer's confidential materials: located on a computer, desktop, printer, etc.

5.4 Explain the fundamentals of dealing with prohibited content/activity: Chapter 11

- First response: identify, report through proper channels, data/device preservation
- Use of documentation/documentation changes
- Chain of custody: tracking of evidence/documenting process

A+ Certification Exam Objectives: 220-802

The following table lists the domains measured by this examination and the extent to which they are represented on the exam.

Domain	Percentage of Exam
1.0 Operating Systems	33%
2.0 Security	22%
3.0 Mobile Devices	9%
4.0 Troubleshooting	36%
Total	100%

1.0 Operating Systems

1.1 Compare and contrast the features and requirements of various Microsoft Operating Systems.

- Windows XP Home, Windows XP Professional, Windows XP Media Center, Windows XP 64-bit Professional: **Chapters 12, 16**
- Windows Vista Home Basic, Windows Vista Home Premium, Windows Vista Business, Windows Vista Ultimate, Windows Vista Enterprise: **Chapters 12, 14, 15**
- Windows 7 Starter, Windows 7 Home Premium, Windows 7 Professional, Windows 7 Ultimate, Windows 7 Enterprise: **Chapter 12**
- Features: 32-bit vs. 64-bit: **Chapters 12, 14, 15**
- Features: Aero, gadgets, user account control, bit-locker, shadow copy, system restore, ready boost, sidebar, compatibility mode, XP mode, easy transfer, administrative tools, defender, Windows firewall, security center, event viewer, file structure and paths, category view vs. classic view: **Chapters 12–16**
- Upgrade paths—differences between in place upgrades, compatibility tools, Windows upgrade OS advisor: **Chapter 14**

1.2 Given a scenario, install, and configure the operating system using the most appropriate method: Chapter 13 except as noted

- Boot methods: USB, CD-ROM, DVD, PXE: **Chapter 14**
- Type of installations: creating image, unattended installation, upgrade, clean install, repair installation, multiboot, remote network installation, image deployment: **Chapters 14–16**
- Partitioning: dynamic, basic, primary, extended, logical
- File system types/formatting: FAT, FAT32, NTFS, CDFS, quick format vs. full format
- Load alternate third party drivers when necessary
- Workgroup vs. Domain setup
- Time/date/region/language settings
- Driver installation, software and windows updates
- Factory recovery partition

1.3 Given a scenario, use appropriate command line tools: Chapter 13

- Networking: PING, TRACERT, NETSTAT, IPCONFIG, NET, NSLOOKUP, NBTSTAT
- OS: TASKKILL, BOOTREC, SHUTDOWN, TLIST, MD, RD, CD, DEL, FDISK, FORMAT, COPY, XCOPY, ROBOCOPY, DISKPART, SFC, CHKDSK; [command name] /?
- Recovery console: fixboot, fixmbr

1.4 Given a scenario, use appropriate operating system features and tools.

- Administrative: computer management, device manager, users and groups, local security policy, performance monitor, services, system configuration, task scheduler, component services, data sources, print management, Windows memory diagnostics, Windows firewall, advanced security: **Chapters 13–16**
- MSCONFIG: general, boot, services, startup, tools: **Chapter 13**
- Task Manager: applications, processes, performance, networking, users: **Chapter 13**
- Disk management: drive status, mounting, extending partitions, splitting partitions, assigning drive letters, adding drives, adding arrays: **Chapter 13**
- Other: User State Migration tool (USMT), File and Settings Transfer Wizard, Windows Easy Transfer: **Chapters 14–16**
- Run line utilities: MSCONFIG, REGEDIT, CMD, SERVICES.MSC, MMC, MSTSC, NOTEPAD, EXPLORER, MSINFO32, DXDIAG: **Chapter 13**

1.5 Given a scenario, use Control Panel utilities (the items are organized by "classic view/large icons" in Windows): Chapter 13 except as noted

- Common to all Microsoft Operating Systems
- Internet options: Connections, Security, General, Privacy, Programs, Advanced
- Display: Resolution
- User accounts
- Folder options: Sharing, View hidden files, Hide extensions, Layout
- System: Performance (virtual memory), Hardware profiles, Remote settings, System protection
- Security center
- Windows firewall
- Power options: Hibernate, power plans, Sleep/suspend, Standby
- Unique to Windows XP: Add/Remove Programs, network connections, printers and faxes, automatic updates, Network Setup wizard: **Chapter 16**
- Unique to Vista: Tablet PC settings, pen and input devices, offline files, problem reports and solutions, printers: **Chapter 15**
- Unique to Windows 7: HomeGroup, Action center, remote applications and desktop applications, troubleshooting: **Chapter 14**

1.6 Setup and configure Windows networking on a client/desktop.

- HomeGroup, file/print sharing: **Chapters 14-15**
- WorkGroup vs. domain setup: **Chapters 14, 16**
- Network shares/mapping drives: **Chapter 14**
- Establish networking connections: VPN, dialups, wireless, wired, WWAN (cellular): **Chapters 14, 16**

- Proxy settings: **Chapters 14, 16**
- Remote desktop: **Chapters 14, 16**
- Home vs. Work vs. Public network settings: **Chapter 14**
- Firewall settings: exceptions, configuration, enabling/disabling Windows firewall: **Chapters 14-15**
- Configuring an alternative IP address in Windows: IP addressing, subnet mask, DNS, gateway: **Chapters 14-15**
- Network card properties: half duplex/full duplex/auto, speed, Wake-on-LAN, PoE, QoS: **Chapters 14-16**

1.7 Perform preventive maintenance procedures using appropriate tools: Chapters 12–13

- Best practices: scheduled backups, scheduled check disks, scheduled defragmentation, Windows updates, patch management, driver/firmware updates, antivirus updates
- Tools: Backup, System Restore, Check Disk, recovery image, defrag

1.8 Explain the differences among basic OS security settings.

- User and groups: Administrator, Power user, Guest, Standard user: **Chapter 13**
- NTFS vs. Share permissions: Allow vs. deny, moving vs. copying folders and files, file attributes: **Chapters 12–13**
- Shared files and folders: administrative shares vs. local shares, permission propagation, inheritance: **Chapter 13**
- System files and folders: **Chapter 12**
- User authentication: single sign-on: **Chapter 13**

1.9 Explain the basics of client-side virtualization: Chapter 12

- Purpose of virtual machines, resource requirements, emulator requirements, security requirements, network requirements, hypervisor

2.0 Security

2.1 Apply and use common prevention methods: Chapter 17

- Physical security: lock doors, tailgating, securing physical documents/passwords/shredding, biometrics, badges, key fobs, RFID badge, RSA token, privacy filters, retinal
- Digital security: antivirus, firewalls, antispyware, user authentication/strong passwords, directory permissions
- User education
- Principle of least privilege

2.2 Compare and contrast common security threats: Chapter 17

- Social engineering, malware, rootkits, phishing, shoulder surfing, spyware, viruses (worms, Trojans)

2.3 Implement security best practices to secure a workstation: Chapter 17

- Setting strong passwords, requiring passwords, restricting user permissions, changing default user names, disabling guest account, screensaver required password, disable autorun

2.4 Given a scenario, use the appropriate data destruction/disposal method: Chapter 17

- Low level format vs. standard format
- Hard drive sanitation and sanitation methods: overwrite, drive wipe
- Physical destruction: shredder, drill, electromagnetic, degaussing tool

2.5 Given a scenario, use the appropriate data destruction/disposal method: Chapter 17

- Change default user-names and passwords
- Changing SSID
- Setting encryption
- Disabling SSID broadcast
- Enable MAC filtering
- Antenna and access point placement
- Radio power levels
- Assign static IP addresses

2.6 Given a scenario, secure a SOHO wired network: Chapter 17

- Change default usernames and passwords
- Enable MAC filtering
- Assign static IP addresses
- Disabling ports
- Physical security

3.0 Mobile Devices

3.1 Explain the basic features of mobile operating systems: Chapter 18

- Android vs. iOS: open source vs. closed source/vendor specific, app source (app store and market), screen orientation (accelerometer/gyroscope), screen calibration, GPS and geotracking

3.2 Establish basic network connectivity and configure email: Chapter 18

- Wireless/cellular data network (enable/disable)
- Bluetooth: enable Bluetooth, enable pairing, find device for pairing, enter appropriate pin code, test connectivity
- Email configuration: server address, POP3, IMAP, port and SSL settings, Exchange, Gmail

3.3 Compare and contrast methods for securing mobile devices: Chapter 18

- Passcode locks, remote wipes, locator applications, remote backup applications, failed login attempts restrictions, antivirus, patching/OS updates

3.4 Compare and contrast hardware differences in regards to tablets and laptops: Chapter 18

- No field serviceable parts
- Typically not upgradeable
- Touch interface: touch flow, multitouch
- Solid state drives

3.5 Execute and configure mobile device synchronization: Chapter 18

- Types of data to synchronize: contacts, programs, email, pictures, music, videos
- Software requirements to install the application on the PC
- Connection types to enable synchronization

4.0 Troubleshooting

4.1 Given a scenario, explain the troubleshooting theory: Chapter 19

- Identify the problem: question the user and identify user changes to computer and perform backups before making changes
- Establish a theory of probable cause (question the obvious)
- Test the theory to determine cause. Once theory is confirmed determine next steps to resolve problem. If theory is not confirmed re-establish new theory or escalate.
- Establish a plan of action to resolve the problem and implement the solution
- Verify full system functionality and if applicable implement preventive measures
- Document findings, actions and outcomes

4.2 Given a scenario, troubleshoot common problems related to motherboards, RAM, CPU and power with appropriate tools: Chapter 20

- Common symptoms: unexpected shutdowns, system lockups, POST code beeps, blank screen on bootup, BIOS time and settings resets, attempts to boot to incorrect device, continuous reboots, no power, overheating, loud noise, intermittent device failure, fans spin—no power to other devices, indicator lights, smoke, burning smell, BSOD
- Tools: multimeter, power supply tester, loopback plugs, POST card

4.3 Given a scenario, troubleshoot hard drives and RAID arrays with appropriate tools: Chapter 20

- Common symptoms: read/write failure, slow performance, loud clicking noise, failure to boot, drive not recognized, OS not found, RAID not found, RAID stops working, BSOD
- Tools: screwdriver, external enclosures, CHKDSK, FORMAT, FDISK, file recovery software

4.4 Given a scenario, troubleshoot common video and display issues: Chapter 20

- Common symptoms: VGA mode, no image on screen, overheat shutdown, dead pixels, artifacts, color patterns incorrect, dim image, flickering image, distorted image, discoloration (degaussing), BSOD

4.5 Given a scenario, troubleshoot wired and wireless networks with appropriate tools: Chapter 20

- Common symptoms: no connectivity, APIPA address, limited connectivity, local connectivity, intermittent connectivity, IP conflict, slow transfer speeds, low RF signal
- Tools: cable tester, loopback plug, punch down tools, toner probes, wire strippers, crimper, PING, IPCONFIG, TRACERT, NETSTAT, NBTSTAT, NET, wireless locator

4.6 Given a scenario, troubleshoot operating system problems with appropriate tools: Chapter 19

- Common symptoms: BSOD, failure to boot, improper shutdown, spontaneous shutdown/restart, RAID not detected during installation, device fails to start, missing dll message, services fails to start, compatibility error, slow system performance, boots to safe mode, file fails to open, missing NTLDR, missing Boot.ini, missing operating system, missing graphical interface, graphical interface fails to load, invalid boot disk
- Tools: fixboot, recovery console, fixmbr, sfc, repair disks, pre-installation environments, MSCONFIG, DEFRAG, REGSRV32, REGEDIT, event viewer, safe mode, command prompt, emergency repair disk, automated system recovery

4.7 Given a scenario, troubleshoot common security issues with appropriate tools and best practices: Chapter 19

- Common symptoms: pop-ups, browser redirection, security alerts, slow performance, internet connectivity issues, PC locks up, Windows updates failures, rogue antivirus, spam, renamed system files, files disappearing, file permission changes, hijacked email, access denied
- Tools: anti-virus software, anti-malware software, anti-spyware software, recovery console, system restore, pre-installation environments, event viewer
- Best practices for malware removal
- Identify malware symptoms
- Quarantine infected system
- Disable system restore
- Remediate infected systems
- Update anti-virus software
- Scan and removal techniques (safe mode, pre-installation environment)
- Schedule scans and updates
- Enable system restore and create restore point
- Educate end user

4.8 Given a scenario, troubleshoot, and repair common laptop issues while adhering to the appropriate procedures: Chapter 20

- Common symptoms: no display, dim display, flickering display, sticking keys, intermittent wireless, battery not charging, ghost cursor, no power, num lock indicator lights, no wireless connectivity, no Bluetooth connectivity, cannot display to external monitor
- Disassembling processes for proper re-assembly: document and label cable and screw locations, organize parts, refer to manufacturer documentation, use appropriate hand tools

4.9 Given a scenario, troubleshoot printers with appropriate tools: Chapter 20

- Common symptoms: streaks, faded prints, ghost images, toner not fused to the paper, creased paper, paper not feeding, paper jam, no connectivity, garbled characters on paper, vertical lines on page, backed up print queue, low memory errors, access denied, printer will not print, color prints in wrong print color, unable to install printer, error codes
- Tools: maintenance kit, toner vacuum, compressed air, printer spooler

Assessment Test

1. Which of the following topologies allows for network expansion with the least amount of disruption for the current network users?
   A. Star
   B. Bus
   C. Ring
   D. Mesh

2. Which layer of the OSI model has the important role of providing error checking?
   A. Session layer
   B. Presentation layer
   C. Application layer
   D. Transport layer

3. Which cable standard is used for Ethernet 10Base2 installations?
   A. RG-6
   B. RG-8
   C. RG-58AU
   D. RJ-45

4. On which port does FTP run by default?
   A. 21
   B. 25
   C. 63
   D. 89

5. Which of the following protocols can be used by a client to retrieve email from a server?
   A. DNS
   B. FTP
   C. SMTP
   D. IMAP

6. Which of the following is a security mechanism used by HTTPS to encrypt web traffic between a web client and server?
   A. IPSec
   B. SSL
   C. L2TP
   D. PPPoE

7. Which of the following is a company that provides direct access to the Internet for home and business computer users?

   A. ASP

   B. ISP

   C. DNS

   D. DNP

8. What is the data throughput provided by one ISDN bearer channel?

   A. 16Kbps

   B. 56Kbps

   C. 64Kbps

   D. 128Kbps

9. Which of the following are 4G technologies? (Choose all that apply.)

   A. LTE

   B. GSM

   C. CDMA

   D. WiMax

10. Which LCD component is responsible for providing brightness?

   A. Backlight

   B. Inverter

   C. Screen

   D. Backdrop

11. Your laptop has 2GB of installed memory and uses shared video memory. If the video card is using 512MB, how much is left for the rest of the system?

   A. 2GB

   B. 1.5GB

   C. 512MB

   D. Cannot determine

12. Which of the following standards is also known as CardBus?

   A. PCMCIA 1.0

   B. PCMCIA 2.0

   C. PCMCIA 5.0

   D. ExpressCard

13. What is the function of the laser in a laser printer?

    A. It heats up the toner so it adheres to the page.

    B. It charges the paper so it will attract toner.

    C. It creates an image of the page on the drum.

    D. It cleans the drum before a page is printed.

14. What is the component called that stores the material that ends up printed to the page in a laser printer?

    A. Toner cartridge

    B. Ink cartridge

    C. Laser module

    D. Laser cartridge

15. The output of a dot-matrix printer is typically measured in what?

    A. CPM

    B. CPS

    C. PPM

    D. PPS

16. Which of the following computer components can retain a lethal electrical charge even after the device is unplugged? (Choose all that apply.)

    A. Monitor

    B. Processor

    C. Power supply

    D. RAM

17. Roughly how much time spent communicating should be devoted to listening?

    A. 23 percent

    B. 40 percent

    C. 50 percent

    D. 80 percent

18. When lifting heavy equipment, what is the proper technique?

    A. Get the heaviest part closest to your body and lift with your legs.

    B. Get the heaviest part closest to your body and lift with your back.

    C. Get the lightest part closest to your body and lift with your legs.

    D. Get the lightest part closest to your body and lift with your back.

19. Your laser printer has recently starting printing vertical white lines on documents it prints. What is the most likely cause of the problem?

   A. The print driver is faulty.

   B. The fuser is not heating properly.

   C. There is toner on the transfer corona wire.

   D. There is a scratch on the EP drum.

20. You are working with a system that is assigned IP information configuration information from a central server. You wish to manually refresh the IP information on the system. Which of the following commands would you use?

   A. `IPCONFIG /REFRESH`

   B `IPCONFIG /ALL`

   C. `IPCONFIG /RENEW`

   D. `WINIPCFG /ALL`

21. One laser printer in your office keeps getting frequent paper jams. What is the most likely cause of the problem?

   A. Worn paper feed rollers

   B. Faulty stepper motor

   C. Faulty fuser assembly

   D. The EP drum not advancing properly

22. Which of the following is *not* considered a system component that can be found inside a computer?

   A. CPU

   B. RAM

   C. PCIe graphics adapter

   D. Motherboard

23. Which of the following is *not* a physical memory format used in desktop computer systems?

   A. DRAM

   B. DIMM

   C. SIMM

   D. RIMM

24. Which of the following are components that can commonly be found on a motherboard? (Choose all that apply.)

   A. Slots

   B. Fan connectors

   C. Gyroscope

   D. Scanner

   E. HDD

25. Which of the following is a chip that is integrated into PATA drives, as opposed to being mounted on a daughter card?

   A. Controller

   B. CPU

   C. Host adapter

   D. IDE

26. What is the name of the power connector that is larger than the connector used for floppy diskette drives and that is commonly used with PATA drives?

   A. AT system connector

   B. Berg

   C. Molex

   D. ATX system connector

27. After SATA was introduced, what was the retroactive term used for the original ATA specification?

   A. EIDE

   B. IDE

   C. PATA

   D. SCSI

28. You are installing a new graphics adapter in a Windows 7 system. Which of the following expansion slots are designed for high-speed, 3D graphics adapters? (Choose all that apply.)

   A. USB

   B. AGP

   C. PCI

   D. ISA

   E. PCIe

29. Which of the following connectors is used for a parallel printer port?

   A. DE9

   B. DA15

   C. DB25

   D. DE25

30. Which of the following are modular ports used in data communications? (Choose all that apply.)

   A. RG-6

   B. RJ-45

   C. RJ-11

   D. DB25

   E. RG-11

31. The _____ is the measurement of the number of pixels an LCD monitor can display without the image appearing distorted.

   A. Native resolution

   B. Contrast ratio

   C. Pixelation

   D. Base frequency

32. Which of the following is *not* a common monitor technology?

   A. CRT

   B. Plasma

   C. OLED

   D. Super PMOLED

33. What can be used at the check-in desk of a doctor's office to prevent patients from viewing confidential information?

   A. An antiglare filter

   B. A privacy filter

   C. An LED display

   D. A thin client

34. Which of the following is a standard computer that can access resources locally as well as from servers but requires no specialized enhancements?

   A. Gaming PC

   B. Home server

   C. Thin client

   D. Thick client

35. Which of the following is a requirement for virtualization workstations?

   A. Enhanced video

   B. Enhanced audio

   C. Maximum RAM and CPU cores

   D. RAID array

36. Which of the following is *not* a requirement for a home server PC?

   A. TV tuner

   B. Print and file sharing services

   C. Gigabit NIC

   D. RAID array

37. Which of the following are popular mobile-device operating systems? (Choose all that apply.)

    A. Android

    B. Windows 7

    C. Ubuntu

    D. iOS

38. Which of the following protocols can be used in close range to transfer data between a mobile device and a computer system or to allow media to stream from the mobile device to an audio system?

    A. SMTP

    B. Bluetooth

    C. POP3

    D. IMAP4

39. What term refers to copying data between a mobile device and a computer system to mirror such things as contacts, programs, pictures, and music?

    A. Calibration

    B. Remote wipe

    C. Pairing

    D. Synchronization

40. Which of the following is a virtual machine manager—the software that allows the virtual machines to exist?

    A. Comptroller

    B. Shell

    C. Kernel

    D. Hypervisor

41. Which of the following would *not* be considered a standard permission in Windows using NTFS?

    A. Full Control

    B. Modify

    C. Allow

    D. Write

42. Which feature is designed to keep Windows current by automatically downloading updates such as patches and security fixes and installing these fixes automatically?

    A. Security Center

    B. Action Center

    C. Windows Update

    D. Windows Anytime

43. With dynamic storage, which of the following partition types are possible?

    A. Complex, bridged, or mirrored

    B. Simple, spanned, or striped

    C. Simple, complex, or interleaved

    D. Spanned, interleaved, or striped

44. Which MSINFO32 option is available only with Windows XP?

    A. /PCH

    B. /COMPUTER

    C. /NFO

    D. /REPORT

45. You have been told to use Task Manager to change the priority of a process to Below Normal. This equates to a base priority of what?

    A. 2

    B. 4

    C. 6

    D. 8

46. Encrypting File System (EFS) is available in which editions of Windows 7? (Choose all that apply.)

    A. Professional

    B. Home Premium

    C. Enterprise

    D. Ultimate

    E. Business

47. Which of the following can provide electrical power over Ethernet cabling?

    A. PoE

    B. QoS

    C. DoS

    D. WoL

48. With which type of duplexing do communications travel in both directions but in only one direction at any given time?

    A. Full

    B. Half

    C. Auto

    D. Mechanical

49. You have just added a new network to your Windows Vista laptop and it is asking you to specify a type of location. With which location types is network discovery on by default? (Choose all that apply.)

A. Home

B. Work

C. Public

D. Private

E. HomeGroup

50. Which applet in Windows Vista is the primary interface for configuring synchronization of offline files?

A. Synchronization Wizard

B. Action Center

C. Merge

D. Sync Center

51. Which of the following Control Panel applets is unique to Windows Vista?

A. Tablet PC Settings

B. Network Setup Wizard

C. Printers and Faxes

D. Action Center

52. Which Control Panel applet allows you to administer, as well as deploy, component services and configure behavior like security?

A. SFC

B. Data Sources

C. Component Services

D. DDR

53. In Windows, the Account Lockout Counter in an Account Lockout policy keeps track of the number of invalid attempts before lockout occurs. The default is 0 (meaning the feature is turned off), but it can be set from 1 to what?

A. 9999

B. 999

C. 99

D. 24

54. What Windows operating system tool can be used to block access from the network (be it internal or the Internet)?

A. Windows Firewall

B. Windows Defender

C. Advanced Security

D. Device Manager

55. Which of the following are programs that enter a system or network under the guise of another program? (Choose the best answer.)

  A. Worms

  B. Trojans

  C. Rootkits

  D. Spyware

56. Which of the following involves applying a strong magnetic field to initialize the media before tossing it away?

  A. Fraying

  B. Fracking

  C. Degaussing

  D. Spreading

57. Which term is synonymous with *MAC filtering*?

  A. Disabling Autorun

  B. Shredding

  C. Port disabling

  D. Network Lock

58. Which of the following is a copy of your system configuration at a given point in time?

  A. Restore point

  B. MBR

  C. Registry

  D. BOOT.INI

59. Your system has issues with locking up intermittently. Because it is running Windows XP, what diagnostic tool can you use that does not exist in Windows Vista or Windows 7?

  A. SFC

  B. Dr. Watson

  C. NTLDR

  D. MSCONFIG

60. Which of the following could be described as a small, deviously ingenious program that replicates itself to other computers, generally causing those computers to behave abnormally? (Choose the best answer.)

  A. Rogue

  B. Redirector

  C. Virus

  D. Pop-up

Answers to Assessment Test

1. A. The star topology is the easiest to modify. A physical star topology branches each net-work device off a central device called a hub or a switch, making it easy to add a new work-station. See Chapter 6 for more information.

2. D. A key role of the Transport layer is to provide error checking. The Transport layer also provides functions such as reliable end-to-end communications, segmentation and reassembly of larger messages, and combination of smaller messages into a single larger message. See Chapter 6 for more information.

3. C. 10Base2 is also known as thinnet, and it uses coaxial cable. The correct cable standard is RG-58AU. RG-6 is for cable television and satellite modems, and RG-8 is for thicknet, or 10Base5. RJ-45 is a connector for twisted pair cabling. See Chapter 6 for more information.

4. A. FTP listens on port 21. See Chapter 7 for more information.

5. D. The IMAP and POP3 protocols can be used to retrieve email from mail servers. See Chapter 7 for more information.

6. B. HTTPS connections are secured using either Secure Sockets Layer (SSL) or Transport Layer Security (TLS). See Chapter 7 for more information.

7. B. An Internet service provider (ISP) provides direct access to the Internet. See Chapter 8 for more information.

8. C. An ISDN B (bearer) channel provides 64Kbps data throughput. A home-based BRI ISDN provides two B channels. See Chapter 8 for more information.

9. A, D. WiMax and LTE are the two current 4G cellular technologies. GSM and CDMA are 3G technologies. See Chapter 8 for more information.

10. A. The backlight provides light to the LCD screen. The inverter provides power to the backlight, and the screen displays the picture. See Chapter 9 for more information.

11. B. If the laptop is using shared video memory, then the system memory is shared with the video card. If the video card is using 512MB (half a gigabyte), then there is 1.5GB left for the system. See Chapter 9 for more information.

12. C. PCMCIA 5.0 is also known as CardBus. See Chapter 9 for more information.

13. C. The laser creates an image on the photosensitive drum that is then transferred to the paper by the transfer corona. The fuser heats up the toner so it adheres to the page. The transfer corona charges the page, and the eraser lamp cleans the drum before a page is printed. A rubber blade is also used to physically remove toner from the drum. See Chapter 10 for more information.

14. A. Laser printers use toner, which they melt to the page in the image of the text and graphics being printed. A toner cartridge holds the fine toner dust until it is used in the printing process. See Chapter 10 for more information.

15. B. The output of impact printers such as dot-matrix printers is measured in characters per second (CPS). Many bubble-jet and laser printers are measured in terms of pages per minute (PPM). See Chapter 10 for more information.

16. A, C. Monitors and power supplies can retain significant electrical charges even after they're unplugged. Don't open the back of a monitor or the power supply unless you are specifically trained to do so. See Chapter 11 for more information.

17. C. Roughly half the time spent communicating should be devoted to listening. See Chapter 11 for more information.

18. A. When lifting heavy equipment, center the weight as close to your body as possible. Then, keep your back straight and lift with your legs. See Chapter 11 for more information.

19. C. White streaks on printouts are most likely caused by toner on the transfer corona wire. Vertical black lines are caused by a scratch or a groove in the EP drum. If the fuser was not heating properly, toner would not bond to the paper and you would have smearing. Faulty print drivers will cause garbage to print or there will be no printing at all. See Chapter 20 for more information.

20. C. The IPCONFIG command can be used with Windows XP (and others) to see the networking configuration values at the command line. It is one of the most commonly used command-line utilities that can be used in troubleshooting and network configurations. To renew IP configuration information, the IPCONFIG /renew command is used to force the DHCP server to renew the IP information assigned to the system. See Chapter 20 for more information.

21. A. The most likely cause of those listed is a worn paper feed roller. Stepper motors control the back-and-forth motion of a print head in a bubble-jet printer. If the fuser assembly were faulty, the images would smear. See Chapter 20 for more information.

22. C. System components are essential for the basic functionality of a computer system. Many of the landmarks found on the motherboard can be considered system components, even expansion slots to a degree. What you plug into those slots, however, must be considered peripheral to the basic operation of the system. For more information, see Chapter 1.

23. A. Although DRAM is a very common type of RAM essentially used in all computer systems today, it does not describe a physical memory format. SIMMs, DIMMs, and RIMMs are all technologies on which memory-module manufacturing is based. For more information, see Chapter 1.

24. A, B. Motherboards commonly have RAM slots and expansion slots. Older motherboards even had CPU slots. Modern motherboards have connectors for powering cooling fans. Gyroscopes are most commonly found in mobile devices. Scanners are external devices. Although there might be one or more types of HDD interfaces built into the motherboard, the HDD itself is not. For more information, see Chapter 1.

25. A. A controller chip is responsible for encoding data to be stored on the disk platters as well as performing geometry translation for the BIOS. Translation is necessary because the true number of sectors per track of the hard disk drive system usually exceeds what is supported by the BIOS. For more information, see Chapter 2.

26. C. The standard peripheral power connector, or Molex connector, is commonly used on larger drives because it allows more current to flow to the drive than does the Berg connector, which is used with floppy diskette drives. For more information, see Chapter 2.

27. C. *IDE* (ATA-1) and *EIDE* (ATA-2 and later) were specific nicknames for the ATA series of standards. Although *ATA* is technically accurate, it refers to legacy IDE standards as well as newer SATA standards. Instead of using the term *ATA* to be synonymous with *IDE* and *EIDE*, as had been done in the past, the term *PATA* was coined, referring to the parallel nature of IDE communications. The term *PATA* differentiates the IDE and EIDE form of ATA from Serial ATA. SCSI is a related yet completely different type of technology. For more information, see Chapter 2.

28. B, E. Although technically PCI and ISA could be used for graphics adapters, AGP was specifically designed for the use of high-speed, 3D graphic video cards. PCIe offers better performance than AGP for graphics adapters. For more information, see Chapter 3.

29. C. Parallel printer ports use a D-subminiature connector known as a DB25. The DE9 port is used for the RS-232 serial port. The DA15 is used for AUI and game/joystick ports. The DE25 is not a common port. For more information, see Chapter 3.

30. B, C. RJ-11 ports are used in analog telephony and allow modems attached to computer serial ports to transmit modulated digital information across the public switched telephone network (PSTN). RJ-45 ports are used by various network interface controller (NIC) cards for attachment to networks such as Ethernet. RG-6 and RG-11 coaxial connectors and DB25 connectors are not modular. For more information, see Chapter 3.

31. A. The native resolution refers to how many pixels an LCD screen can display (across and down) without distortion. The native resolution is based on the placement of the actual transistors that create the image by twisting the liquid crystals. The contrast ratio is the measurement between the darkest color and the lightest color that an LCD screen can display. For more information, see Chapter 4.

32. D. Although there *is* a Super AMOLED display, employing active-matrix technology, there is not a corresponding passive-matrix version. The other technologies exist and are discussed in further detail in Chapter 4.

33. B. Privacy filters are used to limit the viewing angle for a monitor. With such filters, the screen image becomes indiscernible when viewed at just a few degrees from center. For more information, see Chapter 4.

34. D. A thick client is any computer system with a standard configuration. The gaming PC has enhancements over thick clients to their CPU, video, audio, and cooling. The home server PC must have specialized capabilities and services along with a faster NIC than the thick client and a RAID array. The thin client is a lesser device in comparison to the thick client, but that cost-saving feature is its enhancement. These less expensive computers can connect over the network to servers for their operating system images and applications. For more information, see Chapter 5.

35. C. Virtualization workstations require more RAM than standard systems and need to be equipped with as many multicore processors as possible. Video and audio are not resources that need to be enhanced for such workstations. Although a RAID array is a wise addition whenever servers with valuable information are involved, a virtualization workstation does not require one. For more information, see Chapter 5.

36. A. A TV tuner card is a requirement for a home theater PC but not for a home server. The other options are among those features that are required. For more information, see Chapter 5.

37. A, D. Google's Android and Apple's iOS are two of the most popular operating systems for mobile devices on the market. The other two are not. Although some mobile operating systems are based on Linux or UNIX, Ubuntu is a Linux distribution not used for mobile devices. For more information, see Chapter 18.

38. B. Bluetooth allows you to pair a mobile device to a computer or to a device such as an automotive sound system or headset. Data can be transferred between devices and media can be streamed from the mobile device. For more information, see Chapter 18.

39. D. Synchronizing a mobile device with a computer system allows you to mirror personal data between the devices, regardless of which one contains the most current data. Calibration refers to matching the device's and user's perceptions of where the user is touching the screen. Remote wipes allow you to remove personal data from a lost or stolen device. Pairing is what must be done in Bluetooth for two Bluetooth devices to connect and communicate. For more information, see Chapter 18.

40. D. The hypervisor is a virtual machine manager—the software that allows the virtual machines to exist. For more information, see Chapter 12.

41. C. Standard permissions are collections of special permissions, including Full Control, Modify, Read & Execute, Read, and Write. For more information, see Chapter 12.

42. C. Windows includes Windows Update, a feature designed to keep Windows current by automatically downloading updates such as patches and security fixes and installing these fixes automatically. For more information, see Chapter 12.

43. B. Windows 7, Vista, and XP support both basic and dynamic storage. Basic can have a primary and an extended partition, while dynamic can be simple, spanned, or striped. For more information, see Chapter 13.

44. A. The /pch option is available only in Windows XP and is used to display the history view. For more information, see Chapter 13.

45. C. For applications that don't need to drop all the way down to Low, this equates to a base priority of 6. For more information, see Chapter 13.

46. A, C, D. EFS is available in the Professional, Enterprise, and Ultimate editions of Windows 7 allowing for encryption/decryption on files stored in NTFS volumes. For more information, see Chapter 14.

47. A. Power over Ethernet (PoE) is a handy technology to supply both power and an Ethernet connection. The purpose of Power over Ethernet (PoE) is pretty much described in its name: Electrical power is transmitted over twisted-pair Ethernet cable (along with data). For more information, see Chapter 14.

48. B. With half duplex, communications travel in both directions but in only one direction at any given time. For more information, see Chapter 14.

49. A, B. The three location types in Windows Vista for a network are Home, Work, and Public. If you choose one of the first two, network discovery is on by default, allowing you to see other computers and other computers to see you. For more information, see Chapter 14.

50. D. The Sync Center in Windows Vista is the primary interface for configuring synchronization. For more information, see Chapter 15.

51. A. The Tablet PC Settings applet (Start ➢ Control Panel ➢ Tablet PC Settings) in Windows Vista can be used, as the name implies, to configure the device on which the operating system is installed to function as a true tablet. For more information, see Chapter 15.

52. C. Component Services allows you to administer, as well as deploy, component services and configure behavior like security. For more information, see Chapter 15.

53. B. It can be set from 1 to 999. For more information, see Chapter 15.

54. A. Windows Firewall (Start ➢ Control Panel ➢ Windows Firewall) is used to block access from the network (be it internal or the Internet). For more information, see Chapter 15.

55. B. Trojans are programs that enter a system or network under the guise of another program. While rootkits *may* do this, it is not their primary feature and thus not the best answer for this question. For more information, see Chapter 17.

56. C. Degaussing involves applying a strong magnetic field to initialize the media (this is also referred to as disk wiping). This process helps ensure that information doesn't fall into the wrong hands. For more information, see Chapter 17.

57. D. On a number of wireless devices, the term *Network Lock* is used in place of *MAC filtering*, and the two are synonymous. For more information, see Chapter 17.

58. A. A restore point is a copy of your system configuration at a given point in time. It's like a backup of your configuration but not necessarily your data. For more information, see Chapter 12.

59. B. Windows XP includes a special utility known as Dr. Watson. This utility intercepts all error conditions and, instead of presenting the user with a cryptic Windows error, displays a slew of information that can be used to troubleshoot the problem. For more information, see Chapter 19.

60. C. A computer virus is a small, deviously ingenious program that replicates itself to other computers, generally causing those computers to behave abnormally. Generally speaking, a virus's main function is to reproduce. For more information, see Chapter 17.

CompTIA®
A+® Complete
Deluxe Study Guide
Second Edition

220-801

PART

I

Chapter 1

Motherboards, Processors, and Memory

THE FOLLOWING COMPTIA A+ 220-801 OBJECTIVES ARE COVERED IN THIS CHAPTER:

✓ **1.1 Configure and apply BIOS settings.**

- ▪ Install firmware upgrades – flash BIOS

- ▪ BIOS component information: RAM, Hard drive, Optical drive, CPU, Boot sequence, Enabling and disabling devices, Date/time, Clock speeds, Virtualization support

  - ▪ BIOS security (passwords, drive encryption: TPM, lo-jack)

- ▪ Use built-in diagnostics

- ▪ Monitoring: Temperature monitoring, Fan speeds, Intrusion detection/notification, Voltage, Clock, Bus speed

✓ **1.2 Differentiate between motherboard components, their purposes, and properties.**

- ▪ Sizes: ATX, Micro-ATX, ITX

- ▪ Expansion slots: PCI, PCI-X, PCIe, miniPCI, CNR, AGP 1x, AGP2x, 4x, 8x

- ▪ RAM slots

- ▪ CPU sockets

- ▪ Chipsets: Northbridge/Southbridge, CMOS battery

- ▪ Jumpers

- ▪ Power connections and types

- ▪ Fan connectors

- ▪ Front panel connectors: USB, Audio, Power button, Power light, Drive activity lights, Reset button

- ▪ Bus speeds

✓ **1.3 Compare and contrast RAM types and features.**

- Types: DDR, DDR2, DDR3, SDRAM, SODIMM, RAMBUS, DIMM, Parity vs. non-parity, ECC vs. non-ECC, RAM configurations (Single channel vs. dual channel vs. triple channel), Single sided vs. double sided

- RAM compatibility and speed

✓ **1.6 Differentiate among various CPU types and features and select the appropriate cooling method.**

- Socket types: Intel (LGA, 775, 1155, 1156, 1366), AMD (940, AM2, AM2+, AM3, AM3+, FM1, F)

- Characteristics: Speeds, Cores, Cache size/type, Hyperthreading, Virtualization support, Architecture (32-bit vs. 64-bit), Integrated GPU

- Cooling: Heat sink, Fans, Thermal paste, Liquid-based

A personal computer (PC) is a computing device made up of many distinct electronic components that all function together in order to accomplish some useful task, such as adding up the numbers in a spreadsheet or helping you write a letter. Note that this definition describes a computer as having many distinct parts that work together. Most computers today are modular. That is, they have components that can be removed and replaced with another component of the same function but with different specifications in order to improve performance. Each component has a specific function. In this chapter, you will learn about the core components that make up a typical PC, what their functions are, and how they work together inside the PC.

Unless specifically mentioned otherwise, throughout this book the terms *PC* and *computer* can be used interchangeably.

In this chapter, you will learn how to identify system components common to most personal computers, including the following:

- Motherboards
- Processors
- Memory
- Basic input/output systems (BIOS)
- Cooling systems

Identifying Components of Motherboards

The spine of the computer is the *motherboard*, otherwise known as the system board and mainboard. This is the printed circuit board (PCB)—a conductive series of pathways laminated to a nonconductive substrate—that lines the bottom of the computer and is often of a uniform color, such as olive, brown, or blue. It is the most important component in the computer because it connects all the other components together. Figure 1.1 shows a typical PC system board, as seen from above. All other components are attached to this circuit board. On the system board, you will find the central processing unit (CPU), underlying circuitry, expansion slots, video components, random access memory (RAM) slots, and a variety of other chips. We will be discussing each of these components throughout this book.

FIGURE 1.1   A typical system board

System Board Form Factors

System boards are classified by their form factor (design), such as ATX, micro ATX, and ITX. Exercise care and vigilance when acquiring a motherboard and case separately. Some cases are less accommodating than others and might not be physically compatible with the motherboard you choose.

Advanced Technology Extended

The Advanced Technology Extended (*ATX*) motherboard was developed by Intel in the mid-1990s to improve upon the classic AT-style motherboard architecture that had ruled the PC world for many years. The ATX motherboard has the processor and memory slots at right angles to the expansion cards. This arrangement puts the processor and memory in line with the fan output of the power supply, allowing the processor to run cooler. And because those components are not in line with the expansion cards, you can install full-length expansion cards—adapters that extend the full length of the inside of a standard computer case—in an ATX motherboard machine. ATX (and its derivatives) are the primary motherboards in use today. Standard ATX motherboards measure 12″ × 9.6″ (305 × 244 mm).

Micro ATX

One form factor that is designed to work in standard ATX cases, as well as its own smaller cases, is known as *micro ATX* (also referred to as μATX). Micro ATX follows the ATX principle of component placement for enhanced cooling over pre-ATX designs but with a smaller footprint. With this smaller form come some trade-offs. For the compact use of space, you must give up quantity: quantity of memory slots, motherboard headers, expansion slots, integrated components. You also have fewer micro ATX chassis bays, although the same small-scale motherboard can fit into much larger cases if your original peripherals are still a requirement.

Be aware that micro ATX systems tend to be designed with power supplies of lower wattage in order to help keep down power consumption and heat production. This is generally acceptable with the standard, reduced micro ATX suite of components. As more off-board USB ports are added and larger cases are used with additional in-case peripherals, a larger power supply might be required.

Micro ATX motherboards share their width, mounting hole pattern, and rear interface pattern with ATX motherboards but are shallower and square, measuring 9.6″ × 9.6″ (244 × 244 mm). They were designed to be able to fit into full-size ATX cases.

ITX

The *ITX* line of motherboard form factors was developed by VIA as a low-power, small form factor (SFF) board for specialty uses, such as home-theater systems and as embedded components. ITX itself is not an actual form factor but a family of form factors. The family consists of the following form factors:

- Mini-ITX—6.7″ × 6.7″ (170 × 170 mm)
- Nano-ITX—4.7″ × 4.7″ (120 × 120 mm)
- Pico-ITX—3.9″ × 2.8″ (100 × 72 mm)
- Mobile-ITX—2.4″ × 2.4″ (60 × 60 mm)

The mini-ITX motherboard has four mounting holes that line up with three or four of the holes in the ATX and micro ATX form factors. In mini-ITX boards, the rear interfaces are placed in the same location as those on the ATX motherboards. These features make mini-ITX boards compatible with ATX chassis. This is where the mounting compatibility ends because despite the PC compatibility of the other ITX form factors, they are used in embedded systems, such as set-top boxes, and lack the requisite mounting and interface specifications.

System Board Components

Now that you understand the basic types of motherboards and their form factors, it's time to look at the components found on the motherboard and their locations relative to each other. Many of the following components can be found on a typical motherboard:

- Chipsets
- Expansion slots and buses
- Memory slots and external cache
- CPUs and their sockets
- Power connectors
- Onboard disk drive connectors
- Keyboard connectors
- Integrated peripheral ports and headers
- BIOS/firmware
- CMOS battery
- Jumpers and DIP switches
- Front-panel connectors

In the following sections, you will learn about some of the most common components of a motherboard, what they do, and where they are located on the motherboard. We'll show what each component looks like so you can identify it on most any motherboard you run across. In the case of some components, this chapter provides only a brief introduction, with more detail to come in later chapters.

Before we can talk about specific components, however, you need to understand the concepts underlying serial and parallel connectivity, the two main categories of bus architecture.

Bus Architecture

There has been a quiet revolution taking place in the computer industry for quite some time now. Unlike in the early days of personal computing, when parallel communication pathways (made up of multiple synchronized wires or traces) dominated single-file serial connections, this revolution has brought a shift toward serial communications. Once engineers created transmitters and receivers capable of sustaining data rates many times those of parallel connections, they found no need to tie these pathways together in a parallel circuit. The downside of parallel communications is the loss of circuit length and throughput—how far the signal can travel and the amount of data moved per unit of time, respectively—due to the careful synchronization of the separate lines, the speed of which must be controlled to limit skewing the arrival of the individual signals at the receiving end.

The only limitation of serial circuits is in the capability of the transceivers, which tends to grow over time at a refreshing rate due to technical advancements. Examples of specifications that have heralded the migration toward the dominance of serial communications are Serial ATA (SATA), Universal Serial Bus (USB), IEEE 1394/FireWire, and Peripheral Component Interconnect Express (PCIe).

Parallel computer-system components work on the basis of a bus. A *bus*, in this sense, is a common collection of signal pathways over which related devices communicate within the computer system. Expansion buses of various architectures, such as PCI and AGP, incorporate slots at certain points in the bus to allow insertion of external devices, or adapters, into the bus, usually with no regard to which adapters are inserted into which slots; insertion is generally arbitrary. Other types of buses exist within the system to allow communication between the CPU and components with which data must be exchanged. Except for CPU slots and sockets and memory slots, there are no insertion points in such closed buses because no adapters exist for such an environment.

The term *bus* is also used in any parallel or bit-serial wiring implementation where multiple devices can be attached at the same time in parallel or in series (daisy-chained). Examples include Small Computer System Interface (SCSI), USB, and Ethernet.

Chipsets

A *chipset* is a collection of chips or circuits that perform interface and peripheral functions for the processor. This collection of chips is usually the circuitry that provides interfaces for memory, expansion cards, and onboard peripherals and generally dictates how a motherboard will communicate with the installed peripherals.

Chipsets are usually given a name and model number by the original manufacturer. Typically, the manufacturer and model also tell you that your particular chipset has a certain set of features (for example, type of RAM supported, type and brand of onboard video, and so on).

Chipsets can be made up of one or several integrated circuit chips. Intel-based motherboards, for example, typically use two chips. To know for sure, you must check the manufacturer's documentation, especially because today's chipset chips are frequently obscured by cooling mechanisms, sometimes hindering visual brand and model identification.

The functions of chipsets can be divided into two major functional groups, called Northbridge and Southbridge. Let's take a brief look at these groups and the functions they perform.

Northbridge

The *Northbridge* subset of a motherboard's chipset is the set of circuitry or chips that performs one very important function: management of high-speed peripheral communications. The Northbridge is responsible primarily for communications with integrated video using AGP and PCIe, for instance, and processor-to-memory communications. Therefore, it can be said that much of the true performance of a PC relies on the specifications of the Northbridge component and its communications capability with the peripherals it controls.

 When we use the term *Northbridge*, we are referring to a functional subset of a motherboard's chipset. There isn't actually a Northbridge brand of chipset.

The communications between the CPU and memory occur over what is known as the *frontside bus (FSB)*, which is just a set of signal pathways connecting the CPU and main memory, for instance. The clock signal that drives the FSB is used to drive communications by certain other devices, such as AGP and PCIe slots, making them local-bus technologies. The *backside bus (BSB)*, if present, is a set of signal pathways between the CPU and Level 2 or 3 (external) cache memory. The BSB uses the same clock signal that drives the FSB. If no backside bus exists, cache is placed on the frontside bus with the CPU and main memory.

The Northbridge is directly connected to the Southbridge (discussed next). It controls the Southbridge and helps to manage the communications between the Southbridge and the rest of the computer.

Southbridge

The *Southbridge* subset of the chipset is responsible for providing support to the onboard slower peripherals (PS/2, parallel ports, serial ports, Serial and Parallel ATA, and so on), managing their communications with the rest of the computer and the resources given to them. These components do not need to keep up with the external clock of the CPU and do not represent a bottleneck in the overall performance of the system. Any component that would impose such a restriction on the system should eventually be developed for FSB attachment.

In other words, if you're considering any component other than the CPU, memory and cache, AGP slots, or PCIe slots, the Southbridge is in charge. Most motherboards today have integrated PS/2, USB, LAN, analog and digital audio, and FireWire ports for the Southbridge to manage, for example, all of which are discussed in more detail later in this chapter. The Southbridge is also responsible for managing communications with the slower expansion buses, such as PCI, and legacy buses.

Figure 1.2 is a photo of the chipset of a motherboard, with the heat sink of the Northbridge, at the top left, connected to the heat-spreading cover of the Southbridge, at the bottom right.

Figure 1.3 shows a schematic of a typical motherboard chipset (both Northbridge and Southbridge) and the components they interface with. Notice which components interface with which parts of the chipset.

Expansion Slots

The most visible parts of any motherboard are the *expansion slots*. These are small plastic slots, usually from 1 to 6 inches long and approximately ½ inch wide. As their name suggests, these slots are used to install various devices in the computer to expand its capabilities. Some expansion devices that might be installed in these slots include video, network, sound, and disk interface cards.

If you look at the motherboard in your computer, you will more than likely see one of the main types of expansion slots used in computers today:

- PCI
- AGP

- PCIe
- PCI-X
- CNR

FIGURE 1.2   A modern computer chipset

Each type differs in appearance and function. In the following sections, we will cover how to visually identify the different expansion slots on the motherboard. Personal Computer Memory Card International Association (PCMCIA) buses, such as PC Card, Cardbus, Mini PCI, ExpressCard, and PCIe Mini, are related more to laptops than to desktop computers and are covered in Chapter 9, "Understanding Laptops."

FIGURE 1.3 A schematic of a typical motherboard chipset

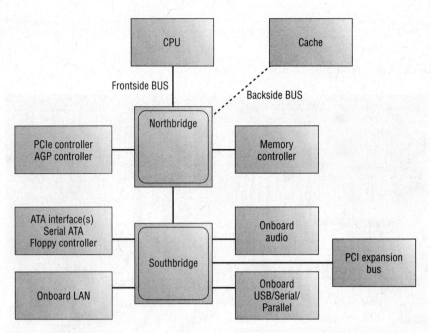

PCI Expansion Slots

Many computers in use today contain 32-bit Peripheral Component Interconnect (*PCI*) slots. They are easily recognizable because they are only around 3 inches long and classically white, although modern boards take liberties with the color. PCI slots became extremely popular with the advent of Pentium-class processors. Although popularity has shifted from PCI to PCIe, the PCI slot's service to the industry cannot be ignored; it has been an incredibly prolific architecture for many years.

PCI expansion buses operate at 33 or 66MHz over a 32-bit (4-byte) channel, resulting in data rates of 133 and 266MBps, respectively, with 133MBps being the most common, server architectures excluded. PCI is a shared-bus topology, however, so mixing 33 and 66MHz adapters in a 66MHz system will slow all adapters to 33MHz. Older servers might have featured 64-bit PCI slots as well, which double the 32-bit data rates. See the sidebar in this chapter titled "Arriving at the Exact Answer" for help with understanding the math involved in frequencies and bit rates.

PCI slots and adapters are manufactured in 3.3 and 5V versions. Universal adapters are keyed to fit in slots based on either of the two voltages. The notch in the card edge of the common 5V slots and adapters is oriented toward the front of the motherboard, and the notch in the 3.3V adapters toward the rear. Figure 1.4 shows several PCI expansion slots. Note the 5V 32-bit slot in the foreground and the 3.3V 64-bit slots. Also notice that a universal 32-bit card, which has notches in both positions, is inserted into and operates fine in the 64-bit 3.3V slot in the background.

FIGURE 1.4   PCI expansion slots

Arriving at the Exact Answer

To get the math exactly right when dealing with frequencies and data rates ending in 33 and 66, you have to realize that every 33 has an associated one-third (⅓), and every 66 has an associated two-thirds (⅔). The extra quantities are left off of the final result but must be added back on to get the math exactly right. The good news is that omitting these small values from the equation still gets you close, and a bit of experience with the numbers leads to being able to make the connection on the fly.

PCI-X Expansion Slots

Visually indistinguishable from 64-bit PCI, because it uses the same slots, PCI-Extended (*PCI-X*) takes the 66MHz maximum frequency of PCI to new heights, to the most common, 133MHz, and the current maximum, 533MHz. With an 8-byte (64-bit) bus, this translates to maximum throughput of 4266MBps, roughly 4.3GBps. Additionally, PCI-X supports a 266MHz bus as well as the only frequency it shares with PCI, 66MHz, making PCI-X slots compatible with PCI adapters.

PCI-X is targeted at server platforms with its speed and support for hot-plugging but is still no match for the speeds available with PCIe, which all but obviates PCI-X today. PCI-X also suffers from the same shared-bus topology as PCI, resulting in all adapters falling back to the frequency of the slowest inserted adapter.

AGP Expansion Slots

Accelerated Graphics Port (*AGP*) slots are known mostly for legacy video card use and have been supplanted in new installations by PCI Express slots and their adapters. Preceding the introduction of AGP, if you wanted a high-speed, accelerated 3D graphics video card, you had to install the card into an existing PCI or ISA slot. AGP slots were designed to be a direct connection between the video circuitry and the PC's memory. They are also easily recognizable because they are usually brown and are located right next to the PCI slots on the motherboard. AGP slots are slightly shorter than PCI slots and are pushed back from the rear of the motherboard in comparison with the position of the PCI slots.

Another landmark to look for when identifying later AGP slots is the tab toward the front of the system that snaps into place on a hook at the "rear" of the adapter. It is necessary to pull the tab away from the adapter before removing it from the slot to avoid breaking the adapter's hook. Figure 1.5 shows an example of an older AGP slot, along with a PCI slot for comparison. Notice the difference in length between the two.

FIGURE 1.5 An AGP slot compared to a PCI slot

AGP performance is based on the original specification, known as AGP 1x. It uses a 32-bit (4-byte) channel and a 66MHz clock, resulting in a data rate of 266MBps. AGP 2x, 4x, and 8x specifications multiply the 66MHz clock they receive to increase throughput linearly. For instance, AGP 8x uses the 66MHz clock to produce an effective clock frequency of 533MHz, resulting in throughput of 2133MBps over the 4-byte channel. Note that this maximum throughput is only half the maximum of PCI-X. In fact, it's only a quarter of the throughput of PCIe x16, which is covered in the following section.

PCIe Expansion Slots

A newer expansion slot architecture that is being used by motherboards is PCI Express (*PCIe*). It was designed to be a replacement for AGP and PCI. PCIe has the advantage of being faster than AGP while maintaining the flexibility of PCI. PCIe has no plug compatibility with either AGP or PCI. As a result, modern PCIe motherboards still tend to have regular PCI slots for backward compatibility, but AGP slots typically are not also included. The lack of AGP means a legacy AGP video card must be replaced with a PCIe video card, often resulting in an appreciable expense. However, because PCI slots tend to be present as well, in general no other adapter requires replacement unless increased performance is desired.

PCIe is casually referred to as a bus architecture to simplify its comparison with other bus technologies. True expansion *buses* share total bandwidth among all slots, each of which taps into different points along the common bus lines. In contrast, PCIe uses a switching component with point-to-point connections to slots, giving each component full use of the corresponding bandwidth and producing more of a star topology versus a bus. Furthermore, unlike other expansion buses, which have parallel architectures, PCIe is a serial technology, striping data packets across multiple serial paths to achieve higher data rates.

PCIe uses the concept of *lanes*, which are the switched point-to-point signal paths between any two PCIe components. Each lane that the switch interconnects between any two intercommunicating devices comprises a separate pair of wires for both directions of traffic. Each PCIe pairing between cards requires a negotiation for the highest mutually supported number of lanes. The single lane or combined collection of lanes that the switch interconnects between devices is referred to as a *link*.

There are seven different link widths supported by PCIe, designated x1 (pronounced "by 1"), x2, x4, x8, x12, x16, and x32, with x1, x4, and x16 being the most common. The x8 link width is less common than these but more common than the others. A slot that supports a particular link width is of a physical size related to that width because the width is based on the number of lanes supported, requiring a related number of wires. As a result, a x8 slot is longer than a x1 slot but shorter than a x16 slot. Every PCIe slot has a 22-pin portion in common toward the rear of the motherboard, which you can see in Figure 1.6, in which the rear of the motherboard is to the left. These 22 pins comprise mostly voltage and ground leads.

There are three major versions of PCIe currently specified: 1.x, 2.x, and 3.0. The beginning of development on version 4.0 was announced in late 2011. During the same period, new motherboards were predominantly produced with PCIe 2.0 slots. For the four versions, a single lane, and hence a x1 slot, operates in each direction (or transmit and receive from either communicating device's perspective), at a data rate of 250MBps (almost twice the rate of the most common PCI slot), 500MBps, 1GBps, and 2GBps respectively.

An associated bidirectional link has a nominal throughput of double these rates. Use the doubled rate when comparing PCIe to other expansion buses because those other rates are for bidirectional communication. This means that the 500MBps bidirectional link of a x1 slot in the first version of PCIe was comparable to PCI's best, a 64-bit slot running at 66MHz and producing throughput of 533MBps.

Combining lanes results in a linear multiplication of these rates. For example, a PCIe 1.1 x16 slot is capable of 4GBps of throughput in each direction, 16 times the 250MBps x1 rate. Bidirectionally, this fairly common slot produces a throughput of 8GBps, quadrupling the data rate of an AGP 8x slot. Later PCIe specifications increase this throughput even more.

FIGURE 1.6   PCIe expansion slots

Up-plugging is defined in the PCIe specification as the ability to use a higher-capability slot for a lesser adapter. In other words, you can use a shorter (fewer-lane) card in a longer slot. For example, you can insert a x8 card into a x16 slot. The x8 card won't completely fill the slot, but it will work at x8 speeds if up-plugging is supported by the motherboard. Otherwise, the specification requires up-plugged devices to operate at only the x1 rate. This is something to be aware of and investigate in advance. Down-plugging is possible only on open-ended slots although not specifically allowed in the official specification. Even if you find or make (by cutting a groove in the end) an open-ended slot that accepts a longer card edge, the inserted adapter cannot operate faster than the slot's maximum rated capability because the required physical wiring to the PCIe switch in the Northbridge is not present.

Because of its high data rate, PCIe is the current choice of gaming aficionados. Additionally, technologies similar to NVIDIA's Scalable Link Interface (SLI) allow such users to combine preferably identical graphics adapters in appropriately spaced PCIe x16 slots with a hardware bridge to form a single virtual graphics adapter. The job of the bridge is to provide non-chipset communication among the adapters. The bridge is not a requirement for SLI to work, but performance suffers without it. SLI-ready motherboards allow two, three, or four PCIe graphics adapters to pool their graphics processing units (GPUs) and memory to feed graphics output to a single monitor attached to the adapter acting as SLI master. SLI implementation results in increased graphics performance over single-PCIe and non-PCIe implementations.

Refer to Figure 1.6, which is a photo of an SLI-ready motherboard with three PCIe x16 slots (every other slot, starting with the top one), one PCIe x1 slot (second slot from the top), and two PCI slots (first and third slots from the bottom). Notice the latch and tab that secures the x16 adapters in place by their hooks. As with later AGP slots, any movement of these high-performance devices can result in temporary failure or poor performance.

CNR Expansion Slots

As is always the case, Intel and other manufacturers are constantly looking for ways to improve the production process. One lengthy process that would often slow down the production of motherboards with integrated analog I/O functions was FCC certification. The manufacturers developed a way of separating the analog circuitry (for example, modem and analog audio) onto its own card. This allowed the analog circuitry to be separately certified (it was its own expansion card) from the already certified digital motherboard, thus reducing time for FCC certification. Eventually this became a nonissue and these cards became extinct.

The Communications and Networking Riser (*CNR*) slot that can be found on some older Intel motherboards was a replacement for Intel's even earlier Audio Modem Riser (AMR) slot, each of which appeared in quantities of no more than one per motherboard. One portion of this slot is the same length as one of the portions of the AMR slot, but the other portion of the CNR slot is longer than that of the AMR slot. The cards made for the CNR slot contained circuitry for sound and analog modem (communications) as well as networking.

Essentially, these legacy 60-pin slots allowed motherboard manufacturers to implement a motherboard chipset with certain integrated features. Then, if the built-in features of that chipset need to be enhanced (by adding Dolby Digital Surround to a standard sound chipset, for example), a CNR riser card could be added to enhance the onboard capabilities. Additional advantages of CNR over AMR include networking support, Plug and Play compatibility, support for hardware acceleration (as opposed to CPU control only), and the fact that there's no need to lose a competing PCI slot for networking unless the CNR slot is in use. Figure 1.7 shows an example of a CNR slot (indicated by the arrow).

FIGURE 1.7   A CNR slot

Memory Slots and Cache

Memory or random access memory (RAM) slots are the next most notable slots on a motherboard. These slots are for the modules that hold memory chips that make up primary memory that is used to store currently used data and instructions for the CPU. Many and varied types of memory are available for PCs today. In this chapter, you will become familiar with the appearance and specifications of the slots on the motherboard so you can identify them.

For the most part, PCs today use memory chips arranged on a small circuit board. A dual inline memory module (*DIMM*) is one type of circuit board. Today's DIMMs differ in the number of conductors, or pins, that each particular physical form factor uses. Some common examples include 168-, 184-, and 240-pin configurations. In addition, laptop memory comes in smaller form factors known as small outline DIMMs (*SODIMMs*) and MicroDIMMs. The single inline memory module (SIMM) is an older memory form factor that began the trend of placing memory chips on modules. More detail on memory packaging and the technologies that use them can be found later in this chapter in the section "Identifying Purposes and Characteristics of Memory." Figure 1.8 shows the form factors for some once popular memory modules. Notice how they basically look the same but the module sizes and keying notches are different.

Memory slots are easy to identify on a motherboard. Classic DIMM slots were usually black and, like all memory slots, were placed very close together. DIMM slots with color coding are more common these days, however. The color coding of the slots acts as a guide to the installer of the memory. See the section "Single-, Dual-, and Triple-Channel Memory" later in this chapter for more on the purpose of this color coding. Consult the motherboard's documentation to determine the specific modules allowed as well as their required orientation. The number of memory slots varies from motherboard to motherboard, but the structure of the different slots is similar. Metal pins in the bottom make contact with the metallic pins on each memory module. Small metal or plastic tabs on each side of the slot keep the memory module securely in its slot.

FIGURE 1.8 Different memory module form factors

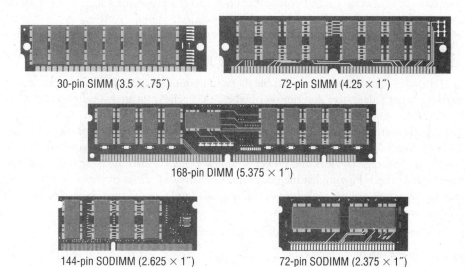

30-pin SIMM (3.5 × .75″)   72-pin SIMM (4.25 × 1″)

168-pin DIMM (5.375 × 1″)

144-pin SODIMM (2.625 × 1″)   72-pin SODIMM (2.375 × 1″)

Sometimes the amount of primary memory installed is inadequate to service additional requests for memory resources from newly launched applications. When this condition occurs, the user may receive an "out of memory" error message and an application may fail to launch. One solution for this is to use the hard drive as additional RAM. This space on the hard drive is known as a swap file or a paging file. The technology in general is known as *virtual memory*. The swap file, `pagefile.sys` in modern Microsoft operating systems, is an optimized space that can deliver information to RAM at the request of the memory controller faster than if it came from the general storage pool of the drive. Note that virtual memory cannot be used directly from the hard drive; it must be paged into RAM as the oldest contents of RAM are paged out to the hard drive to make room. The memory controller, by the way, is the chip that manages access to RAM as well as adapters that have had a few hardware memory addresses reserved for their communication with the processor.

Nevertheless, relying too much on virtual memory (check your page fault statistics in the Reliability and Performance Monitor) results in the entire system slowing down noticeably. An inexpensive and highly effective solution is to add physical memory to the system, thus reducing its reliance on virtual memory. More information on virtual memory and its configuration can be found in Chapter 12, "Operating System Basics."

When it's not the amount of RAM in a system that you need to enhance but its speed, engineers can add *cache memory* between the CPU and RAM. Cache is a very fast form of memory forged from static RAM, which is discussed in detail in the section "Identifying Purposes and Characteristics of Memory" later in this chapter. Cache improves system performance by predicting what the CPU will ask for next and prefetching this information before being asked. This paradigm allows the cache to be smaller in size than the RAM itself. Only the most recently used data and code or that which is expected to be used next is stored in cache. Cache on the motherboard is known as external cache because it is external to the processor; it's also referred to as Level 2 cache (*L2 cache*). Level 1 cache (*L1 cache*), by comparison, is internal cache because it is built into the processor's silicon wafer, or *die*. The word *core* is often interchangeable with the word *die*.

It is now common for chip makers to use extra space in the processor's packaging to bring the L2 cache from the motherboard closer to the CPU. When L2 cache is present in the processor's packaging, but not on-die, the cache on the motherboard is referred to as Level 3 cache (*L3 cache*). Unfortunately, due to the de facto naming of cache levels, the term *L2 cache* alone is not a definitive description of where the cache is located. The terms *L1 cache* and *L3 cache* do not vary in their meaning, however.

The typical increasing order of capacity and distance from the processor die is L1 cache, L2 cache, L3 cache, RAM, HDD/SSD (hard disk drive and solid-state drive—more on these in Chapter 2, "Storage Devices and Power Supplies"). This is also the typical decreasing order of speed. The following list includes representative capacities of these memory types. The cache capacities are for each core of the original Intel Core i7 processor. The other capacities are simply modern examples.

- L1 cache—64KB (32KB each for data and instructions)
- L2 cache—256KB
- L3 cache—4MB–12MB
- RAM—4–16GB
- HDD/SSD—100s–1000s of GB

Central Processing Unit and Processor Socket

The "brain" of any computer is the central processing unit (*CPU*). There's no computer without a CPU. There are many different types of processors for computers—so many, in fact, that you will learn about them later in this chapter in the section "Identifying Purposes and Characteristics of Processors."

Typically, in today's computers, the processor is the easiest component to identify on the motherboard. It is usually the component that has either a fan or a heat sink (usually both) attached to it (as shown in Figure 1.9). These devices are used to draw away and disperse the heat a processor generates. This is done because heat is the enemy of micro-electronics. Theoretically, a Pentium (or higher) processor generates enough heat that without the heat sink it would permanently damage itself and the motherboard in a matter of hours or even minutes.

CPU sockets are almost as varied as the processors they hold. Sockets are basically flat and have several columns and rows of holes or pins arranged in a square, as shown in Figure 1.10. The top socket is known as Socket A or Socket 462, made for earlier AMD processors such as the Athlon, and has holes to receive the pins on the CPU. This is known as a pin grid array (PGA) arrangement for a CPU socket. The holes and pins are in a row/

column orientation, an array of pins. The bottom socket is known as Socket T or Socket *LGA 775*, and there are spring-loaded pins in the socket and a grid of lands on the CPU. The land grid array (*LGA*) is a newer technology that places the delicate pins (yet more sturdy than those on chips) on the cheaper motherboard instead of on the more expensive CPU, opposite to the way the aging PGA does. The device with the pins has to be replaced if the pins become too damaged to function. The PGA and LGA are mentioned again later in this chapter in the section "Identifying Purposes and Characteristics of Processors."

FIGURE 1.9   Two heat sinks, one with a fan

Modern CPU sockets have a mechanism in place that reduces the need to apply the considerable force to the CPU that was necessary in the early days of personal computing to install a processor. Given the extra surface area on today's processors, excessive pressure applied in the wrong manner could damage the CPU packaging, its pins, or the motherboard itself. For CPUs based on the PGA concept, zero insertion force (*ZIF*) sockets are exceedingly popular. ZIF sockets use a plastic or metal lever on one of the two lateral edges to lock or release the mechanism that secures the CPU's pins in the socket. The CPU rides on the mobile top portion of the socket, and the socket's contacts that mate with the CPU's pins are in the fixed bottom portion of the socket. The Socket 462 image in Figure 1.10 shows the ZIF locking mechanism at the edge of the socket along the bottom of the photo.

For processors based on the LGA concept, a socket with a different locking mechanism is used. Because there are no receptacles in either the motherboard or the CPU, there is no opportunity for a locking mechanism that holds the component with the pins in place. LGA-compatible sockets, as they're called despite the misnomer, have a lid that closes over the CPU and is locked in place by an L-shaped arm that borders two of the socket's edges. The nonlocking leg of the arm has a bend in the middle that latches the lid closed when the other leg of the arm is secured. The bottom image in Figure 1.10 shows an LGA socket with no CPU installed and the locking arm secured over the lid's tab (right-hand edge in the photo).

FIGURE 1.10   CPU socket examples

Table 1.1 lists some common socket/CPU relationships.

TABLE 1.1:   Socket types and the processors they support

Socket	Processors
LGA 775 (Socket T)	Intel only: Pentium 4, Pentium 4 Extreme Edition (single core), Pentium D, Celeron D, Pentium Extreme Edition (dual core), Core 2 Duo, Core 2 Extreme, Core 2 Quad, Xeon, Celeron (4xx, Exxxx series)
LGA 1155 (Socket H2)	Intel only: Replacement for LGA 1156 to support CPUs based on the Sandy Bridge (such as Celeron G4xx and G5xx) and eventual Ivy Bridge architectures
LGA 1156 (Socket H)	Intel only: Celeron (G1xxx series), Core i3, Core i5, Core i7 (8xx series), Pentium (G6xxx series), Xeon (34xx series)
LGA 1366 (Socket B)	Intel only: Core i7 (9xx series), Xeon (35xx, 36xx, 55xx, 56xx series), Intel Celeron P1053
Socket 940	AMD only: Athlon 64 FX (FX-51, -53), Opteron
Socket AM2	AMD only: Athlon 64, Athlon 64 X2, Athlon 64 FX, Opteron, Sempron, Phenom
Socket AM2+	AMD only: Often backward compatible with AM2 CPUs as well as Athlon II and Phenom II and forward compatible with AM3 CPUs
Socket AM3	AMD only: DDR3 capable CPUs only (thus not compatible with AM2+ CPUs), such as Phenom II, Athlon II, Sempron, Opteron 138x, and has the potential to accept AM3+ CPUs
Socket AM3+	AMD only: Specified for CPUs based on the Bulldozer microarchitecture and designed to accept AM3 CPUs
Socket FM1	AMD only: Designed to accept AMD Fusion APUs that incorporate CPUs and GPUs, such as the E2-3200 and the A Series
Socket F (LGA)	AMD only: Opteron (2xxx, 8xxx series), Athlon 64 FX (FX-7x series), and replaced by Sockets C32 and G34

Power Connectors

In addition to these sockets and slots on the motherboard, a special connector (the 20-pin block connector shown in Figure 1.11) allows the motherboard to be connected to the power supply to receive power. This connector is where the ATX power connector (mentioned in Chapter 2 in the section "Identifying Purposes and Characteristics of Power Supplies") plugs in.

FIGURE 1.11   An ATX power connector on a motherboard

Firmware

Firmware is the name given to any software that is encoded in hardware, usually a read-only memory (ROM) chip, and can be run without extra instructions from the operating system. Most computers and large printers use firmware in some sense. The best example of firmware is a computer's Basic Input/Output System (BIOS) routine, which is burned in to a chip. Also, some expansion cards, such as SCSI cards and graphics adapters, use their own firmware utilities for setting up peripherals.

BIOS and POST

Aside from the processor, the most important chip on the motherboard is the Basic Input/Output System (*BIOS*) chip, also referred to as the ROM BIOS chip. This special memory chip contains the BIOS system software that boots the system and allows the operating system to interact with certain hardware in the computer in lieu of requiring a more complex device driver to do so. The BIOS chip is easily identified: If you have a brand-name computer, this chip might have on it the name of the manufacturer and usually the word

BIOS. For clones, the chip usually has a sticker or printing on it from one of the major BIOS manufacturers (AMI, Phoenix/Award, Winbond, and so on). On later motherboards, the BIOS might be difficult to identify or even be integrated into the Southbridge, but the functionality remains, regardless of how it's implemented.

BIOS

Figure 1.12 gives you an idea of what a modern BIOS might look like. Despite the 1998 copyright on the label, which refers only to the oldest code present on the chip, this particular chip can be found on motherboards produced as late as 2009. Notice also the Reset CMOS jumper at lower left and its configuration silkscreen at upper left. You might use this jumper to clear the CMOS memory, discussed next, when an unknown password, for example, is keeping you out of the BIOS configuration utility. The jumper in the photo is in the clear position, not the normal operating position. System boot-up is typically not possible in this state.

FIGURE 1.12   A BIOS chip on a motherboard

Most BIOS setup utilities have more to offer than a simple interface for making selections and saving the results. As always, you can enter the utility to check to see if the clock appears to be losing time, possibly due to a dying battery. Today, these utilities also offer diagnostic routines that you can use to have the BIOS analyze the state and quality of the same components it inspects during boot-up, but at a much deeper level.

There is often also a page within the utility that gives you access to such bits of information as current live readings of the temperature of the CPU and the ambient temperature of the interior of the system unit. In such a page, you can set the temperature at which the BIOS sounds a warning tone and the temperature at which the BIOS shuts the system down to protect it. You can also monitor the instantaneous fan speeds, bus speeds, and voltage levels of the CPU and other vital landmarks to make sure they are all within acceptable ranges. You might also be able to set a lower fan-speed threshold at which the system warns you. In many cases, some of these levels can be altered to achieve such phenomena as overclocking or undervolting.

Some BIOS firmware can monitor the status of a contact on the motherboard for intrusion detection. If the feature in the BIOS is enabled and the sensor on the chassis is connected to the contact on the motherboard, the removal of the cover will be detected and logged by the BIOS. This can occur even if the system is off, thanks to the CMOS battery. At the next boot-up, the BIOS will notify you of the intrusion. No notification occurs over subsequent boots unless additional intrusion is detected.

POST

A major function of the BIOS is to perform a process known as a power-on self-test (POST). POST is a series of system checks performed by the system BIOS and other high-end components, such as the SCSI BIOS and the video BIOS. Among other things, the POST routine verifies the integrity of the BIOS itself. It also verifies and confirms the size of primary memory. During POST, the BIOS also analyzes and catalogs other forms of hardware, such as buses and boot devices, as well as manages the passing of control to the specialized BIOS routines mentioned earlier. The BIOS is responsible for offering the user a key sequence to enter the configuration routine as POST is beginning. Finally, once POST has completed successfully, the BIOS selects the boot device highest in the config-ured boot order and executes the master boot record (MBR) or similar construct on that device so that the MBR can call its associated operating system's boot loader and continue booting up.

The POST process can end with a beep code or displayed code that indicates the issue discovered. Each BIOS publisher has its own series of codes that can be gener-ated. Figure 1.13 shows a simplified POST display during the initial boot sequence of a computer.

FIGURE 1.13   An example of a BIOS boot screen

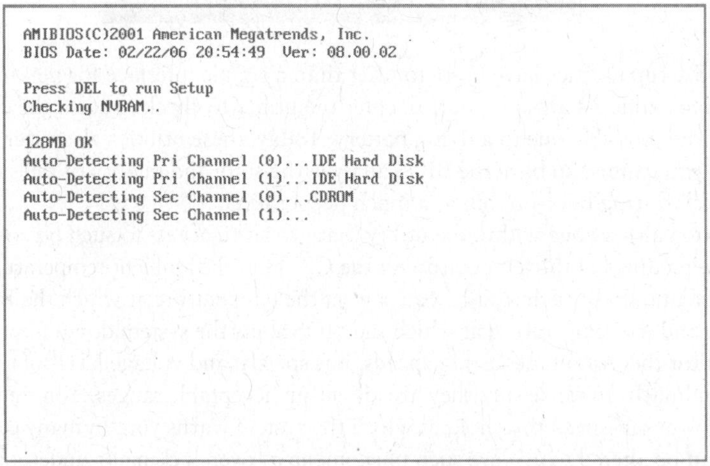

```
AMIBIOS(C)2001 American Megatrends, Inc.
BIOS Date: 02/22/06 20:54:49 Ver: 08.00.02

Press DEL to run Setup
Checking NVRAM..

128MB OK
Auto-Detecting Pri Channel (0)...IDE Hard Disk
Auto-Detecting Pri Channel (1)...IDE Hard Disk
Auto-Detecting Sec Channel (0)...CDROM
Auto-Detecting Sec Channel (1)...
```

Flashing the System BIOS

If ever you find that a hardware upgrade to your system is not recognized, even after the latest and correct drivers have been installed, perhaps a BIOS upgrade, also known as *flashing the BIOS*, is in order. Only certain hardware benefits from a BIOS upgrade, such as drives and a change of CPU or RAM types. Very often, this hardware is recognized immediately by the BIOS and has no associated driver. So, if your system doesn't recognize the new device, and there's no driver to install, the BIOS is a logical target.

Be clear about the fact that we are not talking about entering the BIOS setup utility and making changes to settings and subsequently saving your changes before exiting and rebooting. What we are referring to here is a replacement of the burned-in code within the BIOS itself. You might even notice after the upgrade that the BIOS setup utility looks different or has different pages and entries than before.

On older systems and certain newer ones, a loss of power during the upgrade results in catastrophe. The system becomes inoperable until you replace the BIOS chip, if possible, or the motherboard itself. Most new systems, however, have a failsafe or two. This could be a portion of the BIOS that does not get flashed and has just enough code to boot the system and access the upgrade image. It could be a passive section to which the upgrade is installed and switched to only if the upgrade is successful. Sometimes this is controlled onscreen, and other times, there may be a mechanism, such a jumper, involved in the recovery of the BIOS after a power event occurs. The safest bet is to make sure your laptop has plenty of battery power and is connected to AC power, or your desktop is connected to an uninterruptible power supply (UPS).

In all cases, regardless of BIOS maker, you should not consult BIOS companies—AMI, Award, Phoenix, etc. Instead, go back to the motherboard or system manufacturer; check its website, for example. These vendors have personalized their BIOS code after licensing it from the BIOS publisher. The vendor will give you access to the latest code as well as the appropriate flashing utility for its implementation.

CMOS and CMOS Battery

Your PC has to keep certain settings when it's turned off and its power cord is unplugged:

- Date
- Time
- Hard drive/optical drive configuration
- Memory
- CPU settings, such as overclocking

- Integrated ports (settings as well as enable/disable)
- Boot sequence
- Power management
- Virtualization support
- Security (passwords, trusted platform module settings, LoJack)

Your PC keeps these settings in a special memory chip called the complementary metal oxide semiconductor (*CMOS*) memory chip. Actually, CMOS (usually pronounced *see-moss*) is a manufacturing technology for integrated circuits. The first commonly used chip made from CMOS technology was a type of memory chip, the memory for the BIOS. As a result, the term *CMOS* stuck and is the accepted name for this memory chip.

The BIOS starts with its own default information and then reads information from the CMOS, such as which hard drive types are configured for this computer to use, which drive(s) it should search for boot sectors, and so on. Any overlapping information read from the CMOS overrides the default information from the BIOS. A lack of corresponding information in the CMOS does not delete information that the BIOS knows natively. This process is a merge, not a write-over. CMOS memory is usually *not* upgradable in terms of its capacity and might be integrated into the BIOS chip or the Southbridge.

To keep its settings, integrated circuit-based memory must have power constantly. When you shut off a computer, anything that is left in this type of memory is lost forever. The CMOS manufacturing technology produces chips with very low power requirements. As a result, today's electronic circuitry is more susceptible to damage from electrostatic discharge (ESD). Another ramification is that it doesn't take much of a power source to keep CMOS chips from losing their contents.

To prevent CMOS from losing its rather important information, motherboard manufacturers include a small battery called the *CMOS battery* to power the CMOS memory. The batteries come in different shapes and sizes, but they all perform the same function. Most CMOS batteries look like large watch batteries or small cylindrical batteries. Today's CMOS batteries are most often of a long-life, nonrechargeable lithium chemistry.

Jumpers and DIP Switches

Jumpers and DIP switches are used to configure various hardware options on the motherboard. (DIP stands for dual inline package and will be defined shortly.) For example, some legacy motherboards supported processors that use different core (internal) and I/O (external) voltages. Before this voltage regulation was automated, you had to set the motherboard to provide the correct voltage for the processor it was using. You did so by changing a setting on the motherboard with either a jumper or a DIP switch.

These days, jumpers on motherboards are used for more ancillary purposes, if at all, such as clearing the CMOS memory. Don't be surprised if you discover that the most complex of today's motherboards has no more than just this one jumper present. Figure 1.14 shows both a jumper set and DIP switches. Motherboards often have either several jumpers or one bank of DIP switches. Individual jumpers are often labeled with the moniker JP*x* (where *x* is a unique number for the jumper).

FIGURE 1.14   Jumpers and DIP switches

Jumper   Rocker-type DIP switch   Slide-type DIP switch

 Many of the motherboard settings that were set using jumpers and DIP switches are now either automatically detected or set manually in the BIOS setup program. Additionally, be careful not to place jumper caps (shunts) over pins just because they look like jumpers; they might be connector headers, the shorting of which could lead to widespread circuit or component destruction.

Front-Panel Connectors

From the time of the very first personal computer, there has been a minimum expectation as to the buttons and LEDs that should appear on the front of the case. Users expect a *power button* to use to turn the computer on (although these were on the side or back of very early PCs). The soft power feature available through the front power button, which is no more than a relay, allows access to multiple effects through the contact on the motherboard, based on how long the button is pressed. These effects can be changed through the BIOS or operating system. They expect a *power light*, often a green LED, to assure them that the button did its job. As time progressed, users were introduced to new things on the front panel of their computers. Each of these components depends on connectivity to the motherboard for its functionality. As a result, most motherboards have these standardized connections in common. The following list includes the majority of these landmarks:

- Power button
- Power light
- Reset button
- Drive activity lights
- Audio jacks
- USB ports

Reset Button

The *reset button* appeared as a way to reboot the computer from a cold startup point without removing power from the components. Keeping the machine powered tends to prolong the life of the electronics affected by power cycling. Pressing the reset button also gets around software lockups because the connection to the motherboard allows the system to restart from the hardware level. One disadvantage to power cycling is that certain circuits, such as memory chips, might need time to drain their charge for the reboot to be completely successful. This is why there is always a way to turn the computer off as well.

Drive Activity Light

In the early days of personal computing, the hard disk drive's LED had to be driven by the drive itself. Before long, the motherboard was equipped with drive headers, so adding pins to drive the *drive activity light* was no issue. These days, all motherboards supply this connectivity. The benefit of having one LED for all internal drives is that they are all represented on the front panel when only one LED is provided. The disadvantage might be that you cannot tell which drive is currently active. This tends to be a minor concern because you often know which drive you've accessed. If you haven't intentionally accessed any drive, it's likely the drive that holds the operating system or virtual-memory swap file is being accessed by the system itself. In contrast, external drives with removable media, such as optical drives, supply their own activity light on their faceplate.

Audio Jacks

Early generations of optical drives had to have a special cable attached to the rear of the drive. The cable was then attached to the sound card if audio CDs were to be heard through the speakers attached to the sound card. Sound emanating from a CD-ROM running an application, such as a game, did not have to take the same route and could travel through the same path from the drive as general data. The first enhancement to this arrangement came in the form of a front 3.5mm jack on the drive's faceplate that was intended for headphones but that could have speakers connected to it. The audio that normally ran across the special cable was rerouted to the front jack when something was plugged into it.

Many of today's motherboards have 10-position pin headers designed to connect to standardized front-panel audio modules. Some of these modules have legacy AC'97 analog ports on them while others have high-definition (HD) audio connections. Motherboards that accommodate both have a BIOS setting that allows you to choose which header you want to activate, with the HD setting most often being the default.

USB Ports

So many temporarily attached devices feature USB connectivity, such as USB keys (flash drives) and cameras, that front-panel connectivity is a must. Finding your way to the back of the system unit for a brief connection is hardly worth the effort in some cases. For many years, motherboards have supplied one or more 10-position headers for internal connectivity of front-panel USB ports. Because this header size is popular for many applications, only 9 positions tend to have pins protruding, while the 10th position acts as a key, showing up in different spots for each application to discourage the connection of the wrong cable. Figure 1.15 shows a USB connector on a motherboard.

FIGURE 1.15   A motherboard USB header

Identifying Purposes and Characteristics of Processors

Now that you've learned the basics of the motherboard, you need to learn about the most important component on the motherboard: the CPU. The role of the CPU, or central processing unit, is to control and direct all the activities of the computer using both external and internal buses. It is a processor chip consisting of an array of *millions* of transistors. Intel and Advanced Micro Devices (AMD) are the two largest PC-compatible CPU manufacturers. Their chips were featured in Table 1.1 during the discussion of the sockets in which they fit.

The term *chip* has grown to describe the entire package that a technician might install in a socket. However, the word originally denoted the silicon wafer that is generally hidden within the carrier that you actually see. The external pins you see are structures that can withstand insertion into a socket and that are carefully threaded from the wafer's minuscule contacts. Just imagine how fragile the structures must be that you don't see.

Older CPUs are generally square, with contacts arranged in a pin grid array (PGA). Prior to 1981, chips were found in a rectangle with two rows of 20 pins known as a dual inline package (DIP); see Figure 1.16. There are still integrated circuits that use the DIP form factor. However, the DIP form factor is no longer used for PC CPUs. Most CPUs use either the PGA/SPGA or LGA form factor.

Intel and AMD both make extensive use of an inverted socket/processor combination of sorts. As mentioned earlier, the land grid array (LGA) packaging calls for the pins to be placed on the motherboard, while the mates for these pins are on the processor packaging. As with PGA, LGA is named for the landmarks on the processor, not the ones on the motherboard. As a result, the grid of metallic contact points, called lands, on the bottom of the CPU gives this format its name.

FIGURE 1.16 DIP and PGA

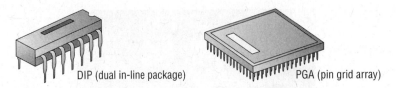

DIP (dual in-line package)   PGA (pin grid array)

You can easily identify which component inside the computer is the CPU because it is a large square lying flat on the motherboard with a very large heat sink and fan (as shown earlier in Figure 1.9). Figure 1.17 shows the location of the CPU in relation to the other components on a typical ATX motherboard. Notice how prominent the CPU is.

FIGURE 1.17 The location of a CPU inside a typical computer

CPU

Modern processors can feature the following characteristics:

Hyperthreading   This term refers to Intel's Hyper-Threading Technology (HTT). HTT is a form of simultaneous multithreading (SMT). SMT takes advantage of a modern CPU's superscalar architecture. Superscalar processors are able to have multiple instructions operating on separate data in parallel.

HTT-capable processors appear to the operating system to be two processors. As a result, the operating system can schedule two processes at the same time, as in the case of symmetric multiprocessing (SMP), where two or more processors use the same system resources. In fact, the operating system must support SMP in order to take advantage of HTT. If the current process stalls because of missing data caused by, say, cache or branch prediction issues, the execution resources of the processor can be reallocated for a different process that is ready to go, reducing processor downtime.

 Real World Scenario

Which CPU Do You Have?

The surest way to determine which CPU your computer is using is to open the case and view the numbers stamped on the CPU, a process that today requires removal of the active heat sink. However, you may be able to get an idea without opening the case and removing the heat sink and fan because many manufacturers place a very obvious sticker somewhere on the case indicating the processor type. Failing this, you can always go to the manufacturer's website and look up the information on the model of computer you have.

If you have a no-name clone, look in the System Properties pages, found by right-clicking My Computer (Computer in Vista and Windows 7) and selecting Properties. The General tab, which is the default, contains this information. Even more detailed information can be found by running the System Information utility from Start ➢ Accessories ➢ System Tools or by entering `msinfo32.exe` in the Start ➢ Run dialog box.

Another way to determine a computer's CPU is to save your work, exit any open programs, and restart the computer. Watch closely as the computer boots back up. You should see a notation that tells you what chip you are using.

Multicore   A processor that exhibits a multicore architecture has multiple completely separate processor dies in the same package. The operating system and applications see multiple processors in the same way that they see multiple processors in separate sockets. As with HTT, the operating system must support SMP to benefit from the separate processors. In addition, SMP is not a benefit if the applications run on the SMP system are not written for parallel processing. Dual-core and quad-core processors are common specific examples of the multicore technology.

Don't be confused by Intel's Core 2 labeling. The numeric component does not imply there are two cores. There was a Core series of 32-bit mobile processors that featured one (Solo) or two (Duo) processing cores on a single die (silicon wafer). The same dual-core die was used for both classes of Core CPU. The second core was disabled for Core Solo processors.

The 64-bit Core 2 product line can be thought of as a second generation of the Core series. Core 2, by the way, reunited Intel mobile and desktop computing—the Pentium 4 family had a separate Pentium M for mobile computing. Intel describes and markets the microcode of certain processors as "Core microarchitecture." As confusing as it may sound, the Core 2 processors are based on the Core microarchitecture; the Core processors are not. Core 2 processors come in Solo (mobile only), Duo, and four-core (Quad) implementations. Solo and Duo processors have a single die; Quad processors have two Duo dies. A more capable Extreme version exists for the Duo and Quad models.

Processors, such as certain models of AMD's Phenom series, can contain an odd number of multiple cores as well. The triple-core processor, which obviously contains three cores, is the most common implementation of multiple odd cores.

Throttling   CPU throttling allows reducing the operating frequency of the CPU during times of less demand or during battery operation. CPU throttling is very common in processors for mobile devices, where heat generation and system-battery drain are key issues of full power usage. You might discover throttling in action when you use a utility that reports a lower CPU clock frequency than expected. If the load on the system does not require full-throttle operation, there is no need to push such a limit.

Speed   The speed of the processor is generally described in clock frequency (MHz or GHz). Since the dawn of the personal computer industry, motherboards have included oscillators, quartz crystals shaved down to a specific geometry so that engineers know exactly how they will react when a current is run through them. The phenomenon of a quartz crystal vibrating when exposed to a current is known as the *piezoelectric effect*. The crystal (XTL) known as the system clock keeps the time for the flow of data on the motherboard. How the clock is used by the frontside bus leads to an *effective* clock rate known as the FSB speed. As shown in the section "Types of Memory" later in this chapter, the FSB speed is computed differently for different types of RAM (DDR, DDR2, etc.). From here, the CPU multiplies the FSB speed to produce its own internal clock rate, producing the third *speed* mentioned thus far.

As a result of the foregoing tricks of physics and mathematics, there can be a discrepancy between the frontside bus frequency and the internal frequency that the CPU uses to latch data and instructions through its pipelines. This disagreement between the numbers comes from the fact that the CPU is capable of splitting the clock signal it receives from the external oscillator that drives the frontside bus into multiple regular signals for its own internal use. In fact, you might be able to purchase a number of processors rated for different (internal) speeds that are all compatible with a single motherboard that has a frontside bus rated, for instance, at 1333MHz. Furthermore, you might be able to adjust the internal clock rate of the CPU you purchased through settings in the BIOS. The successful technician needs to be familiar with more basic information than this, however. The sidebar titled "Matching System Components" explains these basics.

Matching System Components

In a world of clock doubling, tripling, quadrupling, and so forth, it becomes increasingly important to pay attention to what you are buying when you purchase CPUs, memory, and motherboards a la carte. The only well-known relationship that exists in the marketplace among these components is the speed of the FSB (in MHz) and the throughput of the memory (in MBps). Because 8 bytes are transferred in parallel by a processor with a 64-bit (64 bits = 8 bytes) system data bus, you have to know the FSB rating before you choose the RAM for any particular modern motherboard. For example, an FSB of 800MHz requires memory rated at a throughput of 6400MBps (800 million cycles per second × 8 bytes per cycle).

Matching CPUs with motherboards or CPUs with memory requires consulting the documentation or packaging of the components. Generally, the CPU gets selected first. Once you know the CPU you want, the motherboard tends to come next. You must choose a motherboard that features a socket compatible with your chosen CPU. The FSB or QuickPath Interconnect (QPI) used on the selected motherboard/CPU dictates the RAM you should purchase.

32- and 64-bit processors   The set of data lines between the CPU and the primary memory of the system can be 32 or 64 bits wide, among other widths. The wider the bus, the more data that can be processed per unit of time, and hence, more work can be performed. Internal registers in the CPU might be only 32 bits wide, but with a 64-bit system bus, two separate pipelines can receive information simultaneously. For true 64-bit CPUs, which have 64-bit internal registers and can run x64 versions of Microsoft operating systems, the external system data bus will always be 64 bits wide or some larger multiple thereof.

Virtualization support   Many of today's CPUs support virtualization in hardware, which eases the burden on the system that software-based virtualization imposes. For more information on virtualization, see Chapter 12. Unlike AMD's AMD-V (*V* for virtualization) technology, which is widely inclusive of AMD's CPUs, Intel's Virtualization Technology (VT) is used by Intel to segment its market for CPUs made concurrently. For example, you can find Intel VT on the Core 2 Duo processor in the E6000 series and most of the E8000 series but not in the E7000 series. In some cases, you must also first enable the virtualization support in the BIOS before it can be used. If you have an Intel processor and would like to check its support of VT, visit

```
downloadcenter.intel.com/Detail_Desc.aspx?ProductID=1881&DwnldID=7838
```

to download the Intel Processor Identification utility. As shown in Figure 1.18, the CPU Technologies tab of this utility tells you if your CPU supports Intel VT.

FIGURE 1.18   Intel Processor Identification Utility

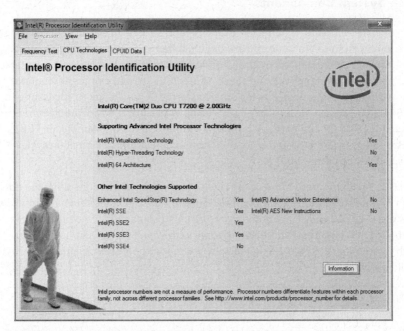

Integrated GPU   Intel and AMD both have a line of low-power CPUs aimed at the net-book and embedded markets that have built-in graphics processing units (GPUs). Building in specialized functionality to CPUs is nothing new, but before now, math coprocessors were some of the most complex features added on to the die of CPUs. A GPU, then, which is normally a large chip on your graphics adapter, is quite a bit more complex than any-thing heretofore integrated into the CPU. Integrated GPUs take much of the burden off of the CPU itself in addition to minimizing the amount of off-package communication that must occur, which improves overall system performance. As if that were not enough, the CPUs in this class are quite a bit smaller than standard CPUs. The Intel Atom and AMD Fusion lines of CPUs have built-in GPUs and open the door for other complex systems to be built into future processors.

Identifying Purposes and Characteristics of Memory

"More memory, more memory, I don't have enough memory!" Today, adding memory is one of the most popular, easy, and inexpensive ways to upgrade a computer. As the com-puter's CPU works, it stores data and instructions in the computer's memory. Contrary to what you might expect from an inexpensive solution, memory upgrades tend to afford the greatest performance increase as well, up to a point. Motherboards have memory limits; operating systems have memory limits; CPUs have memory limits.

To visually identify memory within a computer, look for several thin rows of small circuit boards sitting vertically, potentially packed tightly together near the processor. In situations where only one memory stick is installed, it will be that stick and a few empty slots that are tightly packed together. Figure 1.19 shows where memory is located in a system.

FIGURE 1.19   Location of memory within a system

Important Memory Terms

There are a few technical terms and phrases that you need to understand with regard to memory and its function:

- Parity checking
- Error-correcting code (ECC)
- Single- and double-sided memory
- Single-, dual-, and triple-channel memory

These terms are discussed in detail in the following sections.

Parity Checking and Memory Banks

Parity checking is a rudimentary error-checking scheme that offers no error correction. Parity checking works most often on a byte, or 8 bits, of data. A ninth bit is added at the transmitting end and removed at the receiving end so that it does not affect the actual data transmitted. The four most common parity schemes affecting this extra bit are known as even, odd, mark, and space. Even and odd parity are used in systems that actually compute parity. Mark (a term for a 1 bit) and space (a term for a 0 bit) parity are used in systems that do not compute parity but expect to see a fixed bit value stored in the parity location. Systems that do not support or reserve the location required for the parity bit are said to implement *non-parity* memory.

The most basic model for implementing memory in a computer system uses eight memory chips to form a set. Each memory chip holds millions or billions of bits of information, each in its own *cell*. For every byte in memory, one bit is stored in each of the eight chips. A ninth chip is added to the set to support the parity bit in systems that require it. One or more of these sets, implemented as individual chips or as chips mounted on a memory module, form *memory bank*.

A bank of memory is required for the computer system to electrically recognize that the minimum number of memory components or the proper number of additional memory components has been installed. The width of the system data bus, the external bus of the processor, dictates how many memory chips or modules are required to satisfy a bank. For example, one 32-bit, 72-pin SIMM (single inline memory module) satisfies a bank for an old 32-bit CPU, such as a 386 or 486 processor. Two such modules are required to satisfy a bank for a 64-bit processor, a Pentium, for instance. However, only a single 64-bit, 168-pin DIMM is required to satisfy the same Pentium processor. For those modules that have fewer than eight or nine chips mounted on them, more than one bit for every byte is being handled by some of the chips. For example, if you see three chips mounted, the two larger chips probably handle four bits, a nybble, from each byte stored, and the third, smaller chip probably handles the single parity bit for each byte.

Even and odd parity schemes operate on each byte in the set of memory chips. In each case, the number of bits set to a value of 1 is counted up. If there are an even number of 1 bits in the byte (0, 2, 4, 6, or 8), even parity stores a 0 in the ninth bit, the parity bit; otherwise, it stores a 1 to even up the count. Odd parity does just the opposite, storing a 1 in the parity bit to make an even number of 1s odd and a 0 to keep an odd number of 1s odd. You can see that this is effective only for determining if there was a blatant error in the set of bits received, but there is no indication as to where the error is and how to fix it. Furthermore, the total 1-bit count is not important, only whether it's even or odd. Therefore, in either the even or odd scheme, if an even number of bits is altered in the same byte during transmission, the error goes undetected because flipping two, four, six, or all eight bits results in an even number of 1s remaining even and an odd number of 1s remaining odd.

Mark and space parity are used in systems that want to see nine bits for every byte transmitted but don't compute the parity bit's value based on the bits in the byte. Mark parity always uses a 1 in the parity bit, and space parity always uses a 0. These schemes offer less error detection capability than the even and odd schemes because only changes in the parity bit can be detected. Again, parity checking is not error correction; it's error detection only, and not the best form of error detection at that. Nevertheless, finding an error can lock up the entire system and display a memory parity error. Enough of these errors and you need to replace the memory.

In the early days of personal computing, almost all memory was parity based. As quality has increased over the years, parity checking in the RAM subsystem has become rarer. As noted earlier, if parity checking is not supported, there will generally be fewer chips per module, usually one less per column of RAM.

Error Checking and Correction

The next step in the evolution of memory error detection is known as error-correcting code (*ECC*). If memory supports ECC, check bits are generated and stored with the data. An algorithm is performed on the data and its check bits whenever the memory is accessed. If the result of the algorithm is all zeros, then the data is deemed valid and processing continues. ECC can detect single- and double-bit errors and actually correct single-bit errors.

Single- and Double-Sided Memory

Commonly speaking, the terms *single-sided memory* and *double-sided memory* refer to how some memory modules have chips on one side while others have chips on both sides. Double-sided memory is essentially treated by the system as two separate memory modules. Motherboards that support such memory have memory controllers that must switch between the two "sides" of the modules and, at any particular moment, can access only the side they have switched to. Double-sided memory allows more memory to be inserted into a computer using half the physical space of single-sided memory, which requires no switching by the memory controller.

Single-, Dual-, and Triple-Channel Memory

Standard memory controllers manage access to memory in chunks of the same size as the system bus's data width. This is considered communicating over a single channel. Most modern processors have a 64-bit system data bus. This means a standard memory controller can transfer exactly 64 bits of information at a time. Communicating over a single channel is a bottleneck in an environment where the CPU and memory can both operate faster than the conduit between them. Up to a point, every channel added in parallel between the CPU and RAM serves to ease this constriction.

Memory controllers that support dual- and triple-channel memory implementation were developed in an effort to alleviate the bottleneck between the CPU and RAM. *Dual-channel memory* is the memory controller's coordination of two memory banks to work as a synchronized set during communication with the CPU, doubling the specified system bus width from the memory's perspective. *Triple-channel memory*, then, demands the coordination of three memory modules at a time.

The major difference between dual- and triple-channel architectures is that triple-channel memory employs a form of interleaving that reduces the amount of information transferred by each module. Nevertheless, there is an overall performance increase over that of dual-channel memory because of the ability to access more information per unit of time with triple-channel memory.

Because today's processors largely have 64-bit external data buses, and because one stick of memory satisfies this bus width, there is a 1:1 ratio between banks and modules. This means that implementing dual- and triple-channel memory in today's most popular computer systems requires that pairs or triads of memory modules be installed at a time. Note, however, that it's the motherboard, not the memory, that implements dual- and triple-channel memory (more on this in a moment). *Single-channel memory*, in contrast, is the classic memory model that dictates only that a complete bank be satisfied whenever memory is initially installed or added. One bank supplies only half the width of the effective bus created by dual-channel support, for instance, which by definition pairs two banks at a time.

In almost all cases, multichannel implementations support single-channel installation, but poorer performance should be expected. The same loss of performance occurs when only two modules are installed in a triple-channel motherboard. Multichannel motherboards include slots of different colors, usually one of each color per set of slots. To use only a single channel, you populate slots of the same color, skipping neighboring slots to do so. Filling neighboring slots in a dual-channel motherboard takes advantage of its dual-channel capability.

Because of the special tricks that are played with memory subsystems to improve overall system performance, care must be taken during the installation of disparate memory modules. In the worst case, the computer will cease to function when modules of different speeds, different capacities, or different numbers of sides are placed together in slots of the same channel. If all of these parameters are identical, there should be no problem with pairing modules. Nevertheless, problems could still occur when modules from two different manufacturers or certain unsupported manufacturers are installed, all other parameters being the same. Technical support or documentation from the manufacturer of your motherboard should be able to help with such issues.

Although it's not the make-up of the memory that leads to dual-channel support but instead the technology on which the motherboard is based, some memory manufacturers still package and sell pairs and triplets of memory modules in an effort to give you peace of mind when you're buying memory for a system that implements dual- or triple-channel memory architecture. Keep in mind, the motherboard memory slots have the distinctive color coding, not the memory modules.

Types of Memory

Memory comes in many formats. Each one has a particular set of features and characteristics, making it best suited for a particular application. Some decisions about the application of the memory type are based on suitability; others are based on affordability to consumers or marketability to computer manufacturers. The following list gives you an idea of the vast array of memory types and subtypes:

- DRAM
  - Asynchronous DRAM
    - FPM DRAM

- EDO DRAM
- BEDO DRAM
- Synchronous DRAM
  - SDR SDRAM
  - DDR SDRAM
  - DDR2 SDRAM
  - DDR3 SDRAM
  - DRDRAM
- SRAM
- ROM

I Can't Fill All My Memory Slots

As a reminder, most motherboard manufacturers document the quantity and types of modules that their equipment supports. Consult your documentation, whether in print or online, when you have questions about supported memory. Most manufacturers require that slower memory be inserted in lower-numbered memory slots. This is because such a system adapts to the first module it sees, looking at the lower-numbered slots first. Counterintuitively, however, it might be required that you install modules of larger capacity rather than smaller modules in lower-numbered slots.

Additionally, memory technology continues to advance after each generation of motherboard chipsets is announced. Don't be surprised when you attempt to install a single module of the highest available capacity in your motherboard and the system doesn't recognize the module, either by itself or with others. That capacity of module might not have been in existence when the motherboard's chipset was released. Sometimes flashing the BIOS is all that is required. Consult the motherboard's documentation!

One common point of confusion, not related to capacity, when memory is installed is lack of recognition of four modules when two or three modules work fine, for example. In such a case, let's say your motherboard's memory controller supports a total of four modules. Recall that a double-sided module acts like two separate modules. If you are using double-sided memory, your motherboard might limit you to two such modules comprising four sides (essentially four virtual modules), even though you have four slots on the board. If instead you start with three single-sided modules, when you attempt to install double-sided module in the fourth slot, you are essentially asking the motherboard to accept five modules, which it cannot.

Pay particular attention to all synchronous DRAM types. Note that the type of memory does not dictate the packaging of the memory. Conversely, however, you might notice one particular memory packaging holding the same type of memory every time you come across it. Nevertheless, there is no requirement to this end. Let's detail the intricacies of some of these memory types.

DRAM

DRAM is dynamic random access memory. (This is what most people are talking about when they mention RAM.) When you expand the memory in a computer, you are adding DRAM chips. You use DRAM to expand the memory in the computer because it's a cheaper type of memory. Dynamic RAM chips are cheaper to manufacture than most other types because they are less complex. *Dynamic* refers to the memory chips' need for a constant update signal (also called a refresh signal) in order to keep the information that is written there. If this signal is not received every so often, the information will bleed off and cease to exist. Currently, the most popular implementations of DRAM are based on synchronous DRAM and include SDR SDRAM, DDR, DDR2, DDR3, and DRDRAM. Before discussing these technologies, let's take a quick look at the legacy asynchronous memory types, none of which should appear on modern exams.

Asynchronous DRAM

Asynchronous DRAM (ADRAM) is characterized by its independence from the CPU's external clock. Asynchronous DRAM chips have codes on them that end in a numerical value that is related to (often $\frac{1}{10}$ of the actual value of) the access time of the memory. Access time is essentially the difference between the time when the information is requested from memory and the time when the data is returned. Common access times attributed to asynchronous DRAM were in the 40- to 120-nanosecond (ns) vicinity. A lower access time is obviously better for overall performance.

Because ADRAM is not synchronized to the frontside bus, you would often have to insert wait states through the BIOS setup for a faster CPU to be able to use the same memory as a slower CPU. These wait states represented intervals that the CPU had to mark time and do nothing while waiting for the memory subsystem to become ready again for subsequent access.

Common asynchronous DRAM technologies included Fast Page Mode (FPM), Extended Data Out (EDO), and Burst EDO (BEDO). Feel free to investigate the details of these particular technologies, but a thorough discussion of these memory types is not necessary here. The A+ technician should be concerned with synchronous forms of RAM, which are the only types of memory being installed in mainstream computer systems today.

Synchronous DRAM

Synchronous DRAM (*SDRAM*) shares a common clock signal with the computer's system-bus clock, which provides the common signal that all local-bus components use for each step that they perform. This characteristic ties SDRAM to the speed of the FSB and hence the processor, eliminating the need to configure the CPU to wait for the memory to catch up.

Originally, *SDRAM* was the term used to refer to the only form of synchronous DRAM on the market. As the technology progressed, and more was being done with each clock signal on the FSB, various forms of SDRAM were developed. What was once called simply SDRAM needed a new name retroactively. Today, we use the term *single data rate SDRAM* (SDR SDRAM) to refer to this original type of SDRAM.

SDR SDRAM

With SDR SDRAM, every time the system clock ticks, 1 bit of data can be transmitted per data pin, limiting the bit rate per pin of SDRAM to the corresponding numerical value of the clock's frequency. With today's processors interfacing with memory using a parallel data-bus width of 8 bytes (hence the term *64-bit processor*), a 100MHz clock signal produces 800MBps. That's mega*bytes* per second, not mega*bits*. Such memory modules are referred to as PC100, named for the true FSB clock rate they rely on. PC100 was preceded by PC66 and succeeded by PC133, which used a 133MHz clock to produce 1066MBps of throughput.

Note that throughput in megabytes per second is easily computed as eight times the rating in the name. This trick works for the more advanced forms of SDRAM as well. The common thread is the 8-byte system data bus. Incidentally, you can double throughput results when implementing dual-channel memory.

DDR SDRAM

Double data rate (*DDR*) SDRAM earns its name by doubling the transfer rate of ordinary SDRAM; it does so by double-pumping the data, which means transferring a bit per pin on both the rising and falling edges of the clock signal. This obtains twice the transfer rate at the same FSB clock frequency. It's the increasing clock frequency that generates heating issues with newer components, so keeping the clock the same is an advantage. The same 100MHz clock gives a DDR SDRAM system the impression of a 200MHz clock in comparison to an SDR SDRAM system. For marketing purposes and to aid in the comparison of disparate products (DDR vs. SDR, for example), the industry has settled on the practice of using this effective clock rate as the speed of the FSB.

Module Throughput Related to FSB Speed

There is always an 8:1 module-to-chip (or module–to–FSB speed) numbering ratio because of the 8 bytes that are transferred at a time with 64-bit processors (*not* because of the ratio of 8 bits per byte). The following formula explains how this relationship works:

FSB in MHz	(cycles/second)
X 8 bytes	(bytes/cycle)
throughput	(bytes/second)

Because the actual system clock speed is rarely mentioned in marketing literature, on packaging, or on store shelves for DDR and higher, you can use this advertised FSB frequency in your computations for DDR throughput. For example, with a 100MHz clock and two operations per cycle, motherboard makers will market their boards as having an FSB of 200MHz. Multiplying this effective rate by 8 bytes transferred per cycle, the data rate is 1600MBps. Because DDR made throughput a bit trickier to compute, the industry began using this final throughput figure to name the memory modules instead of the actual frequency, which was used when naming SDR modules. This makes the result seem many times better (and much more marketable), while it's really only twice (or so) as good, or close to it.

In this example, the module is referred to as PC1600, based on a throughput of 1600MBps. The chips that go into making PC1600 modules are named DDR200 for the effective FSB frequency of 200MHz. Stated differently, the industry uses DDR200 memory chips to manufacture PC1600 memory modules.

Let's make sure you grasp the relationship between the speed of the FSB and the name for the related chips as well as the relationship between the name of the chips (or the speed of the FSB) and the name of the modules. Consider an FSB of 400MHz, meaning an actual clock signal of 200MHz, by the way—the FSB is double the actual clock for DDR, remember. It should be clear that this motherboard requires modules populated with DDR400 chips and that you'll find such modules marketed and sold as PC3200.

Let's try another. What do you need for a motherboard that features a 333MHz FSB (actual clock is 166MHz)? Well, just using the 8:1 rule mentioned earlier, you might be on the lookout for a PC2667 module. However, note that sometimes the numbers have to be played with a bit to come up with the industry's marketing terms. You'll have an easier time finding PC2700 modules that are designed specifically for a motherboard like yours, with an FSB of 333MHz. The label isn't always technically accurate, but round numbers sell better, perhaps. The important concept here is that if you find PC2700 modules and PC2667 modules, there's absolutely no difference; they both have a 2667MBps throughput rate. Go for the best deal; just make sure the memory manufacturer is reputable.

DDR2 SDRAM

Think of the 2 in *DDR2* as yet another multiplier of 2 in the SDRAM technology, using a lower peak voltage to keep power consumption down (1.8V vs. the 2.5V of DDR). Still double-pumping, DDR2, like DDR, uses both sweeps of the clock signal for data transfer. Internally, DDR2 further splits each clock pulse in two, doubling the number of operations it can perform per FSB clock cycle. Through enhancements in the electrical interface and buffers, as well as through adding off-chip drivers, DDR2 nominally produces four times the throughput that SDR is capable of producing.

Continuing the DDR example, DDR2, using a 100MHz actual clock, transfers data in four operations per cycle (effective 400MHz FSB) and still 8 bytes per operation, for a total of 3200MBps. Just like DDR, DDR2 names its chips based on the perceived frequency. In this case, you would be using DDR2-400 chips. DDR2 carries on the effective-FSB frequency method for naming modules but cannot simply call them PC3200 modules because those already exist in the DDR world. DDR2 calls these modules PC2-3200 (note the dash to keep the numeric components separate).

As another example, it should make sense that PC2-5300 modules are populated with DDR2-667 chips. Recall that you might have to play with the numbers a bit. If you multiply the well-known FSB speed of 667MHz by 8 to figure out what modules you need, you might go searching for PC2-5333 modules. You might find someone advertising such modules, but most compatible modules will be labeled PC2-5300 for the same marketability mentioned earlier. They both support 5333MBps of throughput.

DDR3 SDRAM

The next generation of memory devices was designed to roughly double the performance of DDR2 products. Based on the functionality and characteristics of DDR2's proposed successor, most informed consumers and some members of the industry surely assumed the forthcoming name would be DDR4. This was not to be, however, and DDR3 was born. This naming convention proved that the 2 in DDR2 was not meant to be a multiplier but instead a revision mark of sorts. Well, if DDR2 was the second version of DDR, then DDR3 is the third. *DDR3* is a memory type that was designed to be twice as fast as the DDR2 memory that operates with the same system clock speed. Just as DDR2 was required to lower power consumption to make up for higher frequencies, DDR3 must do the same. In fact, the peak voltage for DDR3 is only 1.5V.

The most commonly found range of actual clock speeds for DDR3 tends to be from 133MHz at the low end to less than 300MHz. Because double-pumping continues with DDR3 and because four operations occur at each wave crest (eight operations per cycle), this frequency range translates to common FSB implementations from 1066MHz to more than 2000MHz in DDR3 systems. These memory devices are named following the conventions established earlier. Therefore, if you buy a motherboard with a 1600MHz FSB, you know immediately that you need a memory module populated with DDR3-1600 chips because the chips are always named for the FSB speed. Using the 8:1 module-to-chip/FSB naming rule, the modules you need would be called PC3-12800, supporting a 12800MBps throughput.

The earliest DDR3 chips, however, were based on a 100MHz actual clock signal, so we can build on our earlier example, which was also based on an actual clock rate of 100MHz. With eight operations per cycle, the FSB on DDR3 motherboards is rated at 800MHz, quite a lot of efficiency while still not needing to change the original clock our examples began with. Applying the 8:1 rule again, the resulting RAM modules for this motherboard are called PC3-6400 and support a throughput of 6400MBps, carrying chips called DDR3-800, again named for the FSB speed.

DRDRAM

Direct Rambus DRAM (DRDRAM), named for *Rambus*, the company that designed it, is a legacy proprietary SDRAM technology, sometimes called RDRAM, dropping *direct*, and most often associated with server platforms. Although other specifications preceded it, the first motherboard DRDRAM model was known as PC800. As with non-DRDRAM specifications that use this naming convention, PC800 specifies that, using a faster 400MHz actual clock signal and double-pumping like DDR SDRAM, an effective frequency and FSB speed of 800MHz is created.

🌐 Real World Scenario

Choosing the Right Memory for Your CPU

Picking out the right memory for your CPU and motherboard is all about understanding the minimum performance required for the CPU you choose. Sometimes, the motherboard you choose to mate with the CPU makes your decision for you. If you go with the cheaper motherboard, you might find that just a single channel of DDR2 is all you need to worry about. Otherwise, the more expensive boards might support dual- or triple-channel memory and require DDR3 modules. It's usually safe to assume that the higher price of admission gets you better performance. This is generally true on paper, but you might find that the higher-end setup doesn't knock your socks off the way you expected.

Let's say you head down to your local computer store, where motherboards, CPUs, memory, and other computer components are sold a la carte. You're interested in putting together your own system from scratch. Usually, you will have a CPU in mind that you would like to use in your new system. Assume you choose, for example, an Intel Core 2 Quad Q9650 processor. It's fast enough, at 3GHz, but it calls for an older LGA 775 socket, meaning you'll save a bit of money on that performance but you won't be approaching the state of the art. Nevertheless, the FSB this CPU is outfitted with runs at a healthy 1333MHz, and its associated chipsets call for DDR3 memory. As a result, you will need to purchase one or more modules that contain DDR3-1333 chips, especially if you buy a motherboard that supports dual-channel memory. Therefore, you'll be buying PC3-10600 modules (multiplying 1333 by 8 and adjusting for marketing). Recall the 8:1 module-to-chip/FSB naming convention.

Perhaps you'd prefer the pricier Intel Core i7-990X Extreme Edition six-core processor. With a little research, you discover that Intel did away with the FSB by moving the memory controller out of the Northbridge and into the CPU. What remains is what Intel calls the QPI. QPI is a PCIe-like path that uses 20 bidirectional lanes to move data exceedingly fast between the CPU and RAM, requiring less capable RAM than FSB CPUs to do the same amount of work. The Core i7 requires a motherboard that has an LGA 1366 socket and supports a minimum of DDR3-1066 memory chips (chips, not modules). Therefore, you'll be buying at least one stick of your chosen capacity of PC3-8500 (multiplying 1066 by 8), two or three sticks if you decide to take advantage of the chip's ability to access as many as three channels of memory. These days, you'll have better luck starting with a minimum of PC3-10600 modules because PC3-8500s are becoming harder to find. The Core i7 is designed for desktop use; server-level processors that use the Intel QPI include the Xeon and Itanium.

This original naming of DRDRAM modules was based on FSB speed, in a dissimilar fashion to other forms of SDRAM after SDR, which are named for their throughput in MBps. You might recall, for those memory types, that the FSB speed was used to name the actual chips on the modules, not the modules themselves. PC800 DRDRAM, then, features a double-pumped 800MHz FSB. Newer modules, however, such as the 32-bit RIMM 6400, are named for their actual throughput, 6400MBps, in this case. The section "RIMM" later in this chapter details the physical details of the modules.

There are only 16 data pins per channel with DRDRAM, versus 64 bits per channel in other SDRAM implementations. This fact results in a 16-bit (2-byte) channel. A 2-byte packet, therefore, is exchanged during each read/write cycle, bringing the overall transfer rate of PC800 DRDRAM to 1600MBps per channel. DRDRAM chipsets require two 16-bit channels to communicate simultaneously for the same read/write request, creating a mandatory 32-bit dual-channel mode. Two PC800 DRDRAM modules in a dual-channel configuration produce transfer rates of 3200MBps. In motherboards that support 32-bit modules, you would use a single RIMM 3200 to achieve this same 3200MBps of throughput, using the same actual 400MHz clock and 800MHz FSB and transferring 4 bytes (32 bits) at a time.

Despite DRDRAM's performance advantages, it has some drawbacks that kept it from taking over the market in its day. Increased latency, heat output, complexity in the manufacturing process, and cost are the primary shortcomings. The additional heat that individual DRDRAM chips put out led to the requirement for heat sinks on all modules. High manufacturing costs and high licensing fees led to tripling the cost to consumers over SDR. Soon, other SDRAM technologies obviated the need to specialize with DRDRAM. A dual-channel platform using standard PC3200 DDR modules transfers 16 bytes (128 bits) per read/write request, producing the same throughput rate of 6400MBps as high-end RIMM 6400 modules. As a result, and because of the eventual advent of DDR2 and DDR3, DRDRAM no longer held any performance advantage.

To put each of the SDRAM types into perspective, consult Table 1.2, which summarizes how each technology in the SDRAM arena would achieve a transfer rate of 3200MBps, even if only theoretically. For example, PC400 doesn't exist in the SDR SDRAM world.

TABLE 1.2: How some memory types transfer 3200MBps per channel

Memory Type	Actual/Effective (FSB) Clock Frequency (MHz)	Bytes per Transfer
SDR SDRAM PC400*	400/400	8
DDR SDRAM PC3200	200/400	8
DDR2 SDRAM PC2-3200	100/400	8
DDR3 SDRAM PC3-3200**	50/400	8
DRDRAM PC800	400/800	4***

* SDR SDRAM PC400 does not exist.

**PC3-3200 does not exist and is too slow for DDR3.

***Assuming requisite 32-bit dual-channel mode.

SRAM

Static random access memory (SRAM) doesn't require a refresh signal like DRAM does. The chips are more complex and are thus more expensive. However, they are considerably faster. DRAM access times come in at 40 nanoseconds (ns) or more; SRAM has access times faster than 10ns. SRAM is classically used for cache memory.

ROM

ROM stands for read-only memory. It is called read-only because the original form of this memory could not be written to. Once information had been etched on a silicon chip and manufactured into the ROM package, the information couldn't be changed. If you ran out of use for the information or code on the ROM, you added little eyes and some cute fuzzy extras and you had a bug that sat on your desk and looked back at you. Some form of ROM is normally used to store the computer's BIOS because this information normally does not change very often.

The system ROM in the original IBM PC contained the power-on self-test (POST), BIOS, and cassette BASIC. Later IBM computers and compatibles include everything but the cassette BASIC. The system ROM enables the computer to "pull itself up by its boot-straps," or *boot* (find and start the operating system).

Through the years, different forms of ROM were developed that could be altered, later ones more easily than earlier ones. The first generation was the programmable ROM (PROM), which could be written to for the first time in the field using a special programming device, but then no more. You had a new bug to keep the ROM bug company. Liken this to the burning of a CD-R. Don't need it any longer? You've got a handy coaster. Following the PROM came erasable PROM (EPROM), which was able to be erased using ultraviolet light and subsequently reprogrammed using the original programming device. These days, our flash memory is a form of electronically erasable PROM (EEPROM), which does not require UV light to erase its contents but rather a slightly higher than normal electrical pulse.

Although the names of these memory devices are different, they all contain ROM. Therefore, regardless which of these technologies is used to manufacture a BIOS chip, it's never incorrect to say that the result is a ROM chip.

Memory Packaging

First of all, it should be noted that each motherboard supports memory based on the speed of the frontside bus (or the CPU's QPI) and the memory's form factor. For example, if the motherboard's FSB is rated at a maximum speed of 1333MHz and you install memory that is rated at 1066MHz, the memory will operate at only 1066MHz, if it works at all, thus making the computer operate slower than it could. In their documentation, most motherboard manufacturers list which type(s) of memory they support as well as its maximum speeds and required pairings.

The memory slots on a motherboard are designed for particular module form factors or styles. RAM historically evolved from form factors no longer seen for such applications, such as dual inline package (DIP), single inline memory module (SIMM), and single inline pin package (SIPP). The most popular form factors for primary memory modules today are as follows:

- DIMM
- RIMM
- SODIMM
- MicroDIMM

Note also that the various CPUs on the market tend to support only one form of physical memory packaging due to the memory controller in the Northbridge or CPU itself (QPI). For example, the Intel Pentium 4 class of processors was always paired with DIMMs, while certain early Intel Xeon processors mated only with RIMMs. Laptops and smaller devices require SODIMMs or smaller memory packaging. So, in addition to coordinating the speed of the components, their form factor is an issue that must be addressed.

DIMM

One type of memory package is known as a DIMM. As mentioned earlier in this chapter, DIMM stands for dual inline memory module. DIMMs are 64-bit memory modules that are used as a package for the SDRAM family: SDR, DDR, DDR2, and DDR3. The term *dual* refers to the fact that, unlike their SIMM predecessors, DIMMs differentiate the functionality of the pins on one side of the module from the corresponding pins on the other side. With 84 pins per side, this makes 168 independent pins on each standard SDR module, as shown with its two keying notches as well as the last pin labeled 84 on the side shown in Figure 1.20.

FIGURE 1.20   An SDR dual inline memory module (DIMM)

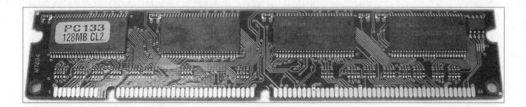

The DIMM used for DDR memory has a total of 184 pins and a single keying notch, while the DIMM used for DDR2 has a total of 240 pins, one keying notch, and possibly an aluminum cover for both sides, called a *heat spreader* and designed like a heat sink to dissipate heat away from the memory chips and prevent overheating. The DDR3 DIMM is similar to that of DDR2. It has 240 pins and a single keying notch, but the notch is in a different location to avoid cross insertion. Not only is the DDR3 DIMM physically incompatible with DDR2 DIMM slots, it's also electrically incompatible.

Figure 1.21 is a photo of a DDR2 module. A matched pair of DDR3 modules with heat spreaders, suitable for dual-channel use in a high-end graphics adapter or motherboard, is shown in Figure 1.22.

FIGURE 1.21 A DDR2 SDRAM module

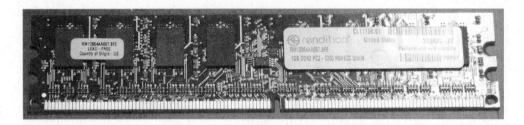

FIGURE 1.22 A pair of DDR3 SDRAM modules

Inserting and Removing Memory Modules

The original single inline memory modules had to be inserted into their slots at a 45° angle. The installer then had to apply slight pressure as the module was maneuvered upright at a 90° angle to the motherboard where a locking mechanism would grip the module and prevent it from returning to its 45° position. This procedure created a pressure that reinforced the contact of the module with its slot. Releasing the clips on either end of the module unlocked it and allowed it to return to 45°, where it could be removed.

DIMM slots, by comparison, have no spring action. DIMMs are inserted straight into the slot with the locking tabs pulled away from the module. The locking tabs are at either end of the module and they automatically snap into place, securing the module. Pulling the tabs away from the module releases the module from the slot, allowing it to be effortlessly removed.

RIMM

Assumed to stand for Rambus inline memory module but not really an acronym, RIMM is a trademark of Rambus Inc. and perhaps a clever play on the acronym DIMM, a competing form factor and by definition, what a RIMM actually is. A RIMM is a custom memory module that carries DRDRAM and varies in physical specification, based on whether it is a 16-bit or 32-bit module. The 16-bit modules have 184 pins and two keying notches, while 32-bit modules have 232 pins and only one keying notch, reminiscent of the trend in SDRAM-to-DDR evolution. Figure 1.23 shows a RIMM module, including the aluminum heat spreaders.

FIGURE 1.23   A Rambus RIMM module

As mentioned earlier, DRDRAM is based on a 16-bit channel. However, dual-channel implementation is not optional with DRDRAM; it's required. The dual-channel architecture can be implemented utilizing two separate 16-bit RIMMs (leading to the generally held view that RIMMs must always be installed in pairs) or the newer 32-bit single-module design.

Typically, motherboards with the 16-bit single- or dual-channel implementation provide four RIMM slots that must be filled in pairs, while the 32-bit versions provide two RIMM slots that can be filled one at a time. A 32-bit RIMM essentially has two 16-bit modules built in (possibly contributing to the persistence of the belief in the "pair" requirement) and requires only a single motherboard slot, albeit a physically different slot. So you must be sure of the module your motherboard accepts before upgrading.

Unique to the use of RIMM modules, a computer must have every RIMM slot occupied. Even one vacant slot will cause the computer not to boot. Any slot not populated with live memory requires an inexpensive blank of sorts called a continuity RIMM, or C-RIMM, for its role of keeping electrical continuity in the DRDRAM channel until the signal can terminate on the motherboard. Think of it like a fusible link in a string of holiday lights. It seems to do nothing, but no light works without it. However, 32-bit modules terminate themselves and do not rely on the motherboard circuitry for termination, so vacant 32-bit slots require a module known as a continuity and termination RIMM (CT-RIMM).

SODIMM

Notebook computers and other computers that require much smaller components don't use standard RAM packages, such as the DIMM. Instead, they call for a much smaller memory form factor, such as a small outline DIMM. SODIMMs are available in many physical implementations, including the older 32-bit (72- and 100-pin) configuration and newer 64-bit (144-pin SDR SDRAM, 200-pin DDR/DDR2, and 204-pin DDR3) configurations.

All 64-bit modules have a single keying notch. The 144-pin module's notch is slightly off-center. Note that although the 200-pin SODIMMs for DDR and DDR2 have slightly different keying, it's not so different that you don't need to pay close attention to differentiate the two. They are not, however, interchangeable. Figure 1.24 shows an example of a 144-pin, 64-bit SDR module. Figure 1.25 is a photo of a 200-pin DDR2 SODIMM.

FIGURE 1.24   144-pin SODIMM

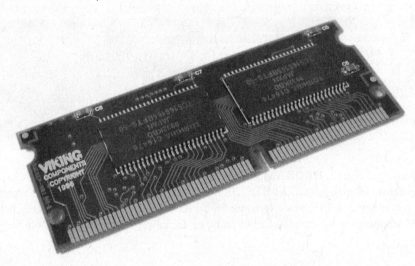

FIGURE 1.25   200-pin DDR2 SODIMM

MicroDIMM

A newer, smaller, and rarer RAM form factor is the MicroDIMM. The MicroDIMM is an extremely small RAM form factor. In fact, it is over 50 percent smaller than a SODIMM, only 45.5 millimeters (about 1.75 inches) long and 30 millimeters (about 1.2 inches—a bit bigger than a quarter) wide. It was designed for the ultralight and portable subnotebook style of computer. Standard versions of these modules have 144 pins for SDR SDRAM, 172 pins for DDR DRAM, and 214 pins for DDR2 SDRAM. MicroDIMMs are similar to a DIMM in that they use a 64-bit data bus. The insertion keying of the MicroDIMM for card-edge versions is reminiscent of the SIMM; only one notch and on one of the two insertion corners of the module instead of somewhere in the middle. Figure 1.26 shows an artist's rendering of a MicroDIMM module. Often employed in laptop computers, SODIMMs and MicroDIMMs are mentioned in Chapter 9 as well.

FIGURE 1.26   172-pin MicroDIMM

Identifying Purposes and Characteristics of Cooling Systems

It's a basic concept of physics: Electronic components turn electricity into work and heat. The excess heat must be dissipated or it will shorten the life of the components. In some cases (like with the CPU), the component will produce so much heat that it can destroy itself in a matter of seconds if there is not some way to remove this extra heat.

Air-cooling methods are used to cool the internal components of most PCs. With air cooling, the movement of air removes the heat from the component. Sometimes, large blocks of metal called heat sinks are attached to a heat-producing component in order to dissipate the heat more rapidly.

Fans

When you turn on a computer, you will often hear lots of whirring. Contrary to popular opinion, the majority of the noise isn't coming from the hard disk (unless it's about to go bad). Most of this noise is coming from the various fans inside the computer. Fans provide airflow within the computer.

Most PCs have a combination of these seven fans:

Front intake fan   This fan is used to bring fresh, cool air into the computer for cooling purposes.

Rear exhaust fan   This fan is used to take hot air out of the case.

Power supply exhaust fan   This fan is usually found at the back of the power supply and is used to cool the power supply. In addition, this fan draws air from inside the case into vents in the power supply. This pulls hot air through the power supply so that it can be blown out of the case. The front intake fan assists with this airflow. The rear exhaust fan supplements the power supply fan to achieve the same result outside of the power supply.

CPU fan   This fan is used to cool the processor. Typically, this fan is attached to a large heat sink, which is in turn attached directly to the processor.

Chipset fan   Some motherboard manufacturers replaced the heat sink on their onboard chipset with a heat sink and fan combination as the chipset became more advanced. This fan aids in the cooling of the onboard chipset (especially useful when overclocking—setting the system clock frequency higher than the default).

Video card chipset fan   As video cards get more complex and have higher performance, more video cards have cooling fans directly attached. Despite their name, these fans don't attach to a chipset in the same sense as a chipset on a motherboard. The chipset here is the set of chips mounted on the adapter, including the GPU and graphics memory. On many late-model graphics adapters, the equivalent of a second slot is dedicated to cooling the adapter. The cooling half of the adapter has vents in the backplane bracket to exhaust the heated air.

Motherboard Fan Power Connectors

It's important to be aware of the two main types of fan connections found on today's motherboards. One of these connectors has only three connections, while the other has four. The fan connectors and motherboard headers are interchangeable between the two pinouts, but if a chassis fan has four conductors, it's a sign that it's calling for connectivity to an extra +5VDC (volts direct current) connection that the most common three-pin header doesn't offer. A rarer three-pin chassis-fan connector features a +12VDC power connection for heavier-duty fans and a rotation pin, used as an input to the motherboard for sensing the speed of the fan.

Four-pin CPU connections place the ground and power connections in pins 1 and 2, respectively, so that two-pin connectors can be used to power older fans. The four-pin header also offers a tachometer input signal from the fan on pin 3 so that the speed of the fan can be monitored by the BIOS and other utilities. Look for markings such as *CPU FAN IN* to identify this function. Pin 4 might be labeled *CPU FAN PWM* to denote the pulse-width modulation that can be used to send a signal to the fan to control its speed. This is the function lost when a three-pin connector is placed in the correct position on a four-pin header. Four-pin chassis-fan connectors can share the tachometer function but replace the speed control function with the extra 5V mentioned earlier.

Other power connections and types will be covered in Chapter 2, including the Molex connector, which can be used to power chassis and CPU fans using an adapter or the built-in connector on mostly older fans manufactured before the motherboard connectors were standardized. The following image shows two three-pin chassis-fan headers on a motherboard.

The following image shows a four-pin CPU fan header with an approaching three-pin connector from the fan. Note that the keying tab is lined up with the same three pins it's lined up with in the three-pin connectors.

This physical aspect and the similar pin functions are what make these connectors interchangeable, provided the header's function matches the role of the fan being connected. The following shows the resulting unused pin on the four-pin header. Again, controlling the fan's speed is not supported in this configuration.

Chipset fan   Some motherboard manufacturers replaced the heat sink on their onboard chipset with a heat sink and fan combination as the chipset became more advanced. This fan aids in the cooling of the onboard chipset (especially useful when overclocking—setting the system clock frequency higher than the default).

Video card chipset fan   As video cards get more complex and have higher performance, more video cards have cooling fans directly attached. Despite their name, these fans don't attach to a chipset in the same sense as a chipset on a motherboard. The chipset here is the set of chips mounted on the adapter, including the GPU and graphics memory. On many late-model graphics adapters, the equivalent of a second slot is dedicated to cooling the adapter. The cooling half of the adapter has vents in the backplane bracket to exhaust the heated air.

Memory module fan   The more capable memory becomes of keeping up with the CPU, the hotter the memory runs. As an extra measure of safety, regardless of the presence of heat spreaders on the modules, an optional fan setup for your memory might be in order. See the following section for more.

Ideally, the airflow inside a computer should resemble what is shown in Figure 1.27.

FIGURE 1.27   System unit airflow

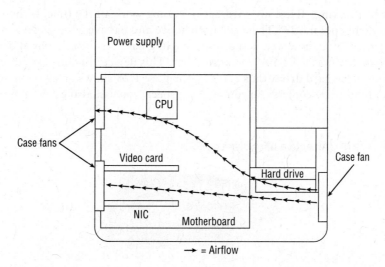

Note that you must pay attention to the orientation of the power supply's airflow. If the power supply fan is an exhaust fan, as assumed in this discussion, the front and rear fans will match their earlier descriptions: front, intake; rear, exhaust. If you run across a power supply that has an intake fan, the orientation of the supplemental chassis fans should be reversed as well. The rear chassis fan(s) should always be installed in the same orientation as the power supply fan runs to avoid creating a small airflow circuit that circumvents the cross flow of air through the case. The front chassis fan and the rear fans should always be installed in the reverse orientation to avoid them fighting against each other and reducing the internal airflow. Reversing supplemental chassis fans is usually no harder than removing four screws and flipping the fan. Sometimes, the fan might just snap out, flip, and then snap back in, depending on the way it is rigged up.

Memory Cooling

If you are going to start overclocking your computer, you will want to do everything in your power to cool all its components, and that includes the memory.

There are two methods of cooling memory: passive and active. The passive memory cooling method just uses the ambient case airflow to cool the memory through the use of enhanced heat dissipation. For this, you can buy either heat sinks or, as mentioned earlier, special "for memory chips only" devices known as heat spreaders. Recall that these are special aluminum or copper housings that wrap around memory chips and conduct the heat away from them.

Active cooling, on the other hand, usually involves forcing some kind of cooling medium (air or water) around the RAM chips themselves or around their heat sinks. Most often, active cooling methods are just high-speed fans directing air right over a set of heat spreaders.

Hard Drive Cooling

You might be thinking, "Hey, my hard drive is doing work all the time. Is there anything I can do to cool it off?" There are both active and passive cooling devices for hard drives. Most common, however, is the active cooling bay. You install a hard drive in a special device that fits into a 5¼″ expansion bay. This device contains fans that draw in cool air over the hard drive, thus cooling it. Figure 1.28 shows an example of one of these active hard drive coolers. As you might suspect, you can also get heat sinks for hard drives.

FIGURE 1.28   An active hard disk cooler

Chipset Cooling

Every motherboard has a chip or chipset that controls how the computer operates. As with other chips in the computer, the chipset is normally cooled by the ambient air movement in the case. However, when you overclock a computer, the chipset may need to be cooled more because it is working harder than it normally would be. Therefore, it is often desirable to replace the onboard chipset cooler with a more efficient one. Refer back to Figure 1.2 for a look at a modern chipset cooling solution.

CPU Cooling

Probably the greatest challenge in cooling is the cooling of the computer's CPU. It is the component that generates the most heat in a computer (aside from some pretty insane GPUs out there). As a matter of fact, if a modern processor isn't actively cooled all the time, it will generate enough heat to burn itself up in an instant. That's why most motherboards have an internal CPU heat sensor and a CPU_FAN sensor. If no cooling fan is active, these devices will shut down the computer before damage occurs.

There are a few different types of CPU cooling methods, but the most important can be grouped into two broad categories: air cooling and advanced cooling methods.

Air Cooling

The parts inside most computers are cooled by air moving through the case. The CPU is no exception. However, because of the large amount of heat produced, the CPU must have (proportionately) the largest surface area exposed to the moving air in the case. Therefore, the heat sinks on the CPU are the largest of any inside the computer.

The CPU fan often blows air down through the body of the heat sink to force the heat into the ambient internal air where it can join the airflow circuit for removal from the case. However, in some cases, you might find that the heat sink extends up farther, using radiator-type fins, and the fan is placed at a right angle and to the side of the heat sink. This design moves the heat away from the heat sink immediately instead of pushing the air down through the heat sink. CPU fans can be purchased that have an adjustable rheostat to allow you to dial in as little airflow as you need, aiding in noise reduction but potentially leading to accidental overheating.

It should be noted that the highest-performing CPU coolers use copper plates in direct contact with the CPU. They also use high-speed and high-CFM cooling fans to dissipate the heat produced by the processor. CFM is short for cubic feet per minute, an airflow measurement of the volume of air that passes by a stationary object per minute.

Most new CPU heat sinks use tubing to transfer heat away from the CPU. With any cooling system, the more surface area exposed to the cooling method, the better the cooling. Plus, the heat pipes can be used to transfer heat to a location away from the heat source before cooling. This is especially useful in cases where the form factor is small and with laptops, where open space is limited.

With advanced heat sinks and CPU cooling methods like this, it is important to improve the thermal transfer efficiency as much as possible. To that end, cooling engineers came up with a compound that helps to bridge the extremely small gaps between the CPU and the heat sink, which avoids superheated pockets of air that can lead to focal damage of the CPU. This product is known as thermal transfer compound or simply thermal compound (alternatively, thermal grease or *thermal paste*) and can be bought in small tubes. Single-use tubes are also available and alleviate the guesswork involved with how much you should apply. Watch out, though; this stuff makes quite a mess and doesn't want to come off your fingers very easily.

Apply the compound by placing a bead in the center of the heat sink, not on the CPU, because some heat sinks don't cover the entire CPU package. That might sound like a problem, but some CPUs don't have heat-producing components all the way out to the edges.

Some CPUs even have a raised area directly over where the silicon die is within the packaging, resulting in a smaller contact area between the components. You should apply less than you think you need because the pressure of attaching the heat sink to the CPU will spread the compound across the entire surface in a very thin layer. It's advisable to use a clean, lint-free applicator of your choosing to spread the compound around a bit as well, just to get the spreading started. You don't need to concern yourself with spreading it too thoroughly or too neatly because the pressure applied during attachment will equalize the compound quite well. During attachment, watch for oozing compound around the edges, clean it off immediately, and use less next time.

Improving and Maintaining CPU Cooling

In addition to using thermal compound, you can enhance the cooling efficiency of a CPU heat sink by lapping the heat sink, which smoothes the mating surface using a very fine sanding element, about 1000-grit in the finishing stage. Some vendors of the more expensive heat sinks will offer this service as an add-on.

If your CPU has been in service for an extended period of time, perhaps three years or more, it is a smart idea to remove the heat sink and old thermal compound and then apply fresh thermal compound and reattach the heat sink. Be careful, though; if your thermal paste has already turned into thermal "glue," you can wrench the processor right out of the socket, even with the release mechanism locked in place. Invariably, this damages the pins on the chip. Try running the computer for a couple of minutes to warm the paste and then try again to remove the heat sink.

Counterintuitively, perhaps, you can remove a sealed heat sink from the processor by gently rotating the heat sink to break the paste's seal. Again, this can be made easier with heat. If the CPU has risen in the socket already, however, rotating the heat sink would be an extremely bad idea. Sometimes, after you realize that the CPU has risen a bit and that you need to release the mechanism holding it in to reseat it, you find that the release arm is not accessible with the heat sink in place. This is an unfortunate predicament that will present plenty of opportunity to learn.

If you've ever installed a brand-new heat sink onto a CPU, you've most likely used thermal compound or the thermal compound patch that was already applied to the heat sink for you. If your new heat sink has a patch of thermal compound preapplied, don't add more. If you ever remove the heat sink, don't try to reuse the patch or any other form of thermal compound. Clean it all off and start fresh.

Advanced CPU Cooling Methods

Advancements in air cooling have led to products like the Scythe Ninja series, which is a stack of thin aluminum fins with copper tubing running up through them. Some of the hottest-running CPUs can be passively cooled with a device like this, using only the existing air-movement scheme from your computer's case. Adding a fan to the side, however, adds to the cooling efficiency but also to the noise level, even though Scythe calls this line Ninja because of how quiet it is.

In addition to standard and advanced air-cooling methods, there are other methods of cooling a CPU (and other chips as well). These methods might appear somewhat unorthodox but often deliver extreme results.

These methods can also result in permanent damage to your computer, so try them at your own risk.

Liquid Cooling

Liquid cooling is a technology whereby a special water block is used to conduct heat away from the processor (as well as from the chipset). Water is circulated through this block to a radiator, where it is cooled.

The theory is that you could achieve better cooling performance through the use of liquid cooling. For the most part, this is true. However, with traditional cooling methods (which use air and water), the lowest temperature you can achieve is room temperature. Plus, with liquid cooling, the pump is submerged in the coolant (generally speaking), so as it works, it produces heat, which adds to the overall liquid temperature.

The main benefit to liquid cooling is silence. There is only one fan needed: the fan on the radiator to cool the water. So a liquid-cooled system can run extremely quietly.

Liquid cooling, while more efficient than air cooling and much quieter, has its drawbacks. Most liquid-cooling systems are more expensive than supplemental fan sets, and require less familiar components, such as reservoir, pump, water block(s), hose, and radiator.

The relative complexity of installing liquid cooling systems, coupled with the perceived danger of liquids in close proximity to electronics, leads most computer owners to consider liquid cooling a novelty or a liability. The primary market for liquid cooling is the high-performance niche that engages in overclocking to some degree. However, developments in active air cooling, including extensive piping of heat away from the body of the heat sink, have kept advanced cooling methods out of the forefront. Nevertheless, advances in fluids with safer electrolytic properties and even viscosities keep liquid cooling viable.

Heat Pipes

Heat pipes are closed systems that employ some form of tubing filled with a liquid suitable for the applicable temperature range. Pure physics are used with this technology to achieve cooling to ambient temperatures; no outside mechanism is used. One end of the heat pipe is heated by the component being cooled. This causes the liquid at the heated end to evaporate and increase the relative pressure at that end of the heat pipe with respect to the cooler end. This pressure imbalance causes the heated vapor to equalize the pressure by migrating to the cooler end, where the vapor condenses and releases its heat, warming the nonheated end of the pipe. The cooler environment surrounding this end transfers the heat away from the pipe by convection. The condensed liquid drifts to the pipe's walls and is drawn back to the heated end of the heat pipe by gravity or by a wicking material or texture that lines the inside of the pipe. Once the liquid returns, the process repeats.

Peltier Cooling Devices

Water- and air-cooling devices are extremely effective by themselves, but they are more effective when used with a device known as a Peltier cooling element. These devices, also known as thermoelectric coolers (TECs), facilitate the transfer of heat from one side of the element, made of one material, to the other side, made of a different material. Thus, they have a hot side and a cold side. The cold side should always be against the CPU surface, and optimally, the hot side should be mated with a heat sink or water block for heat dissipation. Consequently, TECs are not meant to replace air-cooling mechanisms but to complement them.

One of the downsides to TECs is the likelihood of condensation because of the sub-ambient temperatures these devices produce. Closed-cell foams can be used to guard against damage from condensation.

Phase-Change Cooling

With phase-change cooling, the cooling effect from the change of a liquid to a gas is used to cool the inside of a PC. It is a very expensive method of cooling, but it does work. Most often, external air-conditioner-like pumps, coils, and evaporators cool the coolant, which is sent, ice cold, to the heat sink blocks on the processor and chipset. Think of it as a water-cooling system that chills the water below room temperature. Unfortunately, this is easily the noisiest cooling method in this discussion. Its results cannot be ignored, however; it is possible to get CPU temps in the range of −4° F (−20° C). Normal CPU temperatures hover between 104° F and 122° F (40° C and 50° C).

The major drawback to this method is that in higher-humidity conditions, condensation can be a problem. The moisture from the air condenses on the heat sink and can run off onto and under the processor, thus shorting out the electronics. Designers of phase-change cooling systems offer solutions to help ensure that this isn't a problem. Products in the form of foam; silicone adhesive; and greaseless, noncuring adhesives are available to seal the surface and perimeter of the processor. Additionally, manufacturers sell gaskets and shims that correspond to specific processors, all designed to protect your delicate and expensive components from damage.

Liquid Nitrogen and Helium Cooling

In the interest of completeness, there is a novel approach to super-cooling processors that is ill-advised under all but the most extreme circumstances. By filling a vessel placed over the component to be cooled with a liquid form of nitrogen or, for an even more intense effect, helium, temperatures from −100° C to −240° C can be achieved. The results are short lived and only useful in overclocking with a view to setting records. The processor is not likely to survive the incident, due to the internal stress from the extreme temperature changes as well as the stress placed on the microscopic internal joints by the passage of excessive electrons.

Undervolting

Not an attachment, undervolting takes advantage of the property of physics whereby reduction in voltage has an exponential effect on the reduction of power consumption and associated heat production. Undervolting requires a BIOS (where the setting is made) and CPU combination that supports it.

You should monitor the system for unpredictable adverse effects. One of your troubleshooting steps might include returning the CPU voltage to normal and observing the results.

Summary

In this chapter, we took a tour of the system components of a PC. You learned about some of the elements that make up a PC. You'll learn about others in the following chapters. Finally, you learned about the various methods used for cooling a PC. You also saw what many of these items look like and how they function.

Exam Essentials

Know the types of system boards.   Know the characteristics of and differences between ATX, micro ATX, and ITX motherboards.

Know the components of a motherboard.   Be able to describe motherboard components, such as chipsets, expansion slots, memory slots, and external cache; CPUs and processor sockets; power connectors; BIOS (firmware); CMOS batteries; jumpers; and DIP switches.

Understand the purposes and characteristics of processors.   Be able to discuss the different processor packaging, old and new, and know the meaning of the terms *hyperthreading*, *cores*, *cache*, *speed*, *virtualization support*, and *integrated GPU*.

Understand the purposes and characteristics of memory.   Know about the characteristics that set the various types of memory apart from one another. This includes the actual types of memory, such as DRAM (which includes several varieties), SRAM, ROM, and CMOS as well as memory packaging, such as DIMMs, RIMMs, SODIMMs, and MicroDIMMs. Also have a firm understanding of the different levels of cache memory as well as its purpose in general.

Understand the purposes and characteristics of cooling systems.   Know the different ways that internal components can be cooled and how overheating can be prevented.

Review Questions

The answers to the Chapter Review Questions can be found in Appendix A.

1. Which computer component contains all the circuitry necessary for other components or devices to communicate with one another?

    A. Motherboard

    B. Adapter card

    C. Hard drive

    D. Expansion bus

2. Which packaging is used for DDR SDRAM memory?

    A. 168-pin DIMM

    B. 72-pin SIMM

    C. 184-pin DIMM

    D. RIMM

3. What memory chips would you find on a stick of PC3-16000?

    A. DDR-2000

    B. DDR3-2000

    C. DDR3-16000

    D. PC3-2000

4. Which motherboard design style features smaller size and lower power consumption?

    A. ATX

    B. AT

    C. Micro ATX

    D. ITX

5. Which of the following socket types is required for the Intel Core i7-9xx desktop series?

    A. LGA 1366

    B. LGA 1156

    C. LGA 1155

    D. LGA 775

6. Which of the following is a socket technology that is designed to ease insertion of modern CPUs?

    A. Socket 479

    B. ZIF

    C. LPGA

    D. SPGA

7. Which of the following is *not* controlled by the Northbridge?

   A. PCIe

   B. SATA

   C. AGP

   D. Cache memory

8. Which of the following is used to store data and programs for repeated use? Information can be added and deleted at will, and it does *not* lose its data when power is removed.

   A. Hard drive

   B. RAM

   C. Internal cache memory

   D. ROM

9. Which socket type is required for an AMD Phenom II that uses DDR3 RAM?

   A. AM2

   B. AM2+

   C. AM3

   D. Socket 940

10. You press the front power button on a computer and the system boots. Later, you press it briefly and the system hibernates. When you press it again, the system resumes. You press and hold the button and the system shuts down. What is this feature called?

    A. Programmable power

    B. Soft power

    C. Relay power

    D. Hot power

11. Which of the following are the numbers of pins that can be found on DIMM modules used in desktop motherboards? (Choose three.)

    A. 168

    B. 180

    C. 184

    D. 200

    E. 204

    F. 232

    G. 240

12. To avoid software-based virtualization, which two components need to support hardware-based virtualization?

   A. Memory

   B. Hard drive

   C. CPU

   D. BIOS

13. You find out that a disgruntled ex-employee's computer has a boot password that must be entered before the operating system is ever loaded. There is also a password preventing your access to the BIOS utility. Which of the following motherboard components can most likely be used to return the computer to a state that will allow you to boot the system without knowing the password?

   A. Cable header

   B. Power supply connector

   C. Expansion slot

   D. Jumper

14. Your Core i5 fan has a four-pin connector, but your motherboard only has a single 3-pin header with the CPU_FAN label. Which of the following will be the easiest solution to get the necessary cooling for your CPU?

   A. Plug the four-pin connector into the three-pin header.

   B. Buy an adapter.

   C. Leave the plug disconnected and just use the heat sink.

   D. Add an extra chassis fan.

15. What is the combined total speed of a PCIe 2.0 x16 slot?

   A. 500MBps

   B. 16Gbps

   C. 8GBps

   D. 16GBps

16. Which of the following allows you to perform the most complete restart of the computer without removing power?

   A. Start ➢ Restart

   B. Start ➢ Hibernate

   C. Reset button

   D. Power button

17. Which of the following is most helpful when flashing the BIOS on a desktop computer system?

   A. Floppy diskette drive

   B. Uninterruptible power supply

   C. An Internet connection

   D. The Windows administrator password

18. Which of the following have Intel and AMD integrated into their Atom and Fusion processor lines that hasn't been integrated before?

   A. A GPU

   B. A math coprocessor

   C. The frontside bus

   D. The memory controller

19. You have just purchased a motherboard that has an LGA775 socket for an Intel Pentium 4 processor. What type of memory modules will you most likely need for this motherboard?

   A. DIP

   B. SIMM

   C. RIMM

   D. DIMM

20. What type of expansion slot is preferred today for high-performance graphics adapters?

   A. AGP

   B. PCIe

   C. PCI

   D. ISA

Performance-Based Question

On the A+ exams, you will encounter performance-based questions. The questions on the exam require you to perform a specific task, and you will be graded on whether you were able to complete the task. The following requires you to think creatively to measure how well you understand this chapter's topics. You may or may not see similar questions on the actual A+ exams. To see how your answer compares to the authors', refer to Appendix B.

You have been asked to remove a dual inline memory module and insert one with a larger capacity in its place. Describe the process for doing so.

Chapter 2

Storage Devices and Power Supplies

THE FOLLOWING COMPTIA A+ 220-801 EXAM OBJECTIVES ARE COVERED IN THIS CHAPTER:

✓ **1.5 Install and configure storage devices and use appropriate media.**

- Optical drives: CD-ROM, DVD-ROM, Blu-Ray

- Combo drives and burners: CD-RW, DVD-RW, Dual Layer DVD-RW, BD-R, BD-RE

- Connection types

  - External: USB, Firewire, eSATA, Ethernet

  - Internal SATA, IDE and SCSI: IDE configuration and setup (Master, Slave, Cable Select), SCSI IDs (0 – 15)

  - Hot swappable drives

- Hard drives: Magnetic, 5400 rpm, 7200 rpm, 10,000 rpm, 15,000 rpm

- Solid state/flash drives: Compact flash, SD, Micro-SD, Mini-SD, xD, SSD

- RAID types: 0, 1, 5, 10

- Floppy drive

- Tape drive

- Media capacity: CD, CD-RW, DVD-RW, DVD, Blu-Ray, Tape, Floppy, DL DVD

✓ **1.8 Install an appropriate power supply based on a given scenario.**

- Connector types and their voltages: SATA, Molex, 4/8-pin 12v, PCIe 6/8-pin, 20-pin, 24-pin, Floppy

- Specifications: Wattage, Size, Number of connectors, ATX, Micro-ATX

- Dual voltage options

As a PC technician, you need to know quite a bit about hardware. Given the importance and magnitude of this knowledge, the best way to approach it is in sections. The first chapter introduced the topic via the primary core components, and this chapter follows up where it left off. Specifically, this chapter focuses on storage devices and power supplies.

Identifying Purposes and Characteristics of Storage Devices

What good is a computer without a place to put everything? Storage media hold the data being accessed as well as the files the system needs to operate and data that needs to be saved. The many different types of storage differ in terms of their capacity (how much they can store), access time (how fast the computer can access the information), and the physical type of media used.

Hard Disk Drive Systems

Hard disk drive (HDD) systems (hard disks or *hard drives* for short) are used for permanent storage and quick access. Hard disks typically reside inside the computer, where they are semipermanently mounted with no external access (although there are external and removable hard drives) and can hold more information than other forms of storage. Hard drives use a *magnetic* storage medium and are known as conventional drives to differentiate them from newer solid-state storage media.

The hard disk drive system contains three critical components:

Controller   This component controls the drive. The controller chip controls how the drive operates and how the data is encoded onto the platters. It controls how the data sends signals to the various motors in the drive and receives signals from the sensors inside the drive. Most of today's hard disk technologies incorporate the controller and drive into one assembly. The most common and well-known of these are PATA and SATA.

Hard disk   This is the physical storage medium. Hard disk drive systems store information on small discs (from under 1 inch to 5 inches in diameter), also called *platters*, stacked together and placed in an enclosure.

Host bus adapter (HBA)   This is the translator, converting signals from the controller to signals the computer can understand. Most motherboards today incorporate the host adapter into the motherboard's circuitry, offering headers for drive-cable connection. Legacy host adapters and certain modern adapters house the hard drive controller circuitry.

Figure 2.1 shows a hard disk drive and host adapter. The hard drive controller is integrated into the drive in this case, but it could be resident on the host adapter in other hard drive technologies.

FIGURE 2.1   A hard disk drive system

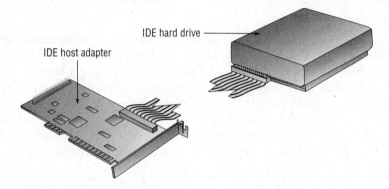

Figure 2.2 shows the 40-pin header (labeled *IDE*) on a motherboard.

FIGURE 2.2   IDE header on a motherboard

IDE (PATA) drives, discussed later, connect to this interface to access the HBA circuitry in the Southbridge. The four similar, smaller headers at the top left of the photo provide a similar connection for SATA drives, also presented later in this chapter.

Anatomy of a Hard Drive

A hard drive is constructed in a cleanroom to avoid the introduction of contaminants into the hermetically sealed drive casing. Once the casing is sealed, most manufacturers seal one or more of the screws with a warning sticker that removal of or damage to the seal will result in voiding the drive's warranty. Even some of the smallest contaminants can damage the precision components if allowed inside the hard drive's external shell. The following is a list of the terms used to describe these components in the following paragraphs:

- Platters
- Read/write heads
- Tracks
- Sectors
- Cylinders
- Clusters (allocation units)

Inside the sealed case of the hard drive lie one or more platters, where the actual data is stored by the read/write heads. The heads are mounted on a mechanism that moves them in tandem across both surfaces of all platters. Older drives used a stepper motor to position the heads at discrete points along the surface of the platters, which spin at thousands of revolutions per minute on a spindle mounted to a hub. Newer drives use voice coils for a more analog movement, resulting in reduced data loss because the circuitry can sense where the data is located through a servo scheme, even if the data shifts due to changes in physical disc geometry. Figure 2.3 illustrates the key terms presented in this discussion. The four stacked discs shown in the illustration are platters.

FIGURE 2.3   Anatomy of a hard drive

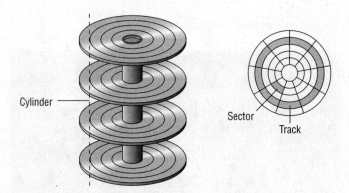

Factory preparation for newer drives or low-level formatting in the field for legacy drives map the inherent flaws of the platters so that the drive controllers know not to place data in these compromised locations. Additionally, this phase in drive preparation creates concentric rings, or *tracks*, which are drawn magnetically around the surface of the platters. Sectors are then delineated within each of the tracks. *Sectors* are the magnetic domains that represent the smallest units of storage on the discs' platters. Magnetic-drive sectors commonly store only 512 bytes (½KB) of data each.

The capacity of a hard drive is a function of the number of sectors it contains. The controller for the hard drive knows exactly how the sectors are laid out within the disk assembly. It takes direction from the BIOS when writing information to and reading information from the drive. The BIOS, however, does not always understand the actual geometry of the drive. For example, the BIOS does not support more than 63 sectors per track. Nevertheless, many hard drives have tracks that contain many more than 63 sectors per track. As a result, a translation must occur from where the BIOS believes it is directing information to be written to where the information is actually written by the controller. When the BIOS detects the geometry of the drive, it is because the controller reports dimensions the BIOS can understand. The same sort of trickery occurs when the BIOS reports to the operating system a linear address space for the operating system to use when requesting that data be written to or read from the drive through the BIOS.

The basic hard disk geometry consists of three components: the number of sectors that each track contains, the number of read/write heads in the disk assembly, and the number of cylinders in the assembly. This set of values is known as CHS (for cylinders/heads/sectors). The number of *cylinders* is the number of tracks that can be found on any single surface of any single platter. It is called a cylinder because the collection of all same-number tracks on all writable surfaces of the hard disk assembly looks like a geometric cylinder when connected together vertically. Therefore, cylinder 1, for instance, on an assembly that contains three platters comprises six tracks (one on each side of each platter), each labeled track 1 on its respective surface.

Because the number of cylinders indicates only the number of tracks on any one writable surface in the assembly, the number of writable surfaces must be factored into the equation to produce the total number of tracks in the entire assembly. This is where the number of heads comes in. There is a single head dedicated to each writable surface, two per platter. By multiplying the number of cylinders by the number of heads, you produce the total number of tracks throughout the disk assembly. By multiplying this product by the number of sectors per track, you discover the total number of sectors throughout the disk assembly. Dividing the result by 2 provides the number of kilobytes the hard drive can store. This works because each sector holds 512 bytes, which is equivalent to ½KB. Each time you divide the result by 1024, you obtain a smaller number but the unit of measure increases from kilobytes to megabytes, from megabytes to gigabytes, and so on. The following equation illustrates this computation:

$$
\begin{array}{c}
\text{cylinders (tracks/surface)} \\
\text{X heads (surfaces/drive)} \\
\hline
\text{total tracks (tracks/drive)} \\
\text{X sectors (sectors/track)} \\
\hline
\text{total sectors (sectors/drive)}
\end{array}
$$

For example, a drive labeled with the maximum allowed CHS geometry of 16383/16/63, respectively, results in only 7.9GB. Using the equation and multiplying the number of cylinders by the number of heads, you arrive at 262,128 total tracks on the drive. Multiplying this number by 63, the result is that there are 16,514,064 total sectors on the drive. Each sector holds ½KB for a total capacity of 8,257,032KB. Dividing by 1024 to convert to MB and again by 1024 to convert to GB, the 7.9GB capacity is revealed. As a result, although drives larger than 8GB still display the 16383/16/63 CHS capacity for devices that must adhere to the CHS geometry, the CHS scheme cannot be used on today's larger drives at the risk of losing the vast majority of their capacity. The solution is to allow the operating system to reference logical blocks of ½KB sectors that can be individually addressed by a 48-bit value, resulting in 128PB of drive capacity, far above the largest drives being manufactured today. A PB is 1024TB; a TB is 1024GB.

File systems laid down on the tracks and their sectors routinely group a configurable number of sectors into equal or larger sets called *clusters* or *allocation units*. This concept exists because operating system designers have to settle on a finite number of addressable units of storage and a fixed number of bits to address them uniquely. Because the units of storage can vary in size, however, the maximum amount of a drive's storage capacity can vary accordingly, but not unless logical drive capacities in excess of 2TB are implemented. Be aware that today's hard drives and volumes created with RAID can certainly exceed 2TB. This is not a hard limit, however. Larger clusters beget larger volumes but result in less efficient usage of space, discussed in the following paragraph.

No two files are allowed to occupy the same sector, so the opportunity exists for a waste of space that defragmenting cannot correct. Clusters exacerbate the problem by having a similar foible: No two files are allowed by the operating system to occupy the same cluster. The larger the cluster size, then, the larger the potential waste. So, although you can increase the cluster size (generally to as large as 64KB, which corresponds to 128 sectors), you should keep in mind that unless you are storing a notable number of very large files, the waste will escalate astoundingly, perhaps negating or reversing your perceived storage-capacity increase. Nevertheless, if you have single files larger than 2TB, increased cluster sizes are for you. A 64KB cluster size results in a maximum volume size in Windows XP Professional's version of NTFS, for example, of 256TB.

HDD Speeds

As the electronics within the HBA and controller get faster, they are capable of requesting data at higher and higher rates. If the platters are spinning at a constant rate, however, the information can only be accessed as fast as a given fixed rate. To make information available to the electronics more quickly, manufacturers increase the speed at which the platters spin from one generation of drives to the next, with multiple speeds coexisting in the marketplace for an unpredictable period until demand dies down for one or more speeds.

The following spin rates have been used in the industry for the platters in conventional magnetic hard disk drives:

- 5400 rpm
- 7200 rpm
- 10,000 rpm
- 12,000 rpm
- 15,000 rpm

While it is true that a higher revolutions per minute (rpm) rating results in the ability to move data more quickly, there are many applications that do not benefit from increased disk-access speeds. As a result, you should choose only faster drives, which are also usually more expensive per byte of capacity, when you have an application for this type of performance, such as for housing the partition where the operating system resides or for very disk-intensive programs. The lower speeds can be ideal in laptops, where heat production and battery usage can be issues with the higher-speed drives.

Solid-State Drives

Conventional hard disk drive platters are still manufactured the same way they have always been. They are metal or glass discs with a magnetic coating on their surface. The read/write heads change the magnetic orientation of each bit location, storing either a binary one or a binary zero. The same head senses the magnetic orientation of each location as the data is read from the disc.

In contrast, solid-state drives (*SSDs*) have no moving parts but use the same solid-state memory technology found in the other forms of flash memory. All solid-state memory is limited to a finite number of write (including erase) operations. Algorithms have been developed to constantly spread the write operations over the entire device. Such "wear leveling" increases the life of the SSD, but lack of longevity remains a disadvantage of this technology.

SSDs read contents more quickly, can consume less power and produce less heat, and are more reliable and less susceptible to damage from physical shock and heat production than their magnetic counterparts. However, the technology to build an SSD is still more expensive per byte, and SSDs are not yet available in capacities high enough to rival the upper limits of conventional hard disk drive technology.

SSDs are separated into two broad categories, volatile DRAM-based and non-volatile flash-based. Flash-based SSDs made with NAND (a transistor-based gate that has the opposite output to an AND gate) memory use considerably less power than HDDs. Those made with DRAM can use every bit as much power as conventional drives, however. The advantage of those made using the standard RAM modules used in desktop motherboards is that the modules can often be upgraded using larger modules, making a larger SSD overall.

When used as a replacement for traditional HDDs, SSDs are most often expected to behave in a similar fashion, mainly by retaining contents across a power cycle. The speed of the HDD is expected to be maintained or exceeded by the SSD as well. The volatility of DRAM-based SSDs can be compensated for by adding a backup power source, such as a battery or capacitor, or by keeping a non-volatile backup of the drive's data that does not detract from the speed of the primary storage location. Flash-based SSDs, while faster during read operations than their HDD counterparts, can be made faster still by including a small amount of DRAM as a cache. DRAM-based SSDs are faster yet.

Floppy Drives

A floppy disk (or floppy diskette) is a magnetic storage medium that uses a diskette made of thin, flexible plastic enclosed in a protective casing. The floppy disk once enabled information to be transported from one computer to another very easily. Today, floppies are a little too small in capacity to be relevant. They were first replaced by writable CDs and DVDs. Today, solid-state storage is the closest analogue to how floppies were originally used. The term *floppy disk* initially referred to the antiquated 8″ medium used with minicomputers and mainframes. The original PC floppy diskette, which used a platter that was 5¼″ in diameter and known as a *minifloppy diskette*, is also obsolete; the *microfloppy diskette* is a diskette that is 3½″ in diameter. A few computers today use microfloppy diskettes, either through internal drives or external USB-attached drives, but most support no floppy at all.

Generally speaking, throughout this book we will use the term *floppy drive* to refer to a 3½″ microfloppy diskette drive. Additionally, it is important to understand that the term *floppy* refers to the enclosed disk platter and not to the external enclosure. A mistake made by many uninformed individuals during the transition from 5¼″ floppies to 3½″ floppies was to refer to the newer, smaller diskettes as "hard disks." The microfloppy diskettes are still considered floppy because of the internal platter. The rigidity of the newer enclosure, in contrast to the flexibility of the older diskettes, had nothing to do with the name of the technology.

A *floppy diskette drive*, or FDD (shown in Figure 2.4), is used to read and write information to and from these disks. The advantage of these drives is that they allow portability of data: you can transfer data from one computer to another on a diskette. The downside of a floppy disk drive is its limited storage capacity. Whereas a hard drive can store hundreds or thousands of gigabytes of information, floppy disks allow storage of only one or two megabytes, although formats of much higher capacity exist, using roughly the same physical form factor but largely incompatible technology. Floptical and SuperDisk are examples.

FIGURE 2.4   A floppy diskette drive

Table 2.1 shows five different floppy-diskette formats with their corresponding data capacities supported in PC systems over the years. The following abbreviations are used: DD means double density, HD means high density. and ED means extended density. A sector holds 512 bytes; call it ½KB to make the math easier. Just remember, all your computations result in kilobytes. Unlike other storage capacities, which shift magnitudes by multiplying or dividing by 1024, floppy storage capacities move up one order of magnitude each time you divide by 1000—for example, kilobytes to megabytes, then megabytes to gigabytes. For instance, the 3½″ HD floppy has two sides to its single platter, yielding a total of 160 tracks. With 18 sectors per track, the total number of sectors on such a floppy diskette totals 2880. Because each sector represents ½KB, the resulting disk capacity totals 1440KB. Dividing by an even 1000 changes the magnitude from kilobytes to megabytes and arrives at the 1.44MB capacity commonly associated with these diskettes.

TABLE 2.1   Floppy diskette capacities

Floppy Drive Size	Tracks per Side	Sectors per Track	Capacity
5¼″ DD	40	9	360KB
5¼″ HD	80	15	1.2MB
3½″ DD	80	9	720KB
3½″ HD	80	18	1.44MB
3½″ ED	80	36	2.88MB

Optical Storage Drives

Most computers today have an optical storage drive, such as the latest *Blu-ray Disc* (*BD*), a digital versatile disc—or digital video disc (*DVD*), or the legacy compact disc (*CD*) drive. Each type of optical drive can be expected to also support the technology that came before it. Such optical storage devices began earnestly replacing floppy diskette drives in the late 1990s. Although, like HDDs, these discs have greater data capacity and increased performance over floppies, it is not intended that they replace hard disk drives. HDDs greatly exceed the capacity and performance of optical drives.

The CDs, DVDs, and BDs used for data storage are virtually the same as those used for permanent recorded audio and video. The way data, audio, and video information is written to consumer-recordable versions makes them virtually indistinguishable from such professionally manufactured discs. Any differences arise from the format used to encode the digital information on the disc. Despite the differences among the professional and consumer formats, newer players have no issue with any type of disc used. The encoding schemes used to store data on such discs are incompatible with the schemes used to record audio and video to the same discs.

CD-ROMs, DVD-ROMs, BD-ROMs, and Capacities

The amount of data that can be stored on the three primary formats of optical disc varies greatly, with each generation of disc exceeding the capacity of all previous generations. The following sections detail the science behind the capacities of all three formats.

CD-ROM

The *CD-ROM* (read-only memory) was designed for long-term storage of data. CD-ROMs are read-only, meaning that information written in the factory can't be erased or changed. CD-ROMs became so popular because they made a great software distribution medium. Programs are always getting larger and increasingly require more room to install, version after version. Instead of installing a program of the day using 100 floppy disks, you could use a single CD-ROM, which can hold approximately 650MB in its original, least-capable format. Although CDs capable of storing 700MB eventually became and continue to be the most common, discs with 800MB and 900MB capacities were standardized as well. See Table 2.2 after the following two sections for a list of optical discs and their capacities.

DVD-ROM

For even more storage capacity, many computers feature some form of DVD or BD drive, such as the original DVD-ROM drive. The basic *DVD-ROM* disc is a single-sided disc that has a single layer of encoded information. These discs have a capacity of 4.7GB, many times the highest CD-ROM capacity. Simple multiplication can sometimes be used to arrive at the capacities of other DVD-ROM varieties. For example, by adding another media surface on the side of the disc where the label is often applied, a double-sided disc is created. Such double-sided discs have a capacity of 9.4GB, exactly twice that of a single-sided disc.

Practically speaking the expected 9.4GB capacity from two independent layers isn't realized when those layers are placed on the same side of a DVD, resulting in only 8.5GB of usable space. (BDs do not have this issue; they make use of the full capacity of each layer.) The loss of capacity is due to the space between tracks on both layers being 10 percent wider than normal to facilitate burning one layer without affecting the other. This results in about 90 percent remaining capacity per layer. This technology is known as DVD DL (*DL* for *dual-layer*), attained by placing two media surfaces on the same side of the disc, one on top of the other, and using a more sophisticated mechanism that burns the inner layer without altering the semitransparent outer layer and vice versa, all from the same side of the disc. Add the DL technology to a double-sided disc and you have a disc capable of holding 17.1GB of information, again twice the capacity of the single-sided version. Figure 2.5 shows an example of an early DVD-ROM drive, which also accepts CD-ROM discs. Modern 5¼″ optical drives are indistinguishable from older ones, aside from obvious markings concerning their capabilities.

FIGURE 2.5   An early DVD-ROM drive

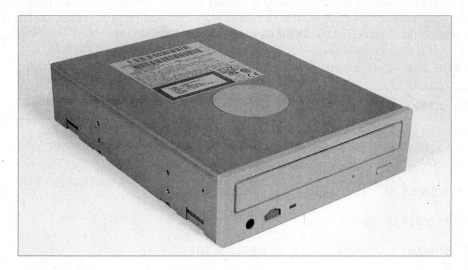

BD-ROM

The next generation of optical storage technology was designed for modern high-definition video sources. The equipment used to read the resulting discs employs a violet laser, in contrast to the red laser used with standard DVD and CD technologies. Taking a bit of creative license with the color of the laser, the Blu-ray Disc Association names itself and the technology Blu-ray Disc (BD), after this "visibly" different characteristic. Blu-ray technology further increases the storage capacity of optical media without changing the form factor. On a 12cm disc, similar to those used for CD-ROMs and DVD-ROMs, BD derives a 25GB storage capacity from the basic disc. When you add a second layer to the same or opposite side of the disc, you attain 50GB of storage. The Blu-ray laser is of a shorter wavelength (405nm) than that of DVD (650nm) and CD (780nm) technologies. As a result, and through the use of refined optics, the laser can be focused on a much smaller area of the disc. This leads to a higher density of information being stored in the same area.

An interesting point to note is that designers of the Blu-ray technology do not have to stop with the common double-layer solution to increasing capacity. Blu-ray discs with more than four layers on a side have been demonstrated, largely owing to the extremely accurate focus attainable with the Blu-ray laser.

In the interest of completeness, it should be mentioned that a high-definition technology directly related to DVD, because it comes from the same forum, and named HD DVD remains only as a footnote to the Blu-ray story. In February 2008, Toshiba, HD DVD's primary champion, gave up the fight, conceding Blu-ray disc as the winner in the high-definition optical-disc race. HD DVD featured red- and blue-laser compatibility and 15GB data storage capacity.

Table 2.2 draws together the most popular optical-disc formats and lists their respective capacities. Some of these formats have already been introduced; others are presented in the upcoming section "Recordable Discs and Burners." Boldfaced capacities in the table are the commonly accepted values for their respective formats.

TABLE 2.2   Optical discs and their capacities

Disc Format	Capacity
CD SS (includes recordable versions)	650MB, **700MB**, 800MB, 900MB
DVD-R/RW SS, SL	4.71GB (**4.7GB**)
DVD+R/RW SS, SL	4.70GB (**4.7GB**)
DVD-R, DVD+R DS, SL	**9.4GB**
DVD-R SS, DL	8.54GB (**8.5GB**)
DVD+R SS, DL	8.55GB (**8.5GB**)
DVD+R DS, DL	17.1GB
BD-R/RE SS, SL	25GB
BD-R/RE SS, DL	50GB
BD-R/RE DS, DL	100GB

SS: single-sided; DS: double-sided; SL: single-layer; DL: dual-layer

Optical Drive Data Rates

CD-ROM drives are rated in terms of their data transfer speed. The first CD-ROM drives transferred data at the same speed as home audio CD players, 150KBps, referred to as 1X. Soon after, CD drives rated as 2X drives that would transfer data at 300KBps appeared. They increased the spin speed in order to increase the data transfer rate. This system of ratings continued up until the 8X speed was reached. At that point, the CDs were spinning so fast that there was a danger of them flying apart inside the drive. So, although future CD drives used the same rating (as in 16X, 32X, and so on), their rating was expressed in terms of theoretical maximum transfer rate; 52X is widely regarded as the highest multiplier for data CDs. Therefore, the drive isn't necessarily spinning faster, but through electronics and buffering advances, the transfer rates continued to increase.

The standard DVD-ROM 1X transfer rate is 1.4MBps, already nine times that of the comparably labeled CD-ROM. As a result, to surpass the transfer rate of a 52X CD-ROM drive, a DVD-ROM drive need only be rated 6X. DVD transfer rates of 16X at the upper end of the scale are common.

The 1X transfer rate for Blu-ray is 4.5MBps, roughly 3¼ times that of the comparable DVD multiplier and close to 30 times that of the 1X CD transfer rate. It takes 2X speeds to properly play commercial Blu-ray videos.

Recordable Discs and Burners

Years after the original factory-made CD-ROM discs and the drives that could read them were developed, the industry, strongly persuaded by consumer demand, developed discs that, through the use of associated drives, could be written to once and then used in the same fashion as the original CD-ROM discs. The firmware with which the drives were equipped could vary the power of the laser to achieve the desired result. At standard power, the laser in these drives allowed inserted discs to be read from. Increasing the power of the laser allowed the crystalline media surface to be melted and changed in such a way that light would reflect or refract from the surface in microscopic increments. This characteristic allowed mimicking of the way in which the original CD-ROM discs stored data.

Eventually, discs that could be written to, erased, and rewritten were developed. Drives that contained the firmware to recognize these discs and control the laser varied the laser's power in three levels. The original two levels closely matched those of the writable discs and drives. The third level, somewhere in between, could neutralize the crystalline material without writing new information to the disc. This medium level of power left the disc surface in a state similar to its original, unwritten state. Subsequent high-power laser usage could write new information to the neutralized locations.

The best algorithms for such drives, which are still available today, allow two types of disc erasure. The entire disc can be erased before new data is written (*erased* or *formatted*, in various application interfaces), or the data can be erased on the fly by one laser, just fractions of a second before new data is written to the same location by a second laser. If not properly implemented in a slow, determined fashion, the latter method can result in write errors because the crystalline material does not adequately return to its neutral state before the write operation. The downside to slowing down the process is obvious, and methods exist to allow a small level of encoding error without data loss. This need to move more slowly adds a third speed rating, the rewrite speed, to the read and write speeds a drive is capable of. The following section delves more deeply into this concept. Updates to the drive's firmware can often increase or equalize these speeds.

Recordable CD Formats

CD-recordable (CD-R) and CD-rewritable (*CD-RW*) drives (also known as CD *burners*) are essentially CD-ROM drives that allow users to create (or *burn*) their own CD-ROMs. They look very similar to CD-ROM drives but feature a logo on the front panel that represents the drive's CD-R or CD-RW capability. Figure 2.6 shows the CD-R and CD-RW logos that you are likely to see on such drives.

FIGURE 2.6   CD-R and CD-RW logos

The difference between these two types of drives is that CD-R drives can write to a CD-R disc only once. A CD-RW drive can erase information from a CD-RW disc and rewrite to it multiple times. Also, CD-RW drives are rated according to their write, rewrite, and read times. So instead of a single rating like 64X, in the case of CD-ROM drives, they have a compound rating, such as 52X-32X-52X, which means it writes at 52X, rewrites at 32X, and reads at 52X.

Recordable DVD Formats

A DVD burner is similar to a CD-R or CD-RW drive in how it operates: It can store large amounts of data onto a special, writable DVD. Single-sided, dual-layer (DL) discs can be used to write 8.5GB of information to one single-sided disc. Common names for the variations of DVD burning technologies include DVD+R, DVD+RW, DVD-R, DVD-RW, DVD-RAM, DVD-R DL, and DVD+R DL. The "plus" standards come from the DVD+RW Alliance, while the "dash" counterparts are specifications of the DVD Forum. The number of sectors per disc varies between the "plus" and "dash" variants, so older drives might not support both types. The firmware in today's drives knows to check for all possible variations in encoding and capability. The "plus" variants have a better chance of interoperability, even without the disc being finalized.

A DVD-ROM or recordable drive looks very similar to a CD-ROM drive. The main difference is the presence of one of the various DVD logos on the front of the drive. CD-ROM and recordable CDs are usually able to be read and, if applicable, burned in DVD burners. Figure 2.7 and Figure 2.8 show the most popular data-oriented logos you are likely to see when dealing with DVD drives suited for computers. Figure 2.7 shows the "dash" logos, while Figure 2.8 shows the "plus" logos.

Table 2.3 lists the main DVD formats used for storing and accessing data in computer systems as well as their characteristics.

TABLE 2.3   DVD formats and characteristics

Format	Characteristics
DVD-ROM	Purchased with data encoded; not able to be changed
DVD-R, DVD+R	Purchased blank; able to be written to once and then treated like a DVD-ROM
DVD-RW, DVD+RW	Purchased blank; able to be written to and erased multiple times; session usually must be closed for subsequent access to stored data
DVD-RAM	Purchased blank; able to be written to and erased just like a hard or floppy disk; no session to close before subsequent access to stored data

FIGURE 2.7   DVD Forum logos

FIGURE 2.8   DVD+RW Alliance logos

Recordable BD Formats

The Blu-ray Disc Association duplicated use of the R suffix to denote a disc capable of being recorded on once by the consumer. Instead of the familiar RW, however, the association settled on RE, short for re-recordable. As a result, watch for discs labeled BD-R and BD-RE. Dual-layer versions of these discs can be found as well.

The Blu-ray Disc Association decided against creating separate logos for each BD type, resolving instead to use the logo in Figure 2.9 solely. Discs are labeled most often in a sans-serif font with the actual type of disc as well as this generic BD logo.

FIGURE 2.9   The Blu-ray Disc logo

Drive Interfaces and RAID

Storage devices come in many shapes and sizes. In addition to IDE/EIDE and SCSI, two of the older standards, there is now Serial ATA (*SATA*), and you can differentiate between internally and externally attached drives. The following sections look at storage devices from a number of those perspectives.

> Parallel ATA (PATA) is nothing new but rather the name retroactively given to the ATA/IDE standards when SATA became available. PATA uses the classic 40-pin connector for parallel data communications, whereas SATA uses a more modern 7-pin card-edge connector for serial data transfer.

AT Attachment Drives

At one time, integrated drive electronics (*IDE*) drives were the most common type of hard drive found in computers. Though so often thought of in relation to hard drives, IDE was much more than a hard drive interface; it was also a popular interface for many other drive types, including optical drives and tape drives. Today, we call IDE PATA and consider it to be a legacy technology. The industry now favors SATA instead.

IDE/PATA Drives

The design of IDE is simple: Put the controller chip and its related electronics right on the drive, and use a relatively short ribbon cable to connect the drive and controller to an interface on the system. This offers the benefits of decreasing signal loss (thus increasing reliability), eliminating the need for low-level formatting in the field, and making the drive easier to install. The IDE interface can be an expansion board (often referred to as a paddle card because it does little more than transfer pins from the drive to pins on the expansion bus; it has no real intelligence onboard), or it can be built into the motherboard, as was the case on almost all systems over quite a few generations in the past, especially nonserver, desktop systems. Today, similar systems tend to have SATA headers exclusively.

IDE generically refers to any drive that has a built-in controller. Enhanced Small Device Interface (ESDI—an antiquated technology) and, to a certain degree, SCSI drives have drive electronics integrated into them. The IDE we know today was once more properly called advanced technology attachment (ATA); the terms *SATA* and *PATA* were derived from *ATA*. Because ATA encompasses both SATA and PATA, but because IDE is synonymous only with PATA, it is no longer appropriate to equate IDE directly with the term ATA.

There have been many revisions of the IDE standard over the years, and each one is designated with a certain AT Attachment number—ATA-1 through ATA-8, so far. Drives that support ATA-2 and higher are generically referred to as Enhanced IDE (EIDE). SATA specifications appeared at the end of this series but then branched off on their own.

With ATA-3, a technology called ATA Packet Interface (ATAPI) was introduced to help deal with IDE devices other than hard disks. ATAPI enables the BIOS to recognize an IDE CD-ROM drive, for example, or a tape backup or Zip drive. ATA-3 also introduced the Self-Monitoring and Reporting Technology (SMART). SMART allows a hard drive to monitor itself and warn the user during and after boot-up of any impending failure. When heeded, these warnings allow you time to salvage data before it is lost. Generally, backing up the potentially ailing drive, before replacing it and restoring your data, is the best route. Note, however, that drives can still fail, and data loss can still occur, even without a warning from SMART.

Starting with ATA-4, a new technology was introduced called UltraDMA, supporting transfer modes capable of rates of up to 33MBps.

ATA-5 supports UltraDMA/66, with transfer modes having rates of up to 66MBps. To achieve this high rate, the drive must have a special 80-wire ribbon cable (still with only 40 pins, however), and the motherboard or IDE controller card must support ATA-5.

ATA-6 supports UltraDMA/100, with transfer modes capable of up to 100MBps.

> If an ATA-5 or ATA-6 drive is used with a normal 40-wire cable or is used on a system that doesn't support the higher-speed modes, it reverts to the ATA-4 performance level.

ATA-7 supports UltraDMA/133, with transfer modes of 133MBps and up to 150MBps for serial ATA.

ATA-8 made only minor revisions to ATA-7 and also supports UltraDMA/133 and 150MBps SATA and has the potential to support SATA 300.

IDE Pros and Cons

The primary benefit of IDE is that it's a mature, well-known technology. At one time, almost every motherboard had IDE connectors. A typical motherboard in those days had two IDE connectors, and each connector supported a single channel of up to two drives on the same cable. That means you were limited to four IDE devices per system, unless you add an expansion board containing another IDE interface. In contrast, with SCSI you can have up to seven devices (including drives) per interface, roughly double or quadruple that on some types of SCSI.

Performance also may suffer when certain IDE devices share an interface. It is recommended that you pair like devices on a channel. Otherwise, the slower device can have a negative impact on the faster one. SCSI drives are much more efficient with this type of transfer.

IDE Installation and Configuration

To install an IDE drive, do the following:

1. Set the master/slave jumper on the drive.

2. Install the drive in the drive bay.

3. Connect the power-supply cable.

4. Connect the ribbon cable to the drive and to the motherboard or IDE expansion board. There is a colored (usually red) stripe down one edge of the ribbon cable that is used to correctly orient the cable both where it connects to the drive and where it connects to the motherboard. If there is no marking for pin 1, you'll usually orient the red stripe toward the drive's power connector. Don't rely on that too much, though. Floppy drives are notorious for placing pin 1 away from its power connector.

5. Configure the drive in BIOS Setup if it isn't automatically detected.

6. Partition and format the drive using the operating system.

Each IDE channel can have only one *master* drive on it. If there are two drives on a single cable, one of them must be the *slave* drive. This setting is accomplished via a jumper on the drive. Some drives have a separate setting for Single (that is, master with no slave) and Master (that is, master with a slave); others use the Master setting generically to configure either case. Figure 2.10 shows a typical master/slave jumper scenario, but different drives may have different jumper positions to represent each state.

Another option is to use the Cable Select setting for master/slave selection. Most cables support Cable Select, but it won't work if the cable is not wired properly. Another caveat is that you must never mix Cable Select with Master and Slave settings. If one drive is set manually as Master, the other on the same cable must be set as Slave. If you set one drive to be configured as master or slave automatically with Cable Select, the other must be set for Cable Select as well. The wiring of the cable will result in the drive at the end of the cable being selected as master.

Most BIOS Setup programs today support Plug and Play, so they detect the new drive automatically at startup. If this doesn't work, the drive may not be installed correctly, the jumper settings may be wrong, or BIOS Setup may have the IDE interface set to None or Disable rather than Auto. Enter BIOS Setup and find out. Setting the IDE interface to Auto and then allowing the BIOS to detect the drive is usually all that is required.

FIGURE 2.10 Master/slave jumpers

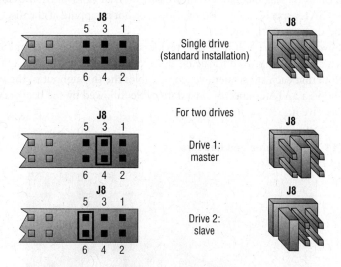

In BIOS Setup for the drive, you might have the option of selecting a DMA or programmed input/output (PIO) setting for the drive. Both are methods for improving drive performance by allowing the drive to write directly to RAM, bypassing the CPU when possible. For modern drives that support UltraDMA, neither of these settings is necessary or desirable.

Now that your drive is installed, you can proceed to partition and format it for the operating system you've chosen. Then, finally, you can install your operating system of choice.

For a modern Windows system, allow the Windows Setup program to partition and format the drive, or use the Disk Management utility in Windows to perform those tasks. To access Disk Management from Control Panel, choose Administrative Tools and then choose Computer Management. You can also right-click Computer (or My Computer in older versions of Windows) and then click Manage.

SATA Drives

Serial ATA began as an enhancement to the original ATA specifications, also known as IDE and, today, PATA. Technology is proving that the orderly progression of data in a single-file path is superior to placing multiple bits of data in parallel and trying to synchronize their transmission to the point that each bit arrives simultaneously. In other words, if you can build faster transceivers, serial transmissions are simpler to adapt to the faster rates than are parallel transmissions.

The first version of SATA, known as SATA 1.5Gbps, and also known by the less-preferred terms SATA I and SATA 150, used an 8b/10b encoding scheme that requires 2 non-data overhead bits for every 8 data bits. The result is a loss of 20 percent of the rated bandwidth, but the silver lining is that the math becomes quite easy. Normally you have to divide by 8 to convert bits to bytes. With 8b/10b encoding, you divide by 10. Therefore, the 150MBps throughput that this version of SATA was nicknamed for is easily derived as ⅒ of the 1.5Gbps transfer rate. The original SATA specification also provided for hot swapping at the discretion of the motherboard and drive manufacturers.

Similar math works for SATA 3Gbps, also recklessly tagged as SATA II and SATA 300, and SATA 6Gbps, which is not approved for being called SATA III or SATA 600, but the damage is already done. Note that each subsequent version doubles the throughput of the version before it. Figure 2.11 shows a SATA connector on a data cable followed by the headers on a motherboard that will receive it.

FIGURE 2.11   SATA cable and headers

The card-edge style connectors for data and power are arranged in such a manner on the back of SATA drives that no cables are required, although desktop and server systems almost certainly employ them. The same interface, however, can be used in laptops without the adapters needed to protect the delicate pins of the parallel interfaces found on the preceding generation of small form factor drives. The lack of the adapter also leads to less space reserved in the bays for drives of the same size, giving designers and consumers the choice between smaller systems or more complex circuitry that can move into the newly available space.

SCSI Drives

Small Computer System Interface (SCSI) devices can be either internal or external to the computer. Eight-bit SCSI-1 and SCSI-2 internal devices use a SCSI A cable, a 50-pin ribbon cable similar to that of an IDE drive. Sixteen-bit SCSI uses a SCSI P cable, with 68 wires and a 68-pin D-subminiature connector. There is also an 80-pin internal SCA connector ideal for use in hot-swapping environments.

Like IDE and floppy-drive cables, 50-pin SCSI ribbon cables have a colored stripe (usually blue or red, but it depends on the color of the rest of the cable) down one side to indicate the orientation of pin 1. The 68-wire ribbon requires no indicator because the connector is keyed by its shape. The cable is often a multicolored ribbon braided for noise reduction. External SCSI connectors depend on the type of standard in use. SCSI-1 uses a 50-pin Centronics connector similar to the 36-pin version used on the older printers with parallel interfaces. SCSI-2 uses a 25-, 50-, or 68-pin connector. SCSI-3 uses a 68- or 80-pin connector.

To configure SCSI, you must assign a unique device number (often called a SCSI address, SCSI ID, or SCSI device ID) to each device on the SCSI bus. These numbers are configured through jumpers, DIP switches, and up/down pushbuttons with the selected ID displayed through a hole on a wheel, among other ways. When the SCSI controller needs to send data to the device, it activates the wire dedicated to signaling that address.

A device called a *terminator* (technically a terminating resistor pack) must be installed at both ends of the bus to keep the signals "on the bus." The device then responds with a signal that contains the number of the device that sent the information and the data itself. The terminator can be built into the device and activated/deactivated with a jumper, or it can be a separate block or connector hooked onto the device when termination is required.

Termination can be either active or passive. A passive terminator works with resistors driven by the small amount of electricity that travels through the SCSI bus. Active termination uses voltage regulators inside the terminator. Active termination is much better, and you should use it whenever you have fast, wide, or Ultra SCSI devices on the chain and/or more than two SCSI devices on the chain. It may not be obvious from looking at a terminator whether it's active or passive.

SCSI Device Installation and Configuration

Installing SCSI devices is more complex than installing an IDE drive. The main issues with installing SCSI devices are cabling, termination, and addressing.

We'll discuss termination and cabling together because they're closely tied. There are two types of cabling:

- Internal cabling uses a 50-, 68-, or 80-wire ribbon cable with several keyed connectors. These connectors are attached to the devices in the computer (the order is unimportant), with one connector connecting to the adapter.

- External cabling uses thick, shielded cables that run from adapter to device to device in a fashion known as *daisy-chaining*. Each device has two ports on it (most of the time). When hooking up external SCSI devices, you run a cable from the adapter to the first device. Then you run a cable from the first device to the second device, from the second to the third, and so on.

Because there are two types of cabling devices, you have three ways to connect them. The methods differ by where the devices are located and whether the adapter has the terminator installed. The guide to remember here is that *both ends* of the bus must be terminated. Let's look briefly at the three connection methods:

Internal devices only   When you have only internal SCSI devices, you connect the cable to the adapter and to every SCSI device in the computer. You then install the terminating resistors on the adapter and terminate the last drive in the chain. All other devices are unterminated. This is demonstrated in Figure 2.12.

FIGURE 2.12   Cabling internal SCSI devices only

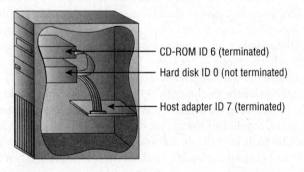

CD-ROM ID 6 (terminated)

Hard disk ID 0 (not terminated)

Host adapter ID 7 (terminated)

Some devices and adapters don't use terminating resistor packs; instead, you use a jumper or DIP switch to activate or deactivate SCSI termination on such devices. Check the documentation to find out what type your device uses.

External devices only   In the next situation, you have external devices only, as shown in Figure 2.13. By external devices, we mean that each has its own power supply. You connect the devices in the same manner in which you connected internal devices, but in this method you use several very short (less than 0.5 meters) *stub* cables to run between the devices in a daisy chain (rather than one long cable with several connectors). The effect is the same. The adapter and the last device in the chain (which has only one stub cable attached to it) must be terminated.

FIGURE 2.13 Cabling external SCSI devices only

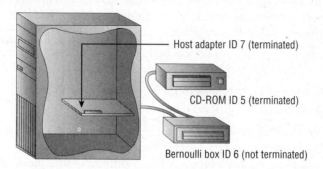

Host adapter ID 7 (terminated)

CD-ROM ID 5 (terminated)

Bernoulli box ID 6 (not terminated)

Both internal and external devices   Finally, there's the hybrid situation in which you have both internal and external devices (Figure 2.14). Most adapters have connectors for both internal and external SCSI devices—if yours doesn't have both, you'll need to see if anybody makes one that will work with your devices. For adapters that do have both types of connectors, you connect your internal devices to the ribbon cable and attach the cable to the adapter. Then you daisy-chain your external devices off the external port. You terminate the last device on each chain, leaving the adapter unterminated.

FIGURE 2.14 Cabling internal and external SCSI devices together

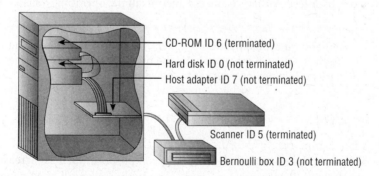

CD-ROM ID 6 (terminated)

Hard disk ID 0 (not terminated)

Host adapter ID 7 (not terminated)

Scanner ID 5 (terminated)

Bernoulli box ID 3 (not terminated)

Even though the third technique described is the technically correct way to install termination for the hybrid situation (in which you have both internal and external devices), some adapter cards still need to have terminators installed. Both ends of a SCSI chain must be terminated.

Each device must also have a unique SCSI ID number. This number can be assigned by the jumper (with internal devices) or with a rotary switch (on external devices). You start by assigning your adapter an address, if necessary. This can be any number from 0 to 7 on an 8-bit bus, 0 to 15 on a 16-bit bus, and 0 to 31 on a 32-bit bus, as long as no other device is using that ID. An ID of 7 is always recommended for the host adapter. This ID has the highest priority for arbitration and therefore the host adapter will always take priority.

Here are some recommendations that are commonly accepted by the PC community. Remember that these are guidelines, not rules:

- Generally speaking, give slower devices higher priority so they can access the bus whenever they need it. Higher numbers are higher priority.

- Set the bootable (or first) hard disk to ID 0.

- Set the CD-ROM to ID 3.

After setting the IDs and the devices are cabled and terminated, you have to get the PC to recognize the SCSI adapter and its devices. The SCSI adapter manages all SCSI device resource allocation, so generally all that is required is to make sure the operating system is able to see the SCSI adapter. This involves installing a driver for the adapter in Windows, for example.

However, if you want to boot from a SCSI drive, the system must be able to read from that drive in order to load the operating system; you must enable the SCSI adapter's own BIOS extension so that the PC can read from it at startup without a driver. Check the documentation for the adapter; sometimes the BIOS Setup program for the SCSI adapter is activated via a function key at startup.

If the SCSI adapter has no BIOS, some versions of Windows will create the NTBOOTDD. SYS file in the root of the system partition. Pressing F6 during Windows setup and installing the driver for the device causes this to happen. Once the drive is installed and talking to the computer, you can high-level format the media and install the operating system.

 If there are problems, double-check the termination and ID numbers. Termination will most likely be the problem, but you might need to make sure no two devices are set to the same ID.

RAID

RAID stands for *Redundant Array of Independent Disks*. It's a way of combining the storage power of more than one hard disk for a special purpose, such as increased performance or fault tolerance. RAID was once more commonly done with SCSI drives, but it can be done with other drives. RAID can be implemented in software or in hardware, but hardware RAID is more efficient and offers higher performance at an increased cost.

There are several types of RAID. The following are the most commonly used RAID levels:

RAID 0   Also known as *disk striping*, where a striped set of equal space from at least two drives creates a larger volume. This is in contrast to unequal space on multiple disks being used to create a simple *volume set*, which is not RAID 0. *RAID 0* is not RAID in every sense because it doesn't provide the fault tolerance implied by the *redundant* component of the name. Data is written across multiple drives, so one drive can be reading or writing while the next drive's read-write head is moving. This makes for faster data access. However, if any one of the drives fails, all content is lost. Some form of redundancy or fault tolerance should be used in concert with RAID 0.

RAID 1   Also known as *disk mirroring. RAID 1* is a method of producing fault tolerance by writing all data simultaneously to two separate drives. If one drive fails, the other contains all the data and will become the primary drive. However, disk mirroring doesn't help access speed, and the cost is double that of a single drive. If a separate host adapter is used for the second drive, the term *duplexing* is attributed to RAID 1. Only two drives can be used in a RAID 1 array.

RAID 5   Combines the benefits of both RAID 0 and RAID 1, creating a redundant striped volume set. Unlike RAID 1, however, *RAID 5* does not employ mirroring for redundancy. Each stripe places data on $n-1$ disks, and parity computed from the data is placed on the remaining disk. The parity is interleaved across all the drives in the array so that neighboring stripes have parity on different disks. If one drive fails, the parity information for the stripes that lost data can be used with the remaining data from the working drives to derive what was on the failed drive and rebuild the set once the drive is replaced.

The same process is used to continue to serve client requests until the drive can be replaced. The loss of an additional drive, however, results in a catastrophic loss of all data in the array. Note that while live requests are served before the array is rebuilt, nothing needs to be computed for stripes that lost their parity. Recomputing parity for these stripes is required only when rebuilding the array. A minimum of three drives is required for RAID 5. The equivalent of one drive is lost for redundancy. The more drives in the array, the less of a percentage this single disk represents.

Although there are other implementations of RAID, such as RAID 3 and RAID 4, the three detailed here are by far the most prolific. RAID 6 is somewhat popular as well because it is essentially RAID 5 with the ability to lose two disks and still function. RAID 6 uses the equivalent of two parity disks as it stripes its blocks across all disks in a fashion similar to the way RAID 5 does. A minimum of four disks is required to make a RAID 6 array.

There are also nested or hybrid implementations, such as *RAID 10* (also known as RAID 1+0), which adds fault tolerance to RAID 0 through the RAID 1 mirroring of each disk in the RAID 0 striped set. Its inverse, known as RAID 0+1, mirrors a complete striped set to another striped set just like it. Both of these implementations require a minimum of four drives and, because of the RAID 1 component, burn half of your purchased storage space for mirroring.

Removable Storage and Media

Many additional types of storage are available for PCs today. Among the other types of storage are tape backup devices, solid-state memory, and advanced optical drives. There are also external hard drives and optical drives as well as new storage media, such as USB keys that can store many gigabytes (more all the time) on a single small plastic device that can be carried on a lanyard around your neck or on a keychain.

Removable storage once meant something vastly different from what it means today. Sequential tape backup is one of the only remnants of the old forms of removable storage that can be seen in the market today. The more modern solution is random-access, solid-state removable storage. The following sections present details of tape backup and the newer removable storage solutions.

Tape Backup Devices

An older form of removable storage is the tape backup. Tape backup devices can be installed internally or externally and use either a digital or analog magnetic tape medium instead of disks for storage. They hold much more data than any other medium but are also much slower. They are primarily used for batch archival storage, not interactive storage.

With hard disks, it's not a matter of "if they fail"; it's "when they fail." So you must back up the information onto some other storage medium. Tape backup devices were once the most common choice in larger enterprises and networks because they were able to hold the most data and were the most reliable over the long term. Today, however, tape backup systems are seeing competition from writable and rewritable optical discs, which continue to advance in technology and size. Nevertheless, when an enterprise needs to back up large amounts of data on a regular basis, some form of tape media is the most popular choice. Table 2.4 lists the best-known tape formats in order of market release dates, oldest first, and capacities they are known for. Note that capacities are not associated with the format names but instead with models of tape within each format family.

TABLE 2.4   Sequential tape formats

Format Name	Representative Capacity
Quarter-inch Cartridge (QIC)	200KB to 525MB
Digital Linear Tape (DLT)	Up to 160GB
Eight Millimeter (Exabyte)	Up to 800GB
Digital Audio Tape (DAT)/Digital Data Storage (DDS)	Up to 300GB
Linear Tape-Open (LTO)	Up to 1.5TB (12.8TB planned)

Flash Memory

Once only for primary memory usage, the same components that sit on your motherboard as RAM can be found in various physical sizes and quantities in today's solid-state storage solutions. These include older removable and nonremovable flash memory mechanisms, Secure Digital (SD) cards and other memory cards, and USB flash drives. Each of these technologies has the potential to reliably store a staggering amount of information in a minute form factor. Manufacturers are using innovative packaging for some of these products to provide convenient transport options (such as keychain attachments) to users. Additionally, recall the SSD alternatives to magnetic hard drives mentioned earlier in this chapter.

For many years, modules and PC Card devices known as *flash memory* have offered low- to mid-capacity storage for devices. The name comes from the concept of easily being able to use electricity to instantly alter the contents of the memory. The original flash memory is still used in devices that require a nonvolatile means of storing critical data and code often used in booting the device, such as routers and switches.

For example, Cisco Systems uses flash memory in various forms to store its Internetwork Operating System (IOS), which is accessed from flash during boot-up and, in certain cases, throughout operation uptime and therefore during an administrator's configuration sessions. Lesser models store the IOS in compressed form on the flash and then decompress the IOS into RAM, where it is used during configuration and operation. In this case, the flash is not accessed again after the boot-up process is complete, unless its contents are being changed, as in an IOS upgrade. Certain devices use externally removable PC Card technology as flash for similar purposes.

The following sections explain a bit more about today's most popular forms of flash memory, memory cards, and USB flash drives.

SD and Other Memory Cards

Today's smaller devices require some form of removable solid-state memory that can be used for temporary and permanent storage of digital information. Gone are the days of using microfloppies in your digital camera. Even the most popular video-camera media, such as mini-DVD and HDD, are giving way to solid-state multi-gigabyte models. These more modern electronics, as well as most contemporary digital still cameras, already use some form of removable memory card to store still images permanently or until they can be copied off or printed out. Of these, the Secure Digital (*SD*) format has emerged as the preeminent leader of the pack, which includes the older *MultiMediaCard (MMC)* format on which SD is based. Both of these cards measure 32mm by 24mm, and slots that receive them are often marked for both. The SD card is slightly thicker than the MMC and has a write-protect notch (and often a switch to open and close the notch), unlike MMC. Figure 2.15 is a photo of an older SD card with size reference.

Even smaller devices, such as mobile phones, have an SD solution for them. One of these products, known as *miniSD*, is slightly thinner than SD and measures 21.5mm by 20mm. The other, *microSD*, is thinner yet and only 15mm by 11mm. Both of these reduced formats have adapters allowing them to be used in standard SD slots.

Table 2.5 lists additional memory card formats, the slots for some of which can be seen in the images that follow the table.

FIGURE 2.15 A typical SD card

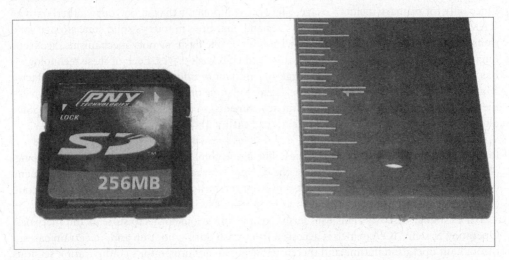

TABLE 2.5 Additional memory card formats

Format	Dimensions	Details	Year Introduced
Subscriber Identity Module (SIM)	25mm by 15mm	Used to store a subscriber's key on a telephone	1991
CompactFlash (CF)	36mm by 43mm	Type I and Type II variants; Type II used by IBM for Microdrive	1994
SmartMedia (SM)	45mm by 37mm	From Toshiba; intended to replace floppies	1995
Memory Stick (MS)	50mm by 21.5mm	From Sony; standard, Pro, Duo, and Micro formats available	1998
xD-Picture Card	20mm by 25mm	Used primarily in digital cameras	2002

Figure 2.16 shows the memory-card slots of an HP PhotoSmart printer, which is capable of reading these devices and printing from them directly or creating a drive letter for access to the contents over its USB connection to the computer. Clockwise from upper left, these slots accommodate CF/Microdrive, SmartMedia, Memory Stick (bottom right), and MMC/SD. The industry provides almost any adapter or converter to allow the various formats to work together.

FIGURE 2.16   Card slots in a printer

   Many other devices exist for allowing access to memory cards. For example, 3½″ form factor devices can be purchased—some of which have multiformat floppy drives embedded—and installed in a standard front-access drive bay. One such device is shown in Figure 2.17. External card readers, such as the USB-attached one shown in Figure 2.18 (front first, then back), are widely available in many different configurations.

FIGURE 2.17   An internal card reader with floppy drive

   Many of today's laptops have built-in memory-card slots, such as the ones shown in Figure 2.19.

USB Flash Drives

USB flash drives are incredibly versatile and convenient devices that allow you to store large quantities of information in a very small form factor. Many such devices are merely extensions of the host's USB connector, extending out from the interface but adding little to its width, making them easy to transport, whether in a pocket or laptop bag. Figure 2.20 illustrates an example of one of these components and its relative size.

FIGURE 2.18   A USB card reader

FIGURE 2.19   Memory-card slots in a laptop

FIGURE 2.20 A USB flash drive

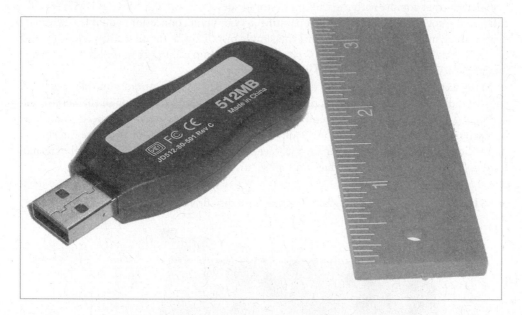

USB flash drives capitalize on the versatility of the USB interface, taking advantage of the Plug and Play feature and the physical connector strength. Upon insertion, these devices announce themselves to Windows Explorer as removable drives and show up in the Explorer window with a drive letter. This software interface allows for drag-and-drop copying and most of the other Explorer functions performed on standard drives. Note that you might have to use the Disk Management (discussed in Chapter 12, "Operating System Basics") utility to manually assign a drive letter to a USB flash drive if it fails to acquire one itself. This can happen in certain cases, such as when the previous letter the drive was assigned has been taken by another device in the USB flash drive's temporary absence.

USB flash drives emerged as the de facto replacement for other, now legacy, removable storage devices such as floppies, edging out Zip and Jaz offerings from Iomega as well as other proprietary solutions for the honor.

Externally Attached Drives

Before USB, an external drive used a SCSI or proprietary adapter and interface/cable combination or the standard RS-232 serial or parallel printer port often built in to the computer. Since USB, there has been a sense that there was no other way to attach drives externally. The fact is, there were and are other ways, but USB remains ubiquitous in today's systems and continues to increase in speed with each new revision. Nevertheless, FireWire and eSATA present higher performance options to those with the interest.

USB-Attached External Disk Drives

USB devices that comply with the USB mass storage device class (USB MSC or UMS) specification are recognized as drives by the operating system upon connection, and if the external drive is to be used as a backup location, you simply install any additional software you want to use. Windows Vista and Windows 7 have built-in backup utilities that are forms of drive imaging software and that work well with external drives.

Many external optical and hard disk drives today are manufactured into their own chassis and have detachable connectivity for USB (and/or FireWire through the Serial Bus Protocol 2 [SBP-2]). If the power requirement for the unit is high enough, there might also be a separate power connection for the device. Otherwise, the USB or FireWire interface on the host provides all the power for the drive. Figure 2.21 is a photo of a small external hard disk drive with a USB interface and no separate power attachment.

FIGURE 2.21   A self-contained external hard disk drive

More flexibly, USB-attached external disk drives can use the same drives that you might install in a drive bay in your chassis; they simply employ a specialty chassis that houses only the drive and the supporting circuitry that converts the drive interface to USB. Almost always, the 3.5″ drive enclosure has a DC power input and a Type-B USB interface, as shown in Figure 2.22. This external chassis has its cover removed, and you can see the internal protective casing, inside of which the hard drive is mounted.

FIGURE 2.22   External drive enclosure

eSATA-Attached External Disk Drives

Having sung the praises of USB as the savior of the external drive market, let's dispense with the illusion. An external drive-attachment technology based on SATA, called *eSATA* for "external" SATA, promises to offer external attachment with no compromises. Where the very nature of USB can hinder the achievement of maximum SATA drive performance, eSATA, by its nature, pledges to represent SATA faithfully, because it *is* SATA. Many enhancements over the SATA physical interface and signal levels, however, were required with eSATA to accommodate the harsher external environment. A different interface, without the recognizable L-shaped key, had to be specified to avoid accidental or intentional insertion of inadequately shielded internal cables.

Did we say "no compromises"? There is one, and it might be a big one, depending on the application. eSATA doesn't provide power the way USB and FireWire do. External power has to be supplied to the drive outside of the 2m or shorter data cable. The eSATA specification is likely to ride the coattails of internal SATA to appreciable success. Figure 2.23 shows an eSATA interface on an external drive chassis from two angles, followed by the associated cable.

FIGURE 2.23 External drive and cable with eSATA interface

Network Attached Storage

Chapter 6, "Networking Fundamentals," discusses network attached storage (NAS) in more detail, but it bears mentioning in this section that you can use the same Ethernet connection you use to put your computer on the network to place a specialty file-serving appliance on the same Ethernet network. This appliance is essentially a stand-alone computer with one or more internal drives and self-contained intelligence for attaching to the network and supporting common file-sharing protocols without the need for an operating system license. If your computer uses server message block (SMB), for instance, to request resources from a file server, the NAS appliance can field that request through its mutual support for SMB.

Hot-Swappable Devices

Many of the removable storage devices mentioned are *hot swappable*. This means that you can insert and remove the device with the system powered on. Most USB-attached devices without a file system fall into this category. Non-hot-swappable devices, in contrast, either cannot have the system's power applied when they are inserted or removed or they have some sort of additional conditions for their insertion or removal. One subset is occasionally referred to as cold swappable, the other as warm swappable. The system power must be off before you can insert or remove cold-swappable devices. An example of a cold-swappable device is anything connected to the PS/2-style mini-DIN connector, such as a keyboard or mouse. Insertion with the power on generally results in lack of recognition for the device and might damage the motherboard. AT keyboards and the full-sized DIN connector have the same restriction.

Warm-swappable devices include USB flash drives and external drives that have a file system. Windows and other operating systems tend to leave files open while accessing them and write cached changes to them at a later time, based on the algorithm in use by the software. Removing such a device without using the Safely Remove Hardware utility can result in data loss. However, after stopping the device with the utility, you can remove it without powering down the system, hence the *warm* component of the category's name. These are officially hot-swappable devices.

RAID systems benefit from devices and bays with a single connector that contains both power and data connections instead of two separate connectors. This is known as Single Connector Attachment (SCA). SCA interfaces have ground leads that are longer than the power leads so that they make contact first and lose contact last. SATA power connectors are designed in a similar fashion for the same purpose. This arrangement ensures that no power leads make contact without their singular ground leads, which would often result in damage to the drive. Drives based on SCA are hot swappable. RAID systems that have to be taken offline before drives are changed out but the system power can remain on are examples of warm swapping.

Installing, Removing, and Configuring Storage Devices

The removal and installation of storage devices, such as hard drives, floppy drives, CD/DVD drives, and tape drives, is pretty straightforward. There really isn't any deviation in the process of installing or exchanging the hardware. Fortunately, with today's operating systems, little to no configuration is required for such devices. The Plug and Play BIOS and operating system work together to recognize the devices. However, you still have to partition and format out-of-the-box hard drives before they will allow the installation of the operating system. Nevertheless, today's operating systems allow for a pain-free partition/format/setup experience by handling the entire process if you let them.

Removing Storage Devices

Removing any component is frequently easier than installing the same part. Consider the fact that most people could destroy a house, perhaps not safely enough to ensure their well-being, but they don't have to know the intricacies of construction to start smashing away. On the other hand, very few people are capable of building a house. Similarly, many could figure out how to remove a storage device, as long as they can get into the case to begin with, but only a few could start from scratch and successfully install one without tutelage.

In Exercise 2.1, you'll remove an internal storage device.

This section details the removal of internal storage devices, and the section "Installing Storage Devices" details their installation. Be aware that external storage devices exist, but today's external storage devices are eSATA-, USB-, and FireWire-attached devices, making them completely Plug and Play. Only the software preparation of external hard drives is a consideration, but the same procedure for the software preparation of internal devices works for external devices as well.

EXERCISE 2.1

Removing an Internal Storage Device

1. With the power source removed from the system, ground yourself and the computer to the same source of ground.

2. Remove the cover from the system, exposing the internal components.

3. Unplug all connections from the storage device you wish to remove. These include data and power connections as well as any others, such as audio connections to the sound card or motherboard. The beveled Molex power connectors fit very tightly, so don't worry about how hard removing them seems to be. There is no clip to release. Do, however, be sure to grip the connector, not the wires.

4. Gather the appropriate antistatic packaging to plan ahead for all static-sensitive components that will be reused in the future, including any adapter cards that the storage device plugs into.

5. Remove any obstructions that might hinder device removal, such as component cables attached to adapter cards or adapter cards themselves, storing them to be reused in antistatic packaging.

6. Remove related adapter cards from the motherboard, storing them to be reused in antistatic packaging.

7. Remove the machine screws holding the storage device to the chassis. These could be on the side of the device or on the bottom.

8. Some devices, especially hard drives because they have no front access from the case, pull out of the chassis toward the rear of the case, while others, such as CD/DVD and floppy drives, generally pull out from the front. A gentle nudge from the rear of the device starts it on its way out the front. Go ahead and remove the device from the case. If you discover other components that obstruct the storage device's removal, repeat step 5.

Installing Storage Devices

An obvious difference among storage devices is their *form factor*. This is the term used to describe the physical dimensions of a storage device. Form factors commonly have the following characteristics:

- 3½″ wide vs. 5¼″ wide
- Half height vs. full height vs. 1″ high and more
- Any of the laptop specialty form factors

You will need to determine whether you have an open bay in the chassis to accommodate the form factor of the storage device you want to install. Adapters exist that allow a device of small size to fit into a larger bay. For obvious reasons, the converse is not also true.

In Exercise 2.2, you'll install an internal storage device.

EXERCISE 2.2

Installing an Internal Storage Device

1. With the power source removed from the system, ground yourself and the computer to the same source of ground.

2. Remove the cover from the system, exposing the internal components.

3. Locate an available bay for your component, paying attention to your device's need for front access. If you do not see one, look around; some cases provide fastening points near the power supply or other open areas of the case. If you still do not see one, investigate the possibility of sacrificing a rarely or never used device to make room.

4. Remove any obstructions that might hinder device installation, such as component cables attached to adapter cards or adapter cards themselves, storing them to be reused in antistatic packaging.

5. Find the proper screws for the storage device and set any jumpers on the drive while it is in-hand. Then insert the device into the bay. Keep in mind that some insert from the rear of the bay and some from the front.

6. Line up the screw holes in the device with the holes in the bay. Note that many devices rarely insert as far as they can before lining up with the chassis's holes. So don't be surprised when pushing the device all the way into the bay results in misalignment. Other devices that require front access stop themselves flush with the front of the case, and still others require you to secure them while holding them flush.

7. Use at least two screws on one side of the device. This keeps the device from sliding in the bay as well as from rotating, which happens when you use only one screw or one screw on each side. If the opposite side is accessible, go ahead and put at least one screw in the other side. Most devices allow for as many as four screws per side, but eight screws are not necessary in the vast majority of situations.

EXERCISE 2.2 *(continued)*

8. Connect the data cable from the device to the adapter card or motherboard header. ATA devices, such as those that are designated as IDE drives (compatible hard drives and CD/DVD drives, for example) use a 40-pin connector. Floppy drives and some tape backup drives that connect through the floppy subsystem use a 34-pin connector. They look the same except for the three rows of two pins that differentiate them. Note that if you use the master/slave and not the Cable Select feature of IDE drives on the same chain, it does not matter which device connects to which connector on the cable. However, with floppy drives, the A: drive must always be attached to the connector after the twist in the cable.

9. Attach a power connector from the power supply to the device, bearing in mind that there are two connector styles that are not very close in appearance. You should have no trouble telling them apart. Be sure to fully insert the connector. Watch out for the smaller connector. (See the sidebar "Do You Smell Something?")

 Real World Scenario

Do You Smell Something?

In 1990, author Toby Skandier started a PC sales and repair business. Those were the days when you could build a computer from scratch for relatively little cost and sell it with a great markup and still come in way under the prices of the name-brand systems.

One customer was especially price conscious. In those days, a floppy drive was not the afterthought that it is today, both in use and price. You needed a floppy drive and could actually save a bit of money if you were buying quite a few units, just by opting for a cheaper model. This customer was buying 45 computers. So, one of the corners that was cut to keep the invoice amount down was floppy-drive quality. They went with a brand that Toby had never heard of but that his distributor listed as the cheapest. How bad could it be? How much of a difference could there be between brands and models? Toby found out. The customer didn't.

The cheaper drive worked just like any other, from the perspective of the user, but the difference showed while they were building the systems. The manufacturer scrimped in the production of the power connector. Where most manufacturers create a casing to receive the power supply's connector with little chance of inserting the connector upside down, this manufacturer allowed the four pins of the connector to protrude in a nondescript manner without any keying or guidance for the power supply's connector.

Unlike the well-keyed, larger Molex power connectors used on hard drives and CD/DVD drives, the Berg connector used with floppy drives can be inserted upside down rather easily if there is no well-thought-out receptacle for it. An upside-down connector causes no problems when the power cable is attached to the system. It causes no problems when the system is turned on. It does, however, "fry" the floppy's 5V circuit board with the 12V meant for the motor the first time the drive is accessed, which is during the boot-up process, emitting the telltale aroma of burning plastic.

When one of Toby's assistants flipped the connector on one of the floppy drives, it wasn't long before Toby realized someone learned a valuable lesson. The lesson was so clear you could smell it. Everyone smelled it. His assistant knew there was a right way and a wrong way to plug the connector, but it was just too easy to invert. Out of 45 floppies, they were lucky to have lost only one. It could have been a lot worse.

Identifying Purposes and Characteristics of Power Supplies

The computer's components would not be able to operate without power. The device in the computer that provides this power is the *power supply* (Figure 2.24). A power supply converts 110V or 220V AC current into the DC voltages that a computer needs to operate. These are +3.3VDC, +5VDC, –5VDC (on older systems), +12VDC, and –12VDC. The jacket on the leads carrying each type of voltage has a different industry-standard color coding for faster recognition. Black ground leads offer the reference that gives the voltage leads their respective magnitudes. The +3.3VDC voltage was first offered on ATX motherboards.

FIGURE 2.24   A power supply

The abbreviation *VDC* stands for *volts DC*. *DC* is short for *direct current*. Unlike alternating current (AC), DC does not alter the direction in which the electrons flow. AC for standard power distribution does so 50 or 60 times per second (50 or 60Hz, respectively).

Power supplies contain transformers and capacitors that can discharge *lethal* amounts of current even when disconnected from the wall outlet for long periods. They are not meant to be serviced, especially by untrained personnel. *Do not* attempt to open them or do any work on them. Simply replace and recycle them when they go bad.

Power supplies are rated in watts. A watt is a unit of power. The higher the number, the more power your computer can draw from the power supply. Think of this rating as the "capacity" of the device to supply power. Most computers require power supplies in the 250- to 500-watt range. Higher wattage power supplies might be required for more advanced systems that employ power-hungry graphics technologies or multiple disk drives, for instance. It is important to consider the draw that the various components and subcomponents of your computer place on the power supply before choosing one or its replacement.

Classic power supplies used only three types of connectors to power the various devices within the computer: floppy drive power connectors, AT system connectors, and standard peripheral power connectors. Each has a different appearance and way of connecting to the device. In addition, each type is used for a specific purpose. Newer systems have a variety of similar, replacement, and additional connectors, such as dedicated power connectors for SATA and PCIe, additional power connectors for the motherboard, and even modular connections for these leads back to the power supply instead of a permanent wiring harness.

Most power supplies have a recessed, two-position slider switch, often a red one, on the rear that is exposed through the case. You can see the one for the power supply in Figure 2.24. Selections read 110 and 220, 115 and 230, or 120 and 240. This dual voltage selector switch is used to adjust for the voltage level used in the country where the computer is in service. For example, in the United States, the power grid supplies anywhere from 110 to 120VAC. However, in Europe, for instance, the voltage supplied is double, ranging from 220 to 240VAC.

Although the voltage is the same as what is used in the United States to power high-voltage appliances, such as electric ranges and clothes driers, the amperage is much lower. The point is, the switch is not there to match the type of outlet used in the same country. If the wrong voltage is chosen in the United States, the power supply expects more voltage than it receives and might not power up at all. If the wrong voltage is selected in Europe, however, the power supply receives more voltage than it is set for. The result could be disastrous for the entire computer. Sparks could also ignite a fire that could destroy nearby property and endanger lives. Always check the switch before powering up a new or recently relocated computer. In the United States and other countries that use the same voltage, check the setting of this switch if the computer fails to power up.

Power Connectors

The connectors coming from the power supply are quite varied these days, but there are also some connectors that are considered legacy connectors that you might not see on modern power supplies. The following sections detail and illustrate the most common of these connectors.

Classic Power Connectors

The classic connectors comprise outdated connectors as well as connectors still in use today despite being found in the original IBM PC.

AT System Connector

The original power connectors attached to the early PC motherboards were known collectively as the *AT system connector*. There are two six-wire connectors, labeled P8 and P9 (as shown in Figure 2.25). They connect to an AT-style motherboard and deliver the power that feeds the electronic components on it. These connectors have small tabs on them that interlock with tabs on the motherboard's receptacle.

FIGURE 2.25   AT power supply system board connectors

The P8 and P9 connectors must be installed correctly or you will damage the motherboard and possibly other components. To do this (on standard systems), place the connectors side by side with their black wires together, and then push the connectors together or separately onto the 12-pin receptacle on the motherboard. Although there is keying on these connectors, they both use the exact same keying structure. In other words, they can still be swapped with one another and inserted. When the black ground leads are placed together when the connectors are side by side, it is not possible to flip the pair 180 degrees and still insert the two connectors without physically defeating the keying. Most technicians would give up and figure out their mistake before any damage occurs if they always place the grounds together in the middle.

Although it's easy to remove this type of connector from the motherboard, the tabs on the connector make it difficult to reinstall it. Here's a hint: Place the connector at an almost right angle to the motherboard's connector, interlocking the tabs in their correct positions. Then tilt the connector to the vertical position. The connector will slide into place more easily.

It is important to note that only legacy computers with AT and baby AT motherboards use this type of power connector.

Most computers today use some form of ATX power connector to provide power to the motherboard. Those connectors are described in later sections of this chapter.

Standard Peripheral Power Connector

The standard peripheral power connector is generally used to power different types of internal disk drives. This type of connector is also called a *Molex* connector. Figure 2.26 shows an example of a standard peripheral power connector. This power connector, though larger than the floppy drive power connector, uses the same wiring color code scheme as the floppy drive connector, although with a heavier gauge of wire. The added copper is for the additional current drawn by most devices that call for the Molex interface.

FIGURE 2.26   A standard peripheral power connector

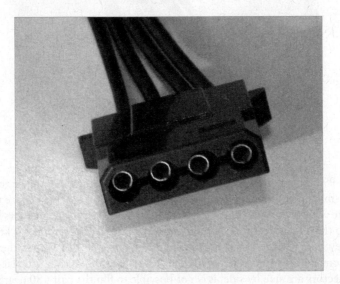

Floppy Drive Power Connectors

Floppy drive power connectors are most commonly used to power floppy disk drives and other small form factor devices. This type of connector is smaller and flatter (as shown in Figure 2.27) than any of the other types of power connectors. These connectors are also called *Berg* connectors. Notice that there are four wires going into this connector. These wires carry the two voltages used by the logic circuits and motors: +5VDC (carried on the red wire) and +12VDC (carried on the yellow wire), respectively; the two black wires are ground wires.

FIGURE 2.27　Floppy drive power connector

Modern Power Connectors

Modern components have exceeded the capabilities of some of the original power supply connectors. The Molex and Berg peripheral connectors remain, but the P8/P9 motherboard connectors have been consolidated and augmented, and additional connectors have sprung up.

ATX, ATX12V, and EPS12V Connectors

With ATX motherboards came a new, single connector from the power supply. PCI Express has power requirements that even this connector could not satisfy, leading to different connectors with different versions of the more advanced ATX12V specifications, which have gone through four 1.x versions and already five 2.x versions. Throughout the versions of

ATX12V, additional 4-, 6-, and 8-pin connectors supply power to components of the motherboard and its peripherals—such as network interfaces, PCIe cards, specialty server components, and the CPU itself—that require a +12V supply in addition to the +12V of the standard ATX connector. These additional connectors follow the ATX12V and EPS12V standards. The ATX connector was further expanded by an additional four pins in ATX12V 2.0.

The original ATX system connector (also known as the ATX motherboard power connector) feeds an ATX motherboard. It provides the six voltages required, plus it delivers them all through one connector: a single 20-pin connector. This connector is much easier to work with than the dual connectors of the AT power supply. Figure 2.28 shows an example of an ATX system connector.

FIGURE 2.28   ATX power connector

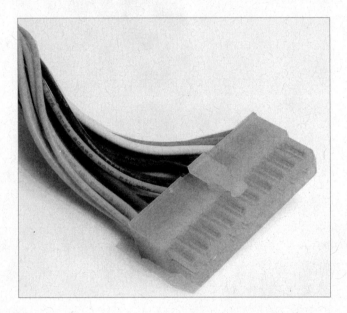

When the Pentium 4 processor was introduced, it required much more power than previous CPU models. Power measured in watts is a multiplicative function of voltage and current. To keep the voltage low meant amperage would have to increase, but it wasn't feasible to supply such current from the power supply itself. Instead, it was decided to deliver 12V at lower amperage to a voltage regulator module (VRM) near the CPU. The higher current at a lower voltage was possible at that shorter distance from the CPU.

As a result of this shift, motherboard and power supply manufacturers needed to get this more varied power to the system board. The solution was the ATX12V 1.0 standard, which added two supplemental connectors. One was a single 6-pin auxiliary connector similar to the P8/P9 AT connectors that supplied additional +3.3V and +5V leads and their grounds. The other was a 4-pin square mini-version of the ATX connector, referred to as a P4 (for the processor that first required them) connector, that supplied two +12V leads and their grounds.

EPS12V uses an 8-pin version, called the processor power connector, that doubles the P4's function with four +12V leads and four grounds. Figure 2.29 illustrates the P4 connector. The 8-pin processor power connector is similar but has two rows of 4 and, despite its uncanny resemblance, is keyed differently from the 8-pin PCIe power connector to be discussed shortly.

FIGURE 2.29   ATX12V P4 power connector

For servers and more advanced ATX motherboards that include PCIe slots, the 20-pin system connector proved inadequate. This led to the ATX12V 2.0 standard and the even higher-end EPS12V standard for servers. These specifications call for a 24-pin connector that adds additional positive voltage leads directly to the system connector. The 24-pin connector looks like a larger version of the 20-pin connector. The corresponding pins of the 24-pin motherboard header are actually keyed to accept the 20-pin connector. Adapters are available if you find yourself with the wrong combination of motherboard and power supply. Many power supplies feature a 20-pin connector that snaps together with a separate 4-pin portion for flexibility, called a 20+4 connector, which can be seen in Figure 2.30. The 6-pin auxiliary connector disappeared with the ATX12V 2.0 specification and was never part of the EPS12V standard.

ATX12V 2.1 introduced a different 6-pin connector, which was shaped more like the P4 connector than the P8/P9-style auxiliary connector from the 1.x standards. See Figure 2.31. This 6-pin connector was specifically designed to give additional dedicated power to PCIe adapters that required it. It provided a 75W power source to such devices.

ATX12V 2.2 replaced the 75W 6-pin connector with a 150W 8-pin connector, shown in Figure 2.32. The plastic bridge between the top two pins on the left side in the photo keeps installers from inserting the connector into the EPS12V processor power header but clears the notched connector of a PCIe adapter. The individual pin keying should avoid this issue, but a heavy-handed installer could defeat that. The bridge also keeps the connector from inserting into a 6-pin PCIe header, which has identically keyed corresponding pins.

FIGURE 2.30   A 24-pin ATX12V 2.x connector in two parts

FIGURE 2.31   A 6-pin ATX12V 2.1 PCIe connector

Proprietary Power Connectors

Although the internal peripheral devices have standard power connectors, manufacturers of computer systems sometimes take liberties with the power interface between the motherboard and power supply of their systems. In some cases, the same voltages required by a standard ATX power connector are supplied using one or more proprietary connectors. This makes it virtually impossible to replace power supplies and motherboards with other units "off the shelf." Manufacturers might do this to solve a design issue or simply to ensure repeat business.

FIGURE 2.32   An 8-pin ATX12V 2.2 PCIe connector

SATA Power Connectors

SATA drives arrived on the market with their own power requirements in addition to their new data interfaces. Refer back to Figure 2.11 and imagine a larger but similar connector for power. You get the 15-pin SATA power connector, a variant of which is shown in Figure 2.33. The fully pinned connector is made up of three +3.3V, three +5V, and three +12V leads interleaved with two sets of three ground leads. Each of the five sets of three common pins is supplied by one of five single conductors coming from the power supply. The same colors are generally used for the conductors as with the Molex and Berg connectors. When the optional 3.3V lead is supplied, it is standard to see it delivered on an orange conductor.

Note that in Figure 2.33, the first three pins are missing. These correspond to the 3.3V pins, which are not supplied by this connector. This configuration works fine and alludes to SATA drives' ability to accept Molex connectors or adapters attached to Molex connectors, thus working without the optional 3.3V lead.

FIGURE 2.33   SATA power connector

Replacing Power Supplies

Sometimes power supplies fail. Sometimes you grow out of your power supply and require more wattage than it can provide. Often, it is just as cost effective to buy a whole new case with the power supply included rather than dealing with the power supply alone. However, when you consider the fact that you must move everything from the old case to the new one, replacing the power supply becomes an attractive proposition. Doing so is not a difficult task.

Regardless of which path you choose, you must make sure the power connection of the power supply matches that of the motherboard to be used. Years ago, a new power supply with the single 20-pin ATX power connector wouldn't do a thing for you if you had a motherboard that had only the older P8/P9 connectors, although there are adapters that allow interconnection. Recall that the 24-pin ATXV2 2.x power supply connection can also be adapted to a motherboard with the 20-pin ATX connector.

Additionally, the physical size of the power supply should factor into your purchasing decision. If you buy a standard ATX-compatible power supply, it might not fit in the petite case you matched up to your micro-ATX motherboard. In that scenario, you should be on the lookout for a smaller form factor power supply to fit the smaller case. Odds are the offerings you find out there will tend to be a little lighter in the wattage department as well.

Exercise 2.3 details the process to remove an existing power supply. Use the reverse of this process to install the new power supply. Just keep in mind that you might need to procure the appropriate adapter if a power supply that matches your motherboard can no longer be found. There is no postinstallation configuration for the power supply, so there is nothing to cover along those lines. Many power supply manufacturers have utilities on their websites that allow you to perform a presale configuration so that you are assured of obtaining the most appropriate power supply for your power requirements.

EXERCISE 2.3

Removing a Power Supply

1. With the power source removed from the system, ground yourself and the computer to the same source of ground.

2. Remove the cover from the system, exposing the internal components.

3. After locating the power supply, which can come in a variety of formats and appear on the left or right side of the case, follow all wiring harnesses from the power supply to their termini, disconnecting each one.

4. Remove any obstructions that appear as if they might hinder removal of the power supply.

5. Using the dimensions of the power supply, detectable from the inside of the case, note which machine screws on the outside of the case correspond to the power supply. There are often four such screws in a nonsquare pattern. If your case has two side panels, and you removed only one, there will likely be one or more screws holding the other panel on that appear to be for the power supply. These do not need to be removed. If all case screws have been removed, pay attention to their location and do not use these holes when securing the new power supply.

6. Remove the screws that you identified as those that hold the power supply in place. Be aware that the power supply is not lightweight, so you should support it as you remove the final couple of screws.

7. Maneuver the power supply past any obstructions that did not have to be removed, and pull the power supply out of the case.

AC Adapters as Power Supplies

Just as the power supply in a desktop computer converts AC voltages to DC for the internal components to run on, the AC adapter of a laptop computer converts AC voltages to DC for the laptop's internal components. And AC adapters are rated in watts and selected for use with a specific voltage just as power supplies are. One difference is that AC adapters are also rated in terms of DC volts out to the laptop or other device, such as certain brands and models of printer.

Because both power supplies and AC adapters go bad on occasion, you should replace them both and not attempt to repair them yourself. When replacing an AC adapter, be sure to match the size, shape, and polarity of the tip with the adapter you are replacing. However, because the output DC voltage is specified for the AC adapter, be sure to replace it with one of equal output voltage, an issue not seen when replacing AT or ATX power supplies, which have standard outputs. Additionally, and as with power supplies, you can replace an AC adapter with a model that supplies more watts to the component because the component uses only what it needs.

You can read more on this subject later in Chapter 9, "Understanding Laptops."

Summary

In this chapter, you learned about two primary classes of personal computer components, specifically storage devices and power supplies. We covered storage devices such as hard drives, both conventional and solid state; floppy drives; optical drives; tape drives; and flash memory. We discussed power supply safety as well as the various connectors and compared and contrasted power supplies and AC adapters. You also learned how to remove, install, and configure storage devices and how to replace power supplies.

Exam Essentials

Be familiar with the components of a conventional hard drive system and the anatomy of a hard drive.   Most of today's hard drive systems consist of an integrated controller and disc assembly that communicates to the rest of the system through an external host adapter. The hard disk drives consist of many components that work together, some in a physical sense and others in a magnetic sense, to store data on the disc surfaces for later retrieval.

Get to know the newer solid-state drives.   SSDs continue to grow in popularity and will likely replace conventional drives as they become more reliable and less expensive.

Know the technology of floppy drives.   Become familiar with the various floppy diskette capacities and the technology behind these drives.

Understand the details surrounding optical storage.   From capacities to speeds, you should know what the varieties of optical storage offer as well as the specifics of the technologies this storage category comprises.

Be able to differentiate among removable storage options.   There are numerous tape and solid-state storage formats as well as a host of external and hot-swappable drives. Know the names of the options in each category.

Know about power supplies and their connectors.   Power supplies are made in AT, ATX, and proprietary form factors. Regardless, they must offer connectors for motherboards and internal devices. Know the differences among the connectors and how power supplies are rated. Also understand why AC adapters are related to power supplies.

Know how to remove, install, and configure storage devices.   Know the difference between the data and power connectors used on storage devices. Be aware of the master/slave relationship used with PATA devices and know the strategy for setting them. Know what it means to partition and format a hard drive. Be aware of the physical differences in storage device form factors.

Know how to remove, install, and configure power supplies.   Know the difference between the modern motherboard power headers, and be aware of when an adapter might be required. Know the two most common device connectors coming from the power supply. Be familiar with how to fasten power supplies to the chassis as well as how to unfasten them.

Review Questions

The answers to the Chapter Review Questions can be found in Appendix A.

1. What is the physical component where data is stored in a HDD?
    A. Read/write head
    B. Platter
    C. Sector
    D. Cluster

2. Which of the following is not one of the three major components of a hard disk drive system?
    A. Drive interface
    B. Controller
    C. Hard disk
    D. Host adapter

3. What is the largest NTFS volume size supported by Windows XP?
    A. 256GB
    B. 2TB
    C. 128TB
    D. 256TB

4. Which technology is based on flash memory and is intended to eventually replace conventional hard disk drives that have moving discs and other mechanisms?
    A. USB flash drives
    B. Memory cards
    C. Solid-state drives
    D. Optical drives

5. What is the formatted capacity of high-density 3½" floppy diskettes?
    A. 360KB
    B. 720KB
    C. 1.44MB
    D. 2.88MB

6. Which optical disc format supports a data capacity of 25GB?
    A. Double-sided, double-layer DVD+R
    B. Single-sided, single-layer Blu-ray disc
    C. Double-sided, single-layer DVD-R
    D. Double-sided, single-layer DVD+R

7. Which of the following best describes the concept of hot-swappable devices?

   A. Power does not need to be turned off before the device is inserted or removed.

   B. The device can be removed with power applied after it is properly stopped in the operating system.

   C. Care must be taken when swapping the device because it can be hot to the touch.

   D. The device can be swapped while still hot, immediately after powering down the system.

8. Of the following voltage pairings, which one accurately represents the input and output, respectively, of power supplies and AC adapters?

   A. AC in, AC out

   B. DC in, DC out

   C. AC in, DC out

   D. DC in, AC out

9. What are the five output voltages that have been commonly produced by PC power supplies over the years? (Choose five.)

   A. +3.3VDC

   B. −3.3VDC

   C. +5VDC

   D. −5VDC

   E. +12VDC

   F. −12VDC

   G. +110VAC

   H. −110VAC

10. Which of the following statements about power supplies is true?

   A. You must make sure the voltage selector switch on the back of the power supply is switched to the lower setting if the computer is going to be used in Europe.

   B. SATA hard drives most often use the same type of power connector PATA hard drives use.

   C. Power supplies supply power to ATX-based motherboards with connectors known commonly as P8 and P9.

   D. Molex connectors are used with PATA hard drives, while Berg connectors are used with floppy drives.

11. Which of the following is not a consideration when installing an internal storage device?

   A. You should match the form factor of the drive or adapt it to an available drive bay or slot.

   B. You should secure the drive with at least two screws on one side and preferably two on each side.

   C. Due to the high revolutions at which modern hard drives spin, you must secure an external power source because the internal power supplies do not have the capacity.

   D. You need to be sure that the routing of the drive's ribbon cable, if applicable, does not obstruct the engineered flow of air across internal components.

12. What kind of media is most commonly used when large amounts of data need to be archived on a regular basis?

    A. Tape

    B. Optical disc

    C. External hard drive

    D. Floppy diskette

13. Which of the following statements regarding floppy drive installation is true?

    A. Like a hard drive, the floppy drive requires no external access.

    B. Like DVD-ROM drives, floppy drives have a 5¼″ form factor and must be installed in the larger drive bays.

    C. Because it is antiquated technology, floppy disk drives can no longer be purchased new.

    D. Although some drives might not clearly key the receptacle for the Berg power connector, you must insert the connector correctly or the drive can be damaged.

14. Which of the following platter spin rates is not commonly associated with conventional magnetic hard disk drives?

    A. 5400 rpm

    B. 7200 rpm

    C. 10,200 rpm

    D. 15,000 rpm

15. Which of the following is not a consideration when upgrading power supplies?

    A. You might find that you do not have a matching motherboard connector on your new power supply.

    B. You might find that your case has a nonremovable power supply.

    C. You might find that your power rating is not adequate on the new power supply.

    D. You might find that you do not have enough of the appropriate connectors coming from the power supply for the devices you have installed.

16. What does the red stripe on a ribbon cable indicate?

    A. Pin 16

    B. Pin 1

    C. The manufacturer's trademark

    D. Parity

17. What do UltraDMA/66 and higher require?

    A. Cable Select configuration

    B. An 80-wire cable

    C. Operating system support

    D. That the BIOS be set for UltraDMA instead of DMA

18. On the primary IDE channel, if a single hard disk is attached, its jumper should be set to _____.

   A. Slave

   B. Single if available, otherwise Master

   C. Master

   D. Boot

19. Which of the following is a concept that applies only to conventional magnetic hard disk drives and not newer solid-state drives?

   A. Storage capacity

   B. External attachment

   C. Access time

   D. 7200 rpm

20. When replacing a power supply, which of the following tends to vary among power supplies and must be chosen properly to support all connected devices?

   A. Wattage

   B. Voltage

   C. Amperage

   D. Resistance

Performance-Based Question

On the A+ exams, you will encounter performance-based questions. The questions on the exam require you to perform a specific task, and you will be graded on whether you were able to complete the task. The following requires you to think creatively to measure how well you understand this chapter's topics. You may or may not see similar questions on the actual A+ exams. To see how your answer compares to the authors', refer to Appendix B.

Detail the process for removing a power supply from a computer chassis.

Chapter 3

Peripherals and Expansion

THE FOLLOWING COMPTIA A+ 220-801 OBJECTIVES ARE COVERED IN THIS CHAPTER:

✓ **1.4 Install and configure expansion cards.**

- ▪ Sound cards
- ▪ Video cards
- ▪ Network cards
- ▪ Serial and parallel cards
- ▪ USB cards
- ▪ FireWire cards
- ▪ Storage cards
- ▪ Modem cards
- ▪ Wireless/cellular cards
- ▪ TV tuner cards
- ▪ Video capture cards
- ▪ Riser cards

✓ **1.7 Compare and contrast various connection interfaces and explain their purpose.**

- ▪ Physical connections
  - ▪ USB 1.1 vs. 2.0 vs. 3.0 speed and distance characteristics (connector types: A, B, mini, micro)
  - ▪ FireWire 400 vs. FireWire 800 speed and distance characteristics
  - ▪ SATA1 vs. SATA2 vs. SATA3, eSATA, IDE speeds

- Other connector types (Serial, Parallel, VGA, HDMI, DVI, Audio, RJ-45, RJ-11)
- Analog vs. digital transmission (VGA vs. HDMI)
- Speeds, distances and frequencies of wireless device connections
  - Bluetooth
  - IR
  - RF

✓ **1.11 Identify connector types and associated cables.**

- Display connector types:
  - DVI-D
  - DVI-I
  - DVI-A
  - DisplayPort
  - RCA
  - HD15 (i.e., DE15 or DB15)
  - BNC
  - miniHDMI
  - RJ-45
  - miniDIN-6
- Display cable types:
  - HDMI
  - DVI
  - VGA
  - Component
  - Composite
  - S-video
  - RGB
  - Coaxial
  - Ethernet

- Device connectors and various connector pin-outs
  - SATA
  - eSATA
  - PATA (IDE, EIDE)
  - Floppy
  - USB
  - IEEE1394
  - SCSI
  - PS/2
  - Parallel
  - Serial
  - Audio
  - RJ-45
- Device cable types
  - SATA
  - eSATA
  - IDE
  - EIDE
  - Floppy
  - USB
  - IEEE1394
  - SCSI (68-pin vs. 50-pin vs. 25-pin)
  - Parallel
  - Serial
  - Ethernet
  - Phone

✓ **1.12 Install and configure various peripheral devices.**

  - Input devices
  - Mouse
  - Keyboard

- Touch screen
- Scanner
- Barcode reader
- KVM
- Microphone
- Biometric devices
- Game pads
- Joysticks
- Digitizer
- Multimedia devices
- Digital cameras
- Microphone
- Webcam
- Camcorder
- MIDI enabled devices
- Output devices
- Printers
- Speakers
- Display devices

With the core system components of the typical personal computer system under your belt, it is time to turn our attention to some of the peripherals that are available for connection to the computer. In doing so, we will also discuss the interfaces and cable assemblies associated with those peripherals.

Installing and Configuring Expansion Cards

An *expansion card* (also known as an *adapter card*) is simply a circuit board you install into a computer to increase the capabilities of that computer. Expansion cards come in varying formats for different uses, but the important thing to note is that no matter what function a card has, the card being installed must match the bus type of the motherboard you are installing it into. For example, you can install a PCI network card into a PCI expansion slot only.

For today's integrated components (those built into the motherboard), you might not need an adapter to achieve the related services, but you will still need to install drivers to make the integrated devices function with the operating system. As the trend toward more integrated components was maturing, many installers found most of the integrated components to be nonfunctional. A quick check in Device Manager showed a small collection of devices to be without their device drivers. Most motherboard manufacturers supply CD-ROM discs with their motherboards that contain all the device drivers needed to get the built-in electronics recognized by the operating system. Execution of the disc's setup program generally results in all components working and Device Manager clearing its warnings.

The following are the four most common categories of expansion cards installed today:

- Video
- Multimedia
- I/O
- Communications

Let's take a quick look at each of these card types, their functions, and what some of them look like.

Video

A video adapter (more commonly called a graphics adapter or even more commonly a *video card*) is the expansion card you put into a computer to allow the computer to display information on some kind of monitor. A video card is also responsible for converting the data sent to it by the CPU into the pixels, addresses, and other items required for display. Sometimes, video cards can include dedicated chips to perform some of these functions, thus accelerating the speed of display.

At a basic level, video adapters that have a PCI interface operate sufficiently. However, because AGP and PCIe slots offer more resources to the adapter, most manufacturers and computer owners prefer not to use PCI slots for video adapters. Although you might be able to find the rare motherboard that still offers an AGP slot, PCIe is the preferred expansion slot for video card attachment. The technology on which PCIe was designed performs better for video than those on which AGP and PCI are based. Figure 3.1 shows an example of a PCIe-based video card.

FIGURE 3.1 A video expansion card

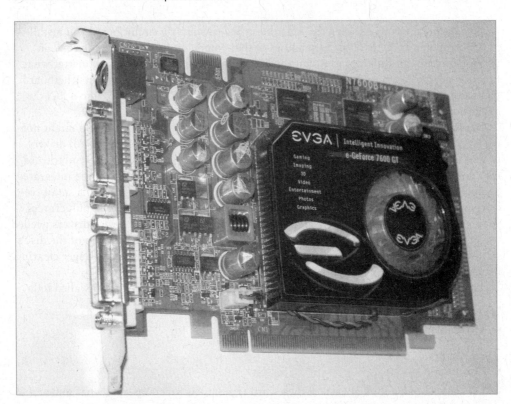

Multimedia

The most basic and prolific multimedia adapter is the sound card. TV tuner cards and video capture cards are newer multimedia adapters that continue to gain in popularity due to decreasing cost and the rise of the Internet as a forum for creative sharing.

Sound Card

Just as there are devices to convert computer signals into printouts and video information, there are devices to convert those signals into sound. These devices are known as *sound cards*. Although sound cards started out as pluggable adapters, this functionality is one of the most common integrated technologies found on motherboards today. A sound card typically has small, round, ⅛″ jacks on the back of it for connecting microphones, headphones, and speakers as well as other sound equipment. Many sound cards used to have a DA15 game port, which can be used for either joysticks or MIDI controllers. Figure 3.2 shows an example of a legacy sound card with a DA15 game port.

FIGURE 3.2 A typical sound card

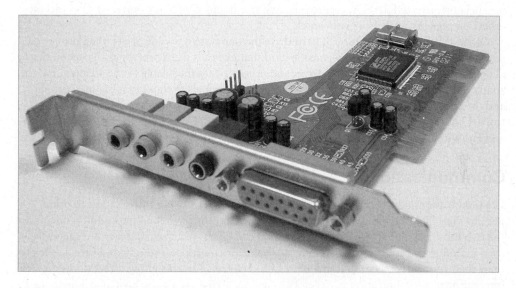

Sound cards today might come with an RCA jack (see the section "Audio/Video Jacks" later in this chapter). This is decidedly not for composite video. Instead, there is a digital audio specification known as the Sony/Philips Digital Interface (S/PDIF). Not only does this format allow you to transmit audio in digital clarity, but in addition to specifying an RCA jack and coaxial copper cabling, it specifies optical fiber connectors (TOSLINK) and cabling for electrically noisy environments, further increasing transmission quality of the digital signal.

TV Tuner Cards and Video Capture Cards

The *TV tuner card* is a class of internal and external devices that allows you to connect a broadcast signal, such as home cable television, to your computer and display the output on the computer monitor. TV tuner cards come in analog, digital, and hybrid varieties. Most TV tuner cards act as video capture cards as well. A *video capture card* can also be a stand-alone device and is often used to save a video stream to the computer for later manipulation or sharing. Video-sharing sites on the Internet make video capture cards quite popular with enterprises and Internet socialites alike. TV tuner cards and video capture cards need and often come with software to aid in the processing of multimedia input.

I/O

I/O card is often used as a catchall phrase for any expansion card that expands the system to interface with devices that offer input to the system, output from the system, or both. Common examples of I/O are the classic serial (RS-232) and parallel (printer) ports and drive interface connections. A popular expansion card of the 1980s and early 1990s was known as the Super I/O card. This one adapter had the circuitry for two standard serial ports, one parallel port, two IDE (PATA) controllers, and one floppy controller. Some versions included other components, such as a game port.

Often, if you want to use a SCSI hard drive in your system or a SCSI-attached printer or scanner, you have to install an expansion card that expands the motherboard's capabilities to allow the use of SCSI devices. The drives and other devices then cable to the adapter, and the adapter performs the requisite conversion of the drive signals to those that the motherboard and the circuits installed on it could use. Today, many server motherboards have SCSI controllers built in for such internal hard drives, and everything else tends to use integrated USB and FireWire interfaces, although expansion cards for these common interfaces exist as well.

Communications

Communications adapters give a computer the ability to transmit information to other devices that might be too distant to cable up to directly. Network adapters and modems are the two most popular types of communications adapter. Network adapters are generally used within the administrative domain of a home or enterprise and rely on other devices to relay their transmissions around the world. In contrast, modems allow direct domestic or international communication between two devices across the Public Switched Telephone Network (PSTN). Although there are other devices in the PSTN, the service provider's network appears as a cloud to the end stations, unlike the intermediate devices of a home or enterprise data network.

Network Interface Card (NIC)

A *network interface card (NIC)* is an expansion card that connects a computer to a network so that it can communicate with other computers on that network. *NIC* can also stand for *network interface controller.* It translates the data from the parallel data stream used inside the computer into the serial data stream that makes up the frames used on the network. It has a connector for the type of expansion bus on the motherboard (PCIe, PCI, and so on) as well as a connector for the type of network (such as fiber connectors, RJ-45 for UTP, antenna for wireless, or BNC for legacy coax). In addition to physically installing the NIC, you need to install drivers for the NIC in order for the computer to use the adapter to access the network. Figure 3.3 shows an example of a NIC.

FIGURE 3.3   A network interface card

 Some computers have NIC circuitry integrated into their motherboards. Therefore, a computer with an integrated NIC wouldn't need to have a NIC expansion card installed unless it was faster or you were using the second NIC for load balancing, security, or fault-tolerance applications.

Wireless NICs

Wireless NICs have the unique characteristic of requiring that you configure their connecting device before configuring the NIC. Wired NICs can generally create a link and begin operation just by being physically connected out of the box to a hub or switch. The wireless access point or ad hoc partner computer must also be configured before secure communication, at a minimum, can occur by using a wireless NIC. These terms will be explained in greater detail in Chapter 8, "Installing Wireless and SOHO Networks."

Cellular Cards

Almost every cellular service provider offers a line of adapters that can be installed into or inserted on the outside of desktop and laptop computers. In addition, depending on your service plan, most smartphones can be tethered to your computer and used as a cellular gateway.

Very often, the cellular adapter comes with a setup program that configures the card for the service provider's network. From that point, anytime you are in a cellular service area, you can use the adapter to gain access to the Internet through the provider or by roaming on the network of a partner or competitor with which an agreement has been reached in that area.

Modem

Any computer that connects to the Internet using an analog dial-up connection needs a modem, or *mo*dulator/*dem*odulator. A *modem* is a device that converts digital signals from a computer into analog signals that can be transmitted over phone lines and back again. These expansion card devices have one connector for the expansion bus being used (PCIe, PCI, and so on) and another for connection to the telephone line. Actually, as you can see in Figure 3.4, which shows an old ISA modem, there might be two RJ-11 ports: one for connection to the telephone line and the other for connection to a telephone. This is primarily so that a phone can gain access to the same wall jack that the computer connects to without swapping their cords. Keep in mind, though, that you won't be able to use the phone while the computer is connected to the Internet.

FIGURE 3.4   A modem

Riser Cards

An alternative motherboard form factor, known as New Low-Profile Extended (NLX), or one of its offshoots have been used in some types of low-profile cases. NLX places the expansion slots sideways on a special *riser card* to use the reduced vertical space optimally. Adapter cards that normally plug into expansion slots vertically in other motherboards plug in parallel to the motherboard, so their second most demanding dimension does not affect case height. Figure 3.5 shows a motherboard with its riser card attached.

FIGURE 3.5   Both sides of a riser card with adapter

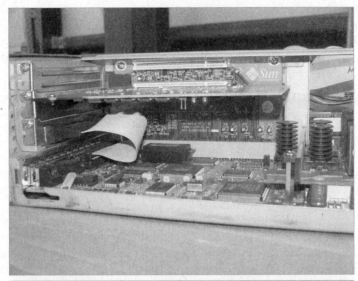

Riser technology also serves to free up valuable motherboard space for circuitry that cannot or should not be placed on adapters. Without the use of the riser, the motherboard would need to be made larger to accommodate the same circuitry. The term *riser* can also be used for any board that combines many functions into a single card, such as AMR and CNR, which were introduced in Chapter 1, "Motherboards, Processors, and Memory," and don't actually allow the attachment of additional cards to themselves the way true risers do.

Adapter Configuration

Expansion cards might require configuration. However, most can be recognized automatically by a Plug and Play operating system. In other words, resources are handed out automatically without jumper settings or the installation of device drivers is handled or requested automatically. Your supplying the drivers might be the only form of configuration required. For example, unlike older ISA adapters, PCI adapters take care of requesting their own resources through Plug and Play. This is especially true of simple I/O adapters, such as those that provide USB, FireWire, parallel, and serial ports.

Some modern adapters, however, require more specific configuration steps during installation. For example, two or more PCIe graphics adapters that support SLI (see Chapter 1) must be bridged together with special hardware that comes with the adapters. Although most sound cards tend to work with no specific configuration, advanced features will need to be implemented through the operating system or through utilities that came with the adapter. Wired network adapters tend to be easier to configure than wireless ones. Wireless adapters often require the installation of a screw-on antenna, which should be postponed until after the card is fully inserted and physically secured in the system. Software configuration that allows these cards to communicate with a wireless access point can be challenging for the novice. Nevertheless, even wired NICs might require static configuration of certain protocol settings, such as IP addressing, duplex, and speed, in order for them to be productive. The functions of TV and video capture cards are sometimes not native to the operating system and therefore come with advanced utilities that must be learned and configured before the adapters will work as expected.

In any event, consult the documentation provided with your adapter for additional configuration requirements or options. The more specialized the adapter, the more likely it will come with specialty-configuration utilities.

Identifying Characteristics of Connectors and Cables

Now that you've learned the various types of items found in a computer, let's discuss the various types of ports and cables used with computers. A *port* is a generic name for any connector on a computer or peripheral into which a cable can be plugged. A cable is simply a way of connecting a peripheral or other device to a computer using multiple copper or fiber-optic conductors inside a common wrapping or sheath. Typically, cables connect two ports: one on the computer and one on some other device.

Let's take a quick look at some of the different styles of port connector types as well as peripheral port and cable types. We'll begin by looking at peripheral port connector types.

Device Connector Types

Computer ports are interfaces that allow other devices to be connected to a computer. Their appearance varies widely, depending on their function. In this section we'll examine the following types of peripheral ports:

- D-subminiature
- RJ-series
- Other types

D-subminiature Connectors

D-sub connectors, for a number of years the most common style of connector found on computers, are typically designated with DXn, where the letter X is replaced by the letters A through E, which refer to the size of the connector, and the letter n is replaced by the number of pins or sockets in the connector. D-sub connectors are usually shaped like a trapezoid and have at least two rows of pins with no other keying structure or landmark, as you can see in Figure 3.6.

The "D" shape ensures that only one orientation is possible. If you try to connect them upside down or try to connect a male connector to another male connector, they just won't go together and the connection can't be made. Table 3.1 lists common D-sub ports and connectors as well as their most common uses. By the way, male interfaces have pins, while female interfaces have sockets. Be on the lookout for the casual use of DB to represent any D-sub connector. This is very common and is accepted as an unwritten de facto standard.

TABLE 3.1 Common D-sub connectors

Connector	Gender	Use
DE9	Male	Serial port
DE9	Female	Connector on a serial cable
DB25	Male	Serial port or connector on a parallel cable
DB25	Female	Parallel port, or connector on a serial cable
DA15	Female	Game port or MIDI port

Connector	Gender	Use
DA15	Male	Connector on a game peripheral cable or MIDI cable
DE15	Female	Video port (has three rows of five pins as opposed to two rows)
DE15	Male	Connector on a monitor cable

At the bottom left in Figure 3.6 is a DE15F 15-pin video port, in the center is a DB25F 25-pin female printer port, and on the right is a DE9M 9-pin male serial port.

FIGURE 3.6   D-sub ports and connectors

RJ-Series

Registered jack (RJ) connectors are most often used in telecommunications. The two most common examples of RJ ports are RJ-11 and RJ-45. RJ-11 connectors are used most often on flat satin cables in telephone hookups; your home phone jack is probably an RJ-11 jack. The ports in older external and internal analog modems are RJ-11.

RJ-45 connectors, on the other hand, are larger and most commonly found on Ethernet networks that use twisted-pair cabling. Your Ethernet NIC likely has an RJ-45 jack on it. See Chapter 6, "Networking Fundamentals," for details on networking interfaces. Although

RJ-45 is a widely accepted description for the larger connectors, it is not correct. Generically speaking, Ethernet interfaces are 8-pin modular connectors, or 8P8C connectors, meaning there are eight pin positions, and all eight of them are connected, or used. RJ-45 specifies the physical appearance of the connector and also how the contacts are wired from one end to the other. Surprisingly the RJ-45 specification does not match the TIA T568A and T568B wiring standards used in data communications.

Figure 3.7 shows an RJ-11 jack on the left and an RJ-45 jack on the right. Notice the size difference. As you can see, RJ connectors are typically square with multiple gold contacts on the flat side. A small locking tab on the other side prevents the connector and cable from falling or being pulled out of the jack casually.

FIGURE 3.7   RJ ports

Other Types of Ports

There are many other types of ports that are used with computers today, including these:

- Universal Serial Bus (USB)
- IEEE 1394 (FireWire)
- Infrared
- Audio jacks
- PS/2 (mini-DIN)
- Centronics

Let's look at each one and how it is used.

Universal Serial Bus (USB)

Most computers built after 1997 have one or more flat ports in place of one DE9M serial port. These ports are Universal Serial Bus (USB) ports, and they are used for connecting multiple (up to 127) peripherals to one computer through a single port (and the use of multiport peripheral hubs). USB version 1.x supports data rates as high as 12Mbps (1.5MBps). USB 2.0 supports data rates as high as 480Mbps (60MBps), 40 times that of its predecessor. USB 3.0 boasts data rates of 5Gbps, more than 10 times the rate of USB 2.0. Figure 3.8 shows an example of a set of Type A USB ports. Port types are explained in the section "Common Peripheral Cables and Their Interfaces" later in this chapter.

FIGURE 3.8   USB ports

USB 2.0 uses the same physical connection as the original USB, but it is much higher in transfer rates and requires a cable with more shielding that is less susceptible to noise. You can tell if a computer, hub, or cable supports USB 2.0 by looking for the red and blue "High Speed USB" graphic somewhere on the computer, device, or cable (or on its packaging). Super Speed USB 3.0 ports are also backward compatible but have additional contacts that only USB 3.0 cable connectors can access for increased performance.

Because of USB's higher transfer rate, flexibility, and ease of use, most devices that in the past used serial or parallel interfaces now come with USB interfaces. It's rare to see a newly introduced PC accessory with a standard serial interface. For example, PC cameras used to come as standard serial-only interfaces. Now, USB and FireWire are the preferred interfaces.

IEEE 1394 (FireWire)

While not as prevalent as USB ports, one other port has crept into the mainstream and is included as a standard attachment in small numbers, often only one, on motherboards and laptops. That port is the *IEEE 1394* port (shown on a desktop PC in Figure 3.9 and on a laptop in Figure 3.10), more commonly known as a *FireWire* port. Its popularity is due to its ease of use, isochronous (synchronized clock) mode, and very high (400Mbps to 3.2Gbps and higher) transmission rates.

FIGURE 3.9   A 6-pin FireWire port on a PC

FIGURE 3.10   A 4-pin FireWire port on a laptop

Originally developed by Apple, it was standardized by IEEE in 1995 as IEEE 1394. It is often used as a way to get digital video into a PC so it can be edited with digital video editing tools. Security applications benefit from FireWire's higher power output, reducing the need for external power to devices such as security cameras. Audio/video enthusiasts like this feature also and rely on the capability of headend devices to control and synchronize the various media sources.

Look for a more thorough discussion of FireWire as a technology in the section "Common Peripheral Cables and Their Interfaces" later in this chapter.

Infrared

Many years ago, increasing numbers of people became fed up with being tethered to their computers by cords. As a result, many computers (especially portable computing devices like laptops and PDAs) hit the market with infrared ports to send and receive data. Modern computers use radio frequency (RF) technologies, such as Bluetooth and WiFi, to accomplish the same and more. RF technologies such as Bluetooth and WiFi are presented in more detail, including their speed and distance limitations, in Chapter 8.

An infrared (IR) port is a small port on the computer that allows data to be sent and received using electromagnetic radiation in the infrared band. The infrared port itself is a small, dark square of plastic (usually a very dark maroon) and can typically be found on the front of a PC or on the side of a laptop or portable. Figure 3.11 shows an example of an infrared port.

FIGURE 3.11   An infrared port

Part of the reason for their fall from grace is that infrared ports send and receive data at a very slow rate (the maximum speed on PC infrared ports is less than 4Mbps). Most infrared ports support the Infrared Data Association (IrDA) standard, which outlines a standard way of transmitting and receiving information by infrared so that devices can communicate with one another.

More information on the IrDA standard can be found at the organization's website: www.irda.org.

Note that although infrared is a wireless technology, it shares characteristics more with light than with radio waves. In fact, infrared pulses can be carried through the air or through optical fiber, just like visible light and laser light. As a result, most infrared communications (especially those that conform to the IrDA standards) are line-of-sight only and take place within a short distance (typically less than four meters). Infrared is generally used for point-to-point communications such as controlling the volume on a device with a handheld remote control.

Audio/Video Jacks

The *RCA* jack (shown in Figure 3.12) was developed by the RCA Victor Company in the late 1940s for use with its phonographs. You bought a phonograph, connected the RCA plug on the back of your phonograph to the RCA jack on the back of your radio or television, and used the speaker and amplifier in the radio or television to listen to records. It made phonographs cheaper to produce and had the added bonus of making sure everyone had an RCA Victor radio or television (or at the very least, one with the RCA jack on the back). Either way, RCA made money.

FIGURE 3.12   An RCA jack (female) and RCA plug (male)

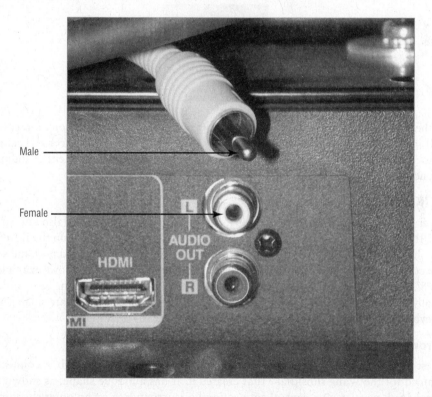

Today, RCA jacks and connectors (or plugs) are used to transmit both audio and video information. Typically, when you see a yellow-coded RCA connector on a PC video card (next to a DE15F VGA connector, perhaps), it's for composite video output (output to a television or VCR). However, digital audio can be implemented with S/PDIF, which can be deployed with an RCA jack. Figure 3.19 later in this chapter shows an S/PDIF RCA jack. RCA jacks are considered coaxial because the outer circular conductor and the center pin that collectively make up the unbalanced single transmit/receive pair have the same axis of rotation, *co-axial*. S/PDIF can also be implemented by TOSLINK fiber connectors. Toshiba's TOSLINK interface is a digital fiber-optic audio technology that is implemented with its own connector.

Although they aren't used for video, it bears mentioning that the 1/8″ stereo minijack and mating miniplug are still commonly used on computers these days for analog audio. Your sound card, microphone, and speakers have them. Figure 3.13 is a photo of a TOSLINK optical interface with a push-in/flip-up cover, pictured to the left of a set of standard analog minijacks.

FIGURE 3.13   The TOSLINK interface

In the spirit of covering interfaces that support both audio and video, don't forget the HDMI interface, which carries both over the same interface. Only CATV coaxial connections to TV cards can boast that on the PC. An RCA jack and cable carry either audio or video, not both simultaneously.

PS/2 (Keyboard and Mouse)

Another common port, as mentioned earlier, is the PS/2 port. A *PS/2 port* (also known as a mini-DIN 6 connector) is a mouse and keyboard interface port first found on the IBM PS/2 (hence the name). It is smaller than previous interfaces (the DIN 5 keyboard port and serial mouse connector), and thus its popularity increased quickly. Figure 3.14 shows examples of both PS/2 keyboard and mouse ports. You can tell the difference because the keyboard port is usually purple and the mouse port is usually green. Also, typically there are small graphics of a keyboard and mouse, respectively, imprinted next to the ports.

Centronics

The last type of port connector is the Centronics connector, a micro ribbon connector named for the Wang subsidiary that created it. It has a unique shape, as shown in Figure 3.15. It consists of a central connection bar surrounding by an outer shielding ring. The Centronics connector was primarily used in parallel printer connections and SCSI interfaces. It is most often found on peripherals, not on computers themselves (except in the case of some older 50-pin SCSI interface cards).

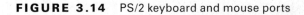

FIGURE 3.14 PS/2 keyboard and mouse ports

Common Peripheral Cables and Their Interfaces

An *interface* is a method of connecting two dissimilar items together. A peripheral interface is a method of connecting a peripheral or accessory to a computer, including the specification of cabling, connector and port type, speed, and method of communication used.

The most common interfaces used in PCs today include (in no particular order):

- Drive interfaces
- SCSI
- Parallel
- Serial
- USB
- IEEE 1394 (FireWire)
- RJ-45
- Audio (RCA and TOSLINK)
- PS/2

Let's look at the cabling and connectors used as well as the type(s) of peripherals that are connected to such interfaces.

FIGURE 3.15   A Centronics connector

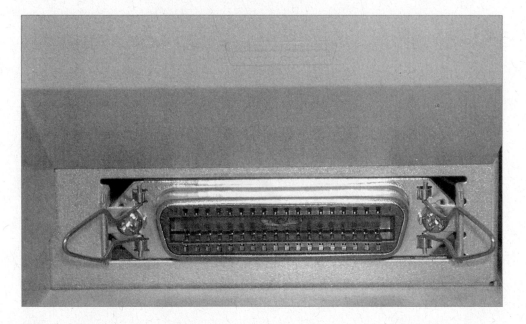

Floppy and Hard Disk Connectors

Almost every computer made today uses some type of disk drive to store data and programs until they are needed. All drives need some form of connection to the motherboard so the computer can "talk" to the disk drive. Regardless of whether the connection is built into the motherboard (*onboard*)—it could reside on an adapter card (*off-board*)—the standard for the attachment is based on the drive's requirements. These connections are known as *drive interfaces*, and there are two main types: floppy disk drive interfaces and hard disk drive interfaces.

Floppy disk drive interfaces allow floppy disk drives (FDDs) and certain other devices, such as some internal tape drives, to be connected to the motherboard, and similarly, hard disk drive interfaces do the same for hard disks and optical drives, among others. The interfaces consist of circuitry and a port, or *header*. Many motherboards produced today lack a header for FDD attachment. Almost all, however, still provide non-SCSI hard disk interfaces on the motherboard, with the latest version of SATA being the most popular. Server motherboards often include SCSI headers and circuitry as well or instead. See Chapter 2, "Storage Devices and Power Supplies," for information on SCSI cables, connectors, and pin-outs.

Today, the headers you will find on most motherboards are for Serial ATA (SATA), the speeds of which were discussed in Chapter 2. Enhanced IDE (EIDE)—also known retroactively as Parallel ATA (PATA)—interfaces have become exceedingly rare, with respect to the number of PATA devices still in force. As a result, you should consider your installed base of PATA drives before upgrading your motherboards. Use Figure 3.16 to compare the size of the 34-wire FDD cable and 34-pin connector to the 40-pin PATA connector underneath it.

FIGURE 3.16   The FDD and PATA cables

The PATA headers on older motherboards will normally be black or some other neutral color if they follow the classic ATA 40-wire standard. If your PATA headers are blue, they represent PATA interfaces that employ the ATA-5 or higher version of the Ultra DMA (UDMA) technology. These headers require 80-wire ribbon cables that allow increased transfer rates by reducing crosstalk in the parallel signal. Many headers and cable connectors are of a corresponding blue color to indicate their capability. The cables reduce crosstalk by alternating among the other wires another 40 ground wires. The connectors and headers still have 40 pins, however, because ground wires can be ganged and do not need separate pins. The color coding of the header alerts you to the enhanced performance. The headers can be downward compatible with the 40-wire technology but at reduced performance. Figure 3.17 shows the 80-wire cable lying on top of the 40-wire cable.

FIGURE 3.17   The 80- and 40-wire PATA cables

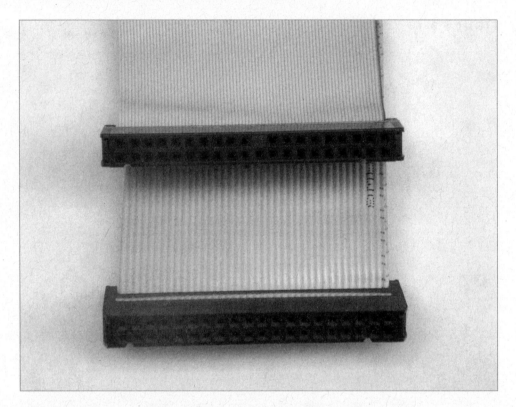

The 40-pin ATA header transfers multiple bits of data between the drive and motherboard in parallel, hence the name Parallel ATA. SATA, in comparison, which came out later and prompted the retroactive PATA moniker, transfers data in series, allowing a higher data throughput because there is no need for the more advanced parallel synchronization of data signals. The SATA headers are vastly different from the PATA headers. Figure 3.18 shows an example of the SATA data connector. Consult Chapter 2 for additional information on SATA and eSATA connectors and their flat data cables.

FIGURE 3.18   The Serial ATA connector

Common Ports and Connectors

For a computer to be useful and have as much functionality as possible, there must be a way to get the data into and out of it. Many different ports are available for this purpose. This section continues the discussion of port and connector types started earlier in the chapter but introduces additional information on those already mentioned and other interfaces.

Briefly, the seven most common types of ports you will see on a computer are Universal Serial Bus (USB), FireWire/IEEE 1394, eSATA, video, Ethernet, digital/analog sound in/out, and PS/2 keyboard and mouse. Figure 3.19 shows some of these and others on a docking station or port replicator for a laptop. From left to right, the interfaces shown are as follows:

- DC power in
- Analog modem RJ-11
- Ethernet NIC RJ-45
- S-video out
- DVI-D (dual-link) out
- SVGA out
- Parallel (on top)
- Standard serial
- Mouse (on top)
- Keyboard

- S/PDIF (out)
- USB

FIGURE 3.19 Peripheral ports and connectors

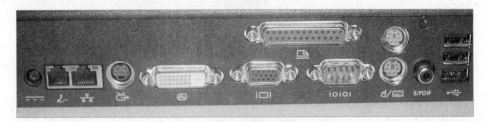

The Classic Game Port

Figure 3.20 shows an example of a game port (also called a joystick port because that was the most common device that connected to it). As discussed later in this chapter, the game port can be used to connect to Musical Instrument Digital Interface (MIDI) devices as well. Game ports connect such peripheral devices to the computer using a DA-15F connector. Legacy sound cards often included a game port. Devices that once connected to the game port have evolved, for the most part, into USB-attached devices.

FIGURE 3.20 A game port

Analog Sound Jacks

Figure 3.21 shows another set of interfaces not shown in Figure 3.19, the sound card jacks. These jacks are known as 1/8″ (3.5mm) stereo minijacks, so called for their size and the fact that they make contact with both the left and right audio channels through their tip, rings (if they have any), and sleeve.

Identifying Characteristics of Connectors and Cables   **151**

FIGURE 3.21   Sound card jacks

Shown in the photo is a six-jack setup capable of 8-channel audio, also known as 7.1 surround sound. The 7 represents the seven full-bandwidth channels and the 1 represents the one low frequency effects (LFE) channel, most often attached to the subwoofer. Each of the full-bandwidth channels is often represented by its own speaker in the system, but not necessarily. If there is a 1:1 channel-to-speaker representation, the eight speakers in 8-channel 7.1 are generally placed equidistant from the audience as follows, with all angles measured from front center (usually where the video source resides):

- One center speaker at 0 degrees (at the video source)
- Left and right front speakers at 22 to 30 degrees
- Left and right side speakers at 90 to 110 degrees
- Left and right rear speakers at 135 to 150 degrees
- One subwoofer possibly hidden anywhere in the room

The right column of jacks in Figure 3.21 represents the classic three minijacks found on sound cards. The middle one is a green output jack used for 2-channel audio, usually manifested as two full-bandwidth speakers, one each on the left and right channels. Both channels are provided by the single green *stereo* minijack. The other two are input interfaces; the top jack is the blue line-in interface, designed for audio sources that lack a specialized interface, less expensive keyboards, and phonographs, for example. The bottom one is the pink microphone input jack.

If you understand the concept of 8-channel 7.1, then 4-channel 3.1 and 6-channel 5.1 will be simpler to understand. The left column of jacks in Figure 3.21 was added for dedicated surround sound use and comprises the orange jack at the top for the *center* and *subwoofer* channels (used for 3.1, 5.1, and 7.1), the black middle jack for the *rear* left and right surround channels (used for 5.1 and 7.1), and the gray jack at the bottom for the *side* left and right surround channels (used only for 7.1 surround sound). With 3.1, 5.1, and 7.1, the green jack is adopted for the *front* stereo channel. Technically, 3.1 is not surround sound because there are only front and center channels and no surround channels.

Most installers place the rear speakers in 5.1 at the rearmost position recommended for the 7.1 side speakers, about 110 degrees from front center. When you're migrating to 7.1, these rear speakers are repurposed as side speakers and new ones are installed as 7.1 rear speakers, at an angle starting from about 135 degrees.

Software can use these interfaces to allow you to record and play back audio content in file—MP3, for instance—or CD/DVD form. Note, however, that the jacks themselves are not distinctive in their physical characteristics. They are uniquely addressable, but it is up to the software's programming to assign their purpose. Most programmers, of course, respect the color code. As a case study, for motherboards that support surround sound but do not supply the black and orange jacks, you have to use the blue jack for both line in and rear surround and the pink jack for both microphone and center/subwoofer. Depending on the software in use, you would need to manually swap one plug for another because the jack functions would change.

Parallel Interfaces

For many years, the most popular type of interface available on computers was the parallel interface. Parallel communications take the interstate approach to data communications. Normally, interstate travel is faster than driving on city roads. This is the case mainly because you can fit multiple cars going the same direction on the same highway by using multiple lanes. On the return trip, you take a similar path, but on a completely separate road. The *parallel printer interface* (an example is shown at the top of Figure 3.6) transfers data 8 bits at a time over eight separate transmit wires inside a parallel cable (1 bit per wire). Normal parallel interfaces use a DB25 female connector on the computer to transfer data to peripherals.

Parallel ports are faster than the original serial ports, which were also once used for printers in electrically noisy environments or at greater distances from the computer. However, the advent of USB has brought serial—fast serial—back to the limelight. As it turns out, firing 1 bit at a time leads to faster bit rates than babysitting a parallel procession of bits.

The most common use of the parallel interface was printer communication. There are three major specifications of parallel port: standard, bidirectional, and enhanced parallel ports. Let's look at the differences among the three.

Standard Parallel Ports

The standard parallel port only transmits data *out* of the computer. It cannot receive data (except for a single wire carrying a Ready signal). The standard parallel port was found on the original IBM PC, XT, and AT. It can transmit data at only 150KBps and was most commonly used to transmit data to printers. This technology also had a maximum transmission distance of 10 feet.

Bidirectional Parallel Ports

As its name suggests, the bidirectional parallel port has one important advantage over a standard parallel port: It can both transmit and receive data. These parallel ports are capable of interfacing with such devices as external CD-ROM drives and external parallel port backup drives (Zip, Jaz, and tape drives). Most computers made since 1994 that included a parallel printer port had this bidirectional parallel port.

> For bidirectional communication to occur properly, the cable must support bidirectional communication as well.

Enhanced Parallel Ports

As more people began using parallel ports to interface with devices other than printers, they started to notice that the available speed wasn't good enough. Double-speed CD-ROM drives had a transfer rate of 300KBps, but the parallel port could transfer data at only 150KBps, thus limiting the speed at which a computer could retrieve data from an external device. To solve that problem, the Institute of Electrical and Electronics Engineers (IEEE) came up with a standard for enhanced parallel ports called IEEE 1284. The IEEE 1284 standard provides for greater data transfer speeds and the ability to send memory addresses as well as data through a parallel port. This standard allows the parallel port to theoretically act as an extension to the main bus. In addition, these ports are backward compatible with the standard and bidirectional ports and support cable lengths of 4.5 meters, which is almost 15 feet.

There are five data transfer implementations of IEEE 1284, two of which are EPP parallel ports and ECP parallel ports. An enhanced parallel port (EPP) increases bidirectional throughput from 150KBps to anywhere from 600KBps to 1.5MBps. An enhanced capabilities port (ECP) is designed to transfer data at even higher speeds, around 2MBps. ECP uses direct memory access (DMA) and buffering to increase printing performance over EPP. IEEE 1284 also allows for backward support of the standard parallel port (SPP) in compatibility mode.

> The cable must also have full support for IEEE 1284 in order for proper communications to occur in both directions and at rated speeds.

Parallel Interfaces and Cables

Most parallel interfaces use a DB25 female connector, as shown earlier in this chapter. Most parallel cables use a DB25 male connector on one end and either a DB25 male connector or, more commonly, a Centronics-36 connector on the other. The original printer cables typically used the DB25M–to–Centronics-36 configuration. Inside a parallel cable, eight wires are used for transmitting data so that 1 byte can be transmitted at a time. Figure 3.22 shows an example of a typical parallel cable (in this case, a printer cable). Note the IEEE 1284 compliance marking on the cable's sheath.

FIGURE 3.22   A typical parallel cable

Figure 3.23 shows the component end of a mini-Centronics cable. The mini-Centronics did not enjoy the success expected due to design issues regarding attachment reliability. Again, however, nothing is more popular today for printer connectivity than USB, so efforts to perpetuate the use of and improve the mini-Centronics were abandoned.

FIGURE 3.23   The mini-Centronics connector

Serial

If standard parallel communications were similar to taking the interstate, then RS-232 serial communications were similar to taking a country road. In serial communications, bits of data are sent one after another (single file, if you will) down one wire, and they return on a different wire in the same cable. Three main types of serial interfaces are available today: standard serial (RS-232), Universal Serial Bus (USB), and FireWire (IEEE 1394). USB and FireWire use increased signaling frequencies to overcome serial's stigma and join other serial technologies, such as PCIe and SATA, as frontrunners in data communications.

Standard Serial

Almost every computer made since the original IBM PC has at least one serial port. These computers are easily identified because they have either a DE9 or DB25 male port (shown in Figure 3.24). Standard serial ports have a maximum data transmission speed of 57Kbps and a maximum cable length of 50 feet.

FIGURE 3.24   Standard DE9 and DB25 male serial ports

Serial cables come in two common wiring configurations: standard serial cable and null modem serial cable. A standard serial cable is used to hook various peripherals such as modems and printers to a computer. A null modem serial cable is used to hook two computers together without a modem. The transmit-centric pins on one end are wired to the receive-centric pins on the other side, so it's as if a modem connection exists between the two computers but without the need for a modem. Figure 3.25 and Figure 3.26 show the *pin-outs* and wiring differences between a standard 9- to 25-pin serial cable and a 9- to 9-pin null modem cable. In the null modem diagram, notice how the transmit (tx) pins on one end are wired to the receive (rx) pins on the other and how certain pins are looped back on each end to fool the computer into believing a modem is ready for its transmission.

FIGURE 3.25   A standard serial cable wiring diagram

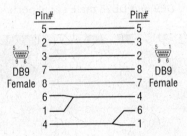

```
                      Pin#              Pin#
                       2 ————————————— 3
                       3 ————————————— 2
        1        13     4 ————————————— 7      5   1
       ·············                          ·····
       ·············                          ·····
        14       25     5 ————————————— 8      9   6
        DB25           6 ————————————— 6    DB9
        Male            7 ————————————— 5    Female
                       8 ————————————— 1
                      20 ————————————— 4
                      22 ————————————— 9
```

FIGURE 3.26   A null modem serial cable wiring diagram

```
                      Pin#              Pin#
                       5 ————————————— 5
                       2 ————————————— 3
        5   1          3 ————————————— 2      5   1
       ·····                                 ·····
       ·····           7 ————————————— 8     ·····
        9   6          8 ————————————— 7      9   6
        DB9            6 ——\    /—— 4    DB9
        Female         1 ——— \/ ——— 6    Female
                       4 ——— /\ ——— 1
```

Finally, because of the two different device connectors (DE9M and DB25M), serial cables have a few different configurations. Table 3.2 shows the most common serial cable configurations.

TABLE 3.2   Common serial cable configurations

First Connector	Second Connector	Description
DE9 female	DB25 male	Standard modem cable
DE9 female	DE9 male	Standard serial extension cable
DE9 female	DE9 female	Null modem cable
DB25 female	DB25 female	Null modem cable
DB25 female	DB25 male	Standard serial cable or standard serial extension cable

Universal Serial Bus (USB)

USB cables are used to connect a wide variety of peripherals to computers, including keyboards, mice, digital cameras, printers, and scanners. Not all USB cables maximize the potential of all USB ports. USB 1.x cables cannot provide USB 2.0 and 3.0 performance; USB 2.0 cables cannot provide USB 3.0 performance. Good or bad, depending on how you look at it, the interfaces accept all cable connectors. So, ensuring that your cable is built to the specification you intend to use, whether version 2.0 or 3.0, is of utmost importance. Otherwise, the connected device will have to fall back to the maximum version supported by the cable. This is usually not an issue, except for the lost performance, but some high-performance devices will refuse to operate at reduced levels.

Table 3.3 details the differences in the maximum speeds defined by the three groups of USB specifications. Note that these speeds are not generally attainable due to a variety of factors, but USB 3.0 has the greatest likelihood of attaining its maximum rate because of its full-duplex nature. Note that all specifications are capable of *Low Speed* 1.5Mbps performance.

TABLE 3.3 USB speed limitations

Specification	Maximum Speed	Speed Trade Name
USB 1.0/1.1	12Mbps	Full Speed
USB 2.0	480Mbps	High Speed
USB 3.0	5Gbps (5000Mbps)	SuperSpeed

The USB technology is fairly straightforward. Essentially, it was designed to be Plug and Play—just plug in the peripheral and it should work, providing the software is installed to support it. Many standard devices have drivers built into the common operating systems. More complex devices come with drivers to be installed before the component is connected.

The USB cable varies most based on the USB peripheral connector on the external-device end. Because there can be quite a number of USB devices on a single system, it helps to have a scheme to clarify their connectivity. The USB standard specifies two broad types of connectors. They are designated Type A and Type B connectors. A standard USB cable has some form of Type A connector on one end and some form of Type B connector on the other end. Figure 3.27 shows four USB 1.x/2.0 cable connectors. From left to right, they are as follows:

- Type A
- Standard Mini-B
- Type B
- Alternate Mini-B

FIGURE 3.27   USB cables and connectors

Modern small form-factor devices, including many phones and smaller digital cameras, use a Micro-B connector, shown in Figure 3.28, that is smaller than the Mini-B shown in Figure 3.27.

FIGURE 3.28   USB Micro-B connector

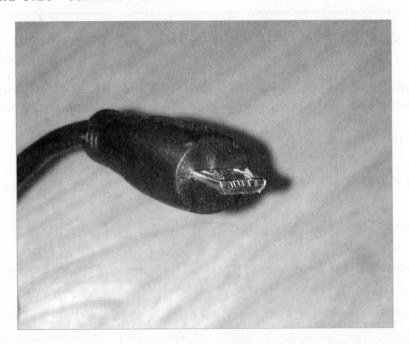

The specification for USB 3.0, also known as SuperSpeed, recommends a standard blue color coding for all interfaces and cables as a way of differentiating them from legacy cables and interfaces. The connectors also feature five additional pins that are not accessible to 1.x/2.0 connectors and receptacles shown in Figure 3.27 and Figure 3.28.

One part of the USB interface specification that makes it so appealing is the fact that if your computer runs out of USB ports, you can simply plug a device known as a *USB hub* into one of your computer's USB ports, which will give you several more USB ports from one original port. Figure 3.29 shows an example of a USB hub.

FIGURE 3.29   A USB hub

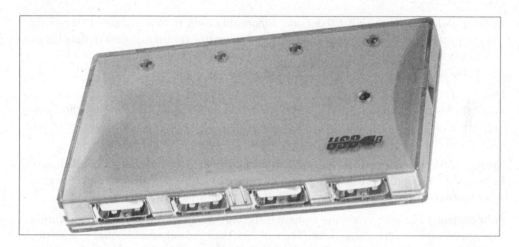

Be aware of the limitations in the USB specification. Table 3.4 details the cable-length limitations for each of the three families of USB. The third column simply shows the combined length of all six cables used with five hubs and a sixth cable connected to the component. If you use hubs, you should never use more than five hubs between the system and any component.

TABLE 3.4   USB cable-length limitations

Specification	Maximum Cable Length	Total Cable with Five Hubs
USB 1.0/1.1	3m	18m
USB 2.0	5m	30m
USB 3.0	3m	18m

In addition to the cable length difference between USB 2.0 and 3.0, there are a host of other differences between these specifications. The following items outline some of the primary differences.

Shielding   USB 3.0 requires that each pair in the cable assembly be shielded to withstand the electromagnetic interference (EMI) inherent with transmissions at higher frequencies.

Connectors   Although all connectors are compatible with all receptacles, to attain SuperSpeed performance, SuperSpeed connectors with five additional pins must be used on cables and receptacles. These pins do not obstruct the four legacy pins required for backward compatibility. Instead, they sit farther back and are accessible only to compatible interfaces.

Bursting and streaming   USB 2.0 does not support bursting, the low-duration, excessively fast transmission of data, nor does it support streaming, the continuous flow of data between two endpoints once the flow has begun. USB 3.0 supports continuous bursting as well as streaming.

Duplex   USB 2.0 is a half-duplex technology, meaning that all devices must share a common bandwidth, making overall performance appear subpar. USB 3.0, on the other hand, supports dual simplex communications pathways that collectively imitate full-duplex transmission, where devices at both ends of the cable can transmit simultaneously.

Media access method   USB 2.0 peripheral devices must wait until polled by the host before transmitting data. USB 3.0 endpoints use an asynchronous transmission mechanism, similar to that of Ethernet, where data is transmitted at will.

Host control   The host (computer system) is the only device in the USB 2.0 specification that can control power management. The endpoints are the only devices that can participate in error detection and recovery as well as flow control. USB 3.0 endpoints can all control when they enter low-power mode to conserve power. Error handling and flow control are performed on each link in USB 3.0, not just at the endpoints.

Power   USB 2.0 provides a maximum of 100 milliamperes (mA) of current at low power and 500mA at high power. USB 3.0 provides 150mA and 900mA, respectively, allowing for the direct powering of some of the same component types that FireWire is capable of powering but that USB 2.0 is not.

Through the use of a 7-bit identifier, providing $2^7 = 128$ possible addresses, no more than 127 devices, including hubs, should be connected back to a single USB host controller in the computer, not that you would ever want to approach this number. The 128th identifier, the highest address, is used for broadcasting to all endpoints. No interconnection of host controllers is allowed with USB; each one and its connected devices are isolated from other host controllers and their devices. As a result, USB ports are not considered networkable ports. Consult your system's documentation to find out if your USB ports operate on the same host controller.

From the perspective of the cable's plug, Type A is always oriented toward the system from the component. As a result, you might notice that the USB receptacle on the computer system that a component cables back to is the same as the receptacles on the USB hub that components cable back to. The USB hub is simply an extension of the system and becomes a component that cables back to the system. Each hub takes one of the 127 available addresses.

Type B plugs connect in the direction of the peripheral component. Therefore, you see a single Type B interface on the hub as well as on the peripheral endpoints to allow them to cable back to the system or another hub. Although they exist, USB cables with both ends of the same type, a sort of extension cable, are in violation of the USB specification. Collectively, these rules make cabling your USB subsystem quite straightforward.

WARNING

USB connectors are keyed and will go into a USB port only one way. If the connector will not go into the port properly, try rotating it.

NOTE

For more information on USB, check out www.usb.org.

IEEE 1394 (FireWire)

The IEEE 1394 interface is about two things, if nothing else: speed and efficiency. Its first iteration, now known as FireWire 400, has a maximum data throughput of 400Mbps in half duplex. Although the numbers imply that USB 2.0 at 480Mbps might outperform FireWire 400, the truth is that FireWire allows a closer saturation of the bandwidth by its devices due to its different encoding mechanism. USB devices are lucky to achieve half of their bus's rated bandwidth during sustained operation. The other major difference between the two technologies is the amount of power accessible to FireWire devices. Whereas USB provides less than an ampere of current at 5VDC, FireWire specifications allow for the provision of 1.5A at up to 30VDC (and slightly more in some implementations). This production of 45W of power allows for larger devices to be powered by the FireWire interface, obviating the need for separate external power.

The next iteration, FireWire 800 (specified under IEEE 1394b), has a maximum data throughput of 800Mbps and works in full duplex. FireWire 400 carries data over a maximum cable length of 4.5 meters with a maximum of 63 devices connected to each interface on the computer. Using new beta connectors and associated cabling, including a fiber-optic solution, FireWire 800 extends to 100 meters. When implemented over copper, FireWire 800, like FireWire 400, is limited to 4.5m cable runs. IEEE 1394c standardized the running of FireWire over the same Category 5e infrastructure that supports Ethernet, including the use of RJ-45 connectors. IEEE 1394b also allows for 1.6Gbps (S1600) and 3.2Gbps (S3200) implementations.

FireWire (also known as i.LINK in Sony's parlance) uses a very special type of six-wire cable, as shown in Figure 3.30 for FireWire 400. Only four wires are used when power is not supplied by the interface. These interfaces are collectively known as *alpha connectors*.

Notice the difference in the system end on the left and the component end on the right. It is difficult to mistake this cable for anything but a FireWire cable. FireWire 800 uses a nine-wire implementation with *beta connectors*. A beta connector and one of the FireWire logos (another is a stylized "1394") are shown on the left of Figure 3.42 later in this chapter. *Alpha* and *beta* originally referred to the different encoding methods used with FireWire 400 and FireWire 800.

FIGURE 3.30   A FireWire (IEEE 1394) 6- to 4-pin alpha cable

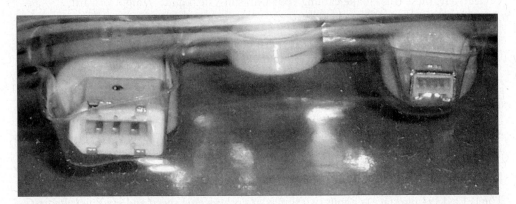

Although most people think of FireWire as a tool for connecting their digital camcorders to their computers, it's much more than that. Because of its high data transfer rate, it is being used more and more as a universal, high-speed data interface for things like hard drives, optical drives, and digital video editing equipment.

Because the FireWire specification was conceived to allow peripherals to be networked together in much the same fashion as intelligent hosts are networked together in LANs and WANs, a quick introduction to the concept of networking is in order; see Chapter 6 for more detail on networking concepts. A topology can be thought of as the layout of the nodes that make up the endpoints and connecting devices of the network. One of the most popular topologies today is the star topology, which uses a central concentrating device that is cabled directly to the endpoints. A tree structure is formed when these concentrating devices are interconnected to one another, each attached to its own set of endpoints. One or few concentrators appear at the first tier of the tree, sort of like the "root system" of the tree. These root devices are expected to carry more traffic than other concentrators because of their position in the hierarchy. In subsequent tiers, other concentrators branch off from the root and each other to complete the tree analogy.

The 1995 IEEE 1394 specification that is equivalent to FireWire 400 allows 1023 buses, each supporting 63 devices, to be bridged together. This networkable architecture supports more than 64,000 interconnected devices that can communicate directly with one another instead of communicating through a host computer the way USB is required to do. Star and tree topologies can be formed as long as no two devices are separated by more than 16 hops. A *hop* can be thought of as a link between any two end devices, repeaters, or bridges, resulting in a total maximum distance between devices of 72 meters.

Through an internal hub, a single end device can use two IEEE 1394 ports to connect to two different devices, creating a daisy-chained pathway that allows the other two devices to communicate with one another as well. The device in the middle, which can be the computer system or any peripheral device, affords a physical pathway between the other two devices but is not otherwise involved in their communication with one another. Contrast this function to that of the USB host, which, prior to version 3.0, had to be involved in all transactions. USB 3.0 does not provide bridged networking the way FireWire does but allows the devices to initiate communication and other transactions.

RCA

The RCA cable is a simple coaxial cable. There are two connectors, usually male, one on each end of the cable. There are two contacts on each connector, the ground ring and the positive data pin in the middle. The male connector connects to the female connector on the equipment. Figure 3.31 shows an example of an RCA cable. An RCA male-to-RCA female connector is also available; it's used to extend the reach of audio or video signals.

FIGURE 3.31   An RCA cable

The RCA male connectors on a connection cable are sometimes plated in gold to increase their corrosion resistance and to improve longevity.

PS/2 (Keyboard and Mouse)

The most important input device for a PC is the keyboard. All PC motherboards contain some sort of connector that allows a keyboard to be connected directly to the motherboard through the case. There are two main types of wired keyboard connectors. Once, these were the AT and PS/2 connectors. Today, the PS/2-style connector remains somewhat popular, but it is quickly being replaced by USB-attached keyboards. The all-but-extinct original AT connector is round, about ½″ in diameter, in a 5-pin DIN configuration. Figure 3.32 shows an example of the AT-style keyboard connector.

The PS/2 connector (as shown in Figure 3.33) is a smaller 6-pin mini-DIN connector. Many new PCs you can purchase today contain a PS/2 keyboard connector as well as a PS/2 mouse connector right above it on the motherboard. Compare your PC's keyboard connector with the connectors in Figure 3.32 and Figure 3.33.

FIGURE 3.32   An AT connector on a motherboard

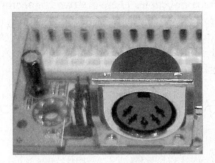

FIGURE 3.33   A PS/2-style keyboard connector on a motherboard

Wireless keyboard and mouse attachment is fairly popular today and is most often achieved with Bluetooth technology or a proprietary RF implementation.

In the past few generations of motherboards, the PS/2 mouse and keyboard connectors have been color-coded to make connection of keyboards and mice easier because they are physically identical but functionally different. PS/2 mouse connectors are green (to match the standard green connectors on some mice), and the keyboard connectors are purple. If you have trouble remembering the difference, think of the fact that mice, not keyboards, exist in nature, and mice might get seasick and turn "green."

Many keyboards and mice today still come with an adapter to change their USB connector into the PS/2 interface. Using the PS/2 connector that most motherboards still come with saves one or two USB interfaces. Manufacturers sometimes opt for a single PS/2 connector with half purple and half green color codes, indicating either device can be attached to the same interface. However, in these situations, only one of the two types of device can be connected at a time. Figure 3.34 shows an example of a PS/2 keyboard cable.

FIGURE 3.34   A PS/2 keyboard cable

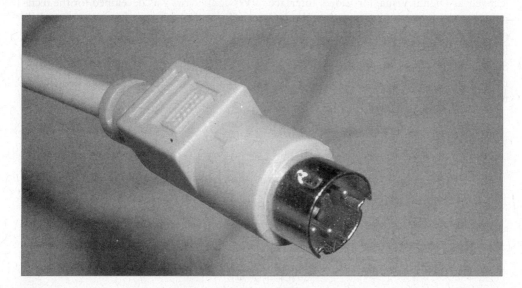

Most often, PS/2 cables have only one connector because the other end is connected directly to the device being plugged in. The only exception is PS/2 extension cables used to extend the length of a PS/2 device's cable.

Video Display Cables and Connectors

While the analog VGA-spawned standards might keep the computing industry satisfied for years to come yet, the sector in the market driving development of non-VGA specifications has become increasingly more prevalent. These high-resolution, high-performance junkies approach video from the broadcast angle. They are interested in the increased quality of digital transmission. For them, the industry responded with technologies like DVI and HDMI. The computing market benefits from these technologies as well. DVI interfaces on graphics adapters and laptops became commonplace. In increasingly more cases, HDMI interfaces take adapters to the next generation.

Other consumers desire specialized methods to connect analog display devices by splitting out colors from the component to improve quality or simply to provide video output to displays not meant for computers. For this group, a few older standards remain viable: component video, S-video, and composite video. The following sections present the details of these five specifications.

DVI

In an effort to leave analog VGA standards and return to digital video, which can typically be transmitted farther and at higher quality than analog, a series of connectors known collectively as Digital Visual (or Video) Interface (*DVI*) connectors was developed for the technology of the same name. These digital interfaces offer much higher performance than the original digital standards, such as CGA and EGA. At first glance, the DVI connector might look like a standard D-sub connector, but on closer inspection, it begins to look somewhat different. For one thing, it has quite a few pins, and for another, the pins it has are asymmetrical in their placement on the connector. Figure 3.35 illustrates the five types of connectors that the DVI standard specifies.

FIGURE 3.35   Types of DVI connector

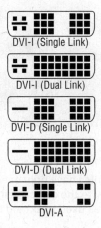

DVI-I (Single Link)

DVI-I (Dual Link)

DVI-D (Single Link)

DVI-D (Dual Link)

DVI-A

One thing to note about analog vs. digital display technologies is that all graphics adapters and all monitors deal with digital information. It is only the connectors and cabling that can be made to support analog transmission. Before DVI and HDMI encoding technologies were developed, consumer digital video display connectors could not afford the space to accommodate the number of pins that would have been required to transmit 16 or more bits of color information per pixel. For this reason the relatively few conductors of the inferior analog signaling in VGA were appealing.

There are three main categories of DVI connectors:

DVI-A   An analog-only connector. The source must produce analog output, and the monitor must understand analog input.

DVI-D   A digital-only connector. The source must produce digital output, and the monitor must understand digital input.

DVI-I   A combination analog/digital connector. The source and monitor must both support the same technology, but this cable works with either a digital or an analog signal.

The DVI-D and DVI-I connectors come in two varieties: single link and dual link. The dual-link options have more conductors—taking into account the six center conductors—than their single-link counterparts, which accommodate higher speed and signal quality. The additional link can be used to increase resolution from 1920×1080 to 2048×1536 for devices with a 16:9 aspect ratio or from WUXGA to WQXGA for devices with a 16:10 aspect ratio. Of course, both components, as well as the cable, must support the dual-link feature. Consult Chapter 4, "Display Devices," for more information on display standards.

DVI-A and DVI-I analog quality is superior to that of VGA, but it's still analog, meaning it is more susceptible to noise. However, the DVI analog signal will travel farther than the VGA signal before degrading beyond usability. Nevertheless, the DVI-A and VGA interfaces are pin-compatible, meaning that a simple passive adapter, as shown in Figure 3.36, is all that is necessary to convert between the two. As you can see, the analog portion of the connector, if it exists, comprises the four separate color and sync pins and the horizontal blade that they surround, which happens to be the analog ground lead that acts as a ground and physical support mechanism even for DVI-D connectors.

It's important to note that DVI-I cables and interfaces are designed to interconnect two analog or two digital devices; they cannot convert between analog and digital. DVI cables must support a signal of at least 4.5 meters, but better cable assemblies, stronger transmitters, and active boosters result in signals extending over longer distances.

HDMI

High-Definition Multimedia Interface (HDMI) is an all-digital technology that advances the work of DVI to include the same dual-link resolutions using a standard HDMI cable but with higher motion-picture frame rates and digital audio right on the same connector. HDMI cabling also supports an optional Consumer Electronics Control (CEC) feature that allows transmission of signals from a remote control unit to control multiple devices without separate cabling to carry infrared signals.

FIGURE 3.36   DVI-A–to–VGA adapter

The HDMI connector is not the same as the one used for DVI. Nevertheless, the two technologies are electrically compatible. In June 2006, revision 1.3 of the HDMI specification was released to support the bit rates necessary for HD DVD and Blu-ray disc. The latest version of the HDMI specification, version 1.4, was released May 28, 2009. The following two years saw the development of revisions 1.4a and 1.4b as well as the creation of the HDMI Forum on October 25, 2011. There will be no more development on version 1.4b, but the next revision will be backward compatible with 1.4b-compliant components.

HDMI is compatible with DVI-D and DVI-I interfaces through proper adapters, but HDMI's audio and remote-control pass-through features are lost. Additionally, 3D video sources work only with HDMI. Figure 3.37 shows a DVI-to-HDMI adapter between DVI-D and the Type A 19-pin HDMI interface. The first image is the DVI-D interface, and the second is the HDMI interface on the other side of the adapter. Compare the DVI-D interface to the DVI-I interface of Figure 3.36 and notice that the ground blade on the DVI-D connector is narrower than that of the DVI-A and DVI-I connectors. The DVI-D receptacle does not accept the other two plugs, for this reason as well as because the four analog pins around the blade have no sockets in the DVI-D receptacle.

FIGURE 3.37   HDMI-to-DVI adapter

There is also a Type B connector that has 29 pins and is intended to support higher resolution for the components that use it. HDMI version 1.3 specified a smaller 19-pin Type C connector for portable devices. The Type C connector, also referred to as a *mini-HDMI* connector, is compatible with the Type A connector but still requires an adapter due to its smaller size. HDMI version 1.4 specified two more interfaces, Type D and Type E. If Type C is a miniHDMI interface, then you might refer to the Type D connector as microHDMI. Figure 3.38 shows a Type D HDMI connector to the right of a Micro-B USB connector on a smartphone. Also compatible with Type A interfaces because they have the same 19 pins, Type D interfaces require but a simple adapter for conversion.

HDMI cables should meet the signal requirements of the latest specification. As a result, and as with DVI, the maximum cable length is somewhat variable. For HDMI, cable length depends heavily on the materials used to construct the cable. Passive cables tend to extend no farther than 15 meters, while adding electronics within the cable to create an active version results in lengths as long as 30 meters. Twisted-pair and fiber cabling options can extend cabling to 50 meters and 100 meters, respectively.

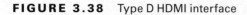

FIGURE 3.38   Type D HDMI interface

Component Video

When analog technologies outside the VGA realm are used for broadcast video, you are generally able to get better-quality video by splitting the red, green, and blue components in the signal into different streams right at the source. The technology known as *component video* performs a signal-splitting function similar to *RGB separation*. However, unlike RGB separation, which requires full-bandwidth red, green, and blue signals as well as a fourth pathway for synchronization, the most popular implementation of component video uses one uncompressed signal and two compressed signals, reducing the overall bandwidth needed. These signals are delivered over coax either as red, green, and blue color-coded RCA plugs or similarly coded *BNC* connectors, the latter being seen mostly in broadcast-quality applications.

The uncompressed signal is called luma (Y), which is essentially the colorless version of the original signal that represents the "brightness" of the source feed as a grayscale image. The component-video source also creates two compressed color-difference signals known as Pb and Pr. These two chrominance (chroma, for short) signals are also known as B – Y and R – Y, respectively, because they are created by subtracting out the luma from the blue and red source signals. It might make sense, then, that the analog technology presented here is most often referred to and labeled as YPbPr. A digital version of this technology, usually found on high-end devices, replaces analog's Pb and Pr with Cb and Cr, respectively, and is most often labeled YCbCr. Figure 3.39 shows the three RCA connectors of a component video cable.

FIGURE 3.39   A component video cable

 As a slightly technical aside, luma is a gamma-correcting, nonlinear display concept related to but not equivalent to luminance, which is a linear, non-gamma-corrected measure of light intensity. Display devices perform nonlinear gamma decompression, which means a complementary nonlinear gamma compression (correction) must have been performed by the transmitter for the resulting image to be displayed properly. Thus, *luma*, not *luminance*, is the appropriate term when discussing component video. Furthermore, although *Y* is commonly used to represent luma, it actually stands for luminance. As a result, if you ever see a reference to Y′PbPr or Y′CbCr, the Y-prime refers correctly to luma. The more common, yet less correct, *Y* is used here to refer to luma.

Note that in the foregoing discussion, there is no mention of a green component-video signal. In fact, the often green-colored lead in the component-video cable carries the luma. There is no need for a separate green color-difference signal. Essentially, the luma signal is used as a colorless map for the detail of the image. The receiving display device adds the luma signal from the Y lead back to the blue and red color-difference signals that were received on the Pb and Pr leads, re-creating compressed versions of the full blue and red source signals. Whatever details in the luma version of the image have weak representation in the blue and red versions of the image are inferred to be green.

Therefore, you can conclude that by providing one full signal (Y) and two compressed signals (Pb and Pr) that are related to the full signal (Pb = B − Y and Pr = R − Y), you can transmit roughly the same information as three full signals (R, G, and B) but with less bandwidth. Incidentally, component video is capable of transmitting HD video at full 1080p (1920×1080, progressive-scan) resolution. However, the output device is at the mercy of the video source, which often is not manufactured to push 1080p over component outputs.

S-video

S-video is a component video technology that, in its basic form, combines the two chroma signals into one, resulting in video quality not quite as high as that of YPbPr. This is because the R, G, and B signals are harder to approximate after the Pb and Pr signals have been combined. One example of an S-video connector, shown in Figure 3.40, is a 7-pin mini-DIN, mini-DIN of various pin counts being the most common connector type. The most basic connector is a 4-pin mini-DIN that has, quite simply, one luma and one chroma (C) output lead and a ground for each. A 4-pin male connector is compatible with a 7-pin female connector, both in fit and pin functionality. The converse is not also true, however. These are the only two standard S-video connectors.

FIGURE 3.40   A 7-pin S-video port

The 6-pin and 7-pin versions add composite video leads, which are discussed next. Some 7-pin ports use the extra pins to provide full Y, Pb, and Pr leads with four ground leads, making those implementations of S-video equivalent to component video. ATI has used 8-, 9-, and 10-pin versions of the connector that include such added features as an S-video input path in addition to output (from the perspective of the video source), bidirectional pin functionality, and audio input/output.

Composite Video

When the preceding component video technologies are not feasible, the last related standard, *composite video*, combines all luma and chroma leads into one. Composite video is truly the bottom of the analog-video barrel. However, the National Television System Committee (NTSC) signal received by over-the-air antennas or by cable-TV feeds is composite video, making it a very common video signal. Unfortunately, once the four signals are combined into one, the display equipment has no way of faithfully splitting them back out, leading to less than optimal quality but great cost efficiency.

A single yellow RCA jack, the composite video jack is rather common on computers and home and industrial video components. While still fairly decent in video quality, composite video is more susceptible to undesirable video phenomena and artifacts, such as aliasing, cross coloration, and dot crawl. If you have a three-connector cable on your home video equipment, such as a DVD player connected to a TV, odds are the tips will be yellow, red, and white. The red and white leads are for left and right stereo audio; the yellow lead is your composite video.

DisplayPort

DisplayPort is a royalty-free digital display interface from the Video Electronics Standards Association (VESA) that uses less power than other digital interfaces and VGA. A simple adapter allows HDMI and DVI voltages to be lowered to those required by DisplayPort because it is functionally similar to HDMI and DVI. DisplayPort cables can extend 3 meters unless an active cable powers the run, in which case the cable can extend to 33 meters.

The DisplayPort connector latches itself to the receptacle with two tiny hooks in the same way that micro-B USB connectors do. Figure 3.41 shows an illustration of the DisplayPort 20-pin interface. Note the keying of the connector in the bottom left of the diagram.

FIGURE 3.41   A full-size DisplayPort connector

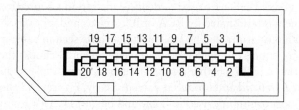

The full-size DisplayPort is being usurped by a smaller compatible version called Thunderbolt, created in collaboration between Intel and Apple. Thunderbolt combines PCI Express with the DisplayPort technology. The Thunderbolt cable is a powered active cable extending as far as 3m and was designed to be less expensive than an active version of the full-size DisplayPort cable of the same length. Figure 3.42 shows a Thunderbolt interface on an Apple MacBook Pro. Note the standard lightning-bolt insignia by the port. To the left of the Thunderbolt port in the image is a 9-pin IEEE 1394b (FireWire) beta port. Despite its diminutive size, the Thunderbolt port has 20 pins around its connector bar, like its larger DisplayPort cousin. Of course, the functions of all the pins do not directly correspond between the two interface types because Thunderbolt adds PCIe functionality.

FIGURE 3.42   A Thunderbolt connector

Coaxial

Two main forms of coaxial cable are used to deliver video from a source to a monitor or television. One of them is terminated by RCA or BNC plugs and tends to serve a single frequency, while the other is terminated by F connectors, those seen in cable television (CATV) settings, and tends to require tuning/demodulation equipment to choose the frequency to display. The terms that refer to whether a single frequency or multiple frequencies are carried over a cable are *baseband* and *broadband*, respectively. Figure 3.43 shows an example of the F connector most commonly used in home and business CATV installations. This is a 75-ohm form of coax known as RG-6.

Ethernet

With the capability of today's data networks, both compressed and even uncompressed audio and video can be digitized and sent over an IP network in packet form. The physical and data-link connectivity is often implemented through devices that connect through a standard Ethernet network. Care must be taken that this new application for the network does not obstruct the normal flow of data or even the possibly recently added voice over IP (VoIP) traffic. As with VoIP applications, quality of service (QoS) must be implemented and supported throughout the data network or audio/video (A/V) quality will surely suffer.

FIGURE 3.43   A CATV F connector and coaxial cable

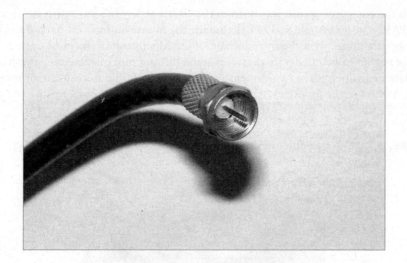

Input Devices

An *input device* is one that transfers information from outside the computer system to an internal storage location, such as system RAM, video RAM, flash memory, or disk storage. Without input devices, computers would be unable to change from their default boot-up state. The following sections detail different classes of input devices and a hub, of sorts, used for switching between the most common of these devices. We will also demonstrate the similarities shared by devices that provide input to computer systems as well as their differences. Installation considerations will be presented where appropriate. The following input devices are covered in the following sections:

- Mouse
- Keyboard
- Barcode reader
- Multimedia devices
- Biometric devices
- Touchscreen
- KVM switch
- Scanner
- Gamepads and joysticks
- Digitizer

Mouse

Although the computer mouse was born in the 1970s at Xerox's Palo Alto Research Center (PARC), it was Apple in 1984 that made the mouse an integral part of the personal computer image with the introduction of the Macintosh. In its most basic form, the mouse is a hand-fitting device that uses some form of motion-detection mechanism to translate its own physical two-dimensional movement into onscreen cursor motion. Many variations of the mouse exist, including trackballs, tablets, touchpads, and pointing sticks. Figure 3.44 illustrates the most recognizable form of the mouse.

FIGURE 3.44   A computer mouse

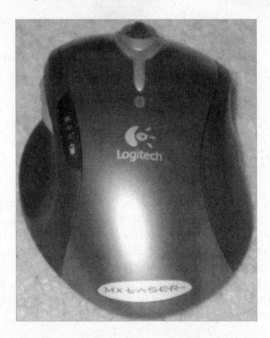

The motion-detection mechanism of the original Apple mouse was a simple ball that protruded from the bottom of the device so that when the bottom was placed against a flat surface that offered a slight amount of friction, the mouse would glide over the surface but the ball would roll, actuating two rollers that mapped the linear movement to a Cartesian plane and transmitted the results to the software interface. This method of motion detection remains available today, although it's fairly unpopular.

Later technologies used optical receptors to catch LED light reflected from specially made surfaces purchased with the devices and used like a mouse pad. A mouse pad is a special surface to improve mechanical mouse traction while offering very little resistance to the mouse itself. As optical science advanced for the mouse, lasers were used to allow a sharper image to be captured by the mouse and more sensitivity in motion detection. Certain surfaces don't lend themselves well to standard laser-mouse functionality, but a higher resolution version exists that can even track across the surface of glass. The mouse today can be wired to the computer system or connected wirelessly. Wireless versions use batteries to power them, and the optical varieties deplete these batteries more quickly than their mechanical counterparts.

The final topic is one that is relevant for any mouse: buttons. The number of buttons you need your mouse to have is dependent on the software interfaces you use. For the Macintosh, one button has always been sufficient, but for a Windows-based computer, at least two are recommended, hence the term *right-click*. Today, the mouse is commonly found to have a wheel on top to aid in scrolling and other specialty movement. The wheel has even developed a click in many models, sort of an additional button underneath the wheel. Buttons on the side of the mouse that can be programmed for whatever the user desires are more common today as well and can alarm the unsuspecting user the first time they grab such a mouse the wrong way.

Touch pads—flat panels below the spacebar—and pointing sticks—eraser-like protrusions in the middle of the keyboard—are found mainly on laptops. A trackball, however, is more like an inverted mouse, so let's look at how they compare to each other. Both devices place the buttons on the top, which is where your fingers will be. A mouse places its tracking mechanism on the bottom, requiring that you move the entire assembly as an analogue for how you want the cursor on the screen to move. In contrast, a trackball places the tracking mechanism, usually a ball that is larger than that of a mouse, on the top with the buttons. In doing so, you have a device that need not be moved around on the desktop and can work in tight spaces and on surfaces that would be incompatible with the use of a mouse. The better trackballs place the ball and buttons in such a configuration that your hand rests ergonomically on the device, allowing effortless control of the onscreen cursor.

Keyboard

More ubiquitous than the mouse, the *keyboard* is easily the most popular input device, so much so that its popularity is more of a necessity. Very few users would even think of beginning a computing session without a working keyboard. Fewer still would even know how. The US English keyboard places keys in the same orientation as the QWERTY typewriter keyboards, which were developed in the 1860s.

In addition to the standard QWERTY layout, modern computer keyboards often have separate cursor-movement and numerical keypads. The numerical keys in a row above the alphabet keys send different scan codes to the computer from those sent by the numerical keypad. At the discretion of the programmer, any given application might require the use of only one of the two sets of numeric keys or allow the use of either. The IBM PC/AT keyboard had only 84 keys, lacking separate cursor-movement keys. These functions were superimposed on the numeric keypad only. The Num Lock key had to be toggled to switch between cursor movement and the numeric keypad. The 101-key keyboard did include these separate keys but still kept the Num Lock arrangement as well, and the popular 104-key Windows keyboard added Windows-specific keys to those 101 keys.

Keyboards have also added function keys (not to be confused with the common laptop key labeled *Fn*), which are often placed in a row across the top of the keyboard above the numerical row. Key functionality can be modified by using one or more combinations of the Ctrl, Alt, Shift, and laptop Fn keys along with the normal QWERTY keys.

Technically speaking, the keys on a keyboard complete individual circuits when each one is pressed. The completion of each circuit leads to a unique scan code that is sent to the keyboard connector on the computer system. The computer uses a keyboard controller chip or function to interpret the code as the corresponding key sequence. The computer then decides what action to take based on the key sequence and what it means to the computer and the active application, including simply displaying the character printed on the key.

In addition to the layout for a standard keyboard, other keyboard layouts exist, some not nearly as popular, however. For example, without changing the order of the keys, an ergonomic keyboard is designed to feel more comfortable to users as they type. To accomplish that goal, manufacturers split the keyboard down the middle, angling keys on each side downward from the center.

The Dvorak Simplified Keyboard, patented in 1936, was designed to reduce fatigue in the hands of typists by placing characters that are more commonly used in the home row, among other physiologic enhancements. The QWERTY layout was designed to keep the hammers of a typewriter from becoming entangled. Although the Dvorak keyboard makes logical sense, especially with the decline in manufacturing and sales of the classic typewriter, the QWERTY keyboard remains dominant. One reason the Dvorak keyboard has failed to take over might be the loss of productivity to a touch-typist as they retrain on the new format.

 Real World Scenario

Installing Your Mouse and Keyboard

In the early days of the mouse for the PC, the original AT keyboard was still in use. The 9-pin D-sub RS-232 serial ports the mouse used looked nothing like the 5-pin DIN to which the keyboard attached. Not long thereafter, the PS/2 product line blurred the distinction; indeed, it removed it. With both interfaces being matching 6-pin mini-DIN connectors, care was paramount during installation. Standard industry color coding has simplified the installation process, but the ports are still easily interchanged during blind insertion. If you have visibility of the ports, remembering that the keyboard interface is coded purple and the mouse green takes much of the guesswork out of analyzing icons stamped into or printed on the case. Of course, graduation to USB-attached devices alleviates the hassle. Consult the accompanying documentation for the installation of all types of wireless input devices.

Scanner

One of the earliest input devices aside from the keyboard and mouse was the *scanner*. Before USB, scanners would routinely connect to computers through a SCSI bus, alongside external drives. Many models supported parallel attachment in the place of a printer, which was helpful for simpler systems with no SCSI interfaces; almost all computers had parallel ports in those days. Look for a menu item in applications capable of scanning that specifies TWAIN, the generic term for the class of drivers associated with scanners, such as Select TWAIN Source. This selection allows you to choose among multiple scanners before initiating the scan job.

More affordable scanners were handheld devices that relied on included or specialty software to intelligently stitch together the scanned ribbons into one cohesive image. Although more easily afforded today, flatbed scanners were once reserved for the computing elite. Regardless of the caliber of scanner, they all use light to reflect off of a surface and measure the relative reflections of the different dots that make up the grid the scanner is able to detect. The tighter the grid (the more dots per inch [DPI] supported), the higher resolution the resulting image. Charge coupled devices (CCDs) are a common choice in today's scanners. CCDs convert light they receive into electrical impulses that is then forwarded to the software producing the scan for further processing into an image that is a facsimile of the original object being scanned.

A flatbed scanner evokes the concept of a copier with the paper handling and printing mechanisms missing. This image is not far off, which is why copiers make wonderful scanners, as long as they can produce a digital image file. It's also why multifunction devices are so prolific; it takes very little to outfit a printer with a scanner component to be used for input to the computer and as a fax-scanning device. Inbound faxes can be printed, or the same digital interface that the scanner uses can be used to transfer the image electronically to software in the computer. Figure 3.45 shows the top flatbed scanner portion of a laser multifunction device that provides a way to print, scan, and fax.

FIGURE 3.45   A flatbed scanner

Figure 3.46 shows you one of numerous brands of portable document scanners. These handy little devices are scarcely more than a foot long and can make short work of scanning anything from a business card to a gas receipt to an 8.5″ × 11″ lodging folio. The associated software that comes with these scanners performs optical character recognition (OCR) and can recognize the orientation of the text and glean pertinent information from the documents scanned to populate the internal database. From this database, you can produce reports for such purposes as expenses, invoicing, and taxes. This model also offers the option to create a PDF during the scan instead.

FIGURE 3.46   A portable document scanner

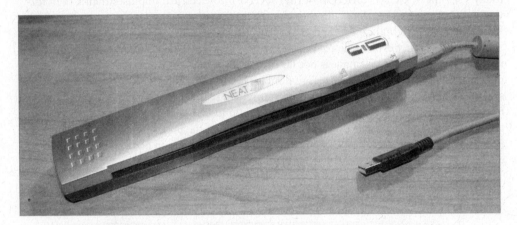

Barcode Reader

A *barcode reader* (or barcode *scanner*) is a specialized input device commonly used in retail and other industrial sectors that manage inventory. The systems that the reader connects to can be so specialized that they have no other input device. Barcode readers can use LEDs or lasers as light sources and can scan one- or two-dimensional barcodes.

Using a Barcode Reader in the VoIP Industry

The VoIP industry relies on barcode readers to quickly scan in the MAC addresses of hundreds or thousands of desk sets from labels on their neatly stacked boxes before their deployment. Depending on the brand of equipment, the MAC addresses might be read in to populate a spreadsheet that is later used as input to the call management system during the identification of which directory numbers will be assigned to which physical devices. The same job done by hand could have untold issues caused by user error.

Barcode readers can connect to the host system in a number of ways, but serial connections, such as RS-232 and USB, are fairly common. If the system uses proprietary software to receive the reader's input, the connection between the two might be proprietary as well. The simplest software interfaces call for the reader to be plugged into the keyboard's PS/2 connector using a splitter, or "wedge," that allows the keyboard to remain connected. The scanner converts all output to keyboard scans so that the system treats the input as if it came from a keyboard. For certain readers, wireless communication with the host is also possible, using IR, RF, Bluetooth, WiFi, and more.

With today's smartphone technology being what it is, the built-in cameras can act as scanners, and the scanning app can interpret what the camera sees. In this way, Universal Product Code (UPC) barcodes and Quick Response (QR) codes and other 2D matrix barcodes can be input and processed. The smartphone can then use its Internet access to launch the application associated with the text, such as a web browser or an email client. A QR code is an encoded image that allows the scanning application to decode large amounts of text and can be used to represent simple text or popular strings, such as a website's URL, a phone number, a GEO location, an email address, or an SMS message. Figure 3.47 is a simple QR code that will direct a QR-code reader app to the www.sybex.com website.

FIGURE 3.47   A QR code

Digitizer

One way to faithfully reproduce incredibly good artwork in digital form for computer use is to place the analog artwork on top of a sensor and use a stylus to trace the artwork after choosing an onscreen "crayon" or "pen." The end result can be a work of art almost as good as the original. The device used to trace an analog source, turning it into a digital representation, is a *digitizer*. Digitizing, in fact, is the act of turning any analog source—artwork, audio, video, slides and photographs—into a binary bit stream. As an input device, however, a digitizer or *digitizing tablet* takes pen strokes in the analog world and turns them into a digital rendering through the software controlling the digitizer. These devices are also commonly used to annotate presentations with the option to save or discard the annotations with each presentation. Figure 3.48 shows an example of a USB-attached digitizing tablet with choice of pen or mouse for input.

FIGURE 3.48   A digitizing tablet

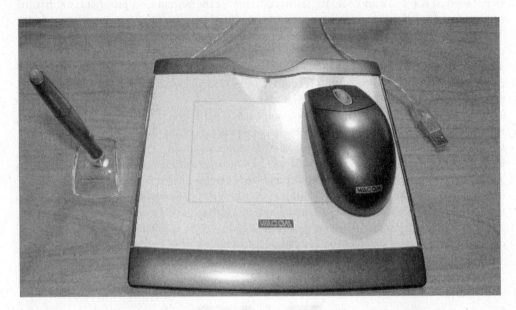

Biometric Devices

Any device that measures one or more physical or behavioral features of an organism is considered a *biometric device*, or literally, a device that measures life. When the same device forwards this biometric information to the computer, it becomes an input device. The list includes fingerprint scanners, retinal and iris scanners, voice recognition devices, and facial recognition devices, to name a few. A computer can use this input to authenticate the user based on preestablished biometric information captured during user setup. Even cipher locks that authenticate personnel before allowing entry to secure environments can be replaced with biometric devices.

Because there are many manufacturers of biometric devices, the installation of any particular model is best performed while consulting that company's documentation. If the device is not built into the computer, at a minimum some form of interface, such as USB, must be used to attach the device, and software must be installed to lock the system until authentication occurs. Many offerings allow multiple forms of authentication to be required in sequence. An example of a highly secure approach to authentication with multiple factors would be a biometric scan, followed by a challenge that requires a code from a token card, followed finally by the opportunity to enter a password. This "something you are, something you have, and something you know" technique works to secure some of the world's most sensitive installations. Further discussion of the concept of multifactor authentication is beyond the scope of this book.

Touchscreens

Touchscreen technology converts stimuli of some sort, which are generated by actually touching the screen, to electrical impulses that travel over serial connections to the computer system. These input signals allow for the replacement of the mouse, simultaneously in movement and in click. With onscreen keyboards, the external keyboard can be retired as well. However, standard computer systems are not the only application for touchscreen enhancement. This technology can also be seen in PDAs and smartphones, point-of-sale venues for such things as PIN entry and signature capture, handheld and bar-mounted games, ATMs, remote controls, appliances, and vehicles. The list continues to grow as technology advances.

For touchscreens, a handful of solutions exist for converting a touch to a signal. Some less-successful ones rely on warm hands, sound waves, or dust-free screens. The more successful screens have optical or electrical sensors that are quite a bit less fastidious. The two most popular with handheld devices are *resistive* and *capacitive*. Capacitive interfaces are generally smoother to the touch than resistive interfaces and can be controlled by the pad of the finger or a special stylus that mimics this soft part of the fingertip. Resistive interfaces usually have to be controlled by the fingernail or a plastic or metal stylus. In any event, the sensory system is added onto a standard monitor at some point, whether in the field by the user or in a more seamless fashion by the manufacturer.

Installing monitors with touch capability on standard computers entails not only attachment to the graphics adapter, but also attachment to a serial interface. The most popular of these has become the USB port, much as it has for the mouse and keyboard.

Calibration is required upon first configuration and whenever there appears to be a misinterpretation by the system as to where the user has touched the screen. This calibration entails displaying a pattern that the user has to touch at certain points to let the system know where these landmarks are perceived to be.

KVM Switch

A KVM switch isn't an input device, but it allows you to switch between sets of input devices. The *KVM switch* is named after the devices among which it allows you to switch. The initials stand for keyboard, video, and mouse. KVM switches come in a variety of models. You can select the switch that accommodates the type of interfaces your components require. For example, your keyboard and mouse might attach with mini-DIN connectors or with USB connectors; your monitor might attach with a VGA, DVI, or HDMI connector.

The purpose of the switch is to allow you to have multiple systems attached to the same keyboard, monitor, and mouse. You can use these three devices with only one system at a time. Some switches have a dial that you turn to select which system attaches to the components, while others feature buttons for each system connected. Common uses of KVM switches include using the same components alternately for a desktop computer and a laptop docking station or having a server room with multiple servers but no need to interface with them simultaneously.

Figure 3.49 shows a four-system VGA/USB switch with analog audio switching as well. If DVI or PS/2 attachments are desired, for example, adapters are required. The buttons on the front (right side of the image) switch the common console connections (on the left side of the image) among the four systems, only three of which are currently attached. A maximum of one of the four LEDs beside the corresponding buttons is lit at a time, only for the system currently in control.

FIGURE 3.49   A KVM switch

Gamepads and Joysticks

As long as there have been gaming applications for the personal computer, there have been standard and specialty controllers for some of those games. For the rest, the keyboard and mouse could be or had to be used for controlling the game. Two popular types of controllers have been the generic *joystick*, a controller with one or more buttons and a stick of varying length and girth, and the often proprietary *gamepad*, usually comprising function and directional buttons specific to the gaming console in use. Standardized PC connections have included the DA15 game port, also known as the joystick port, the DB25/DE9 serial port, and the USB port. Figure 3.50 shows a wired joystick connected through the wireless controller for the Nintendo Wii video game console.

FIGURE 3.50   A proprietary gamepad

Multimedia Input Devices

Multimedia input devices vary in functionality based on the type of input being gathered. Two broad categories of multimedia input are audio and video. Digital motion and still cameras are incredibly popular as a replacement for similar video products that do not transfer information to a computer, making sharing and collaboration so much easier than before. The following sections present information on these multimedia input devices:

- Web cams
- MIDI-enabled devices
- Digital cameras and camcorders

Web Cams

Years ago, owing to the continued growth in the Internet's popularity, video camera-only devices, known as *web cams*, started their climb in esteem. Today, anyone who does a fair amount of instant messaging, whether professional or personal, has likely used or at least been introduced to web cams, often used in conjunction with messaging user interfaces.

Web cams make great security devices as well. Users can keep an eye on loved ones or property from anywhere that Internet access is offered. Care must be taken, however, because the security that the web cam is intended to provide can backfire on the user if the web cam is not set up properly. Anyone who happens upon the web interface for the device can control its actions if there is no authentication enabled. Some web cams provide an activity light when someone is using the camera to watch whatever it's pointed at. Nevertheless, it is possible to decouple the camera's operation and that of its light.

A web cam connects directly to the computer through an I/O interface, such as USB or WiFi, and does not have any self-contained recording mechanism. Its sole purpose is to transfer its captured video directly to the host computer, usually for further transfer over the Internet, hence the term *web*. Web cams that have built-in wired and wireless NIC interfaces for direct network attachment are prevalent as well. A now maturing evolution of the web cam for laptops resulted in manufacturers building the device into the bezel of the display. Connectivity is generally through an internal USB or FireWire interface.

MIDI Devices

Microphones, audio playback, and audio synthesizing devices are common input components connected to a sound card or serial port so that audio from these devices can be collected and processed. As an example, consider Musical Instrument Digital Interface (*MIDI*) devices, called controllers, which create messages describing, and thus synthesizing, the user's intended musical performance. These devices do not make sound that is recorded directly; they are merely designed to somewhat realistically fabricate the music the instruments they represent might produce. MIDI files, therefore, are much smaller than files that contain digitized audio waveforms.

Modern MIDI controllers use 5-pin DIN connectors that look like the original AT keyboard connector. Controllers can be interconnected in one of two ways. The original method is to provide devices with two ports, an input and an output port, and daisy-chain them in a ring. This arrangement introduces a delay caused by devices processing and retransmitting messages that were not destined for them but instead for devices downstream from them. One solution is to replace the output port with one that merely replicates the input signal. If the receiving device is the intended destination, then the unnecessarily repeated message is ignored by downstream recipients. Otherwise, the actual recipient receives its message with far less delay. The second method of connection is another solution that reduces delay. A device with one input and multiple outputs interconnects many devices directly.

Regardless of the controller interconnection method, computers can receive MIDI controllers directly, such as through a sound card with a built-in MIDI interface or through the use of an external MIDI interface that originally connected to the computer's game port. Today, USB and FireWire ports are more commonly used. Ethernet-attached interfaces also exist and require very little processing power to convert the MIDI messages into Ethernet frames.

Digital Cameras and Camcorders

A *digital camera* is a device that takes still pictures and records them to digital media of some sort for later access. A *camcorder* is a video capture device that performs a similar function to that of the digital camera, but for moving video. Most of today's multimedia recording devices perform the functions of both the digital camera and the digital camcorder. Depending on the device, both pictures and video can be stored on the same or different media within the same device. In fact, the most basic smartphone can perform both of these functions, often with exceptional quality.

Early versions of digital cameras relied on the storage media of the day, 3.5″ floppy diskettes, for instance. Eventually, models with internal flash memory were developed, which led to hybrid models that also featured a memory card slot, resulting in the flexibility to grow the camera's storage capacity as the technology produced larger cards.

A similar evolution occurred in the world of camcorders. Originally, camcorders required one of a variety of analog tape formats to record on. This gave way to digital tape formats and then to burnable optical discs, hard disk drives, and today's high-capacity flash storage. Once a removable memory card was added on, the possibilities for what can be recorded and how much became nearly endless. Figure 3.51 shows a digital camcorder on the left and a digital camera on the right.

FIGURE 3.51   A digital camera and camcorder

The mechanism by which the digital information is transferred to a computer varies somewhat among these devices. In some cases, a cable—USB, for instance—can be attached between the device and the computer. A drive icon might then appear in Windows Explorer, or you might have a specific application for access to the content. In other cases, removable media was recorded on and this media can be removed and transferred directly to a reader on the computer system, be it an optical drive or card reader. Certain manufacturers have developed docking stations for their product line. The dock can remain attached to the computer system, and the device can be interfaced to the dock, usually by simply sitting it down on the docking station. In some cases, these stations also charge the device while it is docked.

Output Devices

The process for the installation and configuration of certain output devices varies almost as widely as the number of models within a given category. Nevertheless, certain high-level steps must be taken with nearly each such device. The devices in the following sections are each covered in eye-opening detail elsewhere in this book; two of the three have chapters dedicated to them alone:

- Printers (Chapter 10, "Installing and Configuring Printers")
- Speakers
- Display devices (Chapter 4)

The following sections introduce each of the device categories and any specific issues that exist with their installation and configuration without delving too deeply yet.

Printers

Often immediately behind your monitor in output-device importance, the one or more printers you have attached to your computer become invaluable when you need to produce a hard copy for distribution or for inclusion in a report, for instance. Chapter 10 will detail the various families of printer, such as impact, inkjet, and laser, as well as the details involved in their installation, including connectivity and driver installation. This chapter gives you copious information regarding the interfaces used today and throughout personal-computing history, such as parallel, serial, SCSI, USB, and FireWire.

Speakers

The various audio-related discussions in this chapter present concepts surrounding speakers and their connection to the computer or other device, such as surround-sound processors or A/V receivers. Your operating system's audio controls have settings that can be manipulated, sometimes in very complex ways, to produce software configurations that derive the best performance from the speakers you have installed.

Display Devices

The next chapter presents a wide array of pertinent information on this subject. This chapter also contains considerable interface and cabling information on video display technology. As output devices, the connectivity of display devices can be fixed, with a single type of connection to a video source, or variable, sometimes supporting the connection of multiple sources through similar or different interfaces. In the latter case, input selection is generally a fairly simple process, most often accessible directly from the display device's remote control. In the case of interfaces that have options, such as HDMI, a small amount of onscreen configuration might be in order. In most cases, however, configuration is Plug and Play in nature.

Summary

In this chapter, you learned about various types of expansion cards, the interfaces they are known for, and the peripherals they connect to. The fact that some interfaces have gone through an evolution, changing appearance and capabilities at times, was also presented. No discussion of expansion cards and interfaces would be complete without adding in details of the cables needed, if any, to connect the cards to the peripherals; the discussion in this chapter is no exception.

This chapter also surveyed the details of peripherals from an output vs. input perspective, including specifics on the connections for display devices. Well-known input devices, such as the mouse and keyboard, and less conventional yet popular input devices were also examined in this chapter. You also learned about the KVM switch, a device that allows you to share input devices among computers. The adapter cards highlighted in this chapter fall into four broad categories: video, multimedia, I/O, and communications.

Other output devices were presented, with substantial detail of some and a topical look at others that are covered in more detail elsewhere in this book.

Exam Essentials

Familiarize yourself with installation and configuration of expansion cards.   The variety of expansion cards available leads to the need to know the similarities and differences among them. For example, they all need to insert into the system using an expansion slot. They all perform a specific function or set of functions, based on their type, but not all cards are configured the same way. Some require more configuration than others, while some require no installer interaction at all.

Recognize and understand different peripheral connectors.   Expansion cards and motherboards have external connectivity interfaces. The interfaces have connectors that adhere to some sort of standard for interconnecting with a cable or external device. Knowing these specific characteristics can help you differentiate among the capabilities of the interfaces available to you.

Recognize and be able to describe display connectors specifically.   Although a type of peripheral connector, display connectors are in a class all their own. Technologies continue to be developed to merge display and other peripheral functions, such as serial I/O, but the differences among the various display interfaces are substantial enough for these connectors to warrant their own category.

Know the characteristics of cables used for peripheral attachment.   Whether the connection is internal or external to the computer system, each cable used has specific characteristics, no matter their resemblance to others. Some cables that look similar to others support higher speeds or longer distance. Some have power components, while others are completely passive in nature. Knowing the specific cables that go along with the expansion cards and their interfaces is extremely valuable and important.

Compare and contrast input devices.   Although input devices vary widely in their functionality, they all provide external input to the computer. Familiarize yourself with the specifics of the devices mentioned in this chapter, differentiating between standard input devices and multimedia input devices.

Review Questions

The answers to the Chapter Review Questions can be found in Appendix A.

1. You want to plug a keyboard into the back of a computer. You know that you need to plug the keyboard cable into a PS/2 port. Which style of port is the PS/2?

    A. RJ-11

    B. DE9

    C. DIN 5

    D. Mini-DIN 6

2. What is the maximum speed of USB 2.0 in Mbps?

    A. 1.5

    B. 12

    C. 60

    D. 480

3. Which of the following standards are specified by IEEE 1284? (Choose two.)

    A. SPP

    B. RS-232

    C. EPP

    D. ECP

    E. FireWire

    F. USB

4. What peripheral port type was originally developed by Apple and is currently regarded as the optimal interface for digital video transfers?

    A. DVD

    B. USB 2.0

    C. IEEE 1394

    D. IEEE 1284

5. What peripheral port type is expandable using a hub, operates at 1.5MBps, and is used to connect various devices (from printers to cameras) to PCs?

    A. DVD 1.0

    B. USB 1.1

    C. IEEE 1394

    D. IEEE 1284

6. Which peripheral port type was designed to transfer data at higher speeds over a D-sub interface?

   A. DVD

   B. USB

   C. IEEE 1394

   D. IEEE 1284

7. The surround sound mode known as 5.1 employs how many speakers when only one is used for each channel?

   A. 1

   B. 5

   C. 6

   D. 7

   E. 8

8. Which of the following display interfaces is equivalent to DisplayPort with PCIe added in?

   A. Thunderbolt

   B. WHUXGA

   C. IEEE 1394c

   D. HDMI

9. Which of the following interfaces allows audio to be sent out over the same cabling infrastructure as video?

   A. VGA

   B. DVI

   C. HDMI

   D. Composite

10. How do you connect a DVI-A interface on a peripheral to a DVI-D interface on the computer?

    A. With a DVI-I cable

    B. With a cable that is terminated on one end with a DVI-A connector and on the other end with a DVI-D connector

    C. You wouldn't interconnect those two interfaces

    D. With a standard DVI cable

11. What kind of device uses unique physical traits of the user to authenticate their access to a secure system or location?

    A. Barcode reader

    B. Biometric device

    C. Keyboard

    D. Touch screen

12. Why might you use a KVM switch?

   A. You have multiple Ethernet devices that need to communicate with one another.

   B. You need to be able to switch the voltage supplied to a particular device.

   C. You have a printer that is not attached to the network but you want multiple computers to be able to print to it.

   D. You have more than one server and don't want to buy certain external peripherals separately for each.

13. Which type of input device employs roughly the same connector as the original AT keyboard?

   A. Barcode reader

   B. PS/2 keyboard

   C. MIDI

   D. Touch screen

14. What can you use to convert video to a format that can be uploaded to the Internet, among other things?

   A. A barcode reader

   B. A video capture card

   C. A TV tuner card

   D. A MIDI device

15. Which of the following is not an example of a standard peripheral input-device connector?

   A. ⅛″ jack

   B. Mini-DIN

   C. D-subminiature

   D. USB

16. Which category of adapters includes NICs?

   A. Multimedia

   B. I/O

   C. Communications

   D. Video

17. What category of adapter would you need to install to equip a system with one or more USB ports?

   A. Multimedia

   B. I/O

   C. Communications

   D. Video

18. What type of adapter has an RJ-11 jack built in?

    A. Modem

    B. Video

    C. Sound

    D. NIC

19. What type of pointing device features a ball and buttons on the top and a flat, steady surface on the bottom?

    A. Mouse

    B. Touchpad

    C. Trackball

    D. Trackpad

20. VGA-based video technologies use what type of signal between the adapter and monitor?

    A. Digital

    B. Analog

    C. Compressed

    D. Composite

Performance-Based Questions

On the A+ exams, you will encounter performance-based questions. The questions on the exam require you to perform a specific task, and you will be graded on whether you were able to complete the task. The following require you to think creatively to measure how well you understand this chapter's topics. You may or may not see similar questions on the actual A+ exams. To see how your answers compare to the authors', refer to Appendix B.

1. Looking at the back of a new computer, you see interfaces of the following colors and shapes:

   - Burgundy, DB25
   - Teal, DE9
   - Gray, flat 4-pin
   - Blue, DE15
   - Green, mini-DIN 6
   - Purple, mini-DIN 6
   - Green, 3.5mm TRS

2. List the steps needed to connect the following connectors in order:

   - VGA
   - USB
   - Parallel
   - Mouse
   - RS-232
   - Keyboard
   - Speaker

Chapter

4

Display Devices

THE FOLLOWING COMPTIA A+ 220-801
OBJECTIVES ARE COVERED IN THIS
CHAPTER:

✓ **1.10 Given a scenario, evaluate types and features of
display devices.**

- Types
  - CRT
  - LCD
  - LED
  - Plasma
  - Projector
  - OLED
- Refresh rates
- Resolution
- Native resolution
- Brightness/lumens
- Analog vs. digital
- Privacy/antiglare filters
- Multiple displays

The primary method of getting information out of a computer is to use a computer video display unit (VDU). Display systems convert computer signals into text and pictures and display them on a TV-like screen. As a matter of fact, the first personal computers used television screens because it was simpler to use an existing display technology rather than to develop a new one. Various types of computer displays are in use today, including the TV. Most all of them, projection systems as well, use the same legacy cathode ray tube (*CRT*) technology found in conventional television sets or the liquid crystal display (*LCD*) technology found on nearly all laptop, notebook, and palmtop computers. In fact, it is rare to see a desktop monitor based on CRT technology sold with a computer today. Generally only high-end specialized units (used for enhanced clarity and video performance) are CRT-based.

This chapter introduces you to concepts surrounding display units used with personal computer systems. The previous chapter detailed the technology behind the adapters, interfaces, and connectors used in computer graphics. Other topics covered in this chapter include characteristics of display standards, such as the resolutions and color densities of VGA and the standards that sprung from it, and settings common to most display devices.

Understanding Display Types and Settings

Most display systems work the same way. First, the computer sends a signal to a device called the video adapter—an expansion board installed in an expansion bus slot or the equivalent circuitry integrated into the motherboard—telling it to display a particular graphic or character. The adapter then renders the character for the display—that is, it converts the single instruction into several instructions that tell the display device how to draw the graphic—and sends the instructions to the display device, based on the connection technology between the two. The primary differences after that are in the type of video adapter you are using (digital or analog) and the type of display (CRT, LCD, projector, etc.). We'll talk about some of these differences now.

Video Display Types

To truly understand the video display arena, you must be introduced to a few terms and concepts that you may not be familiar with. The legacy digital transistor-transistor logic (TTL) and the analog technologies that began with video graphics array (VGA) were once the two broad categories of video technologies. These categories have nothing to do with the makeup of the VDU but instead how the graphics adapter communicates with the VDU. You will read about many of the VGA technologies in coming sections of this chapter. First, however, let's explore the different VDU types:

- CRT
- Liquid crystal display
- LED displays
- Plasma
- OLED
- Projection systems

CRT Displays

Legacy and today's specialty computer monitors contain a CRT. In a CRT, a device called an electron gun shoots a beam of electrons toward the back side of the monitor screen (see Figure 4.1). Color CRTs often use three guns, one each for red, green, and blue image components. The back of the screen is coated with special chemical dots called phosphors (often zinc sulfide combined with other elements for color variation, but no phosphorus, ironically) that glow when electrons strike them.

FIGURE 4.1   Cutaway of a CRT monitor

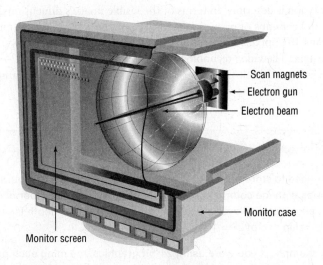

The beam of electrons scans across the monitor from left to right, as you face it, and top to bottom in a raster pattern to create the image. A special metallic screen called a shadow mask (in most implementations) has holes spaced and angled in an extremely precise manner. For color CRTs that employ shadow masks, a trio of dot phosphors is often grouped in a triangle for each hardware picture element. The separate electron beams that control red, green, and blue strike only their own phosphors at the correct angle to cause them to glow. The glow of the phosphors decays very quickly, requiring the electron beam's regular return to each phosphor to sustain the glow. The more dot phosphors that are placed in a given area, the better the image quality at higher resolutions.

There are two ways to measure a CRT monitor's image quality: dot pitch and resolution. Dot pitch is a physical characteristic of the monitor hardware, but resolution is configurable through software.

Dot pitch   *Dot pitch* is the measurement between the same spot in two vertically adjacent dot trios. In other words, it's the height of the trio added to the distance between the closest extremes of it and the next trio above or below it. Expressed in millimeters or dots per inch, the dot pitch tells how "sharp" the picture can be. The lower the measurement in millimeters or the higher the number of dots per inch, the closer together the phosphors are, and as a result, the sharper the image can be. An average dot pitch is 0.28mm to 0.32mm. Anything closer than 0.28mm is considered exceptional. Dot pitch in the flat-panel arena translates to the display's native resolution, discussed later in this chapter. Essentially, software-pixel placement is limited to the hardware's transistor placement, leading to one optimal resolution for each LCD. The transistors that make up the hardware's picture elements are discussed later in the section "Liquid Crystal Displays."

Resolution   *Resolution* is defined by how many software picture elements (pixels) are used to draw the screen. An advantage of higher resolutions is that more information can be displayed in the same screen area. A disadvantage is that the same objects and text displayed at a higher resolution appear smaller and might be harder to see. Up to a point, the added crispness of higher resolutions displayed on high-quality monitors compensates for the negative aspects. The resolution is described in terms of the visible image's dimensions, which indicate how many rows and columns of pixels are used to draw the screen. For example, a resolution of 1024×768 means 1024 pixels across (columns) and 768 pixels down (rows) were used to draw the pixel matrix. The video technology in this example would use 1024×768 = 786,432 pixels to draw the screen. Resolution is a software setting that is common among CRTs, LCDs, and projection systems as well as other display devices.

Resolution's Memory Requirement

Video memory is used to store rendered screen images. The memory required for a screen image varies with the color depth, which is defined as the number of colors in which each pixel can be displayed. A palette with a 24-bit color depth is capable of displaying each pixel in one of $2^{24} = 16,777,216$ distinct colors.

In the preceding example, if you were using 24-bit graphics, meaning each pixel requires 24 bits of memory to store that one screen element, 786,432 pixels would require 18,874,368 bits, or 2,359,296 bytes. Because this boils down to 2.25MB, an early (bordering on ancient) video adapter with only 2MB of RAM would not be capable of such resolution at 24 bits per pixel. Today's adapters have absolutely no trouble displaying such a resolution with a 24- or 32-bit color depth. In fact, they store many screens at a time in order to allow the display of full-motion video.

Liquid Crystal Displays

Portable computers were originally designed to be compact versions of their bigger desktop cousins. They crammed all the components of the big desktop computers into a small, suitcase-like box called (laughably) a portable computer. No matter what the designers did to reduce the size of the computer, the display remained as large as the desktop version's—that is, until an inventor found that when he passed an electric current through a semi-crystalline liquid, the crystals aligned themselves with the current. It was found that by combining transistors with these liquid crystals, patterns could be formed. These patterns could be combined to represent numbers or letters. The first application of these liquid crystal displays was the LCD watch. It was rather bulky, but it was cool.

As LCD elements got smaller, the detail of the patterns became greater, until one day someone thought to make a computer screen out of several of these elements. This screen was very light compared to computer monitors of the day, and it consumed relatively little power. It could easily be added to a portable computer to reduce the weight by as much as 30 pounds. As the components got smaller, so did the computer, and the laptop computer was born.

LCDs are not just limited to laptops; desktop versions of LCD displays and their offshoots are practically all that are seen today. Additionally, the home television market has been enjoying the LCD as a competitor of plasma for years. LCDs used with desktop computer systems use the same technology as their laptop counterparts but potentially on a much larger scale.

These external LCDs are available in either analog or digital interfaces. The analog interface is exactly the same as the VGA interface that was used for analog CRT monitors. Internal digital signals from the computer are rendered and output as analog signals by the video card and are then sent along the same 15-pin connector and associated cable as was used with analog CRT monitors. Digital LCDs with a digital interface, on the other hand, require no analog modulation by the graphics adapter. They require the video card to support digital output using a different interface, such as DVI, for instance. The advantage is that because the video signal never changes from digital to analog, there is less chance of interference and no conversion-related quality loss. Digital displays are generally sharper than their analog counterparts.

Two major types of LCD displays have been implemented over the years: active-matrix screens and passive-matrix screens. Another type, dual scan, is a passive-matrix variant. The main differences lie in the quality of the image. However, when used with computers, each type uses lighting behind the LCD panel (backlighting) to make the screen easier to view. Conventional LCD panels have one or more fluorescent bulbs as backlights. See the section "LED Displays" for details on a better type of backlight. The following discussions highlight the main differences among the pixel-addressing variants.

Active matrix   An active-matrix screen is made up of several independent LCD pixels. A transistor at each pixel location, when switched among various levels, activates two opposing electrodes that align the pixel's crystals and alter the passage of light at that location to produce hundreds or thousands of shades. The front electrode, at least, must be clear. This type of display is very crisp and easy to look at through nearly all oblique angles, and it does not require constant refreshing to maintain an image because transistors conduct current in only one direction and the pixel acts like a capacitor by holding its charge until it is refreshed with new information. Higher refresh rates are not for prevention of pixel discharge, as in the case of CRTs, plasma displays, and passive-matrix LCDs. Higher rates only result in better video quality, not static-image quality.

The major disadvantage of an active-matrix screen is that it requires larger amounts of power to operate all the transistors, one for each grayscale pixel or each red, green, and blue subpixel. Even with the backlight turned off, the screen can still consume battery power at an alarming rate, even more so when conventional fluorescent backlights are employed. The vast majority of LCDs manufactured today are based on active-matrix technology.

Passive matrix   A passive-matrix display does not have a dedicated transistor for each pixel or subpixel but instead a matrix of conductive traces. In simplified terms for a single pixel, when the display is instructed to change the crystalline alignment of a particular pixel, it sends a signal across the x- and y-coordinate traces that intersect at that pixel, thus turning it on. Figure 4.2 illustrates this concept. More realistically, circuits controlling the rows fire in series to refresh or newly activate pixels on each row in succession.

FIGURE 4.2   A passive-matrix display

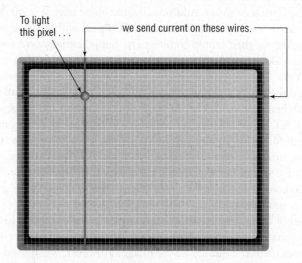

The circuits controlling the columns are synchronized to fire when that row's transistor is active and only for the pixels that should be affected on that row. Once a pixel's charge is gone, the pixel begins to return to normal, or decay, requiring a refresh to make it appear static. Angles of visibility and response times (the time to change a pixel) suffer greatly with passive-matrix LCDs. Because neighboring pixels can be affected through a sort of "crosstalk," passive-matrix displays can look a bit "muddy."

Dual scan   Dual scan is a variation of the passive-matrix display. The classic passive-matrix screen is split in half to implement a dual-scan display. Each half of the display is refreshed separately, leading to increased quality. Although dual scan improves on the quality of conventional passive-matrix displays, it cannot rival the quality produced by active matrix.

The main differences between active matrix and typical passive matrix are image quality and viewing angle. Because the computer takes hundreds of milliseconds to change a pixel in passive-matrix displays (compared with tens of milliseconds or less in active-matrix displays), the response of the screen to rapid changes is poor, causing, for example, an effect known as *submarining*: On a computer with a passive-matrix display, if you move the mouse pointer rapidly from one location to another, it will disappear from the first location and reappear in the new location without appearing anywhere in between. The poor response rate of passive-matrix displays also makes them suboptimal for displaying video.

If you move toward the side of a passive-matrix LCD, you eventually notice the display turning dark. In contrast, active-matrix LCDs have a viewing angle wider than 179 degrees. In fact, if you didn't know better, you'd think a passive-matrix display was a standard display with a privacy filter on it. A *privacy filter* is a panel that fits over the front of a display and, through a polarization affect, intentionally limits the viewing angle of the monitor. The filters were used with CRTs and continue to be produced for the variety of LCD and plasma panels being used as computer monitors. These same filters, as well as specialty versions, can act as *antiglare filters*, brightening and clarifying the image appearing on the monitor's screen.

We'll discuss additional concepts that apply to LCDs and other flat-panel displays later in this chapter.

LED Displays

A source of confusion for users and industry professionals alike, *LED* displays are merely LCD panels with light emitting diodes (LEDs) as light sources instead of the fluorescent bulbs used by conventional LCD monitors. No doubt, the new technology would not be nearly as marketable if they were referred to merely as LCDs. The general consumer would not rush to purchase a new display that goes by the same name as their current display. Nevertheless, calling these monitors LED displays is analogous to calling the conventional LCD monitors fluorescent displays; it's simply the backlight source, not the display technology.

Because there are many individually controlled LEDs in an LED display, sometimes as many as there are transistors in the LCD panel, the image can be intelligently backlit to enhance the quality of the picture. Additionally, there is no need for laptops with LED displays to convert the DC power coming into the laptop to the AC needed to power traditional fluorescent backlights because LEDs operate on DC power like the rest of the laptop. As a result, these systems have no inverter board (discussed later in Chapter 9, "Understanding Laptops"), which are the DC-to-AC conversion devices present in traditionally backlit laptop displays. LED displays rival plasma displays in clarity and variations in luminance. This variation is referred to as *contrast ratio* and is discussed later in this chapter.

Plasma Displays

The word *plasma* refers to a cloud of ionized (charged) particles—atoms and molecules with electrons in an unstable state. This electrical imbalance is used to create light from the changes in energy levels as they achieve balance. Plasma display panels (PDPs) create just such a cloud from an inert gas, such as neon, by placing electrodes in front of and behind sealed chambers full of the gas and vaporized mercury. This technology of running a current through an inert gas to ionize it is shared with neon signs and fluorescent bulbs. Because of the pressurized nature of the gas in the chambers, PDPs are not optimal for high-altitude use, leading to CRTs and LCDs being more popular for high-altitude applications, such as aboard aircraft, where PDPs can be heard to buzz the way fluorescent bulbs sometimes do.

Because of the temporary emission of light that this process produces, plasma displays have more in common with CRTs than they do with LCDs. In fact, as with CRTs, phosphors are responsible for the creation of light in the shade of the three primary colors, red, green, and blue. Because the pixels produce their own light, no backlight is required with plasma displays, also a feature shared with CRTs. The phosphor chemicals in CRTs and PDPs can be "used up" over time, reducing the overall image quality. The heat generated by CRTs and PDPs can lead to a loss of phosphorescence in the phosphor chemicals, which results in images burning into the screen. Advancements in the chemistry of plasma phosphors have reduced this tendency in recent years.

The refresh rate for plasma displays has always been in the 600Hz range so that the decay of the glow of the cells within each pixel (subpixel) is not perceptible until such time as the image calls for that cell to turn off as well as to ensure fluid video motion. See the section "Refresh Rate" later in this chapter for details on these concepts, but note that this rate is approximately 10 times that which is necessary to avoid the human eye's perception of the glow's decay. The result is a display that produces the state of the art in video motion fluidity. Higher refresh rates in LCDs lead to an unwanted artificial or noncinematic quality to video known as the "soap-opera effect." PDPs do not suffer from this effect.

PDPs can also produce deeper black colors than fluorescent-backlit LCD panels because the backlight cannot be completely blocked by the liquid crystal, thus producing hues that are grayer than black. LCDs backlit with LEDs, however, are able to completely dim selective areas or the entire image. Because of the relative cost-effectiveness to produce PDPs of the same size as a given LCD panel, plasma displays historically enjoyed more popularity in the larger-monitor market. That advantage is all but gone today, resulting in more LCDs being sold today than plasma displays.

OLED Displays

Organic light emitting diode (*OLED*) displays, unlike LED displays, really are the image-producing parts of the display, not just the light source. In much the same way as a plasma cell places an excitable material between two electrodes, OLEDs are self-contained cells that use the same principle to create light. An organic light-emitting compound forms the heart of the OLED and is placed between an anode and a cathode, which produce a current that runs through the electroluminescent compound, causing it to emit light. An OLED, then, is the combination of the compound and the electrodes on each side of it. The electrode in the back of the OLED cell is usually opaque, allowing a rich black display when the OLED cell is not lit. The front electrode should be transparent to allow the emission of light from the OLED.

If thin-film electrodes and a flexible compound are used to produce the OLEDs, an OLED display can be made flexible, allowing it to function in novel applications where other display technologies could never. Because of the thin, lightweight nature of the panels, OLED displays can both replace existing heavy full-color LED signs, like the ones you might see in Las Vegas or even at your local car dealer's lot, and carve out new markets, such as integration into clothing and multimedia advertisements on the sides of buses to replace and improve upon the static ads seen today.

LEDs create light and have been used in recent years for business, home, and automotive interior lighting and automotive headlamps. OLEDs are LEDs, organic as they may be, and produce light as well. They, too, have already made their way into the interior lighting market. Because OLEDs create the image in an OLED display *and* supply the light source, there is no need for a backlight with its additional power and space requirements, unlike in the case of LCD panels. Additionally, the contrast ratio of OLED displays exceeds that of LCD panels, regardless of backlight source. This means that in darker surroundings, OLED displays produce better images than do LCD panels. Because OLEDs are highly reflective, however, quite a bit of research and development in optics has been required to produce filters and optical shielding for OLED displays. As unlikely as it seemed from early descriptions of OLED physics, true-black displays that are highly visible in all lighting conditions can now be developed using OLED technology. The foregoing discussion notwithstanding, double transparent-electrode OLEDs, with a sidelight for night viewing, have been demonstrated as a kind of "smart window."

As with LCD panels, OLED panels can be classified as active matrix (AMOLED) or passive matrix (PMOLED). As you might expect, AMOLED displays have better quality than PMOLED displays but, as a result, require more electrodes, a pair for each OLED. AMOLED displays have resolutions limited only by how small the OLEDs can be made, while the size and resolution of PMOLED displays are limited by other factors, such as the need to gang the electrodes for the OLEDs.

The power to drive an OLED display is, on average, less than that required for LCDs. However, as the image progresses toward all white, the power consumption can increase to two or three times that of an LCD panel. Energy efficiency lies in future developments as well as the display of mostly darker images, which is a reason why darker text on lighter backgrounds may give way to the reverse, both in applications and online. For OLEDs, the display of black occurs by default when the OLED is not lit and requires no power at all.

Although the early materials used in OLEDs have demonstrated drastically shorter life spans than those used in LCD and plasma panels, the technology is improving and has given rise to compounds that allow commercially produced OLEDs to remain viable long past the life expectancy of other technologies. The cost of such panels will continue to decrease so that purchases by more than corporations and the elite can be expected. In early January 2012, LG unveiled a 55″ 5mm-thick OLED HDTV. Pricing was not immediately announced, although Samsung's intent to rival LG's model with a dual-core 55″ 3D version with pixel-to-pixel control was.

Two important enhancements to AMOLED technology have resulted in the development of the Super AMOLED and Super AMOLED Plus displays, both owing their existence to Samsung. The Super AMOLED display removes the standard touch sensor panel (TSP) found in the LCD and AMOLED displays and replaces it with an on-cell TSP that is flat and applied directly to the front of the AMOLED panel, adding a mere thousandth of a millimeter to the panel's thickness. The thinner TSP leads to a more visible screen in all lighting conditions and more sensitivity when used with touch panels.

The Super AMOLED Plus display uses the same TSP as the Super AMOLED display. One advantage it has over Super AMOLED is that it employs 1.5 times as many elements (subpixels) in each pixel, leading to a crisper display. Another advantage is that Super AMOLED Plus is 18 percent more energy efficient compared with Super AMOLED. The Super AMOLED and Super AMOLED Plus displays also feature a longer lifetime than that of the standard AMOLED display.

Projection Systems

Another major category of display device is the video projection system, or projector. Portable *projectors* can be thought of as condensed video display units with a lighting system that projects the VDU's image onto a screen or other flat surface for group viewing. Interactive white boards have become popular over the past decade to allow presenters to project an image onto the board as they use virtual markers to electronically draw on the displayed image. Remote participants can see the slide on their terminal as well as the markups made by the presenter. The presenter can see the same markups because the board transmits them to the computer to which the projector is attached, causing them to be displayed by the projector in real time.

To accommodate using portable units at variable distances from the projection surface, a focusing mechanism is included on the lens. Other adjustments, such as keystone, trapezoid, and pincushion, are provided through a menu system on many models as well as a way to rotate the image 180° for ceiling-mount applications.

Rear Projection

Another popular implementation of projection systems has been the rear-projection television, in which a projector is built into a cabinet behind a screen onto which the image is projected in reverse so that an observer in front of the TV can view the image correctly. Early rear-projection TVs as well as ceiling-mounted home-theater units used CRT technology to drive three filtered light sources that worked together to create an RGB image.

Later rear-projection systems, including most modern portable projectors, implement LCD gates. These units shine a bright light through three LCD panels that adjust pixels in the same manner as an LCD monitor, except the projected image is formed as with the CRT projector by synchronizing the combination and projection of the red, green, and blue images onto the same surface.

Digital light processing (DLP) is another popular technology that keeps rear-projection TVs on the market and benefits portable projectors as well, allowing some projectors to be extremely small. Special DLP chips, referred to as optical semiconductors, have roughly as many rotatable mirrors on their surface as pixels in the display resolution. A light source and colored filter wheel or colored light sources are used to rapidly switch among primary, and sometimes secondary, colors in synchronization with the chip's mirror positions, thousands of times per second.

Brightness

Projection systems are required to produce a lighted image and display it many feet away from the system. The inherent challenge to this paradigm is that ambient light tends to interfere with the image's projection. One solution to this problem is to increase the brightness of the image being projected. This *brightness* is measured in lumens. A *lumen* (lm) is a unit of measure for the total amount of visible light that the projector gives off, based solely on what the human eye can perceive and not also on invisible wavelengths. When the rated brightness of the projector, in lumens, is focused on a larger area, the *lux*—a derivative of lumens measuring how much the projector lights up the surface on which it is focused—decreases; as you train the projector on a larger surface (farther away), the same lumens produce fewer lux.

The foregoing discussion notwithstanding, projection systems are rated and chosen for purchase based on lumens of brightness, usually once a maximum supported resolution has been chosen. Sometimes the brightness is even more of a selling point than the maximum resolution the system supports because of the chosen environment in which to operate it. Therefore, this is the rating that must be used to compare the capabilities of projection systems.

Some loose guidelines can help you choose the right projector for your application. Keep in mind that video vs. static image projection requires more lumens, and 3D output requires roughly double the lumens of 2D projection. Additionally, use of a full-screen (4:3 aspect ratio) projector system in a business environment vs. a wide-screen (16:9) home theater projector requires approximately double the lumens of output at the low end and only 1.3 times at the high end.

For example, if you are able to completely control the lighting in the room where the projection system is used, producing little to no ambient light, a projector producing as little as 1300 lumens is adequate in a home theater environment while you would need one producing around 2500 lumens in the office. However, if you can get rid of only most of the ambient light, such as by closing blinds and dimming overhead lights, the system should be able to produce 1500 to 3500 lumens in the home theater and 3000 to 4500 lumens in the office. If you have no control over a very well-lit area, you'll need 4000 to 4500 lumens in the home theater and 5000 to 6000 lumens in the business setting. These measurements assume a screen size of around 120″, regardless of aspect ratio.

By way of comparison, a 60W standard light bulb produces about 800 lumens. Output is not linear, however, because a 100W light bulb produces over double, at 1700lm. Nevertheless, you couldn't get away with using a standard 100W incandescent bulb in a projector. The color production is not pure enough and constantly changes throughout its operation due to deposits of soot from the burning of its tungsten filament during the production of light. High-intensity discharge (HID) lamps like the ones found in projection systems do more with less by using a smaller electrical discharge to produce far more visible light. A strong quartz chamber holds the filament in a projector lamp and can be seen inside the outer bulb. It contains a metal halide (where the word *halogen* comes from) gas that glows bright white when the tungsten filament lights up. Depositing the soot on the inside of the projector bulb is avoided by using a chemical process that attracts the soot created back to the filament where it once again becomes part of the filament, extending its life and reducing changes in light output.

Expect to pay considerably more for projector bulbs than for standard bulbs of a comparable wattage. The metal halide gases used in projector bulbs are more expensive than the noble gases used in standard bulbs. Add to that the fact that the bulb itself might have to be handmade and you can understand the need for higher cost.

Cooling Down

Although it doesn't take long for the fan to stop running on its own, this is a phase that should never be skipped to save time. With projector bulbs one of the priciest consumables in the world of technology, doing so may cost you more than a change in your travel arrangements. See the sidebar titled "Factor In Some Time" for some perspective.

 Real World Scenario

Factor In Some Time

A fellow instructor had his own portable projector that he carried with him on the road. At the end of a week's class, he would power down the projector and get his laptop and other goodies packed away. Just before running out the door, he would unplug the projector and pack it up. As with many instructors, this gentleman's presentations increased in density and length as he became more and more comfortable with the material.

Author Toby Skandier ran into him at a training center some time after this trend had begun. His presentation had been running later and later each Friday afternoon, edging him ever closer to his airline departure time. He admitted he had gotten into the habit of yanking the power plug for his projector from the wall and quickly stuffing the unit into the carrying case before darting out the door. Not long after their meeting, Toby heard that his projector failed catastrophically. Replacing the bulb was not the solution.

One caveat with projectors is that you must never pull the electrical plug from the outlet until you hear the internal fan cut off. There is enough residual heat generated by the projector bulb that damage to the electronics or the bulb itself (discoloration or outright failure) can occur if the fan is not allowed to remove enough heat before it stops running. Without a connection to an electrical outlet, the fan stops immediately. The electronics have the appropriate level of heat shielding that the fan removes enough heat during normal operation to avoid damage to the shielded components.

Adjusting Display Settings

Although most monitors are automatically detected by the operating system and configured to the best quality that they and the graphics adapter support, sometimes manually changing display settings, such as for a new monitor or when adding a new adapter, becomes necessary. Let's start by defining a few important terms:

- Refresh rate
- Resolution
- Multiple displays
- Degauss

Each of these terms relates to settings available through the operating system by way of display-option settings or through the monitor's control panel (degauss).

Refresh Rate

The *refresh rate* is technically the vertical scan frequency and specifies how many times in one second the scanning beam of electrons redraws the screen in CRTs. The phosphors stay bright for only a fraction of a second, so they must constantly be hit with electrons to appear to stay lit to the human eye. Measured in screen draws per second, or Hertz, the refresh rate indicates how much effort is being put into keeping the screen lit. The refresh rate on smaller monitors, say 14 to 16 inches, does fine in the range 60Hz to 72Hz. However, the larger a monitor gets (the more dot phosphors it has), the higher the refresh rate needs to be to reduce eyestrain and perceivable flicker. It is not uncommon to see refresh rates of 85Hz and higher.

Refresh rates apply to LCDs as well. For televisions, the refresh rate is a characteristic of the LCD, generally not an adjustment to be made. LCD televisions that support 120Hz refresh rates are common, but it's easy to find those rated for 60Hz, 240Hz, and 480Hz as well. For computer monitors, you might be able to select among multiple refresh rates because you're in control of the circuitry driving the refresh rate, the graphics adapter. However, because LCDs do not illuminate phosphors, there is no concern of pixel decay (for which refreshing the pixel is necessary). Instead, higher refresh rates translate to more fluid video motion. Think of the refresh rate as how often a check is made to see if each pixel has been altered by the source. If a pixel should change before the next refresh, the monitor is unable to display the change in that pixel. Therefore, for gaming and home-theater systems, higher refresh rates are an advantage.

CRT monitors manufactured today are not susceptible to damage caused by setting the video adapter's refresh rate too high, unlike older monitors. They simply refuse to operate at a rate higher than they are capable of. Refresh rates are set on the video card through the operating system or special utility software. In order for you to see a proper image, however, the monitor must support the rate you select.

The refresh rate is selected for the monitor. Nevertheless, the refresh rate you select must be supported by both your graphics adapter and your monitor because the adapter drives the monitor. If a monitor supports only one refresh rate, it does not matter how many different rates your adapter supports—without overriding the defaults, you will be able to choose only the one common refresh rate. It is important to note that as the resolution you select increases, the higher supported refresh rates begin to disappear from the selection menu. If you want a higher refresh rate, you might have to compromise by choosing a lower resolution. Exercise 4.1 steps you through the process of changing the refresh rate in Windows 7.

EXERCISE 4.1

Changing the Refresh Rate in Windows 7

1. Right-click on a blank portion of the Desktop.

2. Click Screen Resolution.

3. Click the Advanced Settings link.

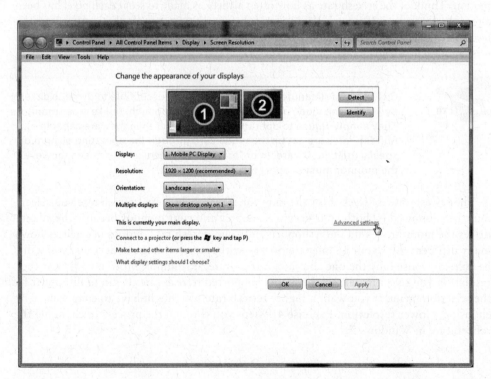

4. Click the Monitor tab.

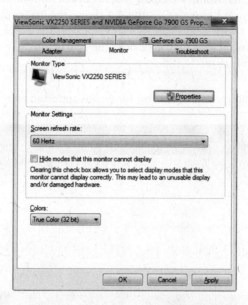

5. Select the desired screen refresh rate from the drop-down menu.

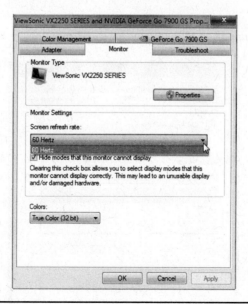

Just because a refresh rate appears in the properties dialog box does not mean that the associated monitor will be able to handle that rate. Figure 4.3 shows a CRT when a refresh rate that is out of range has been selected. Without changing anything, if possible, clear the Hide Modes That This Monitor Cannot Display check box to possibly see other refresh rates not supported by your hardware. Figure 4.4 shows the Properties dialog box for the monitor from Figure 4.3 with additional refresh rates after the check box has been cleared. If you unchecked the box, place a check mark in the box before leaving this dialog box. Click Cancel for good measure.

FIGURE 4.3 An internal monitor error for an unsupported refresh rate

FIGURE 4.4 Unsupported refresh rates for a CRT monitor

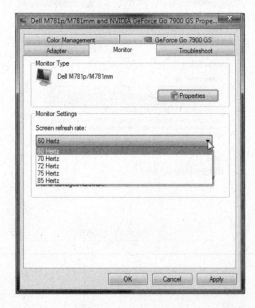

Resolution

Recall that resolution is represented as the number of horizontal dots by the number of vertical dots that make up the rows and columns of your display. There are software and hardware resolutions. Setting the resolution for your monitor is fairly straightforward. If you are using an LCD, for best results you should use the monitor's native resolution, discussed later in this chapter. Some systems will scale the image to avoid distortion, but others will try to fill the screen with the image, resulting in distortion. On occasion, you might find that increasing the resolution beyond the native resolution results in the need to scroll the Desktop in order to view other portions of it. In such instances, you cannot see the entire Desktop all at the same time. The monitor has the last word in how the signal it receives from the adapter is displayed. Adjusting your display settings to those that are recommended for your monitor can alleviate this scrolling effect.

In Windows 7, follow Exercise 4.1 up to step 2. Click the image of the monitor for which you want to alter the resolution, pull down the Resolution menu, and then move the resolution slider up for higher resolutions, as shown in Figure 4.5, or down for lower resolutions.

FIGURE 4.5   Adjusting the resolution in Windows 7

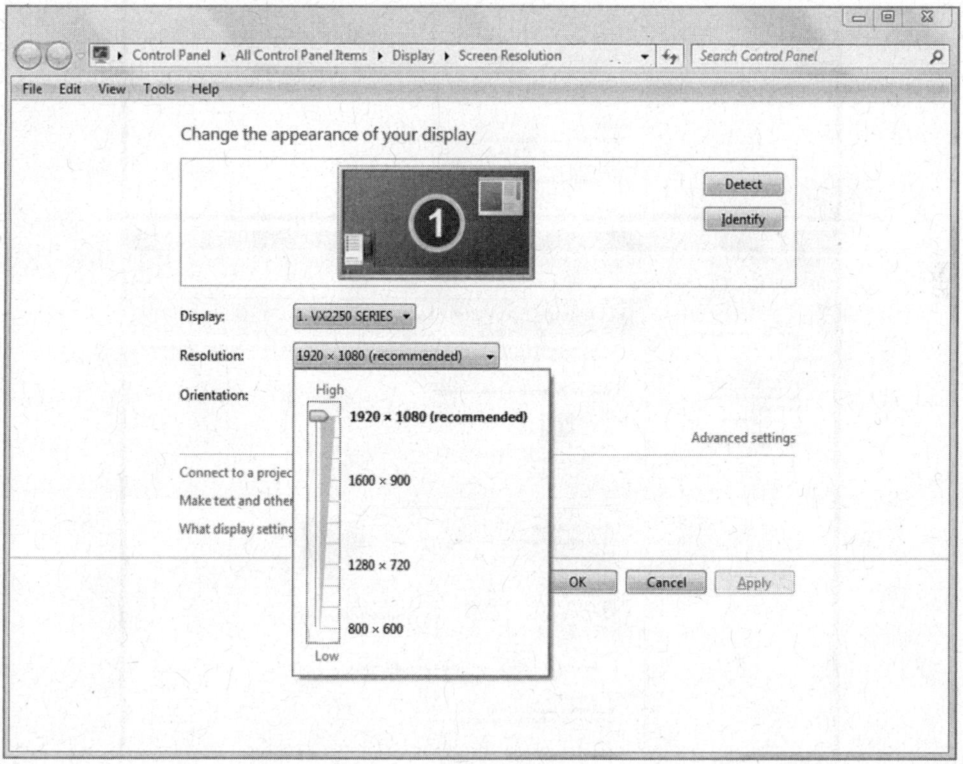

Some adapters come with their own utilities for changing settings such as the refresh rate and resolution. For example, Figure 4.6 shows two windows from the NVIDIA Control Panel. The first window has resolution, color depth, and refresh rate, all in the same spot. The second window shows you the native resolution of the LCD and the current resolution selected. If they are different, you can have the utility immediately make the current resolution match the native resolution.

FIGURE 4.6   The NVIDIA Control Panel

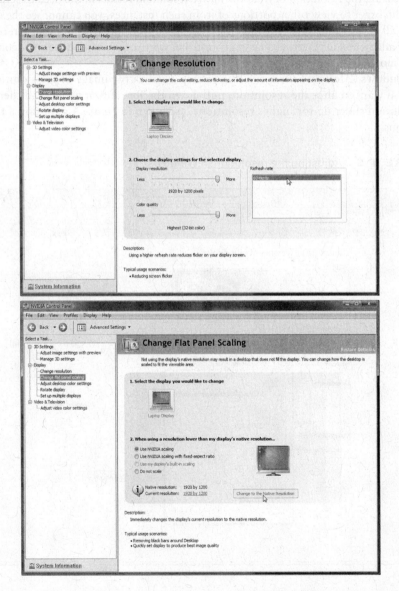

Multiple Displays

Whether regularly or just on occasion, you may find yourself in a position where you need to use two monitors on the same computer simultaneously. For example, if you are giving a presentation and would like to have a presenter's view on your laptop's LCD but need to project a slide show onto a screen, you might need to connect an external projector to the laptop. Simply connecting an external display device does not guarantee it will be recognized and automatically work. You might need to change settings for the external device, such as the resolution or the device's virtual orientation with respect to the built-in display, which affects how you drag objects between the screens. Exercise 4.2 guides you through this process.

Microsoft calls its multimonitor feature Dual View. You have the option to extend your Desktop onto a second monitor or to clone your Desktop on the second monitor. You can use one graphics adapter with multiple monitor interfaces or multiple adapters. However, as of Vista, Windows Display Driver Model (WDDM) version 1.0 required that the same driver be used for all adapters. This doesn't mean that you cannot use two adapters that fit into different expansion slot types, such as PCIe and AGP. It just means that both cards have to use the same driver. Incidentally, laptops that support external monitors use the same driver for the external interface as for the internal LCD attachment. Version 1.1, introduced with Windows 7, relaxed this requirement. WDDM is a graphics-driver architecture that provides enhanced graphics functionality that was not available before Windows Vista, such as virtualized video memory, preemptive task scheduling, and sharing of Direct3D surfaces among processes.

To change the settings for multiple monitors in Windows 7, again perform Exercise 4.1 up to step 2, and then follow the steps in Exercise 4.2 after ensuring that you have a second monitor attached.

EXERCISE 4.2

Changing the Settings for Multiple Monitors

1. Click on the picture of the monitor with the number 2 on it.

EXERCISE 4.2 *(continued)*

2. Pull down the menu labeled Multiple Displays, select Extend These Displays, and click Apply to produce an appropriate image of the second display's size and shape. Note that the Remove This Display option would not be available without completing step 1 but Extend These Displays still would be.

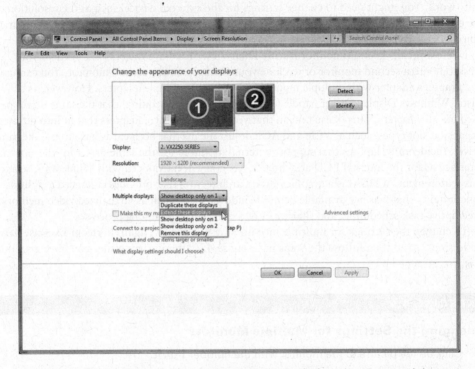

3. Click Keep Changes in the pop-up dialog that appears before the 15-second timer expires.

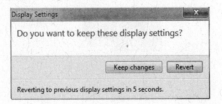

EXERCISE 4.2 *(continued)*

4. Click and drag the second monitor to the desired virtual position around the primary monitor. This affects the direction you drag objects from one display to the other.

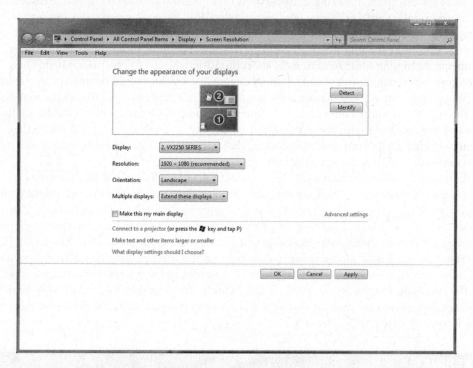

5. While the second monitor is still selected, change its refresh rate and resolution, if necessary, as outlined previously. Note that if you would like for your Desktop to appear on the second monitor, you can check the Make This My Main Display box.

6. Click OK to save your changes and exit.

Degauss

Degaussing is the reduction of the magnetic field of an object. It is generally impossible to completely neutralize an object's magnetic field, so reducing it is the objective. One application of degaussing is to randomize the magnetic domains on the surface of a magnetic storage medium, such as a hard disk drive. Degaussing the drive makes previously saved information all but unrecoverable. This, however, is a discussion of display devices, and as such, degaussing has a related but different implication.

Because CRTs use magnetic fields to guide the electron beams to their intended targets, and LCDs do not, degaussing a monitor is strictly a CRT-related practice. Due to the fact that you cannot completely eradicate the magnetic field of an object, repeated degaussing of a CRT monitor is not advised. In fact, the monitor can be damaged by degaussing it more than once in a short period of time.

The constant bombardment of the metallic shadow mask of a CRT monitor by the electron beams can cause magnetic fields to build up on the mask. These fields affect the paths of the electrons, resulting in distortions that manifest themselves as image discoloration and rainbow effects. Many later-generation CRTs have an internal degaussing coil wrapped around the front portion of the unit near the shadow mask. Newer CRTs activate the coil each time the unit is turned on with the power button, resulting in a sometimes dramatic, humming noise of extremely short duration whenever power is applied. These monitors rarely require intentional manual degaussing by the user or technician as a result.

When these internal degaussing coils are activated manually by a button on the monitor or through the monitor's internal menu system, the same noise can be heard. Additionally, because the monitor is already powered up and displaying an image, you will notice the image shaking at the same time. Unadvised, repeated coil activation results in increasingly less dramatic results with each iteration.

External degaussing devices exist that reduce the magnetic field in the shadow mask. Because these tools can be made considerably stronger than the space-restricted internal coils, they can at once be more effective and more damaging to the sensitive magnetic yokes that guide the electron beams. Excessive electromagnetic energy has been known to permanently damage CRTs. You should take great care when using external degaussing devices on CRTs.

Some monitors have a degaussing button right on the front panel. The CRT used in Exercise 4.3 requires that you degauss from an onscreen menu system that is independent of the operating system. Nevertheless, if this monitor does not detect an attached system, it will not let you into the menu. Exercise 4.3 guides you through using the built-in degaussing feature of a Dell M781 monitor.

EXERCISE 4.3

Degaussing a CRT Monitor

1. Attach the CRT to a working computer system and power on the monitor.

2. Press the Menu button on the front panel of the CRT cabinet (the button on the far right in the following photo).

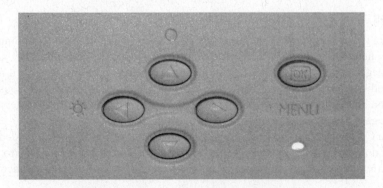

EXERCISE 4.3 *(continued)*

The following screen shot shows the resulting menu. Notice that the monitor detects the signal it is receiving from the graphics adapter. In this case, a resolution of 1600×1200 (UXGA—see Table 4.1 later in this chapter) and a refresh rate of 60Hz are detected. This monitor even offers advice on the recommended resolution for best results. In this case, 1024×768 is recommended. When the recommendation is followed, a better fit to the dot phosphors and a wider selection of refresh rates are likely.

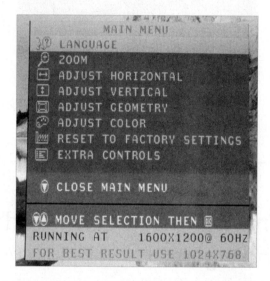

3. Use the up- and down-arrow keys on the front panel of the CRT to select the Extra Controls menu item.

4. Press the Menu button on the front panel to select the Extra Controls submenu, shown here.

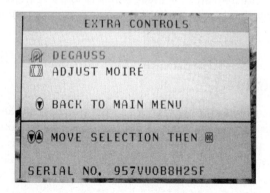

5.   Press the Menu button on the front panel of the CRT because the Degauss menu item is already selected. If degaussing was required, you should hear the distinctive degaussing noise and notice the image distorting as shown here.

Understanding Video Standards and Technologies

The following sections introduce the various video standards, from the earlier digital standards to the later analog standards and the most current digital high-definition standards.

 Pre-VGA standards are presented here to give perspective regarding display technology as a whole. Do not expect to be tested on any standards prior to VGA.

Video Standards

The early video standards differ in two major areas: the highest resolution supported and the maximum number of colors in their palette. The supported resolution and palette size are directly related to the amount of memory on the adapter, which is used to hold the rendered images to be displayed. Display adapters through the years can be divided into five primary groups:

- Monochrome

- CGA

- EGA
- VGA
- DVI, HDMI, and other modern digital video

 See Chapter 3, "Peripherals and Expansion," for more information on DVI, HDMI, and other advanced video standards.

Because the amount of memory used to implement the pre-VGA adapters was fixed, the resolution and number of colors supported by these cards was fixed as well. Newer standards, based on VGA analog technology and connectivity, were eventually developed using adapters with expandable memory or separately priced models with differing fixed memory. Adapters featuring variable amounts of memory resulted in selectable resolutions and color palettes. In time, 24-bit color palettes known as Truecolor and made up of almost 17 million colors, which approached the number of colors the human eye can distinguish, were implemented. As a result, in keeping with growing screen sizes, the latest commercial video standards continue to grow in resolution, their distinguishing trait, but generally not in palette size. These post-VGA resolutions are discussed later in this chapter in the section "Advanced Video Resolutions and Concepts."

Monochrome

The first video technology for PCs was monochrome (from the Latin *mono*, meaning one, and *chroma*, meaning color). This black-and-white video (actually, it was green or amber text on a black background) was fine for the main operating system of the day, DOS. DOS didn't have any need for color. Thus, the video adapter was very basic. The first adapter, developed by IBM, was known as the Monochrome Display Adapter (MDA). It could display text but not graphics and used a resolution of 720×350 pixels.

The Hercules Graphics Card (HGC), introduced by Hercules Computer Technology, had a resolution of 720×350 and could display graphics as well as text. It did this by using two separate modes: a *text mode* that allowed the adapter to optimize its resources for displaying predrawn characters from its onboard library *and* a *graphics mode* that optimized the adapter for drawing individual pixels for onscreen graphics. It could switch between these modes on the fly. These modes of operation have been included in all graphics adapters since the introduction of the HGC.

CGA

The next logical step for displays was to add a splash of color. IBM was the first with color, with the introduction of the Color Graphics Adapter (*CGA*). CGA displays 16-color text in resolutions of 320×200 (40 columns) and 640×200 (80 columns), but it displays 320×200 graphics with only four colors per mode. Each of the six possible modes has 3 fixed colors and a selectable 4th; each of the 4 colors comes from the 16 used for text. CGA's 640×200 graphics resolution has only 2 colors—black and one other color from the same palette of 16.

EGA

After a time, people wanted more colors and higher resolution, so IBM responded with the Enhanced Graphics Adapter (*EGA*). EGA could display 16 colors out of a palette of 64 with CGA resolutions as well as a high-resolution 640×350 mode. EGA marks the end of classic digital-video technology. The digital data pins on the 9-pin D-subminiature connector accounted for six of the nine pins. As a solution, analog technologies, starting with VGA, would all but stand alone in the market until the advent of DVI and HDMI, discussed in Chapter 3.

VGA

With the PS/2 line of computers, IBM wanted to answer the cry for "more resolution, more colors" by introducing its best video adapter to date: the Video Graphics Array (*VGA*). This video technology had a "whopping" 256KB of video memory on board and could display 16 colors at 640×480, 640×350, and 320×200 pixels or, using mode 13h of the VGA BIOS, 256 colors at 320×200 pixels. It became widely used and enjoyed a long reign as at least the base standard for color PC video. For many years, it was the starting point for computers, as far as video is concerned. Until recently, however, your computer likely defaulted to this video technology's resolution and color palette only when there was an issue with the driver for your graphics adapter or when you entered Safe Mode. Today, even these modes display with impressive graphics quality.

One unique feature of VGA (and its offshoots) is that it's an analog technology, unlike the preceding and subsequent standards. Technically, the electronics of all graphics adapters and monitors operate in the digital realm. The difference in VGA-based technologies is that graphics adapters output and monitors receive an analog signal over the cable. Conversely, MDA, CGA, EGA, HDMI, and DVI-D signals arrive at the monitor as digital pulse streams with no analog-to-digital conversion required.

VGA builds a dynamic palette of 256 colors, which are chosen from various shades and hues of an 18-bit palette of 262,114 colors. When only 16 colors are displayed, they are chosen from the 256 selected colors. VGA sold well mainly because users could choose from almost any color they wanted (or at least one that was close). The reason for moving away from the original digital signal is because for every power of 2 that the number of colors in the palette increases, you need at least one more pin on the connector. A minimum of 4 pins for 16 colors is not a big deal, but a minimum of 32 pins for 32-bit graphics become a bit unwieldy. The cable has to grow with the connector, as well, affecting transmission quality and cable length. VGA, on the other hand, requires only 3 pins, one each for red, green, and blue modulated analog color levels, not including the necessary complement of ground, sync, and other control signals. For this application, 12 to 14 of the 15 pins of a VGA connector are adequate.

One note about monitors that may seem rather obvious: You must use a video card that supports the type of monitor you are using. For example, you can't use a CGA monitor on a VGA adapter. Add-on adapters must also have a matching slot in the motherboard to accommodate them.

Advanced Video Resolutions and Concepts

The foregoing display technologies included hardware considerations and resolutions. Adjustments could be made to change the configuration of these technologies. Additional resolutions common in the computing world through the years and characteristics that cannot be adjusted but instead define the quality of the display device are presented in the following sections.

Resolutions

The following sections detail what might, at first, appear to be technologies based on new graphics adapters. However, advancements after the VGA adapter occurred only in the memory and firmware of the adapter, not the connector or its fundamental analog functionality. As a result, the following technologies are distinguished early on by supported resolutions and color palettes and later by resolutions alone. Subsequently, these resolutions have become supported by the newer digital standards with no change in their friendly names.

Super VGA

Up until the late 1980s, IBM set most personal-computer video standards. IBM made the adapters, everyone bought them, and they became a standard. Some manufacturers didn't like this monopoly and set up the Video Electronics Standards Association (VESA) to try to enhance IBM's video technology and make the enhanced technology an open standard. The initial result of this work was Super VGA (*SVGA*). This new standard was indeed an enhancement because it could support 16 colors at a resolution of 800×600 (the VESA standard), but it soon expanded to support 1024×768 pixels with 256 colors.

Since that time, *SVGA* has been a term used loosely for any resolution and color palette to exceed that of standard VGA. This even includes the resolution presented next, XGA. New names still continue to be introduced, mainly as a marketing tool to tout the new resolution du jour. While display devices must be manufactured to support a certain display resolution, one of the benefits of analog video technology was that later VGA monitors could advance along with the graphics adapter, in terms of the color palette. The analog signal is what dictates the color palette, and the standard for the signal has not changed since its VGA origin. This makes VGA monitors' color limitations a nonissue. Such a topic makes sense only in reference to graphics adapters.

XGA

IBM introduced a new technology in 1990 known as the Extended Graphics Array (*XGA*). This technology was available only as a Micro Channel Architecture (MCA) expansion board (vs. ISA or EISA, for instance). XGA could support 256 colors at 1024×768 pixels or 65,536 colors at 800×600 pixels. It was a different design, optimized for GUIs of the day such as Windows or OS/2. It was also an *interlaced* technology when operating at the 1024×768 resolution, meaning that rather than scan every line one at a time on each pass to create the image, it scanned every other line on each pass, using the phenomenon known as *"persistence of vision"* to produce what appears to our eyes as a continuous image.

The *i* in *1080i* refers to interlaced—vs. progressive (*1080p*) scanning.

The advertised refresh rate specifies the frequency with which all odd or all even rows are scanned. The drawback to interlacing is that the refresh rate used on a CRT has to be twice the minimum comfort level for refreshing an entire screen. Otherwise, the human eye will interpret the uncomfortably noticeable decay of the pixels as flicker. Therefore, a refresh rate of 120Hz would result in a comfortable effective refresh rate of 60Hz. Unfortunately, 84Hz was a popular refresh rate for interlaced display signals, resulting in an entire screen being redrawn only 42 times per second, a rate below the minimum comfort level.

More Recent Video Standards

Any standard other than the ones already mentioned are probably extensions of SVGA or XGA. It has becoming quite easy to predict the approximate or exact resolution of a video specification based on its name. Whenever a known technology is preceded by the letter *W*, you can assume roughly the same vertical resolution but a wider horizontal resolution to accommodate 16:10 wide-screen formats (16:9 for LCD and plasma televisions). Preceding the technology with the letter *Q* indicates that the horizontal and vertical resolutions were each doubled, making a final number of pixels 4 times (quadruple) the original. To imply 4 times each, for a final resolution enhancement of 16 times, the letter *H* for *hexadecatuple* is used.

Therefore, if XGA has a resolution of 1024×768, then QXGA will have a resolution of 2048×1536. If Ultra XGA (UXGA) has a resolution of 1600×1200 and an aspect ratio of 4:3, then WUXGA has a resolution of 1920×1200 and a 16:10 aspect ratio. Clearly, there have been a large number of seemingly minute increases in resolution column and row sizes. However, consider that at 1024×768, for instance, the screen will display a total of 786,432 pixels. At 1280×1024, comparatively, the number of pixels increases to 1,310,720—nearly double the pixels for what doesn't sound like much of a difference. As mentioned, you need better technology and more video memory to display even slightly higher resolutions.

The term *aspect ratio* refers to the relationship between the horizontal and vertical pixel counts that a monitor can display. For example, for a display that supports 4:3 ratios, such as 1024×768, if you divide the first number by 4 and multiply the result by 3, the product is equal to the second number. Additionally, if you divide the first number by the second number, the result is approximately 1.3, the same as 4 ÷ 3. Displays with a 16:10 aspect ratio have measurements that result in a dividend of 16 ÷ 10 = 1.6.

Table 4.1 lists the various video technologies, their resolutions, and the maximum color palette they support, if specified as part of the standard. All resolutions, VGA and higher, have a 4:3 aspect ratio unless otherwise noted.

TABLE 4.1 Video display technology comparison

Name	Resolutions	Colors
Monochrome Display Adapter (MDA)	720×350	Mono (text only)
Hercules Graphics Card (HGC)	720×350	Mono (text and graphics)
Color Graphics Adapter (CGA)	320×200	4
	640×200	2
Enhanced Graphics Adapter (EGA)	640×350	16
Video Graphics Array (VGA)	640×480	16
	320×200	256
ATSC 480i/480p, 4:3 or 16:9	704×480	Not specified
Super VGA (SVGA)	800×600	16
Extended Graphics Array (XGA)	800×600	65,536
	1024×768	256
Widescreen XGA (WXGA), 16:10	1280×800	Not specified
Super XGA (SXGA), 5:4	1280×1024	Not specified
ATSC 720p, 16:9	1280×720	Not specified
SXGA+	1400×1050	Not specified
WSXGA+, 16:10	1680×1050	Not specified
Ultra XGA (UXGA)	1600×1200	Not specified
WUXGA, 16:10	1920×1200	Not specified
ATSC 1080i/1080p, 16:9	1920×1080	Not specified
Quad XGA (QXGA)	2048×1536	Not specified
WQXGA, 16:10	2560×1600	Not specified

TABLE 4.1   Video display technology comparison *(continued)*

Name	Resolutions	Colors
WQUXGA, 16:10	3840×2400	Not specified
WHUXGA, 16:10	7680×4800	Not specified

Starting with SXGA, the more advanced resolutions can be paired with 32-bit graphics, which specifies the 24-bit Truecolor palette of 16,777,216 colors and uses the other 8 bits for enhanced noncolor features, if at all. In some cases, using 32 bits to store 24 bits of color information per pixel increases performance because the bit boundaries are divisible by a power of 2; 32 is a power of 2, but 24 is not. That being said, however, unlike with the older standards, the color palette is not officially part of the newer specifications.

Nonadjustable Characteristics

The following sections discuss features that are more selling points for display units and not configurable settings.

Native Resolution

One of the peculiarities of LCD, plasma, OLED, and other flat-panel displays is that they have a single fixed resolution, known as the *native resolution*. Unlike CRT monitors, which can display a crisp image at many resolutions within a supported range, flat-panel monitors have trouble displaying most resolutions other than their native resolution.

The native resolution comes from the placement of the transistors in the hardware display matrix of the monitor. For a native resolution of 1680×1050, for example, there are 1,764,000 transistors (LCDs) or cells (PDPs and OLED displays) arranged in a grid of 1680 columns and 1050 rows. Trying to display a resolution other than 1680×1050 through the operating system tends to result in the monitor interpolating the resolution to fit the differing number of software pixels to the 1,764,000 transistors, often result-ing in a distortion of the image on the screen.

The distortion can take various forms, such as blurred text, elliptical circles, and so forth. SXGA (1280×1024) was once one of the most popular native resolutions for larger LCD computer monitors before use of wide-screen monitors became pervasive. For wide-screen aspects, especially for wide-screen LCD displays of 15.4″ and larger, WSXGA+ (1680×1050) was one of the original popular native resolutions. The ATSC 1080p resolu-tion (1920×1080) is highly common today across all display technologies, largely replacing the popular computer-graphics version, WUXGA (1920×1200).

Contrast Ratio

The *contrast ratio* is the measure of the ratio of the luminance of the brightest color to that of the darkest color the screen is capable of producing. Do not confuse contrast ratio with *contrast.* Contrast ratios are generally fixed measurements that become selling points for the monitors. Contrast, on the other hand, is an adjustable setting on all monitors (usually found alongside brightness) that changes the relative brightness of adjacent pixels. The more contrast, the sharper and edgier the image. Reducing the contrast too much can make the image appear washed out. This discussion is not about contrast but instead contrast ratio.

One of the original problems with LCD displays, and a continuing problem with cheaper versions, is that they have low contrast ratios. Only LED-backlit LCD panels rival the high contrast ratios that plasma displays have always demonstrated. A display with a low contrast ratio won't show a "true black" very well, and the other colors will look washed out when you have a light source nearby. Try to use the device in full sunshine and you're not going to see much of anything, although the overall brightness level is the true key in such surroundings. Also, lower contrast ratios mean that you'll have a harder time viewing images from the side as compared with being directly in front of the display.

Ratios for smaller LCD monitors and televisions typically start out around 500:1. Common ratios for larger units range from 20,000:1 to 100,000:1. In the early days of monitors that used LEDs as backlights, 1,000,000:1 was exceedingly common. Today, vendors advertise 10,000,000:1 and "infinite" as contrast ratios. Anything higher than 32,000:1 is likely a dynamic contrast ratio. Plasma displays have always been expected to have contrast ratios of around 5,000:1 or better.

Once considered a caveat, a dynamic ratio is realized by reducing power to the backlight for darker images. The downside was that the original backlight being a single fluorescent bulb meant that the signal to the brighter LCD pixels had to be amplified to compensate for the uniform dimming of the backlight. This occasionally resulted in over-compensation manifested as areas of extreme brightness, often artificial in appearance. This practice tends to wash out the lighter colors and make white seem like it's glowing, which is hardly useful to the user. Today's LED backlights, however, are controlled either in zones made up of a small number of pixels or individually per pixel, resulting in trust-worthy high dynamic contrast ratios.

The environment where the monitor will be used must be taken into account when considering whether to place a lot of emphasis on contrast ratio. In darker areas, a high contrast ratio will be more noticeable. In brighter surroundings, widely varying contrast ratios do not make as much of a difference. For these environments, a monitor capable of higher levels of brightness is more imperative.

One caveat to contrast ratios that remains is that there is no vendor-neutral regulatory measurement. The contrast ratio claimed by one manufacturer can take into account variables that another manufacturer does not. A manufacturer can boost the ratio simply by increasing how bright the monitor can go, the portion of the monitor tested, or the conditions in the room where the test was performed. This doesn't do anything to help the display of darker colors, though. So, although the contrast ratio is certainly a selling point, don't just take it at face value. Look for independent comparison reviews that use multiple methods of measuring contrast ratio or compare displays in person to see which one works better for the situation in which you intend to use it.

Summary

In this chapter, you read about various display technologies and settings. The primary categories of video display unit were mentioned and explained: CRT, LCD, LED, OLED, plasma, and projector. Concepts unique to each of these categories were explored. Additionally, the similarities among them were highlighted. We identified names and characteristics of display resolutions and explained the process of configuring settings such as resolution, refresh rate, and multimonitor support in Windows.

Exam Essentials

Be able to compare and contrast the main categories of display technology.   Although video display units all have roughly the same purpose—to display images created by the computer and rendered by the graphics adapter—CRTs, LCDs, LEDs, plasmas, OLEDs, and projectors go about the task in slightly different ways.

Be familiar with the key terms and concepts of display units.   Make sure you can differentiate among terms such as *resolution*, *refresh rate*, and *brightness*, and be familiar with terms used in other settings that might be found on the monitor or in the operating system.

Understand key concepts behind LCD and other flat-panel technology.   You need to be familiar with active and passive matrix; resolution standards, such as XGA and UXGA; and terms such as *contrast ratio* and *native resolution*.

Familiarize yourself with the steps that must be taken to configure display settings in Windows.   Most of the settings based on the operating system are found in roughly the same place. However, nuances found in the details of configuring these settings make it important for you to familiarize yourself with the specific configuration procedures.

Review Questions

The answers to the Chapter Review Questions can be found in Appendix A.

1. Which of the following would be the best choice as a personal display technology if a user wants to save desk space and not have to deal with interference from nearby speakers?

    A. CRT

    B. HDMI

    C. LCD

    D. Projector

2. An associate is trying to explain why a particular model of CRT monitor displays images in such high quality but is unable to recall a specific term. The associate mentions that each phosphor is on average only 0.25mm away from the nearest phosphor of the same color. What is the associate trying to describe?

    A. Resolution

    B. Dot pitch

    C. Refresh rate

    D. The number of dots per inch

3. Which of the following is true regarding a monitor's refresh rate?

    A. As long as the graphics adapter can refresh the image at a particular rate, the attached monitor can accommodate that refresh rate.

    B. The refresh rate is normally expressed in MHz.

    C. The refresh rate is normally selected by using the controls on the front panel of the monitor.

    D. As you lower the resolution, the maximum refresh rate allowed tends to increase.

4. Which statement about LCDs is most accurate?

    A. The concept of refresh rate has no meaning with regard to LCDs.

    B. LCDs are preferred to CRTs because they can display a larger range of resolutions.

    C. LCDs tend not to be as clear as CRTs.

    D. LCDs require more power than CRTs.

5. If you are unable to display a given resolution on a monitor, which of the following might explain why?

    A. The graphics adapter does not have enough memory installed.

    B. The video display unit does not have enough memory installed.

    C. You are using a CRT with a single fixed resolution.

    D. You have the refresh rate set too high.

6. Which video technology has a resolution of 1280×1024?

    A. SVGA

    B. SXGA

    C. WSXGA

    D. UXGA

7. What does a *Q* in video resolution names, such as QXGA, refer to?

    A. Both the horizontal and vertical components of the resolution have been quadrupled.

    B. The resolution is cut to one-fourth.

    C. The technology is faster.

    D. Both the horizontal and vertical components of the resolution have been doubled.

8. What is contrast ratio?

    A. The ratio of luminance between the darkest and lightest colors that can be displayed

    B. A term that was used with CRTs but has no meaning with LCDs

    C. The ratio of luminance between two adjacent pixels

    D. Something that can be corrected through degaussing

9. Which of the following display types physically creates the image displayed in a manner most similar to OLED displays?

    A. CRT

    B. LED

    C. LCD

    D. Plasma

10. When approaching an older LCD panel from the side, you don't realize there is actually an image displayed on it until you are almost in front of it. Which two options might explain why you could not detect the image from the side? (Choose two.)

    A. Older LCDs were equipped with a motion sensor.

    B. Multiple monitors are in use, and the LCD is the secondary monitor, resulting in its poor oblique visibility.

    C. The user has a privacy filter in place.

    D. The monitor employs active-matrix pixel addressing.

    E. It is a passive-matrix LCD panel.

11. On which properties tab do you select the refresh rate to use between the graphics adapter and monitor in Windows Vista?

    A. Adapter

    B. Monitor

    C. Advanced

    D. Display Settings

12. After a presentation using a video projector, when in a hurry to pack everything up and head to the airport, which of the following should you avoid doing immediately?

    A. Unplugging the projector's power cable

    B. Unplugging the projector's video cable from your laptop

    C. Powering down the projector

    D. Turning off your laptop

13. What might cause your display to appear in a resolution of 640×480?

    A. You have your resolution set to SVGA.

    B. You added memory to your graphics adapter but have not informed the BIOS of the new memory.

    C. You have your resolution set to XGA.

    D. You have booted XP into Safe Mode.

14. Which of the following results can occur with improper display settings?

    A. The computer spontaneously reboots.

    B. The graphics adapter automatically chooses to use the highest supported resolution.

    C. You might have to scroll to see parts of the Desktop.

    D. The mouse cursor changes or permanently disappears.

15. What is the single, fixed resolution of an LCD called?

    A. Native resolution

    B. Default resolution

    C. Refresh rate

    D. Burned-in resolution

16. Which of the following is it possible to do with multimonitor settings?

    A. Connect multiple monitors to your computer only by using a graphics adapter with two video interfaces.

    B. Cause two different Desktops to merge onto the same monitor.

    C. Connect two laptops together so they display the same Desktop.

    D. Display different parts of your Desktop on different monitors.

17. Which of the following types of LCD has the best performance characteristics?

    A. Active matrix

    B. Passive matrix

    C. Dual matrix

    D. Dual scan

18. Which of the following resolutions is an example of a 16:10 aspect ratio?

  A. 1280×1024

  B. 1920×1200

  C. 800×600

  D. 2048×1536

19. Where can you find the best degaussing tool for modern CRT monitors?

  A. At a computer specialty shop

  B. At a consumer electronics store

  C. Built into the monitor

  D. As a freeware download

20. What is the unit of measure used by manufacturers of projectors to indicate the brightness of their product?

  A. Lux

  B. Lumens

  C. Watts

  D. Candelas

Performance-Based Question

On the A+ exams, you will encounter performance-based questions. The questions on the exam require you to perform a specific task, and you will be graded on whether you were able to complete the task. The following require you to think creatively to measure how well you understand this chapter's topics. You may or may not see similar questions on the actual A+ exams. To see how your answers compare to the authors', refer to Appendix B.

List the steps necessary to extend your main display to a second monitor and adjust their orientation with respect to one another.

Chapter

5

Custom Configurations

THE FOLLOWING COMPTIA A+ 220-801 OBJECTIVES ARE COVERED IN THIS CHAPTER:

✓ **1.9 Evaluate and select appropriate components for a custom configuration, to meet customer specifications or needs.**

- Graphic / CAD / CAM design workstation
  - Powerful processor
  - High-end video
  - Maximum RAM
- Audio/Video editing workstation
  - Specialized audio and video card
  - Large fast hard drive
  - Dual monitors
- Virtualization workstation
  - Maximum RAM and CPU cores
- Gaming PC
  - Powerful processor
  - High-end video/specialized GPU
  - Better sound card
  - High-end cooling
- Home Theater PC
  - Surround sound audio
  - HDMI output
  - HTPC compact form factor
  - TV tuner

- Standard thick client
  - Desktop applications
  - Meets recommended requirements for running Windows
- Thin client
  - Basic application
  - Meets minimum requirements for running Windows
- Home Server PC
  - Media streaming
  - File sharing
  - Print sharing
  - Gigabit NIC
  - RAID array

Not all computers are right for every situation. There are small netbooks that are ideal for portability but that would fail miserably when used for mathematical modeling of complex systems. Supercomputers that are up to the modeling task would have to be completely disassembled to be transported anywhere. While these are extreme examples, dozens more exist that shine the light on the need for custom configurations to perform specific jobs.

This chapter introduces you to some of the custom configurations that have become so popular that they are tantamount to standards, enough so that they can be discussed in a finite way. Such concepts have become requisite knowledge for the A+ certified technician. The following specialized systems are covered in the sections presented in this chapter:

- Graphic and CAD/CAM design workstations

- Audio/video editing workstations

- Virtualization workstations

- Gaming PCs

- Home theater PCs

- Standard thick clients

- Thin clients

- Home server PCs

The topics in the following list are related to the systems discussed in this chapter and are divided into families that sometimes tie many of the custom configurations together. Other of these topics are so specialized that they apply only to a single custom configuration from the previous list. The following major topics are discussed in the sections to come:

- CPU enhancements

- Video enhancements

- Maximized RAM

- Specialized audio

- Specialized drives

- NIC enhancements

- Additional considerations

  - Enhanced cooling

  - Special chassis

  - TV tuner requirement

  - Application specifics

Graphic and CAD/CAM Design Workstations

Workstations used in the design of graphical content place a heavy load on three primary areas of the system:

- CPU enhancements
- Video enhancements
- Maximized RAM

CPU Enhancements

Sometimes it's a matter of how powerful a computer's CPU is. Other times, having multiple lesser CPUs that can work independently on a number of separate tasks is more important. Many of today's PCs have either of these characteristics or a combination of both. Nevertheless, there are enough computers being produced that have neither. As a result, it is necessary to gauge the purpose of the machine when choosing the CPU profile of a computer.

Graphic design workstations and *computer-aided design/computer-aided manufacturing (CAD/CAM) workstations* are computers used for similar yet distinct reasons. Graphic design workstations are used by desktop publishers in the creation of high-quality copy consisting of professional text and graphical images. This output is used in advertising, marketing, and other forms of specialized documentation. CAD/CAM workstations are used in the design of engineering and architectural documentation, including blueprints in both two and three dimensions. Such systems place quite a load on their CPUs. Systems with average CPUs can become overwhelmed by the amount of processing required by professional graphical software. For this reason, such systems must be designed with CPUs of above-average performance.

Graphic Design Workstations

Computers used by graphic-design artists must process a constant flow of colors and detailed shapes, the combination of which can put a strain on the CPU, RAM, and video components.

CAD/CAM Workstations

CAD/CAM systems can carry the designer's vision from conception to design in a 100 percent digital setting. Three-dimensional drawings are also common in this technology. These designs drive or aid in the production of 3D models. Software used for such projects requires a high number of CPU cycles during the rendering of the designs before display on the monitor or output to a printer or plotter. Such systems have been used for decades by professionals in the architecture, surveying, and engineering fields as well as by design engineers in manufacturing firms.

The output of computerized numerical control (CNC) systems used in the manufacturing process following the use of CAD/CAM workstations in the design phase is far different from displays on monitors or printouts. CNC systems take a set of coded instructions and render them into machine or tool movements. The result is often a programmable cutting away of parts of the raw material to produce a finished product. Examples are automotive parts, such as metallic engine parts or wheel rims, crowns and other dental structures, and works of art from various materials.

Video Enhancements

Possibly an obvious requirement for such systems, graphics adapters with better graphics processing units (GPUs) and additional RAM on board have the capability to keep up with the demand of graphic design applications. Such applications place an unacceptable load on the CPU and system RAM when specialized processors and adequate RAM are not present on the graphics adapter.

Maximized RAM

Although such systems take advantage of enhanced video subsystems, all applications still require CPUs to process their instructions and RAM to hold these instructions during processing. Graphics applications tend to be particularly CPU and RAM hungry. Maximizing the amount of RAM that can be accessed by the CPU and operating system will result in better overall performance by graphic design workstations.

Audio/Video Editing Workstations

Professionals that edit multimedia material require workstations that excel in three areas:

- Video enhancements
- Specialized audio
- Specialized drives

The following sections assume the use of nonlinear editing (NLE) schemes for video. NLE differs from linear editing by storing the video to be edited on a local drive instead of editing being performed in real time as the source video is fed into the computer. NLE requires workstations with much higher RAM capacity and disk space than does linear editing. Although maximizing RAM is a benefit to these systems, doing so is considered secondary to the three areas of enhancement mentioned in the preceding list.

Video Enhancements

Although a high-performance video subsystem is a benefit for computer systems used by audio/video (A/V) editors, it is not the most important video enhancement for such systems.

Audio/video editing workstations benefit most from a graphics adapter with multiple video interfaces that can be used simultaneously. These adapters are not rare, but it is still possible to find high-end adapters with only one interface, which are not ideal for A/V editing systems.

When editing multimedia content, or even generalized documents, it is imperative that the editor have multiple views of the same or similar files. The editor of such material often needs to view different parts of the same file. Additionally, many A/V editing software suites allow, and often encourage or require, the editor to use multiple utilities simultaneously. For example, in video editing, many packages optimize their desktop arrangement when multiple monitors are detected, allowing less horizontal scrolling through timelines. The ability to extend the Desktop across multiple monitors is valuable in such a situation. For more on setting up this feature, see the section "Multiple Displays" in Chapter 4, "Display Devices."

To improve video-editing performance, insist on a graphics adapter that supports CUDA and OpenCL. CUDA is Nvidia's Compute Unified Device Architecture, a parallel computing architecture for breaking down larger processing tasks into smaller tasks and processing them simultaneously on a GPU. Open Computing Language (OpenCL) is a similar, yet cross-platform, open standard. Programmers can specify high-level function calls in a programming language they are more familiar with instead of writing specific instructions for the microcode of the processor at hand. The overall performance increase of macro-style application programming interfaces (APIs) like these is an advantage of the technologies as well. The rendering of 2D and 3D graphics occurs much more quickly and fluidly with one of these technologies. CUDA is optimized for Nvidia GPUs, while OpenCL is less specific, more universal, and perhaps, as a result, less ideal when used with the same Nvidia GPUs that CUDA supports.

Furthermore, depending on the visual quality of the content being edited, the professional's workstation might require a graphics adapter and monitor capable of higher resolutions than are readily available in the consumer marketplace. If the accuracy of what the editor sees on the monitor must be as true to life as possible, a specialty CRT monitor might be the best choice for the project. Such CRTs are expensive and are available in high definition and widescreen formats. These monitors might well provide the best color representation when compared to other high-quality monitors available today.

Specialized Audio

The most basic audio controllers in today's computer systems are not very different from those in the original sound cards from the 1980s. They still use an analog codec with a simple two-channel arrangement. Editors of audio information who are expected to perform quality work often require six to eight channels of audio. Many of today's motherboards come equipped with 5.1 or 7.1 analog audio. (See the section "Analog Sound Jacks" in Chapter 3, "Peripherals and Expansion.") Although analog audio is not entirely incompatible with quality work, digital audio is preferred the vast majority of the time. In some cases, an add-on adapter supporting such audio might be required to support an A/V editing workstation.

Specialized Drives

Graphics editing workstations and other systems running drive-intensive NLE software benefit from uncoupling the drive that contains the operating system and applications from the one that houses the media files. This greatly reduces the need for multitasking by a single drive. With the data drive as the input source for video encoding, consider using the system drive as an output destination during the encoding if a third drive is not available. Just remember to move the resulting files to the data drive once the encoding is complete.

Not only should you use separate drives for system and data files, you should also make sure the data drive is large and fast. SATA 6Gbps drives that spin at 7200rpm and faster are recommended for these applications. Editors cannot afford delays and the non-real-time video playback caused by buffering due to inefficient hard-drive subsystems. If you decide to use an external hard drive, whether for convenience or portability or because of the fact that an extremely powerful laptop is being used as an A/V editing workstation, use an eSATA connection when possible. Doing so ensures no loss in performance over internal SATA drives due to conversion delays or slower interfaces, such as USB 2.0.

If you cannot find a drive that has the capacity you require, you should consider implementing RAID 0, disk striping without parity. Doing so has two advantages: You can pay less for the total space you end up with, and RAID 0 improves read and write speeds because multiple drives are active simultaneously. Don't confuse spanned volume sets with RAID 0. Simple volume sets do not read and write to all drives in the set simultaneously; data simply spills over to the next drive when the preceding one is full. The only advantage volume sets share with RAID 0 is the ability to store files larger than a single drive. Consult Chapter 2, "Storage Devices and Power Supplies," for more information on SATA and various RAID levels.

If you would also like to add fault tolerance and prevent data loss, go with RAID 5, which has much of the read/write benefit of RAID 0 with the assurance that losing a single drive won't result in data loss. RAID should be implemented in hardware when possible to avoid overtaxing the operating system, which has to implement or help implement software RAID itself.

Virtualization Workstations

Hardware virtualization has taken the industry by storm and has given rise to entire companies and large business units in existing companies that provide software and algorithms of varying effectiveness for the purpose of minimizing the hardware footprint required to implement multiple servers and workstations. Although virtualization as a technology subculture is discussed in greater detail later in this book, you are ready to investigate the unique requirements for the workstation that will host the guest operating systems and their applications.

Virtualization workstations must exceed the specifications of standard servers and workstations in two primary areas:

- CPU enhancements
- Maximized RAM

Depending on the specific guest systems and processes that the workstation will host, it may be necessary to increase the hard drive capacity of the workstation as well. Because this is only a possibility, increased drive capacity is not considered a primary enhancement for virtualization workstations.

Virtual machines (VMs) running on a host system appear to come along with their own resources. A quick look in the Device Manager utility of a guest operating system leads you to believe it has its own components and does not require nor interfere with any resources on the host. This is not true, however. The following list includes some of the more important components that are shared by the host and all guest operating systems:

- CPU cycles
- System memory
- Drive storage space
- Systemwide network bandwidth

CPU Enhancements

Because the physical host's processor is shared by all operating systems running, virtual or not, it behooves you to implement virtual machines on a host with as many CPUs as possible. The operating system is capable of treating each core in a multicore processor separately and creating virtual CPUs for the VMs from them. Therefore, the more CPUs you can install in a workstation, each with as many cores as possible, the more dedicated CPU cycles that can be assigned to each virtual machine.

Maximized RAM

As you create a virtual machine, even before a guest operating system is installed in the VM, you must decide how much RAM the guest system will require. The same minimum requirements for installing an operating system on a conventional machine apply to the installation of that operating system on a virtual machine.

The RAM you dedicate to that VM is not used until the VM is booted. Once it is booted, though, that RAM is as good as unavailable to the host operating system. As a result, you must ensure that the virtualization workstation is equipped with enough RAM to handle its own needs as well as those of all guests that could run simultaneously. As with a conventional system running a single operating system at a time, you generally want to supply each VM with additional RAM to keep it humming along nicely.

This cumulative RAM must be accounted for in the physical configuration of the virtualization workstation. In most cases, this will result in maximizing the amount of

RAM installed in the computer. The maximum installed RAM hinges on three primary constraints:

- The CPU's address-bus width
- The operating system's maximum supported RAM
- The motherboard's maximum supported RAM

The smallest of these constraints dictates the maximum RAM you will be able to use in the workstation. Attention to each of these limitations should be exercised in the selection of the workstation to be used to host guest operating systems and their applications. Considering the limitations of operating systems leads to preferring the use of server versions over client versions and the use of x64 versions over x86 versions.

 Real World Scenario

What's It Going to Take?

The folks at a medium-sized organization decided to try their hand at virtualization because the IT manager heard they could save money on future infrastructure and go Green at the same time. They already had all the operating systems they needed; they were currently installed on separate machines. The manager envisioned removing the KVM switch and having a single machine in the server room.

The technician in charge did almost everything right. He chose the company's most powerful server and created five virtual machines. The hard drive was large enough that there was plenty of room for the host operating system and the five VMs. The technician knew the minimum requirements for running each of the operating systems and made sure that each VM was configured with plenty of RAM. The dual-core CPU installed in the system was more than powerful enough to handle each operating system.

After a combination of clean installations and image transfers into the VMs, the server was ready to test. The host booted and ran beautifully as always. The first VM was started and was found to be accessible over the network. It served client requests and created a barely noticeable draw on performance. It was the second VM that sparked the realization that the manager and technician missed a crucial point. The processor and the RAM settings for each individual VM were sufficient for the host and at most one VM, but when any second VM was added to the mix, the combined drain on the CPU and RAM was untenable. "What's it going to take to be able to run these servers simultaneously?" the technician wondered.

The solution was to replace the server motherboard with a model containing dual quad-core Xeon processors and to maximize the RAM based on what the motherboard supported. The result was an impressive system with five virtual servers, each of which displayed impressive performance statistics. Before long, the expense of the server was returned in power savings. Eventually, additional savings will be realized when the original physical hardware for the five servers would have had to be replaced.

Gaming PCs

Early video games designed for the PC market were designed to run on the average system available at the time. As is true with all software, there is a push/pull relationship between PC-based games and the hardware they run on. Over time, the hardware improves and challenges the producers of gaming software. Inspired by the possibilities, the programmers push the limits of the hardware, encouraging hardware engineers to create more room for software growth. Today's PC-based gaming software cannot be expected to run on the average system of the day. Specialized gaming PCs, computers optimized for running modern video games, fill a niche in the marketplace, leading to a continually growing segment of the personal-computer market.

Gaming enthusiasts often turn to specialized game consoles for the best performance, but with the right specifications, a personal computer can give modern consoles a run for their money, possibly even eclipsing their performance. For a computer to have a chance, however, four areas of enhancement must be considered:

- CPU enhancements
- Video enhancements
- Specialized audio
- Enhanced cooling

CPU Enhancements

Unlike with A/V editing, gaming requires millions of decisions to be made by the CPU every second. It's not enough that the graphics subsystem can keep up with the action; the CPU must be able to create that action. Some gamers find that they do fine with a high-end stock CPU. Others require that such CPUs perform above their specified rating. They find that overclocking the CPU by making changes in the BIOS to the clock frequency used by the system gains them the requisite performance that allows them to remain competitive against or to dominate competitors. Overclocking was discussed in Chapter 1, "Motherboards, Processors, and Memory," but to reiterate, it means that you are running your CPU at a clock speed greater than the manufacturer's rating to increase performance.

However, this increased performance comes at a price: Their CPU will almost certainly not live as long as if they had used the default maximum speed determined by the manufacturer and detected by the BIOS. Nothing can completely negate the internal damage caused by pushing electrons through the processor's cores faster than should be allowed. Nevertheless, the CPU would scarcely survive days or even hours with standard cooling techniques. Enhancing the cooling system, discussed shortly, is the key to stretching the CPU's life back out to a duration that approaches its original expectancy.

Video Enhancements

Video games have evolved from text-based and simple two-dimensional graphics-based applications into highly complex software that requires everything from real-time high-resolution, high-definition rendering to three-dimensional modeling. Technologies like Nvidia's SLI and ATI's Crossfire are extremely beneficial for such graphics-intensive applications. SLI was discussed in Chapter 1.

No longer can gaming software rely mostly on the system's CPU to process its code and deliver the end result to the graphics adapter for output to the monitor. No longer can this software store a screen or two at a time in the graphics adapter's memory, allowing for adapters with tens of MB of RAM. Today's gaming applications are resource-hungry powerhouses capable of displaying fluid video at 30 frames per second. To keep up with such demands, the RAM installed on graphics adapters has breached the 1GB mark, a capacity not long ago reserved for primary system memory. In the same way that CUDA- and OpenCL-capable GPUs benefit workstations used for video editing, these same standards are indispensable in the world of modern gaming software. Not all GPUs support these standards. Thus, another selling point emerges for high-end graphics adapters.

Of course, all the internal system enhancements in the world are for naught if the monitor you choose cannot keep up with the speed of the adapter or its resolutions and 3D capability. Quite a bit of care must be exercised when comparison shopping for an adequate gaming monitor.

Specialized Audio

Today's video games continue the genre of interactive multimedia spectacles. Not only can your video work in both directions, using cameras to record the image or motion of the player, but so can your audio. It's exceedingly common to find a gamer shouting into a microphone boom on a headset as they guide their character through the virtual world of high-definition video and high-definition digital audio. A lesser audio controller is not acceptable in today's PC gaming world. Technologies such as S/PDIF and HDMI produce high-quality digital audio for the gaming enthusiast. Of course, HDMI provides for state-of-the-art digital video as well.

Enhanced Cooling

As mentioned earlier, the practices of speed junkies, such as modern PC gamers, can lead to a processor's early demise. Although an earlier end to an overclocked CPU can't be totally guaranteed, operators of such systems use standard and experimental cooling methods to reduce the self-destructive effects of the increased heat output from the CPU. Refer back to the section "Advanced CPU Cooling Methods" in Chapter 1 for more information on cooling techniques that give overclocked CPUs a fighting chance. Of course, experimental cooling techniques such as immersion of the system in mineral oil and indirect application of liquid nitrogen or helium to the CPU continue to garner attention from enthusiasts. It remains to be seen, however, if some of these techniques have a shot at making it in the marketplace.

Today's high-end graphics adapters come equipped with their own cooling mechanisms designed to keep such adapters properly cooled under even extreme circumstances. Nevertheless, the use of high-end adapters in advanced ways leads to additional concerns. Graphics adapters that rob a second slot for their cooling mechanism to have space to exhaust heated air through the backplane might be unwelcome in a smaller chassis that have only a single slot to spare. Also, the gaming-PC builder's election to include two or more ganged adapters in one system (SLI or Crossfire) challenges the engineered cooling circuit. When many large adapters are placed in the path of cooler air brought in through one end of the chassis for the purpose of replacing the warmer internal air of the chassis, the overall ambient internal temperature increases.

Home Theater PCs

Home theater PCs (HTPCs) continue to gain in popularity as a specialized computing appliance. An HTPC might have multiple capabilities, such as storing large amounts of video media and streaming it to an output device, streaming it directly from the Internet, or acting as an A/V tuner and receiver, mating input sources with output devices. The versatility of an HTPC makes it a logical choice for people desiring to exercise more control over their existing set-top boxes, most of which do not even offer the option of flexible storage. HTPCs are personal computers with operating systems that allow easy access to local storage, allowing the user to add whatever media they want whenever they feel the need.

The average PC can be turned into a device with similar functionality, but a computer designed for use as such should be built on a chassis that adheres to the HTPC form factor; the average computer would not. In fact, the following list comprises the specializations inherent in true HTPCs:

- Video enhancements
- Specialized audio
- Special chassis
- TV tuner requirement

Video Enhancements

High-definition monitors are as commonplace as television displays in the home today. HTPCs, then, must go a step beyond, or at least not fall a step behind. Because High-Definition Multimedia Interface (HDMI) is an established standard that is capable of the highest-quality audio, video resolution, and video refresh rates offered by consumer electronics and because HDMI has been adopted by nearly all manufacturers, it is the logical choice for connectivity in the HTPC market. Considering the single simple, small-form factor plug and interface inherent to HDMI, more cumbersome video-only choices, such as DVI and YPbPr component video, lose favor on a number of fronts.

Graphics adapters present in HTPCs should have one or more HDMI interfaces. Ideally, the adapter will have both input and output HDMI interfaces, giving the PC the capability to combine and mix signals as well as interconnect sources and output devices. Additionally, internally streamed video will be presented over the HDMI interface to the monitor. Keep in mind that the monitor used should be state-of-the-art to keep up with the output capabilities of the HTPC.

Specialized Audio

Recall that HDMI is capable of eight-channel 7.1 surround sound, which is ideal for the home theater. The fact that the HTPC should be equipped with HDMI interfaces means that surround-sound audio is almost an afterthought. Nevertheless, high-end digital audio should be near the top of the wish list for HTPC specifications. If it's not attained through HDMI, then copper or optical S/PDIF should be employed. At the very least, the HTPC should be equipped with 7.1 analog surround sound (characterized by a sound card with a full complement of six 3.5mm stereo minijacks).

Special Chassis and TV Tuner

As mentioned earlier, HTPCs have their own specialized computer case form factor. These machines should be able to blend well with other home theater appliances, such as digital video recorders (DVRs) from a cable company or satellite provider, or look totally fine taking their place.

Creating a machine that takes up minimal space (perhaps even capable of being mounted on a wall beside or behind the monitor) without compromising storage capacity and performance requires the use of today's smallest components. The following list comprises some of the components you might use when building your own HTPC from separate parts.

- HTPC chassis, typically with dimensions such as 17×17×7″ and 150W HTPC power supply
- Motherboard, typically mini-ITX (6.7×6.7″) with integrated HDMI video
- HDD or SSD, usually 2½″ portable form factor, larger capacity if storage of multimedia content is likely
- RAM—DIMMs for mini-ITX motherboard; SODIMMs for many pre-built models
- Blu-ray drive, player minimum
- PCIe or USB TV tuner card, optionally with capture feature

Many prebuilt offerings exist with all components standard. You need only choose the model with the specifications that match your needs. Barebones systems exist as well, allowing you to provide your own hard drive and RAM modules. Many such units contain smaller ITX boards, such as nano- or pico-ITX, which are not compatible with most do-it-yourself chassis.

TV tuner cards are available as system add-ons and not commonly as integrated motherboard components. HTPCs that will be used only for streaming video from Internet sources and playing music do not require a TV tuner card. Otherwise, such a card might allow one or more sources, including one source split into two inputs, to be watched or recorded.

Standard Thick Clients

A *standard thick client* is not so much a custom configuration but instead the standard configuration that allows the definition of custom configurations. In other words, a thick client is a standard client computer system, and as such, it must meet only the basic standards that any system running a particular operating system and particular applications must meet. Because it's a client, however, the ability to attach to a network and accept a configuration that attaches it to one or more servers is implied. Although most computers today exhibit such capabilities, they cannot be assumed.

Each operating system requires a minimum set of hardware features to support its installation. Each additional desktop application installed requires its own set of features concurrent with or on top of those required for the operating system. For example, the operating system requires a certain amount of RAM for its installation and a certain amount of hard drive space. A typical application might be able to run with the same amount of RAM but will most certainly require enough additional hard-drive space to store its related files.

Keep in mind that minimum specifications are just that, the minimum. Better performance is realized by using recommended specifications or higher.

Thin Clients

Enterprises interested in saving copious amounts in infrastructure cost sometimes turn to thin clients to achieve their goal. A *thin client* is any machine that divests itself of all or most local storage and varying levels of RAM and processing power without necessarily giving up all ability to process instructions and data. In the extreme, a thin client resembles a dumb terminal, only displaying graphical user interface output to the monitor and relaying input from the mouse and keyboard back to the server. The primary difference between these ultra-thin clients and dumb terminals is that the clients feature a true network connection and contain enough intelligence to locate the server before turning over processing control.

The ramification of having clients with low processing and storage capabilities is that there must be one or more servers with increased corresponding capacities. Unfortunately, this leads to a single or centralized point of failure in the infrastructure that can impact productivity to an unacceptable level. Thin clients have no offline capability, requiring constant network connectivity. Workforces that require employees to be independent or mobile with their computing power lean away from thin clients as well, opting for laptops and similar technology.

Thin clients with local storage and basic applications for local execution must be able to accommodate the storage and processing of such applications and the operating systems for which they are designed, including full versions of Windows. Simple designs featuring flash-based storage and small quantities of small-form-factor RAM exist, reducing the need for such systems to resemble thick clients after all.

Home Server PCs

Essentially powerful client systems with standard, nonserver operating systems, home server PCs differ from enterprise servers to the point that they qualify as custom configurations. For many generations, desktop operating systems have run server services and have been capable of allowing limited access by other clients but not enough access to accommodate enterprise networks. Nevertheless, because the home server PC is the center of the home network, fault tolerance considerations should be entertained, which is decidedly not the case for standard home systems.

Recall that fault tolerance differs from redundancy in that fault tolerance seeks to retain accessibility during the failure while redundancy simply ensures recoverability after the failure. Redundancy, in the form of a data backup, does not ensure the continued accessibility of the data, but RAID, for example, seeks to do so. Even the most basic home system should be backed up regularly to avoid total data loss, but only servers in the home environment should be considered for the added expense of fault tolerance.

Home server PCs can be built from the same components that go into today's higher-performance systems. Attention needs to be paid to certain enhanced features, however. The following list outlines these differences:

- Media streaming capabilities
- File sharing services
- Print sharing services
- Gigabit NIC
- RAID array

Media Streaming Capabilities

A popular use for a home server is to stream music photos and videos to other devices, including those that are not PCs. With Windows 7, you can enable media streaming services and configure the computer to stream media. Of course, third-party applications and utilities are also a possibility.

With Windows 7, Microsoft introduced HomeGroups, which are basically workgroups intended to have a smaller scope. HomeGroups work hand in hand with libraries, another feature new to Windows 7. Anything that can be included in a library (documents, pictures, videos, and music) can be shared among the devices in the password-protected HomeGroup.

Additionally, HomeGroups can share installed printers among the member computers. Chapter 14, "Working with Windows 7," discusses HomeGroups in more detail.

You can prepare a Windows 7 computer to stream media through Windows Media Player by accessing the media streaming configuration through the advanced settings of the Network And Sharing Center in Control Panel. Exercise 5.1 walks you through the process.

EXERCISE 5.1

Configuring Windows 7 for Media Streaming

1. In Control Panel, run the Network And Sharing Center applet in classic view.

2. Click the Change Advanced Sharing Settings link in the left frame.

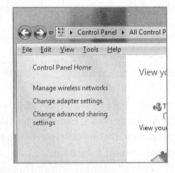

3. Click the down arrow to the right of Home Or Work to expand that configuration section.

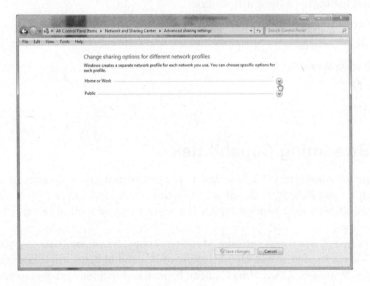

EXERCISE 5.1 *(continued)*

4. In the Media Streaming section, click the Choose Media Streaming Options link.

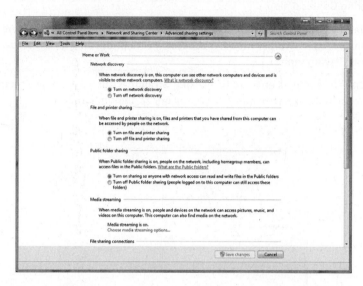

5. In the Media Streaming Options dialog, pull down the buttons labeled Blocked and change them to Allowed for each computer on the network that you want to be able to stream from the local PC.

EXERCISE 5.1 *(continued)*

6. Click OK to leave the Media Streaming Options dialog and then close the Network
    And Sharing Center dialog.

7. Open Windows Media Player (for example, Start ➢ All Programs ➢ Windows Media
    Player) and switch to Library mode, if necessary (the grid icon with the arrow pointing
    left in Now Playing mode).

8. Ensure that streaming is enabled by clicking Stream ➢ Turn On Media Streaming.
    This option is hidden if streaming is already on, as shown here.

9. On one of the remote systems, start Windows Media Player.

10. Scroll down, if necessary, in the left frame until you see Other Libraries.

11. Expand the remote library you just shared and see if you can play music, watch videos
    or recorded TV, or view pictures.

File and Print Sharing Services

In addition to the ability to stream files to remote machines, home servers are expected to allow the static transfer of files to or from the server's hard drive or array. Streaming and file sharing are similar concepts, but streaming occurs in one direction from the server and does not affect the client's file system. File sharing can go in both directions, and it adds to the client's file system during downloads. The server acts as a repository for uploaded files that can then be downloaded from any other machine in the home network.

The difference between home servers and enterprise servers is that all clients in a home environment tend to have equal access to the file server's data store. Enterprise file servers have data stores that are isolated from users that do not have permission to access them. Print servers in the home and enterprise behave in a similar fashion. Each printer attached to the home server should be accessible to anyone on the home network.

File and print sharing are available through classic file sharing in Windows as well as through the Windows 7 HomeGroup.

Gigabit NIC

The home server should be attached to a wired switched port in an Ethernet switch or in the wireless access point. The NIC and the switch port should be capable of gigabit speeds. Providing such speed ensures that clients attached to 100Mbps Fast Ethernet ports and across the wireless network will not create a bottleneck in their attempt to share the server's resources. Running client NICs at gigabit speeds should be avoided, even though the capability is ubiquitous. Running all devices on the network at such speeds guarantees that each device so attached will attempt to saturate the server's gigabit interface with its own traffic.

RAID Array

Because some of the data stored on a home server represents the only copy, such as data that is streamed to all clients or the data included in a crucial backup of client systems, it must be protected from accidental loss. Because the data that comprises the streaming content, shared data store, and client backup sets can become quite expansive, a large capacity of storage is desirable. Even a recoverable server outage results in a home network that is temporarily unusable by any client, so fault tolerance should be included. RAID provides the answer to all of these needs.

By using a hardware RAID solution in the home server PC, the server's operating system is not taxed with the arduous task of managing the array, and additional RAID levels might also be available. The RAID array can extend to many terabytes in size, many times the size of a single drive, and should include hot-swappable drives so that it can be rebuilt on the fly while still servicing client requests during the loss of a single drive.

Windows Home Server 2011

As a specific example of a home server product, Microsoft has released Windows Home Server (WHS) 2011, an operating system intended to be preinstalled on specialized equipment offered by a variety of vendors around the world. WHS 2011 and the systems on which it is installed feature the components and capabilities in the list of the enhanced features a home server PC should have.

In particular, WHS 2011 systems implement a RAID array, typically with four hot-swappable drives in a compact enclosure that operates off of very little power. With the array, you can back up every computer on your network, including the server, on a daily basis. Restoring information from the backups is easy and flexible. Like with Windows 7, you can choose individual files to restore from a complete backup. Of course, you can restore entire systems as well. The entire server can be readily restored also.

File sharing and streaming is highly flexible with the server. It's a simple task to choose what is shared and what is not. Media can be streamed to any compatible network device, which can include network-enabled televisions, monitors, and game consoles. Data flow goes both ways, though, allowing you to keep an eye on the condition and performance level of all networked computers.

With a properly configured and subscribed Internet link, you can access the server from the Internet using a personalized URL, allowing you to remotely upload and download files and access applications.

Summary

In this chapter, you were introduced to seven systems of specific use and how a standard thick client differs from them. The seven systems are graphic and CAD/CAM design work-stations, audio/video editing workstations, virtualization workstations, gaming PCs, home theater PCs, thin clients, and home server PCs.

You learned how some of these systems have very specific needs while others share common requirements for components not found in a standard desktop system. These needs include CPU enhancements, video enhancements, maximized RAM, specialized audio, specialized drives, NIC enhancements, enhanced cooling, special chassis, a TV tuner requirement, and specifics related to applications.

Exam Essentials

Be able to describe graphic and CAD/CAM design workstations and list their components. These workstations require powerful processors, high-end video, and maximum RAM to be able to provide the performance required to allow efficient graphic design and modeling.

Be able to describe audio/video editing workstations and list their components. A/V work-stations call for specialized audio and video, large and fast hard drives, and multiple monitors to allow editors to smoothly play back their media while being able to see all the controls of their utilities and applications.

Be able to describe virtualization workstations and list their components.   Virtualization workstations need plenty of RAM and CPU cores to share among the guest operating systems while still allowing the host to run efficiently and error free.

Be able to describe gaming PCs and list their components.   Gaming PCs make use of high-performance central and graphical processors to bring the ultimate gaming experience to the user. Rounding out the experience is awesome sound production, which comes at the price of increased heat production due to the faster-running components. As a result, enhanced cooling mechanisms must be employed.

Be able to describe home theater PCs and list their components.   Replacing or augmenting other set-top boxes requires features that a home theater PC has. Surround sound, HDMI, and a TV tuner allow such systems to run the show. Place the components in a chassis that conforms to the HTPC form factor and space is not an issue.

Be able to describe thin clients and list their components.   Thin clients should still conform to the basic specifications required to run Windows and basic applications. However, it is possible to go a step further and have the server run all software and feed the client no more than a dumb terminal would receive. The primary difference is that it is fed over an Ethernet connection instead of a classic serial interface.

Be able to describe home server PCs and list their components.   Home server PCs are expected to support media streaming as well as file and print sharing. To stay ahead of the client demand, the server should be connected to a Gigabit Ethernet interface. To ensure fault tolerance, RAID is recommended for home server PCs.

Be able to describe how a standard thick client differs from the custom configurations.   Knowing what the custom configurations require makes it a simple task to differentiate thick clients from a standard desktop client, which needs but be able to run Windows locally and support standard desktop applications.

Review Questions

The answers to the Chapter Review Questions can be found in Appendix A.

1. Which of the following is not a requirement for a graphic design workstation?
   - **A.** Fast hard drive
   - **B.** Maximum RAM
   - **C.** Powerful CPU
   - **D.** High-end video

2. Which of the following is required when constructing an A/V editing workstation?
   - **A.** Gigabit NIC
   - **B.** Powerful processor
   - **C.** Maximum RAM
   - **D.** Fast hard drive

3. Why do virtualization workstations require as many CPU cores as possible?
   - **A.** Each virtual machine has one or more cores installed directly in it.
   - **B.** Each virtual machine makes use of actual CPU resources for processing instructions and data.
   - **C.** Fault tolerance dictates that if one CPU core fails, there should be one or more in line to take its place.
   - **D.** Because each guest operating system runs in its own space, multiple cores are required to store the collective data.

4. Why is high-end cooling a requirement for gaming PCs?
   - **A.** Gaming PCs tend to overclock their CPUs and run multiple high-performance GPUs.
   - **B.** Gaming controllers have components for tactile realism that generate copious amounts of heat.
   - **C.** Digital sound cards generate more heat than analog sound cards.
   - **D.** Placing that many hard drives in such a small space generates too much heat.

5. Which of the following is not a common requirement of a home theater PC?
   - **A.** Surround sound
   - **B.** HDMI
   - **C.** Micro-ATX case
   - **D.** TV tuner

6. Which type of system simply needs to run standard versions of Windows and desktop applications?

   A. Thin client

   B. Thick client

   C. Home server PC

   D. Virtualization workstation

7. Which of the following descriptions most closely matches that of a thin client?

   A. A high-resolution monitor, keyboard, and mouse

   B. A computer with a low-profile case

   C. A laptop

   D. A dumb terminal with a NIC

8. Why should you equip a home server PC with a gigabit NIC?

   A. All systems, including the server, should communicate at the same speed.

   B. The server should not be allowed to communicate at the higher speeds of the rest of the network or it will be overused.

   C. The server should exceed the communication speed of the clients to avoid a bottleneck.

   D. The operating system home servers run is not compatible with Fast Ethernet.

9. Which of the following reasons justifies having a powerful processor in a CAD/CAM workstation?

   A. Only powerful processors can stream graphical information efficiently.

   B. Manufacturing equipment is generally faster than design equipment, which needs faster processors to keep up.

   C. Graphics adapters used in CAD/CAM do not have their own processors, so the CPU performs this job as well.

   D. The algorithms used in rendering graphics can be processor intensive.

10. Why do A/V editing workstations benefit from more than one monitor?

   A. Their software often has enough controls across their width that one monitor seems cramped.

   B. While one graphics adapter works on one rendering project, the other can simply display a normal desktop.

   C. Once the editing is complete, the second monitor is used to present the results to others on the team.

   D. Additional monitors are used for remote collaboration among other editors.

11. Which of the following is required by a virtualization workstation?

   A. Multiple host operating systems

   B. Maximum RAM allowed

   C. File sharing services

   D. Multiple NICs

12. All of the following are recommended for gaming PCs except _____ .

   A. High-end cooling

   B. A RAID array

   C. High-end video

   D. Better sound card

13. Which of the following system types does not require a CPU enhancement of any sort?

   A. A/V editing workstation

   B. Gaming PC

   C. Graphic design workstation

   D. Virtualization workstation

14. Which of the following is the recommended video output technology for home theater PCs?

   A. DVI

   B. WUXGA

   C. HDMI

   D. YCbCr

15. Which of the following is a common feature of a standard thick client?

   A. Has enhanced video capabilities

   B. Has a high-performance hard drive

   C. Has as much RAM installed as is possible

   D. Can run a full version of Windows

16. In a thin client configuration, if the operating system is not resident on the client, where is it normally found?

   A. On a DVD inserted at bootup

   B. On a USB flash drive

   C. On the server for session-by-session client use

   D. Embedded in a flash module on the motherboard

17. Which of the following is not a common requirement in a home server PC?

    A. File and print sharing

    B. Maximum RAM

    C. Gigabit NIC

    D. Media streaming

    E. RAID array

18. All of the following systems benefit from increased RAM except _____ . (Choose two.)

    A. Home theater PC

    B. Virtualization workstation

    C. Graphic design workstation

    D. Gaming PC

19. Which of the following uses would not require a custom configuration for a PC?

    A. A computer running Windows 7 Ultimate with 1TB of data and 250GB of applications installed

    B. A computer running WHS 2011

    C. A design computer used to drive a lathe that makes automotive rims

    D. A computer to replace a BD player and DVR

20. Which of the following system types does not benefit from video enhancements?

    A. CAD/CAM design workstation

    B. Home server PC

    C. A/V editing workstation

    D. Home theater PC

Performance-Based Question

On the A+ exams, you will encounter performance-based questions. The questions on the exam require you to perform a specific task, and you will be graded on whether you were able to complete the task. The following requires you to think creatively to measure how well you understand this chapter's topics. You may or may not see similar questions on the actual A+ exams. To see how your answer compares to the authors', refer to Appendix B.

List the steps required to stream video from one Windows 7 computer to another one in the same house. Assume that the two computers are members of the same HomeGroup.

Chapter 6

Networking Fundamentals

THE FOLLOWING COMPTIA A+ 220-801 EXAM OBJECTIVES ARE COVERED IN THIS CHAPTER:

✓ **2.1 Identify types of network cables and connectors.**

- Fiber
  - Connectors: SC, ST, and LC
- Twisted Pair
  - Connectors: RJ-11, RJ-45
  - Wiring standards: T568A, T568B
- Coaxial
  - Connectors: BNC, F-connector

✓ **2.2 Categorize characteristics of connectors and cabling.**

- Fiber
  - Types (single-mode vs. multi-mode)
  - Speed and transmission limitations
- Twisted Pair
  - Types: STP, UTP, CAT3, CAT5, CAT5e, CAT6, plenum, PVC
  - Speed and transmission limitations
- Coaxial
  - Types: RG-6, RG-59
  - Speed and transmission limitations

✓ **2.8 Identify various types of networks.**

- LAN
- WAN

- PAN
- MAN
- Topologies
  - Mesh
  - Ring
  - Bus
  - Star
  - Hybrid

✓ **2.9 Compare and contrast network devices, their functions and features.**

- Hub
- Switch
- Router
- Access point
- Bridge
- Modem
- NAS
- Firewall
- VoIP phones
- Internet appliance

✓ **2.10 Given a scenario, use appropriate networking tools.**

- Crimper
- Multimeter
- Toner probe
- Cable tester
- Loopback plug
- Punchdown tool

Looking around most homes or offices today, it's kind of hard to imagine a world without networks. Nearly every place of business has some sort of network. Wireless home networks have exploded in popularity in the last few years. Just five or six years ago, if you looked for a wireless signal from a laptop at home you might find one or two. Today it could be a dozen. Even when we're not thinking about networking, it's still likely that we're doing it, with the ubiquitous Internet-enabled smartphones in our pockets and purses.

We take for granted a lot of what we have gained in technology the past few years, much less decades. Twenty years ago, if you wanted to send a memo to everyone in the company, you had to use a photocopier and interoffice mail. Delivery to a remote office could take days. Today, one mistaken click of the Reply All button can result in instantaneous embarrassment. Email is an example of one form of communication that became available only due to the introduction and growth of networks.

This chapter focuses on the basic concepts of how a network works, including the way it sends information, the hardware used, and common types of networks that you might encounter. It used to be that in order to be a PC technician, you needed to focus on only one individual computer at a time. In today's environment, though, you will in all likelihood be asked to troubleshoot both hardware and software problems on existing networks.

 If the material in this chapter interests you, you might consider studying for, and eventually taking, CompTIA's Network+ exam. It is a non-company-specific networking certification similar to A+ but for network-related topics. You can study for it using Sybex's *CompTIA Network+ Study Guide* materials, available at www.sybex.com.

Understanding Networking Principles

Stand-alone personal computers, first introduced in the late 1970s, gave users the ability to create documents, spreadsheets, and other types of data and save them for future use. For the small-business user or home-computer enthusiast, this was great. For larger companies, however, it was not enough. Larger companies had greater needs to share information between offices and sometimes over great distances. Stand-alone computers were insufficient for the following reasons:

- Their small hard-drive capacities were insufficient.

- To print, each computer required a printer attached locally.

- Sharing documents was cumbersome. People grew tired of having to save to a floppy and then take that disk to the recipient. (This procedure was called *sneakernet*.)

- There was no email. Instead, there was interoffice mail, which was slow and unreliable.

To address these problems, networks were born. A *network* links two or more computers together to communicate and share resources. Their success was a revelation to the computer industry as well as businesses. Now, departments could be linked internally to offer better performance and increase efficiency.

You have probably heard the term *networking* in a business context, where people come together and exchange names for future contact and to give them access to more resources. The same is true with a computer network. A computer network allows computers to link to each other's resources. For example, in a network, every computer does not need a printer connected locally in order to print. Instead, you can connect a printer to one computer or directly to the network and allow all of the other computers to access this resource. Because they allow users to share resources, networks can increase productivity as well as decrease cash outlay for new hardware and software.

In the following sections, we will discuss the fundamentals of networking as well as types of networks you are likely to encounter.

Understanding Networking Fundamentals

In many cases, networking today has become a relatively simple plug-and-play process. Wireless network cards can automatically detect and join networks and you're seconds away from surfing the Web or sending email. Of course, not all networks are that simple. Getting your network running may require a lot of configuration, and one messed-up setting can cause the whole thing to fail.

Just as there is a lot of information to know about how to configure your network, there is a lot of background information you should understand about *how* networks work. The following sections cover the fundamentals, and armed with this information, you can then move on to how to make it work *right*. The following basics are covered here:

- LANs, WANs, PANs, and MANs
- Primary network components
- Network operating systems (NOSs)
- Network resource access
- Network topologies
- Rules of communication

LANs, WANs, PANs, and MANs

Local area networks (LANs) were introduced to connect computers in a single office or building. *Wide area networks (WANs)* expanded the LANs to include networks outside the local environment and also to distribute resources across long distances. Generally, it's safe to think of a WAN as multiple, disbursed LANs connected together. Today, LANs exist in many homes (wireless networks) and nearly all businesses. WANs are becoming more common as businesses become more mobile and as more of them span greater distances. WANs were historically used only by larger corporations, but many smaller companies with remote locations now use them as well.

Having two types of network categories just didn't feel like enough, so the industry introduced two more terms. The *personal area network (PAN)* is a very small-scale network designed around one person. The term generally refers to networks using Bluetooth technology. On a larger scale is the *metropolitan area network (MAN)*, which is bigger than a LAN but not quite as big as a WAN.

It is important to understand these concepts as a service professional because when you're repairing computers, you are likely to come in contact with problems that are associated with the computer's connection to a network. Understanding the basic structure of the network can often help you solve a problem.

LANs

The 1970s brought us the minicomputer, which was a smaller version of the mainframe. Whereas the mainframe used *centralized processing* (all programs ran on the same computer), the minicomputer used *distributed processing* to access programs across other computers. As depicted in Figure 6.1, distributed processing allows a user at one computer to use a program on another computer as a *back end* to process and store information. The user's computer is the *front end*, where data entry and minor processing functions are performed. This arrangement allowed programs to be distributed across computers rather than centralized. This was also the first time network cables rather than phone lines were used to connect computers.

FIGURE 6.1   Distributed processing

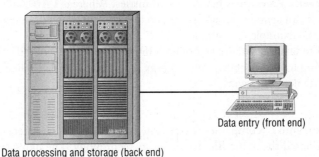

Data entry (front end)

Data processing and storage (back end)

By the 1980s, offices were beginning to buy PCs in large numbers. Portables were also introduced, allowing computing to become mobile. Neither PCs nor portables, however, were efficient in sharing information. As timeliness and security became more important, floppy disks were just not cutting it. Offices needed to find a way to implement a better means to share and access resources. This led to the introduction of the first type of PC local area network (LAN): ShareNet by Novell, which had both hardware and software components. LANs are simply the linking of computers to share resources within a closed environment. The first simple LANs were constructed a lot like the LAN in Figure 6.2.

FIGURE 6.2   A simple LAN

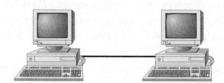

After the introduction of ShareNet, more LANs sprouted. The earliest LANs could not cover large distances. Most of them could only stretch across a single floor of the office and could support no more than 30 users. Further, they were still very rudimentary and only a few software programs supported them. The first software programs that ran on a LAN were not capable of being used by more than one user at a time (this constraint was known as *file locking*). Nowadays, we can see multiple users accessing a program or file at one time. Most of the time, the only limitations will be restrictions at the record level if two users are trying to modify a database record at the same time.

WANs

By the late 1980s, networks were expanding to cover large geographical areas and were supporting thousands of users. Wide area networks (WANs), first implemented with mainframes at massive government expense, started attracting PC users as networks went to this new level. Employees of businesses with offices across the country communicated as if they were only desks apart. Soon the whole world saw a change in the way of doing business, across not only a few miles but across countries. Whereas LANs are limited to single buildings, WANs can span buildings, states, countries, and even continental boundaries. Figure 6.3 gives an example of a simple WAN.

Networks of today and tomorrow are no longer limited by the inability of LANs to cover distance and handle mobility. WANs play an important role in the future development of corporate networks worldwide.

PANs

In 1998, a consortium of companies formed the Bluetooth Special Interest Group (SIG) and formally adopted the name *Bluetooth* for its technology. The name comes from a tenth-century Danish king named Harald Blåtand, known as Harold Bluetooth in English. (One can only imagine how he got that name.) King Blåtand had successfully unified warring factions in the areas of Norway, Sweden, and Denmark. The makers of Bluetooth were trying to unite disparate technology industries, namely computing, mobile communications, and the auto industry.

FIGURE 6.3   A simple WAN

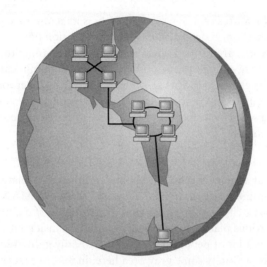

Current membership in the Bluetooth SIG includes Microsoft, Intel, Apple, IBM, Toshiba, and several cell phone manufacturers. The technical specification IEEE 802.15.1 describes a *wireless personal area network (WPAN)* based on Bluetooth version 1.1.

The first Bluetooth device on the market was an Ericsson headset and cell phone adapter, which arrived on the scene in 2000. While mobile phones and accessories are still the most common type of Bluetooth device, you will find many more including wireless keyboards, mice, and printers. Figure 6.4 shows a Bluetooth USB adapter.

FIGURE 6.4   Bluetooth USB adapter

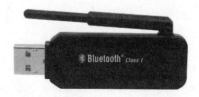

If you want to learn more about Bluetooth you can visit
www.bluetooth.com.

One of the unusual features of a Bluetooth WPAN is its temporary nature. With other popular wireless standards, you need a central communication point, such as a hub or router. Bluetooth networks are formed on an ad hoc basis, meaning that whenever two Bluetooth devices get close enough to each other, they can communicate directly with each other. This dynamically created network is called a *piconet*. A Bluetooth-enabled device can communicate with up to seven other devices in one piconet. Two or more piconets can be linked together in a *scatternet*. In a scatternet, one or more devices would serve as a bridge between the piconets.

MANs

For those networks that are larger than a LAN but confined to a relatively small geographical area, there is the term *metropolitan area network (MAN)*. A MAN is generally defined as a network that spans a city or a large campus. For example, if a city decides to install wireless hotspots in various places, that network could be considered a MAN.

One of the questions a lot of people ask is, "Is there really a difference between a MAN and a WAN?" There is definitely some gray area here; in many cases they are virtually identical. Perhaps the biggest difference is who has responsibility for managing the connectivity. In a MAN, a central IT organization such as the campus or city IT staff is responsible. In a WAN, it's implied that you will be using publicly available communication lines and there will be a phone company or other service provider involved.

Primary Network Components

Technically speaking, two or more computers connected together constitute a network. But networks are rarely that simple. When you're looking at the devices or resources available on a network, there are three types of components to be aware of:

- Servers
- Clients or workstations
- Resources

 Every network requires two more items to tie these three components together: a network operating system (NOS) and some kind of shared medium. These components are covered later in their own sections.

Blurring the Lines

In the 1980s and '90s, LANs and WANs were often differentiated by their connection speeds. For example, if you had a 10Mbps or faster connection to other computers, you were often considered to be on a LAN. WANs were often connected to each other by very expensive T1 connections, which have a maximum bandwidth of 1.544Mbps.

As with all other technologies, networking capacity has exploded. In today's office network, anything slower than 100Mbps is considered archaic. Connections of 1Gbps are fairly common. WAN connectivity, although still slower than LAN connectivity, can easily be several times faster than the T1. Because of the speed increases in WAN connectivity, the old practice of categorizing your network based on connection speed is outdated.

Today, the most common way to classify a network is based on geographical distance. If your network is in one central location, whether that is one office, one floor of an office building, or maybe even one entire building, it's usually considered a LAN. If your network is spread out among multiple distant locations, it's a WAN.

Servers

Servers come in many shapes and sizes. They are a core component of the network, providing a link to the resources necessary to perform any task. The link the server provides could be to a resource existing on the server itself or a resource on a client computer. The server is the critical enabler, offering directions to the client computers regarding where to go to get what they need.

Servers offer networks the capability of centralizing the control of resources and security, thereby reducing administrative difficulties. They can be used to distribute processes for balancing the load on computers and can thus increase speed and performance. They can also compartmentalize files for improved reliability. That way, if one server goes down, not all of the files are lost.

Servers can perform several different critical roles on a network. For example, servers that provide files to the users on the network are called *file servers*. Likewise, servers that host printing services for users are called *print servers*. (Servers can be used for other tasks as well, such as authentication, remote access services, administration, email, and so on.) Networks can include multipurpose and single-purpose servers. A multipurpose server can be, for example, both a file server and a print server at the same time. If the server is a single-purpose server, it is a file server only or a print server only. Another distinction we use in categorizing servers is whether they are dedicated or nondedicated:

Dedicated servers A *dedicated server* is assigned to provide specific applications or services for the network and nothing else. Because a dedicated server specializes in only a few tasks, it requires fewer resources than a nondedicated server might require from the computer that is hosting it. This savings may translate to efficiency and can thus be considered as having a beneficial impact on network performance. A web server is an example of a dedicated server: It is dedicated to the task of serving up web pages and nothing else.

Nondedicated servers Nondedicated servers are assigned to provide one or more network services *and* local access. A *nondedicated server* is expected to be slightly more flexible in its day-to-day use than a dedicated server. Nondedicated servers can be used to direct network traffic and perform administrative actions, but they also often used to serve as a front-end for the administrator to work with other applications or services or perform services for more than one network. For example, a dedicated web server might serve out one or more websites, where a nondedicated web server serves out websites but also might function as a print server on the local network, or the administrator's workstation.

The nondedicated server is not what some would consider a true server because it can act as a workstation as well as a server. The workgroup server at your office is an example of a nondedicated server. It might be a combination file, print, and email server. Plus, because of its nature, a nondedicated server could also function well in a peer-to-peer environment. It could be used as a workstation in addition to being a file, print, and email server.

Many networks use both dedicated and nondedicated servers to incorporate the best of both worlds, offering improved network performance with the dedicated servers and flexibility with the nondedicated servers.

Workstations

Workstations are the computers on which the network users do their work, performing activities such as word processing, database design, graphic design, email, and other office or personal tasks. Workstations are basically everyday computers, except for the fact that they are connected to a network that offers additional resources. Workstations can range from diskless computer systems to desktops or laptops. In network terms, workstations are also known as *client computers*. As clients, they are allowed to communicate with the servers in the network to use the network's resources.

It takes several items to make a workstation into a network client. You must install a *network interface card (NIC)*, a special expansion card that allows the PC to talk on a network. You must connect it to a cabling system that connects to other computers (unless your NIC supports wireless networking). And you must install special software, called *client software*, which allows the computer to talk to the servers and request resources from them. Once all this has been accomplished, the computer is "on the network."

Network client software comes with all operating systems today. When you configure your computer to participate in the network, the operating system utilizes this software.

To the client, the server may be nothing more than just another drive letter. However, because it is in a network environment, the client can use the server as a doorway to more storage or more applications or to communicate with other computers or other networks. To users, being on a network changes a few things:

- They can store more information because they can store data on other computers on the network.

- They can share and receive information from other users, perhaps even collaborating on the same document.

- They can use programs that would be too large or complex for their computer to use by itself.
- They can use hardware not attached directly to their computer, such as a printer.

 Real World Scenario

Is That a Server or a Workstation?

This is one of the things author Quentin Docter does when teaching novice technicians. In the room will be a standard-looking mini-tower desktop computer. He points to it and asks, "Is that a server or a workstation?" A lot of techs will look at it and say it's a workstation because it is a desktop computer. The real answer is, "It depends."

Although many people have a perception that servers are ultra-fancy, rack-mounted devices, that isn't necessarily true. It's true that servers typically need more powerful hardware than workstations do because of their role on the network, but that doesn't have to be the case. (Granted, having servers that are less powerful than your work-stations doesn't make logical sense.) What really differentiates a workstation from a server is what operating system it has installed and what role it plays on the network.

For example, if that system has Windows Server 2008 installed on it, you can be pretty sure it's a server. If it has Windows 7 or XP, it's more than likely going to be a client, but not always. Computers with operating systems such as Windows 7 can be both clients on the network and nondedicated servers, as would be the case if you share your local printer with others on the network.

The moral of the story? Don't assume a computer's role simply by looking at it. You need to understand what is on it and what its role on the network is to make that determination.

Network Resources

We now have the server to share the resources and the workstation to use them, but what about the resources themselves? A *resource* (as far as the network is concerned) is any item that can be used on a network. Resources can include a broad range of items, but the following items are among the most important:

- Printers and other peripherals
- Disk storage and file access
- Applications

When an office has to purchase only a few printers (and all of the associated consumables) for the entire office, the costs are dramatically lower than the costs for supplying printers at every workstation.

Networks also give users more storage space to store their files. Client computers can't always handle the overhead involved in storing large files (for example, database files) because they are already heavily involved in users' day-to-day work activities. Because servers in a network can be dedicated to only certain functions, a server can be allocated to store all the larger files that are worked with every day, freeing up disk space on client computers. In addition, if users store their files on a server, the administrator can back up the server periodically to ensure that if something happens to a user's files, those files can be recovered.

Files that all users need to access (such as emergency contact lists and company policies) can also be stored on a server. Having one copy of these files in a central location saves disk space as opposed to storing the files locally on everyone's system.

Applications (programs) no longer need to be on every computer in the office. If the server is capable of handling the overhead an application requires, the application can reside on the server and be used by workstations through a network connection.

The sharing of applications over a network requires a special arrangement with the application vendor, which may wish to set the price of the application according to the number of users who will be using it. The arrangement allowing multiple users to use a single installation of an application is called a *site license*.

Being on a Network Brings Responsibilities

You are part of a community when you are on a network, which means you need to take responsibility for your actions. First, a network is only as secure as the users who use it. You cannot randomly delete files or move documents from server to server. You do not own your email, so anyone in your company's management can choose to read it. In addition, sending something to the printer does not necessarily mean that it will print immediately—your document may not be the first in line to be printed at the shared printer. Plus, if your workstation has also been set up as a nondedicated server, you cannot turn it off.

Network Operating Systems (NOSs)

PCs use a disk operating system that controls the file system and how the applications communicate with the hard disk. Networks use a *network operating system (NOS)* to control the communication with resources and the flow of data across the network. The NOS runs on the server. Some of the more popular NOSs include UNIX and Linux and Microsoft's Windows Server series (Server 2008, Server 2003, etc.). Several other companies offer network operating systems as well.

Network Resource Access

We have discussed two major components of a typical network, servers and workstations, and we've also talked briefly about network resources. Let's dive in a bit deeper on how those resources are accessed on a network.

There are generally two resource access models: peer-to-peer and client-server. It is important to choose the appropriate model. How do you decide what type of resource model is needed? You must first think about the following questions:

- What is the size of the organization?

- How much security does the company require?

- What software or hardware does the resource require?

- How much administration does it need?

- How much will it cost?

- Will this resource meet the needs of the organization today and in the future?

- Will additional training be needed?

Networks cannot just be put together at the drop of a hat. A lot of planning is required before implementation of a network to ensure that whatever design is chosen will be effective and efficient, and not just for today but for the future as well. The forethought of the designer will lead to the best network with the least amount of administrative overhead. In each network, it is important that a plan be developed to answer the previous questions. The answers will help the designer choose the type of resource model to use.

Peer-to-Peer Networks

In a peer-to-peer network, the computers act as both service providers and service requestors. An example of a peer-to-peer resource model is shown in Figure 6.5.

FIGURE 6.5   The peer-to-peer resource model

Peer-to-peer networks are great for small, simple, inexpensive networks. This model can be set up almost immediately, with little extra hardware required. Many versions of Windows (Windows 7, Vista, XP, 2000), Linux, and Mac OS are popular operating system environments that support a peer-to-peer resource model. Peer-to-peer networks are also referred to as *workgroups*.

Generally speaking, there is no centralized administration or control in the peer-to-peer resource model. Every station has unique control over the resources the computer owns, and each station must be administered separately. However, this very lack of centralized control can make it difficult to administer the network; for the same reason, the network isn't very secure. Moreover, because each computer is acting as both a workstation and server, it may not be easy to locate resources. The person who is in charge of a file may have moved it without anyone's knowledge. Also, the users who work under this arrangement need more training because they are not only users but also administrators.

Will this type of network meet the needs of the organization today and in the future? Peer-to-peer resource models are generally considered the right choice for small companies that don't expect future growth. Small companies that expect growth, on the other hand, should not choose this type of model.

A rule of thumb is that if you have no more than 10 computers and centralized security is not a key priority, a workgroup may be a good choice for you.

Client-Server Resource Model

The client-server (also known as server-based) model is better than the peer-to-peer model for large networks (say, more than 10 computers) that need a more secure environment and centralized control. Server-based networks use one or more dedicated, centralized servers. All administrative functions and resource sharing are performed from this point. This makes it easier to share resources, perform backups, and support an almost unlimited number of users. This model also offers better security. However, the server needs more hardware than a typical workstation/server computer in a peer-to-peer resource model needs. In addition, it requires specialized software (the NOS) to manage the server's role in the environment. With the addition of a server and the NOS, server-based networks can easily cost more than peer-to-peer resource models. However, for large networks, it's the only choice. An example of a client-server resource model is shown in Figure 6.6.

FIGURE 6.6 The client-server resource model

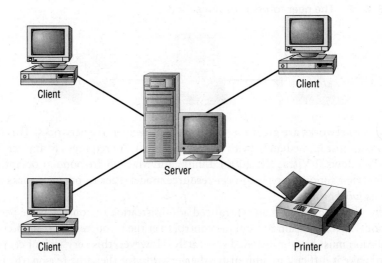

Server-based networks are also known as *domains*. The key characteristic of a domain is that security is centrally administered. When you log in to the network, the login request is passed to the server responsible for security, sometimes known as a *domain controller*. (Microsoft uses the term *domain controller*, whereas other vendors of server products do not.) This is different from the peer-to-peer model, where each individual workstation validates users. In a peer-to-peer model, if the user *jsmith* wants to be able to log in to different workstations, she needs to have a user account set up on each machine. This can quickly become an administrative nightmare! In a domain, all user accounts are stored on the server. User *jsmith* needs only one account and can log on to any of the workstations in the domain.

Client-server resource models are the desired models for companies that are continually growing, need to support a large environment, or need centralized security. Server-based networks offer the flexibility to add more resources and clients almost indefinitely into the future. Hardware costs may be more, but with the centralized administration, managing resources becomes less time consuming. Also, only a few administrators need to be trained, and users are responsible for only their own work environment.

> If you are looking for an inexpensive, simple network with little setup required, and there is no need for the company to grow in the future, then the peer-to-peer network is the way to go. If you are looking for a network to support many users (more than 10 computers), strong security, and centralized administration, consider the server-based network your only choice.

Whatever you decide, always take the time to plan your network before installing it. A network is not something you can just throw together. You don't want to find out a few months down the road that the type of network you chose does not meet the needs of the company—this could be a time-consuming and costly mistake.

Network Topologies

A *topology* is a way of laying out the network. When you plan and install a network, you need to choose the right topology for your situation. Each type differs by its cost, ease of installation, fault tolerance (how the topology handles problems such as cable breaks), and ease of reconfiguration (such as adding a new workstation to the existing network).

There are five primary topologies:

- Bus
- Star
- Ring
- Mesh
- Hybrid

Each topology has advantages and disadvantages. After the following sections, check out Table 6.1, which summarizes the advantages and disadvantages of each topology.

Bus Topology

A *bus topology* is the simplest. It consists of a single cable that runs to every workstation, as shown in Figure 6.7. This topology uses the least amount of cabling. Each computer shares the same data and address path. With a bus topology, messages pass through the trunk, and each workstation checks to see if a message is addressed to itself. If the address of the message matches the workstation's address, the network adapter retrieves it. If not, the message is ignored.

FIGURE 6.7   The bus topology

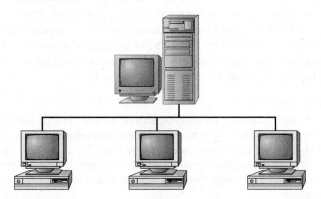

Cable systems that use the bus topology are easy to install. You run a cable from the first computer to the last computer. All the remaining computers attach to the cable somewhere in between. Because of the simplicity of installation, and because of the low cost of the cable, bus topology cabling systems are the cheapest to install.

Although the bus topology uses the least amount of cabling, it is difficult to add a workstation. If you want to add another workstation, you have to completely reroute the cable and possibly run two additional lengths of it. Also, if any one of the cables breaks, the entire network is disrupted. Therefore, such a system is expensive to maintain and can be difficult to troubleshoot. You will rarely run across physical bus networks in use today.

Star Topology

A *star topology* branches each network device off a central device called a *hub*, making it easy to add a new workstation. If a workstation goes down, it does not affect the entire network; if the central device goes down, the entire network goes with it. Because of this, the hub (or switch) is called a *single point of failure*. Figure 6.8 shows a simple star network.

Star topologies are very easy to install. A cable is run from each workstation to the hub. The hub is placed in a central location in the office (for example, a utility closet). Star topologies are more expensive to install than bus networks because several more cables need to be installed, plus the hubs. But the ease of reconfiguration and fault tolerance (one cable failing does not bring down the entire network) far outweigh the drawbacks. This is the most commonly installed network topology in use today.

FIGURE 6.8   The star topology

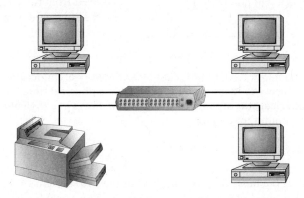

 Although the hub is the central portion of a star topology, many networks use a device known as a switch instead of a hub. Switches are more advanced than hubs, and they provide better performance than hubs for only a small price increase. Colloquially though, many administrators use the terms *hub* and *switch* interchangeably.

Ring Topology

In a *ring topology*, each computer connects to two other computers, joining them in a circle and creating a unidirectional path where messages move from workstation to workstation. Each entity participating in the ring reads a message and then regenerates it and hands it to its neighbor on a different network cable. See Figure 6.9 for an example of a ring topology.

FIGURE 6.9   The ring topology

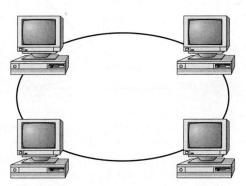

The ring makes it difficult to add new computers. Unlike a star topology network, the ring topology network will go down if one entity is removed from the ring. Physical ring topology systems rarely exist anymore, mainly because the hardware involved was fairly expensive and the fault tolerance was very low.

> You might have heard of an older network architecture called Token Ring. Contrary to its name, it does *not* use a physical ring. It actually uses a physical star topology, but the traffic flows in a logical ring from one computer to the next.

Mesh Topology

The *mesh topology* is the most complex in terms of physical design. In this topology, each device is connected to every other device (Figure 6.10). This topology is rarely found in LANs, mainly because of the complexity of the cabling. If there are x computers, there will be $(x \times (x - 1)) \div 2$ cables in the network. For example, if you have five computers in a mesh network, it will use $5 \times (5 - 1) \div 2 = 10$ cables. This complexity is compounded when you add another workstation. For example, your 5-computer, 10-cable network will jump to 15 cables if you add just one more computer. Imagine how the person doing the cabling would feel if you told them they had to cable 50 computers in a mesh network—they'd have to come up with $50 \times (50 - 1) \div 2 = 1225$ cables!

FIGURE 6.10 The mesh topology

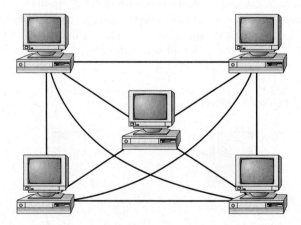

Because of its design, the physical mesh topology is expensive to install and maintain. Cables must be run from each device to every other device. The advantage you gain is high fault tolerance. With a mesh topology, there will always be a way to get the data from source to destination. The data may not be able to take the direct route, but it can take an alternate, indirect route. For this reason, the mesh topology is found in WANs to connect multiple sites across WAN links. It uses devices called *routers* to search multiple routes through the mesh and determine the best path. However, the mesh topology does become inefficient with five or more entities because of the number of connections that need to be maintained.

Hybrid Topology

The *hybrid topology* is simply a mix of the other topologies. It would be impossible to illustrate it because there are many combinations. In fact, most networks today are not only hybrid but heterogeneous (they include a mix of components of different types and brands). The hybrid network may be more expensive than some types of network topologies, but it takes the best features of all the other topologies and exploits them.

Table 6.1 summarizes the advantages and disadvantages of each type of network topology.

TABLE 6.1   Topologies—advantages and disadvantages

Topology	Advantages	Disadvantages
Bus	Cheap. Easy to install.	Difficult to reconfigure. A break in the bus disables the entire network.
Star	Cheap. Very easy to install and reconfigure. Fault tolerant.	More expensive than bus.
Ring	Efficient. Easy to install.	Reconfiguration is difficult. Very expensive.
Mesh	Best fault tolerance.	Reconfiguration is extremely difficult, extremely expensive, and very complex.
Hybrid	Gives a combination of the best features of each topology used.	Complex (less so than mesh, however).

Rules of Communication

Regardless of the type of network you choose to implement, the computers on that network need to know how to talk to each other. To facilitate communication across a network, computers use a common language called a protocol. We'll cover protocols more in Chapter 7, "Introduction to TCP/IP," but essentially they are languages much like English is a language. Within each language, there are rules that need to be followed so that both computers understand the right communication behavior.

To use a human example, within English there are grammar rules. If you put a bunch of English words together in a way that doesn't make sense, no one will understand you. If you just decide to omit verbs from your language, you're going to be challenged to get your point across. And if everyone talks at the same time, the conversation can be hard to follow.

Computers need standards to follow to keep their communication clear. Different standards are used to describe the rules that computers need to follow to communicate with each other. The most important communication framework, and the backbone of all networking, is the OSI model.

> The OSI model is not specifically listed in the CompTIA A+ exam objectives. However, it's a critical piece of networking knowledge and a framework that all technicians should be familiar with.

OSI Model

The International Organization for Standardization (ISO) introduced the *Open Systems Interconnection (OSI)* model to provide a common way of describing network protocols. The ISO put together a seven-layer model providing a relationship between the stages of communication, with each layer adding to the layer above or below it.

> This OSI model is a theoretical model governing computer communication. Even though at one point an "OSI protocol" was developed, it never gained wide acceptance. You will never find a network that is running the "OSI protocol."

Here's how the theory behind the OSI model works: As a transmission takes place, the higher layers pass data through the lower layers. As the data passes through a layer, that layer tacks its information (also called a *header*) onto the beginning of the information being transmitted until it reaches the bottom layer. A layer may also add a trailer to the end of the data. The bottom layer sends the information out on the wire.

At the receiving end, the bottom layer receives and reads the information in the header, removes the header and any associated trailer related to its layer, and then passes the remainder to the next highest layer. This procedure continues until the topmost layer receives the data that the sending computer sent.

The OSI model layers are listed here from top to bottom, as well as descriptions for what each of the layers is responsible for:

7. Application layer   Allows access to network services. This is the layer at which file services, print services, and other applications operate.

6. Presentation layer   Determines the "look," or format, of the data. This layer performs protocol conversion and manages data compression, data translation, and encryption. The character set information also is determined at this level. (The character set determines which numbers represent which alphanumeric characters.)

5. Session layer   Allows applications on different computers to establish, maintain, and end a session. A session is one virtual conversation. For example, all the procedures needed to transfer a single file make up one session. Once the session is over, a new process begins. This layer enables network procedures, such as identifying passwords, logons, and network monitoring.

4. Transport layer   This layer controls the data flow and troubleshoots any problems with transmitting or receiving datagrams. It also takes large messages and segments them into smaller ones and takes smaller segments and combines them into a single, larger message, depending on which way the traffic is flowing. Finally, the TCP protocol (one of the two options at this layer) has the important job of verifying that all packets were received by the destination host, providing error checking and reliable, end-to-end communications.

3. Network layer   Responsible for logical addressing of messages. At this layer, the data is organized into chunks called *packets*. The Network layer is something like the traffic cop. It is able to judge the best network path for the data based on network conditions, priority, and other variables. This layer manages traffic through packet switching, routing, and controlling congestion of data.

2. Data Link layer   Arranges data into chunks called *frames*. Included in these chunks is control information indicating the beginning and end of the datastream. This layer is very important because it makes transmission easier and more manageable and allows for error checking within the data frames. The Data Link layer also describes the unique physical address (also known as the *MAC address*) for each NIC. The Data Link layer is actually subdivided into two sections: Media Access Control (MAC) and Logical Link Control (LLC).

1. Physical layer   Describes how the data gets transmitted over a physical medium. This layer defines how long each piece of data is and the translation of each into the electrical pulses that are sent over the wires. It decides whether data travels unidirectionally or bidirectionally across the hardware. It also relates electrical, optical, mechanical, and functional interfaces to the cable.

Figure 6.11 shows the complete OSI model. Note the relation of each layer to the others and the function of each layer.

 A helpful mnemonic device to remember the OSI layers in order is "All People Seem To Need Data Processing."

IEEE 802 Standards

Continuing with our theme of communication, it's time to introduce one final group of standards. You've already learned that a protocol is like a language; think of the IEEE 802 standards as syntax, or the rules that govern who communicates when and how.

The Institute of Electrical and Electronics Engineers (IEEE) formed a subcommittee to create standards for network types. These standards specify certain types of networks, although not every network protocol is covered by the IEEE 802 committee specifications. This model contains several categories, but the following are the most popularly referenced:

- 802.2 Logical Link Control
- 802.3 CSMA/CD (Ethernet) LAN
- 802.5 Token Ring LAN

- 802.6 Metropolitan Area Network
- 802.11 Wireless Networks

FIGURE 6.11 The OSI model

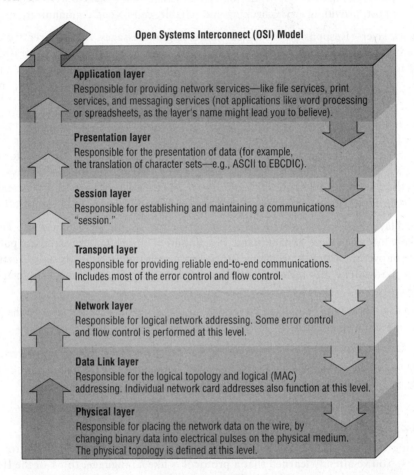

Open Systems Interconnect (OSI) Model

Application layer
Responsible for providing network services—like file services, print services, and messaging services (not applications like word processing or spreadsheets, as the layer's name might lead you to believe).

Presentation layer
Responsible for the presentation of data (for example, the translation of character sets—e.g., ASCII to EBCDIC).

Session layer
Responsible for establishing and maintaining a communications "session."

Transport layer
Responsible for providing reliable end-to-end communications. Includes most of the error control and flow control.

Network layer
Responsible for logical network addressing. Some error control and flow control is performed at this level.

Data Link layer
Responsible for the logical topology and logical (MAC) addressing. Individual network card addresses also function at this level.

Physical layer
Responsible for placing the network data on the wire, by changing binary data into electrical pulses on the physical medium. The physical topology is defined at this level.

The IEEE 802 standards were designed primarily for enhancements to the bottom three layers of the OSI model. The IEEE 802 standard breaks the Data Link layer into two sublayers: a Logical Link Control (LLC) sublayer and a Media Access Control (MAC) sublayer. In the Logical Link Control sublayer, data link communications are managed. The Media Access Control sublayer watches out for data collisions and manages physical (MAC) addresses.

You've most likely heard of 802.11g wireless networking. The rules for communicating with all versions of 802.11 are defined by the IEEE standard. Another very well-known standard is 802.3 CSMA/CD. You might know it by its more popular name, Ethernet.

The original 802.3 CSMA/CD standard defines a bus topology network that uses a 50 ohm coaxial baseband cable and carries transmissions at 10Mbps. This standard groups data bits into frames and uses the Carrier Sense Multiple Access with Collision Detection (CSMA/CD) cable access method to put data on the cable. Currently, the 802.3 standard has been amended to include speeds up to 10Gbps.

Breaking the CSMA/CD acronym apart may help illustrate how it works. First, there is the *Carrier Sense (CS)* part, which means that computers on the network are listening to the wire at all times. *Multiple Access (MA)* means that multiple computers have access to the line at the same time. This is analogous to having five people on a conference call. Everyone is listening, and everyone in theory can try to talk at the same time. Of course, when more than one person talks at once, there is a communication error. In CSMA/CD, when two machines transmit at the same time, a data *collision* takes place and none of the data is received by the intended recipients. This is where the *Collision Detection (CD)* portion of the acronym comes in; the collision is detected and each sender knows they need to send again. Each sender then waits for a short random period of time and tries to transmit again. This process repeats until transmission takes place successfully. The CSMA/CD technology is considered a *contention-based* access method.

The only major downside to 802.3 is that with large networks (more than 100 computers on the same cable), the number of collisions increases to the point where more collisions than transmissions are taking place.

Other examples exist, such as 802.5 token ring, which defines a logical ring on a physical star. On a token ring network, an access packet called a token circles the network. If you have the token, you can send data; otherwise you wait for your turn. It's not important to memorize all of the different IEEE standards for the test. Just know that different ones exist, governing how to transmit data on the wire and making sure all computers co-exist peacefully.

Identifying Common Network Hardware

We have looked at the types of networks, network topologies, and the way communications are handled. That's all of the logical stuff. To really get computers to talk to each other requires hardware. Every computer on the network needs to have a network adapter of some type. In many cases, you also need some sort of cable to hook them together. (Wireless networking is the exception, but at the back end of a wireless network there are still components wired together.) And finally, you might also need connectivity devices to attach several computers or networks to each other.

Network Interface Cards (NICs)

The *network interface card (NIC)* provides the physical interface between computer and cabling. It prepares data, sends data, and controls the flow of data. It can also receive and translate data into bytes for the CPU to understand. NICs come in many shapes and sizes.

Different NICs are distinguished by the PC bus type and the network for which they are used. The following sections describe the role of NICs and how to evaluate them. The following factors should be taken into consideration:

- Compatibility
- Performance
- Sending and controlling data
- Configuration
- Drivers

Compatibility

The first thing you need to determine is whether the NIC will fit the bus type of your PC. If you have more than one type of bus in your PC (for example, a combination PCI/PCI Express), use a NIC that fits into the fastest type (the PCI Express, in this case). This is especially important in servers because the NIC can quickly become a bottleneck if this guideline isn't followed.

More and more computers are using network cards that have either PC Card or USB interfaces. For laptop computers that don't otherwise have a network card built in to them, these small portable cards are very handy.

 A USB network card can also be handy for troubleshooting. If a laptop isn't connecting to the network properly with its built-in card, you may be able to use the USB network card to see if it's an issue with the card or perhaps a software problem.

Network Interface Card Performance

The most important goal of the network adapter card is to optimize network performance and minimize the amount of time needed to transfer data packets across the network. The key is to ensure that you get the fastest card you can for the type of network you're on. For example, if your wireless network supports 802.11b/g/n, make sure to get an 802.11n card because it's the fastest.

Sending and Controlling Data

For two computers to send and receive data, the cards must agree on several things:

- The maximum size of the data frames
- The amount of data sent before giving confirmation
- The time needed between transmissions
- The amount of time to wait before sending confirmation
- The speed at which data transmits

If the cards can agree, the data is sent successfully. If the cards cannot agree, the data is not sent.

To successfully send data on the network, all NICs need to use the same media access method (such as Ethernet or token ring) and be connected to the same piece of cable. This usually isn't a problem because the vast majority of network cards sold today are Ethernet. If you were to try to use cards of different types (for example, one Ethernet and one Token Ring), neither of them would be able to communicate with the other unless you had a separate hardware device between them that could translate.

In addition, NICs can send data using either full-duplex or half-duplex mode. *Half-duplex communication* means that between the sender and receiver, only one of them can transmit at any one time. In *full-duplex communication*, a computer can send and receive data simultaneously. The main advantage of full-duplex over half-duplex communication is performance. NICs (specifically Fast Ethernet NICs) can operate twice as fast (200Mbps) in full-duplex mode as they do normally in half-duplex mode (100Mbps).

Normally you aren't going to have to worry about how your NIC sends or controls data. Just make sure to get the fastest NIC that is compatible with your network as you can. Do know that the negotiations discussed here are happening in the background though.

NIC Configuration

Each card must have a unique hardware address, called a *MAC address*. If two cards on the same network have the same hardware address, neither one will be able to communicate. For this reason, the IEEE has established a standard for hardware addresses and assigns blocks of these addresses to NIC manufacturers, who then hard-wire the addresses into the cards.

Although it is possible for NIC manufacturers to produce multiple NICs with the same MAC address, it happens very rarely. If you do encounter this type of problem, contact the hardware manufacturer.

NIC Drivers

For the computer to use the NIC, it is very important to install the proper device drivers. These drivers communicate directly with the network redirector and adapter. They operate in the Media Access Control sublayer of the Data Link layer of the OSI model.

Cables, Connectors, and Cabling Tools

When the data is passing through the OSI model and reaches the Physical layer, it must find its way onto the medium that is used to physically transfer data from computer to computer. This medium is called the *cable* (or in the case of wireless networks, the air). It is the NIC's role to prepare the data for transmission, but it is the cable's role to properly move the data to its intended destination. There are three main types of physical cabling to discuss: coaxial cable, twisted-pair cable, and fiber-optic cable. (Wireless communications will be covered in Chapter 8, "Installing Wireless and SOHO Networks.") The three cabling types will be discussed in the following sections.

Coaxial

Coaxial cable (or coax) contains a center conductor core made of copper, which is surrounded by a plastic jacket with a braided shield over it (as shown in Figure 6.12). Either Teflon or a plastic coating covers this metal shield.

FIGURE 6.12   Coaxial cable

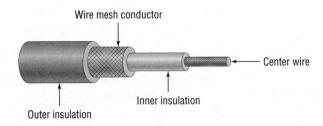

Wire mesh conductor

Center wire

Inner insulation

Outer insulation

Common network cables are covered with a plastic called *polyvinyl chloride (PVC)*. While PVC is flexible, fairly durable, and inexpensive, it has a nasty side effect in that it produces poisonous gas when burned. An alternative is a Teflon-type covering that is frequently referred to as a *plenum-rated* coating. That simply means that the coating does not produce toxic gas when burned and is rated for use in ventilation plenums that carry breathable air. This type of cable is more expensive but may be mandated by electrical code whenever cable is hidden in walls or ceilings.

    Plenum rating can apply to all types of network cabling.

Coax Cable Specifications

Coaxial cable is available in various specifications that are rated according to the Radio Guide (*RG*) system, which was originally developed by the US military. The thicker the copper, the farther a signal can travel—and with that comes a higher cost and a less-flexible cable.

When coax cable was popular for networking, there were two standards that had fairly high use: RG-8 (thicknet) and RG-58A/U (thinnet). Thicknet had a maximum segment distance of 500 meters and was used primarily for network backbones. Thinnet was more often used in a conventional physical bus. A thinnet segment could span 185 meters. Table 6.2 shows the different types of RG cabling and their uses.

TABLE 6.2   Coax RG Types

RG #	Popular Name	Ethernet Implementation	Type of Cable
RG-6	Satellite/cable TV, cable modems	N/A	Solid copper
RG-8	Thicknet	10Base5	Solid copper
RG-58 U	N/A	None	Solid copper
RG-58 AU	Thinnet	10Base2	Stranded copper
RG-59	Cable television	N/A	Solid copper

Coaxial networking has all but gone the way of the dinosaur. The only two coaxial cable types used today are RG-6 and RG-59. Of the two, RG-6 can run longer distances and support digital signals. RG-59 is considered adequate for analog cable TV but not digital.

Coax Connector Types

Thicknet was a bear to work with. Not only was it highly inflexible, but you needed to use a connector called a *vampire tap*. A vampire tap is so named because a metal tooth sinks into the cable, thus making the connection with the inner conductor. The tap is connected to an external transceiver that in turn has a 15-pin AUI connector (also called *DIX* or *DB15* connector) to which you attach a cable that connects to the station (shown in Figure 6.13). DIX got its name from the companies that worked on this format—Digital, Intel, and Xerox.

FIGURE 6.13   Thicknet and vampire taps

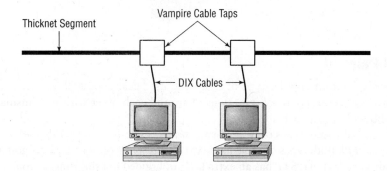

Thinnet coax was much easier to work with. Generally, thinnet cables used a *BNC connector* (see Figure 6.14) to attach to a T-shaped connector that attached to the workstation.

The other side of the T-connector would either continue on with another thinnet segment or be capped off with a terminator. It is beyond our scope to settle the long-standing argument over the meaning of the abbreviation BNC. We have heard Bayonet Connector, Bayonet Nut Connector, and British Naval Connector, among others. What is relevant is that the BNC connector locks securely with a quarter-twist motion.

FIGURE 6.14   Male and female BNC connectors, T-connector, and terminator

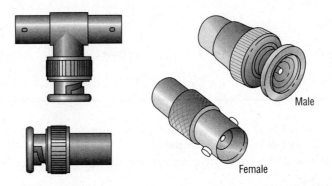

Male

Female

The other type of coax connector is called an *F-connector* (shown in Figure 6.15) and is used with cable TV. The exposed end of the copper cable is pushed into the receptacle, and the connector is threaded so it can screw into place.

FIGURE 6.15   An F-connector

Twisted Pair

Twisted pair is the most popular type of cabling to use because of its flexibility and low cost. It consists of several pairs of wire twisted around each other within an insulated jacket, as shown in Figure 6.16.

There are two different types of twisted-pair: *shielded twisted-pair (STP)* and *unshielded twisted-pair (UTP)*. Both types of cable have two or four pairs of twisted wires going through them. The difference is that STP has an extra layer of braided foil shielding surrounding the wires to decrease electrical interference. UTP has a PVC or plenum coating but no foil shield to protect it from interference.

FIGURE 6.16   Twisted-pair cable

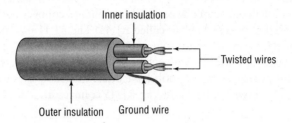

Inner insulation

Twisted wires

Outer insulation   Ground wire

Twisted-Pair Cable Specifications

There aren't any STP standards that you really need to know about, either for the test or real-life situations. UTP is a different animal. It comes in eight grades to offer different levels of performance and protection against electrical interference:

- Category 1 contains two twisted pairs. Is for voice-only transmissions and is in many legacy phone systems today.

- Category 2 is the lowest-grade cable able to have four pairs of wires. (Every other CAT rating since CAT-2 has four pairs.) It can handle data transmission at speeds up to 4Mbps.

- Category 3 is able to transmit data at speeds up to 10Mbps. It was popular for 10BaseT installations before CAT-5 came out.

- Category 4 is able to transmit data at speeds up to 16Mbps.

- Category 5 is able to transmit data at speeds up to 100Mbps.

- Category 5e is able to transmit data at speeds up to 1Gbps. The enhancement over CAT-5 is that the four twisted pairs of copper wire are physically separated and contain more twists per foot. This provides maximum interference protection.

- Category 6 is able to transmit data at speeds up to 10Gbps. Its four twisted pairs of copper wire are oriented differently than in CAT-5e. You can use it as a backbone to connect different parts of your network together, such as those on different floors of a building.

- Category 6a can also handle 10Gbps speed, but at longer distances (up to 100 meters) than CAT-6 can.

   Each of these levels has a maximum transmission distance of 100 meters. Do note, however, that if you want to run 10GBaseT over CAT-6 you won't get that much distance—about 55m.

NOTE   CompTIA (and many others) usually shorten the word *category* to CAT and use the form CAT-5 to refer to Category 5, for example. This is a common way to refer to these categories, and you can feel free to use these terms interchangeably. If you are buying cable today, you shouldn't buy anything older than CAT-5e.

Twisted-Pair Connector Types

Twisted-pair cabling uses a connector type called an *RJ (registered jack)* connector. You are probably familiar with RJ connectors. Most land-line phones connect with an RJ-11 connector. The connector used with UTP cable is called RJ-45. The RJ-11 has room for two pairs (four wires), and the RJ-45 has room for four pairs (eight wires).

In almost every case, UTP uses RJ connectors; a crimper is used to attach an RJ connector to a cable. Higher-quality crimping tools have interchangeable dies for both types of connectors. Figure 6.17 shows an RJ-11 and an RJ-45 connector.

FIGURE 6.17   RJ-11 and RJ-45 connectors

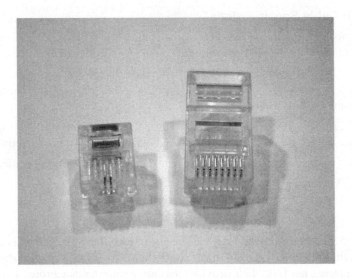

Wiring Standards

Twisted-pair cables are unique in today's network environment in that they use multiple physical wires. Those eight wires need to be in the right places in the RJ-45 connector or it's very likely that the cable will not work properly. To ensure consistency in the industry, two standards have been developed: 568A and 568B.

Older implementations using UTP used only two pairs of wires, and those two pairs were matched to pins 1, 2, 3, and 6 in the connector. Newer applications such as Voice over IP and Gigabit Ethernet use all four pairs of wires, so you need to make sure they're all where they're supposed to be.

If you're creating a regular network *patch cable* to connect a computer to a hub or a switch, both sides need to have the same pinout. For that, follow the 568A standard as shown in Figure 6.18.

If you are going to create a *crossover cable*, you need to cross pin 1 to pin 3 and pin 2 to pin 6 on *one side of the cable only*. This is to get the "send" pins matched up with the "receive" pins on the other side, and vice versa. For easier visualization, look at Figure 6.19.

FIGURE 6.18   568A standard

Pin	Pair	Wire	Color	
1	3	1		white/green
2	3	2		green
3	2	1		white/orange
4	1	2		blue
5	1	1		white/blue
6	2	2		orange
7	4	1		white/brown
8	4	2		brown

FIGURE 6.19   568B standard

Pin	Pair	Wire	Color	
1	2	1		white/orange
2	2	2		orange
3	3	1		white/green
4	1	2		blue
5	1	1		white/blue
6	3	2		green
7	4	1		white/brown
8	4	2		brown

Crossover cables are used to connect a computer to a computer, hub to hub, switch to switch, hub to switch, or computer directly to a router. The key thing to remember is that a patch (straight-through) cable is the same on both ends. A crossover cable is different on each end.

Fiber-Optic

Fiber-optic cabling has been called one of the best advances in cabling. It consists of a thin, flexible glass or plastic fiber surrounded by a rubberized outer coating (see Figure 6.20). It provides transmission speeds from 100Mbps to 10Gbps and a maximum distance of several miles. Because it uses pulses of light instead of electric voltages to transmit data, it is immune to electrical interference and to wiretapping.

FIGURE 6.20   Fiber-optic cable

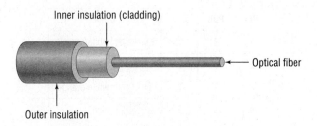

Fiber-optic cable has not been too widely adopted yet for local area networks, however, because of its high cost of installation. Fiber-optic cabling is often used in networks that need extremely fast transmission rates or transmissions over long distances or have had problems with electrical interference in the past.

Fiber-Optic Cable Specifications

Fiber-optic cable comes in two varieties: single-mode or multimode. The term *mode* refers to the bundles of light that enter the fiber-optic cable. *Single-mode fiber (SMF)* cable uses only a single mode of light to propagate through the fiber cable, whereas *multimode fiber* allows multiple modes (paths) of light to propagate simultaneously. In multimode fiber-optic cable, the light bounces off the cable walls as it travels through the cable, which causes the signal to weaken more quickly.

Multimode fiber is most often used as horizontal cable. It permits multiple modes of light to propagate through the cable, which shortens cable distances and delivers less available bandwidth. Devices that use MMF cable typically use light-emitting diodes (LEDs) to generate the light that travels through the cable; however, lasers with multimode fiber-optic cable are now being used in higher-bandwidth network devices such as Gigabit Ethernet. MMF can transmit up to 10Gbps for up to 550 meters, depending on the standard used.

Single-mode fiber cable is commonly used as backbone cabling; it is also usually the cable type used in phone systems. Light travels through single-mode fiber-optic cable using only a single mode, meaning it travels straight down the fiber and does not bounce off the cable walls. Because only a single mode of light travels through the cable, single-mode fiber-optic cable supports higher bandwidth at longer distances than multimode fiber-optic cable does. Devices that use single-mode fiber-optic cable typically use lasers to generate the light that travels through the cable. SMF can transmit up to 10Gbps for up to 40 kilometers, depending on the standard used.

Fiber-Optic Connector Types

There are literally dozens of fiber-optic connectors out there because it seemed that every producer wanted its proprietary design to become "the standard." Three of the most commonly-used ones are ST, SC, and LC.

The *straight tip (ST)* fiber-optic connector, developed by AT&T, is probably the most widely used fiber-optic connector. It uses a BNC attachment mechanism that makes connections and disconnections fairly easy. The ease of use of the ST is one of the attributes that makes this connector so popular. Figure 6.21 shows some examples of ST connectors.

FIGURE 6.21   Examples of ST connectors

The *subscriber connector (SC)*, also sometimes known as a square connector, is a type of fiber-optic connector, as shown in Figure 6.22. SCs are latched connectors, making it virtually impossible for you to pull out the connector without releasing its latch, usually by pressing a button or release. SCs work with either single-mode or multimode optical fibers. They aren't as popular as ST connectors for LAN connections.

FIGURE 6.22   A sample SC

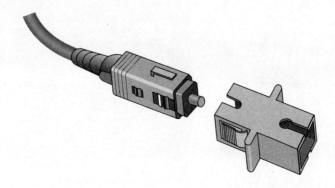

The last type of connector you need to be familiar with is the *local connector (LC)*, which was developed by Lucent Technologies. It is a mini form factor (MFF) connector, especially popular for use with Fibre-Channel adapters, fast storage area networks, and Gigabit Ethernet adapters. It is shown in Figure 6.23.

FIGURE 6.23   LC fiber connector

Cabling Tools

Now that you're familiar with the different types of cables used in networking, let's take a minute to examine a few tools you can use to troubleshoot your cables or your general connectivity.

Crimper

A *crimper* is a very handy tool for helping you put connectors on the end of a cable. Many crimpers will be a combination tool that strips and snips wires as well as crimps the connector on to the end. Figure 6.24 shows you one of these tools.

FIGURE 6.24   A UTP crimper

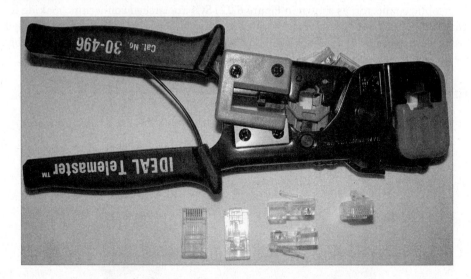

Multimeter

Multimeters are very versatile electronic measuring tools. A *multimeter* can measure voltage, current, and resistance on a wire. There are a wide variety of types and qualities on the market, everywhere, from economical $10 versions to ones that cost several thousand dollars. Figure 6.25 shows a basic multimeter.

FIGURE 6.25   A multimeter

Toner Probe

If you need to trace a wire in a wall from one location to another, a *toner probe* is the tool for you. Shown in Figure 6.26, it consists of two pieces: a tone generator and a probe. Because it's so good at tracking, you will sometimes hear this referred to as a "fox and hound."

Cable Tester

Cable testers are indispensable tools for any network technician. Usually you would use a *cable tester* before you install a cable to make sure it works. Of course, you can also test them after they've been run as well. A decent cable tester will tell you the type of cable, and more elaborate models will have connectors for multiple types of cables.

FIGURE 6.26   A toner probe

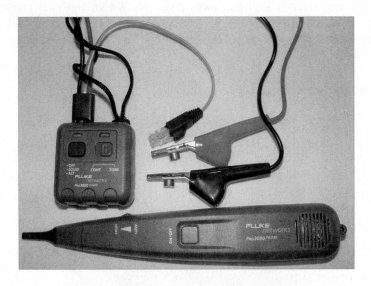

Loopback Plug

Of the devices listed in Objective 2.10, this is the only one that doesn't specifically test cables. Considering that it's part of the objectives though, it makes as much sense to cover it here as it would anywhere else.

A *loopback plug* is for testing the ability of a network adapter to send and receive. The plug gets plugged into the NIC, and then a loopback test is performed using troubleshooting software. You can then tell if the card is working properly or not. Figure 6.27 shows an Ethernet loopback plug, but they are made for fiber-optic NICs as well.

FIGURE 6.27   An Ethernet loopback plug

Punch-Down Tool

Last but not least is the *punch-down tool*. It's not a testing tool but one that allows you to connect (i.e., punch down) the exposed ends of a wire into a wiring harnesses, such as a 110 block (used many times in connectivity closets to help simplify the tangled mess of cables). Figure 6.28 shows the tool and its changeable bit.

FIGURE 6.28   A punch-down tool

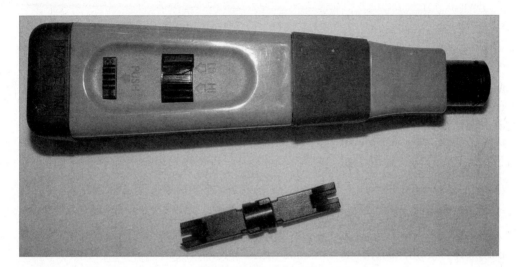

Networking Components

Network cabling can link one computer to another, but most networks are far grander in scale than two simple machines. There are a variety of networking devices that provide connectivity to the network, make the network bigger, and offer auxiliary services to end users.

In the following sections, we're going to classify additional networking components into two broad categories: connectivity devices and auxiliary devices.

Connectivity Devices

We all know that if you want to be part of a computer network, you need to attach to that network somehow. Network cables are one way to accomplish this, but not everyone is in a position to just plug a cable in and go. In addition, if you want to grow your network beyond a few simple connections, you need to use a special class of networking devices known as *connectivity devices*. These devices allow communications to break the boundaries of local networks and really provide the backbone for nearly all computer networks, regardless of size.

There are several categories of connectivity devices, but we are going to discuss the most important and frequently used:

- Modem
- Access point
- Hub
- Bridge
- Switch
- Router

These connectivity devices have made it possible for users to connect to networks and to lengthen networks to almost unlimited distances.

Modems

If you want to connect to a network or the Internet using plain old phone lines and a dial-up connection, a *modem* is the device you'll need. Modems got their name because they modulate and demodulate (mo-dem) digital signals that computers use into analog signals that can be passed over telephone lines. In the early to mid-1990s, modems were practically the only device available to get to the Internet. Many companies also used them to allow users who were not in the office to dial in to the local network.

While modems did provide flexibility, you of course needed to be near a phone line, and speed was an issue. The fastest modems transferred data at 56Kbps. At the time that felt lightning quick, but fortunately our species has moved well beyond that technology. It's horrifically slow by today's standards and therefore rarely used.

Access Points

Technically speaking, an access point is any point that allows a user on to a network. The term is commonly used in reference to a *wireless access point*, which lets users connect to your network via an 802.11 technology. We'll get deeper into wireless access points and how to configure them in Chapter 8.

Hubs

A *hub* is a device used to link several computers together. Hubs are very simple devices that possess no real intelligence. They simply repeat any signal that comes in on one port and copy it to the other ports (a process that is also called *broadcasting*). You'll sometimes hear them referred to as multiport repeaters. They work at the Physical layer (Layer 1) of the OSI model just as repeaters do.

There are two types of hubs: active and passive. *Passive hubs* connect all ports together electrically but do not have their own power source. *Active hubs* use electronics to amplify and clean up the signal before it is broadcast to the other ports.

Bridges

Bridges operate in the Data Link layer (Layer 2) of the OSI model. They join similar topologies and are used to divide network segments into multiple collision domains.

Bridges isolate network traffic, preventing unwanted traffic from entering a segment when there are no recipients on that segment.

For example, with 100 people on one Ethernet segment, performance will be mediocre because of the design of Ethernet and the number of workstations that are fighting to transmit. If you use a bridge to divide the segment into two segments of 50 workstations each, the traffic will be much lower on either side and performance will increase.

Bridges are not able to distinguish one protocol from another because higher levels of the OSI model are not available to them. If a bridge is aware of the destination MAC address, it can forward packets to the correct segment; otherwise, it forwards the packets to all segments.

> Because bridges work at the Data Link layer, they are aware of only hardware (MAC) addresses. They are not aware of and do not deal with IP addresses.

Bridges are more intelligent than repeaters but are unable to move data across multiple networks simultaneously.

The main disadvantage of bridges is that they forward broadcast packets. Broadcasts are addressed to all computers, so the bridge just does its job and forwards the packets. Bridges also cannot perform intelligent path selection, meaning that the path from the sender to the destination will always be the same regardless of network conditions. To stop broadcasts or perform intelligent path selection, you need a router.

Switches

Switches work at Layer 2 as bridges do, and they provide centralized connectivity just as hubs do. They often look similar to hubs, so it's easy to confuse them. There are big performance differences though. Hubs pass along all traffic, but switches examine the Layer 2 header of the incoming packet and forward it properly to the right port and only that port. This greatly reduces overhead and thus improves performance because there is essentially a virtual connection between sender and receiver. The only downside is that switches forward broadcasts because they are addressed to everyone.

> If it helps you to remember their functions, a hub is essentially a multiport repeater, whereas a switch functions like a multiport bridge and, in some cases, a multiport router.

Nearly every hub or switch you will see has one or more status indicator lights on it. If there is a connection to a port of the switch, a light either above the connector or on an LED panel elsewhere on the device will light up. If traffic is crossing the port, the light may flash, or there may be a secondary light that will light up. Many devices can also detect a problem in the connection. If a normal connection produces a green light, a bad connection might produce an amber one.

Routers

Routers are highly intelligent devices that connect multiple network types and determine the best path for sending data. They can route packets across multiple networks and use *routing tables* to store network addresses to determine the best destination. Routers operate at the Network layer (Layer 3) of the OSI model. Because of this, they make their decisions on what to do with traffic based on logical addresses, such as an IP address.

Routers have a few key functions. One, they connect multiple networks to each other, which none of the other devices we have discussed do. Two, routers do not forward broadcasts. (Switches and bridges break up collision domains, whereas routers break up broadcast domains.) Routers are normally used to connect one LAN to another. Typically, when a WAN is set up, at least two routers are used.

In the last few years, wireless routers have become all the rage for small and home networks. They possess all of the functionality of routers historically associated with networking, but they are relatively inexpensive. We'll talk more about these in Chapter 8.

Auxiliary Devices

The devices we just talked about are specialized to provide connectivity. This next group of devices adds in features outside of connectivity that can help network users with their daily tasks and protect them from malicious attacks.

NAS

A *network-attached storage (NAS)* device is a specialized computer that acts like a hard drive directly attached to the network. NAS devices are dedicated for storage only, and while acting as a file server, they can provide additional services such as data backups as well.

Firewall

A *firewall* is a hardware or software solution that serves as your network's security guard. They're probably the most important device on networks that are connected to the Internet. Firewalls can protect you in two ways. They protect your network resources from hackers lurking in the dark corners of the Internet, and they can simultaneously prevent computers on your network from accessing undesirable content on the Internet. At a basic level, firewalls filter packets based on rules defined by the network administrator.

Firewalls can be stand-alone "black boxes," software installed on a server or router, or some combination of hardware and software. Most firewalls will have at least two network connections: one to the Internet, or *public side*, and one to the internal network, or *private side*. Some firewalls have a third network port for a second semi-internal network. This port is used to connect servers that can be considered both public and private, such as web and email servers. This intermediary network is known as a *demilitarized zone (DMZ)*.

Firewalls can be network based in that they protect a group of computers (or an entire network), or they can be host-based. A host-based firewall (such as Windows Firewall) protects only the individual computer on which it's installed.

A firewall is configured to allow only packets that pass specific security restrictions to get through. By default, most firewalls are configured as *default deny*, which means that all traffic is blocked unless specifically authorized by the administrator. The basic method of configuring firewalls is to use an *access control list (ACL)*. The ACL is the set of rules that determines which traffic gets through the firewall and which traffic is blocked. ACLs are typically configured to block traffic by IP address, port number, domain name, or some combination of all three.

VoIP Phones

Voice over Internet Protocol (VoIP) is a term that describes technology that delivers voice communications over the Internet. A good VoIP system will allow users to send data, video, and voice all at the same time over the same Internet connection. To facilitate VoIP, many companies have made telephones that hook directly to your network, otherwise known as *VoIP phones*. It looks like a telephone and acts like a telephone, but it uses your network instead of phone lines.

There are two distinguishing features of VoIP phones. One, they use a network cable instead of a regular phone line with an RJ-11 connector. Two, whenever you make a call with a VoIP phone, you must always dial the area code first.

Internet Appliance

An *Internet appliance* is a specialized hardware device that exists solely to connect to the Internet. It can be used for typical Internet stuff like web browsing and email. Internet appliances were intended to be lower-cost alternatives to laptop computers. Considering that most mobile devices are Internet capable and the price of laptop and tablet computers has continued to drop, you're not likely to see a lot of these devices.

Summary

In this chapter, you learned about a broad variety of networking topics. This chapter has everything you need to get you ready for the networking questions on the A+ 220-801 exam. At the same time, the A+ exam (and consequently this chapter) barely scratches the surface of the things you can learn about networking. If making computers talk to each other effectively is an area of interest to you, we suggest you consider studying for the CompTIA Network+ exam after you pass your A+ tests.

First, we started with networking fundamentals. A lot of the discussion of fundamentals was about understanding the concepts behind networking so you know how to set them up. Topics included LANs versus WANs; clients, servers, and resources; network operating systems; peer-to-peer and server-based resource models; network topologies such as bus, star, and ring; and theoretical networking models and standards, such as the OSI model and IEEE standards.

Next, you learned about hardware devices used in networking. Each computer needs a network adapter (NIC) of some sort to connect to the network. On a wired network, cables are required, and there are several different types, including coaxial, STP, UTP, and fiber-optic. Each cable type has its own specific connector.

Finally, we discussed various types of network connectivity hardware and auxiliary devices and what they're used for. Some users may need a modem or access point to get on to your network. All wired computers will plug into a connectivity device such as a hub or a switch, which in turn is connected to another connectivity device, which may be a bridge or a router. Other devices on your network provide additional services. A NAS device is like a dedicated file server. Firewalls protect your network from intruders. VoIP phones and Internet appliances give end users additional devices for communicating with others.

Exam Essentials

Know the difference between workgroups and domains. A workgroup is often referred to as a peer-to-peer network, and there is no centralized administration. A domain is a server-based network; the server (often called a domain controller) manages user accounts and security for the network. Workgroups are best suited for networks with 10 or fewer computers and low security requirements.

Know the difference between a LAN, a WAN, a PAN, and a MAN. A LAN is a local area network, which typically means a network in one centralized location. A WAN is a wide area network, which means several LANs in remote locations connected to each other.

A PAN is a small Bluetooth network. A network that spans an area such as a city or a campus is a MAN.

Understand the difference between a patch cable and a crossover cable. Patch cables are used to connect hosts to a switch or a hub. Crossover cables switch pins 1 and 3 and 2 and 6 on one end. They are used to connect hubs to hubs, switches to switches, hosts to hosts, and hosts to routers.

Know what hubs, switches, and routers are. These are all network connectivity devices. Hubs and switches are used to connect several computers or groups of computers to each other. Routers are more complex devices that are often used to connect network segments or networks to each other.

Know what types of cables are used in networking and the connectors for each. Common network cables include coaxial, STP, UTP (Category 5/5e and Category 6), and fiber-optic. Coax cables use BNC connectors, STP and UTP use RJ-45 connectors, and fiber-optic uses ST, SC, and LC connectors. (You may also be tested on phone connectors, which are called RJ-11.)

Understand network topologies. Network topologies are bus, star, ring, mesh, and hybrid.

Review Questions

The answers to the Chapter Review Questions can be found in Appendix A.

1. _____ is immune to electromagnetic or radio-frequency interference.
   - **A.** Twisted-pair cabling
   - **B.** CSMA/CD
   - **C.** Broadband coaxial cabling
   - **D.** Fiber-optic cabling

2. Which IEEE 802 standard defines a bus topology using coaxial baseband cable and is able to transmit at 10Mbps?
   - **A.** 802.1
   - **B.** 802.2
   - **C.** 802.3
   - **D.** 802.5

3. Which OSI layer signals "all clear" by making sure the data segments are error free?
   - **A.** Application layer
   - **B.** Session layer
   - **C.** Transport layer
   - **D.** Network layer

4. _____ is the type of media access method used by NICs that listen to or sense the cable to check for traffic and send only when they hear that no one else is transmitting.
   - **A.** Token passing
   - **B.** CSMA/CD
   - **C.** CSMA/CA
   - **D.** Demand priority

5. What model is used to provide a common way to describe network protocols?
   - **A.** OSI
   - **B.** ISO
   - **C.** IEEE
   - **D.** CSMA/CD

6. A physical star topology consists of several workstations that branch off a central device called a _____ .
   - **A.** NIC
   - **B.** Bridge
   - **C.** Router
   - **D.** Hub

7. Of all network cabling options, _____ offers the longest possible segment length.

   A. Unshielded twisted-pair

   B. Coaxial

   C. Fiber-optic

   D. Shielded twisted-pair

8. What devices transfer packets across multiple networks and use tables to store network addresses to determine the best destination?

   A. Routers

   B. Bridges

   C. Hubs

   D. Switches

9. In which network design do users access resources from other workstations rather than from a central location?

   A. Client-server

   B. Star

   C. Ring

   D. Peer-to-peer

10. Which of the following wireless communication standards is often described in terms of a wireless personal area network?

    A. Bluetooth

    B. Infrared

    C. Cellular

    D. Ethernet

11. Which of the following statements are *not* associated with a star network? (Choose all that apply.)

    A. A single cable break can cause complete network disruption.

    B. All devices connect to a central device.

    C. It uses a single backbone computer to connect all network devices.

    D. It uses a dual-ring configuration.

12. If you are going to run a network cable in the space above the drop ceiling in your office, which type of cable should you use?

    A. Plenum

    B. PVC

    C. Coaxial

    D. Fiber-optic

13. Which of the following connector types is an MFF connector?

   A. BNC

   B. ST

   C. SC

   D. LC

14. What troubleshooting device would you use if you needed to trace a cable through a wall?

   A. Toner probe

   B. Cable tester

   C. Multimeter

   D. Loopback plug

15. You have been asked to configure a full mesh network with seven computers. How many connections will this require?

   A. 6

   B. 7

   C. 21

   D. 42

16. Which tool is used by technicians to connect an RJ-45 connector to the end of a cable?

   A. Punch-down tool

   B. Crimper

   C. Cable tester

   D. Loopback plug

17. What type of device will block unwanted traffic from your network using a set of rules called an ACL?

   A. Router

   B. Firewall

   C. Internet appliance

   D. NAS

18. What type of coaxial cable is recommended for digital television cable signals?

   A. RG-6

   B. RG-8

   C. RG-58

   D. RG-59

19. Which of the following devices work at Layer 2 of the OSI model? (Choose two.)

   A. Hub

   B. Router

   C. Bridge

   D. Switch

20. Transmitting at 10Gbps, how far can signals on an MMF cable travel?

   A. 100 meters

   B. 550 meters

   C. 1 kilometer

   D. 40 kilometers

Performance-Based Question

On the A+ exams, you will encounter performance-based questions. The questions on the exam require you to perform a specific task, and you will be graded on if you were able to complete the task. The following requires you to think creatively to measure how well you understand this chapter's topics. You may or may not see similar questions on the actual A+ exams. To see how your answer compares to the authors' refer to Appendix B.

Draw three examples of physical network topologies and explain how each works.

Chapter 7

Introduction to TCP/IP

THE FOLLOWING COMPTIA A+ 220-801 EXAM OBJECTIVES ARE COVERED IN THIS CHAPTER:

✓ **2.3 Explain properties and characteristics of TCP/IP.**

- IP class
  - Class A
  - Class B
  - Class C
- IPv4 vs. IPv6
- Public vs. private vs. APIPA
- Static vs. dynamic
- Client-side DNS
- DHCP
- Subnet mask
- Gateway

✓ **2.4 Explain common TCP and UDP ports, protocols, and their purpose.**

- Ports
  - 21 - FTP
  - 23 - Telnet
  - 25 - SMTP
  - 53 - DNS
  - 80 - HTTP
  - 110 - POP3
  - 143 - IMAP
  - 443 - HTTPS
  - 3389 - RDP

Networking protocols are a lot like human languages in that they are the language that computers speak when talking to each other. If computers don't speak the same language, they won't be able to talk. To complicate matters, there are dozens of different languages out there that computers can use. Just like humans, computers can understand and use multiple languages. Imagine you are on the street and someone comes up to you and speaks in Spanish. If you know Spanish, you will likely reply in kind. It doesn't matter if both of you know English as well because you've already established that you can communicate. On the other hand, it's going to be a pretty quick conversation if you don't know Spanish. This same concept applies to computers that are trying to communicate. They must have a network protocol in common in order for the conversation to be successful.

Throughout the years, hundreds of network protocols have been developed. As the advent of networking exploded, various companies developed their own networking hardware, software, and proprietary protocols. Some were incorporated as an integral part of the network operating system, such as Banyan VINES. One-time networking giant Novell had IPX/SPX. Microsoft developed NetBEUI. Apple created AppleTalk. Others included DECnet, SNA, and XNS. While a few achieved long-term success, most have faded into oblivion. The one protocol suite that has sustained is TCP/IP. While it has some structural plusses such as its modularity, it didn't necessarily succeed because it was inherently superior to other protocols. It succeeded because it is the protocol of the Internet.

This chapter focuses on the TCP/IP protocol. It is the protocol used on the Internet, but it's also the protocol used by the vast majority of home and business networks today. We'll start by taking a quick look at the history of TCP/IP and the model on which it's based. Then, we'll dive deeper into TCP/IP structure and the individual protocols that compose it. From there, we'll spend some time on IP addressing, including IPv4 and IPv6. Entire books have been written on TCP/IP—there's no way we could cover it entirely in one chapter. Instead, we'll give you the foundation you need to understand it well and work effectively with it in the field.

Understanding TCP/IP

As we mentioned in the introduction, computers use a protocol as a common language for communication. A *protocol* is a set of rules that govern communications, much like a language in human terms. Of the myriad protocols out there, the key one to understand is the TCP/IP suite, which is actually a collection of different protocols that work together to deliver connectivity. Consequently, it's the only one listed on the A+ exam objectives. In the following sections, we'll start with a look at its overall structure and then move into key protocols within the suite.

TCP/IP Structure

The *Transmission Control Protocol/Internet Protocol (TCP/IP) suite* is the most popular network protocol in use today, thanks mostly to the rise of the Internet. While the protocol suite is named after two of its hardest-working protocols, *Transmission Control Protocol (TCP)* and *Internet Protocol (IP)*, TCP/IP actually contains dozens of protocols working together to help computers communicate with one another.

TCP/IP is the protocol used on the Internet.

TCP/IP is robust and flexible. For example, if you want to ensure that the packets are delivered from one computer to another, TCP/IP can do that. If speed is more important than guaranteed delivery, then TCP/IP can ensure that too. The protocol can work on disparate operating systems such as UNIX, Linux, and Windows. It can also support a variety of programs, applications, and required network functions. Much of its flexibility comes from its modular nature.

You're familiar with the seven-layer OSI model we discussed in Chapter 6, "Networking Fundamentals." Every protocol that's created needs to accomplish the tasks (or at least the key tasks) outlined in that model. The structure of TCP/IP is based on a similar model created by the United States Department of Defense: the *Department of Defense (DOD) model*. The DOD model has four layers that map to the seven OSI layers, as shown in Figure 7.1.

FIGURE 7.1   The DOD and OSI models

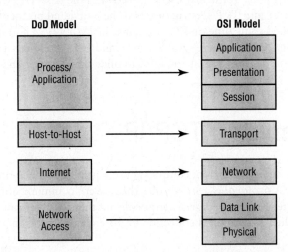

The overall functionality between these two models is virtually identical; the layers just have different names. For example, the Process/Application layer of the DOD model is designed to combine the functionality of the top three layers of the OSI model. Therefore, any protocol designed against the Process/Application layer would need to be able to perform all functions associated with the Application, Presentation, and Session layers in the OSI model.

TCP/IP's modular nature and common protocols are shown in Figure 7.2.

FIGURE 7.2   TCP/IP protocol suite

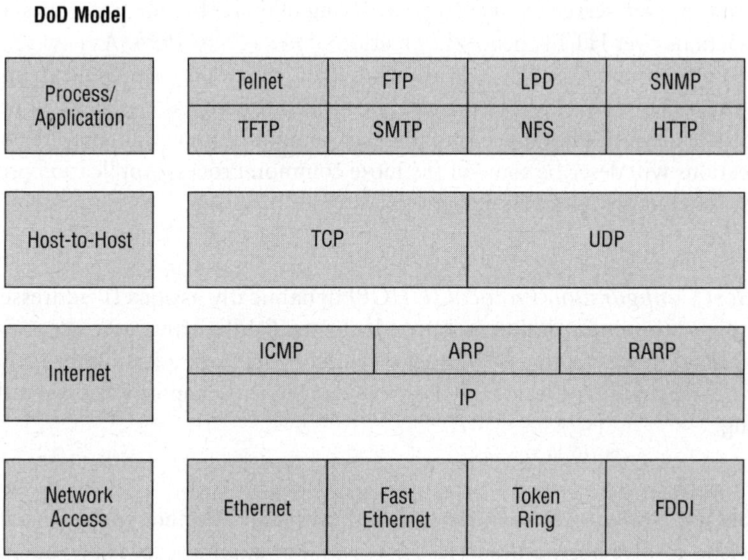

DoD Model

| Process/Application | Telnet | FTP | LPD | SNMP |
| | TFTP | SMTP | NFS | HTTP |

| Host-to-Host | TCP | | UDP | |

| Internet | ICMP | ARP | | RARP |
| | IP | | | |

| Network Access | Ethernet | Fast Ethernet | Token Ring | FDDI |

The majority of TCP/IP protocols are located at the Process/Application layer. These include some protocols you are probably already familiar with, such as *Hypertext Transfer Protocol (HTTP)*, *File Transfer Protocol (FTP)*, *Simple Mail Transfer Protocol (SMTP)*, *Post Office Protocol (POP)*, and others.

At the Host-to-Host layer, there are only two protocols: TCP and *User Datagram Protocol (UDP)*. Most applications will use one or the other to transmit data, although some can use both but will do so for different tasks.

The most important protocol at the Internet layer is IP. This is the backbone of TCP/IP. Other protocols at this layer work in conjunction with IP, such as *Internet Control Message Protocol (ICMP)* and *Address Resolution Protocol (ARP)*.

You'll notice that the Network Access layer doesn't have any protocols per se. This layer describes the type of network access method you are using, such as Ethernet, Token Ring, or others.

Process/Application Layer Protocols

As we mentioned in the previous section, most of the protocols within the TCP/IP suite are at the Process/Application layer. This is the layer of differentiation and flexibility. For example, if you want to browse the Internet, the HTTP protocol is designed for that. FTP is optimized for file downloads, and RDP allows you to connect to a remote computer and manage programs.

Before we get into the protocols themselves, let's take a quick look into a few key points on the TCP/IP suite's flexibility. There are literally dozens of protocols at the Process/Application layer, and they have been created over time as networking needs arose. Take HTTP, for example. The first official version was developed in 1991, nearly 20 years after TCP/IP was first implemented. Before this protocol was created, there weren't any effective client-server request-response protocols at this layer. HTTP let the client (web browser) ask the web server for a page, and the web server would return it. Going one step further, there was a need for secure transactions over HTTP, hence the creation of HTTPS in 1994. As new applications are developed or new networking needs are discovered, developers can build an application or protocol that fits into this layer to provide the needed functionality. They just need to make sure the protocol delivers what it needs to and can communicate with the layers below it. The following sections will describe some of the more common Process/Application protocols—and the ones listed in the A+ exam objectives.

DHCP

Dynamic Host Configuration Protocol (DHCP) dynamically assigns IP addresses and other IP configuration information to network clients. Configuring your network clients to receive their IP addresses from a DHCP server reduces network administration headaches. We'll cover the mechanics of how DHCP works later in this chapter when we talk about IP addressing.

DNS

You probably use *Domain Name System (DNS)* every day whether you realize it or not. Its purpose is to resolve hostnames to IP addresses. For example, let's say you open your web browser and type in a Uniform Resource Locator (URL) such as http://www.sybex.com. Your computer needs to know the IP address of the server that hosts that website in order for you to connect to it. Through a DNS server, your computer resolves the URL to an IP address so communication can happen.

FTP

The *File Transfer Protocol (FTP)* is optimized to do what it says it does—transfer files. This includes both uploading and downloading files from one host to another. FTP is both a protocol and an application. Specifically, FTP lets you copy files, list and manipulate directories, and view file contents. You can't use it to remotely execute applications.

Whenever a user attempts to access an FTP site they will be asked for a login. If it's a public site, you can often just use the login name *anonymous* and then provide your email address as the password. Of course, there's no rule saying you have to give your real email address if you don't want to. If the FTP site is secured, you will need a legitimate login name and password to access it. If you are using a browser such as Internet Explorer to connect via FTP, the correct syntax in the address window is `ftp://`*`username:password`*`@ftp.`*`ftpsite.com`*.

In Windows XP and later, you can type a URL such as the one in the FTP example into the Run box to connect as well.

HTTP

The most commonly used Process/Application layer protocol is HTTP. It manages the communication between a web server and client and lets you connect to and view all of the content you enjoy on the Internet.

HTTPS

The protocol used for most Internet traffic, HTTP, is not secure. To securely encrypt traffic between a web server and client, *Hypertext Transfer Protocol Secure (HTTPS)* can be used. HTTPS connections are secured using either *Secure Sockets Layer (SSL)* or *Transport Layer Security (TLS)*.

From the client side, the most common issue you will encounter when HTTPS is in use on a website is that users may not know what the proper context is. To access most websites, you use http:// in the address bar. To get to a site using HTTPS, you need to use https:// instead.

 Real World Scenario

How Secure Is It?

You have probably heard before that you should not enter personal information (such as a credit card number) into an unsecure website. But what does that really mean?

First, know what to look for. If you are entering information into a website form and the address of the site begins with just http://, you're just asking for someone to steal the information! The HTTP protocol transmits data in plain text, meaning that there is no encryption at all between your computer and the server. On the other hand, HTTPS encrypts the data transmissions as they cross the wire.

To use HTTPS, the website needs to obtain a SSL certificate from a reputable web host, which verifies the identity of the website. So the good news is that if you are accessing a site with https:// in the header, you know that the site is what it says it is (and not a Trojan horse) and that transmissions between your computer and that site are encrypted. Once the data is on the website's server though, HTTPS is no longer relevant and other protection methods are needed to keep your data secure.

Occasionally, you might visit a website that uses HTTPS and get a pop-up error message saying that the certificate has expired or could not be validated. This is most likely a case of the certificate legitimately expiring, but it could be that it's a Trojan horse website. Proceed with caution!

IMAP

Internet Message Access Protocol (IMAP) is a secure protocol designed to download email. Its current version is version 4, or IMAP4. It's becoming more and more common as the client-side email management protocol of choice, replacing the unsecure POP3. Most current email clients, such as Microsoft Outlook and Gmail, are configured to be able to use either IMAP4 or POP3.

IMAP4 has some definite advantages over POP3. First, IMAP4 works in connected and disconnected modes. With POP3, the client makes a connection to the email server, downloads the email, and then terminates the connection. IMAP4 allows the client to remain connected to the email server after the download, meaning that as soon as another email enters the inbox, IMAP4 notifies the email client and is ready to download it. Second, it also lets you store the email on the server, as opposed to POP3, which requires you to download it. Third, IMAP4 allows multiple clients to be simultaneously connected to the same inbox. This can be useful for BlackBerry users who have both Outlook and their BlackBerry operational at the same time or for cases where multiple users monitor the same mailbox, such as on a customer service account. IMAP4 allows each connected user or client to see changes made to messages on the server in real time.

LDAP

The *Lightweight Directory Access Protocol (LDAP)* is a directory services protocol based on the X.500 standard. LDAP is designed to access information stored in an information directory typically known as an LDAP directory or LDAP database.

On your network you probably have a lot of information such as employee phone books and email addresses, client contact lists, and infrastructure and configuration data for the network and network applications. This information might not get updated frequently, but you might need to access it from anywhere on the network, or you might have a network application that needs access to this data. LDAP provides you with the access, regardless of the client platform you're working from. You can also use access control lists (ACLs) to set up who can read and change entries in the database using LDAP. A common analogy is that LDAP provides access to and the structure behind your network's phone book.

POP3

For a long time now, *Post Office Protocol 3 (POP3)* has been the preferred protocol for downloading email. It's being replaced by IMAP4 because IMAP4 includes security and more features than POP3.

RDP

Developed by Microsoft, the *Remote Desktop Protocol (RDP)* allows users to connect to remote computers and run programs on them. When you use RDP, you see the desktop of the computer you've logged in to on your screen. It's like you're really there, even though you're not.

When you use RDP, the computer that you are sitting at is the client, and the computer you're logging in to is the server. The server uses its own video driver to create video output and sends the output to the client using RDP. Conversely, all keyboard and mouse input from the client is encrypted and sent to the server for processing. RDP also supports sound, drive, port, and network printer redirection. In a nutshell, this means that if you could see, hear, or do it if you were sitting at the remote computer, you could see, hear, or do it at the RDP client too.

Services using this protocol can be great for telecommuters. It's also very handy for technical support folks, who can log in and assume control over a remote computer. It's a lot easier to troubleshoot and fix problems when you can see what's going on and "drive"!

SFTP

The *Secure File Transfer Protocol (SFTP)* is used when you need to transfer files over a secure, encrypted connection.

SMB

Server Message Block (SMB) is another Microsoft-developed protocol. It's used to provide shared access to files, printers, and other network resources. In a way, it functions a bit like FTP only with a few more options.

SMTP

We've already looked at a few protocols that are for downloading or receiving email. *Simple Mail Transfer Protocol (SMTP)* is the protocol most commonly used to send email messages. Because it's designed to send only, it's referred to as a *push protocol*. An email client locates its email server by querying the DNS server for a mail exchange (MX) record. After the server is located, SMTP is used to push the message to the email server, which will then process the message for delivery.

SNMP

Simple Network Management Protocol (SNMP) gathers and manages network performance information.

On your network, you might have several connectivity devices such as routers and switches. A management device called an *SNMP server* can be set up to collect data from these devices (called *agents*) and ensure that your network is operating properly. Although it's mostly used to monitor connectivity devices, many other network devices are SNMP compatible as well. The most current version is SNMPv3.

SSH

Secure Shell (SSH) can be used to set up a secure Telnet session for remote logins or for remotely executing programs and transferring files. Because it's secure, it was originally designed to be a replacement for the unsecure `telnet` command. A common client interface using SSH is called OpenSSH (`www.openssh.com`).

Telnet

It seems as though *Telnet* has been around since the beginning of time as a terminal emulation protocol. Someone using Telnet can log into another machine and "see" the remote computer in a window on their screen. Although this vision is text only, the user can manage files on that remote machine just as if they were logged in locally.

The problem with `telnet` and other unsecure remote management interfaces (such as `rcp` and `ftp`) is that the data they transmit, including passwords, is sent in plain text. Anyone eavesdropping on the line can intercept the packets and thus obtain usernames and passwords. SSH overcomes this by encrypting the traffic, including usernames and passwords.

Host-to-Host Layer Protocols

After the myriad protocols at the Process/Application layer, the simplicity of the Host-to-Host layer is welcome. At this layer there are two alternatives within the TCP/IP suite: TCP and UDP. The major difference between the two is that TCP guarantees packet delivery through the use of a virtual circuit and data acknowledgements and UDP does not. Because of this, TCP is often referred to as *connection oriented*, whereas UDP is *connectionless*. Because UDP is connectionless, it does tend to be somewhat faster, but we're talking about milliseconds here.

Another key concept to understand about TCP and UDP is the use of *port numbers*. Imagine a web server that is managing connections from incoming users who are viewing web content and others who are downloading files. TCP and UDP use port numbers to keep track of these conversations and make sure the data gets to the right application and right end user. Conversely, when a client makes a request of a server, it needs to do so on a specific port to make sure the right application on the server hears the request. For example, web servers are listening for HTTP requests on port 80, so web browsers need to make their requests on that port.

A good analogy for understanding port numbers is to think of cable or satellite television. In this analogy, the IP address is your house. The cable company needs to know where to send the data. But once the data is in your house, which channel are you going to receive it on? If you want sports, that might be on one channel, but weather is on a different channel, and the cooking show is on yet another. Those channels are analogous to ports. You know that if you want a cooking show, you need to turn to channel 923 (or whatever). Similarly, the client computer on a network knows that if it needs to ask a question in HTTP, it needs to do it on port 80.

There are 65,536 ports numbered from 0 to 65535. Ports 0 through 1023 are called the *well-known ports* and are assigned to commonly used services, and 1024 through 49151 are called the *registered ports*. Anything from 49152 to 65535 is free to be used by application vendors. Fortunately, you don't need to memorize them all.

TCP/IP applications combine the host's IP address with the port number in order to communicate. This combination is known as a *socket*.

Table 7.1 shows the ports used by some of the more common protocols. You should know each of these for the A+ exam.

TABLE 7.1   Common port numbers

Service	Protocol	Port
FTP	TCP	20, 21
SSH	TCP	22
Telnet	TCP	23
SMTP	TCP	25
DNS	TCP/UDP	53
HTTP	TCP	80
DHCP	UDP	67, 68
POP3	TCP	110
IMAP4	TCP	143
SNMP	UDP	161
LDAP	TCP	389
HTTPS	TCP	443
SMB	TCP	445
RDP	TCP	3389

A complete list of registered port numbers can be found at www.iana.org.

Internet Layer Protocols

At the Internet layer, there's one key protocol and a few helpful support protocols. The main workhorse of TCP/IP is the Internet Protocol (IP), and it can be found here. IP is responsible for managing logical network addresses and ultimately getting data from point A to point B, even if there are dozens of points in between. We'll cover IP addressing more in the next section.

There are three support protocols you should be aware of at this layer as well. *Internet Control Message Protocol (ICMP)* is responsible for delivering error messages. If you're familiar with the ping utility, you'll know that it utilizes ICMP to send and receive packets. *Address Resolution Protocol (ARP)* resolves logical IP addresses to physical MAC addresses built in to network cards. Reverse ARP (RARP) resolves MAC addresses to IP addresses.

Understanding IP Addressing

To communicate on a TCP/IP network, each device needs to have a unique IP address. Any device with an IP address is referred to as a *host*. This can include servers, workstations, printers, and routers. If you can assign it an IP address, it's a host. As an administrator, you can assign the host's IP configuration information manually, or you can have it automatically assigned by a DHCP server.

> The information in this section will cover IPv4. IPv6 will be covered in its own separate section.

An IPv4 address is a 32-bit hierarchical address that identifies a host on the network. It's typically written in dotted-decimal notation, such as 192.168.10.55. Each of the numbers in this example represents 8 bits (or 1 byte) of the address, also known as an *octet*. The same address written in binary (how the computer thinks about it) would be 11000000 10101000 00001010 00110111. As you can see, the dotted-decimal version is a much more convenient way to write these numbers!

The addresses are said to be hierarchical, as opposed to "flat," because the numbers at the beginning of the address identify groups of computers that belong to the same network. Because of the hierarchical address structure, we're able to do really cool things like route packets between local networks and on the Internet.

A great example of hierarchical addressing is your street address. Let's say that you live in apartment 4B on 123 Main Street, Anytown, Kansas, USA. If someone sent you a letter via snail mail, the hierarchy of your address helps the postal service and carrier deliver it to the right place. First and broadest is USA. Kansas helps narrow it down a bit, and Anytown narrows it down more. Eventually we get to your street, the right number on your street, and then the right apartment. If the address space were flat (e.g., Kansas didn't mean anything more specific than Main Street), or you could name your state anything you wanted to, it would be really hard to get the letter to the right spot.

Take this analogy back to IP addresses. They're set up to logically organize networks to make delivery between them possible and then to identify an individual node within a network. If this structure weren't in place, a huge, multinetwork space like the Internet probably wouldn't be possible. It would simply be too unwieldy to manage.

Another example of a hierarchical addressing scheme is telephone numbers. The first three digits, the area code, group all telephone numbers with that area code into one logical network. The second grouping of three numbers defines a local calling area, and the last grouping of numbers is the unique identifier within that local calling area.

A Quick Binary Tutorial

As we mentioned earlier, each IP address is written in four octets in dotted-decimal notation, but each octet represents 8 bits. A binary bit is a value with two possible states: on equals 1, and off equals 0. If the bit is turned on, it has a decimal value based upon its position within the octet. An off bit always equals zero. Take a look at Figure 7.3, which will help illustrate what we mean.

FIGURE 7.3   Binary values

Position in octet	8	7	6	5	4	3	2	1
Bit on	1	1	1	1	1	1	1	1
Has the decimal value of . . .	128	64	32	16	8	4	2	1
Mathematically	2^7	2^6	2^5	2^4	2^3	2^2	2^1	2^0

If all of the bits in an octet are off, or 00000000, the corresponding decimal value is 0. If all bits in an octet are on, you would have 11111111, which is 255 in decimal.

When working with IPv4 addressing, all numbers will be between 0 and 255.

Where it starts to get more entertaining is when you have combinations of zeroes and ones. For example, 10000001 is equal to 129 (128 + 1), and 00101010 is equal to 42 (32 + 8 + 2).

As you work with IPv4 addresses, you'll see certain patterns emerge. For example, you may begin to find yourself able to count quickly from left to right in an octet pattern, such as 128, 192, 224, 240, 248, 252, 254, and 255. That's what you get if you have (starting from the left) 1, 2, 3, and so forth up to 8 bits on in sequence in the octet.

It's beyond the scope of this book to get into too much detail on binary-to-decimal conversion, but this primer should get you started.

Parts of the IP Address

Each IP address is made up of two components: the *network ID* and the *host ID*. The network portion of the address always comes before the host portion. Because of the way IP addresses are structured, the network portion does not have to be a specific fixed length. In other words, some computers will use 8 of the 32 bits for the network portion and the other 24 for the host portion, while other computers might use 24 bits for the network portion and the remaining 8 bits for the host portion. Here are a few rules you should know about when working with IP addresses:

- All host addresses on a network must be unique.

- On a routed network (such as the Internet), all network addresses must be unique as well.

- Neither the network ID nor the host ID can be set to all 0s. A host ID portion of all 0s means "this network."

- Neither the network ID nor the host ID can be set to all 1s. A host ID portion of all 1s means "all hosts on this network," commonly known as a broadcast address.

Computers are able to differentiate where the network ID ends and the host address begins through the use of a *subnet mask*. This is a value written just like an IP address and may look something like 255.255.255.0. Any bit that is set to a 1 in the subnet mask makes the corresponding bit in the IP address part of the network ID (regardless of whether the bit in the IP address is on or off). The rest will be the host ID. The number 255 is the highest number you will ever see in IP addressing, and it means that all bits in the octet are set to 1.

Here's an example based on two numbers we have used in this chapter. Look at the IP address of 192.168.10.55. Let's assume that the subnet mask in use with this address is 255.255.255.0. This indicates that the first three octets are the network portion of the address and the last octet is the host portion, therefore the network portion of this ID is 192.168.10 and the host portion is 55.

To communicate using TCP/IP, each computer is *required* to have an IP address and correct subnet mask. A third component, called a *default gateway*, identifies the IP address of the device that will allow the host to connect outside of the local network. This is typically your router, and it's required if you want to communicate with computers outside of your local network.

IPv4 Address Classes

The designers of TCP/IP designated classes of networks based on the first three bits of the IP address. As you will see, classes differ in how many networks of each class can exist and the number of unique hosts each network can accommodate. Here are some characteristics of the three classes of addresses you will commonly deal with:

Class A Class A networks are defined as those with the first bit set as 0 (decimal values from 0 to 127) and are designed for very large networks. The default network portion for Class A networks is the first 8 bits, leaving 24 bits for host identification. Because the network portion is only 8 bits long (and 0 and 127 are reserved), there are only 126 Class A network addresses available. The remaining 24 bits of the address allow each Class A network to hold as many as 16,777,214 hosts. Examples of Class A networks include telecommunications giants Level 3 Communications and AT&T, and organizations such as General Electric, IBM, Hewlett-Packard, Apple, Xerox, Ford, MIT, and the United States Department of Defense. All possible Class A networks are in use; no more are available.

Class B   Class B networks always have the first two bits set at 10 (decimal values from 128 to 191) and are designed for medium-sized networks. The default network portion for Class B networks is the first 16 bits, leaving 16 bits for host identification. This allows for 16,384 networks, each with as many as 65,534 hosts attached. Examples of Class B networks include the networks of Microsoft, ExxonMobil, and Purdue University. Class B networks are generally regarded as unavailable, but address-conservation techniques have made some of these addresses available from time to time over the years.

Class C   Class C networks have the first three bits set at 110 (decimal values from 192 to 223) and are designed for smaller networks. The default network portion for Class C networks is the first 24 bits, leaving 8 bits for host identification. This allows for 2,097,152 networks, but each network can have a maximum of only 254 hosts. Most companies have Class C network addresses. A few class C networks are still available.

The address assignment examples in this chapter refer to addresses that are used on the Internet. For example, MIT has the network address of 18.0.0.0. No one else on the Internet can use addresses in that network's range. But if you are using IP addresses on an internal network that never connects to the Internet, you are free to use whatever addresses you would like.

Table 7.2 shows the IPv4 classes, their ranges, and their default subnet masks.

TABLE 7.2   IPv4 address classes

Class	First Octet	Default Subnet Mask	Comments
A	1–127	255.0.0.0	For very large networks; 127 reserved for the loopback address
B	128–191	255.255.0.0	For medium-sized networks
C	192–223	255.255.255.0	For smaller networks with fewer hosts
D	224–239	N/A	Reserved for multicasts (sending messages to multiple systems)
E	240–255	N/A	Reserved for testing

The network addresses 0 and 127 are reserved and not available for use. Specifically, the address 127.0.0.1 is called the *loopback address*, and it's used for troubleshooting network adapters. We'll talk more about this in Chapter 20, "Hardware and Network Troubleshooting."

DHCP and DNS

Two critical TCP/IP services you need to be aware of are Dynamic Host Configuration Protocol (DHCP) and Domain Name System (DNS). Both are services that need to be installed on a server and both provide key functionality to network clients.

A DHCP server can be configured to automatically provide IP configuration information to clients. The following configuration information is typically provided:

- IP address
- Subnet mask
- Default gateway (the "door" to the outside world)
- DNS server address

DHCP servers can provide a lot more than the items on this list, but those are the most common. When a DHCP-configured client boots up, it sends out a broadcast on the network (called a *DHCP DISCOVER)* requesting a DHCP server. The DHCP server initially responds to the request and then fulfills the request by returning configuration information to the client.

The alternative to DHCP, of course, is for an administrator to enter in the IP configuration information manually for each host. This is called *static IP addressing* and is very administratively intensive as compared to DHCP's dynamic addressing.

DNS has one function on the network, and that is to resolve host names to IP addresses. This sounds simple enough, but it has profound implications.

Think about using the Internet. You open your browser, and in the address bar, you type the name of your favorite website, something like www.google.com, and press Enter. The first question your computer asks is, "Who is that?" Your machine requires an IP address to connect to the website. The DNS server provides the answer, "That is 72.14.205.104." Now that your computer knows the address of the website you want, it's able to traverse the Internet to find it.

Each DNS server has a database where it stores hostname-to-IP-address pairs. If the DNS server does not know the address of the host you are looking for, it has the ability to query other DNS servers to help answer the request.

Think about the implications of that for just a minute. We all probably use Google several times a day, but in all honesty how many of us know its IP address? It's certainly not something we are likely to have memorized. Much less, how could you possibly memorize the IP addresses of all of the websites you visit? Because of DNS, it's easy to find resources. Whether you want to find Coca-Cola, Toyota, Amazon.com, or thousands of other companies, it's usually pretty easy to figure out how. Type in the name with a .com on the end of it and you're usually right. The only reason this is successful is that DNS is there to perform resolution of that name to the corresponding IP address.

DNS works the same way on an intranet (a local network not attached to the Internet) as it does on the Internet. The only difference is that instead of helping you find www.google.com, it may help you find Jenny's print server or Joe's file server. From a client-side perspective, all you need to do is configure the host with the address of a legitimate DNS server and you should be good to go.

Public vs. Private IP Addresses

All of the addresses that are used on the Internet are called public addresses. They must be purchased, and only one computer can use any given public address at one time. The problem that presented itself was that the world was soon to run out of public IP addresses while the use of TCP/IP was growing. Additionally, the structure of IP addressing made it impossible to "create" or add any new addresses to the system.

To address this, a solution was devised to allow for the use of TCP/IP without requiring the assignment of a public address. The solution was to use private addresses. Private addresses are not routable on the Internet. They were intended to be used on private networks only. Because they weren't intended to be used on the Internet, it freed us from the requirement that all addresses be globally unique. This essentially created an infinite number of IP addresses that companies could use within their own network walls.

While this solution helped alleviate the problem of running out of addresses, it created a new one. The private addresses that all of these computers have aren't globally unique, but they need to be in order to access the Internet.

A service called *Network Address Translation (NAT)* was created to solve this problem. NAT runs on your router and handles the translation of private, nonroutable IP addresses into public IP addresses. There are three ranges reserved for private, nonroutable IP addresses, as shown in Table 7.3.

TABLE 7.3 Private IP address ranges

Class	IP Address Range	Subnet Mask	Number of Hosts
A	10.0.0.0–10.255.255.255	255.0.0.0	16.7 million
B	172.16.0.0–172.31.255.255	255.255.0.0	1 million
C	192.168.0.0–192.168.255.255	255.255.255.0	65,536

These private addresses cannot be used on the Internet and cannot be routed externally. The fact that they are not routable on the Internet is actually an advantage because a network administrator can use them to essentially hide an entire network from the Internet.

This is how it works: The network administrator sets up a NAT-enabled router, which functions as the default gateway to the Internet. The external interface of the router has a public IP address assigned to it that has been provided by the ISP, such as 155.120.100.1. The internal interface of the router will have an administrator-assigned private IP address within one of these ranges, such as 192.168.1.1. All computers on the internal network will then also need to be on the 192.168.1.0 network. To the outside world, any request coming from the internal network will appear to come from 155.120.100.1. The NAT router translates all incoming packets and sends them to the appropriate client. This type of setup is very common today.

By definition, NAT is actually a one-to-one private-to-public IP address translation protocol. There is a type of NAT called NAT Overload, also known as *Port Address Translation (PAT)*, which allows for many private IP addresses to use one public IP address on the Internet.

You may look at your own computer, which has an address in a private range, and wonder, "If it's not routable on the Internet, then how am I on the Internet?" Remember, the NAT router technically makes the Internet request on your computer's behalf, and the NAT router is using a public IP address.

Don't make the mistake of thinking that your internal network can't be hacked if it is using private addresses through NAT. It can. Hackers just have to use more tools and try a little harder to uncover your internal structure. Even if you're using NAT, you still need protective features such as firewalls and antimalware software.

Automatic Private IP Addressing

Automatic Private IP Addressing (APIPA) is a TCP/IP standard used to automatically configure IP-based hosts that are unable to reach a DHCP server. APIPA addresses are in the 169.254.0.0 range with a subnet mask of 255.255.0.0. If you see a computer that has an IP address beginning with 169.254, you know that it has configured itself.

Typically the only time you will see this is when a computer is supposed to receive configuration information from a DHCP server but for some reason that server is unavailable. Even while configured with this address, the client will continue to broadcast for a DHCP server so it can be given a real address once the server becomes available.

APIPA is also sometimes known as *zero configuration networking* or *address auto-configuration*. If you are setting up a small local area network that had no need to communicate with any networks outside of itself, you can use APIPA to your advantage. Set the client computers to automatically receive DHCP addresses, but don't set up a DHCP server. The clients will configure themselves and be able to communicate with each other using TCP/IP. The only downside is that this will create a little more broadcast traffic on your network. This solution is only really effective for a nonrouted network of fewer than 100 computers.

⊕ Real World Scenario

Help! I Can't Get to the Internet!

This is something you will probably hear a lot: A user on your network calls and complains that they can't get their email or get to the Internet. Everything was fine yesterday, but since this morning they have had no connectivity. Of course, they haven't done anything to or changed their computer at all! No one else on the network appears to be affected.

If the computer is otherwise running normally, the first step should always be to run an ipconfig command to look at the IP address configured on the system. More often than not, the user will report back that their IP address is "169 dot 254 dot something dot something." The last two somethings don't really matter—it's the first two numbers that should have your attention. APIPA.

Knowing that the computer is a DHCP client, you know that it's not connecting to the DHCP server for some reason. After getting to the workstation, check the easy stuff first. Are the cables plugged in (if it's wired)? Are there lights on the NIC? Even if they appear to be plugged in, unplug and reconnect them. If that doesn't work, try a different cable. Those simple steps will solve the vast majority of these types of problems. If not, then it's on to more advanced troubleshooting steps! (More TCP/IP troubleshooting is covered in Chapter 20.)

IPv6

The present incarnation of TCP/IP that is used on the Internet was originally developed in 1973. Considering how fast technology evolves, it's pretty amazing to think that the protocol still enjoys immense popularity nearly 40 years later. This version is known as IPv4.

There are a few problems with IPv4 though. One is that we're quickly running out of available network addresses, and the other is that TCP/IP can be somewhat tricky to configure.

If you've dealt with configuring custom subnet masks, you may nod your head at the configuration part, but you might be wondering how we can run out of addresses. After all, IPv4 has 32 bits of addressing space, which allows for nearly 4.3 billion addresses! With the way it's structured, only about 250 million of those addresses are actually usable, and all of those are pretty much spoken for.

A new version of TCP/IP has been developed and it's called IPv6. Instead of a 32-bit address, it provides for 128-bit addresses. That will provide for 3.4×10^{38} addresses, which theoretically should be more than enough that globally they will never run out. (Famous last words, right?)

IPv6 also has many standard features that are optional (but useful) in IPv4. While the addresses may be more difficult to remember, the automatic configuration and enhanced flexibility make the new version sparkle compared to the old one. Best of all, it's backward compatible with and can run on the computer at the same time as IPv4, so networks can migrate to IPv6 without a complete restructure.

Understanding IPv6 Addressing

Understanding the IPv6 addressing scheme is probably the most challenging part of the protocol enhancement. The first thing you'll notice is that, of course, the address space is longer. The second is that IPv6 uses hexadecimal notation instead of the familiar dotted decimal of IPv4. Its 128-bit address structure looks something like this.

```
2001:0db8:3c4d:0012:0000:0000:1234:56ab
_____|___|_____
Global prefix    Subnet      Interface ID
```

The new address is composed of eight 16-bit fields, each represented by four hexadecimal digits and separated by colons. The letters in an IPv6 address are not case sensitive. IPv6 has three address classes: *unicast*, *anycast*, and *multicast*. A unicast address identifies a single node on the network. An anycast address refers to one that has been assigned to multiple nodes. A packet addressed to an anycast address will be delivered to the closest node. Sometimes you will hear this referred to as one-to-nearest addressing. Finally, a multicast address is one used by multiple hosts. Think of it as a controlled, small-scale broadcast. Speaking of broadcasts, IPv6 does not employ broadcast addresses. That functionality is handled by multicasts. Each network interface can be assigned one or more addresses.

Just by looking at them, it's impossible to tell the difference between unicast and anycast addresses. Their structure is the same; it's their functionality that's different. The first four fields, or 64 bits, refer to the network and subnetwork. The last four fields are the interface ID, which is analogous to the host portion of the IPv4 address. Typically, the first 56 bits within the address are the routing (or global) prefix and the next 8 bits refer to the subnet ID. It's also possible to have shorter routing prefixes though, such as 48 bits, meaning the subnet ID will be longer.

The Interface ID portion of the address can be created in one of four ways. It can be created automatically using the interface's MAC address, procured from a DHCPv6 server, assigned randomly, or configured manually.

Multicast addresses can take different forms. All multicast addresses use the first 8 bits as the prefix.

Working with IPv6 Addresses

In IPv4, the length of the network portion of the address was determined by the subnet mask. The network address was often written in an abbreviated form, such as 169.254.0.0/16. The /16 indicates that the first 16 bits are for the network portion and corresponds to a subnet mask of 255.255.0.0. While IPv6 doesn't use a subnet mask, the same convention for stating the network length holds true. An IPv6 network address could be written as 2001:db8:3c4d::/48. The number after the slash indicates how many bits are in the routing prefix.

Because the addresses are quite long, there are a few ways you can write them in shorthand; in the world of IPv6 it's all about eliminating extra zeroes. For example, take the address 2001:0db8:3c4d:0012:0000:0000:1234:56ab. The first common way to shorten it is to remove all leading zeroes. So it could also be written as 2001:db8:3c4d:12:0:0:1234:56ab. The second accepted shortcut is to replace consecutive groups of zeroes with a double colon. So now the example address becomes 2001:db8:3c4d:12::1234:56ab. It's still long, but not quite as long as the original address.

The double-colon shortcut can be used only once in an address. For example, in the 2001:db8:3c4d:12::1234:56ab address, you can count the number of fields (six) and know that the double colon represents two fields of all zeroes. If, for example, you tried to write an address like 2001::1ab4::5468, you would have a big problem. You would know that there are five fields of zeroes, but you would have no way to identify where exactly the 1ab4 portion of the address falls in relation to the all-zero fields.

An increasingly common occurrence is a mixed IPv4-IPv6 network. As mentioned earlier, IPv6 is backward compatible. In the address space, this is accomplished by setting the first 80 bits to 0, the next 16 bits all to 1, and the final 32 bits to the IPv4 address. In IPv6 format, it looks something like ::ffff:c0a8:173. You will often see the same address written as ::ffff:192.168.1.115 to enable easy identification of the IPv4 address.

There are a few more addresses you need to be familiar with. In IPv4, the autoconfiguration (APIPA) address range was 169.254.0.0/16. IPv6 accomplishes the same task with the link-local address fe80::/10. Every IPv6-enabled interface is required to have a link-local address, and they are nonroutable. The IPv4 loopback address of 127.0.0.1 has been replaced with ::1/128 (typically written as just ::1). Global addresses (for Internet use) are 2000::/3, and multicast addresses are FF00::/8.

Summary

In this chapter, you learned about the protocol suite used on the Internet, TCP/IP. It's by far the most common protocol in use worldwide today. We started with TCP/IP structure. It's a modular suite that follows the DOD model, with different protocols performing unique tasks at each layer. We looked at individual protocols and their functions at the Process/Application, Host-to-Host, and Internet layers. We also discussed ports and well-known port numbers for common protocols.

Next, you learned about IP addressing. We started with a brief tutorial on converting binary numbers to decimal to make them easier to read. Then we looked at the different address classes, DHCP and DNS, public vs. private IP addresses, APIPA, and NAT. Each of these services and concepts play a unique role in managing TCP/IP on your network.

We finished the chapter by looking at the next generation of TCP/IP, IPv6. We talked about the seemingly infinite number of addresses, as well as the fact that addresses are written in hexadecimal, which might take some getting used to for experienced technicians. Finally, we looked at working with IPv6 addresses, including shorthand notation and special addresses to be aware of.

Exam Essentials

Understand how IPv4 addressing works.   IP addresses are 32-bit addresses written as four octets in dotted-decimal notation, such as 192.168.5.18. To communicate on an IP network, a host also needs a subnet mask, which may look something like 255.255.255.0.

Understand how IPv6 addressing works.   IPv6 addresses are 128-bit addresses written as eight fields of four hexadecimal characters, such as 2001:0db8:3c4d:0012:0000:0000:1234:56ab. Using shorthand conventions, this address can also be written as 2001:db8:3c4d:12::1234:56ab.

Know what DHCP and DNS do.   On TCP/IP networks, the DHCP server can provide IP configuration information to hosts. A DNS server resolves hostnames to IP addresses.

Know common TCP/IP ports.   Some common protocol and port pairings you should know are HTTP (80), FTP (20 and 21), POP3 (110), SMTP (25), Telnet (23), and HTTPS (443).

Be able to identify IP address classes.   Know how to identify Class A, B, and C IP addresses. Class A addresses will have a *first octet* in the 1 to 126 range. B is from 128 to 191, and C is from 192 to 223.

Know what the private IP addresses ranges are.   Private IP addresses will be in one of three ranges: 10.0.0.0/8, 172.16.0.0/16, or 192.168.0.0/16.

Know what the APIPA range is.   IP addresses in the 169.254.0.0/16 range are APIPA addresses.

Review Questions

The answers to the Chapter Review Questions can be found in Appendix A.

1. You have just set up a network that will use the TCP/IP protocol, and you want client computers to automatically obtain IP configuration information. Which type of server do you need for this?

   A. DNS

   B. DHCP

   C. Domain controller

   D. IP configuration server

2. You have a computer with the IP address 171.226.18.1. What class is this address?

   A. Class A

   B. Class B

   C. Class C

   D. Not a valid IP address

3. Which TCP/IP protocol uses port 80?

   A. HTTP

   B. HTTPS

   C. Telnet

   D. POP3

4. What is the maximum number of IPv6 addresses that can be assigned to one IPv6 interface?

   A. One (unicast)

   B. Two (unicast and anycast)

   C. Three (unicast, anycast, and multicast)

   D. None of the above

5. Which of the following are valid examples of IPv6 addresses? (Choose two.)

   A. 2001:0db8:3c4d:0012:0000:0000:1234:56ab

   B. ::ffff:c0a8:173

   C. 2001:db8:3c4d:12::1234:56ab

   D. 2001::1ab4::5468

6. Which of the following IP addresses would not be valid for a DNS server on the Internet?

   A. 10.25.11.33

   B. 18.33.66.254

   C. 155.118.63.11

   D. 192.186.12.2

7. The workstations on your network are configured to use a DHCP server. One of the workstations can't communicate with other computers. Its IP address is 169.254.1.18. What could be the problem?

   A. The subnet mask is wrong.

   B. It has a private IP address.

   C. The default gateway is wrong.

   D. It can't reach the DHCP server.

8. Which of the following protocols is responsible for sending email?

   A. IMAP4

   B. POP3

   C. SMTP

   D. SNMP

9. What port does the RDP protocol work on?

   A. 53

   B. 143

   C. 389

   D. 3389

10. Which two TCP/IP protocols work at the Host-to-Host layer of the DOD model? (Choose two.)

   A. IP

   B. ARP

   C. TCP

   D. UDP

11. What are two advantages that TCP has over UDP? (Choose two.)

   A. Acknowledged delivery

   B. Faster delivery

   C. Lower overhead

   D. Virtual circuits

12. Your friend is concerned about the security of making an online purchase. What should you tell him to look for in the address bar of the web browser?

   A. HTTP

   B. HTTPS

   C. SSH

   D. SFTP

13. You are manually configuring a TCP/IP host. Another administrator gives you the router's IP address. What is the TCP/IP term for this?

   A. Default gateway

   B. Subnet mask

   C. DNS server

   D. DHCP server

14. Your network is running IPv4. Which of the configuration options are mandatory for your host to communicate on the network? (Choose two.)

   A. IP address

   B. Subnet mask

   C. Default gateway

   D. DNS server address

15. Which of the following protocols is used for secure delivery of email?

   A. SMTP

   B. SNMP

   C. POP3

   D. IMAP4

16. Which protocol was developed to be a secure alternative to Telnet?

   A. SMB

   B. SSH

   C. SNMP

   D. SFTP

17. Which of the following protocols uses TCP port 23?

   A. Telnet

   B. SSH

   C. FTP

   D. DNS

18. Which of the following is an IPv6 broadcast address?

   A. ::1

   B. FE80::

   C. FF00::

   D. ::FFFF

   E. None of the above

19. You are setting up a small network that will not connect to the Internet. You want computers to be able to locate each other by using hostnames. What service will do this?

  A. DNS

  B. DHCP

  C. FTP

  D. APIPA

20. Which of the following protocols is responsible for resolving IP addresses to hardware addresses?

  A. DNS

  B. DHCP

  C. ARP

  D. RARP

Performance-Based Question

On the A+ exams, you will encounter performance-based questions. The questions on the exam require you to perform a specific task, and you will be graded on whether you were able to complete the task. The following require you to think creatively to measure how well you understand this chapter's topics. You may or may not see similar questions on the actual A+ exams. To see how your answers compare to the authors', refer to Appendix B.

You need to use Internet Explorer 8 to connect to the ftp.domain.com FTP site. The username is *jsmith* and the password is *getfiles*. What would you type into the address window to access this ftp site?

Chapter

8

Installing Wireless and SOHO Networks

THE FOLLOWING COMPTIA A+ 220-801 CERTIFICATION EXAM OBJECTIVES ARE COVERED IN THIS CHAPTER:

✓ **2.5 Compare and contrast wireless networking standards and encryption types.**

- Standards: 802.11 a/b/g/n; Speeds, distances, and frequencies
- Encryption types: WEP, WPA, WPA2, TKIP, AES

✓ **2.6 Install, configure, and deploy a SOHO wireless/wired router using appropriate settings.**

- MAC filtering
- Channels (1–11)
- Port forwarding, port triggering
- SSID broadcast (on/off)
- Wireless encryption
- Firewall
- DHCP (on/off)
- DMZ
- NAT
- WPS
- Basic QoS

✓ **2.7 Compare and contrast Internet connection types and features.**

- Cable
- DSL
- Dial-up

- Fiber
- Satellite
- ISDN
- Cellular (mobile hotspot)
- Line of sight wireless internet service
- WiMAX

Over the last two chapters we've talked a lot about foundational networking knowledge. We've discussed theoretical networking models, physical topologies, cables and connectors, and connectivity devices. We also spent an entire chapter devoted to the most common protocol of all, TCP/IP. The one critical technology we haven't covered yet is wireless networking.

Because of the unique technology of wireless networking and its huge spike in popularity, it feels appropriate to talk about it as a separate entity. That said, it's important to remember that wireless networking is just like wired networking only without the wires. You still need to figure out how to get resources connected to each other and give the right people access while keeping the bad people at bay. You're now just playing the game with slightly different rules and many new challenges.

We'll start this chapter off with the last of our key networking "theory" discussions, this one on wireless networking standards and encryption methods. From there, we'll move on to setting up and configuring small networks. This is really where the rubber meets the road. Understanding the theory and technical specifications of networking is fine, but the true value in all of this knowledge comes in being able to make good recommendations and implement the right network for your client's needs.

Understanding Wireless Networking

No area of networking has seen as rapid an ascent as wireless networking has over the last few years. What used to be slow and unreliable is now fast and pretty stable, not to mention convenient. It seems like everywhere you go these days there are Internet cafés or fast food restaurants with wireless hotspots. Even many mobile phones sold today have Internet capabilities. No matter where you go, you're likely just seconds away from being connected to the Grid.

The most common term you'll hear thrown around referring to wireless networking today is *WiFi*. While the term was originally coined as a marketing name for 802.11b, it's now used as a nickname referring to the family of IEEE 802.11 standards. That family comprises the primary wireless networking technology in use today, but there are other wireless technologies out there too. You might hear about Bluetooth, cellular, infrared, or WiMax. Each of these standards has its strengths and weaknesses and fills a role in computing. The A+ exam covers only 802.11 though, so that's what we'll primarily focus on here.

As a technician, it will fall to you to provide users with access to the Grid. You must make sure that their computers and mobile devices can connect and they can get their email and that downtime is something that resides only in history books. To be able to make that a reality, you must understand as much as you can about networking and the topics discussed in the following sections, where we'll take an in-depth look at the 802.11 standards. After that, we'll spend some time on wireless security features as well.

802.11 Networking Standards

In the United States, wireless LAN (WLAN) standards are created and managed by the Institute of Electrical and Electronics Engineers (IEEE). The most commonly used WLAN standards used today are in the IEEE 802.11 family. Eventually, 802.11 will likely be made obsolete by newer standards such as 802.16 or 802.20, but that is some time off. IEEE 802.11 was ratified in 1997 and was the first standardized WLAN implementation. There are over 20 802.11 standards defined, but you will only see a few in common operation: 802.11a, b, g, and n. As mentioned in the introduction, there are several wireless technologies on the market, but 802.11 is the one currently best suited for WLANs.

In concept, an 802.11 network is similar to an Ethernet network, only wireless. At the center of Ethernet networks is a connectivity device such as a hub, switch, or router, and all computers connect to it. Wireless networks are configured in a similar fashion, except they use a wireless router or wireless access point instead of a wired connectivity device. In order to connect to the wireless hub or router, the client needs to know the *service-set identifier (SSID)* of the device. Wireless access points may connect to other wireless access points, but eventually they connect back to a wired connection with the rest of the network.

802.11 networks use the *Carrier Sense Multiple Access/Collision Avoidance (CSMA/CA)* access method instead of Ethernet's Carrier Sense Multiple Access/Collision Detection (CSMA/CD). Packet collisions are generally avoided, but when they do happen, the sender will need to wait a random period of time (called a *back-off time*) before transmitting again.

Since the original 802.11 standard was published in 1997, there have been several upgrades and extensions of the standard released.

802.11

The original *802.11* standard defines WLANs transmitting at 1Mbps or 2Mbps bandwidths using the 2.4GHz frequency spectrum and using either frequency-hopping spread spectrum (FHSS) or direct-sequence spread spectrum (DSSS) for data encoding.

802.11a

The *802.11a* standard provides WLAN bandwidth of up to 54Mbps in the 5GHz frequency spectrum. The 802.11a standard also uses a more efficient encoding system, orthogonal frequency division multiplexing (OFDM), rather than FHSS or DSSS.

This standard was ratified in 1999, but devices didn't hit the market until 2001. Thanks to its encoding system, it was significantly faster than 802.11b (discussed next), but never gained widespread popularity. They were ratified as standards right around the same time, but 802.11b devices beat it to market and were significantly cheaper. Today you will see very few 802.11a devices out in the wild.

802.11b

The *802.11b* standard was ratified in 1999 as well, but device makers were much quicker to market, making this standard the de facto wireless networking standard for several years. 802.11b provides for bandwidths of up to 11Mbps (with fallback rates of 5.5, 2, and 1Mbps) in the 2.4GHz range. The 802.11b standard uses DSSS for data encoding.

The 802.11b and 802.11a standards are incompatible for two reasons: frequency and modulation. 802.11b operates in the 2.4GHz frequency and uses DSSS. 802.11a runs at 5GHz and uses OFDM.

802.11g

Ratified in 2003, the *802.11g* standard provides for bandwidths of 54Mbps in the 2.4GHz frequency spectrum using OFDM or DSSS encoding. Because it operates in the same frequency and can use the same modulation as 802.11b, the two standards are compatible. Because of the backward compatibility and speed upgrades, 802.11g is the most common standard you'll see in use today.

Devices on the market that can operate with both 802.11b and 802.11g standards are labeled as 802.11b/g.

As we mentioned, 802.11g devices are backward compatible with legacy 802.11b devices, and both can be used on the same network. That was initially a huge selling point for 802.11g hardware and helped it gain popularity very quickly. However, you should know that there are some interoperability concerns to be aware of. 802.11b devices are not capable of understanding OFDM transmissions; therefore, they are not able to tell when the 802.11g access point is free or busy. To counteract this problem, when an 802.11b device is associated with an 802.11g access point, the access point reverts back to DSSS modulation to provide backward compatibility. This means that all devices connected to that access point will run at a maximum of 11Mbps. To optimize performance, you should upgrade to all 802.11g devices and set the access point to G-only.

One additional concept you need to know about when working with 2.4GHz wireless networking is channels. We've said before that b/g works in the 2.4GHz range. Within this range, the FCC has defined 14 different 22MHz communication channels. An illustration of this is shown in Figure 8.1.

Although 14 channels have been defined, you're only allowed to configure your wireless networking devices to the first 11. When you install a wireless access point and wireless NICs, they will all auto-configure their channel and this will probably work okay for you. If you are experiencing interference, changing the channel might help. And if you have multiple, overlapping wireless access points, you will need to have non-overlapping channels. (We'll talk about this more in the section "Installing and Configuring SOHO Networks" later in this chapter.) The three non-overlapping channels are 1, 6, and 11.

FIGURE 8.1   2.4GHz communication channels

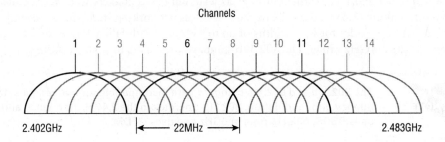

802.11n

The most recent standard to hit the market is *802.11n*, which was ratified in 2010. The standard claims to provide for bandwidth up to 600Mbps, which sounds pretty fast. It works in both the 2.4GHz and 5GHz ranges.

802.11n achieves faster throughput a couple of ways. Some of the enhancements include the use of 40MHz channels, multiple-input multiple-output (MIMO), and channel bonding. Remember how 802.11g uses 22MHz channels? 802.11n combines two channels to (basically) double the throughput. MIMO means using multiple antennas rather than a single antenna to communicate information. (802.11n devices can support up to eight antennas.) Channel bonding allows the device to simultaneously communicate at 2.4GHz and 5GHz and bond the data streams, which increases throughput.

One big advantage to 802.11n is that it is backward compatible with 802.11a/b/g. This is because 802.11n is capable of simultaneously servicing 802.11b/g/n clients operating in the 2.4GHz range as well as 802.11a/n clients operating in the 5GHz range.

Table 8.1 summarizes the 802.11 standards we discussed here.

TABLE 8.1   802.11 standards

Type	Frequency	Maximum Data Rate	Modulation	Indoor Range	Outdoor Range
	2.4GHz	2Mbps	FHSS/DSSS	20m	100m
a	5GHz	54Mbps	OFDM	35m	120m
b	2.4GHz	11Mbps	DSSS	40m	140m
g	2.4GHz	54Mbps	DSSS/OFDM	40m	140m
n	2.4/5GHz	600Mbps	DSSS/OFDM	70m	250m

The ranges provided in Table 8.1 are approximate and may differ based on your environment. For example, thick walls and steel beams will dramatically reduce your range.

Also keep in mind that when discussing ranges, the further away from the WAP you get, the lower your connection speed will be. For example, to get 54Mbps out of your 802.11g router, you need to be within about 100 feet of it. At the far end of its range, your throughput will be only about 6Mbps.

Modulation Techniques

We have mentioned three signal modulation techniques used in the 802.11 standards. Here is how the three in common use today work:

Frequency-hopping spread spectrum (FHSS)   FHSS accomplishes communication by hopping the transmission over a range of predefined frequencies. The changing, or hopping, is synchronized between both ends and appears to be a single transmission channel to both ends.

Direct-sequence spread spectrum (DSSS)   DSSS accomplishes communication by adding the data that is to be transmitted to a higher-speed transmission. The higher-speed transmission contains redundant information to ensure data accuracy. Each packet can then be reconstructed in the event of a disruption.

Orthogonal frequency division multiplexing (OFDM)   OFDM accomplishes communication by breaking the data into subsignals and transmitting them simultaneously. These transmissions occur on different frequencies or subbands.

The mathematics and theories of these transmission technologies are beyond the scope of this book and far beyond the scope of this exam.

 There are many other commercial devices that transmit at the frequencies at which 802.11 operates. When this happens, there can be a lot of interference. Older Bluetooth devices, cordless phones, cell phones, other WLANs, and microwave ovens can all create interference problems for 802.11 networks.

802.11 Devices

If you think about a standard wired network and the devices required on such a network, you can easily determine what types of devices are available for 802.11 networks. Network cards come in a variety of shapes and sizes, including USB and PCMCIA Type II models and wireless print servers for your printers. As for connectivity devices, the most common are wireless routers (as shown in Figure 8.2) and a type of hub called a *wireless access point (WAP)*. WAPs look nearly identical to wireless routers and provide central connectivity like wireless routers, but they don't have nearly as many features. The main one most people worry about is Internet connection sharing. You can share an Internet connection using a wireless router but not with a WAP.

FIGURE 8.2 Wireless router

Most wireless routers and WAPs also have wired ports for RJ-45 connectors. The router shown in Figure 8.2 has four wired connections, but they are on the back side of the device (meaning you can't see them in the figure).

Wireless Encryption Methods

The growth of wireless systems has created several opportunities for attackers. These systems are relatively new, they use well-established communications mechanisms, and they're easily intercepted. Wireless controllers such as 802.11 routers use SSIDs to allow communications with a specific access point. The SSID is basically the network name. Because by default wireless routers will broadcast their SSID, all someone with a wireless client needs to do is search for an available signal. If it's not secured, they can connect within a few seconds.

You can configure the router to not broadcast and then manually set up your clients with the SSID of the device. But using this type of SSID configuration doesn't necessarily prevent your wireless network from being compromised.

We'll discuss more on SSIDs and configuring your wireless routers to be more secure than their default settings in the section "Installing and Configuring SOHO Networks" later in this chapter.

A more effective way of securing your network is to use one of the several encryption methods available. Examples of these are WEP, WPA, and WPA2, which we discuss next.

WEP

Wired Equivalency Protocol (WEP) was one of the first security standards for wireless devices. WEP encrypts data to provide data security. It uses a static key; the client needs to know the right key to gain communication through a WEP-enabled device. The keys are commonly 10, 26, or 58 hexadecimal characters long.

 You may see the use of the notation WEP.*x*, which refers to the key size; 64-bit and 128-bit are the most widely used, and 256-bit keys are supported by some vendors (WEP.64, WEP.128, and WEP.256). WEP.64 uses a 10-character key. WEP.128 uses 26 characters, and WEP.256 uses 58.

The protocol has always been under scrutiny for not being as secure as initially intended. WEP is vulnerable due to the nature of static keys and weaknesses in the encryption algorithms. These weaknesses allow the algorithm to potentially be cracked in a very short amount of time—no more than two or three minutes. This makes WEP one of the more vulnerable protocols available for security.

Because of security weaknesses and the availability of newer protocols, WEP is not used widely. It's still better than nothing though, and it does an adequate job of keeping casual snoops at bay. If you were setting up a home network and wanted a quick and easy security method, it works just fine.

WPA

WiFi Protected Access (WPA) is an improvement on WEP that was first available in 1999 but did not see widespread acceptance until around 2003. Once it became widely available, the WiFi Alliance recommended that networks no longer use WEP in favor of WPA.

This standard was the first to implement some of the features defined in the IEEE 802.11i security specification. Most notably among them was the use of the *Temporal Key Integrity Protocol (TKIP)*. Whereas WEP used a static 40- or 128-bit key, TKIP uses a 128-bit dynamic per-packet key. It generates a new key for each packet sent. WPA also introduced message integrity checking.

When WPA was introduced to the market, it was intended to be a temporary solution to wireless security. The provisions of 802.11i had already been drafted, and a standard that employed all of the security recommendations was in development. The upgraded standard would eventually be known as WPA2.

WPA2

Even though their names might make you assume that WPA and WPA2 are very similar, they are quite different in structure. *WiFi Protected Access 2 (WPA2)* is a huge improvement over WEP and WPA. As mentioned earlier, it implements all of the required elements of the 802.11i security standard. Most notably, it uses Counter Mode CBC-MAC Protocol (CCMP), which is a protocol based on the *Advanced Encryption Standard (AES)* security algorithm. CCMP was created to address the shortcomings of TKIP, so consequently it's much stronger than TKIP.

The terms *CCMP* and *AES* tend to be interchangeable in common parlance. You might also see it written as *AES-CCMP*.

Since 2006, wireless devices have been required to support WPA2 to be certified as WiFi compliant. Of the wireless security options available today, it provides the strongest encryption and data protection.

Installing and Configuring SOHO Networks

Nearly every small office has a network, and it seems like most homes these days have one or more computers that need access to the Internet. As a technician, you may be asked to set up or troubleshoot any number of these types of networks, often collectively referred to as *small office, home office (SOHO) networks*. This part of the chapter will give you the background you need to feel comfortable that you can get the job done. Most of the principles we talk about here apply to larger networks as well, so they're helpful if you're in a corporate environment too.

Before we get into installation and configuration, though, it's critical to introduce a topic that permeates this whole discussion: *planning*. Before installing a network or making changes to it, *always* plan ahead. We'll talk specifically about how to do that, but always keep planning in the back of your mind. Planning ahead of time will help you avoid many problems you could potentially run into, which will save you time in the long run.

In the following sections, we'll look at choosing connection types, network planning and installation, and configuring a wireless router.

Choosing Connection Types

You already know that for computers to talk to each other, they need to be connected in some way. This can be with physical wires or through the air with one of several wireless technologies. The type of connection you choose depends on the purpose of the connection and the needs of the user or users.

You also need to think about the future. Remember that planning concept? When choosing a connection type, think about not only what the needs are today, but what the needs of the individual or organization could be. There is no sense in going overboard and recommending a top-of-the-line expensive solution if it's not needed, but you do want to plan for expansion if that's a possibility.

For our purposes here, we'll break the connection types into two categories. First we'll look at connections designed to facilitate Internet access, and then we'll look at internal network connections.

Choosing an Internet Connection

Internet connections can be broadly broken into two categories: dial-up and broadband. It used to be that you had to weigh the pros and cons and figure out which one was best for your situation. Today, the choice is easy. Go broadband. The only time you would want to use dial-up is if broadband isn't available, and if that's the case, we're sorry!

Your Internet connection will give you online service through an *Internet service provider (ISP)*. The type of service you want will often determine who your ISP choices are. For example, if you want cable Internet, your choices are limited to your local cable companies and a few national providers. We'll outline some of the features of each type of service and discuss why you might or might not recommend a specific connection type based on the situation.

Dial-Up/POTS

One of the oldest ways of communicating with ISPs and remote networks is through dial-up connections. Although this is still possible, dial-up is not used much anymore due to limitations on modem speed, which top out at 56Kbps. Dial-up uses modems that operate over regular phone lines—that is, the *plain old telephone service (POTS)*—and cannot compare to speeds possible with DSL and cable modems. Reputable sources claim that dial-up Internet connections dropped from 74 percent of all US residential Internet connections in 2000 to 15 percent in 2008. Most of the people who still use dial-up do it because it's cheaper than broadband or high-speed access isn't available where they live.

The biggest advantage to dial-up is that it's cheap and relatively easy to configure. The only hardware you need is a modem and a phone cable. You dial in to a server (such as an ISP's server), provide a username and a password, and you're on the Internet.

Companies also have the option to grant users dial-up access to their networks. As with Internet connections, this option used to be a lot more popular than it is today. Microsoft offered a server-side product to facilitate this called Remote Access Service (RAS), as did many other companies. ISPs and RAS servers would use the Data Link layer Point-to-Point Protocol (PPP) to establish and maintain the connection.

It seems that dial-up is considered to be a relic from the Stone Age of Internet access. But there are some reasons it might be the right solution:

- The only hardware it requires is a modem and a phone cord.
- It's relatively easy to set up and configure.
- It's the cheapest online solution (usually $10 to $20 per month).
- You can use it wherever there is phone service, which is just about everywhere.

Of course, there are reasons a dial-up connection might not be appropriate. The big one is speed. If your client needs to download files or has substantial data requirements, dial-up is probably too slow. In addition, with limited bandwidth, it's really good only for one computer. It *is* possible to share a dial-up Internet connection by using software tools, but it's also possible to push a stalled car up a muddy hill. Neither option sounds like much fun.

DSL

One of the two most popular broadband choices for home use is *Digital Subscriber Line (DSL)*. It utilizes existing phone lines and provides fairly reliable high-speed access. To use DSL, you need a DSL modem (shown in Figure 8.3) and a network card in your computer. The ISP usually provides the DSL modem, but you can also purchase them in a variety of electronics stores. You use an Ethernet cable with an RJ-45 connector to plug your network card into the DSL modem (Figure 8.4) and the phone cord to plug the DSL modem into the phone outlet. Typically, you will plug the phone cord into a DSL splitter (such as the one shown in Figure 8.5) and plug the splitter into the wall. The splitter does two things for you. One, it allows you to still plug your phone into the same connection. Two, it filters the "noise" from the DSL modem so you don't hear it when you are on the phone. Your phone line will still work when you have DSL even if you don't use the splitter, but you will hear a lot of static (try it sometime!).

FIGURE 8.3   A DSL modem

  Instead of plugging your computer directly into the DSL modem, you can plug your computer into a router (such as a wireless router) and then plug the router into the DSL modem. Most phone companies will tell you that you can't (or shouldn't) do this, but if you want to connect multiple computers to the Internet and don't mind sharing the bandwidth, there is no reason not to.

There are actually several different forms of DSL, including *high bit-rate DSL (HDSL)*, *symmetric DSL (SDSL)*, *very high bit-rate DSL (VDSL)*, *rate-adaptive DSL (RADSL)*, and *asymmetric DSL (ADSL)*. The most popular in-home form of DSL is ADSL. It's asymmetrical because it supports download speeds that are faster than upload speeds. Dividing up the total available bandwidth this way makes sense because most Internet traffic is downloaded, not uploaded. Imagine a 10-lane highway. If you knew that 8 out of 10 cars that drove the highway went south, wouldn't you make eight lanes southbound and only two lanes northbound? That is essentially what ADSL does.

FIGURE 8.4 The back of the DSL modem

FIGURE 8.5 A DSL splitter

ADSL and your voice communications can work at the same time over the phone line because they use different frequencies on the same wire. Regular phone communications use frequencies from 0 to 4kHz, whereas ADSL uses frequencies in the 25.875kHz to 138kHz range for upstream traffic and in the 138kHz to 1104kHz range for downstream traffic. Figure 8.6 illustrates this.

The first ADSL standard was approved in 1998 and offered maximum download speeds of 8Mbps and upload speeds of 1Mbps. The newest standard supports speeds up to 24Mbps download and 3.5Mbps upload. In practice, the best rate plans typically offered by service providers max out at about 10Mbps to 12Mbps download and 1Mbps upload. Most ADSL communications are full-duplex.

FIGURE 8.6 Voice telephone and ADSL frequencies used

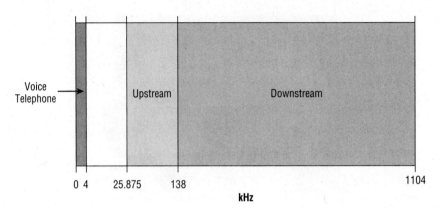

One major advantage that ADSL providers tout is that with DSL you do not share bandwidth with other customers, whereas that may not be true with cable modems.

To summarize, here are some advantages to using DSL:

- It's *much* faster than dial-up.
- Your bandwidth is not shared with other users.
- It's generally very reliable (depending on your ISP).

There are some potential disadvantages as well:

- DSL may not be available in your area. There are distance limitations as to how far away from the phone company's central office you can be to get DSL. Usually this isn't a problem in metro areas, but it could be a problem in rural areas.
- DSL requires more hardware than dial-up: a network card, network cable, a DSL modem, a phone cord, and a noise filter (the splitter). A DSL modem package usually comes with a network cable and noise filters, but many ISPs will make you pay for that package.
- The cost is higher. Lower-speed packages often start off at around $20 to $30 per month, but the ones they advertise with the great data rates can easily run you $100 a month or more.
- If you are in a house or building with older wiring, the older phone lines may not be able to support the full speed you pay for.

That said, DSL is a popular choice for both small businesses and residential offices. If it's available, it's easy to get the phone company to bundle your service with your land line and bill you at the same time. Often you'll also get a package discount for having multiple services. Most important, you can hook the DSL modem up to your router or wireless router and share the Internet connection among several computers. The phone companies don't like the fact that you can do this (they want you to pay for more access), but as of now there's not a lot they can do about it.

> To see if DSL is available in your area, go to www.dslreports.com. You can also talk to your local telephone service provider.

With many people using their cell phones as their home phones and land lines slowly fading into history, you may wonder if this causes a problem if you want DSL. Not really. Many phone providers will provide you DSL without a land line (called *naked DSL*). Of course, you are going to have to pay a surcharge for the use of the phone lines if you don't already use one.

Cable

The other half of the popular home-broadband duet is the *cable modem*. These provide high-speed Internet access through your cable service, much like DSL does over phone lines. You plug your computer into the cable modem using a standard Ethernet cable, just as you would plug into a DSL modem. The only difference is that the other connection goes into a cable TV jack instead of the phone jack. Cable Internet provides broadband Internet access via a specification known as Data Over Cable Service Internet Specification (DOCSIS). Anyone who can get a cable TV connection should be able to get the service.

As advertised, cable Internet connections are faster than DSL connections. You'll see a wide variety of claimed speeds; some cable companies offer packages with download speeds up to 30Mbps, 50Mbps, or even 100Mbps and uploads of 5Mbps. (For business customers, download speeds can be 400Mbps.) If it's that fast, why wouldn't everyone choose it? While cable generally is faster, a big caveat to these speeds is that they are not guaranteed and they can vary.

One of the reasons that speeds may vary is that you are sharing available bandwidth within your distribution network. The size of the network varies, but is usually between 100 and 2,000 customers. Some of them may have cable modems too, and access can be slower during peak usage times. Another reason is that cable companies make liberal use of bandwidth throttling. If you read the fine print on some of their packages that promise the fast speeds, one of the technical details is that they boost your download speed for the first 10MB or 20MB of a file transfer, and then they throttle your speed back down to your normal rate.

To see how this could affect everyone's speed on the shared bandwidth, let's think about a simplified example. Let's say that two users (Sally and John) are sharing a connection that has a maximum capacity of 40Mbps. For the sake of argument, let's assume that they are the only two users and that they share the bandwidth equally. That would mean normally each person gets 20Mbps of bandwidth. If Sally gets a boost that allows her to download 30Mbps, for however long, that leaves John with only 10Mbps of available bandwidth. If John is used to having 20Mbps, that 10Mbps is going to seem awfully slow.

While it may seem as though we are down on cable modems, you just need to understand exactly what you and your customers are getting. In practice, the speeds of a cable modem are pretty comparable to those of DSL. Both have pros and cons when it comes to reliability and speed of service, but a lot of that varies by service provider and isn't necessarily reflective of the technology. When it comes right down to it, the choice you make between DSL and cable (if both are available in your area) may depend on which company you get the best package deal from: phone and DSL through your telephone company or cable TV and cable modem from your cable provider.

To summarize, here are the advantages to using cable:

- It's *much* faster than dial-up, and it can be faster than DSL (particularly for uploads).

- You're not required to have or use a telephone land line.

- It's generally very reliable (depending on your ISP).

As with anything else, there are possible disadvantages:

- Cable may not be available in your area. In metro areas this normally isn't a problem, but it could be in rural areas.

- Cable requires more hardware than dial-up: a network card, network cable, and a cable modem. Most ISPs will charge you a one-time fee or a monthly lease fee for the cable modem.

- Your bandwidth is shared with everyone on your network segment, usually a neighborhood-sized group of homes. Everyone shares the available bandwidth. During peak times, your access speed may slow down.

- Security could be an issue. Essentially you are on a LAN with all the neighbors in your cable segment. Thus, if you (or your cable company) don't protect your connection, theoretically you could see your neighbors' computers and they could see yours. This usually isn't a problem anymore, but know that it is a possibility.

- The cost is higher. Lower-speed packages often start off at around $20 to $30 per month, but the ones they advertise with the great data rates can easily run you $100 a month or more.

Cable modems can be connected directly to a computer but can also be connected to a router or wireless router just as a DSL modem. Therefore, you can share an Internet connection over a cable modem.

For detailed information about cable Internet availability and performance, check out www.highspeedinternet.net.

Integrated Services Digital Network (ISDN)

Integrated Services Digital Network (ISDN) is a digital, point-to-point network capable of maximum transmission speeds of about 2Mbps, although speeds of 128Kbps are more common. ISDN uses the same two-pair UTP wiring as POTS (but it can transmit data at much higher speeds). That's where the similarity ends. What makes ISDN different from a regular POTS line is how it uses the copper wiring. Instead of carrying an analog (voice) signal, it carries digital signals. While not nearly as fast as other broadband services, it still is considered a broadband type of access.

A computer connects to an ISDN line via an *ISDN terminal adapter* (often referred to as an *ISDN TA* or an *ISDN modem*). Like DSL and cable modems, an ISDN terminal adapter is not an actual modem because it does not convert a digital signal to an analog signal; ISDN signals are digital. Computers also need a *network terminator* to connect to the ISDN TA, but most TAs have them built in. If you have multiple users on the network who need Internet access through the ISDN line, you need an ISDN router.

An ISDN line has two types of channels. The data is carried on a channel called a *Bearer channel*, or *B channel*, which can carry 64Kbps of data. The second type of channel is used for call setup and link management and is known as the *signal channel*, or *D channel*. This channel has only 16Kbps of bandwidth. A typical 144Kbps *basic rate interface (BRI)* ISDN line has two B channels and one D channel. One B channel can be used for a voice call while the other is being used for data transmissions, or both can be used for data. When the B channels are combined to maximize data throughput (which is common), the process is called *bonding* or *inverse multiplexing*. Multiple BRI ISDN lines can also be bonded together to form higher throughput channels.

BRI ISDN is also known as 2B+D because of the number and type of channels used. BRI ISDN is more common in Europe than it is in the United States.

You can also obtain a *primary rate interface (PRI)*, also known as 23B+D, which means it has 23 B channels and one D channel. The total bandwidth of a 23B+D ISDN line is 1536Kbps (23 B channels × 64Kbps per channel + 64Kbps for the D channel). This is typically carried on a dedicated T1 connection and is fairly popular in the United States.

The main advantages of ISDN are as follows:

- The connection is faster than dial-up.

- It runs over phone lines.

- It's flexible. Each B channel can support voice or data. If you have a BRI ISDN connection, you can have two separate voice conversations happening at once, two datastreams, a voice conversation and a data stream, or both channels bridged into one.

- Support for video teleconferencing is easy to obtain.

- There is no conversion from digital to analog.

However, ISDN does have a few disadvantages:

- It's more expensive than POTS.

- You need an ISDN modem and perhaps an ISDN router.

- ISDN is a type of dial-up connection and therefore the connection must be initiated before use.

BRI ISDN connections were starting to become popular in home applications in the mid- to late-1990s as an alternative to dial-up before broadband really took off. Today you'll rarely see it used in a home, but it's occasionally used in an office. You will find PRI ISDN to be more common in office environments. BRI rates start at about $20 to $40 per month, while PRI solutions typically start in the $300-per-month range.

If you need a dedicated Internet connection, which will serve as an Internet-only connection, then one of the other broadband services is likely a better choice. If you want a line that can support both Internet and voice and provide flexibility to go between the two, then ISDN could be the right solution (although VoIP could be as well—but that is beyond the scope of this chapter).

Fiber-Optic Internet

Fiber-optic cable is pretty impressive with the speed and bandwidth it delivers. For nearly all of fiber-optic cable's existence, it's been used mostly for high-speed telecommunications and network backbones. This is because it is much more expensive than copper to install and operate. The cables themselves are pricier, and so is the hardware at the end of the cables.

Technology follows this inevitable path of getting cheaper the longer it exists, and fiber is really starting to embrace its destiny. Some phone and media companies are now offering fiber-optic Internet connections for home subscribers.

An example of one such option is FiOS, offered by Verizon. It offers *Fiber-to-the-Home (FTTH)* service, which means that the cables are 100 percent fiber from their data centers to your home. At the time we were writing this book, the fastest speeds offered were 150Mbps download and 35Mbps upload. That means you could download a two-hour HD movie in about four and a half minutes. That's sick. What's even better is that 400Mbps implementations are being planned.

Other companies may offer a service called *Fiber-to-the-Node (FTTN)*, sometimes called Fiber to the Curb. This runs fiber to the phone or cable company's utility box near the street and then runs copper from there to your house. Maximum speeds for this type of service are around 25Mbps. These options are probably best suited for small businesses or home offices with significant data requirements, unless online gaming is *really* important to you.

Some cable companies promise a high-speed, fiber-optic connection for your TV cable as well as cable Internet service. In the vast majority of cases, the fiber is FTTN, and the fiber runs only from their network to the junction box at the entrance to your neighborhood or possibly to your curb. From there, the cable is coaxial copper. If you're paying for a fiber connection, be sure you're actually *getting* a fiber connection.

Are there any downsides to a fiber Internet connection? Really only two come to mind. The first is availability. It's still pretty spotty on where you can get it. The second is price. That great 150Mbps connection will run you about $200 a month.

Satellite

One type of broadband Internet connection that does not get much fanfare is satellite Internet. *Satellite Internet* is not much like any other type of broadband connection. Instead of a cabled connection, it uses a satellite dish to receive data from an orbiting satellite and relay station that is connected to the Internet. Satellite connections are typically a lot slower than wired broadband connections, often maxing out at around 4Mbps.

The need for a satellite dish and the reliance upon its technology is one of the major drawbacks to satellite Internet. People who own satellite dishes will tell you that there are occasional problems due to weather and satellite alignment. You must keep the satellite dish aimed precisely at the satellite or your signal strength (and thus your connection reliability and speed) will suffer. Plus, cloudy or stormy days can cause interference with the signal, especially if there are high winds that could blow the satellite dish out of alignment. Receivers are typically small satellite dishes (like the ones used for DirecTV or DishNetwork) but can also be portable satellite modems (modems the size of a briefcase) or portable satellite phones.

Satellite Internet is often referred to as "line of sight" wireless because it does require a clear line of sight between the user and the transmitter.

Another drawback to satellite technology is the delay (also called *propagation delay*), or *latency*. The delay occurs because of the length of time required to transmit the data and receive a response via the satellite. This delay (between 250 and 350 milliseconds) comes from the time it takes the data to travel the approximately 35,000 kilometers into space and return. To compare it with other types of broadband signals, cable and DSL have a delay between customer and ISP of 10 to 30 milliseconds. With standard web and email traffic, this delay, while slightly annoying, is acceptable. However, with technologies like VoIP and live Internet gaming, the delay is intolerable.

Online gamers are especially sensitive to propagation delay. They often refer to it as *ping time*. The higher the ping time (in milliseconds), the worse the response time in the game. It sometimes means the difference between winning and losing an online game.

Of course, satellite also has advantages or no one would use it. First, satellite connections are incredibly useful when you are in an area where it's difficult or impossible to run a cable or if your Internet access needs are mobile and cellular data rates just don't cut it.

The second advantage is due to the nature of the connection. This type of connection is called *point-to-multipoint* because one satellite can provide a signal to a number of receivers simultaneously. It's used in a variety of applications from telecommunications and handheld GPSs to television and radio broadcasts and a host of others.

Here are a few considerations to keep in mind regarding satellite:

Installation can be tricky.   When installing a satellite system, you need to ensure that the satellite dish on the ground is pointed at precisely the right spot in the sky. This can be tricky to do if you're not trained, but some have a utility that helps you see how close you are to being right on (you're getting warmer… warmer…).

Line of sight is required.   Satellite communications also require line of sight. A tree between you and your orbiting partner will cause problems. Rain and other atmospheric conditions can cause problems as well.

Latency can be a problem.   Because of the long distance the message must travel, satellites can be subject to long latency times. While it happens with wired connections, it disproportionately affects satellite transmissions. Have you ever watched a national news channel when a reporter is reporting from some location halfway across the world? The anchor behind the desk will ask a question, and the reporter will nod, and nod, and finally about five excruciating seconds after the anchor is done, the reporter will start to answer. That's latency.

Most satellite connections are also pretty slow compared to the other broadband methods. Average speed for downloads is often 256Kbps to 1.5Mbps, and uploads are in the 128Kbps to 256Kbps range. In addition, many providers set thresholds on the amount of data you can download per month. Going over that amount can result in extra charges.

 Real World Scenario

All in the Name of Entertainment

Several years ago (and we do mean several) as a teenager, one of the authors worked for a local television station during the summers. Each summer, the television station would broadcast a Senior PGA golf tournament that was held on a nearby mountain course.

Before the tournament, the crew would spend three days setting up the control truck, cameras, and link back to the station. (It was a network with TV cameras instead of workstations!) Because of the remote location, the crew had to set up a satellite uplink to get the signals back to civilization. From the control truck, a transmitter was pointed at a relay station on the side of the mountain, which in turn was pointed at a satellite orbiting the earth. It took a team of four engineers to get it set up. Two engineers would stay at the truck, and two others would board ATVs and journey up the remote mountainside. Once in position, they would set up the relay station, which looked a lot like a keg of beer with a few antennas. The engineers at the truck would adjust their directional microwave transmitter until the relay station received a strong signal. Then the engineers on the mountainside would perform the arduous task of pointing their transmitter at the satellite.

It was a long and tedious process, and that's really the point of the story. Satellite was the *only* option available to complete the network, but satellite networks can be a challenge to set up and configure.

Cellular (Cellular WAN)

The cell phone, once a clunky brick-like status symbol of the well-to-do, is now pervasive in our society. It seems that everyone—from kindergarteners to 80-year-old grandmothers—has a cell. The industry has revolutionized the way we communicate and, some say, contributed to furthering an attention-deficit-disorder-like, instant-gratification-hungry society. In fact, the line between cell phones and computers has blurred significantly with all of the new smartphones on the market. It used to be that the Internet was reserved for "real" computers, but now anyone can be online at almost any time.

Regardless of your feelings about cell phones, whether you are fanatical about checking in every time you visit a local eatery to ensure you're the "mayor" or you long for the good old days when you could escape your phone because it had a functional radius as long as your cord, you need to understand the basics of cell technology.

CELLULAR TECHNICAL SPECIFICATIONS

There are two major cell standards in the United States. The *Global System for Mobile Communications (GSM)* is the most popular, boasting over 1.5 billion users in 210 countries. The other standard is *Code Division Multiple Access (CDMA)*, which was developed by Qualcomm and is available only in the United States. GSM and CDMA are not compatible with each other.

GSM uses a variety of bands to transmit. The most popular are 900MHz and 1800MHz, but 400MHz, 450MHz, and 850MHz are also used. Because of this, an individual GSM phone might not be fully compatible with all of the GSM networks in the world. GSM splits up its channels by time division, in a process called Time Division Multiple Access (TDMA).

The maximum rate for GSM is about 270 kilobits per second (Kbps). While this is incredibly low based on current networking standards, it's ample for voice communications. The maximum functional distance of GSM is about 22 miles (35 kilometers). For security, GSM uses the A5/1 and A5/2 stream ciphers.

A newer enhancement to GSM is called General Packet Radio Service (GPRS). It's designed to provide data transmissions over a GSM network at up to 171Kbps.

CDMA is considered superior to GSM because it doesn't break up its channels by time but rather by a code inserted into the communicated message. This allows for multiple transmissions to occur at the same time without interference. CDMA was first used by the English in World War II, and today it is used in global positioning systems (GPSs) as well.

Takeoffs of the CDMA technology include Wideband Code Division Multiple Access (W-CDMA), CDMA2000, and Evolution Data Optimized (EVDO). EVDO rev B supports peak download rates of 14.7Mbps. Not only does CDMA have better transmission speeds than GSM, it works in ranges up to 100 kilometers.

MOBILE HOTSPOTS

Many cell phone providers offer network cards (or they will incorrectly call them modems) that allow your laptop computer or other device to connect to the Internet from anywhere you can get a cell signal. Some will bundle that service with your normal monthly cell service at no additional charge, while others will charge you an incremental fee. The term you'll hear a lot in connection with this is *MiFi*. Figure 8.7 shows a Verizon MiFi hotspot.

FIGURE 8.7   MiFi hotspot

What Is 3G?

Whenever you turn on the TV, you can't help but be bombarded with commercials (if you don't fast-forward through them) from cell providers pitching the fastest or widest or whatever-est 3G network. What does it all mean?

To be specific, 3G refers to a generation of standards for mobile phones and telecommunication services that fulfill the International Mobile Telecommunications-2000 (IMT-2000) specifications as adopted by the International Telecommunication Union (ITU). In more practical terms, it's simply a standard for wireless telephone, Internet, video, and mobile TV. To meet IMT-2000 standards, the service must provide peak data rates of at least 200Kbps.

There are two major branches of 3G standards worldwide. The first is Universal Mobile Telecommunications System (UMTS), which is used in Europe, Japan, and China. It's basically an outgrowth of the GSM standard. The second is CDMA2000, which is used in the United States and South Korea.

Believe it or not, there actually were 1G and 2G standards as well. You probably just never heard anything about them. Now that you understand 3G, just wait. Historically, the ITU releases new standards about every 10 years, and 4G devices are now on the market!

A MiFi card such as this allows you to connect up to five WiFi-enabled devices (802.11b/g) as a MiFi cloud to get Internet access. The connection the MiFi card will make back to the cell phone provider will most likely be EVDO based.

After you purchase a MiFi device, you first connect it to your laptop via USB cable for activation and setup. Once that step is complete, you can go entirely wireless. MiFi supports WiFi security such as WEP, WPA, and WPA2.

WiMAX

We mentioned that 4G technologies are here, and *World Wide Interoperability for Microwave Access (WiMAX)* is the first example. In concept, think about WiMAX as a fast network run over cell towers. Because of its acronym, a lot of people think of WiMAX as WiFi's big brother, but that's not actually very accurate. First, WiMAX is based on IEEE 802.16, not IEEE 802.11. Second, WiMAX was intended to be an alternative to DSL or cable modems as an Internet access method, whereas WiFi is clearly entrenched as a LAN standard. WiMAX has seen its greatest successes so far in MAN-type settings and has a practical range of about 5 miles.

There are a few problems with WiMAX. First, it's not backward compatible with existing 2G and 3G technologies. Second, while it's relatively fast (5Mbps to 6Mbps downloads and 2Mbps to 3Mbps uploads), it's not as fast as originally promised. Third, it costs a lot and requires a lot of power.

A competitive technology called Long Term Evolution (LTE) actually looks to be a more promising 4G alternative. It's faster than WiMAX (up to 12Mbps down and 5Mbps up), backward compatible with 3G and WiMAX, and more stable than WiMAX. As this book was being written, the newest TV commercials for smartphones talked about 4G LTE service.

Table 8.2 summarizes the connection types we have just discussed.

TABLE 8.2   Common Internet connection types and speeds

Designation	Download Speed Range	Description
Dial-up	2400bps to 56Kbps	Plain old telephone service. A regular analog phone line.
DSL	256Kbps to 12Mbps	Digital subscriber line. Shares existing phone wires with voice service.
Cable	128Kbps to 50Mbps	Inexpensive broadband Internet access method with wide availability.
ISDN	64Kbps to 1.5Mbps	Integrated Services Digital Network. Once popular for home office Internet connections.
Fiber	Up to 150Mbps	Incredibly fast and just as expensive.
Cellular	Up to 14.7Mbps	Great range; supported by cell phone providers. Best for a very limited number of devices.
WiMAX	Up to 6Mbps	4G technology; not backward compatible with 3G.
Satellite	128Kbps to 4Mbps	Great for rural areas without cabled broadband methods.

Real World Scenario

Sometimes, the Choices Are Limited...

Before you decide which broadband connection sounds the most appealing to you, you should also factor in something very important: what is available in your area. DSL is available at different rates of connectivity based on distance from a central station. If you live far enough from a central station, or near a central station that has not been updated lately (such as in the middle of rural America), DSL may not be an option.

Similarly, not all cable providers are willing to take the steps necessary to run a connection in all situations. One of the authors once had a small business in a section of an old industrial building. The cable provider said the office where the modem was desired was too far from their nearest pole and there was nothing that could be done about it. He offered to pay the expense to have an additional pole placed closer to the location, but they would not discuss it further.

Make certain you know the available options—not just the technological options—before you spend too much time determining what is best for you.

Choosing Internal Network Connections

Along with deciding how your computers will get to the outside world, you need to think about how your computers will communicate with each other on your internal network. The choices you make will depend on the speed you need, distance and security requirements, and cost involved with installation and maintenance. It may also depend some on the abilities of the installer or administrative staff. You may have someone who is quite capable of making replacement Category 6 cables but for whom making replacement fiber-optic cables is a much more daunting task. Your choices for internal connections can be lumped into two groups: wired and wireless.

 Many networks today are a hybrid of wired and wireless connections. Understand the fundamentals of how each works separately; then you can understand how they work together. Every wireless connection eventually connects back to a wired network point somehow.

Wired Network Connections

Wired connections form the backbone of nearly every network in existence. Even as wireless becomes more popular, the importance of wired connections still remains strong. In general, wired networks are faster and more secure than their wireless counterparts.

When it comes to choosing a wired network connection type, you need to think about speed, distance, and cost. You learned about several types of wired connections in Chapter 6, "Networking Fundamentals," such as coaxial, UTP, STP, and fiber-optic, but the only two you'll want to go with today are twisted pair and fiber. You'll run one of the two (or maybe a combination of the two), with UTP being by far the most common choice, as an Ethernet star network. Table 8.3 shows a summary of the more common Ethernet standards along with the cable used, speed, and maximum distance.

TABLE 8.3   Common Ethernet standards

Types	Cables Used	Maximum Speed	Maximum Distance
10BaseT	UTP CAT-3 and above	10Mbps	100m (~300 feet)
100BaseTX	UTP CAT-5 and above	100Mbps	100m
100BaseFX	Multi-mode fiber	100Mbps	2000m
1000BaseT	UTP CAT-5e and above	1Gbps	100m
10GBaseT	UTP CAT-6a and above	10Gbps	100m
10GBaseSR	Multi-mode fiber	10Gbps	300m
10GBaseLR	Single-mode fiber	10Gbps	10km (6.2 miles)
10GBaseER	Single-mode fiber	10Gbps	40km (~25 miles)

The first question you need to ask yourself is, "How fast does this network need to be?" There really is no point installing a 10BaseT network these days because even the slowest wireless LAN speeds can deliver that. For most networks, 100Mbps is probably sufficient. If the company has higher throughput requirements, then you can start looking into Gigabit Ethernet (1Gbps) or faster (10Gbps).

The second question is then, "What is the maximum distance I'll need to run any one cable?" In most office environments, you can configure your network in such a way that 100 meters will get you from any connectivity device to the end user. If you need to go longer than that, you'll definitely need fiber for that connection unless you want to mess with repeaters.

As you're thinking about what type of cable you will go with, also consider the hardware you'll need. If you are going to run fiber to the desktop, you'll need fiber network cards, routers, and switches. If you are running UTP, you need network cards, routers, and switches with RJ-45 connectors. If you're going to run Gigabit, all of your devices need to support it.

The third question to ask yourself is, "How big of a deal is security?" Most of the time, the answer lies somewhere between "very" and "extremely"! Copper cable is pretty secure, but it does emit a signal that can be intercepted, meaning people can tap into your transmissions (hence the term *wiretap*). Fiber-optic cables are immune to wiretapping. Normally this isn't a big deal because copper cables don't exactly broadcast your data all over as a wireless connection does. But if security is of the utmost concern, then fiber is the way to go.

Fourth, "Is there a lot of electrical interference in the area?" Transmissions across a copper cable can be ravaged by the effects of electromagnetic interference (EMI). Fiber is immune to those effects.

Finally, ask yourself about cost. Fiber cables and hardware are more expensive than their copper counterparts. Table 8.4 summarizes your cable choices and provides characteristics of each.

TABLE 8.4 Cable types and characteristics

Characteristics	Twisted-Pair	Fiber-Optic
Transmission rate	CAT-5: 100Mbps	100Mbps to 10Gbps
	CAT-5e: 1Gbps	
	CAT-6a: 10Gbps	
Maximum length	100 meters (328 feet)	~25 miles
Flexibility	Very flexible	Fair
Ease of installation	Very easy	Difficult
Connector	RJ-45	Special (SC, ST, and others)
Interference (security)	Susceptible	Not susceptible
Overall cost	Inexpensive	Expensive
NIC cost	100Mbps: $15–$40	$100–$150; easily $600–$800 for server NICs
	1Gbps: $30 and up	
10m cable cost	CAT-5/5e: $8–$12 CAT-6: $12–$15	Depends on mode and connector type, but generally $20–$40
8-port switch cost	100Mbps: $30–$100	$350 and up
	1Gbps: $70–$400	

Understand that the costs shown in Table 8.4 are approximate and are for illustrative purposes only. The cost for this equipment in your area may differ. Fiber has gotten considerably cheaper in the last 5 to 10 years, but it's still far more expensive than copper.

Fiber-optic cabling has some obvious advantages over copper, but as you can see it may be prohibitively expensive to run fiber to the desktop. What a lot of organizations will do is use fiber sparingly, where it is needed the most, and then run copper to the desktop. Fiber will be used in the server room and perhaps between floors of a building as well as any place where a very long cable run is needed.

Wireless Network Connections

People love wireless networks for one major reason: convenience. Wireless connections enable a sense of freedom in users. They're not stuck to their desk; they can work from anywhere! (We're not sure if this is actually a good thing or not.) Wireless isn't as fast and it tends to be a bit more expensive than wired copper networks, but the convenience factor far outweighs the others.

WIRELESS LAN (WLAN)

When thinking about using wireless for network communications, the only real technology option available today is IEEE 802.11. Bluetooth and infrared (which we'll cover in just a bit) can help mobile devices communicate, but they aren't designed for full Wireless LAN (WLAN) use. Your choice becomes which 802.11 standard you want to use. Table 8.5 summarizes your options.

TABLE 8.5   802.11 standards

Type	Frequency	Maximum Data Rate	Indoor Range	Outdoor Range
a	5GHz	54Mbps	35m	120m
b	2.4GHz	11Mbps	40m	140m
g	2.4GHz	54Mbps	40m	140m
n	2.4/5GHz	600Mbps	70m	250m

So how do you choose which one is right for your situation? You can apply the same thinking you would for a wired network in that you need to consider speed, distance, security, and cost. Generally speaking though, with wireless it's best to start with the most robust technology and work your way backwards.

Security concerns on wireless networks are similar regardless of your choice. You're broadcasting network signals through air; there will be some security concerns. It comes down to range, speed and cost.

In today's environment it's almost silly to consider 802.11a or 802.11b. Deciding that you are going to install an 802.11b network from the ground up at this point is a bit like saying you are going to use 10BaseT. You could, but why? In fact, it will be a challenge to even find 802.11b-only devices for your network. Most devices that support 802.11b are branded as 802.11b/g (or 802.11g/b), meaning they support both network types. 802.11a never really got too popular even when it *was* the best technology, so why use it now?

That brings us to your most likely choices: 802.11g and 802.11n. Devices are plentiful, and both are backward compatible with 802.11b. (If you happen to have 802.11a devices, then 802.11n makes more sense. But really, you should upgrade those devices!) It will come down to cost. Network cards will run you anywhere between $20 to $100, and you can get wireless access points and wireless routers for as little as around $40. Shop around to see what kind of deal you can get.

BLUETOOTH

Bluetooth is not designed to be a WLAN but rather a wireless personal area network (WPAN). In other words, it's not the right technology to use if you want to set up a wireless network for your office. It is, however, a great technology to use if you have wireless devices that you want your computer to be able to communicate with. Examples include smartphones, mice, keyboards, headsets, and printers.

Nearly every laptop comes with built-in WiFi capabilities, but they don't necessarily come Bluetooth enabled. To use Bluetooth devices, you will need to add an adapter, such as the one shown in Figure 8.8.

FIGURE 8.8   Bluetooth USB adapter

There are two Bluetooth standards you might run across. Version 1.2 was adopted in 2003 and supports data rates of up to 1Mbps. Version 2.1+EDR, adopted in 2007, supports data rates of up to 3Mbps. Version 2.1+EDR is backward compatible with older Bluetooth standards. Most mobile Bluetooth devices are Class 2 devices, which have a maximum range of 10 meters.

Like 802.11b/g, Bluetooth uses the unlicensed 2.4GHz range for communication. To avoid interference, Bluetooth can "signal hop" at different frequencies to avoid conflicts with devices using other technologies in the area. Thanks to technology improvements, interference with WiFi is unlikely, but it can still occur.

One of the unusual features of Bluetooth networks is their temporary nature. With WiFi, you need a central communication point, such as a WAP or router. Bluetooth networks are formed on an ad hoc basis, meaning that whenever two Bluetooth devices get close enough to each other, they can communicate directly with each other. This dynamically created network is called a *piconet*. A Bluetooth-enabled device can communicate with up to seven other devices in one piconet.

INFRARED

Infrared waves have been around since the beginning of time. They are longer than light waves but shorter than microwaves. The most common use of infrared technology is the television remote control, although infrared is also used in night-vision goggles and medical and scientific imaging.

In 1993 the *Infrared Data Association (IrDA)* was formed as a technical consortium to support "interoperable, low-cost infrared data interconnection standards that support a walk-up, point-to-point user model." The key terms here are *walk-up* and *point-to-point*, meaning you need to be at very close range to use infrared and it's designed for one-to-one communication. Infrared requires line of sight, and generally speaking, the two devices need to be pointed at each other to work. If you point your remote away from the television, how well does it work?

 More information on the IrDA standard can be found at the organization's website: http://www.irda.org.

Some laptops have a built-in infrared port, which is a small, dark square of plastic, usually black or dark maroon. For easy access, infrared ports are located on the front or sides of devices that have them. Figure 8.9 shows an example of an infrared port.

Current IrDA specifications allow transmission of data up to 16Mbps, and IrDA claims that 100Mbps and 500Mbps standards are on the horizon. Because it does not use radio waves, there are no concerns of interference or signal conflicts. Atmospheric conditions can play a role in disrupting infrared waves, but considering that the maximum functional range of an IrDA device is about 1 meter, weather is not likely to cause you any problems.

Security is not an issue with infrared. The maximum range is about 1 meter with an angle of about 30 degrees, and the signal does not go through walls, so hacking prospects are limited. If someone is making an attempt to intercept an infrared signal, it's going to be pretty obvious. The data is directional, and you choose when and where to send it.

FIGURE 8.9   Infrared port

Installing the Network

Before you run your first cable or place your first wireless router, know exactly where everything is supposed to go on the network. The only way you'll be able to do this is to plan ahead. If you have planned the installation before you begin, the actual physical work of installing the network will be much easier.

Keys to Planning a Network

Every network is going to be somewhat different, but there are some general things to keep in mind as you go through your planning process:

Get a map.   Understand the layout of the space in which you're installing the network. Get a map of the office or draw one yourself. Add distances or a scale if possible so you can determine how far you'll need to run cables or how many wireless access points you'll need. Label power locations and their capacity. Mark any potential obstacles or hazards that you may run into when you try to run cable, such as your fluorescent lights, water pipes, or cinder block walls.

Locate your server(s).   If you are installing a small network, you may not have to worry about this. But if you have a network with one or more dedicated servers, decide where they will be located. They need to be in a secured location where only authorized people have access to them. This can be anything from a small closet to an elaborate server room with raised, antistatic floors. Just make sure it's temperature controlled because server closets tend to get very hot, and we know that heat and computers don't mix well.

Identify where client computers will be.   If you are setting up an office in a cubicle farm, just assume one computer (or more, depending on the cubicle type) per cube. This will help you determine where you need shared network resources as well as cable placement.

Locate network resources.   If your network users are going to share resources such as printers, where will they be located? If there are dozens or even hundreds of users, you may need multiple printer locations or *printer banks*. Locate these and other shared resources in enough places so that users don't have to walk from one end of the office to the other just to pick up printouts.

Determine how you are going to connect.   If you are going to go all wireless, you can start figuring out how many wireless routers or access points you'll need. If you are going to have wired connections, start determining how long the cable runs will be. Remember that UTP has a maximum segment distance of 100 meters. If you have to go up from a patch panel, into a ceiling, and down through a wall or conduit, take that into account too!

Designate additional connectivity areas if needed.   If you are running cables and some systems are outside of your maximum cable length, you will need to install a repeater of some sort. The best choice is probably a switch, which repeats signals. If you have several hundred computers, though, and you want to separate out networks, then a router is the best choice. These connectivity locations can be just a small closet. Other times, if no space is available, some administrators will put the switch in the drop ceiling. Although there is nothing wrong with this (as long as it's secured), it can be challenging to find power up there and it does make it more difficult to add to that switch. Finally, if there's no way to run power into the area where you need the switch, you could buy one that uses Power over Ethernet (PoE). Generally the number of ports these devices support is limited, but it beats having no connectivity at all.

Physical Installation

You shouldn't begin to physically install the network until all of your plans are complete and you've double-checked them. There are few things more annoying than getting halfway through an installation and determining that your plans need to change drastically. Here we'll look at installation of three groups of items: network cards, cables, and connectivity devices.

Installing and Configuring Network Interface Cards

In the old days (1980s) of personal computers, NICs were a pain to install. Not only did you have to configure the hardware manually, you had to configure the network protocol stack manually. This usually involved a configuration program of some kind and was very cumbersome. Fortunately, installing a NIC today is pretty straightforward.

INSTALLING A NIC

Before you can begin communicating on your network, you must have a NIC installed in the machine. Installing a NIC is a fairly simple task if you have installed any expansion card before; a NIC is just a special type of expansion card. In Exercise 8.1, you will learn how to install a NIC.

EXERCISE 8.1

Installing a NIC in Windows 7

Follow these steps to install a NIC:

1. Power off the PC, remove the case and the metal or plastic blank covering the expansion slot opening, and insert the expansion card into an open slot.

2. Secure the expansion card with the screw provided.

3. Put the case back on the computer and power it up (you can run software configuration at this step, if necessary). If there are conflicts, change any parameters so that the NIC doesn't conflict with any existing hardware.

Note that these first three steps may not be necessary if you have an onboard NIC.

4. Install a driver for the NIC for the type of operating system that you have. Windows Plug and Play (PnP) will recognize the NIC and install the driver automatically. It may also ask you to provide a copy of the necessary driver if it does not recognize the type of NIC you have installed. If Windows does not start the installation routine immediately, open Control Panel, and choose Add A Device under Hardware And Sound. A list of hardware devices will appear. Choose the NIC and continue the installation.

5. After installing a NIC, you must hook the card to the network using the appropriate cable (if using wired connections). Attach this patch cable to the connector on the NIC and to a port in the wall (or connectivity device), thus connecting your PC to the rest of the network.

CONFIGURING A NIC

Now that your NIC is installed, it's time to configure it with the right IP address and TCP/IP configuration information. There are two ways to do this. The first is to automatically obtain IP configuration information from a Dynamic Host Configuration Protocol (DHCP) server, if one is available on the network. The other way is to manually enter in the configuration information yourself.

If you have a small network of no more than 10 computers and do not have a DHCP server but want your computers to configure themselves automatically, set the NIC up to get its IP information from the DHCP server anyway. Microsoft Windows operating systems will automatically configure themselves with an APIPA address if they are unable to locate a DHCP server, and with the APIPA address the computers on a local network will be able to communicate with one another.

To configure your NIC in Windows 7, open Control Panel in Category View and click View Network Status And Tasks under Network And Internet. In the left pane, click Change

Adapter Settings. You'll see the name of a connection, such as Local Area Connection. Right-click that, and click Properties. Figure 8.10 shows you what this screen will look like.

FIGURE 8.10   Local Area Connection properties

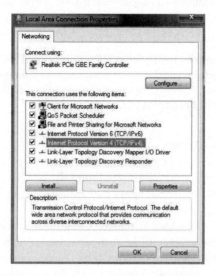

On that screen, highlight Internet Protocol Version 4 (TCP/IPv4) and click Properties. This will take you to a screen similar to the one in Figure 8.11.

FIGURE 8.11   TCP/IP properties

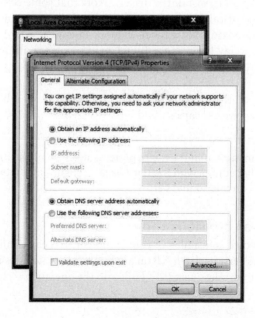

As you can see in Figure 8.11, this computer is configured to obtain its information from a DHCP server. (If you have a wireless router, as many people do on their home networks, it can function as a DHCP server. We'll talk more about that in a few sections.) If you wanted to configure the client manually, you would click Use The Following IP Address and enter in the correct information. To supply the client with a DNS server address manually, click Use The Following DNS Server Addresses.

If you manually configure the IP address, you must also configure the DNS server address manually. Otherwise, the client will not have access to a DNS server. Client computers can broadcast to find a DHCP server, but they cannot broadcast to find a DNS server.

WIRELESS CARD INSTALLATION

Installing a wireless NIC is just like installing a normal, wired NIC. The only difference is in the configuration of the NIC. You must configure the NIC to connect to your preferred wireless network (by its SSID) and configure any security settings (such as wireless encryption keys).

To configure a wireless card under Windows 7, you must first install the wireless card. For a desktop, this means powering off the computer, removing the case cover, and inserting the card into an open slot (assuming the wireless card expansion card type and bus slot type match). Then you can power the computer back up, and the computer should recognize that a new card was installed and prompt you to install the driver. The process will be nearly identical to the one you followed in Exercise 8.1.

On a laptop, simply insert the wireless PC Card or USB NIC into any open PC Card slot or USB port with the laptop powered up. Once you have done this, Windows PnP will recognize the card and ask you to install the driver. (Note that some NIC manufacturers ask you to insert the CD and install the drivers before physically installing the NIC. Not doing so could cause installation issues. Always check your documentation!) Nearly every laptop processor chipset made today (such as the Intel Core i5) comes with integrated wireless, so no external adapter needs to be added. USB-attached NICs are an option for desktop computers as well.

Once the NIC is in and the driver is installed, you may have to reboot (but only in very unique cases). Then the wireless card should be ready to use.

Bear in mind that these are general steps. Always consult the documentation that comes with the hardware to ensure that there isn't a special step that is unique to that card.

WIRELESS CONNECTION CONFIGURATION

Now that your wireless card is installed in your computer, you can configure the connection so you can use it. Windows versions from XP on are beautiful for wireless use because they have utilities for connecting to wireless networks built into the operating system. Windows uses the Wireless Zero Configuration Service (also called Wireless Auto Configuration or WLAN AutoConfig) to automatically connect to wireless access points using IEEE 802.11 standards.

To configure a wireless connection, you can simply bring a Windows (XP or newer) laptop or computer within range of a wireless access point and Windows will detect and alert you to the presence of the access point. Alternatively, if you would like control over the connection, in Windows XP, you can open the network control panel (Start ➢ Control Panel ➢ Network Connections), right-click the wireless card, and choose View Available Wireless Connections. This will bring up the screen shown in Figure 8.12. In Windows 7, you can get to a similar screen by choosing Start ➢ Control Panel ➢ Network And Internet and then choosing Connect To A Network.

FIGURE 8.12   Available wireless connections

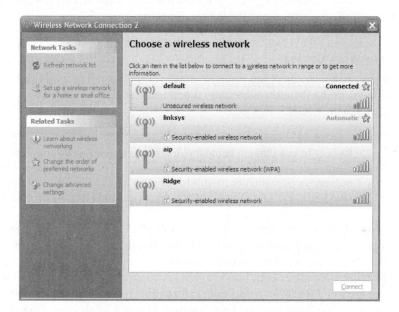

From this screen you can view the SSIDs of the available wireless networks, including the one to which you are connected (the one that says "Connected" next to it). The bars in the far-right column indicate the relative signal strength of each connection. The more green bars showing, the stronger the signal and the better (and faster) the connection.

 If the connection shows a lock icon underneath it, it is a secured wireless network and you will need to enter some sort of password to gain access to it.

To connect to any network, double-click it and Windows will try to connect. You'll see a window similar to the one in Figure 8.13 that shows you the connection attempt is in progress. Once you are connected, Windows will display "Connected" next to that connection.

FIGURE 8.13 Connecting to a wireless network

> The weaker the signal, the longer the connection will take. Authentication will also slow down the initial connection time.

Installing Network Cables

Network cables are not the most fun thing to install. Proper installation of network cables generally means running them through ceilings and walls and making a mess of the office. Thank goodness for wireless!

> Be sure to use plenum cable if you are running cables through spaces where there is air ventilation, such as drop ceilings. PVC-coated cables will produce poisonous gas when burned. Also be sure that you have the proper permission to run the cables and that you aren't violating any building codes.

If you are installing a wired network in an existing office space, you may want to look into hiring out the cable installation to a third party. You'll find many companies that have the tools needed to properly install a wired network.

When installing a wired network yourself, always be aware of the maximum cable lengths, as outlined in Table 8.3. In addition, utilize cable troughs in ceilings and walls or other conduit in walls to keep your cables organized. Figure 8.14 shows a cable trough; they come in a variety of lengths and quality.

FIGURE 8.14 Cable trough

Finally, if you must run cables across the floor in a walkway (which isn't recommended), use a floor cable guard to avoid creating a trip hazard and to protect your cables. A floor cable guard is shown in Figure 8.15.

FIGURE 8.15   Floor cable guard

 When running cables through a ceiling, never run the cables directly across fluorescent lights. These lights emit electromagnetic radiation (EMI) that can interfere with network communications. Utilize your cable troughs to keep cables in one place and away from lights. Also remember that fiber-optic cables are immune to EMI!

Installing and Configuring Wireless Access Points and Wireless Routers

Instead of using switches and hubs, wireless networks use either a *wireless access point (WAP)* or a *wireless router* to provide central connectivity. A WAP functions essentially like a wireless hub, whereas wireless routers provide more functionality, similar to that of a wired router. Based on looks alone, they are pretty much identical, and physically installing them is similar. The differences come in configuring them because they will have different options.

In the following sections, we're going to talk about installing and configuring WAPs and wireless routers interchangeably; just remember that a lot of the features available in a wireless router may not be available in a WAP.

PHYSICALLY INSTALLING A WIRELESS ACCESS POINT OR ROUTER

After unwrapping the device from its packaging (and reading the instructions, of course), you must choose a place for it. If it is supplying wireless access to your home network and the Internet, locate it where you can receive access in the most places. Keep in mind that the more walls the signal has to travel through, the lower the signal strength.

In addition, you may choose to have some computers plug directly into the device using a CAT-5 or other UTP cable. If so, it makes sense to locate the device near the computer or computers you will want to physically connect.

 Place the WAP in the center of your home, close to a network connection. Or if you have only one computer, place it close to the broadband Internet connection you are using (i.e., the cable modem or DSL line).

In many offices, WAPs and wireless routers are often placed in the ceiling, with the antennae pointed downward through holes in the ceiling tiles. You can purchase metal plates designed to replace ceiling tiles to hold these devices. The plates have holes precut in them for the antennae to stick through, are designed to securely hold the device and easily open for maintenance, and often lock for physical security. There are also WiFi ceiling antennas you can purchase that basically look like a little dome hanging from the ceiling.

For wireless connectivity devices placed in a ceiling (or other places with no easy access to an electrical outlet), *Power over Ethernet (PoE)* is a very handy technology to supply both power and an Ethernet connection.

Once you have chosen the location, plug the unit into a wall outlet and connect the two antennae that come with the unit (as needed; many newer devices contain built-in antennae). They will screw onto two bungs on the back of the unit. Once the unit is plugged in, you need to connect it to the rest of your network.

If you are connecting directly to the Internet through a cable modem or DSL or to a wired hub or router, you will most likely plug the cable into the Internet socket of the device, provided it has one. If not, you can use any of the other wired ports on the back of the device to connect to the rest of your network. Make sure that you get a link light on that connection.

At this point, the device is configured for a home network, with a few basic caveats. First, the default SSID (for example, Linksys) will be used, along with the default administrative password and the default IP addressing scheme. Also, there will be no encryption on the connection. This is known as an *open access point*. Even if you have nothing to protect except for the Internet connection, you shouldn't just leave that off. It just makes you an easy and inviting target for neighbors who want to siphon off your bandwidth or even worse. Many wireless manufacturers have made their devices so easy to configure that for most networks it is Plug and Play.

If you have personal data on your home network and more than one computer, you should never keep the default settings. Anyone could snoop your access point from the road in front of or behind your house and possibly get on your home network. It's too easy for identity theft!

From a computer on the home network, insert the device's setup CD into the computer's CD-ROM drive. It will automatically start and present you with a wizard that will walk you through setting the name of the SSID of this new access point as well as changing the default setup password, setting any security keys for this connection, and generally configuring the unit for your network's specific configuration. Then you're done!

Configuring a Wireless Router

Each wireless router manufacturer uses different software, but you can usually configure their parameters with the built-in, web-based configuration utility that's included with the product. While the software is convenient, you still need to know which options to config-ure and how those configurations will affect users on your networks. The items that require configuration depend on the choices you make about your wireless network. We will divide the configuration section into three parts: basic configuration, security options, and addi-tional services.

Basic Configuration

The WiFi Alliance (www.wi-fi.org) is the authoritative expert in the field of wireless LANs. It lists five critical steps to setting up a secured wireless router:

1. Change the router's SSID.

2. Change the administrator username and password. Make sure it's a strong password.

3. Select AES.

4. Choose a high quality security passphrase.

5. From the clients, select WPA2 and enter the security passphrase to connect.

The parameter that needs immediate attention is the SSID. An SSID is a unique name given to the wireless network. All hardware that is to participate on the network must be configured to use the same SSID. Essentially, the SSID is the network name. When you are using Windows to connect to a wireless network, all available wireless networks will be listed by their SSID when you select View Available Wireless Networks.

When you first install the wireless network, the default SSID is used and there is no security enabled. In other words, it's pretty easy to find your network (Linksys), and any-one within range of your signal can get on your network with no password required. This is obviously a security risk, so you want to change that.

For the rest of this example, we'll use a Linksys WRT54G wireless router. First, you need to log in to your device. The default internal address of the router is 192.168.1.1, so to log in, open Internet Explorer (or your preferred Internet browser) and type **192.168.1.1** into the address bar. You'll get a screen similar to the one in Figure 8.16.

You should have already set up the username and password using the CD provided with the device. If not, look in the manual for the default username and password. You'll defi-nitely want to change these as soon as possible. Once you're logged in, the first screen you'll see is similar to the one in Figure 8.17. On this screen, you can see two basic sections along the left-hand side: Internet Setup and Network Setup. The Internet Setup portion identi-fies how you configure your incoming connection from the ISP. In most cases, your cable or DSL provider will just have you use DHCP to get an external IP address from its DHCP server, but there are options to configure this manually as well. The hostname is the name of your device, and some ISPs require that you put in a domain name as well. If it's needed, the ISP will tell you what to put in.

FIGURE 8.16 Logging in to the wireless router

FIGURE 8.17 Basic setup screen

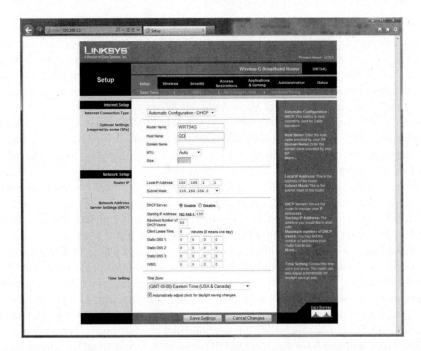

The Network Setup portion lets you configure your router's internal IP address, in this case 192.168.1.1, and subnet mask. On this router, DHCP is also configured on this screen. If you want the device to act as a DHCP server for internal clients, enable it here, specify the starting IP address, and specify the maximum number of DHCP users. (Author's note: I just realized that I have my router set up to allow 50 DHCP leases at once. In my home, I have three computers that connect to my network and need a DHCP lease, so having it set to 50 is overkill. I should probably change that!) Disabling DHCP makes your network a bit more secure because random clients can't obtain an IP address automatically. Disabling DHCP means that clients will have to use a static IP address.

Most wireless routers (like the one used in this example) describe each setting on the configuration pages to the right of the setting. So if you're not totally sure what a setting does, you may get some help from the information on the right. If not, there's always the manual or online help!

By clicking the Wireless tab, you'll be taken to the Basic Wireless Settings screen, as shown in Figure 8.18.

FIGURE 8.18   Basic Wireless Settings screen

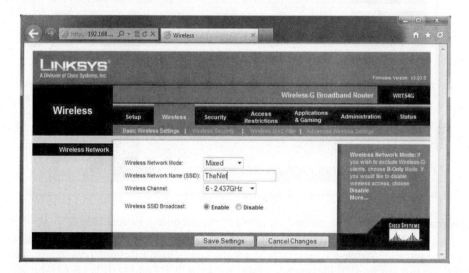

There are a couple of critical settings here. The first is your SSID. Always change it from the default to something else. The second is Wireless SSID Broadcast. By default this is enabled, which means that anyone within range can detect your signal and see your SSID. By disabling this, your router no longer broadcasts the SSID. This is recommended because it increases security, but the reality is that it only makes you less vulnerable to casual hackers.

Disabling your SSID broadcast makes you less susceptible to *wardriving*, which is when someone drives through your neighborhood looking for a wireless signal. If you're not broadcasting, you're not as likely to be found. The downside to disabling your SSID broadcasts is that doing so can make it more challenging for legitimate clients to connect to the network.

Still on the Wireless tab, under the Wireless Security section, you'll find more key configuration options. The first is the security mode. In Figure 8.19, this router is configured to use WEP at 64-bit encryption. You can see the four WEP keys the system generated.

FIGURE 8.19   Wireless Security section

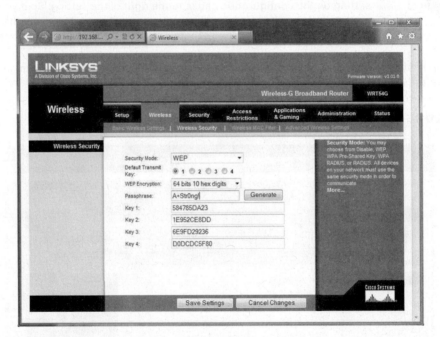

If security is enabled and you are using WEP, the client will be required to know the passphrase as well as the WEP key to connect to the wireless router. As we discussed earlier in the section "Wireless Encryption Methods," though, WEP is not very secure (again, something this author should change!). Changing from WEP 64-bit to WEP 128-bit will help, but WEP is still a problem. Many routers will also let you choose more secure security methods, such as WPA, WPA2, or a RADIUS server.

Remote Authentication Dial-In User Service (RADIUS) is a service that provides centralized authentication on a network. For your wireless router to use RADIUS, you need to have a RADIUS server on your network. The A+ exam won't test you on RADIUS, but other exams will, such as Network+.

With that, the router-side setup recommendations have been taken care of. Now it's just a matter of setting up the clients with the same security method and entering in the passphrase. Before we move on to specific security options, there are a few more basic setup concepts we need to cover.

Wireless Channels

Earlier in the chapter in the section on 802.11g, we brought up the concept of wireless channels. There are 11 configurable channels in the 2.4GHz range, which is what 802.11b/g uses to communicate. If you look back at Figure 8.18, you'll see that the default channel is 6. Most of the time, you won't have a need to change that.

But let's say you're in a situation where you have too many users for one WAP to adequately service (about 30 or more) or your physical layout is too long and you need multiple access points. Now you need to have more than one access point. In a situation like this, here's how you should configure it:

- Set up the WAPs so they have overlapping ranges. The recommended overlap is 10 percent. This way, if users roam from one area to another, they don't lose their signal.
- Configure the WAPs with the same SSID.
- Configure the WAPs with non-overlapping channels.

Channels need to be at least five numbers apart to not overlap. So, for example, channels 2 and 7 do not overlap, nor do 4 and 10. There are 11 configurable channels, so you can have a maximum of three overlapping ranges on the same SSID, configured with channels 1, 6, and 11, and not have any interference. Wireless clients are configured to auto-detect a channel by default, but they can be forced to use a specific channel as well.

Network Address Translation (NAT)

Network Address Translation (NAT) is a very cool service that translates private IP addresses on your internal network to a public IP address on the Internet. If you are using your wireless router to allow one or more clients to access the Internet but you have only one external public IP address, your router is using NAT.

Most routers have NAT enabled by default, and there might not be any specific configuration options for it. That's true in the case of the WRT54G router we've been using as an example. The only options you can configure are the internal IP addresses that the router hands out to clients.

To be technically correct, NAT is specifically a one-to-one translation of a private IP address to a public IP address. If you have multiple client computers with private addresses accessing the Internet using one public address (called many-to-one), that is a specific form of NAT known as overloading, or port address translation (PAT). The A+ exam does not test you on the differences between NAT and PAT, but other tests do, such as the Network+ exam.

Real World Scenario

Sharing an Internet Connection

Wireless routers have many advantages over wireless access points. One of the biggest advantages is the ability to share an Internet connection. By doing this, you pay for only one connection but you can connect as many computers as you would like (or is reasonable) to your wireless router. Here is how to do that.

First, ensure that your DSL modem or cable modem is connected properly. Then, connect your wireless router to your cable modem or DSL modem using a UTP cable (CAT-5 or better). In most cases, the wireless router will have a wired Internet port on the back of it. Connect the cable here and plug it into your broadband modem. Finally, you can connect computers to your wireless router.

Many ISPs, in an attempt to prohibit this sort of behavior, will restrict access through the modem to one MAC address. This isn't a problem. You can do one of two things. The first option is, when you first make your connection to the ISP, just make sure your computer is already connected through your router. The ISP will see the MAC address of the router and assume that is your computer. The second option is that most wireless routers will allow you to clone your computer's MAC address (see the following screen shot). Your router will simply tell the ISP that it has the same MAC address as your computer, which was previously connected directly to the cable or DSL modem. ISPs may not like it, but sharing a wireless Internet connection is very economical option for a small office or home network.

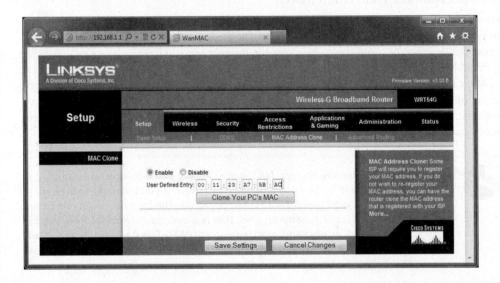

WiFi Protected Setup (WPS)

In 2007, the WiFi Alliance created *WiFi Protected Setup (WPS)* as an easy way for novice users to set up and configure a secure wireless network. With literally the push of a button on the wireless router, client computers would be able to connect to the router using the secure WPA2 encryption method. It's a very similar concept to configuring a remote for your garage door opener. Figure 8.20 shows an example of a WPS button.

FIGURE 8.20   WPS button on a wireless router

In December 2011, a major security flaw was discovered in WPS. Essentially, it allows a hacker to obtain the WPS security code (PIN) and therefore get the network's WPA2 security key.

 As this book was being written, there was not a security fix for this flaw. The WiFi Alliance web site (www.wi-fi.org) should have the most current information on WPS.

Wireless Router Security

By their very nature, wireless routers are less secure than their wired counterparts. The fact that their signals travel through air makes them a little harder to contain. Here we'll review a few things you can do to increase the security of your wireless installation. Specifically, you can implement the following:

- Disabling SSID broadcasts
- Wireless encryption
- MAC filtering

We've already covered the first two. Disabling the SSID broadcast makes it a little harder to find your network—not impossible, just harder. (Figure 8.18 shows you where to disable this on our example router.) Someone with a wireless packet sniffer could still detect your network transmissions and attempt to hack in. It does help thwart casual hackers or those who would wardrive to try to find a network. The only downside to disabling your SSID broadcast is that you will have to configure legitimate client computers manually with the name.

Wireless encryption is highly recommended if you want to secure your network. In the section "Wireless Encryption Methods" earlier in this chapter, we reviewed your current security options. If all of your devices support it, WPA2 (or AES from the router side) is the best way to go. Take a look back at Figure 8.19 for an example of where to configure this on a router (this device is configured for WEP).

The last one to look at is MAC filtering. If you'll recall, the MAC address is the unique hardware address associated with the network adapter. All NICs, wired or wireless, have a unique MAC. By enabling MAC filtering, you can limit the computers that have access to your network.

On this router, the MAC filter is on the Wireless tab under Wireless MAC Filter. You click the Enable button, choose to prevent or permit those on the list, and then click Edit MAC Filter List to enter your MAC addresses. These options with a sample MAC list are shown in Figure 8.21.

FIGURE 8.21   MAC filtering

As with most other security options, MAC filtering isn't totally foolproof either. We showed you earlier how your router can spoof your PC's MAC address to fool your ISP. You can guess that if a hacker wanted to badly enough, they could spoof a MAC address of your wireless clients as well. Still, it's a good, solid security option to utilize.

 Always be sure that your router has the most current firmware. Older firmware versions may have security holes, and newer versions will patch those as well as possibly offer you new features. To upgrade the firmware, you first download the newest version from the manufacturer's website and save it to a local computer. Then you can update the firmware from a screen similar to one shown in the following screen shot.

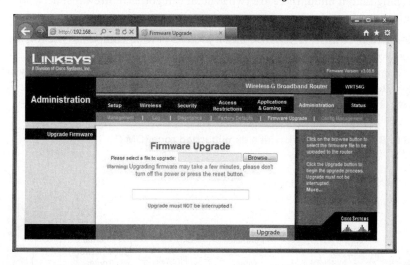

Additional Wireless Router Services

Wireless routers offer many more services than we've been able to cover to this point, and most of them are out of the scope of A+ exam training. We want to finish off this chapter with two things that routers can provide and are in scope: firewalls and QoS.

Understanding Firewall Basics

Before we get into configuring your wireless router as a firewall, let's be sure you know what firewalls can do for you. A *firewall* is a hardware or software solution that serves as your network's security guard. For networks that are connected to the Internet, they're probably the most important device on the network. Firewalls can protect you in two ways. They protect your network resources from hackers lurking in the dark corners of the Internet, and they can simultaneously prevent computers on your network from accessing undesirable content on the Internet. At a basic level, firewalls filter packets based on rules defined by the network administrator.

Firewalls can be stand-alone "black boxes," software installed on a server or router, or some combination of hardware and software. Most firewalls will have at least two network connections: one to the Internet, or *public side*, and one to the internal network, or *private side*. Some firewalls have a third network port for a second semi-internal network. This port is used to connect servers that can be considered both public and private, such as web and email servers. This intermediary network is known as a *demilitarized zone (DMZ)*, an example of which is shown in Figure 8.22. Personal software-based firewalls will run on computers with only one NIC.

TYPES OF FIREWALLS

We've already stated that firewalls can be software or hardware based or a combination of both. Keeping that in mind, there are two general categories of firewalls: network based and host based.

Network-based firewalls   A *network-based firewall* is what companies use to protect their private network from public networks. The defining characteristic of this type of firewall is that it's designed to protect an entire network of computers instead of just one system. It's generally a stand-alone hardware device with specialized software installed on it to protect your network.

FIGURE 8.22   A network with a demilitarized zone (DMZ)

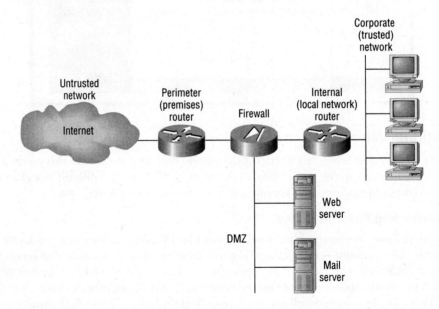

Host-based firewalls   In contrast to network-based firewalls, a *host-based firewall* is implemented on a single machine so it protects only that one machine. This type of firewall is usually a software implementation because you don't need any additional hardware in your personal computer to run it. All current Windows client operating systems come with Windows Firewall, which is a great example of a host-based solution. Host-based firewalls are generally not as secure as network firewalls, but for small businesses or home use, they're an adequate, cheap solution.

HOW FIREWALLS WORK

Firewalls are configured to allow only packets that pass specific security restrictions to get through them. They can also permit, deny, encrypt, decrypt, and proxy all traffic that flows through them, most commonly between the public and private parts of a network. The network administrator decides on and sets up the rules a firewall follows when deciding to forward data packets or reject them.

The default configuration of a firewall is generally *default deny*, which means that all traffic is blocked unless specifically authorized by the administrator. While this is very secure, it's also time consuming to configure the device to allow legitimate traffic to flow through it. The other option is *default allow*, which means all traffic is allowed through unless the administrator denies it. If you have a default allow firewall and don't configure it, you might as well not have a firewall at all.

The basic method of configuring firewalls is to use an *access control list (ACL)*. The ACL is the set of rules that determines which traffic gets through the firewall and which traffic is blocked. ACLs are typically configured to block traffic by IP address, port number, domain name, or some combination of all three. How you configure your ACLs is sometimes referred to as *port assignment* or setting up rules.

Packets that meet the criteria in the ACL are passed through the firewall to their destination. This is known as *port forwarding*. For example, let's say you have a computer on your internal network that is set up as a web server. To allow Internet clients to access the system, you need to allow data on port 80 (HTTP) to get to that computer.

The final concept you may be tested on in the A+ exam is *port triggering*. Port triggering is essentially an automated form of port forwarding. It allows traffic to enter the network on a specific port after a computer makes an outbound request on that specific port. For example, if a computer on your internal network makes an outbound Telnet request (port 23), subsequent inbound traffic destined for the originating computer on port 23 would be allowed through.

Configuring Your Wireless Firewall

Nearly every wireless router sold today provides you with some level of firewall protection. On the router used in this example, the firewall options are on two separate tabs. Enabling the firewall and setting a few basic options is done from the Security tab, as shown in Figure 8.23.

For more advanced options, we move to the Access Restrictions tab, shown in Figure 8.24. Here you can set an Internet access policy; block services such as HTTP, FTP, and Telnet; block websites by URL; and block website traffic by keyword.

FIGURE 8.23 Enabling the firewall

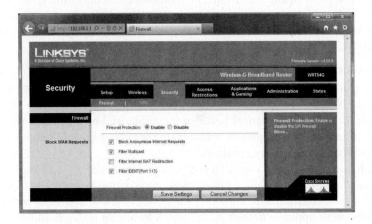

FIGURE 8.24 Access restrictions

Quality of Service (QoS)

Quality of Service (QoS) is a strategy that allows an administrator to control resources to maintain a certain service level. By using QoS, an administrator can set different priorities for one or more types of network traffic based on different applications, data flows, or users. For example, if the engineering group needs to have a certain amount of guaranteed network bandwidth, QoS can make that happen. This is not typically implemented on small or home office networks but rather for larger enterprise networks.

QoS focuses on dealing with five different types of problems that can affect data on a network:

- Delay, usually caused by congested routes that prevent critical data from arriving on time
- Dropped packets, which often causes delay
- Error, or corrupted data
- Jitter, or variation in packet delay in a data stream
- Out-of-order delivery, which can cause performance issues in time-sensitive applications such as VoIP.

Before each session, a QoS level is established as part of a service-level agreement (SLA). This is a simply priority setting. Higher-level numbers indicate higher priority, and administrators can set priority levels 0 through 5. Table 8.6 shows the eight levels of QoS.

TABLE 8.6   QoS levels

Level	Description
0	Best effort
1	Background
2	Standard
3	Excellent load (business-critical applications)
4	Controlled load (streaming media)
5	Interactive voice and video (less than 100ms latency)
6	Layer 3 network control reserved traffic (less than 10ms latency)
7	Layer 2 network control reserved traffic (lowest latency)

As more and more real-time business-critical applications hit the market, QoS will become a bigger topic.

Summary

In this chapter, you learned about wireless networking and configuring a small office, home office (SOHO) network. We started with wireless networking. We introduced the key wireless networking standards 802.11a, 802.11b, 802.11g, and 802.11n and talked about their characteristics, such as speed, distances, frequencies, and modulation. Then, we moved into wireless security. Important security protocols to remember are WEP, WPA, and WPA2.

Next, you learned the fundamentals of installing a small network. We started this section off looking at the myriad possibilities for Internet connections, from the archaic dial-up to broadband options such as DSL, cable modems, fiber, ISDN, and satellite. After that, we talked about choosing internal network connections in both wired and wireless environments.

From there, we dove in to physical network installation. The first critical step is planning. Don't be the one who forgets that! After covering elements of good planning, we looked at how to install network adapters, cabling, and connectivity devices.

Finally, we looked at how to configure a router. The WiFi Alliance has some great practical steps on how to configure a secure wireless network, and we looked at other basic configuration options, such as DHCP, communication channels, and NAT. After that, we talked specifically about security options like MAC filtering, SSID broadcasts, and wireless encryption. We finished up by looking at your wireless router as a firewall and taking a quick look at basic QoS.

Exam Essentials

Know the different 802.11 standards.   Standards you should be familiar with are 802.11a, 802.11b, 802.11g, and 802.11n. 802.11a transmits up to 54Mbps in the 5GHz range. 802.11b transmits up to 11Mbps in the 2.4GHz range. 802.11g is backward compatible with 802.11b and transmits 54Mbps in the 2.4GHz range. The newest one, 802.11n, is backward compatible with all of them and can achieve throughput of 600Mbps communicating in both the 2.4GHz and 5GHz ranges.

Understand security protocols used for wireless networking.   Listed in order from least to most secure, the common wireless security protocols include WEP, WPA, and WPA2. WPA uses TKIP and WPA2 uses AES.

Know the different types of available broadband connections.   Broadband connections include DSL, cable, satellite, ISDN, cellular, and fiber optic.

Know the three non-overlapping wireless channels.   The three non-overlapping channels are 1, 6, and 11.

Understand ways you can secure your network with a wireless router. Security options include using a good security protocol such as WPA2, using MAC filtering, disabling SSID broadcasts, setting up a DMZ, and using a firewall.

Know what WPS is. WiFi Protected Setup is designed to enable novice users to set up a WPA2-secured network and easily add clients literally through the push of a button.

Review Questions

The answers to the Chapter Review Questions can be found in Appendix A.

1. Which of the following wireless IEEE standards operate on the 2.4GHz radio frequency and are directly compatible with each other? (Choose two.)

   A. 802.11a

   B. 802.11b

   C. 802.11d

   D. 802.11g

2. What is the primary function of the SSID?

   A. Secure communication between a web server and browser

   B. Secure communication between a server and remote host

   C. A type of password used to help secure a wireless connection

   D. A type of password used to secure an Ethernet 802.3 connection

3. Which two of the following are standards for cellular communications?

   A. GSM

   B. SIG

   C. CDMA

   D. CCFL

4. What is the most secure wireless encryption standard for 802.11 networks?

   A. WEP

   B. WPA

   C. WPA2

   D. SAFER+

5. What level of QoS is designated for interactive voice and video?

   A. 1

   B. 4

   C. 5

   D. 6

6. You have just installed a wireless router on your home network. Which of the following should you do to make it highly secure? (Choose two.)

   A. Change the default administrator name and password.

   B. Change the SSID.

   C. Enable WEP.

   D. Configure it to channel 11.

7. You are setting up a small office network for a client. Which Internet service would you recommend to provide the best speed?

   A. DSL

   B. Dial-up

   C. Satellite

   D. BRI ISDN

   E. PRI ISDN

8. Which service allows users with private IP addresses to access the Internet using a public IP address?

   A. DHCP

   B. DNS

   C. DMZ

   D. NAT

9. You are installing a single 802.11g wireless network. The office space is large enough that you need three WAPs. What channels should you configure the WAPs on to avoid communication issues?

   A. 2, 5, and 7

   B. 1, 8, and 14

   C. 1, 6, and 11

   D. 3, 6, and 9

10. You are setting up a wireless network. Which wireless standards would give the users over 40Mbps throughput? (Choose three.)

    A. 802.11a

    B. 802.11b

    C. 802.11g

    D. 802.11n

11. Which of the following are 4G standards? (Choose two.)

    A. LTE

    B. GSM

    C. CDMA

    D. WiMAX

12. Which of the following wireless communication methods has an operational range of 1 meter with a viewing angle of 30 degrees?

    A. Bluetooth

    B. Infrared

    C. WiMAX

    D. Satellite

13. Which of the following are advantages to using dial-up Internet service? (Choose two.)

    A. High speed

    B. Broad availability

    C. Low cost

    D. High security

14. Which of the following security standards was the first to introduce a dynamic 128-bit per-packet security key?

    A. WEP

    B. TKIP

    C. AES

    D. CCMP

15. You are running an 802.11g wireless router in mixed mode. You have three 802.11g wireless NICs using the router. A new user connects using an 802.11b wireless NIC. What will happen?

    A. The user with 802.11b will access the network at 11Mbps while the users with 802.11g will access the network at 54Mbps.

    B. The user with 802.11b will not be able to communicate on the network.

    C. The user with 802.11b will access the network at 11Mbps. The users with 802.11g will access the network at 54Mbps unless they are communicating with the 802.11b device, which will be at 11Mbps.

    D. All users will access the network at 11Mbps.

16. When enabled, which feature of a wireless router allows only specified computers to access the network?

    A. Port forwarding

    B. WPS

    C. SSID

    D. MAC filtering

17. A firewall operates by using a set of rules known as what?

    A. SLA

    B. ACL

    C. Default deny

    D. DMZ

18. You have set up a wireless router on your network and configured it to use AES. What configuration option do you need to choose on the client computers?

    A. WEP

    B. WPA

    C. WPA2

    D. TKIP

19. Besides 802.11 standards, which wireless communication method works in the 2.4GHz range?

   A. Bluetooth

   B. Infrared

   C. Satellite

   D. Cellular

20. Which of the following broadband technologies provides two dedicated, digital data channels that can be combined for greater throughput?

   A. DSL

   B. Cable

   C. Satellite

   D. BRI ISDN

   E. PRI ISDN

Performance-Based Question

On the A+ exams, you will encounter performance-based questions. The questions on the exam require you to perform a specific task, and you will be graded on whether you were able to complete the task. The following require you to think creatively to measure how well you understand this chapter's topics. You may or may not see similar questions on the actual A+ exams. To see how your answers compare to the authors', refer to Appendix B.

You just purchased a new PCI network card for a Windows 7 desktop computer. How would you install it?

Chapter

9

Understanding Laptops

THE FOLLOWING COMPTIA A+ EXAM 220-801 OBJECTIVES ARE COVERED IN THIS CHAPTER:

✓ **3.1 Install and configure laptop hardware and components.**

- Expansion options: Express card/34, Express card/54, PCMCIA, SODIMM, Flash

- Hardware/device replacement: Keyboard, Hard Drive (2.5 vs. 3.5), Memory, Optical drive, Wireless card, Mini-PCIe, Screen, DC jack, Battery, Touchpad, Plastics, Speaker, System board, CPU

✓ **3.2 Compare and contrast the components within the display of a laptop.**

- Types: LCD, LED, OLED, Plasma

- Wi-Fi antenna connector/placement

- Inverter and its function

- Backlight

✓ **3.3 Compare and contrast laptop features.**

- Special function keys: Dual displays, Wireless (on/off), Volume settings, Screen brightness, Bluetooth (on/off), Keyboard backlight

- Docking station vs. port replicator

- Physical laptop lock and cable lock

As recently as the early 1990s, portable computers were luxuries that were affordable to only the wealthy or the select few businesspeople who traveled extensively. As with all other technologies, though, portable systems have gotten smaller, lighter (more portable), more powerful, and less expensive. Because the technology and price disparity between the two platforms has decreased significantly, laptops have outsold desktops since the mid-2000s.

Every indication is that the movement toward mobile computing will continue, so you definitely need to be well versed in portable technologies, which contain both nifty features and frustrating quirks. For this discussion, assume that a *portable computer* is any computer that contains all the functionality of a desktop computer system but is portable. Most people define *portable* in terms of weight and size. So that we can discuss things on the same level, let's define *portable* as less than 10 pounds and smaller than an average desktop computer.

Of course, laptops are not the only types of portable computers in the market today. There are netbooks, tablets, and a variety of handheld smartphones that can lay claim to being called computers too. For the purpose of this chapter, we'll specifically look at laptops, but many of the principles will be applicable to other other, smaller portable computers as well. For specific material on smaller mobile devices, see Chapter 18, "Mobile Devices."

The original portable computers were hardly portable, hence the unofficial term *luggable*. They were the size of a small suitcase and could weigh 50 pounds. Not only were they greatly inferior to desktops in technology, they were also outrageously expensive. It's no wonder few people purchased them. Compaq, Kaypro, and Osborne made some of the first luggable computers.

Laptops were the next type of portable computer. They contain a built-in keyboard, pointing device, and LCD screen in a clamshell design. They are also called *notebook* computers because they resemble large notebooks. Most portable computers in use today are laptop computers.

In this chapter, you will learn about laptop computer architecture and how it differs from desktop computer architecture, including specific laptop hardware technologies. We'll then talk about management features unique to laptops and how to replace laptop components.

Understanding Laptop Architecture

Laptops are similar to desktop computers in architecture in that they contain many parts that perform similar functions. However, the parts that make up a laptop are completely different from those in desktop computers. The obvious major difference is size; laptops are space challenged. Another primary concern is heat. Restricted space means less airflow, meaning parts can heat up and overheat faster.

To overcome space limitations, laptop parts are physically much smaller and lighter, and they must fit into the compact space of a laptop's case. It might not sound like much, but there really is a major difference between a 4.5-pound laptop and a 5.5-pound laptop if you're hauling it around in its carrying case all day. Also, laptop parts are designed to consume less power and to shut themselves off when not being used, although many desktops also have components that go into a low-power state when not active, such as video circuitry. Finally, most laptop components are proprietary—the motherboard is especially proprietary, and the LCD screen from one laptop will not necessarily fit on another.

A more recent development in the laptop arena has been the netbook computer. A *netbook* is an extremely small laptop computer that is lighter in weight and more scaled down in features than a standard laptop. Users are attracted to netbooks because of their enhanced portability and affordability. The features that remain are ideal for Internet access and emailing. However, many users would find netbooks insufficient for mainstream usage.

In the following sections, you will learn about the various components that make up laptops and how they differ from desktop computer components. If you don't remember exactly what each component does, it may help you to refer back to earlier hardware chapters occasionally as you read this chapter.

Laptops vs. Desktops

If you've ever shopped for a laptop, you have no doubt noticed that the prices of desktop PCs are often quite a bit lower than those for notebook computers, yet the desktops are faster and more powerful. If you've ever wondered what makes a laptop so much different than a PC, here are the primary differences between laptops and desktops:

Portability   This is probably the most obvious difference. Laptops are designed to be portable. They run on batteries, so you aren't tied to one spot at home or at the office. Networking options are available that allow you to connect to a network wirelessly and do work from just about anywhere, including malls, airports, coffee shops, and so on. As anyone who's tried to bring their full-tower PC to a LAN party can tell you, desktops just aren't that portable.

Cost   Laptops tend to cost more than desktop computers with similar features. The primary reason is that portability requires small components and unique proprietary designs so that those components fit into the small size necessary. Miniature versions of components cost more money than standard-sized (desktop) versions. The cost discrepancy between desktops and laptops has shrunk considerably in the last few years, but it still exists.

Performance   By and large, laptops are always going to lose out somewhere in the performance department. Compromises must often be made between performance and portability, and considering that portability is the major feature of a laptop, performance is what usually suffers. While it is possible to have a laptop with comparable performance to a desktop, the amount of money one would have to spend for a "desktop replacement" laptop is considerable. This is not to say that a laptop can't outperform a desktop, it's just that the "bang for the buck" factor is higher in a desktop.

Expandability   Because desktop computers were designed to be modular, their capabilities can be upgraded quite easily. It is next to impossible to upgrade the processor or motherboard on most laptops. Other than memory and hard drives, most laptop upgrades consist of adding an external device through one of the laptop's ports, such as a USB port.

Quality of construction   Considering how much abuse laptops get, it is much more important that the materials used to construct the laptop case and other components be extremely durable. Durability is important in a desktop too, but it won't be tested as much as in a laptop.

Building Your Own

This anecdote comes from one of the authors: "During an A+ course, I gave the class the assignment to go out on the Web and put together the most powerful and complete computer they could for under a thousand dollars. The class was for non-degree-seeking adults, so nothing was graded; it was simply to provide experience with speccing out and pricing the parts that go into making a complete system.

"One of the students had her eye on a new laptop for personal use. Because she noticed the trend toward being able to build a desktop computer for less than she could buy one, the student assumed the same about laptops. Unfortunately, I had not specifically mentioned the fact that there are no standards for building complete laptop clones, unlike with desktops.

"You can't reliably build your own laptop. Because laptop components are designed to exacting specifications to fit properly inside one manufacturer's notebook, there generally are no universal motherboards, video boards, and so on for laptops. Memory and hard drives are the exception. You can get different brands of memory and hard drives for laptops, but you can't buy a motherboard from one company and the video circuitry from another. Even things as common as optical drives are usually designed to work only with a specific brand or model."

Now that we've illustrated the primary differences between laptops and desktops, let's examine the parts of the laptop and what they do.

Laptop Case

A typical laptop case is made up of three main parts:

- The display—usually an LCD or LED display
- The case frame, which is the metal reinforcing structure inside the laptop that provides rigidity and strength and that most components mount to
- The case, or the plastic cover that surrounds the components and provides protection from the elements

The cases are typically made of some type of plastic (usually ABS plastic or ABS composite) to provide for light weight as well as strength.

 A few notebooks have cases made of a strong, lightweight metal, such as aluminum or titanium. However, the majority of laptop cases are made of plastic.

Laptop cases are made in what is known as a clamshell design. In a clamshell design, the laptop has two halves, hinged together at the back. Usually, the display is the top half and everything else is in the bottom half.

Occasionally, part of the laptop's case will crack and need to be replaced. However, you usually can't just replace the cracked section. Most often, you must remove every component from inside the laptop's case and swap the components over to the new case. This is a labor-intensive process because the screws in laptops are often very small and hard to reach. Often, repairing a cracked case may cost several hundred dollars in labor alone. Most times, people who have cracked laptop cases wait until something else needs to be repaired before having the case fixed. Or, they just wait until it's time to upgrade to a new system. The decision on when to repair or replace the laptop boils down to a few factors. The primary one is if the user can live with the damage. While they can be annoying, most case problems don't inhibit the operation of the machine. The secondary factor is money. The user (or company) needs to decide if it's really worth spending the money needed to fix the issue immediately.

Motherboards and Processors

As with desktop computers, the motherboard of a laptop is the backbone structure to which all internal components connect. However, with a laptop, almost all components must be integrated onto the motherboard, including onboard circuitry for the serial, parallel, USB, IEEE 1394, video, expansion, and network ports of the laptop. With desktop systems, the option remains to not integrate such components. Because of the similarities between laptop and desktop components, some material in the next few sections will be familiar to you if you have read Chapter 1, "Motherboards, Processors, and Memory."

Laptop Motherboards

The primary differences between a laptop motherboard and a desktop motherboard are the lack of standards and the much smaller form factor. As mentioned earlier, most motherboards are designed along with the laptop case so that all the components will fit inside. Therefore, the motherboard is nearly always proprietary, and that's what we mean by "lack of standards." They all use the technologies you're used to such as USB and 802.11, but it's very unlikely you're going to be able to swap a motherboard from one laptop into another, even if both laptops are from the same manufacturer. Figure 9.1 shows an example of a laptop motherboard.

FIGURES 9.1   A laptop motherboard

To save space, components of the video circuitry (and possibly other circuits as well) are placed on a thin circuit board that connects directly to the motherboard. This circuit board is often known as a riser card or a *daughterboard*.

Having components performing different functions (such as video, audio, and networking) integrated on the same board is a mixed bag. On one hand, it saves a lot of space. On the other hand, if one part goes bad, you have to replace the entire board, which is more expensive than just replacing one expansion card.

Laptop Processors

Just as with desktop computers, the processor is the brain of the laptop computer. And just like everything else, compared to desktop hardware devices, laptop hardware devices are smaller and not quite as powerful. The spread between the speed of a laptop CPU and that of a desktop motherboard can be a gigahertz or more.

Laptops have less space, and thus, heat is a major concern. Add to that the fact that processors are the hottest-running component and you can see where cooling can be an issue. To help combat this heat problem, laptop processors are engineered with the following features:

Streamlined connection to the motherboard   Nearly all desktop processors mount using pin connectors, whether on the CPU or on the motherboard (as is the case with LGA sockets). Pins and sockets are big and bulky, meaning they're not a laptop's friends. Laptop processors are generally either soldered directly to the motherboard or attached using the Micro-FCBGA (Flip Chip Ball Grid Array) standard, which uses balls instead of pins. In most cases, this means that the processor cannot be removed, meaning no processor upgrades are possible.

Lower voltages and clock speeds   Two ways to combat heat are to slow the processor down (run it at a lower speed) or give it less juice (run it at a lower voltage). Again, performance will suffer compared to a desktop processor, but lowering heat is the goal here.

Active sleep and slowdown modes   Most laptops will run the processor in a lower power state when on battery power, in an effort to extend the life of the battery. This is known as processor throttling. The motherboard works closely with the operating system to determine if the processor really needs to run at full speed. If it doesn't, it's slowed down to save energy and to reduce heat. When more processing power is needed, the CPU is throttled back up.

One of the best features of many laptop processors is that they include built-in wireless networking. One of the earliest laptop-specific chipsets that gained a ton of popularity was the Pentium M chip made by Intel. The Pentium M consists of three separate components:

- The Mobile Intel Express chipset (such as the Mobile Intel 915GM Express or the Mobile Intel 910GML), which is the graphics memory controller hub

- The Intel/PRO Wireless Network Connection, providing an integrated wireless LAN connection

- The Intel Centrino chipset, which is the "brain" of the chipset, designed to run on lower power than the desktop processor

Depending on the manufacturer, motherboard, and processor used, the features described as part of the Pentium M will be built into the motherboard rather than the processor itself. Regardless of where it's built in to, it's a great set of features to have for mobile computers!

Some portable computers will simply use stripped-down versions of desktop processors such an Intel Pentium or Core series processor. While there's nothing wrong with this, it makes sense that components specifically designed for notebooks fit the application better than components that have been retrofitted for notebook use. Consider an analogy to the automobile industry: It's better to design a convertible from the ground up than to simply cut the top off an existing coupe or sedan.

Memory

Notebooks don't use standard desktop computer memory chips, because they're too big. In fact, for most of the history of laptops, there were no standard types of memory chips. If you wanted to add memory to your laptop, you had to order it from the laptop manufacturer. Of course, because you could get memory from only one supplier, you got the privilege of paying a premium over and above a similar-sized desktop memory chip.

However, there are now two common types of laptop memory package: SODIMM and MicroDIMM. Nevertheless, modern laptop manufacturers may still opt to go the proprietary route due to design considerations that favor a custom solution. To see what kind of memory your laptop uses, check either the manual or the manufacturer's website. You can also check third-party memory producers' websites (such as www.crucial.com).

SODIMM

The most common memory form factor for laptops is called a Small Outline DIMM (SODIMM). They're much smaller than standard DIMMs, measuring about 67 millimeters (2.6″) long and 32 millimeters (1.25″) tall. SODIMMs are available in a variety of configurations, including 32-bit (72-pin) and 64-bit (144-pin SDRAM, 200-pin DDR, 200-pin DDR2, and 204-pin DDR3) options. Figure 9.2 shows an example of the classic 144-pin variety.

 NOTE   You'll also see SODIMM spelled as SO–DIMM as well.

Just as with desktop computers, make sure the SODIMM you want to put into the laptop is compatible with the motherboard. The same standards that apply to desktop memory compatibility apply to laptops. This means you can find DDR, DDR2, and DDR3 SODIMMs for laptops. DDR has all but topped out at 1GB per module, while DDR2 and DDR3 SODIMM modules can be purchased in sizes up to 8GB (at the time this book was being written), which lags desktop DIMM capacity by a bit.

FIGURE 9.2   144-pin SODIMM

MicroDIMM

Although no longer new, the MicroDIMM is the most recent form factor for laptop memory modules. The MicroDIMM is an extremely small RAM form factor. In fact, it is over 50 percent smaller than a SODIMM—only about 45.5mm (about 1.75″) long and 30mm (about 1.2″, a bit bigger than a US quarter) wide. Another major difference is that the MicroDIMM does not have any notches on the bottom. Figure 9.3 shows a 172-pin MicroDIMM. It was designed for the ultralight and portable subnotebook style of computer. Popular MicroDIMM form factors include 64-bit modules with 172 or 214 pins for DDR2.

FIGURE 9.3   144-pin MicroDIMM

Storage

Nearly all laptops have a hard drive, but not all laptops have both a floppy drive and an optical drive. Many times there just isn't room for both, and considering floppy drives are practically obsolete, why have one anyway? Often there is a multipurpose bay that can be used to hold either drive or an extra battery. If this drive bay exists, users generally keep the optical drive installed most of the time and leave out the floppy drive. In some cases, the floppy drive is an external device that you connect with a special cable to a proprietary connector. Figure 9.4 shows an example of one of these connectors, and Figure 9.5 shows an example of a laptop floppy drive with a proprietary connector. Notice how thin the floppy drive is and how compact the electronics are. When used at all, floppy drives that attach to the laptop through a USB port are more common today.

Laptops don't have the room for the full-sized 3½″ hard drives that desktop computers use. Instead, they use a hard drive with a 2½″ form factor that is less than ½″ thick. These drives share the same controller technologies as desktop computers; however, they use smaller connectors. Figure 9.6 shows an example of a standard hard drive compared to a laptop hard drive.

Optical drives on laptops are necessarily smaller than their desktop counterparts as well. Figure 9.7 shows an example of a desktop CD-ROM drive compared to a laptop CD-ROM drive. Note that the laptop drive is very small, but it has all the functionality of a desktop unit. The drive mechanism and circuits have all been miniaturized to save space. As a result, the functionality is basically the same, but the cost is usually higher. Any time a component's functionality remains the same while its size decreases, you will notice an increase in price over the standard-sized item.

FIGURE 9.4 A proprietary floppy connector

FIGURE 9.5 A laptop floppy drive

FIGURE 9.6 A desktop hard drive compared to a laptop hard drive

CD, DVD, and Blu-ray burners are great to have on laptops as backup devices. Simply copy the contents of the hard drive (or just important files) to the optical discs and store them in a safe location.

FIGURE 9.7   A desktop DVD drive compared to a laptop DVD drive

Input Devices

Because of the small size of laptops, getting data into them presents unique challenges to designers. They must design a keyboard that fits within the case of the laptop. They must also design some sort of pointing device that users can use in graphical interfaces like Windows. The primary challenge in both cases is to design these peripherals so they fit within the design constraints of the laptop (low power and small form factor) while remaining usable.

Keyboards

A standard-sized desktop keyboard wasn't designed to be portable. It wouldn't fit well with the portable nature of a laptop. That usually means laptop keys are not normal size; they must be smaller and packed together more tightly. People who learned to type on a typewriter or regular computer often have a difficult time adjusting to a laptop keyboard.

Laptop keyboards are built into the lower portion of the clamshell. Sometimes, they can be removed easily to access peripherals below them like memory and hard drives, as in the Lenovo ThinkPad series.

Special Function Keys

Because of the much smaller space available for keys, some laptop keys (like the number pad, Home, Insert, PgUp, and PgDn keys) are consolidated into special multifunction keys. These keys are accessed through the standard keys by using a special *function (Fn) key*. It's typically near the Windows key on the keyboard and labeled in lettering of an alternate color (usually blue) that matches the lettering of the labels for alternate functions on other keys. To use a multifunction key, you press and hold the Fn key (as you would the Shift, Ctrl, and Alt keys) and then tap the key labeled with the function you want, finally releasing the Fn key. Figure 9.8 shows an example of a function key.

The function key combinations can control many laptop functions, but the most common are video, audio, and networking settings. The specific keys used will vary by laptop model, but there are usually icons on the keys that perform the functions to help you out.

FIGURE 9.8 Function (Fn) key

Video adjustments come in two varieties: changing the video output and dimming or brightening the screen. Dimming and brightening the screen is pretty straightforward, but the video output function can throw people off. Remember that nearly every laptop has a video connector on the back to plug in an external monitor or a projector. You will need to use the video toggle key to get this external port to work. Usually there are three states: laptop only, external output only, and both displays. Figure 9.9 shows examples of the keys that handle video functions.

FIGURE 9.9 Video adjustment keys F4 (LCD toggle), F7 (dim), and F8 (brighten)

Note that the LCD toggle (the F4 key in Figure 9.9) has the same symbol on it as the external video connector. The dimming key has a sun with an arrow pointing down, and the brightening key has a sun with an arrow pointing up. (Some manufacturers will use a small sun on the dimming key and a large sun on the brightening key.)

The audio setting can often be adjusted using the function keys too. To lower the volume, look for an icon with a speaker with only one "wave" coming out of it. The volume is increased with the speaker with several waves, and the mute button will have a speaker with an *X*. Figure 9.10 shows an example.

FIGURE 9.10   Audio adjustment keys F10 (mute), F11 (quieter), and F12 (louder)

Finally, there are the network settings. There aren't really a lot of choices here; it's a matter of turning the network adapter on or off. The symbol for WiFi usually looks like a small antenna. If you're using Bluetooth, the symbol will be Bluetooth's trademarked *B*. Sometimes disabling these options is handled by the F*n* keys, and other times they are handled by separate switches near the keyboard. For example, Figure 9.11 shows a WiFi switch on the front of a laptop, and Figure 9.12 shows a WiFi toggle above the keyboard. The switch in Figure 9.12 looks like an indicator light only, but the strip is touch-sensitive.

FIGURE 9.11   Network card toggle switch on the front of the computer

FIGURE 9.12   Network card toggle switch above the keyboard

The point is, look around if you don't see the right function key on the keyboard itself. It's bound to be there somewhere.

Some laptops include a backlight for the keyboard as well. These can also be dimmed or brightened, or turned off and on, with the use of a function key. For example, on the Toshiba P205, the right combination is Fn+Z. Keep in mind that on laptop models with an ambient light sensor, such as the MacBook Pro, the backlight settings will be controlled automatically by the operating system; you won't be able to turn it off unless it's already on.

Mice and Pointing Devices

In addition to using the keyboard, you must have a method of controlling the onscreen pointer in the Windows interface. There are many methods of doing this, but there are some that are more common:

- Trackball
- Touchpad
- Point stick
- Touchscreen

Because of different pointing-device preferences, some laptops use multiple pointing devices to appeal to a wider variety of people.

Most laptops today include a mouse/keyboard port, a USB port, or both. Either of these ports can be used to add an input device like a mouse or a standard-sized keyboard.

Trackball

Many early laptops used trackballs as pointing devices. A *trackball* is essentially the same as a mouse turned upside down. The onscreen pointer moves in the same direction and at the same speed you move the trackball with your thumb or fingers.

Trackballs are cheap to produce. However, the primary problem with trackballs is that they do not last as long as other types of pointing devices; a trackball picks up dirt and oil from operators' fingers, and those substances clog the rollers on the trackball and prevent it from functioning properly.

Touchpad

To overcome the problems of trackballs, a newer technology that has become known as the Touchpad was developed. *Touchpad* is actually the trade name of a product. However, the trade name is now used to describe an entire genre of products that are similar in function.

A Touchpad is a device that has a pad of touch-sensitive material. The user draws with their finger on the Touchpad, and the onscreen pointer follows the finger motions. Included with the Touchpad are two buttons for left- or right-clicking (although with some Touchpads, you can perform the functions of the left-click by tapping on the Touchpad). Figure 9.13 shows a Touchpad.

FIGURE 9.13   Laptop Touchpad

Point Stick

With the introduction of the ThinkPad series of laptops, IBM introduced a new feature known as the Touchpoint, generically known as a *point stick*. The point stick is a pointing device that uses a small rubber-tipped stick. When you push the point stick in a particular direction, the onscreen pointer goes in the same direction. The harder you push, the faster the onscreen pointer moves. The point allows fingertip control of the onscreen pointer, without the reliability problems associated with trackballs.

Point sticks have their own problems, however. Often, the stick does not return to center properly, causing the pointer to drift when not in use. You might also notice the rubber cover for the stick becoming a bit gummy with extended use. Most manufacturers supply replacement covers of varying textures with new systems. Some later systems employ a concave version of the cover and updated workings that tend to minimize a lot of these concerns.

Touchscreen

The last type of pointing device we'll discuss can be found in use at many department stores: the informational *kiosks* with screens that respond to your touch and give you information about product specials or bridal registries. Instead of a keyboard and mouse, these computer screens have a film over them that is sensitive to touch. This technology is known as a *Touchscreen* (see Figure 9.14). With most of the interfaces in use on Touchscreens, touching a box drawn on the monitor does the same thing as double-clicking that box with a mouse. These screens are most commonly found on monitors; however, with the advent of the *tablet PC* (a laptop designed to be held like a pad of paper), the Touchscreen is becoming more popular as an input device for a laptop.

Cleaning a Touchscreen is usually just as easy as cleaning a regular monitor. With optical Touchscreens, the monitor *is* a regular monitor, so it can be cleaned with glass cleaner. However, if the screen has a capacitive coating, glass cleaner may damage it. Instead, use a cloth dampened with water to clean the dirt, dust, and fingerprints from the screen.

FIGURE 9.14   A typical Touchscreen

Expansion Buses and Ports

Although laptop computers are less expandable than their desktop counterparts, they can be expanded to some extent. Laptops have expansion ports similar to those found on desktop computers as well as a couple that are found only on laptops.

PCMCIA (PC Card) Expansion Bus

The tongue-twister *PCMCIA* stands for Personal Computer Memory Card International Association. The PCMCIA was organized to provide a standard way of expanding portable computers. The PCMCIA bus was originally designed to provide a way of expanding the memory in a small, handheld computer, referred to generically as a PCMCIA host. The PCMCIA bus has been renamed *PC Card* to make it easier to pronounce. PC Card uses a small expansion card (about the size of a credit card). The interface is a thin, 68-pin connector that has remained relatively unchanged from the original specification. Although this form factor is primarily used in portable computers, PC Card adapters (converters) are available for desktop PCs. The PC Card bus now serves as a universal expansion bus that can accommodate nearly any device.

In addition to the card, the PC Card architecture includes two other components:

- Socket Services software is a BIOS-level interface to the PCMCIA bus slot. When loaded, it hides the details of the PC Card hardware from the computer. This software can detect when a card has been inserted and what type of card it is.

- Card Services software is the interface between the application and Socket Services. It tells the applications which interrupts and I/O ports the card is using. Applications that need to access the PC Card don't access the hardware directly; instead, they tell Card Services that they need access to a particular feature, and Card Services gets the appropriate feature from the PC Card.

This dual-component architecture allows the PCMCIA architecture to be used in different types of computer systems (that is, not just x86/x64-based PCs). For example, Apple laptop computers based on Motorola processors could use PC Cards for modems and for LAN interface cards.

The first release of the PCMCIA standard (PCMCIA 1.0, circa 1990) defined a 16-bit ISA-like bus to be used for memory expansion only. PCMCIA 1.0 supported 5V memory cards. The second major release (PCMCIA 2.*x*) introduced 3.3V cards and host slots. PCMCIA 2.*x* was designed to be backward compatible with version 1, so 5V memory cards can be used in version 2 host slots. Cards that are only capable of 3.3V operation are keyed to prevent damage from insertion into older 5V-only host slots. PCMCIA version 2.01 was released in 1992 to specify the use of Card and Socket Services as a standard driver platform.

PCMCIA 5.0 (aka CardBus) increased the bus width to 32 bits and the bus speed from 8MHz to a maximum of 33MHz. In addition, the new CardBus PC Card adapters used PCI-like access methods, and the throughput speeds increased dramatically, up to a maximum of 133MBps (1.06Gbps). These cards are differentiated from the 16-bit cards by a metal grounding strip, often gold in color, along the insertion edge of the card. You can insert 16-bit PC Cards in a CardBus slot, but the converse is not also true.

PCMCIA standards jumped from PCMCIA 2.1 to PC Card 5.0 as PCMCIA and JEIDA standards were merged. At the same time, the name *CardBus* was introduced to differentiate the new 32-bit cards from their 16-bit ancestors.

The bus width of these cards and slots is either 16 or 32 bits, as previously discussed. Also, the original PCMCIA specification supported only one interrupt request, or IRQ (a problem if you needed to install two devices that both need interrupts in the same PC Card bus). Card and Socket Services took care of this deficiency. PC Cards also support bus mastering and Direct Memory Access (DMA), but only as of PC Card 5.0. DMA support was eventually removed in version 7.2. PC Card 8.0, released in 2001, specifies a newer CardBay standard designed to integrate USB functionality into the PC Card format. The benefit would be for devices that have PC Card slots but no USB ports. The reverse is more common, however.

Three major types of PC Cards (and slots) have been specified. Each has different uses and physical characteristics, although each one measures 54mm in width and 85.6mm in length. They are called Type I, Type II, and Type III:

- Type I cards are 3.3mm thick and are most commonly used for memory cards.

- Type II cards are 5mm thick and are mostly used for modems and LAN adapters but for sound cards, SCSI controllers, and other devices as well. This is the most common PC Card type found today, and most systems have at least two Type II slots (or one Type III slot).

- The Type III slot is 10.5mm thick. Its most common application is PC Card hard disks. These slots are all but extinct.

ExpressCard

ExpressCard was launched by PCMCIA as a way to support USB 2.0 and PCI Express (hence the term *Express*Card) connectivity for portable computers. In fact, with support for transfer rates 2.5 times that of CardBus, ExpressCard is capable of transferring data at 2.5Gbps, approximately the rate of a single lane of PCIe. Cards can be created that support either specification or both. The manufacturer chooses the option that matches the application. ExpressCard 1.0 was published in 2003 and updated in 2006 to Release 1.1. Version 2 of the ExpressCard specification is designed to support USB 3.0 and PCIe 2.0.

With ExpressCard technology, portable computers can be adapted to support faster versions of legacy technologies. Standards not supported by CardBus, such as Gigabit Ethernet, IEEE 1394b, and eSATA, are accessible through the use of ExpressCard. Whereas CardBus required additional hardware and software to support nonnative hot swapping through the ISA and PCI buses, ExpressCard takes advantage of hot swapping natively through the USB and PCIe buses. As an added bonus, the ExpressCard adapters are smaller than their CardBus cousins. The smaller size can be attributed to the PCIe-based serial technology on which ExpressCard is based. The PCI-based parallel communications used by CardBus require the larger 68-pin and -socket interface, while ExpressCard is implemented on a 26-contact blade interface.

ExpressCard adapters are 75mm in length and 5mm thick. The standard ExpressCard, known as ExpressCard/34, is only 34mm wide. A 54mm-wide version, known appropriately as ExpressCard/54, is still only 34mm at its insertion point, but 22mm from that end, it expands to 54mm to accommodate more internal electronics. The additional space allows for better heat dissipation and the support of applications such as 1.8″ disk drives, card readers, and CompactFlash readers. While a Universal ExpressCard host slot appears to be able to accept a CardBus adapter, the card inserts not even an inch before stopping on the internal guide that assures correct ExpressCard/34 insertion. ExpressCard shares with CardBus the use of 3.3V to power some cards but swaps the 5V versions for a new, lower 1.5V offering.

You may see the term *ExpressBus* used in reference to this technology. Despite the source, it's not a valid term.

Mini PCI and Mini PCIe

Mini PCI is an adaptation of the Peripheral Component Interconnect (PCI) standard used in desktop computers. As its name implies, it's just a smaller version (about ¼ the size of PCI cards) designed primarily for laptops.

These cards reside internally in the laptop, with their connection ports generally lining up with the edge of the outside of the case.

Mini PCI is functionally identical to the PCI version 2.2, meaning it's a 32-bit, 33MHz bus with a 3.3V-powered connection. It also supports bus mastering and DMA. There are three different Mini PCI form factors: Type I, Type II, and Type III. The size and connector types are listed in Table 9.1.

TABLE 9.1 Mini PCI form factors

Type	Connector	Size
IA	100-pin, stacking	7.5 x 70 x 45 millimeters
IB	100-pin, stacking	5.5 x 70 x 45 millimeters
IIA	100-pin, stacking	17.44 x 78 x 45 millimeters
IIB	100-pin, stacking	5.5 x 78 x 45 millimeters
IIIA	124-pin, card edge	2.4 x 59.6 x 50.95 millimeters
IIIB	124-pin, card edge	2.4 x 59.6 x 44.6 millimeters

The extra 24 pins on Type III connectors allow for routing information back to the system, which is required for audio, phone line, or network connections.

Common Mini PCI devices include sound cards, modems, networking cards, and SCSI, ATA, and SATA controllers. Adapters are available that allow you to use a Mini PCI adapter in a standard PCI slot.

Mini PCIe cards are physically similar to ExpressCard devices without the external cover, measuring a few millimeters less in length and width as a result. In reality, however, they have a completely different, 52-pin edge connector. Nevertheless, like ExpressCard, Mini PCIe cards support USB 2.0 and PCIe x1 functionality. Additionally, Mini PCIe cards have the 1.5V and 3.3V power options in common with ExpressCard.

USB Ports

Like desktops, laptops use USB ports for expansion. However, because of the lack of internal expansion in laptops, most peripherals for laptops are found as either PC Cards or USB expansion devices.

The USB port is the most common type for portable memory devices known as flash drives. These handy little sticks can hold up to 32GB of data (at the time of this writing) and have basically made floppy drives completely obsolete.

For more information about USB ports and their function, refer to Chapter 3, "Peripherals and Expansion."

Mouse/Keyboard Port

Just in case you don't like using your laptop's built-in keyboard or pointing device, some laptops come with a combination *keyboard/mouse port* that allows you to connect either an external keyboard or an external mouse. On laptops that don't have USB ports, this port is most often used for a standard PS/2 mouse. On those laptops that do have USB ports, this port is used for an external keypad or keyboard (because the USB port can accommodate an external mouse).

Communications Ports

Laptops are built to make computing mobile. And in this world where it seems as if you always need to be in touch with others while you're mobile, it makes sense that laptops have a variety of methods to communicate while you're on the go. Several communication methods are available; nearly all new laptops come equipped with some version of an 802.11 wireless card. Others may have connections for an analog dial-up modem or an infrared, cellular, Bluetooth, or Ethernet device. Each of these can also be added to laptops through USB or PC Card connection.

Docking Stations

Some laptops are designed to be desktop replacement laptops. That is, they will replace a standard desktop computer for day-to-day use and are thus more full-featured than other laptops. These laptops often have a proprietary docking port. A docking port (as shown in Figure 9.15) is used to connect the laptop to a special laptop-only peripheral known as a *docking station*. A docking station is basically an extension of the motherboard of a laptop. Because a docking station is designed to stay behind when the laptop is removed, it can contain things like a full-sized drive bay and expansion bus slots. Also, the docking station can function as a port replicator.

FIGURE 9.15   A docking port

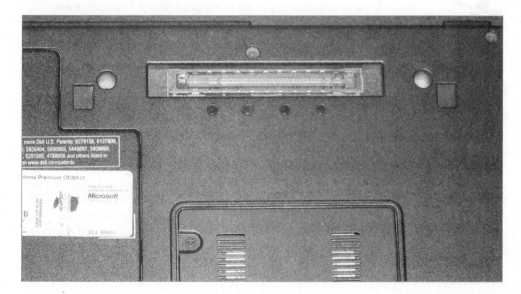

A port replicator reproduces the functions of the ports on the back of a laptop so that peripherals such as monitors, keyboards, printers, and so on that don't travel with the laptop can remain connected to the dock and don't have to all be physically unplugged each time the laptop is taken away. Figure 9.16 is a photo of the back of a docking station, showing the replicated ports, some of which are only available on the docking station and not on the laptop. Finally, there are accessory bays (also called media bays). These external bays allow you to plug your full-sized devices into them and take your laptop with you (for example, a full-sized hard drive that connects to an external USB or FireWire port). As a point of clarification (or perhaps confusion), media bays and accessory bays are sometimes used to refer to laptop drive bays.

FIGURE 9.16 Ports on a docking station

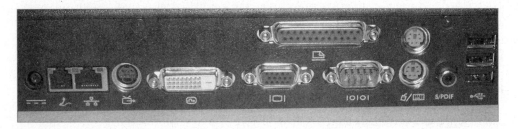

Docking ports and docking stations are *proprietary*. That is, the port works only with docking stations designed by the laptop's manufacturer and vice versa.

Power Systems

Because portable computers have unique characteristics as a result of their portability, they have unique power systems as well. Portable computers can use either of two power sources: batteries or adapted power from an AC or DC source. Regardless the source of their power, laptops utilize DC power to energize their internal components. Therefore, any AC power source needs to be rectified (converted) to DC. Most laptop display backlights, on the other hand, require high-voltage, low-amperage AC power. To avoid a separate external AC input, an inverter is used to convert the DC power that is supplied for the rest of the system to AC for the backlight. In case it's not obvious, rectifiers and inverters perform opposite functions, more or less.

Batteries

There are many different battery chemistries that come in various sizes and shapes. Nickel cadmium (NiCd), lithium-ion (Li-ion), and nickel-metal hydride (NiMH) have been the most popular chemistries for laptop batteries. A newer battery chemistry, lithium-polymer (Li-poly), has been gaining in prominence over recent years for limited categories of devices, mostly the smaller ones. Li-poly still has issues that need to be worked out before mainstream acceptance for a wider range of applications is seen. Figure 9.17 is a photo of a Li-ion battery for a Dell laptop. Notice the meter on the left side in the bottom view.

Battery chemistries can be compared by energy density and power density. Energy density measures how much energy a battery can hold. Power density measures how quickly the stored energy can be accessed, focusing on access in bursts, not prolonged runtime. An analogy to the storage and distribution of liquids might help solidify these concepts. A gallon bucket has a higher "energy density" and "power density" than a pint bottle; the bucket holds more and can pour its contents more quickly. Another common metric for battery comparison is rate of self-discharge, or how fast an unused battery reduces its stored charge.

FIGURE 9.17   A laptop Li-ion battery

🌐 Real World Scenario

Is That Battery Really Dead?

Some batteries, such as nickel cadmium (NiCd) ones, suffer from a performance-affecting chemical memory loss. Others, such as lithium-ion, don't suffer from this affliction but do suffer from so-called digital memory loss that plagues the built-in gauges that monitor the charge left in the battery. This effect can be observed in software gauges that read the battery's charge level. The digital memory effect manifests itself as a sudden loss of power when the gauges register, say, 30 percent remaining capacity. The fix, much like the fix for chemical memory in NiCd batteries, is to allow a full discharge once a month or so. This is called *battery calibration* and can be performed right in the device being powered by the battery. Other than this occasional full discharge, Li-ion batteries last longer when you partially discharge them and then recharge them, making them ideal for laptops and personal handheld devices, such as cell phones, that tend to get used sporadically on battery power before being plugged back in to charge.

Power Adapters

Most notebook computers can also use AC power with a special adapter (called an *AC adapter*) that converts AC-power input to DC output. The adapter can be integrated into the notebook, but more often it's a separate "brick" with two cords, one that plugs into the back of the laptop and another that plugs into a wall outlet. Figure 9.18 is a photo of the latter.

FIGURE 9.18 A laptop AC adapter

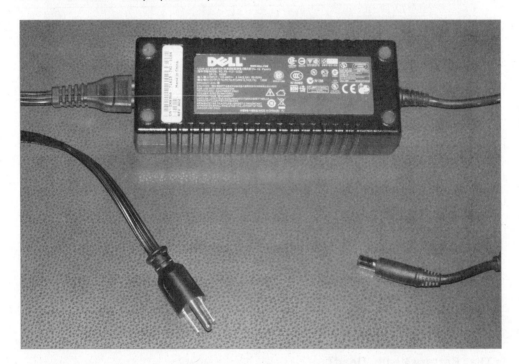

Another power accessory that is often used is a *DC adapter*, which allows a user to plug the laptop into the power source (usually a cigarette lighter) inside a car or on an airplane. These adapters allow people who travel frequently to use their laptops while on the road (literally).

Use caution when selecting a replacement AC adapter for your laptop. You should choose one rated for the same or higher wattage than the original. You must also pay special attention to the polarity of the plug that interfaces with the laptop. If the laptop requires the positive lead to be the center conductor, for instance, then you must take care not to reverse the polarity.

Regarding the input voltage of the adapter, care must also be taken to match the adapter to the power grid of the surrounding region. Some adapters have a fixed AC input requirement. Purchasing the wrong unit can result in lack of functionality or damage to the laptop. Other adapters are autoswitching, meaning they are able to automatically switch the input voltage they expect based on the voltage supplied by the wall outlet. These units are often labeled with voltage-input ranges, such as 100 to 240V, and frequency ranges, such as 50 to 60Hz, and are able to accommodate deployment in practically any country around the world. Nevertheless, you should still ascertain whether some sort of converter is required, even for autoswitching adapters.

Laptop Displays

The display system is the primary component in the top half of the clamshell case. (The wireless antenna often resides here too, and we'll get to that in just a bit.) Much like all other laptop components, the display is more or less a smaller version of its desktop counterpart. What is unique to laptop displays, though, is that for some time, the technology used in them was actually more advanced than what was commonly used in desktops. This is due to liquid crystal display (LCD) technology.

Before LCD technology, computer displays used cathode-ray tube (CRT) technology (like old-school televisions) and were big, bulky, and hardly mobile. We talked about LCD standards and concepts (in addition to LED, OLED, and plasma) in Chapter 4, "Display Devices," so there's not really a need to dive into the technical specs again. Instead, we'll focus here on the different components that are required to make these types of displays work.

Video Card

The video card in a laptop or desktop with an LCD monitor does the same thing a video card supporting a CRT monitor would do. It's responsible for generating and managing the image sent to the screen. The big difference is that most LCD monitors are digital, meaning you need a video card that puts out a digital image. Laptop manufacturers put video cards that are compatible with the display in laptops, but with desktops it can get a bit confusing. Figure 9.19 shows an ABIT video card, with a digital video interface (DVI) port on the right and an analog (VGA) port on the left. The port in the middle is an S-video/composite video port.

The video card in Figure 9.19 is obviously for a desktop. Most laptop manufacturers choose to integrate the LCD circuitry on the motherboard to save space.

On the market, you can find digital-to-analog video converters if you need to plug in an older analog monitor to a digital video card.

FIGURE 9.19   Video card

Real World Scenario

Video Memory Sharing

If your video card is built into your motherboard, odds are that it doesn't have its own memory but shares system memory with the processor. Note that there is nothing wrong with this type of setup; in fact, it often brings the cost of the laptop down. It's just that instead of having 4GB of RAM and 512MB of video RAM (for example), you would have only 4GB total. So if your video card were using 512MB, the system would be left with only 3.5GB.

How much of a difference does all of this make? Well, it depends on what you're doing with your laptop. If you're using it for the Internet and light work, probably not much difference. If you're working with more video-intensive applications, using a computer with shared memory might slow you down some. This usually brings up two questions: One, what's the optimal balance? Two, where do I change this?

To answer question one, again, it depends on what you are doing. If you perform more video-intensive operations (or if you're gaming), then you might want to set aside more memory for the video card. If you're not as concerned with rapid pixilation, then less is fine. Which brings us to the second question: Where do you set it? Shared memory is configured in the system BIOS. Each BIOS is different, so be sure to consult your owner's manual if you have any questions. Keep in mind that some BIOSs will allow you to set aside a only certain amount of memory—say, 512MB—for video memory.

How does this affect your computer when you upgrade the memory? First, keep in mind that some of your memory will be taken by the video card, so you might want to upgrade to more than you originally planned for. Second, after upgrading the memory, you will need to go into the BIOS and reconfigure how much you want allocated to the video card.

Backlight

LCD displays do not produce light, so to generate brightness, LCD displays have a *backlight*. A backlight is a small fluorescent lamp placed behind, above, or to the side of an LCD display. The light from the lamp is diffused across the screen, producing brightness. The typical laptop display uses a *cold cathode fluorescent lamp (CCFL)* as its backlight. They're generally about 8 inches long and slimmer than a pencil. Best of all, they generate little heat, which is always a good thing to avoid with laptops.

Inverter

The only problem with fluorescent lighting, and LCD backlights in particular, is that they require fairly high-voltage, high-frequency energy. Another component is needed to provide the right kind of energy, and that's the *inverter*.

The inverter is a small circuit board installed behind the LCD panel that takes DC current and inverts it to AC for the backlight. If you are having problems with flickering screens or dimness, it's more likely that the inverter is the problem and not the backlight itself.

There are two things to keep in mind if you are going to replace an inverter. One, they store and convert energy, so they have the potential to discharge that energy. To an inexperienced technician, they can be dangerous. Two, make sure the replacement inverter was made to work with the LCD backlight you have. If they weren't made for each other, you might have problems with a dim screen or poor display quality.

 Inverters can discharge energy, which can cause severe injury to you. Be careful when working with them!

Screen

The screen on a laptop does what you might expect—it produces the image that you see. The overall quality of the picture depends a lot on the quality of the screen and the technology your laptop uses. Current options include LCD, LED, OLED, and plasma.

 For more information on LCD, LED, OLED, and plasma technologies, see Chapter 4.

WiFi Antenna

The vast majority of laptops produced today include built-in WiFi capabilities. Considering how popular wireless networking is today, it only makes sense to include 802.11 functionality without needing to use an expansion card. With laptops that include built-in WiFi, the wireless antenna is generally run up through the upper half of the clamshell case. This is to get the antenna higher up and improve signal reception. The wiring will run down the side of the display, through the hinge of the laptop case, and plug in somewhere on the motherboard.

The WiFi antenna won't affect what you see on the screen, but if you start digging around in the display, know that you'll likely be messing with your wireless capabilities as well.

Cable Locks

Portability defines what makes laptops truly useful. They're not as fast or as strong as their desktop cousins, but the fact that we can easily haul them around wherever we go gives them a special status within our hearts. It also presents less-scrupulous types with ample opportunity to quickly make away with our prized possessions and personal data. Laptop theft is a major concern for companies and individual owners alike.

One way you can help physically secure your laptop is through the use of a cable lock. Essentially, a cable lock anchors your device to a physical structure, making it nearly impossible for someone to walk off with it. Figure 9.20 shows a cable lock with a number combination lock. With others, small keys are used to unlock the lock. If you grew up using a bicycle lock, these will look really familiar.

FIGURE 9.20   Cable lock

Here's how it works. First, find a secure structure, such as the permanent metal supports of your workstation at work. Then, wrap the lock cord around the structure, putting the lock through the loop at the other end. Finally, secure the lock into your cable lock hole on the back or side of your laptop (Figure 9.21), and you're secure. If you forget your combination or lose your key, you're most likely going to have to cut through the cord, which will require a large cable cutter or a hack saw.

If someone wants your laptop bad enough, they can break the case and dislodge your lock. Having the lock in place will deter most people looking to make off with it though.

FIGURE 9.21   Cable lock insertion point

Disassembling and Reassembling Laptops

Desktop computers often have a lot of empty space inside their cases. This lets air circulate and also gives the technician some room to maneuver when troubleshooting internal hardware. Space is at a premium in laptops, and rarely is any wasted. With a desktop computer, if you end up having an extra screw left over after putting it together, it's probably not a big deal. With laptops, every screw matters, and you'll sometimes find yourself trying to visually identify miniscule differences between screws to make sure you get them back into the right places.

Even though repairing a laptop poses unique issues, most of the general troubleshooting and safety tips you use when troubleshooting a desktop still apply. For example, always make sure you have a clean and well-lit work space and be cautious of electrostatic discharge (ESD). General safety tips and ESD prevention is covered in Chapter 11, "Understanding Operational Procedures." Here, we'll get in to specific objectives for tearing apart laptops.

Throughout this section, we'll use the word *laptop* almost exclusively. The principles covered here apply to nearly all portable devices, though, such as notebooks, handhelds, and netbooks.

Using the Right Tools

It's doubtful that any technician goes into a job thinking, "Hey, I'm going to use the wrong tools just to see what happens." With laptops, though, it's especially important to ensure that you have exactly the tools you need for the job. Two critical camps of materials you need are the manufacturer's documentation and the right hand tools.

Using the Manufacturer's Documentation

Most technicians won't bat an eye at whipping out their cordless screwdriver and getting into a desktop's case. The biggest difference between most desktops is how you get inside the case. Once it's opened, everything inside is pretty standard fare.

Laptops are a different story. Even experienced technicians will tell you to not remove a single screw until you have the documentation handy unless you're incredibly familiar with that particular laptop. Most laptop manufacturers give you access to repair manuals on their website; Table 9.2 lists the service and support websites for some of the top laptop manufacturers.

TABLE 9.2 Laptop manufacturers' service and support websites

Company	URL	QR Code
Asus	http://support.asus.com/ServiceHome.aspx	
Compaq	http://www.compaq.com/country/cpq_support.html	
Dell	http://support.dell.com/support/index.aspx	
HP	http://www8.hp.com/us/en/support-drivers.html	
Lenovo	http://support.lenovo.com/en_US/	
Sony	http://esupport.sony.com/US/perl/select-system.pl?DIRECTOR=DOCS	
Toshiba	http://www.csd.toshiba.com/cgi-bin/tais/support/jsp/home.jsp	

Once you are at the right website, search for the manual using the laptop's model number.

> Some laptop manufacturers have a policy that if you open the case of a laptop, the warranty is voided. Be sure to understand your warranty status and implications of cracking the case before you do it.

Using the Right Hand Tools

Once you have the manual in hand or on your screen, you need to gather the right hand tools for the job. For some laptops, you only need the basics, such as small Phillips-head and straight-edge screwdrivers. For others, you may need a Torx driver. Gather the tools you need and prepare to open the case. A small flashlight might also come in handy.

 Real World Scenario

The Consequences of Using the Wrong Tools

It's been said once, but it's important to say it again: Always use the right tool for the job when repairing laptops. If the documentation says you need a T-10 Torx driver, make sure you have a T-10 Torx driver.

Not using the right tools can result in the stripping of the screw head. If you strip a screw head in a desktop, you might have alternative methods of removing the screw. Laptops are far less forgiving. If you strip a screw head and are unable to turn the screw, you may never be able to remove it. That could result in needing to scrap the device.

Organization and Documentation

Before you crack the case of your laptop, have an organization and documentation plan in place. Know where you are going to put the parts. Have a container set aside for the screws. You can purchase small plastic containers that have several compartments in them with lids that snap tightly shut, to place screws in. You can also use containers designed to organize prescription pills. The bottom of an egg carton works well too, provided you don't need to be mobile to fix the laptop.

For documentation, many technicians find it handy to draw a map of the computer they're getting into, such as the one shown in Figure 9.22. It can be as complex as you want it to be, as long as it makes sense to you.

The drawing in Figure 9.22 shows the locations of the screws, and also calls out where the screws should be placed once they're removed. Again, this type of documentation can be as simple or complex as you want it to be, as long as it makes sense and helps you stay organized.

Replacing Laptop Components

You have your manual, screwdrivers, and screw container handy and are ready to go. Now you just need to figure out how to get to the defective component to replace it. It would be nice if we could just tell you one simple way to do this for all laptops, but that's not going to happen. Internal laptop structure, components that can be replaced, and how to get to those components varies widely between models. It's impractical to list steps to remove all of these devices because the steps we would list here will only help you if you're working on the same model of laptop we're using for an example.

FIGURE 9.22 Laptop repair "road map"

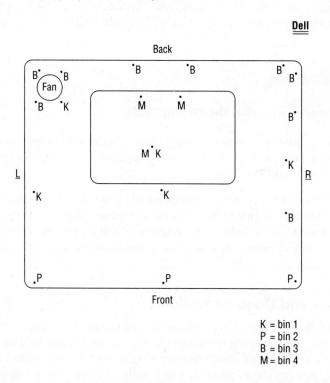

The list of components that may be replaceable could include input devices such as the keyboard and Touchpad; storage devices, including hard drives and optical drives; core components such as memory, the processor, and the motherboard; expansion options, including wireless cards and mini-PCIe cards; and integrated components such as the screen, plastics, speakers, battery, and DC jack. Again, depending on the make and model of the laptop you're working on, the list of replaceable components might be longer or shorter.

In the following sections, we're going to assume you've figured out what's defective and needs to be replaced. We'll stay away from describing components and what they do, unless it's not been covered elsewhere in the book. The model we're going to use in the examples in the rest of this chapter is a Dell Latitude C640. Admittedly, this particular model is a bit dated, but all of the procedures we're going to walk you through will still be similar for newer systems. For other models, please consult the manufacturer's documentation.

Replacing Hard Drives and Memory

Hard drives and memory are the two most common components people usually upgrade in a laptop. We'll look at how to accomplish replacing both of them.

Replacing Hard Drives

External storage devices are more popular now than they ever have been. On the small end, you can get postage-stamp-sized SD memory sticks or ultra-portable thumb drives that hold a few gigabytes each. If you need more storage, you can get external hard drives that hold in excess of one terabyte and connect to your laptop using a USB cable.

Even with all of those options, a laptop still needs an internal hard drive. Exercise 9.1 shows you how to remove and replace an internal hard drive.

We could start off each of these exercises by saying, "Check your documentation," because that is realistically what you're going to have to do for the specific model of laptop you're working on. Obviously, each of these exercises is intended to be an example of how to replace a part. Instead of telling you to check your documentation each time for the exact steps, we'll assume that it's understood.

EXERCISE 9.1

Replacing a Laptop Hard Drive

1. Turn off the computer.

2. Disconnect the computer and any peripherals from their power sources, and remove any installed batteries.

3. Locate the hard drive door and remove the screw holding it in place.

4. Lift the hard drive door until it clicks.

5. Slide the hard drive out to remove it.

EXERCISE 9.1 *(continued)*

6. Remove the two screws holding the hard drive to the hard drive door.

7. Attach a new hard drive to the hard drive door.

8. Slide the new hard drive back into the hard drive bay.

9. Snap the hard drive door back into place, and insert and tighten the screw to hold the door in place.

Replacing Memory

No matter how much memory your laptop has, it's probably not enough. Most laptops share their system memory with the video card, meaning that memory on a laptop might not go as far as you think.

Not long ago there weren't any standards for the physical size of laptop memory. Manufacturers weren't in a hurry to conform to each other either. After all, if they were the only ones producing memory for their systems, then they could pretty much charge what they wanted.

Fortunately, standards do exist today, and most manufacturers will use memory that conforms to SODIMM (or MicroDIMM) standards. Only occasionally will you run into a laptop that uses proprietary memory modules. Your documentation will tell you what type of memory your system takes. Exercise 9.2 shows you how to access the memory bay so you can upgrade or replace memory chips.

EXERCISE 9.2

Replacing Laptop Memory

1. Turn off the computer.

2. Disconnect the computer and any peripherals from their power sources, and remove any installed batteries.

EXERCISE 9.2 *(continued)*

3. Remove the screws holding the memory door in place.

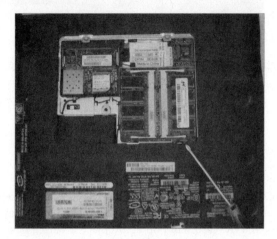

4. Use your fingers to gently separate the plastic tabs holding the memory module in place. The module should pop up so you can grab it.

5. Align the notch in the new memory module to the one in the connector.

6. Insert the new memory module into the socket at a 45-degree angle. Once full contact is made, press the module down. It should click into place.

7. Replace the memory door and fasten the screws.

Replacing Internal Laptop Expansion Cards

As we covered earlier in the chapter, laptops have their own proprietary architecture for internal expansion. The two most common standards are Mini PCI and Mini PCIe, and they're covered in detail in the section "Expansion Buses and Ports" earlier in this chapter.

Most laptops will come with only one Mini PCI or Mini PCIe port, and common Mini PCI devices include SCSI controllers, SATA controllers, network cards, sound cards, and modems. Refer back to Table 9.1 for the dimensions of the various Mini PCI form factors.

Figure 9.23 shows you the Type IIIA Mini PCI network card installed in this laptop, which happens to be in the same bay as the system memory. The connector is on the top side of the figure.

You can tell that the card in Figure 9.23 is a Type IIIA card by looking at two things. First, it has a card edge connector, making it Type III. Second, the card looks almost like a square, making it Type IIIA. Type IIIB cards are about ¼" shorter and look more rectangular.

FIGURE 9.23   Mini PCI card installed in a laptop

Removing the Mini PCI card is just like removing the memory, except that this one has antenna cables you need to disconnect first. After that, spread the retaining clips just as you would for the memory and the card will pop up. Replace it with a new card the same way you would replace a memory module.

Mini PCIe cards have a 52-pin card edge connector, and removing and replacing them is similar to removing and replacing Mini PCI cards.

Upgrading Wireless and Video Systems

What do wireless network cards and video cards have in common in laptops? Most of the time, they're integrated into your system motherboard. If either one fails, you need to replace the entire motherboard. A few laptops have these components as separate *field-replaceable units (FRUs),* and you can remove them as needed. The only way to know for sure is to consult your trusty service manual. The following sections look at some ways you may be able to upgrade these devices.

Upgrading Wireless Network Cards

Wireless network cards and laptops are a perfect match for each other, much like peanut butter and chocolate. You can have one without the other, but what's the point, really?

Most network cards are built into the motherboard chipset of laptops. In other words, if it fails, you likely need to replace the motherboard. Network cards are special, though, in that you have many other easier ways to upgrade if you want to.

On the market you can find several external portable network cards. You often have choices that range from network cards that look like a thumb drive and have a USB connector to slightly bulkier PC Card network cards. These are even valid options if your built-in network card is still working but you want to upgrade. For example, if you have an older laptop with an 802.11b network card in it but you want to upgrade to 802.11g or 802.11n, it may be more economical to purchase an external card and use it in your system. Windows should disable the old device automatically to avoid conflicts, but if not, you can do it manually through Device Manager.

Upgrading Laptop Video Cards

Odds are that the laptop you're working on has an integrated video card. If the video card fails, you're likely looking at a motherboard replacement. Some laptops do have a replaceable video card. If it fails or if you choose to upgrade it, the procedure will probably resemble replacing system memory. The Dell Latitude C640 we've been using as an example has a built-in video card, so there's no way to upgrade that specific device. For an example of what it might take to replace a video card, we'll use a Dell Inspiron 6000 in Exercise 9.3.

EXERCISE 9.3

Removing a Laptop Video Card

1. Turn off the computer.

2. Disconnect the computer and any peripherals from their power sources, and remove any installed batteries.

3. Remove the Mini PCI card and the optical drive.

4. Remove the hard drive, the hinge cover, the keyboard, the display assembly, and the palm rest.

5. Loosen the two captive screws holding the video card/thermal cooling assembly in place.

6. Lift up on the video card/thermal cooling assembly to remove it from the motherboard.

Replacing LCD Components

Besides the video card, many of the LCD components (the screen, backlight, and inverter) in a laptop can be replaced. Replacing these components often means removing the LCD display from the main chassis of the laptop. When doing so, just be careful of the video circuitry that connects the two, and the wireless network card antenna wires, which are usually threaded through one of the laptop case hinges.

 Be particularly careful working with inverters. They can store and discharge energy, which can cause severe injury to you!

Replacing Other Internal Components

By now you have probably gotten the idea that in order to know how to replace components inside your laptop, you need to check the laptop's manual. The upshot is that nearly every component you can think of replacing in a desktop computer is also replaceable in a laptop. It just might require a bit more work to fix the laptop than it would to fix a desktop.

As a rule of thumb, you can either access components from the bottom of your laptop, such as the memory, Mini PCI card, and modem in the Latitude C640, or you're going to need to remove the keyboard to access the components from the top.

As the keyboard is often the gateway to the guts of a laptop, we will include an example of removing it. We'll also include a few other examples of components you may need to replace in your line of work. Exercise 9.4 shows you how to remove a keyboard.

Laptop keyboards aren't as easy to switch out as desktop keyboards. If your laptop keyboard has failed, however, you can very easily attach an external keyboard to it. If you have the wrong type of connector, most electronics stores will have USB-to-PS/2 or PS/2-to-USB converters. Of course, if your goal is to remove the keyboard to get to the laptop's guts, then you need to perform surgery like the example in Exercise 9.4.

EXERCISE 9.4

Removing a Laptop Keyboard

1. Turn off the computer.

2. Disconnect the computer and any peripherals from their power sources, and remove any installed batteries.

3. Remove the hard drive.

4. On the bottom of the laptop, remove the five screws marked with the letter *K*.

5. Turn the laptop over and open the display.

6. Remove the center control cover by inserting a small flat-edged screwdriver into the notch at the right end of the center control cover and prying it loose.

EXERCISE 9.4 *(continued)*

7. To release the keyboard, use a small flat-edged screwdriver to pry up on its right edge, near the blank key.

8. Lift the keyboard up about an inch and rotate it forward so the keys are facing on the palm rest. Don't pull the keyboard too far or you might damage the connector cable.

9. Pull up on the keyboard connector to disconnect it from the keyboard interface connector on the motherboard.

10. Set the keyboard aside.

Now that the keyboard is off, you can remove several other components with relative ease. Exercise 9.5 looks at removing the processor cooling assembly and the processor.

Removing the Processor Cooling Assembly and Processor

1. Turn off the computer.

2. Disconnect the computer and any peripherals from their power sources, and remove any installed batteries.

3. Remove the hard drive.

4. Remove the keyboard.

5. Loosen the four captive screws that hold the cooling assembly in place.

6. Insert a small screwdriver into the recess in the front left side of the assembly and pry the assembly from the motherboard. If this is the first time removing the assembly, it might take some force because it's likely glued to the processor. Set the assembly aside.

7. Use a small flat-edged screwdriver to loosen the processor's ZIF socket by rotating the cam screw counterclockwise until it reaches the cam stop. (It should take about a one-quarter turn.)

EXERCISE 9.5 *(continued)*

8. Use a microprocessor extraction tool to remove the microprocessor. If you don't have an extraction tool, you can try to use your hands. Make sure you're grounded first, and always pull straight up to avoid bending pins.

9. Set the processor aside on an antistatic mat or place in an antistatic bag.

The last internal device we'll look at removing is the CMOS battery. If the BIOS isn't maintaining system information such as the date and time or boot sequence, you will want to replace this component. Exercise 9.6 shows you how to replace the CMOS battery.

Many laptops use the same type of round, silver watch-style batteries that desktop motherboards use. Others use packaged batteries that more closely resemble cell phone batteries, such as this laptop.

EXERCISE 9.6

Replacing the CMOS Battery

1. Turn off the computer.

2. Disconnect the computer and any peripherals from their power sources, and remove any installed batteries.

3. Remove the hard drive.

4. Remove the keyboard.

5. Disconnect the CMOS battery from the motherboard.

EXERCISE 9.6 *(continued)*

6. Pry the battery from its seat with a small straight-edged screwdriver. Note that it's adhered to the EMI shield below it, so removing it might require some force.

7. Connect the new battery to the appropriate connector on the motherboard.

8. Peel away the backing from the adhesive bottom of the new CMOS battery. Press the battery into the battery tray.)

9. Upgrade the BIOS using a flash BIOS CD.

Flashing the system BIOS is usually a pretty straightforward process. You can get a BIOS update from the manufacturer and burn it to a CD. Once you have the CD, you just need to boot the laptop from the CD, and the disc will automatically flash the BIOS. Exercise 9.7 shows you the steps to flash the BIOS on this model.

EXERCISE 9.7

Flashing the System BIOS

1. Turn off the computer.

2. Ensure that the computer is plugged into AC power and that the main battery is installed properly.

3. Turn on the computer and press F2 to enter the BIOS setup.

4. Reset the system boot order to ensure that the system boots from the CD first.

5. Insert the flash BIOS update CD, and reboot the computer. The disc will flash the BIOS and automatically reboot.

6. Upon reboot, press F2 again to enter the BIOS setup. Verify that the settings are correct, and change the boot sequence to your preferred setting.

7. Remove the flash BIOS CD.

Removing External Hardware

In the grand scheme of things, there are two types of peripherals: internal and external. We've already discussed removing internal hardware, and compared to that, removing external components is very easy. If you have USB-type devices plugged in, removing them is as easy as disconnecting them, but other peripherals require a bit more work.

Devices that can be removed when the computer is powered on are called hot-swappable devices. If you need to turn the computer off first, then the device is not hot swappable. There are several different hot-swappable peripherals, including mice, keyboards, some hard drives, network cards, printers, and others. Good examples of non-hot-swappable devices include motherboards and internal IDE hard drives. Odds are if it's internal to your computer case, then it's not hot swappable. Always be sure to check your hardware documentation to see if it's safe to plug in or disconnect the device with the system powered on.

WARNING   Although most of the time you can just remove a USB device, make sure it's not in use when you remove it.

In Exercise 9.8, we will show you the recommended method to remove a device.

EXERCISE 9.8

Removing External Devices

1. You need to stop the device first (this is good policy even for USB devices), using the Safely Remove Hardware icon in the system tray here (it looks like a card with a green arrow over it).

2. Once you've clicked the icon, you will get a screen similar to the one shown here:

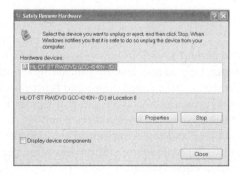

3. Highlight the device you want to remove, and click Stop. Windows will then notify you that it's safe to remove the device. If it's a cabled device, just detach it. If it's PCMCIA, you can press the Eject button next to the slot in which the card is located. Other types of hardware in some laptops require you to release a latch. The following photo shows a modular front-load bay, and the right side has a CD-ROM in it:

4. Turn the computer over, and you can see the release latch. Slide it to the side, and pull on the grip on the underside of the CD-ROM. Out it comes.

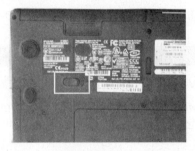

Adding an external device to a laptop generally means that the computer will automatically recognize and enable the device for you, unless there's no compatible driver available. In cases like these, Windows will tell you that it detected new hardware and ask you to provide an appropriate driver.

Summary

In this chapter, you learned about the various laptop issues that face the A+ technician. We discussed differences between laptops and desktops, including the various components that make up a laptop and how they differ in appearance and function from those on a desktop.

Input devices, expansion buses, and interfaces found in laptops were presented in detail. We also discussed special laptop function keys and the components of an LCD screen.

Then, we looked at repairing and replacing laptop components. We started off by quickly talking about finding laptop documentation and using the right tools. We then discussed organization and documentation.

Next, we discussed replacing hard drives and memory and also looked at upgrading internal expansion cards. After that, we explored upgrading wireless, video cards, and other internal components. Finally, we explained how to safely remove an external device from your laptop.

Exam Essentials

Know the differences between laptop processors and desktop processors.   Laptops have less room in them, so it makes sense that laptop processors are smaller than their desktop brethren. They also operate at lower voltages, have more advanced power-down or sleep modes, and are often soldered directly to the motherboard. Finally, chipsets such as the Intel Pentium M chipset also include built-in video processing and networking capabilities.

Understand the differences between laptop memory standards and desktop memory standards.   Continuing a main theme of this chapter, memory in laptops needs to be smaller than in desktops, and so it is. The two main standards for laptop memory are SODIMM and MicroDIMM.

Understand the various power sources for laptops.   You should know that the Li-ion battery is the preferred rechargeable power source for laptops and that active power supplies that plug into AC and DC power sources are available. Additionally, knowing the difference between autoswitching and fixed power supplies is essential.

Know the various input devices and expansion buses and ports found on laptop computers. Although many of these technologies are available in desktop computers as well, the science behind outfitting laptops with similar functionality presents unique details the A+ technician should know. PC Card–based expansion buses have their own specific traits, which you should be familiar with.

Know where to get service manuals for laptops.   Service manuals can be found at the laptop manufacturers' websites.

Be familiar with the components of an LCD.   LCDs are made up of the video card, backlight, inverter, and screen.

Know how to recognize internal laptop expansion slot types.   Two types of internal expansion slots are Mini PCI and Mini PCIe. There are six Mini PCI form factors. Mini PCIe has a 52-pin card edge connector.

Know how to replace hardware devices from laptops.   Components are typically accessed either from the bottom of the case or by removing the keyboard and accessing them from the top. Each laptop is different, so be sure to consult your documentation.

Review Questions

The answers to the Chapter Review Questions can be found in Appendix A.

1. Where can you obtain the service manual for a laptop computer?
    A. By pressing F1 while in Windows
    B. By pressing F2 while the system is booting up
    C. With the laptop, as a paper copy
    D. From the manufacturer's website

2. Which of the following is *not* a benefit of laptop design?
    A. Portability
    B. Increased performance
    C. Desktop replacement
    D. Higher-quality construction

3. Which of the following are components of an LCD? (Choose two.)
    A. Inverter
    B. Screen
    C. CRT
    D. Backdrop

4. Which laptop input device was released with the IBM ThinkPad series of laptops?
    A. Touchpad
    B. Mouse
    C. Point stick
    D. Trackball

5. Which laptop accessory allows you to power your laptop from a car or airplane?
    A. AC adapter
    B. DC adapter
    C. Battery converter
    D. Automotive Wizard

6. How many pins does a MicroDIMM memory module have?
    A. 72
    B. 144
    C. 172
    D. 198

7. _____ is the fastest and most modern interface used as an expansion method for external peripherals, such as mice, web cams, scanners, and printers, and is popular on laptops and desktops alike.

   A. Parallel

   B. PS/2

   C. USB

   D. ATA

8. What type of connector does the Mini PCI IIIA standard use?

   A. 100-pin card edge

   B. 100-pin stacking

   C. 124-pin card edge

   D. 124-pin stacking

9. Which laptop component is often upgraded with an external PCMCIA device?

   A. Video card

   B. Motherboard

   C. Network card

   D. Keyboard

10. Which type of PC Card is used most often for expansion devices like NICs, sound cards, and so on?

    A. Type I

    B. Type II

    C. Type III

    D. Type IV

11. Which of the following expansion buses uses serial communications and is capable of operating in USB and PCIe modes?

    A. ExpressCard

    B. CardBus

    C. Mini PCI

    D. FireWire

12. What should you do first to remove external devices from your laptop?

    A. Just remove the device.

    B. Unplug the power to the device, then remove the device.

    C. Click the Safely Remove Hardware icon.

    D. Click the Remove Hardware Now icon.

13. PC Cards rely on which type of software to operate? (Choose two.)

   A. Cardmember Services

   B. Card Services

   C. Modem Services

   D. Socket Services

14. What component allows you to keep desktop devices such as keyboard, monitor, and mouse permanently connected so they can be used by an attached laptop?

   A. Docking station

   B. Keyboard, video, mouse (KVM) switch

   C. Print server

   D. USB hub

15. The process by which the processor slows down to conserve power is officially called _____.

   A. Underclocking

   B. Cooling

   C. Disengaging

   D. Throttling

16. When replacing your laptop's AC adapter, which of the following purchases is acceptable to obtain the same or better results?

   A. An AC adapter with a higher voltage rating than the original

   B. An AC adapter with a higher wattage rating than the original

   C. A DC adapter with the same voltage rating as the original

   D. An AC adapter with a lower voltage and wattage rating than the original

17. What should you do for a Li-ion battery that appears to charge fully but does not last as long as the battery's meter indicates it will last?

   A. Replace the battery.

   B. Exercise the battery.

   C. Calibrate the battery.

   D. Short the terminals to discharge the battery.

18. How do laptop hard drives differ from desktop hard drives?

   A. Laptop hard drives use completely different standards from those used by desktop hard drives for communication with the host.

   B. Laptop hard drives are solid state; desktop hard drives have spinning platters.

   C. Laptop hard drives require a separate power connection; desktop hard drives are powered through the drive interface.

   D. The most common form factor of a laptop hard drive is about an inch smaller than that of a desktop hard drive.

19. What type of connector does a Mini PCI type IIA card have?

    A. 52-pin card edge

    B. 100-pin stacking

    C. 100-pin card edge

    D. 124-pin card edge

20. Which of the following memory types has the smallest form factor?

    A. RIMM

    B. DIMM

    C. MicroDIMM

    D. SODIMM

Performance-Based Question

On the A+ exams, you will encounter performance-based questions. The questions on the exam require you to perform a specific task, and you will be graded on if you were able to complete the task. The following requires you to think creatively to measure how well you understand this chapter's topics. You may or may not see similar questions on the actual A+ exams. To see how your answer compares to the authors' refer to Appendix B.

The hard drive on a Dell Latitude C640 computer failed. You have an extra hard drive of the exact same type. What would you do to replace it?

Chapter

10

Installing and Configuring Printers

- Printer sharing:
    - Sharing local/networked printer via Operating System settings

✓ 4.3 Given a scenario, perform printer maintenance.

- Laser:
    - Replacing toner, applying maintenance kit, calibration, cleaning
- Thermal:
    - Replace paper, clean heating element, remove debris
- Impact:
    - Replace ribbon, replace print head, replace paper

Let's face it. No matter how much we try to get away from it, our society is dependent on paper. When we conduct business, we use different types of paper documents, such as contracts, letters, and, of course, money. And because most of those documents are created on computers, printers are inherently important. Even with electronic business being the norm in many situations, you will likely still have daily situations that require an old-fashioned hard copy of something.

Printers are electromechanical output devices that are used to put information from the computer onto paper. They have been around since the introduction of the computer. Other than the display monitor, the printer is the most popular peripheral purchased for a computer because a lot of people want to have paper copies of the documents they create.

In this chapter, we will discuss the details of each major type of printer, including impact printers, inkjet printers, laser printers, and thermal printers. Once we cover the different types, we'll talk about installing and configuring printers and finish up with a section on printer maintenance.

Take special note of the section on laser printers. The A+ exams test these subjects in detail, so we'll cover them in depth.

Printer troubleshooting is an objective of the 220-802 exam and consequently is covered in Chapter 20, "Hardware Troubleshooting."

Understanding Printer Types and Processes

Several types of printers are available on the market today. As with all other computer components, there have been significant advancements in printer technology over the years. Most of the time when faced with the decision of purchasing a printer, you're going to be weighing performance versus cost. Some of the higher-quality technologies, such as color laser printing, are rather expensive for the home user. Other technologies are less expensive but don't provide the same level of quality.

In the following sections, you will learn about the various types of printers that you will see as a technician as well as their basic components and how they function. Specifically, we are going to look at four classifications of printers: impact, inkjet (bubble-jet), laser, and thermal.

Impact Printers

The most basic type of printer is in the category known as *impact printers*. Impact printers, as their name suggests, use some form of impact and an inked *ribbon* to make an imprint on the paper. Impact printers also use a paper feed mechanism called a *tractor feed* that requires special paper. Doubtless you've seen it before—it's continuous feed paper with holes running down both edges. In a manner of speaking, typewriters are like impact printers. Both use an inked ribbon and an impact head to make letters on the paper. The major difference is that the printer can accept input from a computer.

There are two major types of impact printers: daisy wheel and dot matrix. Each type has its own service and maintenance issues.

Daisy-Wheel Printers

The first type of impact printer we're going to discuss is the *daisy-wheel printer*. This is one of the oldest printing technologies in use. These impact printers contain a wheel (called the daisy wheel because it looks like a daisy) with raised letters and symbols on each "petal" (see Figure 10.1). When the printer needs to print a character, it sends a signal to the mechanism that contains the wheel. This mechanism is called the *print head*. The print head rotates the daisy wheel until the required character is in place. An electromechanical hammer (called a *solenoid*) then strikes the back of the petal containing the character. The character pushes up against an inked ribbon that ultimately strikes the paper, making the impression of the requested character.

FIGURE 10.1   A daisy-wheel printer mechanism

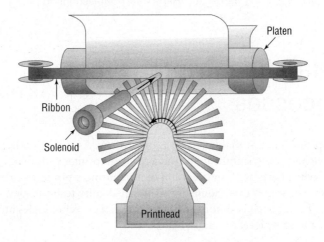

You may see the term *print head* written as one word: *printhead*. There doesn't seem to be a specific convention one way or the other, so know that either way is fine.

Daisy-wheel printers were among the first types of impact printer developed. Their speed is rated by the number of *characters per second (cps)* they can print. The earliest printers could print only two to four characters per second. Aside from their poor speed, the main disadvantage to this type of printer is that it makes a lot of noise when printing—so much, in fact, that special enclosures were developed to contain the noise.

The daisy-wheel printer has a few advantages, of course. First, because it is an impact printer, you can print on multipart forms (like carbonless receipts), assuming they can be fed into the printer properly. Sometimes you will hear this type of paper referred to as *impact paper*. Second, it is relatively inexpensive compared to the price of a laser printer of the same vintage. Finally, the print quality is comparable to that of a typewriter because it uses a very similar technology. This typewriter level of quality was given a name: *letter quality (LQ)*. Today, LQ might refer to quality that's better than a typewriter but not up to inkjet standards.

Dot-Matrix Printers

The other type of impact printer we'll discuss is the *dot-matrix printer*. These printers work in a manner similar to daisy-wheel printers, but instead of a spinning, character-imprinted wheel, the print head contains a row of pins (short, sturdy stalks of hard wire). These pins are triggered in patterns that form letters and numbers as the print head moves across the paper (see Figure 10.2).

FIGURE 10.2 Formation of images in a dot-matrix printer

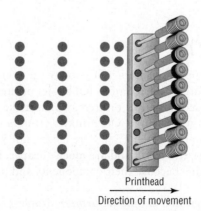

Printhead

Direction of movement

The pins in the print head are wrapped with coils of wire to create a solenoid and are held in the rest position by a combination of a small magnet and a spring. To trigger a particular pin, the printer controller sends a signal to the print head, which energizes the wires around the appropriate print wire. This turns the print wire into an electromagnet, which repels the print pin, forcing it against the ink ribbon and making a dot on the paper. The arrangement of the dots in columns and rows creates the letters and numbers you see on the page. Figure 10.2 shows this process.

The main disadvantage of dot-matrix printers is their image quality, which can be quite poor compared to the quality produced with a daisy wheel. Dot-matrix printers use patterns of dots to make letters and images, and the early dot-matrix printers used only nine pins to make those patterns. The output quality of such printers is referred to as *draft quality*—good mainly for providing your initial text to a correspondent or reviser. Each letter looked fuzzy because the dots were spaced as far as they could be and still be perceived as a letter or image. As more pins were crammed into the print head (17-pin and 24-pin models were eventually developed), the quality increased because the dots were closer together. Dot-matrix technology ultimately improved to the point that a letter printed on a dot-matrix printer was *almost* indistinguishable from typewriter output. This level of quality is known as *near letter quality (NLQ)*.

Dot-matrix printers are noisy, but the print wires and print head are covered by a plastic dust cover, making them quieter than daisy-wheel printers. They also use a more efficient printing technology, so the print speed is faster (typically starting around 72cps). Some dot-matrix printers (like the Epson DFX series) can print at close to a page per second! Finally, because dot-matrix printers are also impact printers, they can use multipart forms. Because of these advantages, dot-matrix printers quickly made daisy-wheel printers obsolete.

Most impact printers have an option to adjust how close the print head rests from the ribbon. So if your printing is too light, you may be able to adjust the print head closer to the ribbon. If it's too dark or you get smeared printing, you may be able to move the print head back.

Inkjet (Bubble-Jet)

One of the most popular types of printers in use today are *inkjet printers*. You might also hear these types of printers referred to as bubble-jet printers, but that term is copyrighted by Canon. As opposed to impact printers, which strike the page, these printers spray ink on the page to form the image. Older inkjet printers used a reservoir of ink, a pump, and a nozzle to accomplish this. They were messy, noisy, and inefficient. Bubble-jet printers work much more efficiently and are much cheaper. For purposes of the exam, consider them one in the same because their components and printing processes are nearly identical.

The main difference is that in a *bubble-jet printer*, droplets of ink are sprayed onto a page and form patterns that resemble the items being printed. You can think of it as spraying droplets of ink in a very high-definition dot-matrix pattern, although printer manufacturers would likely scoff at the comparison to an older technology. In the following sections, you will learn the parts of a bubble-jet printer as well as how bubble-jet printers work.

Parts of a Typical Bubble-Jet Printer

Bubble-jet printers are simple devices. They contain very few parts (even fewer than dot-matrix printers) and, as such, are inexpensive to manufacture. It's common today to have a $40 to $50 bubble-jet printer with print quality that rivals that of basic laser printers.

The printer parts can be divided into the following categories:

- Print head/ink cartridge
- Head carriage, belt, and stepper motor
- Paper-feed mechanism
- Control, interface, and power circuitry

Print Head/Ink Cartridge

The first part of a bubble-jet printer is the one people see the most: the *print head*. This part of a printer contains many small nozzles (usually 100 to 200) that spray the ink in small droplets onto the page. Many times the print head is part of the *ink cartridge*, which contains a reservoir of ink and the print head in a removable package. Most color bubble-jet printers include multiple print heads, one for each of the *CMYK (cyan, magenta, yellow, and black)* print inks. The print cartridge must be replaced as the ink supply runs out.

Inside the ink cartridge are several small chambers. At the top of each chamber are a metal plate and a tube leading to the ink supply. At the bottom of each chamber is a small pinhole. These pinholes are used to spray ink on the page to form characters and images as patterns of dots, similar to the way a dot-matrix printer works but with much higher resolution.

There are two methods of spraying the ink out of the cartridge. The first was popularized by Hewlett-Packard (HP): When a particular chamber needs to spray ink, an electric signal is sent to the heating element, energizing it. The elements heat up quickly, causing the ink to vaporize. Because of the expanding ink vapor, the ink is pushed out the pinhole and forms a bubble. As the vapor expands, the bubble eventually gets large enough to break off into a droplet. The rest of the ink is pulled back into the chamber by the surface tension of the ink. When another drop needs to be sprayed, the process begins again. The second method, developed by Epson, uses a piezoelectric element (either a small rod or a unit that looks like a miniature drum head) that flexes when energized. The outward flex pushes the ink from the nozzle; on the return, it sucks more ink from the reservoir.

When the printer is done printing, the print head moves back to its maintenance station. The *maintenance station* contains a small suction pump and ink-absorbing pad. To keep the ink flowing freely, before each print cycle the maintenance station pulls ink through the ink nozzles using vacuum suction. This expelled ink is absorbed by the pad. The station serves two functions: to provide a place for the print head to rest when the printer isn't printing and to keep the print head in working order.

Head Carriage, Belt, and Stepper Motor

Another major component of the bubble-jet printer is the head carriage and the associated parts that make it move. The *print head carriage* is the component of a bubble-jet printer that moves back and forth during printing. It contains the physical as well as electronic connections for the print head and (in some cases) the ink reservoir. Figure 10.3 shows an example of a head carriage. Note the clips that keep the ink cartridge in place and the electronic connections for the ink cartridge. These connections cause the nozzles to fire, and if they aren't kept clean, you may have printing problems.

FIGURE 10.3   A print head carriage (holding two ink cartridges) in a bubble-jet printer

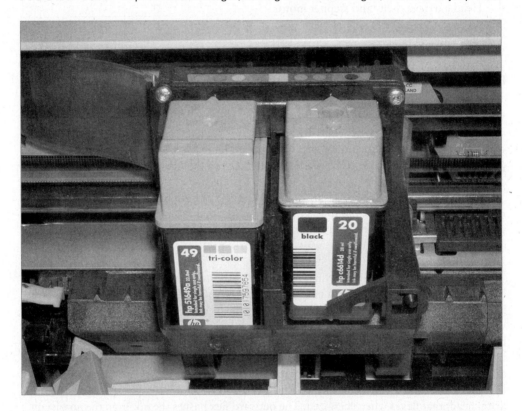

The stepper motor and belt make the print head carriage move. A *stepper motor* is a precisely made electric motor that can move in the same very small increments each time it is activated. That way, it can move to the same position(s) time after time. The motor that makes the print head carriage move is also often called the *carriage motor* or *carriage stepper motor*. Figure 10.4 shows an example of a stepper motor.

In addition to the motor, a belt is placed around two small wheels or pulleys and attached to the print head carriage. This belt, called the *carriage belt*, is driven by the carriage motor and moves the print head back and forth across the page while it prints. To keep the print head carriage aligned and stable while it traverses the page, the carriage rests on a small metal *stabilizer bar*. Figure 10.5 shows the stabilizer bar, carriage belt, and pulleys.

FIGURE 10.4 A carriage stepper motor

FIGURE 10.5 Stabilizer bar, carriage belt, and pulleys in a bubble-jet printer

Pulley   Stabilizer bar   Belt

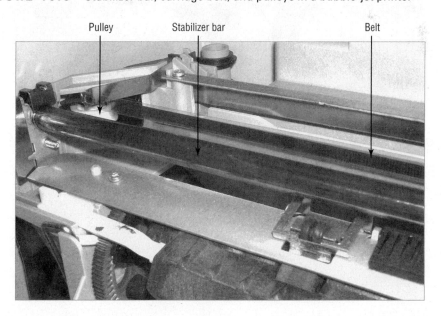

Paper-Feed Mechanism

In addition to getting the ink onto the paper, the printer must have a way to get the paper into the printer. That's where the paper-feed mechanism comes in. The *paper-feed mechanism* picks up paper from the paper drawer and feeds it into the printer. This component consists of several smaller assemblies. First are the *pickup rollers* (Figure 10.6), which are several rubber rollers with a slightly flat spot; they rub against the paper as they rotate, and feed the paper into the printer. They work against small cork or rubber patches known as *separator pads* (Figure 10.7), which help keep the rest of the paper in place so that only one sheet goes into the printer. The pickup rollers are turned on a shaft by the *pickup stepper motor*.

FIGURE 10.6   Bubble-jet pickup rollers

FIGURE 10.7   Bubble-jet separator pads

Clean pickup rollers (and other rubber rollers) with mild soap and water and not alcohol. Alcohol can dry out the rollers, making them brittle and ineffective.

Sometimes the paper that is fed into a bubble-jet printer is placed into a *paper tray*, which is simply a small plastic tray in the front of the printer that holds the paper until it is fed into the printer by the paper-feed mechanism. On smaller printers, the paper is placed vertically into a *paper feeder* at the back of the printer; it uses gravity, in combination with feed rollers and separator pads, to get the paper into the printer. No real rhyme or reason dictates which manufacturers use these different parts; some models use them, and some don't. Generally, more expensive printers use paper trays because they hold more paper. Figure 10.8 shows an example of a paper tray on a bubble-jet printer.

FIGURE 10.8 A paper tray on a bubble-jet printer

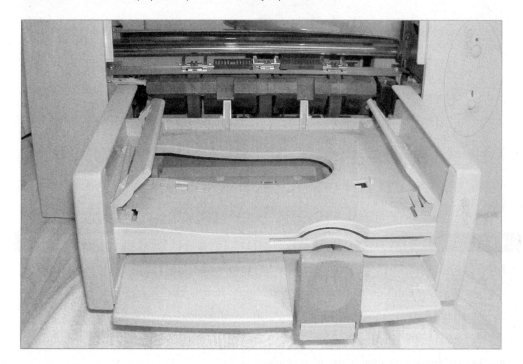

The final parts of the paper-feed mechanism are the *paper-feed sensors*. These components tell the printer when it is out of paper as well as when a paper jam has occurred during the paper-feed process. Figure 10.9 shows an example of a paper-feed sensor.

Being able to identify the parts of a bubble-jet printer is an important skill for an A+ candidate. In Exercise 10.1 you will identify the parts of a bubble-jet printer. For this exercise, you'll need a bubble-jet printer.

FIGURE 10.9 A paper-feed sensor on a bubble-jet printer

EXERCISE 10.1

Identifying the Parts of a Bubble-jet Printer

1. Unplug the bubble-jet printer from the power source and the computer.

2. Open the top cover to expose the inner print mechanism.

3. Locate and identify the paper tray.

4. Locate and identify the paper-feed sensor.

5. Locate and identify the pickup roller(s).

6. Locate and identify the separator pad(s).

7. Locate and identify the print head and carriage assembly.

Control, Interface, and Power Circuitry

The final component group is the electronic circuitry for printer control, printer interfaces, and printer power. The *printer control circuits* are usually on a small circuit board that contains all the circuitry to run the stepper motors the way the printer needs them to work (back and forth, load paper and then stop, and so on). These circuits are also responsible for monitoring the health of the printer and reporting that information back to the PC.

The second power component, the interface circuitry (commonly called a port), makes the physical connection to whatever signal is coming from the computer (parallel, serial, network, infrared, and so on) and also connects the physical interface to the control circuitry. The interface circuitry converts the signals from the interface into the datastream that the printer uses.

The last set of circuits the printer uses is the *power circuits*. Essentially, these conductive pathways convert 110V (in the United States) or 220V (in most of the rest of the world) from a standard wall outlet into the voltages the bubble-jet printer uses, usually 12V and 5V, and distribute those voltages to the other printer circuits and devices that need it. This is accomplished through the use of a *transformer*. A transformer, in this case, takes the 110V AC current and changes it to 12V DC (among others). This transformer can be either internal (incorporated into the body of the printer) or external. Either design can be used in today's bubble-jets, although the integrated design is preferred because it is simpler and doesn't show the bulky transformer.

The Bubble-Jet Printing Process

Just as with other types of printing, the bubble-jet printing process consists of a set of steps the printer must follow in order to put the data onto the page being printed. The following steps take place whenever you click the Print button in your favorite software (like Microsoft Word or Internet Explorer):

1. You click the Print button (or similar) that initiates the printing process.

2. The software you are printing from sends the data to be printed to the printer driver you have selected.

 The function and use of the printer driver are discussed later in this chapter.

3. The printer driver uses a page-description language to convert the data being printed into the format that the printer can understand. The driver also ensures that the printer is ready to print.

4. The printer driver sends the information to the printer via whatever connection method is being used (USB, network, parallel, and so on).

5. The printer stores the received data in its onboard *print buffer* memory. A print buffer is a small amount of memory (typically 512KB to 16MB) used to store print jobs as they are received from the printing computer. This buffer allows several jobs to be printed at once and helps printing to be completed quickly.

6. If the printer has not printed in a while, the printer's control circuits activate a cleaning cycle. A *cleaning cycle* is a set of steps the bubble-jet printer goes through to purge the print heads of any dried ink. It uses a special suction cup and sucking action to pull ink through the print head, dislodging any dried ink or clearing stuck passageways.

7. Once the printer is ready to print, the control circuitry activates the paper-feed motor. This causes a sheet of paper to be fed into the printer until the paper activates the paper-feed sensor, which stops the feed until the print head is in the right position and the leading edge of the paper is under the print head. If the paper doesn't reach the paper-feed sensor in a specified amount of time after the stepper motor has been activated, the Out Of Paper light is turned on and a message is sent to the computer.

8. Once the paper is positioned properly, the print head stepper motor uses the print head belt and carriage to move the print head across the page, little by little. The motor is moved one small step, and the print head sprays the dots of ink on the paper in the pattern dictated by the control circuitry. Typically, this is either a pattern of black dots or a pattern of CMYK inks that are mixed to make colors. Then the stepper motor moves the print head another small step; the process repeats all the way across the page. This process is so quick, however, that the entire series of starts and stops across the page looks like one smooth motion.

9. At the end of a pass across the page, the paper-feed stepper motor advances the page a small amount. Then the print head repeats step 8. Depending on the model, either the print head returns to the beginning of the line and prints again in the same direction only or it moves backward across the page so that printing occurs in both directions. This process continues until the page is finished.

10. Once the page is finished, the feed-stepper motor is actuated and ejects the page from the printer into the output tray. If more pages need to print, the process for printing the next page begins again at step 7.

11. Once printing is complete and the final page has been ejected from the printer, the print head is *parked* (locked into rest position) and the print process is finished.

Some nicer models of bubble-jet printers will have a *duplexing assembly* attached to them, usually at the back of the printer. It's used for two-sided printing. After the first page is printed, it's fed into the duplexing assembly, turned over, and fed back into the paper feed assembly. Then the second page can be printed on the back side of the original piece of paper. It's a fancy attachment that gives your bubble-jet more functionality.

Laser Printers

Laser printers and inkjet printers are referred to as *page printers* because they receive their print job instructions one page at a time rather than receiving instructions one line at a time. There are two major types of page printers that use the electrophotographic (EP) print process. The first uses a laser to scan the image onto a photosensitive drum, and the second uses an array of light-emitting diodes (LEDs) to create the image on the drum. Even though they write the image in different ways, both types still follow the EP print process. Since the A+ exam focuses on the EP print process and not on differences between laser and LED, we'll focus on the same here.

Xerox, Hewlett-Packard, and Canon were pioneers in developing the laser printer technology we use today. Scientists at Xerox developed the electrophotographic (EP) process in 1971. The first successful desktop laser printer was introduced by HP in 1984 using Canon hardware that used the EP process. This technology uses a combination of static electric charges, laser light, and a black powdery ink-like substance called *toner*. Printers that use this technology are called EP process laser printers, or just *laser printers*. Every laser printer technology has its foundations in the EP printer process.

Let's discuss the basic components of the EP laser printer and how they operate so you can understand the way an EP laser printer works.

Basic Components

Most printers that use the EP process contain nine standard assemblies: the toner cartridge, laser scanner, high-voltage power supply, DC power supply, paper transport assembly (including paper-pickup rollers and paper-registration rollers), transfer corona, fusing assembly, printer controller circuitry, and ozone filter. Let's discuss each of the components individually before we examine how they all work together to make the printer function.

The Toner Cartridge

The EP toner cartridge (Figure 10.10), as its name suggests, holds the toner. Toner is a black carbon substance mixed with polyester resins to make it flow better and iron oxide particles to make it sensitive to electrical charges. These two components make the toner capable of being attracted to the photosensitive drum and of melting into the paper. In addition to these components, toner contains a medium called the developer (also called the carrier), which carries the toner until it is used by the EP process. The toner cartridge also contains the EP print drum. This drum is coated with a photosensitive material that can hold a static charge when not exposed to light but *cannot* hold a charge when it *is* exposed to light—a curious phenomenon and one that EP printers exploit for the purpose of making images. Finally, the drum assembly contains a cleaning blade that continuously scrapes the used toner off the photosensitive drum to keep it clean.

Exposing a photosensitive drum to dust or light can damage it, but touching it will most likely render the drum inoperable! It's best to just not mess around with them.

In most laser printers, *toner cartridge* means an EP toner cartridge that contains toner and a photosensitive drum in one plastic case. In some laser printers, however, the toner and photosensitive drum can be replaced separately instead of as a single unit. If you ask for a toner cartridge for one of these printers, all you will receive is a cylinder full of toner. Consult the printer's manual to find out which kind of toner cartridge your laser printer uses.

WARNING Never ship a printer anywhere with a toner cartridge installed! If the printer is a laser printer, remove the toner cartridge first. If it's an LED page printer, there is a method to remove the photosensitive drum and toner hopper (check your manual for details).

FIGURE 10.10 An EP toner cartridge

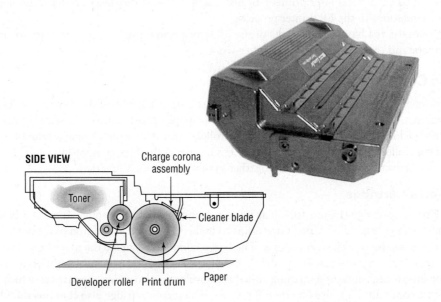

SIDE VIEW — Charge corona assembly — Toner — Cleaner blade — Developer roller — Print drum — Paper

The Laser Scanning Assembly

As we mentioned earlier, the EP photosensitive drum can hold a charge if it's not exposed to light. It is dark inside an EP printer, except when the laser scanning assembly shines on particular areas of the photosensitive drum. When it does that, the drum discharges, but only in the area that has been exposed. As the drum rotates, the laser scanning assembly scans the laser across the photosensitive drum, writing the image onto it. Figure 10.11 shows the laser scanning assembly.

WARNING Laser light is damaging to human eyes. Therefore, the laser is kept in an enclosure and will operate only when the laser printer's cover is closed.

High-Voltage Power Supply (HVPS)

The EP process requires high-voltage electricity. The high-voltage power supply (HVPS) provides the high voltages used during the EP process. This component converts AC current from a standard wall outlet (120V and 60Hz) into higher voltages that the printer can use. This high voltage is used to energize both the charging corona and the transfer corona.

WARNING Anything with the words *high voltage* in it should make you pause before opening a device and getting your hands into it. The HVPS can hurt or kill you if you're inside a laser printer and don't know what you're doing.

FIGURE 10.11 The EP laser scanning assembly (side view and simplified top view)

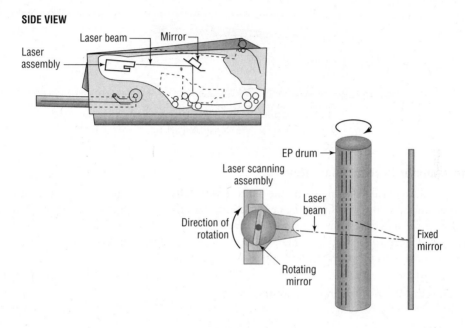

DC Power Supply (DCPS)

The high voltages used in the EP process can't power the other components in the printer (the logic circuitry and motors). These components require low voltages, between +5 VDC and +24VDC. The DC power supply (DCPS) converts house current into three voltages: +5VDC and −5VDC for the logic circuitry and +24VDC for the paper-transport motors. This component also runs the fan that cools the internal components of the printer.

Paper-Transport Assembly

The paper-transport assembly is responsible for moving the paper through the printer. It consists of a motor and several rubberized rollers that each performs a different function.

The first type of roller found in most laser printers is the *feed roller*, or *paper-pickup roller* (Figure 10.12). This D-shaped roller, when activated, rotates against the paper and pushes one sheet into the printer. This roller works in conjunction with a special rubber separator pad to prevent more than one sheet from being fed into the printer at a time.

Another type of roller that is used in the printer is the *registration roller* (also shown in Figure 10.12). There are actually two registration rollers, which work together. These rollers synchronize the paper movement with the image-formation process in the EP cartridge. The rollers don't feed the paper past the EP cartridge until the cartridge is ready for it.

Both of these rollers are operated with a special electric motor known as an *electronic stepper motor*. This type of motor can accurately move in very small increments. It powers all the paper-transport rollers as well as the fuser rollers.

FIGURE 10.12   Paper-transport rollers

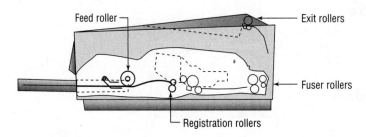

The Transfer Corona Assembly

When the laser writes the images on the photosensitive drum, the toner then sticks to the exposed areas; we'll cover this in the next section, "Electrophotographic (EP) Print Process." How does the toner get from the photosensitive drum onto the paper? The *transfer corona assembly* (Figure 10.13) is given a high-voltage charge, which is transferred to the paper, which in turn pulls the toner from the photosensitive drum.

FIGURE 10.13   The transfer corona assembly

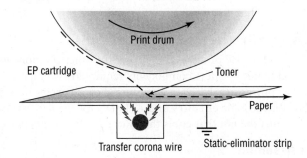

Included in the transfer corona assembly is a *static-charge eliminator strip* that drains away the charge imparted to the paper by the corona. If you didn't drain away the charge, the paper would stick to the EP cartridge and jam the printer.

There are two types of transfer corona assemblies: those that contain a transfer *corona wire* and those that contain a transfer *corona roller*. The transfer corona wire is a small-diameter wire that is charged by the HVPS. The wire is located in a special notch in the floor of the laser printer (under the EP print cartridge). The transfer corona roller performs the same function as the transfer corona wire, but it's a roller rather than a wire. Because the transfer corona roller is directly in contact with the paper, it supports higher speeds. For this reason, the transfer corona wire is infrequently used in laser printers today.

Fusing Assembly

The toner in the EP toner cartridge will stick to just about anything, including paper. This is true because the toner has a negative static charge and most objects have a net positive charge. However, these toner particles can be removed by brushing any object across the page. This could be a problem if you want the images and letters to stay on the paper permanently!

To solve this problem, EP laser printers incorporate a device known as a *fuser* (Figure 10.14), which uses two rollers that apply pressure and heat to fuse the plastic toner particles to the paper. You may have noticed that pages from either a laser printer or a copier (which uses a similar device) come out warm. This is because of the fuser.

FIGURE 10.14   The fuser

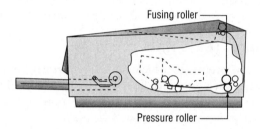

The fuser is made up of three main parts: a halogen heating lamp, a Teflon-coated aluminum fusing roller, and a rubberized pressure roller. The fuser uses the halogen lamp to heat the fusing roller to between 329° F (165° C) and 392° F (200° C). As the paper passes between the two rollers, the pressure roller pushes the paper against the fusing roller, which melts the toner into the paper.

 The fuser can cause severe burns! Be careful when working with it.

Printer Controller Circuitry

Another component in the laser printer we need to discuss is the *printer controller assembly*. This large circuit board converts signals from the computer into signals for the various assemblies in the laser printer, using a process known as *rasterizing*. This circuit board is usually mounted under the printer. The board has connectors for each type of interface and cables to each assembly.

When a computer prints to a laser printer, it sends a signal through a cable to the printer controller assembly. The controller assembly formats the information into a page's worth of line-by-line commands for the laser scanner. The controller sends commands to each of the components, telling them to wake up and begin the EP print process.

Ozone Filter

Your laser printer uses various high-voltage biases inside the case. As anyone who has been outside during a lightning storm can tell you, high voltages create ozone. Ozone is a chemically reactive gas that is created by the high-voltage coronas (charging and transfer) inside the printer. Because ozone is chemically reactive and can severely reduce the life of laser printer components, many older laser printers contain a filter to remove ozone gas from inside the printer as it is produced. This filter must be removed and cleaned with compressed air periodically (cleaning it whenever the toner cartridge is replaced is usually sufficient). Most newer laser printers don't have ozone filters. This is because these printers don't use transfer corona wires but instead use transfer corona rollers, which dramatically reduce ozone emissions.

Duplexing Assembly

Any laser printer worth its money today can print on both sides of the paper. This is accomplished through the use of a *duplexing assembly*. Usually located inside or on the back of the printer, the assembly is responsible for taking the paper, turning it over, and feeding back into the printer so the second side can be printed.

Electrophotographic (EP) Print Process

The *EP print process* is the process by which an EP laser printer forms images on paper. It consists of six major steps, each for a specific goal. Although many different manufacturers call these steps different things or place them in a different order, the basic process is still the same. Here are the steps in the order you will see them on the exam:

1. Cleaning
2. Charging
3. Writing (exposing)
4. Developing
5. Transferring
6. Fusing

 To help you remember the steps of the EP print process in order, learn the first letter of each step: CCWDTF. The most often used mnemonic sentence for this combination of letters is "Charlie Can Walk, Dance, and Talk French."

Before any of these steps can begin, however, the controller must sense that the printer is ready to start printing (toner cartridge installed, fuser warmed to temperature, and all covers in place). Printing cannot take place until the printer is in its ready state, usually indicated by an illuminated Ready LED light or a display that says something like 00 READY (on HP printers). The computer sends the print job to the printer, which begins processing the data. As it's processing the data, the print process steps begin.

Step 1: Cleaning

In the first part of the laser print process, a rubber blade inside the EP cartridge scrapes any toner left on the drum into a used toner receptacle inside the EP cartridge, and a fluorescent lamp discharges any remaining charge on the photosensitive drum (remember that the drum, being photosensitive, loses its charge when exposed to light). This step is called the *cleaning step* (Figure 10.15).

FIGURE 10.15   The cleaning step of the EP process

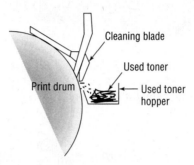

The EP cartridge is constantly cleaning the drum. It may take more than one rotation of the photosensitive drum to make an image on the paper. The cleaning step keeps the drum fresh for each use. If you didn't clean the drum, you would see ghosts of previous pages printed along with your image.

The amount of toner removed in the cleaning process is quite small. The cartridge will run out of toner before the used toner receptacle fills up.

Step 2: Charging

The next step in the EP process is the *charging step* (Figure 10.16). In this step, a special wire or roller (called a *charging corona*) within the EP toner cartridge (above the photosensitive drum) gets a high voltage from the HVPS. It uses this high voltage to apply a strong, uniform negative charge (around −600VDC) to the surface of the photosensitive drum.

Step 3: Writing

Next is the *writing step*. In this step, the laser is turned on and scans the drum from side to side, flashing on and off according to the bits of information the printer controller sends it as it communicates the individual bits of the image. Wherever the laser beam touches, the photosensitive drum's charge is severely reduced from −600VDC to a slight negative charge (around −100VDC). As the drum rotates, a pattern of exposed areas is formed, representing the image to be printed. Figure 10.17 shows this process.

FIGURE 10.16 The charging step of the EP process

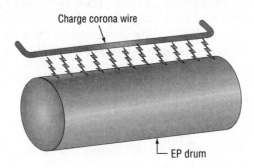

FIGURE 10.17 The writing step of the EP process

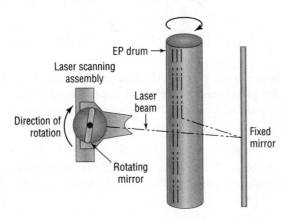

 You might also hear this step called the exposing step because it's when the drum is exposed to the laser.

At this point, the controller sends a signal to the pickup roller to feed a piece of paper into the printer, where it stops at the registration rollers.

Step 4: Developing

Now that the surface of the drum holds an electrical representation of the image being printed, its discrete electrical charges need to be converted into something that can be transferred to a piece of paper. The EP process step that accomplishes this is the *developing step* (Figure 10.18). In this step, toner is transferred to the areas that were exposed in the writing step.

A metallic roller called the *developing roller* inside an EP cartridge acquires a –600VDC charge (called a *bias voltage*) from the HVPS. The toner sticks to this roller because there is a magnet located inside the roller and because of the electrostatic charges between the toner and the developing roller. While the developing roller rotates toward the photosensitive drum, the toner acquires the charge of the roller (–600VDC). When the toner comes between the developing roller and the photosensitive drum, the toner is attracted to the areas that have been exposed by the laser (because these areas have a lesser charge, –100VDC). The toner also is repelled from the unexposed areas (because they are at the same –600VDC charge and like charges repel). This toner transfer creates a fog of toner between the EP drum and the developing roller.

FIGURE 10.18   The developing step of the EP process

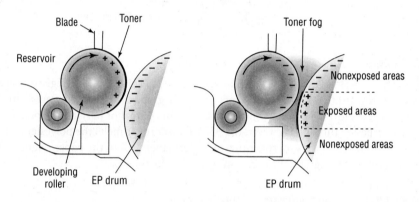

The photosensitive drum now has toner stuck to it where the laser has written. The photosensitive drum continues to rotate until the developed image is ready to be transferred to paper in the next step.

Step 5: Transferring

At this point in the EP process, the developed image is rotating into position. The controller notifies the registration rollers that the paper should be fed through. The registration rollers move the paper underneath the photosensitive drum, and the process of transferring the image can begin; this is the *transferring step*.

The controller sends a signal to the charging corona wire or roller (depending on which one the printer has) and tells it to turn on. The corona wire/roller then acquires a strong *positive* charge (+600VDC) and applies that charge to the paper. The paper, thus charged, pulls the toner from the photosensitive drum at the line of contact between the roller and the paper because the paper and toner have opposite charges. Once the registration rollers move the paper past the corona wire, the static-eliminator strip removes all charge from that line of the paper. Figure 10.19 details this step. If the strip didn't bleed this charge away, the paper would attract itself to the toner cartridge and cause a paper jam.

The toner is now held in place by weak electrostatic charges and gravity. It will not stay there, however, unless it is made permanent, which is the reason for the fusing step.

FIGURE 10.19   The transferring step of the EP process

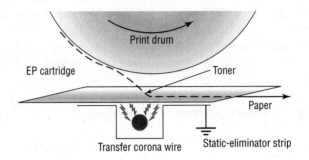

Step 6: Fusing

In the final step, the *fusing step*, the toner image is made permanent. The registration rollers push the paper toward the fuser rollers. Once the fuser grabs the paper, the registration rollers push for only a short time more. The fuser is now in control of moving the paper.

As the paper passes through the fuser, the 350° F fuser roller melts the polyester resin of the toner, and the rubberized pressure roller presses it permanently into the paper (Figure 10.20). The paper continues through the fuser and eventually exits the printer.

FIGURE 10.20   The fusing step of the EP process

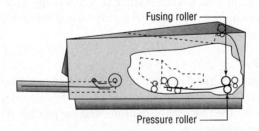

Once the paper completely exits the fuser, it trips a sensor that tells the printer to finish the EP process with the cleaning step. At this point, the printer can print another page, and the EP process can begin again.

Summary of the EP Print Process

Figure 10.21 summarizes all the parts involved in the EP printing process. First, the printer uses a rubber scraper to clean the photosensitive drum. Then the printer places a uniform −600VDC charge on the photosensitive drum by means of a charging corona. The laser "paints" an image onto the photosensitive drum, discharging the image areas to a much lower voltage (–100VDC). The developing roller in the toner cartridge has charged (–600VDC) toner stuck to it. As it rolls the toner toward the photosensitive drum, the toner is attracted to (and sticks to) the areas of the photosensitive drum that the laser has discharged. The image is then transferred from the drum to the paper at its line of contact by means of the transfer corona wire (or corona roller) with a +600VDC charge. The static-eliminator strip removes the high, positive charge from the paper, and the paper, now holding the image, moves on. The paper then enters the fuser, where a fuser roller and the pressure roller make the image permanent. The paper exits the printer, and the printer begins printing the next page or returns to its ready state.

FIGURE 10.21   The EP print process

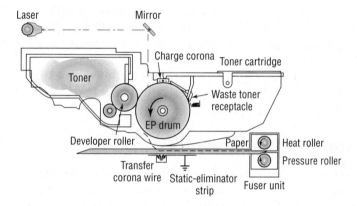

Thermal Printers

The types of printers you have learned about so far in this chapter account for 90 percent of all printers that are used with home or office computers and that you will see as a repair technician. The other 10 percent consist of other types of printers that primarily differ by the method they use to put colored material on the paper to represent what is being printed. Examples of these include solid ink, dye sublimation, and thermal printers. Keep in mind that for the most part, these printers operate like other printers in many ways: They all have a paper-feed mechanism (sheet-fed or roll); they all require consumables such as ink or toner and paper; they all use the same interfaces, for the most part, as other types of printers; and they are usually about the same size.

Thermal printing technology is used in many Point of Sale terminals and older fax machines (newer fax machines usually use inkjet or laser technology). They print on a kind of special, waxy paper that comes on a roll; the paper turns black when heat passes over it. *Thermal printers* work by using a print head the width of the paper. When it needs to print, a heating element heats certain spots on the print head. The paper below the heated print head turns black in those spots. As the paper moves through the printer, the pattern of blackened spots forms an image on the page of what is being printed. Another type of thermal printer uses a heat-sensitive ribbon instead of heat-sensitive paper. A thermal print head melts wax-based ink from the ribbon onto the paper. These are called thermal transfer or thermal wax-transfer printers.

Thermal direct printers typically have long lives because they have few moving parts. The only unique part that you might not be as familiar with is the paper feed assembly, which oftentimes needs to accommodate a roll of paper instead of sheets. The paper is somewhat expensive, doesn't last long (especially if it is left in a very warm place, like a closed car in summer), and produces poorer-quality images than most of the other printing technologies.

Installing and Configuring Printers

Odds are that if someone owns a computer they own a printer as well. If they don't, they have easy access to a printer at a library, work, or some other place. Many retailers and computer manufacturers make it incredibly easy to buy a printer because they often bundle a printer with a computer system as an incentive to get you to buy.

The A+ 220-801 exam will test your knowledge of the procedures to install printers. We're going to break this section into two parts: printer interface components and installing and sharing printers.

Printer Interface Components

A printer's *interface* is the collection of hardware and software that allows the printer to communicate with a computer. The hardware interface is commonly called a port. Each printer has at least one interface, but some printers have several to make them more flexible in a multiplatform environment. If a printer has several interfaces, it can usually switch between them on the fly so that several computers can print at the same time.

An interface incorporates several components, including its interface type and the *interface software*. Each aspect must be matched on both the printer and the computer. For example, if you have an older HP LaserJet 4L, it only has a parallel port. Therefore, you must use a parallel cable as well as the correct software for the platform being used (for example, a Macintosh HP LaserJet 4L driver if you connect it to a Macintosh computer).

Interface Types

When we say *interface types*, we're talking about the ports used in getting the printed information from the computer to the printer. There are two major classifications here: wired and wireless. Wired examples are serial, parallel, USB, and Ethernet. Wireless options include 802.11, Bluetooth, and infrared. You've learned about these connections in earlier chapters, but now you will learn how they apply to printers.

Serial

When computers send data serially, they send it 1 bit at a time, one after another. The bits stand in line like people at a movie theater, waiting to get in. Just as with modems, you must set the communication parameters (baud, parity, start and stop bits) on both entities—in this case, the computer and its printer(s)—before communication can take place.

It's very rare to find a serial printer in use today due to slow data transmission speed.

Parallel

When a printer uses parallel communication, it is receiving data 8 bits at a time over eight separate wires (one for each bit). Parallel communication was the most popular way of communicating from computer to printer for many years, mainly because it's faster than serial.

A parallel cable consists of a male DB25 connector that connects to the computer and a male 36-pin Centronics connector that connects to the printer. Most of the cables are less than 10′ long. Parallel cables should be IEEE 1284 compliant.

Keep printer cable lengths to less than 10′. Some people try to run printer cables more than 50′. If the length is greater than 10′, communications can become unreliable due to crosstalk.

Universal Serial Bus (USB)

The most popular type of printer interface as this book is being written is the Universal Serial Bus (USB). In fact, it is the most popular interface for just about every peripheral. The convenience for printers is that it has a higher transfer rate than either serial or parallel and it automatically recognizes new devices. And of course, USB is very easy to physically connect.

Ethernet

Many printers sold today have a wired Ethernet interface that allows them to be hooked directly to an Ethernet cable. These printers have an internal network interface card (NIC) and ROM-based software that allow them to communicate on the network with servers and workstations.

As with any other networking device, the type of network interface used on the printer depends on the type of network to which the printer is being attached. It's likely that the only connection type you will run into is RJ-45 for an Ethernet connection.

Wireless

The latest boom in printer interface technology is wireless. Clearly, people love their WiFi because it enables them to roam around an office and still remain connected to one another and to their network. It logically follows that someone came up with the brilliant idea that it would be nice if printers could be that mobile as well—after all, many are on carts with wheels. Some printers have built-in WiFi interfaces, while others can accept wireless network cards.

The wireless technology that is especially popular among peripheral manufacturers is *Bluetooth*. Bluetooth is a short-range wireless technology; most devices are specified to work within 10 meters (33 feet). Printers such as the HP Officejet 100 mobile printer have Bluetooth capability.

When printing with a Bluetooth-enabled device (like a PDA or cell phone) and a Bluetooth-enabled printer, all you need to do is get within range of the device (that is, move closer), select the print driver from the device, and choose Print. The information is transmitted wirelessly through the air using radio waves and is received by the device.

 WiFi is used to connect printers to a network, whereas Bluetooth can be used to connect a printer to a single computer (or mobile device).

Infrared

With the explosion of personal digital assistants (PDAs) and other handheld devices, the need grew for printing under the constraints they provide. The biggest hurdle faced by handheld device owners who need to print is the lack of any kind of universal interface. Most interfaces are too big and bulky to be used on handheld computers such as PDAs. The solution was to incorporate the standardized technology used on some remote controls: infrared transmissions. *Infrared transmissions* are simply wireless transmissions that use radiation in the infrared range of the electromagnetic spectrum. Some laser printers come with infrared transmitter/receivers (transceivers) so that they can communicate with the infrared ports on handhelds. This allows the user of a PDA, handheld, or laptop to print to that printer by pointing the device at the printer and initiating the print process.

As far as configuring the interface is concerned, very little needs to be done. The infrared interfaces are generally enabled by default on the computers, handhelds, and printers equipped with them. The only additional item that must be configured is the print driver on the PDA, handheld, or computer. The driver must be the correct one for the printer to which you are printing. In order to make infrared work, you need clear line of sight between the two devices and the devices need to be within about 3 feet of each other.

Interface Software

Now that we've looked at the ways you can connect your printer, it's time to face a grim reality: Computers and printers don't know how to talk to each other. They need help. That help comes in the form of interface software used to translate software commands into commands the printer can understand.

There are two major components of interface software: the page-description language and the driver software. The page-description language (PDL) determines how efficient the printer is at converting the information to be printed into signals the printer can understand. The driver software understands and controls the printer. It is very important that you use the correct interface software for your printer. If you use either the wrong page-description language or the wrong driver software, the printer will print garbage—or possibly nothing at all.

Page-Description Languages

A *page-description language* works just as its name implies: It describes the whole page being printed by sending commands that describe the text as well as the margins and other settings. The controller in the printer interprets these commands and turns them into laser pulses (or pin strikes). There are several printer communication languages in existence, but the three most common ones are PostScript, Printer Command Language (PCL), and Graphics Device Interface (GDI).

The first page-description language was PostScript. Developed by Adobe, it was first used in the Apple LaserWriter printer. It made printing graphics fast and simple. Here's how PostScript works: The PostScript printer driver describes the page in terms of "draw" and "position" commands. The page is divided into a very fine grid (as fine as the resolution of the printer). When you want to print a square, a communication like the following takes place:

```
POSITION 1,42%DRAW 10%POSITION 1,64%DRAW10D% . . .
```

These commands tell the printer to draw a line on the page from line 42 to line 64 (vertically). In other words, a page-description language tells the printer to draw a line on the page, gives it the starting and ending points, and that's that. Rather than send the printer the location of each and every dot in the line and an instruction at each and every location to print that location's individual dot, PostScript can get the line drawn with fewer than five instructions. As you can see, PostScript uses commands that are more or less in English. The commands are interpreted by the processor on the printer's controller and converted into the print-control signals.

PCL was developed by Hewlett-Packard in 1984 and originally intended for use with ink-jet printers as a competitor to PostScript. Since then, its role has been expanded to virtually every printer type, and it's a de facto industry standard.

GDI is actually a Windows component and is not specific to printers. Instead, it's a series of components that govern how images are presented to both monitors and printers. GDI printers work by using computer processing power instead of their own. The printed image is rendered to a bitmap on the computer and then sent to the printer. This means that the printer hardware doesn't need to be as powerful, which results in a less expensive printer. Generally speaking, the least expensive laser printers on the market are GDI printers.

Many newer printers can handle both PS and PCL (and GDI) and will automatically translate for you. Therefore, it's less likely that you'll install the "wrong" print driver than it was several years ago.

The main advantage of page-description languages is that they move some of the processing from the computer to the printer. With text-only documents, they offer little benefit. However, with documents that have large amounts of graphics or that use numerous fonts, page-description languages make the processing of those print jobs happen much faster. This makes them an ideal choice for laser printers, although nearly every type of printer uses them.

If you're working with an older laser printer and it's printing garbage, check the driver. It might have the letters *PS* or *PCL* at the end of the name. If a PS driver is installed for a printer that wants PCL (or vice versa), garbage output could be the result.

 Real World Scenario

Life Without a Page-Description Language

The most basic page-description language is no page-description language. The computer sends all the instructions the printer needs in a serial stream, like so: Position 1, print nothing; Position 2, strike pins 1 and 3; Position 3, print nothing. This type of description language works great for dot-matrix printers, but it can be inefficient for laser printers. For example, if you wanted to print a page using a standard page-description language and there was only one character on the page, there would be a lot of wasted signal for the "print nothing" commands.

With graphics, the commands to draw a shape on the page are relatively complex. For example, to draw a square, the computer (or printer) has to calculate the size of the square and convert that into lots of "strike pin *x*" (or "turn on laser") and "print nothing" commands. This is where the other types of page-description languages come into the picture.

Driver Software

The *driver* software controls how the printer processes the print job. When you install a printer driver for the printer you are using, it allows the computer to print to that printer correctly (assuming you have the correct interface configured between the computer and printer).

 If you're working with a Windows-based operating system, Microsoft refers to the software that is installed on the computer and lets you print as the "printer." The physical device where the paper comes out is referred to as the "print device." Here, when we say "printer," we mean the physical device.

When you need to print, you select the printer driver for your printer from a preconfigured list. The driver you select has been configured for the type, brand, and model of printer as well as the computer port to which it is connected. You can also select which paper tray the printer should use as well as any other features the printer has (if applicable). Also, each printer driver is configured to use a particular page-description language.

WARNING

If the wrong printer driver is selected, the computer will send commands in the wrong language. If that occurs, the printer will print several pages full of garbage (even if only one page of information was sent). This "garbage" isn't garbage at all but the printer page-description language commands printed literally as text instead of being interpreted as control commands.

Installing and Sharing Printers

Although every device is different, there are certain accepted methods used for installing any device. The following procedure works for installing many kinds of devices:

1. Attach the device using a local or network port and connect the power.
2. Install and update the device driver and calibrate the device.
3. Configure options and settings.
4. Print a test page.
5. Verify compatibility with the operating system and applications.
6. Educate users about basic functionality.

TIP

Before installing any device, read your device's installation instructions. There are exceptions to every rule.

Step 1: Attach the Device Using a Local or Network Port and Connect Power

When installing a printer, you must first take the device out of its packaging and set it up on a flat, stable surface. Then, with it powered off, connect the device to either the host computer (if it is a local printer device) or to the network (if it is a network device).

Once you have connected the device, connect power to it using whatever supplied power adapter comes with it. Some devices have their own built-in power supply and just need an AC power cord connecting the device to the wall outlet, while others rely on an external transformer and power supply. Finally, turn on the device.

Step 2: Install and Update the Device Driver and Calibrate the Device

Once you have connected and powered up the device, boot up the computer and wait for Windows to recognize the device. Windows will pop up a screen similar to the one shown in Figure 10.22. This wizard will allow you to configure the driver for the printer (depending on the device). You can insert the driver CD or DVD that comes with the device and the wizard will guide you through the device driver installation. If Windows fails to recognize the device, you can use the Add a Printer (in Windows 7) or the Add Printer Wizard (in older Windows versions) to troubleshoot the installation and to install the device drivers.

This might go without saying at this point, but it bears repeating: You need the right driver, one that matches both your printer and your operating system, for everything to work right.

FIGURE 10.22 Adding a printer in Windows 7

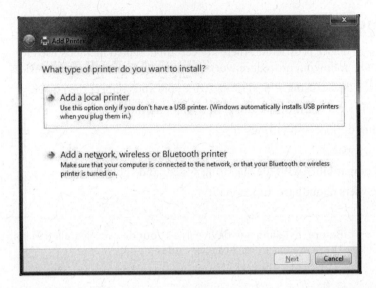

Once the driver is installed, the device will function. But some devices, such as inkjet printers, must be calibrated. *Calibration* is the process by which a device is brought within functional specifications. For example, inkjet printers need their print heads aligned so they print evenly and don't print funny-looking letters and unevenly spaced lines. The process is part of the installation of all inkjet printers.

When working with print media, it is especially important to calibrate all your hardware, including your monitor, scanner, printer, and digital camera, to ensure color matching.

Each manufacturer's process is different, but a typical alignment/calibration works like this:

1. During software installation, the installation wizard asks you if you would like to calibrate now, to which you respond Yes or OK.

2. The printer prints out a sheet with multiple sets of numbered lines. Each set of lines represents an alignment instance.

3. The software will ask you which set(s) looks the best. Enter the number and click OK or Continue.

4. Some alignment routines end at this point. Others will reprint the alignment page and see if the alignment "took." If not, you can reenter the number of which one looks the best.

5. Click Finish to end the alignment routine.

Step 3: Configure Options and Settings

Once you have installed the software and calibrated the device, you can configure any options you would like for the printer. All of the settings and how to change them can be found online or in your user manual.

Where you configure specific printer properties depends a lot on the printer itself. As a rule of thumb, you're looking for the Printer Properties or Printing Preferences applet. In Windows 7, if you click Start and then Devices And Printers, you will get a window similar to the one shown in Figure 10.23. At the top there is an option to add a device or a printer. If you double-click the printer icon, you will get another window (like the one in Figure 10.24) that lets you get to the printer's configuration options.

FIGURE 10.23 Devices And Printers

If you don't see the options you're looking for, be sure to highlight the printer first.

FIGURE 10.24   Printer information and options

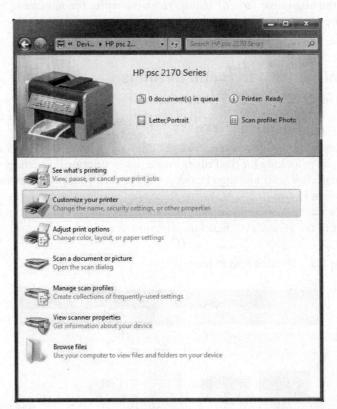

Various configuration features can be set from each menu option. The first two options in this example are the ones you would probably be the most interested in. The first one, See What's Printing, lets you look at and manage the print queue. This is something we'll talk more about in Chapter 20. The second one, Customize Your Printer, is where you find the printer's properties, shown in Figure 10.25.

From this dialog box, you can configure nearly any option you want to for your printer. The Properties dialog box will be pretty much the same for any printer you install, and we'll cover a few options here in a minute. First though, notice the Preferences button on the General tab. Clicking this will produce a new window like the one in Figure 10.26. That window will have configuration options based on the specific model of printer you're working with.

Now back to the Properties dialog box. The printer's Properties dialog box is less about how the printer does its job and more about how people can access the printer. From the Properties dialog box, you can share the printer, set up the port that it's on, configure when the printer will be available throughout the day, and specify who can use it. Let's take a look at a few key tabs. We've already taken a look at the General tab, which has the Preferences button as well as the all-important Print Test Page button. It's handy for troubleshooting!

FIGURE 10.25   Printer Properties dialog box

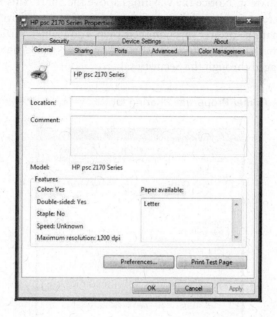

FIGURE 10.26   Printing Preferences window

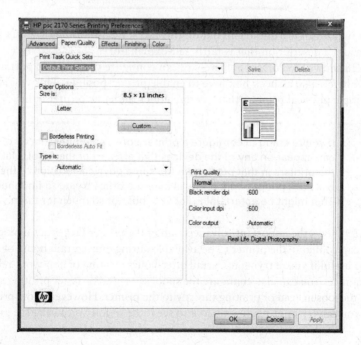

Figure 10.27 shows the Sharing tab. If you want other users to be able to print to this printer, you need to share it. Notice the warnings above the Share This Printer check box. Those are important to remember. When you share the printer, you give it a share name. Network users can map the printer through their own Add Printer Wizard (choosing a networked printer) and by using the standard \\computer_name\share_name convention. User permissions are managed through the Security tab.

FIGURE 10.27   Printer Properties Sharing tab

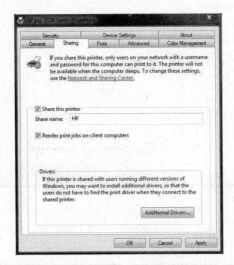

One other important feature to call out on this tab is the Additional Drivers button. This one provides a description that is fairly self-explanatory.

Figure 10.28 shows the Ports tab. Here you can configure your printer port and add and delete ports. There's also a check box here to enable printer pooling. This would be used if you have multiple physical printers that operate under the same printer name.

If you're going to configure a printer pool, remember that all of the output can appear on any of the devices that are part of that pool. Make sure all of the printers in that pool are in the same physical location! Otherwise, you will have people wandering all over the office trying to find their printouts. That might be entertaining for you, but not so much for them.

Figure 10.29 shows the important Advanced tab of the printer Properties dialog box. On this tab, you can configure the printer to be available during only certain hours of the day. This might be useful if you're trying to curtail after-hours printing of non-work-related documents, for example. You can also configure the spool settings. For faster printing, you should always spool the jobs instead of printing directly to the printer. However, if the printer is printing garbage, you can try printing directly to it to see if the spooler is causing the problem.

FIGURE 10.28 Printer Properties Ports tab

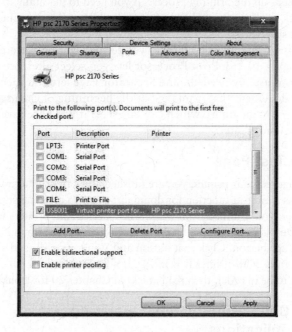

FIGURE 10.29 Printer Properties Advanced tab

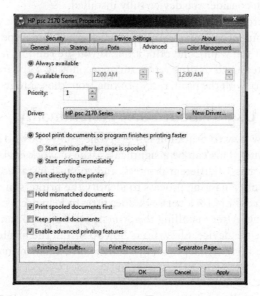

Regarding the check boxes at the bottom, you will want to always print spooled documents first because that speeds up the printing process. If you need to maintain an electronic copy of all printed files, check the Keep Printed Documents check box. Keep in mind that this will eat up a lot of hard disk space.

Finally, the Printing Defaults button takes you to the Printing Preferences window (shown earlier in Figure 10.26). Print Processor lets you select alternate methods of processing print jobs (not usually needed), and Separator Page lets you specify a file to use as a separator page (a document that prints out at the beginning of each separate print job, usually with the user's name on it), which can be useful if you have several (or several dozen) users sharing one printer.

Step 4: Print a Test Page

Once you have configured your printer, you are finished and can print a test page to test its output. Windows has a built-in function for doing just that. To print a test page, right-click the icon for the printer you installed from within the Devices And Printers window and click Printer properties. On the General tab of the Printer properties (shown in Figure 10.25), there will be a Print Test Page button. Click that button and Windows will send a test page to the printer. If the page prints, your printer is working. If not, double-check all of your connections. If they appear to be in order, then read ahead to Chapter 20 for troubleshooting tips.

Step 5: Verify Compatibility with Operating System and Applications

Once your printer is installed and you have tried out a test page, everything else should work well, right? That's usually true, but it's good practice to verify compatibility with applications before you consider the device fully installed.

With printers, this process is rather straightforward. Open the application you wonder about and print something. For example, open up Microsoft Word, type in some gibberish (or open a real document if you want), and print it out. If you are running non-Microsoft applications (such as a computer-aided drafting program or accounting software) and have questions about their compatibility with the printer, try printing from those programs as well.

Step 6: Educate Users About Basic Functionality

Most users today know how to print, but not everyone knows how to install the right printer or print efficiently. This can be a significant issue in work environments.

Say your workplace has 10 different printers, and you just installed number 11. First, your company should use a naming process to identify the printers in a way that makes sense. Calling a printer HPLJ4 on a network does little to help users understand where that printer is in the building. After installing the printer, offer installation assistance to those who might want to use the device. Show users how to install the printer in Windows (or if printer installation is automated, let them know they have a new printer and where it is).

Also let the users know the various options available on that printer. Can it print double-sided? If so, you can save a lot of paper. Show users how to configure that. Is it a color printer? Do users really need color for rough drafts of documents or presentations? Show users how to print in black and white on a color printer to save the expensive color ink or toner cartridges.

In Exercise 10.2 we'll step through the process of installing a USB printer in Windows 7; the process will work in Windows XP or Vista as well.

EXERCISE 10.2

Installing a USB printer in Windows 7

For this exercise, you will need the following items:

- A USB printer
- A USB printer cable
- The software driver CD or DVD that came with the printer
- A computer with a free USB port and a CD-ROM drive

    1. Turn on the computer.

    2. Plug the printer in to the wall outlet and turn it on.

    3. Insert the CD into the computer's CD-ROM drive. The driver CD's autorun feature should automatically start the installation program. If not, click Start ➢ Run and type in **D:\setup** or **D:\install** (if your CD-ROM drive letter is different, substitute that letter for *D*).

    4. Follow the prompts in the installation program to install the driver.

    5. Once the software has been installed, plug one end of the USB cable into the printer and the other end into the free USB port. Some installation programs will prompt you for this step.

    6. Windows will automatically detect the new printer, install the driver, and configure it automatically. Windows will display a balloon in the lower-right corner of the screen saying *Your hardware is now installed and is ready to use*. If Windows doesn't properly detect the printer, open Add a Printer to begin the installation process again, and manually specify the location of the print driver (such as the CD-ROM).

    7. Print a test page to see if the printer can communicate and print properly.

Real World Scenario

Which Printer Did That Go To?

One of the authors used to work at a satellite office in Salt Lake City for a company whose headquarters were in Houston. Because of printer problems, a new network printer has been installed, and it had a different network name from the previous printer.

At the end of the month, one of the accountants printed off her monthly reconciliation report, which typically ran about 400 pages. (A hard copy was required for regulatory reasons.) Puzzled when it didn't come out on the printer, she printed it again. And again. And again. After the fourth failed attempt, and several hours later, she decided to ask someone in IT what the problem was.

It turns out that she had mapped (installed) the new network printer but had gotten a few letters wrong in the printer name. Instead of being at her office, all of her print jobs were sent to a printer in the Houston office. And of course, there were people in Houston trying to print similar reports and who just kept refilling the printer with paper because they didn't want to cut someone else's report off in the middle.

While this wasn't a catastrophic failure, it was annoying. She had unintentionally wasted three reams of paper, the associated toner, and hours of printer life. It wasn't a malicious act and she was a literate computer user, but it's illustrative of the need to educate and help users with installing and configuring devices. Had the printer been mapped correctly the first time, the waste could have been avoided.

Performing Printer Maintenance and Upgrades

Considering the amount of work they do, printers last a pretty long time. Some printers can handle over 100,000 pages per month, yet they're usually pretty reliable devices. You can help your printers live a long and fulfilling life by performing the right maintenance, and smoothly running printers always makes your officemates happy. After all, going to get your print job from the printer and discovering that the printer is in the shop is a very frustrating experience! In addition, there may be ways you can upgrade a slower printer or add functionality without breaking the bank. In the following sections, we'll look at performing printer maintenance and upgrading your printers.

Performing Printer Maintenance

Regardless of the type of printer you use, giving it a regular check-up is a good idea. You're probably familiar with some of the activities that fall under maintenance, such as replacing paper, ink or toner cartridges, and ribbons. We'll look at those as well as some additional, more involved maintenance procedures.

Replacing Consumables

To properly maintain a printer, you need to replace consumables such as toner or ink cartridges, assemblies, filters, and rollers on occasion. Trying to cut costs by buying cheaper supplies rarely pays off.

Whenever purchasing supplies for your printer, always get supplies from the manufacturer or from an authorized reseller. This way, you'll be sure that the parts are of high quality. Using unauthorized parts can damage your printer and possibly void your warranty.

Printer Paper

Most people don't give much thought to the kind of paper they use in their printers. It's a factor that can have tremendous effect on the quality of the hard-copy printout, however, and the topic is more complex than people think. For example, if the wrong paper is used, it can cause frequent paper jams and possibly even damage components.

Several aspects of paper can be measured; each gives an indication as to the paper's quality. The first factor is *composition*. Paper is made from a variety of substances. Paper used to be made from cotton and was called rag stock. It can also be made from wood pulp, which is cheaper. Most paper today is made from the latter or a combination of the two.

Another aspect of paper is the property known as *basis weight* (or simply *weight* for short). The weight of a particular type of paper is the actual weight, in pounds, of a ream (500 sheets) of the standard size of that paper made of that material. For regular bond paper, that size is 17×22.

The final paper property we'll discuss is the *caliper* (or thickness) of an individual sheet of paper. If the paper is too thick, it may jam in feed mechanisms that have several curves in the paper path. (On the other hand, a paper that's too thin may not feed at all.)

These are just three of the categories we use to judge the quality of paper. Because there are so many different types and brands of printers as well as paper, it would be impossible to give the specifications for the "perfect" paper. However, the documentation for any printer will give specifications for the paper that should be used in that printer.

For best results, store paper in an area where it will not get wet or be exposed to excessive humidity.

Ink and Toner

The area in which using recommended supplies is the biggest concern is ink and toner cartridges. Using the wrong ink or toner supplies is the easiest way to ruin a perfectly good printer.

Dot-matrix printers use a cloth or polyester ribbon soaked in ink and coiled up inside a plastic case. This assembly is called a *printer ribbon* (or *ribbon cartridge*). It's very similar to a typewriter ribbon, but instead of being coiled into the two rolls you'd see on a typewriter, the ribbon is continuously coiled inside the plastic case. Once the ribbon has run out of ink, it must be discarded and replaced. Ribbon cartridges are developed closely with their respective printers. For this reason, ribbons should be purchased from the same manufacturer as the printer. The wrong ribbon could jam in the printer as well as cause quality problems.

It is possible to re-ink a ribbon. Some vendors sell a bottle of ink solution that can be poured into the plastic casing, where the cloth ribbon will soak up the solution. This can be a messy process, and you should do this only if the manufacturer recommends it.

Bubble-jet cartridges have a liquid ink reservoir. The ink in these cartridges is sealed inside. Once the ink runs out, the cartridge must be removed and discarded. A new, full one is installed in its place. Because the ink cartridge contains the printing mechanism as well as ink, it's like getting a new printer every time you replace the ink cartridge.

In some bubble-jet printers, the ink cartridge and the print head are in separate assemblies. This way, the ink can be replaced when it runs out, and the print head can be used several times. This works fine if the printer is designed to work this way. However, some people think they can do this on their integrated cartridge/print head system, using special ink cartridge refill kits. These kits consist of a syringe filled with ink and a long needle. The needle is used to puncture the top of an empty ink cartridge, and the syringe is then used to refill the reservoir.

Do not use ink cartridge refill kits! There are several problems with these kits (the ones you see advertised with a syringe and a needle). First, the kits don't use the same kind of ink that was originally in the ink cartridges. The new ink may be thinner, causing it to run out or not print properly. Also, the print head is oftentimes supposed to be replaced around this same time. Refilling the cartridge doesn't replace the print head, so you'll have print-quality problems. Finally, the hole the syringe leaves cannot be plugged and may allow ink to leak out. These problems can happen with do-it-yourself kits as well as with cartridges refilled by office supply stores or private printer supply sellers. Here's the bottom line: *Buy new ink cartridges from the printer manufacturer.* Yes, they are a bit more expensive, but in the long run you will save money because you won't have any of the problems described here.

The final type of consumable is toner. Each model of laser printer uses a specific toner cartridge. You should check the printer's manual to see which toner cartridge your printer needs. Many businesses will recycle your toner or ink cartridges for you, refill them, and sell them back to you at a discount. Don't buy them. While some businesses that perform this "service" are more legitimate than others, using recycled parts is more dangerous to your hardware than using new parts. The reason for this is that refilled cartridges are more likely to break or leak than new parts, and this leakage could cause extensive damage to the inside of your printer. And again, using secondhand parts can void your warranty, so you're left with a broken printer that you have to pay for. Avoid problems like this by buying new parts.

 Real World Scenario

Think Before You Refill

Just as with ink cartridges, you should always buy the exact model recommended by the manufacturer. The toner cartridges have been designed specifically for a particular model. Additionally, *never* refill toner cartridges, for most of the same reasons we don't recommend refilling ink cartridges. The printout quality will be poor, and the fact that you're just refilling the toner means you might *not* be replacing the photosensitive drum (which is usually inside the cartridge), and the drum might *need* to be replaced. Simply replacing refilled toner cartridges with proper, name-brand toner cartridges has solved most laser printer quality problems we have run across. We keep recommending the right ones, but clients keep coming back with the refilled ones. The result is that we take our clients' money to solve their print-quality problems when all it involves is a toner cartridge, our (usually repeat) advice to buy the proper cartridge next time, and the obligatory minimum charge for a half hour of labor (even though the job of replacing the cartridge takes all of 5 minutes!).

 Always properly recycle your used ink and toner cartridges. Just don't buy recycled cartridges!

Performing Scheduled Maintenance

When shopping for a printer, one of the characteristics you should look for is the printer's capacity, which is often quoted in monthly volume. This is particularly important if the printer will be serving in a high-load capacity. Every printer needs periodic maintenance, but printers that can handle a lot of traffic typically need it less frequently. Check the printer specifications to see how often scheduled maintenance is suggested. Never, ever fall behind on performing scheduled maintenance on a printer.

Many laser printers have LCD displays that provide useful information, such as error messages or notices that you need to replace a toner cartridge. The LCD display will also tell you when the printer needs scheduled maintenance. How does it know? Printers keep track of the number of pages they print, and when the page limit is reached, they display a message, usually something simple like *Perform user maintenance*. The printer will still print, but you should perform the maintenance.

Being the astute technician that you are, you clean the printer with the recommended cleaning kit or install the maintenance kit you purchased from the manufacturer. Now, how do you get the maintenance message to go away? Reset the page count using a menu option. For example, on many HP laser printers, you press the Menu button until you get to the Configuration menu. Once there, you press the Item key until the display shows *Service Message = ON*. Then press the plus key (+) to change the message to *Service Message = OFF*. Bring the printer back online, and you're ready to go.

Using Cleaning Solutions

With all of the ink or toner they use, printers get dirty. If printers get too dirty or if the print heads get dirty, you'll notice print problems. No one wants this to happen.

Most printers have a self-cleaning utility that is activated through a menu option or by pressing a combination of buttons on the printer itself. It's recommended that you run the cleaning sequence every time you replace the toner or ink cartridges. If you experience print-quality problems, such as lines in the output, run the cleaning routine.

Sometimes the self-cleaning routines aren't enough to clear up the problem. If you are having print-quality issues, you might want to consider purchasing a cleaning kit, which frequently comes with a cleaning solution.

 Cleaning kits are often designed for one specific type of printer and should be used only on that type of printer. For example, don't apply an inkjet cleaning solution to a laser printer.

Each cleaning kit comes with its own instructions for use. Exercise 10.3 walks you through the steps of using an inkjet cleaning solution. Note that the steps for your printer might differ slightly; please consult your manual for specific instructions.

EXERCISE 10.3

Using an Inkjet Cleaning Solution

1. Power on the printer, and open the top cover to expose the area containing the print cartridges.

2. Initiate a self-cleaning cycle. When the print head moves from its resting place, pull the AC power plug. This lets you freely move the print heads without damaging them.

3. Locate the sponge pads on which to apply the cleaning solution. They'll be in the area where the print heads normally park. Use a cotton swab or paper towel to gently soak up any excess ink in the pads.

4. Using the supplied syringe, apply the cleaning solution to the sponge pads until they are saturated.

5. Plug the printer back into the wall outlet, and turn it on. The print heads will park themselves.

6. Turn the printer back off. Let the solution sit for at least 3 hours.

7. Power the printer back on, and run three printer cleaning cycles. Print a nozzle check pattern (or a test page) after each cleaning cycle to monitor the cleaning progress.

That should take care of it! If not, again, refer to your printer's manual for more instructions.

Thermal printers require special attention because they contain a heating element. Always unplug the device and ensure that it's cooled off before trying to clean it. Thermal printer cleaning cards, cleaning pens, and kits are widely available in the marketplace. If you need to remove any debris (from any printer), use compressed air or a specialized computer vacuum.

Ensuring a Suitable Environment

Printers won't complain if the weather outside is too hot or too cold, but they are susceptible to environmental issues. Here are some things to watch out for in your printer's environment:

Heat Laser printers can generate a lot of heat. Because of this, ensure that your laser printer is in a well-ventilated area. Resist the temptation to put the laser printer in the little cubbyhole in your desk; overheating will reduce the shelf life of your printer.

Light The laser printer's toner cartridge contains a photosensitive drum. Exposing that drum to light could ruin the drum. While the drum is encased in plastic, it's best to avoid exposing the printer or toner cartridges to extreme light sources. Under no circumstance should you open the toner cartridge, unless you're ready to get rid of it as well as clean up a big mess.

Ozone Laser printers that use corona wires produce ozone as a by-product of the printing process. In offices, ozone can cause respiratory problems in small concentrations, and it can be seriously dangerous to people in large amounts. Ozone is also a very effective oxidizer and can cause damage to printer components.

Fortunately, laser printers don't produce large amounts of ozone, and most laser printers have an ozone filter. Ozone is another reason to ensure that your printer area has good ventilation. Also, replace the ozone filter periodically; check your printer's manual for recommendations on when to do this.

Ammonia Ammonia isn't produced by the printer, but it is contained in many cleaning products. Ammonia can greatly reduce the printer's ability to neutralize ozone and can cause permanent damage to toner cartridges. It's best to avoid using ammonia-based cleaners near laser printers.

Installing Printer Upgrades

The printer market encompasses a dizzying array of products. You can find portable printers, photo printers, cheap black-and-white printers for under $30, high-end color laser printers for over $5,000, and everything in between. Most of the cheaper printers do not have upgrade options, but higher-end printers will have upgrade options, including the memory, network cards, and firmware.

Installing Printer Memory

When purchasing a memory upgrade for your printer, you need to make sure of two things. First, buy only memory that is compatible with your printer model. Most printers today use a standard computer dual in-line memory module (DIMM), but check your manual or the manufacturer's website to be sure. If you're not sure, purchasing the memory through the manufacturer's website (or an authorized reseller) is a good way to go. Second, be sure that your printer is capable of a memory upgrade. It's possible that the amount of memory in your printer is the maximum that it can handle.

Once you have obtained the memory, it's time to perform the upgrade. The specific steps required to install the memory will depend on your printer. Check with the manual or the manufacturer's website for instructions tailored to your model.

Exercise 10.4 walks you through the general steps for installing memory into a laser printer.

EXERCISE 10.4

Installing Memory into a Laser Printer

1. Turn off the printer.

2. Disconnect all cables from the printer (power and interface cables).

3. Find the area in which you need to install the memory.

   On most HP LaserJet printers, this is in the back, on a piece of hardware called the formatter board. The formatter board is held in by tabs near the top and bottom of the board. Remove the formatter board from the printer. Other brands have different configurations. For example, on many Xerox laser printers you remove a panel on the top of the unit (underneath the paper output tray) to get to the memory.

   If your printer requires you to remove a component (such as the formatter board) to upgrade the memory, place that component on a grounded surface, such as an anti-static work mat. Otherwise, proceed to step 6.

4. If you are replacing an existing memory module, remove the old module, being careful not to break off the latches at the end of the module that hold it in.

5. Insert the new memory module, making sure that any alignment notches on the memory module are lined up with the device before inserting the memory module.

6. Replace the removable component (if necessary).

7. Reconnect the power and interface cables.

EXERCISE 10.4 *(continued)*

8. Power on the printer.

9. Follow the printer manual's instructions on running a self-test to ensure that the memory is recognized.

Some printers require that you manually enable the added memory. Here are the steps to do that in Windows:

1. Open the Devices and Printers (in Windows 7), Printers and Faxes (in Windows XP), or Printers (in Windows Vista) window.

2. Right-click the printer and choose Properties.

3. On the Device Settings tab, click the Printer Memory button in the Installable Options section.

4. Select the amount of memory that is now installed.

5. Click OK.

Installing a Network Interface Card

Installing a NIC directly into a printer has become popular as more and more people need their printers to be on the network but don't want to hassle with a host computer The NIC in a printer is similar to the NIC in a computer, with a couple of important differences. First, the NIC in a printer has a small processor on it to perform the management of the NIC interface (functions that the software on a host computer would do). This software is usually referred to as a print server, but be careful because that term can also refer to a physical computer that hosts many printers. Second, the NIC in a printer is proprietary, for the most part. It is made by the same manufacturer as the printer.

When a person on the network prints to a printer with a NIC, they are printing right to the printer and not going through any third-party device (although in some situations, that is desirable and possible with NICs). Because of its dedicated nature, the NIC option installed in a printer makes printing to that printer faster and more efficient—that NIC is dedicated to receiving print jobs and sending printer status to clients.

> Most printer NICs come with management software installed that allows clients to check their print jobs' status as well as toner levels from any computer on the network. You access the configuration options by typing the IP address of the printer into your web browser and generally entering an authorized username and password.

Your manual is the best place to check to see if you can install a print server. Specific steps for installing the print server will also be in the manual or on the manufacturer's website. Generally speaking, it's very similar to installing a NIC into a computer.

Upgrading Printer Firmware

As with upgrading memory, methods to upgrade a printer's firmware depend on the model of printer you have. Most of the time, upgrading a printer's firmware is a matter of downloading and/or installing a free file from the manufacturer's website. Printer firmware upgrades are generally done from the machine hosting the printer (usually called the print server).

Firmware is usually upgraded for one of two reasons. One, if you are having compatibility issues, a firmware upgrade might solve them. Two, firmware upgrades can offer newer features not available on previous versions.

Installing Other Upgrades

While we've covered some of the most important upgrades, most printers (especially laser printers) can be upgraded with additional capabilities as well. Each manufacturer, with the documentation for each printer, includes a list of all the accessories, options, and upgrades available. The following options can be included on that list:

- Hard drives
- Trays and feeders
- Finishers

Hard Drives

For a printer to print properly, the type style or *font* being printed must be downloaded to the printer along with the job being printed. Desktop publishing and graphic design businesses that print color pages on slower color printers are always looking for ways to speed up their print jobs. So they install multiple fonts into the onboard memory of the printer to make them *printer-resident fonts*.

But there's a problem: Most printers have a limited amount of storage space for these fonts. To solve this problem, printer manufacturers made it possible for hard drives to be added to many printers. These hard drives can be used to store many fonts used during the print process and are also used to store the large document file while it is being processed for printing.

Trays and Feeders

One option that is popular in office environments is the addition of paper trays. Most laser and bubble-jet printers come with at least one paper tray (usually 500 sheets or less). The addition of a paper tray allows a printer to print more sheets between paper refills, thus reducing its operating cost. In addition, some printers can accommodate multiple paper trays, which can be loaded with different types of paper, stationery, and envelopes. The benefit is that you can print a letter and an envelope from the same printer without having to leave your desk or change the paper in the printer.

Related to trays is the option of *feeders*. Some types of paper products need to be watched as they are printed to make sure the printing happens properly. One example is envelopes: You usually can't put a stack of envelopes in a printer because they won't line up straight or they may get jammed. An accessory that you might add for this purpose is the *envelope feeder*. An envelope feeder typically attaches to the front of a laser printer and feeds in envelopes, one at a time. It can hold usually between 100 and 200 envelopes.

Finishers

A printer's *finisher* does just what its name implies: It finishes the document being printed. It does this by folding, stapling, hole punching, sorting, or collating the sets of documents being printed into their final form. So rather than printing out a bunch of paper sheets and then having to collate and staple them, you can have the finisher do it. This particular option, while not cheap, is becoming more popular on laser printers to turn them into multifunction copiers. As a matter of fact, many copiers are now digital and can do all the same things a laser printer can but much faster and for a much cheaper cost per page.

Summary

In this chapter, we discussed how different types of printers work as well as the most common methods of connecting them to computers. You learned how computers use page-description languages to format data before they send it to printers and drivers to talk to them. You also learned about the various types of consumable supplies and how they relate to each type of printer.

The most basic category of printer currently in use is the impact printer. Impact printers form images by striking something against a ribbon, which in turn makes a mark on the paper. You learned how these printers work and the service concepts associated with them.

One of the most popular types of printer today is the bubble-jet printer, so named because of the mechanism used to put ink on the paper.

The most complex type of printer is the laser printer. The A+ 220-801 exam covers this type of printer more than any other. You learned about the steps in the electrophotographic (EP) process, the process that explains how laser printers print. We also explained the various components that make up this printer and how they work together.

You then learned about the interfaces used to connect printers to PCs and how to install and share a printer. Proper steps include connecting the device, installing the driver, configuring options, validating application and operating system compatibility, and educating users on how to use the device. Installing the device is the first step, but you're not done until you ensure that it works properly and that users know how to access it.

Finally, we looked at how to perform printer maintenance, including the importance of using recommended supplies and various types of upgrades you can install in printers.

Exam Essentials

Know the differences between types of printer technologies (e.g., laser, inkjet, thermal, impact).   Laser printers use a laser and toner to create the page. Inkjet printers spray ink onto the page. Thermal printers use heat to form the characters on the page. Impact printers use a mechanical device to strike a ribbon, thus forming an image on the page.

Know the names, purposes, and characteristics of interfaces used by printers, including port and cable types.   Most printers today use the same interfaces, no matter what their type. Printers use serial, parallel, USB, Ethernet, WiFi, Bluetooth, or infrared to connect to their host computers. By far the most common is USB.

Know how to install and configure printers.   The basic procedure is as follows:

1. Attach the device using a local or network port and connect the power.
2. Install and update the device driver and calibrate the device.
3. Configure options and default settings.
4. Print a test page.
5. Verify compatibility with the operating system and applications.
6. Educate users about basic functionality.

Know the six steps in the laser printing print sequence.   The six steps are cleaning, conditioning, writing, developing, transferring, and fusing.

Understand the importance of using recommended supplies.   Using consumables (paper, ink, toner) that are recommended for your printer is important. Using bad supplies could ruin your printer and void your warranty.

Understand how to upgrade printer memory and firmware.   Printer memory is upgraded by installing an additional or replacement memory module. To do this, you must remove a panel from the printer. The specific steps depend on your printer model. Firmware is upgraded by downloading a file from the manufacturer's website and installing it.

Know what environmental hazards to watch out for around printers.   Heat, excessive light, ozone, and ammonia are all bad things for printers to be around.

Review Questions

The answers to the Chapter Review Questions can be found in Appendix A.

1. Which voltage is applied to the paper to transfer the toner to the paper in an EP process laser printer?

    A. +600VDC

    B. −600VDC

    C. +6000VDC

    D. −6000VDC

2. Which types of printers are referred to as page printers because they receive their print job instructions one page at a time? (Choose two.)

    A. Daisy wheel

    B. Dot matrix

    C. Bubble-jet

    D. Laser

    E. Thermal

3. Which of the following is *not* an advantage of a Universal Serial Bus (USB) printer interface?

    A. It has a higher transfer rate than a serial connection.

    B. It has a higher transfer rate than a parallel connection.

    C. It automatically recognizes new devices.

    D. It allows the printer to communicate with networks, servers, and workstations.

4. Which type of printers can be used with multipart forms?

    A. Bubble-jet printers

    B. Laser printers

    C. Thermal printers

    D. Dot-matrix printers

5. Which step in the EP print process uses a laser to discharge selected areas of the photosensitive drum, thus forming an image on the drum?

    A. Writing

    B. Transferring

    C. Developing

    D. Cleaning

6. Which of the following are page-description languages? (Choose two.)

    A. Page Description Language (PDL)

    B. PostScript

    C. PageScript

    D. Printer Control Language (PCL)

7. What voltage does the corona wire or corona roller hold?

    A. +600VDC

    B. −600VDC

    C. 0VDC

    D. −100VDC

8. Which device in a bubble-jet printer contains the print head?

    A. Toner cartridge

    B. Ink cartridge

    C. Daisy wheel

    D. Paper tray

9. What is the correct order of the steps in the EP print process?

    A. Developing, writing, transferring, fusing, charging, cleaning

    B. Charging, writing, developing, transferring, fusing, cleaning

    C. Transferring, writing, developing, charging, cleaning, fusing

    D. Cleaning, charging, writing, developing, transferring, fusing

10. Any printer that uses the electrophotographic process contains how many standard assemblies?

    A. Five

    B. Six

    C. Four

    D. Nine

11. What is typically included in the EP laser printer toner cartridge? (Choose three.)

    A. Toner

    B. Print drum

    C. Laser

    D. Cleaning blade

12. What happens during the developing stage of laser printing?

    A. An electrostatic charge is applied to the drum to attract toner particles.

    B. Heat is applied to the paper to melt the toner.

    C. The laser creates an image of the page on the drum.

    D. An electrostatic charge is applied to the paper to attract toner particles.

13. Which of the following are possible interfaces for printers? (Choose three.)

   A. Parallel

   B. PS/2

   C. Serial

   D. Network

14. You have just installed a new printer. After it is installed, it prints only garbled text. Which of the following is likely the problem?

   A. Wrong IP address

   B. Worn print head

   C. Incorrect print drivers

   D. Unsupported printer

15. Which printer contains a wheel that looks like a flower with raised letters and symbols on each petal?

   A. Bubble-jet printers

   B. Daisy-wheel printer

   C. Dot-matrix printer

   D. Laser printer

16. What part of a laser printer supplies the voltages for the charging and transfer corona assemblies?

   A. High-voltage power supply (HVPS)

   B. DC power supply (DCPS)

   C. Controller circuitry

   D. Transfer corona

17. Which printer part gets the toner from the photosensitive drum onto the paper?

   A. Laser-scanning assembly

   B. Fusing assembly

   C. Corona assembly

   D. Drum

18. Which step in the laser printer printing process occurs immediately after the writing phase?

   A. Charging

   B. Fusing

   C. Transferring

   D. Developing

19. Which assembly permanently presses the toner into the paper?

    A. Transfer corona

    B. Fuser

    C. Printer controller circuitry

    D. Paper transport assembly

20. Which of the following most accurately describes how to obtain a firmware upgrade for your laser printer?

    A. Download the firmware upgrade for free from the manufacturer's website.

    B. Pay to download the firmware upgrade from the manufacturer's website.

    C. Have a certified laser printer technician come to your site and install a new firmware chip.

    D. Contact the manufacturer of the printer, and they will send you the firmware upgrade on a CD.

Performance-Based Question

On the A+ exams, you will encounter performance-based questions. The questions on the exam require you to perform a specific task, and you will be graded on whether you were able to complete the task. The following requires you to think creatively to measure how well you understand this chapter's topics. You may or may not see similar questions on the actual A+ exams. To see how your answer compares to the authors', refer to Appendix B.

Your network has several inkjet printers in use. A user is complaining that on one of them, their documents are consistently printing with extra smudges along the lines of print. What steps would you take to clean the printer?

Chapter

11

Understanding Operational Procedures

THE FOLLOWING COMPTIA A+ 220-801 EXAM OBJECTIVES ARE COVERED IN THIS CHAPTER:

✓ **5.1 Given a scenario, use appropriate safety procedures.**

- ESD straps
- ESD mats
- Self-grounding
- Equipment grounding
- Personal safety
    - Disconnect power before repairing PC
    - Remove jewelry
    - Lifting techniques
    - Weight limitations
    - Electrical fire safety
    - CRT safety – proper disposal
    - Cable management
- Compliance with local government regulations

✓ **5.2 Explain environmental impacts and the purpose of environmental controls.**

- MSDS documentation for handling and disposal
- Temperature, humidity level awareness and proper ventilation

- Power surges, brownouts, blackouts
  - Battery backup
  - Surge suppressor
- Protection from airborne particles
  - Enclosures
  - Air filters
- Dust and debris
  - Compressed air
  - Vacuums
- Component handling and protection
  - Antistatic bags
- Compliance with local government regulations

✓ **5.3 Given a scenario, demonstrate proper communication and professionalism.**

- Use proper language—avoid jargon, acronyms, slang when applicable.
- Maintain a positive attitude.
- Listen and do not interrupt a customer.
- Be culturally sensitive.
- Be on time (if late contact the customer).
- Avoid distractions.
  - Personal calls.
  - Talking to co-workers while interacting with customers.
  - Personal interruptions.
- Dealing with a difficult customer or situation.
  - Avoid arguing with customers and/or being defensive.
  - Do not minimize customer's problems.
  - Avoid being judgmental.
  - Clarify customer statements (ask open-ended questions to narrow the scope of the problem, restate the issue or question to verify understanding).

- Set and meet expectations/timeline and communicate status with the customer.

  - Offer different repair/replacement options if applicable.

  - Provide proper documentation on the services provided.

  - Follow up with customer/user at a later date to verify satisfaction.

- Deal appropriately with customers confidential materials.

  - Located on computer, desktop, printer, etc.

✓ **5.4 Explain the fundamentals of dealing with prohibited content/activity.**

- First response

  - Identify

  - Report through proper channels

  - Data/device preservation

- Use of documentation/documentation changes

- Chain of custody

  - Tracking of evidence/documenting process

This chapter looks at the foundations of two key operational procedures. While these two topics might not be top-of-mind issues for you every day (hopefully you don't go to work every day thinking "Okay, don't get killed by a monitor" or "Let's see if I can be nice to someone today"), they should be integrated into your work processes.

In this chapter, we will start off talking about safety, which includes the safety of you and your co-workers as well as environmental concerns. Observing proper safety procedures can help prevent injury to yourself or others.

A discussion about the environment is two sided. The environment affects computers (via things like dust, sunlight, and water), but computers can also potentially harm the environment. We'll consider both sides as we move through this chapter.

In the final part of this chapter, we'll switch to discussing professionalism and communication and focus on topics you need to know for your exam study. Applying the skills learned here will help you pass the exam, but on a more practical level, it will help you become a better technician and possibly further advance your career.

Understanding Safety Procedures

The proliferation of computers in today's society has created numerous jobs for technicians. Presumably that's why you're reading this book: You want to get your CompTIA A+ certification. Many others who don't fix computers professionally do like tinkering with them as a hobby. Years ago, only the most expert users dared crack the case on a computer. Oftentimes repairing the system meant using a soldering iron. Today, thanks to the cheap cost of parts, repair is not quite as involved. Regardless of your skill or intent, if you're going to be inside a computer, you always need to be aware of safety issues. There's no sense in getting yourself hurt or killed—literally.

As a provider of a hands-on service (repairing, maintaining, or upgrading someone's computer), you need to be aware of some general safety tips because if you are not careful, you could harm yourself or the equipment. Clients expect you to solve their problems, not make them worse by injuring yourself or those around you. In the following sections, we'll talk about identifying safety hazards and creating a safe working environment.

Identifying Potential Safety Hazards

Anything can be a potential safety hazard, right? Okay, maybe that statement is a bit too paranoid, but there *are* many things, both man-made and environmental, that can cause safety problems when working with and around computers.

Perhaps the most important aspect of computers that you should be aware of is that they not only *use* electricity, they also *store* electrical charge after they're turned off. This makes the power supply and the monitor pretty much off-limits to anyone but a repair person trained specifically for those devices. In addition, the computer's processor and various parts of the printer run at extremely high temperatures, and you can get burned if you try to handle them immediately after they've been in operation.

Those are just two general safety measures that should concern you. There are plenty more. When discussing safety issues with regard to PCs, let's break them down into four general areas:

- Computer components
- Electrostatic discharge
- Electromagnetic interference
- Natural elements

Computer Components

As mentioned earlier, computers use electricity. And as you're probably aware, electricity can hurt or kill you. The first rule when working inside a computer is to always make sure it's powered off. So if you have to open the computer to inspect or replace parts (as you will with most repairs), be sure to turn off the machine before you begin. Leaving it plugged in is usually fine, and many times actually preferred because it grounds the equipment and can help prevent electrostatic discharge.

There's one exception to the power-off rule: you don't have to power off the computer when working with hot-swappable parts, which are designed to be unplugged and plugged back in when the computer is on. Most of these components have an externally accessible interface (such as USB devices or hot-swappable hard drives), so you don't need to crack the computer case.

The Power Supply

Do not take the issue of safety and electricity lightly. Removing the power supply from its external casing can be dangerous. The current flowing through the power supply normally follows a complete circuit; when your body breaks the circuit, your body becomes part of that circuit. Getting inside the power supply is the most dangerous thing you can do as an untrained technician.

The two biggest dangers with power supplies are burning yourself and electrocuting yourself. These risks usually go hand in hand. If you touch a bare wire that is carrying current, you could get electrocuted. A large-enough current passing through you can cause severe burns. It can also cause your heart to stop, your muscles to seize, and your brain to stop functioning. In short, it can kill you. Electricity always finds the best path to ground. And because the human body is basically a bag of saltwater (an excellent conductor of electricity), electricity will use us as a conductor if we are grounded.

Although it is possible to open a power supply to work on it, doing so is *not* recommended. Power supplies contain several capacitors that can hold *lethal* charges *long after they have been unplugged!* It is extremely dangerous to open the case of a power supply. Besides, power supplies are pretty cheap. It would probably cost less to replace one than to try to fix it, and this approach would be much safer.

In the late 1990s, a few mass computer manufacturers experimented with using open power supplies in their computers to save money. I don't know if any deaths occurred because of such incompetence, but it was definitely a very bad idea.

Current vs. Voltage: Which Is More Dangerous?

When talking about power and safety, you will almost always hear the saying, "It's not the volts that kill you, it's the amps." That's mostly true. However, an explanation is in order.

The number of volts in a power source represents its potential to do work. But volts don't do anything by themselves. Current (amperage, or amps) is the force behind the work done by electricity. Here's an analogy to help explain this concept: Say you have two boulders; one weighs 10 pounds, the other 100 pounds, and each is 100 feet off the ground. If you drop them, which one will do more work? The obvious answer is the 100-pound boulder. They both have the same potential to do work (100 feet of travel), but the 100-pound boulder has more mass and thus more force. Voltage is analogous to the distance the boulder is from the ground, and amperage is analogous to the mass of the boulder.

This is why you can produce static electricity on the order of 50,000 volts and not electrocute yourself. Even though this electricity has a great *potential* for work, it does very little work because the amperage is so low. This also explains why you can weld metal with 110 volts. Welders use only 110 (sometimes 220) volts, but they also use anywhere from 50 to 200 amps!

If you ever have to work on a power supply, for safety's sake you should discharge all capacitors within it. To do this, connect a resistor across the leads of the capacitor with a rating of 3 watts or more and a resistance of 100 ohms (Ω) per volt. For example, to discharge a 225-volt capacitor, you would use a 22.5kΩ resistor (225 volts times 100Ω = 22,500Ω, or 22.5kΩ).

The Monitor

Other than the power supply, the most dangerous component to try to repair is a cathode-ray tube (CRT) monitor. In fact, we recommend that you *do not* try to repair monitors of any kind.

To avoid the extremely hazardous environment contained inside the monitor—it can retain a high-voltage charge for hours after it's been turned off—take it to a certified monitor technician or television repair shop. The repair shop or certified technician will know the proper procedures for discharging the monitor, which involve attaching a resistor to the flyback transformer's charging capacitor to release the high-voltage electrical charge that builds up during use. They will also be able to determine whether the monitor can be repaired or needs to be replaced. Remember, the monitor works in its own extremely protected environment (the monitor case) and may not respond well to your desire to try to open it.

 The CRT is vacuum sealed. Be extremely careful when handling the CRT. If you break the glass, it will implode, which can send glass in any direction.

Even though we recommend not repairing monitors, the A+ exam tests your knowledge of the safety practices to use when you need to do so. If you have to open a monitor, you must first discharge the high-voltage charge on it by using a *high-voltage probe*. This probe has a very large needle, a gauge that indicates volts, and a wire with an alligator clip. Attach the alligator clip to a ground (usually the round pin on the power cord). Slip the probe needle underneath the high-voltage cup on the monitor. You will see the gauge spike to around 15,000 volts and slowly reduce to 0 (zero). When it reaches zero, you may remove the high-voltage probe and service the high-voltage components of the monitor.

 Do *not* use an ESD strap when discharging the monitor; doing so can lead to a fatal electric shock.

Working with LCD monitors or any device with a fluorescent or LCD backlight presents a unique safety challenge. These types of devices require an *inverter*, which provides the high-voltage, high-frequency energy needed to power the backlight.

The inverter is a small circuit board installed behind the LCD panel that takes AC power and converts (inverts) it for the backlight. If you've ever seen a laptop or handheld device with a flickering screen or perpetual dimness, it was likely an inverter problem. Inverters store energy even when their power source is cut off, so they have the potential to discharge that energy if you mess with them. Be careful!

The Case

One component people frequently overlook is the case. Cases are generally made of metal, and some computer cases have very sharp edges inside, so be careful when handling them. You can, for example, cut yourself by jamming your fingers between the case and the frame when you try to force the case back on. Also of particular interest are drive bays. Countless technicians have scraped or cut their hands on drive bays when trying in vain to plug a drive cable into the motherboard. Particularly sharp edges can be covered with duct tape—just make sure you're covering only metal and nothing with electrical components on it.

The Printer

If you've ever attempted to repair a printer, you might have sometimes thought there was a little monster in there hiding all the screws from you. Besides missing screws, here are some things to watch out for when repairing printers:

- When handling a toner cartridge from a laser printer or page printer, do not turn it upside down. You will find yourself spending more time cleaning the printer and the surrounding area than fixing the printer.

- Do not put any objects into the feeding system (in an attempt to clear the path) when the printer is running.

- Laser printers generate a laser that is hazardous to your eyes. Do not look directly into the source of the laser.

- If it's an inkjet printer, do not try to blow in the ink cartridge to clear a clogged opening—that is, unless you like the taste of ink.

- Some parts of a laser printer (such as the EP cartridge) will be damaged if you touch them. Your skin produces oils and has a small surface layer of dead skin cells. These substances can collect on the delicate surface of the EP cartridge and cause malfunctions. Bottom line: Keep your fingers out of places they don't belong!

- Laser printers can get extremely hot. Don't burn yourself on internal components.

Using an egg carton (or other container with small compartments) is a great way to store and keep track of screws you take out of a device when you're working on it.

When working with printers, we follow some pretty simple guidelines. If there's a messed-up setting, paper jam, or ink or toner problem, we will fix it. If it's something other than that, we call a certified printer repair person. The inner workings of printers can get pretty complex, and it's best to call someone trained to make those types of repairs.

The Keyboard and Mouse

Okay, we know you're thinking, "What danger could a keyboard or mouse cause?" We admit that not much danger is associated with these components, but there are a couple of safety concerns you should always keep in mind.

First, if your mouse has a cord, you can trip over it, so make sure it's safely out of the way. Second, you could short-circuit your keyboard if you accidentally spill liquid on it. Keyboards don't function well with half a can of cola in their innards!

Electrostatic Discharge

So far we've talked about how electricity can hurt people, but it can also pose safety issues for computer components. One of the biggest concerns for components is *electrostatic discharge (ESD)*. For the most part, ESD won't do serious damage to a person other than provide a little shock. But little amounts of ESD can cause serious damage to computer components, and that damage can manifest itself by causing computers to hang or reboot or fail to boot at all. ESD happens when two objects of dissimilar charge come in contact with one another. The two objects exchange electrons in order to standardize the electrostatic charge between them. This charge can, and often does, damage electronic components.

> CPU chips and memory chips are particularly sensitive to ESD. Be extremely cautious when handling them.

When you shuffle your feet across the floor and shock your best friend on the ear, you are discharging static electricity into the ear of your friend. The lowest static voltage transfer you can feel is around 3,000 volts; it doesn't electrocute you because there is extremely little current. A static transfer that you can *see* is at least 10,000 volts! Just by sitting in a chair, you can generate around 100 volts of static electricity. Walking around wearing synthetic materials can generate around 1,000 volts. You can easily generate around 20,000 volts simply by dragging your smooth-soled shoes across a shag carpet in the winter. (Actually, it doesn't have to be winter to run this danger. This voltage can occur in any room with very low humidity—like a heated room in wintertime.)

> Relative humidity has a significant impact on the electricity you generate. Walking around can generate 1,500 volts at 65 to 90 percent relative humidity, but it can produce 35,000 volts if the relative humidity is in the 10 to 25 percent range.

It makes sense that these thousands of volts can damage computer components. However, a component can be damaged with under 100 volts! That means if a small charge is built up in your body, you could damage a component without realizing it.

> Do you have long hair or (gasp!) have to wear a tie when fixing computers? Tie it back. Letting long hair or dangling cloth get inside an open computer case is asking for trouble because both are notorious for carrying and conducting static electricity.

The good news is that there are measures you can implement to help contain the effects of ESD. The first and easiest item to implement is the antistatic wrist strap, also referred to as an ESD strap. We will look at the antistatic wrist strap, as well as other ESD prevention tools, in the following sections.

Antistatic Wrist Straps

To use the ESD strap, you attach one end to an earth ground (typically, the ground pin on an extension cord) or the computer case and wrap the other end around your wrist. This strap grounds your body and keeps it at a zero charge. Figure 11.1 shows the proper way to attach an antistatic strap. There are several varieties of wrist straps available. The one in Figure 11.1

uses a banana clip, while others use alligator clips and are attached to the computer case itself. If the grounding strap is attached to the case rather than an outlet, the computer needs to be plugged in (but turned off!) for the grounding system to be effective.

 Real World Scenario

ESD Symptoms

Symptoms of ESD damage may be subtle, but they can be detected. One of the authors relates this experience:

"When I think of ESD, I always think of the same instance. A few years ago, I was working on an Apple Macintosh. This computer seemed to have a mind of its own. I would troubleshoot it, find the defective component, and replace it. The problem was that as soon as I replaced the component, it failed. I thought maybe the power supply was frying the boards, so I replaced both at the same time, but to no avail.

"I was about to send the computer off to Apple when I realized that it was winter. Normally this would not be a factor, but winters where I live are extremely dry. Dry air promotes static electricity. At first I thought my problem couldn't be that simple, but I was at the end of my rope. So, when I received my next set of new parts, I grounded myself with an antistatic strap for the time it took to install the components, and prayed while I turned on the power. Success! The components worked as they should, and a new advocate of ESD prevention was born."

FIGURE 11.1   One possible way to use an ESD strap

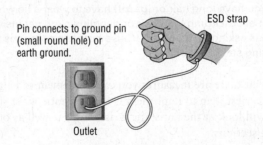

Pin connects to ground pin
(small round hole) or
earth ground.

ESD strap

Outlet

For an antistatic wrist strap to work properly, the computer must be plugged in but turned off. When the computer is plugged in, it is grounded through the power cord. When you attach yourself to it with the wrist strap, you are grounded through the power cord as well. If the computer is not plugged in, there is no ground and any excess electricity on you will just discharge into the case, which is not good.

An ESD strap is a device that is specially designed to bleed electrical charges away *safely*. It uses a 1 megohm resistor to bleed the charge away slowly. A simple wire wrapped around your wrist will not work correctly and you could be electrocuted!

Never wear an ESD strap if you're working inside a monitor or inside a power supply. If you wear one while working on the inside of these components, you increase the chance of getting a lethal shock.

ESD Antistatic Mats

It is possible to damage a device by simply laying it on a bench top. For this reason, you should have an ESD mat in addition to an ESD strap. This mat drains excess charge away from any item coming in contact with it (see Figure 11.2). ESD mats are also sold as mouse/keyboard pads to prevent ESD charges from interfering with the operation of the computer. Many wrist straps can be connected to the mat, thus causing the technician and any equipment in contact with the mat to be at the same electrical potential and eliminating ESD. There are even ESD bootstraps and ESD floor mats, which are used to keep the technician's entire body at the same potential.

FIGURE 11.2   Proper use of an ESD antistatic mat

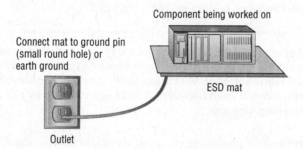

Component being worked on

Connect mat to ground pin
(small round hole) or
earth ground

ESD mat

Outlet

Antistatic Bags for Parts

Antistatic bags are important tools to have at your disposal when servicing electronic components because they protect the sensitive electronic devices from stray static charges. These silver or pink bags are designed so that the static charges collect on the outside of the bags rather than on the electronic components.

Unlike antistatic mats, antistatic bags do not "drain" the charges away, and they should never be used in place of an antistatic mat.

You can obtain the bags from several sources. The most direct way to acquire antistatic bags is to go to an electronics supply store and purchase them in bulk. Most supply stores have several sizes available. Perhaps the easiest way to obtain them, however, is simply to hold on to the ones that come your way. That is, when you purchase any new component, it usually comes in an antistatic bag. After you have installed the component, keep the bag. It may take you a while to gather a collection of bags if you take this approach, but eventually you will have a fairly large assortment.

Self-Grounding

First of all, we recommend that you include a grounding strap in your technician toolkit so you're never without it. But we also realize that things happen and you might find yourself in a situation where you don't have your strap or an ESD mat. In cases like that, you should self-ground.

Self-grounding is not as effective as using proper anti-ESD gear, but it makes up for that with its simplicity. To self-ground, make sure the computer is turned off but plugged in. Then, touch an exposed (but not hot or sharp!) metal part of the case. That will drain electrical charge from you. Better yet is if you can maintain constant contact with that metal part. That should keep you at the same bias as the case. Yes, it can be rather challenging to work inside a computer one-handed, but it can be done.

Additional Methods

Another preventive measure you can take is to maintain the relative humidity at around 50 percent. Be careful not to increase the humidity too far—to the point where moisture begins to condense on the equipment. Also, use antistatic spray, which is available commercially, to reduce static buildup on clothing and carpets.

If you don't have any antistatic spray, you can always use the "Downy solution." In a spray bottle, combine one part water with one part liquid fabric softener. Mist areas such as carpet and clothing that cause problems. If used regularly, it will keep static away and keep your office smelling nice too!

Vendors have methods of protecting components in transit from manufacture to installation. They press the pins of integrated circuits (ICs) into antistatic foam to keep all the pins at the same potential. In addition, most circuit boards are shipped in antistatic bags, as discussed earlier.

Antistatic foam looks a lot like Styrofoam. However, there are huge differences between the two. While antistatic foam helps reduce the transfer of electricity, Styrofoam does not. Styrofoam holds a charge on its surface quite easily. Have you ever tried to get some of those small packing "peanuts" off your hands? Be careful to not mix the two up, lest you fry your components.

At the very least, you can be mindful of the dangers of ESD and take steps to reduce its effects. Beyond that, you should educate yourself about those effects so you know when ESD is becoming a major problem.

> If an ESD strap or mat is not available, you can discharge excess static voltage by touching the metal case of the power supply. However, the power supply *must be plugged into a properly grounded outlet* for this technique to work as intended. Also, for this to work you need to maintain contact to continuously drain excess charge away. As you can see, it's easier to have an antistatic wrist strap.

Electromagnetic Interference

When compared to the other dangers we've discussed in this chapter, *electromagnetic interference (EMI)*, also known as *radio frequency interference (RFI)*, is by far the least dangerous. EMI really poses no threats to you in terms of bodily harm. What it can do is make your equipment or network malfunction.

EMI is an unwanted disturbance caused by electromagnetic radiation generated by another source. In other words, some of your electrical equipment may interfere with other equipment. Here are some common sources of interference:

Network devices   The popularity of wireless networking devices has introduced the possibility of interference. The most popular wireless networking standards, 802.11b/g/n, use the 2.4GHz range for transmissions. Bluetooth devices happen to use the same frequency. In theory, they won't interfere with each other because they use different modulation techniques. In practice, interference between the two types of devices can happen.

Magnets   Magnets work by generating an electromagnetic field. It might make sense, then, that this field could cause electromagnetic interference. For the most part, you don't need to worry about this unless you have huge magnets at work. Do note, however, that many motors use magnets, which can cause interference. For example, one of our friends used to have his computer on the opposite side of a wall from his refrigerator. Whenever the compressor kicked in, his monitor display would become wavy and unreadable. It was time to move his home office. Another common culprit is desk fans. Put a desk fan next to a CRT and turn the fan on. What happens to the display? It will become wavy. This is another example of EMI.

Cordless phones   Cordless phones can operate at a variety of frequencies. Some of the more common ones are 900MHz, 1.9GHz, 2.4GHz, and 5.8GHz. Many of these are common ranges for computer equipment to operate in as well.

Microwave ovens   Microwave ovens are convenient devices to heat food and beverages. The radiation they generate is typically in the 2.45GHz range, although it can vary slightly. If a microwave is being used near your computer, you'll often see a distorted display just as if a fan or motor were being run next to your computer. You may also experience interference with wireless network communications.

NOTE Copper wires are susceptible to EMI. Fiber-optic cables, which use light to transmit data, are not susceptible to EMI.

Natural Elements

Computers should always be operated in cool environments away from direct sunlight and water sources. This is also true when you're working on computers. We know that heat is an enemy of electrical components. Dirt and dust act as great insulators, trapping heat inside components. When components run hotter than they should, they have a greater chance of breaking down faster.

 Real World Scenario

Play It Safe with Common Sense

When you're repairing a PC, do not leave it unattended. Someone could walk into the room and inadvertently bump the machine, causing failure. Worse, they could step on pieces that may be lying around and get hurt. It is also not a good idea to work on the PC alone. If you're injured, someone should be around to help if you need it. Finally, if you're fatigued, you may find it difficult to concentrate and focus on what you are doing. There are real safety measures related to repairing PCs, so the most important thing to remember is to pay close attention to what you are doing.

It pretty much should go without saying, but we'll say it anyway: Water and electricity don't mix. Keep liquids away from computers. If you need your morning coffee while fixing a PC, make sure the coffee has a tight and secure lid.

Creating a Safe Workplace

Benjamin Franklin was quoted as saying, "An ounce of prevention is worth a pound of cure." That sage advice applies to a lot in life and certainly to computer safety. Knowing how to properly work with and handle computer equipment is a good first start. It's also important to institutionalize and spread the knowledge though and make sure your company has the proper policies and procedures in place to ensure everyone's safety.

Moving Computer Equipment

We've already talked about some of the hazards posed by computer parts. Many times it's the more mundane tasks that get us though, such as moving stuff around. One of the most common ways IT employees get hurt is by moving equipment in an improper way.

Changing the location of computers is a task often completed by IT personnel, and you can avoid injury by moving things the right way.

 Real World Scenario

Water and Servers Don't Mix

This situation happened at a company one of the authors used to work for. The building needed some roof repairs. Repairs went on for several days, and then the weekend came. It just so happened that the area they were working on was over the server room. That weekend was a particularly rainy one, and of course over the weekend no one was in the office.

Monday morning came, and the IT staff arrived to find that the server room was partially flooded. Rain had come in through weaknesses in the roof caused by the maintenance and had flooded through the drop ceiling and into the server room. Nearly half a million dollars of equipment was ruined.

Although this is an extreme example, it illustrates an important point: Always be aware of the environment you're working in, and be alert to potential sources of problems for your computer equipment.

To ensure your personal safety, here are some important techniques to always consider before moving equipment:

- The first thing to always check is that it's unplugged. There's nothing worse (and potentially more dangerous) than getting yanked because you're still tethered.
- Securely tie the power cord to the device, or remove it altogether if possible.
- Remove any loose jewelry and secure long hair or neckties.
- Lift with your legs, not your back (bend at the knees when picking something up, not at the waist).
- Do not twist when lifting.
- Maintain the natural curves of the back and spine when lifting.
- Keep objects close to your body and at waist level.
- Push rather than pull if possible.

The muscles in the lower back aren't nearly as strong as those in the legs or other parts of the body. Whenever lifting, you want to reduce the strain on those lower-back muscles as much as possible. If you want, use a back belt or brace to help you maintain the proper position while lifting.

Monitors can be heavy. (Thank goodness for flat screens!) When lifting and carrying a monitor, always keep the glass face toward your body. The front of the monitor is the heaviest part, and you want the heavy part closest to your body to reduce strain on your muscles.

If you believe the load is too much for you to carry, don't try to pick it up! Get assistance from a co-worker. Another great idea is to use a cart. It will save you trips if you have multiple items to move, and it saves you the stress of carrying components.

When moving loads, always be aware of your surrounding environment. Before you move, scout out the path to see whether there are any trip hazards or other safety concerns such as spills, stairs, uneven floors (or ripped carpet), tight turns, or narrow doorways.

Using Appropriate Repair Tools

A big part of creating a safe working environment is having the right tools available for the job. There's no sense implementing a sledgehammer solution to a ball-peen hammer problem. Using the wrong tool might not help fix the problem, and it could very possibly hurt you or the computer in the process.

Most of the time, computers can be opened and devices removed with nothing more than a simple screwdriver. But if you do a lot of work on PCs, you'll definitely want to have additional tools on hand.

Computer toolkits are readily available on the Internet or at any electronics store. They come in versions from inexpensive (under $10) kits that have around 10 pieces to kits that cost several hundred dollars and have more tools than you will probably ever need. Figure 11.3 shows an example of a basic 11-piece PC toolkit. All of these tools come in a handy zippered case so it's hard to lose them.

FIGURE 11.3   PC toolkit

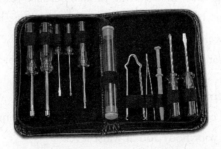

Looking at Figure 11.3, from left to right you have two nut drivers (¼″ and ³⁄₁₆″), a ⅛″ flat screwdriver, a #0 Phillips screwdriver, a T-15 Torx driver, a screw tube, an integrated circuit (IC) extractor, tweezers, a three-claw retriever, a #1 Phillips screwdriver, and a ³⁄₁₆″ flat screwdriver. A favorite of ours is the three-claw retriever because screws like to fall and hide in tiny places. While most of these tools are incredibly useful, an IC extractor probably won't be. In today's environment, it's rare to find an IC that you can extract, much less find a reason to extract one.

The following sections look at some of the tools of the PC troubleshooting trade.

Screwdrivers

Every PC technician worth their weight in pocket protectors needs to have a screwdriver. At least one. There are three major categories of screwdrivers: flat-blade, Phillips, and Torx. In addition, there are devices that look like screwdrivers, except they have a hex-shaped indented head on them. They're called hex drivers and belong to the screwdriver family.

Whenever picking a screwdriver, always keep in mind that you want to match the size of the screwdriver head to the size of the screw. Using a screwdriver that's too small will cause it to spin inside the head of the screw, stripping the head of the screw and making it useless. And if the screwdriver is too large, you won't be able to get the head in far enough to generate any torque to loosen the screw. Of course, if the screwdriver is way too big, it won't even fit inside the screw head at all. Common sizes for Phillips-head screws are 000, 00, 0, 1, 2, and 3. When dealing with Torx screws, the two most common sizes are T-10 and T-15.

When tightening screws, you don't need to make them so tight that they could survive the vibrations of an atmospheric reentry. Snug is fine. Making them too tight can cause problems loosening them, which could cause you (or someone else not so strong) to strip the head. Using an electric screwdriver is fine if you have one. The only problem with them is that they tend to be larger than manual screwdrivers and can be difficult to get inside a case.

Using magnetic-tipped screwdrivers is not recommended. Many computer disks contain magnetically coded information, and the magnetic tip of a screwdriver could cause a problem. Keep a retrieving tool handy instead, just in case you drop a screw.

Antistatic Wrist Straps

We've already talked about these, but they are important, so we'll mention them again. An antistatic wrist strap is essential to any PC technician's arsenal. They don't typically come with smaller PC toolkits, but you should always have one or two handy.

Other Useful Tools

PC techs also commonly carry the following tools:

Pliers   Pliers are useful for a variety of tasks, especially gripping something. Long-nose or needle-nose pliers extend your reach.

Wire cutters   Wire cutters come in a variety of forms but are primarily used for cutting cables. It's not likely you'll need any sort of heavy-duty metal cutters.

Strippers   If you are making your own network cables or fixing them, having a cable stripper (and crimper) is essential.

Mirrors   Mirrors are handy inside tight spaces. Many techs like to use a dentist-style mirror because of its compact size and good reach.

Flashlight   Never underestimate the utility of a good flashlight. You never know what your lighting situation will be like when you're at a repair site. Smaller flashlights with good output are great to have because they can fit into tight spaces.

Compressed air   For as much as computers and dust don't get along, it sure seems like they are attracted to each other. In all seriousness, computer components are powered by electricity, which causes the components to have a slight electrical charge. Dust is also electrically charged, so it's attracted to computer components. Compressed air can help you clean off components, especially in hard-to-reach places.

> Be judicious about your use of compressed air. Often, you will find yourself just blowing the dust from one part of a computer to another.

Multimeter   If you're having power issues, a multimeter is an invaluable tool that measures electrical current, voltage, and resistance. You'll also hear of voltmeters, and while the two have somewhat different functions, both of them can be used to troubleshoot power problems. Using a voltmeter, you can see if a computer power supply is producing the right amount of current for the devices that depend on it.

Creating a Safe Work Environment

We've already talked about some work environment issues to be aware of. For example, don't put a computer next to the break room sink, and keep computers out of direct sunlight (even if the desk location is great). A couple of other things to watch out for include trip hazards, atmospheric conditions, and high-voltage areas.

Cables are a common cause of tripping. If at all possible, run cables through drop ceilings or through conduits to keep them out of the way. If you need to lay a cable through a trafficked area, use a cable floor guard to keep the cables in place and safe from crushing. Floor guards come in a variety of lengths and sizes (for just a few cables or for a lot of cables). Figure 11.4 shows a cable guard.

FIGURE 11.4   Floor cable guard

Another useful tool to keep cables under control is a cable tie, like the one shown in Figure 11.5. It's simply a plastic tie that holds two or more cables together. They come in different sizes and colors so you're bound to find one that suits your needs.

FIGURE 11.5 Cable ties

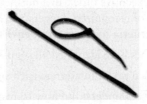

In a pinch, and without a floor cable guard, you can use tape such as duct tape to secure your cables to the floor. This is recommended only as a temporary fix for two reasons. First, it's not much less of a trip hazard than just having the cables run across the floor. Second, duct tape doesn't protect the cables from being crushed if people step on them or heavy objects are moved over them.

Exercise 11.1 is a simple exercise that you can modify and use as needed. Its purpose is to illustrate the hazards that are around your office that you may have not realized were there.

EXERCISE 11.1

Finding Trip Hazards

1. Walk around the server room and count how many cables are lying on the floor.

2. Walk around the client areas and see how many cables are lying on the floor or are exposed underneath cubicles.

Maybe you're fortunate and don't find any, but odds are you found at least one area that has exposed cables that should not be exposed. You can reapply this exercise for other dangerous items such as exposed wires and exposed sharp edges.

Atmospheric conditions that you need to be aware of include areas with high static electricity or excessive humidity. This is especially important for preventing electrostatic discharge, as we've already discussed.

Finally, be aware of high-voltage areas. Computers do need electricity to run but only in measured amounts. Running or fixing computers in high-voltage areas can cause problems for the electrical components and can cause problems for you if something should go wrong.

Implementing Safety Policies and Procedures

The Occupational Safety and Health Act states that every working American has the right to a safe and healthy work environment. To enforce the act, the Occupational Safety and Health Administration (OSHA) was formed. OSHA covers all private sector employees and post office workers. Public sector employees are covered by state programs, and federal employees are covered under a presidential executive order. In a nutshell, OSHA requires employers to "provide a workplace that is free of recognized dangers and hazards."

There are three overarching criteria to a safe work environment:

- The company and its employees have identified all significant hazards in the work setting.
- Preventive measures have been taken to address each significant hazard.
- The company and its employees understand how to respond to accidents or near-miss accidents if or when they occur.

The following sections explore specific responsibilities and how to create a safe work environment plan.

 Always ensure that your company's safety policies and procedures comply with all government regulations.

Employer and Employee Responsibilities

Maintaining workplace safety is the responsibility of employers as well as employees. Here are some of the important responsibilities of employers:

- Provide properly maintained tools and equipment.
- Provide a warning system, such as codes or labels, to warn employees of potential hazards or dangerous chemicals.
- Post the OSHA poster in a prominent location.
- Keep records of workplace injuries or illnesses.
- Continuously examine workplace conditions to ensure OSHA compliance.

It's also the responsibility of the employee to help maintain a safe work environment. Specifically, employees are charged with the following tasks:

- Read and understand OSHA posters.
- Follow all employer-implemented health and safety rules and safe work practices.
- Use all required protective gear and equipment.
- Report hazardous conditions to the employer.
- Report hazardous conditions that the employer does not correct to OSHA.

As you can see, both employers and employees need to work together to keep the workplace safe. It is illegal for an employee to be punished in any way for exercising their rights under the Occupational Safety and Health Act.

Safety Plans

We recommend that your company create and follow a workplace safety plan. Having a safety plan can help avoid accidents that result in lost productivity, equipment damage, and employee injury or death.

A good safety plan should include the following elements:

- A written document that states, among other things, who is responsible for implementing and managing the plan
- Systematic periodic inspections to identify workplace hazards
- Procedures for eliminating hazards once identified
- Processes for investigating the cause of accidents, injuries, or illnesses
- A safety and health training program specific to the job duties performed
- A system for employees to communicate safety or health concerns, without fear of reprisal
- A system to ensure that employees comply with safety and health rules
- A system to maintain safety and health records, including steps taken to implement accident prevention initiatives

It might seem like a laundry list of items to consider, but a good safety program needs to be holistic in nature for it to be effective.

Many companies are also incorporating rules against drug or alcohol use in their safety and health plans. Specifically, employees are not allowed to come to work if under the influence of alcohol or illegal drugs. Employees who do come to work under the influence may be subject to disciplinary action up to and including termination of employment.

After your safety plan has been created, you need to ensure that all employees receive necessary training. Have each employee sign a form at the end of training to signify that they attended, and keep the forms in a central location (such as with or near the official safety policy). In addition to the training record, you should make available and keep records of the following:

- Safety improvement suggestion form
- Accident and near-accident reporting form
- Injury and illness log
- Safety inspection checklist
- Hazard removal form
- Material Safety Data Sheets

Safety rules and regulations will work only if they have the broad support of management from the top down. Everyone in the organization needs to buy into the plan or it won't be a success. Make sure everyone understands the importance of a safe work environment, and make sure the culture of the company supports safety in the workplace.

Incident Management

Accidents happen. Hopefully, they don't happen too often, but we know that they do. Details on how to handle accidents are a key part of any safety plan. That way when an accident does happen, you and your co-workers know what to do. Good plans should include steps for handling the situation as well as reporting the incident. Two major classifications of accidents are environmental and human.

ENVIRONMENTAL ACCIDENTS

When related to computers, environmental accidents typically come in one of two forms: electricity or water. Too much electricity is bad for computer components. If lightning is striking in your area, you run a major risk of frying computer parts. Even if you have a surge protector, you could still be at risk.

The best bet in a lightning storm is to power off your equipment and unplug it from outlets. Make the lightning have to come inside a window and hit your computer directly in order to fry it.

 WARNING   Those cheap $10 surge suppressors will fry right along with your computer. And don't be fooled—most power strips do *not* protect against power surges.

 TIP   Modems are particularly susceptible to surges in electricity. If you're still using modems, be sure to unplug them from the wall outlet during an electrical storm, just as you would a power cord.

Water is obviously also bad for computer components. If there is water in the area and you believe it will come in contact with your computers, it's best to get the machines powered off as quickly as possible. If components are not powered on but get wet, they may still work after thoroughly drying out. But if they're on when they get wet, they're likely cooked. Water + electronic components = bad. Water + electronic components + electricity = *really* bad.

Many server rooms have raised floors. Although this serves several purposes, one is that equipment stored on the raised floor is less susceptible to water damage if flooding occurs.

HUMAN ACCIDENTS

Human nature dictates that we are not infallible, so of course we're going to make mistakes and have accidents. The key is to minimize the damage caused when an accident happens.

If a chemical spill occurs, make sure the area gets cordoned off as soon as possible. Then clean up the spill. The specific procedure on how to do that depends on the chemical, and that information can be found on Material Safety Data Sheets (MSDS). Depending on the severity of the spill or the chemical released, you may also need to contact the local authorities. Again, the MSDS should have related information.

Physical accidents are more worrisome. People can trip on wires and fall, cut or burn themselves repairing computers, and incur a variety of other injuries as well. Computer components can be replaced, but that's not always true of human parts (or lives). The first thing to keep in mind is to always be careful and use common sense. If you're trying to work inside a computer case and you see sharp metal edges inside the case, see whether the metal (or component you are working on) can be moved to another location until you finish. Before you stick your hand into an area, make sure nothing is hot or could cut you.

When an accident does happen (or almost happens), be sure to report it. Many companies pay for workers' compensation insurance. If you're injured on the job, you're required to report the incident, and you might also get temporary payments if you are unable to work because of the accident. Also, if the accident was anything but minor, seek medical attention. Just as victims in auto accidents might not feel pain for a day or two, victims in other physical accidents might be in the same position. If you never reported the accident, the insurance companies may find it less plausible that your suffering was work related.

 Real World Scenario

Fire Safety

Repairing a computer isn't often the cause of an electrical fire. However, you should know how to extinguish such a fire properly. Four major classes of fire extinguishers are available, one for each type of flammable substance: A for wood and paper fires, B for flammable liquids, C for electrical fires, and D (metal powder or NaCl [salt]) for flammable metals such as phosphorus and sodium.

The most popular type of fire extinguisher today is the multipurpose, or ABC-rated, extinguisher. It contains a dry chemical powder (e.g., sodium bicarbonate, monoammonium phosphate) that smothers the fire and cools it at the same time. For electrical fires (which may be related to a shorted-out wire in a power supply), make sure the fire extinguisher will work for class C fires. If you don't have an extinguisher that is specifically rated for electrical fires (type C), you can use an ABC-rated extinguisher.

Understanding Environmental Controls

It is estimated that more than 25 percent of all the lead (a poisonous substance) in landfills today is a result of consumer electronics components. Because consumer electronics (televisions, VCRs, stereos) contain hazardous substances, many states require that they be disposed of as hazardous waste. Computers are no exception. Monitors contain several carcinogens and phosphors as well as mercury and lead. The computer itself may contain several lubricants and chemicals as well as lead. Printers contain plastics and chemicals such as toners and inks that are also hazardous. All of these items should be disposed of properly.

Remember all those 386 and 486 computers that came out in the late 1980s and are now considered antiques? Where did they all go? Is there an Old Computers Home somewhere that is using these computer systems for good purposes, or are they lying in a junkyard somewhere? Or could it be that some folks just cannot let go and have a stash of old computer systems and computer parts in the dark depths of their basements? Regardless of where they are today, all of those old components have one thing in common: They are hazardous to the environment.

On the flip side, the environment is also hazardous to our computers. We've already talked about how water and computers don't mix well, and that's just the beginning. Temperature, humidity, and air quality can have dramatic effects on a computer's performance. And we know that computers require electricity; too much or too little can be a problem.

With all of these potential issues, you might find yourself wondering, "Can't we all just get along?" In the following sections, we will talk about how to make our computers and the environment coexist as peacefully as possible.

Managing the Physical Environment

Some of our computers sit in the same dark, dusty corner for their entire lives. Other computers are carried around, thrown into bags, and occasionally dropped. Either way, the physical environment in which our computers exist can have a major effect on how long they last. It's smart to periodically inspect the physical environment to ensure that there are no working hazards. Routinely cleaning components will also extend their useful life, and so will ensuring that the power supplying them is maintained as well.

Maintaining Power

As electronics, computers need a power source. Laptops can free you from your power cord leash for a while, but only temporarily. Power is something we often take for granted until we lose it, then we twiddle our thumbs and wonder what people did before the Internet. Most people realize that having too much power (a power surge) is a bad thing because it can fry electronic components. Having too little power, such as when a *blackout* occurs, can also wreak havoc on electrical circuits.

Power blackouts are generally easy to detect. Power sags without a complete loss, called a *brownout*, are also very damaging to electrical components but oftentimes go unnoticed.

Power strips come in all shapes and sizes and are convenient for plugging multiple devices into one wall outlet. Most of them even have an on/off switch so you can turn all of the devices on or off at the same time. A simple one is shown in Figure 11.6.

FIGURE 11.6 A power strip

Don't make the mistake of thinking that power strips will protect you from electrical surges, though. If you get a strong power surge through one of these $10 devices, the strip and everything plugged into it can be fried. Some people like to call power strips "surge protectors" or "surge suppressors," but power strips do nothing to protect or suppress.

Devices that actually attempt to keep power surges at bay are called *surge protectors*. They often look just like a power strip so it's easy to mistake them for each other, but protectors are more expensive, usually starting in the $25 range. They have a fuse inside them that is designed to blow if it receives too much current and not transfer the current to the devices plugged into it. Surge protectors may also have plug-ins for RJ-11 (phone), RJ-45 (Ethernet), and BNC (coaxial cable) connectors as well. Figure 11.7 shows a surge protector.

FIGURE 11.7 Surge protector

The best device for power protection is called an *uninterruptible power supply (UPS)*. These devices can be as small as a brick, like the one in Figure 11.8, or as large as an entire server rack. Some just have a few indicator lights, while others have LCD displays that show status and menus and come with their own management software.

FIGURE 11.8 An uninterruptible power supply

Inside the UPS is one or more batteries and fuses. Much like a surge suppressor, a UPS is designed to protect everything that's plugged into it from power surges. UPSs are also designed to protect against power sags and even power outages. Energy is stored in the batteries, and if the power fails, the batteries can power the computer for a period of time so the administrator can then safely power it down. Many UPSs and operating systems will also work together to automatically (and safely) power down a system that gets switched to UPS power. These types of devices may be overkill for Uncle Bob's machine at home, but they're critically important fixtures in server rooms.

The UPS should be checked periodically as part of the preventative maintenance routine to make sure its battery is operational. Most UPSs have a test button you can press to simulate a power outage. You will find that batteries wear out over time, and you should replace the battery in the UPS every couple of years to keep the UPS dependable.

Managing the Environment

Sometimes we can't help how clean—or unclean—our environments are. A computer in an auto body shop is going to face dangers that one in a receptionist's office won't. Still, there are things you can do to help keep your systems clean and working well. We're going to break these concepts down into two parts. In the first, we'll look at common issues to be aware of, and in the second we'll discuss proper cleaning methods.

Avoiding Common Problems

In a nutshell, water and other liquids, dirt, dust, rogue power sources, and heat and humidity aren't good for electronic components. Inspect your environment to eliminate as many of these risks as possible. Leaving your laptop running outside in a rainstorm? Not such a good idea. (Been there, done that.)

Computers in manufacturing plants are particularly susceptible to environmental hazards. One technician reported a situation with a computer that had been used on the manufacturing floor of a large equipment manufacturer. The computer and keyboard were covered with a black substance that would not come off. (It was later revealed to be a combination of paint mist and molybdenum grease.) There was so much diesel fume residue in the power supply fan that it would barely turn. The insides and components were covered with a thin, greasy layer of muck. To top it all off, the computer *smelled terrible*!

Despite all this, the computer still functioned. However, it was prone to reboot itself every now and again. The solution was (as you may have guessed) to clean every component thoroughly and replace the power supply. The muck on the components was able to conduct a small current. Sometimes that current would go where it wasn't wanted, and zap!—a reboot. In addition, the power supply fan is supposed to partially cool the inside of the computer. In this computer, the fan was detrimental to the computer because it got its cooling air from the shop floor, which contained diesel fumes, paint fumes, and other chemical fumes. Needless to say, those fumes aren't good for computer components.

Computers and humans have similar tolerances to heat and cold, although computers like the cold better than we do. In general, anything comfortable to us is comfortable to a computer. They don't, however, require food or drink (except maybe a few RAM chips now and again)—keep those away from the computer.

WARNING   It's bad practice to eat, drink, or smoke around your computer. Smoke particles contain tar that can get inside the computer and cause problems similar to those described earlier.

Computers need lots of clean, moving air to keep them functioning. One way to ensure that the environment has the least possible effect on your computer is to always leave the blanks in the empty slots on the back of your box. These pieces of metal are designed to keep dirt, dust, and other foreign matter out of the inside of the computer. They also maintain proper airflow within the case to ensure that the computer does not overheat.

You can also purchase computer enclosures to keep the dust out—just make sure they allow for proper air ventilation. Many times these devices use air filters, in much the same way a furnace or a car engine does.

Cleaning Systems

The cleanliness of a computer is extremely important. Buildup of dust, dirt, and oils can prevent various mechanical parts of a computer from operating. Cleaning them with the right cleaning compounds is equally important. Using the wrong compounds can leave residue behind that is more harmful than the dirt you are trying to remove.

Most computer cases and monitor cases can be cleaned by using mild soapy water on a clean, lint-free cloth. Do *not* use any kind of solvent-based cleaner on either monitor or LCD screens because doing so can cause discoloration and damage to the screen surface. Most often, a simple dusting with a damp cloth (moistened with water) will suffice. Make sure the power is off before you put anything wet near a computer. Dampen (don't soak) a cloth in mild soap solution and wipe the dirt and dust from the case. Then wipe the moisture from the case with a dry, lint-free cloth. Anything with a plastic or metal case can be cleaned in this manner.

WARNING   Don't drip liquid into any vent holes on equipment. Monitors in particular have vent holes in the top.

Additionally, if you spill anything on a keyboard, you can clean it by soaking it in distilled, *demineralized water* and drying it off. The extra minerals and impurities have been removed from this type of water, so it will not leave any traces of residue that might interfere with the proper operation of the keyboard after cleaning. The same holds true for the keyboard's cable and its connector.

The electronic connectors of computer equipment, on the other hand, should never touch water. Instead, use a swab moistened in distilled, *denatured isopropyl alcohol* (also known as electronics or contact cleaner and found in electronics stores) to clean contacts. Doing so will take oxidation off the copper contacts.

Finally, the best way to remove dust and dirt from the inside of the computer is to use compressed air instead of vacuuming. Compressed air can be more easily directed and doesn't easily produce ESD damage as a vacuum could. Simply blow the dust from inside the computer by using a stream of compressed air. However, make sure to do this outside so you don't blow dust all over your work area or yourself. If you need to use a vacuum, a nonstatic *computer vacuum* that is specially made for cleaning computer components is recommended. Their nozzles are grounded to prevent ESD from damaging the components of the computer. One is pictured in Figure 11.9.

One unique challenge when cleaning printers is spilled toner. It sticks to everything and should not be inhaled. Use an electronics vacuum that is designed specifically to pick up toner. A normal vacuum's filter isn't fine enough to catch all the particles, so the toner may be circulated into the air. Normal electronics vacuums may melt the toner instead of picking it up.

FIGURE 11.9   A computer vacuum

 If you get toner on your clothes, use a magnet to get it out (toner is half iron).

Table 11.1 summarizes the most common cleaning tools and their uses.

TABLE 11.1   Computer cleaning tools

Tool	Purpose
Computer vacuum	Sucking up dust and small particles.
Mild soap and water	Cleaning external computer and monitor cases.
Demineralized water	Cleaning keyboards or other devices that have contact points that are not metal.
Denatured isopropyl alcohol	Cleaning metal contacts, such as those on expansion cards.
Monitor wipes	Cleaning monitor screens. Do *not* use window cleaner!
Lint-free cloth	Wiping down anything. Don't use a cloth that will leave lint or other residue behind.
Compressed air	Blowing dust or other particles out of hard-to-reach areas.

Periodically cleaning equipment is one of the easiest ways to prevent costly repairs, but it's also one of the most overlooked tasks. We're often too busy solving urgent crises to deal with these types of tasks. If possible, block time every week for the sole purpose of cleaning your equipment.

Handling and Disposing of Computer Equipment

Each piece of computer equipment you purchase comes with a manual. In the manual are detailed instructions on the proper handling and use of that component. In addition, many manuals give information on how to open the device for maintenance or on whether you should even open the device at all.

   If you have the luxury of having paper manuals, don't throw them away. Keep a drawer of a file cabinet specifically for hardware manuals (and keep it organized!). You can always look up information on the Internet as well, but having paper manuals on hand is useful for two reasons. One, you may need to fix something when Internet access isn't readily available (router problems, anyone?). Two, some companies are required to keep hardware documentation in case of an audit (such as for ISO 9000–compliant organizations). In the following sections, we'll cover two topics: using safety documentation and following safety and disposal procedures.

Using Safety Documentation

Besides your product manuals, another place to find safety information is in *Material Safety Data Sheets (MSDSs)*. MSDSs include information such as physical product data (boiling point, melting point, flash point, and so forth), potential health risks, storage and disposal recommendations, and spill/leak procedures. With this information, technicians and emergency personnel know how to handle the product as well as respond in the event of an emergency.

   MSDSs are typically associated with hazardous chemicals. Indeed, chemicals do not ship without them. MSDSs are not intended for consumer use; rather, they're made for employees or emergency workers who are consistently exposed to the risks of the particular product.

   The United States *Occupational Safety and Health Administration (OSHA)* mandates MSDSs only for products that

- meet OSHA's definition of *hazardous* (it poses a physical or health hazard); *and*

- are "known to be present in the workplace in such a manner that employees may be exposed under normal conditions of use or in a foreseeable emergency."

One of the interesting things about MSDSs is that OSHA does not require companies to distribute them to consumers. Most companies will be happy to distribute one for their products, but again, they are under no obligation to do so.

   If employees are working with materials that have MSDSs, those employees are required by OSHA to have "ready access" to MSDS sheets. This means that employees need to be able to get to the sheets without having to fetch a key, contact a supervisor, or submit a procedure request. Remember the file cabinet drawer you have for the hardware manuals? MSDSs should also be kept readily accessible. Exercise 11.2 helps you find your MSDS sheets and get familiar enough with them to find critical information.

EXERCISE 11.2

Finding MSDS Sheets

1. Locate the MSDS sheets in your workplace. You might have to ask a manager. (Do you even have them?)

2. Find one for a product you're interested in.

3. Are there any potential health effects listed for this item? What are they?

4. What is the proper disposal procedure for this item?

It's not likely that you're going to memorize or need to memorize everything on an MSDS sheet. The key is knowing where to find them and knowing how to quickly find information on them. If you have a spill of a potentially dangerous chemical, the last thing you need to spend time on is figuring out how to handle the spill without causing injury to yourself or others.

At this point, you might stop to think for a second: Do computers really come with hazardous chemicals? Do I really need an MSDS? Consider this as an example: oxygen. Hardly a dangerous chemical, considering we need to breathe it to live, right? In the atmosphere, oxygen is at 21 percent concentration. At 100 percent concentration, oxygen is highly flammable and can even spontaneously ignite some organic materials. In that sense, and in the eyes of OSHA, nearly everything can be a dangerous chemical.

If you are interested in searching for free MSDSs, several websites are available, such as www.msds.com. Many manufacturers of components will also provide MSDSs on their websites.

The sections within an MSDS sheet will be the same regardless of the product; the information inside each section changes. Here is a truncated sample MSDS for ammonium hydrogen sulfate.

```
**** MATERIAL SAFETY DATA SHEET ****

Ammonium Hydrogen Sulfate
90009
```

**** SECTION 1—CHEMICAL PRODUCT AND COMPANY IDENTIFICATION ****

MSDS Name: Ammonium Hydrogen Sulfate
Catalog Numbers:
   A/5400
Synonyms:
   Sulfuric acid, monoammonium salt; Acid ammonium sulfate; Ammonium
   acid sulfate.

**** SECTION 2—COMPOSITION, INFORMATION ON INGREDIENTS ****

CAS#	Chemical Name	%	EINECS#
7803-63-6	Ammonium hydrogen sulfate	100 %	232-265-5
	Hazard Symbols: C		
	Risk Phrases: 34		

**** SECTION 3—HAZARDS IDENTIFICATION ****

EMERGENCY OVERVIEW

Causes burns. Corrosive. Hygroscopic (absorbs moisture from the air).

Potential Health Effects
   Skin:
         Causes skin burns.
   Ingestion:
 May cause severe gastrointestinal tract irritation with nausea, vomiting,
and possible burns.
   Inhalation:
 Causes severe irritation of upper respiratory tract with coughing, burns,
breathing difficulty, and possible coma.

**** SECTION 4—FIRST-AID MEASURES ****

   Skin:
 Get medical aid immediately. Immediately flush skin with plenty of water for at
least 15 minutes while removing contaminated clothing and shoes.
   Ingestion:
 Do not induce vomiting. If victim is conscious and alert, give 2-4 cupfuls of
milk or water. Never give anything by mouth to an unconscious person. Get medical
aid immediately.
   Inhalation:

Get medical aid immediately. Remove from exposure and move to fresh air immediately.

If not breathing, give artificial respiration. If breathing is difficult, give oxygen.

**** SECTION 5-FIREFIGHTING MEASURES ****

**** SECTION 6-ACCIDENTAL RELEASE MEASURES ****

General Information: Use proper personal protective equipment as indicated in Section 8.

**** SECTION 7-HANDLING and STORAGE ****

Handling:

Wash thoroughly after handling. Wash hands before eating. Use only in a well-ventilated area. Do not get in eyes, on skin, or on clothing. Do not ingest or inhale.

Storage:

Store in a cool, dry place. Keep container closed when not in use.

**** SECTION 8-EXPOSURE CONTROLS, PERSONAL PROTECTION ****

Engineering Controls:

Use adequate general or local exhaust ventilation to keep airborne concentrations below the permissible exposure limits.

Respirators:

Follow the OSHA respirator regulations found in 29 CFR 1910.134 or European Standard EN 149. Always use a NIOSH or European Standard EN 149 approved respirator when necessary.

**** SECTION 9-PHYSICAL AND CHEMICAL PROPERTIES ****

Physical State: Solid
Color: White
Odor: Not available

**** SECTION 10-STABILITY AND REACTIVITY ****

Chemical Stability:

Stable under normal temperatures and pressures.

Conditions to Avoid:

Incompatible materials, dust generation, exposure to moist air or water.

**** SECTION 11—TOXICOLOGICAL INFORMATION ****

RTECS#:
        CAS# 7803-63-6: BS4400500

**** SECTION 12—ECOLOGICAL INFORMATION ****

**** SECTION 13—DISPOSAL CONSIDERATIONS ****

Products which are considered hazardous for supply are classified as Special Waste, and the disposal of such chemicals is covered by regulations which may vary according to location. Contact a specialist disposal company or the local waste regulator for advice. Empty containers must be decontaminated before returning for recycling.

**** SECTION 14—TRANSPORT INFORMATION ****

**** SECTION 15—REGULATORY INFORMATION ****

European/International Regulations
        European Labeling in Accordance with EC Directives
                Hazard Symbols: C
                Risk Phrases:
                                R 34 Causes burns.
                Safety Phrases:
 S 26 In case of contact with eyes, rinse immediately with plenty of water and seek medical advice. S 28 After contact with skin, wash immediately with...

**** SECTION 16—ADDITIONAL INFORMATION ****

MSDS Creation Date: 6/23/2004 Revision #0 Date: Original.

Following Proper Disposal Procedures

It is relatively easy to put old components away, thinking you might be able to put them to good use again someday, but doing so is not realistic. Most computers are obsolete as soon as you buy them. And if you have not used them recently, your old computer components will more than likely never be used again.

We recycle cans, plastic, and newspaper, so why not recycle computer equipment? The problem is that most computers contain small amounts of hazardous substances. Some countries are exploring the option of recycling electrical machines, but most have still not enacted appropriate measures to enforce their proper disposal. However, we can do a few things as consumers and caretakers of our environment to promote the proper disposal of computer equipment:

- Check with the manufacturer. Some manufacturers will take back outdated equipment for parts (and may even pay you for them).

- Properly dispose of solvents or cleaners (as well as their containers) used with computers at a local hazardous waste disposal facility.

- Disassemble the machine and reuse the parts that are good.

- Check out businesses that can melt down the components for the lead or gold plating.

- Contact the Environmental Protection Agency (EPA) for a list of local or regional waste disposal sites that accept used computer equipment. The EPA's web address is www.epa.gov.

- Check with the EPA to see if what you are disposing of has a Material Safety Data Sheet (MSDS). These sheets contain information about the toxicity of a product and whether it can be disposed of in the trash. They also contain lethal-dose information.

- Check with local nonprofit or education organizations that may be interested in using the equipment.

- Check out the Internet for possible waste disposal sites. Table 11.2 lists a few websites we came across that deal with disposal of used computer equipment. A quick web search will likely locate some in your area.

TABLE 11.2   Computer recycling websites

Site Name		Web Address
Computer Recycle Center		http://www.recycles.com
Computer Recycling Center		http://www.crc.org

Site Name		Web Address
RE-PC		http://www.repc.com
Tech Dump		http://www.techdump.org

Following the general rule of thumb of recycling your computer components and consumables is a good way to go. In the following sections, we'll look at three classifications of computer-related components and proper disposal procedures for each.

Batteries

The EPA estimates that there are over 350 million batteries purchased annually in the United States. One can only imagine what the worldwide figure is. Batteries contain several heavy metals and other toxic ingredients, including alkaline, mercury, lead acid, nickel cadmium, and nickel metal hydride.

> **WARNING** *Never* burn a battery to destroy it. That will cause the battery to explode, which could result in serious injury.

When batteries are thrown away and deposited into landfills, the heavy metals inside them will find their way into the ground. From there, they can pollute water sources and eventually find their way into the supply of drinking water. In 1996, the United States passed the Battery Act to address two issues: to phase out the use of mercury in disposable batteries and to provide collection methods and recycling procedures for batteries.

> **NOTE** There are several countries around the world with battery recycling programs. Information on battery recycling in the United States can be found at www.ibm.com/ibm/environment/products/battery_us.shtml.

There are five types of batteries most commonly associated with computers and hand-held electronic devices: alkaline, nickel cadmium (NiCd), nickel metal hydride (NiMH), lithium ion, and button cell.

Alkaline batteries   Alkaline batteries have been incredibly popular portable batteries for several decades now. Before 1984, one of the major ingredients in this type of battery was mercury, which is highly toxic to the environment. In 1984, battery companies began reduction of mercury levels in batteries, and in 1996 mercury was outlawed in alkaline batteries in the United States. Still, it's strongly recommended that you recycle these batteries at a recycling center. Although newer alkaline batteries contain less mercury than their predecessors, they are still made of metals and other toxins that contaminate the air and soil.

Nickel cadmium (NiCd)   Nickel cadmium is a popular format for rechargeable batteries. As their name indicates, they contain high levels of nickel and cadmium. Although nickel is only semitoxic, cadmium is highly toxic. These types of batteries are categorized by the EPA as hazardous waste and should be recycled.

Nickel metal hydride (NiMH) and lithium ion   Laptop batteries are commonly made with NiMH and lithium ion. Unlike the previous types of batteries we have discussed, these are not considered hazardous waste, and there are no regulations on recycling them. However, these batteries do contain elements that can be recycled, so it's still a good idea to go that route.

Button cell   These batteries are named because they look like a button. They're commonly used in calculators and watches as well as portable computers. They often contain mercury and silver (and are environmental hazards due to the mercury) and need to be recycled.

You may have noticed a theme regarding disposal of batteries: recycling. Many people just throw batteries in the trash and don't think twice about it. However, there are several laws in the United States that require recycling of many types of batteries, and recycling does indeed help keep the environment clean. For a list of recycling centers in your area, use your local yellow pages (under Recycling Centers) or do an Internet search.

If you're ever exposed to the electrolyte (the inside "juice") of the battery, immediately flush the exposed area with water. If it gets on your eye, wash the eye for 15 minutes and immediately contact a physician.

Display Devices

Computer monitors (CRT monitors, not LCD ones) are big and bulky, so what do you do when it's time to get rid of them? As we mentioned earlier in this chapter, monitors have capacitors in them that are capable of retaining a lethal electric charge after they've been unplugged. You wouldn't want anyone to accidentally set off the charge and die. But the thing we didn't mention earlier, which is important now, is that most CRT monitors contain high amounts of lead. Most monitors contain several pounds of lead, in fact. Lead is very dangerous to humans and the environment and must be dealt with carefully. Other harmful elements found in CRTs include arsenic, beryllium, cadmium, chromium, mercury, nickel, and zinc.

If you have a monitor to dispose of, contact a computer recycling firm. It's best to let professional recyclers handle the monitor for you.

 Real World Scenario

How *Not* to Dispose of Your Monitors

This story comes from the technical support division of a now-defunct major computer manufacturer, which used a lot of computers at its own facility. At one time, the company had as many as 500 technicians working the phones. So you can imagine that they burned out a lot of equipment.

Here's how they disposed of dead monitors. An IT staff member would take the monitor out to the dumpster and bring along a sledgehammer. Setting the monitor on its back, he would take one good swing at the glass panel with the hammer to shatter the screen. (This was done, by policy, to ensure that no one would want to go out to the dumpster and try to salvage the dead monitor.) After spraying glass everywhere, he picked up the monitor and threw it in the dumpster.

One employee made an observation that it probably wasn't good to be spreading glass all over the parking lot by shattering monitors. That advice was taken, and the sledge-hammer was done away with. Instead, an IT staff member would use a permanent black marker and draw all over the screen (again, so no one would want to try to salvage it), and again, it was thrown in the dumpster.

In our enlightened state today (as opposed to the mid-1990s), we can see how this was not a good plan for disposing of broken monitors. In fact, many states today have laws prohibiting the disposal of computer monitors in trash bins. This is a good law because with the amount of harmful elements in monitors, they're every bit the environmental hazard that batteries are.

Chemical Solvents and Cans

Nearly every chemical solvent you encounter will have a corresponding MSDS. On the MSDS you will find a section detailing the proper methods for disposing of that chemical. These chemicals were not designed to be released into the environment because they could cause significant harm to living organisms if they're ingested. If in doubt, contact a local hazardous materials handler to find out the best way to dispose of a particular chemical solvent.

Cans are generally made from aluminum or other metals, which are not biodegradable. It's best to always recycle these materials. If the cans were used to hold a chemical solvent or otherwise hazardous material, contact a hazardous materials disposal center instead of a recycling center.

Always be sure that you are following all applicable laws and regulations when disposing of computer equipment!

Demonstrating Professionalism

As a professional technician you need to possess a certain level of technical competence or you'll quickly find yourself looking for work. Technical ability alone isn't enough though; there are many people out there with skills similar to yours. One thing that can set you apart is acting like a true professional and building a solid reputation. As the noted investor Warren Buffet said, "It takes 20 years to build a reputation and 5 minutes to ruin it. If you think about that, you'll do things differently."

You could probably break down professionalism a hundred different ways. For the A+ 220-801 exam and the purposes of this chapter, we're going to break it down into three parts: communication, behavior, and dealing with prohibited content.

Good communication includes listening to what the user or manager or developer is telling you and making certain that you understand completely: Approximately half of all communication should be listening. Even though a user or customer may not fully understand the terminology or concepts, that doesn't mean they don't have a real problem that needs addressing. You must, therefore, be skilled at not only listening but also translating.

Professional behavior encompasses politeness, guidance, punctuality, and accountability. Always treat the customer with the same respect and empathy you would expect if the situation were reversed. Likewise, guide the customer through the problem and the explanation. Tell them what has caused the problem they are currently experiencing and the best solution for preventing it from reoccurring in the future.

On the surface, dealing with prohibited content or activity might seem like a strange fit here, but it is definitely a part of being a professional. It's a part of dealing with problems in general. You'll come across problems like this more often than you will probably want to, and everyone involved will be noticing your conduct as well as how you deal with the problem. Dealing with it fairly and appropriately in a timely fashion will strengthen your standing in the eyes of others.

Communicating with Customers

The act of diagnosis starts with the art of customer relations. Go to the customer with an attitude of trust: Believe what the customer is saying. At the same time, retain an attitude of hidden skepticism; *don't* believe that the customer has told you everything. This attitude of hidden skepticism is not the same as distrust, but just remember that what you hear isn't always the whole story, and customers may inadvertently forget to give some crucial detail.

One of the best ways to become proficient in communicating with customers is to put yourself in the shoes of the novice user. None of us are experts in every field, so think of an area where you are weak—auto repair or home repair, for example—and imagine how you would want a professional in that area to discourse with you.

For example, a customer may complain that their CD-ROM drive doesn't work. What they fail to mention is that it has never worked and that they installed it. On examining the machine, you realize that they mounted it with screws that are too long and that these prevent the tray from ejecting properly.

Here are a few suggestions for making your communication with the customer easier:

Have the customer reproduce the error.   The most important part of this step is to have the customer show you what the problem is. The best method we've seen of doing this is to ask, "Show me what 'not working' looks like." That way, you see the conditions and methods under which the problem occurs. The problem may be a simple matter of doing an operation incorrectly or performing the operation in the wrong order. During this step, you have the opportunity to observe how the problem occurs, so pay attention.

Identify recent changes.   The user can give you vital information. The most important question is, "What changed?" Problems don't usually come out of nowhere. Was a new piece of hardware or software added? Did the user drop some equipment? Was there a power outage or a storm? These are the types of questions you can ask a user in trying to find out what is different.

If nothing changed, at least outwardly, then what was going on at the time of failure? Can the problem be reproduced? Is there a workaround? The point here is to ask as many questions as you need to in order to pinpoint the source of the trouble.

Use the collected information.   Once the problem or problems have been clearly identified, your next step is to isolate possible causes. If the problem cannot be clearly identified, then further tests will be necessary. A common technique for hardware and software problems alike is to strip the system down to bare-bones basics. In a hardware situation, this could mean removing all interface cards except those absolutely required for the system to operate. In a software situation, this may mean disabling elements within Device Manager.

Generally, then, you can gradually rebuild the system toward the point where the trouble started. When you reintroduce a component and the problem reappears, you know that component is the one causing the problem.

Customer satisfaction goes a long way toward generating repeat business. If you can *meet* the customer's expectations, you will most likely hear from them again when another problem arises. However, if you can *exceed* the customer's expectations, you can almost guarantee that they will call you the next time a problem arises.

Real World Scenario

Communication Is Key

Marriages disintegrate when couples do not communicate effectively, or so many experts proclaim. Communication is ranked as one of the most important skills needed to make a marriage work. The same can be said for business partnerships—it is important to make certain you are listening to your customers, whether they are truly customers in the traditional sense of the word or internal users that you support. You also need to listen carefully to managers and vendors and make sure you understand them before beginning a project.

Similarly, you need to make certain that the parties in question understand what you are saying to them. It isn't acceptable to resort to the "But I told you ..." excuse when customers or partners aren't pleased with the results. Making certain they understand what you are telling them is as equally important as making certain you understand what they are telling you.

Customer satisfaction is important in all communication media—whether you are on site, providing phone support, or communicating through e-mail or other correspondence. If you are on site, follow these rules:

- When you arrive, immediately look for the person (user, manager, administrator, and so on) who is affected by the problem. Announce that you are there and assure that person that you will do all you can to remedy the problem.

- Listen intently to what your customer is saying. Make it obvious that you are listening and respecting what they are telling you. If there is a problem with understanding the client, go to whatever lengths you need to in order to remedy the situation. Look for verbal and nonverbal cues that can help you isolate the problem.

- Share the customer's sense of urgency. What may seem like a small problem to you can appear to your customer as if the whole world were collapsing around them.

- Be honest and fair with the customer and try to establish a personal rapport. Explain what the problem is, what you believe is the cause, and what can be done in the future to prevent it from recurring.

- Handle complaints as professionally as possible. Accept responsibility for errors that may have occurred on your part, and never try to pass the blame elsewhere. Avoid arguing with a customer; it serves no purpose. Resolve the customer's anger with as little conflict as possible. Remember, the goal is to keep the customer and not to win an argument.

- When you finish a job, notify the user that you have finished. Make every attempt to find the user and inform them of the resolution. If it is impossible to find them, leave a note explaining the resolution. You should also leave a means by which the customer can contact you should they have a question about the resolution or a related problem. In most cases, you should leave your business number and, if applicable, your cell phone number in case the customer needs to contact you after hours. Notification should also be given to both managers—yours and the user's—that the job has been completed.

If you are providing phone support, keep these guidelines in mind:

- Always answer the telephone in a professional manner, announcing the name of the company and yourself.

- Using the customer's name can help build rapport. Using it in every sentence can sound condescending, but using it once in a while can make you seem more personable.

- Make a concentrated effort to ascertain the customer's technical level and communicate at that level, not above or below it.

- The most important skill you can have is the ability to listen. You have to rely on the customer to tell you the problem and describe it accurately. They cannot do that if you are second-guessing or jumping to conclusions before the whole story is told. Ask broad questions to begin, and then narrow them down to help isolate the problem. It is your job to help guide the description of the problem from the user. For example, you might ask the following questions:

  - Is the printer plugged in?

  - Is it online?

  - Are there any lights flashing on it?

- Complaints should be handled in the same manner they would be handled if you were on site. Make your best effort to resolve the problem and not argue. Again, your primary goal is to keep the customer.

- Close the incident only when the customer is satisfied that the solution is the correct one and the problem has gone away.

- End the telephone call in a courteous manner—thanking the customer for the opportunity to serve them is often the best way.

Talking to the user is an important first step in the troubleshooting process. Your first contact with a computer that has a problem is usually through the customer, either directly or by way of a work order that contains the user's complaint. Often, the complaint is something straightforward, such as "There's smoke coming from the back of my monitor." At other times, the problem is complex, and the customer does not mention everything that has been going wrong. Regardless of the situation, always approach the situation calmly and professionally, and remember that you only get one chance to make a good first impression.

Real World Scenario

Communication Is Everywhere

Communication, and problems that can occur with it, are not isolated to the IT world. Almost every profession stresses the importance of good communication. Jamie Walters, founder and chief vision and strategy officer for Ivy Sea, Inc., and Sarah Fenson, Ivy Sea's guide to client services, wrote an article for Inc.com on steps to smooth conversations (`www.inc.com/articles/2000/08/20000.html`) that included this advice:

- Don't take things personally. If someone acts inappropriately toward you, just react in a calm manner. They are likely responding that way because of outside factors.

- Admit when you don't know the answer to something. It's okay to defer to somebody else or tell the user or customer that you'll have to look into their complaint and will get back with them as soon as possible.

- It is better to validate someone's feeling or respond to the information they have given you than to react to them. For instance, if somebody complains that a help ticket has not been responded to in a timely manner, tell them you understand how they feel and will look into it instead reacting in a defensive manner.

- Don't let your personal opinions or feelings get in the way of what the real complaint is. Try to put yourself in the user's or customer's shoes.

- Be sympathetic. If you need a user to leave their laptop with you overnight, tell them you realize it's frustrating and apologize.

- Try to provide a solution that you both can benefit from. Look for commonalities between you and the client, and work to find a solution that is agreeable to both of you.

- Try to be as informative as possible when discussing a solution to their problem. Most people are uncomfortable with change, so explaining the benefits of a particular solution might help ease this discomfort.

- Try to keep a positive attitude and be optimistic.

- Always work on your listening skills!

Using Appropriate Behavior

Critical to appropriate behavior is to treat the customer, or user, the way you would want to be treated. Much has been made of the Golden Rule—treating others the way you would have them treat you. Six key elements to this, from a business perspective, are punctuality, accountability, flexibility, confidentiality, respect, and privacy. The following sections discuss these elements in detail.

Punctuality

Punctuality is important and should be a part of your planning process: If you tell the customer you will be there at 10:30 a.m., you need to make every attempt to be there at that time. If you arrive late, you have given them false hope that the problem will be solved by a set time. That can lead to anger if you arrive late because it can appear that you are not taking the problem seriously. Punctuality continues to be important throughout the service call and does not end with your arrival. If you need to leave to get parts and return, tell the customer when you will be back, and be there at that time. If for some reason you cannot return at the expected time, alert the customer and tell them when you can return.

Along those same lines, if a user asks how much longer the server will be down and you respond that it will up in 5 minutes only to have it down for 5 more hours, the result can be resentment and possibly anger. When estimating downtime, always allow for more time than you think you will need just in case other problems occur. If you greatly underestimate the time, always inform the affected parties and give them a new time estimate. To use an analogy that will put it in perspective, if you take your car to get an oil change and the counter clerk tells you it will be "about 15 minutes," the last thing you want is to be still sitting there four hours later.

Exercise 11.3 is a simple exercise that you can modify as needed. Its purpose is to illustrate the importance of punctuality.

EXERCISE 11.3

Understanding Punctuality

1. Consider this scenario: You call someone important in your life—your spouse, a parent, an in-law, or a close friend—and tell them you have something very important you need to discuss. You give that person no other details, but ask them to meet you in exactly 1 hour at a location familiar to both of you.

2. Now imagine that you waited 2 hours before showing up.

3. What would that person's reaction be? How would that person feel about having to wait for you? What kind of an impact would it have on the person's mood and behavior?

This is an interaction with someone who matters in your life. Imagine how it would affect a customer who does not know you. Punctuality can go a long way toward keeping dialogue pleasant between two parties.

Accountability

Accountability is a trait every technician should possess. When problems occur, you need to be accountable for them and not attempt to pass the buck to someone else. For example, suppose you are called to a site to put a larger hard drive into a server. While performing this operation, you inadvertently scrape your feet across the carpeted floor, build up energy, and zap the memory in the server. Some technicians would pretend the electrostatic discharge (ESD) never happened, put the new hard drive in, and then act completely baffled by the fact that problems unrelated to the hard drive are occurring. An accountable technician would explain to the customer exactly what happened and suggest ways of proceeding from that point—addressing and solving the problem as quickly and efficiently as possible.

Accountability also means you do what you say you're going to do and ensure that expectations are set and met. Here are some examples of ways to be accountable:

- Offer different repair or replacement options if they're available.
- Provide documentation on the services you provided.
- Follow up with the customer at a later date to ensure satisfaction.

The last one is the most overlooked, yet it can be the most important. Some technicians fix a problem and then develop an "I hope that worked and I never hear from them again" attitude. Calling your customer back (or dropping by their desk) to ensure that everything is still working right is an amazing way to quickly build credibility and rapport.

Flexibility

Flexibility is another equally important trait for a service technician. While it is important that you respond to service calls promptly and close them (solve them) as quickly as you can, you must also be flexible. If a customer cannot have you on site until the afternoon, you must make your best effort to work them into your schedule around the time most convenient for them. Likewise, if you are called to a site to solve a problem and the customer brings another problem to your attention while you are there, you should make every attempt to address that problem as well. Under no circumstances should you ever give a customer the cold shoulder or not respond to additional problems because they were not on an initial incident report.

You should always follow the express guidelines of the company for which you work as they relate to flexibility, empowerment, and other issues.

It's also important that you are flexible in dealing with challenging or difficult situations. When someone's computer has failed, they likely aren't going to be in a good mood and that can make them a "difficult customer" to deal with. In situations like these, keep in mind the following principles:

Avoid arguing.   Arguing with the customer—about anything—is only going to make the situation worse. The customer may be mad and may be yelling at you, but don't argue back or take their comments personally. Try to diffuse the situation by calmly reminding them that you're here to help and you want to understand what's going on so you can do that.

They may need to vent for a bit, so let them to do that. Just focus on doing what you need to do to resolve the problem.

Don't minimize their problems. While the customer's problem might seem trivial to you, it isn't to them. Treat the problem as seriously as they're treating it. Keep in mind that facial expressions and body language are also important. If someone tells you their problem and you look at them like they're delusional, they're probably going to pick up on that, which can make the situation worse.

Avoid being judgmental. Don't blame or criticize. As stated earlier, just focus on what needs to happen to fix the problem. Accusing the user of causing the problem does not build rapport.

Focus on your communication skills. If you have a difficult customer, treat it as an opportunity to see how good a communicator you really are. (Maybe your next job will be a foreign ambassador!) Ask nonconfrontational, open-ended questions. "When was the last time it worked?" is more helpful than "Did it work yesterday" or "Did you break it this morning?"

Another good tactic here is to restate the issue or question to verify that you understand. Starting with "I understand that the problem is…" and then repeating what the customer said can show empathy and proves you were listening. If you have it wrong, it's also a good opportunity to let your customer correct you so you're on track to solve the right problem.

Confidentiality

The goal of *confidentiality* is to prevent or minimize unauthorized access to files and folders and disclosure of data and information. In many instances, laws and regulations require confidentiality for specific information. For example, Social Security records, payroll and employee records, medical records, and corporate information are high-value assets. This information could create liability issues or embarrassment if it fell into the wrong hands. Over the last few years, there have been a number of cases in which bank account and credit card numbers were published on the Internet. The cost of these types of breaches of confidentiality far exceed the actual losses from the misuse of this information.

Confidentiality entails ensuring that data expected to remain private is seen only by those who should see it. Confidentiality may be implemented through authentication and access controls.

As a computer professional you are expected to uphold a high level of confidentiality. Should a user approach you with a sensitive issue—telling you their password, asking for assistance obtaining access to medical forms, and so on—it is your obligation as a part of your job to make certain that information goes no further.

Confidential materials on work spaces and printers should always be protected.

Respect

Much of the discussion in this chapter is focused on respecting the customer as an individual. However, you must also respect the tangibles that are important to the customer. While you may look at a monitor they are using as an outdated piece of equipment that should be scrapped, the business owners may see it as a gift from their children when they first started their business.

Treat the customers' property as if it had value, and you will win their respect. Their property includes the system you are working on (laptop/desktop computer, monitor, peripherals, and the like) as well as other items associated with their business. Do not use their telephone to make personal calls or call other customers while you are at this site. Do not use their printers or other equipment, unless it is in a role associated with the problem you've been summoned to fix.

The Customer Respect Group, www.customerrespect.com, measures the behavior of corporations and the respect they give to customers through their websites. Such items as privacy, responsiveness, attitude, simplicity, transparency, and business principles are combined to create a Customer Respect Index (CRI) ranking. The items they rank in the online world are just as important in the offline world and mirror those presented here.

Respecting the customer is not rocket science. All you need to do—for this exam and in the real world—is think of how you would want someone to treat you. Exercise 11.4 explores this topic further. This exercise, like Exercise 11.3, can be modified to fit your purpose or constraints. Its goal is to illustrate the positive power of the unexpected.

EXERCISE 11.4

Surprise Someone

1. Pick a random, toll-free number used for business solicitation and call it.

2. Chat with the operator for a few moments about the company's product or service, and then ask to speak to the supervisor.

3. When the supervisor comes on, commend the operator you have been speaking with for the job that he has done.

EXERCISE 11.4 *(continued)*

It is likely the operator became confused when you asked to speak to the supervisor; this almost always occurs only in a negative situation. How did the operator handle the request? Did it change the tone of the communication that was taking place? Did they fulfill your request even though they feared they could lose from it? Did the supervisor respond by expecting negative comments? How was the positive information you offered accepted?

Ideally, this illustrated the importance of staying professional and keeping the channel of communication open even in a tough situation. You should be able to adapt this to the workplace when a customer asks to speak to your superior or has another request that is difficult for you to fulfill.

One last area to consider that directly relates to this topic is that of ethics. Ethics is the application of morality to situations. While there are different schools of thought, one of the most popular areas of study is known as normative ethics, focusing on what is normal or practical (right versus wrong and so on). Regardless of religion, culture, and other influences, there are generally accepted beliefs that some things are wrong (stealing, murder, and the like) and some things are right (for example, the Golden Rule). You should always attempt to be ethical in everything you do because it reflects not only on your character but also on the company for which you work.

Privacy

While there is some overlap between confidentiality and privacy, privacy is an area of computing that is becoming considerably more regulated. As a computing professional, you must stay current with applicable laws because you're often one of the primary agents expected to ensure compliance.

Although the laws provide a minimal level of privacy, you should go out of your way to respect the privacy of your users beyond what the law establishes. If you discover information about a user that you should not be privy to, you should not share it with anyone, and you should alert the customers that their data is accessible and encourage them—if applicable—to remedy the situation.

Dealing with Prohibited Content/Activity

This is a situation that no one really wants to deal with, but it happens more often than we would care to admit. A computer you are fixing has content on it that is inappropriate or illegal, or you see someone on your network performing an action that is against policy or laws. How you respond in such a situation can have a significant bearing on your career, the other people involved, and depending on the situation, the well-being of your company. The lynchpin to dealing with *prohibited content* or activity is to have a comprehensive policy in place that covers appropriate behavior. After that, it's a matter of executing the proper steps per the plan when something happens.

🌐 Real World Scenario

A Little Goes a Long Way

The following examples of respecting and disrespecting the customer come from one of the authors' own experiences:

"My wife and I were in an unfamiliar part of Chicago without ready access to a vehicle when we started to get hungry. I am a meat-and-potatoes man and rarely take a chance on anything else. There were no restaurants of that type around, however, and we wound up in an Asian grill. Expecting not to like the buffet, we ordered a side of lettuce wraps and then two buffets and drinks. As it turned out, I liked the buffet a great deal and went back through the line many times. We also liked the drinks and got several of those. Everything was great, except the waiter forgot to bring the lettuce wraps. I dismissed it and made a mental note to inform the waiter when he brought the bill and have him deduct them from our tab. Instead, the manager brought the bill over when we were finished eating, and he had scribbled on it 'no charge.' When I asked him why, he apologized that no one brought the wraps and said he hoped we would come back another time. I was beside myself with disbelief and thanked him profusely, and since then I have told many people about that restaurant, describing it as the best place in Chicago I know of to eat.

"In a very different situation, while driving home one night, the 'low tire pressure' dash-board light came on. Upon inspection, I could hear the right-rear tire hissing. I drove to a tire store and explained the situation. I had used this same tire store over the past 14 years for tires, oil changes, exhaust, maintenance, and a number of other things on the vehicles I've owned. The manager came out and said they found a nail in the tire. They removed the nail, patched the tire, and charged me $13. I was delighted, expecting it to cost much more, and so I paid the bill and went on my way. The next morning, I woke up to find the right-rear tire completely flat. I canceled the morning's appointment, filled the tire with an air compressor, and drove back to the tire store. Shortly, the manager came out and told me that they found another nail in that tire; they were going to eat the $13 on this one, but it had better not happen again. I could not believe the insinuation—that I was driving about looking for nails to hit with that one tire just so I could spend my morning taking them for $13! Instead of offering the possibility that they had overlooked a nail the previous night, apologizing for the inconvenience, or anything of that sort, he shifted the responsibility to me. Needless to say, I have not been back since, and all of my repair business is now done elsewhere."

These two examples illustrate two different approaches to treating the customer. In the first example, the customer is well respected and treated better than expected. In the second example, the customer is disrespected and is treated as an inconvenience. Given the lifetime value of customers, it is always better to respect them—and retain them—than to offhandedly dismiss them.

Creating a Prohibited Content Policy

As mentioned, creating a policy is the most important part of dealing with prohibited content or actions. Without a policy in place that specifically defines what is and isn't allowed, and what actions will be taken when a violation of the policy occurs, you don't really have a leg to stand on when a situation happens.

What is on the policy depends on the company you work for. Generally speaking, if something violates an existing federal or local law, it probably isn't appropriate for your network either. Many companies also have strict policies against the possession of pornographic or hate-related materials on company property. Some either go further than that, banning any personal files such as downloaded music or movies on work computers. Regardless of what is to be on your policy, always ensure that you have buy-in from very senior management so that the policy will be considered valid. Here are some specific examples of content that might be prohibited:

- Adult content
- Content that advocates against an individual, group, or organization
- Unlicensed copyrighted material
- Content related to drug, alcohol, tobacco, or gambling
- Content about hacking, cracking, or other illegal computer activity
- Violent or weapons-related content

A good policy will also contain the action steps to be taken if prohibited content or activity is spotted. For example, what should you do if you find porn on someone's work laptop?

The policy should explicitly outline the punishment for performing specific actions or possessing specific content. The appropriate penalty may very well be based upon the type of content found. Something that is deemed mildly offensive might result in a verbal or written warning the first time and a more severe sentence the second time. If your company has a zero tolerance policy, then employees may be terminated and possibly subject to legal action.

Finally, after the policy has been established, it's critical to ensure that all employees are aware of it and have the proper training. In fact, it's highly recommended that you have all employees sign a disclosure saying they have read and understand the policy and that the signed document be kept in their human resources file. Many companies also require that employees review the policy yearly and resign the affidavit as well.

Handling Specific Situations

If you have your policy in place, then this part should be relatively scripted. It might not be easy to deal with, but the steps you should take should be outlined for you. Because we're talking about professionalism, now is a good time to remind you that people will be looking at your reaction as well as your actions. If you see prohibited content and start giggling and walk away, that probably doesn't reflect well. Always remember that others are watching you.

The specific steps you take will depend on your policy, but here are some general guidelines:

Follow your policies exactly as they are written. Yes, we've already said this several times. It's crucial that you do this. Not following the policies and procedures can derail your case against the offender and possibly set you up for problems as well.

If you are the first responder, get a verifier. Your first priority as the first responder is to identify the improper activity or content. Then, you should always get someone else to verify the material or action so it doesn't turn into a situation of your word against someone else's. Immediately report the situation through proper channels.

Preserve the data or device. The data or device should immediately be removed from the possession of the offending party and preserved. This will ensure that the data doesn't mysteriously disappear before the proper parties are notified.

Follow the right chain of custody. The removed materials should be secured and turned over to the proper authorities. Depending on the situation, materials may be held in a safe, locked location at the office, or they may need to be turned over to local authorities. Always document the findings and who has custody of the offensive materials.

Once this first part is complete, then it's a matter of levying the right punishment for the infraction.

Situations involving prohibited content or activities are not easy to deal with. The accused person might get angry or confrontational, so it's important to always have the right people there to help manage and diffuse the situation. If you feel that the situation is severe enough and are worried about your own personal safety, don't be afraid to involve the police if needed. While the situation needs to be dealt with, there's no sense in putting yourself in direct danger to do so.

Putting It All in Perspective

Whether you are dealing with customers in person or on the phone, there are rules to which you should adhere. These were implied and discussed in the previous sections, but you must understand them and remember them for the exam:

- Use proper language and avoid using jargon, abbreviations, and acronyms. Every field has its own language, and outsiders feel lost when they start hearing it. Put yourself in the position of someone not in the field and explain what is going on by using words they can relate to.

- Maintain a positive attitude and tone of voice. The customer is counting on you to fix their problem. The last thing they want is for you to sound defeated when you hear the problem.

- Listen to your customers. Allow them to complete their statements and avoid interrupting them. People like to know they are being heard, and as simple an act as it is, this can make all the difference in making them feel at ease with your work. Everyone has been in a situation where they have not been able to fully explain their problem without being interrupted or ignored. It is not enjoyable in a social setting, and it is intolerable in a business setting.

- Be culturally sensitive. Some people may have a language barrier that makes it difficult to explain their problem. (Think about how much computer language you learned in your high school language courses!) Others may have different habits or practices in their workplace. Be respectful of their world.

- Be on time. If you're going to be late, be sure to contact your customer. Not doing so indicates that you think their problem isn't important.

- Avoid distraction and/or interruptions when talking with customers. You need to make them feel like their problem is important and that it has your full attention.

- Exercise patience with difficult customers and situations:
    - Avoid arguing with customers and/or becoming defensive.
    - Do not minimize customers' problems. While it may be a situation you see every day, it is a crisis to them.
    - Avoid being judgmental and/or insulting or calling the customer names.
    - Clarify customer statements and ask pertinent questions. The questions you ask should help guide you toward isolating the problem and identifying possible solutions. Don't be afraid to nod, ask questions, and repeat to the customer what you think they are saying to make sure you are understanding it correctly.

- Set and meet—or exceed—expectations and communicate timelines and status. Customers want to know what is going on. They want to know that you understand the problem and can deal with it. Being honest and direct is almost always appreciated.

- Deal appropriately with confidential materials. Don't look at files or printouts that you have no business looking at. Make sure the customer's confidential materials stay that way.

- Create a policy that covers appropriate use and prohibited content. Ensure that everyone who uses the company's computers is trained on and understands the policy.

Summary

This chapter covered two areas of operational procedures that you should integrate into your work: (1) safety procedures and (2) professionalism and communication.

First, we looked at the importance of safety procedures. Safety is about protecting you from harm as well as protecting your computer components from getting damaged. We outlined some methods to apply safe working environment policies and procedures and identified potential safety hazards. Included were preventing electrostatic discharge (ESD) and electromagnetic interference (EMI), creating a safe work environment, and handling computer equipment properly.

Safety involves you and your co-workers, but it also includes environmental issues. The environment can have a harmful effect on our computers, but computers can also greatly harm the environment. You also need to be familiar with Material Safety Data Sheets (MSDSs) and their importance as well as proper disposal procedures for batteries, display devices, and chemical solvents and cans. These items need to be kept out of the environment because of the damage they can cause.

Finally, we moved on to professionalism and communication. You should treat your customers as you would want to be treated and let them know that you respect them and their business through your actions and behavior.

Exam Essentials

Know which computer components are particularly dangerous to technicians.   The most dangerous are the power supply and the monitor. Both are capable of storing lethal charges of electricity, even when unplugged. You also need to be aware of parts that get incredibly hot, such as the processor, which can cause severe burns if touched.

Understand where to find safety information regarding chemicals.   You can find this information on a Material Safety Data Sheet (MSDS). An MSDS might not have come with your purchase, but most suppliers will gladly supply one if requested.

Know which tool to use for which job.   The majority of computer repair jobs can be handled with nothing more than a Phillips-head screwdriver. However, you might need cutters, extra light, or a mirror for some jobs. Avoid using magnetically tipped tools.

Understand methods to help prevent ESD.   One of the biggest and most common dangers to electronic components is electrostatic discharge (ESD). There are several methods you can employ to help avoid ESD problems, such as grounding yourself; using an antistatic wrist strap, bag, or mat; and controlling the humidity levels.

Know proper disposal procedures for used computer parts, batteries, and chemical solvents. The specific disposal procedure depends on what you are trying to dispose of. However, the safe answer is to always recycle the component and not throw it in the trash bin.

Use good communication skills.   Listen to your customers. Let them tell you what they understand the problem to be, and then interpret the problem and see if you can get them to agree to what you are hearing them say. Treat your customers, whether they be end users or colleagues, with respect, and take their issues and problems seriously.

Use job-related professional behavior.   The Golden Rule should govern your professional behavior. Five key elements to this, from a business perspective, are punctuality, accountability, flexibility, confidentiality, and privacy.

Understand how to handle prohibited content or activity.   First, always have policies and procedures in place to deal with prohibited content or activity. When an incident happens, follow the procedures, report through proper channels, preserve the data or device, and follow the chain of custody.

Review Questions

The answers to the Chapter Review Questions can be found in Appendix A.

1. A computer is experiencing random reboots and phantom problems that disappear after reboot. What should you do?

   A. Replace the motherboard.

   B. Boot clean.

   C. Replace the power supply.

   D. Open the cover, clean the inside of the computer, and reseat all cards and chips.

2. Which of the following is used to properly discharge voltage from an unplugged computer monitor?

   A. Antistatic wrist strap

   B. Screwdriver

   C. High-voltage probe

   D. Power cord

3. Which of the following must contain information about a chemical solvent's emergency cleanup procedures?

   A. OSHA

   B. MSDS

   C. Product label

   D. CRT

4. You are purchasing, for home use, an inkjet printer cartridge that you know has an MSDS. How do you obtain the MSDS for this product?

   A. The store is required to give you one at the time of purchase.

   B. It's contained in the packaging of the printer cartridge.

   C. You are not legally allowed to have an MSDS for this product.

   D. Visit the website of the printer cartridge manufacturer.

5. In the interest of a safe work environment, which of the following should you report? (Choose two.)

   A. An accident

   B. A near-accident

   C. Dirt on the floor inside a building

   D. Rain forecasted for a work day

6. What is the approximate minimum level of static charge for humans to feel a shock?

    A. 300 volts

    B. 3,000 volts

    C. 30,000 volts

    D. 300,000 volts

7. Which of the following measures can be implemented to reduce the risk of ESD? (Choose two.)

    A. Antistatic wrist strap

    B. Antistatic bag

    C. Antistatic hair net

    D. Shuffling your feet

8. Which of the following are OSHA requirements for a safe work environment that must be followed by employers? (Choose two.)

    A. Attend yearly OSHA safe work environment seminars.

    B. Provide properly maintained tools and equipment.

    C. Have an OSHA employee stationed within 5 miles of the facility.

    D. Display an OSHA poster in a prominent location.

9. What is the proper way to dispose of a broken CRT monitor?

    A. Take it to a computer recycling center.

    B. Discharge it with a high-volt probe and throw it away.

    C. Remove the glass screen and throw it away.

    D. Cut off the power cord and throw the monitor away.

10. When moving computer equipment, which of the following are good procedures to follow? (Choose two.)

    A. Lift by bending over at the waist.

    B. Carry monitors with the glass face away from your body.

    C. Use a cart for heavy objects.

    D. Ensure that there are no safety hazards in your path.

11. You have four AA alkaline batteries that you just removed from a remote-control device. What is the recommended way to dispose of these batteries?

    A. Throw them in the trash.

    B. Incinerate them.

    C. Take them to a recycling center.

    D. Flush them down the toilet.

12. You have discovered prohibited material on a user's laptop computer. What two things should you do first? (Choose two.)

A. Destroy the prohibited material.

B. Confiscate and preserve the prohibited material.

C. Confront the user about the material.

D. Report the prohibited material through the proper channels.

13. While working on a user's system, you discover a sticky note attached to the bottom of the keyboard that has their username and password written on it. The user is not around, and you need to verify that the network connection is working. What should you do?

A. Log in, verify access, and log out.

B. Log in and stay logged in when you are finished.

C. Page the user.

D. Log in and change the user's password.

14. You promised a customer that you would be out to service their problem before the end of the day but have been tied up at another site. As it now becomes apparent that you will not be able to make it, what should you do?

A. Arrive first thing in the morning.

B. Wait until after hours and then leave a message that you were there.

C. Call the customer and inform them of the situation.

D. Send an e-mail letting them know you will be late.

15. A customer is trying to explain a problem with their system. Unfortunately, the customer has such a thick accent that you are unable to understand what the problem is. What should you do?

A. Just start working on the system and looking for obvious errors.

B. Call your supervisor.

C. Ask that another technician be sent in your place.

D. Apologize and find another user or manager who can help you translate.

16. You have been trying to troubleshoot a user's system all day when it suddenly becomes clear that the data is irretrievably lost. Upon informing the customer of this, he becomes so angry that he shoves you against a wall. What should you do?

A. Shove the user back, only a little harder than he shoved you.

B. Shove the user back, only a little easier than he shoved you.

C. Try to calm the user down, and leave the site if you cannot.

D. Yell for everyone in the area to come quickly.

17. A customer tells you that the last technician who was there spent three hours on the phone making personal calls. What should you do with this information?

    A. Nothing.

    B. Inform your manager.

    C. Talk to the technician personally.

    D. Ask the customer to prove it.

18. You arrive at the site of a failed server to find the vice president nervously pacing and worrying about lost data. What should you do?

    A. Offer a joke to lighten things up.

    B. Downplay the situation and tell him that customers lose data every day.

    C. Keep your head down and keep looking at manuals to let him know you are serious.

    D. Inform him that you've dealt with similar situations and will let him know what needs to be done as soon as possible.

19. You're temporarily filling in on phone support when a caller tells you that he is sick and tired of being bounced from one hold queue to another. He wants his problem fixed, and he wants it fixed now. What should you do?

    A. Inform him up front that you are only filling in temporarily and won't be of much help.

    B. Transfer him to another technician who handles phone calls more often.

    C. Try to solve his problem without putting him on hold or transferring him elsewhere.

    D. Suggest that he call back at another time when you are not there.

20. At the end of the day, you finish a job only to find the user you were doing it for had to leave. What should you do? (Choose two.)

    A. Clean up and leave no evidence that you were there.

    B. Leave a note for the user detailing what was done and how to contact you.

    C. Notify the user's manager and your own that you have finished.

    D. Put the system back to its original state.

Performance-Based Question

On the A+ exams, you will encounter performance-based questions. The questions on the exam require you to perform a specific task, and you will be graded on whether you were able to complete the task. The following require you to think creatively to measure how well you understand this chapter's topics. You may or may not see similar questions on the actual A+ exams. To see how your answers compare to the authors', refer to Appendix B.

Recently, one of your office co-workers tripped on a power cord and injured himself. What should you do to find potential trip hazards in your office? Once the hazards are identified, what actions should you take?

220-802

PART

II

Chapter

12

Operating System Basics

THE FOLLOWING A+ 220-802 EXAM OBJECTIVES ARE COVERED IN THIS CHAPTER:

✓ **1.1 Compare and contrast the features and requirements of various Microsoft Operating Systems.**

- Windows XP Home, Windows XP Professional, Windows XP Media Center, Windows XP 64-bit Professional

- Windows Vista Home Basic, Windows Vista Home Premium, Windows Vista Business, Windows Vista Ultimate, Windows Vista Enterprise

- Windows 7 Starter, Windows 7 Home Premium, Windows 7 Professional, Windows 7 Ultimate, Windows 7 Enterprise

- Features: 32-bit vs. 64-bit; Aero, gadgets, user account control, system restore, sidebar, compatibility mode, administrative tools, security center, event viewer, file structure and paths, category view vs. classic view

✓ **1.4 Given a scenario, use appropriate operating system features and tools.**

- Run line utilities: NOTEPAD

✓ **1.7 Perform preventive maintenance procedures using appropriate tools.**

- Best practices: Windows updates

- Tools: System restore

✓ **1.8 Explain the differences among basic OS security settings.**

- NTFS vs. Share permissions: File attributes

- System files and folders

✓ **1.9 Explain the basics of client-side virtualization.**

- Purpose of virtual machines
- Resource requirements
- Emulator requirements
- Security requirements
- Network requirements
- Hypervisor

The previous chapters mostly focused on the hardware and physical elements of the computing environment. We looked at the physical components, or hardware, of personal computers and laptops as well as networking, printers, and operational procedures. That completes the coverage of the topics on the 220-801 exam, and this chapter marks a departure from that.

In this chapter—and several to come—the focus is on operating systems (OS). To be specific, the focus is on Microsoft Windows operating systems, which you must know well for the 220-802 certification exam.

Understanding Operating Systems

Computers are pretty much useless without software. A piece of hardware might just as well be used as a paperweight or doorstop unless you have an easy way to interface with it. Software provides that way. While there are many types of software, or programs, the most important application you'll ever deal with is the operating system. Operating systems have many different, complex functions, but two of them jump out as being critical: interfacing with the hardware and providing a platform on which other applications can run.

Here are three major distinctions of software you should be aware of:

Operating system (OS)   Provides a consistent environment for other software to execute commands. The OS gives users an interface with the computer so they can send commands (input) and receive feedback or results (output). To do this, the OS must communicate with the computer hardware to perform the following tasks, as illustrated in Figure 12.1:

- Disk and file management
- Device access
- Memory management
- Output format

Once the OS has organized these basic resources, users can give the computer instructions through input devices (such as a keyboard or a mouse). Some of these commands are built into the OS, whereas others are issued through the use of applications. The OS becomes the center through which the system hardware, other software, and the user communicate; the rest of the components of the system work together through the OS, which coordinates their communication.

FIGURE 12.1 The operating system interacts with resources.

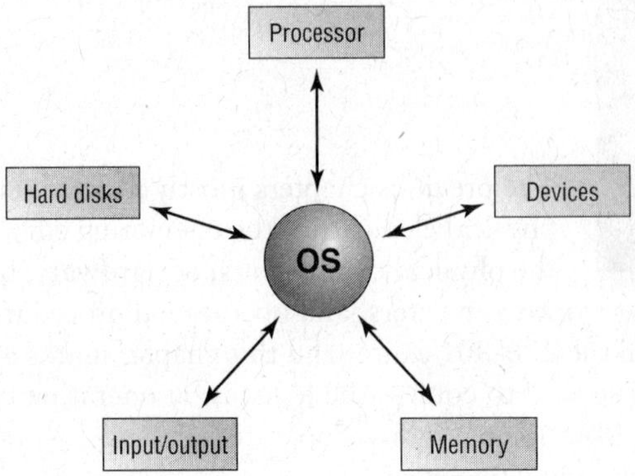

```
                    ┌───────────┐
                    │ Processor │
                    └───────────┘
                         ↑
                         │
                         ↓
┌───────────┐         ╭─────╮         ┌─────────┐
│ Hard disks │ ←─────→ │ OS  │ ←─────→ │ Devices │
└───────────┘         ╰─────╯         └─────────┘
              ↙                   ↘
    ┌──────────────┐         ┌─────────┐
    │ Input/output │         │ Memory  │
    └──────────────┘         └─────────┘
```

Application Used to accomplish a particular task, an application is software that is written to supplement the commands available to a particular OS. Each application is specifically compiled (configured) for the OS on which it will run. For this reason, the application relies on the OS to do many of its basic tasks. Examples of applications include complex programs such as Microsoft Word and Internet Explorer as well as simple programs such as a command-line FTP program. Either way, when accessing devices and memory, the programs can simply request that the OS do it for them. This arrangement saves substantially on programming overhead because much of the executable code is *shared*—it is written into the operating system and can therefore be used by multiple applications running on that OS.

Driver Extremely specific software written for the purpose of instructing a particular OS on how to access a piece of hardware. Each modem or printer has unique features and configuration settings, and the driver allows the OS to properly understand how the hardware works and what it is able to do.

In the following sections, we'll look at some terms and concepts central to all operating systems. Then we'll move into specific discussions on Windows operating systems.

 Real World Scenario

Is Windows the Only Operating System?

In the workplace, it is likely that you will encounter operating systems beyond just Windows 7, Windows Vista, and Windows XP. Linux, for example, is a popular operating system for servers while Mac OS rules the Apple world. This exam focuses only on the three Windows operating systems mentioned and thus they are the only ones we cover in this book. It is highly recommended that you become familiar with other operating systems as your job requires, but you will not need to know them for the A+ certification exam.

Operating System Terms and Concepts

Before we get too far into our discussion of PC operating systems, it will be useful to define a few key terms. The following are some terms you will come across as you study this chapter and work in the computer industry:

Version   A particular revision of a piece of software, normally described by a number that tells you how new the product is in relation to other versions of the product.

Source   The actual code that defines how a piece of software works. Computer operating systems can be *open source*, meaning the OS can be examined and modified by anyone, or they can be *closed source*, meaning that only an owner or developer can modify or examine the code.

   A word often used interchangeably with *closed source* is *proprietary*.

Shell   A program that runs on top of the OS and allows the user to issue commands through a set of menus or other interface (which may or may not be graphical). Shells make an OS easier to use by changing the user interface.

Graphical user interface (GUI)   A method by which a person communicates with a computer using graphical images, icons, and methods other than text. GUIs allow a user to use a mouse, touchpad, or another mechanism (in addition to the keyboard) to interact with the computer to issue commands.

Network   Any group of computers that have a communication link between them. Networks allow computers to share information and resources quickly and securely.

Cooperative multitasking   A multitasking method that depends on the application itself to be responsible for using the processor and then freeing it for access by other applications. This is the way very early versions of Windows managed multiple applications. If any application locked up while using the processor, the application was unable to properly free the processor to do other tasks and the entire system locked, usually forcing a reboot.

Preemptive multitasking   A multitasking method in which the OS allots each application a certain amount of processor time and then forcibly takes back control and gives another application or task access to the processor. This means that if an application crashes, the OS takes control of the processor away from the locked application and passes it on to the next application, which should be unaffected. Although unstable programs still lock, only the locked application will stall—not the entire system. This is what is used today in modern operating systems.

Multithreading   The ability of a single application to have multiple requests in to the processor at one time. This results in faster application performance because it allows a program to do many things at once.

32-bit   An operating system that is 32-bit is one that can not only run on 32-bit processors but can utilize the capabilities of the processor fully. While this may sound simple, the truth of the matter is that it took many years after the 32-bit processor became available before operating systems (which were 16-bit at the time) were able to utilize their features. Just as you could not mix racecars with a country road, you cannot mix 64-bit software with 32-bit hardware.

64-bit   A 64-bit operating system is one that is written to utilize the instructions possible with 64-bit processors. Originally, these were more common with servers than desktops, but with prices dropping, 64-bit processors have become more common on the desktop, as have operating systems that will run on them. As mentioned earlier, you cannot mix 64-bit software with 32-bit hardware (but you can run most 32-bit software on 64-bit hardware).

*x*86   The terms *x*86 is commonly used to refer to operating systems intended to run on the Intel processor because Intel initially identified its 32-bit processors with numbers ending in 86 prior to switching to the Pentium line.

*x*64   The term *x*64 is commonly used to denote operating systems that can run on 64-bit processors. This is also commonly referred to as AMD64 since AMD defined the 64-bit instruction set used today.

Minimum System Requirements

In the chapters to come, we'll explore how to install and upgrade each of the operating systems you need to know for the exam, but one of the things that can prevent you from even considering these options is the hardware requirements of the operating system you are thinking of installing. Before you can begin to install an OS, there are several items you must consider. You must perform the following tasks before you even put the OS installation disc into your computer's optical drive. These items essentially set the stage for the procedure you are about to perform:

- Determining hardware compatibility and minimum requirements
- Determining installation options
- Determining the installation method
- Preparing the computer for installation

Let's begin our discussion by talking about hardware compatibility issues and requirements for installing the various versions of Windows.

Determining Hardware Compatibility and Minimum Requirements

Before you can begin to install any version of Windows, it is important that you determine whether the hardware you will be using is supported by the Windows version you will be running. That is, will the version of Windows have problems running any device drivers for the hardware you have?

To answer this question, Microsoft first came up with several versions of its *Hardware Compatibility List (HCL)*. This was intended to be a list of all the hardware that worked with Windows and the versions of Windows with which the hardware worked. With the release of Windows XP, Microsoft expanded the idea of the HCL to include software as well, and a list that includes both hardware and software can hardly be called a Hardware Compatibility List. The new term was the *Windows Catalog*, and it replaced HCLs. This gave way to the *Compatibility Center*, and the one for Windows 7 can be found at the following location:

www.microsoft.com/windows/compatibility/windows-7/en-us/default.aspx.

The point is, before you install Windows, you should check all your computer's components against this list and make sure each item is compatible with the version of Windows you plan to install. Just because a product is not on the list does not mean that it will not work; it merely means that it has not been tested. The list represents tested software and hardware that vendors have stated are compatible, but it is by no means all inclusive.

In addition to general compatibility, it is important that your computer have enough "oomph" to run the version of Windows you plan to install. For that matter, it is important for your computer to have enough resources to run any software you plan to use. Toward that end, Microsoft (as well as other software publishers) publishes a list of both minimum and recommended hardware specifications that you should follow when installing Windows.

"Minimum specifications" are the absolute minimum requirements for hardware your system should meet in order to install and run the OS you have chosen. "Recommended hardware specifications" are what you should have in your system to realize usable performance. Always try to have the recommended hardware (or better) in your system. If you don't, you may have to upgrade your hardware before you upgrade your OS if you're running more than just a minimal environment. Table 12.1 lists the minimum and recommended hardware specifications for Windows XP Professional. Note that in addition to these minimum requirements, the hardware chosen must be compatible with the selected version of Windows. Also, be aware that additional hardware may be required if certain features are installed (for example, a NIC is required for networking support).

TABLE 12.1   Windows XP Professional minimum and recommended hardware

Hardware	XP Professional Requirement	XP Professional Recommendation
Processor	233MHz Pentium/Celeron or AMD K6/Athlon/Duron	300MHz or higher Intel-compatible processor
Memory	64MB	128MB
Free hard disk space	1.5GB	1.5GB

TABLE 12.1 Windows XP Professional minimum and recommended... *(continued)*

Hardware	XP Professional Requirement	XP Professional Recommendation
Floppy drive	Not required	Not required
CD-ROM or DVD drive	Required	Required
Video	SuperVGA or better	SuperVGA or better
Mouse	Required	Required
Keyboard	Required	Required

Table 12.2 lists the minimum system requirements for various versions of Windows Vista.

TABLE 12.2 Windows Vista minimum hardware requirements

Hardware	Minimum Supported for All Versions	Home Basic Recommendation	Home Premium/Business/ Enterprise/Ultimate Recommendation
Processor	800MHz	1GHz 32-bit (x86) or 64-bit (x64) processor	1GHz 32-bit (x86) or 64-bit (x64) processor
Memory	512MB	512MB	1GB
Free hard disk space	15GB free on a 20GB drive	15GB free on a 20GB drive	15GB free on a 40GB drive
CD-ROM or DVD	CD-ROM	DVD-ROM	DVD-ROM
Video	SVGA	Support for DirectX 9 graphics and 32MB graphics memory	Support for DirectX 9 with WDDM driver, 128MB of graphics memory, Pixel Shader 2.0 in hardware, 32 bits per pixel
Mouse	Required (but not listed as a requirement)	Required (but not listed as a requirement)	Required (but not listed as a requirement)

Hardware	Minimum Supported for All Versions	Home Basic Recommendation	Home Premium/Business/ Enterprise/Ultimate Recommendation
Keyboard	Required (but not listed as a requirement)	Required (but not listed as a requirement)	Required (but not listed as a requirement)
Internet access	Not listed as a requirement	Required	Required

Table 12.3 lists the minimum system requirements for Windows 7. It should be noted that Windows XP Mode requires an additional 1GB RAM and 15GB hard drive space.

TABLE 12.3   Windows 7 minimum hardware requirements

Hardware	Minimum Supported for All Versions
Processor	1GHz
Memory	1GB for 32-bit; 2GB for 64-bit
Free hard disk space	16GB free for 32-bit; 20GB free for 64-bit
CD-ROM or DVD drive	DVD-ROM
Video	DirectX 9 with WDDM 1.0 (or higher) driver
Mouse	Required (but not listed as a requirement)
Keyboard	Required (but not listed as a requirement)
Internet access	Not listed as a requirement

If there is one thing to be learned from Table 12.1, Table 12.2, and Table 12.3, it is that Microsoft is nothing if not optimistic. For your own sanity, though, we strongly suggest that you always take the minimum requirements with a grain of salt. They are *minimum requirements*. Even the recommended requirements should be considered minimum requirements. The bottom line is make sure you have a good margin between your system's performance and the minimum requirements listed. Always run Windows on more hardware rather than less!

Other hardware—sound cards, network cards, modems, video cards, and so on—may or may not work with Windows. If the device is fairly recent, you can be relatively certain that it was built to work with the newest version of Windows. But if it is older, you may need to find out who made the hardware and check their website to see if there are drivers available for the version of Windows you are installing.

Windows 7 Upgrade Advisor

The easiest way to see if your current hardware can run Windows 7 is to download and run the Windows 7 Upgrade Advisor available at the following location:

`http://windows.microsoft.com/en-us/windows/downloads/upgrade-advisor`

There's one more thing to consider when evaluating installation methods. Some methods only work if you're performing a clean installation and not an upgrade. We'll discuss this in greater detail in the next chapter.

The Windows Interface

The interface of a machine running Windows XP is shown in Figure 12.2. If you've worked with older versions of Windows, you'll notice that it looks only a bit different than the older interfaces. Most basic tasks, however, are accomplished in almost identical fashion on everything from a Windows 95 workstation computer to a Windows 2008 Server computer and a Windows 7 computer. Also, although the tools that are used often vary between the different OSs, the way you use those tools remains remarkably consistent across platforms.

This changed a bit with Windows Vista and the Aero interface, as Figure 12.3 shows, but not as dramatically as many in the media have made it out to be. It was tweaked a bit more with Windows 7, as shown in Figure 12.4.

We will begin with an overview of the common elements of the Windows GUI. We will then look at some tasks that are similar across Windows operating systems. If you have a copy of Windows 7, Windows Vista, or Windows XP available, you may want to follow along by exploring each of the elements as they are discussed.

 If you are able to follow along, you may notice that there are numerous icons and options we do not mention. Quite honestly, there are too many to cover, and they're out of the scope of this chapter. For now, simply ignore them, or browse through them on your own and then return to the text.

FIGURE 12.2   The Windows XP interface

FIGURE 12.3   The Windows Vista interface

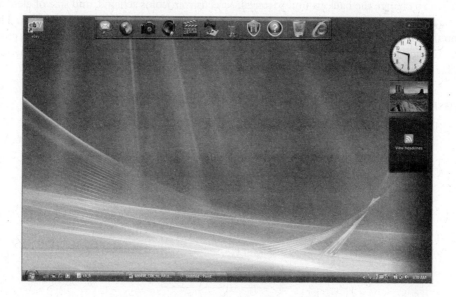

FIGURE 12.4   The Windows 7 interface

The Desktop

The Desktop is the virtual desk on which all of your other programs and utilities run. By default it contains the *Start menu*, the *Taskbar*, and a number of *icons*. The Desktop can also contain additional elements, such as shortcuts or links to web page content. Because it is the base on which everything else sits, the way the Desktop is configured can have a major effect on how the GUI looks and how convenient it is for users.

You can change the background patterns, screensaver, color scheme, and size of elements on the Desktop by right-clicking any area of the Desktop that doesn't contain an icon. The menu that appears allows you to do several things, such as create new Desktop items, change how your icons are arranged, or select a special command called Properties or Personalize, similar to the one shown for Windows 7 in Figure 12.5.

FIGURE 12.5   The Windows 7 Desktop context menu

The Three Clicks in Windows

When it comes to interacting with a mouse in Windows, there are three possibilities:

- *Primary mouse click*—A single click (typically the left mouse button) used to select an object or place a cursor.

- *Double-click*—Two primary mouse clicks in quick succession. Used to open a program through an icon or for other application-specific functions.

- *Secondary mouse click (or alternate click)*—Most mice have two buttons. Clicking once on the secondary button (usually the one on the right, although that can be modified) is interpreted differently from a left mouse click. Generally, in Windows this click displays a context-sensitive menu from which you can perform tasks or view object properties.

When you right-click the Desktop and choose Personalize, then Display, you will see the Display Properties screen shown in Figure 12.6 (for Windows 7).

FIGURE 12.6   The Display Properties screen for Windows 7

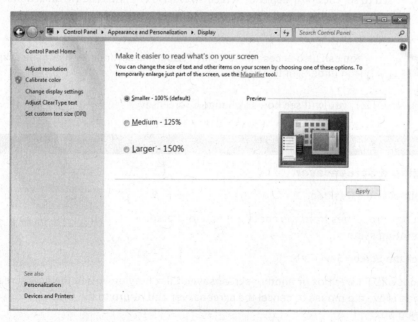

This screen will differ slightly based on the operating system, but you either click the various options at the top to move to the different screens of information about the way Windows looks (non–Windows 7) or choose the options on the left to do the same (Windows 7) . While the options will differ based on the operating system, the main ones in the Display Properties window of most are listed here:

Personalization (or Themes)   Used to select a theme that enables you to quickly customize the look and feel of your machine. Selecting a theme sets several items at once, such as a picture to display on the Desktop, the look of icons, sounds to use, and so on. All of these options can also be selected individually through the other Desktop Properties tabs. For example, if you're more comfortable with the look and feel of previous versions of Windows, you can select the Windows Classic theme.

Background or Desktop   The Background tab is used to select an HTML document or a picture to display on the Desktop. In addition, you can configure other items through the Customize Desktop button. Examples include changing which default icons to display on the Desktop and configuring web content for the Desktop.

Screen Saver   Sets up an automatic screensaver to cover your screen if your computer has not been active for a certain period of time. Originally used to prevent burned-in monitors, screen-savers are now generally used for entertainment or to password-protect users' Desktops. The Screen Saver tab also gives you access to other power settings.

Appearance   Used to select a color scheme for the Desktop or to change the color or size of other Desktop elements.

Settings   Used to set the color depth or screen size. Also contains the Advanced button, which leads to graphics driver and monitor configuration settings.

 You can also access the Display Properties settings by using the Display icon under Control Panel.

In Exercise 12.1, you will see how to change a screensaver.

EXERCISE 12.1

Changing a Screensaver

1.   Right-click the Desktop.

2.   Choose Properties from the context menu (or Personalize, depending on your operating system).

3.   Click the Screen Saver tab.

4.   Choose 3D Flower Box or another screensaver. Click Preview to see the new screen-saver. Move the mouse to cancel the screensaver and return to the Display Properties dialog box.

5.   Click the OK button or the Apply button. (OK performs two tasks—Apply and Exit Window—whereas Apply leaves the window open.)

The Taskbar

The Taskbar (see Figure 12.7) is another standard component of the Windows interface. Note that although the colors and feel of the Desktop components, including the Taskbar, have changed throughout the operating systems, the components themselves are the same. The Taskbar contains two major items: the Start menu and the *system tray* (systray). The Start menu is on the left side of the Taskbar and is easily identifiable: It is a button that has the word *Start* on it, or in the case of Windows 7/Vista, it is the large Windows icon. The *system tray* is located on the right side of the Taskbar and contains only a clock by default, but other Windows utilities (for example, screensavers or virus-protection utilities) may put their icons here to indicate that they are running and to provide the user with a quick way to access their features.

FIGURE 12.7   The Taskbar

Windows also uses the middle area of the Taskbar. When you open a new window or program, it gets a button on the Taskbar with an icon that represents the window or program as well as the name of the window or program. To bring that window or program to the front (or to maximize it if it was minimized), click its button on the Taskbar. As the middle area of the Taskbar fills with buttons, the buttons become smaller so they can all be displayed.

A special area on the Taskbar to the right of the Start button is known as the Quick Launch area, and it appears with some Windows OSs (including Windows XP and Windows Vista). Icons of commonly used programs can appear here, and the programs can be started with a single click. If the icons are in the Quick Launch area—as opposed to on the Desktop, or elsewhere—they are always visible and accessible. In Windows 7 the Quick Launch area was replaced with a mechanism where commonly used programs can be pinned to the Task bar.

You can increase the size of the Taskbar by moving the mouse pointer to the top of it and pausing until the pointer turns into a double-headed arrow. Once this happens, click the mouse and move it up to make the Taskbar bigger. Or move it down to make the Taskbar smaller. You can also click the Taskbar and drag it to the top or side of the screen.

In Windows, once you've configured the Taskbar position and layout to your liking, you can configure it so that it can't be changed accidentally. To do so, right-click the Taskbar and select Lock The Taskbar. To unlock the Taskbar and make changes, right-click the Taskbar and select Lock The Taskbar again.

You can make the Taskbar automatically hide itself when it isn't being used (thus freeing that space for use by the Desktop or other windows). In Exercise 12.2, we will show you how.

EXERCISE 12.2

Auto-Hiding the Taskbar

1. Right-click the Taskbar.

2. Choose Properties, which will bring up the Taskbar And Start Menu Properties screen.

3. Check the Auto-Hide The Taskbar option on the Taskbar tab of the Taskbar And Start Menu Properties dialog box.

4. Click OK.

5. The Taskbar retracts as soon as you click OK.

6. Move the mouse pointer to the bottom of the screen and the Taskbar will pop up and be available for normal use.

In addition to the Taskbar, Windows Vista includes the Sidebar, shown in Figure 12.8. This provides a quick interface that allows you to access common utilities (such as the headlines) and *gadgets*. While the Sidebar existed only for Windows Vista, the concept of gadgets persists and they can be placed directly on the Desktop in Windows 7.

FIGURE 12.8 The Windows Vista Sidebar

The Start Menu

Back when Microsoft officially introduced Windows 95, it bought the rights to use the Rolling Stones's song "Start Me Up" in its advertisements and at the introduction party. Microsoft chose that particular song because the Start menu was the central point of focus in the new Windows interface, as it has been in all subsequent versions.

To display the Start menu, click the Start button in the Taskbar. You'll see a Start menu similar to that shown in Figure 12.9 for Windows XP and Figure 12.10 for Windows 7/Vista. You'll notice that in Windows XP the look of the Start menu is slightly different than that in Windows 7/Vista, but they all behave the same. Regardless of the operating system, the Start menu always serves the same function: providing quick access to important features and programs.

FIGURE 12.9   The Windows XP Start menu

From the Start menu, you can select any of the various options the menu presents. An arrow pointing to the right indicates that a submenu is available. To select a submenu, move the mouse pointer over the submenu title and pause. The submenu will appear; you don't even have to click. (You have to click to choose an option on the submenu, though.) We'll discuss each of the Start menu's submenu options and how to use them.

All Programs Submenu

The All Programs submenu holds icons for the program groups. When you select this submenu, you will be shown a submenu for each program group. In Windows 7, Vista, and XP, the look is again a little different, but the functionality is the same. You can navigate through this menu and its submenus and click the icon for program you wish to start.

You can check which OS you are using by right-clicking the My Computer icon on the Desktop and selecting Properties. The OS type and version are displayed on the first tab. Note that the My Computer icon may not display on the Desktop by default (if the icon does not appear on the Desktop, you can find it on the Start menu instead). In Windows XP, you can add the icon to the Desktop by using Display Properties (click Customize Desktop on the Desktop tab, select My Computer on the General tab, and apply your changes), or you can click Start and then right-click the My Computer option (known as just Computer in Windows 7 and Windows Vista) and select Properties.

If you are running Windows XP or Vista and are attached to the look and feel of the pre–Windows XP Start menu, you can configure XP to use the old Start menu layout. To do so, right-click the Taskbar and select Properties. Click the Start Menu tab, select Classic Start Menu, and click OK.

FIGURE 12.10   The Windows 7/Vista Start menu

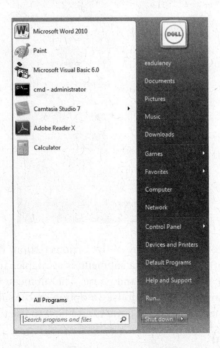

The most common way to add programs to this submenu is by using an application's installation program. In Windows XP, if you're using the Classic Start menu, you can also add programs to this submenu by using the Taskbar Properties screen (right-click the Taskbar and choose Properties). Additionally, items can be added by dragging and dropping icons onto these menus.

My Recent Documents (Windows XP)/Recent Items (Windows 7 and Windows Vista) Submenu

The My Recent Documents/Recent Items submenu has only one function: to keep track of the last data files you opened. Whenever you open a file, a shortcut to it is automatically made in this menu. To open the document again, click the shortcut in the Documents menu to open it in its associated application.

In some versions of Windows XP, this feature is not enabled by default. To enable it, in the Taskbar And Start Menu Properties screen, click the Start Menu tab and then click Customize (next to Start Menu). Click the Advanced tab, select the List My Most Recently Opened Documents option, and then click OK. An option called My Recent Documents is added to the Start menu; it lists the 15 most recently opened data files.

> To clear the list of documents shown in the My Recent Documents/
> Recent Items submenu, open the Taskbar And Start Menu Properties
> screen. Then use the Clear button on the Advanced tab. (Remember that
> you access the Advanced tab in Windows XP via the Customize button
> on the Start Menu tab.)

Search (Find) Submenu/Option

The name of this Start menu option differs between Search and Find in the various versions of Windows, but its purpose doesn't. In all cases, it's used to locate information on your computer or on a network.

In Windows XP, to find a file or directory, click the Search option in the Start menu. Doing so opens the Search Results dialog box. In the left pane, click All Files And Folders, and then enter the appropriate information in the text fields. Expand the down-pointing double arrows to access advanced search options. To start the search, click Search. The search results appear in the right pane.

In Windows 7 and Windows Vista, the Search menu choice has disappeared, but you can search by typing into the Search box that always appears in the upper-right corner of Windows Explorer (technically, searching is still available from the Start menu in the Search Programs And Files bar, but Explorer's works better). You can search through file content by using the filter **contents:** followed by the word/phrase/text you are seeking. More importantly, though, to quickly find commands start typing into the Start menu find field and the system displays matching commands. This is sometimes the quickest way of getting to a particular command especially when you can't remember the exact name (for example, the Disk Management tools can be accessed by typing "ntfs"; the command appears as Create and format hard disk partitions).

Help And Support Command

Windows has always included a very good Help system. In addition, the Help system was updated with a new interface and new tools in Windows 7, Vista, and XP. Because of its usefulness and power, it was placed in the Start menu for easy access.

When you click Help And Support, the Help And Support Center home page opens. This screen may have been slightly customized by a hardware vendor if the operating system was preinstalled on your machine. However, all the options and available tools will still be present.

A quick way to access Help is to press the F1 key.

The Run Command

You can use the Run command to start programs if they don't have a shortcut on the Desktop or in the Programs/All Programs submenu. When you choose Run from the Start menu, a pop-up window appears. To execute a particular program, type its name in the Open field. If you don't know the exact path, you can browse to find the file by clicking the Browse button. Once you have typed in the executable name, click OK to run the program.

To open a command prompt, you can type CMD or COMMAND into the Run box and click OK. You might need to run this as Administrator if you want to change system settings in Vista and Win7. From the Start menu type cmd into the search field then type Ctrl-Shift-Enter to run as administrator.

Applications can easily be started from the Run window; often you will find it faster to open programs this way than search for their icons in the Start menu maze. In Exercise 12.3, you will see how to start a program from the Run window.

EXERCISE 12.3

Starting a Program from the Run Window

1. Click Start ➤ Run.

2. In the Open field, type **notepad**.

3. Click OK. Notepad will open in a new window.

If the program you want to run has been run from the Run window before, you can find it on the Open field's drop-down list. Click the down arrow to display the list, and then select the program you want by clicking its name and clicking OK.

While this functionality did not disappear from Windows Vista, it is a bit different. A blank dialog box appears at the bottom of the Start menu with the default phrase *Start Search* within. Type the name of the command you want to run in here, and press Enter. Vista will look for the executable and run it.

Turn Off Computer Command

Windows operating systems are very complex. At any one time, many files are open in memory. If you accidentally hit the power switch and turn off the computer while these files are open, there is a good chance they will be corrupted. For this reason, Microsoft has added the Turn Off Computer command under the Start menu (in 7/Vista it appears as Shut Down or as an icon of an on/off button and does not have a label). Note that with a configuration called Fast User Switching, Windows XP also displays Shut Down rather than Turn Off Computer. When you select this option, Windows presents you with several choices. Exactly which options are available depends on the Windows version you are running.

The possible choices are as follows:

Turn Off/Shut Down   This option writes any unsaved data to disk, closes any open applications, makes a copy of the Registry, and gets the computer ready to be powered off. Depending on the OS, the computer is then powered down automatically, or you'll see a black screen with the message *It's now safe to turn off your computer.* In this case, you can power off the computer or press Ctrl+Alt+Del to reboot the computer. In Windows 7, the Turn Off option is known as Shut Down.

Restart   This option works the same as the first option, but instead of causing the computer to shut down completely and shut off, it automatically reboots it with a warm reboot.

Sleep (Windows 7 and Windows Vista only)   This option places the computer into a hibernation state. The session is saved and can be restored, but monitor and hard disks are turned off.

Stand By (Windows XP only)   This option places the computer into a low-power state. The monitor and hard disks are turned off, and the computer uses less power. To resume working, press a key on the keyboard; the computer is returned to its original state. In this state, information in memory is not saved to hard disk, so if a power loss occurs, any data in memory will be lost.

If you enable Hibernation on a Windows XP machine, you can place the computer into hibernation by holding down the Shift key while clicking Stand By in the Turn Off Computer screen. When you use the Hibernation feature, any information in memory is saved to disk before the computer is put into a low power state. Thus, if power is lost while the machine is in hibernation, your data is not lost. However, going into and coming out of hibernation takes more time than going into and coming out of stand-by mode.

Icons

Icons are shortcuts that allow a user to open a program or a utility without knowing where that program is located or how it needs to be configured. Icons consist of several major elements:

- Icon label
- Icon graphic
- Program location or path

The label and graphic of the icon typically tell the user the name of the program and give a visual hint about what that program does. The icon for the Solitaire program, for instance, is labeled *Solitaire*, and its icon graphic is a deck of cards. By right-clicking an icon once, you make that icon the active icon and a drop-down menu appears. One of the selections is Properties. Clicking Properties brings up the icon's attributes (see Figure 12.11) and is the only way to see exactly which program an icon is configured to start and where the program's executable is located. You can also specify whether to run the program in a normal window or maximized or minimized.

FIGURE 12.11 The Properties window of an application with its icon above it

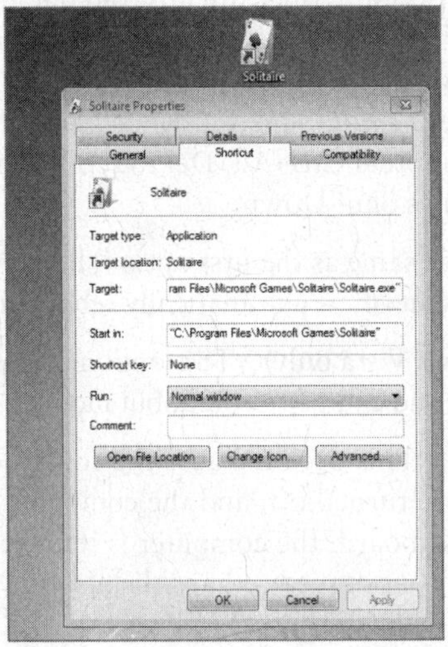

Additional functionality has been added to an icon's properties to allow for backward compatibility with older versions of Windows (known as *compatibility mode*). To configure this, click the Compatibility tab and specify the version of Windows for which you want to configure compatibility. Note that you cannot configure compatibility if the program is part of this version of Windows. Figure 12.12 shows the settings available for an older program.

This feature is helpful if you own programs that used to work in older versions of Windows but no longer run under the current Windows version. In addition, you can specify different display settings that might be required by older programs.

Standard Desktop Icons

In addition to the options in your Start menu, a number of icons are placed directly on the Desktop in Windows. The Recycle Bin icon is one of these. In addition to the Recycle Bin icon, two of the most important icons are Computer/My Computer and Network/Network Neighborhood/My Network Places. However, although they are important, they no longer display by default on the Desktop. You can add them if you want to (in Windows 7, for example, choose Personalization from Control Panel, and then choose Change Desktop Icons).

FIGURE 12.12   The Compatibility settings possible with an older program

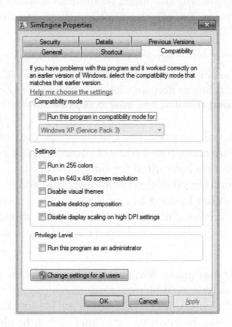

THE COMPUTER/MY COMPUTER ICON

If you double-click the Computer icon, it displays a list of all the disk drives installed in your computer. In addition to displaying disk drives, it displays a list of other devices attached to the computer, such as scanners, cameras, and mobile devices. The disk devices are sorted into categories such as Hard Disk Drives, Devices With Removable Storage, Scanners And Cameras, and so on.

You can delve deeper into each disk drive or device by double-clicking its icon. The contents are displayed in the same window. You can select Tools ➢ Folder Options to configure each folder to open in a new window. Having multiple windows open makes it easy to copy and move files between drives and directories.

In addition to allowing you access to your computer's files, the Computer icon on the Desktop lets you view your machine's configuration and hardware, also called the System Properties.

With Windows 7, Vista, and XP, right-clicking Computer in the Start menu allows you to choose Properties and see the same information (choosing Manage, instead of Properties, brings up the Computer Management interface, in which you can make a plethora of changes).

NETWORK/MY NETWORK PLACES

Another icon in Windows relates to accessing other computers to which the local computer is connected, and it's called Network or My Network Places. (In Windows 7 and Vista, the label for this icon has been changed from My Network Places to simply Network.)

Opening Network enables you to browse for and access computers and shared resources to which your computer is connected. This might be another computer in a workgroup, domain, or other network environment. You can also use Network to establish new connections to shared resources.

For the exam, know that the two types of networks you can choose from are workgroup or domain. Other chapters in this book focus more on the networking specifics and how to set up each.

Through the properties of Network, you can configure your network connections, including LAN and dial-up connections (should you still live in an area where a now antiquated dial-up connection is required for Internet access).

You can choose Network from the Start menu or you can add it—and other common icons—to the Windows 7/Vista Desktop by choosing Start ➢ Control Panel, clicking Appearance And Personalization, and then clicking Personalization. Choose Change Desktop Icons from the choices on the left to open the dialog box shown in Figure 12.13.

THE RECYCLE BIN

All files, directories, and programs in Windows are represented by icons, and these icons are generally referred to as *objects*. When you want to remove an object from Windows, you do so by deleting it. Deleting doesn't just remove the object, though; it also removes the ability of the system to access the information or application the object represents. For this reason, Windows includes a special directory where all deleted files are placed: the Recycle Bin. The Recycle Bin holds the files until it is emptied or until you fill it, and it gives users the opportunity to recover files that they delete accidentally. By right-clicking the Recycle Bin icon, you can see how much disk space is allocated, and some larger files that cannot fit in the Recycle Bin will be erased after a warning.

FIGURE 12.13 Common icons can easily be added to the Desktop.

You can retrieve a file you have deleted by opening the Recycle Bin icon and then dragging the file from the Recycle Bin to where you want to restore it. Alternatively, you can right-click a file and select Restore, and the file will be restored to the location from which it was deleted.

 The Recycle Bin offers an interesting anomaly: In Windows XP (and previous NTFS-based operating systems), the "deleted" files are stored in the \RECYCLER folder. With Windows 7 and Windows Vista, the folder is called \$Recycle.Bin.

To permanently erase files, you need to empty the Recycle Bin, thereby deleting any items in it and freeing the hard drive space they took up. If you want to delete only specific files, you can select them in the Recycle Bin, right-click, and choose Delete. You can also permanently erase files (bypassing the Recycle Bin) by holding down the Shift key as you delete them (by dragging the file and dropping it in the Recycle Bin, pressing the Del key, or clicking Delete on the file's context menu). If the Recycle Bin has files in it, its icon looks like a full trash can; when there are no files in it, it looks like an empty trash can.

What's in a Window?

We have now looked at the nature of the Desktop, the Taskbar, the Start menu, and icons. Each of these items was created for the primary purpose of making access to user applications easier, and these applications are in turn used and managed through the use of *windows*, the rectangular application environments for which the Windows family of operating systems is named. We will now examine how windows work and what they are made of.

A program window is a rectangular area created on the screen when an application is opened within Windows. This window can have a number of different forms, but most windows include at least a few basic elements.

Elements of a Window

Several basic elements are present in a standard window. Figure 12.14 shows the control box, title bar, Minimize/Maximize button, Restore button, Close button, and resizable border in a text editor called Notepad (NOTEPAD.EXE) that has all the basic window elements—and little else.

The basic window elements are as follows:

Control box   Located in the upper-left corner of the window, the control box is used to control the state of the application. It can be used to maximize, minimize, and close the application. Clicking it once brings into view a selection menu. Double-clicking it closes the window and shuts down the application.

Minimize and Maximize/Restore buttons   Used to change the state of the window on the Desktop. They are discussed in the section "States of a Window" later in this chapter.

FIGURE 12.14   The basic elements of a window

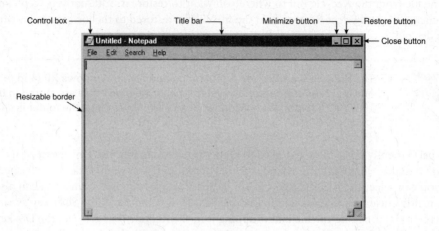

Close button   Used to easily end a program and return any resources it was using to the system. It essentially does the same thing as double-clicking the control box, but with one less click.

Title bar   The area between the control box and the Minimize button. It states the name of the program and in some cases gives information about the particular document being accessed by that program. The color of the title bar indicates whether the window is the active window. Clicking on it is an easy way to move the window on the screen.

Menu bar   Used to present useful commands within an application in an easily accessible format. Clicking one of the menu choices displays a list of related options you may choose from.

Active window   The window that is currently being used. It has two attributes. First, any keystrokes that are entered are directed into the active window by default. Second, any other windows that overlap the active window are pushed behind it.

Border   A thin line that surrounds the window in its restored down state and allows it to be resized.

Not every element is found on every window because application programmers can choose to eliminate or modify each item. Still, in most cases they will be constant, with the rest of the window filled in with menus, toolbars, a workspace, or other application-specific elements. For instance, Microsoft Word, the program with which this book was written, adds an additional control box and Minimize and Maximize buttons for each document. It also has a menu bar, a number of optional toolbars, scroll bars at the right and bottom of the window, and a status bar at the very bottom. Application windows can become quite cluttered.

Notepad is a very simple Windows program. It has only a single menu bar and the basic elements seen previously in Figure 12.14. It also starts a simple editor, where you can edit a file that already exists or create a new one. Figure 12.15 shows a Microsoft Word window. Both Word and Notepad are used to create and edit documents, but Word is far more configurable and powerful and therefore has many more optional components available within its window.

FIGURE 12.15   A window with more components

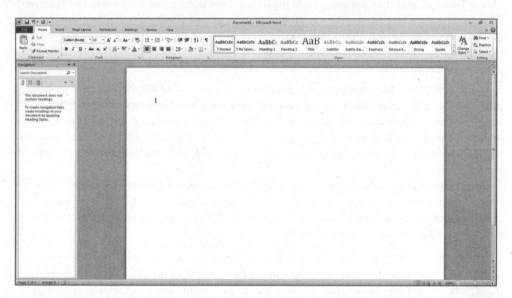

States of a Window

There is more to the Windows interface than the specific parts of a window. Windows also are movable, stackable, and resizable, and they can be hidden behind other windows (often unintentionally!).

When an application window has been launched, it exists in one of three states:

Maximized   A maximized window takes up all available space on the screen. When it is in front of other programs, it is the only thing visible—even the Desktop is hidden. It takes up the entire space of the Desktop, and the middle button in the upper-right corner displays two rectangles rather than one. The sides of the window no longer have borders. The window is flush with the edges of the screen. Maximizing a window provides the maximum workspace possible for that window's application, and the window can be accessed actively by the user. In general, maximized mode is the preferred window size for most word processing, graphics-creation, and other types of user applications.

Restored   A restored window can be used interactively and is identical in function to a maximized window, with the simple difference that it does not necessarily take up the entire screen. Restored windows can be very small, or they can take up almost as much space as maximized windows. Generally, how large the restored window becomes is the user's choice. Restored windows display a Maximize button (the middle button in the upper-right corner) with a single rectangle in it; this is used to maximize the window. Restored windows have a border.

Minimized   Minimized program windows are represented by nothing but an icon and title on the Taskbar, and they are not usable until they have been either maximized or restored. The difference between a minimized program and a closed program is that a minimized program is out of the way but is still taking up resources and is therefore ready to use if you need it. It also leaves the content of the window in the same place when you return to it as when you minimized it.

When one program is open and you need to open another (or maybe you need to stop playing a game because your boss has entered the room), you have two choices. First, you can close the program currently in use and choose to simply reopen it later. If you do this, however, the contents of the window (your current game, for example) will be lost and you will have to start over. Once the program has been closed, you can move on to open the second program.

The second option is to minimize the active window. Minimizing the game window, for example, removes the open window from the screen and leaves the program open but displays nothing more than an icon and title on the Taskbar. Later, you can restore the window to its previous size and finish the game in progress.

Keep in mind that applications in the background are still running. Therefore, if you minimize your game, you might return to find that you've been
eaten by whatever monster you were running from in the game. A program
running while minimized can be a good thing, however, if you're running a
useful utility such as a long search or a disk defrag.

Updating Windows

Windows includes *Windows Update*, a feature designed to keep Windows current by automatically downloading updates such as patches and security fixes and installing them automatically.

By default, Windows Update will run automatically when any administrator user is logged in. However, if you want to run it manually, you can do so by clicking Start ➢ All Programs ➢ Windows Update. With Windows XP, you can also go to `http://windowsupdate` `.microsoft.com` to start the process. In Windows 7/Vista, it just tells you to start Windows Update from the Start menu.

Often, major updates to Windows are called *service packs*.

Here is an overview of how Windows Update works:

1. Windows Update starts (either by itself or manually).

2. Windows Update goes online to check to see what updates are available. It compares the update list to the updates that have already been applied to the computer or have been refused by the administrator.

3. If updates are available, they may be downloaded automatically in the background.

4. Once the updates are downloaded, Windows Update notifies you that the download is complete and asks you if you want to install them, assuming you have that behavior configured (settings can be used to control the behavior).

If you choose not to install the updates right away, Windows will do so for you when you shut off the computer. Instead of shutting off right away, Windows Update will install the updates first and then perform a proper shutdown.

By default, Windows Update is enabled. But there might be times you want to configure it. Exercise 12.4 steps through the process of configuring Windows Update in Windows 7/Vista, while Exercise 12.5 does the same for Windows XP.

EXERCISE 12.4

Configuring Windows Update in Windows 7/Vista

1. Click the Start button, and choose All Programs. Scroll down the list and choose Windows Update.

2. Click the Change Settings entry on the left to open the Choose How Windows Can Install Updates window.

EXERCISE 12.4 *(continued)*

3. Choose the option that best suits your needs. You have four choices:

    ▪ Install Updates Automatically (Recommended)

    ▪ Download Updates But Let Me Choose Whether To Install Them

    ▪ Check For Updates But Let Me Choose Whether To Download And Install Them

    ▪ Never Check For Updates (Not Recommended)

4. Click OK. You will be prompted by User Account Control (UAC) to verify that you want to make that change.

EXERCISE 12.5

Configuring Windows Update in Windows XP

1. Open the System Properties box (right-click My Computer and choose Properties, or double-click the System icon in Control Panel).

2. Select the Automatic Updates tab.

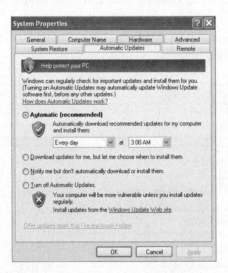

3. Choose the option that best suits your needs. You have four choices:

    ▪ Automatically Download Recommended Updates For My Computer And Install Them.

    ▪ Download Updates For Me, But Let Me Choose When To Install Them.

EXERCISE 12.5 *(continued)*

- Notify Me But Don't Automatically Download Or Install Them.

- Turn Off Automatic Updates.

It's not a problem if you want to choose to have control over which updates get installed and when. However, it is in your best interest to have Windows Update enabled to ensure that you have the most current updates available.

 Microsoft has an update server, Windows Server Update Services (WSUS), for large organizations that controls the update process for all hosts in the company.

Creating Restore Points

Almost everyone, no matter how hard they've tried to keep their computer running properly, will experience a computer crash at some point. Many of the ways to get your computer back up and running (such as reinstalling the operating system) take a lot of time. In Windows 7, Vista, and XP, System Restore allows you to create restore points to make recovery of the operating system easier.

A *restore point* is a copy of your system configuration at a given point in time. Restore points are created one of three ways. One, Windows creates them automatically by default. Two, you can manually create them yourself (which is highly recommended before you make any significant changes to the system, such as installing new drivers). Three, during the installation of some programs, a restore point is created before the installation; that way, if the install fails, you can "roll back" the system to a preinstallation configuration.

Restore points are useful for when Windows fails to boot but the computer appears to be fine otherwise or if Windows doesn't seem to be acting right and you think it was because of a recent configuration change.

To open System Restore, click Start ➢ All Programs ➢ Accessories ➢ System Tools ➢ System Restore. In Windows 7, it will open a screen like the one shown in Figure 12.16.

 If you need to use a restore point and Windows won't boot, you can reboot into Safe Mode. After Safe Mode loads, you will have the option to work in Safe Mode or use System Restore. Choose System Restore and you'll be presented with restore points (if any) you can use.

This tool can be used to configure System Restore settings. You can also get to the same place by opening the System control panel (right-clicking Computer and choosing Properties) and selecting the System Restore tab.

FIGURE 12.16   System Restore

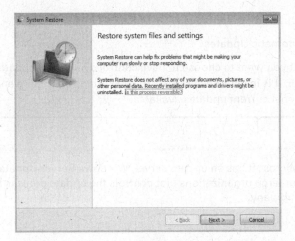

FIGURE 12.16   System Restore

It is possible for you to turn off System Restore. Don't, unless you really don't care if your computer crashes and you can't recover it without a reinstall. The other option is to select how much disk space is available for System Restore. The less disk space you make available, the fewer restore points you will be able to retain. If you have multiple hard drives, you can allocate a different amount of space per hard drive.

Exercise 12.6 demonstrates how to manually create a restore point in Windows 7.

EXERCISE 12.6

Manually Creating a Restore Point in Windows 7

1. Assuming you are using Category view, click Start ➢ Control Panel ➢ System And Security ➢ System ➢ System Protection.

2. If prompted, type in the administrator password (and account name, if needed), or confirm that you want to continue.

3. Choose the System Protection tab and then click Create.

4. Fill in a description for the restore point and then click Create (you cannot click Create without putting text in for a description).

5. When the process is finished, click OK and then exit out of the Control Panel windows.

A factory recovery partition may exist on a machine. A vendor has a great deal of freedom with what they put here, but usually it contains copies of drivers and preinstalled programs. This partition—if it exists—may serve as a last resort for stabilizing a system if all else has failed.

File Management

File management is the process by which a computer stores data and retrieves it from storage. Although some of the file-management interfaces across Windows may have a different look and feel, the process of managing files is similar across the board.

Files and Folders

For a program to run, it must be able to read information off the hard disk and write information back to the hard disk. To be able to organize and access information—especially in larger new systems that may have thousands of files—it is necessary to have a structure and an ordering process.

Windows provides this process by allowing you to create *directories*, also known as *folders*, in which to organize files. Windows also regulates the way that files are named and the properties of files. Each file created in Windows has to follow certain rules, and any program that accesses files through Windows must also comply with these rules:

- Each file has a filename of up to 255 characters.

- Certain characters, such as a question mark (?) and slash (\ or /), are reserved for other uses and cannot be used in the filename. Periods are used to separate the filename from the extension, and the backslash is used to separate the directories in a path from the filename.

- A filename extension (generally three or four characters) can be added to identify the file's type.

- Filenames are not case sensitive. (You can create files with names that use both upper- and lowercase letters, but to identify the file within the file system, it is not necessary to adhere to the capitalization in the filename.) Thus, you cannot have a file named working.txt and another called WORKING.TXT in the same directory. To Windows, these filenames are identical, and you can't have two files with the same filename in the same directory. We'll get into more detail on this topic a little later.

In Windows 3.*x* and DOS, filenames were limited to eight characters and a three-character extension, separated by a period. This is also called the 8.3 file-naming convention. With Windows 95, long filenames were introduced, which allowed the 255-character filename convention.

The Windows file system is arranged like a filing cabinet. In a filing cabinet, paper is placed into folders, which are inside dividers, which are in a drawer of the filing cabinet. In the Windows file system, individual files are placed in subdirectories that are inside directories, which are stored on different disks or different partitions.

Windows also protects against duplicate filenames, so no two files on the system can have exactly the same name and *path*. A path indicates the location of the file on the disk; it is composed of the letter of the logical drive the file is on and, if the file is located in a directory or subdirectory, the names of those directories. For instance, if a file named AUTOEXEC.BAT is located in the root of the C: drive—meaning it is not within a directory—the path to the file is C:\AUTOEXEC.BAT. If, as another example, a file called FDISK.EXE is located in the Command

directory under Windows under the root of C:, then the path to this file is `C:\WINDOWS\`
`COMMAND\FDISK.EXE`.

> The *root directory* of any drive is the place where the hierarchy of folders
> for that drive begins. On a C: drive, for instance, `C:\` is the root directory of
> the drive.

Common filename extensions you may encounter are `.EXE` for executable files (applications), `.DLL` for dynamic linked library (DLL) files, `.SYS` for system files, `.LOG` for log files, `.DRV`
for driver files, and `.TXT` for text files. Note that DLL files contain additional functions and
commands applications can use and share. In addition, specific filename extensions are used
for the documents created with each application. For example, the filenames for documents
created in Microsoft Word have a `.DOC` or `.DOCX` extension. You'll also encounter extensions
such as `.MPG` for video files, `.MP3` for music files, `.png` and `.tif` for graphics files, `.HTM` and
`.HTML` for web pages, and so on. Being familiar with different filename extensions is helpful
in working with the Windows file system.

Capabilities of Windows Explorer

Although it is technically possible to use the command-line utilities provided within the command prompt to manage your files, this generally is not the most efficient way to accomplish
most tasks. The ability to use drag-and-drop techniques and other graphical tools to manage
the file system makes the process far simpler, and Windows Explorer is a utility that allows
you to accomplish a number of important file-related tasks from a single graphical interface.

Here are some of the tasks you can accomplish using Windows Explorer:

- View files and directories
- Open programs or data files
- Create directories and files
- Copy objects to other locations
- Move objects to other locations
- Delete or rename objects
- Change file attributes

You can access many of these functions by right-clicking a file or folder and selecting the
appropriate option, such as Copy or Delete, from the context menu.

Navigating and Using Windows Explorer

Using Windows Explorer is simple. A few basic instructions are all you need to start working
with it. First, the Windows Explorer interface has a number of parts, each of which serves
a specific purpose. The top area of Windows Explorer is dominated by a set of menus and
toolbars that give you easy access to common commands. The main section of the window is
divided into two panes: The left pane displays the drives and folders available, and the right

pane displays the contents of the currently selected folder. The following list includes some common actions in Explorer:

Expanding a folder   You can double-click a folder in the left pane to expand it (show its sub-folders in the left pane) and display its contents in the right pane. Clicking the plus sign (+) to the left of a folder expands the folder without changing the display in the right pane.

The status bar is available in XP (Click View, then Status Bar). The Windows 7/Vista Details pane has similar information.

Collapsing a folder   Clicking the minus sign (–) next to a folder collapses it.

Selecting a file   If you click the file in the right pane, Windows highlights the file by marking it with a darker color.

Selecting multiple files   The Ctrl or Shift keys allow you to select multiple files at once. Holding down Ctrl while clicking individual files selects each new file while leaving the currently selected file(s) selected as well. Holding down Shift while selecting two files selects both of them and all files in between.

Opening a file   Double-clicking a file in the right pane opens the program if the file is an application; if it is a data file, it will open using the application for which the filename extension is configured.

Changing the view type   Windows XP has several different view types: Icons (you cannot choose between large and small icons), List, Details, Thumbnail, and Tiles. The choices in Windows Vista are Extra Large Icons, Large Icons, Medium Icons, Small Icons, List, Details, and Tile. In Windows 7, the Content option was added to those existing with Vista. You can move between these views by clicking the View menu and selecting the view you prefer.

Finding specific files   You access this option by using the Search button or bar. You can search for files based on their name, file size, file type, and other attributes.

When you're searching, you can also use wildcards. *Wildcards* are characters that act as placeholders for a character or set of characters, allowing, for instance, a search for all files with a .TXT filename extension. To perform such a search, you'd type an asterisk (*) as a stand-in for the filename: *.TXT. An asterisk takes the place of any number of characters in a search. A question mark (?) takes the place of a single number or letter. For example, AUTOEX??.BAT would return the file AUTOEXEC.BAT as part of its results.

Creating new objects   To create a new file, folder, or other object, navigate to the location where you want to create the object, and then right-click in the right pane (without selecting a file or directory). In the menu that appears, select New and then choose the object you want to create.

Deleting objects   Select the object and press the Del key on the keyboard, or right-click the object and select Delete from the menu that appears.

 The simplicity of deleting in Windows makes it likely that you or one of the people you support will delete or misplace a file or a number of files that are still needed. In such a case, the Recycle Bin (mentioned earlier) is a lifesaver.

Besides simplifying most file-management commands as shown here, Windows Explorer allows you to easily complete a number of disk-management tasks. You can format and label removable media and, in some cases, copy the Windows system files to said media so that you can boot from a device other than the hard drive.

Changing File Attributes

File attributes determine what specific users can do to files or directories. For example, if a file or directory is flagged with the Read Only attribute, then users can read the file or directory but not make changes to it or delete it. Attributes include Read Only, Hidden, System, and Archive as well as Compression, Indexing, and Encryption. Not all attributes are available with all versions of Windows. We'll look at this subject in more detail in a moment.

 Some attributes date back to DOS—such as Read Only, Hidden, System, and Archive. All others, such as Compression, Indexing, and Encryption, are a part of NTFS.

You can view and change file attributes either by entering **ATTRIB** at the command prompt or by changing the properties of a file or directory. To access the properties of a file or directory in the Windows GUI, right-click the file or directory and select Properties. Figure 12.17 shows the Properties screen of a file in Windows XP. In Windows XP, you can view and configure the Read Only and Hidden file attributes on the General tab. To view and configure additional attributes, click Advanced.

System files are usually flagged with the Hidden attribute, meaning they don't appear when a user displays a directory listing. You should not change this attribute on a system file unless absolutely necessary. System files are required for the OS to function. If they are visible, users might delete them (perhaps thinking they can clear some disk space by deleting files they don't recognize). Needless to say, that would be a bad thing!

File System Advanced Attributes

Windows 7, Vista, and XP may use the NT File System (NTFS), which gives you a number of options that are not available on earlier file systems such as FAT and FAT32. A number of these options are implemented through the use of the Advanced Attributes window, shown in Figure 12.18. To reach these options in Windows, right-click the folder or file you wish to modify and select Properties from the menu. On the main Properties page of the folder or file, click the Advanced button in the lower-right corner.

FIGURE 12.17   The General tab of a file's Properties screen

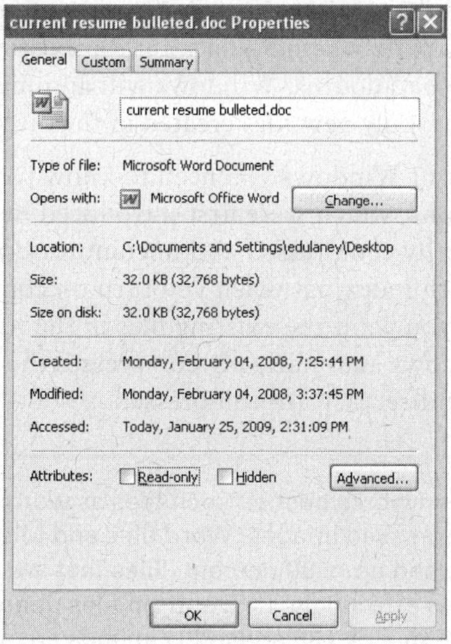

Properties dialog — "current resume bulleted.doc Properties":

General | Custom | Summary

current resume bulleted.doc

Type of file: Microsoft Word Document
Opens with: Microsoft Office Word   [Change...]

Location: C:\Documents and Settings\edulaney\Desktop
Size: 32.0 KB (32,768 bytes)
Size on disk: 32.0 KB (32,768 bytes)

Created: Monday, February 04, 2008, 7:25:44 PM
Modified: Monday, February 04, 2008, 3:37:45 PM
Accessed: Today, January 25, 2009, 2:31:09 PM

Attributes: ☐ Read-only   ☐ Hidden   [Advanced...]

[OK] [Cancel] [Apply]

> FAT32 does not have as many options as NTFS, such as Encryption and Compression. These attributes are available only on NTFS partitions.

On the Advanced Attributes window, you have access to the following settings:

Archiving   The archiving option can be used to tell the system whether or not the file has changed since the last time it was backed up. Technically it is known as the Archive Needed attribute; if this bit is on, the file should be backed up. If it is not selected, a current version of the file is already backed up.

FIGURE 12.18   The Advanced Attributes window

Advanced Attributes dialog:

Choose the options you want for this file.

Archive and Index attributes
☑ File is ready for archiving
☑ For fast searching, allow Indexing Service to index this file

Compress or Encrypt attributes
☐ Compress contents to save disk space
☐ Encrypt contents to secure data   [Details]

[OK] [Cancel]

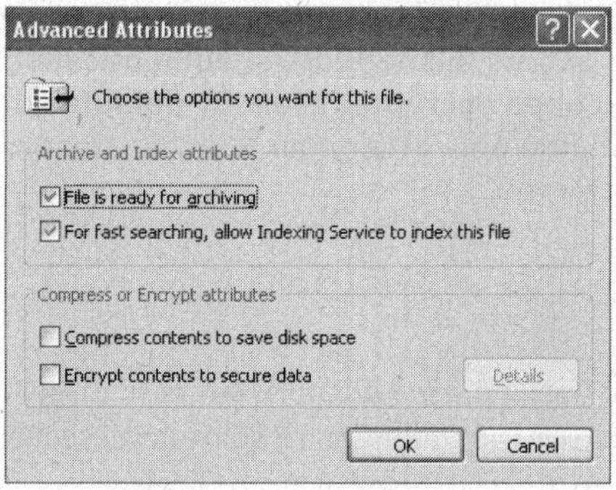

Indexing   Windows implements a feature called the Indexing Service to catalog and improve the search capabilities of your drive. Once files are indexed, you can search for them more quickly by name, date, or other attributes. Setting the index option on a folder causes a prompt to appear, asking whether you want the existing files in the folder to be indexed as well. If you choose to do this, Windows will automatically reset this attribute on subfolders and files. If not, only new files created in the directory are indexed.

Compression   The versions of Windows you need to know for the exam support advanced *compression* options, which were first introduced in Windows NT. NTFS files and folders can be dynamically compressed and uncompressed, often saving a great deal of space on the drive. As with indexing, when you turn on compression for a folder, you'll be prompted as to whether you want the existing files in the folder to be compressed. If you choose to do this, Windows automatically compresses the subfolders and files. If not, only new files created in the directory are compressed.

Compression works best on such files as word processing documents and uncompressed images. Word files and Microsoft Paint bitmaps can be compressed up to 80 percent. Files that are already packed well do not compress as effectively; EXE and zip files generally compress only about 2 percent. Similarly GIF and JPEG images are already compressed (which is why they are used in Internet web pages), so they compress a little or not at all.

Encryption   *Encryption* lets you secure files so that no one else can view them; you encrypt files by encoding them with a key that only you have access to. This can be useful if you're worried about extremely sensitive information, but in general, encryption is not necessary on the network. NTFS local file security is usually enough to provide users with access to what they need and prevent others from getting to what they shouldn't. If you want to encrypt a file, go through the same process you would for indexing or compression.

Encryption and Compression are mutually exclusive—you can set one but not both features on a file or folder. Not all features are available in all versions of the operating systems (for example, neither feature is available in XP Home Edition). If a user forgets their password or is unable to access the network to authenticate their account, they will not be able to open encrypted files. By default, if the user's account is lost or deleted, the only other user who can decrypt the file is the Administrator account.

File Permissions

Windows also supports the use of *file permissions* because these OSs use NTFS, which includes file-level file system security (along with share-level security). Permissions serve the purpose of controlling who has access and what type of access to what files or folders. Several permissions are available, such as Read, Write, Execute, Delete, Change Permissions, Take Ownership, Full Control, and more. The list is quite extensive. For a complete list, consult the Windows Help files.

Assigning special permissions individually could be a tedious task. To make it easier for administrators to assign multiple permissions at once, Windows incorporates *standard permissions*. Standard permissions are collections of special permissions, including Full Control, Modify, Read & Execute, Read, and Write. As we said, each of these standard permissions automatically assigns multiple special permissions at once. To see which special permissions are assigned by the different standard permissions refer to http://technet .microsoft.com/en-us/library/cc732880.

Note that you can assign permissions to individual users or to groups. You assign standard permissions on the Security tab of a file or folder, which you access through the file or folder's properties.

Being able to set file permissions is a great reason to use NTFS. In Exercise 12.7, we will show you how to examine file permissions.

EXERCISE 12.7

Examining File Permissions

1. Open Windows Explorer.

2. Right-click a file or folder and choose Properties.

3. Select and then examine the Security tab. The Security tab will not appear if Simple File Sharing (Windows XP only) is selected. If this is the case, you can turn off Simple File Sharing by selecting Tools ➢ Folder Options and clicking the View tab in the resulting dialog box. Then scroll down to the Advanced Settings area and deselect Use Simple File Sharing.

4. You'll see the users and/or groups to which permissions have been assigned. Select a user or group in the list and examine the list of standard permissions. (To add a new user or group, click Add and follow the prompts.) Any standard permissions that are checked in the Allow column are applied. If a check box is grayed out, this means the permission was inherited. To revoke a set of standard permissions, click the appropriate check box in the Deny column. If you click the check box in the Deny column for the Full Control permission, all other standard permissions are denied also.

5. Click Advanced to examine advanced options.

6. Click Cancel twice to close the file or folder's properties.

Be sure you don't accidentally make any changes you didn't intend to make. Changing permissions without understanding the ramifications can have negative consequences, such as losing access to files or folders. It is a best practice to assign Deny permissions sparingly. Unchecking Allow is better (you may need to turn off Inheritance).

Going Virtual

Thanks to the ability to create virtual machines (VMs), it is becoming far less common to need dual-boot machines today than in the past. Using VMs, you can run multiple operating systems (or multiple instances of the same operating system) on the same hardware at the same time and not need to reboot the system each time you want a different OS.

The *hypervisor* is a virtual machine manager—the software that allows the virtual machines to exist. In the Microsoft client OS realm, the built-in hypervisor is the Microsoft Virtual PC. Other options include VMware and Xen, which are two other well-known hypervisors.

There have been a number of virtualization-specific threats that have cropped up focusing on the hypervisor, but updates have fixed the issues as they have become known. The solution to most virtual machine threats is to always apply the most recent updates and keep the system(s) up-to-date.

An excellent white paper from Microsoft on desktop virtualization can be found at `http://bit.ly/vKTROF`.

From a networking standpoint, each of the virtual desktops will typically need full network access, and configuring the permissions for each can sometimes be tricky. The virtual desktop is often called a *virtual desktop interface (VDI)*, and that term encompasses the software and hardware needed to create the virtual environment.

Virtual desktops are often used with remote administration, allowing a remote administrator to work on the workstation with or without the knowledge of the user sitting in front of the machine.

The resource requirements for virtualization are largely based upon what environments you are creating. The hardware on the machine must have enough memory, hard drive space, and processor capability to support the virtualization. You also need the software to make virtualization possible. XP Mode has been mentioned earlier in this chapter and is a free emulator from Microsoft that you can download and it supplies a pre-configured virtual machine, which is run in the Windows Virtual PC emulator (the hypervisor). A number of others are also available. In most cases, the motherboard and associated BIOS settings need no alteration to provide services to these virtual machines. Some of the newer virtualization products, however (such as Microsoft's Hyper-V), require that the motherboard support *hardware-assisted virtualization*. The benefit derived from using hardware-assisted virtualization is that it allows the *hypervisor* (the virtualization product) to dynamically allocate memory and CPU to the VMs as required.

VMware Player allows you to work in multiple environments on one system. For more information, go to www.vmware.com/products/player/.

Summary

In this chapter, you learned about Windows, the basics of Windows structure, and window management. Because Windows is a graphical system, the key to success in learning to use it is to explore the system to find out what it can do. You will then be better prepared to later decipher what a user has done.

First, we covered the Windows interface. Next, we covered what the component that gives Windows its name (the window) actually is and how windows are used.

Finally, we covered some basic Windows management concepts. Concepts included using file systems and managing files as well as understanding directory structure. We discussed using approved hardware, updating Windows, and creating restore points.

With the basic knowledge gained in this chapter, you are now ready to learn how to interact with the most commonly used tools, the subject of the following chapter.

Exam Essentials

Know what file systems are available in Windows and the differences between them.   The most commonly used file system on Windows hard drives is NTFS. FAT32 is older and perhaps a bit quicker for smaller hard drives, but NTFS adds a plethora of important features, including security and auditing.

Understand how to manage files in Windows.   Nearly all file management is accomplished through Windows Explorer, including moving, copying, renaming, and deleting files and changing file attributes, advanced attributes, and permissions.

Know where files are located.   The various versions of Windows that you need to know for this exam store files in multiple locations. You should be able to identify the location of those files mentioned in this chapter and be able to identify subtle differences—such as where the Recycle Bin files are on each Windows operating system.

Review Questions

The answers to the Chapter Review Questions can be found in Appendix A.

1. You just clicked Start ➢ Run on a Windows XP workstation. Which of the following can you type to open a command prompt? (Choose two.)

    A. RUN

    B. CMD

    C. COMMAND

    D. OPEN

2. Which part of the operating system can be described as extremely specific software written for the purpose of instructing the OS on how to access a piece of hardware?

    A. Source

    B. Application

    C. Kernel

    D. Driver

3. The Taskbar can be increased in size by _____.

    A. Right-clicking the mouse and dragging the Taskbar to make it bigger

    B. Left-clicking the mouse and double-clicking the Taskbar

    C. Moving the mouse pointer to the top of the Taskbar, pausing until the pointer turns into a double-headed arrow, and then clicking and dragging

    D. Highlighting the Taskbar and double-clicking in the center

4. Which of the following file attributes are available to files on a FAT32 partition?

    A. Hidden, Read Only, Archive, System

    B. Compression, Hidden, Archive, Encryption, Read Only

    C. Read Only, Hidden, System, Encryption

    D. Indexing, Read Only, Hidden, System, Compression

5. The Windows Explorer program can be used to do which of the following? (Choose two.)

    A. Browse the Internet

    B. Copy and move files

    C. Change file attributes

    D. Create backup jobs

6. Standard permissions are _____.
   A. The same as special permissions
   B. Only the Read, Write, and Execute permissions
   C. Permissions assigned to users but not to groups
   D. Permissions grouped together for easy assignment

7. Which of the following is a program that runs on top of the OS and allows the user to issue commands through a set of menus or some other graphical interface?
   A. Taskbar
   B. Shell
   C. GUI
   D. Source

8. If a program doesn't have a shortcut on the Desktop or in the Programs submenu, you can start it by _____. (Choose the best answer.)
   A. Using the Shut Down command
   B. Typing **CMD** in the Start Run box
   C. Using the RUN command and typing in the name of the program
   D. Typing **CMD** in the Start box followed by the program name

9. What operating system feature offers the ability for a single application to have multiple requests in to the processor at one time?
   A. Multiuser mode
   B. Dystopia
   C. Preemption
   D. Multithreading

10. In Windows, a deleted file can be retrieved using which of the following?
    A. My Computer icon
    B. Recycle Bin
    C. Control Panel
    D. Settings panel

11. To turn off a Windows 7 machine, you should _____.
    A. Run the Shut Down (Turn Off) command at a command prompt.
    B. Turn off the switch and unplug the machine.
    C. Press Ctrl+Alt+Del.
    D. Select Start ➤ Shut Down, choose Shut Down, and turn off the computer.

12. What is the minimum amount of memory recommended for XP Professional?

   A. 128MB

   B. 256MB

   C. 512MB

   D. 1GB

13. What is the minimum amount of free hard drive space recommended for the installation of Windows Vista Home Basic?

   A. 1.5GB

   B. 15GB

   C. 30GB

   D. 60GB

14. What is the minimum recommended memory for a 32-bit installation of Windows 7?

   A. 512MB

   B. 1GB

   C. 2GB

   D. 4GB

15. In Windows, a quick way to access Help is to press which keyboard key?

   A. F12

   B. The Windows button on the keyboard

   C. F1

   D. Alt

16. Which of the following was installed to the Desktop by default only in Windows Vista?

   A. Gadgets

   B. Sidebar

   C. System tray

   D. Recycle Bin

17. Which of the following is located on the rightmost portion of the Taskbar?

   A. Start menu

   B. Quick Launch

   C. System tray

   D. Shutdown options

18. In addition to right-clicking on the Desktop, how else can you access the Display Properties settings in Windows XP?

   A. Display icon under Control Panel

   B. System icon under Control Panel

   C. Pressing Ctrl+Alt+Esc

   D. Pressing Ctrl+Alt+Tab

19. Which of the following is the name of the graphical interface included with Windows Vista?

   A. Start

   B. Aero

   C. KDE

   D. GNOME

20. What is the minimum recommended memory for a 64-bit installation of Windows 7?

   A. 512MB

   B. 1GB

   C. 2GB

   D. 4GB

Performance-Based Question

On the A+ exams, you will encounter performance-based questions. The questions on the exam require you to perform a specific task, and you will be graded on whether you were able to complete the task. The following requires you to think creatively to measure how well you understand this chapter's topics. You may or may not see similar questions on the actual A+ exams. To see how your answer compares to the authors', refer to Appendix B.

You have been told that a number of workstations in your department may be upgraded in the near future and you've been assigned the task of locally logging on to each and collecting basic data on them. All workstations on this floor run Windows 7. How would you most efficiently collect the following information?

Windows Edition:

Service Pack installed:

Processor:

Installed Memory:

Total paging file size for all drives:

Chapter

13

Operating System Administration

THE FOLLOWING COMPTIA A+ 220-802 EXAM OBJECTIVES ARE COVERED IN THIS CHAPTER:

✓ **1.1 Compare and contrast the features and requirements of various Microsoft Operating Systems.**

- Features: User account control, compatibility mode, administrative tools, security center, event viewer, file structure and paths, category view vs. classic view

✓ **1.2 Given a scenario, install, and configure the operating system using the most appropriate method.**

- Partitioning: Dynamic, Basic, Primary, Extended, Logical

    - File system types/formatting: FAT, FAT32, NTFS, CDFS, Quick format vs. full format

    - Load alternate third party drivers when necessary

    - Workgroup vs. Domain setup

    - Time/date/region/language settings

    - Driver installation, software and windows updates

    - Factory recovery partition

✓ **1.3 Given a scenario, use appropriate command line tools.**

- Networking: PING, TRACERT, NETSTAT, IPCONFIG, NET, NSLOOKUP, NBTSTAT

    - OS: TASKKILL, BOOTREC, SHUTDOWN, TASKLIST, MD, RD, CD, DEL, FDISK, FORMAT, COPY, XCOPY, ROBOCOPY, DISKPART, SFC, CHKDSK, [command name] /?

    - Recovery Console: Fixboot, Fixmbr

✓ **1.4 Given a scenario, use appropriate operating system features and tools.**

- Administrative: Computer management, Device manager, Performance monitor, Services, Task Scheduler

- MSCONFIG: General, Boot, Services, Startup, Tools

- Task Manager: Applications, Processes, Performance, Networking, Users

- Disk management: Drive Status, Mounting, Extending partitions, Splitting partitions, Assigning drive letters, Adding drives, Adding Arrays

- Run line utilities: MSCONFIG, REGEDIT, CMD, SERVICES.MSC, MMC, MSTSC, EXPLORER, MSINFO32, DXDIAG

✓ **1.5 Given a scenario, use Control Panel utilities.**

- Common to all Microsoft Operating Systems

  - Internet options (Connections, Security, General, Privacy, Programs, Advanced)

  - Display (Resolution)

  - User accounts

  - Folder options (Sharing, View hidden files, Hide extensions, Layout)

  - System (Performance (virtual memory), Hardware profiles, Remote settings, System protection

  - Security center

  - Windows firewall

  - Power options (Hibernate, Power plans, Sleep/suspend, Standby

✓ **1.7 Perform preventive maintenance procedures using appropriate tools.**

- Best practices (Scheduled backups, Scheduled check disks, Scheduled defragmentation)

- Tools

  - Backup

  - Check disk

  - Defrag

✓ **1.8 Explain the differences among basic OS security settings.**

- NTFS vs. Share permissions (Allow vs. deny, Moving vs. copying folders and files, File attributes)
- System files and folders
- Shared files and folders (Administrative shares vs. local shares, Permission propagation, Inheritance)
- User Authentication (Single sign-on)

The previous chapter introduced the basic components of the Windows operating systems. This chapter builds upon that and focuses more on the administration of those operating systems. All of the content is generic to the three operating systems you'll be tested on in the 220-802 certification exam: Windows 7, Windows Vista, and Windows XP.

Some of the tools covered are network-specific rather than OS-specific; the `ping` command, for example, will work the same in many operating systems, but this exam focuses on only Microsoft Windows operating systems. In the three chapters that follow, we will dive into specifics for each of the three end-user operating systems, one per OS.

Interacting with Operating Systems

In the following sections, we will look at the Microsoft GUI from the ground up. In Chapter 12, "Operating System Basics," we took a detailed look at its key components, and we will build on that with an exploration of basic tasks common across Windows 7, Vista, and XP. The following general topics will be covered:

- Control Panel
- The command prompt
- The Windows Registry
- Virtual memory

Control Panel

Although for the most part the Windows system is functional from the time it is installed, Microsoft realized that if someone were going to use computers regularly, they would probably want to be able to customize their environment so it would be better suited to their needs—or at least more fun to use. As a result, the Windows environment has a large number of utilities that are intended to give you control over the look and feel of the operating system.

This is, of course, an excellent idea. It is also a bit more freedom than some less-than-cautious users seem to be capable of handling, and you will undoubtedly serve a number of customers who call you in to restore their configuration after botched attempts at changing one setting or another.

More than likely, you will also have to reinstall Windows yourself a few times because of accidents that occur while you are studying or testing the system's limits. This is actually a good thing because no competent computer technician can say that they have never had to reinstall because of an error. You can't really know how to fix Windows until you are experienced at breaking it. So it is extremely important to experiment and find out what can be changed in the Windows environment, what results from those changes, and how to undo any unwanted results. To this end, we will examine the most common configuration utility in Windows: Control Panel. The names of some of the applets, icons, categories, and tasks are different in various versions of Windows; different names are indicated in parentheses. And not all applets are available in all versions. You'll see some of the more popular applets described in Table 13.1.

TABLE 13.1   Selected Windows Control Panel applets

Applet Name	Function
Add Hardware	Adds and configures new hardware.
Add Or Remove Programs (Add/ Remove Programs)	Changes, adds, or deletes software.
Administrative Tools	Performs administrative tasks on the computer.
Date And Time (Date/Time)	Sets the system time and configures options such as time zone.
Display	Configures screensavers, colors, display options, and monitor drivers.
Folder Options	Configures the look and feel of how folders are displayed in Windows Explorer.
Fonts	Adds and removes fonts.
Internet Options	Sets a number of Internet connectivity options.
Sounds And Multimedia; Sounds And Audio Devices; also Scanners And Cameras (Multimedia)	Configures audio, video, or audio and video options.
Network And Dial-Up Connections; Network Connections (Network)	Sets options for connecting to other computers.
Phone And Modem Options (Modems)	Sets options for using phone lines to dial out to a network or the Internet.
Power Options	Configures different power schemes to adjust power consumption.

TABLE 13.1 Selected Windows Control Panel applets *(continued)*

Applet Name	Function
Printers And Faxes (Printers)	Configures printer settings and print defaults.
System	Allows you to view and configure various system elements. We'll look at this in more detail later in this chapter.

In current version of Windows, when you first open Control Panel, it appears in Category view. Control Panel programs have been organized into different categories, and this view provides you with the categories to choose from. Once you choose a category, you can pick a task and the appropriate Control Panel program is opened for you, or you can select one of the Control Panel programs that is part of the category. However, you can change this view to Classic view, which displays all the Control Panel programs in a list, as in older versions of Windows. The specific wording of the CompTIA objective for this exam reads, "Given a scenario, use Control Panel utilities (the items are organized by 'classic view/large icons' in Windows)." Because of this, we *strongly* suggest that administrators change to this view. To do so, click Switch To Classic View in the left pane. Throughout this chapter, when we refer to accessing Control Panel programs, we will assume that you have changed the view to Classic view.

For a quick look at how the Control Panel programs work, in Exercise 13.1 you'll examine some of the settings in the Date/Time applet (TIMEDATE.CPL). The Date/Time applet is used to configure the system time, date, and time zone settings, which can be important for files that require accurate time stamps or to users who don't have a watch. Because it is a simple program, it's a perfect example to use. Current versions of Windows have an Internet Time tab, which enables you to synchronize time on the computer with an Internet time server (the options in Windows 7 are shown in Figure 13.1).

EXERCISE 13.1

Changing the Time Zone

1. Click Start ➢ Control Panel.

2. From Control Panel, double-click the Date/Time (Date And Time) icon (by default, the programs are listed alphabetically).

3. Click the Time Zone tab and use the drop-down menu to select (GMT −03:30) Newfoundland.

4. Hop a plane to Newfoundland, secure in the knowledge that you will know what time it is once you get there.

5. If you skipped step 4, change the time zone back to where it should be before closing the window.

FIGURE 13.1 System time can be configured to be retrieved from an Internet time server.

The Regional and Language Options

Regional settings are configured through the Control Panel applet called Region And Language (in Windows 7) or Regional And Language Options (in Vista and XP). From this applet (INTL.CPL), you can choose what format is used for numbers (see Figure 13.2), what the layout is of the keyboard you are using, your geographic location, and the language to be used for non-Unicode programs.

The ability to support so many languages is provided through the use of the Unicode standard. In Unicode, and the Unicode Character Set (UCS), each character has a 16-bit value. This allows the same character to be interpreted/represented by 65,536 different entities.

The Internet Options Applet

The Internet Options applet (INETCPL.CPL) brings up the Internet properties, shown in Figure 13.3. The tabs here include General, Security, Privacy, Content, Connections, Programs, and Advanced. This applet is used when you want to configure the browser environment and such things as the programs used to work with files found online.

The Folder Options Applet

Some of the more important files you will need to work on are hidden by default as a security precaution. To make certain folders or files visible, you need to change the display properties of Windows Explorer. We will show you how to do this in Exercise 13.2.

FIGURE 13.2 Set the format used for numbers with the options in the Regional And Language applet.

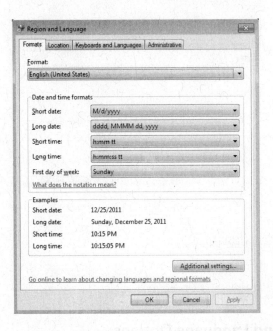

FIGURE 13.3 The Internet properties are accessed through the Internet Options applet.

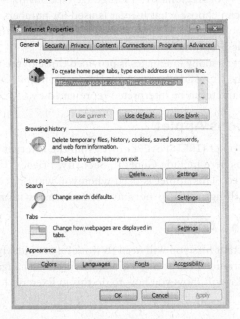

EXERCISE 13.2

Showing Hidden Files and Folders

1. Open Windows Explorer on a Windows XP system.

2. Browse to the root of the C: drive. Look for the IO.SYS system file. It should be hidden and will not appear in the file list.

3. Choose Tools ➢ Folder Options. The Folder Options window opens.

4. Select the View tab, and scroll until you find the Hidden Files option.

5. Select Show All Files.

6. Deselect Hide Protected Operating System Files (Recommended).

7. Uncheck Hide File Extensions For Known File Types.

8. Click OK. You will now be able to see the Windows system files discussed in the following sections. For security reasons, you should set these attributes back to the defaults after you've read this chapter.

The System Control Applet

The System Control Panel applet (see Figure 13.4 for the Windows 7 System applet) is one of the most important, and it's nearly all business. It usually appears with System Properties in the title bar. From within this one relatively innocuous panel (SYSDM.CPL), you can make a large number of configuration changes to a Windows machine. The different versions of Windows have different options available in this applet, but they can include some of the following options:

- General
- Network Identification
- Device Manager
- Hardware
- Hardware Profiles
- User Profiles
- Environment Variables
- Startup and Recovery
- Performance
- System Restore
- Automatic Updates
- Remote
- Computer Name
- Advanced

The General tab (in Windows XP) gives you an overview of the system, such as OS version, registration information, basic hardware levels (processor and RAM), and the service pack level that's installed, if any. In the following sections, we will look a bit more closely at the functionality of the rest of the tabs (we identify which versions of Windows contain each tab).

FIGURE 13.4 The System Properties control panel applet on a Windows 7 computer with the Advanced tab selected

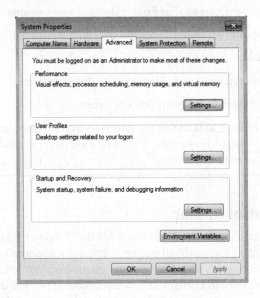

Computer Name

This tab is used to define whether the machine is in a workgroup or a domain environment. We will talk more about networking in a separate chapter, but in general terms, here's the difference between a workgroup and a domain:

Workgroup Loosely associated computers, each of which is its own security authority, that share a common workgroup name.

Domain A group of computers that is tightly connected or associated and share a common domain name. Has a single authority (called a *domain controller*) that manages security for all the computers.

Hardware

This tab includes a number of tools, all of which allow you to change how the hardware on your machine is used:

Driver Signing To minimize the risks involved with adding third-party software to your machine, Microsoft came up with a technique called *driver signing*. Installing new hardware drivers onto the system is a situation in which both viruses and badly written software can threaten your system's health. To minimize the risks, you can choose to use only drivers that have been signed. The signing process is meant to ensure that you are getting drivers that have been checked with Windows 7/Vista/XP and that those drivers have not been modified maliciously.

WARNING   Even in a Plug and Play system, it is important to properly unplug a device if you wish to remove it while the system is running. If you don't do this, nothing may go wrong, but you can sometimes damage the device or cause the system to become unstable.

NOTE   For the exam, understand that loading alternate third-party drivers when necessary can be a solution to problems. Know, as well, that it is preferred that those drivers be signed.

When you purchase a hardware device, odds are it's been in that box for a while. By the time it gets made, packaged, stored, delivered to the store, stored again at the retailer, and then purchased by you, it's entirely likely that the company that made the device has updated the driver—even possibly a few times if there have been a lot of reported problems.

When you install a device, always go to the manufacturer's website to see if a newer driver is available. The old driver might work fine, but the newest driver is the one most likely to be bug-free and have all of the most current bells and whistles for your device.

Advanced

The Advanced tab has three subheadings, each of which can be configured separately. They're not identical in Windows versions, however, and this could also be called the Etc. tab rather than the Advanced tab. The following options are among those on this tab:

- Performance
- Environment Variables
- User Profiles
- Startup And Recovery

Performance   Although it is hidden in the backwaters of Windows's system configuration settings, the Performance option holds some important settings you may need to configure on a system. To access it, on the Advanced tab, click Settings in the Performance area.

In the Performance window, you can set the size of your virtual memory and how the system handles the allocation of processor time. In Windows 7/Vista/XP, you also use Performance to configure visual effects for the GUI.

How resources are allocated to the processor is normally not something you will need to modify. It is set by default to optimize the system for foreground applications, making the system most responsive to the user who is running programs. This is generally best, but it means that any applications (databases, network services, and so on) that are run by the system are given less time by the system.

> If the Windows machine will be working primarily as a network server, you may want to change the Performance option to Background Services. Otherwise, leave it as is.

Environment Variables   There are two types of *environment variables*, and you can access either one by clicking the Environment Variables button:

User Variables   Specify settings that are specific to an individual user and do not affect others who log on to the machine.

System Variables   Set for all users on the machine. System variables are used to provide information needed by the system when running applications or performing system tasks.

> System and user variables were extremely important in the early days of DOS and Windows. Their importance has been more subdued with recent Windows versions, but this is the interface where TEMP variables, the location of the OS, and other important settings for Windows can be found.

User Profiles   In Windows 7, Vista, and XP, every user is automatically given a user profile when they log on to the workstation. This profile contains information about their settings and preferences. Although it does not happen often, occasionally a user profile becomes corrupted or needs to be destroyed. Alternatively, if a particular profile is set up appropriately, you can copy it so that it is available for other users. To do either of these tasks, use the User Profiles settings to select the user profile you want to work with. You will be given three options:

Delete   Removes the user's profile entirely. When that user logs on again, they will be given a fresh profile taken from the system default. Any settings they have added will be lost, as will any profile-related problems they have caused.

Change Type   Allows you to configure a profile as local (the default) or roaming. If a user works at two machines, each machine will use a different profile. Updates to one machine will not be reflected on the other. If you have a network, roaming profiles can be configured to allow a user to have a single profile anywhere on the network. Further discussion of this topic is beyond the scope of this book.

Copy To   Copies a profile from one user to another. Often the source profile is a template set up to provide a standard configuration.

Startup And Recovery   The Windows Startup And Recovery options are relatively straightforward. They involve two areas: what to do during system startup and what to do in case of unexpected system shutdown:

System Startup   The System Startup option defaults to the Windows OS you installed, but you can change this default behavior if you like. Unless you are *dual-booting*, only one option is available, but if you have another OS installed, you can change the Windows boot manager to load that as the default. You can also reduce the time the menu is displayed or remove the menu entirely. In Windows XP, you can also click Edit to edit the BOOT.INI file.

If you choose to completely disable the menu on a dual-boot system, you will find that doing so may cause you annoyance in the future when you want to boot into a different OS but no longer have a choice to do so. Thus, you should always let the boot menu appear for at least 2 to 5 seconds if you are dual-booting.

System Failure   A number of options are available in the Startup And Recovery screen for use in case of problems. These include writing an event about the problem, sending out an alert to the network, and saving information about the problem to disk. These options come into play only in case of a major system problem, though.

Your options for handling system failures will be covered along with trouble-shooting information later in this chapter.

System Protection/System Restore

The System Protection (or System Restore) tab lets you disable/enable and configure the System Restore feature. When it's enabled on one or more drives, the operating system monitors the changes you make on your drives. From time to time it creates what is called a *restore point*. Then, if you have a system crash, it can restore your data back to the restore point. You can turn on System Restore for all drives on your system or for individual drives. Note that turning off System Restore on the system drive (the drive on which the OS is installed) automatically turns it off on all drives.

For more on System Restore, see the section "Creating Restore Points" in Chapter 12.

Remote

The Remote tab lets you enable or disable Remote Assistance and Remote Desktop. Remote Assistance permits people to access this system in response to requests issued by the local user using the Windows Remote Assistance tool. Remote Desktop permits people to log into the system at any time using the Remote Desktop Connection tool.

This can help an administrator or other support person troubleshoot problems with the machine from a remote location.

Remote Assistance is enabled by default. It is handled at two levels. Having just Remote Assistance turned on allows the person connecting to view the computer's screen. To let that person take over the computer and be able to control the keyboard and mouse, click Advanced, and then in the Remote Control section, click Allow This Computer To Be Controlled Remotely. You can also configure Remote Desktop here.

Automatic Updates (Windows XP Only)

The Automatic Updates tab in Windows lets you configure how you want to handle updating the OS. You can specify that you want to automatically download updates or notify the user when updates are available (but not automatically install them), or you can turn off the feature. You can also specify that you want the operating system to notify you again of updates you declined to download at an earlier point in time.

For more on automatic updates, see the section "Updating Windows" in Chapter 12.

The Security Center Applet

The Security Center applet, knows as Action Center in Windows 7 (`WSCUI.CPL`) is used to manage the firewall, automatic updates, and virus protection. From here, you can manage settings for Internet options as well and see any maintenance or troubleshooting issues that you need to attend to.

The Windows Firewall Applet

As the name implies, the Windows Firewall applet (`FIREWALL.CPL`) can be used to manage the firewall included with the operating system. Figure 13.5 shows the interface for Windows 7.

The Power Options Applet

The Power Options applet (`POWERCFG.CPL`) allows you to configure a power plan dictating when devices, namely the display and the computer, will to turn off or be put to sleep. Through the advanced settings, you can configure the need to enter a password to revive the devices as well as configure wireless adapter settings, Internet options (namely JavaScript), and the system cooling policy.

The Command Prompt

Although the exam focuses on the Windows operating systems, it tests a great deal of concepts that carry over from the Microsoft Disk Operating System (MS-DOS). MS-DOS was never meant to be extremely user friendly. Its roots are in CP/M, which in turn has its roots in UNIX. Both of these older OSs are command line based, and so is MS-DOS. In other words, they all use long strings of commands typed in at the computer keyboard to perform operations. Some people prefer this type of interaction with the computer, including many folks with technical backgrounds. Although Windows has left the full command-line interface behind, it still contains a bit of DOS, and you get to it through the command prompt.

FIGURE 13.5   The Windows Firewall control panel applet on a Windows 7 computer

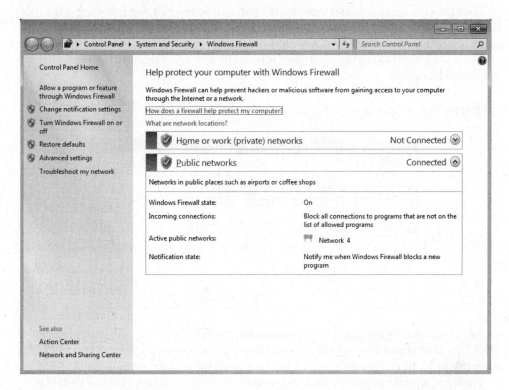

Although you can't tell from looking at it, the Windows command prompt is actually a Windows program that is intentionally *designed* to have the look and feel of a DOS command line. Because it is, despite its appearance, a Windows program, the command prompt provides all the stability and configurability you expect from Windows. You can access a command prompt by running CMD.EXE.

A number of diagnostic utilities are often run at the command prompt, and they can be broken into two categories: networking and operating system. Because knowledge of each is required for the exam, they are discussed in the order in which they appear in the exam objectives, starting with the networking command-line tools.

Networking Command-Line Tools

The networking command-line tools you are expected to know for this exam are PING, TRACERT, NETSTAT, IPCONFIG, NET, NSLOOKUP, and NBTSTAT.

PING Command

The PING command is one of the most useful commands in the TCP/IP protocol. It sends a series of packets to another system, which in turn sends back a response. This utility can be extremely useful for troubleshooting problems with remote hosts. Pings are also called ICMP echo requests/replies because they use the ICMP protocol.

The PING command indicates whether the host can be reached and how long it took for the host to send a return packet. Across wide area network links, the time value will be much larger than across healthy LAN links.

The syntax for PING is ping *hostname* or ping *IP address*. Figure 13.6 shows what a ping should look like.

FIGURE 13.6 A successful ping

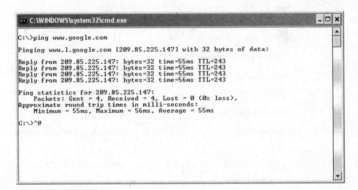

As you can see, by pinging with the hostname, we found the host's IP address thanks to DNS. The time is how long in milliseconds it took to receive the response. On a LAN, you want this to be 10 milliseconds (ms) or less, but 55ms for an Internet ping isn't too bad.

There are several options for the PING command, and you can see them all by typing **ping /?** at the command prompt. Table 13.2 lists some of the more useful ones.

TABLE 13.2 PING options

Option	Function
-t	Persistent ping. Will ping the remote host until stopped by the client (by using Ctrl+C).
-n *count*	Specifies the number of echo requests to send.
-l *size*	Specifies the packet size to send.
ping -4 / ping -6	Use either the IPv4 or IPv6 network explicitly.

Some webmasters have configured their routers to block pings in order to avoid problems such as someone trying to eat up bandwidth with a *ping of death* (sending a persistent ping with a huge buffer to overwhelm the recipient). For example, if you ping www.microsoft.com, you won't get a response, even though the site is functional.

TRACERT Command

Tracert (trace route) is a command-line utility that enables you to verify the route to a remote host. Execute the command TRACERT *hostname*, where *hostname* is the computer name or IP address of the computer whose route you want to trace. Tracert returns the different IP addresses the packet was routed through to reach the final destination. The results also include the number of hops needed to reach the destination. If you execute the TRACERT command without any options, you see a help file that describes all the TRACERT switches.

This utility determines the intermediary steps involved in communicating with another IP host. It provides a road map of all the routing an IP packet takes to get from host A to host B.

Timing information from TRACERT can be useful for detecting a malfunctioning or overloaded router. Figure 13.7 shows what a TRACERT output looks like.

FIGURE 13.7   TRACERT output

```
C:\WINDOWS\system32\cmd.exe                                    _ □ ×
C:\>tracert www.google.com

Tracing route to www.l.google.com [209.85.225.147]
over a maximum of 30 hops:

  1    1 ms   <1 ms   <1 ms  192.168.1.1
  2    3 ms    1 ms    1 ms  192.168.0.1
  3   33 ms   33 ms   33 ms  mpls-dsl-gw02-194.mpls.qwest.net [207.225.140.19
4]
  4   33 ms   32 ms   32 ms  mpls-agw1.inet.qwest.net [65.103.30.9]
  5   33 ms   33 ms   33 ms  min-core-01.inet.qwest.net [205.171.128.129]
  6   43 ms   42 ms  100 ms  chp-brdr-03.inet.qwest.net [67.14.8.190]
  7   43 ms   43 ms   43 ms  63.146.27.22
  8   44 ms   43 ms   44 ms  ae-11-53.car1.Chicago1.Level3.net [4.68.101.66]

  9   44 ms   44 ms   44 ms  GOOGLE-INC.car1.Chicago1.Level3.net [4.79.208.18
]
 10   45 ms   48 ms   44 ms  209.85.240.158
 11   60 ms   54 ms   54 ms  72.14.232.141
 12   58 ms   68 ms   54 ms  209.85.241.35
 13   67 ms   54 ms   55 ms  209.85.248.102
 14   55 ms   54 ms   54 ms  iy-in-f147.google.com [209.85.225.147]

Trace complete.

C:\>^@
```

NETSTAT Command

The Netstat utility is used to check out the inbound and outbound TCP/IP connections on your machine. It can also be used to view packet statistics, such as how many packets have been sent and received and the number of errors.

When used without any options, the NETSTAT command produces output similar to what you see in Figure 13.8, which shows all the outbound TCP/IP connections.

FIGURE 13.8 NETSTAT output

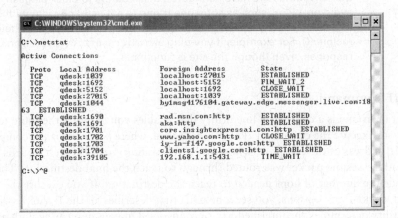

There are several useful command-line options for NETSTAT, as shown in Table 13.3.

TABLE 13.3 NETSTAT options

Option	Function
–a	Displays all connections and listening ports.
–b	Displays the executable involved in creating each connection or listening port. In some cases, well-known executables host multiple independent components, and in these cases the sequence of components involved in creating the connection or listening port is displayed. In this case, the executable name is in brackets, [ ], at the bottom; at the top is the component it called; and so forth until TCP/IP was reached. Note that this option can be time consuming and will fail unless you have sufficient permissions.
–e	Displays Ethernet statistics. This may be combined with the –s option.
–f	Displays fully qualified domain names (FQDNs) for foreign addresses.
–n	Displays addresses and port numbers in numerical form.
–o	Displays the owning process ID associated with each connection.
–p proto	Shows connections for the protocol specified by proto; proto may be any of the following: TCP, UDP, TCPv6, or UDPv6. If used with the –s option to display per-protocol statistics, proto may be IP, IPv6, ICMP, ICMPv6, TCP, TCPv6, UDP, or UDPv6.

Option	Function
-r	Displays the routing table.
-s	Displays per-protocol statistics. By default, statistics are shown for IP, IPv6, ICMP, ICMPv6, TCP, TCPv6, UDP, and UDPv6; the -p option may be used to specify a subset of the default.

IPCONFIG Command

With Windows-based operating systems, you can determine the network settings on the client's network interface cards, as well as any that a DHCP server has leased to your computer, by typing the following at a command prompt: **ipconfig /all**.

IPCONFIG /ALL also gives you full details on the duration of your current lease. You can verify whether a DHCP client has connectivity to a DHCP server by releasing the client's IP address and then attempting to lease an IP address. You can conduct this test by typing the following sequence of commands from the DHCP client at a command prompt:

```
ipconfig /release
ipconfig /renew
```

IPCONFIG is one of the first tools to use when experiencing problems accessing resources because it will show you whether an address has been issued to the machine. If the address displayed falls within the 169.254.*x*.*x* category, this means the client was unable to reach the DHCP server and has defaulted to Automatic Private IP Addressing (APIPA), which will prevent the network card from communicating outside its subnet, if not altogether. Table 13.4 lists useful switches for IPCONFIG.

TABLE 13.4   IPCONFIG switches

Switch	Purpose
/ALL	Shows full configuration information
/RELEASE	Releases the IP address, if you are getting addresses from a Dynamic Host Configuration Protocol (DHCP) server
/RELEASE6	Releases the IPv6 addresses
/RENEW	Obtains a new IP address from a DHCP server

TABLE 13.4   IPCONFIG switches *(continued)*

Switch	Purpose
/RENEW6	Obtains a new IPv6 address from a DHCP server
/FLUSHDNS	Flushes the domain name server (DNS) name resolver cache

In the Linux world, a utility similar to ipconfig is ifconfig.

Figure 13.9 shows output from IPCONFIG, and Figure 13.10 shows you the output from IPCONFIG /ALL.

FIGURE 13.9   IPCONFIG output

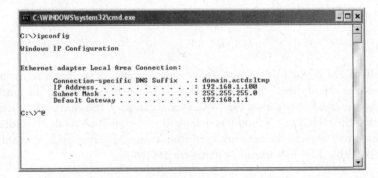

In Exercise 13.3, you will renew an IP address on a Windows XP system within the graphical interface. In Exercise 13.4, you will perform this same operation in Windows 7/ Vista, and Exercise 13.5 shows you how to renew your lease from the command line.

EXERCISE 13.3

Renew an IP Address in Windows XP System

1. Choose Start ➢ Control Panel and then click the Network Connections icon. A list of the LAN or high-speed Internet connections presently known appears. (This exercise assumes you are using Windows XP and dynamic IP assignments from a DHCP server.)

2. Right-click your connection and choose Status. In the connection status box, the first tab that appears is General, and it displays information such as whether you are connected, the speed of the connection, and how long the connection has been there.

3. Click the Support tab. Here, you can see whether the address is static or assigned by DHCP, the present address, the subnet mask, and the default gateway values.

EXERCISE 13.3 *(continued)*

4. Click the Details button. This expands the information by also showing you the physical (MAC) address and lease information, among other things. Note the date and time of the Lease Obtained values. Click Close.

5. Back at the Support tab, click the Repair button. This will attempt to establish or renew the connection. If the network (DHCP) is functioning properly, a notification that it finished will appear in a short time. Click the Details button again. The Lease Obtained values should reflect the current date and time.

FIGURE 13.10   IPCONFIG /ALL output

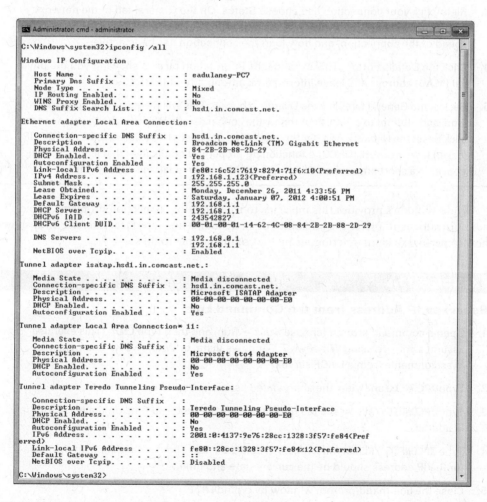

The interface in Windows XP provides a convenient way to interact with the network components. Exercise 13.4 shows how to perform a similar action in Windows Vista.

EXERCISE 13.4

Renew an IP Address in Windows 7/Vista

1. From the Start menu, right-click on Network to open the Network and select Properties and Sharing Center. (This exercise assumes the use of Windows 7 or Vista and dynamic IP assignments from a DHCP server.)

2. In the left-hand pane, click Manage Network Connections (in Windows 7 this is Change Adapter Settings). This will open a new window displaying your network connections.

3. Right-click your connection and choose Status. On the General tab of the network connection's status you will see information such as whether you are connected, the speed of the connection, and how long the connection has been active.

4. Click the Details button. This expands the information by also showing you the physical (MAC) address and lease information, among other things.

5. Back at the General tab, click the Diagnose button. This will diagnose any network problems and attempt to establish or renew the connection (in Windows Vista you need to click Reset the Network Adapter for Local Area Connection to release/renew the DHCP lease.) If the network (DHCP) is functioning properly, a notification that it finished will appear in a short time. If not, Windows will attempt to repair the connection.

While Windows provides this interface to troubleshoot connection problems, some administrators still prefer the reliability of a command-line interface. Exercise 13.5 shows how to perform a similar action, using the command line to do so.

EXERCISE 13.5

Renew an IP Address from the Command Line

1. Open a command prompt (choose Start ➢ Run, and then type **CMD**). (This exercise assumes you are using Windows 7, Windows Vista, or Windows XP and dynamic IP assignments from a DHCP server.)

2. Type **IPCONFIG** and view the abbreviated list of information.

3. Type **IPCONFIG /ALL** to see the full list. Notice the date and time on the lease for the IP address.

4. Type **IPCONFIG /RENEW** followed by **IPCONFIG /ALL**. The date and time on the lease for the IP address should be the current date and time.

5. Close the command-prompt window by typing **EXIT**.

NET Command

Depending on the version of Windows you are using, NET can be one of the most powerful commands at your disposal. While all Windows versions include a NET command, the capabilities of it differ based on whether it is server or workstation based and the version of the operating system.

While always command line based, this tool allows you to do almost anything you want with the operating system.

Table 13.5 shows common NET switches.

TABLE 13.5 NET switches

Switch	Purpose
NET ACCOUNTS	Set account options (password age, length, etc.).
NET COMPUTER	Add and delete computer accounts.
NET CONFIG	See network-related configuration.
NET CONTINUE, NET PAUSE, NET START, NET STATISTICS, and NET STOP	Control services.
NET FILE	Close open files.
NET GROUP and NET LOCALGROUP	Create, delete, and change groups.
NET HELP	See general help.
NET HELPMSG	See specific message help.
NET NAME	See the name of the current machine and user.
NET PRINT	Interact with print queues and print jobs.
NET SEND	Send a message to user(s).
NET SESSION	See session statistics.
NET SHARE	Create a share.
NET TIME	Set the time to that of another computer.
NET USE	Connect to a share.
NET USER	Add, delete, and see information about a user.
NET VIEW	See available resources.

These commands are invaluable troubleshooting aids when you cannot get the graphical interface to display properly. You can also use them when interacting with hidden ($) and administrative shares that do not appear within the graphical interface.

The NET command used with the SHARE parameter enables you to create shares from the command prompt, using this syntax:

NET SHARE <share_name>=<drive_letter>:<path>

To share the C:\EVAN directory as SALES, you would use the following command:

NET SHARE SALES=C:\EVAN

You can use other parameters with NET SHARE to set other options. Table 13.6 summarizes the most commonly used parameters.

TABLE 13.6 NET SHARE parameters

Parameter	Purpose
/DELETE	Stop sharing a folder.
/REMARK	Add a comment for browsers.
/UNLIMITED	Set the user limit to Maximum Allowed.
/USERS	Set a specific user limit.

The NET /? command is basically a catch-all help request. It will instruct you to use the NET command you are interested in for more information. Sample output from this command is shown in Figure 13.11.

FIGURE 13.11 NET /? output

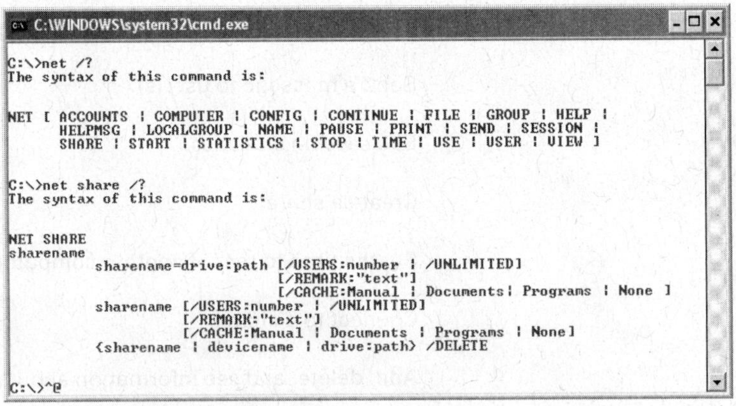

NSLOOKUP Command

Nslookup is a command-line utility that enables you to verify entries on a DNS server. You can use the NSLOOKUP command in two modes: interactive and noninteractive. In interactive mode, you start a session with the DNS server in which you can make several requests. In noninteractive mode, you specify a command that makes a single query of the DNS server. If you want to make another query, you must type another noninteractive command.

One of the key things that must take place to effectively use TCP/IP is that a hostname must resolve to an IP address—an action usually performed by a DNS server.

NBTSTAT Command

Nbtstat is a command-line utility that shows NetBIOS over TCP/IP information. While not used as often as other entries in this category, it can be useful when trying to diagnose a problem with NetBIOS name resolution. The /? parameter can be used to see the available switches. Sample output from this command is shown in Figure 13.12.

FIGURE 13.12   NBTSTAT /? output

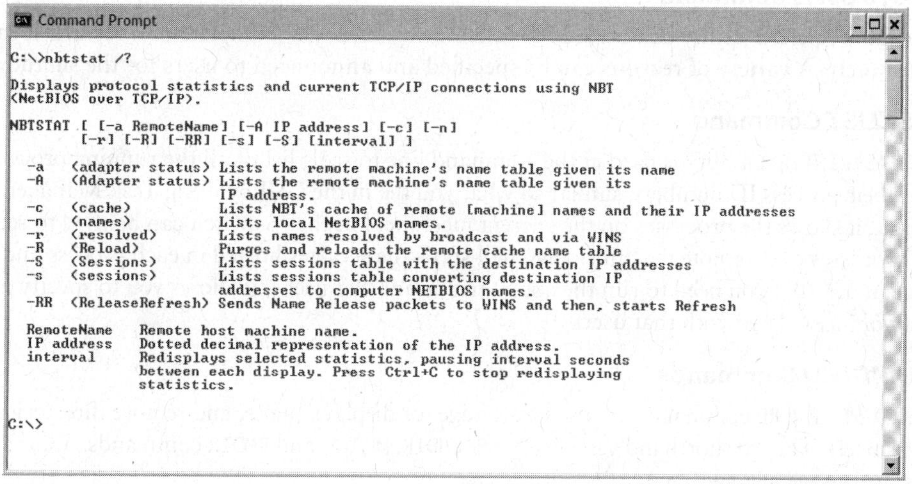

OS Command-Line Tools

The OS command-line tools you are expected to know for this exam are TASKKILL, BOOTREC, SHUTDOWN, TASKLIST, MD, RD, CD, DEL, FDISK, FORMAT, COPY, XCOPY, ROBOCOPY, DISKPART, SFC, CHKDSK, and /?. They are discussed in the sections that follow.

TASKKILL Command

The TASKKILL.EXE utility is used to terminate processes. Those processes can be identified by either name or process ID number (PID). The process can exist on the machine where the administrator is sitting (the default) or on another machine, in which case you signify the other system by using the /S switch.

The /IM name is used to specify an (image) name of a process to kill and can include the wildcard (*) characters. If the process ID number is used in place of the name, then the /PID switch is needed. The processes in question are the same which can be killed through the Task Manager. There are two signals that can be sent: the default is SIGTERM (a gentle kill, related to code 15) and the /F switch issues a SIGKILL (a terminate at all cost kill, related to code 9).

BOOTREC Command

The BOOTREC.EXE utility can be run in Windows 7 or Windows Vista to interact with the Master Boot Record (MBR), boot sector, or Boot Configuration Data (BCD) store. It cannot be used with Windows XP because it uses a different boot structure.

To run the tool, you must boot from the installation disk, choose the Repair Your Computer option and enter the *Recovery Console*. Choose Command Prompt from System Recovery Options and then type **bootrec.exe**.

The options for BOOTREC are /Fixboot (to write a new boot sector), /Fixmbr (to write a new MBR), /RebuildBCD (to rebuild the BCD store), and /ScanOS (to scan all disks for installations the Boot Manager menu is not listing).

SHUTDOWN Command

The SHUTDOWN.EXE utility can be used to schedule a shutdown (complete or a restart) locally or remotely. A variety of reasons can be specified and announced to users for the shutdown.

TASKLIST Command

The TASKLIST.EXE utility is used at the command line to see a list of all the running processes (and their process ID number), similar to what you see in the GUI by using Task Manager. By default, it shows the processes on the current machine, but the /S switch can be used to see the processes on a remote machine. /SVC will show the services hosted in each process and you can use /U if you need to run the command as another user (/P allows you to specify a password associated with that user).

CD/MD/RD Commands

The CD, MD, and RD commands are used to change (or display), make, and remove directories, respectively. They're shorthand versions of the CHDIR, MKDIR, and RMDIR commands. Table 13.7 lists their usage and switches.

TABLE 13.7 CD/MD/RD usage and switches

Command	Purpose
CD [path]	Changes to the specified directory.
CD /D [drive:][path]	Changes to the specified directory on the drive.
CD ..	Changes to the directory that is up one level.
CD\	Changes to the root directory of the drive.

Command	Purpose
MD *[drive:][path]*	Makes a directory in the specified path. If you don't specify a path, the directory will be created in your current directory.
RD *[drive:][path]*	Removes (deletes) the specified directory.
RD /S *[drive:][path]*	Removes all directories and files in the specified directory, including the specified directory itself.
RD /Q *[drive:][path]*	Quiet mode. You won't be asked whether you're sure you want to delete the specified directory when you use /S.

Now that you've looked at the available switches, let's use them in Exercise 13.6.

EXERCISE 13.6

Command-Line Directory Management

1. Open a command prompt. To do this, click Start ➢ Run, type **CMD** in the Open field, and click OK.

2. Change to the root of your C: drive by typing **CD /D C:** and pressing Enter. (Note: If you are already in C:, all you have to do is type **CD** and press Enter.)

3. Create a directory called C14 by typing **MD C14** and pressing Enter.

4. Change to the C14 directory by typing **CD C14** and pressing Enter.

5. Create several layers of subdirectories at once. Type **MD A1\B2\C3\D4** and press Enter.

Notice that these commands created each of the directories you specified. You now have a directory structure that looks like this: C:\C14\A1\B2\C3\D4.

6. Change back to your root directory by typing **CD**.

7. Attempt to delete the C14 directory by typing **RD C14** and pressing Enter.

Windows won't let you delete the directory because the directory is not empty. This is a safety measure. Now let's really delete it.

8. Delete the C14 directory and all subdirectories by typing **RD /S C14** and pressing Enter. You will be asked whether you're sure you want to delete the directory. If you are, type **y** and press Enter. To close the command prompt window, type **EXIT**.

Note that if you had used the /Q option in addition to /S, your system wouldn't have asked whether you were sure; it would have just deleted the directories.

DEL Command

The DEL command is used to delete files and directories at the command line. Wildcards can be used with it and ERASE performs the same operations.

FDISK Command

The FDISK command used to be included with earlier operating systems to make disk partitioning possible. This command does not exist in Windows 7, Vista, or XP, having been replaced with DISKPART. CompTIA lists it as a command to know, and for the exam you should know that it is not included with the current versions of Windows.

FORMAT Command

The FORMAT command is used to wipe data off disks and prepare them for new use. Before a hard disk can be formatted, it must have partitions created on it. (Partitioning was done in the DOS days with the FDISK command, but that command does not exist in Windows 7, Vista, or XP, having been replaced with DISKPART.) The syntax for FORMAT is as follows:

FORMAT [*volume*] [*switches*]

The *volume* parameter describes the drive letter (for example, D:), mount point, or volume name. Table 13.8 lists some common FORMAT switches.

TABLE 13.8 FORMAT switches

Switch	Purpose
/FS:[*filesystem*]	Specifies the type of file system to use (FAT, FAT32, or NTFS).
/V:[*label*]	Specifies the new volume label.
/Q	Executes a quick format.

There are other options as well to specify allocation sizes, the number of sectors per track, and the number of tracks per disk size. However, we don't recommend that you use these unless you have a very specific need. The defaults are just fine.

So, if you wanted to format your D: drive as NTFS, with a name of HDD2, you would type the following:

FORMAT D: /FS:NTFS /V:HDD2

Before you format any drive, be sure you have it backed up or are prepared to lose whatever is on it!

COPY Command

The COPY command does what it says: It makes a copy of a file in a second location. (To copy a file and then remove it from its original location, use the MOVE command.) Here's the syntax for COPY:

COPY [filename] [destination]

It's pretty straightforward. There are several switches for COPY, but in practice they are rarely used. The three most used ones are /A, which indicates an ASCII text file; /V, which verifies that the files are written correctly after the copy; and /Y, which suppresses the prompt asking whether you're sure you want to overwrite files if they exist in the destination directory.

The COPY command cannot be used to copy directories. Use XCOPY for that function.

One useful tip is to use wildcards. For example, in DOS (or at the command prompt), the asterisk (*) is a wildcard that means *everything*. So you could type **COPY** *.**EXE** to copy all files that have an .EXE filename extension, or you could type **COPY** *.* to copy all files in your current directory.

XCOPY Command

If you are comfortable with the COPY command, learning XCOPY shouldn't pose too many problems. It's basically an extension of COPY with one notable exception—it's designed to copy directories as well as files. The syntax is as follows:

XCOPY [source] [destination][switches]

There are 26 XCOPY switches; some of the more commonly used ones are listed in Table 13.9.

TABLE 13.9 XCOPY switches

Switch	Purpose
/A	Copies only files that have the Archive attribute set and does not clear the attribute. (Useful for making a quick backup of files while not disrupting a normal backup routine.)
/E	Copies directories and subdirectories, including empty directories.
/F	Displays full source and destination filenames when copying.
/G	Allows copying of encrypted files to a destination that does not support encryption.

TABLE 13.9   XCOPY switches *(continued)*

Switch	Purpose
/H	Copies hidden and system files as well.
/K	Copies attributes. (By default, XCOPY resets the Read-Only attribute.)
/O	Copies file ownership and ACL information (NTFS permissions).
/R	Overwrites read-only files.
/S	Copies directories and subdirectories but not empty directories.
/U	Copies only files that already exist in the destination.
/V	Verifies the size of each new file.

Perhaps the most important switch is /O. If you use XCOPY to copy files from one location to another, the file system creates a new version of the file in the new location without changing the old file. In NTFS, when a new file is created, it inherits permissions from its new parent directory. This could cause problems if you copy files. (Users who didn't have access to the file before might have access now.) If you want to retain the original permissions, use XCOPY /O.

ROBOCOPY Command

The ROBOCOPY utility (Robust File Copy for Windows) is included with Windows 7 and has the big advantage of being able to accept a plethora of specifications and keep NTFS permissions intact in its operations. The /MIR switch, for example, can be used to mirror a complete directory tree.

An excellent TechNet article on how to use Robocopy can be found at the following location:

http://technet.microsoft.com/en-us/magazine/ee851678.aspx.

DISKPART Command

The DISKPART utility shows the partitions and lets you manage them on the computer's hard drives.

SFC Command

The System File Checker (SFC) is a command-line-based utility that checks and verifies the versions of system files on your computer. If system files are corrupted, the SFC will replace the corrupted files with correct versions.

The syntax for the SFC command is as follows:

SFC [switch]

Table 13.10 lists the switches available for SFC.

TABLE 13.10 SFC switches

Switch	Purpose
/CACHESIZE=X	Sets the Windows File Protection cache size, in megabytes.
/PURGECACHE	Purges the Windows File Protection cache and scans all protected system files immediately.
/REVERT	Reverts SFC to its default operation.
/SCANFILE (Windows 7 and Vista only)	Scans a file that you specify and fixes problems if they are found.
/SCANNOW	Immediately scans all protected system files.
/SCANONCE	Scans all protected system files once.
/SCANBOOT	Scans all protected system files every time the computer is rebooted.
/VERIFYONLY	Scans protected system files and does not make any repairs or changes.
/VERIFYFILE	Identifies the integrity of the file specified, and does make any repairs or changes.
/OFFBOOTDIR	Does a repair of an offline boot directory.
/OFFFWINDIR	Does a repair of an offline windows directory.

To run the SFC, you must be logged in as an administrator or have administrative privileges. If the System File Checker in Windows XP discovers a corrupted system file, it will automatically overwrite the file by using a copy held in the %systemroot%\system32\ dllcache directory. If you believe that the dllcache directory is corrupted, you can use SFC /SCANNOW, SFC /SCANONCE, SFC /SCANBOOT, or SFC /PURGECACHE to repair its contents. Both Windows Vista and Windows 7 store the files in c:\windows\winsxs\Backup (where they are now protected by the system and only TrustedInstaller is allowed direct access to them—the cache is not rebuildable).

The C:\WINDOWS\SYSTEM32 directory is where many of the Windows system files reside.

If you attempt to run SFC from a standard command prompt in Windows Vista, for example, you will be told that you must be an administrator running a console session in order to continue. Rather than opening a standard command prompt, choose Start ➤ All Programs ➤ Accessories, then right-click Command Prompt and choose Run as administrator. The UAC will prompt you to continue, and then you can run SFC without a problem.

CHKDSK Command

You can use the Windows Chkdsk utility to create and display status reports for the hard disk. Chkdsk can also correct file system problems (such as cross-linked files) and scan for and attempt to repair disk errors. You can manually start Chkdsk by right-clicking the problem disk and selecting Properties. This will bring up the Properties dialog box for that disk, which shows the current status of the selected disk drive.

By clicking the Tools tab at the top of the dialog box and then clicking the Check Now button in the Error-Checking section, you can start Chkdsk. Exercise 13.7 walks you through starting Chkdsk in the GUI, while Exercise 13.8 does the same from the command line.

EXERCISE 13.7

Running Chkdsk within Windows

1. Open Windows Explorer by holding down the Windows key and pressing E.

2. Right-click C: and choose Properties.

3. Click the Tools tab and then click the Check Now button.

4. Choose your options: You can automatically fix file system errors and/or scan for and attempt recovery of bad sectors.

5. After you have selected your options, click Start.

EXERCISE 13.8

Running Chkdsk at the Command Line

1. Open a command prompt by clicking the Start button and typing **CMD** in the Start Search box of 7/Vista or in the Run box on XP.

2. Type **CHKDSK /f** and press Enter. The system will now scan for, and fix, file system errors.

/? Command

The HELP command does what it says: it gives you help. Actually, if you just type **HELP** and press Enter, your computer gives you a list of system commands you can type. To get more information, type the name of a command you want to know about after typing HELP. For example, type **HELP RD** and press Enter and you will get information about the RD command. You can also get the same help information by typing **/?** after the command.

The /? switch is slightly faster and provides more information than the HELP command. The HELP command provides information for only system commands (it does not include network commands). For example, if you type **HELP IPCONFIG** at a command prompt, you get no useful information (except to try /?); however, typing **IPCONFIG /?** provides the help file for the IPCONFIG command.

The Windows Registry

Windows configuration information is stored in a special configuration database known as the *Registry*. This centralized database contains environmental settings for various Windows programs. It also contains registration information that details which types of filename extensions are associated with which applications. So, when you double-click a file in Windows Explorer, the associated application runs and opens the file you double-clicked.

The Registry was introduced with Windows 95. Most OSs up until Windows 95 were configured through text files, which can be edited with almost any text editor. However, the Registry database is contained in a special binary file that can be edited only with the special Registry Editor provided with Windows.

Windows 7, Vista, and XP have what appear to be two applications that can be used to edit the Registry, REGEDIT and REGEDT32 (with no *I*), but in reality, REGEDT32 opens REGEDIT. They work similarly, but each has slightly different options for navigation and browsing.

The Registry is broken down into a series of separate areas called hives. The keys in each hive are divided into two basic sections—user settings and computer settings. In Windows, a number of files are created corresponding to each of the different hives. The names of most of these files do not have extensions, and their names are SYSTEM, SOFTWARE, SECURITY, SAM, and DEFAULT. One additional file whose name does have an extension is NTUSER.DAT.

The basic hives of the Registry are as follows:

HKEY_CLASSES_ROOT   Includes information about which filename extensions map to particular applications.

HKEY_CURRENT_USER   Holds all configuration information specific to a particular user, such as their Desktop settings and history information.

HKEY_LOCAL_MACHINE   Includes nearly all configuration information about the actual computer hardware and software.

HKEY_USERS   Includes information about all users who have logged on to the system. The HKEY_CURRENT_USER hive is actually a subkey of this hive.

HKEY_CURRENT_CONFIG   Provides quick access to a number of commonly needed keys that are otherwise buried deep in the HKEY_LOCAL_MACHINE structure.

Modifying a Registry Entry

If you need to modify the Registry, you can modify the values in the database or create new entries or keys. You will find the options for adding a new element to the Registry under the Edit menu. To edit an existing value, double-click the entry and modify it as needed. You need administrative-level access to modify the Registry.

WARNING   Windows uses the Registry extensively to store all kinds of information. Indeed, the Registry holds most, if not all, of the configuration information for Windows. Modifying the Registry in Windows is a potentially danger-ous task. Control Panel and other configuration tools are provided so you have graphical tools for modifying system settings. Directly modifying the Registry can have unforeseen—and unpleasant—results. You should modify the Registry only when told to do so by an extremely trustworthy source or if you are absolutely certain you have the knowledge to do so without causing havoc in the Registry.

Restoring the Registry

Windows stores Registry information in files on the hard drive. You can restore this infor-mation using the *Last Known Good Configuration* option, which restores the Registry from a backup of its last functional state. This can be used if—and only if—you have not logged in again since a change was made (otherwise, the Last Known Good Configuration option is useless).

To use this option, press F8 during startup and then select Last Known Good Configuration from the menu that appears. You can also back up the Registry files to the systemroot\repair directory by using the Windows Backup program, or you can save them to tape during a normal *backup*. To repair the Registry from a backup, overwrite the Registry files in systemroot\system32\config.

 Real World Scenario

Beware Editing the Registry

Just in case it hasn't sunk in yet, be careful editing the Registry. There is no Undo button, nor do you have the safety net of choosing not to save your edits before you close. Once you make the change, it's made, for better or for worse.

There have been countless examples throughout our careers of people going in to edit the Registry without really knowing what they were doing. In many cases, making small changes to the Registry, without having a viable backup, means having to reinstall Win-dows. At the very least, this is inconvenient.

Windows can help in this regard if you are in a networked environment with Windows-based servers. You can create system policies that prevent users from performing cer-tain tasks, and the most important task to restrict is running Registry editors.

Automated System Recovery (ASR), which is accessible through the Backup utility, can be used as a last-resort option for system recovery in Windows XP. Both Windows Vista and Windows 7 use the WinRE recovery environment to do a Complete PC Restore to achieve the same goal.

Virtual Memory

Another thing you may need to configure is *virtual memory*. Virtual memory uses what's called a swap file, or paging file. A swap file is actually hard drive space into which idle pieces of programs are placed while other active parts of programs are kept in or swapped into main memory. The programs running in Windows believe that their information is still in RAM, but Windows has moved the data into near-line storage on the hard drive. When the application needs the information again, it is swapped back into RAM so that it can be used by the processor.

Random access memory (RAM) is the computer's physical memory. The more RAM you put into the machine, the more items it can remember without looking anything up. And the larger the swap file, the fewer times the machine has swapped out the contents of what it is holding in memory. The maximum possible size of your swap file depends on the amount of disk space you have available on the drive where the swap file is placed. Windows configures the minimum and maximum swap file size automatically, but if you want Windows to handle the size of the swap file dynamically, you have to change the default setting by selecting System Managed Size in the Virtual Memory dialog box. We'll show you how to get there in a moment.

In Windows, the swap file is called PAGEFILE.SYS, and it's located in the root directory of the drive on which you installed the OS files. The swap file is a hidden file, so to see the file in Windows Explorer you must have the folder options configured to show hidden files. Typically, there's no reason to view the swap file in the file system because you'll use Control Panel to configure it. However, you may want to check its size, and in that case you'd use Windows Explorer.

The moral of the story: As with most things virtual, a swap file is not nearly as good as actual RAM, but it is better than nothing!

To modify the default Virtual Memory settings, follow these steps: Click Start ➤ Control Panel. Double-click the System icon, and select the Advanced tab in Windows XP (select Advanced System Settings from the left panel in Windows Vista and Windows 7). In the Performance area, click Settings. Next, click the Advanced tab (yes, another Advanced tab), and then, in the Virtual Memory area, click Change. Note that in addition to changing the swap file's size and how Windows handles it, you can specify the drive on which you want to place the file.

You should place the swap file on a drive with plenty of empty space. As a general rule, try to keep 20 percent of your drive space free for the overhead of various elements of the OS, like the swap file. Do not set the swap file to an extremely small size. If you make the swap file too small, the system can become unbootable, or at least unstable. In general, the swap file should be at least 1.5x the amount of RAM in the machine.

Administrative Tools

Microsoft has included a number of tools with each iteration of Windows to simplify system administration. While some tools have very specific purposes and are used only on rare occasions, you will come to rely on a number of them and access them on a regular basis. It is this latter set that we will examine in the following sections.

Task Manager

Task Manager lets you shut down nonresponsive applications selectively in all Windows versions. In current versions of Windows, it can do so much more, allowing you to see which processes and applications are using the most system resources, view network usage, see connected users, and so on. To display Task Manager, press Ctrl+Alt+Delete and click the Task Manager button (in earlier Windows versions, you only needed to press Ctrl+Alt+Delete). In Windows XP, whether the Security screen appears depends on whether you're using the Windows XP Welcome screen (you can change this setting on the Screen Saver tab of the computer's Display Properties dialog box). By default, in Windows 7, Vista, and XP, the Windows Security screen does not display if you press Ctrl+Alt+Del (unless it is a member of a domain); instead, Task Manager opens right away or you are given a set of tasks, among them Start Task Manager.

You can also right-click on an empty spot in the Taskbar and choose it from the pop-up menu that appears.

To get to Task Manager directly in any of the Windows versions that include it, you can press Ctrl+Shift+Esc.

Task Manager has at least five tabs: Applications, Processes, Performance, Networking, and Users. A sixth tab, Services, appears in Windows 7 and Windows Vista.

The Networking tab is shown only if your system has a network card installed (it is rare to find one that doesn't). The Users tab is displayed only if the computer you are working on is a member of a workgroup or is a stand-alone computer. The Users tab is unavailable on some computers that are members of a network domain (depending on the OS and the configuration). Let's look at these tabs, in the order of their appearance, in more detail:

Applications   The Applications tab lets you see which tasks are open on the machine. You also see the status of each task, which can be either Running or Not Responding. If a task/ application has stopped responding (that is, it's hung), you can select the task in the list and click End Task. Doing so closes the program, and you can try to open it again. Often, although certainly not always, if an application hangs you have to reboot the computer to prevent the same thing from happening again shortly after you restart the application. You can also use the Applications tab to switch to a different task or create new tasks.

Processes   The Processes tab lets you see the names of all the processes running on the machine. You also see the user account that's running each process as well as how much CPU and RAM resources each process is using. To end a process, select it in the list and click End Process. Be careful with this choice because ending some processes can cause Windows to shut down. If you don't know what a particular process does, you can look for it in any search engine and find a number of sites that will explain it.

You can also change the priority of a process in Task Manager's Processes display by right-clicking on the name of the process and choosing Set Priority. The six priorities, from lowest to highest, are as follows:

Low   For applications that need to complete sometime but that you don't want interfering with other applications. On a numerical scale from 0 to 31, this equates to a base priority of 4.

Below Normal   For applications that don't need to drop all the way down to Low. This equates to a base priority of 6.

Normal   The default priority for most applications. This equates to a base priority of 8.

Above Normal   For applications that don't need to boost all the way to High. This equates to a base priority of 10.

High   For applications that must complete soon, when you don't want other applications to interfere with the applications' performance. This equates to a base priority of 13.

Realtime   For applications that must have the processor's attention to handle time-critical tasks. Applications can be run at this priority only by a member of the Administrators group. This equates to a base priority of 24.

If you decide to change the priority of an application, you'll be warned that doing so may make it unstable. You can generally ignore this option when changing the priority to Low, Below Normal, Above Normal, or High, but you should heed this warning when changing applications to the Realtime priority. Realtime means that the processor gives precedence to this process over all others—over security processes, over spooling, over everything—and this is sure to make the system unstable.

Task Manager changes the priority only for that instance of the running application. The next time the process is started, priorities revert back to that of the base (typically Normal).

Services (Windows 7 and Vista only)   The Services tab lists the name of each running service as well as the process ID associated with it and its description, status, and group. A button labeled Services appears on this tab, and clicking it will open the MMC console for Services, where you can configure each service. Within Task Manager, right-clicking a service will open a context menu listing three choices: Start Service, Stop Service, and Go To Process (this takes you to the Processes tab).

Performance   The Performance tab contains a variety of information, including overall CPU usage percentage, a graphical display of CPU usage history, page-file usage in MB, and a graphical display of page-file usage. This tab also provides you with additional memory-related information such as physical and kernel memory usage as well as the total number of handles, threads, and processes. Total, limit, and peak commit-charge information also appears. Some of the items are beyond the scope of this book, but it's good to know that you can use the Performance tab to keep track of system performance. Note that the number of processes, CPU usage percentage, and commit-charge information always appear at the bottom of the Task Manager window, regardless of which tab you have currently selected.

Networking   The Networking tab provides you with a graphical display of the performance of your network connection. It also tells you the network adapter name, link speed, and state. If you have more than one network adapter installed in the machine, you can select the appropriate adapter to see graphical usage data for that adapter. Bluetooth would show up on this screen as well.

Users   The Users tab provides you with information about the users connected to the local machine. You'll see the username, ID, status, client name, and session type. You can right-click the name of any connected user to perform a variety of functions, including sending the user a message, disconnecting the user, logging off the user, and initiating a remote-control session to the user's machine.

Use Task Manager whenever the system seems bogged down by an unresponsive application.

MMC

Microsoft created the Microsoft Management Console (MMC) interface as a front end in which you can run administrative tools. Many administrators don't even know that applications they use regularly run within an MMC.

Computer Management

Windows includes a piece of software to manage computer settings: the Computer Management Console. The Computer Management Console can manage more than just the installed hardware devices; the Computer Management Console can manage all the services running on a computer, in addition to a Device Manager that functions almost identically to the one that has existed since Windows 9x. It contains an *Event Viewer* to show any system errors and events as well as methods to configure the software components of all the computer's hardware.

To access the Computer Management Console, you can go through Administrative Tools in Control Panel or just right-click the Computer/My Computer icon and choosing Manage.

After you are in Computer Management, you will see all of the tools available. This is one power-packed interface, which includes the following system tools:

Device Manager Lets you manage hardware devices.

Event Viewer A link to the tool that allows you to view application error logs, security audit records, and system errors. This tool is shown in Figure 13.13 as it would appear in Windows 7.

FIGURE 13.13 Event Viewer's opening screen

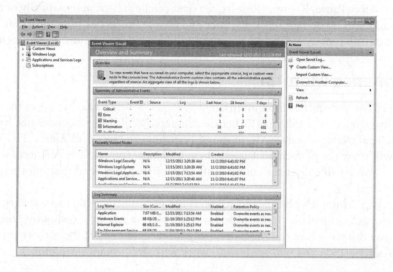

Shared Folders Allows you to manage all of your computer's shared folders.

Local Users And Groups Allows you to create and manage local user and group accounts.

Performance Logs And Alerts Shows you how your system hardware is performing, and alerts you if system performance goes under a threshold you set.

Computer Management also has the Storage area, which lets you manage removable media, defragment your hard drives, or manage partitions through the Disk Management utility. Finally, you can manage system services and applications through Computer Management as well.

Administrative Shares vs. Local Shares

Administrative shares are created on servers running Windows on the network for administrative purposes. These shares can differ slightly based on which OS is running, but end with a dollar sign ($) to make them hidden. There is one for each volume on a hard drive (C$, D$, etc.) as well as admin$ (the root folder – usually C:\WINDOWS), and print$ (where the print drivers are located). These are created for use by administrators and usually require administrator privileges to access.

Local shares, as the name implies, are those that are created locally and are visible with the icon of a hand beneath them.

Services

This tool (SERVICES.MSC) is an MMC snap-in that allows you to interact with the services running on the computer. Select Start ➢ Control Panel ➢ Administrative Tools and choose Services and you will see those configured on the system. The status of the services will typically either be started or stopped, and you can right-click and make a choice from the context menu: Start, Stop, Pause, Resume, Restart. Services can be started automatically or manually or be disabled. If you right-click a service and choose Properties from the menu, you can choose the startup type as well as see the path to the executable and any dependencies.

Performance Monitor

Performance Monitor differs a bit in different versions of Windows, but it has the same purpose throughout: to display performance counters. While lumped under one heading, two tools are available—System Monitor and Performance Logs And Alerts. The System Monitor will show the performance counters in graphical format. The Performance Logs And Alerts utility will collect the counter information and then send that information to a console or event log.

Performance Monitor's objects and counters are very specific; you can use Performance Monitor as a general troubleshooting tool as well as a security troubleshooting tool. For instance, you can see where resources are being utilized and where the activity is coming from. In Exercise 13.9, you will see how to work with Performance Monitor.

EXERCISE 13.9

Working with Performance Monitor

1. Select Start ➢ Control Panel ➢ Administrative Tools, and choose Performance. (Windows 7 calls it Performance Monitor, while Windows Vista calls it Reliability and Performance Monitor.)

2. Click the Add Counters button (depending on the OS, you may need to choose the Performance Monitor section before the Add Counters button will show), and choose to add the Processor Performance object.

3. Add the %Processor Time counter (if it is not added by default), and then click Close.

4. Choose Start ➢ Search ➢ For Files And Folders and click the Search Now button without specifying any particular files to look for. Quickly change to Performance Monitor and watch the impact of this search on the processor. This action is time consuming and therefore will help you notice the changes that take place in Performance Monitor.

EXERCISE 13.9 *(continued)*

5. Run the same operation again, but this time change your view within Performance Monitor to histogram (click the two buttons to the left of the plus sign [+]).

6. Run the same operation again, and change your view within Performance Monitor to report (click the button directly to the left of the plus sign [+]).

7. Exit Performance Monitor.

Task Scheduler

Accessible either beneath Computer Management or via Start ➢ All Programs ➢ Accessories ➢ System Tools, the Task Scheduler (Scheduled Tasks in Windows XP) allows you to configure an application to run automatically or at any regular interval (see Figure 13.14). There are a number of terms used to describe the options for configuring tasks: *action* (what the task actually does), *condition* (an optional requirement that must be met before a task runs), *setting* (any property that affects the behavior of a task), and *trigger* (the required condition for the task to run).

For example, you could configure a report to automatically run (action) every Tuesday (trigger) when the system has been idle for 10 minutes (condition), and only when requested (setting). Figure 13.15 shows the dialog boxes used to configure the task.

FIGURE 13.14   Windows Task Scheduler in Windows Vista

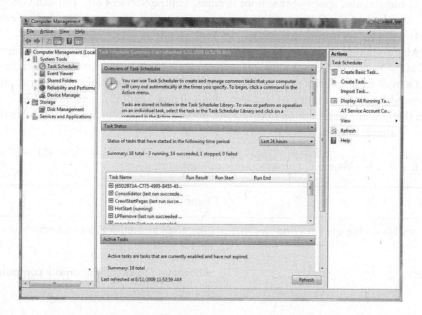

FIGURE 13.15   Task configuration dialog boxes in Windows Vista

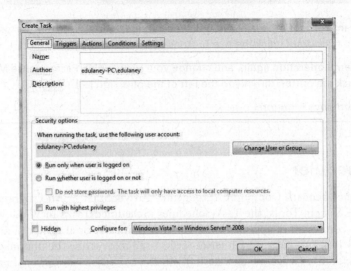

Windows System Configuration Tools

The Msconfig system configuration tool differs a bit in the tabs that it has based on the Windows version you are running, but the key ones are General, Boot, Services, Startup, and Tools. In Windows XP, Boot is actually Boot.ini, and this tab lets you modify the BOOT.INI file and also specify other boot options. On the Services tab, you can view the services installed on the system and their current status (running or stopped). You can also enable and disable services as necessary.

The Msinfo32 tool, shown in Figure 13.16, displays a fairly thorough list of settings on the machine. You cannot change any values from here, but you can search, export, save, and run a number of utilities (accessed through the Tools menu option). There are a number of command-line options that can be used when starting Msinfo32, and Table 13.11 summarizes them; with the exception of three that are available in Windows 7 and Vista as well, most are available only in Windows XP.

TABLE 13.11   Msinfo32 command-line options

Option	Function
/category (available only in Windows XP)	Specifies a category to be selected when the utility starts
/computer	Allows you to specify a remote computer to run the utility on

Option	Function
/nfo	Creates a file and saves it in .NFO format
/pch (available only in Windows XP)	Displays the history view
/report	Creates a file and saves it in .TXT format
/showcategories (available only in Windows XP)	Shows category IDs instead of friendly names
/? (available only in Windows XP)	Shows the command-line options available for use with the utility

FIGURE 13.16   The Msinfo32 interface shows configuration values for the system.

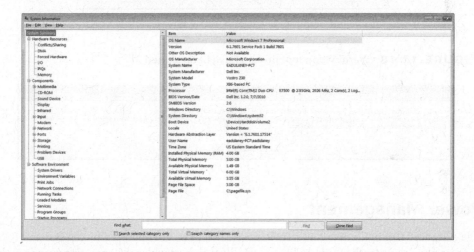

Another utility to know is the *DxDiag* (DirectX Diagnostic) tool, shown in Figure 13.17. This tool (which can be summoned alone or from the Tools menu of Msinfo32) allows you to test DirectX functionality. When you start it, you can also verify that your drivers have been signed by Microsoft, as shown in Figure 13.18. DirectX is a collection of application programming interfaces (APIs) related to multimedia.

Finally, *MSTSC* (Remote Desktop Connection) is used to configure remote desktop connections. It offers a glut of options, as shown in Figure 13.19.

FIGURE 13.17 The DxDiag tool lets you test functionality with DirectX components.

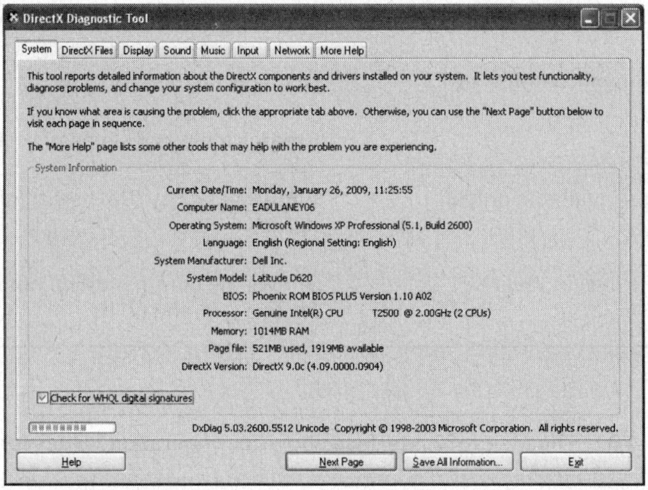

FIGURE 13.18 Verification that drivers have been signed

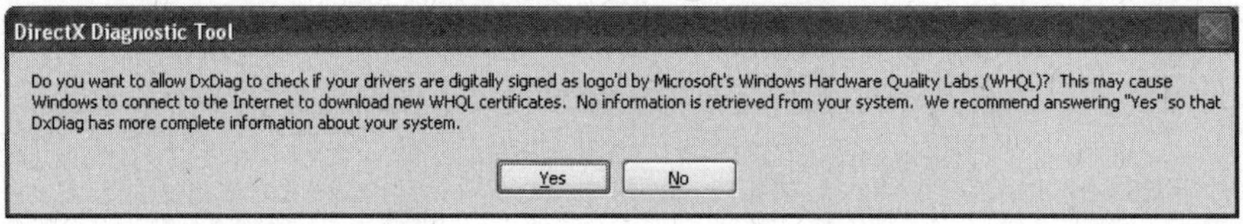

Power Management

The Advanced Configuration Power Interface (ACPI) must be supported by the system BIOS in order to work properly. With ACPI, it is the BIOS that provides the operating system with the necessary methods for controlling the hardware. This is in contrast to Advanced Power Management (APM), which only gave a limited amount of power to the operating system and let the BIOS do all the real work. Because of this, it is not uncommon to find legacy systems that can support APM but not ACPI.

There are three main states of power management common in most operating systems:

Hibernate This state saves all the contents of memory to the hard drive, preserves all data and applications exactly where they are, and allows the computer to completely power off. When the system comes out of hibernation, it returns to its previous state.

Standby This state leaves memory active but saves everything else to disk.

Suspend/Sleep In most operating systems, Sleep is used interchangeably with *Hibernate*. In Windows XP, Hibernate is used instead of Suspend. Windows 7 and Windows Vista offer both Hibernate and Sleep (not Suspend). Sleep puts the system in a low-power state, while Hibernate turns it off.

FIGURE 13.19 Options for MSTSC

If you are interested in saving power with a system that is not accessed often, one option is to employ Wake on LAN (WoL). Wake on LAN is an Ethernet standard implemented via a card that allows a "sleeping" machine to awaken when it receives a wakeup signal. Wake on LAN cards have more problems than standard network cards. In our opinion, this is because they're always on. In some cases, you'll be unable to get the card working again unless you unplug the PC's power supply and reset the card.

Windows offers quite a range of choices from the Shut Down (non–Windows XP/ Vista) or Turn Off Computer (Windows XP and Vista) command under the Start menu (in Vista, it appears as an icon of an on/off button and does not have a label). Note that with a configuration called Fast User Switching, Windows XP also displays Shut Down rather than Turn Off Computer. When you select this option, Windows presents you with several choices. Exactly which options are available depends on the Windows version you are running.

Whether you see Shut Down or Turn Off Computer has a lot to do with the way your user interface is configured (Classic View, for example). Regardless of the name of the option, it performs the same function.

The possible choices are as follows:

Shut Down/Turn Off (Windows XP and Vista)   This option writes any unsaved data to disk, closes any open applications, makes a copy of the Registry, and gets the computer ready to be powered off. Depending on the OS, the computer is then powered down automatically, or you'll see a black screen with the message *It's now safe to turn off your computer.* In this case, you can power off the computer or press Ctrl+Alt+Del to reboot the computer.

Restart   This option works the same as the first option, but instead of shutting down completely, it automatically reboots the computer with a warm reboot.

Stand By (Windows XP only)   This option places the computer into a low-power state. The monitor and hard disks are turned off, and the computer uses less power. To resume working, press a key on the keyboard; the computer is returned to its original state. In this state, information in memory is not saved to hard disk, so if a power loss occurs, any data in memory will be lost.

Switch User   This option allows you to switch users on a machine without closing programs. This is generally not recommended in a work environment for the security reasons associated with leaving programs running.

Log Off   This option is recommended over Switch User because it closes all open programs and then logs off the user—allowing another user to then log on.

Lock   This option leaves programs running but locks the computer and requires the user's password to be entered again before the session can continue.

Hibernate   This option saves the session to disk and turns off the computer so no power is used. When the computer is powered back up, the session resumes.

Sleep   This option keeps the session in memory and puts the computer in a low-power state from which you can quickly resume. This is like Hibernate, but without fully powering down the computer.

If you enable Hibernation on a Windows XP machine, you can place the computer into hibernation by holding down the Shift key while clicking Stand By on the Turn Off Computer screen. Using the Hibernation feature, any information in memory is saved to disk before the computer is turned off. Going into and coming out of hibernation takes more time than going into and coming out of Stand By/Sleep mode.

Sleep timers allow you to configure a system to sleep for certain periods of time to conserve power. While not included with the operating system, a number of downloadable programs can be found that will turn the machine off at a certain time or after some specified condition is met.

Disk Management

Where there are files, there are disks. That is to say, all the files and programs we've talked about so far reside on disks. Disks are physical storage devices, and they also need to be managed. There are several aspects to disk management. One is concerned with getting disks ready to be able to store files and programs; another deals with backing up your data. Yet another involves checking the health of disks and optimizing their performance. We'll look at these aspects in more detail.

Getting Disks Ready to Store Files and Programs

For a hard disk to be able to hold files and programs, it has to be partitioned and formatted. Partitioning is the process of creating logical divisions on a hard drive. A hard drive can have one or more partitions. Formatting is the process of creating and configuring a file allocation table (FAT) and creating the root directory. Several file system types are supported by the various versions of Windows, such as FAT16, FAT32, and NTFS.

New Technology Filesystem (NTFS) is available with all the versions of Windows you need to know for the exam, but they also recognize and support FAT16 and FAT32. The file table for the NTFS is called the Master File Table (MFT).

The following is a list of the major file systems that are used with Windows and the differences among them:

File allocation table (FAT)   An acronym for the file on this file system used to keep track of where files are. It's also the name given to this type of file system, introduced in 1981. The file systems for many OSs have been built on the design of FAT, but without its limitations. A FAT file system uses the *8.3 naming convention* (eight letters for the name, a period, and then a three-letter file identifier). This later became known as *FAT16* (to differentiate it from FAT32) because it used a 16-bit binary number to hold cluster-numbering information. Because of that number, the largest FAT disk partition that could be created was approximately 2GB.

Virtual FAT (VFAT)   An extension of the FAT file system that was introduced with Windows 95. It augmented the 8.3 file-naming convention and allowed filenames with up to 255 characters. It created two names for each file: a long name and an 8.3-compatible name so that older programs could still access files. When VFAT was incorporated into Windows 95, it used 32-bit code for improved disk access while keeping the 16-bit naming system for backward compatibility with FAT. It also had the 2GB disk partition limitation.

FAT32   Introduced along with Windows 95 OEM Service Release 2. As disk sizes grew, so did the need to be able to format a partition larger than 2GB. FAT32 was based more on VFAT than on FAT16. It allowed for 32-bit cluster addressing, which in turn provided for a maximum partition size of 2 terabytes (2048GB). It also included smaller cluster sizes to avoid wasted space. FAT32 support is included in current Windows versions.

NT File System (NTFS)   Introduced along with Windows NT (and available on 7/Vista/XP). NTFS is a much more advanced file system in almost every way than all versions of the FAT file system. It includes such features as individual file security and *compression* and RAID support as well as support for extremely large file and partition sizes and disk transaction monitoring. It is the file system of choice for higher-performance computing.

CD-ROM File System (CDFS)   While not a file system that can be used on a hard drive, CDFS is the file system of choice for CD media and has been used with 32-bit Windows versions since Windows 95. A CD mounted with the CDFS driver appears as a collection.

When you're installing any Windows OS, you will be asked first to format the drive using one of these disk technologies. Choose the disk technology based on what the computer will be doing and which OS you are installing.

To format a partition, you can use the FORMAT command. FORMAT.EXE is available with all versions of Windows. You can run FORMAT from a command prompt or by right-clicking a drive in Windows Explorer and selecting Format. However, when you install Windows it performs the process of partitioning and formatting for you if a partitioned and formatted drive does not already exist. You can usually choose between a *quick format* or a *full format*. With both formats, files are removed from the partition; the difference is that a quick format does not then check for bad sectors (a time-consuming process).

Be extremely careful with the Format command! When you format a drive, all data on the drive is erased.

In Windows, you can manage your hard drives through the Disk Management component. To access Disk Management, open Control Panel and double-click Administrative Tools. Then, double-click Computer Management. Finally, double-click Disk Management.

The Disk Management screen lets you view a host of information regarding all the drives installed in your system, including CD-ROM and DVD drives. The list of devices in the top portion of the screen shows you additional information for each partition on each drive, such as the file system used, status, free space, and so on. If you right-click a partition in either area, you can perform a variety of functions, such as formatting the partition and changing the name and drive-letter assignment. For additional options and information, you can also access the properties of a partition by right-clicking it and selecting Properties.

Windows 7, Vista, and XP support both basic and dynamic storage. Basic storage can have a primary and an extended partition, while dynamic storage can be simple, spanned, or striped. The partition that the operating system boots from must be designated as *active*. Only one partition on a disk may be marked active. With basic storage, Windows drives can be partitioned with *primary* or *extended* partitions. The difference is that extended partitions can be divided into one or more logical drives and primary partitions cannot be further subdivided. Each hard disk can be divided into a total of four partitions, either four primary partitions or three primary and one extended partition.

Basic partitions are a fixed size and are always on a single physical disk. Dynamic partitions can increase in size (without reformatting) and can span multiple physical disks.

Finally, there is the concept of a *logical partition*. In reality, all partitions are logical in the sense that they don't necessarily correspond to one physical disk. One disk can have several logical divisions (partitions). A logical partition is any partition that has a drive letter.

 Sometimes, you will also hear of a logical partition as one that spans multiple physical disks. For example, a network drive that you know as drive H: might actually be located on several physical disks on a server. To the user, all that is seen is one drive, or H:.

Backing Up the Data on Your Drives

Another very important aspect of disk management is backing up the data on your drives. Sooner or later, you can count on running into a situation where a hard drive fails or data becomes corrupted. Without a backup copy of your data, you're facing a world of trouble trying to recreate it, if that's even possible or economically feasible. You also shouldn't rely on the Recycle Bin. Although it is a good utility to occasionally restore a file or directory that a user has accidentally deleted, it will not help you if your drives and the data on them become unusable.

Toward that end, Windows has a built-in backup feature called, you guessed it, Backup. To access Backup in Windows 7 or Windows Vista, click Start ➢ Control Panel ➢ Backup And Restore, then click either Set Up Backup or select another backup to restore files from. To access Backup in Windows XP, click Start ➢ Programs/All Programs) ➢ Accessories ➢ System Tools ➢ Backup. This will open the Backup Wizard. To move on to the Backup utility, click Advanced Mode.

The Backup utility in each of the different versions of Windows has different capabilities, with newer versions having greater capabilities. In general, you can either run a wizard to create a backup job or manually specify the files to back up. You can also run backup jobs or schedule them to run at specific time at a specific interval. Refer to the Windows Help system for in-depth information on how to use Backup.

Checking the Health of Hard Disks and Optimizing Their Performance

As time goes on, it's important to check the health of Windows computers' hard disks and optimize their performance. Windows provides you with several tools to do so, some of which we've already mentioned in this chapter. One important tool is Disk Defragmenter, which has existed in almost all versions of Windows.

When files are written to a hard drive, they're not always written contiguously, or with all the data located in a single location. Files are stored on the disk in numbered blocks similar to PO boxes—when they are written, they are written to free blocks. As a result, file data is spread out over the disk, and the time it takes to retrieve files from the disk increases. Defragmenting a disk involves analyzing the disk and then consolidating fragmented files and folders so they occupy a contiguous space (consecutive blocks), thus increasing performance during file retrieval.

To access Disk Defragmenter, click Start ➢ Programs/All Programs ➢ Accessories ➢ System Tools ➢ Disk Defragmenter. In the list of drives, select the drive you want to defragment, and then click Analyze. When the analysis is finished, Disk Defragmenter tells you how much the drive is fragmented and whether defragmentation is recommended. If it is, click Defragment. Be aware that for large disks with a lot of fragmented files, this process can take quite some time to finish.

> In Windows 7/Vista/XP, you can also access Disk Defragmenter through the properties of any partition listed in Disk Management. Click the Tools tab and then click Defragment.

User Authentication

One of the big problems that larger systems must deal with is the need for users to access multiple systems or applications. This may require a user to remember multiple accounts and passwords. The purpose of a *single sign-on (SSO)* is to give users access to all the applications and systems they need when they log on. This is becoming a reality in many environments, including Kerberos, Microsoft Active Directory, Novell eDirectory, and some certificate model implementations.

> Single sign-on is both a blessing and a curse. It's a blessing in that once the user is authenticated, they can access all the resources on the network and browse multiple directories. It's a curse in that it removes the doors that otherwise exist between the user and various resources.

In the case of Kerberos, a single token allows any "Kerberized" applications to accept a user as valid. The important thing to remember in this process is that each application that wants to use SSO must be able to accept and process the token presented by Kerberos.

Active Directory (AD) works off a slightly different method. A server that runs AD retains information about all access rights for all users and groups in the network. When a user logs on to the system, AD issues the user a globally unique identifier (GUID). Applications that support AD can use this GUID to provide access control.

Using AD simplifies the sign-on process for users and lowers the support requirements for administrators. Access can be established through groups, and it can be enforced through group memberships. Active Directory can be implemented using a Windows Server (such as Windows Server 2008) computer. All users will then log in to the Windows domain using their centrally created AD account. On a decentralized network, SSO passwords are stored on each server and can represent a security risk. It's important to enforce password changes and make certain passwords are updated throughout the organization on a frequent basis.

While single sign-on is not the opposite of multi-factor authentication, they are often mistakenly thought of that way. One-, two-, and three-factor authentication merely refers to the number of items a user must supply to authenticate. Authentication can be based on something they have (a smart card), something they know (a password), something unique (biometric), and so forth. After factor authentication is done, then single sign-on can still apply throughout the user's session.

Summary

In this chapter, you learned about some of the tools that can be used with Windows. We covered basic Windows management concepts. Concepts included managing disks, using file systems, and understanding directory structure. Keeping your computer healthy will save you a lot of stress. Examples we discussed included performing backups.

With the basic knowledge gained in this chapter, you are now ready to learn how to interact with the most popular operating systems in use today. These topics are covered in the next three chapters.

Exam Essentials

Know what the critical Windows interfaces are and how to use them. This list includes the Desktop, Taskbar, Start menu, icons, windows, Control Panel, the command prompt, Computer (My Computer), Network (My Network Places), the system tray, and the Registry editor.

Know what file systems are available in Windows and what the differences between them are. The most commonly used file system on Windows hard drives is NTFS. FAT32 is older and perhaps a bit quicker for smaller hard drives, but NTFS adds a plethora of important features, including security and auditing.

Understand what each of the following commands does: CMD, COPY, XCOPY, /?, MD, CD, and RD. Many utilities that come with Windows help you navigate through or manage files and directories from a command prompt. The CMD command opens a command line, where you can type the rest of the commands. If you're not sure which utility to use, /? will give you information. The MD, CD, and RD commands make, change, and delete (remove) directories, respectively. Both COPY and XCOPY are used to copy files.

Know what the IPCONFIG and PING commands are for. Both IPCONFIG and PING are network troubleshooting commands. You can use IPCONFIG to view your computer's IP configuration and PING to test connectivity between two network hosts.

Know the main administrative tools. You should know the primary graphical tools for troubleshooting Windows and working with the operating system. These include the disk management tools, Administrative Tools, Device Manager, Task Manager, System Information, System Restore, and Task Scheduler.

Review Questions

The answers to the Chapter Review Questions can be found in Appendix A.

1. Which switch can be used with PING to specify a packet size?

   A. -t

   B. -l

   C. -c

   D. -o

2. In Windows, which of the following is the file system of choice for CD media?

   A. NTFS

   B. JFS

   C. FAT32

   D. CDFS

3. Which utility works like ping but returns the different IP addresses the packet was routed through to reach the final destination?

   A. Ipconfig

   B. Nbtstat

   C. Tracert

   D. Netstat

4. You have been told to use the /FIXBOOT switch to write a new boot sector on a Windows 7 machine. Which command does this switch work with?

   A. BOOTREC

   B. SFC

   C. BCEDIT

   D. ROBOCOPY

5.   Which command is shown in the following screen shot?

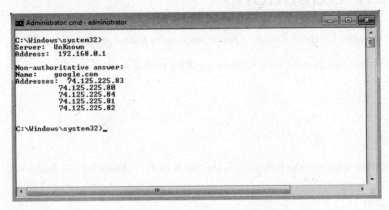

A.   TASKLIST

B.   TRACERT

C.   NETSTAT

D.   NSLOOKUP

6.   Which command lists at the command line all running processes?

A.   WLIST

B.   ALIST

C.   PLIST

D.   TASKLIST

7.   Virtual memory is configured through which system tool?

A.   Taskbar

B.   System control applet

C.   Memory Manager

D.   Virtual Configuration

8.   Within the Services snap-in, services can be in any state except which of the following?

A.   Started automatically

B.   Started manually

C.   Disabled

D.   Detached

9. What can you do if a program is not responding to any commands and appears to be locked up?

A. Open the System control panel applet and choose Performance to see what process is causing the problem.

B. Add more memory.

C. Press Ctrl+Alt+Del to reboot the computer.

D. Open Task Manager, select the appropriate task, and click End Task.

10. Which of the following can be used to configure a remote connection?

A. REGEDIT

B. MSTSC

C. REGSRV32

D. SPL

11. Which tool is shown in the following screen shot?

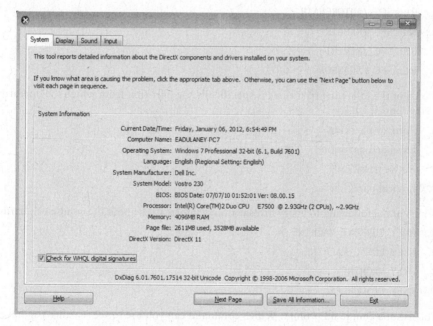

A. DXDIAG

B. MSINFO

C. MSCONFIG

D. MSINFO32

12. Which type of resource do you configure in Device Manager?

    A. Hardware

    B. Files and folders

    C. Applications

    D. Memory

13. To back up the files on your disks in Windows XP, which Windows program can you use?

    A. Disk Management

    B. Backup

    C. My Computer

    D. No backup program in Windows

14. You believe that your system files are corrupted in Windows XP. You run System File Checker. What do you do to make System File Checker automatically repair your system files if repair is needed?

    A. Run SFC /AUTOREPAIR

    B. Run SFC /REPAIR

    C. Run SFC /REVERT

    D. Run SFC /SCANNOW

15. Which of the following partitions is specifically the partition from which the operating system boots?

    A. Primary partition

    B. Extended partition

    C. Active partition

    D. Logical partition

16. Which of the following Registry hives contains information about the computer's hardware?

    A. HKEY_CURRENT_MACHINE

    B. HKEY_LOCAL_MACHINE

    C. HKEY_MACHINE

    D. HKEY_RESOURCES

17. You are at a command prompt. Which command can you use to see whether you have a network connection to another computer?

    A. IPCONFIG

    B. CONNECT

    C. PING

    D. IP

18. Which of the following utilities will rearrange the files on your hard disk to occupy contiguous chunks of space?

    A. Disk Defragmenter

    B. Windows Explorer

    C. Scandisk

    D. Windows Backup

19. Which of the following switches can be used with ROBOCOPY to mirror a complete directory tree?

    A. /S

    B. /MIR

    C. /CDT

    D. /AH

20. Which of the following tools allows you to test DirectX functionality?

    A. Msinfo32

    B. Ping

    C. Telnet

    D. DxDiag

Performance-Based Question

On the A+ exams, you will encounter performance-based questions. The questions on the exam require you to perform a specific task, and you will be graded on whether you were able to complete the task. The following require you to think creatively to measure how well you understand this chapter's topics. You may or may not see similar questions on the actual A+ exams. To see how your answers compare to the authors', refer to Appendix B.

You are working at a Windows 7 workstation when the phone rings and it is your superior. He tells you that there has been a problem with the DHCP server but it is fixed now. He wants you to release the configuration information (mainly the IP address) currently leased to your workstation and obtain a new lease. How should you approach this?

Chapter

14

Working with Windows 7

THE FOLLOWING COMPTIA A+ 220-802 EXAM OBJECTIVES ARE COVERED IN THIS CHAPTER:

✓ **1.1 Compare and contrast the features and requirements of various Microsoft Operating Systems.**

- Windows 7 Starter, Windows 7 Home Premium, Windows 7 Professional, Windows 7 Ultimate, Windows 7 Enterprise

- Features: 32-bit vs. 64-bit; Aero, gadgets, user account control, bit-locker, shadow copy, system restore, ready boost, compatibility mode, administrative tools, defender, Windows firewall, security center

- Upgrade paths – differences between in place upgrades, compatibility tools, Windows 7 Upgrade Advisor

✓ **1.2 Given a scenario, install, and configure the operating system using the most appropriate method.**

- Boot methods: USB, CD-ROM, DVD, PXE

- Types of installations: Creating image, Upgrade, Clean install

✓ **1.4 Given a scenario, use appropriate operating system features and tools.**

- Administrative: Users and groups, Local security policy, System configuration, Component services, Data sources, Print management, Windows memory diagnostics, Windows firewall, Advanced security

- Other: User State Migration Tool (USMT), Windows Easy Transfer

✓ **1.5 Given a scenario, use Control Panel utilities.**

- Unique to Windows 7: HomeGroup, Action center, Remote applications and desktop applications, Troubleshooting

✓ **1.6 Setup and configure Windows networking on a client/desktop.**

- HomeGroup, file/print sharing

- Workgroup vs. domain setup

- Network shares/mapping drives

- Establish network connections: VPN, Dialups, Wireless, Wired, WWAN (Cellular)

- Proxy settings

- Remote desktop

- Home vs. Work vs. Public network settings

- Firewall settings: Exceptions, Configuration, Enabling/disabling Windows firewall

- Configuring an alternate IP address in Windows: IP addressing, Subnet mask, DNS, Gateway

- Network card properties: Half duplex/full duplex/auto, Speed, Wake-on-LAN, PoE QoS

The previous two chapters looked at operating systems in general and briefly touched on the three that you need to know for the 220-802 exam. This chapter focuses on Windows 7 exclusively.

Some of the tools covered in this chapter have been addressed in the previous chapters, but care has been taken to attempt to avoid redundancy wherever possible. Be certain you know the specifics of Windows 7 and the differences in how this operating system stands out from its predecessors.

Windows 7 Editions

Windows 7 has been released in six different editions, only three of which are available in the retail channel. The three retail versions are Windows 7 Home Premium, Windows 7 Professional, and Windows 7 Ultimate. In addition to these, there is also Windows 7 Enterprise, which offers more features than Professional and less than Ultimate but is licensed with a Software Assurance contract and not available in the retail channel; for all intents and purposes, Ultimate and Enterprise are functionally identical. Windows 7 Starter was created for OEMs to install on netbooks. The sixth edition, Windows 7 Home Basic, is not listed on the CompTIA objectives and is marketed only in emerging technology countries.

Table 14.1 lists the five editions of Windows 7 you need to know for the 220-802 exam and key features of each.

TABLE 14.1 Windows 7 features and editions

Edition	Maximum RAM Supported	Maximum Physical CPUs Supported (Multiple Cores)	Notes
Starter	2GB (x86)	1	Lacks support for Aero, cannot join a Windows Server domain, no parental controls, Remote Desktop client only, can join HomeGroup but not create

TABLE 14.1 Windows 7 features and editions *(continued)*

Edition	Maximum RAM Supported	Maximum Physical CPUs Supported (Multiple Cores)	Notes
Home Premium	16GB	1	Includes support for multitouch, cannot join a Windows Server domain, Remote Desktop client only, can join or create HomeGroup
Professional	192GB	2	Can join a Windows server domain, includes Remote Desktop Server, includes EFS, includes Windows XP mode, can create HomeGroup if not domain joined, supports offline files/folders and Group Policy
Enterprise	192GB	2	Includes BitLocker, not available in retail or OEM channels (volume licensing only), includes Multilingual User Interface (MUI), can create HomeGroup if not domain joined, supports offline files/folders and Group Policy
Ultimate	192GB	2	Includes BitLocker, available in retail and OEM channels, includes MUI, can create HomeGroup if not domain joined, supports offline files/folders and Group Policy, Functionally, identical to Enterprise.

There are 32-bit and 64-bit versions available for each of the editions listed except Starter. Except where indicated, the RAM support in the table is for the 64-bit versions. As a successor to Windows Vista, Windows 7 was released by Microsoft with the key goals of overcoming the sluggishness in Vista as well as the incompatibilities with applications written for previous versions.

 There are some features of the operating system that are available, or not available, only if certain conditions exist. For example, Parental Controls ceases to be available if the workstation is part of a domain.

Table 14.2 lists a number of features associated with the Windows 7 operating system that CompTIA wants you to know for the exam, along with a brief description of each.

If you don't know what edition of Windows 7 is running on a particular machine, you can click Start and type **winver** in the search box. The screen that is returned will identify the edition as well as the service pack installed.

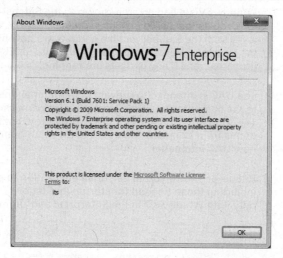

TABLE 14.2 Windows 7 features

Feature	Significance
Aero	The Aero interface offers a glass design that includes translucent windows. It was new with Windows Vista and is available in every edition of Windows 7 except Starter.
Gadgets	These are mini programs, introduced with Windows Vista, that can be placed on the Desktop, allowing them to run quickly and personalize the PC (clock, weather, etc.). Windows 7 renamed these Windows Desktop Gadgets (right-click on the Desktop, click Gadgets in the context menu, then double-click on the one you want to add). In 2011, Microsoft announced it is no longer supporting development or uploading of new gadgets.

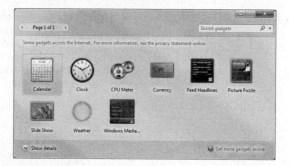

TABLE 14.2 Windows 7 features *(continued)*

Feature	Significance
Sidebar	Windows Vista had an area known as the Sidebar that was designed for gadgets that could be placed on the Desktop. Windows 7 did away with the Sidebar and the gadgets are now placed directly on the Desktop. Interestingly enough, though, SIDEBAR.EXE is the program that runs if any gadgets are running.
User Account Control	The UAC is intended to prevent unintentional/unauthorized changes to the computer by either prompting for permission to continue or requiring the administrator password before continuing. Changes to this from Windows Vista now allow more granular control over how UAC intercedes.
BitLocker	BitLocker allows you to use drive encryption to protect files, including those needed for startup and logon. This is available only with Windows 7 in the Enterprise and Ultimate editions. 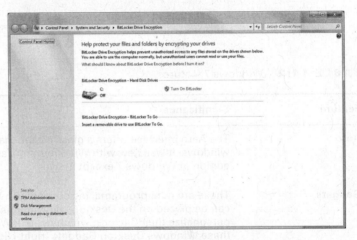 For removable drives, BitLocker To Go provides the same encryption technology to help prevent unauthorized access to the files stored on them.
Shadow Copy	The Volume Shadow Copy Service creates copies that you can recover from should a file be accidentally deleted or overwritten. Windows 7 adds to what Vista included: an interface for configuring storage used by volume shadow copies. The Properties dialog box for a file contains a Previous Versions tab that can be used to return to another version of the file.

TABLE 14.2   Windows 7 features *(continued)*

Feature	Significance
ReadyBoost	This feature allows you to use free space on a removable drive to speed up a system by caching content. In Windows 7, it can work with a USB drive, flash memory, SD card, or CompactFlash. Up to eight devices can employ ReadyBoost in Windows 7 (each needing a minimum of 256MB of free space). ReadyBoost is configured from the ReadyBoost tab of the properties for the removable media device.
Compatibility Mode	Program Compatibility is included with Windows 7 to configure programs to believe they are running with an older version of Windows: Choose Start ➢ Control Panel ➢ Programs, and then click Run programs made for previous versions of Windows.
XP Mode	Included with Windows 7 Professional, Enterprise, and Ultimate is the ability to run applications in Windows XP Mode (XPM). This is a virtual client (emulating Windows XP Professional with Service Pack 3) and you must download and install Windows Virtual PC to use it. This can be downloaded from the Windows Virtual PC site at: www.microsoft.com/windows/virtual-pc/. You should have 2GB RAM and 15GB hard drive space for each virtual Windows instance.
Windows Defender	Windows 7 includes Windows Defender antispyware program.
Windows Firewall	Windows 7 incorporates Windows Firewall, which can be used to stop incoming and outgoing traffic. There are only three basic settings: On, Off, and Block All Incoming Connections.

While the items in Table 14.2 are specifically listed in the objectives, CompTIA also wants you to know these key features of Windows 7:

Jump lists   This is a quick way to access files you've been working on through their association with the application that has been using them. Right-click on the application and a list of current files appears.

Pinning to the Taskbar   The context menu for each application allows you to choose whether you want to pin (add) it to the Taskbar or remove it if it is already there.

Windows Taskbar   This has been redesigned to include thumbnail previews.

Snap   This is a quick way to resize windows on the Desktop.

HomeGroup   This is a simplified way to set up a home network. It allows you to share files and prevent changes from being made to those files by those sharing them (unless you give them permission to do so).

Windows Search   Instantly find anything on your PC as soon as you start typing into the search box.

Windows Touch   This feature adds touchscreen functionality to the operating system, allowing you to make selections without using a keyboard or mouse.

Libraries   You can logically (as opposed to physically) group files and folders that are not in the same location and make them appear as if they are. For example, suppose you have to rewrite four chapters of a book. There can be one chapter stored in a folder beneath C:\BOOK, another beneath C:\REWRITES, and images beneath C:\USERS\PUBLIC\ PICTURES, and all can be grouped into a library so that when you open C:\A_PLUS, all the entities appear to be beneath there.

 Real World Scenario

ReadyBoost or ReadyDrive?

In addition to ReadyBoost, Windows offers another similar technology: ReadyDrive. You are not required to know about ReadyDrive for the exam, but it's a feature worth knowing about. Included with Windows Vista as well as Windows 7, ReadyDrive is the acceleration technology used with hybrid drives (H-HDD) that combines flash drives and mobile PC hard drives for better performance and battery life.

There have been problems with ReadyDrive. For example, when the first partition is small, the hybrid drive is not recognized. When the technology works, the results are nothing short of impressive. When it does not work, absence is noticeable.

Installing Windows 7

As of this writing, Windows 7 is the most current Windows version available. Like every new operating system, it requires more (newer, better, etc.) hardware than previous operating systems. Make sure the hardware you plan to install Windows 7 on can support the OS.

Checking Hardware Compatibility

The easiest way to see if your current hardware can run Windows 7 is to download and run the Windows 7 Upgrade Advisor available at:

`http://windows.microsoft.com/en-US/windows/downloads/upgrade-advisor`

You can also always check hardware in the Windows 7 Compatibility Center at:

`www.microsoft.com/windows/compatibility/windows-7/en-us/default.aspx`

If you are installing an operating system on more than one computer, it is always worth the effort to master an automated tool that can simplify this process. In the case of Windows 7, Microsoft has released the Microsoft Assessment and Planning (MAP) Toolkit which can be downloaded from the Microsoft Download Center (`www.microsoft.com/downloads`). Using this tool, you can get an inventory of computers on your network and plan a rollout of the new operating system. The current version of MAP (5.5) requires a 1.6GHz or faster processor, 1.5GB of RAM, a network adapter card, and a graphics adapter that supports 1024×768 or higher resolution.

Windows 7 can be installed as an upgrade or a clean installation—accomplished with the Custom option (think custom = clean). When you choose Custom, you can choose whether or not to format the hard disk. If you choose to not format the hard disk, the old operating system is placed in a folder called `WINDOWS.OLD`; if you choose to format, the Custom option will erase your files, programs, and settings. On a standard, default, installation, the /BOOT directory holds the boot file configuration for Windows.

The installation can be started from an installation disc or from a download (preferably to a USB drive). If the installation does not begin immediately on boot, look for the SETUP.EXE file and run it. When the Install Windows page appears, click Install Now.

You'll be asked if you want to get any updates (recommended) and to agree to the license agreement. After you've done so, choose Custom (advanced) for the installation type and specify where you want to install Windows (C: is the most common). Follow the steps to walk through the remainder of the installation, and it is highly recommended that after the installation is complete, you run Windows Update to get the latest system updates and drivers.

Just as with its two predecessors, you will need to activate Windows 7. Activation is required, but registration is not. You have 30 days in which to do the activation or Windows 7 stops working, and all you truly need to complete the process is the product key.

Upgrading to Windows 7

If you want to do an upgrade instead of a clean installation, then review the upgrade options in Table 14.3 (it is worth noting that a "No" does not mean you can't buy the upgrade version of Windows 7 but rather that you can't keep your files, programs, and settings).

TABLE 14.3 Windows 7 upgrade options

Existing Operating System	Windows 7 Home Premium 32-bit	Windows 7 Home Premium 64-bit	Windows 7 Professional 32-bit	Windows 7 Professional 64-bit	Windows 7 Ultimate 32-bit	Windows 7 Ultimate 64-bit
Windows XP	No	No	No	No	No	No
Windows Vista Starter 32-bit	No	No	No	No	No	No
Windows Vista Starter 64-bit	No	No	No	No	No	No
Windows Vista Home Basic 32-bit	Yes	No	No	No	Yes	No

Existing Operating System	Windows 7 Home Premium 32-bit	Windows 7 Home Premium 64-bit	Windows 7 Professional 32-bit	Windows 7 Professional 64-bit	Windows 7 Ultimate 32-bit	Windows 7 Ultimate 64-bit
Windows Vista Home Basic 64-bit	No	Yes	No	No	No	Yes
Windows Vista Home Premium 32-bit	Yes	No	No	No	Yes	No
Windows Vista Home Premium 64-bit	No	Yes	No	No	No	Yes
Windows Vista Business 32-bit	No	No	Yes	No	Yes	No
Windows Vista Business 64-bit	No	No	No	Yes	No	Yes
Windows Vista Ultimate 32-bit	No	No	No	No	Yes	No
Windows Vista Ultimate 64-bit	No	No	No	No	No	Yes

Operating systems not listed in Table 14.3 do not include any options to upgrade to Windows 7; that is, an upgrade package cannot be used (you must buy the full version of Windows 7). It should be noted that an easy way to remember upgrade options for the exam is that you must have at least Windows Vista in order to be able to upgrade to Windows 7. In the real world, the Windows Vista machine should be running Service Pack 1 at a minimum, and you can always take an earlier OS and upgrade it to Vista SP1 and then upgrade to Windows 7.

Is the Operating System Current?

As of this writing, Service Pack 1 is the latest available service pack for Windows 7, Service Pack 2 is the latest available for Windows Vista, and Service Pack 3 is the latest available for Windows XP. You can find the latest at:

http://windows.microsoft.com/en-US/windows/downloads/service-packs

In the past, all service packs were cumulative, meaning you needed to load only the last one. Starting with XP SP3, however, all Windows service packs released have been incremental, meaning that you must install the previous one(s) before you can install the new one.

Microsoft created the Windows 7 Upgrade Advisor to help with the upgrade to this operating system. You can download the advisor from www.microsoft.com/downloads; if the installation is started from the previous OS, it offers an option to Check compatibility online. It will scan your hardware, devices, and installed programs for any known compatibility issues. Once it is finished, it will gives you advice on how to resolve the issues found and recommendations on what to do before you upgrade. The reports are divided into three categories: System Requirements, Devices, and Programs. Figure 14.1 shows the opening screen.

Figure 14.2 shows an example of a report generated by the Windows 7 Upgrade Advisor.

After all incompatibilities have been addressed, the upgrade can be started from an installation disc or from a download (preferably to a USB drive). If the setup routine does not begin immediately on boot, look for the SETUP.EXE file and run it. When the Install Windows page appears, click Install Now.

You'll be asked if you want to get any updates (recommended) and to accept the license agreement. After you've done so, choose Upgrade for the installation type and follow the steps to walk through the remainder of the installation. It is highly recommended that after the installation is complete, you run Windows Update to get the latest drivers.

FIGURE 14.1   Run the Windows 7 Upgrade Advisor before beginning the upgrade of a machine.

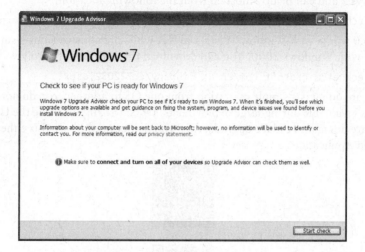

FIGURE 14.2   Incompatibilities are highlighted by the Windows 7 Upgrade Advisor.

Microsoft Windows User State Migration Tool (USMT) allows you to migrate user file settings related to the applications, Desktop configuration, and accounts. Version 4.0 works with Windows 7 and can be downloaded from the following location:

http://technet.microsoft.com/en-us/library/dd560801(WS.10).aspx

Version 3.0 works with Windows Vista and XP, while previous versions—such as 2.6— also worked with Windows 2000. You can download this tool from the following location:

http://technet.microsoft.com/en-us/library/cc722032.aspx

If all you are doing is a simple migration from one OS to another, you do not need this tool, but it is invaluable during large deployments. Of course, if you chose the Upgrade option and are doing an in-place upgrade, then you do not need to use this either because User files and Applications are preserved.

If you are migrating only a few accounts, Microsoft recommends Windows Easy Transfer (WET) instead of USMT. When you're transferring to Windows 7, a version of Windows Easy Transfer can be downloaded in either 32-bit or 64-bit versions for Windows Vista or Windows XP from www.microsoft.com/downloads.

Upgrading Editions of Windows 7

Like Windows Vista, Windows 7 has the ability to upgrade at any time from one edition of the operating system to a higher one (for example, from Home Premium to Professional) using the Windows Anytime Upgrade utility in Control Panel (it can also be accessed by clicking the Start button and choosing All Programs. Scroll down the list and choose Windows Anytime Upgrade). Figure 14.3 shows the opening screen of this utility.

FIGURE 14.3   Change to a higher edition of Windows 7 using Windows Anytime Upgrade.

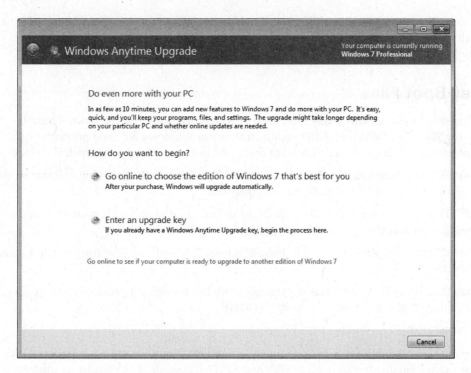

Installation/Upgrade Boot Options

You can begin the installation or upgrade process by booting from a number of sources. There are four in particular that CompTIA wants you to be familiar with: CD-ROM, DVD, USB, and PXE. The one most commonly used for an attended installation is the CD-ROM/DVD boot (they are identical). Because Windows 7 only comes on DVD, though, the CD-ROM option applies to older operating systems and not this one.
You can boot a PC over the network (rather than from a DVD, USB or hard disk) with Windows Preinstallation Environment (WinPE), which is a stub operating system creating a *Pre-boot Execution Environment (PXE)*.

WinPE can be installed onto a bootable CD, USB, or network drive using the COPYPE.CMD command. This can be used in conjunction with a Windows deployment from a server for unattended installations, and also to host the Windows Recovery Environment (WinRE).

The Windows 7 Boot Sequences

Both for the exam and for real life, you should know how to recognize common problems with the OS and make certain it is booting correctly. The sections that follow look at a number of topics related to keeping your OS booting and running properly.

Key Boot Files

Windows 7 requires only a few files, each of which performs specific tasks. These mirror Windows Vista and differ significantly from Windows XP (and previous Windows operating systems). They are discussed next in the order in which they load:

BOOTMGR   The Windows Boot Manager (BOOTMGR) bootstraps the system. In other words, this file starts the loading of an OS on the computer.

BCD   The Boot Configuration Data (BCD) holds information about OSs installed on the computer, such as the location of the OS files.

WINLOAD.EXE   The program used to boot Windows 7. It loads the operating system kernel (NTOSKRNL.EXE).

WINRESUME.EXE   If the system is not starting fresh but resuming a previous session, then WINRESUME.EXE is called by the BOOTMGR.

NTOSKRNL.EXE   The Windows OS kernel.

System files   In addition to the previously listed files, Windows needs a number of files from its system directories (e.g., SYSTEM and SYSTEM32), such as the hardware abstraction layer (HAL.DLL), session manager (SMSS.EXE), user session (WINLOGON.EXE) and security subsystem (LSASS.EXE).

Windows 7 Features

There are a number of features that make Windows 7 notable. In the following sections, we will look first at some of the tools and then focus on the ones you need to know for the A+ exam.

Tools in Windows 7

The tools that stand out in Windows 7, and that CompTIA expects you to know for the exam, include System Restore, Windows Defender, Windows Firewall, and Action Center. Each of these are discussed in the sections that follow.

System Restore

Chapter 12, "Operating System Basics," explored System Restore as it appears in all three versions of Windows. It allows you to restore the system to a previous point in time. This feature is accessed from Start ➢ All Programs ➢ Accessories ➢ System Tools ➢ System Restore and can be used to roll back as well as to create a restore point. Figure 14.4 shows the opening dialog box.

FIGURE 14.4   System Restore in Windows 7

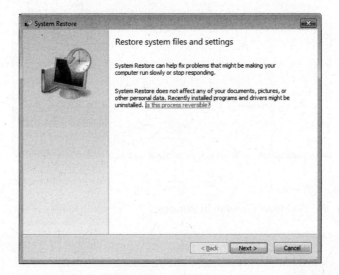

After clicking Next, pick a restore point to return to, as shown in Figure 14.5.

In Windows XP, you could also choose to create a restore point manually from here. With Windows 7 and Vista, you can no longer create a restore point manually from here; you must use the System Protection tab of System Properties.

Windows Defender

Windows Defender can identify spyware and is included with all versions of Windows 7 (with small/large icons, choose Start ➢ Control Panel ➢ Windows Defender). As with similar programs, for Windows Defender to function properly, you need to keep the definitions current and scan on a regular basis.

Windows Firewall

Windows Firewall (with small/large icons, choose Start ➢ Control Panel ➢ Windows Firewall) is used to block access from the network, and in Windows 7, it is divided into separate settings for private networks and public networks as well as Domain Networks if connected to a domain (see Figure 14.6). If you are using Category view (instead of small/large icons), you have to click System and Security before getting to the Firewall.

FIGURE 14.5 Choose a restore point in Windows 7

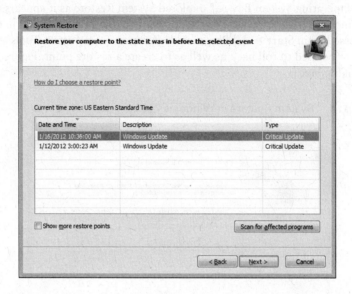

FIGURE 14.6 Windows Firewall in Windows 7

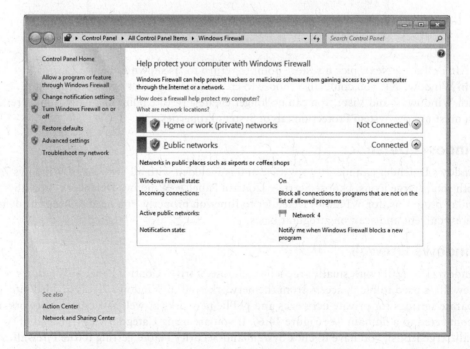

While host-based firewalls are not as secure as other types of firewalls, this provides much better protection than previously and is turned on by default. It is also included in the Security component of the Action Center (discussed in the next section) and can be tweaked significantly using the advanced settings. Once you click Advanced Settings, *Windows Firewall with Advanced Security* opens (see Figure 14.7).

FIGURE 14.7 Windows Firewall with Advanced Security in Windows 7

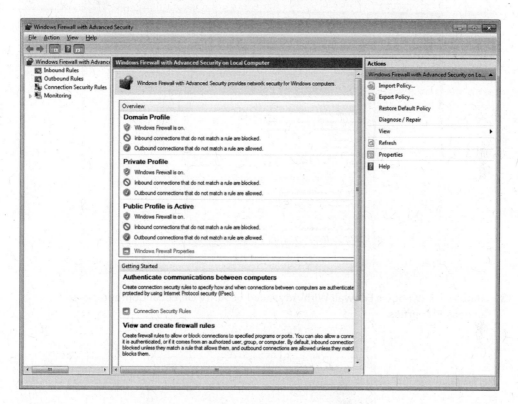

Here, you can configure inbound and outbound rules as well as import and export policies and monitor the security of your system. Monitoring is not confined to the firewall; you can also monitor security associations and connection security rules. In short, Windows Firewall with Advanced Security is an incredibly powerful tool that builds upon what Windows Vista started. Not only can this MMC snap-in do simple configuration, but it can configure remote computers and work with Group Policy.

Firewall logging is not on by default in Windows 7. In Exercise 14.1, we will look at the firewall log settings in Windows 7 and turn them on.

EXERCISE 14.1

Turning On Windows 7 Firewall Logs

1. From the Start menu, choose Control Panel ➢ System And Security ➢ Windows Firewall.

2. Click Advanced Settings.

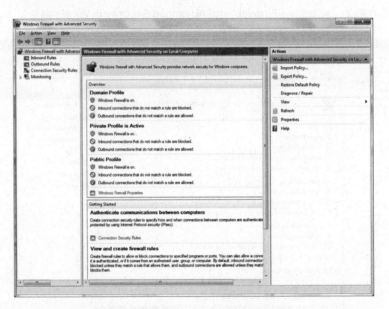

3. Right-click Windows Firewall With Advanced Security On Local Computer and choose Properties.

EXERCISE 14.1 *(continued)*

4. Click Customize beneath Logging to open the Customize Logging Settings For The Domain Profile dialog box. Note that unless connected to a domain, the logging option will have no effect.

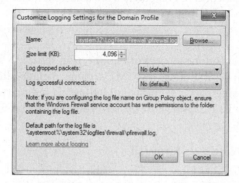

5. Change the setting for Log Dropped Packets to Yes; this will log why and when a packet was dropped. Note that you can also elect to change the setting on Log Successful Connections, but that can create quite a few more entries and you'll need to check the log files more often; it logs why and when a connection was allowed.

6. Change Size Limit from the default of 4,096KB to 8,192KB. Note that this value is limited to sizes between 1KB and 32,767KB.

7. Click OK. Events, as they occur, can now be found in Event Viewer beneath Applications And Services Logs (choose Windows, and then choose Windows Firewall With Advanced Security).

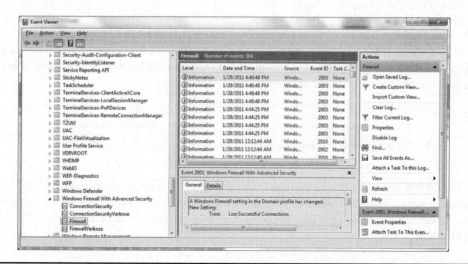

Exceptions

Exceptions are configured as variations from the rules. Windows Firewall will block incoming network connections except for the programs and services you choose to allow through. For example, you can make an exception for Remote Assistance to allow communication from other computers when you need help (the scope of the exception can be set to allow any computer, only those on the network, or computers from a custom list of allowed addresses you create). Exceptions can include programs as well as individual ports.

Configuration

Most of the configuration is done as network connection settings. You can configure both ICMP and Services settings. Examples of ICMP settings include allowing incoming echo requests, allowing incoming router requests, and allowing redirects. Examples of services often configured include FTP Server, Post Office Protocol Version 3 (POP3), and Web Server (HTTP).

Enabling/Disabling Windows Firewall

On the General tab of Windows Firewall, it is possible to choose the Off radio button (not recommended). As the name implies, this turns Windows Firewall completely off. The other radio button option—On (recommended)—enables the firewall. You can also toggle a check box labeled Don't Allow Exceptions. This should be enabled when you're connecting to a public network in an unsecure location (airport, library, etc.) and it will then ignore any exceptions that were configured.

Action Center

What was previously known as the Security Center has been modified in Windows 7 to become the Action Center (Start ➤ Control Panel ➤ Action Center). This interface (shown in Figure 14.8) still includes security, but it has been expanded to include such maintenance issues as problem reports and backup settings.

The Security settings show the status of, and allow you to configure, the firewall, Windows Update, virus protection, spyware and unwanted software protection, Internet security settings, UAC, and Network access protection. The solutions portion of Maintenance rolls in the problem reporting features from earlier versions of Windows. In Windows 7, there are four options for error reporting settings that can be chosen:

- "Automatically check for solutions (recommended)"
- "Automatically check for solutions and send additional data, if needed"
- "Each time a problem occurs, ask me before checking for solutions"
- "Never check for solutions (not recommended)"

The setting you want can be configured in the Action Center by choosing Problem Report Settings. The administrator may choose to set one universal setting for the machine (not the default) or allow each user to make their own setting (the default), as shown in Figure 14.9.

FIGURE 14.8   Windows Action Center in Windows 7

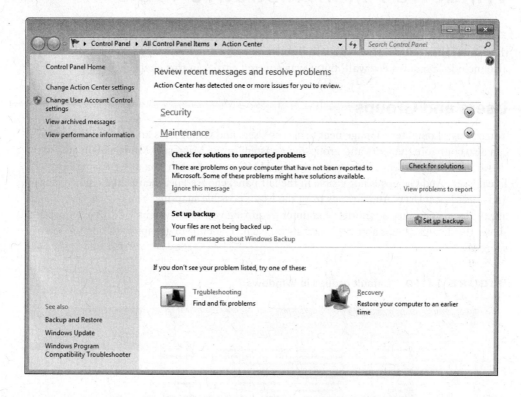

FIGURE 14.9   Configuring Windows Error Reporting options in Windows 7

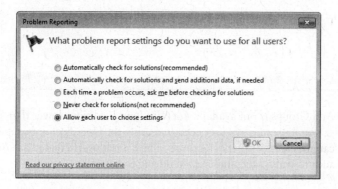

Windows 7 Administrative Tools

There are a number of system tools included with Windows 7 that you need to know for the exam. These administrative tools, discussed in the order they appear in the objectives, also include Windows Firewall, but it was covered earlier in this chapter.

Users and Groups

You can use Computer Management to access Users and Groups. As an administrator, you can also configure the users and groups on a system in the Microsoft Management Console (MMC). Start by clicking Start ➤ and typing **MMC** in the Search box and pressing Enter. If Local Users And Groups is not visible in the left pane, choose File, then Add/Remove Snap-in, and select Local Users And Groups from the list of possible snap-ins. You can choose to manage the local computer or another computer (requiring you to provide its address). Figure 14.10 shows the default groups and explanations for each. The built-in groups for a domain are a superset of this set.

FIGURE 14.10   Default groups in Windows 7

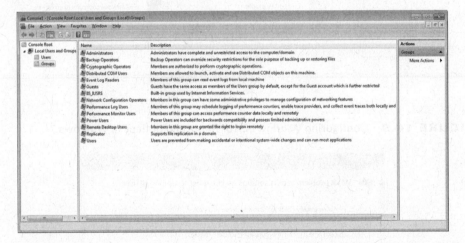

Local Users And Groups is not available for Windows 7 editions lower than Professional. In all other editions, you must manage user accounts using the User Accounts applet in Control Panel, and you cannot create or manage groups. The default users created are Administrator, Guest, and the administrative account created during the install.

Local Security Policy

Local Security Policy (choose Start ➤ and then enter **secpol.msc**) allows you to set the default security settings for the system. This feature is not available for Windows 7 in any edition other than Windows 7 Professional, Windows 7 Ultimate, and Windows 7 Enterprise. Figure 14.11 shows the utility.

FIGURE 14.11   Local Security Policy in Windows 7

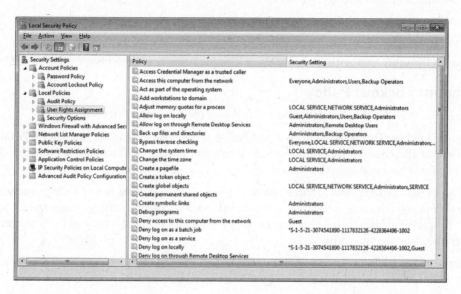

The following sections examine some of the Security Settings choices.

Account Policies

Account Policies further divides into Password Policy and Account Lockout Policy. The following choices are available under Password Policy:

Enforce Password History   This allows you to require unique passwords for a certain number of iterations. The default number is 0, but it can go as high as 24.

Maximum Password Age   The default is 42 days, but values range from 0 to 999.

Minimum Password Age   The default is 0 days (the password can be changed immediately), but values range from 0 to 998.

Minimum Password Length   The default is 0 characters (meaning no passwords are required), but you can specify a number up to 14.

Password Must Meet Complexity Requirements   The default is disabled. When this is turned on, the password must include at least three of the following criteria: uppercase characters, lowercase characters, numerical characters, nonalphanumeric characters, Unicode characters.

Store Password Using Reversible Encryption   The default is disabled. When enabled, it provides support for applications that require knowledge of the password.

Because the likelihood of laptops being stolen always exists, it's strongly encouraged that you use good password policies for this audience. Here's an example:

- Enforce Password History: 8 passwords remembered
- Maximum Password Age: 42 days
- Minimum Password Age: 3 days
- Minimum Password Length: 6 to 8 characters

Leave the other two settings disabled.

Account Lockout Policy

The Account Lockout Policy setting is divided into the following three values:

Account Lockout Duration   This is a number of minutes ranging from 1 to 99999. A value of 0 is also allowed here and signifies that the account never unlocks itself—administrator interaction is always required.

Account Lockout Threshold   This is the number of invalid attempts before lockout occurs. The default is 0 (meaning the feature is turned off). Invalid attempt settings range from 1 to 999. A number greater than 0 changes the values of the following two options to 30 minutes; otherwise, they are "not defined."

Reset Account Lockout Counter After   This is a number of minutes, ranging from 1 to 99999, that each failed login attempt remains on the counter.

When you're working with a mobile workforce, you must weigh the choice of users calling you in the middle of the night when they've forgotten their password against keeping the system from being entered if the wrong user picks up the laptop. A good recommendation for a medium to low security environment may be to use a lockout after five attempts for a period of time between 30 and 60 minutes.

Local Policy Settings

The Local Policies section divides into three subsections:

Audit Policy   The Audit Policy section contains nine settings; the default value for each is No Auditing. Valid options are Success and/or Failure. The Audit Account Logon Events entry is the one you should consider turning on for mobile users to see how often they log in and out of their machines. When auditing is turned on for an event, the entries are logged in the Security log file.

User Rights Assignment   The User Rights Assignment subsection of Local Policies is where the meat of the old System Policies comes into play. User Rights Assignment has many options, most of which are self-explanatory. Not Defined indicates that no one is specified for this operation. You can add groups and users. (This functionality isn't needed.) If you want to "remove" users or groups from the list, uncheck the box granting them access. The Power User group has no more rights than a standard user in Windows 7; the group has only been left to provide backwards compatibility.

Security Options   The Security Options section includes a great many options, which, for the most part, are Registry keys. The default for each is Not Defined; the two main definitions that can be assigned are Enabled and Disabled, or a number (as with the number of previous logons to cache) can be entered.

System Configuration

The System Configuration tool (MSCONFIG.EXE) in Windows 7 is unchanged from Windows Vista. The five tabs it offers are General, Boot, Services, Startup, and Tools. The "tools" you can run, and the executables associated with them, are as follows:

- **About Windows:** WINVER.EXE
- **Change UAC Settings:** USERACCOUNTCONTROLSETTINGS.EXE
- **Action Center:** WSCUI.CPL
- **Windows Troubleshooting:** CONTROL.EXE /NAME MICROSOFT.TROUBLESHOOTING
- **Computer Management:** COMPMGMT.MSC
- **System Information:** MSINFO32.EXE
- **Event Viewer:** EVENTVWR.EXE
- **Programs:** APPWIZ.CPL
- **System Properties:** CONTROL.EXE SYSTEM
- **Internet Options:** INETCPL.CPL
- **Internet Protocol Configuration:** IPCONFIG.EXE
- **Performance Monitor:** PERFMON.EXE
- **Resource Monitor:** RESMON.EXE
- **Task Manager:** TASKMGR.EXE
- **Command Prompt:** CMD.EXE
- **Registry Editor:** REGEDT32.EXE
- **Remote Assistance:** MSRA.EXE
- **System Restore:** RSTRUI.EXE

Each of these should be considered troubleshooting utilities that you can use to solve system problems. Know what they do and the executable associated with each to solve the majority of problems you will encounter when working with Windows 7.

Component Services

Component Services is an MMC snap-in in Windows 7 that allows you to administer, as well as deploy, component services and configure behavior like security. Figure 14.12 shows an example of the interface (Start ➢ Control Panel ➢ Administrative Tools ➢ Component Services).

FIGURE 14.12 Component Services in Windows 7

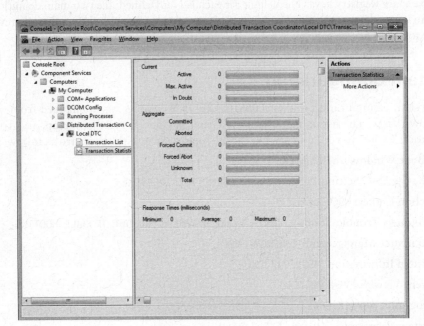

Data Sources

ODBC Data Source Administrator—Start ➤ Control Panel ➤ Administrative Tools ➤ Data Sources (ODBC)—allows you to interact with database management systems. Figure 14.13 shows an example of the screen.

FIGURE 14.13 Data Sources in Windows 7

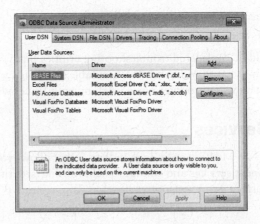

Database drivers that are added to the system will show up here and can be shared between applications.

Print Management

Carrying over from Windows Vista, Print Management (Start ➢ Control Panel ➢ Administrative Tools ➢ Print Management) allows you to manage multiple printers and print servers from a single interface (see Figure 14.14).

FIGURE 14.14   Print Management in Windows 7

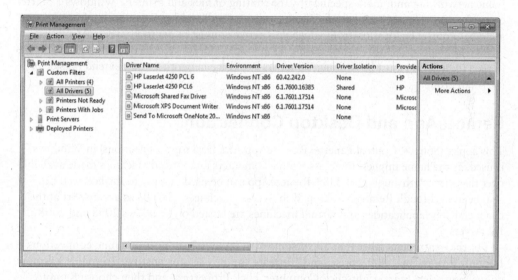

Print Management is not available for Windows 7 in any edition lower than Windows 7 Professional. In all other editions, you must manage individual printers using the Printers applet in Control Panel, and you are very limited in what you can manage.

Windows Memory Diagnostics

The Windows Memory Diagnostics Tool (Start ➢ Control Panel ➢ Administrative Tools ➢ Memory Diagnostics Tool) can be used to check a system for memory problems. For the tool to work, the system must be restarted. The two options that it offers are to restart the computer now and check for problems and wait and check for problems on the next restart.

When the computer reboots, the test will take several minutes and the display screen will show which pass number is being run and the overall status of the test (percent complete). When the memory test concludes, the system will restart again and nothing related to it is apparent until you log in. If the test is without error, you'll see a message that no errors were found. If any issues have been detected, the results will be displayed.

Unique Control Panel Utilities

There are four Control Panel applets unique to Windows 7 to be aware of. One of these, Action Center, was addressed earlier in this chapter. The other three are discussed here and include HomeGroup, RemoteApp And Desktop Connections, and Troubleshooting.

HomeGroup

The purpose behind HomeGroup (Start ➤ Control Panel ➤ HomeGroup) is to simplify home networking and, more specifically, the sharing of files and printers. Windows 7 Starter can only join a HomeGroup, while all other editions of Windows 7 can both join and create a HomeGroup. The location from which you network must be set to Home.

Shared files can include libraries (a big feature of Windows 7). All computers participating in the HomeGroup must be running Windows 7 and the network cannot extend outside of the small group.

RemoteApp and Desktop Connections

This applet (Start ➤ Control Panel ➤ RemoteApp And Desktop Connections) in Windows 7 is used, as the name implies, to access remote computers and virtual machines made available over the network through port 3389. RemoteApp can be used directly to the host and can also be used through Remote Desktop Web Access which uses HTTPS as a transport at the client end. The applications and virtual machines are hosted on Windows 2008 and 2008 R2 servers.

For the exam, remember that all versions of Windows 7 support outgoing connections but only Professional, Enterprise, and Ultimate can be used for hosting. To enable a remote connection, click Start, right-click Computer, click Properties, and then choose Remote Settings. You can now turn on Remote Assistance and/or Remote Desktop.

Remote Assistance is either on or off, while Remote Desktop offers three options:

- "Don't allow connections to this computer"
- "Allow connections from computers running any version of Remote Desktop (less secure)"
- "Allow connections only from computers running Remote Desktop with Network Level Authentication (more secure)"

Troubleshooting

This applet (Start ➤ Control Panel ➤ Troubleshooting) in Windows 7 is used, as the name implies, to provide a simple interface to use to attack many common problems. Figure 14.15 shows the opening screen.

All links preceded by a shield require administrator permissions to run and are often tied to UAC prompts before they will continue. Most of the problems found will be "automatically fixed" without any prompts. For example, clicking the link Improve Power Usage on the machine shown in Figure 14.15 started the Power troubleshooter, which then fixed problems. Clicking to see the detailed report of what was done brings up the screen shown in Figure 14.16.

FIGURE 14.15   The Troubleshooting applet in Windows 7

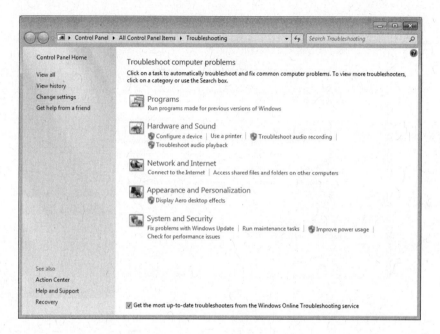

FIGURE 14.16   Report of the Power troubleshooter's changes

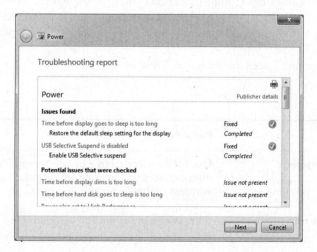

Note in Figure 14.15 the link Get help from a friend. Selecting this brings up Remote Assistance, allowing someone to connect to this computer. You can also offer to be the one helping another, as shown in Figure 14.17.

FIGURE 14.17 Windows Remote Assistance in Windows 7

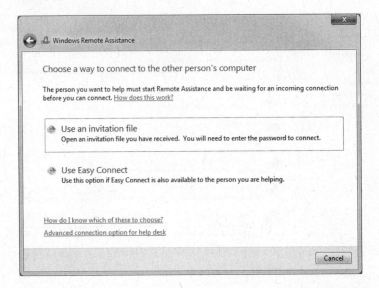

Networking and Windows 7

There are a number of things CompTIA expects you to know when it comes to the topic of networking and Windows 7. Most of the networking topics are covered in the chapters dedicated to that and thus the discussion here is limited only to those topics specifically tied to Windows 7.

Connection option choices are shown in Table 14.4.

TABLE 14.4 Network connection options

Option	Purpose
Connect to the Internet	Use for connection to a proxy server or other device intended to provide Internet access. This includes wireless, broadband and dial-up.
Set up a wireless router or access point	If the wireless device will be connected to this machine, this is the option to use.

Option	Purpose
Manually connect to a wireless network (this option is only visible if a wireless adapter is installed)	If you have a wireless network already in place and the device (router, etc.) is not directly connected to this machine, then use this option.
Set up a wireless ad hoc (computer-to-computer) network (this option is only visible if a wireless adapter is installed)	This is meant for peer-to-peer resource sharing and is typically a temporary connection.
Set up a dial-up connection	If you live in the middle of nowhere and the only way to access a network is by using a dial-up modem, then this is the option to select.
Connect to a workplace	If you are needing to connect to a virtual private network (VPN) from a remote location, this is the option to use.

 A wireless wide area network (WWAN) connection is one that uses cellular to connect the host to the network. A wireless service provider (such as AT&T, Sprint, or T-Mobile) will provide a card that is plugged into the host to make the cellular connection possible.

Regardless of which option you choose, you will need to fill out the appropriate fields for the device to be able to communicate on the network. With TCP/IP, required values are an IP address for the host, subnet mask, address for the gateway, and DNS information.

You also need to specify one of the types of locations for this network: Home, Work, or Public. If you choose one of the first two, *network discovery* is on by default, allowing you to see other computers and other computers to see you. If you choose Public, network discovery is turned off.

Configuring an Alternative IP Address in Windows

Windows 7, Windows Vista, and Windows XP all allow the use of an alternate IP address. This is an address that is configured for the system to use in the event the first choice is not available. To set an Alternate Configuration, the first choice has to be dynamic, the tab only becomes visible when the General configuration is set to Obtain an IP address automatically, and the alternate is used only if the primary address cannot be found/used, such as when the DHCP server is down.

The Properties dialog box for each instance of IPv4—on any of the Windows operating systems this exam focuses on—contains an Alternate Configuration tab. To make changes, you must click on it.

IP Addressing

Two radio buttons exist on the Alternate Configuration tab: Automatic Private IP Address and User Configured. The default is the first, meaning that the alternate address used is one in the APIPA range (169.254.*x.x*). Selecting User Configured requires you to enter a static IP address to be used in the IP Address field. The entry entered must be valid for your network in order for it to be usable (see Chapter 6, "Networking Fundamentals," for more information on IP addressing).

Subnet Mask

When the User Configured radio button is chosen on the Alternate Configuration tab, you must enter a value in the Subnet mask field. This value must correspond with the subnet values in use on your network and work with the IP address you enter in the IP Address field (see Chapter 6 for more information on subnet addresses).

DNS

When the User Configured radio button is chosen on the Alternate Configuration tab, you should enter values in the Preferred DNS Server and Alternate DNS Server fields. These entries are needed in order to translate domain names into IP addresses (see Chapter 6 for more information on DNS).

Gateway

When the User Configured radio button is chosen on the Alternate Configuration tab, you must enter a value in the Default Gateway field. This value must correspond with the subnet values and the IP address you enter. This address identifies the router to be used to communicate outside the local network (see Chapter 6 for more information on default gateways).

Network Card Properties

Like other devices, network cards can be configured to optimize performance. Configuration is done through the Properties dialog box for each card.

Half Duplex / Full Duplex / Auto

Duplexing is the means by which communication takes place:

- With *full duplexing*, everyone can send and receive at the same time. The main advantage of full-duplex over half-duplex communication is performance. NICs can operate twice as fast in full-duplex mode as they do normally in half-duplex mode.

- With *half duplexing*, communications travel in both directions but in only one direction at any given time. Think of a road where construction is being done on one lane—traffic can go in both directions but in only one direction at a time at that location.

- With *auto duplexing*, the mode is set to the lowest common denominator. If a card senses another card is manually configured to half duplex, then it also sets itself at that.

Speed

You can configure whether the card should run at its highest possible setting or not. You often need to be compatible with the network on which the host resides. If, for example, you are connecting a workstation with a 10/100BaseT card to a legacy network, you will need to operate at 10MBps to match the rest of the network.

Wake-on-LAN

Wake-on-LAN (WoL) is an Ethernet standard implemented via a card that allows a "sleeping" machine to awaken when it receives a wakeup signal.

PoE

If the device you are networking is in a remote location (such as a wireless access point in a ceiling or other place with no easy access to an electrical outlet), *Power over Ethernet (PoE)* is a handy technology to supply both power and an Ethernet connection. The purpose of Power over Ethernet (PoE) is pretty much described in its name: Electrical power is transmitted over twisted-pair Ethernet cable (along with data). A key advantage of PoE is that a UPS is required only in the main facility instead of at each device.

QoS

Quality of Service (QoS) implements packet scheduling to control the flow of traffic and help with network transmission speeds. No properties can be configured for the service itself.

Windows 7 System Performance and Optimization

Windows 7 went beyond Windows Vista in configurability and allows you choose between four UAC settings:

- Always Notify
- Notify me only when programs try to make changes to my computer (the default)
- Notify me only when programs try to make changes to my computer (do not dim my desktop)
- Never Notify

To access the Change User Account Control settings, click Start ➢ Control Panel ➢ User Accounts ➢ Change User Account Control settings. This opens the slider shown in Figure 14.18.

Encrypting File System (EFS) is available in the Professional, Enterprise, and Ultimate editions of Windows 7, allowing for encryption/decryption on files stored in NTFS volumes. EFS can be used by all users (whereas BitLocker can be turned on only by administrators) and does not require any special hardware. While BitLocker benefits from the *Trusted Platform Module (TPM)*, it doesn't need it; it can also be operated using a USB key to store the encryption keys. Last, EFS can encrypt just one file, if so desired, while BitLocker encrypts the whole volume and whatever is stored on it. EFS can be used in conjunction with BitLocker to further increase security.

FIGURE 14.18 Changing UAC settings in Windows 7

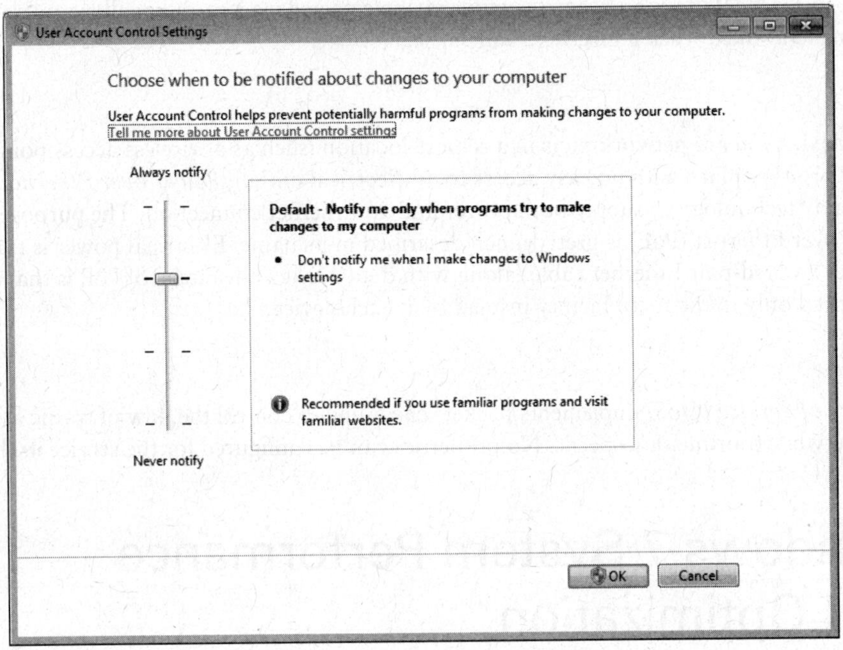

Summary

This chapter focused on Windows 7. This is the newest operating system on the exam, and CompTIA expects you to be familiar with it and able to answer questions on everything from installing it to managing it.

We looked at the various features of Windows 7, some that exist in other versions of Windows and some that are unique to this operating system. The latter category includes the following: HomeGroup, Action Center, RemoteApp and Desktop Applications, and Troubleshooting.

Exam Essentials

Know what types of installations are possible with Windows 7.   You should know which operating systems can be upgraded to Windows 7 and which require a clean installation.

Understand upgrading.   You should know that a custom installation either wipes the old system or replaces the existing system putting the old files into WINDOWS.OLD—applications have to be reinstalled and user data has to be migrated from the old system using WET or USMT. An upgrade preserves the existing applications and user data moving them into the new system.

Know the editions of Windows 7.   Windows 7 Starter is available for netbooks. The retail channel options are Windows 7 Home Premium, Windows 7 Professional, and Windows 7 Ultimate. Windows 7 Enterprise is available only through volume licensing.

Know what Control Panel utilities are unique to Windows 7.   The Control Panel applets unique to Windows 7 are HomeGroup, Action Center, RemoteApp and Desktop Applications, and Troubleshooting. You should be familiar with the purpose and options of each.

Review Questions

The answers to the Chapter Review Questions can be found in Appendix A.

1. Which editions of Windows 7 can create a HomeGroup? (Choose four.)

    A. Windows 7 Starter

    B. Windows 7 Home Premium

    C. Windows 7 Professional

    D. Windows 7 Enterprise

    E. Windows 7 Ultimate

2. What is the name of the file that runs if there are any gadgets placed on the Windows 7 Desktop?

    A. NTOS

    B. GADCONFIG

    C. GADGET

    D. SIDEBAR

3. Which of the following is used by BitLocker to be able to encrypt a drive?

    A. EFS

    B. TPM

    C. HPM

    D. Aero

4. Which feature of Windows 7 allows files and folders to be grouped logically and appear as if they are in the same location even when they are not?

    A. HomeGroup

    B. Touch

    C. Libraries

    D. Snap

5. As an administrator, you need to get an inventory of computers on your network and plan a rollout of Windows 7. Which tool can be used for this purpose?

    A. UDMT

    B. Microsoft Assessment and Planning (MAP) Toolkit

    C. USMT

    D. MigWiz

6. Which of the following editions of Windows Vista can be upgraded to Windows 7 Professional?

   A. Windows Vista Starter

   B. Windows Vista Home Basic

   C. Windows Vista Home Premium

   D. Windows Vista Business

   E. Windows Vista Ultimate

7. Which utility is shown in the following screen shot?

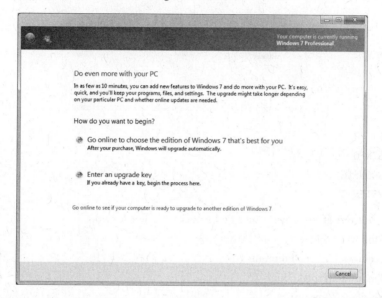

   A. Windows State Mover

   B. Windows Easy Transfer

   C. Windows Anytime Upgrade

   D. Windows Edition Roller

8. You need to do an installation of Windows 7 in a PXE environment. Which of the following can be used?

   A. WinLoad

   B. BOOTMGR

   C. WinPE

   D. WinResume

9. Which utility is shown below?

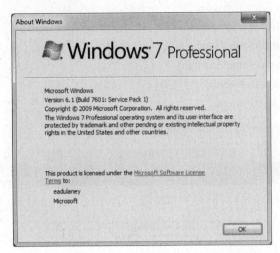

A. WINVER

B. MSINFO

C. MSCONFIG

D. SYSTEM32

10. Which editions of Windows 7 include BitLocker? (Choose two.)

A. Windows 7 Starter

B. Windows 7 Home Premium

C. Windows 7 Professional

D. Windows 7 Enterprise

E. Windows 7 Ultimate

11. Where, in Windows 7, can you manually create a restore point?

A. System Restore option beneath System Tools.

B. System Protection tab of System Properties.

C. In Backup, beneath Administrative Tools.

D. Windows 7 does not allow the manual creation of restore points.

12. Which utility is shown in the following screen shot?

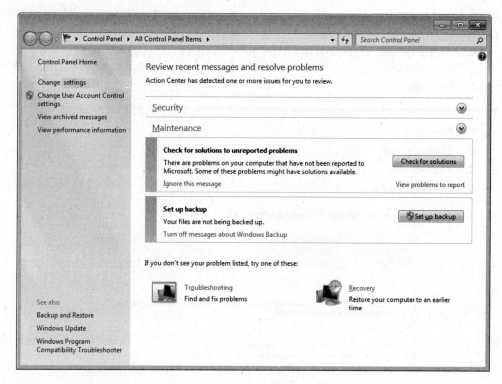

A. Action Center

B. Security Center

C. HomeGroup

D. Windows Vista Enterprise

13. After installation of the operating system, what does Windows 7 require in order to curb software piracy?

A. Certification

B. Confirmation

C. Activation

D. Substantiation

14. What is the maximum number of physical CPUs supported by Windows 7 Enterprise edition?

A. One

B. Two

C. Three

D. Four

15. In Windows 7, what is the default setting for the UAC?

   A. Always notify.

   B. Notify me only when programs try to make changes to my computer.

   C. Notify me only when programs try to make changes to my computer (do not dim my desktop).

   D. Never notify.

16. Which feature allows you to use free space on an SD card to speed up a system?

   A. ReadyDrive

   B. Shadow Copy

   C. ReadyBoost

   D. BitLocker to Go

17. Which utility is shown in the following screen shot?

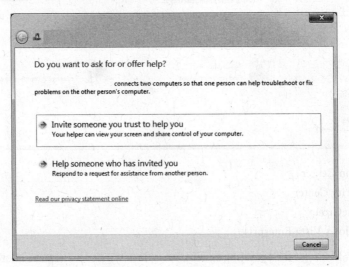

   A. Remote Control

   B. Remote Applications

   C. Remote Desktop

   D. Remote Assistance

18. Remote computers and virtual machines are made available with Windows 7 using which port?

   A. 80

   B. 139

   C. 3389

   D. 13742

19. Which directory on a standard Windows 7 installation holds the boot file configuration?

 A. /BOOT

 B. /START

 C. /SYSTEM32

 D. /WINDOWS

20. What is the maximum amount of RAM supported in the 64-bit Enterprise edition of Windows 7?

 A. 8GB

 B. 16GB

 C. 128GB

 D. 192GB

Performance-Based Question

On the A+ exams, you will encounter performance-based questions. The questions on the exam require you to perform a specific task, and you will be graded on whether you were able to complete the task. The following require you to think creatively to measure how well you understand this chapter's topics. You may or may not see similar questions on the actual A+ exams. To see how your answers compare to the authors', refer to Appendix B.

You have been sent to a client's Windows 7 workstation with specific directions to follow. They are using only IPv4 and they are to use DHCP for their normal configuration information. In the event that the DHCP server is not accessible, however, APIPA should not be used. An alternate configuration needs to be assigned with the following values:

IP address: 192.16.68.4

Subnet mask: 255.255.255.0

Default gateway: 192.16.68.1

How would you configure this?

Chapter

15

Working with Windows Vista

THE FOLLOWING COMPTIA A+ 220-802 EXAM OBJECTIVES ARE COVERED IN THIS CHAPTER:

✓ **1.1 Compare and contrast the features and requirements of various Microsoft Operating Systems.**

- Windows Vista Home Basic, Windows Vista Home Premium, Windows Vista Business, Windows Vista Ultimate, Windows Vista Enterprise

- Features:

  - 32-bit vs. 64-bit

  - Aero, gadgets, user account control, bit-locker, shadow copy, system restore, ready boost, sidebar, compatibility mode, administrative tools, defender, Windows firewall, security center

✓ **1.2 Given a scenario, install, and configure the operating system using the most appropriate method.**

- Types of installations

  - Creating image

  - Upgrade

  - Clean install

✓ **1.4 Given a scenario, use appropriate operating system features and tools.**

- Administrative

  - Users and groups

  - Local security policy

  - System configuration

  - Component services

  - Data sources

  - Print management

- Windows memory diagnostics
- Windows firewall
- Advanced security
- Other
  - User State Migration Tool (USMT), File and Settings Transfer Wizard, Windows Easy Transfer

✓ **1.5 Given a scenario, use Control Panel utilities.**

- Unique to Vista
  - Tablet PC settings
  - Pen and input devices
  - Offline files
  - Problem Reports and solutions
  - Printers

✓ **1.6 Setup and configure Windows networking on a client/desktop.**

- HomeGroup, file/print sharing
- Home vs. Work vs. Public network settings
- Firewall settings
  - Exceptions
  - Configuration
  - Enabling/disabling Windows firewall
- Configuring an alternate IP address in Windows
  - IP addressing
  - Subnet mask
  - DNS
  - Gateway
- Network card properties
  - Half duplex/full duplex/auto
  - Speed
  - Wake-on-LAN
  - QoS

Whereas the previous chapter examined the operating system features unique and worth noting about Windows 7, this one does the same thing with Windows Vista. Windows Vista was a vast departure, in many ways, from Windows XP, and it failed to live up to the adoption expectations set for it. Although it was not widely adopted, it is not uncommon to find it in use, and you must be familiar with it for the 220-802 certification exam.

Some of the tools covered have been addressed in the previous chapters for Windows 7 (Chapter 14, "Working with Windows 7") and operating systems in general (Chapter 12, "Operating System Basics," and Chapter 13, "Operating System Administration"), but be certain you know the differences in how they operate in Windows Vista.

Windows Vista Editions

Windows Vista was released in six different editions, four of which have been available in the retail channel since 2006. The four retail versions are Windows Vista Home Basic, Windows Vista Home Premium, Windows Vista Business, and Windows Vista Ultimate. In addition to these, there is Windows Vista Enterprise, which offers more features than Business and less than Ultimate but is not available in the retail channel. A sixth edition, Windows Vista Starter, is also available but is not listed for the CompTIA exam objectives. This version is not marketed in countries such as the United States or the European Union in which technology is more developed than in other countries.

Table 15.1 lists the five editions of Windows Vista you need to know for the 220-802 exam and the key features of each.

TABLE 15.1   Windows Vista editions and features

Edition	Maximum RAM Supported (in 64-bit Versions)	Maximum Physical CPUs Supported (Multiple Cores)	Notes
Home Basic	8GB	1	Lacks support for Aero, cannot join a Windows Server domain, does not support Shadow copies
Home Premium	16GB	1	Includes support for HDTV, cannot join a Windows Server domain, does not support Shadow copies

TABLE 15.1   Windows Vista editions and features *(continued)*

Edition	Maximum RAM Supported (in 64-bit Versions)	Maximum Physical CPUs Supported (Multiple Cores)	Notes
Business	128GB	2	Does not support parental controls, premium games disabled by default
Enterprise	128GB	2	Includes BitLocker, not available in retail or OEM channels (volume licensing only), premium games disabled by default
Ultimate	128GB	2	Includes BitLocker, available in retail and OEM channels

There are 32-bit and 64-bit versions available for each of the editions listed here. Table 15.2 lists a number of features associated with the Windows Vista operating system that CompTIA wants you to know for the exam, along with a brief description of each.

If you don't know what edition of Windows Vista is running on a particular machine, you can click Start and type **winver** in the search box. The screen returned will identify the edition as well as the service pack installed.

TABLE 15.2   Windows Vista features

Feature	Description
Aero	The Aero interface was new with Windows Vista. The main difference between it and the previous Windows interface is the glass design that offers translucent windows.
Gadgets	These are mini-programs that can be placed on the desktop, which allows them to run quickly and personalize the PC. Commonly used gadgets are the Calendar, Clock, and news/weather feeds.

Feature	Description
Sidebar	Gadgets can be placed on a bar that appears on the desktop known as the Sidebar (Windows 7 kept the gadgets but did away with the Sidebar). The main selling point for using Sidebar is that the bar can provide one location for the common gadgets and be configured to always be visible.
User Account Control (UAC)	New to Vista, the UAC is intended to prevent unintentional/unauthorized changes to the computer by either prompting for permission or requiring the administrator password.
BitLocker	Referenced by CompTIA as "Bit-Locker," Microsoft calls it BitLocker, and this allows you to use drive encryption to protect files, including those needed for startup and logon.
Shadow Copy	The Volume Shadow Copy Service is used to create the copies you can use should a file be accidentally deleted or overwritten.
ReadyBoost	This feature allows you to use free space on a removable drive (usually USB) as virtual memory and speed up a system. For the option to even be possible, at least 256MB of space must be available on the removable media. ReadyBoost is configured from the ReadyBoost tab of the Properties dialog box for the removable media device.
Compatibility Mode	The Program Compatibility Wizard was included with Vista to configure programs to believe they are running with Windows XP or earlier versions of Windows: Choose Start ➢ Control Panel ➢ Programs, and then click Use An Older Program With This Version Of Windows.
Windows Defender	While available for other operating systems, Windows Vista was the first to ship with the Windows Defender antispyware program.
Windows Firewall	Windows Vista incorporates Windows Firewall, which can be used to stop incoming and outgoing traffic. There are three basic settings: On, Off, and Block All Incoming Connections.
Security Center	Windows Security Center provides a single interface for firewall settings, automatic updating, malware protection, and other security settings.

⊕ **Real World Scenario**

Helpful or Just Plain Annoying?

One of the most derided features of Windows Vista is User Account Control (UAC). This feature was first introduced in Windows Vista, and it has carried on in Windows 7. While the purpose behind it is brilliant—to keep users from accidentally messing up their configuration settings—it turned out to be more a source of frustration than ever anticipated.

Whenever a configuration change is possible—such as starting a utility that could make one or almost anything system related—the UAC either requires an administrator password or prompts the user to verify that they are sure that they really want to go on. The problem lies not with the concept but with the annoyance of constantly having to respond to it. With Windows 7, there are four settings you can choose from to tighten or loosen the hold UAC has on the system. In Windows Vista, it is either on or off.

While turning UAC off is not recommended, you can do so by choosing Start ➢ Control Panel ➢ User Accounts and clicking Turn User Account Control On Or Off. Naturally, UAC prompts you one last time to make sure you really want to make the change. After confirming that you do, or entering the administrator password, clear the check box to turn UAC off.

Installing Windows Vista

As of this writing, Windows 7 is the most current Windows version available and the one you will likely install in new situations. However, you may still need to install Windows Vista if, for example, it needs to be reinstalled on a machine or used as an upgrade over an older operating system. You can install Windows Vista on a machine as a clean install or upgrade the existing operating system to Vista.

Clean Install

There are two methods of running a clean installation. Clean installing Vista over a previous operating system results in the user's data being moved to a folder call WINDOWS.OLD. The first option is to start the computer with the bootable Windows Vista DVD (CDs were available if you needed them) and begin the installation.

The second method—the one Microsoft recommends—is to run Setup from the DVD within your current Windows version. Once the DVD is inserted, the Setup program should automatically begin. If it does not, setup.exe can be manually run from the root folder and the menu will appear. On the menu, choose Install Now and then select Custom (Advanced) when the Which Type Of Installation Do You Want? screen appears. Answer the prompts to walk through and complete the installation.

If booting from the DVD, you will get the message *Press any key to boot from CD or DVD* upon startup, and at this point you simply press a key and then begin the installation.

Windows Activation

To curb software piracy, Microsoft requires that each copy of Windows now be *activated* (either by phone or Internet) after installation. Activation is the validation of the product key. Without activation, you can run the operating system, but only for a limited number of days. During that period of time, Windows will frequently remind you to activate the product.

In addition, the activation records what kind(s) of hardware are in your system, and if three or more pieces change, it requires you to activate again. It's somewhat of a hassle on the part of a system owner if they are constantly upgrading systems. However, some types of Windows distributions don't require activation (such as those under volume license agreements with Microsoft).

The activation process is simple. After installation is complete, a wizard pops up asking if you want to activate Windows. You can choose either the Internet or Phone option. If you have a connection to the Internet, the Activation Wizard asks you only which country you live in. No other personal information is required. You can then click Activate, and the Activation Wizard will send a unique identifier built from the different types of hardware in your system across the Internet to Microsoft's activation servers. These servers will send back a code to the Activation Wizard that activates your copy of Windows. The phone process is similar, but you must enter the code manually after calling Microsoft and receiving it.

Upgrading to Windows Vista

Whereas installation can typically be done over any existing OS, upgrading can only be done from an OS that is generally compatible with the one to which you're upgrading. In other words, the current operating system you are using determines which version of Windows Vista you can upgrade to, if any. Table 15.3 lists the upgrade paths for each Windows Vista 32-bit version based on the existing operating system. Those listed as No must be clean installations.

For the exam, recognize that no version of Windows older than Windows XP can be upgraded to Windows Vista.

TABLE 15.3   Windows Vista upgrade options

Existing Operating System	Vista Home Basic	Vista Home Premium	Vista Business	Vista Ultimate
Windows XP Home	Yes	Yes	Yes	Yes
Windows XP Professional	No	No	Yes	Yes
Windows XP Professional x64	No	No	No	No
Windows XP Media Center 2004/2005	No	Yes	No	Yes
Windows XP Tablet PC	No	No	Yes	Yes
Windows Vista Home Basic	N/A	Yes	No	Yes
Windows Vista Home Premium	No	N/A	No	Yes
Windows Vista Business	No	No	N/A	Yes
Windows Vista Ultimate	No	No	No	N/A

Note that Windows Vista Enterprise does not appear in the table because it is typically installed as a clean install. It can only be installed as an "upgrade" to Windows Vista Business. Note that where N/A appears in the table, an upgrade is not possible, However a repair installation or clean installation can still be performed.

To begin the upgrade, insert the DVD. The Setup program should automatically begin (if it does not, run setup.exe from the root folder) and a menu will appear. On the menu, choose Install Now and then select Upgrade when the Which Type Of Installation Do You Want? screen appears. Answer the prompts to walk through the upgrade. On a standard, default installation, the /boot directory holds the boot file configuration for Windows Vista.

 You could once obtain CDs instead of the Windows Vista DVD from Microsoft, but they are no longer available.

Booting from the DVD is also possible but recommended only if the method just described does not work. When you boot, you will get a *Press any key to boot from CD or DVD* message upon startup, and at this point you simply press a key and begin the upgrade.

Transferring to Windows Vista

The *User State Migration Tool (USMT)* can be downloaded from Microsoft. It is intended to be used by administrators and requires a client computer connected to a Windows Server–based domain controller. It allows you to migrate user file settings related to applications, desktop configuration, and accounts for USMT 2.6 (USMT 3.0 does not require domain controller access except to transfer domain accounts). More information on USMT can be found at the following location:

`http://technet.microsoft.com/en-us/library/cc722032(WS.10).aspx.`

Windows Easy Transfer is also available for transferring items to Windows Vista (Start ➢ All Programs ➢ Accessories ➢ System Tools ➢ Windows Easy Transfer). This tool is intended for the one-time transfer of user settings, as well as applications and files, to Vista whereas USMT is meant for wide-scale migrations. A key difference is that USMT allows transfers to be scripted whereas WET uses a GUI that requires user interaction.

The Windows Vista Boot Sequences

Both for the exam and for practical application, you should know how to recognize common problems with the OS and be able to make certain it is booting correctly. The sections that follow look at a number of topics related to keeping your OS booting and running properly.

Key Boot Files

Windows Vista requires only a few files, each of which performs specific tasks. These files differ from the files for Windows XP and all previous Windows operating systems. These are discussed next in the order in which they load:

BOOTMGR   The Windows Boot Manager (BOOTMGR) bootstraps the system. In other words, this file starts the loading of an OS on the computer. This file replaces NTLDR (used in previous operating systems) and is responsible for switching from real to protected mode during the boot process. The latter mode provides memory protection, multitasking, and other features you expect from the operating system.

BCD   The Boot Configuration Data (BCD) file holds information about OSs installed on the computer, such as the location of the OS files.

WINLOAD.EXE   The program used to boot Windows Vista. It loads the operating system kernel (NTOSKRNL.EXE).

WINRESUME.EXE   If the system is not starting fresh, but resuming a previous session, then WINRESUME.EXE is called by the BOOTMGR.

NTOSKRNL.EXE   The Windows OS kernel. The solution to a corrupted NTOSKRNL.EXE file is to boot from a startup disk and replace the file from the setup disks or CD.

System files   In addition to the previously listed files, Windows needs a number of files from its system directories (e.g., system and system32), such as the hardware abstraction layer (HAL.DLL), session manager (SMSS.EXE), user session (WINLOGON.EXE) and security subsystem (LSASS.EXE).

We'll now look at the Windows Vista boot process from start to finish:

1. The system self-checks and enumerates hardware resources. BIOS looks for the Master Boot Record.

2. The Master Boot Record (MBR) loads and finds the volume boot sector. The MBR finds the bootable partition and searches it for the NT boot sector of that partition.

3. The MBR determines the file system and loads BOOTMGR. Information in the boot sector allows the system to locate the system partition and to find and load into memory the file located there.

4. BOOTMGR checks to see if WINRESUME.EXE is needed.

5. BOOTMGR processes BCD.

6. BOOTMGR loads and runs WINLOAD.EXE.

7. WINLOAD.EXE loads NTOSKRNL.EXE and HAL.DLL.NTOSKRNL.EXE holds the OS kernel and also what's known as the *executive subsystems*. Executive subsystems are software components that parse the Registry for configuration information and start needed services and drivers. HAL.DLL enables communication between the OS and the installed hardware.

8. The HKEY_LOCAL_MACHINE\SYSTEM Registry hive and device drivers are loaded and control is transferred to NTOSKRNL.EXE to complete the boot process. It calls the WIN32K.SYS subsystem and the session manager SMSS.EXE.

9. WINLOGON.EXE loads. At this point, you are presented with the Logon screen. After you enter a username and password, you're taken to the Windows Desktop.

Windows Vista Features

There are a number of features that make Windows Vista an operating system worth noting. In the following sections, we will look first at some of the tools; we'll focus on the ones you need to know for the A+ exam. By default, Vista displays a user friendly screen for the Control Panel; clicking on Classic View will show all the available Control Panel items discussed in the following descriptions.

Tools in Windows Vista

The tools that stand out in Windows Vista, and that CompTIA expects you to know for the exam, include System Restore, Windows Defender, Windows Firewall, and Security Center. They are discussed in the sections that follow.

System Restore

Chapter 12 explored System Restore as it appears in all three versions of Windows that you are tested on. System Restore is arguably the most powerful tool in Windows Vista. It allows you to restore the system to a previous point in time. This feature is accessed from Start ➢ All Programs ➢ Accessories ➢ System Tools ➢ System Restore and can be used to roll back as well as to create a restore point. Figure 15.1 shows the opening screen of the dialog box.

In the operating system preceding this one, Windows XP, you could also choose to create a restore point manually from the opening screen of the System Restore dialog box. With Windows Vista, the manual creation of the restore point can no longer be accessed from this screen, and instead the restore point must be manually created from the System Protection tab of System Properties (Start ➢ Control Panel ➢ System). Depending on the view you are using, you may need to select System and Maintenance before it shows you the System option, shown in Figure 15.2.

Windows Defender

Windows Defender can identify spyware and unwanted software and is native to all versions of Vista (Start ➢ Control Panel ➢ Windows Defender). Depending on the view you are using, you may need to select Security before it shows you the Windows Defender option. As with similar programs, in order for Windows Defender to function properly, you need to keep the definitions current and scan the system on a regular basis.

Windows Firewall

Windows Firewall (Start ➢ Control Panel ➢ Windows Firewall) is used to block access from the network (be it internal or the Internet). While host-based firewalls are not as secure as other types of firewalls, this was a great move in the right direction and has been a component of Windows ever since Windows XP Service Pack 2.

FIGURE 15.1   System Restore in Windows Vista

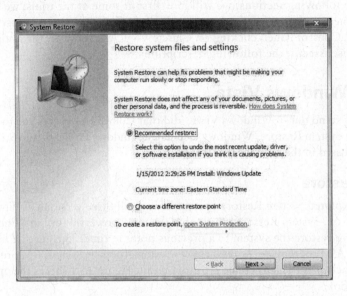

FIGURE 15.2   The option for creating a restore point in Windows Vista

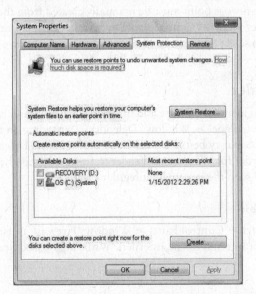

Figure 15.3 shows the opening screen of Windows Firewall in Windows Vista. Windows Firewall is turned on by default and it is also included in the Security Center (discussed in the next section).

FIGURE 15.3   Windows Firewall can block unwanted traffic.

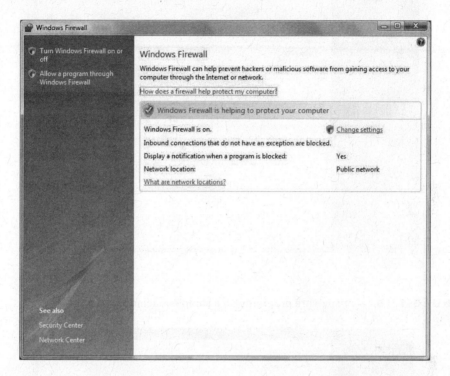

By default, Windows Firewall blocks incoming traffic. Clicking the Change Settings link opens the Windows Firewall Settings screen, which has three tabs: General, Exceptions, and Advanced. Using the Exceptions tab, you can configure which incoming traffic you want to allow through.

Security Center

Security Center (Start ➢ Control Panel ➢ Security Center) provides a single interface where you can administer Windows Firewall, Automatic Updates, Malware Protection, and other security settings. Figure 15.4 shows the opening screen.

You can expand any of the four main categories to offer information on what is installed and make configuration changes. For example, as shown in Figure 15.5, by expanding Malware Protection and clicking Show Me The Antispyware Programs On This Computer, it is possible to see that on this particular machine, there are three tools, and one of them—Windows Defender—is not turned on.

FIGURE 15.4   Windows Security Center in Windows Vista

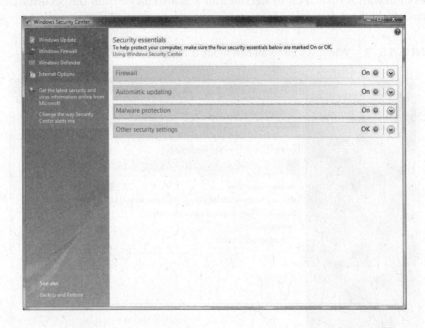

FIGURE 15.5   Antispyware programs on a sample machine

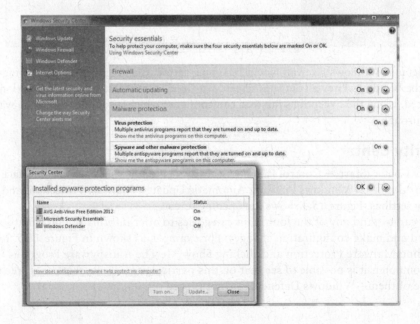

Windows Vista Administrative Tools

There are a number of system tools included with Windows Vista that you need to know for the exam. These administrative tools, discussed in the order they appear in the objectives, also include Windows Firewall, but it was covered earlier in this chapter.

Users and Groups

As an administrator, you can configure the users and groups on a system in the Microsoft Management Console (MMC). Start by clicking Start ➢ and typing MMC in the Search box and pressing Enter. If Local Users And Groups is not visible in the left pane, choose File, then Add/Remove Snap-In, and then select Local Users And Groups from the list of possible snap-ins. You can choose to manage the local computer or another computer (requiring you to provide its address).

Local Users And Groups is not available for Windows Vista in any edition other than Windows Vista Business, Windows Vista Ultimate, and Windows Vista Enterprise. In all other editions, you must manage user accounts using the User Accounts applet in Control Panel and you cannot create or manage groups.

Local Security Policy

The Local Security Policy (Choose Start ➢ and then enter **secpol.msc**) (also available as Control Panel ➢ Administrative Tools ➢ Local Security Policy) allows you to set the default security settings for the system. This feature is not available for Windows Vista in any edition other than Windows Vista Business, Windows Vista Ultimate, and Windows Vista Enterprise.

The following sections examine some of the Security Settings choices.

Account Policies

Account Policies further divides into Password Policy and Account Lockout Policy.

Password Policy

The following choices are available under Password Policy:

Enforce Password History This allows you to require unique passwords for a certain number of iterations. The default number is 0, but it can go as high as 24.

Maximum Password Age This variable defines the maximum number of days a password can be used. The default is 42 days, but values range from 0 to 999.

Minimum Password Age This variable defines the minimum number of days that a password must be used between password changes. The default is 0 days, but values range from 0 to 999.

Minimum Password Length This variable defines the least number of characters that must be used in a password. The default is 0 characters (meaning no passwords are required), but you can specify a number up to 14.

Password Must Meet Complexity Requirements   This setting is disabled by default. When it is turned on, the password must include at least three of the following criteria: uppercase characters, lowercase characters, numerical characters, nonalphanumeric characters, Unicode characters.

Store Password Using Reversible Encryption For All Users In The Domain   This setting is disabled by default. When it's enabled, it provides support for applications that require knowledge of the password.

Because the likelihood of laptops being stolen always exists, it's strongly encouraged that you implement strong password policies. Here's an example:

- Enforce Password History: 8 passwords remembered
- Maximum Password Age: 42 days
- Minimum Password Age: 3 days
- Minimum Password Length: 6 to 8 characters

Leave the other two settings disabled.

Account Lockout Policy

The Account Lockout Policy setting is divided into the following three values:

Account Lockout Threshold   This is the number of invalid attempts before lockout occurs. The default is 0 (meaning the feature is turned off). Invalid attempt settings range from 1 to 999. A number greater than 0 changes the values of the following two options to 30 minutes; otherwise, they are "not defined."

Account Lockout Duration   This is a number of minutes an account lockout lasts, ranging from 1 to 99999. A value of 0 is also allowed here and signifies that the account never unlocks itself—administrator interaction is always required. When the number is greater than 0, the user must wait that many minutes before being allowed to try to log in again.

Reset Account Lockout Counter After   This is a number of minutes, ranging from 1 to 99999, that each failed login attempt remains on the counter. For example, if the value is set at 5, then after 5 minutes, one of the failed attempts is removed from the counter.

When you're working with a mobile workforce, you must weigh the choice of users calling you in the middle of the night when they've forgotten their password against keeping the system from being entered if the wrong user picks up the laptop. A good recommendation is to use a lockout after five attempts for a period of time between 30 and 60 minutes.

Local Policy Settings

The Local Policies section is divided into three subsections: Audit Policy, User Rights Assignment, and Security Options. The Audit Policy section contains nine settings; the default value for each is No Auditing. When auditing is enabled, log entries are created for interactions with the item specified by the setting. Valid options are Success and Failure. The Audit Account Logon Events entry is the one you should consider turning on for mobile users to see how often they log in and out of their machines.

When auditing is turned on for an event, the entries are logged in the Security log file.

The User Rights Assignment subsection of Local Policies is where the meat of what was once called System Policies comes into play. User Rights Assignment has many options, most of which are self-explanatory. Part of what is shown in the list of user rights are the defaults for who can perform each action; a value of Not Defined indicates that no one is specified for the corresponding operation.

The Security Options section includes a great many options, which, for the most part, are representative of various Registry keys. The default for each is Not Defined; the two definitions that can be assigned are Enabled and Disabled, or a physical number can be assigned (as with the number of previous logons to cache).

System Configuration

The System Configuration tool (`msconfig.exe`) in Windows Vista is used to control the way the system behaves at startup and includes a number of tabs and options, as shown in Figure 15.6.

FIGURE 15.6   The System Configuration tool in Windows Vista

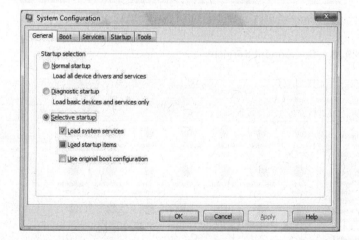

By clicking the Boot tab, you can see configuration options for the BCD and make some minor changes, as shown in Figure 15.7. The Advanced Options button allows you to configure the number of processors, maximum memory, and global debug settings.

Component Services

Component Services is an MMC snap-in in Windows Vista that allows you to administer and deploy component services. It can be used to configure various settings, such as security settings. With this tool, it is possible for administrators to manage components while developers configure routine component and application behavior (object pooling, for example). Figure 15.8 shows an example of the interface.

FIGURE 15.7   Options available on the Boot tab

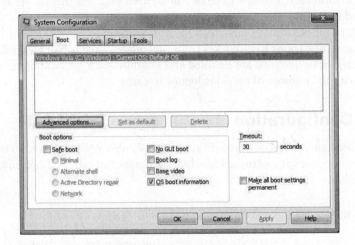

FIGURE 15.8   Component Services

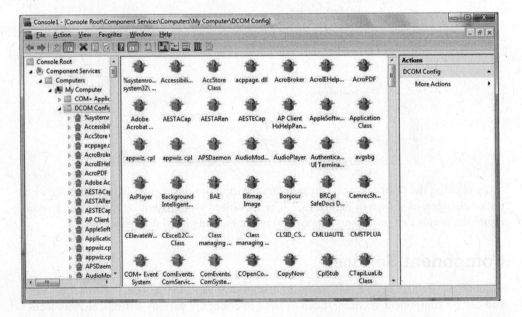

Data Sources

ODBC Data Source Administrator, accessed via Start ➢ Control Panel ➢ Administrative Tools ➢ Data Sources (ODBC), allows you to interact with database management systems. Figure 15.9 shows an example of the screen.

FIGURE 15.9   Data Sources in Vista

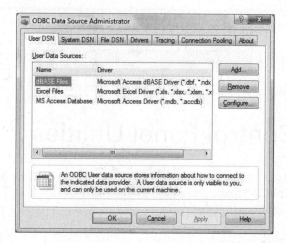

Database drivers that are added to the system will show up here and can be shared between applications.

Print Management

New to Windows Vista, Print Management (Start ➢ Control Panel ➢ Administrative Tools ➢ Print Management) allows you to manage multiple printers and print servers from a single interface. Print Management is not available for Windows Vista in any edition other than Windows Vista Business, Windows Vista Ultimate, and Windows Vista Enterprise. In all other editions, you must manage individual printers using the Printers applet in Control Panel, and you are very limited in what you can manage.

Windows Memory Diagnostics

The Windows Memory Diagnostics tool (Start ➢ Control Panel ➢ Administrative Tools ➢ Memory Diagnostics Tool) can be used to check a system for memory problems. For the tool to work, the system must be restarted. The two options that it offers are to restart the computer now and check for problems or wait and check for problems on the next restart.

Upon reboot, the test will take several minutes and the display screen will show the number of which pass is being run and the overall status of the test (percent complete). When the memory test concludes, the system will restart again and nothing related to it having run is apparent until you log in. If the test is without error, you'll see a message that no errors were found (see Figure 15.10). If any issues have been detected, the results will be displayed.

FIGURE 15.10   Memory test results

Unique Control Panel Utilities

There are a number of Control Panel applets unique to Windows Vista to be aware of. These include Tablet PC Settings, Pen And Input Devices, Offline files, Problem Reports And Solutions, and Printers.

Tablet PC Settings

The Tablet PC Settings applet (Start ➢ Control Panel ➢ Tablet PC Settings) in Windows Vista can be used, as the name implies, to configure the device on which the operating system is installed to function as a true tablet. You can tweak handwriting recognition, handedness (left versus right), and other tablet-relevant settings.

Figure 15.11 shows the interface when Tablet PC Settings is first opened.

The Home Basic edition of Windows Vista does not support a tablet PC input panel, but all other editions of the operating system do.

Pen and Input Devices

The Pen And Input Devices applet (Start ➢ Control Panel ➢ Pen And Input Devices) in Windows Vista is used in conjunction with the Tablet PC Settings applet. It is used to configure the pen and pointer options, as shown in Figure 15.12.

The Home Basic edition of Windows Vista does not support a tablet PC or have this applet, but all other editions of the operating system do.

Offline Files

Only some editions of Windows Vista (Business Ultimate and Enterprise) support offline files. Beginning with Windows 2000, the Windows-based operating systems added the capability to work with resources that are "online" (accessed through the network or other connection) and "offline" (replicated copies of the resource stored locally). The key is to keep the files in synchronization so that multiple copies of the same file stored in different locations match each other.

FIGURE 15.11   Tablet PC Settings

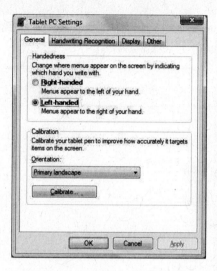

FIGURE 15.12   Pen And Input Device Settings

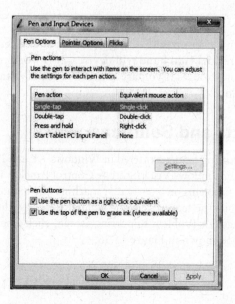

Windows Vista includes a Sync Center (Start ≻ Control Panel, then click Sync Center), as shown in Figure 15:13.

FIGURE 15.13   The Sync Center in Windows Vista is the primary interface for configuring synchronization.

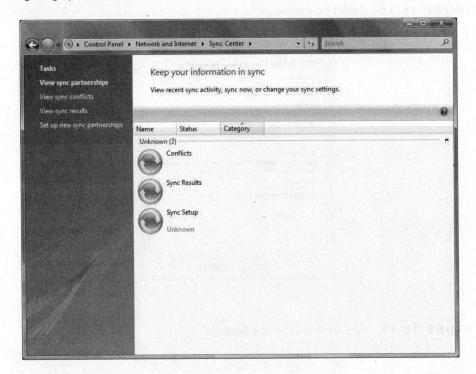

Sync partnerships can be set up with a large number of devices, ranging from a flash drive (as shown in Figure 15.14) to handheld devices. It is worth noting again that you cannot sync with network folders if you are using Windows Vista Starter, Home Basic, or Home Premium editions.

Problem Reports and Solutions

Building on the error reporting features offered in Windows XP, the Problem Reports And Solutions applet with Windows Vista (Start ≻ Control Panel ≻ Problem Reports And Solutions) can help solve problems on a particular machine (see Figure 15.15).

To configure (or disable) the feature, choose Change Settings, then Advanced Settings. On the Advanced Settings For Problem Reporting screen, click Change Setting to open a window similar to the one shown in Figure 15.16.

FIGURE 15.14 Establish a partnership with the device you want to sync with in Sync Center.

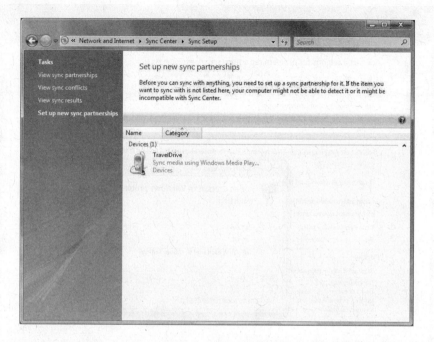

FIGURE 15.15 Problem Reports And Solutions in Windows Vista

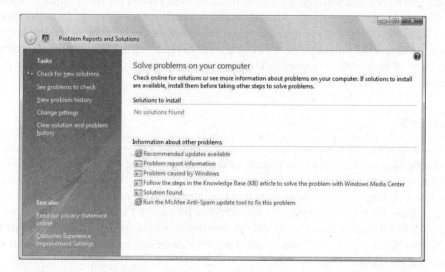

FIGURE 15.16 Windows error reporting options in Windows Vista

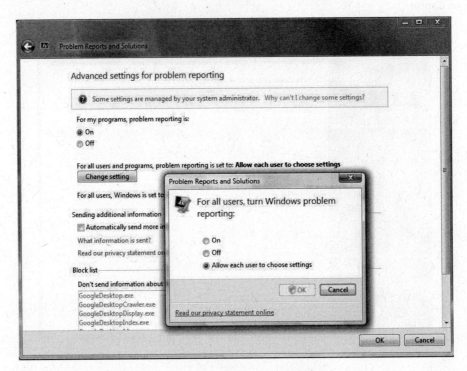

Your two major choices are to disable or enable error reporting. If you choose to disable it, you can still be notified when errors occur. Windows Vista offers the third choice of allowing each user to choose their settings. After choosing to enable error reporting, you can choose to report Windows operating system and/or program errors. By clicking the program's button, you can configure the programs on which you want to report errors. By default, all program errors from all programs are reported, but you can configure the reporting of errors on a program-by-program basis.

Printers

The Printers applet in Windows Vista (Start ➤ Control Panel ➤ Printers) provides a simple interface for adding a new printer or managing existing ones. Figure 15.17 shows an example.

By right-clicking on any printer shown in the interface, you can choose to make it the default printer from the options menu that appears (in Figure 15.17, the check mark on the Epson NX510 indicates that it is the default printer). Clicking Add A Printer will start the Add Printer Wizard and allow you to add a network, wireless, or Bluetooth printer as well as one that is locally connected.

FIGURE 15.17   The Printers applet in Windows Vista

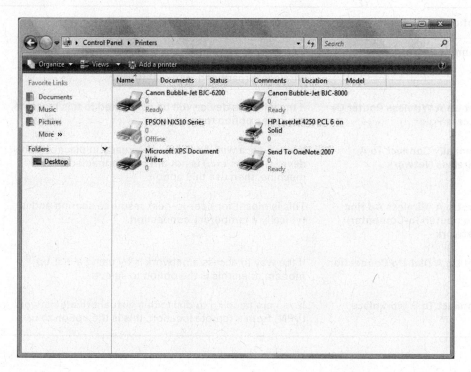

Networking and Windows Vista

There are a number of things CompTIA expects you to know when it comes to the topic of networking and Windows Vista. Most of the networking topics are covered in the chapters dedicated to that and thus the discussion here is limited only to those topics specifically tied to Windows Vista.

HomeGroups is a feature in Windows 7 and not Windows Vista, but you can easily configure almost any other type of network you want with Vista. By choosing the Network And Sharing Center (Start ➤ Control Panel ➤ Network And Sharing Center), you can choose to connect to an existing network, see (and manage) your current connections, and set up a new network. Choosing to set up a new network offers the choices shown in Figure 15.18.

The choices that are available are elaborated on in Table 15.4.

TABLE 15.4   Network Connection Options

Option	Purpose
Connect To The Internet	Use for connection to a proxy server or other device intended to provide Internet access. This includes wireless, broadband, and dial-up.
Set Up A Wireless Router Or Access Point	If the wireless device will be connected to this machine, this is the option to use.
Manually Connect To A Wireless Network	If you have a wireless network already in place and the device (router, etc.) is not directly connected to this machine, then use this option.
Set Up A Wireless Ad Hoc (Computer-To-Computer) Network	This is meant for peer-to-peer resource sharing and is typically a temporary connection.
Set Up A Dial-Up Connection	If the way to access a network is by using a dial-up modem, then this is the option to select.
Connect To A Workplace	If you are needing to dial in to a virtual private network (VPN) from a remote location, this is the option to use.

FIGURE 15.18   Creating a new network connection in Windows Vista

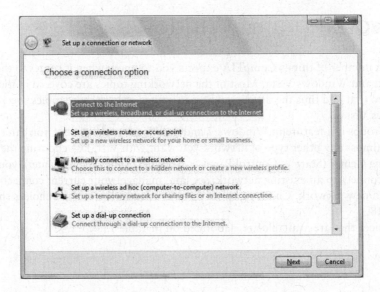

Regardless of which option you choose, you will need to fill out the appropriate fields for the device to be able to communicate on the network. With TCP/IP, the only required values needed are an IP address for the host and a subnet mask to function. At the bare minimum, though, an address for the gateway, and DNS information is recommended to be able to access other networks or the Internet.

You also need to specify one of the types of locations for this network: Home, Work, or Public. If you choose one of the first two, *network discovery* is on by default, allowing you to see other computers and other computers to see you. If you choose Public, network discovery is turned off. Exercise 15.1 walks through the process of changing a network location type.

EXERCISE 15.1

Changing the Network Location Type in Windows Vista

1. Click the Start button, and choose Control Panel.

2. Choose Network And Sharing Center.

3. Click the Customize link to the right of the network connection.

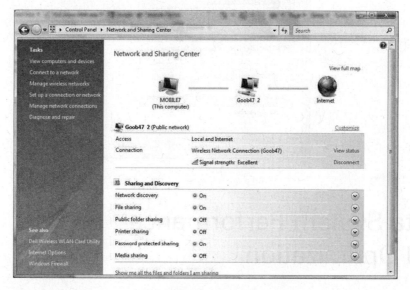

4. Change the setting for the connection. You have two choices, one of which will already be selected:

   - Public

   - Private

5. Click Next.

6. Click Close and exit the Network And Sharing Center.

Network card properties that may be required include the speed at which the card will communicate and whether it is *half duplex* (data going one direction at a time), *full duplex* (data going both directions at a time), or automatic. There may be extra features to configure, including *Wake-on-LAN (WoL)*, an Ethernet standard implemented via a card that allows a "sleeping" machine to awaken when it receives a wakeup signal. *Quality of Service (QoS)*, another extra feature, implements packet scheduling to control the flow of traffic and help with network transmission speeds. Figure 15.19 shows the QoS packet scheduler installed on a card. No properties can be configured for the service itself.

FIGURE 15.19 QoS scheduling on a network card in Windows Vista

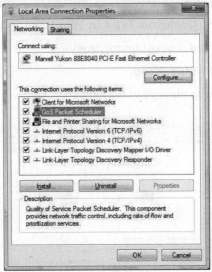

Vista System Performance and Optimization

Windows Vista introduced a number of features that an administrator should be aware of to understand how to better optimize a system. Some of these were mentioned at the beginning of the chapter, but only in passing. These include the *Aero* interface, the *User Account Control* feature, indexing, and *Sidebar*.

Aero

An acronym for *Authentic, Energetic, Reflective, and Open*, Aero differs from previous GUIs in that its windows are translucent and it allows the ability to create a 3D stack of open windows and cycle through them (known as *Flip 3D*); while Flip 3D is nice, it relies on a more important feature of Aero that provides live thumbnails of each window, as demonstrated in Windows Flip (the standard task window) and on the Taskbar. To configure Aero, right-click on the Desktop and choose Personalize from the context menu, and then choose Window Color And Appearance, as shown in Figure 15.20.

FIGURE 15.20   Configuring Aero

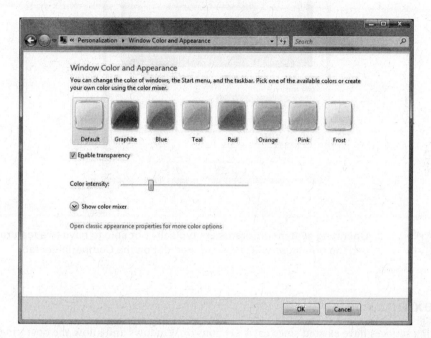

Here, you can turn off the transparency, as well as change the colors used for windows. Aero can be turned off altogether by clicking Open Classic Appearance Properties For More Color Options. This brings up the Appearance Settings dialog box shown in Figure 15.21, from which you can choose to use Windows Standard, Windows Classic, or another interface (choosing anything but the default of Windows Aero turns Aero off).

User Account Control

The User Account Control (UAC) feature was mentioned earlier in this chapter and has the sole purpose of keeping the user from running programs that could pose a potential threat by requiring escalating privileges for many actions. While turning UAC off is an option, it is not a recommended option. If you have a program you regularly run and do not want to be prompted each time, you can right-click the icon for that program and then click Properties. Choose the Compatibility tab and then select the Run This Program As An Administrator check box. This will prevent the prompt from occurring each time you use the program.

FIGURE 15.21   Choosing an interface besides Aero

Operating system programs are typically not able to have this feature set and the privileges will stayed grayed out on the Compatibility tab.

Indexing

Indexing services have existed since early versions of Windows and allow the operating system to quickly find files by looking through a database of entries rather than having to start from scratch each time. The primary interface for configuring indexing is the Indexing Options applet in Control Panel. Figure 15.22 shows this interface for Windows Vista, and it differs from previous OS versions simply in the addition of the Pause button.

The Advanced button takes you to the heart of the configuration. From here, you can choose whether to include encrypted files, and what types of files to include in the index. Most meaningful is the ability to choose whether the index should include properties only (the default) or also include file contents. While choosing to include contents in the index greatly decreases search time, it can also slow the system down on a regular basis as it builds the index.

Sidebar

The Sidebar is a feature that allows easy access to gadgets. To configure the Sidebar, right-click on an area of it and choose Properties (if the Sidebar is not visible, click Start ➢ All Programs ➢ Accessories ➢ Windows Sidebar). This will bring up the dialog box shown in Figure 15.23.

FIGURE 15.22   Configuring Indexing

FIGURE 15.23   Configuring the Sidebar

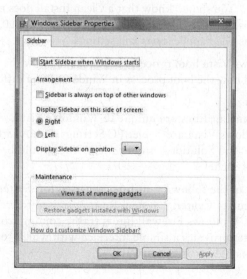

In addition to choosing Properties from the context menu, you can choose Close Sidebar, Bring Gadgets To Front, and Add Gadgets. To remove a gadget, right-click it and choose Close Gadget. You can also drag any gadget from the Sidebar directly onto the Desktop and drag them from the Desktop into the Sidebar as you wish.

Summary

This chapter focused on Windows Vista. Even though it is not the newest Windows operating system on the market, CompTIA expects you to be familiar with it and be able to answer questions on everything from installing it to managing it.

We looked at the various features of Windows Vista, some that exist in other versions of Windows and some that are unique to this operating system. The latter category includes Tablet PC Settings, Pen And Input Devices, Offline Files, Problem Reports And Solutions, and Printers.

Exam Essentials

Know what types of installations are possible with Windows Vista.   You should know which operating systems can be upgraded to Windows Vista and which require a clean installation.

Understand upgrading.   You should know that a Clean Install does not preserve installed applications and will push old data files and setting into WINDOWS.OLD, while an in-place upgrade will preserve installed applications and settings.

Understand the Windows Vista boot process, and order.   Know the purpose and role of BOOTMGR and BCD and how the boot process in Windows Vista differs from that of Windows XP.

Know what Control Panel utilities are unique to Windows Vista.   The Control Panel applets unique to Windows Vista are Tablet PC Settings, Pen And Input Devices, Offline Files, Problem Reports And Solutions, and Printers. You should be familiar with the purpose and options of each.

Understand what each of the following utilities are used for: System Restore, Windows Firewall, Security Center.   System Restore is used to create, and revert back to, restore points. Windows Firewall limits traffic coming from the network to the host. Security Center provides a simple interface with which to interact with virus scanners and other installed security software.

Review Questions

The answers to the Chapter Review Questions can be found in Appendix A.

1. Which version of Windows Vista does *not* include offline folder capabilities?

   A. Business

   B. Enterprise

   C. Home Premium

   D. Ultimate

2. What is the first file used in the boot-up of Windows Vista?

   A. NTOSKRNL.EXE

   B. CONFIG.SYS

   C. AUTOEXEC.BAT

   D. BOOTMGR

3. What is the maximum amount of RAM supported in the 64-bit Home Premium edition of Windows Vista?

   A. 8GB

   B. 16GB

   C. 128GB

   D. 256GB

4. Which of the following is an Ethernet standard implemented via a card that allows a "sleeping" machine to awaken when it receives a wakeup signal?

   A. Sleep timer

   B. WEP

   C. Wake-on-LAN

   D. WPA

5. Which editions of Windows Vista include BitLocker support? (Choose two.)

   A. Business

   B. Enterprise

   C. Home Premium

   D. Ultimate

6. Which Windows Vista feature allows you to recover from an accidental deletion or overwrite?

   A. BitLocker

   B. User Account Control

   C. Security Center

   D. Shadow Copy

7. You are migrating one stand-alone machine from Windows XP to Window Vista. Which of the following tools should you consider for transferring user state data and application files?

   A. Windows State Mover

   B. UDMT

   C. Windows Easy Transfer

   D. USMT

8. In Windows Vista, which of the following utilities can be used to see the edition and service pack installed on a system?

   A. info

   B. spm

   C. winver

   D. msall

9. Which utility is shown in the following screen shot?

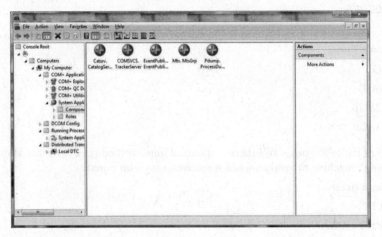

   A. Windows Memory Diagnostics

   B. Print Management

   C. Data Sources

   D. Component Services

10. Which of the following files is at the end of the boot process and presents the user with the Logon screen?

   A. SMSS

   B. Winlogon

   C. HAL

   D. SIR

11. Where is the Windows Memory Diagnostics utility found in Windows Vista?

  A. In the `Accessories` folder

  B. In the `System` folder, beneath `Accessories`

  C. Beneath `Administrative Tools`

  D. Not available in Windows Vista

12. Which editions of Windows Vista support Local Security Policy (`secpol.msc`)? (Choose three.)

  A. Windows Vista Home Basic

  B. Windows Vista Home Premium

  C. Windows Vista Business

  D. Windows Vista Enterprise

  E. Windows Vista Ultimate

13. After installation of the Windows Vista operating system, what is required in order to curb software piracy?

  A. Certification

  B. Confirmation

  C. Activation

  D. Substantiation

14. What is the maximum number of physical CPUs supported by Windows Vista Business edition?

  A. One

  B. Two

  C. Three

  D. Four

15. Which utility is the System Configuration tool in Windows Vista?

  A. `msinfo32.exe`

  B. `msconfig.exe`

  C. `sysconfig.cpl`

  D. `config.cpl`

16. Which feature allows you to use free space on a removable drive (usually USB) to speed up a system?

  A. USB Speed

  B. Shadow Copy

  C. ReadyBoost

  D. Screamer

17. Spencer is currently running Windows XP Professional and wants to upgrade to Windows Vista. Which of the following upgrades are possible? (Choose two.)

    A. Windows Vista Business

    B. Windows Vista Enterprise

    C. Windows Vista Home Premium

    D. Windows Vista Ultimate

18. Which of the following network locations disables network discovery in Windows Vista?

    A. Home

    B. Work

    C. Public

    D. Personal

19. Which directory on a standard Windows Vista installation holds the boot file configuration?

    A. /boot

    B. /start

    C. /system32

    D. /windows

20. What is the maximum amount of RAM supported in the 64-bit Ultimate edition of Windows Vista?

    A. 8GB

    B. 16GB

    C. 128GB

    D. 256GB

Performance-Based Question

On the A+ exams, you will encounter performance-based questions. The questions on the exam require you to perform a specific task, and you will be graded on whether you were able to complete the task. The following require you to think creatively to measure how well you understand this chapter's topics. You may or may not see similar questions on the actual A+ exams. To see how your answers compare to the authors', refer to Appendix B.

You are trying to troubleshoot a Windows Vista machine and think memory may be an issue. How can you run the Windows Memory Diagnostics Tool?

Chapter

16

Working with Windows XP

THE FOLLOWING COMPTIA A+ 220-802 EXAM OBJECTIVES ARE COVERED IN THIS CHAPTER:

✓ **1.1 Compare and contrast the features and requirements of various Microsoft Operating Systems.**

- Windows XP Home, Windows XP Professional, Windows XP Media Center, Windows XP 64-bit Professional

- Features:

  - System restore, defender, Windows firewall, security center

✓ **1.2 Given a scenario, install, and configure the operating system using the most appropriate method.**

- Types of installations:

  - Creating image

  - Unattended installation

  - Upgrade

  - Clean install

  - Repair installation

  - Multiboot

  - Remote network installation

  - Image deployment

✓ **1.4 Given a scenario, use appropriate operating system features and tools.**

- Administrative:

  - Users and groups

  - Local security policy

- System configuration
- Component services
- Data sources
- Windows firewall

- Other:
  - User State Migration Tool (USMT), File and Settings Transfer Wizard, Windows Easy Transfer

✓ **1.5 Given a scenario, use Control Panel utilities.**

- Unique to Windows XP:
  - Add/remove programs
  - Network connections
  - Printers and faxes
  - Automatic updates
  - Network setup wizard

✓ **1.6 Setup and configure Windows networking on a client/desktop.**

- Workgroup vs. domain setup
- Establish networking connections:
  - VPN
  - Dialups
  - Wireless
  - Wired
  - WWAN (Cellular)
- Proxy settings
- Remote desktop
- Network card properties:
  - Wake-on-LAN

This is the final chapter of the set that examines operating systems. In this chapter, Windows XP is explored in detail.

While this operating system has been out for a while, it is still widely used in legacy installations and is an operating system that you must know well for the 220-802 certification exam. Some of the tools covered have been addressed in the previous chapters for Windows 7 and Windows Vista, but be certain you know the differences in how they operate in Windows XP.

Installing the Operating System

Operating system installations can be lumped into two generic methods: attended or unattended. During an attended installation, you walk through the installation manually and answer the questions as prompted. Questions about the product key, the directory in which you want to install the operating system (OS), and relevant network settings are typically asked.

As simple as attended installations may be, they're time consuming and administrator intensive in that they require someone to fill in a fair number of fields to move through the process. Unattended installations allow you to configure the OS with little or no human intervention.

Working in the computing field, you may know that Windows XP is aging and that it is unlikely you would install it on a system today, let alone "upgrade" another operating system to it. Sadly, that reality can cost you valuable points on this exam if you don't take the time to study properly. CompTIA specifically wants you to know about Windows XP and the intricacies of it. Take the time to read the Windows XP material carefully; the time you spend doing this will be rewarded when you pass this exam.

Windows XP offers a number of methods for performing unattended installations, with the primary ones being Remote Installation Service (RIS), Windows Deployment Services (WDS), and the System Preparation tool (Sysprep). Both RIS and WDS are services that run on Windows Server. Client machines that are to have Windows XP installed must connect to a server service and run the installation across the network.

The System Preparation tool takes a completely different approach. SYSPREP.EXE is used to prepare a preconfigured Windows XP workstation so that an image can be made from it using third-party software. That image, which lacks user/computer-specific information and security identifiers (SIDs), can then be deployed to other client computers, typically also through the use of third-party software.

Setup Manager is not an unattended installation method in and of itself but is used to create answer files (known as uniqueness database files [UDFs]) for automatically providing computer or user information during setup. Setup Manager, like Sysprep, isn't installed on the system by default but is stored within the `Deploy` cabinet file on the CD beneath `Support\Tools`.

For the exam, you should be familiar with the attended installation and know that the other methods exist.

Determining OS Installation Options

One of the first steps in preparing to install an OS is to make sure you have appropriate hardware that meets at least the minimum system specifications. (see Chapter 12, "OS Basics," for information on compatibility and minimum system requirements). In addition, you must make decisions about a few of the Windows installation options. These options control how Windows will be installed as well as which Windows components will be installed:

- Installation type
- Network configuration
- File system type
- Dual-boot support

Installation Type

When you install an application, an OS, or any software, you almost always have options as to how it is installed. Especially with OSs, there are usually many packages that make up the software. You can choose how to install the many different components; these options are usually labeled something like Typical, Full, Minimal, and Custom:

- A typical installation installs the most commonly used components of the software but not all of the components.

- A full installation installs every last component, even those that may not be required or used frequently.

- A minimal installation (also known as a compact installation) installs only those components needed to get the software functional.

- A custom installation usually allows you to choose exactly which components are installed.

All Windows versions use these installation types, or derivations of them, and you should decide ahead of time which method you are going to use (which may be dictated by the amount of disk space you have available).

Network Configuration

With Windows XP, you can choose whether to install networking options. If you do install networking, you can also choose which networking components you want installed. With Windows XP, you also must know whether the machine will join a workgroup or a domain.

File System Type

As Windows has evolved, a number of changes have been made to the basic architecture, as you might expect. One of the architecture items that had changed the most is the disk system structure. When you're installing any Windows OS, you will be asked first to select a partition on which to install it and then to format the drive using one of the available file systems. Choose based on what the computer will be doing and which OS you are installing. NTFS is generally used (and strongly recommended) unless you will be creating a dual-boot machine.

Dual-Boot Support

Occasionally, a mission-critical program (one you or your business can't function without) doesn't support the OS to which you are upgrading. There may be a newer release in the future, but when you need to upgrade, it may not be supported. In that case, you may have to install the new OS in a dual-boot configuration.

In a *dual-boot configuration*, you install two OSs on the same computer (Windows XP and a legacy copy of Windows 2000, for example). At boot time, you have the option of selecting which OS you want to use.

It is possible to multiboot to all Microsoft OSs, including old versions of DOS and all versions of Windows. Microsoft recommends that each installation target a separate disk or partition in order to avoid conflicts with built-in programs like Internet Explorer. In addition, it is important to install the oldest OS first and then proceed in chronological order to the newest.

For more information on dual-boot and multiboot configurations, visit the Microsoft support website at http://support.microsoft.com.

Thanks to the ability to create virtual machines (VMs), it is becoming far less common to need dual-boot machines today than in the past. Using VMs, you can run multiple operating systems (or multiple instances of the same operating system) on the same hardware at the same time and not need to reboot the system each time you want a different OS.

Determining the Installation Method

Another decision you must make is which method you are going to use to install Windows. Windows XP is still small enough that it comes on a single CD (Windows Vista added DVDs). It is possible to boot to this disc and begin the installation process. However, your system must be capable of supporting bootable media.

If you don't have a bootable CD, you must first boot the computer using some other bootable media (such as the hard drive, flash drive, etc.), which then loads the driver for the CD-ROM drive so that you can access the installation program on the CD.

There's one more thing to consider when evaluating installation methods. Some methods can be used only if you're performing a clean installation and not an upgrade. Table 16.1 shows you four common unattended installation methods and when they can be utilized. In the following sections, we'll look at each of these methods in a bit more detail.

TABLE 16.1   Windows unattended installation methods

Method	Clean Installation	Upgrade
Unattended install	Yes	Yes
Bootable media	Yes	No (except for scenarios involving legacy operating systems you do not need to know for the exam)
Sysprep	Yes	No
Remote install	Yes	No

Unattended Installation

Answering the myriad questions posed by Windows Setup doesn't qualify as exciting work for most people. Fortunately, there is a way to answer the questions automatically: through an unattended installation. In this type of installation, an *answer file* is supplied with all of the correct parameters (time zone, regional settings, administrator username, and so on), so no one needs to be there to tell the computer what to choose or to click Next 500 times.

Unattended installations are great because they can be used to upgrade operating systems to Windows XP. The first step is to create an answer file. Generally speaking, you'll want to run a test installation using that answer file first before deploying it on a large scale because you'll probably need to make some tweaks to it. After you create your answer file, place it on a network share that will be accessible from the target computer. Most people put it in the same place as the Windows XP installation files for convenience.

Boot the computer that you want to install on using a boot disk or CD, and establish the network connection. Once you start the setup process from the network location, everything should run automatically.

Sysprep

Another tool that can aid in performing unattended installations is the System Preparation tool, or *Sysprep*. The Sysprep utility works by making an exact image or replica of an operating system installation (called the *master computer*), which can then be installed on other computers. Sysprep removes the master computer's security ID and will automatically generate new security IDs for each computer the image is used to install.

> All Sysprep does is create the system image. You still need a third-party cloning utility to copy the image and deploy it to other computers.

Perhaps the biggest caveat to using Sysprep is that because you are making an exact image of an installed computer, the computers that you will be installing the image on need to be identical (or very close) to the configuration of the master computer. Sysprep images can be installed across a network or copied to a CD for local installation. Sysprep cannot be used to upgrade a system; plan on all data on the system (if there is any) being lost after a Sysprep image is deployed.

> One of the big benefits of integrating Sysprep usage into the image capturing process (over traditional image capture methods) is that a "sysprepped" image will run plug-and-play when deployed and it will discover devices and install any drivers automatically. The HAL (Hardware Abstraction Layer) must be the same (or *very* similar) for XP images, but peripherals do not have to be.

There are several third-party vendors that provide similar services, and you'll often hear the process referred to as *disk imaging* or *drive imaging*. The process works the same way as Sysprep, except that the third-party utility will create the image while Sysprep only prepares a source machine so that it can be captured as an image. When a new machine is targeted for deployment, the image file must be transferred to the computer. Typically this is accomplished by booting the target system with the imaging software and then starting the image download. The new system's disk drive is made into an exact sector-by-sector copy of the original system.

Imaging has major upsides. The biggest one is speed. In larger networks with multiple new computers, you can configure hundreds of computers by using imaging in just hours rather than the days it would take to individually install the OS, applications, and drivers.

Bootable Media

For computers not connected to a network, images can be copied to a CD or DVD for local installation with an answer file you create. This is a quick way to perform a clean installation of an operating system without consuming all of your network bandwidth.

NOTE   For any purists that may be curious: If you are working with legacy equipment, you can do an upgrade from the XP CD (think coming from Windows 98, for example), and an answer file on a floppy can be incorporated to even make it an unattended installation.

Remote Install/Windows Deployment Service

Older Windows Server operating systems have a feature called Remote Installation Service (RIS), which allows you to perform several network installations at one time. Beginning with Windows Server 2003 SP2, RIS was replaced by Windows Deployment Service (WDS). This utility offers the same functionality as RIS.

A *network installation* is handy when you have many installs to perform and installing by CD is too much work. To prepare for a network installation, the installation CD is copied to a shared location on the network. Then individual workstations boot and access the network share to execute the installation. The workstations can boot either through a boot disk or through a built-in network boot device known as a *boot ROM* (which is where PXE comes in). Boot ROMs essentially download a small file that contains an OS and network drivers and has enough information to boot the computer in a limited fashion. At the very least, it can boot the computer so it can access the network share and begin the installation.

Preparing the Computer for Installation

Once you have verified that the machine on which you are planning to install Windows is capable of running it properly, you're sure all hardware is supported, and you have chosen your installation options, you need to make certain that the system is ready for the install. The primary question is whether you are planning to perform a fresh install of Windows or whether you are going to upgrade an existing system. We'll deal with upgrading later in the chapter; for now, we'll focus on new installations.

Preparing the Hard Drive

If you are installing Windows onto a system that does not already have a functioning OS, you have a bit of work to do before you get to the installation itself. New disk drives need two critical functions performed on them before they can be used:

- *Partitioning* is the process of dividing part or all of a hard drive into sections, or partitions, for use by the computer.

- *Formatting* is the process of preparing the partitions to store data in a particular fashion.

With older operating systems, you dealt with these two procedures by using the `FDISK.EXE` and `FORMAT.COM` commands (from Windows XP onwards, the `DISKPART.EXE` program replaced them). Running any sort of command on a machine that has no OS is impossible, though. You need a way to boot the computer—usually with a disk that is bootable.

For Windows XP, the process is to boot up using the Windows XP CD, which starts the installation process, and then utilize the installation process to partition and format the hard drive.

Partitioning the Hard Drive

Partitioning refers to establishing large allocations of hard drive space to create logical disks. A partition is a continuous section of sectors that are next to each other. In DOS and Windows, a partition is typically referred to, once mounted, by a drive letter, such as C: or D:. Partitioning a hard drive into two or more parts gives it the appearance of being two or more physical hard drives. At the beginning of each hard drive is a special file called the *master boot record (MBR)*. The MBR contains the partition information for the hard drive and includes the beginning and end of each partition that has been defined on the drive.

When you're formatting a partition, there are multiple choices for file systems to use. The file system you choose will determine certain limitations. NTFS partitions are less wasteful of space than FAT partitions are because of limitations in FAT cluster sizes.

Formatting the Hard Drive

The next step in management of a hard drive is formatting, initiated by the FORMAT or DISKPART command (or automatically by selecting to format a partition during the installation program). When formatting is performed, the surface of the hard drive platter is briefly scanned to find any possible bad spots, and the areas surrounding a bad spot are marked as bad sectors. Then magnetic tracks are laid down in concentric circles. These tracks are where information is eventually encoded. These tracks are split into pieces of 512 bytes called *sectors*. Some space is reserved in between the sectors for error-correction information, referred to as cyclic redundancy check (CRC) information. The OS may use CRC information to recreate data that has been partially lost from a sector. An operating system boot record is created along with the root directory. Finally, the File Allocation Table (FAT) or Master File Table (MFT) is created. This table is used to store and retain information about the location of files as they are placed onto the hard drive.

Starting the Installation

The installation processes for operating systems has arguably gotten easier over time. Being able to boot to a CD and automatically begin the installation is a good example of this ease of use. Although modern operating systems have more options for you to choose from, care has also been taken to minimize the stress involved in the process. In the next sections, we will look at the installation of Windows XP specifically.

Installing Windows XP

Installing Windows XP is a breeze compared to previous editions of Windows. As a matter of fact, you can install it with a minimal amount of user interaction. Microsoft has designed Windows XP to be incredibly simple to install.

As with other versions of Windows, you will go through various phases of the installation:

- Installation preparation phase
- Text-based installation phase
- Graphical installation phase

Windows XP, however, does almost everything for you. It is a very quick OS installation.

This installation process assumes that there is no OS on the computer already. If there is an existing OS, check out "Upgrading to Windows XP" later in this chapter.

Installation Preparation Phase

During this phase, you begin the installation of Windows XP, which includes configuring the disk system to accept Windows XP and then starting the graphical phase of Windows XP Setup.

To start a Windows XP installation, as with the other Windows OSs, you must first check your prerequisites (hardware support, available disk space, and so on). Additionally, you must ensure that your computer supports booting to a CD-ROM. Most systems do these days, especially those that are able to support Windows XP.

Once you have validated these things, you are ready to start the installation. First power up the computer and quickly insert the Windows XP CD into the CD-ROM drive. If you don't do this quickly enough, you may get an *Operating system not found* message because the CD-ROM wasn't ready as a boot device because it hadn't spun up yet. If this happens, leave the CD in the drive and reboot the computer.

You may have to press a key on some systems. A phrase like *Press any key to boot from CD-ROM* may appear. If it does, press a key to do just that so you can begin the installation. In some cases, you may need to reconfigure the BIOS to ensure that the CD-ROM is set to be a boot device and placed in order above anything else that may boot first.

If the CD is inserted successfully, the screen clears, and the words *Setup is inspecting your computer's configuration* appear. After that, you'll see the Windows XP Setup main screen. Then the Windows XP main Setup screen appears, shown in Figure 16.1.

FIGURE 16.1   Windows XP main Setup screen

```
Windows XP Professional Setup

Welcome to Setup.

This portion of the Setup program prepares Microsoft(R)
Windows(R) XP to run on your computer.

    •  To set up Windows XP now, press ENTER.

    •  To repair a Windows XP installation using
       Recovery Console, press R.

    •  To quit Setup without installing Windows XP, press F3.




ENTER=Continue   R=Repair   F3=Quit
```

If your computer was produced after the release of Windows XP and you
need to install a third-party SCSI, IDE, or RAID driver to recognize the disk
drives, press F6 as soon as the screen turns from black to blue to provide
the drivers. Setup will prompt you to act at the bottom of the screen.

Text-Based Installation Phase

When the Setup screen appears, you can press Enter to begin the installation. The End User
License Agreement (EULA) is then displayed, which you must accept (otherwise you can't
install Windows XP—as with other versions of Windows). Windows Setup then presents you
with a series of screens where you can prepare the disk to accept Windows XP by partitioning
it and then formatting it with either FAT or NTFS. It is best to choose NTFS for performance
and security reasons.

Windows Setup will format the partition as you specified and then copy the files to
the selected partition, which is needed to start the graphical portion of Setup. When
it's finished copying and unpacking the files, Setup reboots the computer and starts the
graphical portion of Windows XP Setup. If the text-based installation phase has been
successful, you will see a screen similar to that in Figure 16.2.

Graphical Installation Phase

During the graphical installation phase, Windows XP Setup performs almost all of the
actions necessary to bring Windows XP to a functional level. The first thing it does is
copy files to the hard disk and begin installing device drivers (as shown in Figure 16.3).
This process takes several minutes and should not be interrupted.

FIGURE 16.2 Windows XP Setup

FIGURE 16.3 Installing devices in Windows XP Setup

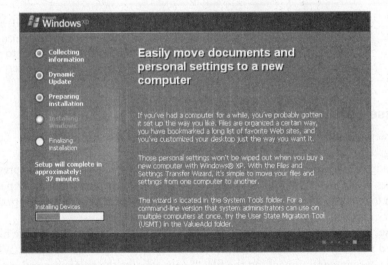

Proceed with the installation with the following steps:

1. Setup asks you for regional and language settings. The defaults are English (United States) for the language, United States for the location, and US Keyboard Layout for the default text-input method. If you are in a different location or prefer a different input method, you can change either item by clicking the button next to it (Customize for language and location, Details for text-input method). If you accept the displayed options, click Next to continue the installation.

2. Identify yourself to Windows XP Setup by entering your name and company.

3. Windows asks you for the product key. You must enter the product key that comes with your version of Windows XP. This product key can be used only on this computer. To prevent product key theft, Microsoft requires that you go through product activation to validate the product key after the installation is complete.

4. Enter a computer name to identify this computer. Use something that will be completely unique on the entire network. Windows XP Setup suggests a name automatically, but you can overwrite it and choose your own. You also must enter a password for the built-in Administrator user account.

5. Set the time, date, and time zone as well as whether to adjust for daylight saving time. Click Next.

6. Setup prompts you for the network setup information. You can either have Setup install the network for you or choose the settings yourself. Our preference is to accept the Typical Settings option and to go back and configure them later if they don't work. The typical settings include TCP/IP configured to obtain an IP address automatically via DHCP (most networks are configured this way).

7. Setup asks you if you want to use a workgroup or a domain. Choose either option and continue. Selecting a workgroup has no implications, but selecting a domain prompts for account authentication to join the computer to the domain.

8. Windows finishes the installation by copying all the remaining necessary files, putting items on the Start menu, building the Registry, and cleaning up after itself. This last step should take several minutes to complete. When it's finished, Setup reboots the computer.

Upon reboot, Windows automatically adjusts the screen size for optimum use. You are presented with a screen welcoming you to Windows XP. It walks you through connecting your computer to the Internet (to register and activate your copy of Windows XP), asks you for the names of people who are going to use this computer, and then presents you with the login screen (Figure 16.4 shows the screen for a machine that is a member of a workgroup). Click a username you want to use to log in and Windows XP will present you with a Desktop (Figure 16.5).

Postinstallation Routines

Even though you have now installed your OS, there are a few items you must do to be truly finished:

- Updating drivers
- Restoring user data files
- Verifying installation

If you don't perform these tasks, you will find using the newly installed OS less than enjoyable.

Updating Drivers

After you have gotten the OS up and running, you may find that a few items aren't configured or working properly. That is somewhat typical. The drivers for some hardware aren't found on the Windows installation disc, which may cause the driver installation to fail even though the device was detected properly. Or, more commonly, the drivers on the installation disc are installed successfully but are horribly out-of-date. In either situation, it is a good idea to search for and install or update the drivers for your hardware.

FIGURE 16.4 A Windows XP login screen

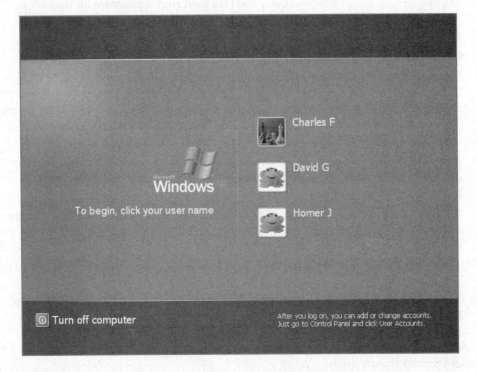

You should check the version of drivers for the following hardware against their manufacturer's website and ensure that you have the most current driver for each item:

- Motherboard and chipset
- Video adapter
- Network adapter
- Sound card
- Disk controller

To update a driver, use the Update Driver button accessible from Device Manager. You can also download the appropriate driver file package from the hardware manufacturer's website, extract it, and either run the setup utility that is included or use the Add Hardware Wizard that comes with Windows XP.

FIGURE 16.5   A Windows XP Desktop

 Adding the /sos option to the operating system option in the BOOT.INI file will enable you to see the drivers as they're loaded in Windows XP.

The easiest way to see or change drivers in Windows XP is to click the Driver tab in the properties for the device. For example, to see the driver associated with the hard drive in Windows XP, double-click the hard drive in Device Manager (Start ➤ Control Panel ➤ System, and then click the Hardware tab and the Device Manager button), and choose the Driver tab. Among other things, this shows the driver's provider, date, version, and signer. You can choose to view details about it, update it, roll it back to a previous driver, or uninstall it. We'll talk more drivers later in this chapter.

Restoring User Data Files

After you have installed an OS, you will want to use the computer. This involves installing applications and (if applicable) restoring data from either an older computer or this computer if you are reinstalling the OS.

Most often, restoring data files simply involves copying them from a different medium (such as thumb drives, a floppy disk, external hard drive, magnetic tape, or other removable media). However, it can also involve copying the older data files from another computer. Windows XP includes a utility known as the *Files and Settings Transfer Wizard* that will transfer most of your files and individual application settings from an old computer to a new one. To prepare to run the wizard, you must first connect the two computers either by LAN or by null modem serial cable. Then, to start the transfer, execute the wizard on both computers. The files and settings are automatically transferred to the new computer without much trouble.

While the Files and Settings Transfer Wizard can be used by individual users, there is also a *User State Migration Tool (USMT)* that can be downloaded from Microsoft and offers the same functionality and more. It is intended to be used by administrators and requires a client computer connected to a Windows Server–based domain controller. More information on USMT can be found at http://support.microsoft.com/kb/321197.

 Windows Easy Transfer can be used to transfer data from Windows XP, but is not supported for transferring it to Windows XP.

Verifying Installation

The last thing you should do after installing any operating system is perform a verification. It sounds easy enough, but many people forget to do it, and not doing it can come back to haunt you later. Simply reboot (not that the installation didn't reboot a few times already), and log in as a user. Make sure all of the appropriate programs are there and all of the devices (such as the network card and video card) are working properly.

Upgrading the Operating System

If you add an OS to a machine that doesn't currently have one (recently formatted, built from scratch, and so on), that is referred to as *installing*. If you add an OS so that you can dual-boot (choose which one to run at start), that is *installing*. If you replace one OS with another while attempting to keep the same data/application files intact, that is referred to as *upgrading*.

Whereas installations can typically be performed over any existing OS, upgrading can be performed only from an OS that is compatible with the one to which you are upgrading. With Windows XP, you can upgrade to the Home version only from Windows 98 or Windows Me. You can upgrade to the Professional version from Windows 98, Windows Me, Windows NT Workstation 4.0, Windows 2000 Professional, or even from Windows XP Home.

> Step-by-step upgrade information for Windows XP can be found at
> `http://windows.microsoft.com/en-US/windows-xp/help/setup/`
> `install-windows-xp`.

`WINNT32.EXE` is the utility to use to initiate the upgrade. The Setup Wizard automatically creates a report of devices that can't be upgraded. Uncompression of compressed volumes must occur before you start an upgrade.

Upgrading to Windows XP

Upgrading to XP is quite simple:

1. Insert the CD and choose Install Windows XP from the menu that appears.

2. The Setup program detects that you already have an OS installed and presents you with a menu that says Upgrade (Recommended). Click Next to begin the upgrade.

3. Setup asks you to agree to the EULA, enter the product key, and download an updated version of the Setup program (if necessary).

4. Setup copies several files over, reboots a couple of times, and continues like a standard Windows XP installation.

Once you have finished the installation, you must activate it as you would a standard installation of Windows XP. Windows XP Setup makes most of the decisions about the upgrade for you, so only a minimal amount of interaction is necessary.

 Real World Scenario

Should You Be Upgrading to Windows XP?

While you need to know installation and upgrade options involving Windows XP for the exam, in the real world you should avoid upgrading to Windows XP whenever possible. Microsoft announced many years ago that extended support for Windows XP SP3 will end in 2014 (April 8, to be exact).

The "end of support" from Microsoft's standpoint means that it will not issue anything new for the product after that date. That means there will not be any security updates, hotfixes, or support from Microsoft (paid or unpaid). No administrator should be installing what will soon be an unsupported/unsecure client operating system on workstations.

Know the material in this chapter for the exam, but in the real world, know that Windows 7 should be the choice you consider.

Finalizing Your Upgrade

Now that you've completed your upgrade, you need to think about making this computer functional, as you would have if you had just installed a new operating system. The first step after a reboot should always be to make sure that the newest service packs and system updates are applied. Fortunately, Windows XP participates in the *Windows Update* program, which will automatically download new updates if you allow it to. Still, when you've just performed an upgrade (or new installation), it's best to force this action by manually initiating Windows Update from the Start menu.

After your updates and patches are applied, verify that the user's data and software was carried forward into the new operating system properly, including checking for files and folders and ensuring that critical programs work. Finally, install any additional services that might be necessary—and the computer is ready to go!

Migrating User Data

Installing an operating system would be simple if it weren't for users and the data that they want to bring with them. To simplify the task of migrating user data, Microsoft offers a free tool for administrators: Microsoft Windows User State Migration Tool (USMT). It allows an administrator to migrate user files settings related to applications, desktop configuration, and accounts to a new operating system installation for an end user.

Version 3.0 works with Windows XP, while previous versions—such as 2.6—also worked with Windows 2000. You can download this tool from `http://technet.microsoft.com/en-us/library/cc722032.aspx`. If all you are doing is a simple upgrade from one OS to another, you do not need this tool, but it is invaluable during large deployments.

Performing a Repair Install

There are occasions when a system will become unstable and the operating system is suspected as a likely culprit. When this happens, you can attempt what is known as a *repair install*. The concept behind a repair install is simple: You want to fix the operating system but keep all of your user and data files. This is accomplished by running a repair install of the operating system over the operating system already running.

Windows XP includes an option to press R during installation to repair the operating system. You see this as soon as you boot from the installation media as an option in the first text-based screen of the installation.

There are two Repair options in the Windows XP installation process. The first appears on the Welcome to Setup screen (shown in Figure 16.1) but it doesn't do a re-install; it opens the Recovery Console, which is a restricted option CMD prompt interface. To get to the option described here, you need to hit Enter to continue, F8 to accept the EULA, and then type R.

Adding Hardware in Windows XP

There is a difference between physically installing hardware (adding it to the machine) and logically installing the drivers that make the hardware work with the operating system. As with previous versions of Windows, there are a few options to install hardware from the OS standpoint:

- Let Windows recognize new hardware on boot-up and install drivers then.
- Use the manufacturer's installation program.
- Manually install hardware using the Add Hardware Wizard.

When you install some hardware under Windows XP, the operating system will warn you to install software before installing the device. You will notice this requirement mainly on USB devices and some other PnP devices.

To begin installing a driver for a new piece of hardware, follow these steps:

1. Install the hardware (either insert the expansion card or plug in the device).

2. Boot the computer and wait for Windows to recognize the new hardware. If Windows recognizes the presence of new hardware, it displays a screen similar to the one shown in Figure 16.6, which asks if you want Windows to install the driver automatically or if you want to pick the driver from a list. If you go with the default choice of having Windows install the driver automatically, Windows attempts to locate the driver in its database of drivers that come with the operating system or that have already been installed. It then proceeds to install the driver and activate the new hardware.

FIGURE 16.6   XP detecting new hardware

You may see a warning telling you that if your hardware came with an installation CD, you should insert the CD now. That way, Windows can find the driver automatically on the CD.

3. Once Windows has found the driver, it determines whether it is properly signed (and gives you the chance to stop the installation if it's not).

4. Windows tells you that the device has been installed.

If Windows XP can't find the right driver for the device, it will start a troubleshooting wizard to help you along with the installation.

 Always check Device Manager to make sure that the device is recognized by the system and the driver is working properly! Device Manager shows a list of all installed hardware and lets you add items, remove items, update drivers, and more. This is a Windows-only utility. With Windows XP, open the System Properties dialog box, click the Hardware tab, and then click the Device Manager button to display the tool.

The XP Boot Sequences

Both for the test and for real life, you should know how to recognize common problems with the OS and make certain it is booting correctly. The sections that follow look at a number of topics related to keeping your OS booting and running properly.

Key Boot Files

Windows XP requires only a few files to boot properly, each of which performs specific tasks. These are discussed next in the order in which they load:

NTLDR Bootstraps the system. In other words, this file starts the loading of an OS on the computer. Windows XP uses NTLDR, while subsequent versions of the operating system use BOOTMGR. This file is responsible for switching from real to protected mode during the boot process.

BOOT.INI Holds information about the location of the OS files for Windows XP.

BOOTSECT.DOS In a dual-boot configuration, keeps a copy of the DOS or Windows 9x boot sector so that the Windows 9x environment can be restored and loaded as needed.

NTDETECT.COM Parses the system for hardware information each time Windows XP is loaded. This information is then used to create dynamic hardware information in the Registry.

NTBOOTDD.SYS On a system with a SCSI boot device, this file is used to recognize and load the SCSI interface. On EIDE systems, this file is not needed and is not even installed.

NTOSKRNL.EXE   The Windows OS kernel. The solution to a corrupted NTOSKRNL.EXE file is to boot from a startup disk and replace the file from the setup disks or CD.

NTBTLOG.TXT   While not an executable file, this log file is very important; it holds the information collected if you choose to boot using the Boot Logging startup option. The file is created in the %SYSTEM_ROOT% directory (usually c:\windows).

System files   In addition to the previously listed files, all of which (except NTOSKRNL.EXE) are located in the root of the C: partition on the computer, Windows XP needs a number of files from its system directories (e.g., system and system32), such as the hardware abstraction layer (HAL.DLL).

Numerous other dynamic link library (DLL) files are also required, but usually the lack or corruption of one of them produces a noncritical error, whereas the absence of HAL.DLL causes the system to be nonfunctional.

The Windows XP Boot Process

We'll now look at the Windows XP boot process. It's a pretty long and complicated process, but keep in mind that these are complex operating systems, providing you with a lot more functionality than older versions of Windows could offer:

1. The system self-checks and enumerates hardware resources. Each machine has a different startup routine, called the power-on self-test (POST), which is executed by the commands written to the motherboard of the computer. Newer Plug and Play (PnP) boards not only check memory and processors, they also poll the systems for other devices and peripherals.

2. The Master Boot Record (MBR) loads and finds the boot sector. Once the system has finished with its housekeeping, the MBR is located on the first hard drive and loaded into memory. The MBR finds the active partition and searches it for the boot sector of that partition.

3. The MBR determines the file system and loads NTLDR. Information in the boot sector allows the system to locate the system partition and to find and load into memory the NTLDR file located there.

4. NTLDR switches the system from real mode to protected mode and enables paging. Protected mode enables the system to address all of the available physical memory. It's also referred to as *32-bit flat mode*. At this point, the file system is also started.

5. NTLDR processes BOOT.INI. BOOT.INI is a text file that resides in the root directory. It specifies what OSs are installed on the computer and where each OS resides on the disk. During this step of the boot process, you may be presented with a list of the installed OSs (depending on how your startup options are configured and whether you have multiple OSs installed). If you're presented with the list, you can choose an OS, or if you don't take any action, the default selection is chosen automatically. If you have multiple OSs installed and you choose a DOS-based OS from the list (such as Windows 9x), NTLDR processes BOOTSECT.DOS and does a warm boot. The MBR code contained in BOOTSECT.DOS is run after the computer goes through the POST, and IO.SYS is loaded, starting the DOS-based OS's boot process. We will, however, continue with the XP boot process.

6. NTLDR loads and runs NTDETECT.COM. NTDETECT.COM checks the system for installed devices and device configurations and initializes the devices it finds. It passes the information to NTLDR, which collects this information and passes it to NTOSKRNL.EXE after that file is loaded.

7. NTLDR loads NTOSKRNL.EXE and HAL.DLL. NTOSKRNL.EXE holds the OS kernel and also what's known as the *executive subsystems*. Executive subsystems are software components that parse the Registry for configuration information and start needed services and drivers. HAL.DLL enables communication between the OS and the installed hardware.

8. NTLDR loads the HKEY_LOCAL_MACHINE\SYSTEM Registry hive and loads device drivers. The drivers that load at this time serve as boot drivers, using an initial value called a *start value*.

9. NTLDR transfers control to NTOSKRNL.EXE. NTOSKRNL.EXE initializes loaded drivers and completes the boot process.

10. WINLOGON.EXE loads. At this point, you are presented with the Logon screen. After you enter a username and password, you're taken to the Windows Desktop.

Working with the Boot Sequence

Under a normal boot, these files are accessed as needed, and the system is brought to its ready state. If problems are occurring, however, you may need to alter the boot method used. Windows offers a number of choices of alternative boot sequences:

Safe Mode   To access Safe Mode, you must press F8 when the OS menu is displayed during the boot process. A menu of Safe Mode choices appears, and you can select the mode you want to boot into. This is the mode to boot into if you suspect driver problems and want to load with a minimal set of device drivers while you diagnose the problem.

Recovery Console   This is a command-line utility used for troubleshooting. From it, you can format drives, stop and start services, and interact with files stored on FAT, FAT32, or NTFS. The Recovery Console isn't installed on a system by default, but you can add it as a menu choice at the bottom of the startup menu.

Restore points   System Restore allows you to restore the system to a previous point in time. Restore points are created automatically in Windows XP by default. You can also use the System Restore utility to create them manually.

Automated System Recovery (ASR)   It's possible to automate the process of creating a system recovery set by choosing the ASR Wizard on the Tools menu of the Backup utility (Start ➢ All Programs ➢ Accessories ➢ System Tools ➢ Backup). This wizard walks you through the process of creating a disk that can be used to restore parts of the system in the event of a major system failure.

Windows XP Features

There are a number of features that make Windows XP a solid operating system that has been around—and widely used—as long as it has been. Even when Windows Vista came out, a majority of users and enterprises opted to stick with Windows XP because it offered what they needed. In the following sections, we will look first at some of the tools available within Windows XP, then Windows Error Reporting, and finally, Remote Desktop Connection and Assistance.

Tools in Windows XP

The tools that stand out in Windows XP, and that CompTIA expects you to know for the exam, include System Restore, Windows Defender, Windows Firewall, and Security Center. Each of these are discussed in the sections that follow.

System Restore

Chapter 12 explored System Restore as it appears in all three versions of Windows. System Restore is arguably the most powerful tool in Windows XP. It allows you to restore the system to a previous point in time. This feature is accessed from Start ➢ All Programs ➢ Accessories ➢ System Tools ➢ System Restore and can be used to roll back as well as to create a restore point. Figure 16.7 shows the opening dialog box, while Figure 16.8 shows the prompt for a restore point that can be created manually.

FIGURE 16.7   System Restore in Windows XP

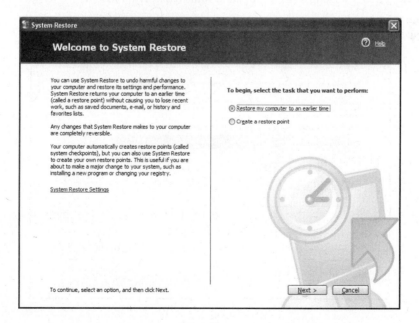

Restore points are created automatically in Windows XP by default, though you can create them manually. Figure 16.9 shows the restore options.

FIGURE 16.8   Providing a name for the restore point in Windows XP

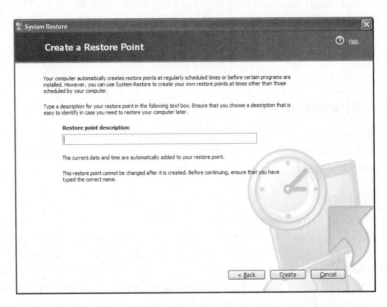

FIGURE 16.9   Picking a restore point to return to in Windows XP

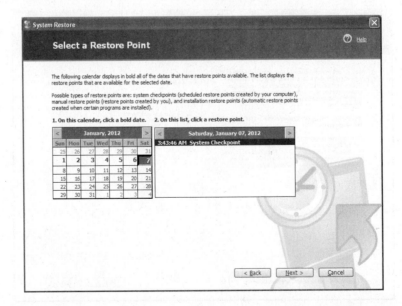

Windows Defender

Windows Defender can identify unwanted spyware software. While Defender is native to all versions of Vista and Windows 7, it must be downloaded and installed for XP Service Pack 2 or later. As with similar programs, in order for Windows Defender to function properly (see Figure 16.10), you need to keep the definitions current and scan on a regular basis. In Exercise 16.1, you'll run Windows Defender in Windows XP.

FIGURE 16.10 Windows Defender can identify security threats.

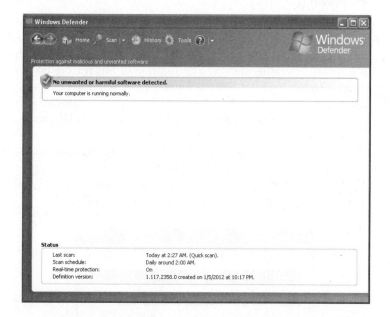

EXERCISE 16.1

Run Windows Defender in Windows XP

1. Choose Start ➤ All Programs ➤ Windows Defender.

2. From the drop-down list next to help (a question mark in a blue circle), choose Check For Updates.

3. Click Scan.

4. Upon completion, the message *Your computer is running normally* should appear within the frame No Unwanted Or Harmful Software Detected. If anything else appears, resolve those issues.

5. Exit Windows Defender.

Windows Defender is not the only security tool available from Microsoft for Windows XP (as well as Windows 7 and Windows Vista). While Windows Defender is focused on spyware, Security Essentials expands that to include a great deal more malicious software. When Security Essentials is running, Defender should be disabled because it is a subset of the protection included in Security Essentials.

Windows Firewall

Windows Firewall (Start ≻ Control Panel ≻ Windows Firewall) is used to block access to the network (be it from an internal source or the Internet). While host-based firewalls are not as secure as other types of firewalls, this was a great move toward enhancing the security of the Windows operating system. The addition of this feature is considered to be a move in the right direction and has been a component of Windows ever since.

Figure 16.11 shows the opening screen of Windows Firewall in Windows XP. As of Service Pack 2, Windows Firewall is turned on by default and it is also included in the Security Center (discussed in the next section).

By default, Windows Firewall blocks incoming traffic. Using the Exceptions tab, you can configure which incoming traffic you want to allow through.

FIGURE 16.11   Windows Firewall can block unwanted traffic.

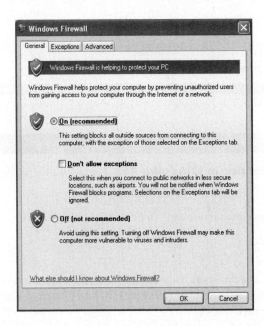

Security Center

Security Center (Start ➤ Control Panel ➤ Security Center) provides a single interface where you can administer Windows Firewall, Automatic Updates, and virus protection. Figure 16.12 shows the opening screen.

FIGURE 16.12   Windows Security Center in Windows XP

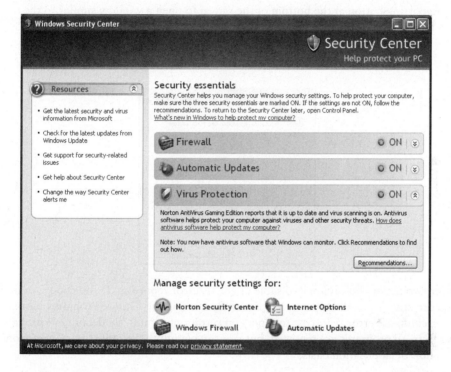

On the machine shown in the example, a version of Norton AntiVirus (Norton AntiVirus Gaming Edition, in this case) has been installed and that is appearing in the Security Center window. Other security-related products installed on the machine should appear in the Security Center window as well.

Windows Reporting

Error reporting is a feature in Windows XP. If a program error occurs (such as Internet Explorer crashing), a window will pop up asking if you want to report the problem to Microsoft. This may occur for non-Microsoft programs as well. If you choose to report the problem, you must have an active Internet connection. If you do have an active Internet connection, technical information about the problem is gathered and sent to

Microsoft. If others have reported the same problem, then additional technical information may be available to suggest how to solve the problem.

According to Microsoft, the information gathered is only used by programming groups to help solve technical problems. Your individual information is not stored or tracked in any way.

To configure (or disable) Windows reporting with Windows XP, open System Properties by right-clicking My Computer and selecting Properties. On the Advanced tab, click the Error Reporting button at the bottom of the screen to open a window similar to the one shown in Figure 16.13.

FIGURE 16.13   Windows Error Reporting options in Windows XP

Your two major choices are to disable or enable error reporting. If you choose to disable it, you can still be notified when errors occur. By clicking the Choose Programs button, you can configure error reporting to report on certain programs. By default, all program errors from all programs are reported, but you can configure the reporting of errors on an application-by-application basis.

Remote Desktop Connection and Remote Assistance

Windows contains two remote connectivity applications, called Remote Desktop Connection and Remote Assistance. The following sections describe each in more detail.

Remote Desktop Connection

The *Remote Desktop* feature of Windows would probably be more accurately named remote control. Remote Desktop allows you to connect to another computer and take control over it as if you were sitting in front of it. This utility allows you to connect to your work computer from home, for example, and it can also work as a great troubleshooting tool by allowing connection from an administrator's workstation to other workstations or servers in the network. On the flip side, it can also be a huge security risk.

Remote Desktop classifies computers into two categories: home computer and remote computer. The *home computer* is the one that you are sitting at. For it to use Remote Desktop, it needs to have *Remote Desktop Connection* installed, which is present by default in Windows XP. The *remote computer* is the one you are connecting to. It must have Remote Desktop enabled in order to accept incoming connections. Remote Desktop is separate from Remote Desktop Connection.

> Windows XP Home edition does not have Remote Desktop, only Remote Desktop Connection. Therefore, Windows XP Home computers can be only home computers, not remote computers.

When you're using Remote Desktop, keystrokes and mouse movements are transmitted from the home computer to the remote computer. Programs that you open on the remote computer (from the home computer) run locally on the remote computer. You (from the home computer) can see the Desktop of the remote computer, just as if you were sitting there. Finally, sound can also be passed from the remote computer to the home computer. This is enabled by default, but it consumes a lot of bandwidth so you might not want to use it.

> Know that with Remote Desktop Connection, you can connect to more than one remote computer at a time.

By default, users are not allowed to remotely connect to your computer. To change this and allow connections into a system, you must open System Properties (right-click My Computer and select Properties) and click the Remote tab, shown in Figure 16.14.

FIGURE 16.14   System Properties Remote tab

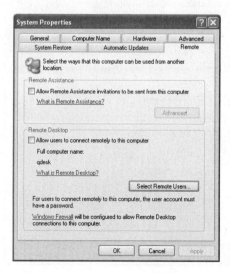

Check the Allow Users To Connect Remotely To This Computer check box to enable access. Then to choose which users can connect remotely, click the Select Remote Users button. For users to be able to access your computer, they must have a user account and password on your computer or domain.

To configure Remote Desktop Connection options, open Remote Desktop Connection by clicking Start ➢ All Programs ➢ Accessories ➢ Communications ➢ Remote Desktop Connection (with SP3 it is on the level above, in the Accessories menu). This opens a window like the one in Figure 16.15.

This is the window you would use to connect to another computer. By clicking the Options button, you can configure desired settings. Looking at Figure 16.16, you can see that there are five tabs of configuration options.

On the bottom of the General tab, you'll notice that you can save these settings into different profiles. This might be handy if you connect to different computers.

FIGURE 16.15 Remote Desktop Connection

FIGURE 16.16 Remote Desktop Connection options

On the Display tab, you can set the size of your Remote Desktop window, up to full screen. It also allows you to configure the depth of color used, much like when you configure your own Desktop.

On the Local Resources tab (shown in Figure 16.17), you configure sound (good to leave off unless absolutely necessary), keyboard settings, and connectivity to local devices.

FIGURE 16.17   Local Resources tab

On the Programs tab, you can choose to start applications when the remote connection is made.

Finally, on the Experience tab, you can choose your connection speed as well as a few graphical options (such as allowing themes or the Desktop background) designed to help optimize your connection.

Remote Assistance

Have you ever tried explaining a computer problem you're having to someone else and it just isn't sinking in? Or how about being on the other end and having a user trying in vain to explain a problem to you but they just can't seem to get their point across?

The Remote Assistance feature of Windows allows you to access someone else's computer in an effort to repair it. You can act as an expert to their novice and walk through problems that can be corrected with your additional knowledge.

Looking back at Figure 16.14, you will see a check box marked Allow Remote Assistance Invitations To Be Sent From This Computer. By checking that box, you are able to send an invitation to a person on another computer that would allow them to connect to yours, ideally with the intention of fixing a problem. By clicking the Advanced button, you can choose whether or not to allow remote users to be able to take control over your machine. If you want them to fix the problem, it may be helpful to allow them to take control of the system. If giving them control is unwelcome or not possible, you can just give them a guided tour once they're connected and have them provide verbal instructions instead.

 For Remote Assistance to work, you should be running either Windows Messenger or a MAPI-compliant email system such as Outlook or Outlook Express. Alternatively, the request can also be saved as a file and shared using any of the ways in which a file can be exchanged.

Once you have enabled Remote Assistance on the Remote tab of System Properties, you can send an invitation to others to connect to your computer. Here's how:

1. Click Start ➢ Help And Support (or Start ➢ All Programs ➢ Remote Assistance).

2. Click the link that says Invite A Friend To Connect To Your Computer With Remote Assistance. That will take you to another Help And Support menu.

3. Click Invite Someone To Help You.

4. If you use Windows Messenger (or MSN Messenger), highlight the person's name on your contacts list and click Invite This Person. If you do not use Messenger, type their email address in the Type An E-mail Address box and click Invite This Person.

Upon receiving the invitation, the user (expert) will be given the opportunity to accept. After they accept, you (novice) will be notified that they have accepted and the session is started.

To end a Remote Assistance session, click the Disconnect button in the Remote Assistance window or close the session.

Differences Between Remote Desktop and Remote Assistance

Both remote programs use the same base technology, but there are differences. Remote Desktop was designed to give you remote access to a Windows system running on a computer even if you're not physically there in front of that machine. For example, you can be at home and log in to your work computer to access files or applications.

Remote Assistance allows a friend or a technician to use an Internet connection to access your computer to provide help. By default, the friend sees your Desktop and communicates with you through a messenger window. If you choose, you can allow that friend to have control over your computer.

Is Wake on LAN Right for You?

If you are interested in saving power with a system that is not accessed often, one option Windows XP supports is to employ Wake on LAN (WoL). Wake on LAN is an Ethernet standard implemented via a card that allows a "sleeping" machine to awaken when it receives a wakeup signal. Wake on LAN cards cause more problems than standard network cards. In our opinion, this is because they're always on. In some cases, you'll be unable to get the card working again unless you unplug the PC's power supply and reset the card.

Windows XP Administrative Tools

There are a number of system tools included with Windows XP that you need to know for the exam. These administrative tools are discussed in the order in which they appear in the objectives and also include Windows Firewall, which was covered earlier in this chapter.

Users and Groups

As an administrator, you can configure the users and groups on a Windows XP system by clicking Start ➢ Control Panel ➢ Administrative Tools ➢ Computer Management ➢ Local Users And Groups. The two folders—one for users, and the other for groups—provide an interface through which you can add and delete users and groups and set the password or properties for them. Figure 16.18 shows the users on a sample system, while Figure 16.19 shows the groups. The groups shown are the standard defaults (except the group PasswordPropDeny) for a Windows XP system, and you should know them for the exam.

FIGURE 16.18   Users in Windows XP

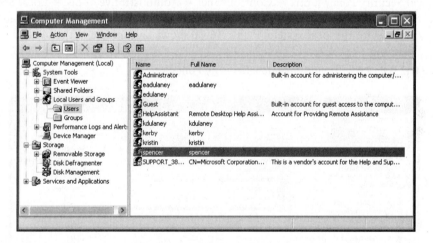

The standard users are Administrator and Guest. The standard groups are Administrators, Backup Operators, Guests, HelpServicesGroup (used to provide rights to accounts used by support applications such as Remote Assistance), Network Configuration Operators, Power Users (which have most of the rights of the Administrators group but not all), Remote Desktop Users, Replicator (which exists only for file replication in the domain), and Users.

FIGURE 16.19   Groups in Windows XP

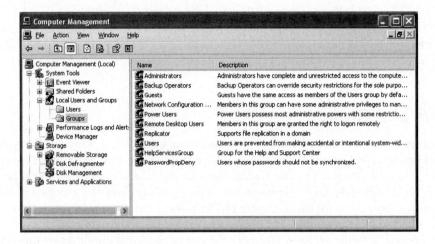

Local Security Policy

The Local Security Policy (Start ➤ Control Panel ➤ Administrative Tools ➤ Local Security Policy or choose Start ➤ Run, and then enter **secpol.msc**) allows you to set the default security settings for the local system. Figure 16.20 shows an example of the screen.

FIGURE 16.20   Setting the Local Security Policy

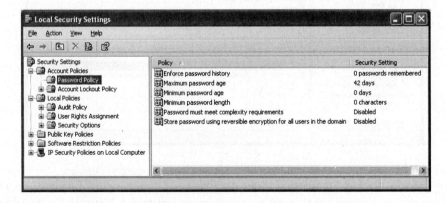

The following sections examine some of the Security Settings choices.

Account Policies

Account Policies further divides into Password Policy and Account Lockout Policy. The following choices are available under Password Policy:

Enforce Password History   This allows you to require unique passwords for a certain number of iterations. The default number is 0, but it can go as high as 24.

Maximum Password Age   The default is 42 days, but values range from 0 to 999.

Minimum Password Age   The default is 0 days, but values range from 0 to 999.

Minimum Password Length   The default is 0 characters (meaning no passwords are required), but you can specify a number up to 14.

Password Must Meet Complexity Requirements   The default is disabled. When this is turned on, the password must include at least three of the following criteria: uppercase characters, lowercase characters, numerical characters, nonalphanumeric characters, and Unicode characters.

Store Password Using Reversible Encryption For All Users In The Domain   The default is disabled. When enabled, it provides support for applications that require knowledge of the password.

Because the likelihood of laptops being stolen always exists, it's strongly encouraged that you use good password policies for this audience. Here's an example:

- Enforce Password History: 8 passwords remembered
- Maximum Password Age: 42 days
- Minimum Password Age: 3 days
- Minimum Password Length: 6 to 8 characters

Leave the other three settings disabled.

Account Lockout Policy

The Account Lockout Policy setting divides into the following three values:

Account Lockout Threshold   This is the number of invalid attempts before lockout occurs. The default is 0 (meaning the feature is turned off). Invalid attempt numbers range from 1 to 999. A number greater than 0 changes the values of the following two options to 30 minutes; otherwise, they are "not defined."

Account Lockout Duration   This is a number of minutes ranging from 1 to 99999. A value of 0 is also allowed here and signifies that the account never unlocks itself—administrator interaction is always required.

Reset Account Lockout Counter After   This is a number of minutes, ranging from 1 to 99999 that each failed login attempt counts as. For example, if the value is set at 5, then after 5 minutes one of the failed attempts is removed from the counter.

When you're working with a mobile workforce, you must weigh the choice of users calling you in the middle of the night when they've forgotten their password against keeping the system from being entered if the wrong user picks up a laptop. A possible configuration for a medium to low security environment is to use a lockout after five attempts for a period of time between 30 and 60 minutes.

Local Policy Settings

The Local Policies section divides into three subsections: Audit Policy, User Rights Assignment, and Security Options. The Audit Policy section contains nine settings; the default value for each is No Auditing. Valid options are Success and/or Failure. The Audit Account Logon Events entry is the one you should consider turning on for mobile users to see how often they log in and out of their machines.

When auditing is turned on for an event, the entries are logged in the Security log file and can be viewed with Event Viewer.

The User Rights Assignment subsection of Local Policies is where the meat of the old System Policies comes into play. User Rights Assignment has many options, most of which are self-explanatory. Also shown in the list that follows are the defaults for who can perform these actions; Not Defined indicates that no one is specified for this operation. If your mobile users need to be able to install, delete, and modify their environment, make them a member of the Power Users group.

The Security Options section includes a great many options, which for the most part are Registry keys. The default for each is Not Defined; the two definitions that can be assigned are Enabled and Disabled, or a physical number (as with the number of previous logons to cache) can be assigned. In some cases, you can make a selection from a dropdown (such as Devices: Unsigned driver installtion behavior) or a text message (such as Interactive logon: Message text for users attempting to log in).

System Configuration

The System Configuration tool (MSCONFIG.EXE) in Windows XP is used to control the way the system behaves at startup, and it includes a number of tabs and options not present in subsequent versions of Windows, as shown in Figure 16.21.

Among the options not present in Windows Vista or Windows 7 are the ability to interact with and minimally edit the INI files (BOOT.INI as well as SYSTEM.INI and WIN.INI) because these files are not used in those operating systems.

Component Services

Component Services (Start ≻ Control Panel ≻ Administrative Tools ≻ Component Services) allows you to administer, as well as deploy, component services and configure behavior like security. In this tool, it is possible for administrators to manage components while developers configure routine component and application behavior (object pooling, for example). Figure 16.22 shows an example of the screen.

FIGURE 16.21   The System Configuration tool in Windows XP

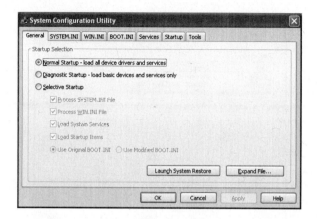

FIGURE 16.22   Component Services

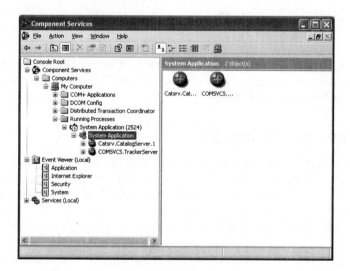

Data Sources

Data Sources, accessed by choosing Start ➢ Control Panel ➢ Administrative Tools ➢ Data Sources (ODBC), allows you to interact with database management systems. Figure 16.23 shows an example of the ODBC Data Source Administrator dialog box.

Database drivers that are added to the system will show up here and can be shared between applications.

FIGURE 16.23   Data Sources in Windows XP

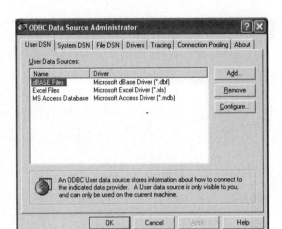

Unique Control Panel Utilities

There are a number of Control Panel applets unique to Windows XP to be aware of. These include Add or Remove Programs, Network Connections, Printers and Faxes, Automatic Updates, and the Network Setup Wizard.

Add or Remove Programs

The Add Or Remove Programs applet (Start ➣ Control Panel ➣ Add Or Remove Programs) in Windows XP can be used, as the name implies, to add or delete programs. It can also be used to add and delete Windows components, to set program access and defaults, and to change programs (add or remove portions of them, for example).

When first opened, it (APPWIZ.CPL) shows the currently installed programs, as shown in Figure 16.24.

If you click Add/Remove Windows Components, it will open the Windows Components Wizard, shown in Figure 16.25. As the name implies, the Windows Components Wizard walks you through the process of adding or removing Windows components.

Network Connections

The Network Connections applet (Start ➣ Control Panel ➣ Network Connections) in Windows XP can be used, as the name implies, to add or remove network connections. It can also be used to set up a home/small office network and change Windows Firewall settings.

When first opened, it (NCPA.CPL) shows the currently configured connections, as shown in Figure 16.26.

FIGURE 16.24   Add Or Remove Programs

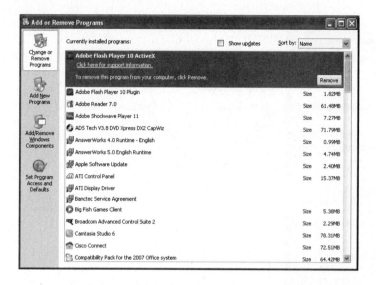

FIGURE 16.25   The Windows Components Wizard

FIGURE 16.26   Network Connections

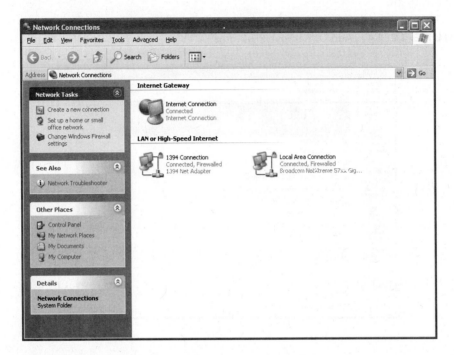

If you choose the option Set Up A Home Or Small Office Network, it brings up the Network Setup Wizard (`NETSETUP.CPL`) which is discussed a bit later.

Clicking a connection will change the network tasks to those that are relevant to that type of connection, thus adding to what is currently shown: such choices as Disable This Network Device, Rename This Connection, and so on. By right-clicking the connection, you can bring up the properties and change the settings for the connection.

Printers and Faxes

The Printers And Faxes applet (Start ➢ Control Panel ➢ Printers And Faxes) in Windows XP can be used, as the name implies, to add, delete, and manage printers and fax devices. When first opened, it shows the currently configured devices, as shown in Figure 16.27.

When you select a device, the tasks that apply to that device will appear in the left frame. For example, clicking the icon for an installed printer will list such options as Pause Printing, Share This Printer, Rename This Printer, and Set Printer Properties. The latter option will bring up a dialog box similar to that shown in Figure 16.28. In this figure, the Advanced tab has been selected to show the options available for a shared printer. Note the check box to the upper left of the printer icon in Figure 16.27 signifying that it is the default printer.

FIGURE 16.27   Printers And Faxes

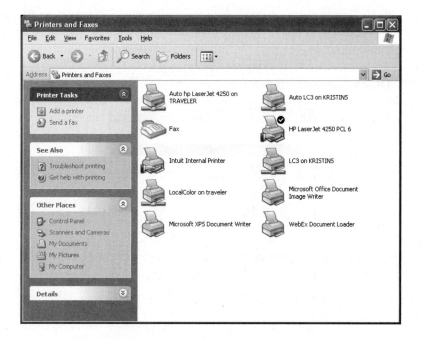

FIGURE 16.28   The Advanced tab of a shared printer's properties

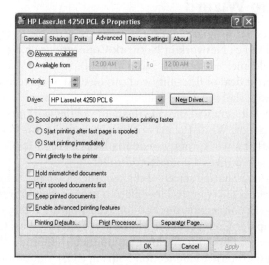

Automatic Updates

The Automatic Updates applet (Start ➢ Control Panel ➢ Automatic Updates) in Windows XP can be used to configure how often a check is done for new software and what to do when updates are found. Figure 16.29 shows the simple interface (WUAUCPL.CPL).

FIGURE 16.29   Configuring Automatic Updates

Network Setup Wizard

The Windows Network Setup Wizard (NETSETUP.CPL) is available by clicking the option Set Up A Home Or Small Office Network in Network Connections or directly from Control Panel (Start ➢ Control Panel ➢ Network Setup Wizard).

This tool offers a great deal of flexibility and can be used to share an Internet connection, set up Windows Firewall, share files and folders, or share a printer.

As you walk through it, you will provide the name of the workgroup or domain that the system will be a part of. While the networking chapters of this book spend more time on the subject, know that a workgroup essentially lacks a server (creating a peer-based network) while a domain utilizes a domain controller.

Use the File And Printer Sharing screen of the wizard, shown in Figure 16.30, to configure Windows Firewall to either allow or disallow file and printer sharing traffic to pass.

When configuring the connection method for accessing the Internet, the three simple choices are This Computer Connects Directly To The Internet, This Computer Connects Through A Residential Gateway Or Another Computer, and Other. If the first option is chosen, you can turn on Internet Connection Sharing (ICS) and allow this machine to service as a proxy. The network connection you configure can be wireless or wired, dial-up, or even a virtual private network (VPN).

FIGURE 16.30   Configuring file and printer sharing

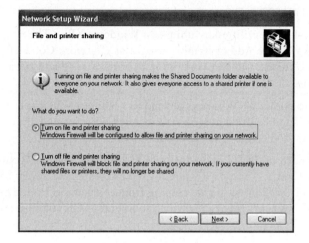

Summary

This chapter focused on Windows XP. Although the operating system has been out for many years, it is still very popular in many workplaces and homes. We looked at the various features of Windows XP, some that exist in other versions of Windows and some that are unique to this operating system. The latter category includes Add or Remove Programs, Network Connections, Printers And Faxes, Automatic Updates, and Network Setup Wizard.

We also looked at the installation process, for both a clean installation and an upgrade, and we looked at Administrative Tools. Among the Administrative Tools for this operating system discussed were Users And Groups, Local Security Policy, System Configuration, Component Services, Data Sources, and Windows Firewall.

Exam Essentials

Know what types of installations are possible with Windows XP.   All installations fall into the categories of being either attended or unattended and either clean installations or upgrades. You should know which operating systems can be upgraded to Windows XP and which require a clean installation.

Understand upgrading.   You should know that an installation overwrites any existing files, whereas an upgrade keeps the same data and application files.

Understand the Windows XP boot process, in order. The NTLDR utility bootstraps Windows and calls the BOOT.INI file. Then, NTLDR loads NTDETECT.COM, NTOSKRNL.EXE, HAL.DLL, NTOSKRNL.EXE, and WINLOGON.EXE.

Know what Control Panel utilities are unique to Windows XP. The Control Panel applets unique to Windows XP are Add or Remove Programs, Network Connections, Printers And Faxes, Automatic Updates, and Network Setup Wizard. You should be familiar with the purpose and options of each.

Understand how to configure Windows Defender. Windows Defender is not native to Windows XP, but it can be downloaded and installed. Once installed, it provides a tool that can be used to protect against malware.

Understand what each of the following utilities are used for: System Restore, Windows Firewall, Security Center. System Restore is used to create, and revert back to, restore points. Windows Firewall limits traffic coming from the network to the host. Security Center provides a simple interface with which to interact with virus scanners and other installed security software.

Review Questions

The answers to the Chapter Review Questions can be found in Appendix A.

1. What do you use in Windows XP to create a recovery disk?

   A. Automated System Recovery (ASR)

   B. RDISK.EXE

   C. Enhanced Startup Disk (ESD)

   D. Emergency Recovery System (ERS)

2. What is the first file used in the boot process of Windows XP?

   A. NTOSKRNL.EXE

   B. CONFIG.SYS

   C. AUTOEXEC.BAT

   D. NTLDR

   E. NTBOOTD.SYS

3. What does Safe Mode allow you to do?

   A. Run Windows without processing AUTOEXEC.BAT and CONFIG.SYS.

   B. Boot the system without scanning drives.

   C. Start Windows using only basic files and drivers.

   D. Skip loading the Registry.

4. Which of the following is an Ethernet standard implemented via a card that allows a "sleeping" machine to awaken when it receives a wakeup signal?

   A. Sleep timer

   B. WEP

   C. Wake on LAN

   D. WPA

5. What is the quickest solution to fixing a corrupted NTOSKRNL.EXE file?

   A. Reinstall Windows.

   B. Replace the corrupted file with a new one.

   C. Modify the BOOT.INI file to point to the backup NTOSKRNL.EXE file.

   D. Boot from a startup disk and replace the file from the setup disks or CD.

6. During what type of installation must a user be present to choose all options as they appear?

   A. Attended

   B. Existing

   C. Bootstrap

   D. Denote

7. In Windows XP, how do you access advanced startup options?

    A. By pressing the spacebar when prompted to do so

    B. By holding down Ctrl+Alt+Del after the Windows logo displays for the first time

    C. By pressing Esc after the OS menu displays

    D. By pressing F8 during the first phase of the boot process

8. In Windows XP, which of the following utilities is responsible for finding, downloading, and installing Windows service packs?

    A. Update Manager

    B. Service Pack Manager

    C. Windows Update

    D. Download Manager

9. In Windows XP, which of the following files is specifically responsible for enabling communication between the system hardware and the operating system?

    A. NTDETECT.COM

    B. NTOSKRNL.EXE

    C. NTBOOTDD.SYS

    D. HAL.DLL

    E. NTLDR

10. Which of the following is a replacement for RIS?

    A. STIR

    B. UAC

    C. WDS

    D. SIR

11. What is the first step when installing Windows onto a system that doesn't already have a functioning operating system?

    A. Formatting

    B. Partitioning

    C. Redirecting

    D. Installing the OS

12. Which of the following is/are performed by formatting the hard drive? (Choose four.)

    A. Formatting scans the surface of the hard drive platter to find bad spots and marks the areas surrounding a bad spot as bad sectors.

    B. Formatting lays down magnetic tracks in concentric circles.

    C. The tracks are split into pieces of 512 bytes called sectors.

    D. Formatting creates a File Allocation Table that contains information about the location of files.

13. After installation of the operating system, what does Windows XP require in order to curb software piracy?

   A. Certification

   B. Confirmation

   C. Activation

   D. Substantiation

14. Windows XP includes a feature called a _____, which is a copy of your system configuration that can be used to roll back the system to a previous state if a configuration error occurs.

   A. Restore point

   B. Repair point

   C. Roll back point

   D. Registry

15. Which utility is the System Configuration tool in Windows XP?

   A. MSINFO32.EXE

   B. MSCONFIG.EXE

   C. SYSCONFIG.CPL

   D. CONFIG.CPL

16. If Plug and Play does not work with a particular device on a Windows XP machine, what Control Panel applet can you use?

   A. Update

   B. System

   C. Add/Remove Hardware

   D. Add Hardware

17. Which utility that comes with Windows XP Professional is used to prepare a machine that can then be used to create an image to use for network installation?

   A. Ghost

   B. Sysprep

   C. Sysimage

   D. RIS

18. Adding which option to the `operating system` option in the `BOOT.INI` file will show the drivers as they're loaded in Windows XP?

   A. `/show`

   B. `/sos`

   C. `/all`

   D. `/flag`

19. Setup Manager is used to create answer files for automatically providing computer or user information during setup. These files are also known as what?

   A. UDFs

   B. INIs

   C. DLLs

   D. BTKs

20. Where would you configure a workstation to boot from the USB drive first and the hard drive only if there is not a bootable USB device attached?

   A. NTLDR

   B. C:\WINDOWS\TEMP\1st.txt

   C. BOOT.INI

   D. None of the above

Performance-Based Question

On the A+ exams, you will encounter performance-based questions. The questions on the exam require you to perform a specific task, and you will be graded on whether you were able to complete the task. The following require you to think creatively to measure how well you understand this chapter's topics. You may or may not see similar questions on the actual A+ exams. To see how your answers compare to the authors', refer to Appendix B.

You are working on an older Windows XP workstation that seems to be exhibiting some trouble every now and then and you aren't sure what is causing it. You want to configure the machine such that when a system failure occurs, it writes an event to the system log, sends an administrative alert, and automatically restarts. The debugging information should be configured so that it writes a complete memory dump (overwriting any existing file) to %SystemRoot%/TROUBLE.DMP. What steps would you take?

Chapter

17

Security

THE FOLLOWING COMPTIA A+ 220-802 EXAM OBJECTIVES ARE COVERED IN THIS CHAPTER:

✓ **2.1 Apply and use common prevention methods.**

- Physical security: Lock doors, Tailgating, Securing physical documents/passwords/shredding, Biometrics, Badges, Key fobs, RFID badge, RSA token, Privacy filters, Retinal

- Digital security: Antivirus, Firewalls, Antispyware, User authentication/strong passwords, Directory permissions

- User education

- Principle of least privilege

✓ **2.2 Compare and contrast common security threats.**

- Social engineering

- Malware

- Rootkits

- Phishing

- Shoulder surfing

- Spyware

- Viruses: Worms, Trojans

✓ **2.3 Implement security best practices to secure a workstation.**

- Setting strong passwords

- Requiring passwords

- Restricting user permissions

- Changing default user names

- Disabling guest account

- Screensaver required password

- Disable autorun

✓ **2.4 Given a scenario, use the appropriate data destruction/disposal method.**

- Low level format vs. standard format
- Hard drive sanitation and sanitation methods: Overwrite, Drive wipe
- Physical destruction: Shredder, Drill, Electromagnetic, Degaussing tool

✓ **2.5 Given a scenario, secure a SOHO wireless network.**

- Change default user-names and passwords
- Changing SSID
- Setting encryption
- Disabling SSID broadcast
- Enable MAC filtering
- Antenna and access point placement
- Radio power levels
- Assign static IP addresses

✓ **2.6 Given a scenario, secure a SOHO wired network.**

- Change default usernames and passwords
- Enable MAC filtering
- Assign static IP addresses
- Disabling ports
- Physical security

Think of how much simpler an administrator's life was in the days before every user had to be able to access the Internet. Think of how much simpler it must have been when you only had to maintain a number of dumb terminals connected to a minitower. Much of what has created headaches for an administrator since then is the inherent security risk that comes about as the network expands. As our world—and our networks—have become more connected, the need to secure data and keep it away from the eyes of those who can do harm has increased exponentially.

Realizing this, CompTIA added the security domain to the A+ exams a few years back. Security is now a topic that every administrator and technician must not only be aware of and care about but also be actively involved in. In the world of production, quality may be job one, but in the IT world, it is security.

This chapter looks at security primarily from the standpoint of what you need to know to pass the exam. All of the topics relevant to the security domain of the 220-802 exam are covered, and a thorough overview of each topic is provided.

Common Prevention Methods

A great many of the security issues that plague networks today can be solved through the implementation of basic security elements. Some of those elements are physical (locked doors) and others digital (antivirus software), but all share in common the goal of keeping the problems out.

Four topic areas are key: physical security, digital security, user education, and the principle of least privilege. As you study for the exam, know what types of physical security elements you can add to an environment to secure it. Know, as well, what types of digital security you should implement to keep malware at bay. Understand that the first line of defense is the users. You need to educate them to understand why security is important, and you need to impose the principle of least privilege to prevent them from inadvertently causing harm.

Physical Security

Physical security is a grab bag of elements that can be added to an environment to aid in securing it. It ranges from key fobs to retinal scanners. In the following sections, we will examine the list of components in the order in which they are listed by CompTIA.

Lock Doors

One of the easiest ways to prevent those intent on creating problems from physically entering your environment is to lock your doors and keep them out. A key aspect of access control involves *physical barriers*. The objective of a physical barrier is to prevent access to computers and network systems. The most effective physical barrier implementations require that more than one physical barrier be crossed to gain access. This type of approach is called a *multiple barrier system*.

Ideally, your systems should have a minimum of three physical barriers. The first barrier is the external entrance to the building, referred to as a *perimeter*, which is protected by burglar alarms, external walls, *fencing*, surveillance, and so on. An *access list* should exist to specifically identify who can enter and can be verified by a guard or someone with authority. The second barrier is the entrance into the building, and it could rely upon such items as *ID badges* to gain access. The third barrier is the entrance to the computer room itself (and could require key fobs, or just keys to locks). Each of these entrances can be individually secured, monitored, and protected with alarm systems.

Think of the three barriers this way: (1) outer, such as a fence; (2) middle, such as guards, locks, and mantraps; and (3) inner, such as key fobs.

Although these three barriers won't always stop intruders, they will potentially slow them down enough that law enforcement can respond before an intrusion is fully developed. Inside, a truly secure site should be dependent upon a *physical security token* for access to the actual network resources.

Tailgating

Tailgating refers to being so close to someone when they enter a building that you are able to come in right behind them without needing to use a key, a card, or any other security device. Many social engineering intruders needing physical access to a site will use this method of gaining entry. Educate users to beware of this and other social engineering ploys and prevent them from happening.

Using mantraps, which are devices such as small rooms that limit access to one or a few individuals, is a great way to stop tailgating.

Securing Physical Documents/Passwords/Shredding

It is amazing the information that can be gleaned from physical documents even in the age when there is such a push to go paperless. *Dumpster diving* is a common problem that puts systems at risk. Companies normally generate a huge amount of paper, most of which eventually winds up in dumpsters or recycle bins. Dumpsters may contain information that is highly sensitive in nature (such as a password a user has written on a piece of paper because they haven't memorized it yet). In high-security and government environments, sensitive papers should be either shredded or burned. Most businesses don't do this. In addition, the advent of "green" companies has created an increase in the amount of recycled paper, which can often contain all kinds of juicy information about a company and its individual employees.

Biometrics

Biometric devices use physical characteristics to identify the user. Such devices are becoming more common in the business environment. Biometric systems include fingerprint/palm/hand scanners, retinal scanners, and soon, possibly, DNA scanners. To gain access to resources, you must pass a physical screening process. In the case of a hand scanner, this may include identifying fingerprints, scars, and markings on your hand. Retinal scanners compare your eye's retinal pattern to a stored retinal pattern to verify your identity. DNA scanners will examine a unique portion of your DNA structure to verify that you are who you say you are.

With the passing of time, the definition of *biometrics* is expanding from simply identifying physical attributes about a person to being able to describe patterns in their behavior. Recent advances have been made in the ability to authenticate someone based on the key pattern they use when entering their password (how long they pause between each key, the amount of time each key is held down, and so forth). A company adopting biometric technologies needs to consider the controversy they may face (some authentication methods are considered more intrusive than others). The error rate also needs to be considered and an acceptance of the fact that errors can include both false positives and false negatives.

Badges

Badges can be any form of identification intended to differentiate the holder from everyone else. This can be as simple as a name badge or photo ID.

Smart cards are difficult to counterfeit, but they're easy to steal. Once a thief has a smart card, they have all the access the card allows. To prevent this, many organizations don't put any identifying marks on their smart cards, making it harder for someone to utilize them. A password or PIN is required to activate many modern smart cards, and encryption is employed to protect the card's contents.

Key Fobs

Key fobs are named after the chains that used to hold pocket watches to clothes. They are security devices that you carry with you; they display a randomly generated code that you can then use for authentication. This code usually changes very quickly (every 60 seconds is probably the average), and you combine this code with your PIN for authentication. RSA is one of the most well-known vendors of these.

RFID Badges

A *smart card* is a type of badge or card that gives you access to resources, including buildings, parking lots, and computers. It contains information about your identity and access privileges. Each area or computer has a card scanner or a reader in which you insert your card. RFID (Radio Frequency Identification) is the wireless, no-contact technology used with these cards and their accompanying reader.

The reader is connected to the workstation and validates against the security system. This increases the security of the authentication process because you must be in physical possession of the smart card to use the resources. Of course, if the card is lost or stolen, the person who finds the card can access the resources it allows.

RSA Tokens

Physical tokens are anything that a user must have on them to access network resources and are often associated with devices that enable the user to generate a one-time password authenticating their identity. SecurID, from RSA, is one of the best-known examples of a physical token, and information on it can be found at www.rsa.com/node.aspx?id=1156.

Privacy Filters

Privacy filters are either film or glass add-ons that are placed over a monitor or laptop screen to prevent the data on the screen from being readable when viewed from the sides. Only the user sitting directly in front of the screen is able to read the data.

Retinal

As mentioned earlier, retinal scanners are one form of biometric devices that can be used to identify a user. As the name implies, matches are made based upon identification of the blood vessels in an individual's retina. Though highly reliable, the equipment needed is still rather expensive.

Digital Security

Whereas the topic of physical security, from CompTIA's standpoint, focuses on keeping individuals out, digital security focuses on keeping harmful data and malware out as well as on authorization and permissions. The areas of focus are antivirus software, firewalls, antispyware, user authentication/strong passwords, and directory permissions. Each of these are addressed in the sections that follow.

Antivirus Software

The primary method of preventing the propagation of malicious code involves the use of *antivirus software*. Antivirus software is an application that is installed on a system to protect it and to scan for viruses as well as worms and Trojan horses. Most viruses have characteristics that are common to families of virus. Antivirus software looks for these characteristics, or fingerprints, to identify and neutralize viruses before they impact you.

More than 200,000 known viruses, worms, bombs, and other malware have been defined. New ones are added all the time. Your antivirus software manufacturer will usually work very hard to keep the definition database files current. The definition database file contains the currently known viruses and countermeasures for a particular antivirus software product. You probably won't receive a virus that hasn't been seen by one of these companies. If you keep the virus definition database files in your software up-to-date, you probably won't be overly vulnerable to attacks.

 The best method of protection is to use a layered approach. Antivirus software should be at the gateways, at the servers, and at the desktop. If you want to go one step further, you can use software at each location from different vendors to make sure you're covered from all angles.

Firewalls

Firewalls are among the first lines of defense in a network. There are different types of firewalls, and they can be either stand-alone systems or included in devices such as routers or servers. You can find firewall solutions that are marketed as hardware only and others that are software only. Many firewalls, however, consist of add-in software that is available for servers or workstations.

 Although solutions are sold as "hardware only," the hardware still runs some sort of software. It may be hardened and in ROM to prevent tampering, and it may be customized, but software is present nonetheless.

The basic purpose of a firewall is to isolate one network from another. Firewalls are becoming available as appliances, meaning they're installed as the primary device separating two networks. *Appliances* are freestanding devices that operate in a largely self-contained manner, requiring less maintenance and support than a server-based product.

Firewalls function as one or more of the following:

- Packet filter
- Proxy firewall
- Stateful inspection firewall

 To understand the concept of a firewall, it helps to know where the term comes from. In days of old, dwellings used to be built so close together that if a fire broke out in one, it could easily destroy a block or more before it could be contained. To decrease the risk of this happening, firewalls were built between buildings. The firewalls were huge brick walls that separated the buildings and kept a fire confined to one side. The same concept of restricting and confining is true in network firewalls. Traffic from the outside world hits the firewall and isn't allowed to enter the network unless it's invited.

The firewall shown in Figure 17.1 effectively limits access from outside networks while allowing inside network users to access outside resources. The firewall in this illustration is also performing proxy functions.

FIGURE 17.1 A proxy firewall blocking network access from external networks

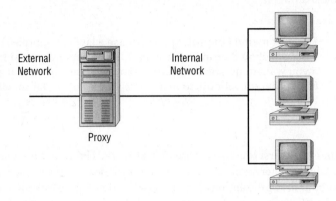

> Although firewalls are often associated with outside traffic, you can place a firewall anywhere. For example, if you want to isolate one portion of your internal network from others, you can place a firewall between them.

The following list includes discussions of three of the most common functions that firewalls perform:

Packet filter firewalls   A firewall operating as a *packet filter* passes or blocks traffic to specific addresses based on the type of application and the port used. The packet filter doesn't analyze the data of a packet; it decides whether to pass it based on the packet's addressing information. For instance, a packet filter may allow web traffic on port 80 and block Telnet traffic on port 23. This type of filtering is included in many routers. If a received packet request asks for a port that isn't authorized, the filter may reject the request or simply ignore it. Many packet filters can also specify which IP addresses can request which ports and allow or deny them based on the security settings of the firewall.

Packet filters are growing in sophistication and capability. A packet filter firewall can allow any traffic that you specify as acceptable. For example, if you want web users to access your site, then you configure the packet filter firewall to allow data on port 80 to enter. If every network were exactly the same, firewalls would come with default port settings hard-coded, but networks vary, so the firewalls don't include such settings (though Deny All is the most common default).

Proxy firewalls   A *proxy firewall* can be thought of as an intermediary between your network and any other network. Proxy firewalls are used to process requests from an outside network; the proxy firewall examines the data and makes rule-based decisions about whether the request should be forwarded or refused. The proxy intercepts all the packages and reprocesses them for use internally. This process may include hiding IP addresses.

The proxy firewall provides better security than packet filtering because of the increased intelligence that a proxy firewall offers. Requests from internal network users are routed through the proxy. The proxy, in turn, repackages the request and sends it along, thereby isolating the user from the external network. The proxy can also offer caching, should the same request be made again, and can increase the efficiency of data delivery.

A proxy firewall typically uses two network interface cards (NICs). This type of firewall is referred to as a *dual-homed* firewall. One of the cards is connected to the outside network, and the other is connected to the internal network. The proxy software manages the connection between the two NICs. This setup segregates the two networks from each other and offers increased security. Figure 17.2 illustrates a dual-homed firewall segregating two networks from each other.

FIGURE 17.2   A dual-homed firewall segregating two networks from each other

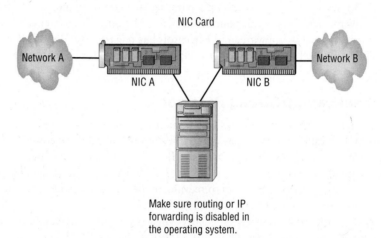

The proxy function can occur at either the application level or the circuit level. *Application-level proxy* functions read the individual commands of the protocols that are being served. This type of server is advanced and must know the rules and capabilities of the protocol used. An implementation of this type of proxy must know the difference between GET and PUT operations, for example, and have rules specifying how to execute them. A *circuit-level proxy* creates a circuit between the client and the server and doesn't deal with the contents of the packets that are being processed.

A unique application-level proxy server must exist for each protocol supported. Many proxy servers also provide full *auditing, accounting* and other usage information that wouldn't normally be kept by a circuit-level proxy server.

Stateful inspection firewalls   *Stateful inspection* is also referred to as *stateful packet filtering.* Most of the devices used in networks don't keep track of how information is routed or used. After a packet is passed, the packet and path are forgotten. In stateful inspection (or stateful packet filtering), records are kept using a state table that tracks every communications channel. Stateful inspections occur at all levels of the network and provide additional security, especially in connectionless protocols such as *User Datagram Protocol (UDP)* and *Internet Control Message Protocol (ICMP)*. This adds complexity to the process. Denial of service (DoS) attacks present a challenge because flooding techniques are used to overload the state table and effectively cause the firewall to shut down or reboot. When multiple computers are aimed at the target, it is known as a distributed denial of service (DDoS) attack. A *smurf* attack attempts to use a broadcast ping (ICMP) on a network. The return address of the ping may be a valid system in your network. This system will be flooded with responses in a large network.

Antispyware

Just as antivirus software seeks out and stops viruses from entering and spreading, so too is the purpose of antispyware software. One thing separating spyware from most other malware is that it almost always exists to provide commercial gain. The operating systems from Microsoft are the ones most affected by spyware, and Microsoft has released Windows Defender and Security Essentials (as well as System Center Endpoint Protection for the enterprise) to combat the problem.

User Authentication/Strong Passwords

You can set up many different parameters and standards to force the people in your organization to conform. In establishing these parameters, it's important that you consider the capabilities of the people who will be working with them. If you're working in an environment where people aren't computer savvy, you may spend a lot of time helping them remember and recover passwords. Many organizations have had to reevaluate their security guidelines after they've invested great time and expense to implement high-security systems.

Enforcing authentication security, especially when supporting users, can become a high-maintenance activity for network administrators. On one hand, you want people to be able to authenticate easily; on the other hand, you want to establish security that protects your company's resources. In a Windows domain, password policies can be configured at the domain level using Group Policy objects. Variables you can configure include password complexity and length and the time between allowed changes to passwords. A good password includes both upper- and lowercase letters as well as numbers and symbols. Educate users to not use personal information that one could easily guess about them, such as their pet names, anniversaries, or birthdays.

Directory Permissions

There is not much users can do to improve or change the security of the directory services deployed. However, you can ensure that they don't become a tool for an attacker bent on compromising your organization's security:

- Ensure that the most secure form of authentication encryption is used and supported by both the client and the authentication servers.
- Use encrypted software and protocols whenever possible, even for internal communications.

- Require users to change their password according to the company's password policy.

- Establish a minimum character limit for passwords. While many companies set the minimum at 8 characters, it is not uncommon to see this set at 16.

- Instruct user to never write their password down, or if they do, divide it up into several pieces and store each in a different secure location (such as a home safe, a gun cabinet, a chemical supply locker, or safety deposit box).

- Tell users to never share their password or logon session with another person; this includes friends, spouse, and children.

- Make sure users allow all approved updates and patches to be installed onto their client.

- Ensure that users copy all company data back to a central file server before disconnecting from a logon session.

- Users should back up any personal data onto verified removable media.

- Users should never walk away from a logged-on workstation without first locking it (requiring a password to continue the session).

- Require users to employ a password-protected screensaver.

- Don't let users use auto-logon features.

- Tell users to be aware of who is around them (and may be watching them) when they log on and when they work with valuable data.

- Users should never leave a company notebook, cell phone, or PDA in a position where it can be stolen or compromised while they are away from the office. Cable locks should be used to keep notebooks securely in place whenever they are off site.

 Real World Scenario

Check the Movie Listings

Be wary of popular names or current trends that make certain passwords predictable. For example, during the first release of *Star Wars*, two of the most popular passwords used on college campuses were C3PO and R2D2. This created a security problem for campus computer centers.

A few years back, characters from the *Matrix* trilogy became popular passwords as those working in offices tried to live out their lives in fantasy. While you may truly like a movie or character that is popular at the moment, you need to understand that names associated with popular movies will be tried as password possibilities very quickly.

 As for the permission on directories themselves, that is governed by NTFS and share permissions.

The protection of a directory service is based on the initial selection of network operating system and its deployment infrastructure. After these foundational decisions are made, you need to fully understand the technologies employed by your selected directory services system and learn how to make the most functional, yet secure, environment possible. This will usually require the addition of third-party security devices, applications, services, and solutions.

User Education

The most effective method of preventing viruses, spyware, and harm to data is education. Teach your users not to open suspicious files and to open only those files that they're reasonably sure are virus free. They need to scan every disk, email, and document they receive before they open them. You should also have all workstations scheduled to be automatically scanned on a regular basis.

Principle of Least Privilege

The concept of least privilege is a simple one: When assigning permissions, give users only the permissions they need to do their work and no more. This is especially true with administrators. Users who need administrative-level permissions should be assigned two accounts: one for performing nonadministrative, day-to-day tasks and the other to be used only when performing administrative tasks that specifically require an administrative-level user account. Those users should be educated on how each of the accounts should be used.

The biggest benefit to following this policy is the reduction of risk. The biggest headache with following this policy is trying to deal with users who may not understand it. Managers, for example, may assert that they should have more permission that those who report to them, but giving those permissions to them also opens up all the possibilities for inadvertently deleting files, misconfiguring resources, and so on.

A least privilege policy should exist, and be enforced, throughout the enterprise. Users should have only the permissions and privileges needed to do their jobs and no more. The ISO standard 27002 (which updates 17799) sums it up well: "Privileges should be allocated to individuals on a need-to-use basis and on an event-by-event basis, i.e., the minimum requirement for their functional role when needed." Adopting this as the policy for your organization is highly recommended.

Common Security Threats

In the following sections, we discuss a number of very important topics that fall into the realm of two broad categories: social engineering and malware. We'll look at these topics as well as some of the reasons your network is vulnerable. The discussion is far from inclusive because new variants of malware and social engineering attacks are being created by miscreants on a regular basis. We will cover, however, everything CompTIA expects you to know for the exam.

Social Engineering

Social engineering is a process in which an attacker attempts to acquire information about your network and system by social means, such as talking to people in the organization. A social engineering attack may occur over the phone, by email, or in person. The intent is to acquire access information, such as user IDs and passwords. When the attempt is made through email or instant messaging, this is known as *phishing* (discussed later), and it's often made to look as if a message is coming from sites where users are likely to have accounts (eBay and PayPal are popular).

These are relatively low-tech attacks and are more akin to con jobs. Take the following example: Your help desk gets a call at 4:00 a.m. from someone purporting to be the vice president of your company. They tells the help desk personnel that they are out of town to attend a meeting, their computer just failed, and they are sitting in a FedEx office trying to get a file from their desktop computer back at the office. They can't seem to remember their password and user ID. They tell the help desk representative that they need access to the information right away or the company could lose millions of dollars. Your help desk rep knows how important this meeting is and gives the user ID and password over the phone. At this point, the attacker has just successfully socially engineered an ID and password that can be used for an attack.

Another common approach is initiated by a phone call or email from someone who pretends to be your software vendor, telling you that they have a critical fix that must be installed on your computer system. It may state that if this patch isn't installed right away, your system will crash and you'll lose all your data. For some reason, you've changed your maintenance account password and they can't log on. Your system operator gives the password to the person. You've been hit again.

In Exercise 17.1, you'll test your users to determine the likelihood of a social engineering attack. The steps are suggestions for tests; you may need to modify them slightly to be appropriate at your workplace. Before proceeding, make certain your manager knows that you're conducting such a test and approves of it.

EXERCISE 17.1

Testing Social Engineering

1. Call the receptionist from an outside line when the sales manager is at lunch. Tell her that you're a new salesperson, that you didn't write down the username and password the sales manager gave you last week, and that you need to get a file from the email system for a presentation tomorrow. Does she direct you to the appropriate person or attempt to help you receive the file?

2. Call the human resources department from an outside line. Don't give your real name, but instead say that you're a vendor who has been working with this company for years. You'd like a copy of the employee phone list to be emailed to you, if possible. Do they agree to send you the list, which would contain information that could be used to try to guess usernames and passwords?

3. Pick a user at random. Call them and identify yourself as someone who does work with the company. Tell them that you're supposed to have some new software ready for them by next week and that you need to know their password to finish configuring it. Do they do the right thing?

The best defense against any social engineering attack is education. Make certain the employees of your company would know how to react to the requests presented here.

Malware

We've all been battling malicious, invasive software since we bought our first computers. This software can go by any number of names—virus, malware, and so on—but if you aren't aware of its presence, these uninvited intruders may damage the data on your hard disk, destroy your operating system, and possibly spread to other systems.

Make certain your systems, and the data within them, are kept as secure as possible by using antivirus and antispyware programs. Doing so prevents others from changing the data, destroying it, or inadvertently harming it.

Rootkits

Rootkits have become the software exploitation program du jour. Rootkits are software programs that have the ability to hide certain things from the operating system; they do so by obtaining (and retaining) administrative-level access. With a rootkit, there may be a number of processes running on a system that don't show up in Task Manager, or connections that don't appear in a Netstat display may be established or available—the rootkit masks the presence of these items. It does this by manipulating function calls to the operating system and filtering out information that would normally appear.

Unfortunately, many rootkits are written to get around antivirus and antispyware programs that aren't kept up-to-date. The best defense you have is to monitor what your system is doing and catch the rootkit in the process of installation.

Phishing

Phishing is a form of social engineering in which you simply ask someone for a piece of information that you are missing by making it look as if it is a legitimate request. An email might look as if it is from a bank and contain some basic information, such as the user's name. These types of messages often state that there is a problem with the person's account or access privileges. They will be told to click a link to correct the problem. After they click the link—which goes to a site other than the bank's—they are asked for their username, password, account information, and so on. The person instigating the phishing can then use this information to access the legitimate account.

One of the best countermeasures to phishing is to simply mouse over the Click Here link and read the URL. Almost every time the URL is an adaptation of the legitimate URL as opposed to a link to the real thing.

The only preventive measure in dealing with social engineering attacks is to educate your users and staff to never give out passwords and user IDs over the phone or via email or to anyone who isn't positively verified as being who they say they are.

When you combine phishing with Voice over IP (VoIP), it becomes known as *vishing* and is just an elevated form of social engineering. While crank calls have been in existence since the invention of the telephone, the rise in VoIP now makes it possible for someone to call you from almost anywhere in the world, without the worry of tracing/caller ID/and other features of the land line, and pretend to be someone they are not in order to get data from you.

Two other forms of phishing to be aware of are *spear phishing* and *whaling*, and they are very similar in nature. With spear phishing, the attacker uses information that the target would be less likely to question because it appears to be coming from a trusted source. Suppose, for example, you receive a message that appears to be from your spouse and it says to click here to see that video of your children from last Christmas. Because it appears far more likely to be a legitimate message, it cuts through your standard defenses like a spear, and the likelihood that you would click the link is higher. Generating the attack requires much more work on the part of the attacker and often involves using information from contact lists, friend lists from social media sites, and so on.

Whaling is nothing more than phishing, or spear phishing, for so-called "big" users, thus the reference to the ocean's largest creatures. Instead of sending out a To Whom It May Concern message to thousands of users, the whaler identifies one person from whom they can gain all the data they want—usually a manager or business owner—and targets the phishing campaign at them.

Shoulder Surfing

One form of social engineering is known as *shoulder surfing* and involves nothing more than watching someone when they enter their sensitive data. They can see you entering a password, typing in a credit card number, or entering any other pertinent information. The best defense against this type of attack is simply to survey your environment before entering personal data.

Spyware

Spyware differs from other malware in that it works—often actively—on behalf of a third party. Rather than self-replicating, like viruses and worms, spyware is spread to machines by users who inadvertently ask for it. The users often don't know they have asked for it, but have done so by downloading other programs, visiting infected sites, and so on. In a replay attack, an expired certificate is being used repeatedly to gain logon privileges.

The spyware program monitors the user's activity and responds by offering unsolicited pop-up advertisements (sometimes known as *adware*), gathers information about the user to pass on to marketers, or intercepts personal data such as credit card numbers.

Viruses

Viruses can be classified as polymorphic, stealth, retrovirus, multipartite, armored, companion, phage, and macro viruses. Each type of virus has a different attack strategy and different consequences.

 Estimates for losses due to viruses are in the billions of dollars. These losses include financial loss as well as lost productivity.

The following sections will introduce the symptoms of a virus infection, explain how a virus works, and describe the types of viruses you can expect to encounter and how they generally behave. We'll also discuss how a virus is transmitted through a network and look at a few hoaxes.

Symptoms of a Virus/Malware Infection

Many viruses will announce that you're infected as soon as they gain access to your system. They may take control of your system and flash annoying messages on your screen or destroy your hard disk. When this occurs, you'll know that you're a victim. Other viruses will cause your system to slow down, cause files to disappear from your computer, or take over your disk space.

 Because viruses are the most common malware, the term *virus* is used in this section.

You should look for some of the following symptoms when determining if a virus infection has occurred:

- The programs on your system start to load more slowly. This happens because the virus is spreading to other files in your system or is taking over system resources.

- Unusual files appear on your hard drive, or files start to disappear from your system. Many viruses delete key files in your system to render it inoperable.

- Program sizes change from the installed versions. This occurs because the virus is attaching itself to these programs on your disk.

- Your browser, word-processing application, or other software begins to exhibit unusual operating characteristics. Screens or menus may change.

- The system mysteriously shuts itself down or starts itself up and does a great deal of unanticipated disk activity.

- You mysteriously lose access to a disk drive or other system resources. The virus has changed the settings on a device to make it unusable.

- Your system suddenly doesn't reboot or gives unexpected error messages during startup.

This list is by no means comprehensive. What is an absolute, however, is the fact that you should immediately quarantine the infected system. It is imperative that you do all you can to contain the virus and keep it from spreading to other systems within your network, or beyond.

How Viruses Work

A virus, in most cases, tries to accomplish one of two things: render your system inoperable or spread to other systems. Many viruses will spread to other systems given the chance and then render your system unusable. This is common with many of the newer viruses.

If your system is infected, the virus may try to attach itself to every file in your system and spread each time you send a file or document to other users. Figure 17.3 shows a virus spreading from an infected system either through a network or by removable media. When you give removable media to another user or put it into another system, you then infect that system with the virus.

FIGURE 17.3   Virus spreading from an infected system using the network or removable media

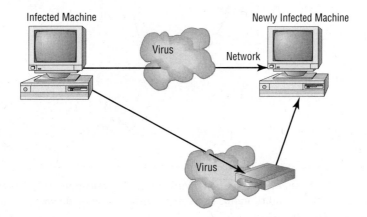

Many viruses today are spread using email. The infected system attaches a file to any email that you send to another user. The recipient opens this file, thinking it's something you legitimately sent them. When they open the file, the virus infects the target system. The virus might then attach itself to all the emails the newly infected system sends, which in turn infects computers of the recipients of the emails. Figure 17.4 shows how a virus can spread from a single user to literally thousands of users in a very short time using email.

Types of Viruses

Viruses take many different forms. The following list briefly introduces these forms and explain how they work.

FIGURE 17.4   An email virus spreading geometrically to other users

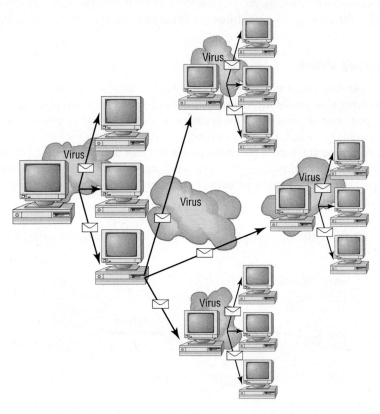

 The best defense against a virus attack is up-to-date antivirus software installed and running. The software should be on all workstations as well as the server.

These are the most common types of viruses, but this isn't a comprehensive list:

Armored virus   An *armored virus* is designed to make itself difficult to detect or analyze. Armored viruses cover themselves with protective code that stops debuggers or disassemblers from examining critical elements of the virus. The virus may be written in such a way that some aspects of the programming act as a decoy to distract analysis while the actual code hides in other areas in the program.

From the perspective of the creator, the more time it takes to deconstruct the virus, the longer it can live. The longer it can live, the more time it has to replicate and spread to as many machines as possible. The key to stopping most viruses is to identify them quickly and educate administrators about them—the very things that the armor makes difficult to accomplish.

Companion virus   A *companion virus* attaches itself to legitimate programs and then creates a program with a different filename extension. This file may reside in your system's temporary directory. When a user types the name of the legitimate program, the companion virus executes instead of the real program. This effectively hides the virus from the user. Many of the viruses that are used to attack Windows systems make changes to program pointers in the Registry so that they point to the infected program. The infected program may perform its dirty deed and then start the real program.

Macro virus   A *macro virus* exploits the enhancements made to many application programs. Programmers can expand the capability of applications such as Microsoft Word and Excel. Word, for example, supports a mini-BASIC programming language that allows files to be manipulated automatically. These programs in the document are called *macros*. For example, a macro can tell your word processor to spell-check your document automatically when it opens. Macro viruses can infect all the documents on your system and spread to other systems via email or other methods. Macro viruses are one of the fastest-growing forms of exploitation today.

Multipartite virus   A *multipartite virus* attacks your system in multiple ways. It may attempt to infect your boot sector, infect all of your executable files, and destroy your application files. The hope here is that you won't be able to correct all the problems and will allow the infestation to continue. The multipartite virus depicted in Figure 17.5 attacks a system's boot sector, infects application files, and attacks Word documents.

Phage virus   A *phage virus* alters other programs and databases. The virus infects all of these files. The only way to remove this virus is to reinstall the programs that are infected. If you miss even a single incident of this virus on the victim system, the process will start again and infect the system once more.

FIGURE 17.5   A multipartite virus commencing an attack on a system

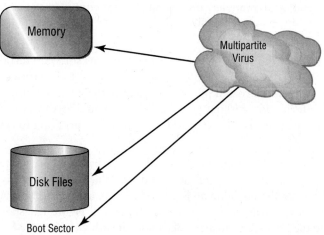

Polymorphic virus *Polymorphic viruses* change form to avoid detection. These types of viruses attack your system, display a message on your computer, and delete files on your system. The virus will attempt to hide from your antivirus software. Frequently, the virus will encrypt parts of itself to avoid detection. When the virus does this, it's referred to as *mutation*. The mutation process makes it hard for antivirus software to detect common characteristics of the virus. Figure 17.6 shows a polymorphic virus changing its characteristics to avoid detection. In this example, the virus changes a signature to fool antivirus software.

FIGURE 17.6 The polymorphic virus changing its characteristics

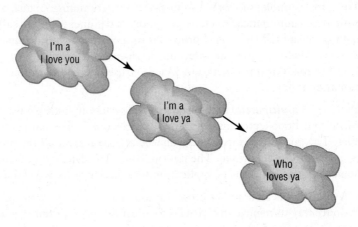

 A *signature* is an algorithm or other element of a virus that uniquely identifies it. Because some viruses have the ability to alter their signature, it is crucial that you keep signature files current, whether you choose to manually download them or configure the antivirus engine to do so automatically.

Retrovirus A *retrovirus* attacks or bypasses the antivirus software installed on a computer. You can consider a retrovirus to be an anti-antivirus. Retroviruses can directly attack your antivirus software and potentially destroy the virus definition database file. Destroying this information without your knowledge would leave you with a false sense of security. The virus may also directly attack an antivirus program to create bypasses for itself.

Stealth virus A *stealth virus* attempts to avoid detection by masking itself from applications. It may attach itself to the boot sector of the hard drive. When a system utility or program runs, the stealth virus redirects commands around itself to avoid detection. An infected file may report a file size different from what is actually present. Figure 17.7 shows a stealth virus attaching itself to the boot sector to avoid detection. Stealth viruses may also move themselves from file A to file B during a virus scan for the same reason.

FIGURE 17.7   A stealth virus hiding in a disk boot sector

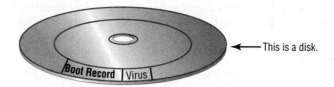

Virus Transmission in a Network

Upon infection, some viruses destroy the target system immediately. The saving grace is that the infection can be detected and corrected. Some viruses won't destroy or otherwise tamper with a system; they use the victim system as a carrier. The victim system then infects servers, file shares, and other resources with the virus. The carrier then infects the target system again. Until the carrier is identified and cleaned, the virus continues to harass systems in this network and spread.

Present Virus Activity

New viruses and threats are released on a regular basis to join the cadre of those already in existence. From an exam perspective, you need only be familiar with the world as it existed at the time the questions were written. From an administrative standpoint, however, you need to know what is happening today.

To find this information, visit the CERT/CC Current Activity web page at `www.us-cert` `.gov/current/current_activity.html`. Here you'll find a detailed description of the most current viruses as well as links to pages on older threats.

Worms

A *worm* is different from a virus in that it can reproduce itself, it's self-contained, and it doesn't need a host application to be transported. Many of the so-called viruses that have made the news were actually worms. However, it's possible for a worm to contain or deliver a virus to a target system.

By their nature and origin, worms are supposed to propagate, and they use whatever services they're capable of to do that. Early worms filled up memory and bred inside the RAM of the target computer. Worms can use TCP/IP, email, Internet services, or any number of possibilities to reach their target.

Trojans

Trojan horses are programs that enter a system or network under the guise of another program. A Trojan horse may be included as an attachment or as part of an installation program. The Trojan horse can create a back door or replace a valid program during installation. It then accomplishes its mission under the guise of another program. Trojan horses can be used to compromise the security of your system, and they can exist on a system for years before they're detected.

The best preventive measure for Trojan horses is to not allow them entry into your system. Immediately before and after you install a new software program or operating system, back it up! If you suspect a Trojan horse, you can reinstall the original programs, which should delete the Trojan horse. A port scan may also reveal a Trojan horse on your system. If an application opens a TCP or UDP port that isn't supported in your network, you can track it down and determine which port is being used.

Workstation Security Best Practices

The user represents the weakest link in the security chain, whether harm comes to them in the form of malware, social engineering, or simply avoidable mistakes. The workstation represents the digital arm of the user and must be properly and adequately secured to keep the user—and the network—protected.

There a number of best practices involved with securing a workstation. While a checklist could take many pages, depending upon your environment, CompTIA has identified seven that should appear on any roster:

- Set strong passwords.
- Require passwords.
- Restrict user permissions.
- Change default usernames.
- Disable the guest account.
- Make the screensaver require a password.
- Disable autorun functionality.

The following sections will explore these best practices in more detail.

Setting Strong Passwords

One of the strongest ways to keep a system safe is to employ strong passwords and educate your users in the best practices associated with them. Many password-generation systems are based on a one-way hashing approach. You can't take the hash value and reverse it to guess the password. In theory, this makes it harder to guess or decrypt a password.

Passwords should be as long as possible. Most security experts believe a password of 10 characters is the minimum that should be used if security is a real concern. If you use only the lowercase letters of the alphabet, you have 26 characters with which to work. If you add the numeric values 0 through 9, you'll get another 10 characters. If you go one step further and add the uppercase letters, you'll then have an additional 26 characters, giving you a total of 62 characters with which to construct a password.

> Most vendors recommend that you use nonalphabetic characters such as #, $, and % in your password, and some go so far as to require it.

If you used a 4-character password, this would be $62 \times 62 \times 62 \times 62$, or approximately 14 million password possibilities. If you used 5 characters in your password, this would give you 62 to the 5th power, or approximately 920 million password possibilities. If you used a 10-character password, this would give you 62 to the 10th power, or 8.4×10^{17} (a very big number) possibilities. As you can see, these numbers increase exponentially with each position added to the password. The 4-digit password could probably be broken in a fraction of a day, while the 10-digit password would take considerably longer and much more processing power.

If your password consisted of only the 26 lowercase letters from the alphabet, the 4-digit password would have 26 to the 4th power, or 456,000 password combinations. A 5-character password would have 26 to the 5th power, or over 11 million, and a 10-character password would have 26 to the 10th power, or 1.4×10^{14}. This is still a big number, but it would take considerably less time to break it.

> To see tables on how quickly passwords can be surmised, visit www.lockdown.co.uk/?pg=combi&s=articles.

Mathematical methods of encryption are primarily used in conjunction with other encryption methods as part of authenticity verification. The message and the hashed value of the message can be encrypted using other processes. In this way, you know that the message is secure and hasn't been altered.

Requiring Passwords

Make absolutely certain you require passwords (such a simple to thing to overlook in a small network) for all accounts, and change the default passwords on system accounts.

Restricting User Permissions

When assigning user permissions, follow the principle of least privilege (discussed earlier): Give users only the bare minimum they need to do their job. Assign permissions to groups rather than users, and make users member of groups (or remove them from groups) as they change roles or positions.

Changing Default Usernames

Default accounts represent a huge weakness because everyone knows they exist. When an operating system is installed—whether on a workstation or a server—certain default accounts are created., Knowing the names of those accounts simplifies the process of potential attackers accessing them because they only have to supply the password.

Disabling the Guest Account

When Windows is installed, one of the default accounts it creates is Guest and this represents a weakness that can be exploited by an attacker. While the account cannot do much, it can provide initial access to a system and the attacker can use that to find another account or acquire sensitive information about the system.

To secure the system, disable all accounts that are not needed, especially the Guest account. Next, rename the accounts if you can (Microsoft won't allow you to rename some). Finally, change the passwords from the defaults and add them to the cycle of passwords that routinely get changed.

Screensaver Required Password

A screensaver should automatically start after a short period of idle time, and a password should be required before the user can begin the session again. This method of locking the workstation adds one more level of security.

Disable Autorun

It is never a good idea to put any media in a workstation if you do not know where it came from or what it is. The simple reason being that said media (CD, DVD, USB) could contain malware. Compounding matters, that malware could be referenced in the AUTORUN.INF file, causing it to be summoned when the media is inserted in the machine and requiring no other action. AUTORUN.INF can be used to start an executable, access a website, or do any of a large number of different tasks. The best way to prevent a user from falling victim to such a ploy is to disable the autorun feature on the workstation.

Microsoft has changed (by default, disabled) the function on Windows Vista and Windows 7, though running it remains the default action for PCs running Windows XP through Service Pack 3. The reason Microsoft changed the default action can be summed up in a single word: security. That text-based AUTORUN.INF file can not only take your browser to a web page, it can also call any executable file, pass along variable information about the user, or do just about anything else imaginable. Simply put, it is never a good idea to plug any media into your system if you have no idea where it came from or what it holds. Such an action opens up the user's system—and the network—to any number of possible risks. An entire business's data could be jeopardized by such a minuscule act if a harmful CD were placed in a computer at work by someone with elevated privileges.

Destruction and Disposal Methods

Think of all the sensitive data written to a hard drive. Said drive can contain information about students, about clients, about users, about anyone and anything. That hard drive can be in a desktop PC, in a laptop, or even in a printer (many laser printers above consumer grade offer the ability to add a hard drive to store print jobs), and if it falls into the wrong hands, you can not only lose valuable data but also risk a lawsuit for not properly protecting privacy. An appropriate data destruction/disposal plan should be in place to avoid any potential problems.

Since data on media holds great value and liability, that media should never be simply tossed away for prying eyes to stumble upon. For the purpose of this objective, the media in question is hard drives, and there are three key concepts to understand in regard to them: formatting, sanitation, and destruction. Formatting prepares the drive to hold new information (which can include copying over data already there). Sanitation involves wiping the data on the drive off of it, while destruction renders the drive no longer usable.

While this objective is heavily focused on hard drives, it is also possible to have data stored on portable flash drives, backup tapes, CDs, or DVDs. In the interest of security, it is recommended you destroy them before disposing of them as well.

Low-Level Format vs. Standard Format

There are multiple levels of formatting that can be done on a drive. A standard format, accomplished using the operating system's FORMAT utility (or similar), can mark space occupied by files as available for new files without truly deleting what was there. Such erasing—if you want to call it that—doesn't guarantee that the information isn't still on the disk and recoverable.

A low-level format (typically only accomplished in the factory) can be performed on the system, or a utility can be used to completely wipe the disk clean. This process helps ensure that information doesn't fall into the wrong hands.

A low-level format is performed on integrated device electronics (IDE) hard drives by the manufacturer. Low-level formatting must be performed even before a drive can be partitioned. In low-level formatting, the drive controller chip and the drive meet for the very first time and learn to work together. Because IDE drives have their controllers integrated into the drive, low-level formatting is a factory process with these drives. Low-level formatting is not operating system dependent.

Never perform a low-level format on IDE or SCSI drives! They're formatted at the factory, and you may cause problems by using low-level utilities on these types of drives.

The main thing to remember for the exams is that most forms of formatting included with the operating system do not actually completely erase the data. Formatting the drive and then disposing of it has caused many companies problems when the data has been retrieved by individuals who never should have seen it using applications that are commercially available.

Hard Drive Sanitation and Sanitation Methods

A number of vendors offer hard drives with Advanced Encryption Standard (AES) cryptography built in, but it's still better to keep these secure hard drives completely out of the hands of others than to trust their internal security mechanisms once their usable life span has passed for the client. Some vendors include utilities to erase the hard drive, and if it is a Serial ATA (SATA) drive, you can always run HDDERASE, but you are still taking your chances.

In addition to HDDERASE, you can find a number of other software "shredders" by doing a quick Web search. It is important to recognize and acknowledge that many of these do not meet military or GSA specifications, and those specifications should be considered as guidelines that you also adhere to when dealing with your own, or a client's, data. The only sure-fire method of rendering the hard drive contents completely eradicated is physical destruction.

Overwrite

Overwriting the drive entails copying over the data with new data. A common practice is to replace the data with 0s. A number of applications allow you to recover what was there prior to the last write operation, and for that reason, most overwrite software will write the same sequence and save it multiple times.

Drive Wipe

If it's possible to verify beyond a reasonable doubt that a piece of hardware that's no longer being used doesn't contain any data of a sensitive or proprietary nature, then that hardware can be recycled (sold to employees, sold to a third party, donated to a school, and so on). That level of assurance can come from wiping a hard drive or using specialized utilities.

NOTE   Degaussing hard drives is difficult and may render the drive unusable.

If you can't be assured that the hardware in question doesn't contain important data, then the hardware should be destroyed. You cannot, and should not, take a risk that the data your company depends on could fall into the wrong hands.

Physical Destruction

Physically destroying the drive involves rendering the component no longer usable. While the focus is on hard drives, you can also physically destroy other forms of media, such as flash drives and CD/DVDs.

Shredder

Many commercial paper shredders include the ability to destroy DVDs and CDs. Paper shredders, however, are not able to handle hard drives, and you need a shredder created for just such a purpose: Jackhammer makes a low-volume unit that will destroy eight drives a minute and carries a suggested list price of just under $30,000.

Drill

If you don't have the budget for a hard drive shredder, you can accomplish similar results in a much more time-consuming way with a power drill. The goal is to physically destroy the platters in the drive. Start the process by removing the cover from the drive—this is normally done with a Torx driver (while #8 does not work with all, it is a good one to try first). You can remove the arm with a slotted screwdriver and then the cover over the platters using a Torx driver. Don't worry about damaging or scratching anything—nothing is intended to be saved. Everything but the platters can be tossed away.

As an optional step, you can completely remove the tracks using a belt sander, grinder, or palm sander. The goal is to turn the shiny surface into fine powder. Again, this step is optional, but it adds one more layer of assurance that nothing usable remains. Always wear eye protection and be careful not to breathe in any fine particles that you generate during the grinding/destruction process.

Following this, use the power drill to create as small a set of particles as possible. A drill press works much better for this task than trying to hold the drive and drill it with a handheld model.

Do You Really Want to Do it Yourself?

Even with practice, you will find that manually destroying a hard drive is time consuming. There are companies that specialize in this and can do it efficiently. One such company is Shred-it, which will pick it up and provide a chain-of-custody assurance and a certificate of destruction upon completion. You can find out more about what they offer at the following location:

www.shredit.com/shredding-service/What-to-shred/Hard-drive-destruction.aspx

---

Electromagnet

A large electromagnet can be used to destroy any magnetic media, such as a hard drive or backup tape set. The most common of these is the degaussing tool, discussed next.

Degaussing Tool

Degaussing involves applying a strong magnetic field to initialize the media (this is also referred to as *disk wiping*). This process helps ensure that information doesn't fall into the wrong hands.

Degaussing involves using a specifically designed electromagnet to eliminate all data on the drive, and that destruction also includes the factory prerecorded servo tracks. You can find wand model degaussers priced at just over $500 or desktop units that sell for up to $30,000.

Securing a SOHO Wireless Network

CompTIA wants administrators of small office, home office (SOHO) networks to be able to secure those networks in ways that protect the data stored on them. This objective looks at the security protection that can be added to a wireless SOHO network, while the one that follows examines similar procedures for a wired network.

The wireless network is not and never will be secure. Use wireless only when absolutely necessary. If you must deploy a wireless network, here are some tips to make some improvements to wireless security:

- Change the default SSID.
- Disable SSID broadcasts.
- Disable DHCP or use reservations.
- Use MAC filtering.
- Use IP filtering.
- Use the strongest security available on the wireless access point.
- Change the static security keys every two to four weeks.
- When new wireless protection schemes become available (and reasonably priced), consider migrating to them.
- Limit the user accounts that can use wireless connectivity.
- Use a preauthentication system, such as RADIUS.
- Use remote access filters against client type, protocols used, time, date, user account, content, and so forth.
- Use IPSec tunnels over the wireless links.
- Turn down the signal strength to the minimum needed to support connectivity.
- Seriously consider removing wireless access from your LAN.

Change Default Usernames and Passwords

In addition to those created with the installation of the operating system(s), default accounts are also often associated with hardware. Wireless access points, routers, and similar devices often include accounts for interacting with, and administering, those devices. You should always change the passwords associated with those devices and, where possible, change the usernames.

If there are accounts that are not needed, disable them or delete them. Make certain you use strong password policies and protect the passwords with the same security you use for users or administrators (in other words, don't write the router's password on an address label and stick it to the bottom of the router).

Changing the SSID

All radio frequency signals can be easily intercepted. To intercept 802.11a/b/g/n traffic, all you need is a PC with an appropriate 802.11a/b/g/n card installed. Many networks will regularly broadcast their name (known as an *SSID broadcast*) to announce their presence. Simple software on the PC can capture the link traffic in the wireless AP and then process this data to decrypt account and password information.

You should change the SSID—whether or not you choose to disable its broadcast or not—to keep it from being a value that many outsiders come to know. If you use the same SSID for years, then the number of individuals who will have left the company or otherwise learned of its value will only increase. Changing the variable adds one more level of security.

Setting Encryption

The types of wireless encryption available (WEP, WPA, WPA2, etc.) were discussed in Chapter 6, "Networking Fundamentals." It's important to remember that you should always enable encryption for any SOHO network you may administer, and you should choose the strongest level of encryption you can work with.

Disabling SSID Broadcast

One method of "protecting" the network that is often recommended is to turn off the SSID broadcast. The access point is still there and can still be accessed by those who know of it, but it prevents those who are looking at a list of available networks from finding it. This should be considered a very weak form of security because there are still ways, albeit a bit more complicated, to discover the presence of the access point besides the SSID broadcast.

Enable MAC Filtering

Most APs offer the ability to turn on *MAC filtering*, but it is off by default. In the default stage, any wireless client that knows of the existence of the AP can join the network. When MAC filtering is used, the administrator compiles a list of the MAC addresses associated with the users' computers and enters them. When a client attempts to connect, an additional check of the MAC address is performed. If the address appears in the list, the client is allowed to join, otherwise they are forbidden from so doing. On a number of wireless devices, the term *network lock* is used in place of *MAC filtering*, and the two are synonymous.

Adding port authentication to MAC filtering takes security for the network down to the switch port level and increases your security exponentially.

Antenna and Access Point Placement

Antenna placement can be crucial in allowing clients to reach the access point. For security reasons, you do not want to overextend the reach of the network so that people can get onto the network from other locations (the parking lot, the building next door, etc.). Balancing security and access is a tricky thing to do.

There isn't any one universal solution to this issue, and it depends on the environment in which the access point is placed. As a general rule, the greater the distance the signal must travel, the more it will attenuate, but you can lose a signal quickly in a short space as well if the building materials reflect or absorb it. You should try to avoid placing access points near metal (which includes appliances) or near the ground. They should be placed in the center of the area to be served and high enough to get around most obstacles.

Radio Power Levels

On the chance that the signal is actually traveling too far, some access points include *power level controls* that allow you to reduce the amount of output provided.

Power Value Information

A great source for information on RF power values and antenna can be found on the Cisco site at the following location:

www.cisco.com/en/US/tech/tk722/tk809/
technologies_tech_note09186a00800e90fe.shtml

Assign Static IP Addresses

While DHCP can be a godsend, a SOHO network is small enough that you can get by without it issuing IP addresses to each host. The advantage to statically assigning the IP addresses is that you can make certain which host is associated with which IP address and then utilize filtering to limit network access to only those hosts.

Securing a SOHO Wired Network

While a wired network can be more secure than a wireless one, there are still a number of procedures you should follow to leave as little to chance as possible. Among them, change the default usernames and passwords to different values and secure the physical environment. You should also disable any ports that are not needed, assign static IP addresses, and use MAC filtering to limit access to only those hosts you recognize.

Change Default Usernames and Passwords

Make sure the default password is changed after the installation of any network device. Failure to do so leaves that device open for anyone recognizing the hardware to access it using the known factory password.

In Windows, the Guest account is automatically created with the intent that it is to be used when someone must access a system but lacks a user account on that system. Because it is so widely known to exist, it is recommended that you not use this default account and create another one for the same purpose if you truly need one. The Guest account leaves a security risk at the workstation and should be disabled to deter those attempting to gain unauthorized access.

Change *every* username and password that you can so they vary from their default settings.

Enable MAC Filtering

Limit access to the network to MAC addresses that are known and filter out those that are not. Even in a home network, you can implement MAC filtering with most routers and typically have an option of choosing to allow only computers with MAC addresses that you list or deny only computers with MAC addresses that you list.

If you don't know a workstation's MAC address, use IPCONFIG /ALL to find it in the Windows-based world (it is listed as *physical address*) and ifconfig in UNIX/Linux.

Assign Static IP Addresses

Static IP addresses should be used (avoid having them dynamically issued by DHCP) on small office, home office networks to keep from issuing addresses to hosts other than those you recognize and want on the network.

Disabling Ports

Disable all unneeded protocols/ports. If you don't need them, remove the additional protocols, software, or services or prevent them (disable them) from loading. Ports not in use present an open door for an attacker to enter.

> Many of the newer SOHO router solutions (and some of the personal firewall solutions on end-user workstations) close down the ICMP ports by default. Keep this in mind because it can drive you nuts when you are trying to see if a brand-new station/server/router is up and running.

Physical Security

Just as you would not park your car in a public garage and leave its doors wide open with the key in the ignition, you should educate users to not leave a workstation that they are logged in to when they attend meetings, go to lunch, and so forth. They should log out of the workstation or lock it: "Lock when you leave" should be a mantra they become familiar with. A password (usually the same as their user password) should be required to resume working at the workstation.

You can also lock a workstation by using an operating system that provides file system security. Microsoft's earliest file system was referred to as File Allocation Table (FAT). FAT was designed for relatively small disk drives. It was upgraded first to FAT-16 and finally to FAT-32. FAT-32 (also written as FAT32) allows large disk systems to be used on Windows systems.

FAT allows only two types of protection: share-level and user-level access privileges. If a user has write or change access to a drive or directory, they have access to any file in that directory. This is very unsecure in an Internet environment.

New Technology Filesystem (NTFS) was introduced with Windows NT to address security problems. Before Windows NT was released, it had become apparent to Microsoft that a new file system was needed to handle growing disk sizes, security concerns, and the need for more stability. NTFS was created to address those issues.

With NTFS, files, directories, and volumes can each have their own security. NTFS's security is flexible and built in. Not only does NTFS track security in access control lists (ACLs), which can hold permissions for local users and groups, but each entry in the ACL can also specify what type of access is given—such as Read-Only, Change, or Full Control. This allows a great deal of flexibility in setting up a network. In addition, special file-encryption programs can be used to encrypt data while it is stored on the hard disk.

Microsoft strongly recommends that all network shares be established using NTFS. While NTFS security is important, though, it doesn't matter at all what file system you are using if you log in to your workstation and leave, allowing anyone to sit down at your desk and use your account.

> Because NTFS and share permissions are operating system specific, they were discussed in the chapters on operating systems.

Last, don't overlook the obvious need for physical security. Adding a cable to lock a laptop to a desk prevents someone from picking it up and walking away with a copy of your customer database. Every laptop case we are aware of includes a built-in security slot in which a cable lock can be added to prevent it from being carried off the premises easily, like the one shown in Figure 17.8.

FIGURE 17.8   A cable in the security slot keeps a laptop from being taken easily.

When it comes to desktop models, adding a lock to the back cover can prevent an intruder with physical access from grabbing the hard drive or damaging the internal components. You should also physically secure network devices, such as routers, access points, and the like. Place them in locked cabinets, if possible, for if they are not physically secured, the opportunity exists for them to be absconded with or manipulated in such a way to allow someone unauthorized to connect to the network.

Summary

In this chapter, you learned about the various issues related to security that appear on the A+ 220-802 exam. Security is a popular topic in computing, and the ways in which a miscreant can cause harm increase regularly. Because of this, CompTIA expects everyone who is A+ certified to understand the basic principles of security and be familiar with solutions that exist.

In this chapter, you learned of security problem areas and issues that can be easily identified. Problem areas include viruses, Trojans, worms, and spyware. Security solutions include implementing encryption technology, using authentication, implementing firewalls, and incorporating security at many levels.

Security is a set of processes and products. For a security program to be effective, all of its parts must work and be coordinated by the organization.

Exam Essentials

Be able to describe why antivirus software is needed.   Antivirus software looks at a virus and takes action to neutralize it based on a virus definition database. Virus definition database files are regularly made available on vendor sites.

Understand the need for user education.   Users are the first line of defense against most threats, whether physical or digital. They should be trained on the importance of security and how to help enforce it.

Know the characteristics and types of viruses used to disrupt systems and networks.   Several different types of viruses are floating around today. The most common ones are polymorphic viruses, stealth viruses, retroviruses, multipartite viruses, and macro viruses.

Know the various types of social engineering.   Social engineering variants include shoulder surfing (watching someone work) and phishing (tricking someone into believing they are communicating with a party other than the one they are communicating with). Variations on phishing include vishing and whaling as well as spear phishing.

Understand the need for good passwords.   Passwords are the first line of defense for protecting an account. A password should be required for every account and strong passwords should be enforced. Users need to understand the basics of password security and work to keep their accounts protected by following company policies regarding passwords.

Disable what you don't need.   All accounts that are not in use—especially the guest account—should be disabled. You should also disable the Autorun feature to prevent it from running programs or commands that could inflict harm without your knowledge.

Understand the difference between standard and low-level formatting.   Standard formatting uses operating system tools and marks the drive as available for holding data without truly removing what was on the drive (thus the data can be recovered). A low-level format is operating system independent and destroys any data that was on the drive.

Understand how to physically destroy a drive.   A hard drive can be destroyed by tossing it into a shredder designed for such a purpose, or it can be destroyed with an electromagnet in a process known as degaussing. You can also disassemble the drive and destroy the platters with a drill or other tool that renders the data irretrievable.

Know the names, purpose, and characteristics of wireless security technologies.   Wireless networks can be encrypted through WEP, WPA, and WPA2 technologies. Wireless controllers use Service Set IDentifiers (SSIDs)—32-character case sensitive strings—and must be configured in the network cards to allow communications. However, using ID sring configurations doesn't necessarily prevent wireless networks from being monitored, and there are vulnerabilities specific to wireless devices.

Understand the basics of antenna placement and radio power levels.   Antenna placement can be crucial in allowing clients to reach an access point. Place access points near the center of the area to be served and high enough to get around most obstacles. Know that power level controls allow you to reduce the amount of output provided.

Understand why ports should be disabled.   Disable all unneeded protocols/ports. If you don't need them, remove them or prevent them from loading. Ports not in use present an open door for an attacker to enter.

Understand the purpose of MAC filtering.   MAC filtering allows you to limit access to a network to MAC addresses that are known and filter out (deny access to) those that are not.

Review Questions

The answers to the Chapter Review Questions can be found in Appendix A.

1. Which component of physical security addresses outer-level access control?

    A. Perimeter security

    B. Mantraps

    C. Security zones

    D. Strong passwords

2. Which technology uses a physical characteristic to establish identity?

    A. Biometrics

    B. Surveillance

    C. Smart card

    D. CHAP authenticator

3. As part of your training program, you're trying to educate users on the importance of security. You explain to them that not every attack depends on implementing advanced technological methods. Some attacks, you explain, take advantage of human shortcomings to gain access that should otherwise be denied. What term do you use to describe attacks of this type?

    A. Social engineering

    B. IDS system

    C. Perimeter security

    D. Biometrics

4. You're in the process of securing the IT infrastructure by adding fingerprint scanners to your existing authentication methods. This type of security is an example of which of the following?

    A. Access control

    B. Physical barriers

    C. Biometrics

    D. Softening

5. Which type of attack denies authorized users access to network resources?

    A. DoS

    B. Worm

    C. Logic bomb

    D. Social engineering

6. As the security administrator for your organization, you must be aware of all types of attacks that can occur and plan for them. Which type of attack uses more than one computer to attack the victim?

    A. DoS

    B. DDoS

    C. Worm

    D. UDP attack

7. A server in your network has a program running on it that bypasses authentication. Which type of attack has occurred?

    A. DoS

    B. DDoS

    C. Back door

    D. Social engineering

8. You've discovered that an expired certificate is being used repeatedly to gain logon privileges. Which type of attack is this most likely to be?

    A. Man-in-the-middle attack

    B. Back door attack

    C. Replay attack

    D. TCP/IP hijacking

9. A junior administrator comes to you in a panic. After looking at the log files, he has become convinced that an attacker is attempting to use a duplicate IP address to replace another system in the network to gain access. Which type of attack is this?

    A. Man-in-the-middle attack

    B. Back door attack

    C. Worm

    D. TCP/IP hijacking

10. Which of the following is different from a virus in that it can reproduce itself, it's self-contained, and it doesn't need a host application to be transported?

    A. Worm

    B. Smurf

    C. Phish

    D. Trojan

11. A smurf attack attempts to use a broadcast ping on a network; the return address of the ping may be that of a valid system in your network. Which protocol does a smurf attack use to conduct the attack?

    A. TCP

    B. IP

    C. UDP

    D. ICMP

12. Your system log files report an ongoing attempt to gain access to a single account. This attempt has been unsuccessful to this point. What type of attack are you most likely experiencing?

    A. Password-guessing attack

    B. Back door attack

    C. Worm attack

    D. TCP/IP hijacking

13. One of the vice presidents of the company calls a meeting with the information technology department after a recent trip to competitors' sites. She reports that many of the companies she visited granted access to their buildings only after fingerprint scans, and she wants similar technology employed at this company. Of the following, which technology relies on a physical attribute of the user for authentication?

    A. Smart card

    B. Biometrics

    C. Mutual authentication

    D. Tokens

14. Your company provides medical data to doctors from a worldwide database. Because of the sensitive nature of the data you work with, it's imperative that authentication be established on each session and be valid only for that session. Which of the following authentication methods provides credentials that are valid only during a single session?

    A. Tokens

    B. Certificate

    C. Smart card

    D. Kerberos

15. Your help desk has informed you that they received an urgent call from the vice president last night requesting his logon ID and password. When talking with the VP today, he says he never made that call. What type of attack is this?

    A. Spoofing

    B. Replay attack

    C. Social engineering

    D. Trojan horse

16. Internal users suspect repeated attempts to infect their systems as reported to them by pop-up messages from their virus-scanning software. According to the pop-up messages, the virus seems to be the same in every case. What is the most likely culprit?

    A. A server is acting as a carrier for a virus.

    B. You have a caterpillar virus.

    C. Your antivirus software has malfunctioned.

    D. A DoS attack is under way.

17. You're working late one night, and you notice that the hard disk on your new computer is very active even though you aren't doing anything on the computer and it isn't connected to the Internet. What is the most likely suspect?

    A. A disk failure is imminent.

    B. A virus is spreading in your system.

    C. Your system is under a DoS attack.

    D. TCP/IP hijacking is being attempted.

18. You're the administrator for a large bottling company. At the end of each month, you routinely view all logs and look for discrepancies. This month, your email system error log reports a large number of unsuccessful attempts to log on. It's apparent that the email server is being targeted. Which type of attack is most likely occurring?

    A. Software exploitation attack

    B. Backdoor attack

    C. Worm

    D. TCP/IP hijacking

19. Upper management has decreed that a firewall must be put in place immediately, before your site suffers an attack similar to one that struck a sister company. Responding to this order, your boss instructs you to implement a packet filter by the end of the week. A packet filter performs which function?

    A. Prevents unauthorized packets from entering the network

    B. Allows all packets to leave the network

    C. Allows all packets to enter the network

    D. Eliminates collisions in the network

20. Which media is susceptible to viruses?

    A. Tape

    B. Memory stick

    C. CD-R

    D. All of the above

Performance-Based Question

On the A+ exams, you will encounter performance-based questions. The questions on the exam require you to perform a specific task, and you will be graded on whether you were able to complete the task. The following require you to think creatively to measure how well you understand this chapter's topics. You may or may not see similar questions on the actual A+ exams. To see how your answers compare to the authors', refer to Appendix B.

Pop-ups are proving to be a security concern—as well as an annoyance—throughout the office. Configure your Windows 7/IE 9 machine to block pop-ups but to allow www.sybex.com through so you can access the material you are studying for the A+ exams.

Chapter

18

Mobile Devices

THE FOLLOWING COMPTIA A+ 220-802
OBJECTIVES ARE COVERED IN THIS
CHAPTER:

✓ **3.1 Explain the basic features of mobile operating systems.**

- Android vs. iOS (Open source vs. closed source/vendor specific, App source (app store and market), Screen orientation (accelerometer/gyroscope), Screen calibration, GPS and geotracking

✓ **3.2 Establish basic network connectivity and configure email.**

- Wireless/cellular data network (enable/disable)

- Bluetooth (Enable Bluetooth, Enable pairing, Find device for pairing, Enter appropriate pin code, Test connectivity)

- Email configuration

  - Server address (POP3, IMAP, Port and SSL settings)

  - Exchange

  - Gmail

✓ **3.3 Compare and contrast methods for securing mobile devices.**

- Passcode locks

- Remote wipes

- Locator applications

- Remote backup applications

- Failed login attempts restrictions

- Antivirus

- Patching/OS updates

✓ **3.4 Compare and contrast hardware differences in regards to tablets and laptops.**

- No field serviceable parts

- Typically not upgradeable

- Touch interface (Touch flow, Multitouch)

- Solid state drives

✓ **3.5 Execute and configure mobile device synchronization.**

- Types of data to synchronize (Contacts, Programs, Email, Pictures, Music, Videos)

- Software requirements to install the application on the PC

- Connection types to enable synchronization

There are two primary trends for the advancement of computer technology: Computers become faster with each generation, and computer technology continually allows for smaller components with the same or better performance. Because more components can fit in the same space with each successive generation, these trends can make for state-of-the-art performance with the same footprint. However, the other manifestation over the last decade has been to create smaller computers with comparable performance. Today, powerful devices that fit in your pocket can be purchased from a wide variety of vendors at affordable prices. This chapter focuses on two popular platforms, Apple's iOS and Google's Android operating system.

Comparing Android to iOS

By far the two most prolific mobile operating systems in the world, Google's Android and Apple's iOS are produced by organizations that both approach the market from the viewpoint of being a one-stop shop for almost everything their customers will need for their mobile computing and communications experience.

The two companies go about their quest for market domination in slightly different ways. Although they both provide a site for downloading applications compatible with their respective operating systems, Apple keeps its applications a little closer to the vest and manufactures its own handsets. Google prefers to let the developers dictate what applications are available to consumers and to let a wide variety of handset manufacturers produce the hardware on which its operating system runs.

The following sections discuss these particulars as well as the proprietary nature of the operating systems, how the two platforms determine the orientation of the device, how to calibrate their screens, and how Android and iOS track your position geographically.

Throughout this chapter, unless otherwise stated, it is assumed that no jailbreaking or rooting of your mobile device has been performed. Customizing devices in this way is outside the scope of the A+ exams. These concepts will be introduced shortly, however, for informational purposes.

Source Code Classification

Source code is the programming code used in the creation of software. In the early days of personal computing, software was either free or for sale. Nothing has changed, except the terms we use for describing these two categories. Now, software is either proprietary or *open source*. Proprietary software—also known as *closed-source* and *vendor-specific* software—is licensed to others for use but kept within the control of the original publisher. Open-source software, on the other hand, is licensed to the community to be further developed, shared, and sometimes marketed, depending on the language of the licensing agreement. In any event, no money changes hands during the procurement of open-source software.

Google offers the Android operating system to the mobile community under an open-source license. Apple keeps its iOS closed source and manages all development and marketing of the operating system.

The Android operating system was developed in 2003 by Android, Inc., which was acquired by Google in 2005. Later versions of Android are based on the Linux operating system. Android is currently under the developmental control of the Open Handset Alliance, of which Google is a founding member. Android is protected by the Apache v2 license, which allows developers to alter the original code in any way they see fit, including adding and removing code, requiring only a simple referral to the license instead of spelling out the license in detail. The Apache license allows developers to create proprietary versions of the protected software without the need to contribute back to the original platform. The result is a similar mobile experience with the differential advantage being the applications and functionality of the individual platform.

The Apple iPhone OS was introduced in 2007 and rebranded in 2010 as iOS, after an agreement with Cisco that avoided infringement lawsuits for using a name too similar to the abbreviation for Cisco's Internetwork Operating System (IOS). Apple iOS is based on the same Darwin distribution of UNIX that Mac OS X is based on. Although iOS code originates from open source, the modifications made by Apple are proprietary, making iOS closed source. The open-source roots, however, led to standardized development tools that non-Apple developers might be familiar with.

Source of Applications

Both Apple and Google maintain online sources for downloading applications written for their respective operating systems. Links can be supplied on the web pages of application publishers and marketers to forward customers to these locations where they can begin downloading their application. More commonly, customers use an application on the mobile device—or on the computer used to synchronize software with the mobile device—to search for and download the application they are interested in.

Downloading Apps for iOS

Apple's *App Store* opened for business in 2008 just ahead of the introduction of the iPhone 3G, which was natively capable of accessing the App Store. The App Store was designed to market and serve applications created with the iOS and Mac software development kits (SDKs). The term *app* was coined long ago as shorthand for *application*, but in the period during the naming of Apple's store, the term saw resurgence and is now most associated with mobile applications.

Apple requires annual fees from developers (Android requires only a one-time fee) and each app must be submitted to Apple for approval before being added by Apple to the App Store, which is the only way they can be made available for installation. Note that any iPhone app can be run on Apple's line of iPads, but if an iPad-optimized app is available, iPad users should opt for these instead. If a user has an iPhone/iPod Touch and an iPad on the same Apple account, both classes of device can install the same app after paying only once. The price, by the way, is the same for either platform.

A few months after the Apple App Store opened in 2008, Google's *Android Market* was launched and available to users. In 2012, the Market and the Google Music service were combined to form Google Play, which took the place of both component services. Google does not guard apps for Android as closely as Apple guards its apps. In fact, you can use third-party utilities to find and download Android apps. You can also download them directly from the developer's website or use the Android SDK to create your own and install them yourself. Neither Google nor the Open Handset Alliance needs to approve apps before installation. Enterprises benefit from the resulting quick turnaround from in-house development to deployment for their proprietary apps.

Exercise 18.1 details the steps required to search for and download an app from the Apple App Store. The procedure downloads iHandy's Flashlight app. If you already have this app, you can substitute any search criteria you like and adjust the remaining steps accordingly. The iPhone examples and exercises in this chapter reference procedures required on an iPhone 4S with iOS version 5.1.1.

EXERCISE 18.1

Downloading an App from the App Store

1. Find the App Store icon on the Home screens.

2. Tap the icon to open the app to the last page you visited.

EXERCISE 18.1 *(continued)*

3. Tap the Search icon at the bottom.

4. Type **ihandy flashlight** in the search field and tap the Search button on the keyboard.

5. Select the app with the icon that matches the second one from the top in the following image.

6. Tap the Free button to change it to an Install App button.

7. Tap the Install App button to be asked for your Apple ID password.

8. Enter your password and tap OK. You'll be taken back to a Home screen as the app installs.

9. Tap the app's icon to open it.

If your apps are ever updated in the App Store, the App Store icon will develop a little red badge in the upper-right corner with the number of apps that have updates that are ready for you to download, as shown in Figure 18.1.

FIGURE 18.1   Updates available

Downloading Apps for Android

Exercise 18.2 walks you through the steps required to use Google Play to search for and download an app. The Android examples and exercises in this chapter reference procedures required on a Sprint HTC EVO 4G with Android version 2.3.5.

If at any time you are unable to find an Android icon mentioned in this chapter, you can add it to one of the device's home screens or run it from the All Apps list. To add it to a home screen, find a blank area large enough to accommodate it—sometimes, what you add is larger than an icon and more like a mini app. Then, press and hold that area until you are transferred to the Add To Home list. You'll need to know or investigate whether you are trying to add a widget, an app, a shortcut, or a folder and choose it from that list.

To run an app directly from the All Apps list, press the All Apps button to the left of the Phone button at the bottom of the home screens and then find it alphabetically in the list. Figure 18.2 shows the All Apps button on the left as an up arrow in a circle.

FIGURE 18.2   Placement of the All Apps button

EXERCISE 18.2

Downloading an App from Google Play

1. Find the Play Store icon on the home screens or in the All Apps list.

2. Tap the icon to open Google Play.

3. Tap the Apps area on the left side.

4. Tap the magnifying glass in the upper-left corner to start a search.

5. Type in **instagram** and tap the Search button on the keyboard.

6. Tap the line with the Instagram icon on it, shown here at the top of the list

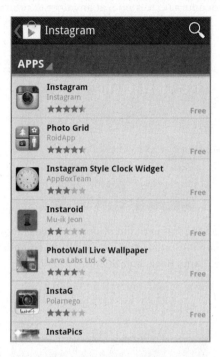

7. Tap the Download button.

8. Tap the Accept & Download button.

After the app downloads and installs, you will see a screen like the following one. You can repeat this procedure up to step 6 at any time to return to this screen to open or uninstall the app.

9.   Tap the Home button on the frame of the phone to leave Google Play. This is not a soft button on the screen but rather a touch-sensitive icon built into the phone. The other hard buttons are Menu, Back, and Search.

10. Find a blank area on a home screen and tap and hold it.

11. Select App from the Add To Home menu.

12. Scroll down until you see Instagram in the list and select it. It then appears on the home screen where you indicated it should.

Screen Orientation

Most mobile devices can automatically detect their position and use the detected information to reorient the screen to match the orientation of the device. Most devices, especially handsets, are built for being used most often in an orientation that corresponds to the display of screen images in portrait mode (higher than wide). For screens of information that are displayed best in portrait mode, no change in orientation is required. Some devices, such as Apple's iPad, can even display images in portrait mode when the device is held upside down. This aids in collaboration with someone positioned across from you, which is more common with pads than with handsets. For images that display best in landscape mode, merely turning most devices sideways reorients the screen image in landscape mode.

The method of detecting device orientation varies somewhat, but the following two popular methods exist and are presented here with their characteristic detection capabilities:

- Accelerometer—forward/backward, left/right, up/down
- Gyroscope—roll, pitch, yaw

Use of multiple or all methods by the same device increases the accuracy of orientation and positioning. The simple combination of an accelerometer and gyroscope, for example, makes for optimal orientation detection. The following sections detail the strengths previously listed beside the two methods.

Accelerometer

An *accelerometer* measures the acceleration—change in velocity, which is a function of speed and direction—of an object. The original iPhone used only an accelerometer. In fact, only an accelerometer was used until the iPhone 4 introduced the addition of a gyroscope, discussed next, in 2011.

Picture an iPhone lying flat on a desk. If you push the device in any of the four square directions—up, down, left, right—or diagonally without also rotating the phone on any of its various axes, the accelerometer will detect the precise movement. If you lift the phone up and then place it back down on the desk, the accelerometer can track this motion as well. These three axes (x, y, and z) of movement make up the totality of an accelerometer's capabilities.

Gyroscope

The accelerometer cannot detect if you lift any edge of the iPhone or give it a good spin as it lies flat on the desk. For these motions, a gyroscope is called for. A *gyroscope* is a sensor that detects rotation around any of three axes, known as roll, pitch, and yaw.

For example, pick up the iPhone from the desk and hold it in your hand. Now, without changing the position of the absolute center of the phone, lift the left side upward, as if to flip the phone over toward the right, until the phone is facedown and right side up in your hand. Then, flip it back in the reverse direction until it is faceup again. A gyroscope would detect both of these motions as *roll*.

From the starting position, a gyroscope would sense a change in *pitch* if you lifted the top or bottom edge of the phone and flipped it toward the opposite end until the phone is once again facedown, except now also upside-down, in your hand.

If you place the phone back on the desk and give it a clockwise or counterclockwise spin, the gyroscope would detect such a rotation as *yaw*. These three new axes of movement complement those detected by the accelerometer, producing a high level of accuracy when detecting the device's orientation.

Positioning and Geolocation

Screen orientation is only part of the story. *Geolocation*, the relative and absolute positioning of your device from the viewpoint of the planet and space, is an important capability that allows effective navigation and access to personalized services and security features. Two technologies are used by most modern smartphones to accomplish positioning and geolocation:

- Magnetometer—compass heading
- Global positioning system—absolute position on the earth

Magnetometer

To detect the position of a device relative to a landmark on the planet, we use a compass. A *magnetometer* allows a device to sense magnetic fields, such as the one our planet exhibits at the magnetic north pole. Using a magnetometer, iPhones and Android devices allow for apps that act as compasses, giving you instantaneous access to the direction in which the top of your phone is pointing with respect to magnetic north. Orient the back (or the front, if you're lying down looking up) of your device as flat to the ground as possible to get the most accurate reading. All iPads and all iPhones beginning with the 3GS have included a magnetometer for relative positioning.

Global Positioning System

To detect the absolute position of a device with respect to the manmade latitude and longitude markings on the surface of the earth, triangulation is required. Using three satellites at a fixed distance above the earth's surface, devices with global positioning system (*GPS*) capability can determine their own absolute position. Add a magnetometer or use the change in GPS information over time, and the compass heading of the device can also be determined. The magnetometer can detect the compass heading at all times when sources of magnetic interference are not present, and the GPS sensor can detect the heading in magnetic noise but only while in motion.

Apple iPhones and cellular-equipped iPads have used assisted GPS, which uses information from the cellular network to help with geolocation, in all versions except the first iPhone. Assisted GPS is helpful when the satellite signals are being interfered with or partially blocked. When satellites are completely unavailable, cellular or WiFi alone can be used to give slightly less accurate positioning. All Apple iOS products over all versions have supported geolocation over WiFi. The Android operating system supports these forms of geolocation as well.

The Russian form of GPS, known as the Global Navigation Satellite System (GLONASS), is also supported by the Apple iPhone 4S. Sony Ericsson was one of the first providers to bring GLONASS support to Android phones and tablets. Theoretically, GLONASS and GPS can be used in tandem to provide better positioning. In practice, however, access to three satellites in each system simultaneously is an issue. The upside is that satellite-based global positioning will be available in more parts of the world with newer devices.

Geotracking and Geotagging

Geolocation information collected by your mobile device can be used in various ways, some welcome and some less so. For example, you might perceive as a blessing being able to locate your child using real-time geolocation information from a phone they are carrying. However, you might consider it a curse when someone else can locate your child in the same way.

In mid 2010, Apple added a controversial feature to iOS, starting with version 4, that collects your position and stores it locally on the phone in a file that is never harvested but also reports it twice a day back to Apple. This *geotracking* feature has understandably come under scrutiny by privacy advocates.

You must jailbreak your iOS device—or in other words, gain full root access to its UNIX file system—to be able to find the file that holds the geolocation information, which can be used by forensic investigators and privacy invaders alike. Utilities exist, however, that can use the file to overlay the raw data on a world map, showing a visual record of the device's positioning over time, even months earlier.

Since the inception of its geotracking, Apple has progressively dialed down the amount of data that is collected by the iOS. Apple has also stopped allowing this information to be backed up and has begun encrypting the related file, as of iOS version 5, making casual access to the file and its contents impossible.

Geotagging uses similar information to add location information to various forms of media, such as photographs taken with the device and messages sent with the device. Geotagging information is also sent by many mobile devices to social networking sites when updates are posted by default. Although often welcomed as a convenience by users with a pronounced Internet presence that would invariably identify their location anyway, geotagging is generally quite easy to disable on any given device for those who would rather not have their location automatically identified. Many parents, for example, would not want their children's current location advertised to the Internet.

Screen Calibration

Any device that, for input, relies on the user pressing against and flexing the outermost layer of material covering the screen occasionally requires the recalibration of the user's interface with the device's touch sensors. If the user places their finger squarely in the middle of an icon from the perspective of their visible interface but selects a different icon from the perspective of the sensors, the touch interface might require calibration. The need for recalibration varies between the two primary technologies used, resistive and capacitive. The following sections elaborate on this fact.

Resistive Touchscreens

The need for recalibration is expected in devices that use a resistive technology to detect touch. This is because they have an almost unperceivably flexible outer surface that eventually wears and changes over time due to repeated flexion. As a result, pressing the location where the image displays from the perspective of the user eventually generates an incorrect resistance based on the original calibration of the screen. Recalibration of resistive displays entails displaying an image with known touch points and asking the user to touch them all in succession. In this manner, the resistance across the entire screen is adjusted to compensate for the physical change in the outer surface.

Such devices are built using two layers of sturdy panels separated by an air pocket. One panel is flexible, usually made of plastic, and the other panel is often rigid, usually made of glass. Both panels are coated with indium tin oxide (ITO), which is conductive, and separated by an air pocket. When the user presses against the flexible outer surface, the two layers of ITO make contact and change the resistance detected by electrode strips along the edges of the panels. The computer is able to take the resistance reading from the electrodes and calculate two-dimensional coordinates.

Either a firm, often pointed, stylus or your fingernail is highly effective on resistive touchscreens. The optimal effect is achieved by applying pinpoint pressure to the outer surface without causing damage to the surface. Of course, damage is being caused, but on a minor level. Nevertheless, the cumulative damage caused by the required pressure is what leads to the need for calibration and eventual replacement of the screen or device.

Capacitive Touchscreens

With capacitive touchscreens, the same two layers of ITO as used with resistive screens are placed between two pieces of glass, resulting in a very smooth, silky surface to the touch. The same electrode placement is also used. The difference is in what electrical property the electrodes are monitoring. A uniform capacitive field can be projected through the top layer of glass. The faint electromagnetic charge of a human fingertip can change the capacitance to a measurable level at the point of contact. The two-dimensional coordinates of the point touched can be calculated by the device in the same manner that they are calculated from the changes in resistance for the resistive display.

The padded tip of the finger is the preferred method of touch for such displays. A stylus that emulates the fingertip and its electromagnetic charge can be used in place of the fingertip. Because of the physics involved, with capacitive interfaces, such as that used by all of Apple's mobile devices and many non-Apple devices, dry environments and other conditions favorable to the buildup of excess static electricity can lead to the touch sensors responding before the user's finger touches the surface. This phenomenon can be confused with poor calibration.

However, because capacitive touchscreens do not wear as quickly as do resistive screens, due to the fact that the user does not apply pressure to complete a circuit, capacitive screens do not tend to require recalibration. In fact, if you feel that you need to recalibrate an Apple display, there are more serious issues afoot. If neither restarting the device or performing a reset by holding the sleep and home buttons simultaneously solves the problem, it is likely that a certified Apple repair is in order because it is more probable that you have a hardware issue than a calibration issue.

Regardless of whether you have a resistive or capacitive display, or both, some devices give you the option to improve the ability of the computer to recognize how you personally actuate the sensors. Exercise 18.3 walks you through the procedure of recalibrating (actually retraining) the onscreen touch keyboard of the HTC EVO 4G running the Android operating system. Other Android devices may vary in their ability to be recalibrated or in the method of doing so.

EXERCISE 18.3

Recalibrating an Onscreen Android Keyboard

1. Tap the Menu button on the frame of the phone (not a soft button in this Android version).

2. Tap the Settings button in the menu.

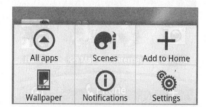

3. Scroll down to and tap the Language & Keyboard selection in the menu.

4. Tap the Touch Input selection in the menu.

5. Tap the Text Input selection in the menu.

6. Tap the Calibration Tool selection near the bottom of the menu.

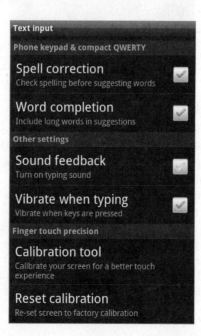

EXERCISE 18.3 *(continued)*

7. Type the phrase shown as naturally as you can without thinking too much about the typing itself until you see the Calibration Is Complete message, as seen in the next image. Although typing with both thumbs is often the most effective method on such keyboards, just ensure that you are typing naturally.

8. Tap the Home button to leave the calibration tool.

Combination Touchscreens

Early resistive touchscreens were obvious to the touch. They had a matte finish that you could feel by running your fingertip across it. This finish made them more durable and allowed the use of a pointed stylus without the likelihood of the stylus sliding across the screen's surface, which would have resulted in less accuracy.

Many manufacturers migrated to a smoother surface and a stylus with a softer tip. With such a surface, some manufacturers created touchscreens that were both resistive *and* capacitive. If you used the stylus or your fingernail to press down on the screen, the resistive nature reacted. If you instead glided your fingertip or special capacitive stylus across the surface, the capacitive features of the display took over. Because the outer panel on the screen is flexible, frequent use of pressure to actuate the sensors will result in the need to recalibrate the screen.

Network Connectivity and Email

Mobile devices like the iPhone and Android phones are well known for their cellular connectivity and ability to access data networking services over the cellular network. However, many subscribers still pay a premium for such access. To assuage the expense involved in data-network access, nearly all manufacturers provide alternate access methods in their devices. No additional expense is levied by the service provider for WiFi or Bluetooth data access, for example.

Bluetooth access to other devices is designed mainly for short-range applications, such as between the mobile device and a nearby computer with which it can exchange or synchronize data. Other applications of Bluetooth generally do not involve the exchange of data but rather the use of a nearby resource, such as a stereo system for the playback of the mobile device's audio media. WiFi, on the other hand, is capable of offering full Internet access to the mobile device and at speeds in excess of the average cellular rates.

It's not as common to access noncellular voice or instant messaging services, but many phones have the option to do so. For example, Internet calls over WiFi can be configured on many Android phones using the Session Initiation Protocol (SIP) and a simple Internet calling utility. Apple's iMessage allows instant messaging over WiFi between capable devices running iOS version 5 and higher or Mac OS X Mountain Lion (10.8) and higher. The iMessage service allows larger single messages than Short Message Service (SMS), the mechanism used for standard cellular instant messaging, and does not count against your monthly messaging limits.

As you can see, there is a distinct advantage to being able to connect your mobile device to a noncellular network. Mobile devices will use WiFi when connected instead of cellular for data operations. Android devices will ask you during an important update if you would like to use WiFi only or if cellular is okay to use. Figure 18.3, for example, shows the Google Play Settings screen on an Android device that clearly offers the option to prohibit updates over anything other than WiFi.

The following sections detail the concepts of attaching to noncellular networks on iPhones and Android devices. Additionally, you will be introduced to the tasks required to establish email connectivity over these mobile units.

Establishing WiFi Connectivity

Before you can transfer data over a WiFi network, you have to attach to the network in the same manner as you would attach a laptop, for instance, to the same wireless network. You have to find the network by its service-set identifier (SSID) or you have to enter the SSID if it is not being broadcast. You must then satisfy any security requirements that might be in place, such as 802.1x authentication or security keys. Exercise 18.4 steps you through the procedure on an iPhone.

FIGURE 18.3   Google Play Settings

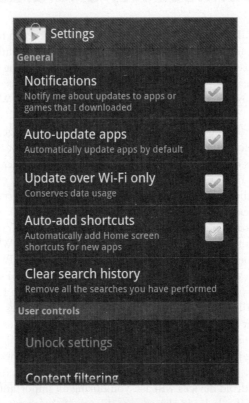

EXERCISE 18.4

Connecting an iPhone to a WiFi Network

1.   Tap the Settings app on the Home screens.

EXERCISE 18.4 *(continued)*

2. Select Wi-Fi from the Settings menu.

3. Swipe the Wi-Fi switch to the right to turn it on if it is off. Tapping switches also works to toggle them to the opposite state.

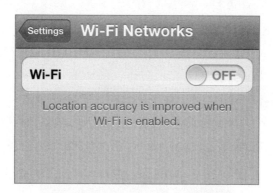

EXERCISE 18.4 *(continued)*

4. Tap the name of the wireless network that you want to join.

5. Enter the password or key for the wireless network, if you are asked for one, and then tap the Join button.

EXERCISE 18.4 *(continued)*

6. Tap the Settings back button at the top left to return to the previous screen.

Notice on this screen that the network you selected has a check mark beside it. If not, something went wrong. Also take note of the Ask To Join Networks switch at the bottom. Turning this off means you will never be interrupted with offers to join new wireless networks that are in range of the device. Regardless of the setting of this switch, the device will still automatically reconnect to remembered WiFi networks as they come into range.

7. Click the Home hard button at the bottom in the frame of the phone to return to the Home screens after noting that the network you joined is now listed next to Wi-Fi on the menu.

 You can use the Home button to return to the Home screens at any time, but the app you leave will continue to open in the same screen as when you left it until you restart the iOS device or manually force the app to end.

 Throughout this chapter, the practice of tapping successive back buttons in the upper-left corner of the screen, instead of clicking the Home button prematurely, will be referred to as *backing out of the app*.

A similar series of tasks is required when attaching an Android phone to the same type of network. Exercise 18.5 details that procedure.

Connecting an Android Phone to a WiFi Network

1. Tap the Menu button on the frame of the phone.

2. Tap the Settings button in the menu.

3. Select Wireless & Networks from the Settings menu.

4. Place a check in the box beside Wi-Fi in the Wireless & Networks menu, if it is unchecked.

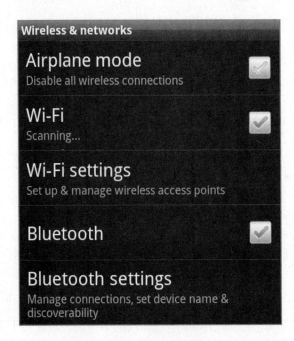

5. Select Wi-Fi Settings from the Wireless & Networks menu to be taken to a screen with a list of wireless networks that are in range.

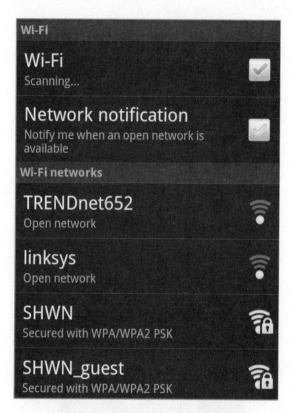

6. Tap the name of the wireless network that you want to join.

7. Enter the password or key for the wireless network, if you are asked for one, and then tap the Connect button.

8. Confirm that the network you selected connects successfully.

9. Tap the Home hard button to return to the home screens.

Now that the phones are connected to a WiFi network, let's see how to disable use of the cellular network at all times on the iPhone. Exercise 18.6 walks you through the steps. When the device is connected to a WiFi network or when paired with a Bluetooth peer, data access will be possible. Otherwise, no data-network access will occur.

In case you wish to disable cellular use just for specific functions, look at the settings for the app performing that function under Settings. It might so happen that there is a way to turn off the use of cellular data for that function alone. For example, Figure 18.4 shows the Use Cellular Data switch found in the settings for the App Store, known only as Store in the Settings app.

EXERCISE 18.6

Disabling Cellular Use for Data Networking on an iPhone

1. Tap the Settings app on the Home screens.

2. Scroll down, if necessary, and select General from the Settings menu.

3. Select Network from the General Settings menu.

4. Turn off the switch labeled Cellular Data, shown next.

If you would like to keep cellular data usage enabled but not allow roaming into other pro-viders' data networks, you can tap the Roaming button, shown in the preceding graphic with a Voice & Data tag. The following Roaming screen is produced, allowing you to turn off the Data Roaming switch.

Note that if you have already turned cellular data off, as shown in the next screen capture, the tag on the Roaming button reads Voice Only, and if you tap the button to enter the Roaming screen, the Data Roaming switch is not visible.

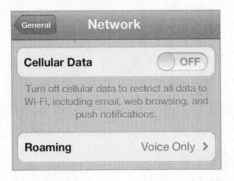

5.   Back out of the Settings app and then press the Home button.

Establishing Bluetooth Connectivity

Wireless personal area networks (WPANs) that use Bluetooth for data-link transport are specified by IEEE 802.15. The concept is that certain paired devices will be capable of exchanging or synchronizing data over the Bluetooth connection, such as between a mobile device and a desktop or laptop computer.

In other cases, the Bluetooth pairing can be used to simply control one device with another, allowing information to flow bidirectionally, even if that transfer does not result in its permanent storage on the destination. Examples of this latter functionality include a Bluetooth headset for a cell phone, a Bluetooth-attached keyboard and mouse, and pairing a smartphone or MP3 player with a vehicle's sound system.

In general, connecting a mobile device to another device requires that both devices have Bluetooth enabled. Pairing subsequently requires that at least one of the devices be discoverable and the other perform a search for Bluetooth devices. Once the device performing the search finds the other device, a sometime-configurable pairing code must often be entered on the device that performed the search. The code must match the one configured on the device that was found in order for pairing to occur. In some cases, this pairing will work in only one direction. Usually, it is the mobile device that should search for the other device. If both devices have the same basic capability and will be able to readily exchange data, then it's not as important which device performs the search. Regardless, the pairing code must be known for entry into the device that requests it.

FIGURE 18.4   App Store settings

The truth about pairing mobile devices with conventional computers is that the results are hit or miss. There's never any guarantee that a given pairing will be successful to the point of data transfer capability. Both devices must agree on the same Bluetooth specification. This turns out to be the easy part because devices negotiate during the connection. The part that is out of our control is what software services the manufacturer decided to include in the devices. If one device is not capable of file transfers over Bluetooth, then the pairing may go off without a hitch, but the communication process will stop there.

For example, in our exercises, we use a MacBook Pro and an Android-based HTC EVO 4G. Given the MacBook, the Android, an iPhone, and an iPad to choose from, no other pairing among the four devices will result in a file-transfer capability. Most users would assume the Apple products would communicate with one another at a very high level, but alas, Bluetooth is not a technology that has received as much attention from Apple as, say, WiFi. Third-party solutions that involve jailbreaking the iPhone do exist, however.

In Exercise 18.7, the steps are shown for how to connect an Android device to a MacBook Pro over Bluetooth and then to transfer a file back and forth between the two. This exercise is split into four sections so that you can concentrate on individual stages of the pairing and file sharing processes. Exercise 18.8 steps you through the process of pairing an iPhone with a vehicle to stream music to the vehicle's sound system. Note that the procedures shown here are based on the specific non-mobile devices used—a MacBook Pro and a 2010 Lexus. The procedure is roughly the same with other remote devices, but will likely vary in the fine details.

EXERCISE 18.7

Pairing an Android Device with a MacBook Pro

Enabling Bluetooth and Pairing

1. On the Android, tap the Menu button.

2. Tap the Settings button.

3. Select Wireless & Networks from the Settings menu.

4. Select Bluetooth Settings in the Wireless & Networks menu.

5. Check the box next to Bluetooth in the Bluetooth Settings menu, if it is not already checked.

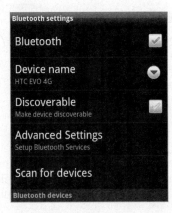

Note that you could have checked the Bluetooth box in the previous screen, but you would have needed to complete step 4 anyway to make the device discoverable or to scan for other devices. If this device does not scan for other devices or enable itself to be scanned by other devices, pairing cannot occur.

6. Select Advanced Settings from the Bluetooth Settings menu.

7. Check the box labeled FTP Server, if it is not already checked. If the FTP server on the Android is not enabled, file transfers can still occur, such as pushing files back and forth between the devices, but you will not be able to browse the Android file system from the MacBook, which will also prevent your using the MacBook to pull files from the Android.

8. Tap the Back hard button to return to the Bluetooth Settings screen.

9. On the MacBook, click System Preferences in the Dock.

10. Click Bluetooth in the Internet & Wireless section of System Preferences.

11. Check the box labeled On in the Bluetooth dialog, if it is not already checked.

12. Click the Sharing Setup button at the bottom of the Bluetooth dialog.

13. Check the File Sharing and Bluetooth Sharing boxes in the Sharing dialog, if not already checked, and click the onscreen back button (left arrow) to return to the Bluetooth dialog (or click the Bluetooth Preferences button at the bottom).

Note the folders listed on the right side. The DOWNLOADS folder is set as the folder accessed by actions along the lines of "send via Bluetooth." The remote device cannot see the contents of this folder; it can only add to it. Any transfer to the folder set here must be approved on a file-by-file basis, or a box can be checked during the transfer to allow all. The PUBLIC folder is set as the one accessed by actions that mention "uploading" and "downloading." The remote device can actually see the contents of this folder.

14. On the Android, check the box next to Discoverable. Note that scanning for devices to find the MacBook Pro is not helpful in this case. That would be useful for finding the car stereo system, for example.

15. On the MacBook, click the Set Up New Device button in the Bluetooth dialog.

16. Select the device you want to pair from the list in the Bluetooth Setup Assistant and click the Continue button.

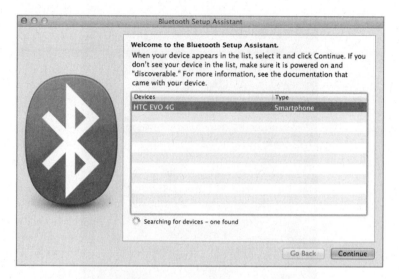

17. On the MacBook, make note of the code that is generated in the Bluetooth Setup Assistant dialog shown here.

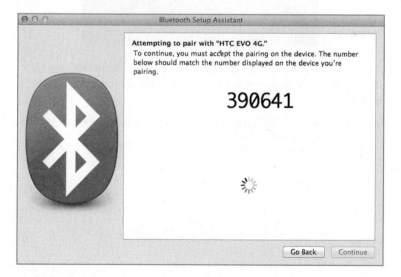

When the approval to pair is granted on the Android, the Bluetooth Setup Assistant will automatically advance to the Conclusion dialog.

EXERCISE 18.7 *(continued)*

18. On the Android, compare the code in the pop-up generated when the MacBook Pro requests the pairing. If there is a match, tap the Pair button.

Notice that the MacBook's name has populated the Bluetooth Devices section behind the pop-up. This happens automatically when a remote device requests a pairing session.

19. On the MacBook, click the Quit button in the Bluetooth Setup Assistant to close that dialog and return your attention to the Bluetooth dialog.

EXERCISE 18.7 *(continued)*

20. Select the Android device—doing so is only necessary if there are multiple devices found—and then click the gear icon, revealing that there are options. We will refer to this menu as the Bluetooth task list.

In case you noticed that the Android device is not connected, this is the default behavior because FTP is used for the file transfers. FTP works in bursts over multiple successive connections. There is currently no need for a connection because data is not flowing.

MacBook: Transferring Files—Pulling from Android

1. Click Browse Device on the MacBook Bluetooth task list to produce a listing of the root file structure of the Android's SD card. This is the step that requires completion of step 7 of the section in this exercise titled "Enabling Bluetooth and Pairing."

2. Navigate to a file to download to the MacBook.

EXERCISE 18.7 *(continued)*

3. Drag and drop the file to the location of your choice. The following screen shot shows a file dropped onto the Desktop.

Notice the Android is shown as Connected now. This will remain as long as you are browsing and turn off in a matter of seconds after the browsing window is closed. The Connected state will also occur briefly when you push a file to the Android using Send File on the Bluetooth task list, discussed next.

Transferring Files—Pushing to Android

1. On the MacBook, click Send File on the Bluetooth task list to open the Finder.

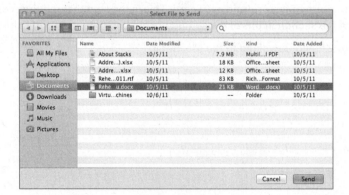

2. Navigate to a file to upload to the Android.

3. Select the file and then click the Send button. The result indicates something must be done on the Android.

4. On the Android, check the box labeled Always in the pop-up and tap Accept to start the transfer.

If you do not check the box labeled Always, you will see this pop-up each time a file is pushed to the Android. That might be desirable, but you will have to confirm each transfer anyway, so checking the box makes each transfer a bit easier.

EXERCISE 18.7 *(continued)*

5. Use your finger to pull down—like a window shade—the status bar with the time on it above the home screens on the Android.

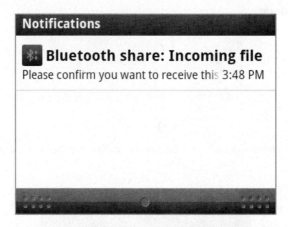

6. Tap the Bluetooth Share notification to begin the confirmation process.

7. Tap the Accept button in the resulting pop-up.

The file pushed to the Android is stored in a folder named BLUETOOTH, which is created, if it doesn't already exist, under the top-level folder named DOWNLOADS. You might have to install an app to be able to view the local file structure of the Android. The following screen shot is from an app called ES File Explorer and shows the transferred file on the SD memory card at /SDCARD/DOWNLOADS/BLUETOOTH.

EXERCISE 18.7 *(continued)*

Transferring Files—Pushing to and Pulling from MacBook

This procedure might require installing a third-party Android app, such as Bluetooth File Transfer. The Android operating system includes the functionality to put—or upload—files to the remote device but not to get—or download—them. It also does not have a remote file browser built in.

Most apps have a remote or Bluetooth tab that acts as your browser tab to the remote device. With this tab, you can upload and download with MacBook approval required only during each new connection establishment phase, not for each file transferred. This is in contrast to transferring using the "send via Bluetooth" mechanism, in which case approval is required for each individual object transferred in addition to the initial approval. The following dialog box is an example of the approval you have to give for "send via Bluetooth" transfers.

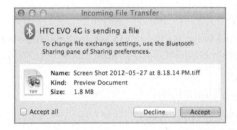

Because "send via Bluetooth" transfers are placed in the "Accepted Items" folder from the Bluetooth Sharing dialog, you will find the transferred file in the DOWNLOADS folder, not the PUBLIC folder.

If you attempt to browse the MacBook's file system from the Android, you will have to click the Allow button in the following pop-up on the MacBook to allow browsing. Notice the folder name is the name that was chosen earlier for the Browse field in the MacBook's Bluetooth Sharing dialog.

In true FTP form, the Android will display the MacBook's PUBLIC folder for the currently logged-in user as the root of a directory tree. If you upload from the Android while browsing, it is this folder on the MacBook that will contain the transferred files.

To reiterate, the procedure in Exercise 18.8 is from the perspective of an iPhone pairing with a 2010 Lexus vehicle. Actual steps to pair an iPhone with a vehicle's sound system are likely to vary somewhat on the vehicle side of the process, but the iPhone procedure should be fairly close to the steps described in Exercise 18.8.

EXERCISE 18.8

Pairing an iPhone with a Vehicle's Sound System

1. Enter the vehicle's Bluetooth setup.

2. Confirm that the vehicle's hands-free power is enabled. Hands-free power might be referred to in other ways, including simply as Bluetooth. Alternatively, the Bluetooth module in certain vehicles might be "always on" and not configurable. The key is to make sure the vehicle is ready to accept incoming Bluetooth requests.

3. Note the vehicle's Bluetooth passcode. It might be required that you enter this passcode on the iPhone to complete the pairing.

4. Confirm that the vehicle has vacant pairing positions for Bluetooth devices.

5. Select the control in the vehicle's Bluetooth setup that adds a new device. This places the vehicle's Bluetooth module in discoverable mode. The iPhone should now be able to locate the vehicle.

6. Run the Settings app on the iPhone.

7. Select General from the Settings menu.

8. Select Bluetooth from the General menu and confirm that Bluetooth is on. The vehicle should be visible in this screen.

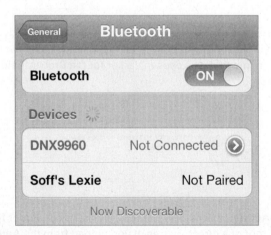

Bluetooth pairings in this list can be Connected, Not Connected (pairing was, however, successful), or Not Paired. The vehicle should be in a Not Paired state, meaning it has been discovered but there are additional steps, such as entering the passcode, required for pairing.

9. Tap the vehicle's entry in the Devices list.

10. Enter the vehicle's passcode that you noted in step 3 and tap the Pair button.

11. Confirm the iPhone's connection from the vehicle's perspective. If the vehicle has the ability to use the iPhone for voice calls, this feature might be presented to you automatically after pairing is complete. If so, this is a perfect way to confirm connectivity, as shown in the following photo.

You will also be able to see a change in the vehicle's Bluetooth status on the iPhone. It should now be Connected.

12. Switch to the vehicle's Bluetooth audio mode. The iPhone might still need to be "connected" for this use. The pairing allows you to select the connection feature in the vehicle and see the iPhone as a connection option. Depending on the vehicle, selecting the iPhone should cause music to begin playing either from its default playlist or the last position where playback was stopped over another output source, including the iPhone's internal speaker or headset jack. Future connection to the iPhone from this vehicle should be automatic when the vehicle's Bluetooth mode is selected, and the iPhone should begin playing from the point where it last stopped playing over any output source. The specific initial and subsequent interactions between the vehicle and iPhone may vary from this description.

Configuring Email Accounts

Because the vast majority of the world's email traffic flows over TCP/IP internetworks, which includes the Internet, it is exceedingly simple to set up mobile devices to access email accounts. Sometime the most difficult part is finding the server settings that are used only during establishment of the connection, which tends to occur only once for each device. Users that hang on to devices and accounts for many years can be challenged to come up with the correct accounts when the situation presents itself. The following sections detail the automatic and manual establishment of a connection to various types of email services.

Automatic Internet Email Configuration

It never hurts to attempt automatic configuration of your email account. If it's on a common web-based service, such as Gmail or Hotmail, for example, your email address and password are often all that are required. If, however, you have a custom domain, even if it's hosted and accessible through Gmail, Live, or the other popular services, it may not be possible to achieve an automatic connection. For the purposes of trying out a common service, you can always make a dummy account on their website and play around with that, as was done here in Gmail for the purpose of the exercises. Exercise 18.9 and Exercise 18.10 detail the steps required for automatic configuration of a Gmail account on the iPhone and on an Android standard email client, respectively.

EXERCISE 18.9

Automatic Internet Email Configuration on an iPhone

1. Run the Settings app on the iPhone.

2. Select Mail, Contacts, Calendars from the Settings menu.

3. Select Add Account from the Mail, Contacts, Calendar menu.

EXERCISE 18.9 *(continued)*

4. Select the account's service provider. A Gmail account is used in this exercise.

5. Enter a name recipients will see only when you send them email from this device, the email address you created on the provider's website, the password you used when you created the account, and a description that will be used on the iPhone to differentiate this account from any others you configure the iPhone to connect to.

6. Tap the Next button and look for check marks beside each item you entered indicating there were no issues with any of your entries. Only the address and password are authenticated against the provider's server. The others are checked only for formatting.

7. Enable only the features that you want to synchronize between your iPhone and the server and then tap the Save button.

8. Click the Home hard button on the iPhone to return to the Home screens, leaving the Settings app in its current state.

9. Tap the Mail app to open it.

10. Select the inbox for the account you just created.

You should already see messages in the inbox, if any exist. Complete the remaining steps only if you want to delete the account you just configured from the iPhone.

11. Press the Home hard button on the iPhone to return to the Home screens.

12. Tap the icon to run the Settings app, returning to where you left it in Mail, Contacts, Calendars.

13. Select the account you want to delete.

14. Tap the Delete Account button at the bottom of the screen.

15. Confirm your choice in the pop-up.

16. Back out to Settings and then click the Home hard button.

Exercise 18.10, as stated earlier, details the steps required for automatic configuration of a Gmail account on an Android standard email client. If the Android device does not have the Mail app on the home screens, you can add it or run it directly from the All Apps list. The procedure for doing so was discussed earlier in this chapter.

This exercise is written for an Android Mail app that is not configured for any accounts. If accounts are already configured, from within the Mail app, tap the down arrow in the circle at the upper-left corner and then select New Account from the resulting pop-up.

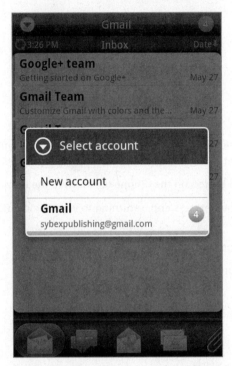

EXERCISE 18.10

Automatic Internet Email Configuration on an Android Phone

1. Run the Mail app.

2. Select Other (POP3/IMAP) from the Choose A Mail Provider menu.

3. Enter the email address and password for the account you want to configure and then tap the Next button.

4. Enter the name you want this account known by on this device and the name you would like to appear to recipients as the sender.

Immediately after authorizing your account, the Mail app takes you into your inbox.

This is the screen from which you delete accounts from the device. If you configured an account that you want to keep, the exercise is complete. The following steps continue from the current screen to delete the account.

5. Tap the Menu button and then tap the More soft button.

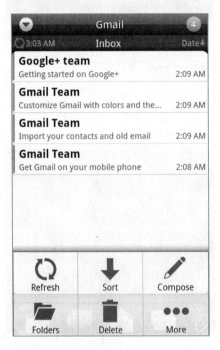

6. Select Settings from the resulting menu.

7. Select Delete Account from the Settings menu.

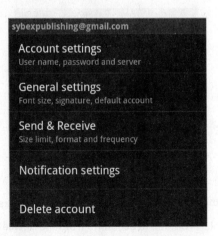

8. Tap the OK button in the pop-up to confirm the deletion.

Manual Internet Email Configuration

In those situations when you find your email account cannot be automatically configured for you by your email client, there are very often manual settings for the protocols required for sending and receiving emails. Table 18.1 might remind you of these protocols and their uses.

TABLE 18.1   TCP/IP mail protocols

Mail Protocol	Description	Default Port Number
Simple Mail Transfer Protocol (SMTP)	Used to communicate between client and server and between servers to send mail to a recipient's account	TCP 25
Post Office Protocol (POP)	Used to communicate between a client and the client's mail server to retrieve mail with little interaction	TCP 110
Internet Message Access Protocol (IMAP)	Used to communicate between a client and the client's mail server to retrieve mail with extensive interaction	TCP 143

In a TCP/IP network using only the protocols in Table 18.1 (there are other less common options), you must always use SMTP for sending mail. You must decide between the use of POP and IMAP for interacting with the mail server to retrieve your mail with the client. IMAP is a clear choice when it is supported because of its extensive interaction with the server, allowing the client to change the state or location of a mail item on the server without the need to download and delete it from the server. Many users who are familiar with Exchange might get the impression that Exchange is at work behind the scenes because of the ability to control items on the server from one client and then go to another local or web-based client and see the items in the exact same state as they left them in the previous client.

Conversely, POP limits client interaction with the server to downloading and deleting items from the server, not allowing their state to be changed by the client. In fact, the use of POP as your receive-mail protocol can lead to confusion because copies of the same items appear in multiple client locations, some marked as read and others unread. Additionally, where IMAP changes the state of a mail item on the server and leaves the item on the server for later access by the same or different client, POP settings must be configured to *not* delete the item from the server on download to each client. This, however, is what leads to the choice of multiple copies among the clients or only one client being able to download the item.

Most, if not all, Internet mail services require secure connections using Secure Sockets Layer (SSL) or Transport Layer Security (TLS). You might recognize these protocols from their use on TCP port 443 for the HTTPS protocol. The common port numbers listed in Table 18.1 are not secure and are rarely used. Instead, the TCP port numbers in Table 18.2

are more commonly used by most webmail services for securing the protocols in Table 18.1. When you're establishing a manual email client connection, these are the ones you are most likely to require.

TABLE 18.2 Secure mail ports

Mail Protocol	TCP Port Number
SMTP with SSL	465
SMTP with TLS	587
IMAP with SSL/TLS	993
POP with SSL/TLS	995

Additionally, you will need to know the server names for your service. Sometimes they are the same for inbound and outbound mail handling, but usually they are different. Table 18.3 lists the servers in the United States for Gmail, Live (Hotmail), and Yahoo Mail. Unless otherwise specified, the ports in Table 18.2 should be used throughout Table 18.3 for the protocols listed.

TABLE 18.3 Secure mail servers for common webmail services

Service	Direction and Protocol	Server Name
Gmail	Outbound on SMTP with SSL or TLS	smtp.gmail.com
	Inbound on IMAP with SSL	imap.gmail.com
	Inbound on POP with SSL	pop.gmail.com
Live (no IMAP)	Outbound on SMTP with SSL (port 25) or TLS	smtp.live.com
	Inbound on POP with SSL	pop3.live.com
Yahoo	Outbound on SMTP with SSL	smtp.mail.yahoo.com
	Inbound on IMAP with SSL	imap.mail.yahoo.com
	Inbound on POP with SSL	pop.mail.yahoo.com

If you are using the newer Yahoo Mail Plus, add the word *plus* followed by a period to the beginning of the Yahoo server names.

Exercise 18.11 and Exercise 18.12 use the details in Table 18.3 to perform manual Gmail configuration on an iPhone and an Android phone, respectively.

EXERCISE 18.11

Manual Internet Email Configuration on an iPhone

1. Tap Settings.

2. Tap Mail, Contacts, Calendars.

3. Select Add Account.

4. Scroll down to the bottom of the list and tap Other.

5. Select Add Mail Account.

6. Complete the form on the New Account screen with the same information used earlier for the automatic configuration of the same account (Exercise 18.9) and then tap the Next button.

EXERCISE 18.11 *(continued)*

7.   Select IMAP as the protocol to use for incoming mail. Use POP only if your server does not support IMAP.

8.   Scroll down and complete the incoming server information to match your provider's required settings.

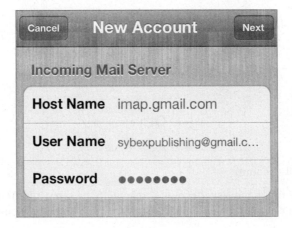

9. Scroll to the bottom of the screen and complete the outgoing server information and then tap the Next button.

10. Tap the Save button after verification completes. Note that you might have fewer synchronization choices as compared to those you had when automatic configuration was performed. In this case, the contacts switch is missing.

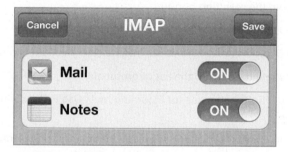

11. Leave the Settings app and enter the Mail app. Entries that meet the download policy for date and number of downloads are shown in the Inbox screen.

EXERCISE 18.11 *(continued)*

---

12. Back out one screen and notice that the icon next to your account is generic, unlike the icon that appeared there when automatic configuration was performed.

13. Delete the account using the procedure outlined at the end of Exercise 18.9, if so desired.

EXERCISE 18.12

Manual Internet Email Configuration on an Android Phone

1. Run the Mail app.

2. Skip to step 3 if no accounts are currently configured. Otherwise, from within the Mail app, tap the down arrow in the circle at the upper-left corner and then select New Account from the resulting pop-up.

3. Select Other (POP3/IMAP) from the Choose A Mail Provider menu.

4. Tap the Manual Setup button at the bottom of the New Account screen.

5. Tap the Protocol field to bring up the list of protocols.

6. Select IMAP as the protocol to use for incoming mail. Use POP only if the server does not support IMAP.

7. Fill in the Incoming Settings form for secure IMAP or secure POP, entering the email address of the account as both the email address and the username.

8. Select the security protocol used by the server and confirm the port number that the Android fills in automatically, and then tap the Next button.

9. Fill in the Outgoing Server Settings form with the secure settings for the mail server, confirm the defaults, and then tap the Next button.

10. Enter the name you want the account to be labeled with on the local device and the name you want to be displayed to recipients of outgoing mail and then tap the Finish Setup button to be taken to the account's inbox.

11. Delete the account from the device, at your discretion, by using the Android account deletion procedure detailed in Exercise 18.10.

Automatic and Manual Exchange Configuration

Exchange is a proprietary client-server messaging platform from Microsoft. Many enterprises rely on Exchange for their entire suite of email services. Exchange connectivity to Internet mail services such as Hotmail/Live and Office 365 is steadily becoming more popular, a public form of the longstanding capability of enterprises to offer Exchange access to intranet users using Webmail over HTTP or through Outlook Web App (OWA).

The procedure for establishing connectivity to a Microsoft Exchange server is not much different from how you established connectivity to an Internet mail service. In fact, the same server can be configured to support Exchange. Microsoft Exchange servers support access by proprietary Exchange messaging as well as by the Internet mail protocols. When a mail client that does not support Exchange has to be used, or when an Exchange client account might cost the user money (as in the use of the newer public Exchange accounts), it is possible that the protocols and ports in Table 18.2 can be used to establish a connection.

When an Exchange or Exchange ActiveSync client is used in the enterprise, there is sometimes no need to supply information beyond the user's account name and password along with their email address. Sometimes, however, this is not enough to establish the connection. Unlike the need for picky details for an Internet mail connection, Exchange is likely to require only the server name to complete a manual configuration. Therefore, the automatic and manual procedures are presented together in Exercise 18.13 for the iPhone and Exercise 18.14 for an Android phone.

EXERCISE 18.13

Automatic and Manual Exchange Configuration on an iPhone

1. Tap Settings.

2. Tap Mail, Contacts, Calendars.

3. Select Add Account.

4. Select Microsoft Exchange from the list.

5. Enter the email address for the Exchange account along with the username and password and a descriptive local label for the account, and then tap the Next button.

EXERCISE 18.13 *(continued)*

The username could be the email address for public Exchange accounts or just the portion before the @ symbol for enterprise accounts. Other variables exist, so confirm the required username if problems arise.

This is an attempt at automatic Exchange configuration. The remaining steps are required for manual configuration and will appear only if verification fails during automatic configuration.

6. Complete the field labeled Server with the DNS name of the Exchange server where this account exists and then tap the Next button.

7. Inspect your mailboxes and account to confirm the existence of the Exchange account.

8. Delete the account using the procedure outlined at the end of Exercise 18.9, if so desired.

EXERCISE 18.14

Automatic and Manual Exchange Configuration on an Android Phone

1. Run the Mail app.

2. Skip to step 3 if no accounts are currently configured. Otherwise, from within the Mail app, tap the down arrow in the circle at the upper-left corner and then select New Account from the resulting pop-up.

3. Select Exchange ActiveSync from the Choose A Mail Provider menu.

4. Enter the Exchange account's email address and password to attempt an automatic configuration and then tap the Next button.

If you know manual configuration is required, you can opt to enter the information requested and then tap the Manual Setup button to bypass the attempt at verification. If, instead, you tap the Next button and are met with a popup warning about an invalid certificate, tap the Cancel button to enter the server name manually. The following steps assume manual configuration is being performed.

5. Confirm the fields with data entered, enter the correct server name if the default is incorrect, and then tap the Next button. It is likely that the Android-assumed server name is not correct, leading to the need for manual configuration.

6. Choose the features you would like to have synced with the Android through the Exchange service and then tap the Finish Setup button. The Mail app takes you directly to your Exchange inbox where the first synchronization occurs.

7. Delete the account from the device, at your discretion, by using the Android account deletion procedure detailed in Exercise 18.10.

Mobile Device Security

Apple computers have a pretty decent reputation in the industry for being somewhat resistant to malware. Whether or not this is because of the relatively small installed base or the ease with which hackers penetrate "other" operating systems, this characteristic carries over to Apple's mobile devices. In fact, hackers don't seem to be as interested in attacking the legions of mobile devices as much as they have gone after the Windows operating system that drives the vast majority of laptops, desktops, and servers in the world. Nevertheless, attacks occur. Coupled with how easy mobile devices are to misplace or steal, it behooves users to have proactive monitoring and contingency plans in place.

The following sections detail the built-in security utilities that are common in today's mobile devices. Furthermore, for threats not covered by the software the devices ship with, the protection available from third-party utilities is worth discussing.

Passcode Locks

Apple and Android mobile devices include a requisite passcode locking mechanism that is off by default but that the user on the go is encouraged to set. If your device acts more as a home computing device and rarely goes with you out the door, there is very little reason to set such a passcode, but knowing how to do so is important. Exercise 18.15 outlines the steps for creating a code for your iPhone. The same general concept for the Android is presented in Exercise 18.16.

EXERCISE 18.15

Setting the Passcode Lock on an iPhone

1. Tap Settings.

2. Select General.

3. Select Passcode Lock.

4. Tap Turn Passcode On. If you'd like to use a passcode that requires use of the keyboard, you need to turn off the Simple Passcode switch. Otherwise, a simple four-digit PIN is required.

5. Enter the passcode of your choosing. The display will slide automatically, implying that you need to enter it a second time to confirm. Doing so sets the passcode.

6. Set the amount of time that must pass while the phone is asleep before the passcode will be required and whether the Erase Data feature should be enabled. Setting the Required Passcode field to Immediately requires entering the passcode each time the device is woken up.

Make note of the fact that there is a switch on the final screen shown in Exercise 18.15 that, when on, destroys all local data on the phone if incorrect passcodes are entered 10 times in a row. While this is recommended for users with phones that contain sensitive data and that are frequently taken into public venues or placed in compromising positions, the casual user should not turn this feature on unless they can be sure there will always be a recent backup available in iTunes.

Imagine a user's child or mischievous, yet harmless, friend poking away at passcodes until the device informs them that it is being wiped clean. It's not for everyone. Restoring from a backup is easy enough, but will there be a recent backup available when disaster strikes? Apple performs a backup to the computer running iTunes that the iOS device syncs with. Conditions required for synchronization to occur are discussed later in this chapter.

Apple imposes cooling-off time-out periods of increasing duration even if the Erase Data feature is disabled and you or someone else repeatedly enters the wrong code over multiple lockouts. The final penalty with the Erase Data feature disabled is that you cannot unlock the device until it is connected to the computer with which it was last synced. Synchronization is discussed later in this chapter. The screen shot in Figure 18.5 is from an iPhone after the first such period has been imposed. Note that emergency calls are still allowed.

FIGURE 18.5   Lockout screen on an Apple iPhone

EXERCISE 18.16

Setting the Passcode Lock on an Android Phone

1. Tap the Menu button.

2. Tap the Settings soft button.

3. Select Security from the Settings menu.

4. Tap Set Up Screen Lock from the Security menu.

5. Select Pattern from the Screen Unlock Security list.

6. Use your finger to draw a continuous pattern of four or more dots and then tap the Continue button.

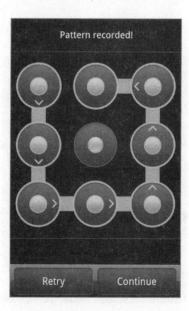

EXERCISE 18.16 *(continued)*

7. Repeat the same pattern and then tap the Confirm button.

8. Adjust the Lock Phone After field to set how long the device needs to be asleep before requiring the passcode.

When a passcode is set, Android devices take a less punitive approach to failed login attempts when compared to their Apple counterparts, where the static "destroy after 10 failed attempts" feature is your only option. Most Android systems have no adjustment for their default behavior, aside from turning off security. Figure 18.6 shows the screen you might see after five failed attempts to unlock one of these devices. This is similar to the time-out Apple devices impose.

FIGURE 18.6   An Android lockout screen

The difference is that if waiting the time-out period won't help because you've forgotten the pattern or code, these devices can tie your access back to the Google account you used when setting up the device. This is also the account where you receive purchase notifications from the Market or Google Play and does not have to be a Gmail account (one of the benefits of the open-source nature of Android). If you remember how to log in to that account, you can still get into your phone, as shown in Figure 18.7. At least you can investigate the credentials to that account on a standard computer and return to the device to enter those credentials.

FIGURE 18.7   An Android account unlock screen

Remote Wipes and Locators

Should your work or personal mobile device disappear or fall into the wrong hands, it's always nice to have a backup plan for making sure no company secrets or personal identifiers get misused by anyone who would use the information with ill will. Apple supplies a free app called Find My iPhone that, together with iCloud or the erstwhile choice, MobileMe (deactivated as of June 30, 2012), allows multiple mobile devices and Macs to be located if powered on and attached to the Internet (via 4G, 3G, WiFi, Ethernet, etc.). The app allows the device to be controlled remotely to lock it, play a sound (even if audio is off), display a message, or wipe it clean.

Within a newer iPhone's Settings screen, you can find an iCloud settings page, shown in Figure 18.8. Note the Find My iPhone switch. With this switch off, the Find My iPhone app and iCloud web page will be unable to find your device.

FIGURE 18.8   Settings page for iCloud

On the login screen, shown in Figure 18.9 for the iPhone app, you must enter the iCloud account information that includes the device you are attempting to control remotely.

The same applies for your MobileMe account. Note that when you change the password for your Apple ID, it affects your iCloud account but does not transfer automatically within your device. Always remember to update your iCloud account information on each device when you update the associated Apple ID.

 Although iCloud has its own settings page, you can also create an iCloud or MobileMe account— or change their settings—through the path Settings ➢ Mail, Contacts, Calendar.

The website's login page at www.icloud.com, shown in Figure 18.10, calls for the same credentials as the app requires. You are signing in with HTTPS, so your username and password are not traversing the Internet in the clear.

FIGURE 18.9   Find My iPhone app login page

FIGURE 18.10   Login page for iCloud website

With the switch in the iCloud settings screen set to off for all devices on your account, when you sign on to the app with your iCloud account credentials, you are met with the message in Figure 18.11.

FIGURE 18.11 Result of disabling the Find My iPhone switch

You do not need to go to the website if you have another device with the Find iPhone app or borrow one from someone else. Your credentials are forgotten by the device when you log out, so the owner will not be able to control your device the next time they use the app.

After logging into the iCloud website, you can click the icon shown in Figure 18.12 that matches the icon for the find iPhone app in iOS.

Assuming you've made it into the app on another device and your Find My iPhone feature is turned on in your missing device, the Info screen shown in Figure 18.13 tells you that your device has been found and gives you options for the next step you take.

Tapping the Location button in the upper left shows you a map of where your device is currently located. You have three options for how to view the location: two-dimensional map, satellite, and a hybrid version where the two-dimensional street-name information is laid over the satellite view. Figure 18.14 shows the satellite view on the app.

FIGURE 18.12   Find My iPhone icon on the iCloud website

FIGURE 18.13   Find My iPhone app Info screen

Figure 18.15 shows a similar view, but from the website.

If you tap the Play Sound Or Send Message button on the Info screen shown in Figure 18.13 instead of the Location button, the screen shown in Figure 18.16 pops up and allows you to display a message remotely.

You might consider first displaying a message without the sound, which is at maximum volume. Ask in the message to be called at another number. If you hear from someone in possession of your device, the hunt is over. Otherwise, send another message with the tone to get the attention of the nearest person. If you are at the reported location when you generate the sound, it can help you home in on the device.

FIGURE 18.14   Find My iPhone app Location screen

FIGURE 18.15   Location screen from the iCloud website

FIGURE 18.16   Send Message screen in the Find My iPhone app

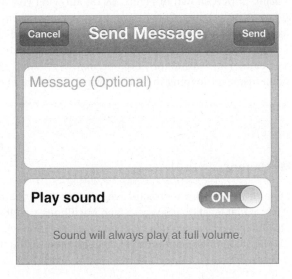

If you do decide to use the remote-lock feature of the app, you'll have the opportunity to reconsider before locking it. You should have no issue with locking the device; doing so does not prevent you from using the app further. It simply makes sure that the device is harder to break into. Figure 18.17 shows the confirmation message you receive before locking the device.

FIGURE 18.17   Find My iPhone lock confirmation

Should you decide to take the sobering step of destroying the contents of the device remotely, you get a solemn notice, shown in Figure 18.18, allowing you the opportunity to reassess the situation before proceeding. Sometimes there's just no other option.

For Android devices, the app called Lookout is a critically acclaimed application that performs some of the same functions as Apple's Find My iPhone, including the emission of an extremely loud scream. The website for Lookout, www.mylookout.com, is shown in Figure 18.19 at the point just after logging in and choosing the device of interest.

 Real World Scenario

Uh-Oh. Where's My Phone?

During a recent visit to a car dealership, a prospective new-car owner named Rotimi departed without his iPhone; at least, that's where Find My iPhone said it was. Luckily he had the foresight to set up his free iCloud account and log that phone into it. Upon his return to the dealership, Rotimi was temporarily disheartened to find that no one had seen his phone.

It occurred to him that he had laid his phone down on the counter in the men's room as he was washing his hands. He didn't recall having it after that point. A cursory look around the facilities turned up nothing. The app was not accurate enough to tell him where exactly the phone was at the time of its location on the Find My iPhone website, which he checked from home. It did indicate that it was still somewhere at the dealership, though.

Rotimi noticed that the salesperson assisting him had an iPhone. Upon recalling that fact, he asked her if she used the same app. She said she absolutely did. He asked if he could borrow her phone for a brief instant. She obliged, and Rotimi entered his iCloud credentials into the salesperson's app and proceeded to enter the message, "I'm in the showroom." He left the Play Sound switch on and tapped the Send button.

In less than 5 minutes, a manager that had been back at the loading dock came to the showroom with a story. He said he heard a disturbing noise coming from the dumpster, which was quite full and scheduled for pick-up the next morning. The trash bag containing Rotimi's phone was conveniently right at the top of the heap and easily retrieved by the manager.

Rotimi recalled being in a bit of a fluster as he left the men's room. He was about to finalize the terms of the deal he had been working on for more than an hour. In his haste to get back to the table, apparently his phone slipped from his hand as he was disposing of the wad of paper towels he used to dry his hands and the area around the sink that was quite wet and laced with liquid soap from a long day's use. Evidently, it's true that no good deed goes unpunished, but also the cliché "all's well that ends well" has a shred of truth. He owed this happy ending to the features of the Find My iPhone app and tells his story to anyone who will listen.

FIGURE 18.18   Find My iPhone Erase All Data button

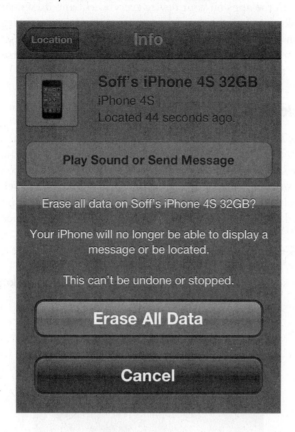

FIGURE 18.19   Lookout Mobile Security web page

On an Android phone, the Lookout app automatically scans every app you install, performs a full scan of all the apps on your device every week, and downloads the latest definitions regularly. Lookout Labs provides virus scanning of all apps on a regular basis in this product as well as in some of its more specialized offerings. Among these specialized apps, the company produces the Plan B app that boasts the ability to install itself after the device is lost, subsequently turning on location services remotely.

Remote Backup

Software companies like Lookout Labs also produce apps that are capable of backing your device's contents up over the Internet so that in case of a catastrophic failure, your information is easily restored to a new device. The app known as MyBackup Pro is designed exclusively for the purpose of backing up your data and storing the backup sets either locally on the device or remotely on the company's servers. You can choose the type of information to be backed up, and restoration is quite painless, resulting in your device returning to its predisaster state.

Figure 18.20 shows the Lookout iPhone app with its backup feature at the bottom of the list.

Figure 18.21 is a screen shot showing the services offered by MyBackup Pro on an Android phone.

FIGURE 18.20   Lookout app

FIGURE 18.21  MyBackup Pro app

Apple iOS devices automatically back themselves up to the computer running iTunes that they sync with. In the sense that this backup exists on a system other than the iOS device, this can be considered a remote backup as well.

Operating System Updates

It's easy to forget that these tiny yet powerful mobile devices we've been talking about are running operating systems that play the same role as the operating systems of their larger brethren. As such, users must be careful not to let the operating systems go too long without updates. Occasionally, mobile devices will notify the user of an important update to the operating system. Too often, however, these notifications never come. Therefore, each user should develop the habit of checking for updates on a regular basis.

Not keeping up with software updates creates an environment of known weaknesses and unfixed bugs. Mobile devices operate on a very tight tolerance of hardware and software performance. Not maintaining the device for performance at the top of its game will tend to have more pronounced repercussions than those seen in larger systems.

For the iPhone, iPod Touch, and iPad, you can check for the most important level of updates by tapping Settings ➤ General ➤ Software Update. For the Android operating system, there are multiple updates that can be checked for manually. All of them are accessible by following Menu ➤ Settings ➤ System Updates. The resulting menu includes options for updating the firmware, the profile, the preferred roaming list (PRL), and the manufacturer's specific software.

Larger Mobile Devices

Once upon a time, in the era of using a desktop as your personal computer and looking to "luggables" if you needed portability, mobility was a luxury, if not a novelty. In stark contrast, today's mobile devices can be so small that the likelihood of misplacing your computing device is a real and ongoing concern. Furthermore, the physical size of the smaller devices is not conducive to comfortable computing.

When a larger screen and more convenient controls are desired, there are two popular solutions: laptops/netbooks and tablets. These two broad families of larger mobile devices are similar in their portability but differ in other aspects. For instance, you can use a laptop when a real keyboard, desktop-class operating system, external connections, and larger display are in order. Otherwise, and when maximum portability is key, a tablet, such as Apple's iPad, can often get the job done with maximum convenience. However, certain functionality has to be left behind to pay for the handiness. The following sections will illuminate the characteristics that either bind the technologies or set them apart.

Field Servicing and Upgrading

Ever since the dawn of the portable computer, manufacturers and service providers have based a percentage of their success on warranties and "house calls" to repair devices on the fritz. It's a fact that quasi-fixed components, such as displays and motherboards, are widely considered replaceable with only identical components in laptops and similar devices. However, technically minded users could take it upon themselves to expand the capabilities of their own system by, for instance, upgrading the hard drive, increasing RAM, using PC Cards and flash devices, attaching wired peripherals, and inserting discs.

Although the ability to repair and expand the functionality of portable devices in the field has become all but obviated, it has been shown with current and past generations of mobile devices that users are not averse to giving up these capabilities as long as functionality and convenience outshine the loss.

Although many Android and other non-Apple devices allow the replacement of batteries and the use of removable memory cards as primary storage, even this basic level of access is removed in Apple's mobile devices, including its iPad line of tablets. In an effort to produce a sleeker mobile phone, even Android devices have been developed without user access to the battery. For Apple, however, in addition to producing a nice compact package, it is all part of keeping the technology as closed to adulteration as possible. Supporters of this practice recognize the resulting long-term quality. Detractors lament the lack of options.

To service closed mobile devices of any size, it is necessary to seek out an authorized repair facility and take or send your device to them for service. Attempting your own repairs will not only void any remaining warranty but likely render the device unusable. Apple's devices, for example, require a special tool to open them. You cannot simply dig between the seams of the case to pop the device open. Even if you get such a device open, there is no standard consumer pipeline for parts, whether for repair or upgrading.

Anyone who has been around the business for more than just a few years has likely seen their fair share of components and systems with no user-serviceable parts. For these situations, an authorized technician can be dispatched to your location, home or work, with the appropriate tools, parts, and skill to field-service the system for you. On a slightly different, perhaps subtle, note, the bottom line here is that many of today's mobile devices, including some of the larger tablet-style devices, have no field-serviceable parts inside, let alone user-serviceable parts. In some extremes, special work environments similar to the original clean manufacturing environment have to be established for servicing.

Input Methods

With decreased size come increased interaction difficulties. Human interfaces can become only so small without the use of projection or virtualization. In other words, a computer the size of a postage stamp is fine as long as it can project a full-sized keyboard and a 60″ display, for example. Using microscopic real interfaces would not sell much product. So, the conundrum is that users want smaller devices but do not want to have to wear a jeweler's loupe or big-screen virtualization glasses to interact with their petite devices.

As long as the size of the devices remains within the realm of human visibility and interaction, modern technology allows for some pretty convenient methods of user input. All devices from the tablet size down are equipped with the touchscreens discussed earlier in this chapter, supplying onscreen keyboards and other virtual input interfaces. On top of that, more and more of the screens are developing the ability to detect more than one contact point.

Generically, this technology is referred to in the industry as *multi-touch* and is available on all Apple devices with touch input, including the touch pads of the Apple laptops. Apple, through its acquisition of the company Fingerworks, holds patents for the capacitive multi-touch technology featured on its products. Today, multi-touch is more about functionality than novelty. Nevertheless, the markets for both business and pleasure exist for multi-touch.

Certainly, touchscreens with the ability to sense 300 separate points of contact can allow large-scale collaboration or fun at parties. Imagine a coffee table that can allow you to pull out the jigsaw puzzle, with the touch of an icon, remembering where you and three friends left off. Imagine all of you being able to manipulate pieces independently and simultaneously and being able to send the puzzle away again as quickly as you brought it out so that you can watch the game on the same surface. This technology exists and is for sale today. Check out products built on Microsoft's PixelSense technology, including the Samsung SUR40, once marketed as Microsoft Surface.

On a smaller scale, our mobile devices allow us to pinch and stretch images on the screen by placing multiple fingers on the screen at the same time. Even touch pads on laptops can be made to differentiate any number of fingers being used at the same time, each producing a different result, including pointing and clicking, scrolling and right-clicking, and dragging, all one-handed with no need to press a key or mouse button while gesturing.

HTC created an early touchscreen software interface called *TouchFLO* that has matured into HTC Sense and is still in use today on its Android and Windows line of mobile devices. TouchFLO is not multi-touch capable, nor does it specify the physical technology behind the touchscreen, only the software application for it. Theoretically, then, TouchFLO and multi-touch could be combined.

The primary contribution of TouchFLO was the introduction to the market of an interface that the user perceives as multiple screens, each of which is accessible by an intuitive finger gesture on the screen to spin around to a subsequent page. On various devices using this concept, neighboring pages have been constructed as side by side as well as above and below one another. Apple's mobile devices employ gestures owing to the contributions of TouchFLO, bringing the potential of combining TouchFLO-like technology and multi-touch to bear.

Users of early HTC devices with resistive touchscreen technology met with difficulty and discord when flowing to another screen. The matte texture of the early resistive screens was not conducive to smooth gesturing. The capacitive touchscreen technology is a welcome addition to such a user interface, making gestures smooth and even more intuitive than ever.

Secondary Storage

Computers of all sizes and capabilities use similar forms of RAM for primary storage—the storage location for currently running instructions and data. Secondary storage—the usually nonvolatile location where these instructions and data are stored on a more permanent basis—is another story. Larger systems still favor conventional hard disk drives—with magnetic spinning disks, larger overall capacity, and less cost per byte—over the newer solid state drives. This discussion was presented first in Chapter 2, "Storage Devices and Power Supplies."

The primary concern with smaller devices is the shock they tend to take as the user makes their way through a typical day. Simply strapping a phone to your hip and taking the Metro to work presents a multitude of opportunities for a spinning disk to meet with catastrophe. The result would be the frequent loss of users' information from a device that they count on more and more as technology advances.

Just as many telephony subscribers migrate from a home landline that stays put to a cell phone that follows them everywhere, many casual consumers are content to use their mobile device as their primary or only computing system, taking it wherever they go. As a result, the data must survive conditions more brutal than most laptops because laptops are most often shut down before being transported.

The most popular solution is to equip mobile devices with solid-state drives (SSDs) in the place of traditional magnetic disk drives. There are no moving parts; the drive stays cooler and resists higher temperature extremes; and SSDs require less power to run than their conventional counterparts.

Mobile Device Synchronization

The preceding discussion notwithstanding, most users do not consider their mobile devices to be islands unto themselves. Instead, they treat their devices as an extension of their primary computing device that, even if it happens to be portable, stays at work or at home while the mobile computing device goes on the road with the user. However, because many of the same changes to a user's calendar, contacts, and personal files can be made from the mobile device as easily as from the primary computer, frequent synchronization of the two devices is in order. *Synchronization* is the act of mirroring all unique changes and additions from each device to the other.

In most cases, there are multiple options as to how the mobile device will connect to the computer system. Some connections allow synchronization; others do not. Common connections include over USB or FireWire, across WiFi, and over a Bluetooth connection. While the wired serial connections tend to be the most reliable, the convenience of wireless connections and their automatic unattended synchronizations cannot be ignored.

Because each manufacturer of mobile devices must approach synchronization of data in the best manner for their devices, generalized discussions of data to be synchronized can *only* include the common types. The tabs in iTunes and their purpose are detailed in the next section, but the following list comprises the most common types of data to be synchronized by all such utilities:

- Contacts
- Apps
- Email
- Photos
- Music
- Videos

Syncing Apple iOS Devices

As for Apple devices—iPhones, for instance—iTunes must be installed on a compatible non-iOS computer. The iOS devices will automatically sync each time they are connected by USB and, in some cases, WiFi and are recognized under the Devices section in the left frame of iTunes. The exception is when iTunes is set to prevent automatic synchronization. Figure 18.22 shows the dialog from iTunes attained by clicking Edit ➢ Preferences ➢ Devices. Notice syncing is set to occur automatically because the Prevent iPods, iPhones, And iPads From Syncing Automatically check box is cleared.

FIGURE 18.22   Devices Preferences in iTunes

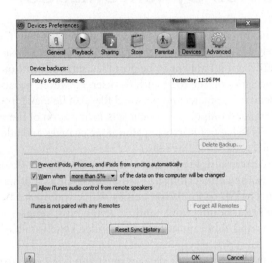

The selection of what is to be synchronized is a task unto itself, but with specific tabs for each class of data, iTunes allows you to make very granular choices about what you want to sync. The following list gives the basic characteristics of each tab:

- Info—contacts, calendars, mail, and bookmarks to be synced
- Apps—apps to be synced, their orientation on the different Home screens, and documents, if any, available through apps that support file sharing
- Tones—ringtones to be synced
- Music—music to be synced and playlist, artist, album, and genre sections for making selections in partial syncing
- Movies—movies and video clips to be synced
- TV Shows—TV shows to be synced
- Books—books to be synced
- Photos—photos to be synced

If the iOS device is running iOS version 5 or higher and the computer it syncs with is running iTunes version 10.5 or higher, you can sync your iOS device by using WiFi. Besides these minimum version requirements, a few things have to come together before this will work. The following list outlines these requirements.

- Apple states the iOS device must be plugged in to a source of power before sync will occur. It has been demonstrated that given enough battery power, the iOS device will sync without being plugged in.

- The iOS device should not be plugged into the USB port of the computer it syncs with. USB synchronization overrides WiFi synchronization.

- The iOS device and the computer it syncs with must be on the same WiFi network, which means the SSID of the WiFi network they are attached to is the same and you are sure the wireless network is not misconfigured to produce a false positive result, such as with two unconnected WAPs configured with the same SSID.

- The computer the iOS device syncs with must have iTunes running. Otherwise, the Sync Now button on the iOS device will be dimmed. When in this state, however, once iTunes is opened and all other requirements are met, WiFi sync will begin automatically if not disabled in Devices Preferences.

For syncing over WiFi to occur, it is not necessary to remove the wired connection of the computer running iTunes, if one exists. Although the computer will favor the use of the wired connection over the wireless link for regular network traffic, iTunes forces the communication to the iOS device to occur over the WiFi link during establishment of the connection and synchronization.

You can tell the difference between when a device is connected over WiFi versus when it is charging while connected by USB. Figure 18.23 shows a device after its WiFi synchronization has run. The eject icon changes to a rotating sync icon when sync is running.

FIGURE 18.23   An iOS device connected by WiFi

You can also see in Figure 18.24 that iTunes states in the Version section of the Summary tab that updating software on the iOS device or restoring from a backup must occur over a USB connection, implying that it cannot occur over WiFi. When connected by USB, regardless of whether the device is charging, this same section contains a Restore button and a Check For Update button.

Figure 18.25 shows the same device connected to the iTunes computer with a USB cable. Notice the battery charging indicator that was not there when there was only WiFi connectivity. While the device is connected by USB, the indicator will also disappear when the battery fully charges.

FIGURE 18.24   Apple iTunes requesting USB connectivity

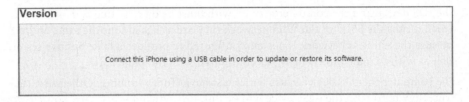

FIGURE 18.25   An iOS device connected by USB

If automatic synchronization is disabled in Devices Preferences, manual synchronization of an iOS device can be started by clicking the iOS device in the left frame in iTunes and then clicking the Sync button at the bottom-right corner of its Summary tab. Alternatively, you can right-click the device in the left frame and choose Sync from that menu, as shown in Figure 18.26.

FIGURE 18.26   Manual synchronization in iTunes

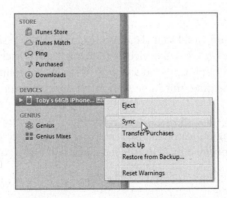

Regardless of whether you are connected to the iTunes computer over WiFi or by USB, you can also force a manual sync to begin by running the Settings app, selecting General, then selecting iTunes Wi-Fi Sync. Doing so takes you to the screen in Figure 18.27. In this example, there is an issue connecting to the last computer with which the iOS device synced. The Sync Now button is not selectable. This likely means that the device is attached by WiFi. As counterintuitive as it sounds, if a USB connection exists, the Sync Now button will be lit and can be used to start the wired synchronization.

As soon as the issue is resolved, a screen similar to the one in Figure 18.28 appears. Notice the selectable Sync Now button.

FIGURE 18.27   Disabled button in iTunes Wi-Fi Sync screen

FIGURE 18.28   Enabled button in iTunes Wi-Fi Sync screen

Tapping the Sync Now button eventually changes it to read Cancel Sync, as shown in Figure 18.29, and shows you the progress of the wireless or wired sync. The progress can also be followed from iTunes.

FIGURE 18.29 Cancel Sync button in iTunes Wi-Fi Sync screen

Syncing Android Devices

Just as with Apple's devices, mobile devices built for the Android operating system can be synced to a traditional computer. Apple's iTunes is proprietary and has been designated as the application that performs synchronization of iOS devices. In a similar way, manufacturers of Android devices have their own syncing utilities. Because this software and the connection methods allowed vary widely from one manufacturer to another, it is difficult to predict exactly what one manufacturer will offer in its utility and if each Android device it produces will interact the same way and over the same connections.

It should be assumed that, at a minimum, the same items that can be synced with iOS devices and iTunes can likely be synced for Android devices as well. What is also safe to assume is that no utility with the popularity and well-designed integration and features of iTunes exists for the Android market. Many manufacturers, however, create utilities that can tap into the playlists of iTunes and the data structures of Microsoft Outlook to obtain quite a bit of what they are looking for without the need to supply the same features in their own utilities. Don't be surprised when you see an Android device with an exact replica of a computer's iTunes playlists, names as well as contents.

Software Installation Requirements

As with any software, minimum hardware and disk-space requirements exist for installing the software that allows synchronization of mobile devices. Any computer that a user would install these software applications on should have USB and WiFi for connectivity. It never hurts to make sure, though. Here we'll outline the minimum requirements for installing iTunes and HTC Sync, a utility for the devices made by the popular manufacturer HTC.

Installation Requirements for iTunes

Apple's iTunes is available for Mac OS and Windows. The following sections list the hardware and software requirements for installing iTunes on each of these operating systems.

Windows Requirements

The following list details the minimum hardware requirements that a Windows machine must have to support the installation of iTunes version 10.6.1:

- 1GHz Intel or AMD processor
- 512MB of RAM
- To play standard definition video
  - Intel Pentium D processor
  - 512MB of RAM
  - DirectX 9.0–compatible video card
- To play 720p HD video, an iTunes LP, or iTunes Extras
  - 2.0GHz Intel Core 2 Duo processor
  - 1GB of RAM
  - Intel GMA X3000, ATI Radeon X1300, or NVIDIA GeForce 6150 video card
- To play 1080p HD video
  - 2.4GHz Intel Core 2 Duo processor
  - 2GB of RAM
  - Intel GMA X4500HD; ATI Radeon HD 2400; NVIDIA GeForce 8300 GS video card
- Screen resolution of 1024×768 or greater; 1280×800 or greater to play an iTunes LP or iTunes Extras
- 16-bit sound card and speakers
- Broadband Internet connection
- iTunes-compatible CD or DVD recorder

Only certain versions of Windows support iTunes. The following list contains the software requirements for installing iTunes in Windows:

- Windows XP Service Pack 2; 32-bit editions of Windows Vista; 32-bit editions of Windows 7
- The iTunes 64-bit installer for 64-bit editions of Windows Vista or Windows 7
- 200MB of available disk space

Mac Requirements

Apple includes iTunes in its operating system and on each of its new machines. Nevertheless, Apple publishes minimum hardware and software requirements for the installation of iTunes 10.6.1 on a Macintosh. The following list includes hardware requirements:

- Mac computer with an Intel, PowerPC G5 or G4 processor
- 512MB of RAM
- To play standard definition video
  - 1.0GHz PowerPC G4
  - 512MB of RAM
- To play 720p HD video, an iTunes LP, or iTunes Extras
  - 2.0GHz Intel Core 2 Duo processor
  - 1GB of RAM
- To play 1080p HD video
  - 2.4GHz Intel Core 2 Duo processor
  - 2GB of RAM
- Screen resolution of 1024×768 or greater; 1280×800 or greater to play an iTunes LP or iTunes Extras
- Broadband Internet connection
- Apple combo drive or SuperDrive; possibly some non-Apple CD-RW recorders)

The Macintosh software requirements are shown in the following list:

- Mac OS X version 10.5.8
- Safari 4.0.3
- 200MB of available disk space

Installation Requirements for HTC Sync

A very popular manufacturer of mobile devices, HTC produces its own utilities for syncing its devices to your computer. Its ever-popular and widely supported HTC Sync application has been joined by HTC Sync Manager for a small subset of devices. In the past, HTC allowed syncing over Bluetooth, but today, syncing with HTC Sync requires a USB 2.0 connection.

The following list outlines the capabilities of HTC Sync. Note the similarity to general syncing interests as well as to those particular to iTunes:

- Synchronize Outlook contacts and calendar or Outlook Express contacts
- Synchronize web browser bookmarks
- Install third-party Android applications

- Bring the following items to your phone:
  - Photos
  - Videos
  - Documents
  - Songs
  - Playlists

Because we are interested in establishing the basic functionality that allows synchronization to occur, let's take a look at the system requirements for installing HTC Sync. You'll notice they are in line with those for installing iTunes. HTC Sync is not supported for Mac at this time, so only Windows requirements are listed in this section.

This list specifies the minimum hardware requirements that a Windows machine must have to support the installation of HTC Sync version 3.2.10:

- Intel Pentium III processor
- 1GB of RAM
- XGA (1024×768) resolution video adapter and monitor
- 300MB of available free hard disk space
- USB 2.0

The software requirements in the following list are similar as well:

- Windows XP Home/Professional/Media Center Edition Service Pack 2 and 3 (x86)
- Windows Vista Ultimate/Enterprise/Business/Home Premium/Home Basic Edition (x86 or x64) Service Pack 1
- Windows 7 Ultimate/Professional/Home Premium/Home Basic Edition (x86 or x64)
- Microsoft Office Outlook 2000, XP, 2003, 2007 or 2010 (x86 or x64)

HTC reminds you to enable USB debugging to make sure HTC Sync works properly. This setting is for developers and for applications to gain a deeper access to the resources of the device. Most apps don't require it, but some, such as HTC Sync, cannot function properly or consistently without it. To make sure USB debugging is enabled on your HTC Android device, select Settings ➤ Applications ➤ Development and check the box beside USB Debugging. You should disconnect and reconnect the device after making this change.

Summary

This chapter introduced you to mobile devices in general and specifically to two popular mobile platforms in Apple's iOS and Google's Android. The primary concepts demonstrated in the course of this chapter included the basic features of the two operating systems, how to establish network connectivity and configure email clients, how to secure these mobile devices, and how to synchronize mobile devices with conventional computer systems. The differences and similarities between tablets and laptops were also discussed.

Exam Essentials

Be able to explain the differences and similarities between iOS and Android operating systems.   Although all mobile devices inherently resemble one another, there are enough differential features that set each major platform apart from the others. It is important that you are able to discuss such differences as well as what is similar.

Know how to connect a mobile device to a wireless network.   WiFi networks have a strict set of guidelines for connectivity. This means that the procedure for connecting disparate devices is quite similar. However, each mobile operating system has its own sequence of screens and selections to make the connection to wireless networks. Familiarize yourself with the procedure in each platform.

Familiarize yourself with configuring email clients on mobile devices.   Similar to the way that you can configure a laptop or desktop computer to access popular email services, you can configure mobile devices. Be able to interface automatically and manually with Internet mail services as well as with Exchange mail servers.

Demonstrate the ability to secure mobile devices against security threats.   The initial securing of mobile devices is crucial, but knowing how to find lost devices and destroy sensitive information remotely is of paramount importance because of the relative ease with which highly portable devices seem to part ways with their owners. You should also never forget that keeping operating systems up-to-date is as important with mobile devices as it is with larger systems.

Know the basic differences between laptops and the smaller tablet computers.   Although laptops are potentially small devices, especially in the form of netbooks, tablets are often smaller and lighter still. Tablets have no lids to add weight and often have very few, if any, components that can be upgraded or repaired in the field.

Know how to synchronize mobile devices with larger computer systems.   Mobile devices are marvels of modern computing science, but their portability lends itself to loss and damage. Synchronization affords the user the ability to recover from even the most disastrous of circumstances. The key is to synchronize often, which should include the creation of full-system backups that are stored on a computer system separate from the mobile device and the ability to restore to the same or new mobile device if the need arises.

Review Questions

The answers to the Chapter Review Questions can be found in Appendix A.

1. Which of the following is *not* a difference between iOS and Android?

   A. Android is not a proprietary operating system.

   B. You can download iOS apps from only one place.

   C. You can make a cellular phone call from all Android devices.

   D. It costs more to be a developer of iOS apps.

2. By what name was Google Play formerly known?

   A. Google Market

   B. Android Market

   C. Android Play

   D. App Store

3. Bob's iPhone 4S cannot detect when he turns his device to the left and right like it's a steering wheel. Games and other apps that require this motion will not work correctly as a result. Which component has failed in Bob's phone?

   A. Gyroscope

   B. Accelerometer

   C. Magnetometer

   D. GPS

4. Which of the following is more likely to be associated with a resistive touchscreen versus a capacitive one?

   A. You won't have to apply as much pressure.

   B. You will need to recalibrate it.

   C. You will have to clean it more often for optimal functionality.

   D. You can use the pad of your finger instead of your fingernail.

5. Which of the following are text-messaging services used with mobile devices? (Choose two.)

   A. SMS

   B. SIP

   C. Androtext

   D. iOS Messaging

   E. iMessage

6. Which of the following is *not* a valid reason to disable cellular data networking?

   A. You have a limited amount of data in your monthly plan.

   B. You have access to a reliable WiFi signal.

   C. You are about to download an update to your phone.

   D. Your phone calls are going out over your carrier's cellular network.

7. Which of the following is a characteristic of Bluetooth?

   A. Bluetooth connections support wireless device control but not file transfers.

   B. Bluetooth is not yet a fully standardized protocol.

   C. Bluetooth connections do not reach as far as WiFi connections.

   D. You must reboot paired devices to complete connection establishment.

8. What is the default TCP port number for SMTP?

   A. 25

   B. 110

   C. 143

   D. 995

9. Which mail protocol commonly uses TCP port 587?

   A. SMTP with SSL

   B. SMTP with TLS

   C. IMAP4 with SSL/TLS

   D. POP3 with SSL/TLS

10. Which of the following is *not* a type of Android passcode lock that can be set?

   A. Spoken passphrase

   B. Drawn pattern

   C. Numeric PIN

   D. Password

11. If you do not have your iPhone 4S set to erase data after too many failed login attempts but your phone still locks you out after making the maximum allowable attempts, how can you unlock the phone?

   A. By having it send you an email with the passcode

   B. Only by taking into an Apple Store

   C. By plugging it into the last computer that it synced with in iTunes

   D. By holding down the sleep/wake and home buttons simultaneously

12. Which of the following can Apple's Find My iPhone application *not* do?

   A. Remotely lock the device

   B. Remotely wipe the device

   C. Locate the device

   D. Alert the authorities

13. Directly under which of the following iOS menus can you find the Software Update utility?

   A. General

   B. iCloud

   C. Notifications

   D. Security

14. Which of the following are you most likely to be able to do to a larger mobile device, such as Apple's iPad?

   A. Replace the internal SSD

   B. Add additional RAM

   C. Upgrade the processor

   D. Print over WiFi or Bluetooth

15. Which of the following features is not supported when you are unable to zoom in on a picture or screen of information by placing two fingers together on the screen and spreading them?

   A. Multi-touch

   B. TouchFLO

   C. SuperPinch

   D. Resistive touchscreen

16. Which of the following are universally common items that are synced between a mobile device and a larger computer? (Choose three.)

   A. Office documents

   B. Contacts

   C. Operating system files

   D. Email

   E. Configuration settings

   F. Apps

17. Which of the following is *not* a requirement for installing iTunes on a Windows machine?

   A. A 1GHz processor or better

   B. 512MB of RAM or higher

   C. 200MB of available disk space

   D. The x64 versions of Windows

18. Which of the following statements about configuring email access on a mobile device is true?

    A. Most Internet mail services offer an Exchange option.

    B. The TCP ports used for configuring access are usually standard port numbers.

    C. Most ports used for access are UDP ports.

    D. You must download third-party apps for connecting to email services.

19. Which of the following built-in components is used by location services to find a lost mobile device?

    A. Gyroscope

    B. Accelerometer

    C. Global positioning system

    D. Magnetometer

20. Which of the following do modern mobile devices most likely have?

    A. SSD

    B. Keyboard connector

    C. Optical disc drive

    D. Video connector

Performance-Based Question

On the A+ exams, you will encounter performance-based questions. The questions on the exam require you to perform a specific task, and you will be graded on whether you were able to complete the task. The following require you to think creatively to measure how well you understand this chapter's topics. You may or may not see similar questions on the actual A+ exams. To see how your answers compare to the authors', refer to Appendix B.

Explain how to establish WiFi connectivity on an Apple iPhone.

Chapter

19

Troubleshooting Theory, OSs, and Security

THE FOLLOWING COMPTIA A+ 220-802 EXAM OBJECTIVES ARE COVERED IN THIS CHAPTER:

✓ **4.1 Given a scenario, explain the troubleshooting theory.**

- Identify the problem: Question the user and identify user changes to computer and perform backups before making changes

- Establish a theory of probable cause (question the obvious)

- Test the theory to determine cause: Once theory is confirmed determine next steps to resolve problem; If theory is not confirmed re-establish new theory or escalate

- Establish a plan of action to resolve the problem and implement the solution

- Verify full system functionality and if applicable implement preventive measures

- Document findings, actions, and outcomes

✓ **4.6 Given a scenario, troubleshoot operating system problems with appropriate tools.**

- Common symptoms: BSOD, Failure to boot, Improper shutdown, Spontaneous shutdown/restart , RAID not detected during installation, Device fails to start, Missing dll message, Services fails to start, Compatibility error, Slow system performance, Boots to safe mode, File fails to open, Missing NTLDR, Missing Boot.ini, Missing operating system, Missing Graphical Interface, Graphical Interface fails to load, Invalid boot disk

- Tools: Fixboot, Recovery console, Fixmbr, Sfc, Repair disks, Pre-installation environments, MSCONFIG, DEFRAG, REGSVR32, REGEDIT, Event viewer, Safe mode, Command prompt, Emergency repair disk, Automated system recovery

✓ **4.7 Given a scenario, troubleshoot common security issues with appropriate tools and best practices.**

- Common symptoms: Pop-ups, Browser redirection, Security alerts, Slow performance, Internet connectivity issues, PC locks up, Windows update failures, Rogue antivirus, Spam, Renamed system files, Files disappearing, File permission changes, Hijacked email, Access denied

- Tools: Anti-virus software, Anti-malware software, Anti-spyware software, Recovery console, System restore, Pre-installation environments, Event viewer

- Best practices for malware removal

  - Identify malware symptoms

  - Quarantine infected system

  - Disable system restore

  - Remediate infected systems

    - Update anti-virus software

    - Scan and removal techniques (safe mode, pre-installation environment)

  - Schedule scans and updates

  - Enable system restore and create restore point

  - Educate end user

Mentioning the words *troubleshooting theory* to many technicians can cause their eyes to roll back in their heads. It doesn't sound glamorous or sexy, and a lot of techs believe the only way to solve a problem is to just dive right in and start working on it. Theories are for academics. In a way they're right; you do need to dive in to solve problems because they don't just solve themselves. But to be successful at troubleshooting, you must take a systematic approach.

You may hear people say, "Troubleshooting is as much of an art as it is a science," and our personal favorite, "You just need to get more experience to be good at it." While there is an art to fixing problems, you can't ignore science. And if you need experience to be any good, why are some less experienced folks incredibly good at solving problems while their more seasoned counterparts seem to take forever to fix anything? More experience is good, but it's not a prerequisite to being a good troubleshooter. It's all about a systematic approach.

Applying a systematic approach to troubleshooting is key; systematic solutions also work well in preventing problems in the first place. Many of the computer problems you stress over can be prevented.

Preventive maintenance tends to get neglected at many companies because technicians are too busy fixing problems. Spending some time on keeping those problems from occurring in the first place is a good investment of resources.

In this chapter, we'll look at the two systematic methods we just talked about. First, we'll cover troubleshooting theory and the steps you need to take to successfully solve problems. Then, we'll look at some ways to help keep your systems running in top shape.

Understanding Troubleshooting Theory

When troubleshooting, you should assess every problem systematically and try to isolate the root cause. Yes, there is a lot of art to troubleshooting, and experience plays a part too. But regardless of how "artful" or experienced you are, haphazard troubleshooting is doomed to fail. Conversely, even technicians with limited experience can be effective troubleshooters if they stick to the principles. The major key is to start with the issue and whittle away at it until you can get down to the point where you can pinpoint the problem—this often means eliminating, or verifying, the obvious.

Although everyone approaches troubleshooting from a different perspective, a few things should remain constant. First, always back up your data before making any changes to a system. Hardware components can be replaced but data often can't be. For that reason, always be vigilant about making data backups.

Second, establish priorities—one user being unable to print to the printer of their choice isn't as important as a floor full of accountants unable to run payroll. Prioritize every job and escalate it (or de-escalate it) as you need to.

Third, but perhaps most important, document everything—not just that there was a problem but also the solution you found, the actions you tried, and the outcomes of each. In the next few sections we'll take you through each step of the troubleshooting process.

Identifying the Problem

While this may seem obvious, it can't be overlooked: If you can't define the problem, you can't begin to solve it. Sometimes problems are relatively straightforward, but other times they're just a symptom of a bigger issue. For example, if a user isn't able to connect to the Internet from their computer, it could indeed be an issue with their system. But if other users are having similar problems, then the first user's difficulties might just be one example of the real problem.

Ask yourself, "Is there a problem?" Perhaps "the problem" is as simple as a customer expecting too much from the computer.

Problems in computer systems generally occur in one (or more) of four areas, each of which is in turn made up of many pieces:

- A *collection of hardware pieces* integrated into a working system. As you know, the hardware can be quite complex, what with motherboards, hard drives, video cards, and so on. Software can be equally perplexing.

- An *operating system*, which in turn is dependent on the hardware.

- An *application* or software program that is supposed to do something. Programs such as Microsoft Word and Excel are bundled with a great many features.

- A *computer user*, ready to take the computer system to its limits (and beyond). A technician can often forget that the user is a very complex and important part of the puzzle.

Talking to the Customer

Many times you can define the problem by asking questions of the user. One of the keys to working with your users or customers is to ensure, much like a medical professional, that you have good bedside manner. Most people are not as technically hip as you, and when something goes wrong they become confused or even fearful that they'll take the blame. Assure them that you're just trying to fix the problem but that they can probably help because they know what went on before you got there. It's important to instill trust with your customer. Believe what they are saying, but also believe that they might not tell you everything right away. It's not that they're necessarily lying; they just might not know what's important to tell.

⊕ **Real World Scenario**

Is the Power On?

It's a classic IT story that almost sounds like a joke, but it's happened. A customer calls technical support because their computer won't turn on. After 20 minutes of troubleshooting, the technician is becoming frustrated...maybe it's a bad power supply? The technician asks the user to read some numbers off of the back of his computer, and the user says, "Hold on, I need to get a flashlight. It's dark in here with the power out."

Help clarify things by having the customer show you what the problem is. The best method I've seen of doing this is to say, "Show me what 'not working' looks like." That way, you see the conditions and methods under which the problem occurs. The problem may be a simple matter of an improper method. The user may be performing an operation incorrectly or performing the operation in the wrong order. During this step, you have the opportunity to observe how the problem occurs, so pay attention.

Here are a few questions to ask the user to aid in determining what the problem is:

Can you show me the problem?   This question is one of the best. It allows the user to show you exactly where and when they experience the problem.

How often does this happen?   This question establishes whether this problem is a one-time occurrence that can be solved with a reboot or whether a specific sequence of events causes the problem to happen. The latter usually indicates a more serious problem that may require software installation or hardware replacement.

Has any new hardware or software been installed recently?   New hardware or software can mean compatibility problems with existing devices or applications. For example, a newly installed device may want to use the same resource settings as an existing device. This can cause both devices to become disabled. When you install a new application, that application is likely to install several support files. If those support files are also used by an existing application, then there could be a conflict.

Has the computer recently been moved?   Moving a computer can cause things to become loose and then fail to work. Perhaps all of the peripherals of the computer didn't complete — or weren't included on—the move, meaning there's less functionality than the user expects.

Has someone who normally doesn't use the computer recently used it?   That person could have mistakenly (or intentionally) done something to make the computer begin exhibiting the irregular behavior.

Have any other changes been made to the computer recently?   If the answer is yes, ask if the user can remember approximately when the change was made. Then ask them approximately when the problem started. If the two dates seem related, there's a good chance the problem is related to the change. If it's a new hardware component, check to see that it was installed correctly.

Be careful of how you ask questions so you don't appear accusatory. You can't assume that the user did something to mess up the computer. Then again, you also can't assume that they don't know anything about why it's not working.

 Real World Scenario

The Social Side of Troubleshooting

When you're looking for clues as to the nature of a problem, no one can give you more information than the person who was there when it happened. They can tell you what led up to the problem, what software was running, and the exact nature of the problem ("It happened when I tried to print"), and they can help you re-create the problem, if possible.

Use questioning techniques that are neutral in nature. Instead of saying, "What were you doing when it broke?" be more compassionate and say, "What was going on when the computer decided not to work?" Frame the question in a way that makes it sound like the computer did something wrong, and not the person. It might sound silly, but these things can make your job a lot easier!

While it's sometimes frustrating dealing with end users and computer problems, such as the user who calls you up and gives you the "My computer's not working" line (okay, and what *exactly* is that supposed to mean?), even more frustrating is when no one was around to see what happened. In cases like this, do your best to find out where the problem is by establishing what works and what doesn't work.

Gathering Information

Let's say that you get to a computer and the power light is on and you can hear the hard drive spinning but there is no video and the system seems to be unresponsive. At least you know that the system has power and you can start investigating where things start to break down. (We sense a reboot in your future!)

The whole key to this step is to identify, as specifically as possible, what the problem is. The more specific you can be in identifying what's not working, the easier it will be for you to understand why it's not working and fix it. If you have users available who were there when the thing stopped working, you can try to gather information from them. If not, you're on your own to gather clues. It's like *CSI* but not as gory.

So now instead of having users to ask questions of, you need to use your own investigative services to determine what's wrong. The questions you would have otherwise asked the user are still a good starting point. Does anything appear amiss or seem to have been changed recently? What is working and what's not? Was there a storm recently? Can I reboot? If I reboot, does the problem seem to go away?

If a computer seems to have multiple problems that appear to be unrelated, identify what they are one at a time and fix them one at a time. For example, if the sound is not working and you can't get on the Internet, deal with those separately. If they seem related, such as not being able to get on the Internet and you can't access a network file server, then one solution might solve both problems.

The key is to find out everything you can that might be related to the problem. Document exactly what works and what doesn't and, if you can, why. If the power is out in the house, as in the story related earlier, then there's no sense in trying the power plug in another outlet.

Determining If the Problem Is Hardware or Software Related

This step is important because it determines the part of the computer on which you should focus your troubleshooting skills. Each part requires different skills and different tools.

To determine whether a problem is hardware or software related, you can do a few things to narrow down the issue. For instance, does the problem manifest itself when the user uses a particular piece of hardware (a DVD-ROM or USB hard drive, for example)? If it does, the problem is more than likely hardware related.

This step relies on personal experience more than any of the other steps do. You'll without a doubt run into strange software problems. Each one has a particular solution. Some may even require reinstallation of an application or the operating system. If that doesn't work, you may need to resort to restoring the entire system (operating system, applications, and data) from a data backup done when the computer was working properly.

Determining Which Component Is Failing (for Hardware Problems)

Hardware problems are usually pretty easy to figure out. Let's say the sound card doesn't work, you've tried new speakers that you know do work, and you've reinstalled the driver. All of the settings look right but it just won't respond. The sound card is probably the piece of hardware that needs to be replaced.

With many newer computers, several components such as sound, video, and networking cards are integrated into the motherboard. If you troubleshoot the computer and find a hardware component to be bad, there's a good chance that the bad component is integrated into the motherboard and the whole motherboard must be replaced—an expensive proposition, to be sure.

Laptops and a lot of desktops have components (network card, sound card, video adapter) integrated into the motherboard. If an integrated component fails, you may be able to use an expansion device (such as a USB or PC Card network adapter) to give the system full functionality without a costly repair.

Establishing a Theory

Way back when, probably in your middle school or junior high school years, you learned about the scientific method. In a nutshell, scientists develop a hypothesis, test it, and then figure out if their hypothesis is still valid. Troubleshooting involves much the same process.

Once you have determined what the problem is, you need to develop a theory as to why it is happening. No video? It could be something to do with the monitor or the video card. Can't get to your favorite website? Is it that site? Is it your network card, the cable, your IP address, DNS server settings, or something else? Once you have defined the problem, establishing a theory about the cause of the problem—what is wrong—helps you develop possible solutions to the problem.

Eliminating Possibilities

Theories can either state what can be true or what can't be true. However you choose to approach your theory generation, it's usually helpful to take a mental inventory to see what is possible and what's not. Start eliminating possibilities and eventually the only thing that can be wrong is what's left. This type of approach works well when it's an ambiguous problem; start broad and narrow your scope. For example, if the hard drive won't read, there is likely one of three culprits: the drive itself, the cable it's on, or the connector on the motherboard. Try plugging the drive into the other connector or using a different cable. Narrow down the options.

 A common troubleshooting technique is to strip the system down to the bare bones. In a hardware situation, this could mean removing all interface cards except those absolutely required for the system to operate. In a software situation, this usually means booting up in Safe Mode so most of the drivers do not load.

Once you have isolated the problem, slowly rebuild the system to see if the problem comes back (or goes away). This helps you identify what is really causing the problem and determine if there are other factors affecting the situation. For example, we have seen memory problems that are fixed by switching the slot that the memory chips are in.

Using External Resources

Sometimes you can figure out what's not working, but you have no idea why or what you can do to fix it. That's okay. In situations like those, it may be best to fall back on an old trick called reading the manual. As they say, "When all else fails, read the instructions." The service manuals are your instructions for troubleshooting and service information. Virtually every computer and peripheral made today has service documentation on the company's website, or on a DVD, or even in a paper manual. Don't be afraid to use them!

If you're lucky enough to have experienced, knowledgeable, and friendly co-workers, be open to asking for help if you get stuck on a problem.

Before starting to eliminate possibilities, check the vendor's website for any information that might help you. For example, typing in a specific error message on a vendor's website might take you directly to specific steps to fix the problem.

Testing Solutions

You've eliminated possibilities and developed a theory as to what the problem is. Your theory may be pretty specific, such as "the power cable is fried," or it may be a bit more general, like "the hard drive isn't working" or "there's a connectivity problem." No matter your theory, now is the time to start testing solutions. Again, if you're not sure where to begin to find a solution, the manufacturer's website is a good place to start!

Check the Simple Stuff First

This step is the one that even experienced technicians overlook. Often, computer problems are the result of something simple. Technicians overlook these problems because they're so simple that the technicians assume they *couldn't* be the problem. Here are some examples of simple problems:

Is it plugged in? And plugged in at both ends? Cables must be plugged in at *both ends* to function correctly. Cables can easily be tripped over and inadvertently pulled from their sockets.

 Real World Scenario

"Is It Plugged In?" and Other Insulting Questions

Think about how you feel if someone asks you this question. Your likely response is, "Of course it is!" After all, you're not an idiot, right? You'll often get the same reaction to similar questions about the device being turned on. The problem is, making sure it's plugged in and turned on are the first things you should always do when investigating a problem.

When asking these types of questions, it's not what you say but how you say it. For example, instead of asking if it's plugged in, you could say something like, "Can you do me a favor and check to see what color the end of the keyboard plug is? Is that the same color of the port where it's plugged into on the computer?" That generally gets the user to at least look at it without making them feel dumb. For power, something like, "What color are the lights on the front of the router? Are any of them blinking?" can work well.

Ask neutral and nonthreatening questions. Make it sound like the computer is at fault, not the user. These types of things will help you build rapport and be able to get more information so you can solve problems faster.

Is it turned on?   This one seems the most obvious, but we've all fallen victim to it at one point or another. Computers and their peripherals must be turned on to function. Most have power switches with LEDs that glow when the power is turned on.

Is the system ready?   Computers must be ready before they can be used. *Ready* means the system is ready to accept commands from the user. An indication that a computer is ready is when the operating system screens come up and the computer presents you with a menu or a command prompt. If that computer uses a graphical interface, the computer is ready when the mouse pointer appears. Printers are ready when the Online or Ready light on the front panel is lit.

Do the chips and cables need to be reseated?   You can solve some of the strangest problems (random hang-ups or errors) by opening the case and pressing down on each socketed chip (known as *reseating*). This remedies the chip-creep problem, which happens when computers heat up and cool down repeatedly as a result of being turned on and off, causing some components to begin to move out of their sockets. In addition, you should reseat any cables to make sure they're making good contact.

WARNING   Always be sure you're grounded before operating inside the case! If you're not, you could create a static charge (ESD) that could damage components.

Check to See If It's User Error

User error is common but preventable. If a user can't perform some very common computer task, such as printing or saving a file, the problem is likely due to user error. As soon as you hear of a problem like this, you should begin asking questions to determine if the solution is as simple as teaching the user the correct procedure. A good question to ask is, "Were you *ever* able to perform that task?" If the answer is no, it means they are probably doing the procedure wrong. If they answer yes, you must ask additional questions to get at the root of the problem.

If you suspect user error, tread carefully in regard to your line of questioning to avoid making the user feel defensive. User errors provide an opportunity to teach the users the right way to do things. Again, what you say matters. Offer a "different" or "another" way of doing things instead of the "right" way.

Restart the Computer

It's amazing how often a simple computer restart can solve a problem. Restarting the computer clears the memory and starts the computer with a clean slate. Whenever we perform phone support, we always ask the customer to restart the computer and try again. If restarting doesn't work, try powering down the system completely and then powering it up again (rebooting). More often than not, that will solve the problem.

Establishing a Plan of Action

If your fix worked, then you're brilliant! If not, then you need to reevaluate and look for the next option. After testing solutions, your plan of action may take one of three paths:

- If the first fix didn't work, try something else.
- If needed, implement the fix on other computers.
- If everything is working, document the solution.

 Real World Scenario

Reboot First, Ask Questions Later

If you're running into a software problem on a computer, the first step (after understanding what the problem is and getting any relevant error messages written down or captured in a screen grab) should always be to reboot. Many times, the problem will go away, and your work there is done. If it goes away, then it's not a problem!

Try, Try Again

So you tried the hard drive with a new (verified) cable and it still doesn't work. Now what? Your sound card won't play and you've just deleted and reinstalled the driver. Next steps? Move on and try the next logical thing in line.

 When trying solutions to fix a problem, make only one change to the computer at a time. If the change doesn't fix the problem, revert the system back to the way it was and then make your next change. Making more than one change at a time is not recommended for two reasons: One, you are never sure which change actually worked. Two, by making multiple changes at once, you might actually cause additional problems.

When evaluating your results and looking for that golden "next step," don't forget other resources you might have available. Use the Internet to look at the manufacturer's website. Read the manual. Talk to your friend who knows everything about obscure hardware (or arcane versions of Windows). When fixing problems, two heads can be better than one.

Spread the Solution

If the problem was isolated to one computer, this step doesn't apply. But some problems you deal with may affect an entire group of computers. For example, perhaps some configuration information was entered incorrectly into the DHCP server, giving everyone the wrong

DNS server address. The DHCP server is now fixed, but all of the clients need to renew their IP addresses.

Document the Solution

Once everything is working, you'll need to document what happened and how you fixed it. If the problem looks to be long and complex, we suggest taking notes as you're trying to fix it. It will help you remember what you've already tried and what didn't work. We'll discuss documenting in more depth in the section "Documenting the Work" later in this chapter.

Verifying Functionality

After fixing the system, or all of the systems, affected by the problem, go back and verify full functionality. For example, if the users couldn't get to any network resources, check to make sure they can get to the Internet as well as internal resources.

Some solutions may actually cause another problem on the system. For example, if you update software or drivers, you may inadvertently cause another application to have problems. There's obviously no way you can or should test all applications on a computer after applying a fix, but know that these types of problems can occur. Just make sure that what you've fixed works and that there aren't any obvious signs of something else not working all of a sudden.

Another important thing to do at this time is to implement preventive measures, if possible. If it was a user error, ensure that the user understands ways to accomplish the task that don't cause the error. If a cable melted because it was too close to someone's space heater under their desk, resolve the issue. If the computer overheated because there was an inch of dust clogging the fan...you get the idea.

Documenting the Work

Lots of people can fix problems. But can you remember what you did when you fixed a problem a month ago? Maybe. Can one of your co-workers remember something you did to fix the same problem on that machine a month ago? Unlikely. Always document your work so that you or someone else can learn from the experience. Good documentation of past troubleshooting can save hours of stress in the future.

Documentation can take a few different forms, but the two most common are personal and system based.

We always recommend that technicians carry a personal notebook and take notes. The type of notebook doesn't matter—use whatever works best for you. The notebook can be a lifesaver, especially when you're new to a job. Write down the problem, what you tried, and the solution. The next time you run across the same or a similar problem, you'll have a better idea of what to try. Eventually you'll find yourself less and less reliant on it, but it's incredibly handy to have!

System-based documentation is useful to both you and your co-workers. Many facilities have server logs of one type or another, conveniently located close to the machine. If someone makes a fix or a change, it gets noted in the log. If there's a problem, it's noted in the log. It's critical to have a log for a few reasons. One, if you weren't there the first time it was fixed, you might not have an idea of what to try and it could take you a long time using trial and error. Two, if you begin to see a repeated pattern of problems, you can make a permanent intervention before the system completely dies.

We've seen several different forms of system-based documentation. Again, the type of log doesn't matter as long as you use it! Often it's a notebook or a binder next to the system or on a nearby shelf. If you have a rack, you can mount something on the side to hold a binder or notebook. For client computers, one way is to tape an index card to the top or side of the power supply (don't cover any vents!) so if a tech has to go inside the case, they can see if anyone else has been in there to fix something too. In larger environments, there is often an electronic knowledge base or incident repository available for use; it is just as important to contribute to these systems as it is to use them to help diagnose problems.

 Real World Scenario

If It Ain't Broke...

When doctors take the Hippocratic oath, they promise to not make their patients any sicker than they already were. Technicians should take a similar oath. It all boils down to "if it ain't broke, don't fix it." When you troubleshoot, make one change at a time. If the change doesn't solve the problem, revert the computer to its previous state before making a different change. Otherwise, you could cause more problems than you started with. There's no sense in making things more difficult than they need to be!

Troubleshooting Operating Systems

Windows is mind-bogglingly complex. Other operating systems are too, but the mere fact that Windows 7 has nearly 50 million lines of code (and over 2,000 developers worked on it!) makes you pause and shake your head.

 Operating systems other than Windows can have issues that are not covered in this chapter. The CompTIA A+ exam asks questions on only Windows operating systems, so that's all we'll cover here. There are several good books on the market on UNIX, Linux, or MAC OS X, that are handy references to have if you work on those operating systems.

Windows-based issues can be grouped into several categories based on their cause, such as boot problems, missing files (such as system files), configuration files, and virtual memory. If you're troubleshooting a boot problem, it's imperative that you understand the Windows boot process. Some common Windows problems don't fall into any category other than "common Windows problems." We cover those in the following sections, followed by a discussion of the tools that can be used to fix them.

Common Symptoms

There are numerous "common symptoms" that CompTIA asks you be familiar with for the exam. The range from the dreaded Blue Screen of Death (BSOD) to spontaneous restarts and everything in between. They are discussed here in the order in which they appear in the objective list.

BSOD

The *Blue Screen of Death (BSOD)*—not a technical term, by the way—is another way of describing the blue-screen error condition that occurs when Windows fails to boot properly or quits unexpectedly. Because it is at this stage that the device drivers for the various pieces of hardware are installed/loaded, if your Windows GUI fails to start properly, more than likely the problem is related to a misconfigured driver or misconfigured hardware.

There are a few things you can try if you believe that a driver is causing the problem. One is to try booting Windows in *Safe Mode*. In Safe Mode, Windows loads only basic drivers, such as a standard VGA video driver and the keyboard and mouse. Once in Safe Mode, you can uninstall the driver you think is causing the problem. Another option is to boot into the last known good configuration. Doing this will revert the system drivers back to the state they were in when the last login was successfully completed. Bear in mind that the Last Known Good Configuration option is useful only if the user has not logged in again since the problem began occurring. If the problem is with a driver and the user has logged in since the driver went "bad," the last known good configuration will include the bad driver.

Failure to Boot

To troubleshoot boot problems, you must understand the Windows boot process. Windows requires only a few files to boot, each of which performs specific tasks. These are discussed next in the order in which they load:

NTLDR/BOOTMGR   Bootstraps the system. In other words, this file starts the loading of an OS on the computer. While Windows 7 and Vista uses BOOTMGR, Windows XP uses NTLDR. Whichever of the two files the operating system uses, that file is responsible for switching from real to protected mode during the boot process.

BOOT.INI   Holds information about which OSs are installed on the computer. This file also contains the location of the OS files with Windows XP. Windows 7 and Vista uses Boot Configuration Data (BCD) in place of the BOOT.INI file and is configured with BCDEDIT.EXE.

NTDETECT.COM   In Windows XP, parses the system for hardware information each time Windows is loaded. This information is then used to create dynamic hardware information in the Registry.

NTBOOTDD.SYS   On a Windows XP system with a SCSI boot device, this file is used to recognize and load the SCSI interface. On EIDE systems, this file is not needed and is not even installed.

NTOSKRNL.EXE   The Windows OS kernel. The solution to a corrupted NTOSKRNL.EXE file is to boot from a startup disk and replace the file from the setup media.

NTBTLOG.TXT   While not an executable file, this log file is very important; it holds the information collected if you choose to boot using the Boot Logging startup option.

System files   In addition to the previously listed files, all of which (except NTOSKRNL.EXE) are located in the root of the C: partition on the computer, Windows needs a number of files from its system directories (e.g., system and system32), such as the hardware abstraction layer (HAL.DLL). In Windows 7 and Windows Vista, WINLOAD.EXE and WINRESUME.EXE replace NTLDR/NTDETECT.COM.

Numerous other dynamic link library (DLL) files are also required, but usually the lack or corruption of one of them produces a noncritical error, whereas the absence of HAL.DLL causes the system to be nonfunctional.

We'll now look at the Windows XP boot process. It's a pretty long and complicated process, but keep in mind that these are complex operating systems, providing you with a lot more functionality than older versions of Windows could offer:

1. The system self-checks and enumerates hardware resources. Each machine has a different startup routine, called the POST (power-on self-test), which is executed by the commands written to the motherboard of the computer. Newer PnP boards not only check memory and processors, they also poll the systems for other devices and peripherals.

2. The Master Boot Record (MBR) loads and finds the boot sector. Once the system has finished with its housekeeping, the MBR is located on the first hard drive and loaded into memory. The MBR finds the bootable partition and searches it for the boot sector of that partition.

3. The MBR determines the file system and loads NTLDR. Information in the boot sector allows the system to locate the system partition and to find and load into memory the NTLDR file located there.

4. NTLDR switches the system from real mode (which lacks multitasking, memory protection, and those things that make Windows so great) to protected mode (which offers memory protection, multitasking, etc.) and enables paging. Protected mode enables the system to address all of the available physical memory. It's also referred to as *32-bit flat mode*. At this point, the file system is also started.

5. NTLDR processes BOOT.INI. BOOT.INI is a text file that resides in the root directory. It specifies what OSs are installed on the computer and where they reside on the disk. During this step of the boot process, you may be presented with a list of the installed OSs (depending on how your startup options are configured and whether you have multiple OSs installed). If you're presented with the list, you can choose an OS; if you don't take any action, the default selection is chosen automatically. If you have multiple OSs installed and you choose a DOS-based OS from the list (such as Windows 9*x*), NTLDR processes BOOTSECT.DOS and does a warm boot. The MBR code contained in

BOOTSECT.DOS is run after the computer goes through the POST, and IO.SYS is loaded, starting the DOS-based OS's boot process.

6. NTLDR loads and runs NTDETECT.COM. NTDETECT.COM checks the system for installed devices and device configurations and initializes the devices it finds. It passes the information to NTLDR, which collects this information and passes it to NTOSKRNL.EXE after that file is loaded.

7. NTLDR loads NTOSKRNL.EXE and HAL.DLL. NTOSKRNL.EXE holds the OS kernel and also what's known as the *executive subsystems*. Executive subsystems are software components that parse the Registry for configuration information and start needed services and drivers. HAL.DLL enables communication between the OS and the installed hardware.

8. NTLDR loads the HKEY_LOCAL_MACHINE\SYSTEM Registry hive and loads device drivers. The drivers that load at this time serve as boot drivers, using an initial value called a *start value*.

9. NTLDR transfers control to NTOSKRNL.EXE. NTOSKRNL.EXE initializes loaded drivers. It loads the Session Manager, which then loads the Windows subsystem, and completes the boot process.

10. Winlogon loads. At this point, you are presented with the Logon screen. After you enter a username and password, you're taken to the Windows Desktop.

Improper Shutdown

Not shutting down properly can result in lost data from open applications or corrupted operating system files. Neither option is good.

You would think that people are pretty aware of how to shut down, but sadly it's not always true. When it comes to your own computers, always shut down properly by clicking Start ➤ Turn Off Computer in Windows XP or the Shut Down icon on the Start menu in Windows 7/Vista.

If you are a technician at a company, it's your responsibility to train all users on how to properly shut down as well.

Spontaneous Shutdown/Restart

Occasionally, a rogue system will begin automatically shutting down and/or restarting while in use. While it could be indicative of a hardware problem (malfunctioning motherboard, for example), it can also indicate a setting misconfiguration problem. Check the sleep settings for hibernation and disable those to see if it makes a difference. If the problem continues, start looking at drivers.

 On server systems, check to see if any of the services have a recovery setting configured to restart the computer if a service failure is encountered.

To begin ruling out possibilities, boot the system into Safe Mode and see if the problem continues. If the problem does not occur while in Safe Mode, then boot normally and begin testing what occurs as you eliminate drivers/devices one by one (sound, video, etc.) until you find the culprit.

RAID Not Detected During Installation

A hardware RAID array is possible with Windows but occasionally is not recognized during the installation. A likely possibility is that the correct drivers for the version of Windows being used is not located. Download the drivers from the vendor and install them. During the Detect Hardware phase of the installation process, you can click Install Drivers (in Windows XP) or the button labeled Where Do You Want To Install Windows? (in Windows 7 and Windows Vista) and then choose the downloaded drivers (saved on a USB drive or other media).

Device Fails to Start

When you are using Windows, you are constantly interacting with pieces of hardware. Each piece of hardware has a Windows driver that must be loaded in order for Windows to be able to use it. In addition, the hardware must be installed and functioning properly. If the device driver is not installed properly or the hardware is misconfigured, the device won't function properly.

If you have just updated a driver and the device isn't functioning, rolling back the driver installation can sometimes solve the problem. To roll back a driver, right-click on the device name in Device Manager and choose Properties. On the Drivers tab, click the Roll Back Driver button.

Missing DLL

The dynamic link library (DLL) files are required (they were mentioned earlier in the section "Failure to Boot"). The problem of missing DLL files can also occur with applications when you attempt to start them and the solution involves finding a copy of the DLL (online, on a backup, etc.) and replacing it. A great article on the topic can be found at the following location:

www.makeuseof.com/tag/how-to-fix-missing-dll-file-errors/

Service Fails to Start

Once you have an application successfully installed, you may run into a problem getting it to start properly. This problem can come from any number of sources, including an improper installation, a software conflict, or system instability. If your application was installed incorrectly, the files required to properly run the program may not be present, and the program can't function without them. If a shared file that's used by other programs is installed, installation of the wrong (usually older) version can cause conflicts with other already installed programs. Finally, if one program causes a general protection fault (GPF), it can result in memory problems that can destabilize the system and cause other programs to crash. The solution to these problems is to uninstall and reinstall the offending application, first making sure that all programs are closed.

 Real World Scenario

Did You Reboot Your Computer?

Quick quiz: You just got an error in Windows, and it appears that you are on the verge of a crash (of your application or the whole system). What do you do?

The first thing is to write down any error messages that appear. Then, save your work (if possible) and reboot your computer.

Anyone who has called tech support, or who has been a tech support person, knows how demeaning the question, "Did you restart your computer?" can seem. Most people respond with an indignant, "Of course!" when the reality is they might or might not have actually done it.

Whenever there's a software problem, always, always reboot the computer before trying to troubleshoot. Often, the problem will disappear, and you'll have just saved yourself half an hour of frustration. If the same problem reappears, then you know you have work to do.

Why does rebooting help? When an application is running, it creates one or more temporary files that it uses to store information, and it also stores information in memory (RAM). If a temporary file or information in RAM becomes corrupted (such as by application A writing its information into application B's memory space), the application can have problems. Rebooting will clear the memory registers and most often remove problematic temporary files, thus eliminating the issue.

It might sound trite, but the first axiom in troubleshooting software really is to reboot. Even if the user says they did, ask them to reboot again. (Tell them you want to see the opening screen for any possible error messages, or make up another good excuse.) If the problem doesn't come back, it's not a problem. If it does, then you can use your software skills to fix it.

Compatibility Error

Device drivers are software programs that tell the operating system how to work with the hardware. When you purchase a hardware device, odds are it's been in that box for a while. By the time it gets made, packaged, stored, delivered to the store, stored again at the retailer, and then purchased by you, it's entirely likely that the company that made the device has updated the driver—even possibly a few times if there have been a lot of reported problems.

If your device driver is not digitally signed by Microsoft—that is, it hasn't been tested for *compatibility* with your version of Windows—then you will get a warning message when you attempt to install it. You can tell Windows to continue the installation, and most of the time this doesn't cause any problems. Be aware, though, that if the driver isn't signed or isn't compatible, that means that there could be problems with it after you complete the installation. We've installed dozens of unsigned drivers without problems, but we've also run across a few that didn't work as advertised.

In Windows 7/Vista, the User Account Control (UAC) feature has the sole purpose of keeping the user from running programs that could pose a potential threat by escalating privileges to that of Administrator. While turning UAC off is an option, it is not a recommended option. If you have a program you regularly run and do not want to be prompted each time, you can right-click the icon for that program and then click Properties. Choose the Compatibility tab and then select the Run This Program As An Administrator check box. This will prevent the prompt from occurring each time you use the program.

You are typically not able to set the UAC feature for operating system programs and the privileges will stayed grayed out on the Compatibility tab.

Slow System Performance

Over time, systems seem to run slower than they once did. This can be due to a plethora of drivers, lots of background processes, memory hogs, or many other possibilities. The first place to turn to help troubleshoot this problem is the Performance Troubleshooter.

In Windows 7, choose Start ➢ Control Panel ➢ Troubleshooting ➢ Check For Performance Issues (under System And Security). The Performance Troubleshooter will look for common problems such as more than one virus detection program running, multiple users logged into the same machine, visual settings affecting performance, and so on.

If no problems are found, then take the usual steps: deleting programs that are never run, removing items from startup, defragmenting the hard drive, and so on. Disk Cleanup can help you free up space by deleting unneeded files.

Boots to Safe Mode

At times a system will become corrupted to the point where it will only boot into Safe Mode and not allow a normal boot. While this can be caused by a hardware issue, it can often be associated with a damaged/missing driver. To address the problem, boot into the Recovery Console (see the section "Recovery Console" later in this chapter) and scan for problems. You can choose to boot to the last known good configuration or resort to the recovery DVD.

File Fails to Open

When a file fails to open, it is often due to corruption. The corruption can be caused from improperly shutting down the application or system. The best solution to this problem is to recover the file from a backup.

Missing *NTLDR*

The NTLDR loader file is a key component of the Windows XP boot process and the system will not boot without it. Occasionally, a message that the file is missing will occur if you change your active partition (which may be done if you are dual-booting with another operating system, such as Windows 7, for example). This message can also be triggered by a BOOT.INI file that points to the wrong location. In this case, the problem is not with the NTLDR file at all but with the misconfigured BOOT.INI.

The file can be retrieved from the Recovery Console or from bootable media (recovery DVD, repair disk, and so on).

Windows 7 and Windows Vista use the BOOTMGR instead and a similar message that will appear is that this file is missing. To resolve the problem, you can boot into System Recovery Options and choose Startup Repair (or type **bootrec /fixboot** at the command prompt).

Missing *BOOT.INI*

Windows XP uses the BOOT.INI file to identify the operating systems installed, their locations, and the boot options to use. It is a text-based file that can be (re)created using any text editor. When it is missing or damaged, you can recover it by booting into the Recovery Console.

Windows 7 and Windows Vista use the Windows Boot Configuration Data (BCD) file instead and a similar message that will appear is that this file is missing. To resolve the problem, you can boot into the System Recovery Options and choose Startup Repair (or type **bootrec /rebuildbcd** at the command prompt).

Missing Operating System

The first thing to check when it's reported that an operating system is missing is that there is not media in the machine (DVD, CD, and so on) that the system is reading during boot prior to accessing the hard drive. If that is the case, remove the media and reboot (down the road, change the BIOS settings to boot from the hard drive before any other media).

If there is no removable media attempting to boot, then turn to the installation DVD (you may have to set the BIOS to use the DVD drive as your primary boot device) or the Windows Repair CD. In Windows 7 or Windows Vista, go to System Recovery Options and choose Startup Repair.

Missing Graphical Interface/GUI Fails to Load

Occasionally, the Windows graphical user interface (GUI) won't appear. The system will hang just before the GUI appears. This is caused by missing or corrupt files, and the best tool to turn to is the Windows Repair CD or the installation DVD. In Windows 7 or Windows Vista, go to System Recovery Options and choose Startup Repair.

Invalid Boot Disk

Remove any media in the machine (DVD, CD, and so on) that the system is reading during boot prior to accessing the hard drive and reboot. If that solves the problem, change the BIOS settings to make the hard drive the primary boot device. If that does not solve the problem, turn to the installation DVD (you may have to set the BIOS to use the DVD drive as your primary boot device) or the Windows Repair CD. In Windows 7 or Windows Vista, go to System Recovery Options and choose Startup Repair.

Operating System Tools

Many of the tools needed for troubleshooting appear in the objectives pertaining to the operating systems as well. Chapter 12, "Operating System Basics," and Chapter 13, "Operating System Administration," introduced and discussed many of the operating system tools. To avoid needless repetition, only new information or topics not previously fully covered are addressed here.

Recovery Console

The Recovery Console is a Windows XP command-line utility used for troubleshooting (System Recovery Options serve a similar purpose with Windows 7 and Windows Vista). From it, you can format drives, stop and start services, and interact with files. The latter is extremely important because many boot/command-line utilities bring you into a position where you can interact with files stored on FAT or FAT32 but not NTFS. The Recovery Console can work with files stored on all three file systems.

The Recovery Console isn't installed on a system by default. To install it, use the following steps:

1. Place the Windows CD in the system.

2. From a command prompt, change to the i386 directory of the CD.

3. Type `winnt32 /cmdcons`.

4. A prompt appears alerting you to the fact that 7MB of hard drive space is required and asking if you want to continue. Click Yes.

Upon successful completion of the installation, the Recovery Console is added as a menu choice at the bottom of the startup menu. To access it, you must choose it from the list at startup. If more than one installation of Windows exists on the system, another boot menu will appear, asking which you want to boot into, and you must make a selection to continue.

To perform this task, you must enter the administrator password. You'll then arrive at a command prompt. You can give a number of commands from this prompt, two of which are worth special attention: EXIT restarts the computer, and HELP lists the commands you can give. Table 19.1 lists the other commands available, most of which will be familiar to administrators who have worked with MS-DOS.

TABLE 19.1 Recovery Console commands

Command	Purpose
ATTRIB	Shows the current attributes of a file or folder, and lets you change them.
BATCH	Runs the commands within an ASCII text file.
BOOTCFG	Build or rebuild BOOT.INI.
CD	Used without parameters, it shows the current directory. Used with parameters, it changes to the directory specified.
CHDIR	Works the same as CD.
CHKDSK	Checks the disk for errors.
CLS	Clears the screen.
COPY	Allows you to copy a file (or files, if used with wildcards) from one location to another.
DEL	Deletes a file.
DELTREE	Recursively deletes files and directories.
DIR	Shows the contents of the current directory.
DISABLE	Allows you to stop a service/driver.
DISKPART	Shows the partitions on the drive, and lets you manage them.
EXPAND	Extracts compressed files.
ENABLE	Allows you to start a service/driver.
FIXBOOT	Writes a new boot sector.
FIXMBR	Checks and fixes (if possible) the master boot record.

Command	Purpose
FORMAT	Allows you to format media or a partition.
LISTSVC	Shows the services/drivers on the system.
LOGON	Lets you log on.
MAP	Shows the maps currently created.
MD	Makes a new folder/directory.
MKDIR	Works the same as MD.
MORE	Shows only one screen of a text file at a time.
NET USE	Map network drives.
RD	Removes a directory or folder.
REN	Renames a file or folder.
RENAME	Works the same as REN.
RMDIR	Works the same as RD.
SYSTEMROOT	Works like CD but takes you to the system root of whichever OS installation you're logged on to.
TYPE	Displays the contents of an ASCII text file.

During the installation of the Recovery Console, a folder named CMDCONS is created in the root directory to hold the executable files and drivers it needs. A file named CMLDR, with attributes of System, Hidden, and Read-Only, is also placed in the root directory.

If you want to delete the Recovery Console (to prevent users from playing around, for example), you can do so by deleting the CMLDR file and the CMDCONS folder, and removing the entry from the BOOT.INI file.

For the exam, know that *FIXBOOT* is an option in the Recovery Console that writes a new boot sector on the system partition. *FIXMBR* is another option that checks and fixes the master boot record. With Windows 7 and Windows Vista, use the command-line commands BOOTREC /FIXBOOT and BOOTREC /FIXMBR to accomplish the same. Lastly, BOOTCFG does a similar job to BOOTREC /REBUILDBCD.

SFC

The purpose of this utility is to keep the operating system alive and well. SFC.EXE automatically verifies system files after a reboot to see if they were changed to unprotected copies. If an unprotected file is found, it's overwritten by a stored copy of the system file. In Windows 7 and Windows Vista, that comes from C:\Windows\winsxs\Backup, and in Windows XP it comes from %systemroot%\system32\dllcache. (%systemroot% is the folder into which the operating system was installed.)

Storing system files (some of which can be quite large) in two locations consumes a large amount of disk space. When you install an operating system, make sure you leave ample hard drive space on the drive where %systemroot% resides for growth.

Only users with the administrative permissions can run SFC. It also requires the use of a parameter. The valid parameters are as follows:

Parameter	Function
/CACHSIZE=	Sets the size of the file cache
/CANCEL	Stops all checks
/ENABLE	Returns to normal mode
/PURGECACHE	Clears the cache
/QUIET	Replaces files without prompting
/SCANBOOT	Checks system files on every boot
/SCANNOW	Checks system files now
/SCANONCE	Checks system files at the next boot

Repair Disks

If you want to recover your computer and bring it back to the point where it was when it was new (minus any files you added since purchasing the machine), you can use the recovery CD set or DVD. With Dell computers, for example, this is known as the Reinstallation DVD and accompanies each machine shipped; it can be used only to reinstall the operating system on the machine. After the Reinstallation DVD finishes, you must then use a similar DVD to reinstall the applications that were on the machine when it shipped.

Use the recovery sets only when nothing else seems to work and you are ready to start from scratch.

In Windows 7, you can create a system repair disc from the Backup and Restore interface (beneath the Control Panel options for System And Security). The system repair disc can be used to boot the computer and will contain the system recovery tools.

Pre-installation Environments

The Windows Pre-installation Environment (Windows PE) is a minimal Win32 OS running the Windows 7 kernel that is intended to be a stub that can be run on a machine to allow it to then begin an installation. As such, you can think of it as a bootable OS for the Windows Recovery Environment or installation deployment through System Center Configuration Manager (SCCM), Systems or Windows Deployment Services (WDS).

This is the operating system booted into when recovery or installation is necessary.

The technical reference for Windows PE can be found at the following location:

`http://technet.microsoft.com/en-us/library/dd744322(WS.10).aspx`

MSCONFIG

This utility helps troubleshoot startup problems by allowing you to selectively disable individual items that normally are executed at startup. There is no menu command for this utility; you must run it with the Run command (on the Start menu). Choose Start ➢ Run, and type **MSCONFIG**. It works in most versions of Windows, although the interface window is slightly different among versions.

DEFRAG

When you save files to a hard drive, Windows will generally write the file into the first available space on the disk. So let's say you create an Excel spreadsheet and save it. It will be written to the disk. Next, you create a dozen new Word documents and save them as well. Then, you go back and add a ton of data to your spreadsheet. Now the Excel file is much bigger. Instead of moving it all to a space on the hard drive big enough to handle the file, Windows will keep part of the file in its original location and write the rest of the data to another available space on the hard drive. When a file is in several places on a disk, it's called a *fragmented* file. Excessive fragmentation of your files can slow down your computer's performance.

Defragmenting a disk involves analyzing the disk and then consolidating fragmented files and folders so they occupy a contiguous space, thus increasing performance during file retrieval. In Windows there are a few different ways you can get to the Disk Defragmenter:

- In Windows 7/Vista, click Start and type **defrag** into the Start Search box. Choose Disk Defragmenter from the Programs list.

- In Windows, open Computer or My Computer, right-click on a hard drive, choose Properties, select the Tools tab, and click Defragment Now (Figure 19.1).

- In Windows XP, open Computer Management (right-click My Computer and choose Manage) and select Disk Defragmenter from the Storage section.

When you open Disk Defragmenter in Windows 7 or Vista, the first page gives you options for scheduling defragmentation, as shown in Figure 19.2.

FIGURE 19.1   Click Defragment Now.

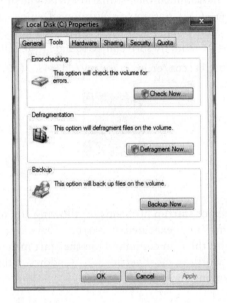

FIGURE 19.2   Disk Defragmenter

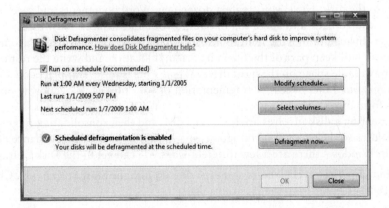

Microsoft recommends that you enable scheduled defragmentation. If you want to defragment immediately, click the Defragment Now button.

Windows XP does not give you the option to schedule defragmentation through Disk Defragmenter. To run a defrag in XP, highlight the appropriate drive, as shown in Figure 19.3, and click the Defragment button. If you're not sure whether the drive needs to be defragmented, you can click Analyze instead, which will provide you with a report on how fragmented your drive is.

There are two versions of Disk Defragmenter: a command-line version and a Windows version that runs from within Windows. The Windows version is located on the System Tools submenu on the Start menu (Start ➤ All Programs ➤ Accessories ➤ System Tools ➤ Disk Defragmenter). In Exercise 19.1, you will run the Disk Defragmenter in Windows 7; Exercise 19.2 mirrors these actions in Windows XP.

FIGURE 19.3   Disk Defragmenter in Windows XP

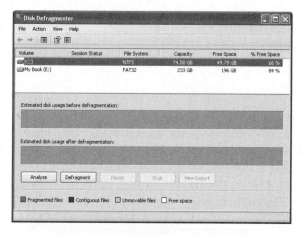

EXERCISE 19.1

Run Disk Defragmenter in Windows 7

1. Choose Start ➤ All Programs ➤ Accessories ➤ System Tools ➤ Disk Defragmenter.

2. If you are prompted by UAC to continue, choose to do so. The Disk Defragmenter utility will appear.

3. Click the Defragment Now button. This will work only if this is the first time the tool has been used. If you have already used it, you have the Analyze option available and can pick a drive and then click Defragment disk.

4. Choose the disks to defragment and click OK.

5. Exit Disk Defragmenter.

EXERCISE 19.2

Run Disk Defragmenter in Windows XP

1. Choose Start ➢ All Programs ➢ Accessories ➢ System Tools ➢ Disk Defragmenter. The Disk Defragmenter utility will appear.

2. Choose the disks to defragment and click Analyze. The results will tell you if the possible changes are worth doing.

3. If the analysis suggests that you should defragment, click the Defragment button.

4. Upon completion, exit Disk Defragmenter.

These are some of the available switches for the command-line version (`defrag.exe`):

-a   Analyze only

-f   Force defragmentation even if disk space is low

-v   Verbose output

REGSVR32

`REGSVR32.EXE`, known as the RegSvr32 tool, allows you to register and unregister modules and controls for troubleshooting purposes. It is often associated with Internet Explorer, but it can be used with any control or module. The command-line syntax is `regsvr32 dllname` and Figure 19.4 shows the options that are available with it.

FIGURE 19.4   RegSvr32 options

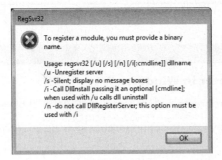

REGEDIT

The Registry Editor is used to change values and variables stored in a configuration database known as the Registry. This centralized database contains environmental settings for various Windows programs along with registration information, which details the types of filename extensions associated with applications so when you double-click a file in Windows Explorer, the associated application runs and opens the file.

The Registry Editor, shown in Figure 19.5, enables you to make changes to the large hierarchical database that contains all of Windows's settings. These changes can potentially disable the entire system, so they should not be made lightly.

There is no menu command for the Registry Editor. You must run it with the Run command. Regedit is the name of the program. Windows also includes a second Registry Editor program called Regedt32. This alternative program accesses the same Registry but does so in a slightly different way; it shows each of the major key areas in a separate window. In Windows XP and newer operating systems, the command REGEDT32 is present, but running it launches Regedit; they have been rolled into a single utility.

FIGURE 19.5 The Registry Editor in Windows XP

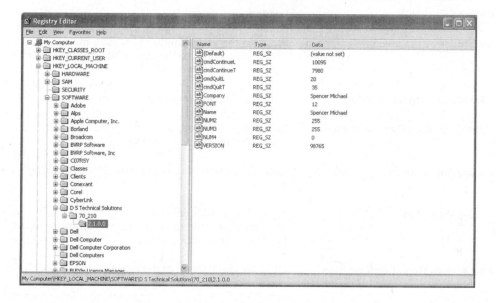

The Registry holds great power but can also cause great harm. Never edit the Registry without being completely sure what you're doing.

Event Viewer

This utility provides information about what's been going on with the whole system to help you troubleshoot problems. Event Viewer shows warnings, error messages, and records of things that have happened successfully. It's found in all current versions of Windows (which include Windows 7, Windows XP, and Windows Vista). You can access it through Computer Management, or you can access it directly from the Administrative Tools in Control Panel.

Safe Mode

If, when you boot, Windows won't load completely (it hangs or is otherwise corrupted), you can often solve the problem by booting into Safe Mode. Safe Mode is a concept borrowed from Windows 95 wherein you can bring up part of the operating system by bypassing the settings, drivers, or parameters that may be causing it trouble during a normal boot. The goal of Safe Mode is to provide an interface with which you're able to fix the problems that occur during a normal boot and then reboot in normal mode.

To access Safe Mode, you must press F8 when the operating system menu is displayed during the boot process. You'll then see a menu of Safe Mode choices, listed in Table 19.2. Select the mode you want to boot into.

TABLE 19.2   Windows Advanced Boot Options

Choice	Loaded
Safe Mode	Provides the VGA monitor, Microsoft mouse drivers, and basic drivers for the keyboard (storage system services, no networking).
Safe Mode With Networking	Same as Safe Mode, but with networking.
Safe Mode With Command Prompt	Same as Safe Mode, but without the interface and drivers/services associated with it.
Enable Boot Logging	Creates NTBTLOG.TXT in the root directory during any boot.
Enable VGA Mode	Normal boot with only basic video drivers. In Windows 7 and Windows Vista, this option is called Enable low-resolution video.
Last Known Good Configuration	Uses the last backup of the Registry to bypass corruption caused during the previous session.
Disable automatic restart on system failure	Disables automatic restarting and is helpful when troubleshooting.
Debugging Mode	Sends information through the serial port for interpretation/troubleshooting at another computer.
Start Windows Normally	Bypasses any of the options here.
Return To OS Choices Menu	Gives you an out in case you pressed F8 by accident.

You need to keep a few rules in mind when booting in different modes:

- If problems don't exist when you boot to Safe Mode but do exist when you boot to normal mode, the problem isn't with basic services/drivers.
- If the system hangs when you load drivers, the log file can show you the last driver it attempted to load, which is usually the cause of the problem.
- If you can't solve the problem with Safe Mode, restore the Registry to a state known to be good. Bear in mind that in doing so you will lose all changes that have occurred since the last ERD was made.

Command Prompt

The command prompt has been mentioned numerous times in this chapter and is the environment in which you can run many troubleshooting utilities. This can be started by typing CMD at the Run prompt on the Start menu. Figure 19.6 shows an example of the command prompt interface.

If you will be regularly running commands as Administrator, you can create an icon on the desktop for the executable (CMD.EXE) and configure on the Advanced section of the Shortcut tab to run the program as Administrator.

FIGURE 19.6   The command prompt interface in Windows 7

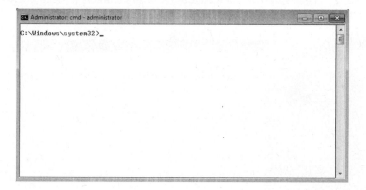

Automated System Recovery

It's possible to automate the process of creating a system recovery set by choosing the ASR Wizard on the Tools menu of the Backup utility (Start ➢ All Programs ➢ Accessories ➢ System Tools ➢ Backup).

In Windows 7, the option Backup And Restore appears beneath the Control Panel options for System And Security. To make it equally confusing, in Windows Vista, Backup appears as Backup Status And Configuration.

This wizard walks you through the process of creating a disk that can be used to restore parts of the system in the event of a major system failure.

The default name of this file is BACKUP.BKF. The backup set contains all the files necessary for starting the system.

Troubleshooting Security Issues

Many viruses will announce that your system is infected as soon as they gain access to it. They may take control of your system and flash annoying messages on your screen or destroy your hard disk. When this occurs, you'll know that you're a victim. Other viruses will cause your system to slow down, cause files to disappear from your computer, or take over your disk space. The Windows Security Center, shown in Figure 19.7, can show you what security measures are set on your system.

Viruses are the most common type of malware. In this section, we use the term *virus* to refer to many types of malware.

FIGURE 19.7   The Windows Security Center offers a quick glimpse of current protection settings.

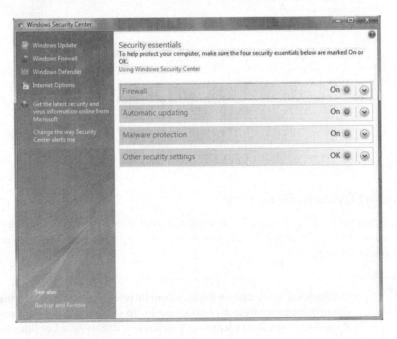

You should look for some of the following symptoms when determining if a virus infection has occurred:

- The programs on your system start to load more slowly. This happens because the virus is spreading to other files in your system or is taking over system resources.

- Unusual files appear on your hard drive, or files start to disappear from your system. Many viruses delete key files in your system to render it inoperable.

- Program sizes change from the installed versions. This occurs because the virus is attaching itself to these programs on your disk.

- Your browser, word processing application, or other software begins to exhibit unusual operating characteristics. Screens or menus may change.

- The system mysteriously shuts itself down or starts itself up and a great deal of unanticipated disk activity occurs.

- You mysteriously lose access to a disk drive or other system resources. The virus has changed the settings on a device to make it unusable.

- Your system suddenly doesn't reboot or gives unexpected error messages during startup.

- You notice an *X* in the system tray over the icon for your virus scanner, or the icon for the scanner disappears from the system tray altogether.

This list is by no means comprehensive. What is an absolute, however, is the fact that you should immediately quarantine the infected system. It is imperative that you do all you can to contain the virus and keep it from spreading to other systems within your network, or beyond. Many enterprises have a no-tolerance (zero tolerance) policy for infected systems and they are always flattened.

 Establishing security policies and procedures, updating your operating systems, updating your applications, and updating your network devices are all good measures to take to help eliminate potential security problems and cannot be overstated.

Common Symptoms

There are a number of common symptoms CompTIA expects you to know for the 220-802 exam when it comes to security issues. Many of these issues also appear in other CompTIA certification exams, namely Security+. Rest assured that for the 220-802 exam, you do not need to know the content as well as you would if you were preparing for the Security+ exam.

Pop-Ups

Pop-ups (also commonly known as popups) are both frustrating and chancy. When a user visits a website and another instance (either another tab or another browser window) is opened in the foreground, it is called a pop-up; if it opens in the background, it is called a pop-under. Both pop-ups and pop-unders are pages or sites that you did not specifically request and may only display ads or bring up applets that should be avoided.

Pop-up blockers are used to prevent both pop-ups and pop-unders from appearing. While older browsers did not incorporate an option to block pop-ups, most newer browsers, including the latest versions of Internet Explorer, now have that capability built in.

Browser Redirection

Pharming is a form of redirection in which traffic intended for one host is sent to another. This can be accomplished on a small scale by changing entries in the hosts file, and on a large scale by changing entries in a DNS server (poisoning). In either case, when a user attempts to go to a site, they are redirected to another. For example, suppose Illegitimate Company ABC creates a site to look exactly like the one for Giant Bank XYZ. The pharming is done (using either redirect method) and users trying to reach Giant Bank XYZ are tricked to going to Illegitimate Company ABC's site, which looks enough like what they are used to seeing that they give username and password data.

As soon as Giant Bank XYZ realizes that the traffic is being redirected, it will immediately move to stop it. But while Illegitimate Company ABC will be shut down, it was able to collect data for the length of time the redirection occurred, which could vary from minutes to days.

Security Alerts

Users have plenty of real viruses and other issues to worry about. Yet some people find it entertaining to issue phony threats disguised as *security alerts* to keep people on their toes. Some of the more popular hoaxes that have been passed around are the Good Time and the Irina viruses. Millions of users received emails about these two viruses, and the symptoms sounded awful.

Both of these warnings claimed that the viruses would do things that are impossible to accomplish with a virus. When you receive a virus warning, you can verify its authenticity by looking on the website of the antivirus software you use, or you can go to several public systems. One of the more helpful sites to visit to get the status of the latest viruses is the CERT organization (`www.cert.org`). CERT monitors and tracks viruses and provides regular reports on this site.

Though the names are similar, there is a difference between cert.org and us-cert.gov. While the latter is a government site for the United States Computer Emergency Readiness Team, the former is a federally funded research and development center at Carnegie Mellon University.

When you receive an email you suspect is a hoax, check the CERT site before forwarding the message to anyone else. The creator of the hoax wants to create widespread panic, and if you blindly forward the message to co-workers and acquaintances, you're helping the creator accomplish this task. For example, any email that includes "forward to all your friends" is a candidate for hoax research. Disregarding the hoax allows it to die a quick death and keeps users focused on productive tasks. Any concept that spreads quickly through the Internet is referred to as a *meme*.

Identifying a Hoax

Symantec and other vendors maintain pages devoted to bogus hoaxes:

www.symantec.com/business/security_response/threatexplorer/risks/ hoaxes.jsp

You can always check there to verify whether an email you've received is indeed a hoax.

Slow Performance

Slow performance was addressed previously in this chapter in relation to operating system issues. Viruses, worms, and other malware can slow performance because they rob resources from the other applications and services forced to share.

Internet Connectivity Issues

If your computer is hooked up to a network (and more and more computers today are), you need to know when your computer is not functioning on the network properly and what to do about it. In most cases, the problem can be attributed to either a malfunctioning network interface card (NIC) or improperly installed network software. The biggest indicator in Windows that some component of the network software is nonfunctional is that you can't log on to the network or access any network service. To fix this problem, you must first fix the underlying hardware problem (if one exists) and then properly install or configure the network software.

PC Locks Up

It is obvious when a system lockup occurs. The system simply stops responding to commands and stops processing completely. System lockups can occur when a computer is asked to process too many instructions at once with too little memory. Usually, the cure for a system lock-up is to reboot. If the lockups are persistent, it may be a hardware-related problem instead of a software problem.

Remember that there are two universal solutions to Windows problems: rebooting and obtaining an update from the software manufacturer. If neither of these solutions work, it could be hardware causing the problem.

Real World Scenario

Dr. Watson?

Windows XP includes a special utility known as Dr. Watson. This utility intercepts all error conditions and, instead of presenting the user with a cryptic Windows error, displays a slew of information that can be used to troubleshoot the problem. This is probably most useful if you have programming skills and want to debug the program that caused the error. Windows 7 and Windows Vista do not include Dr. Watson for debugging. In those versions of Windows, the program is called Problem Reports And Solutions.

Windows Update Failures

Failed updates for Windows—assuming they are not caused by connectivity issues—can often be traced to setting misconfigurations. These settings can also cause the operating system to report that an update needs to be installed when it has already been installed. The best solution is to find the error code being reported in Windows Update Troubleshooter, solve the problem, and download the update.

For information on addressing this problem with both Windows Update and Microsoft Office, see the knowledge base article at `http://support.microsoft.com/kb/906602`.

Rogue Antivirus

One of the more clever ways of spreading a virus is to disguise it so that it looks like an antivirus program. When it alerts the user to a fictitious problem, the user then begins interacting with the program and allowing the rogue program to do all sorts of damage. One of the more tricky things for miscreants to do is make the program look as if it came from a trusted source—such as Microsoft—and mimic the Windows Security Center interface enough to fool an unsuspecting user.

Microsoft offers a page on fake virus alerts that can be helpful in sharing with employees to help educate them of what to be aware of at the following location:

`http://www.microsoft.com/security/pc-security/antivirus-rogue.aspx`

Spam

While *spam* is not truly a virus or a hoax, it is one of the most annoying things an administrator can contend with. Spam is defined as any unwanted, unsolicited email, and not only can the sheer volume of it be irritating, it can often open the door to larger problems. For instance, some of the sites advertised in spam may be infected with viruses, worms, and other unwanted programs. If users begin to respond to spam by visiting those sites, then viruses and other problems will multiply in your system.

There are numerous antispam programs available, and they can be run by users as well as administrators. One of the biggest problems with many of these applications is false positives: They will occasionally flag legitimate email as spam and stop it from being delivered. You should routinely check your spam folders and make sure legitimate email is not being flagged and held there.

Just as you can, and must, install good antivirus software programs, you should also consider similar measures for spam. Filtering the messages out and preventing them from ever entering the network is the most effective method of dealing with the problem. Recently, the word *spam* has found its way into other forms of unwanted messaging beyond email, giving birth to the acronyms SPIM (spam over Instant Messaging) and SPIT (spam over Internet Telephony).

Renamed System Files/Disappearing Files/Permission Changes/Access Denied

Creators of malware have a number of methods by which they can wreak havoc on a system. One of the simplest ways is to delete key system files. When this occurs, the user can no longer perform the operation associated with the file, such as print, save, and so on. Just as harmful as deleting a file is to rename it or change the permissions associated with it so the user can no longer access it or perform those operations.

Hijacked Email

One of the easiest ways to spread malware is to capture the email contacts of a user and send it as an attachment to all of those in their circle. The recipient is more likely to open the attachment because it seemingly comes from a trusted source.

Security Tools

Recovery Console, pre-installation environments, and Event Viewer were all discussed earlier in the chapter.

Antivirus Software

This type of preventive maintenance is absolutely critical these days if you have a connection to the Internet. A *computer virus* is a small, deviously ingenious program that replicates itself to other computers, generally causing those computers to behave abnormally. Generally speaking, a virus's main function is to reproduce. A virus attaches itself to files on a hard disk and modifies those files. When the files are accessed by a program, the virus can infect the program with its own code. The program may then, in turn, replicate the virus code to other files and other programs. In this manner, a virus may infect an entire computer.

When an infected file is transferred to another computer (via disk or download), the process begins on the other computer. Because of the frequency of downloads from the Internet, viruses can run rampant if left unchecked. For this reason, antivirus programs were developed. They check files and programs for any program code that shouldn't be there and either eradicate it or prevent the virus from replicating. An antivirus program is generally run in the background on a computer, and it examines all the file activity on that computer. When it detects a suspicious activity, it notifies the user of a potential problem and asks the user what to do about it. Some antivirus programs can also make intelligent decisions about what to do. The process of running an antivirus program on a computer is known as *inoculating* the computer against a virus.

For a listing of most of the viruses that are currently out there, refer to Symantec's AntiVirus Research Center (SARC) at `www.symantec.com/security_response/`.

You may notice that a lot of the language surrounding computer viruses sounds like language we use to discuss human illness. The moniker *virus* was given to these programs because a computer virus functions much like a human virus, and the term helped to anthropomorphize the computer a bit. Somehow, if people can think of a computer as getting sick, it breaks down the computer phobia that many people have.

There are two categories of viruses: benign and malicious. Benign viruses don't do much besides replicate themselves and exist. They may cause the occasional problem, but it is usually an unintentional side effect. Malicious viruses, on the other hand, are designed to destroy things. Once a malicious virus (for example, the Michelangelo virus) infects your machine, you can usually kiss the contents of your hard drive goodbye.

To prevent virus-related problems, you can install one of any number of antivirus programs (Norton AntiVirus or McAfee VirusScan, for example). These programs will periodically scan your computer for viruses, monitor regular use of the computer, and note any suspicious activity that might indicate a virus. In addition, these programs have a database of known viruses and the symptoms each one causes.

Antivirus databases should be updated frequently (about once a week, although more often is better) to keep your antivirus program up to date with all the possible virus definitions. Most antivirus programs will automatically update themselves (if configured properly) just as Windows Update will update Windows, provided that the computer has a live Internet connection. It's a good idea to let them automatically update, just in case you forget to do it yourself.

Anti-Malware Software

There are many other forms of malware in addition to viruses. While a true antivirus program will scan for viruses, anti-malware programs are a superset of virus scanners and will look for more than just traditional viruses. One program included with Windows that falls into this category is Windows Defender, which is mainly a spyware detector (Microsoft Security Essentials is also available for Windows XP/Vista/7).

As with similar programs, for Windows Defender to function properly, you need to keep the definitions current and scan on a regular basis. In Exercise 19.3, you'll run Windows Defender (shown in Figure 19.8) in Windows 7; Exercise 19.4 mirrors these actions using Windows XP.

FIGURE 19.8   Windows Defender can identify security threats.

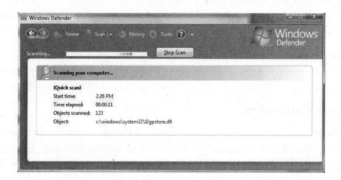

EXERCISE 19.3

Run Windows Defender in Windows 7

1.   Choose Start ➢ Control Panel ➢ Security ➢ Windows Defender.

2.   If you are prompted that Defender is not configured, choose to turn it on (this will bring up a UAC prompt to continue if UAC is toggled on).

3.   From the drop-down list next to Help (a question mark in a blue circle), choose Check For Updates (again, if UAC is toggled on, you will be prompted to continue).

EXERCISE 19.3 *(continued)*

4. Click Scan.

5. Upon completion, the message *Your computer is running normally* should appear within the frame labeled No Unwanted Or Harmful Software Detected. If anything else appears, resolve those issues.

6. Exit Windows Defender.

EXERCISE 19.4

Run Windows Defender in Windows XP

1. Choose Start ➢ Control Panel ➢ Security ➢ Software Explorers. Windows Defender will appear. If Windows Defender is not currently installed on the XP workstation, download it from Microsoft.

2. From the drop-down list next to Help (a question mark in a blue circle), choose Check For Updates.

3. Click Scan.

4. Upon completion, the message *Your computer is running normally* should appear within the frame labeled No Unwanted Or Harmful Software Detected. If anything else appears, resolve those issues.

5. Exit Windows Defender.

Anti-Spyware Software

A subset of malware is spyware. *Spyware* differs from other malware in that it works—often actively—on behalf of a third party. Rather than self-replicating, like viruses and worms, spyware is spread to machines by users who inadvertently ask for it. The users often do not know they have asked for it but have acquired it by downloading other programs, visiting infected sites, and so on.

The spyware program monitors the user's activity and responds by offering unsolicited pop-up advertisements (which fit into the category known as *adware*), gathers information about the user to pass on to marketers, or intercepts personal data such as credit card numbers. One thing separating spyware from most other malware is that it almost always exists to provide commercial gain. The operating systems from Microsoft are the ones most affected by spyware, and Microsoft has released Microsoft Security Essentials and Windows Defender to combat the problem. This spyware/adware interface works similar to most antivirus programs and uses a definition file that must be updated regularly to locate malware. You can also join the SpyNet community to help with isolating and reducing the problem. In Exercise 19.5, we'll show you how to join the Microsoft SpyNet using Windows Defender.

EXERCISE 19.5

Join Microsoft SpyNet using Windows Defender

1. Click the Windows Start button.

2. Type **Windows Defender** in the Start Search box and choose it from the list of programs that appear. If it is not currently running, click the link to turn it on.

3. In Windows Defender, click Tools.

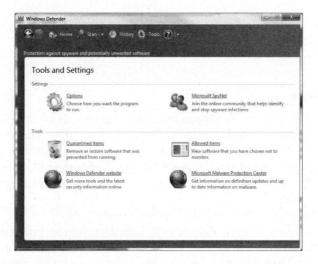

4. Click Microsoft SpyNet.

5. If Join With A Basic Membership or Join With An Advanced Membership is not already selected, read the options and make the choice you are comfortable with.

6. Click Save.

7. Exit Windows Defender.

System Restore

There are times when bad things happen to good computers. No matter how hard you've tried to keep a system running flawlessly, your computer crashes. There are several ways to get your computer back up and running, but many of them (such as reinstalling the operating system) take a lot of time. A new feature called System Restore was introduced with Windows XP, and it allows you to create restore points to make recovery of the operating system easier.

A *restore point* is a copy of your system configuration at a given point in time. It's like a backup of your configuration but not necessarily your data. Restore points are created one of three ways. One, Windows creates them automatically by default. Two, you can manually create them yourself. Three, during the installation of some programs, a restore point is created before the installation (that way, if the install fails, you can "roll back" the system to a preinstallation configuration). Restore points are useful for when Windows fails to boot but the computer appears to be fine otherwise or if Windows doesn't seem to be acting right and you think it was because of a recent configuration change.

To open System Restore, click Start ➤ All Programs ➤ Accessories ➤ System Tools ➤ System Restore. It will open a screen like the one in Figure 19.9. By clicking Next, you can choose a restore point.

You'll notice that checkpoints are included in the list of restore points along with backups that you have performed.

If you need to use a restore point and Windows won't boot, you can reboot into Safe Mode. After Safe Mode loads, you will have the option to work in Safe Mode or to use System Restore. Choose System Restore and you'll be presented with restore points (if any) you can use.

Creating a restore point manually is easy to do using the System Restore utility. In Exercise 19.6, we'll walk through the process of creating a restore point in Windows Vista.

FIGURE 19.9   System Restore

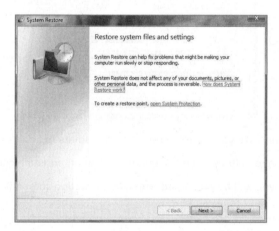

EXERCISE 19.6

Creating a Restore Point in Windows Vista

1. Open System Restore by clicking Start ➤ All Programs ➤ Accessories ➤ System Tools ➤ System Restore.

EXERCISE 19.6 *(continued)*

2. Click the Open System Protection link. (You can also get to System Protection by right-clicking My Computer, choosing Properties, and then selecting the System Protection tab. This is the method to use with Windows 7.)

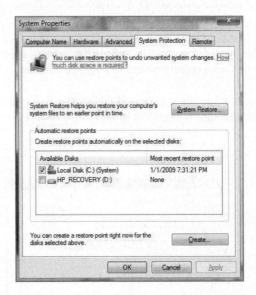

3. Choose the disk or disks you want to create restore points for, and then click Create.

4. Type a description to help you identify the restore point, and then click Create.

5. Within a minute, you will be presented with a confirmation screen with the time, date, and name of your restore point.

Exercise 19.7 shows you how to create restore points in Windows XP.

EXERCISE 19.7

Creating a Restore Point in Windows XP

1. Open System Restore by clicking Start ➢ All Programs ➢ Accessories ➢ System Tools ➢ System Restore.

2. Choose Create A Restore Point, and click Next.

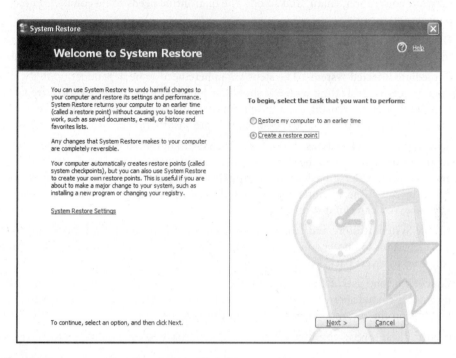

3. Provide a restore point description. Click Create.

4. Within a minute, you will be presented with a confirmation screen with the time, date, and name of your restore point.

Best Practices of Malware Removal

Rounding out this chapter is a discussion of the best practices for malware removal. The best way to think of this is as a seven-item list of what CompTIA wants you to consider when approaching a possible malware infestation. The following discussion presents the information you need to know in just that fashion.

1. **Identify malware symptoms.** Before doing anything major, it is imperative to first be sure that you are dealing with the right issue. If you suspect malware, then try to identify the type (spyware, virus, and so on) and look for the proof needed to substantiate that it is indeed the culprit.

2. **Quarantine infected system.** Once you have confirmed that malware is at hand, then quarantine the system infected to prevent it from spreading the malware to other systems. Bear in mind that malware can spread any number of ways, including through a network connection, email, and so on. The quarantine needs to be complete enough to prevent any spread.

3. **Disable System Restore.** This is a necessary step because you do not want to have the infected system create a restore point—or return to one—where the infection exists.

4. **Remediate infected systems.** The steps taken here need to be dependent upon the type of malware you're dealing with but should include updating antivirus software with the latest definitions and using the appropriate scan and removal techniques. The latter can include booting into safe mode, booting to a pre-installation environment, and so on.

5. **Schedule scans and updates.** The odds of the system never being confronted by malware again are slim. To reduce the chances of it being infected again, though, schedule scans and updates to run regularly. Most anti-malware programs can be configured to automatically run at specific intervals, but should you encounter one that does not have such a feature, you can run it through Task Scheduler.

6. **Enable System Restore and create a restore point.** Once everything is working properly, it is important to once again create restore points should a future problem occur and you need to revert back.

7. **Educate the end user.** Education should always be viewed as the final step. The end user needs to understand what led to the malware infestation and what to avoid, or look for, in the future to keep it from happening again.

Together, these seven steps offer a best practices approach to confronting malware removal.

Summary

This chapter was about systematic approaches to working with computers as well as troubleshooting operating systems and security issues. The first topic was troubleshooting theory, the second was operating system issues, and the third was security-related.

In our discussion of troubleshooting theory, you learned that you need to take a systematic approach to problem solving. There is both art and science involved, and experience in troubleshooting is helpful but not a prerequisite to being a good troubleshooter. You learned that in troubleshooting, the first objective is to identify the problem. Many times this can be the most time-consuming task!

Once you've identified the problem, you need to establish a theory of why the problem is happening, test your theories, establish a plan of action, verify full functionality, and then document your work. Documentation is frequently the most overlooked aspect of working with computers, but it's an absolutely critical step!

Next we discussed operating system troubleshooting issues. First, we looked at common symptoms of trouble and followed that by discussing tools that can be helpful in solving problems.

Last, we looked at security troubleshooting issues. Again, we started by looking at common issues, then turned to tools. The discussion concluded by looking at the best practices for malware removal.

Exam Essentials

Know the steps to take in troubleshooting computers. First identify the problem. Then establish a theory of probable cause, test your theory, establish a plan of action to resolve the problem, verify full system functionality, and finally, document your findings.

Understand how to talk to the customer. Questions should be nonaccusatory and neutral in tone. Seek to understand what happened, but be careful to not blame the users because they may become defensive and not give you the information you need to solve the problem.

Know how to create restore points. Restore points in Windows 7, Vista, and XP are created through the System Restore utility and the System Protection tab.

Review Questions

The answers to the Chapter Review Questions can be found in Appendix A.

1. In Windows 7, which utility is responsible for finding, downloading, and installing Windows service packs?

   A. Update Manager

   B. Service Pack Manager

   C. Download Manager

   D. Windows Update

2. Which boot mode loads only basic drivers?

   A. Limited Mode

   B. Safe Mode

   C. Feature Mode

   D. Windows Mode

3. Which BOOTREC option can be used in Windows 7 to rebuild the boot configuration file?

   A. /FIXBOOT

   B. /REBUILDBCD

   C. /FIXBCD

   D. /FIXMBR

4. What is the first step in the troubleshooting process?

   A. Document findings

   B. Identify the problem

   C. Establish a theory

   D. Verify functionality

5. Which tool do you use to create a restore point in Windows XP?

   A. Backup

   B. System Restore

   C. Restore Point

   D. Emergency Repair

6. Which of the following operating systems use the BOOT.INI file during boot?

   A. Windows XP

   B. Windows Vista

   C. Windows 7

   D. All of the above

7. One of the users you support has a Windows 7 laptop that continues to spontaneously shut down and restart. What should you try first?

    A. Swap the motherboard.

    B. Begin disabling drivers one by one until you find the culprit.

    C. Disable the sleep settings for hibernation.

    D. Reinstall Windows 7.

8. Windows 7 includes a feature called a _____, which is a copy of your system configuration that can be used to roll back the system to a previous state if a configuration error occurs.

    A. Restore point

    B. Repair point

    C. Rollback point

    D. Registry point

9. Which of the following are used to prevent pop-unders from appearing?

    A. Anti-malware utilities

    B. Pop-up blockers

    C. Phishing sites

    D. Antivirus software

10. In general, how often should you update your antivirus definitions?

    A. Once a week

    B. Once a month

    C. Once a year

    D. Antivirus definitions do not need to be updated

11. One of your users claims that their hard drive seems to be running slowly. What tool can you use to check to see how fragmented the hard drive is?

    A. Disk Analyzer

    B. Disk Cleanup

    C. Disk Defragmenter

    D. Chkdsk

12. You want to ensure that your Windows XP computer receives automatic updates to Windows and Microsoft Office. Which tool will take care of this for you?

    A. Windows Update

    B. Microsoft Update

    C. System Update

    D. None of the above

13. Which of the following programs could be considered anti-malware?

    A. Windows Defender

    B. Microsoft Monitor

    C. System Watchdog

    D. None of the above

14. Which of the following allows you to register and unregister modules and controls for troubleshooting purposes?

    A. RegSvr32

    B. SFC

    C. Fixboot

    D. Fixmbr

15. Which of the following can you do to help eliminate security problems? (Choose four.)

    A. Establish security policies and procedures.

    B. Update your operating systems.

    C. Update your applications.

    D. Update your network devices.

16. Internal users are seeing repeated attempts to infect their systems as reported to them by pop-up messages from their virus scanning software. According to the pop-up messages, the virus seems to be the same in every case. What is the most likely culprit?

    A. A server is acting as a carrier for a virus.

    B. You have a worm virus.

    C. Your antivirus software has malfunctioned.

    D. A DoS attack is under way.

17. Which of the following tools can you use to delete temporary Internet files and other unneeded files to free up disk space?

    A. Disk Analyzer

    B. Disk Cleanup

    C. Disk Defragmenter

    D. CHKDSK

18. Which of the following tools automatically verifies system files after a reboot to see if they were changed to unprotected copies?

    A. DAZR

    B. NTLDR

    C. REGEDIT

    D. SFC

19. To open System Restore, click Start ➤ All Programs ➤ Accessories, and then:

    A. Advanced

    B. System Tools

    C. Backup

    D. TCP/IP

20. Which utility is shown in the following figure?

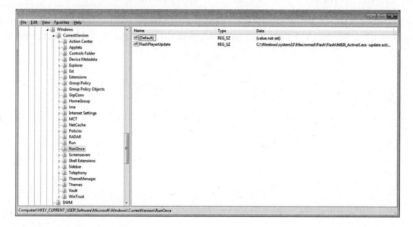

    A. Regedit

    B. RegSrv32

    C. Msconfig

    D. Event Viewer

Performance-Based Question

On the A+ exams, you will encounter performance-based questions. The questions on the exam require you to perform a specific task, and you will be graded on whether you were able to complete the task. The following require you to think creatively to measure how well you understand this chapter's topics. You may or may not see similar questions on the actual A+ exams. To see how your answers compare to the authors', refer to Appendix B.

You are running an older Windows XP system and need to run the Recovery Console. After looking around for that option, however, you do not find it. What must you do to install it?

Chapter

20

Hardware and Network Troubleshooting

THE FOLLOWING COMPTIA A+ EXAM 220-802 OBJECTIVES ARE COVERED IN THIS CHAPTER:

✓ **4.2 Given a scenario, troubleshoot common problems related to motherboards, RAM, CPU and power with appropriate tools.**

- Common symptoms

  - Unexpected shutdowns

  - System lockups

  - POST code beeps

  - Blank screen on bootup

  - BIOS time and settings resets

  - Attempts to boot to incorrect device

  - Continuous reboots

  - No power

  - Overheating

  - Loud noise

  - Intermittent device failure

  - Fans spin – no power to other devices

  - Indicator lights

  - Smoke

  - Burning smell

  - BSOD

- Tools
  - Multimeter
  - Power supply tester
  - Loopback plugs
  - POST card

✓ **4.3 Given a scenario, troubleshoot hard drives and RAID arrays with appropriate tools.**

- Common symptoms
  - Read/write failure
  - Slow performance
  - Loud clicking noise
  - Failure to boot
  - Drive not recognized
  - OS not found
  - RAID not found
  - RAID stops working
  - BSOD
- Tools
  - Screwdriver
  - External enclosures
  - CHKDSK
  - FORMAT
  - FDISK
  - File recovery software

✓ **4.4 Given a scenario, troubleshoot common video and display issues.**

- Common symptoms
  - VGA mode
  - No image on screen
  - Overheat shutdown

- Dead pixels
- Artifacts
- Color patterns incorrect
- Dim image
- Flickering image
- Distorted image
- Discoloration (degaussing)
- BSOD

✓ **4.5 Given a scenario, troubleshoot wired and wireless networks with appropriate tools.**

- Common symptoms
  - No connectivity
  - APIPA address
  - Limited connectivity
  - Local connectivity
  - Intermittent connectivity
  - IP conflict
  - Slow transfer speeds
  - Low RF signal
- Tools
  - Cable tester
  - Loopback plug
  - Punch down tools
  - Toner probes
  - Wire strippers
  - Crimper
  - PING
  - IPCONFIG
  - TRACERT
  - NETSTAT

- NBTSTAT
- NET
- Wireless locator

✓ **4.8 Given a scenario, troubleshoot, and repair common laptop issues while adhering to the appropriate procedures.**

- Common symptoms
  - No display
  - Dim display
  - Flickering display
  - Sticking keys
  - Intermittent wireless
  - Battery not charging
  - Ghost cursor
  - No power
  - Numlock indicator lights
  - No wireless connectivity
  - No Bluetooth connectivity
  - Cannot display to external monitor
- Disassembling processes for proper re-assembly
  - Document and label cable and screw locations
  - Organize parts
  - Refer to manufacturer documentation
  - Use appropriate hand tools

✓ **4.9 Given a scenario, troubleshoot printers with appropriate tools.**

- Common symptoms
  - Streaks
  - Faded prints
  - Ghost images
  - Toner not fused to the paper

By now, you've probably gotten the feeling that troubleshooting is really hard. To be clear, it definitely can be. With all of the integration between software applications and hardware components, it can be challenging to understand where one stops and the other starts or how their interoperation affects one another. To top it all off, you're probably going to be working in an environment that requires you to understand not just one computer but a network full of workstations, servers, switches, routers, and other devices and how they play nice together. Situations will arise that make even the most experienced technicians shake their heads in confusion.

The best way to tackle any problem, as we talked about in the previous chapter, is to take a systematic approach to resolving it. This applies to the software and security issues we covered in Chapter 19, "Troubleshooting Theory, OSs, and Security," as well as the hardware and networking ones we'll talk about here. Troubleshooting becomes a lot easier if you follow logical procedures and develop a little bit of experience.

Before we get into the details of specific problems, remember that in order to troubleshoot anything, you need to have a base level of knowledge. For example, if you've never opened the hood of a car, it will be a bit challenging for you to figure out why your car won't start in the morning. If you're not a medical professional, you might not know why that body part hurts or how to make it feel better. In the same vein, if you don't know how data is stored and accessed on a computer, it's unlikely you'll be able to fix related computer problems. So, before you get too heavy into troubleshooting, make sure you understand how the systems you are working on are supposed to function in the first place!

Because this chapter is at the end of the book, we're going to assume that you've read all of the other chapters, including the troubleshooting steps outlined in Chapter 19. Therefore, we're not going to get into a lot of detail about how things work—it's implied that you know those details by now. (If you're still not certain, this book is a great reference manual!) Instead, we'll talk more about what happens when things don't work the way they're supposed to: what signs to look for and what to do to fix the problem. The first part of this chapter will cover key internal hardware components. After that, we'll look at issues specific to laptops and printers and then finish off the book with a section on network troubleshooting.

Troubleshooting Core Hardware Issues

To many who are not familiar with computers, that whirring, humming box sitting under their desk is an enigma. They know what shows up on the screen, where the power button is, where to put DVDs, and what not to spill on their keyboard. But the insides are shrouded in mystery.

Fortunately for them, we're around. We can tell the difference between a hard drive and a motherboard and have a pretty good idea of what each part inside that box is supposed to do. When the computer doesn't work like it's supposed to, we can whip out our trusty screwdriver, crack the case, and perform surgery. And most of the time, we can get the system running just as good as new.

In the following sections, we're going to focus our troubleshooting efforts on the key hardware components inside the case, but we're also going to include monitors (which are attached to video cards, which are inside the case, so close enough for our purposes). We will start off with motherboards, processors, memory, and power. Then we will look at storage devices, and finish off the discussion with video and display issues.

Troubleshooting Motherboards, CPUs, RAM, and Power Problems

These components are the brains, backbone, and nervous system of your computer. Without a network card, you won't be able to surf the Web. Without a processor, well, you won't be able to surf the Web. Or do much of anything else for that matter. So we'll get started with these components.

As you continue to learn and increase your troubleshooting experience, your value will increase as well. This is because, if nothing else, it will take you less time to accomplish common repairs. Your ability to troubleshoot by past experiences and gut feelings will make you more efficient and more valuable, which in turn will allow you to advance and earn a better income. We will give you some guidelines you can use to evaluate common hardware issues that you're sure to face.

Identifying Hardware Symptoms and Causes

Before we get into specific components, let's take a few minutes to talk about hardware symptoms and causes at a general level. This discussion can apply to a lot of different hardware components.

Some hardware issues are pretty easy to identify. If there are flames shooting out of the back of your computer, then it's probably the power supply. If the power light on your monitor doesn't turn on, it's the monitor itself, the power cord, or your power source. Other hardware symptoms are a bit more ambiguous. We'll now look at some hardware-related symptoms and their possible causes.

Excessive Heat

Electronic components produce heat; it's a fact of life. While they're designed to withstand a certain amount of the heat that's produced, excessive heat can drastically shorten the life of components. There are two common ways to reduce heat-related problems in computers: heat sinks and case fans.

Any component with its own processor will have a heat sink. Typically these look like big, finned hunks of aluminum or other metal attached to the processor. Their job is to dissipate heat from the component so it doesn't become too hot. Never run a processor without a heat sink!

WARNING   One way to ensure that your processor dies quickly is to overclock it. Overclocking is running the processor faster than it was designed to run. While it may work in the short run, it's never a good idea to do this!

Case fans are designed to take hot air from inside the case and blow it out of the case. There are many different designs, from simple motors to high-tech liquid-cooled models. Put your hand up to the back of your computer at the case fan and you should feel warm air. If there's nothing coming out, you either need to clean your fan or replace your power supply. Some cases come with additional cooling fans to help dissipate heat.

TIP   Computers are like human beings: They have similar tolerances to heat and cold. In general, anything comfortable to us is comfortable to computers. They need lots of clean, moving air to keep them functioning.

We've mentioned dust before and now is a good time to bring it up again. Dust, dirt, grime, paint, smoke, and other airborne particles can become caked on the inside of the components. This is most common in automotive and manufacturing environments. The contaminants create a film that coats the components, causing them to overheat and/or conduct electricity on their surface. Blowing out these exposed systems with a can of compressed air from time to time can prevent damage to the components. While you're cleaning the components, be sure to clean any cooling fans in the power supply or on the heat sink.

TIP   To clean the power supply fan, blow the air from the inside of the case. When you do this, the fan will blow the contaminants out the cooling vents. If you spray from the vents toward the inside of the box, you'll be blowing the dust and grime inside the case or back into the fan motor.

One way to ensure that dust and grime don't find their way into your computer is to always leave the *blanks* in the empty slots on the back of your box. Blanks are the pieces of metal or plastic that come with the case and cover the expansion slot openings. They are designed to keep dirt, dust, and other foreign matter from the inside of the computer. They also maintain proper airflow within the case to ensure that the computer doesn't overheat.

Noise

Have you ever been working on a computer and heard a noise that resembles fingernails on a chalkboard? If so, you will always remember that sound, along with the impending feeling of doom as the computer stopped working.

Some noises on a computer are normal. The POST beep (which we'll talk about in a few pages) is a good sound. The whirring of your hard drive and power supply fan are familiar sounds. Some techs get so used to their "normal" system noises that if anything is slightly off pitch, they go digging for problems even if none are readily apparent.

Real World Scenario

Creeping Chips

The inside of a computer is a harsh environment. The temperature inside the case of many computers is well over 100° F! When you turn on your computer, it heats up. Turn it off, and it cools down. After several hundred such cycles, some components can't handle the stress and begin to move out of their sockets. This phenomenon is known as *chip creep*, and it can be really frustrating.

Chip creep can affect any socketed device, including ICs, RAM chips, and expansion cards. The solution to chip creep is simple: Open the case, and reseat the devices. It's surprising how often this is the solution to phantom problems of all sorts, particularly intermittent device failures, random reboots, and unexpected shutdowns.

For the most part, the components that can produce noise problems are those that move. Hard drives have motors that spin the platters. Power supply fans spin. CD and DVD drives spin the disks. If you're hearing excessive noise, these are the likely culprits.

If you hear a whining sound and it seems to be fairly constant, it's more than likely a fan. Either it needs to be cleaned (desperately) or replaced. Power supplies that are failing can also sound louder and quieter intermittently because a fan will run at alternating speeds.

The "fingernails on a chalkboard" squealing could be an indicator that the hard drive heads have crashed into the platter. This thankfully doesn't seem to be as common today as it used to be, but it still happens. Note that this type of sound can also be caused by a power supply fan's motor binding up. A rhythmic ticking sound is also likely to be the hard drive.

Problems with the CD-ROM or DVD-ROM drive tend to be the easiest to diagnose. Those drives aren't constantly spinning unless you put some media in them. If you put a disc in and the drive makes a terrible noise, you have a good idea what the problem is.

So what do you do if you hear a terrible noise from the computer? If it's still responsive, shut it down normally as soon as possible. If it's not responsive, then shut off the power as quickly as you can. Examine the power supply to see if there are any obvious problems such as excessive dust, and clean as needed. Power the system back on. If the noise was caused by the hard drive, odds are that the drive has failed and the system won't boot normally. You may need to replace some parts.

If the noise is mildly annoying but doesn't sound drastic, boot up the computer with the case off and listen. By getting up close and personal with the system you can often tell where the noise is coming from and then troubleshoot or fix the appropriate part.

WARNING   Never touch internal components when the case is off and the power is on! Doing so could result in a severe electrical shock to you and/or the components.

Odors and Smoke

Bad smells or smoke coming from your computer are never good things. While it normally gets pretty warm inside a computer case, it should never be hot enough inside there to melt plastic components, but it does happen from time to time. And power problems can sometimes cause components to get hot enough to smoke.

If you smell an odd odor or see smoke coming from a computer, shut it down immediately. Open the case and start looking for visible signs of damage. Things to look for include melted plastic components and burn marks on circuit boards. If components appear to be damaged, it's best to replace them before returning the computer to service.

 If you have scorch marks on a component, say a video card or a mother-board, it could be that the specific component went bad. It could also be a sign of a problem with the power supply. If you replace the component and a similar problem occurs, definitely replace the power supply.

Status Light Indicators

Many hardware devices have status light indicators that can help you identify when there is a problem. Obviously, when you power on a system you expect the power light to come on. If it doesn't, you have a problem. The same holds true for other external devices, such as wireless routers, external hard drives, and printers. In situations in which the power light doesn't come on and the device has no power, always obey the first rule of troubleshooting: Check your connections first!

Beyond power indicators, several types of devices have additional lights that can help you troubleshoot. If you have a hub, switch, or other connectivity device, you should have an indicator for each port that lights up when there is a connection. Some devices will give you a green light for a good connection and a yellow or red light if they detect a problem. A lot of connectivity devices will also have an indicator that blinks or flashes when traffic is going through the port. Sometimes it's the same light that indicates a connection, but other times it's a separate indicator.

If you have a device with lights and you're not sure what they mean, it's best to check the manual or the manufacturer's website to learn.

 The manufacturer's website is generally a great place to go for trouble-shooting tips!

Alerts

An alert is a message generated by a hardware device. In some cases, the device has a display panel that will tell you what the alert is. A good example of this is an office printer. Many have an LCD display that can tell you if something is wrong.

Other alerts will pop up on the computer screen. If the device is attached to a specific computer, the alert will generally pop up on that computer's screen. Some devices can be configured to send an alert to a specific user account or system administrator, so the administrator will get the alert regardless of which computer they are logged in to.

Visible Damage

The good news about visible damage is that you can usually figure out which component is damaged pretty quickly. The bad news is it often means you need to replace parts.

Visible damage to the outside of the case or the monitor casing might not matter much as long as the device still works. But if you're looking inside a case and see burn marks or melted components, that's a sure sign of a problem. Replace damaged circuit boards or melted plastic components immediately. After replacing the part, it's a good idea to monitor the new component for a while too. It could be the power supply causing the problem. If the new part fries quickly too, it's time to replace the power supply as well.

POST Routines

Every computer has a diagnostic program built into its basic input/output system (BIOS) called the *power-on self-test (POST)*. When you turn on the computer, it executes this set of diagnostics. Many steps are involved in the POST, but they happen very quickly, they're invisible to the user, and they vary among BIOS versions. The steps include checking the CPU, checking the RAM, checking for the presence of a video card, and verifying basic hardware functionality. The main reason to be aware of the POST's existence is that if it encounters a problem, the boot process stops. Being able to determine at what point the problem occurred can help you troubleshoot.

If the computer doesn't POST as it should, one way to determine the source of a problem is to listen for a *beep code*. This is a series of beeps from the computer's speaker. A successful POST generally produces a single beep. If there's more than one beep, the number, duration, and pattern of the beeps can sometimes tell you what component is causing the problem. However, the beeps differ depending on the BIOS manufacturer and version, so you must look up the beep code in a chart for your particular BIOS. The beeping is different for different BIOS manufacturers. AMI BIOS, for example, relies on a raw number of beeps and uses patterns of short and long beeps.

Another way to determine a problem during the POST routine is to use a *POST card*. This is a circuit board that fits into an ISA or PCI expansion slot in the motherboard and reports numeric codes as the boot process progresses. Each of those codes corresponds to a particular component being checked. If the POST card stops at a certain number, you can look up that number in the manual that came with the card to determine the problem.

 Motherboard manufacturers tend to use different beep codes to indicate different error messages. If you're getting a beep code during POST, check the motherboard manufacturer's website for information on what the beep code means.

Identifying BIOS Issues

Because we just talked about the POST routine, which is a function of the BIOS, let's look at a few other BIOS issues as well. First, computer BIOSs don't go bad; they just become out-of-date. This isn't necessarily a critical issue—they will continue to support the hardware that came with the box. It *does*, however, become an issue when the BIOS doesn't support some component that you would like to install—a larger hard drive, for instance.

Most of today's BIOSs are written to an EEPROM and can be updated through the use of software. This process is called flashing the BIOS. Each manufacturer has its own method for accomplishing this. Check the documentation for complete details.

 If you make a mistake in the upgrade process, the computer can become **WARNING** unbootable. If this happens, your only option may be to ship the box to a manufacturer-approved service center. Be careful!

A fairly common issue with the BIOS is when it fails to retain your computer's settings, such as time and date and hard drive configuration. The BIOS uses a small battery (much like a watch battery) on the motherboard to help it retain settings when the system power is off. If this battery fails, the BIOS won't retain its settings. Simply replace the battery to solve the problem.

Finally, remember that your BIOS also contains the boot sequence for your system. You probably boot to the first hard drive in your system, but you can also set your BIOS to boot from the CD-ROM, the floppy drive (if you have one), or the network. If your computer is attempting to boot from the wrong device, you need to change the boot sequence in the BIOS. To do this, reboot the system, and look for the message telling you to press a certain key to enter the BIOS (usually something like F2). Once you're in the BIOS, find the menu with the boot sequence and set it to the desired order. If the changes don't hold the next time you reboot, check the battery!

 There may be times that you want to boot to an alternate device such as **TIP** the CD-ROM. During the part of the boot process when the BIOS entry key is shown, most systems will also show you an alternate key to press (such as the spacebar) to boot from the CD-ROM. This can be very helpful when troubleshooting a system that won't load the OS properly, as long as you have the installation disc handy.

Identifying Motherboard and CPU Problems

Most motherboard and CPU problems manifest themselves by the system appearing to be completely dead. However, "completely dead" can be a symptom of a wide variety of problems, not only with the CPU or motherboard but also with the RAM or the power supply. Other times, a failing motherboard or CPU will cause the system to completely lock up, or "hang," requiring a hard reboot, or cause continuous reboots. A POST card may be helpful in narrowing down the exact component that is faulty.

When a motherboard fails, it's usually because it has been damaged. Most technicians can't repair motherboard damage; the motherboard must be replaced. Motherboards can become damaged due to physical trauma, exposure to electrostatic discharge (ESD), or short-circuiting. To minimize the risk, observe the following rules:

- Handle a motherboard as little as possible, and keep it in an antistatic bag whenever it's removed from the PC case.
- Keep all liquids well away from the motherboard; water can cause a short circuit.
- Wear an antistatic wrist strap when handling or touching a motherboard.
- When installing a motherboard in a case, make sure you use brass standoffs with paper or plastic washers to prevent any stray solder around the screw holes from causing a short circuit with the metal of the screw.

A CPU may fail because of physical trauma or short-circuiting, but the most common cause for a CPU not to work is failure to install it properly. With a PGA- or LGA-style CPU, ensure that the CPU is oriented correctly in the socket. With an SECC-style CPU, make sure the CPU is completely inserted into its slot.

Identifying I/O Port and Cable Problems

Input/output (I/O) ports are most often built into the motherboard and include legacy parallel and serial, USB, and FireWire ports. All of them are used to connect external peripherals to the motherboard. When a port doesn't appear to be functioning, make sure the following conditions are met:

- The cables are snugly connected.
- The port has not been disabled in BIOS Setup.
- The port has not been disabled in Device Manager in Windows.
- No pins are broken or bent on the male end of the port or on the cable being plugged into it.

If you suspect it's the port, you can purchase a loopback plug to test its functionality. If you suspect that the cable, rather than the port, may be the problem, swap out the cable with a known good one. If you don't have an extra cable, you can test the existing cable with a multimeter by setting it to ohms and checking the resistance between one end of the cable and the other.

Use a pin-out diagram, if available, to determine which pin matches up to which at the other end. There is often—but not always—an inverse relationship between the ends. In other words, at one end pin 1 is at the left, and at the other end it's at the right on the same row of pins. You see this characteristic with D-sub connectors where one end of the cable is male and the other end is female.

Identifying Memory Issues

Isolating memory issues on a computer is one of the more difficult tasks to do properly because so many memory problems manifest themselves as software issues. For example, memory problems can cause applications to fail and produce error messages such as general protection faults (GPFs). Memory issues can also cause a fatal error in Windows, producing the infamous Blue Screen of Death (BSOD) that we discussed in Chapter 19. Sometimes these are caused by the physical memory failing. Other times they are caused by bad programming, when an application writes into a memory space reserved for the operating system or another application.

In short, memory problems can cause system lockups, unexpected shutdowns or reboots, or the errors mentioned in the preceding paragraph. They can be challenging to pin down. If you do get an error message related to memory, be sure to write down the memory address if the error gives you one. If the error happens again, write down the memory address again. If it's the same or a similar address, then it's very possible that the physical memory is failing. You can also use one of several hardware- or software-based RAM testers to see if your memory is working properly.

Identifying Power Supply and Cooling Problems

Power supply problems can manifest themselves as a system that doesn't respond in any way when the power is turned on. When this happens, open the case, remove the power supply, and replace it with a new one. Partial failures, or intermittent power supply problems, are much less simple. A completely failed power supply gives the same symptoms as a malfunctioning wall socket, uninterruptible power supply (UPS) or power strip; a power cord that is not securely seated; or some motherboard shorts (such as those caused by an improperly seated expansion card, memory stick, CPU, and the like). You want to rule out those items before you replace the power supply and find you still have the same problem as when you started. Be aware that different cases have different types of on/off switches. The process of replacing a power supply is a lot easier if you purchase a replacement with the same mechanism.

 Real World Scenario

Hot, Hot, Hot

Several years ago, the company one of the authors was working for got in a batch of hardware it had purchased from another company. He and another tech were building Frankensteins out of the plethora of parts they had.

They put RAM into one of the systems and powered it on. Immediately there was an electrical arc from the RAM to the motherboard, so they shut it back off. The arc was present for a split second, and they had the box powered down within a second or two after that.

The RAM module had a pretty obvious burn mark on it, so the author went to take it out and promptly scorched his fingers when he touched it. It was searing hot! They let it cool down for about 20 minutes before going back to take it out. The moral of the story: Be careful not to burn yourself on fried components.

Incidentally, they put a new motherboard and new RAM into the same case and powered it up only to see the exact same thing happen. Fried. (Fortunately the author was smart enough not to burn himself a second time!) The verdict? Bad power supply. After replacing the power supply and trying a third motherboard and RAM combination, they had a functioning system.

If you're curious as to the state of your power supply, you can buy hardware-based power supply testers online starting at about $10 and running up to several hundred dollars. Multimeters are also effective devices for testing your power supplies.

WARNING   Never try to repair or disassemble a power supply. There is a high risk of electrocution, and the relatively low cost of a new power supply makes working on them something to avoid.

Identifying Cooling Issues

A PC that works for a few minutes and then locks up is probably experiencing overheating because of a heat sink or fan not functioning properly. To troubleshoot overheating, first check all fans inside the PC to ensure they're operating, and make sure any heat sinks are firmly attached to their chips.

In a properly designed, properly assembled PC case, air flows in a specific path driven by the power supply fan and using the power supply's vent holes. Make sure you know the direction of flow and that there are limited obstructions and no dust buildup. Cases are also designed to cool by making the air flow in a certain way. Therefore, operating a PC with the cover removed can make a PC more susceptible to overheating, even though it's "getting more air."

Similarly, operating a PC with expansion-slot covers removed can inhibit a PC's ability to cool itself properly because the extra holes change the airflow pattern from what was intended by its design.

Although CPUs are the most common component to overheat, occasionally other chips on the motherboard, such as the chipset, or chips on other devices, particularly video cards, may also overheat. Extra heat sinks or fans may be installed to cool these chips.

Liquid cooling systems have their own set of issues. The pump that moves the liquid through the tubing and heat sinks can become obstructed or simply fail. If this happens, the liquid's temperature will eventually equalize with that of the CPU and other components, resulting in their damage. Dust in the heat sinks has the same effect as with nonliquid cooling systems, so keep these components clean as you would any such components. Check regularly for signs of leaks that might be starting and try to catch them before they result in damage to the system.

Exercise 20.1 walks you through the steps of troubleshooting a few specific hardware problems. The exercise will probably end up being a mental one for you, unless you have the exact problem that we're describing here. As practice, you can write down the steps you would take to solve the problem and then check to see how close you came to our steps. Clearly, there are several ways to approach a problem, so you might use a slightly different process, but the general approach should be similar. Finally, when you have found the problem, you can stop. This exercise assumes that each step didn't solve the issue so you need to move on to the next step.

EXERCISE 20.1

Troubleshooting Practice

Issue One: Blank screen on bootup. You turn the computer on, and there's nothing on the screen.

1. Check to make sure the monitor is on. Is its power light on?

   Seriously. Check it. Sometimes 5 seconds of checking the obvious can save you an hour of wasted time.

2. Is the monitor getting a signal?

   Some monitors will go into sleep mode if they don't get a signal. Check the connections. If all the connections are good and you're not getting a signal, it could be the video card.

3. Did the system POST properly? Did you get a POST beep or a beep code?

   No POST likely indicates a bigger problem than just the video card or the monitor. If you do get a POST beep but never see anything, try a different monitor.

4. Did you ever see anything on the screen? BIOS information? Did the OS start to load and then it went blank?

The key to troubleshooting an ambiguous situation like this is to ask yourself, "What is the last thing that worked as it was supposed to?" That will help you determine what you need to fix.

Issue Two: The power supply fan spins, but no other devices have power.

1. Did you hear a POST beep or a beep code?

   Odds are you didn't get any sounds, but it's always good to reboot and double-check.

2. Disconnect all internal and external peripherals so that the only component drawing power is the motherboard (with CPU and RAM, of course). Does it POST then?

   If you disconnect everything and it still doesn't POST, odds are that your motherboard is fried. If it POSTs, then start plugging components back in one at a time, starting with your hard drive and other internal devices and working your way to the external peripherals. You'll eventually get to the part that's causing the problem.

3. If you have a power supply tester or multimeter, now would be a good time to make sure the power supply is working properly. There's no sense in replacing components such as the motherboard if the power supply is just going to fry them!

Again, with all troubleshooting, it's imperative to narrow down the problem to isolate the cause. If you can do that, then fixing it should be the easy part.

Troubleshooting Storage Device Problems

Storage devices present unique problems simply due to their nature. They're devices with moving parts, which means they are more prone to mechanical failure than a motherboard or a stick of RAM. In the following sections, we'll discuss hard disk problems, including RAID arrays. Then we'll take a quick look at CD-ROM/DVD and floppy drive issues.

Identifying Hard Disk System Problems

Hard disk system problems usually stem from one of three causes:

- The adapter (that is, the SATA, IDE, or SCSI interface) is bad.
- The disk is bad.
- The adapter and disk are connected incorrectly.

The first and last causes are easy to identify, because in either case the symptom will be obvious: the drive won't work. You won't be able to get the computer to communicate with the disk drive.

However, if the problem is a bad disk drive, the symptoms aren't as obvious. As long as the POST routines can communicate with the disk drive, they're usually satisfied. But the POST routines may not uncover problems related to storing information. Even with healthy POST results, you may find that you're permitted to save information to a bad disk, but when you try to read it back, you get errors. Or the computer may not boot as quickly as it used to because the disk drive can't read the boot information successfully every time.

Software utilities used to manage hard drives include Chkdsk, Format, and Fdisk. These are covered in detail in Chapter 13, "Operating System Administration."

Let's take a look at some specific hard-drive-related issues, the likely culprits, and actions to take:

Loud clicking or scratching noises   These are usually caused by a physical malfunction within the drive itself. If the drive is still usable, back up the information on it as soon as possible. The drive is going to stop working in short order. It's time to brandish the screwdriver and replace the hard drive.

Slow performance or read/write failures   A failing hard drive might exhibit these symptoms. They can also be a symptom of the hard drive being too full. Hard drives move information around a lot, especially temporary files. If the drive doesn't have enough free space (at least 10 percent), it can slow down dramatically. The solution here is to remove files to free up space and look at defragmenting the hard drive. If problems persist, consider formatting the hard drive and reinstalling the OS. If the issues don't go away, assume that the hard drive is on its last legs.

Boot problems   This could be any of a number of problems, such as a complete failure to boot, the hard drive not being recognized by the BIOS, or the OS not being found. Failure to boot at all likely means the drive is dead. Do your due diligence and reseat your connections and make sure the BIOS recognizes the drive before replacing it. Most BIOSs today auto-detect the hard drive. If that auto-detection fails, it's bad news for the hard drive unless there's a cable or connection issue. Finally, if the system boots fine but it can't find the OS, it could indicate a problem with the Master Boot Record (MBR). You can boot from a bootable disk and repair the MBR with FDISK (pre-Windows XP), FIXMBR (Windows XP), or BOOTREC /FIXMBR (Windows Vista and 7).

> Never perform a low-level format on SATA, IDE, or SCSI drives! A low-level format is done at the factory, and you may cause problems by using low-level utilities on these types of drives.

If you are using a Redundant Array of Independent Disks (RAID) system, you have additional challenges to deal with. First, you have more disks, so the chance of having a single failure increases. Second, you more than likely have one or more additional hard disk controllers, so again you introduce more parts that can fail. Third, there will likely be a software component that manages the RAID array.

Boiling it down, though, dealing with RAID issues is just like dealing with a single hard drive issue, except you have more parts that make up the single storage unit. If your RAID array isn't found or stops working, try to narrow down the issue. Is it one disk that's failed, or is the whole system down, indicating a problem with a controller or the software? Along with external enclosures, which require a separate connection to the computer, most external RAID systems have status indicators and troubleshooting utilities to help you identify problems. Definitely use those to your advantage.

Finally, the problem could be dependent on the type of RAID you're using. If you are using RAID 0 (disk striping), you actually have more points of failure than a single device, and your fault tolerance has decreased. One drive failure will cause the set to fail. RAID 1 (disk mirroring) increases your fault tolerance; if one drive fails, the other has an exact replica of the data. You'll need to replace the failed drive, but unless both drives unexpectedly fail, you shouldn't lose any data. If you're using RAID 5 (disk striping with parity), a single drive failure usually means that your data will be fine, provided you replace the failed drive.

> If your hard drive fails completely and you need to get critical data off of it, there are third-party companies that provide file recovery software and services. These services are generally very expensive. (And you should have been backing up the drive in the first place!)

Identifying CD-ROM/DVD Issues

CD-ROM and DVD problems are normally media related. Although compact disc technology is much more reliable than that for floppy disks, it's not perfect. One factor to consider is the cleanliness of the disc. On many occasions, if a disc is unreadable, cleaning it with an approved cleaner and a lint-free cleaning towel will fix the problem. The next step might be to use a commercially available scratch-removal kit. If that fails, you always have the option to send the disc to a company that specializes in data recovery.

If the operating system doesn't see the drive, start troubleshooting by determining whether the drive is receiving power. If the tray will eject, you can assume there is power to it. Next, check BIOS Setup (SATA or IDE drives) to make sure the drive has been detected. If not, check the master/slave jumper on the drive, and make sure the IDE adapter is set to Auto, CD-ROM, or ATAPI in BIOS Setup. Once inside the case, ensure that the ribbon cable is properly aligned with pin 1 and that both the drive and motherboard ends are securely connected.

To play movies, a DVD drive must have MPEG decoding capability. This is usually built in to the drive, video card, or sound card these days, but it may require a software decoder. If DVD data discs will play but not movies, suspect a problem with the MPEG decoding.

If a CD-RW or DVD drive works normally as a regular CD-ROM drive but doesn't perform its special capability (doesn't read DVD discs or doesn't write to blank discs), perhaps you need to install software to work with it. For example, with CD-RW drives, unless you're using an operating system that supports CD writing, you must install CD-writing software to write to CDs.

Identifying Floppy and Other Removable Disk Drive Problems

Like CD-ROM/DVD drives, most floppy-drive problems result from bad media. Your first troubleshooting technique with floppy drive issues should be to try a new disk.

One of the most common problems that develops with floppy drives is misaligned read-write heads. The symptoms are fairly easy to recognize—you can read and write to a floppy on one machine but not on any others. This is normally caused by the mechanical arm in the floppy drive becoming misaligned. When the disk was formatted, it wasn't properly positioned on the drive, thus preventing other floppy drives from reading it.

Numerous commercial tools are available to realign floppy drive read-write heads. They use a floppy drive that has been preformatted to reposition the mechanical arm. In most cases, though, this fix is temporary—the arm will move out of place again fairly soon. Given the inexpensive nature of the problem, the best solution is to spend a few dollars and replace the drive.

Another problem you may encounter is a phantom directory listing. For example, suppose you display the contents of a floppy disk and then you swap to another floppy disk but the listing stays the same. This is almost always a result of a faulty ribbon cable; a particular wire in the ribbon cable signals when a disk swap has taken place, and when that wire breaks, this error occurs.

Troubleshooting Video Issues

Troubleshooting video problems is usually fairly straightforward because there are a limited number of issues you might face. You can sum up nearly all video problems with two simple statements:

- There is either no video or bad video.
- Either the video card or the monitor is to blame.

In the vast majority of cases when you have a video problem, a good troubleshooting step is to check the monitor by transferring it to another machine that you know is working. See if it works there. If the problem persists, you know it's the monitor. If it goes away, you know it's the video card (or possibly the driver). Is the video card seated properly? Is the newest driver installed?

WARNING   Remember that CompTIA recommends not working on a CRT monitor because of the electrical charge stored within.

Let's take a look at some common symptoms and their causes:

Booting into VGA mode   Video graphics array (VGA), as you will recall from Chapter 4, "Display Devices," is a basic mode for displaying video. Pretty much all you get is 640×480 with 16 colors. (Remember, that used to be awesome!) When your system refuses to boot into anything other than VGA mode, it indicates one of two problems. Either the video card is set to a resolution it can't handle, or the video card driver isn't loading properly. When in VGA mode, reset the video resolution to something you know the card can handle and reboot. If that doesn't solve it, reinstall the driver. If it still doesn't work, replace the video card.

No image on the screen   Troubleshooting this one is usually pretty easy. Try another monitor or try this monitor on another computer. That will narrow it down pretty quickly. Remember, if it's not the monitor it's probably the video card. (Don't forget to make sure the system POSTed!)

Monitor that keeps shutting down   Monitors have their own internal power supply, and they can overheat. Overheating was more common with CRT displays than LCDs, but it still happens. Make sure the air vents on the back of the monitor are dust and debris free. If the problem persists, it's best to replace the monitor.

Dead pixels or artifacts   These two problems are definitely monitor related. Dead pixels are spots on the screen that never "fire" or light up. You can check for these by setting the background to white and seeing if any spots don't light up. With artifacts, no matter what you have on your screen, you can still see the outlines of a different image. That image has been "burned" into the monitor and isn't going away. In either case, the only resolution is to replace the monitor.

Incorrect colors   This too is most likely a monitor issue, but you should confirm it by switching monitors. This can happen when the LCD monitor's controller board starts to fail and doesn't perform color mapping correctly. It also used to happen on CRTs, and you used a process called *degaussing* (decreasing or eliminating an unwanted magnetic field), which was done through a utility built in to the menu on the monitor, to try to fix the problem. Finally, this can also happen if the pins on the connector are damaged. If switching the monitor makes the problems go away, it's probably time to replace the monitor.

Dim or flickering images   In LCD monitors, these issues are most commonly caused by the backlight starting to fail. In those cases, replace the backlight.

Distorted images   This used to be more of a problem on CRT monitors if they were near a motor or other device that produced a magnetic field. If your office is a cubicle farm, desk fans can be a major culprit. If you can eliminate the possibility of any sort of external interference, and you've confirmed it's the monitor and not the video card, then replace the monitor.

Other graphics issues can be attributed to the memory installed on the video card. This is the storage location of the screens of information in queue to be displayed by the monitor. Problems with the memory modules on the video card have a direct correlation to how well it works. It follows, then, that certain unacceptable video-quality issues can be remedied by adding additional memory to a video card. Doing so generally results in an increase in both quality and performance. If you can't add memory to the video card, you can upgrade to a new one.

Troubleshooting Laptops, Printers, and Networking

Now that we've taken a whirlwind tour of troubleshooting the inside of a computer, it's time to change our focus. First, we will cover unique challenges to troubleshooting laptops. They have most of the same components as desktop computers, so a lot of what we've already covered still applies. Because of their small size and features, though, they introduce a whole host of new potential problems. After we discuss laptops, we'll move into troubleshooting two services that most computer users are fond of: printing and networking.

Troubleshooting Common Laptop Issues

Laptops use essentially the same types of devices as desktops, but troubleshooting the two can feel very different. While the general troubleshooting philosophies never change—steps such as gathering information, isolating the problem, and then testing one fix at a time— the space and configuration limitations can make laptop troubleshooting more frustrating.

Before getting into specific laptop-type issues, remember that good troubleshooting means acting in a methodical manner. You need to find out if the device or software ever worked, what happened before the problem occurred, and what changes were made (if any). Then you must try to isolate the problem and test one fix at a time.

There are four typical areas where laptops could have different problems than their desktop counterparts: power, video, input, and wireless networking.

Working on Laptops

Don't forget these key concepts when working on laptops:

- Document and label screw and cable locations.

- Have a clear organization method for your parts and screws.

- Refer to the manufacturer's documentation.

- Use the appropriate hand tools.

For a review of these four concepts, see Chapter 9, "Understanding Laptops."

Power Issues

Is it plugged in? Everyone hates getting asked that question if their computer doesn't work. But it's the critical first question to ask. After all, if it's not plugged in, who knows whether or not it will work? You can't assume that the battery is working (or is attached) as it's supposed to. Always check power and connections first!

 If the laptop works while it's plugged in but not while on battery power, the battery itself may be the culprit. As batteries get older, they are not able to hold as much of a charge, and in some cases, they are not able to hold a charge at all. If the battery won't charge while the laptop is plugged in, try removing the battery and reinserting it. If it still won't charge, you might want to replace the battery.

Most laptop power adapters have a light on them indicating that they're plugged in. If there's no light, check to make sure the outlet is working, or switch outlets. Also, most laptops have a power-ready indicator light when plugged into a wall outlet as well. Check to see if it's lit. If the outlet is fine, try another power adapter. They do fail on occasion.

If you're working on a DC adapter, the same thing applies. Check for lights, try another adapter if you have one, or try changing plugs if possible. For example, if you're using a DC outlet in a car, many newer models have secondary power sources, such as ones in the console between the seats.

Another thing to remember when troubleshooting power problems is to remove all external peripherals. Strip your laptop down to the base computer so there isn't a short or other power drain coming from an external device.

 Windows has built-in power management features to help conserve laptop battery life. In Windows, open the Power Options applet in Control Panel. Once there you can configure different power-saving settings to maximize the battery life of your laptop.

Video Difficulties

Video problems are usually caused by the video card (built into the motherboard on most laptops) or the display unit. Video problems on laptops can also occur if the connection between the motherboard and the LCD screen becomes damaged. This connection typically passes through the hinges of the case, which is the weakest part.

The coverage for video problems follows the section on power problems for a reason: Make sure the computer is on before diagnosing the issue as a video problem!

Here are a few things to try:

- Plug in an external monitor that you know works. On most laptops, you need to press the function key and another key known as the LCD cutoff switch (often F4 or F8) to direct the video output to an external monitor. This is called toggling the display. You might need to do this a few times. Figure 20.1 shows a laptop keyboard where F4 is the appropriate toggle key. Look for the box with the vertical lines next to it.

FIGURE 20.1 Video adjustment keys F4 (LCD toggle), F9 (dim), and F10 (brighten)

- Check the *LCD cutoff switch*. Remember the function+F4 idea? Try toggling it a few times, waiting a few seconds between each press of the toggle key to let the display power up. Most laptops have three display states: LCD only, external only, and both.

- Raise or lower the brightness level. This is usually done with a function key combination as well, such as Fn+F9 or Fn+F10. Check your keyboard for function keys that have a sun on them.

- If you have a handheld computer, try turning the backlight feature on or off. For specifics on how to do this, check your manual.

If the display is not working, you can order a new one from the laptop manufacturer—although it may be cheaper to just buy a new laptop. If the computer won't output a display to an external monitor, it means one of two things: Either the external VGA port is shot, or the function keys aren't working. In either case, you likely need to replace the motherboard if you want to display to an external device.

Dim or flickering displays on laptops are usually caused by a faulty backlight in the display panel. A failing inverter can cause these problems too.

Input Problems

Laptop keyboards aren't as easy to switch out as desktop keyboards. You can, however, very easily attach an external keyboard to your laptop if the keys on your laptop don't appear to work. If you have the wrong type of connector, most electronics stores will have USB-to-PS/2 or PS/2-to-USB converters.

If the keyboard doesn't seem to respond at all, try pressing the NumLock or CapsLock keys, to see if they toggle the NumLock or CapsLock lights on and off. If the lights don't respond, the keyboard isn't functioning properly. Try rebooting the system. (You will probably have to press and hold the power button for five seconds, and the system will shut off. Wait 10 seconds, and press the power button again to turn it back on.) If that doesn't fix the problem, you probably have faulty hardware.

Another problem unique to laptop keyboards is the *Fn key*. (It can be your friend or your enemy.) You can identify it on your laptop keyboard because it's in the lower-left corner and has the letters *Fn* on it (often in blue), as shown in Figure 20.2. If the Fn key is "stuck" on, the only keys that will work are those with functions on them. If you look at other keys on your laptop, several of them will have blue lettering too. Those are the functions the keys may perform if you press and hold the Fn key before pressing the function key you want. If the Fn key is stuck on, try toggling it just as you would a Caps Lock or Num Lock key.

If another key on your laptop keyboard is stuck, you need to determine if the contact is having problems or if the key itself is stuck. If the key is not physically stuck but the laptop thinks it is, rebooting generally solves the problem. If the key physically sticks, you can try blowing out underneath the key with compressed air, or use a cotton swab slightly dampened with water (or rubbing alcohol) to clean underneath the key. Make sure to clean the entire surface underneath the sticking key. If none of this resolves the issue, you might need to replace the keyboard.

FIGURE 20.2   The Fn key on a laptop

One of the conveniences that users often take advantage of in laptops is built-in pointing devices. A lot of laptops now have touchpads or point sticks that function much like a mouse. They're nice because you don't need to carry an external mouse around with you. While these types of devices are usually considered very handy, some people find them annoying. For example, when you are typing your palm might rest on the touchpad, causing erratic pointer behavior. This is referred to as a *ghost cursor* because it seems like the cursor just randomly jumps all over the screen. You can turn the touchpad off through Control Panel. While understanding that you can turn it off on purpose, remember that it can be turned off accidentally as well. Check to make sure it's enabled. Some laptops allow you to disable or change the sensitivity of the touchpoint as well, just as you can adjust the sensitivity of your mouse.

Networking Troubles

Nearly all modern laptops are equipped with wireless networking built into the computer. WiFi is prevalent, and many laptops natively support Bluetooth as well. In many cases, the wireless antenna is run into the LCD panel. This allows the antenna to stand up higher and pick up a better signal.

If your wireless isn't working, check to make sure that the LEDs on your network card are functioning. If there are no lights, it could indicate a problem with the card itself or, on some cards, that there is no connection or signal. First, make sure the wireless card is enabled through Windows. You generally do this in Windows by right-clicking My Network Places, selecting Properties, right-clicking the wireless network connection, and selecting Properties to look at the network card properties. However, some network cards have their own proprietary configuration software. You can also often check here by clicking a tab (often called Wireless Networks) to see if you're getting a signal and, if so, the strength of that signal.

A weak signal is the most common cause of intermittent wireless networking connection problems. If you have intermittent connectivity and keep getting dropped, see if you can get closer to the WAP or remove obstructions between you and the WAP. Failing network cards and connectivity devices can also cause intermittent wireless networking connection failures.

A lot of laptops now also come with an external switch on the front, side, or above the keyboard that can toggle the network card on and off. Be sure that this is set to the on position! Figure 20.3 shows a toggle above the keyboard (it's the one on the left that looks like an antenna).

FIGURE 20.3   Network card toggle switch above the keyboard

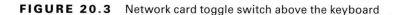

If you have a USB network adapter, try unplugging it and plugging it back in. Make sure Windows recognizes the card properly.

When the wireless connection fails but the network card appears to be working, try plugging it in. Most laptops with wireless cards also have wired RJ-45 network ports. Plug the card in and see if you get lights, and see if the network works.

 Real World Scenario

Potential Wireless and Wired Conflicts

A short time ago, a friend of ours was frustrated because he couldn't get to the network in his office with his laptop plugged into his docking station. He had used the laptop at home the night before and gotten on his wireless network without a problem. But this day, his wired connection would not work. He checked his cables (always your first step!) and saw that there were lights (a good sign). He had tried to access both the Internet and intranet sites but to no avail.

We opened a command prompt and ran IPCONFIG. He didn't have an IP address, but we noticed that his built-in wireless card was listed and active.

What he needed to do was to disable his built-in wireless card. He had enabled the wireless to work at home, and it was still enabled. Because it was enabled, the wireless card was trying to obtain an IP address, and it refused to let the wired "portion" of the card pick up an address from the company DHCP server (there was no wireless in the building). After disabling his wireless card, his wired connection picked up an IP address, and all was well.

Most laptop network cards have a wired connection in addition to their wireless capabilities. For many (but not all) of them, the wired connection will not work if the wireless is enabled. It's an attempt to prevent conflicts if both connection types are active.

Troubleshooting Printer Problems

Other than the monitor (which every computer needs), the most popular peripheral purchased for computers today is the printer. Printers are also the most complex peripheral as far as troubleshooting is concerned; this arises from complications in putting ink to paper. There are several different ways that this can be accomplished, but the end result is all pretty much the same.

Different types of printers work in different ways, so you would expect that laser printers might have different issues than impact printers have. Because problems are often dependent upon the type of printer you're working with, we've chosen to break down this discussion by printer type. We'll start with a quick review of the technology and then get into specific issues. At the end, we'll look at the process of managing the print spooler, which is the same regardless of the printer type in use.

Printer manufacturer websites are great places to look to find trouble-shooting information. They often provide descriptions of problems and detailed instructions for resolving the issue. Most printers also come with management software that you can install on your computer, which may be able to assist you in troubleshooting any issues you have.

For a more detailed description of each type of printer's components and inner workings, see Chapter 10, "Installing and Configuring Printers."

Dot-Matrix Printer Problems

Dot-matrix printers are impact printers, meaning that they rely upon making a physical impact in order to print. A dot-matrix printer contains a print head, which has a row of short, sturdy pins made of a hard wire. The pins in the print head are wrapped with coils of wire to create a solenoid and are held in the rest position by a combination of a small magnet and a spring. To trigger a particular pin, the printer controller sends a signal to the print head, which energizes the wires around the appropriate print wire. This turns the print wire into an electromagnet, which repels the print pin, forcing it against the ink ribbon and making a dot on the paper.

Although this might sound complex, dot-matrix printers are relatively simple devices. Therefore, only a few problems usually arise. We will cover the most common problems and their solutions here.

Low Print Quality

Problems with print quality are easy to identify. When the printed page comes out of the printer, the characters may be too light or have dots missing from them. Table 20.1 details some of the most common print quality problems, their causes, and their solutions.

TABLE 20.1   Common dot-matrix print quality problems

Characteristics	Cause	Solution
Consistently faded or light characters	Worn-out printer ribbon	See if you can adjust the print head to be closer to the ribbon. If not (or if it doesn't help), replace the ribbon with a new, vendor-recommended ribbon.

TABLE 20.1 Common dot-matrix print quality problems *(continued)*

Characteristics	Cause	Solution
Print lines that go from dark to light as the print head moves across the page	Printer ribbon-advance gear slipping	Replace the ribbon-advance gear or mechanism.
A small, blank line running through a line of print (consistently)	Print head pin stuck inside the print head	Replace the print head.
A small, blank line running through a line of print (intermittently)	A broken, loose, or shorting print head cable	Secure or replace the print head cable.
A small, dark line running through a line of print	Print head pin stuck in the out position	Replace the print head. (Pushing the pin in may damage the print head.)
Printer making a printing noise, but no print appears on the page	Worn, missing, or improperly installed ribbon cartridge	Replace the ribbon cartridge correctly.
Printer printing garbage	Cable partially unhooked, wrong driver selected, or bad printer control board (PCB)	Hook up the cable correctly, select the correct driver, or replace the PCB (respectively).

Printout Jams inside the Printer

Printer jams (aka "the printer crinkled my paper") are very frustrating because they always seem to happen more than halfway through your 50-page print job, requiring you to take time to remove the jam before the rest of your pages can print. A paper jam happens when something prevents the paper from advancing through the printer evenly. There are generally two causes of printer jams: an obstructed paper path and stripped drive gears.

Obstructed paper paths are often difficult to find. Usually it means disassembling the printer to find the bit of crumpled-up paper or other foreign substance that's blocking the paper path. A common obstruction is a piece of the "perf"—the perforated sides of tractor-feed paper—that has torn off and gotten crumpled up and then lodged in the paper path. It may be necessary to remove the platen roller and feed mechanism to get at the obstruction.

Use extra caution when printing peel-off labels in dot-matrix printers. If a label or even a whole sheet of labels becomes misaligned or jammed, *do not* roll the roller backward to realign the sheet. The small plastic paper guide that most dot-matrix printers use to control the forward movement of the paper through the printer will peel the label right off its backing if you reverse the direction of the paper. Once the label is free, it can easily get stuck under the platen, causing paper jams. A label stuck under the platen is almost impossible to remove without disassembling the paper-feed assembly. If a label is misaligned, try realigning the whole sheet of labels *slowly* using the feed roller, with the power off, moving it in very small increments.

Stepper Motor Problems

Printers use stepper motors to move the print head back and forth as well as to advance the paper. The carriage motor is responsible for the back-and-forth motion while the main motor advances the paper. These motors get damaged when they are forced in any direction while the power is on. This includes moving the print head over to install a printer ribbon as well as moving the paper-feed roller to align paper. These motors are very sensitive to stray voltages. If you are rotating one of these motors by hand, you are essentially turning it into a small generator and thus damaging it.

A damaged stepper motor is easy to detect. Damage to the stepper motor will cause it to lose precision and move farther with each step. If the main motor is damaged (which is more likely to happen), lines of print will be unevenly spaced. If the print head motor goes bad, characters will be scrunched together. If a stepper motor is damaged badly enough, it won't move at all in any direction; it may even make high-pitched squealing noises. If any of these symptoms appear, it's time to replace one of these motors.

Stepper motors are usually expensive to replace—about half the cost of a new printer! Damage to them is easy to avoid; the biggest key is to not force them to move when the power is on.

Inkjet Printer Problems

An Inkjet printer has many of the same types of parts that a dot-matrix printer does. In this sense, it's almost as if the inkjet technology is simply an extension of the technology used in dot-matrix printers. The parts on an inkjet can be divided into four categories:

- Print head/ink cartridge
- Print head carriage, belt, and stepper motor
- Paper-feed mechanism
- Control, interface, and power circuitry

Perhaps the most obvious difference between inkjet and dot-matrix printers is that dot-matrix printers often use tractor-feed paper while inkjets use normal paper. The differences don't end there, though. Inkjet printers work by spraying ink (often in the form of a bubble, hence their name) onto a page. The pattern of the bubbles forms images on the paper.

Inkjet printers are the most common type of printer found in homes because they are inexpensive and produce good-quality images. For this reason, you need to understand the most common problems with these printers so your company can service them effectively. Let's take a look at some of the most common problems with inkjet printers and their solutions.

Print Quality

The majority of inkjet printer problems are quality problems. Ninety-nine percent of these can be traced to a faulty ink cartridge. With most inkjet printers, the ink cartridge contains the print head and the ink. The major problem with this assembly can be described by "If you don't use it, you lose it." The ink will dry out in the small nozzles and block them if they are not used at least once a week.

An example of a quality problem is when you have thin, blank lines present in every line of text on the page. This is caused by a plugged hole in at least one of the small, pinhole ink nozzles in the print cartridge. Replacing the ink cartridge solves this problem easily.

As we warned in Chapter 10, some people try to save a buck by refilling their ink cartridge when they need to replace it. If you are one of them, *stop!* Don't refill your ink cartridges! Almost all ink cartridges are designed *not* to be refilled. They are designed to be used once and thrown away. By refilling them, you make a hole in them—ink can leak out, and the printer will need to be cleaned. The ink will probably also be of the wrong type, and print quality can suffer. Finally, using a refilled cartridge may void the printer's warranty.

If an ink cartridge becomes damaged or develops a hole, it can put too much ink on the page and the letters will smear. Again, the solution is to replace the ink cartridge. (You should be aware, however, that a very small amount of smearing is normal if the pages are laid on top of each other immediately after printing.)

One final print quality problem that does not directly involve the ink cartridge occurs when the print quickly goes from dark to light and then prints nothing. As we already mentioned, ink cartridges dry out if not used. That's why the manufacturers include a small suction pump inside the printer that primes the ink cartridge before each print cycle. If this priming pump is broken or malfunctioning, this problem will manifest itself and the pump will need to be replaced.

If the problem of the ink quickly going from dark to light and then disappearing ever happens to you, and you really need to print a couple of pages, try this trick. First, take the ink cartridge out of the printer. Then squirt some window cleaner on a paper towel and gently tap the print head against the wet paper towel. The force of the tap plus the solvents in the window cleaner should dislodge any dried ink, and the ink will flow freely again. Just be careful to not rub the paper towel across the print head because this could damage the nozzles.

After you install a new cartridge into many inkjet printers, the print heads in that cartridge must be aligned. *Print head alignment* is the process by which the print head is calibrated for use. A special utility that comes with the printer software is used to do this. You run the alignment utility, and the printer prints several vertical and horizontal lines with numbers next to them. It then shows you a screen and asks you to choose the horizontal and vertical lines that are the most "in line." Once you enter the numbers, the software understands whether the print head(s) are out of alignment, which direction, and by how much. The software then makes slight modifications to the print driver software to tell it how much to offset when printing. Occasionally alignment must be done several times to get the images to align properly.

Most new inkjet printers automatically align the print head, and no interaction is required on your part. Even if this is the case, your printer software may have an option for you to be able to manually align the print heads.

Color Output Problems

Sometimes when you print a color document, the colors might not be the same colors you expected based on what you saw on the screen. This could be caused by a few different issues. First, ink could be bleeding from adjacent areas of the picture, causing the color to be off. A leaking cartridge can cause this, as can using the wrong type of paper for your printer.

If you know you're using the right paper, try cleaning the print cartridges using the software utility that should have been included with the printer software. Once you do that, print a test page to confirm that the colors are correct. On most color printers, the test page will print colors in a pattern from left to right that mirrors the way the ink cartridges are installed. That brings us to our second potential problem, which is the ink cartridges are installed in the wrong spot. (This is for printers with multiple color ink cartridges.) That should be easy to check. Obviously, if that's the problem, put the right color cartridges where they're supposed to be!

Third, if the ink that comes out of the cartridge doesn't match the label on the cartridge, try the self-cleaning utility. If that doesn't help, replace the cartridge. Finally, if one of the colors doesn't come out at all, and self-cleaning doesn't help, just replace the cartridge.

Paper Jams

Inkjet printers have pretty simple paper paths. Therefore, paper jams due to obstructions are less likely than they are on dot-matrix printers. They are still possible, however, so an obstruction shouldn't be overlooked as a possible cause of jamming.

Paper jams in inkjet printers are usually due to one of two things:

- A worn pickup roller
- The wrong type of paper

The pickup roller usually has one or two D-shaped rollers mounted on a rotating shaft. When the shaft rotates, one edge of the D roller rubs against the paper, pushing it into the printer. When the roller gets worn, it gets smooth and doesn't exert enough friction against the paper to push it into the printer.

If the paper used in the printer is too smooth, it can cause the same problem. Pickup rollers use friction, and smooth paper doesn't offer much friction. If the paper is too rough, on the other hand, it acts like sandpaper on the rollers, wearing them smooth. Here's a rule of thumb for paper smoothness: paper slightly smoother than a new dollar bill will work fine.

Creased paper is a common culprit in paper jams. The paper can be creased by the printer if there are obstructions in the paper path or problems with the paper feed mechanism.

Paper-Feeding Problems

You will normally see one of two paper-feeding options on an inkjet printer. The first is that the paper is stored in a paper tray on the front of the printer. The second, which is more common on smaller and cheaper models, is for the paper to be fed in vertically from the back of the printer in a paper feeder.

Regardless of the feed style, the printer will have a paper-feed mechanism, which picks up the paper and feeds it into the printer. Inside the paper-feed mechanism are pickup rollers, which are small rubber rollers that rub up against the paper and feed it into the printer. They press up against small rubber or cork patches known as separator pads. These help keep the rest of the paper in the tray so that only one sheet gets picked up at a time. The pickup rollers are turned by a pickup stepper motor.

If your printer fails to pick up paper, it could indicate that the pickup rollers are too worn. If your printer is always picking up multiple sheets of paper, it could be a couple of things, such as problems with the separator pads or your paper being too "sticky," damp, or rough. Some printers that use vertical paper feeders have a lever with which you can adjust the amount of tension between the pickup rollers and the separator pads. If your printer is consistently pulling multiple sheets of paper, you might want to try to increase the tension using this lever.

The final component is the paper-feed sensor. This sensor is designed to tell the printer when it's out of paper, and they rarely fail. When they do, the printer will refuse to print because it thinks it is out of paper. Cleaning the sensor might help, but if not, you should replace the printer.

Stepper Motor Problems

Inkjet printers use stepper motors, just as dot-matrix printers do. On an inkjet, the print head carriage is the component containing the print head that moves back and forth. A carriage stepper motor and an attached belt (the carriage belt) are responsible for the movement. To keep the print head carriage horizontally stable, it rests on a metal stabilizer bar. Another stepper motor is responsible for advancing the paper.

Stepper motor problems on an inkjet will look similar to the ones on a dot-matrix printer. That is, if the main motor is damaged, lines of print will be unevenly spaced, and if the print head motor goes bad, characters will be scrunched together. A lot of damage may cause the stepper motor to not move at all and possibly make high-pitched squealing noises. If any of these symptoms appear, it's time to replace one of these motors. As with dot-matrix printers, stepper motors can be expensive. It may make more economical sense to replace the printer.

Power Problems

Inkjet printers have internal power circuits that convert the electricity from the outlet into voltages that the printer can use, typically 12V and 5V. The specific device that does this is called the transformer. If the transformer fails, the printer will not power up. If this happens, it's time to get a new printer.

Laser Printer Problems

The process that laser printers use to print, called the electrophotographic (EP) print process, is the most complex process of all commonly used printers. You should have memorized the six-step EP process for the A+ Exam 220-801, but perhaps you've forgotten a bit. Table 20.2 gives you the six steps and a short description of what happens in each step.

The descriptions in Table 20.2 are summaries of the process. For detailed descriptions, please see Chapter 10.

TABLE 20.2   The EP printing process

Step	Action
Cleaning	A rubber blade scrapes any remaining toner off of the drum and a fluorescent lamp discharges any remaining charge on the photosensitive drum.
Charging	The charging corona gets a high voltage from the high voltage power supply (HVPS). It uses the voltage to apply a strong uniform negative charge (–600VDC) to the photosensitive drum.
Writing	The laser scans the drum. Wherever it touches the drum, the charge is reduced from –600VDC to around –100VDC. The pattern formed on the drum will be the image that is printed.
Developing	The developing roller acquires a –600VDC charge from the HVPS and picks up toner, which gets the same –600VDC charge. As the developing toner rolls by the photosensitive drum, the toner is attracted to the lesser-charged (–100VDC) areas on the photosensitive drum and sticks to it in those areas.

TABLE 20.2   The EP printing process *(continued)*

Step	Action
Transferring	The charging corona wire or roller acquires a strong positive charge (+600VDC) and transfers it to the paper. As the photosensitive drum with ink on it rolls by, the ink is attracted to the paper.
Fusing	The 350° F fuser roller melts the toner paper and the rubberized pressure roller presses the melted toner into the paper, making the image permanent.

Looking at the steps involved in laser printing, it's pretty easy to tell that laser printers are the most complex printers that we have discussed. There is good news, though—most laser printer problems are easily identifiable and have specific fixes. Let's discuss the most common laser and page printer problems and their solutions.

Don't forget to perform periodic preventative maintenance on your laser printers. It can help eliminate many potential problems before they happen. Preventative maintenance includes cleaning the printer and using manufacturer-recommended maintenance kits.

Power Problems

If you turn your laser printer on and it doesn't respond normally, there could be a problem with the power it's receiving. Of course, the first thing to do is to ensure that it's plugged in!

A laser printer's DC power supply provides three different DC voltages to printer components. This can all be checked at a power interface labeled J210, which is a 20-pin female interface. Pin 1 will be in the lower-left corner, and the pins along the bottom will all be odd numbers, increasing from left to right.

Printer voltages can be tested with a multimeter.

Using the multimeter, you should find the following voltages:

- Pin 1 +5v
- Pin 5 −5v
- Pin 9 +24v

If none of the voltages are reading properly, then you probably need to replace the fuse in the DC power supply. If one or more (but not all) of the voltages aren't reading properly, then the first thing to do is remove all optional hardware in the printer (including memory) and test again. If the readings are still bad, it's likely you need to replace the DC power supply.

No Connectivity (IP Issues)

You can connect many laser printers directly to your network by using a network cable (such as Category 5e or 6) or by using a wireless network adapter with the printer. In cases like these, the printer acts as its own print server (typically print server software is built into the printer), and it can speed up printing because you don't have a separate print server translating and then sending the directions to the printer.

For printers such as these, no connectivity can be a sign of improperly configured IP settings such as the IP address. While each printer is somewhat different, you can manually configure most laser printers' IP settings a number of ways, such as:

- Through the printer's LCD control panel. For example, on several HP LaserJet models, you press Menu, navigate to the Network Config menu, select TCP/IP Config, select Manual, and then enter the IP address. You would then also configure the subnet mask and default gateway.

- By using Telnet to connect to the printer's management software from your computer.

- By using the management software that came with your printer.

You can also configure most IP printers to automatically obtain an IP address from a Dynamic Host Configuration Protocol (DHCP) server. Whenever the printer is powered up, it will contact the server to get its IP configuration information just like any other client on the network. While this may be convenient, it's usually not a good idea to assign printers random IP addresses. Client computers will have their printer mapped to a specific IP address; if that address is changed, you will have a lot of people complaining about no connectivity. If you are using the DHCP server to manage all of your network's IP addresses, be sure to reserve a static address for the printers.

> To see what a printer's IP address is set at, print off a configuration page from the printer's control panel. Then post the IP information near the printer so that users can easily connect to it.

Nothing Prints

You tell your computer to print, but nothing comes out of the printer. That problem is probably the most challenging to solve because it could be caused by several different things. Are you the only one affected by the problem or are others having the same issue? Is the printer plugged in, powered on, and online? As with any troubleshooting, check your connections first.

Other times when nothing prints, you get a clue as to what the problem is. The printer may give you an "out of memory" error or something similar. Another possibility is that the printer will say "processing data" (or something similar) on its LCD display and nothing will print. It's likely that the printer has run out of memory while trying to process the print job. If your printer is exhibiting these symptoms, it's best to power the printer off and then power it back on.

Be aware that large print jobs may cause the printer to say "processing data" for several minutes before the print job starts. There is nothing wrong with this, although it's possible that your printer could stand a memory upgrade. But if the printer exhibits this behavior for a long time, say 20 or 30 minutes, it may be best to cycle the power.

Paper Jams

Laser printers today run at copier speeds. Because of this, their most common problem is paper jams. Paper can get jammed in a printer for several reasons. First, feed jams happen when the paper-feed rollers get worn (similar to feed jams in inkjet printers). The solution to this problem is easy: Replace the worn rollers.

Another cause of feed jams is related to the drive gear of the pickup roller. The drive gear (or clutch) may be broken or have teeth missing. Again, the solution is to replace it. To determine if the problem is a broken gear or worn rollers, print a test page, but leave the paper tray out. Look into the paper-feed opening with a flashlight and see if the paper pickup roller(s) are turning evenly and don't skip. If they turn evenly, the problem is probably worn rollers.

If your paper-feed jams are caused by worn pickup rollers, there is something you can do to get your printer working while you're waiting for the replacement pickup rollers. Scuff the feed roller(s) with a Scotch-Brite pot-scrubber pad (or something similar) to roughen up the feed rollers. This trick works only once. After that, the rollers aren't thick enough to touch the paper.

Worn exit rollers can also cause paper jams. These rollers guide the paper out of the printer into the paper-receiving tray. If they are worn or damaged, the paper may catch on its way out of the printer. These types of jams are characterized by a paper jam that occurs just as the paper is getting to the exit rollers. If the paper jams, open the rear door and see where the paper is. If the paper is very close to the exit roller, the exit rollers are probably the problem.

The solution is to replace all the exit rollers. You must replace all of them at the same time because even one worn exit roller can cause the paper to jam. Besides, they're inexpensive. Don't be cheap and skimp on these parts if you need to have them replaced.

Paper jams can also be the fault of the paper. If your printer consistently tries to feed multiple pages into the printer, the paper isn't dry enough. If you live in an area with high humidity, this could be a problem. We've heard some solutions that are pretty far out but that work (like keeping the paper in a Tupperware-type airtight container or microwaving it to remove moisture). The best all-around solution, however, is humidity control and keeping the paper wrapped until it's needed. Keep the humidity around 50 percent or lower (but above 25 percent if you can, in order to avoid problems with electrostatic discharge).

⊕ Real World Scenario

Printer Triage

One of the authors relates the following story. He was in the local hospital ER a while ago having his hand looked at (he had cut it pretty badly on some glass). The receptionist asked him a few questions, filled out a report in the medical database on her computer, and printed it. When the paper starting coming out of the laser printer, she grabbed it and "ripped" it from the printer as you might do if the paper were in an old typewriter! The printer's exit rollers complained bitterly and made a noise that made him cringe. She did this for every sheet of paper she printed.

The following week, that printer came in for service because it was jamming repeatedly. The problem? Worn exit rollers.

He had a word with the person in charge of computer repair at that hospital and saved them from many future repairs. The lesson? Printers don't have to be treated with kid gloves, but using them properly can prolong life and reduce need for service repairs.

Finally, a grounded metal strip called the static-eliminator strip inside the printer drains the transfer corona charge away from the paper after it has been used to transfer toner from the EP cartridge. If that strip is missing, broken, or damaged, the charge will remain on the paper and may cause it to stick to the EP cartridge, causing a jam. If the paper jams after reaching the transfer corona assembly, this may be the cause.

Blank Pages

There's nothing more annoying than printing a 10-page contract and receiving 10 pages of blank paper from the printer. Blank pages are a somewhat common occurrence in laser printers. Somehow, the toner isn't being put on the paper. There are three major causes of blank pages:

- The toner cartridge
- The transfer corona assembly
- The high-voltage power supply (HVPS)

TONER CARTRIDGE

The toner cartridge is the source of most quality problems because it contains most of the image-formation pieces for laser printers. Let's start with the obvious. A blank page will come out of the printer if there is no toner in the toner cartridge. It might sound simple, but some people think these things last forever. Many laser printers give some sort of warning if the toner cartridge is low, but it's easy to check. Just open the printer, remove the toner cartridge, and shake it. You will be able to hear if there's toner inside the cartridge. If it's empty, replace it with a known, good, manufacturer-recommended toner cartridge. If it is not yet empty, shaking it redistributes the toner and may provide better printing for some time.

> When you're shaking a toner cartridge, loose toner can fall out of the cartridge and get on your clothing. Always hold the toner cartridge away from your body when shaking it.

Another issue that crops up rather often is the problem of using refilled or reconditioned toner cartridges. During their recycling process, these cartridges may be filled with the wrong kind of toner (for example, one with an incorrect composition). This can cause toner to be repelled from the EP drum instead of attracted to it. Thus, there's no toner on the page because there was no toner on the EP drum to begin with. The solution once again is to replace the toner cartridge with the type recommended by the manufacturer.

A third problem related to toner cartridges happens when someone installs a new toner cartridge and forgets to remove the sealing tape that is present to keep the toner in the cartridge during shipping. The solution to this problem is as easy as it is obvious: Remove the toner cartridge from the printer, remove the sealing tape, and reinstall the cartridge.

> Most of the time if you have dust or debris in a printer, you can go ahead and use compressed air to blow it away. Don't do that with toner though, because if you do you'll make a huge mess. If you have a toner spill, use a specialized toner vacuum to pick it up.

TRANSFER CORONA ASSEMBLY

The second cause of the blank-page problem is a damaged or missing transfer corona wire or damaged transfer corona roller. If a wire is lost or damaged, the developed image won't transfer from the EP drum to the paper. Thus, no image appears on the printout. To determine if this is causing your problem, do the first half of the self-test (described later in this chapter in the section "Self-Tests"). If there is an image on the drum but not on the paper, you know that the transfer corona assembly isn't doing its job.

To check if the transfer corona assembly is causing the problem, open the cover and examine the wire (or roller, if your printer uses one). The corona wire is hard to see, so you may need a flashlight. You will know if it's broken or missing just by looking (it will either be in pieces or just not be there). If it's not broken or missing, the problem may be related to the high voltage power supply.

The transfer corona wire (or roller) is a relatively inexpensive part and can be easily replaced with the removal of two screws and some patience.

HIGH-VOLTAGE POWER SUPPLY (HVPS)

The HVPS supplies high-voltage, low-current power to both the charging and transfer corona assemblies in laser printers. If it's broken, neither corona will work properly. If the self-test shows an image on the drum but none on the paper, and the transfer corona assembly is present and not damaged, then the HVPS is at fault.

All-Black Pages

Only slightly more annoying than 10 blank pages are 10 black pages. This happens when the charging unit (the charging corona wire or charging corona roller) in the toner cartridge malfunctions and fails to place a charge on the EP drum. Because the drum is grounded, it has no charge. Anything with a charge (like toner) will stick to it. As the drum rotates, all the toner is transferred to the page and a black page is formed.

This problem wastes quite a bit of toner but can be fixed easily. The solution (again) is to replace the toner cartridge with a known, good, manufacturer-recommended one. If that doesn't solve the problem, then the HVPS is at fault (it's not providing the high voltage that the charging corona needs to function).

Repetitive Small Marks or Defects

Repetitive marks occur frequently in heavily used (as well as older) laser printers. The problem may be caused by toner spilled inside the printer. It can also be caused by a crack or chip in the EP drum (this mainly happens with recycled cartridges), which can accumulate toner. In both cases, some of the toner gets stuck onto one of the rollers. Once this happens, every time the roller rotates and touches a piece of paper, it leaves toner smudges spaced a roller circumference apart.

The solution is relatively simple: Clean or replace the offending roller. To help you figure out which roller is causing the problem, the service manuals contain a chart like the one in Figure 20.4. (Some larger printers will also have the roller layout printed inside the service door.) To use the chart, place the printed page next to it. Align the first occurrence of the smudge with the top arrow. The next smudge will line up with one of the other arrows. The arrow it lines up with tells you which roller is causing the problem.

FIGURE 20.4   Laser printer roller circumference chart

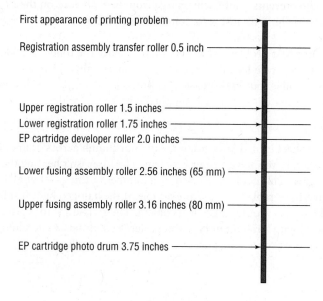

Remember that the chart in Figure 20.4 is only an example. Your printer may have different-sized rollers and thus need a different chart. Check your printer's service documentation for a chart like this. It is valuable in determining which roller is causing a smudge.

Vertical White Lines on the Page

Vertical white lines running down all or part of the page are a relatively common problem on older printers, especially ones that don't see much maintenance. They are caused by foreign matter (more than likely toner) caught on the transfer corona wire. The dirty spots keep the toner from being transmitted to the paper (at those locations, that is), with the result that streaks form as the paper progresses past the transfer corona wire.

The solution is to clean the corona wires. LaserJet Series II printers contain a small corona wire brush to help in this procedure. It's usually a small, green-handled brush located near the transfer corona wire. To use it, remove the toner cartridge and run the brush in the charging corona groove on top of the toner cartridge. Replace the cartridge and use the brush to remove any foreign deposits on the transfer corona. Be sure to put it back in its holder when you're finished.

Vertical Black Lines on the Page

A groove or scratch in the EP drum can cause the problem of vertical black lines running down all or part of the page. Because a scratch is lower than the surface, it doesn't receive as much (if any) of a charge as the other areas. The result is that toner sticks to it as though it were discharged. The groove may go around the circumference of the drum, so the line may go all the way down the page.

Another possible cause of vertical black lines is a dirty charging corona wire. A dirty charging corona wire prevents a sufficient charge from being placed on the EP drum. Because the charge on the EP drum is almost zero, toner sticks to the areas that correspond to the dirty areas on the charging corona.

The solution to the first problem is, as always, to replace the toner cartridge (or EP drum, if your printer uses a separate EP drum and toner). You can also solve the second problem with a new toner cartridge, but in this case that would be an extreme solution. It's easier to clean the charging corona with the brush supplied with the cartridge.

Image Smudging

If you can pick up a sheet from a laser printer, run your thumb across it, and have the image come off on your thumb, you have a fuser problem. The fuser isn't heating the toner and fusing it into the paper. This could be caused by a number of things—but all of them can be taken care of with a fuser replacement. For example, if the halogen light inside the heating roller has burned out, that would cause the problem. The solution is to replace the fuser. The fuser can be replaced with a rebuilt unit, if you prefer. Rebuilt fusers are almost as good as new ones, and some even come with guarantees. Plus, they cost less.

The whole fuser may not need to be replaced. Fuser components can be ordered from parts suppliers and can be rebuilt by you. For example, if the fuser has a bad lamp, you can order a lamp and replace it in the fuser.

A similar problem occurs when small areas of smudging repeat themselves down the page. Dents or cold spots in the fuser heat roller cause this problem. The only solution is to replace either the fuser assembly or the heat roller.

Ghosting

Ghosting is what you have when you can see light images of previously printed pages on the current page. This is caused by one of two things: a broken cleaning blade or bad erasure lamps. A broken cleaning blade causes old toner to build up on the EP drum and consequently present itself in the next printed image. If the erasure lamps are bad, then the previous electrostatic discharges aren't completely wiped away. When the EP drum rotates toward the developing roller, some toner sticks to the slightly discharged areas.

Replacing the toner cartridge solves the first problem. Replacing the erasure lamps in the printer solves the second. Because the toner cartridge is the least expensive cure, you should try that first. Usually, replacing the toner cartridge will solve the problem. If it doesn't, you will have to replace the erasure lamps.

Printer Prints Pages of Garbage

This has happened to everyone at least once. You print a one-page letter, but instead of the letter you have 10 pages of what looks like garbage or many more pages with one character per page come out of the printer. This problem comes from one of two different sources: the printer driver software or the formatter board.

PRINTER DRIVER

The correct printer driver needs to be installed for the printer you have. For example, if you have an HP LaserJet III, then that is the driver you need to install. Once the driver has been installed, it must be configured for the correct page-description language: PCL or PostScript. Most HP LaserJet printers use PCL (but can be configured for PostScript). Determine what page-description language your printer has been configured for and set the printer driver to the same setting. If this is not done, you will get garbage out of the printer.

Most printers that have LCD displays will indicate that they are in Post-Script mode with a *PS* or *PostScript* somewhere in the display.

If the problem is the wrong driver setting, the garbage the printer prints will look like English. That is, the words will be readable, but they won't make any sense.

FORMATTER BOARD

The other cause of several pages of garbage being printed is a bad formatter board. This circuit board takes the information the printer receives from the computer and turns it into commands for the various components in the printer. Usually, problems with the formatter board produce wavy lines of print or random patterns of dots on the page.

It's relatively easy to replace the formatter board in a laser printer. Usually this board is installed under the printer and can be removed by loosening two screws and pulling it out. Typically, replacing the formatter board also replaces the printer interface, which is another possible source of garbage printouts.

Example Printer Testing: HP LaserJet

Now that we've defined some of the possible sources of problems with laser printers, let's discuss a few of the testing procedures you use with them. We'll discuss HP LaserJet laser printers because they are the most popular type of laser printer, but the topics covered here apply to other types of laser printers as well.

We'll look at two ways to troubleshoot laser printers: self-tests and error codes (for laser printers with LCD displays).

SELF-TESTS

You can perform three tests to narrow down which assembly is causing the problem: the engine self-test, the engine half self-test, or the secret self-test. These tests, which the printer runs on its own when directed by the user, are internal diagnostics for printers and are included with most laser printers.

Engine self-test   The engine self-test tests the print engine of the LaserJet, bypassing the formatter board. This test causes the printer to print a single page with vertical lines running its length. If an engine self-test can be performed, you know the laser print engine can print successfully. To perform an engine self-test, you must press the printer's self-test button, which is hidden behind a small cover on the side of the printer (see Figure 20.5). The location of the button varies from printer to printer, so you may have to refer to the printer manual. Using a pencil or probe, press the button, and the print engine will start printing the test page.

FIGURE 20.5   Print engine self-test button location. The location may vary on different printers.

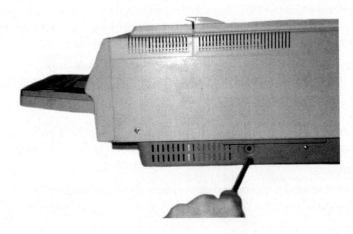

Half self-test A print engine half self-test is performed the same way as the self-test, but you interrupt it halfway through the print cycle by opening the cover. This test is useful in determining which part of the print process is causing the printer to malfunction. If you stop the print process and part of a developed image is on the EP drum and part has been transferred to the paper, you know that the pickup rollers, registration rollers, laser scanner, charging roller, EP drum, and transfer roller are all working correctly. You can stop the half self-test at various points in the print process to determine the source of a malfunction.

Secret self-test To activate this test, you must first put the printer into service mode. To accomplish this, turn on the printer while simultaneously holding down the On Line, Continue, and Enter buttons (that's the first secret part, because nobody knows it unless somebody tells them). When the screen comes up blank, release the keys and press, in order, Continue and then Enter. The printer will perform an internal self-test and then display 00 READY. At this point you are ready to initiate the rest of the secret self-test. Take the printer offline, press the Test button on the front panel, and hold the button until you see the 04 Self Test message. Then release the Test button. This will cause the printer to print one self-test page. (If you want a continuous printout, instead of releasing the Test button at the 04 Self Test message, keep holding the Test button. The printer will print continuous self-test pages until you power off the printer or press On Line or until it runs out of paper.)

ERROR CODES

In addition to the self-tests, you have another tool for troubleshooting HP laser printers. Error codes are a way for the LaserJet to tell the user (and a service technician) what's wrong. Table 20.3 details some of the most common codes displayed on an HP LaserJet.

TABLE 20.3 HP LaserJet error messages

Message	Description
00 Ready	The printer is in standby mode and ready to print.
02 Warming Up	The fuser is being warmed up before the 00 Ready state.
05 Self-Test	A full self-test has been initiated from the front panel.
11 Paper Out	The paper tray sensor is reporting that there is no paper in the paper tray. The printer will not print as long as this error exists.
13 Paper Jam	A piece of paper is caught in the paper path. To fix this problem, open the cover and clear the jam (including all pieces of the jam). Close the cover to resume printing. The printer will not print as long as this error exists.
14 No EP Cart	There is no EP cartridge (toner cartridge) installed in the printer. The printer will not print as long as this error exists.
15 Engine Test	An engine self-test is in progress.

TABLE 20.3   HP LaserJet error messages *(continued)*

Message	Description
16 Toner Low	The toner cartridge is almost out of toner. Replacement will be necessary soon.
50 Service	A fuser error has occurred. This problem is most commonly caused by fuser lamp failure. Power off the printer and replace the fuser to solve the problem. The printer will not print as long as this error exists.
51 Error	There is a laser-scanning assembly problem. Test and replace, if necessary. The printer will not print as long as this error exists.
52 Error	The scanner motor in the laser-scanning assembly is malfunctioning. Test and replace as per the service manual. The printer will not print as long as this error exists.
55 Error	There is a communication problem between the formatter and the DC controller. Test and replace as per the service manual. The printer will not print as long as this error exists.

Troubleshooting Tips for HP LaserJet Printers

Printer technicians usually use a set of troubleshooting steps to help them solve HP LaserJet printing problems. Let's detail each of them to bring our discussion of laser printer troubleshooting to a close:

1. **Is the exhaust fan operational?** This is the first component to receive power when the printer is turned on. If you can feel air coming out of the exhaust fan, this confirms that AC voltage is present and power is turned on, that +5VDC and +24VDC are being generated by the AC power supply (ACPS), and that the DC controller is functional. If there is no power to the printer (no lights, fan not operating), the ACPS is at fault. Replacement involves removing all printer covers and removing four screws. You can purchase a new ACPS module, but it is usually cheaper to replace it with a rebuilt unit.

 If you are into electronics, you can probably rebuild the ACPS yourself simply and cheaply. The main rectifier is usually the part that fails in these units; it can easily be replaced if you know what you're doing.

2. **Do the control panel LEDs work?** If so, the formatter board can communicate with the control panel. If the LEDs do not light, it could mean the formatter board is bad, the control panel is bad, or the wires connecting the two are broken or shorting out.

3. **Does the main motor rotate at power up?** Turn off the power. Remove the covers from the sides of the printer. Turn the printer back on and carefully watch and listen for main motor rotation. If you see and hear the main motor rotating, this indicates that a toner cartridge is installed, all photosensors are functional, all motors are functional, and the printer can move paper (assuming there are no obstructions).

4. **Does the fuser heat lamp light after the main motor finishes its rotation?** You will need to remove the covers to see this. The heat lamp should light after the main motor rotation and stay lit until the control panel says 00 Ready.

5. **Can the printer perform an engine test print?** A sheet of vertical lines indicates that the print engine works. This test print bypasses the formatter board and indicates whether the print problem resides in the engine. If the test print is successful, you can rule out the engine as a source of the problem. If the test print fails, you will have to further troubleshoot the printer to determine which engine component is causing the problem.

6. **Can the printer perform a control panel self-test?** This is the final test to ensure printer operation. If you can press the Test Page control panel button and receive a test printout, this means the entire printer is working properly. The only possibilities for problems are outside the printer (interfaces, cables, and software problems).

Most printers will print a test page, which contains both colors and patterns, based on your printer's capabilities. Although the exact style of pattern may vary, the idea is the same for all printers. You're checking to ensure that the printer can do what it's capable of. Many test patterns will measure gradients and resolution as well as letter qualities at various font sizes. Color printers will also print color sections, whereas black-and-white printers will often produce patterns in grayscale. If you are experiencing print-quality issues, running a test pattern is a good way to check to see what's wrong with the printer.

Managing Print Jobs

Most people know how to send a job to the printer. Clicking File, then Print, or pressing Ctrl+P on your keyboard generally does the trick. But once the job gets sent to the printer, what do you do if it doesn't print?

Keep in mind that in a networked environment, users need the proper permissions to both install and print to the printer. Not having permission will result in denied access.

When you send a job to the printer, that print job ends up in a line with all other documents sent to that printer. The line of all print jobs is called the *print queue*. In most cases, the printer will print jobs on a first-come, first-served basis. (There are exceptions if you've enabled printing priorities in Printer Properties.) Once you send the job to the printer, a small printer icon will appear in the system tray in the lower-right corner of your desktop, near the clock. By double-clicking it (or by right-clicking it and selecting the printer name), you will end up looking at the jobs in the print queue, like the one shown in Figure 20.6.

FIGURE 20.6 Print jobs in the print queue

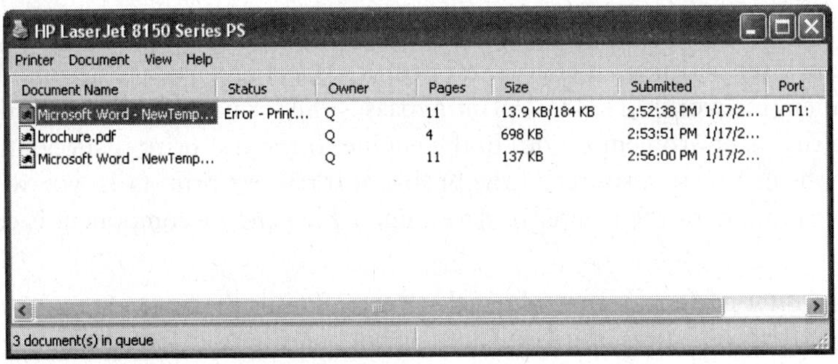

In Figure 20.6 you can see that the first document submitted has an error, which may explain why it hasn't printed. All of the other documents in the queue are blocked until the job with the error is cleared. You can clear it one of two ways. Either right-click on the document and choose Cancel or select Document ➢ Cancel, as shown in Figure 20.7.

FIGURE 20.7 Printer documents menu

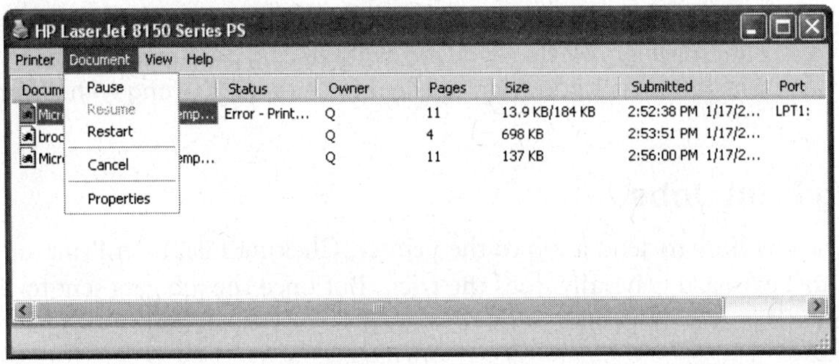

Note that from the menu you see in Figure 20.7, you can pause, resume, restart, and cancel print jobs as well as see properties of the selected print job. If you wanted to pause or cancel all jobs going to a printer, you would do that from the Printer menu, as shown in Figure 20.8.

Once you have cleared the print job causing the problem, the next job will move to the top of the queue. It should show its status as Printing, like the one shown in Figure 20.9.

But what if it shows it's printing but it still isn't working? (We're assuming the printer is powered on, connected properly, and online.) It could be a problem with the print spooler.

FIGURE 20.8   Printer menu

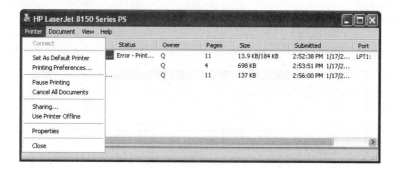

 If print jobs are processed very slowly, or if you are continually seeing "low memory" error messages, it might be a good time to upgrade the memory in the printer.

FIGURE 20.9   Print job printing correctly

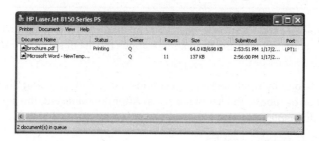

Managing the Print Spooler

The *print spooler* is a service that formats print jobs in the language that the printer needs. Think of it as a holding area where the print jobs are prepared for the printer. In Windows, the spooler is a service that's started automatically when Windows loads.

If jobs aren't printing and there's no apparent reason why, it could be that the print spooler has stalled. To fix the problem, you need to stop and restart the print spooler. Exercise 20.2 walks you through stopping and restarting the spooler in Windows 7.

EXERCISE 20.2

Stopping and Restarting the Print Spooler in Windows 7

1. Open Computer Management and navigate to Services (right-click the Computer icon and choose Manage; if necessary, click on the arrow next to Services And Applications to expand the list).

2. Find the Print Spooler service, shown in the middle pane.

3. Stop the spooler. There are several ways you can do this. You can right-click the service name and choose Stop, click the Stop square above the list of services, or use the More Actions menu on the right.

4. Restart the spooler by right-clicking the service name and choosing Start or by clicking the Start arrow above the list of services. After it's restarted, the service's Status column should display Started.

5. Close Computer Management.

If you have a different version of Windows, the steps to stop and restart the spooler are the same as in Exercise 21.2; the only difference might be in how you get to Computer Management.

Printing a Test Page

If your printer isn't spitting out print jobs, it may be a good idea to print a test page and see if that works. The test page information is stored in the printer's memory, so there's no formatting or translating of jobs required. It's simply a test to make sure your printer hears your computer.

When you install a printer, one of the last questions it asks you is if you want to print a test page. If there's any question, go ahead and do it. If the printer is already installed, you can print a test page from the printer's Properties window (right-click the printer and choose Printer Properties). Just click the Print Test Page button and it should work. If nothing happens, double-check your connections and stop and restart the print spooler. If garbage prints, there is likely a problem with the printer or the print driver.

Troubleshooting Networking Problems

As a technician, you are going to be called on to solve a variety of issues, including hardware, software, and networking problems. Networking problems can sometimes be the most tricky to solve considering that it could be either a software or a hardware problem or a combination of the two causing your connectivity issue.

The first adage for troubleshooting any hardware problem is to check your connections. That holds true for networking as well, but then your troubleshooting will need to go far deeper than that in a hurry. As with troubleshooting anything else, follow a logical procedure when troubleshooting and be sure to document your work.

Nearly all of the issues tested by CompTIA have something to do with connectivity, which makes sense because that's what networking is all about. Connectivity issues, when not caused by hardware, are generally the result of a messed-up configuration. And because the most common protocol in use today, TCP/IP, has a lot of configuration options, you can imagine how easy it is to configure something incorrectly.

In the following sections, we'll look at connectivity issues and how to resolve them. We'll also review several tools that we've talked about elsewhere in the book but are handy for network troubleshooting as well.

CompTIA 220-802 objective 4.5 combines wired and wireless networking. We'll cover them together and note when specific differences exist.

Resolving Connectivity Issues

The whole purpose of using a network is to connect to other resources, right? So when networks don't work like they're supposed to, users tend to get a bit upset. With the explosion of wireless networking over the last 5 to 10 years, our job as technicians has only gotten more complicated. Let's take a look at some common issues you might run across and how to deal with them.

No Connectivity

Let's start with the most dire situation: no connectivity. Taking a step back to look at the big picture, think about all of the components that go into networking. On the client side you need a network card and drivers, operating system, protocol, and the right configuration. Then you have a cable of some sort or a wireless connection. At the other end is a switch or wireless router. That device connects to other devices, and so forth. The point is, if someone is complaining of no connectivity, there could be one of several different things causing it. So start with the basics.

The most common issue that prevents network connectivity on a wired network is a bad or unplugged patch cable. Cleaning crews and the rollers on the bottoms of chairs are the most common threats to a patch cable. In most cases, wall jacks are placed 4 to 10 feet away from the desktop. The patch cables are normally lying exposed under the user's desk, and from time to time damage is done to the cable or it's inadvertently snagged and unplugged. Tightly cinching the cable, while tying it up out of the way, is no better solution. Slack must be left in the cable to allow for some amount of equipment movement and to avoid altering the electrical characteristics of the cable. When you troubleshoot connectivity, start with the most rudimentary explanations first. Make sure the patch cable is tightly plugged in, and then look at the card and see if any lights are on. If there are lights on, use the NIC's documentation to help troubleshoot. More often than not, shutting down the machine, unplugging the patch and power cables for a moment, and then reattaching them and rebooting the PC will fix an unresponsive NIC.

A properly connected NIC should typically have one light illuminated (the link light). If the link light is not illuminated, it indicates a problem with the NIC, the patch cable, or the device the patch cable is connecting to (hub, switch, server, and so on). Other lights that may be illuminated include a speed light, duplex light, and/or activity light.

If you don't have any lights, you don't have a connection. It could be that the cable is bad or it's not plugged in on the other side, or it could also be a problem with the NIC or the connectivity device on the other side. Is this the only computer having problems? If everyone else in the same area is having the same problem, that points to a central issue.

Most wireless network cards have indicators on them as well that can help you troubleshoot. For example, a wireless card might have a connection light and an activity light, much like a wired network card. On one particular card we've used, the lights will alternate blinking if the card isn't attached to a network. Once it attaches, the connection light will be solid and the link light will blink when it's busy. Other cards may operate in a slightly different manner, so be sure to consult your documentation.

If you don't have lights, try reseating your cables and rebooting. It might also help to reseat the card. If you're using a USB or PC Card wireless adapter, this is pretty easy. If it's inside your desktop, it will require a little surgery. If it's integrated into your laptop, you could have serious issues. Try rebooting first. If that doesn't help, see if you can use an expansion NIC and make that one light up.

So let's assume that you have lights and that no one else is having a problem. (Yes, it's just you.) That means the hardware is probably okay, so it's time to check the configuration. Open a command prompt, type **IPCONFIG**, and press Enter. You should get an IP address. (If it starts with 169.254.*x*.*x*, that's an APIPA address. We'll talk about those later.) If you don't have a valid IP address, that's the problem.

Remember that in order to communicate on a network using TCP/IP, you need to have a unique IP address and a valid subnet mask. If you want to communicate on a network outside of your own local network, you also need a default gateway.

If you do have a valid IP address, it's time to see how far your connectivity reaches. With your command prompt open, use the PING command to ping a known, remote working host. If that doesn't work, start working backward. Can you ping the outside port of your router? The inside port? A local host? (Some technicians recommend pinging your loopback address first with PING 127.0.0.1 and then working your way out to see where the connectivity ends. Either way is fine. The advantage to starting with the loopback is that if it doesn't work, you know nothing else will either.) Using this methodology, you'll be able to figure out where your connectivity truly begins and ends.

APIPA Addresses

As we talked about in Chapter 7, "Introduction to TCP/IP," Automatic Private IP Addressing (APIPA) is a service that auto-configures your network card with an IP address. APIPA kicks in only if your computer is set to receive an IP address from the Dynamic Host Configuration Protocol (DHCP) server and that server doesn't respond. You can always tell an APIPA address because it will be in the format of 169.254.*x.x*.

When you have an APIPA address, you will be able to communicate with other computers that also have an APIPA address but not with any other resources. The solution is to figure out why you're not getting an answer from the DHCP server and fix that problem.

IP Address Conflicts

Every host on a network needs to have a unique IP address. If two or more hosts have the same address, communication problems will occur. The good news is nearly every operating system today will warn you if it detects an IP address conflict with your computer. The bad news is it won't fix it by itself.

The communication problems will vary. In some cases the computer will seem nearly fine, with intermittent issues. In others, it will appear as if you have no connectivity.

The most common cause of this is if someone configures a computer with a static IP address that's part of the DHCP server's range. The DHCP server, not knowing that the address has been statically assigned somewhere, doles out the address and now there's a conflict. Rebooting the computer won't help, and neither will releasing the address and getting a new lease from the DHCP server—it's just going to hand out the same address again because it doesn't know that there's a problem.

As the administrator, you need to track down the offending user. A common way to do this is to use a packet sniffer to look at network traffic and determine the computer name or MAC address associated with the IP address in question. Most administrators don't keep network maps of MAC addresses, but everyone should have a network map with hostnames. If not, it could be a long, tedious process to check everyone's computer to find the culprit.

Usually the person who manually configured their address didn't intend to cause any problems. This would be a good time to show your professionalism and communication skills and educate the user as to why they shouldn't have done what they did.

Limited or Local Connectivity

In a way, limited connectivity problems are a bit of a blessing. You can immediately rule out client-side hardware issues because they can connect to some resources. You just need to figure out why they can't connect to others. This is most likely caused by one of two things: a configuration issue or a connectivity device (such as a router) problem.

Check the local configuration first. Use **IPCONFIG /ALL** to ensure that the computer's IP address, subnet mask, and default gateway are all configured properly. After that, use the ping utility to see what the range of connectivity is. In situations like this, it's also good to check with other users in the area. Are they having the same connectivity issues? If so, it's more likely to be a central problem rather than one with the client computer.

Intermittent Connectivity

Under this heading, we're going to consider intermittent connectivity, slow transfer speeds, and low radio frequency (RF) signal because they are all pretty similar.

On a wired network, if you run into slow speeds or intermittent connectivity, it's likely a load issue. There's too much traffic for the network to handle, and the network is bogging down. (You obviously don't need to worry about RF signals on a wired network.) Solutions include adding a switch, replacing your hubs with switches, and even creating virtual LANs (VLANs) with switches. If the network infrastructure is old (for example, if it's running on Cat 3 cable or you only have 10Mbps switches), then it might be time for an upgrade.

Wireless networks can get overloaded too. It's recommended that no more than 30 or so client computers use one wireless access point (WAP) or wireless router. Any more than that can cause intermittent access problems. The most common reason that users on wireless networks experience any of these issues though is distance. The further away from the WAP the user gets, the weaker the signal becomes. When the signal weakens, the transfer rates drop dramatically. For example, the signal from an 802.11g wireless router has a maximum range of about 300 feet barring any obstructions. At that distance though, 802.11g will support transfer rates of only 6Mbps—far less than the 54Mbps the users think they're getting! The solutions here are to move closer or install more access points. Depending on the configuration of your working environment, you could also consider adding a directional antenna to the WAP. It will increase the distance the signal travels, but only in a limited direction.

Using Network Troubleshooting Tools

The CompTIA A+ 220-802 will test you on your knowledge of troubleshooting tools for networks. There are two categories of tools that you need to know: hardware devices and software commands. We've covered all (but one) of these tools in depth earlier in the book. The hardware tools are in Chapter 6, "Networking Fundamentals," and the software commands are in Chapter 13. Here we'll provide a quick review.

Here are the hardware tools you need to know:

- *Wire strippers* and *crimpers*. Wire strippers take the protective plastic coating off of wires, and crimpers put ends on cables. Any crimper worth what it cost has a wire stripper built in to it as well.

- *Punch-down tools* are used to connect individual wires from an unshielded twisted pair (UTP) cable into a wiring harness, such as a 110 block.

- *Cable testers* are used to make sure cables work.

- A *toner probe* is great for tracing cables from one end to the other, such as when they are run through a wall. For example, say you have a 25-pair cable and you suspect one of the pairs is bad. You can trace that specific pair to the other end with a toner probe.

- *Loopback plugs* are for testing network cards. You plug it in, and it tests the card by simulating sending and receiving data.

The one hardware tool we didn't talk much about earlier is a wireless locator. A *wireless locator* can be either a handheld hardware device or specialized software that is installed on a laptop and whose purpose is to detect WiFi signals. Anyone interested in wardriving will definitely have one of these, but they're also handy for locating wireless hot spots.

Here are the software commands you need to know:

- IPCONFIG displays IP configuration information. IPCONFIG /ALL is useful for showing more options. IPCONFIG /RELEASE and IPCONFIG /RENEW release and renew the lease from a DHCP server.

- The PING command tests connectivity.

- TRACERT traces the path from the local host to the destination host, showing all of the hops (routers) in between.

- The NET command by itself doesn't do a lot. NET /? shows you NET options. You can use NET USE to establish network connections, NET VIEW to see established connections, and NET STOP to disconnect them. Other options are available as well.

- NETSTAT checks inbound and outbound TCP/IP connections on the local host, and you can use it to view packet statistics.

- NBTSTAT shows NetBIOS over TCP/IP statistics.

Summary

In this chapter, we discussed hardware and network troubleshooting. First, we looked at general hardware troubleshooting. We investigated the causes for hardware problems, such as excessive heat, and signs of problems, such as noise, odors, and visible damage. We also discussed alerts and status lights.

After the discussion of general hardware, we talked about issues specific to internal components, including the motherboard, CPU, RAM, power supply, storage systems, and video cards. Next, we covered problems that are unique to laptop computers. Because of their compact nature, they have unique issues relating to heat, power, and input and output. Laptops also typically have built-in wireless networking, which is a blessing but occasionally needs to be fixed.

We followed that with a discussion on troubleshooting printers. Specifically, we discussed problems with three major classes of printers, including dot-matrix, inkjet, and laser, and then talked about managing print jobs, the print spooler, and printing a test page.

Finally, we ended the chapter with a section on troubleshooting issues that are specific to networking. We talked about connectivity issues and looked at tools and commands you can use to troubleshoot network problems.

Exam Essentials

Understand what happens during the POST routine.   During the power-on self-test (POST), the BIOS checks to ensure that the base hardware is installed and working. Generally, one POST beep is good. Any more than that and you might have an error.

Understand the types of symptoms that misbehaving hardware can cause.   Hardware problems cause symptoms that include excessive heat, noise, odors, and visible damage. Some devices can also warn of problems with status light indicators or alerts.

Know how to stop and restart the print spooler.   Open the Services applet of Computer Management. Find Print Spooler on the right side. Right-click it and click Stop, or highlight it and click the stop square above the list of services. To restart it, right-click and select Start or click the start triangle above the list of services.

Understand what to do for laptop video issues.   If you have no video, you can try an external monitor or try toggling the LCD cutoff switch. For screens that are too dim or too bright, you can raise and lower the brightness by using the Fn key plus the appropriate function key on your keyboard.

Know what to check if your wireless networking card isn't working.   Make sure the card has lights indicating it's working. You might also have an external toggle switch to turn the card on and off. Finally, if your computer has an external RJ-45 connection, you can plug it in and see if it works when wired.

Know how to set IP addresses on a printer.   The IP address can often be obtained automatically from a DHCP server, but this is not recommended for corporate networks. Instead, you may be able to use the printer's control panel, Telnet, or printer management software to configure the IP address.

Know what could cause the printer to print garbage.   Most often this is caused by the print driver. Deleting and reinstalling it should fix the problem. It can also be caused by a defective formatter board.

Understand what could cause print-quality issues on a dot-matrix printer. Print-quality issues are generally related to either the ribbon or the print head. The specific problem you are having will help determine the culprit.

Know what can cause unevenly spaced lines or characters on a dot-matrix or inkjet printer. This is usually caused by a failing stepper motor. For line spacing problems, it's the main stepper motor. For character spacing, it will be the carriage stepper motor.

Know what causes printers to have paper jams. In a dot-matrix printer, jams are usually caused by material getting into the rollers, such as extra perf from the tractor-feed paper. On inkjets and laser printers, this problem is often caused by worn pickup rollers.

Review Questions

The answers to the Chapter Review Questions can be found in Appendix A.

1. If the video on your laptop is not working, what should you do to troubleshoot it? (Choose two.)

    A. Toggle the video function key.

    B. Try using an external monitor.

    C. Remove the display unit and reattach it.

    D. Power the system off and back on.

2. While inspecting a motherboard, you notice a discolored area. What is usually a cause of this?

    A. Spilled liquid

    B. Improper manufacture

    C. Power surge

    D. Underclocking

3. You need to connect a client computer to a shared network drive from the command prompt. Which command should you use?

    A. NET USE

    B. NETSTAT

    C. NSLOOKUP

    D. IPCONFIG

4. Every computer has a diagnostic program built into its BIOS called the _____.

    A. CMOS

    B. BIOS

    C. POST

    D. DNS

5. While troubleshooting a client computer, you decide to obtain a new IP address from the DHCP server. After releasing the existing address, which command do you use to get new IP information from the DHCP server?

    A. IPCONFIG /REFRESH

    B. IPCONFIG /RENEW

    C. IFCONFIG /RELEASE

    D. IFCONFIG /START

6. Users are complaining that their print jobs are not printing. You open the print queue and see 50 jobs lined up. The printer is connected properly and online. What should you do?

   A. Open Printer Troubleshooting and have it diagnose the problem.

   B. Stop and restart the print spooler.

   C. Delete and reinstall the printer.

   D. Delete and reinstall Windows.

7. What two devices are commonly used to cool components within a PC? (Choose two.)

   A. Fans

   B. Compressed air

   C. Freon

   D. Heat sinks

8. You are having problems with the video card in one of your computers. Where could you check for troubleshooting information?

   A. Another computer with the same video card

   B. The video card manufacturer's website

   C. The manual that came with the card

   D. The server log

9. Your laser printer keeps printing vertical black lines on its output pages. What is the most likely cause of the problem?

   A. There is a groove or scratch in the EP drum.

   B. The EP drum cleaning blade is broken.

   C. The printer is low on toner.

   D. The transfer corona wire is not working properly.

10. The display on your laptop appears warped and fuzzy. You plug in an external monitor, and the image on it is fine. What is the most likely cause of the problem?

    A. The video card

    B. The LCD display

    C. The motherboard

    D. The video driver

11. You have an inkjet printer. Recently, papers are being printed with excessive amounts of ink, and the ink is smearing. What is the most likely cause of the problem?

    A. A faulty ink cartridge

    B. A corrupt print driver

    C. A faulty fuser

    D. Too much humidity in the air

12. You are working with a system that is assigned IP information configuration information from a central server. You wish to view the IP information on the system. Which of the following commands would you use from the command prompt?

A. IPCONFIG /REFRESH

B IPCONFIG /ALL

C. IPCONFIG /RENEW

D. WINIPCFG /ALL

13. When you print documents on your laser printer, you see residue from previous images on the output. What two things are the most likely causes of this problem? (Choose two.)

A. A faulty transfer corona wire

B. An overheating printer

C. A bad erasure lamp

D. A broken cleaning blade

14. You turn a computer on, but nothing shows up on the monitor. Instead of one beep, you hear one long beep followed by three short beeps. What is the problem?

A. The video card is dead.

B. The motherboard is dead.

C. The BIOS is not functioning.

D. Not enough information; you need to look up the beep code to determine the problem.

15. Which of the following command-line utilities is used to verify the route a data packet takes to a remote host?

A. Trace

B. Tracert

C. TraceRoute

D. Tracepacket

16. You turn a computer on and it doesn't boot up properly. From inside the case you hear a rhythmic ticking sound. What is most likely the problem?

A. The motherboard

B. The power supply fan

C. The hard drive

D. The video card

17. You support an old dot-matrix printer at work. When the printer prints, there is always a blank horizontal line in the middle of each line of output. What is the most likely cause of the problem?

A. The print ribbon is old and needs to be replaced.

B. The print ribbon is not advancing properly.

C. The print head needs to be replaced.

D. The wrong print driver is installed.

18. A user calls saying his laptop won't power on. He charged it all night so he knows the battery is fine. What should you have him do first?

    A. Plug the laptop in using an AC adapter and try to power it on.

    B. Replace the battery with a spare and try to power it on.

    C. Toggle the battery power switch on the front of the laptop, and then try to power it on.

    D. Send the laptop in for service.

19. You suspect a faulty network card on a client machine. Which tool can you use to test your hypothesis?

    A. Wireless locator

    B. Cable tester

    C. Toner probe

    D. Loopback plug

20. You are troubleshooting a server and discover that one of the hard drives in the RAID 0 array has failed. Which statement is true?

    A. You need to replace the failed drive, but the data is okay because it is configured as a mirror.

    B. You need to replace the failed drive, but the data is okay because it is configured as a disk stripe with parity.

    C. You need to replace the failed drive, and the data on the array is lost.

    D. You do not need to replace the failed drive; the system will function normally.

Performance-Based Question

On the A+ exams, you will encounter performance-based questions. The questions on the exam require you to perform a specific task, and you will be graded on whether you were able to complete the task. The following require you to think creatively to measure how well you understand this chapter's topics. You may or may not see similar questions on the actual A+ exams. To see how your answers compare to the authors', refer to Appendix B.

Your network users are sending print jobs to the printer, but they are stacking up in the queue and not printing. The printer appears to be online and has paper. How would you stop and restart the print spooler in Windows 7?

Appendix A

Answers to Review Questions

Chapter 1: Motherboards, Processors, and Memory

1. **A.** The spine of the computer is the system board, otherwise known as the motherboard. On the motherboard you will find the CPU, underlying circuitry, expansion slots, video components, RAM slots, and various other chips.

2. **C.** DDR SDRAM is manufactured on a 184-pin DIMM. DIMMs with 168 pins were used for SDR SDRAM. The SIMM is the predecessor to the DIMM, on which SDRAM was never deployed. RIMM is the Rambus proprietary competitor for the DIMM that carries DRDRAM instead of SDRAM.

3. **B.** Remember the 8:1 rule. Modules greater than but not including SDR SDRAM are named with a number eight times larger than the number used to name the chips on the module. The initials *PC* are used to describe the module, the initials *DDR* are used for the chips, and a single-digit number after PC and DDR is used to represent the level of DDR. The lack of a single-digit number represents DDR as long as the number that is present is greater than 133 (such as PC1600). Otherwise, you're dealing with SDR (such as PC133). This means that PC3-16000 modules are DDR3 modules and are populated with chips named DDR3 and a number that is one-eighth of the module's numeric code: 2000.

4. **D.** The ITX motherboard family consists of smaller boards that fit in standard or miniature cases and use less power than their larger counterparts.

5. **A.** The lower-end Core i7 desktop (nonmobile) processors call for the LGA 1156 socket, but the 9xx series requires the LGA 1366 socket.

6. **B.** ZIF sockets are designed with a locking mechanism that, when released, alleviates the resistance of the socket to receiving the pins of the chip being inserted. Make sure you know your socket types so that the appearance of a specific model, such as Socket 479, in a question like this does not distract you from the correct answer. Only LGA would be another acceptable answer to this question because with a lack of pin receptacles, there is no insertion resistance. However, no other pin-layout format, such as SPGA, addresses issues with inserting chips. LPGA might have evoked an image of LGA, leading you to that answer, but that term means nothing outside of the golfing community.

7. B. The Northbridge is in control of the local-bus components that share the clock of the frontside bus. SATA and all other drive interfaces do not share this clock and are controlled by the Southbridge.

8. A. A hard drive stores data on a magnetic medium, which does not lose its information after the power is removed and can be repeatedly written to and erased.

9. C. This processor requires an AM3 socket. The only other version of Phenom II was for the AM2+ and is not compatible with DDR3 RAM.

10. B. Soft power is the feature whereby the front power button acts as a relay to initiate various system power changes, depending on the duration that the button is held.

11. A, C, G. DIMMs used in desktop-motherboard applications have one of three possible pin counts. SDR SDRAM is implemented on 168-pin modules. DDR SDRAM and 16-bit RIMMs are implemented on 184-pin modules. DDR2 and DDR3 are implemented on 240-pin modules with different keying. Dual-channel RIMM modules have 232 pins. Modules with 200 and 204 pins are used in the SODIMM line, and there are no modules with 180 pins.

12. C, D. Both the CPU and BIOS have to be designed to support virtualization in hardware.

13. D. Most motherboards have a jumper or similar momentary closure mechanism that will allow you to clear the CMOS memory of any user settings and cause the BIOS to use factory defaults, including no user or supervisor passwords.

14. A. The easiest solution that works to cool your CPU is to connect the four-pin connector into the three-pin header. The missing pin allows you to control the speed of the fan. Without it, the fan will run at top speed, which is fine, albeit a little noisier. The heat sink alone should not be relied upon for proper cooling of modern CPUs.

15. D. The PCIe 1.1 specification provided 250MBps of throughput per lane per direction. With the 2.x versions of PCIe, this rate was doubled to 500MBps. As a result, each v2.0 lane is capable of a combined 1GBps. A x16 slot consists of 16 lanes, for a total bidirectional throughput of 16GBps.

16. C. The reset button causes the computer to return to nearly the same point it is in when you power it on, but without the need for power cycling. Using Restart in the Start menu does not reboot as deeply as the reset button. Hibernation is a power state that completely removes power after saving the contents of RAM to the hard drive; pressing the power button is required to resume the session in the same manner as starting the computer after a complete shutdown. The power button cannot be used as a method of restarting the system.

17. B. None of the options are required, but a UPS is by far the most helpful among the answers in that loss of power during this procedure can range from annoying to devastating.

18. A. These CPUs integrate the graphics processing unit. The Core i7 before them integrated the memory controller, eliminating the FSB. Math coprocessors have been integrated since the 80486DX.

19. D. Pentium 4 processors are always mated with memory mounted on DIMMs.

20. B. Although technically all slots listed could be used for video adapters, PCIe excels when compared to the other options and offers technologies such as SLI, which only make PCIe's advantage more noticeable.

Chapter 2: Storage Devices and Power Supplies

1. B. A conventional HDD contains discs called platters, on which data is stored magnetically through read/write heads by way of a magnetic coating.

2. A. A conventional hard disk drive system consists of the hard disk and its often-integrated controller as well as a host adapter to gain access to the rest of the computer system. The drive interface is a common component of the controller and host adapter.

3. D. A fixed number of clusters is supported by each operating system, leading to a corresponding maximum volume size. If the maximum NTFS cluster size of 64KB is used, Windows XP can support a single-volume size of 256TB. When a cluster size of one sector, or 512 bytes (½KB), is used, the maximum volume size reduces to 2TB.

4. C. Solid-state disks (SSDs) are capable of replacing conventional HDDs, contingent upon cheaper components and higher capacities.

5. C. High-density 3½" floppy diskettes have a formatted capacity of 1.44MB. Double-density 5¼" floppies can be formatted to a capacity of 360KB, while double-density floppies support 720KB. The extended-density 3½" floppy diskettes can be formatted to 2.88MB.

6. B. Blu-ray discs have a single-sided, single-layer capacity of 25GB. The best the other options achieve is no more than roughly 17GB.

7. A. Hot-swappable devices can be removed while the power to the system is still on. Warm-swappable devices need to be stopped in the operating system before being removed. The term has nothing to do with the heat level of the device.

8. C. Power supplies and AC adapters use standard wall outlets for an input of AC voltage, which they convert to the DC voltages required by the components they supply power to.

9. A, C, D, E, F. A PC's power supply produces +3.3VDC, +5VDC, –5VDC, +12VDC, and –12VDC from a 110VAC input.

10. D. Molex power connectors have been used with larger internal devices since the original PCs hit the market. When the 3½" floppy diskette drives were launched, they used the newer Berg connectors. Europe requires the voltage selector switch be set at the higher setting. SATA drives most often use a specific power connector that is not compatible with the Molex connector used by PATA drives. AT-based motherboards call for P8 and P9 connectors; ATX motherboards have a newer 20- or 24-pin single power connector.

11. C. Today's hard drives, regardless of their rpm, have standard internal power connections. Each of the other options are valid concerns when installing an internal drive.

12. A. Although inefficient as an interactive medium, sequential tape-based storage continues to be developed in increasing capacities. Tape remains the best choice for frequently backing up large amounts of data for redundancy and archival purposes.

13. D. Inserting the Berg connector upside down will damage the drive the first time the motor is activated. Floppy drives require front access for floppy disk insertion. Their form factor is only 3.5″, and you can still buy them new. (See the sidebar "Do You Smell Something?" in this chapter.)

14. C. The other common spin rates are 10,000 rpm and 12,000 rpm.

15. B. Personal computers do not have permanently installed power supplies. Like other electrical and electronic components, power supplies can and do fail on a regular basis. Permanently mounting a power supply to a chassis would be a disservice to the consumer. You should consider the cumulative power needs of your installed components, and you might have to obtain adapters and splitters if you do not have enough or you have the wrong types of connectors coming from the power supply.

16. B. The red stripe on the cable indicates pin 1.

17. B. UltraDMA/66 requires a special ribbon cable with extra wires to cut down on cross-talk. It does not require Cable Select to be in use, and it does not require specific operating system support because it operates at a lower level than the OS. There is no special setting in the BIOS for UltraDMA drives.

18. B. If there is a Single setting, it should be used. Otherwise, use Master. Slave is never appropriate for a single drive. There is no such jumper setting as Boot.

19. D. Each concept applies to both HDDs and SSDs except for platter spin rates. Revolutions per minute (rpm) measurements refer to drives with moving parts. SSDs have none.

20. A. Power supplies are rated in watts. When you purchase a power supply, you should make sure the devices inside the computer do not require more wattage than the chosen power supply can offer. The voltage is fairly standard among power supplies and has nothing to do with the devices connected to the power supply. Amperage and resistance are not selling points for power supplies.

Chapter 3: Peripherals and Expansion

1. D. A PS/2 port is also known as a mini-DIN 6 connector.

2. D. The USB 2.0 spec provides for a maximum speed of 480 megabits per second (Mbps—not megabytes per second, or MBps).

3. C, D. Bidirectional parallel ports can both transmit and receive data. EPP and ECP are IEEE 1284 standards that were designed to transfer data at higher speeds in both directions so that devices could return status information to the system. The standard parallel port only transmits data out of the computer. It cannot receive data. FireWire is specified by IEEE 1394. IEEE 1284 does not specify serial protocols, such as RS-232 and USB.

4. C. The IEEE 1394 standard provides for greater data transfer speeds, increased power, and the ability to send memory addresses as well as data through a serial port. USB 3.0 proves to threaten more competition in these areas, but USB 2.0 could not compare to the overall performance of IEEE 1394.

5. B. USB hubs are used to connect multiple peripherals to one computer through a single port. They support data transfer rates as high as 12Mbps, or 1.5MBps (for USB 1.1, which is the option listed here).

6. D. The IEEE 1284 standard specifies that the ECP parallel port use a DMA channel and the buffer be able to transfer data at higher speeds to printers.

7. C. The description 5.1 refers to six channels of audio. The 5 in the name refers collectively to the single center channel, the right and left front channels, and the right and left rear channels. The 1 in the name refers to the single LFE channel connected to the subwoofer.

8. A. Intel and Apple collaborated on Thunderbolt to add PCIe to VESA's DisplayPort and to make the resulting interface smaller and less expensive to connect.

9. C. HDMI is a digital interface and cabling specification that allows digital audio to be carried over the same cable as video.

10. C. Such a connection should not be made. DVI-I cables act like universal cables; they can connect two DVI-A interfaces or two DVI-D interfaces with adapters. Natively, they are used to connect two DVI-I interfaces, both of which are configured as either analog or digital. They are unable to convert the analog signal to a digital one, however. Analog and digital DVI interfaces are too disparate to interconnect.

11. B. Biometric input devices scan a physical trait of the user, such as voice, fingerprint, and retina, for authentication purposes when the user attempts to access computer systems and other property.

12. D. KVM switches are ideal when you have multiple computers situated near one another and do not want to commit the extra desk space to each computer having its own keyboard, mouse, and monitor.

13. C. MIDI devices use a 5-pin DIN connector similar to the one used with the original AT keyboard.

14. B. A video capture card is used to convert raw video input to a format that can be shared electronically. Although many TV tuner cards provide this functionality, it is their video-capture component that gives them this capability. Any adapter that is strictly a TV tuner cannot capture video.

15. A. Multimedia input devices, not standard input devices, use 1/8″ jacks. Standard input devices include human interface devices, such as keyboards and mice. The other three options can be used for such devices.

16. C. Network interface cards are considered to be a form of communications adapter.

17. B. Interfaces, such as USB ports, are considered input/output ports. If you have to add USB capability to a computer, an I/O adapter with USB ports on it would meet the need.

18. A. Modems have RJ-11 jacks for interface to the Public Switched Telephone Network (PSTN). The modular jacks that Ethernet NICs have are known as RJ-45 jacks.

19. C. A trackball is a sort of stationary mouse that has the ball for movement detection on the top of the device along with the keys. The ball is actuated by the thumb or fingers, not by moving the device along a flat surface or mouse pad. Trackballs are ideal where desk space is limited. There is no such thing as a trackpad.

20. B. VGA signals are analog, uncompressed, component signals that carry all the video information for all three components of the original RGB signal.

Chapter 4: Display Devices

1. C. LCDs do not have electron guns that are aimed by magnets as CRTs do. This difference makes LCDs more compatible with nearby speaker magnets. Additionally, the cathode ray tube for which CRT monitors are named is a rather bulky component, requiring more desk space to accommodate the CRT's cabinet. Projectors are not common personal display devices; they are used more in group environments. HDMI is a standard for connecting display devices, not a type of display device.

2. B. The associate is trying to think of the term *dot pitch*. Essentially, dot pitch is the height of a dot-phosphor trio added to the distance between the next dot trio in the same direction. It works out to be the distance from any point on one dot to the same point on the next dot of the same color. The smaller this number, the better the display quality. The number of dots per inch is a similar concept but inversely proportional and not measured in fractions of a millimeter. Resolution is a software concept; dot phosphors are hardware related. The refresh rate has nothing to do with how close the chemical dots are to one another.

3. D. The maximum allowable refresh rate does tend to be affected by the resolution you choose in the operating system. The refresh rate is most often expressed in cycles per second (Hz), not millions of cycles per second (MHz). You must usually select the refresh rate you want from the display settings dialog boxes, not through the monitor's built-in menu system, although the monitor's system can often tell you which refresh rate you're using. Finally, both the monitor and adapter must agree on the refresh rate you select. If either device does not support a particular refresh rate, such a rate cannot be used.

4. C. At the same resolution, CRTs are more likely to display a clearer image than LCDs. LCDs are normally limited to a fixed, native resolution but require less power than CRT monitors. Although LCD screens are not regularly and systematically refreshed the way CRTs are, the LCD refresh rate dictates how often any one pixel is allowed to change.

5. A. The amount of memory installed on a graphics adapter is directly related to how many pixels can be displayed at one time and how many colors the pixels can be set to. Monitors don't have memory installed in them. LCDs, not CRTs, have a single, fixed resolution called the native resolution. By default, you might be limited to a particular refresh rate because the resolution is too high, but the refresh rate is automatically adjusted down, if necessary, when you select a resolution.

6. B. SXGA has a resolution of 1280×1024. Consult Table 4.1 for the resolutions that characterize other technologies.

7. D. Although the Q stands for *quad*, the pixel count for each axis is only doubled, resulting in four times as many total pixels.

8. A. Contrast ratio is a selling point for LCDs. Higher contrast ratios mean darker blacks and brighter whites. The measure of luminance between adjacent pixels is known as contrast, not contrast ratio.

9. D. Both OLED and plasma displays use electrodes to excite the material in a sealed chamber to produce light. Each in its own way uses that light to create red, green, or blue light within individual subpixels. Plasma is more akin to CRT in that they both use chemical phosphors to create the red, green, and blue hues. In contrast to the way CRTs and PDPs produce color, OLEDs natively produce these colors of light without the use of filters or phosphors.

10. C, E. Older LCD panels might have employed a passive-matrix addressing for their pixels, resulting in a poorer viewing angle than that created by active-matrix LCD panels. Additionally, privacy filters intentionally limit the angle of screen visibility by changing the light's polarization when viewed from the side. Antiglare filters might unintentionally do the same thing.

11. B. Although it's true that you must start with the Display Settings dialog box, which ironically shows a single tab labeled Monitor, and that you subsequently click the Advanced Settings button, it's on the Monitor properties tab thereafter that you select the refresh rate. The Adapter tab in those same properties pages has no selection for refresh rate.

12. A. Unplugging the power to the projector before the projector's fan has had the opportunity to cool the unit and stop running on its own can lead to expensive repairs on the projector or to the cost of replacing the projector outright.

13. D. Safe Mode in XP disables as many nonessential drivers and services as possible. One of the nonessential drivers it disables is the driver for the graphics adapter. Windows uses its standard VGA driver to control the graphics adapter while you are in Safe Mode. Another reason for defaulting back to standard VGA is that you might have a corrupt or incorrect driver for your adapter.

14. C. If your monitor allows you to change the resolution, it might not actually allow you to change the resolution. As confusing as that sounds, your monitor might maintain its optimal hardware resolution, such as an LCD's native resolution, and force you to scroll to see any pixels created by the chosen software resolution that it cannot fit on the hardware screen at that particular moment.

15. A. An LCD's native resolution is the single, fixed resolution that provides optimal clarity.

16. D. The multimonitor feature allows two monitors to display exactly the same thing (clone) or to extend your Desktop onto the second monitor. There is no need to use one adapter to achieve this result. In fact, the two adapters don't even have to use the same expansion-bus architecture. The two cards must, however, use the same graphics-adapter driver.

17. A. Active matrix technology is superior to passive matrix. Dual scan is merely an enhanced form of passive matrix but is not on par with active matrix. Dual matrix isn't an LCD type.

18. B. Dividing 16 by 10 produces a value of 1.6. Dividing the first number of a 16:10 resolution by the second number always results in 1.6. Resolutions with a 4:3 aspect ratio produce the value 1.333, while 5:4 resolutions such as 1280×1024 produce the value 1.25.

19. C. The built-in degaussing tool of the latest CRT monitors is designed to work with the monitor in which it is found. External degaussing tools, while effective, can be a little hard on the delicate inner workings of the CRT. Software alone cannot degauss a CRT monitor.

20. B. A lumen is a unit of measure for the total amount of visible light that the projector gives off, based solely on what the human eye can perceive.

Chapter 5: Custom Configurations

1. A. Graphics design and CAD/CAM design workstations do not require a fast hard drive because the artist works with static images that do not stream from the drive. However, RAM in which to hold the highly detailed, sometimes 3D artwork before saving, a powerful processor for implementing complex algorithms on a small amount of information during rendering, and high-end video for assisting in the rendering and display of the images are necessary.

2. D. A/V editing workstations require specialized audio and video cards and large and fast hard drives and benefit from dual monitors. A fast NIC, extra RAM, and a faster than normal processor do not support the requirements of A/V editors.

3. B. Virtual machines do not imply virtual processing. The data storage, processing cycles, and RAM usage are all real. The separate hard drive and chassis for each operating system are virtual. The other answers all have at least one fundamental problem with their logic. CPU cores are not installed in virtual machines but in CPU packages within physical machines. CPU cores do not take over for each other. There is no fault tolerance among them. Storing data is the job of RAM, which should also be maximized for virtualization workstations.

4. A. The processors found in a gaming PC are many, and the CPU is often overclocked. Such a configuration generates too much heat for conventional cooling to dissipate before the system is damaged. These machines don't have unusual hard-drive requirements. The cooling has no effect on external controllers, and sound cards don't generate much heat, but analog would certainly generate more than digital.

5. C. Home theater PCs are based on the mini-ITX motherboard and have their own form factor, HTPC, a more compact form factor than chassis made for micro-ATX boards.

6. B. Thick clients are standard desktop PCs. They stand in contrast to systems with specialized requirements, such as the remaining options.

7. D. Although not all thin clients are devoid of local processing capability, some are. High-resolution graphics are not a requirement of thin clients, but even such systems require a system unit with a NIC.

8. C. Optimally, the server should communicate across a link that is the aggregate of all client links, but at the least, the server's link should be a faster one to alleviate the potential bottleneck when all clients try to access the server simultaneously.

9. D. Quite simply, the rendering of 2D and 3D graphics makes use of complex algorithms that need all the processing power they can get to remain usable. These stations deal with static images, not streaming video. Manufacturing equipment is generally slower than computers used for the design phase. These workstations call for high-end video, which includes graphics adapters with GPUs often more powerful than the system's CPU.

10. A. Editors of this type of media have numerous controls and timelines to keep track of. These constructs often lie along the bottom of the application and run horizontally. Subsequent monitors allow the editor to spread out without shrinking the view excessively.

11. B. Maximum RAM and CPU cores are the primary requirements for such systems. Although there are multiple guest operating systems, generally there is but one host to those guests. File sharing may be a service the administrator decides to offer, and multiple NICs might prove advantageous with virtual machines that are popular among the clients, but these workstations do not require either.

12. B. Gaming PCs are not known for requiring fault tolerance or data persistence. RAID arrays, therefore, are generally not included. The other components are a benefit for gaming PCs, however.

13. A. A/V editing workstations require video enhancements and a hard drive capable of storing a large quantity of data and accessing it quickly. The other system types require faster or more plentiful processors.

14. C. Because of its exceptional capabilities of digital video and audio output as well as its potential for support of future standards, HDMI is the home-theater video output technology of choice. Neither DVI nor component (YCbCr and YPbPr) can make the same claims. WUXGA is a resolution of 1920×1200 and not a video output technology.

15. D. These standard systems do not have any special requirements, just that they can run Windows and desktop applications.

16. C. Clients request services of servers. Thin clients can request software services from their servers, whether in the form of running the software and passing the results to the client or passing the code of the software to the client to be executed by its processor and kept only in RAM.

17. B. Additional RAM in the home server PC offers no advantage for the performance of the server past a certain point. The tasks the server is asked to perform do not require high performance.

18. A, D. Virtualization and graphic design workstations benefit from as much RAM as can be installed. Home theater PCs and gaming PCs do not require a large amount of temporary storage of instructions and data. They are more about the rapid movement of graphical data toward an output device.

19. A. The Windows 7 computer can be built as a normal system with a 2TB or 3TB drive. WHS 2011 needs a home server PC. The rims are crafted by a type of CAD/CAM workstation capable of CNC. A home theater PC is an ideal choice to take the place of both the BD player and DVR.

20. B. The clients of the home server PC that use the server for streaming video content might benefit from enhanced video, but the server will not.

Chapter 6: Networking Fundamentals

1. D. Companies that want to ensure the safety and integrity of their data should use fiber-optic cable because it cannot be affected by electromagnetic or radio-frequency interference. Even though some copper cables have shielding, they are not immune to EMI or RFI. This eliminates twisted-pair and coaxial. CSMA/CD is an access method, not a cable type.

2. C. The IEEE 802.3 standard originally specified the use of a bus topology with coaxial baseband cable and can transmit data up to 10Mbps.

3. C. It is the responsibility of the Transport layer to signal an "all clear" by making sure the data segments are error free. It also controls the data flow and troubleshoots any problems with transmitting or receiving data frames.

4. B. Carrier Sense Multiple Access with Collision Detection (CSMA/CD) specifies that the NIC pause before transmitting a packet to ensure that the line is not being used. If no activity is detected, then it transmits the packet. If activity is detected, it waits until it is clear. In the case of two NICs transmitting at the same time (a collision), both NICs pause to detect and then retransmit the data.

5. A. The Open Systems Interconnection (OSI) model is used to describe how network protocols should function. The OSI model was designed by the International Organization for Standardization (ISO).

6. D. At the center of a star topology is a hub or a switch. A NIC is a network card, which each computer must have to be on the network. Bridges and routers are higher-level connectivity devices that connect network segments or networks together.

7. C. Fiber-optic cable can span distances of several kilometers because it has much lower attenuation, crosstalk, and interference in comparison to copper cables.

8. A. Routers are designed to route (transfer) packets across networks. They are able to do this routing, and determine the best path to take, based on internal routing tables they maintain.

9. D. A peer-to-peer network has no servers, so all of the resources are shared from the various workstations on which they reside. This is the opposite of a client-server network, in which the majority of resources are located on servers that are dedicated to responding to client requests.

10. A. Bluetooth networks are often called wireless personal area networks (WPANs).

11. A, C, D. In a star network, all systems are connected using a central device such as a hub or a switch. The network is not disrupted for other users when more systems are added or removed. The star network design is used with today's UTP-based networks.

12. A. For areas where a cable must be fire retardant, such as in a drop ceiling, you must run plenum-grade cable. Plenum refers to the coating on the sleeve of the cable, not the media (copper or fiber) within the cable itself. PVC is the other type of coating typically found on network cables, but it produces poisonous gas when burned.

13. D. The local connector (LC) is a mini form factor (MFF) fiber-optic connector developed by Lucent Technologies. If it helps, think of LC as "Little Connector."

14. A. A toner probe will allow you to check the physical path of a cable through something like a wall. Cable testers will test to see if the cable works. Multimeters can test voltage and see if a cable is operational as well. Loopback plugs are used to test network adapters.

15. C. In a mesh network, the number of connections is determined by the formula n(n-1)/2. With seven computers, that means 21 connections.

16. B. A crimper can attach connectors to the end of a network cable. A punch-down tool will attach a cable to a wiring frame such as a 110 block. Cable testers will see if the cable works properly after you've created it. A loopback plug is for testing network cards.

17. B. The job of a firewall is to block unwanted traffic. Firewalls do this by using a list of rules called an access control list (ACL). Routers connect networks to each other. Internet appliances give the user Internet access. A network attached storage (NAS) device is like a dedicated file server.

18. A. The two RG standards used for cable television are RG-6 and RG-59. Of the two, RG-6 is better and can handle digital signals. RG-59 is for analog signals only. RG-8 is thicknet coax, and RG-58 is thinnet coax.

19. C, D. Bridges and switches are Layer 2 devices. Hubs work at Layer 1, and routers work at Layer 3. Note that some switches are called multilayer switches and will work at Layer 3 as well.

20. B. Multimode fiber (MMF) can transmit up to 550 meters, depending on the Ethernet specification. Other standards using MMF can transmit only up to 300 meters. If you need to transmit up to 40 kilometers, you will need to use single-mode fiber (SMF).

Chapter 7: Introduction to TCP/IP

1. B. A Dynamic Host Configuration Protocol (DHCP) server provides IP configuration information to hosts when they join the network. A Domain Name System (DNS) server resolves hostnames to IP addresses. A domain controller may provide login authentication, but it does not provide IP configuration information. There is no IP configuration server.

2. B. Class A addresses have a first octet between 1 and 126, Class B between 128 and 191, and class C between 192 and 223. With a first octet of 171, this is a Class B address.

3. A. HTTP uses port 80. HTTPS uses 443, Telnet 23, and POP3 110.

4. D. An IPv6 interface is not limited in the number of addresses it can be assigned, although there could be limitations based upon practicality.

5. A, B, C. An IPv6 address contains 128 bits, written in eight 16-bit fields represented by four hexadecimal digits. Option A contains all eight fields expressed in full. Option B is an IPv4 address expressed in IPv6 form. Option C is the same address as option A but written in accepted shorthand. Option D is not valid because the double colons (::) can be used only once within an address.

6. A. DNS servers resolve hostnames to IP addresses. On the Internet, a DNS server needs to have a public IP address. The address 10.25.11.33 is in a private address space, so that address would not be valid for a DNS server on the Internet.

7. D. The address assigned to the computer is an APIPA address. Microsoft client computers (and others) will configure themselves with an address in this range if they are unable to reach a DHCP server.

8. C. Simple Mail Transfer Protocol (SMTP) is responsible for sending email. IMAP4 and POP3 both receive email. SNMP is a network management protocol.

9. D. Remote Desktop Protocol (RDP) works on port 3389. DNS works on port 53, IMAP4 works on 143, and LDAP works on 389.

10. C, D. The two protocols that work at the Host-to-Host layer are TCP and UDP. IP and ARP both work at the Internet layer.

11. A, D. TCP is a connection-oriented protocol that establishes virtual circuits and acknowledges delivery of packets. Because of these features, it has higher overhead than UDP and is a little slower.

12. B. The HTTP protocol is inherently unsecure, but the HTTPS protocol is secure. (SSH and SFTP are secure as well, but they are not protocols used to connect to websites.)

13. A. The router is your doorway out into other networks and is known in TCP/IP terms as the default gateway. Without this configuration option, you will not be able to get to external networks.

14. A, B. The only mandatory IPv4 configuration items are an IP address and a subnet mask. If you are not connecting to another network, you do not need a default gateway. DNS servers resolve hostnames to IP addresses but they are not mandatory.

15. D. IMAP4 and POP3 are the two protocols that are used for email delivery. Of the two, only IMAP4 provides security features. SMTP sends email. SNMP is a network management protocol.

16. B. The Secure Shell (SSH) was developed as a secure alternative to Telnet. SMB is Server Message Block, which is a network file system. SNMP is for network management. SFTP is designed for secure file downloads. It's a secure alternative to FTP, not a replacement for Telnet.

17. A. Telnet uses port 23. SSH uses port 22. FTP uses ports 21 and 20. DNS uses port 53.

18. E. IPv6 does not have broadcasts. IPv6 does have multicasts, which are a bit like targeted broadcasts. FF00:: is the first part of a multicast address.

19. A. DNS is typically known as a name resolver on the Internet, but it will work on private networks as well. DNS resolves hostnames to IP addresses. DHCP automatically configures clients with IP address information. FTP is for file downloads. APIPA is a process used to automatically assign clients a private IP address when they can't reach the DHCP server.

20. C. The Address Resolution Protocol (ARP) resolves IP addresses to hardware (MAC) addresses. RARP does the reverse—it resolves MAC addresses to IP addresses. DNS resolves hostnames to IP addresses. DHCP automatically configures TCP/IP clients.

Chapter 8: Installing Wireless and SOHO Networks

1. B, D. Both 802.11b and 802.11g operate in the 2.4GHz range and use similar transmission standards. Many devices on the market are listed as 802.11b/g, meaning they will work with either system. Alternatively, 802.11a operates in the 5GHz range. Finally, 802.11d is not a commonly implemented standard.

2. C. A service-set identifier (SSID) is the unique name given to the wireless network. All hardware that is to participate on the network must be configured to use the same SSID. Essentially, it is the network name. When you are using Windows to connect to a wireless network, all available wireless networks will be listed by their SSID.

3. A, C. The Global System for Mobile Communications (GSM) and Code Division Multiple Access (CDMA) are cellular standards. A SIG is a special interest group, and cold cathode fluorescent lamp (CCFL) is a backlight on a laptop.

4. C. WEP was the original encryption standard developed for WiFi networks, but it is easily hacked. WPA is an upgrade, but WPA2 is more secure and incorporates the entire 802.11i standard. SAFER+ is used to encrypt Bluetooth communications.

5. C. QoS level 5 is designated for interactive voice and video, with less than 100ms delay. Level 1 is for background applications and is low priority. Level 4 is known as controlled load, which is lower priority than interactive voice and video. Level 6 only has 10ms latency but is reserved for control traffic.

6. A, B. You should always change the default administrator name and password as well as the default SSID when installing a new wireless router. Enabling encryption is also a good idea, but WPA and WPA2 are better options than WEP. The channel has nothing to do with security.

7. A. Of the options listed, DSL provides the fastest speed. DSL can easily provide 12Mbps downloads. Dial-up is limited to 56Kbps, and ISDN BRI (128Kbps) and PRI (about 1.5Mbps) don't even come close. Satellite is also much slower than DSL.

8. D. Network Address Translation (NAT) allows users to have a private IP address and still access the Internet with a public IP address. NAT is installed on a router and translates the private IP address into a public one for the user to access the Internet. DHCP assigns IP configuration information to clients. DNS resolves hostnames to IP addresses. A DMZ is an area on a network between an external router and an internal router.

9. C. There are 14 communication channels in the 2.4GHz range, but only the first 11 are configurable. The three non-overlapping channels are 1, 6, and 11.

10. A, C, D. Three current standards, 802.11a (54Mbps), 802.11g (54Mbps), and 802.11n (600Mbps) give users the required throughput.

11. A, D. LTE and WiMAX are 4G standards. GSM and CDMA are cell phone communication standards. (CDMA 2000 is the same as LTE, and it's 4G, but CDMA by itself is not 4G.)

12. B. Infrared is limited to about 1 meter, with a viewing angle of about 30 degrees. Most Bluetooth devices can transmit up to 10 meters. WiMAX has a maximum range of about 5 miles. Satellite signals can travel from the surface of the Earth to a small metal can orbiting the planet.

13. B, C. Dial-up Internet is archaic by today's standards, but it is widely available (anywhere there is phone service) and it's generally lower in cost than other Internet access methods. It's definitely not high speed, and its security is really no different than that of broadband Internet access methods.

14. B. WEP could use a 64-bit or 128-bit security key, but it was a static key. TKIP introduced a dynamic per-packet key. AES and CCMP came after TKIP.

15. D. The good news is that 802.11g is backward compatible with 802.11b. The bad news is if you run in a mixed environment, all devices that communicate with the WAP (or router) will be forced to slow down to accommodate the older technology.

16. D. MAC filtering is a security option that can specify that only computers with specific MAC (hardware) addresses can access the network. Port forwarding is a feature of firewalls. WPS is an easy setup mechanism for wireless networks. SSID is the wireless network name.

17. B. The set of rules for access on a firewall is called an access control list (ACL). An SLA is an agreement on service level for QoS. Default deny is a good policy for firewalls because it doesn't let any traffic through. A DMZ is a subnet located between an external network router and an internal router.

18. C. If your router is using AES, the clients will need to use WPA2. TKIP is a protocol utilized by WPA. WEP is the weakest of the encryption options.

19. A. Bluetooth also operates in the 2.4GHz range.

20. D. Basic rate interface ISDN (BRI ISDN) provides two separate 64Kbps B channels for data transmissions. These channels can be combined to increase throughput. A PRI ISDN uses 23 B channels. DSL, cable, and satellite do not offer multiple dedicated digital channels.

Chapter 9: Understanding Laptops

1. D. Laptop service manuals can be obtained from the manufacturer's website. It's very rare that paper service manuals are shipped with the laptop. Pressing F1 while in Windows will open Windows Help, and pressing F2 on many laptops during the system boot will take you into the BIOS.

2. B. By and large, compromises always must be made when comparing laptops to desktops. Although laptops can be used as desktop replacements, their performance is almost always lower than comparably priced desktops.

3. A, B. The components of an LCD screen are the inverter, screen, and backlight. The video card is also a key component of the LCD system. A CRT is a different technology than LCD.

4. C. The Touchpoint point stick was released with the IBM ThinkPad series of laptops.

5. B. A DC adapter converts the DC output from a car or airplane accessory power plug into the DC voltages required by your laptop.

6. C. MicroDIMMs can have 144 or 172 pins.

7. C. USB is used most often in laptops as an expansion bus for external peripherals. Although parallel and PS/2 allow for connection of external peripherals, they are not as flexible or widely used for expansion as USB.

8. C. Mini PCI IIIA uses a 124-pin card edge connector, as does Mini PCI IIIB. Mini PCI standards IA, IB, IIA, and IIB use 100-pin stacking connectors.

9. C. Network cards are available in PCMCIA forms. If your network card fails or you need an upgrade, you can easily install an external PCMCIA NIC.

10. B. A Type II PC Card is the type used most often for expansion devices like NICs, sound cards, SCSI controllers, modems, and so on.

11. A. The ExpressCard bus brings USB 2.0 and PCIe to the small-form-factor computing industry. CardBus supports USB 1.1 and PCI only. Mini PCI *is* PCI, not PCIe.

12. C. Before removing external hardware, you should click the Safely Remove Hardware icon.

13. B, D. The PC Card architecture has two components. The first is the Socket Services software, and the second is the Card Services software.

14. A. A docking station made specifically for its associated brand and model of laptop can host desktop components permanently, regardless of whether the laptop is attached to the docking station. When the laptop's portability is not required, but instead use of the desktop components is the priority, attaching the laptop to the docking station makes such components available to the laptop without separately attaching each component.

15. D. The processor can reduce how fast it's working, which is called throttling, to help conserve battery life.

16. B. Think of wattage as a "bucket" of power that the attached device can draw on. A bigger bucket simply holds more power but does not force the power on the device. Less wattage is not advised, however. Voltage can be thought of as the pressure behind the power to the device. Anything but the proper voltage is dangerous for the device. When you replace a laptop's AC adapter, you should match the voltage ratings of the original adapter. This also means you should use an adapter with a fixed voltage if that matches the characteristics of the original; otherwise, obtain one that automatically switches voltages at the levels needed.

17. C. Battery calibration for Li-ion batteries allows the powered device to drain the battery's power before recharging. Battery exercising is the initial charging and discharging of nickel-based batteries so that they will function as expected. You should never short a battery's terminals, and replacement is a last resort when any battery has reached the end of its life.

18. D. Laptop hard drives commonly have a 2½″ form factor. The most common form factor for desktop hard drives is 3½″. Laptop hard drives use the same drive technologies as their desktop counterparts, such as serial and parallel ATA. As with desktop hard drives, laptop hard drives are available in both solid-state and conventional varieties. Unlike desktop hard drives, laptop hard drives do not have separate power connectors.

19. B. Mini PCI cards have either a 100-pin stacking connector or a 124-pin card edge connector. Type II cards have a 100-pin stacking connector. Mini PCIe cards have 52-pin card edge connectors.

20. C. The SODIMM and MicroDIMM are the common laptop small-form factor memory standards. Of the two, MicroDIMM is smaller.

Chapter 10: Installing and Configuring Printers

1. A. Because the toner on the drum has a slight negative charge (–100VDC), it requires a positive charge to transfer it to the paper; +600VDC is the voltage used in an EP process laser printer.

2. C, D. A page printer is a type of computer printer that prints a page at a time. Common types of page printers are the laser printer and the inkjet (or bubble-jet) printer.

3. D. The rate of transfer and the ability to automatically recognize new devices are two of the major advantages that make USB the current most popular type of printer interface. However, it is the network printer interface that allows the printer to communicate with networks, servers, and workstations.

4. D. Dot-matrix printers are impact printers and therefore can be used with multipart forms. Daisy wheel printers can be used with multipart forms as well.

5. A. The writing step uses a laser to discharge selected areas of the photosensitive drum, thus forming an image on the drum.

6. B, D. Of those listed, only PostScript and PCL are page-description languages. There is no PDL or PageScript.

7. A. For the toner (which has a charge of –600VDC) to be transferred from the print drum (which has a charge of –600VDC) to the paper, there must be a positive, or opposite, charge of greater difference to break the –600VDC charge from the drum.

8. B. In a bubble-jet printer, the ink cartridge is the actual print head. This is where the ink is expelled to form letters or graphics. Toner cartridges are used by laser printers to store toner. A daisy wheel is the device that impacts the letters on the paper in a daisy-wheel printer. Paper trays are the storage bins in laser printers and bubble-jet printers that allow the pickup rollers to feed the paper into the printer.

9. D. The correct sequence in the EP print process is cleaning, charging, writing, developing, transferring, and fusing.

10. D. There are nine standard assemblies in an electrophotographic process printer. Early laser printers using the electrographic process contained nine standard assemblies. Newer laser printers do not require an ozone filter and contain only eight standard assemblies.

11. A, B, D. In an electrophotographic (EP) laser printer toner cartridge, the toner, print drum, and cleaning blade are all contained in the toner cartridge. The laser is usually contained within the printer, not within the toner cartridge.

12. A. After a laser has created an image of the page, the developing roller uses a magnet and electrostatic charges to attract toner to itself and then transfers the toner to the areas on the drum that have been exposed to the laser. The toner is melted during the fusing stage. The laser creates an image of the page on the drum in the writing stage. An electrostatic charge is applied to the paper to attract toner in the transferring stage, which happens immediately after the developing stage.

13. A, C, D. Printers can communicate via parallel, serial, USB, infrared, wireless, and network connections.

14. C. If a printer is using out-of-date or incorrect printer drivers, the printer may produce pages of garbled text. The solution is to ensure that the most recent printer drivers are downloaded from the manufacturer's website.

15. B. The daisy-wheel printer gets its name because it contains a wheel with raised letters and symbols on each "petal."

16. A. The high-voltage power supply is the part of the laser printer that supplies the voltages for the charging and transfer corona assemblies.

17. C. The transfer corona assembly gets the toner from the photosensitive drum onto the paper. For some printers, this is a transfer corona wire, and for others, it is a transfer corona roller.

18. D. Developing happens after writing. The correct order is cleaning, charging, writing, developing, transferring, and fusing.

19. B. The fuser assembly presses and melts the toner into the paper. The transfer corona transfers the toner from the drum to the paper. The printer controller circuitry converts signals from the PC into signals for the various printer assemblies. The paper transport assembly controls the movement of the paper through the printer.

20. A. Firmware upgrades for laser printers are downloaded for free from the manufacturer's website. A technician does not need to install a new chip because firmware is upgraded via software. It's unlikely that the manufacturer will send you the upgrade on a CD; it will refer you to its website to download it.

Chapter 11: Understanding Operational Procedures

1. D. When a computer is experiencing random reboots and phantom problems that disappear after reboot, you should open the cover, clean everything (if it's dirty), and reseat all cards and chips. Some components could have gunk on them that carries an electrical charge or could have experienced "chip creep," where they slowly work themselves out of their sockets.

2. C. A high-voltage probe is designed to release the electricity from high-voltage components, which are found in the back of CRT computer monitors. Wearing an antistatic wrist strap when working on a computer monitor can cause the stored-up electric current to be released through your body, which could result in serious injury or death!

3. B. The Material Safety Data Sheet (MSDS) contains information about chemical properties, including what to do if an accident occurs.

4. D. Companies are not legally required to provide MSDSs to consumers. However, most will if you ask. The best place to look is the manufacturer's website.

5. A, B. Accidents and near-accidents should always be reported. Dirt isn't usually a safety issue. Rain could be, but hopefully that doesn't affect the inside of your building.

6. B. Most people can feel an electric shock at about 3,000 volts. However, computer equipment can be damaged with as little as 100 volts.

7. A, B. Antistatic wrist straps, bags (for parts), and floor mats can all help reduce the risk of ESD. There are no antistatic hair nets (but if you have long hair, it's best to tie it back so it doesn't contact the computer parts). Shuffling your feet on the floor will actually increase the risk of ESD.

8. B, D. Private sector employers are required by OSHA to maintain a safe work environment. This includes maintaining tools and equipment, keeping records of accidents, and displaying a safety information poster.

9. A. Monitors should be recycled after the end of their useful life. They contain many harmful elements, including lead, that can cause environmental problems.

10. C, D. You should always lift with your legs, not your back. This means bending at the knees and not the waist. Monitors should be carried with the glass face toward your body. Using carts for heavy objects is a good idea, as is ensuring that your path is free of safety hazards, such as trip hazards.

11. C. Alkaline batteries should always be recycled. Throwing them in the trash means they'll end up in a landfill where they can contaminate the environment. Burning batteries is always a bad idea because they will explode.

12. B, D. If you encounter prohibited material, you should confiscate and preserve the material and report it through the correct channels. Confronting the issue directly with the user before you have established a proper case could cause problems.

13. C. You should page the user and let them know they need to verify access. You also should tell them that you saw the sticky note and highly recommend that they change their password and not write it down. Logging in to the system using the information you found would be violating the privacy of that user and should not be done. Further, logging in with someone else's information makes you a potential scapegoat for any data that is corrupted or missing until the user changes the password.

14. C. While calling and sending e-mail are both solutions to this situation, calling the customer provides an immediate means of communication that you know will get there. Inform the customer of the situation and offer to be out the first opportunity you can, which will hopefully be first thing in the morning.

15. D. While there is no perfect solution to problems of this type, the best solution is to find someone else who can mediate and help you understand the problem.

16. C. Physical abuse violates respect and should be avoided at all costs. You should try to calm the user down. If you cannot do this, you should leave the site immediately and not return until it is safe to do so. You may also want to report the incident to your management so that they're aware of the situation.

17. B. The customer is expressing a concern that she was not shown respect by a technician from your company. You should apologize and make your manager aware of the situation or concern. Unless you are a supervisor, which is not implied in the question, you should not personally talk to the technician about the issue.

18. D. You should always act with confidence and in a way similar to how you would want to be treated if you were in the customer's situation. Ignoring, downplaying, and joking about the vice president's obvious concern are very poor choices.

19. C. The best solution is to meet the customer's needs and solve his problem. If that means you have to summon additional help or resources, you should do so.

20. B, C. You should leave a note for the user explaining what you did and include your contact information. You should also notify your manager and the user's manager that you have completed your task.

Chapter 12: Operating System Basics

1. B, C. To open a command prompt, you can use CMD or COMMAND (though the latter does not work in Windows 7).

2. D. A driver is extremely specific software written for the purpose of instructing a particular OS on how to access a piece of hardware.

3. C. You can increase the Taskbar's size by moving the mouse pointer to the top of it, pausing until the pointer turns into a double-headed arrow, and then clicking and dragging. Keep in mind that in Windows XP, you have to unlock the Taskbar first by right-clicking on it and deselecting Lock The Taskbar.

4. A. FAT32 does not have as many options as NTFS, such as Encryption and Compression. These attributes are available only on NTFS partitions.

5. B, C. The Windows Explorer program can be used to copy and move files and to change file attributes.

6. D. Standard permissions, unlike special permissions, have been grouped together to make it easier for administrators to assign permissions.

7. B. The shell is a program that runs on top of the OS and allows the user to issue commands through a set of menus or some other graphical interface.

8. C. To run any program, select Start ➤ Run and type the name of the program in the Open field. If you don't know the exact name of the program, you can find the file by clicking the Browse button. Once you have typed in the executable name, click OK to run the program.

9. D. Multithreading offers the ability for a single application to have multiple requests in to the processor at one time.

10. B. All deleted files are placed in the Recycle Bin. Deleted files are held there until the Recycle Bin is emptied. Users can easily recover accidentally deleted files from the Recycle Bin.

11. D. To turn off a Windows 7 machine, select Start ➤ Shut Down, choose Shut Down, and turn off the computer.

12. A. The minimum amount of memory recommended for XP Professional is 128MB.

13. B. The minimum amount of free hard drive space recommended for the installation of Windows Vista Home Basic is 15GB.

14. B. The minimum recommended memory for a 32-bit installation of Windows 7 is 1GB.

15. C. In Windows, a quick way to access Help is to press the F1 key.

16. B. The Sidebar existed only in Windows Vista and provided a quick interface that allowed you to access common utilities such as the headlines.

17. C. The System Tray is located on the right side of the Taskbar.

18. A. In addition to right-clicking on the Desktop, you can access the Display Properties settings by using the Display icon under Control Panel as long as you are not using Category view.

19. B. The interface included with Windows Vista is called Aero.

20. C. The minimum recommended memory for a 64-bit installation of Windows 7 is 2GB.

Chapter 13: Operating System Administration

1. B. The −1 switch can be used with PING to specify a packet size.

2. D. In Windows, CDFS is the file system of choice for CD media.

3. C. Tracert works like ping but returns the different IP addresses the packet was routed through to reach the final destination.

4. A. The BOOTREC /FIXBOOT command can be used to write a new boot sector.

5. D. The screen shows the results of the NSLOOKUP GOOGLE.COM command.

6. D. The TASKLIST utility will list at the command line all running processes.

7. B. Virtual memory settings are accessed through the Performance tab or area of the System control panel applet.

8. D. Services can be started automatically or manually or be disabled.

9. D. You can use Task Manager to deal with applications that have stopped responding.

10. B. MSTSC can be used to configure a remote connection.

11. A. The screen shot shows DXDIAG with the name of the utility purposely obscured.

12. A. Device Manager is used in Windows to configure all hardware resources that Windows knows about.

13. B. The Backup utility is provided with all versions of Windows, but it has different levels of functionality in the different versions.

14. D. The SFC command will run System File Checker. The /SCANNOW option will scan files, and SFC automatically repairs files it detects as corrupted.

15. C. The operating system boots from the active partition. Active partitions must be primary partitions, but a primary partition does not have to be active (there can be up to four primary partitions per hard drive).

16. B. There are five basic hives in the Windows Registry: HKEY_CLASSES_ROOT, HKEY_CURRENT_USER, HKEY_LOCAL_MACHINE, HKEY_USERS, and HKEY_CURRENT_CONFIG. HKEY_LOCAL_MACHINE stores information about the computer's hardware. HKEY_CURRENT_MACHINE, HKEY_MACHINE, and HKEY_RESOURCES do not exist.

17. C. The PING command tests to see whether you can reach a remote host on the network.

18. A. Windows Disk Defragmenter rearranges files on your hard disk so they occupy contiguous spaces (as much as possible). Windows Explorer lets you view and manage files but not manage their location on the physical hard disk. Scandisk will check the hard drive for errors, and Windows Backup backs up files but does not manage their physical location.

19. B. The /MIR switch can be used with ROBOCOPY to mirror a complete directory tree.

20. D. The DxDiag utility (DirectX Diagnostics) is used to test DirectX functionality. Telnet is used to establish a remote connection, Msinfo32 shows configuration settings, and ping can let you know if a remote host can be reached.

Chapter 14: Working with Windows 7

1. B, C, D, E. While all editions of Windows 7 can join a HomeGroup, only Home Premium, Professional, Enterprise, and Ultimate can create one.

2. D. Even though Windows 7 does not have Sidebar (a feature that lived and died only with Windows Vista), the file that runs for gadgets is SIDEBAR.EXE.

3. B. BitLocker uses (if it is present) the Trusted Platform Module (TPM).

4. C. Libraries allow files and folders to be grouped logically and appear as if they are in the same location even when they are not.

5. B. The Microsoft Assessment and Planning (MAP) Toolkit can be used to get an inventory of computers on your network and plan a rollout of the new operating system.

6. D. Only Windows Vista Business can be upgraded to Windows 7 Professional.

7. C. The utility shown is Windows Anytime Upgrade, which can be accessed from Control Panel. Portions of the screen that would reveal the name of the utility have been hidden in the screen shot.

8. C. Windows Preinstallation Environment (WinPE), which is a stub operating system creating a Pre-boot Execution Environment (PXE).

9. A. The utility shown is WINVER. This utility will show the operating system, the edition, and the service pack installed on any Windows operating system.

10. D, E. Only Windows 7 Enterprise and Windows 7 Ultimate support BitLocker drive encryption.

11. B. In Windows 7 (and Windows Vista), the ability to do this has been moved to the System Protection tab of System Properties.

12. A. The Action Center replaces the Security Center (which existed in Vista) and adds the Maintenance portion.

13. C. Windows 7 requires the installation to be followed by a process known as product activation to curb software piracy.

14. B. The maximum number of physical CPUs supported by Windows 7 Enterprise edition is two.

15. B. The UAC default in Windows 7 is "Notify me only when programs try to make changes to my computer."

16. C. The ReadyBoost feature allows you to use free space on a removable drive (such as an SD card) to speed up a system.

17. D. The utility shown is Windows Remote Assistance. Portions of the utility that show its name have been obscured in the screen shot.

18. C. When remote computers and virtual machine utilities are used in Windows 7 networking, port 3389 is the default port used.

19. A. On a standard, default, installation, the /BOOT directory holds the boot file configuration for Windows 7.

20. D. The Professional, Enterprise, and Ultimate editions support 192GB. The maximum amount of RAM supported by Home Premium is 16GB. The Starter edition supports only 2GB.

Chapter 15: Working with Windows Vista

1. C. The two biggest modifications to offline folders in Windows Vista are the inclusion of the Sync Center and the restriction of offline file support to the Business, Enterprise, and Ultimate versions.

2. D. The first file used in the Windows Vista boot process is BOOTMGR.

3. B. The maximum amount of RAM supported by 64-bit Home Premium is 16GB. The Business, Enterprise, and Ultimate editions support 128GB. The Home Basic edition supports only 8GB.

4. C. Wake-on-LAN is an Ethernet standard implemented via a card that allows a "sleeping" machine to awaken when it receives a wakeup signal.

5. B, D. Only the Enterprise and Ultimate editions of Windows Vista include support for BitLocker.

6. D. Shadow Copy is a Windows Vista feature allowing you to recover from an accidental deletion or overwrite.

7. C. For just one machine, Windows Easy Transfer should be used for transferring user state data and application files. For a mass rollout across a network, USMT can be used.

8. C. In Windows Vista, and all Windows versions you need to be familiar with for the A+ exam, the winver utility can be used to see the edition and service pack installed on a system.

9. D. The utility shown is Component Services (with the name of the utility obscured). This MMC snap-in allows you to deploy and administer component services.

10. B. Winlogon presents the Logon screen and wraps up the boot process.

11. C. The Windows Memory Diagnostics utility (Start ➢ Control Panel ➢ Administrative Tools ➢ Memory Diagnostics Tool) can be used to check a system for memory problems.

12. C, D, E. Only the Business, Enterprise, and Ultimate editions of Windows Vista support Local Security Policy (secpol.msc).

13. C. Windows Vista requires the installation to be followed by a process known as product activation to curb software piracy.

14. B. The maximum number of physical CPUs supported by Windows Vista Business edition is two. Both Home Basic and Home Premium editions support only one, while Business, Enterprise, and Ultimate support two.

15. B. The System Configuration tool is `msconfig.exe` in Windows Vista.

16. C. The ReadyBoost feature allows you to use free space on a removable drive (usually USB) to speed up a system.

17. A, D. Windows XP Professional can only be upgraded to Windows Vista Business and Windows Vista Ultimate. Know the upgrade options well for the exam.

18. C. When the network location is set to Public, network discovery is disabled. Network discovery is enabled for both Home and Work. There is no such location as Personal in Windows Vista.

19. A. On a standard, default installation, the `/boot` directory holds the boot file configuration for Windows Vista.

20. C. The 64-bit, Enterprise, and Ultimate editions support 128GB. The maximum amount of RAM supported by Home Premium is 16GB. The Home Basic edition supports only 8GB.

Chapter 16: Working with Windows XP

1. A. Windows XP uses Automated System Recovery (ASR). It makes a backup of your system partition and creates a recovery disk.

2. D. The first file used in the Windows XP boot process is NTLDR. Both the `NTOSKRNL.EXE` and `NTBOOTDD.SYS` files are used in the boot process, but neither is the first file run. Neither `AUTOEXEC.BAT` nor `CONFIG.SYS` is involved in the Windows XP boot process.

3. C. Safe Mode is a good option to choose to restore files that are missing or to fix a configuration error. With only basic files and drivers loaded, you can more easily identify the source of the problem.

4. C. Wake on LAN is an Ethernet standard implemented via a card that allows a "sleeping" machine to awaken when it receives a wakeup signal.

5. D. The solution to a corrupted `NTOSKRNL.EXE` file is to boot from a startup disk and replace the file from the setup disks or CD.

6. A. In an attended installation, a user must be present to choose all of the options when the installation program gets to that point.

7. D. Pressing F8 during the first phase of the boot process brings up the Advanced Startup Options menu in Windows.

8. C. Windows Update is responsible for finding updates, patches, and service packs, downloading them, and installing them on your computer.

9. D. HAL, or the Hardware Abstraction Layer, is the translator between the hardware and the operating system.

10. C. Beginning with Windows Server 2003, RIS was replaced by Windows Deployment Service (WDS). This utility offers the same functionality as RIS.

11. B. New disk drives or PCs with no OS need to have two critical functions performed on them before they can be used: partitioning first and then formatting. These two functions are performed by two commands, `FDISK.EXE` and `FORMAT.COM`, or by the Windows installation program itself.

12. A, B, C, D. Formatting performs all of the listed processes.

13. C. Windows XP requires the installation to be followed by a process known as product activation to curb software piracy.

14. A. Windows XP automatically creates restore points, which are copies of your system configuration. You can also create them manually through the System Restore utility.

15. B. The System Configuration tool is `MSCONFIG.EXE`, and in Windows XP it includes a number of tabs and options not present in subsequent versions of Windows.

16. D. When Plug and Play does not work, the Add Hardware Wizard applet in Control Panel can be used. There is not an Add/Remove option with hardware, but Add or Remove Programs is used with software.

17. B. The Sysprep utility comes with Windows XP Professional and is used to prepare a machine so that an image can then be created of the computer. Ghost is a third-party utility made by Norton that can be used to create images. Sysimage is not a known Windows utility, and RIS comes only with Windows Server operating systems.

18. B. Adding the `/sos` option to the `operating system` option in the `BOOT.INI` file will show the drivers as they're loaded in Windows XP.

19. A. Setup Manager is used to create answer files (known as uniqueness database files [UDFs]) for automatically providing computer or user information during setup.

20. D. Boot order is configured in the BIOS of the workstation and not in a Windows-related file.

Chapter 17: Security

1. A. The first layer of access control is perimeter security. Perimeter security is intended to delay or deter entrance into a facility.

2. A. Biometrics is a technology that uses personal characteristics, such as a retinal pattern or fingerprint, to establish identity.

3. A. Social engineering uses the inherent trust in the human species, as opposed to technology, to gain access to your environment.

4. C. A fingerprint scanner, or any device that identifies a person by a physical trait, is considered a biometric security control.

5. A. Although the end result of any of these attacks may be denying authorized users access to network resources, a DoS attack is specifically intended to prevent access to network resources by overwhelming or flooding a service or network.

6. B. A distributed denial of service (DDoS) attack uses multiple computer systems to attack a server or host in the network.

7. C. In a back door attack, a program or service is placed on a server to bypass normal security procedures.

8. C. A replay attack attempts to replay the results of a previously successful session to gain access.

9. D. TCP/IP hijacking is an attempt to steal a valid IP address and use it to gain authorization or information from a network.

10. A. A worm is different from a virus in that it can reproduce itself, it's self-contained, and it doesn't need a host application to be transported.

11. D. A smurf attack attempts to use a broadcast ping (ICMP) on a network. The return address of the ping may be that of a valid system in your network. This system will be flooded with responses in a large network.

12. A. A password-guessing attack occurs when a user account is repeatedly attacked using a variety of passwords.

13. B. Biometrics relies on a physical characteristic of the user to verify identity. Biometric devices typically use either a hand pattern or a retinal scan to accomplish this.

14. A. Tokens are created when a user or system successfully authenticates. The token is destroyed when the session is over.

15. C. Someone trying to con your organization into revealing account and password information is launching a social engineering attack.

16. A. Some viruses won't damage a system in an attempt to spread into all the other systems in a network. These viruses use that system as the carrier of the virus.

17. B. A symptom of many viruses is unusual activity on the system disk. This is caused by the virus spreading to other files on your system.

18. A. A software exploitation attack attempts to exploit weaknesses in software. A common attack attempts to communicate with an established port to gain unauthorized access.

19. A. Packet filters prevent unauthorized packets from entering or leaving a network. Packet filters are a type of firewall that block specified traffic based on IP address, protocol, and many other attributes.

20. D. All of these devices can store and pass viruses to uninfected systems. Make sure that all files are scanned for viruses before they're copied to these media.

Chapter 18: Mobile Devices

1. C. There is no requirement of either operating system that the devices they are on have cellular calling capability.

2. B. Google Play used to be called the Android Market. The App Store is Apple's equivalent.

3. A. Three gyroscopes are used to detect roll, pitch, and yaw. The problem is with the gyroscope that detects yaw. The accelerometer would be suspect if the iPhone were not detecting flat movement to the side or forward and backward. The magnetometer can only help with compass headings and the GPS with geographical positioning.

4. B. Resistive touchscreens require pressure to actuate them, while capacitive ones do not and instead can be actuated by the fleshy part of the human finger. Body oils, moisture, and dirt are not as detrimental to the effectiveness of resistive screens as they are to capacitive screens.

5. A, E. SMS is the most widely supported text-messaging service, across all platforms and service providers. Apple's iMessage is a proprietary service that does not require cellular access to send text messages.

6. D. Whenever you have a reliable WiFi signal available that you do not pay for as you go, you should feel free to disable your cellular access to data networking. The wireless network is often faster and does not cost you anything to use. If data networking works better when you leave the cellular network available to fall back on, you can choose to disable it only for certain large downloads or disable it completely until the download is complete. Phone calls will continue to be sent out over the cellular network. This does not imply that your data is not using an available WiFi connection. Therefore, unless you are particularly sensitive to the situation or know that data is going out over your cell access, you might not need to disable the cellular data networking feature.

7. C. The range of Bluetooth connections is considered short compared to WiFi connections. Bluetooth is a fully standardized protocol that supports file transfers using FTP. Rebooting, or even restarting, paired devices is not a requirement for Bluetooth connection.

8. A. SMTP sends mail to the server at TCP port 25. POP3 uses port 110. IMAP4 uses 143, and port 995 is used by POP3 securely over SSL or TLS.

9. B. SMTP with TLS uses port 587 by default. With SSL, SMTP uses port 465. IMAP4 with SSL/TLS uses port 993, while POP3 with SSL/TLS uses port 995.

10. A. All of these options can be used to set a passcode on an Android mobile device except speaking a passphrase.

11. C. The fact that the iPhone is attached to the computer with which it last synced indicates that the owner is likely in possession of it. Servicing the phone is not required, and performing an Apple reset will still have you locked out as a security precaution.

12. D. Locator applications tend to leave reporting thefts to the user. Because not all losses are due to theft and because the user would need to determine the authorities to contact, this feature is not seen in such applications. The location information can certainly be relayed to the authorities. These applications tend to allow messages to be displayed on the device's screen as well.

13. A. Software Update is a selection found under Settings ≻ General in the iOS. There is no Security menu per se, although keeping your iOS updated is considered a proactive security measure.

14. D. You should not count on being able to do anything that involves opening the device. Many tablets and phones offer options for printing wirelessly, sometimes with the purchase of additional software or hardware to assist.

15. A. Multi-touch is the feature that allows pinch-to-zoom technology. Spreading your fingers apart zooms in, while pinching your fingers together zooms out. TouchFLO is the HTC technology that features multiple screens that you can flip between. SuperPinch does not exist, and as unpopular an idea as it may seem, even resistive touchscreens are technically capable of multi-touch.

16. B, D, F. The items most often able to be synchronized are contacts, apps, email, photos, music, and videos.

17. D. You can install iTunes on the supported x86 versions of Windows as well.

18. B. Mail access uses standard secure or insecure TCP ports, not UDP ports. Exchange access to such mail services is not unheard of, but it is exceedingly rare. Mobile devices tend to have email clients built in.

19. C. The GPS transceiver, WiFi connection, and cellular network are used to home in on the geographical location of a missing mobile device.

20. A. Most modern devices use a solid-state drive (SSD), called internal storage, instead of a traditional magnetic drive to store permanent information. Memory cards can often be used to augment the SSD's storage capacity.

Chapter 19: Troubleshooting Theory, OSs, and Security

1. D. Windows Update automatically (by default) finds, downloads, and installs service packs and other Windows updates. None of the other options are real utilities.

2. B. Safe Mode only loads basic drivers, such as a standard VGA video driver and the keyboard and mouse.

3. B. Windows 7 and Windows Vista use the Windows Boot Configuration Data (BCD) file instead of the `BOOT.INI` file. This can be rebuilt with the `/REBUILDBCD` option.

4. B. The first step is to identify the problem. Once you have done that, you should (in order) establish a theory of probable cause, test the theory, establish a plan of action to resolve the problem, verify full system functionality, and document your findings.

5. B. The System Restore tool is used to create restore points. Backup creates backups of your hard drive. You can use Backup to create copies of your configuration (like a restore point) along with other data, but to specifically create a restore point, use System Restore. There are no Restore Point or Emergency Repair tools (although there is an emergency repair disk).

6. A. Only Windows XP uses the `BOOT.INI` file. Windows 7 and Windows Vista use the Boot Configuration Data (BCD) file.

7. C. Check the sleep settings for hibernation and disable those first to see if that makes a difference. If it does not, then you can begin disabling drivers and making other changes.

8. A. Windows can use restore points to roll back the system configuration to a previous state. None of the other options exist.

9. B. *Pop-up blockers* are used to prevent both pop-ups and pop-unders from appearing. While older browsers did not incorporate an option to block pop-ups, most newer browsers, including the latest versions of Internet Explorer, now have that capability built in.

10. A. It's critical to keep your antivirus software up-to-date, so you should update your definitions at least once per week.

11. C. Disk Defragmenter will analyze the hard drive to determine how fragmented it is and will allow you to defragment it. There is no Disk Analyzer tool. Disk Cleanup can help you free up space by deleting unneeded files. Checkdisk (Chkdsk) can help you find problems on the hard drive, but it does not look for fragmentation.

12. B. Windows Update downloads patches for the Windows operating system. Microsoft Update downloads patches for Windows as well as Microsoft applications.

13. A. Windows Defender is an anti-malware program. It checks for harmful, or unwanted, software installed on the machine.

14. A. The Regsvr32 tool (REGSVR32.EXE) allows you to register and unregister modules and controls for troubleshooting purposes.

15. A, B, C, D. Establishing security policies and procedures, updating your operating systems, updating your applications, and updating your network devices are all good measures to take to help eliminate potential security problems.

16. A. Some viruses won't damage a system in an attempt to spread into all the other systems in a network. These viruses use that system as the carrier of the virus.

17. B. Disk Cleanup can help you free up space by deleting unneeded files. Disk Defragmenter will analyze the hard drive to determine how fragmented it is and will allow you to defragment it. There is no Disk Analyzer tool. Checkdisk (Chkdsk) can help you find problems on the hard drive, but it does not delete files.

18. D. SFC automatically verifies system files after a reboot to see if they were changed to unprotected copies.

19. B. To open System Restore, click Start ➢ All Programs ➢ Accessories ➢ System Tools ➢ System Restore.

20. A. The figure shows Regedit, but the name of the utility has been purposely obscured.

Chapter 20: Hardware and Network Troubleshooting

1. A, B. Two helpful things to try are toggling the video output function key (usually Fn+F8) and plugging an external monitor into the laptop. Removing the display is possible but not recommended. Powering the system off and back on isn't likely to correct the problem.

2. C. Discolored areas on the board are often caused by overheating. This can be the result of power surges.

3. A. The NET USE command allows you to connect to shared resources such as shared drives and printers on the network.

4. C. Every computer has a diagnostic program built into its BIOS called the power-on self-test (POST). The BIOS is the software stored on the CMOS chip. DNS is Domain Name Service, which in networking resolves hostnames to IP addresses.

5. B. Explanation: The IPCONFIG command is perhaps the most used utility in troubleshooting and network configuration. The IPCONFIG /RENEW command will send a query to the DHCP server asking it to resend and renew all DHCP information. For a more detailed look at the IPCONFIG command, type **IPCONFIG /?** at the command prompt.

6. B. If print jobs are seemingly getting "stuck" in the printer queue, you should stop and restart the print spooler service. There is no Printer Troubleshooting utility that will diagnose printer problems. Deleting and reinstalling is not necessary.

7. A, D. Heat sinks and fans are commonly used to cool components within a PC. Compressed air can be used to blow out small particles or dust. Freon is a coolant used in some air conditioners but is not typically used for personal computers.

8. B. The manufacturer's website is the first place you should go for information on your products, including troubleshooting information. Many years ago, manufacturers would provide paper manuals with their products, but that's almost unheard of today. Server logs can show error codes but won't tell you how to fix anything.

9. A. The most likely cause is a groove or a scratch in the EP drum. Toner is collecting in that groove or scratch and then being deposited on to the page.

10. B. It has to be a problem with the LCD display. If it were the video card, then the display would appear warped and fuzzy on the external monitor as well. While many motherboards contain video circuitry, this answer is not specific enough. If the video driver were corrupted, you would have the same problem on all displays.

11. A. If an ink cartridge is faulty or develops a hole, it can release excessive amounts of ink, which will lead to smearing. A corrupt print driver would result in printing garbage. Inkjet printers do not have a fuser. Excessive humidity may cause smearing, but it wouldn't cause the disbursement of too much ink.

12. B. The ipconfig utility can be used with Windows to see the networking configuration values at the command line. It is one of the most commonly used command-line utilities that can be used in troubleshooting and network configurations. To view IP configuration information, use the `IPCONFIG /all` command.

13. C, D. Seeing images from previous print jobs is a phenomenon called ghosting. It's most likely due to a bad erasure lamp or a broken cleaning blade.

14. D. It may well be that the video card is dead. Different BIOS manufacturers use different beep codes, though, so you'll want to look it up to be sure. If the motherboard was dead or the BIOS wasn't functioning, you wouldn't get to the POST routine, so you wouldn't get a beep code.

15. B. Tracert is a command-line utility that enables you to verify the route to a remote host. It is often used in the troubleshooting process to verify the path a data packet takes toward its final destination.

16. C. The only components that typically make noise are the ones that have moving parts, such as fans and hard drives. In most cases, a rhythmic ticking sound will be something that's generated by the hard drive.

17. C. If there is a consistent blank space, it likely means that a pin is not firing properly and the print head needs to be replaced. If the print ribbon was old, you would have consistently faded printing. If the ribbon was not advancing properly, you would get light and dark printing. If the wrong driver is installed, you will get garbage.

18. A. If a laptop won't power up on battery, always try to use AC power. You never know when a battery could have failed. If he had a spare and didn't have an AC power cord, trying a spare might work, but trying AC power is the best bet. There is no battery power switch on laptops.

19. D. Loopback plugs are used to test the sending and receiving ability of network cards. Wireless locators find wireless network signals. Cable testers validate cables, and toner probes are used to trace a cable from one end to the other.

20. C. A RAID 0 array is also known as disk striping. RAID 0 actually decreases your fault tolerance versus one hard drive because there are more points of failure. You need to replace the drive, and hopefully you had it backed up so you can restore the data.

Appendix

B

Answers to Performance-Based Questions

Chapter 1: Motherboards, Processors, and Memory

1. Unplug the power cable from the computer.
2. Open the system cover to gain access to the memory slots.
3. Pull the tabs on either end of the DIMM away from the DIMM.
4. Pull the loose DIMM straight out of the slot and away from the motherboard.
5. Ensure that the locking tabs are completely opened and out of the way of the slot.
6. Insert the new DIMM straight down into the slot.
7. Apply firm and even pressure downward until the locking tabs automatically snap into place.
8. Nudge the tabs inward toward the module to make sure they are tight.
9. Close the system cover.
10. Reconnect all necessary cables.
11. Boot the system to confirm that the new module is recognized and working properly.

Chapter 2: Storage Devices and Power Supplies

1. Remove the power source from the system.
2. Ground yourself and the computer to the same source of ground.
3. Remove the cover from the system.
4. Locate the power supply.

5. Follow all wiring harnesses from the power supply to their termini, disconnecting each one.

6. Remove any obstructions that appear as if they might hinder removal of the power supply.

7. Locate and remove the machine screws on the outside of the case that that are used to secure the power supply.

8. Pull the power supply out of the case.

Chapter 3: Peripherals and Expansion

1. Plug the VGA cable into the blue, DE15 interface.
2. Plug the USB cable into the gray, flat 4-pin interface.
3. Plug the parallel cable into the burgundy, DB25 interface.
4. Plug the mouse into the green, mini-DIN 6 interface.
5. Plug the RS-232 cable into the teal, DE9 interface.
6. Plug the keyboard into the purple, mini-DIN 6 interface.
7. Plug the speaker into the green, 3.5mm TRS interface.

Chapter 4: Display Devices

1. Right-click a blank portion of the Desktop.
2. Click Screen Resolution.

3. Click on the picture of the monitor with the number 2 on it.

4. Pull down the menu labeled Multiple Displays; select Extend These Displays.

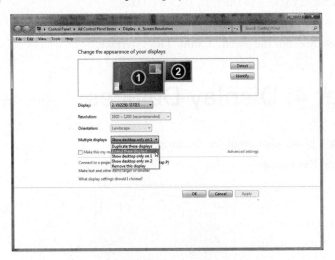

5. Click Keep Changes in the popup dialog that results.

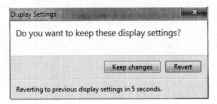

6. Click and drag the second monitor to the desired virtual position around the primary monitor.

7. Click OK to save changes and exit or click Cancel to exit without saving changes.

Chapter 5: Custom Configurations

1. Run Network And Sharing Center.

2. Click the Change Advanced Sharing Settings link in the left frame.

3. Expand the Home Or Work configuration section.

4. Click the Choose Media Streaming Options link.

5. Change desired Blocked buttons to Allow.

6. Open Windows Media Player and switch to Library mode, if necessary.

7. Ensure that streaming is enabled.

8. On the remote system, start Windows Media Player.

9. Expand the remote library you just shared under Other Libraries to play music, watch videos or recorded TV, and view pictures.

Chapter 6: Networking Fundamentals

Possible answers could include bus, ring, star, mesh, and hybrid. The simplest topology, and the one that uses the least amount of cable, is a bus. It consists of a single cable that runs to every workstation, as shown in the following illustration.

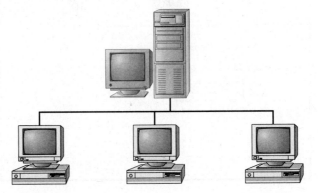

In a star topology, shown in the next illustration, each network device branches off a central device called a hub or a switch, making it easy to add a new workstation. If the hub or switch fails, the entire network fails.

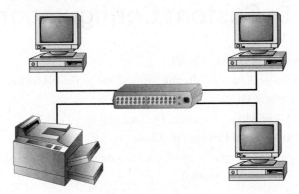

In a physical ring, each computer connects to two other computers, joining them in a circle and creating a unidirectional path where messages move from workstation to workstation. These are very rarely implemented.

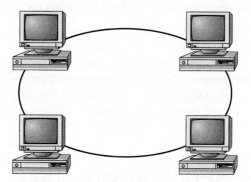

The mesh topology is the most complex in terms of physical design. In a mesh, each device is connected to every other device as shown in the following illustration. This provides redundancy but costs more to implement.

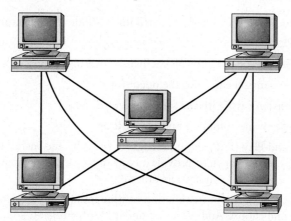

A hybrid topology combines two or more other topologies into one network. An example might be a server room that has a partial mesh for redundancy but the clients are all connected to switches in a star.

Chapter 7: Introduction to TCP/IP

First, open Internet Explorer. Then, in the address window, type the following:

    ftp://jsmith:getfiles@ftp.domain.com

Some older versions of IE, such as IE 5 and 6, won't pass passwords through a URL. If you're using one of these older browsers, open IE and type **ftp://ftp.domain.com** into the address window and press Enter. You will get a message telling you that you're not authorized to view the page. Click OK to remove the security dialog box. Then, right-click in the blank browser window and select Login As. In the dialog box that pops up, enter your username and password.

Chapter 8: Installing Wireless and SOHO Networks

Here are the steps to install a PCI network card for a Windows 7 desktop:

1. Power off the PC.
2. Remove the case and the metal or plastic blank covering the expansion slot opening.
3. Insert the new expansion card into the open slot.
4. Secure the expansion card with the screw provided.
5. Put the case back on the computer and power it up.
6. Windows Plug and Play (PnP) should recognize the NIC and install the driver automatically. It may also ask you to provide a copy of the necessary driver if it does not recognize the type of NIC you have installed.
7. If Windows does not start the installation routine immediately, open Control Panel in Category view and choose Add A Device under Hardware And Sound. A list of hardware will appear. Choose the NIC and continue the installation.
8. After installing a NIC, you must hook the card to the network using the appropriate cable (if you're using wired connections). Attach a patch cable to the connector on the NIC and to a port in the wall (or connectivity device), thus connecting your PC to the rest of the network.

Chapter 9: Understanding Laptops

1. Turn off the computer.
2. Disconnect the computer and any peripherals from their power sources, and remove any installed batteries.

3. Locate the hard drive door and remove the screw holding it in place.

4. Lift the hard drive door until it clicks.

5. Slide the hard drive out to remove it.

6. Remove the two screws holding the hard drive to the hard drive door.

7. Attach a new hard drive to the hard drive door.

8. Slide the new hard drive back into the hard drive bay.

9. Snap the hard drive door back into place, and insert and tighten the screw to hold the door in place.

Chapter 10: Installing and Configuring Printers

1. Power on the printer, and open the top cover to expose the area containing the print cartridges.
2. Initiate a self-cleaning cycle.
3. When the printhead moves from its resting place, pull the AC power plug.
4. Locate the sponge pads on which to apply the cleaning solution.
5. Using the supplied syringe, apply the cleaning solution to the sponge pads until they are saturated.
6. Plug the printer back into the wall outlet, and turn it on. The printheads will park themselves.
7. Turn the printer back off. Let the solution sit for at least three hours.
8. Power the printer back on, and run three printer cleaning cycles. Print a nozzle check pattern (or a test page) after each cleaning cycle to monitor the cleaning progress.

Chapter 11: Understanding Operational Procedures

1. Walk around the server room and count how many cables are lying on the floor.
2. Walk around the client areas and see how many cables are lying on the floor or are exposed underneath cubicles.
3. Devise a plan to secure the cables and prevent them from being hazards. For example, purchase and install floor guards, use cable ties, or install conduit as necessary to secure all loose cables.

Chapter 12: Operating System Basics

Given the information you need to collect, the easiest method is to use the System applet in Control Panel:

1. Choose Start
2. Select Control Panel

3. Choose System

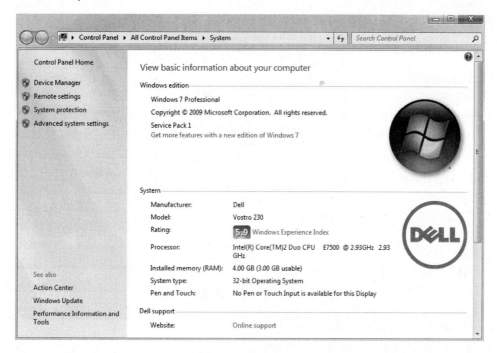

4. Write down the information for every item except that related to the paging file.

5. Click Advanced system settings. The System Properties dialog box appears.

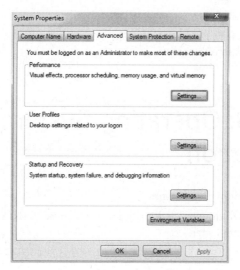

6. Click on the Settings button beneath Performance and choose the Advanced tab.

7. Write down the paging file information.
8. Click OK to exit the Performance Options.
9. Click OK to exit the System Properties.
10. Close the System applet.

The msinfo32.exe (System Information) tool also presents all this information in one screen.

Chapter 13: Operating System Administration

To perform this task, follow these steps:

1. Open a command window by clicking Start, typing **cmd** in the Search Programs And Files box and pressing Enter.

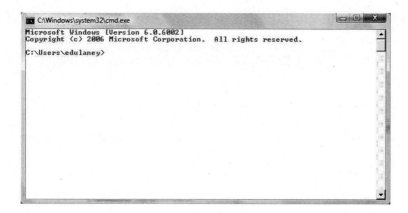

2. To release the current address, type **IPCONFIG /RELEASE** and press Enter.

3. To obtain a new lease, type **IPCONFIG /RENEW** and press Enter.

4. To make certain all is working, type **IPCONFIG /ALL** and press Enter. You should see a valid IP address, subnet mask, and related configuration information.

5. Close the command window by typing **EXIT** and pressing Enter or clicking the close window button in the top-right corner.

Chapter 14: Working with Windows 7

To configure the values given:

1. Choose Start ➢ Control Panel ➢ Network And Sharing Center.

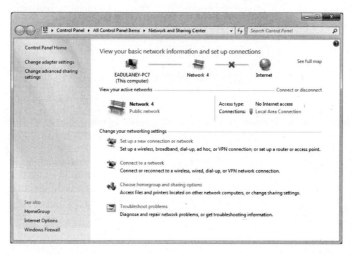

2. Click Change Adapter Settings.

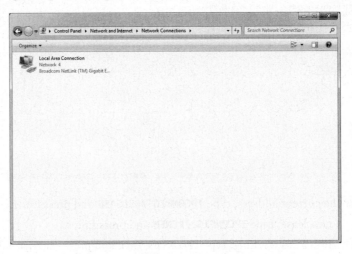

3. Right-click the icon and choose Properties.

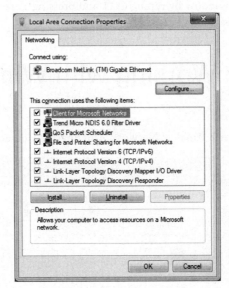

4. Click Internet Protocol Version 4 (TCP/IPv4) and then click the Properties button.

5. On the General tab, make certain the radio button Obtain An IP Address Automatically is selected.

6. Click the Alternate Configuration tab.

7. Click the User Configured radio button.

8. Enter the three values given for the IP address, the subnet mask, and the default gateway

9. Click OK to close the dialog box. Click Close to exit the Local Area Connection Properties dialog box. Click the close icon in the upper-right corner of the Network Connections window.

Chapter 15: Working with Windows Vista

1. Choose Start ➣ Control Panel ➣ Administrative Tools.

2. Choose Memory Diagnostics Tool.

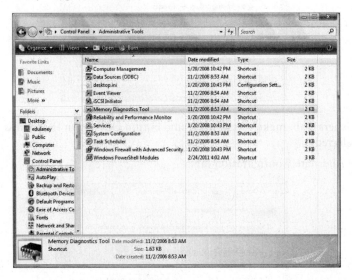

3. Click Restart Now And Check For Problems.

4. Upon reboot, the test will take several minutes and the display screen will show which pass number is being run and the overall status of the test (percent complete).

Chapter 16: Working with Windows XP

1. Choose Start ➢ Control Panel ➢ System.

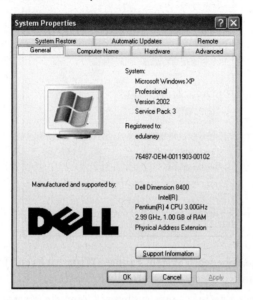

2. Click the Advanced tab.

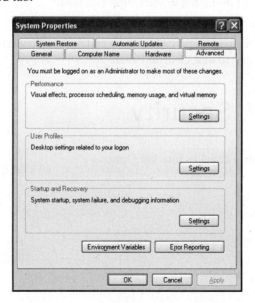

3. Click Settings beneath Startup And Recovery.

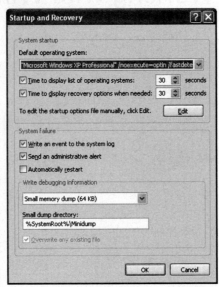

4. Check the three boxes beneath System Failure (Write An Event To The System Log, Send An Administrative Alert, Automatically Restart).

5. Beneath Write Debugging Information, choose Complete Memory Dump.

6. Enter the name of the dump file in the Dump File field.

7. Check the Overwrite Any Existing File box.

8. Click OK to exit the dialog box. Click OK to exit System Properties. Click the close icon in the upper right to exit Control Panel.

Chapter 17: Security

1. Click Start ➤ Control Panel ➤ Internet Options.

2.   Click the Privacy tab.

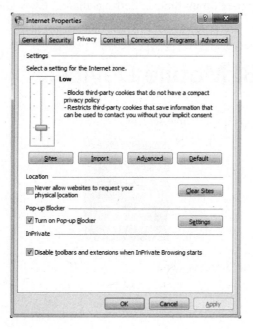

3. Click the Turn On Pop-up Blocker check box, and then click the Settings button.

4. Type in the address **www.sybex.com** and click Add.

5. Click Close to exit the Pop-up Blocker Settings dialog. Click OK to exit Internet Properties.

Chapter 18: Mobile Devices

1. Tap the Settings app on the Home screens.

2. Select Wi-Fi from the Settings menu.

3. Turn on the Wi-Fi switch.

4. Tap the name of the wireless network that you want to join.

5. Enter the password or key for the wireless network, if you are asked for one, and then tap the Join button.

6. Tap the Settings back button at the top left to return to the previous screen.

7. Tap the hard Home button at the bottom in the frame of the phone to return to the Home screens after noting that the network you joined is now listed next to Wi-Fi on the menu.

Chapter 19: Troubleshooting Theory, OSs, and Security

The Recovery Console isn't installed on a system by default. To install it, use the following steps:

1. Place the Windows CD in the system.

2. From a command prompt, change to the i386 directory of the CD.

3. Type `winnt32 /cmdcons`.

4. A prompt appears, alerting you to the fact that 7MB of hard drive space is required and asking if you want to continue. Click Yes.

Chapter 20: Hardware and Network Troubleshooting

1. Open Computer Management and navigate to Services by right-clicking on the Computer icon and choosing Manage. If necessary, click the arrow next to Services And Applications to expand the list.

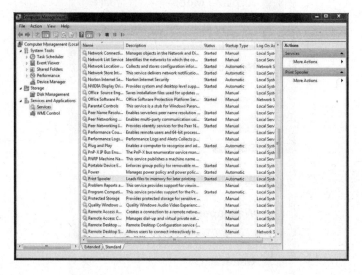

2. Find the Print Spooler service.

3. Stop the spooler service. There are several ways you can do this:

> Right-click the service name and choose Stop.
>
> Click the Stop square above the list of services.
>
> Use the More Actions menu on the right.

4. Restart the spooler by right-clicking the service name and choosing Start or by clicking the Start arrow above the list of services.

5. Close Computer Management.

Appendix C

About the Companion CD

IN THIS APPENDIX:

✓ What you'll find on the CD

✓ System requirements

✓ Using the CD

✓ Troubleshooting

What You'll Find on the CD

The following sections are arranged by category and summarize the software and other goodies you'll find on the CD. If you need help with installing the items provided on the CD, refer to the installation instructions in the section "Using the CD" at the end of this appendix.

Sybex Test Engine

The CD contains the Sybex test engine, which includes the eight bonus practice exams.

Electronic Flashcards

These handy electronic flashcards are just what they sound like. One side contains a question or fill-in-the-blank statement, and the other side shows the answer.

Companion Author Videos

We've included over an hour's worth of author videos showing some of the more critical tasks you will need to know how to perform as well as some of the components of a computer and laptop, storage devices and cables, and the tools you'll need as a technician.

E-Book in All Formats

The CD that accompanies this book also contains electronic versions of the book. You can copy any of these files to your computer and read them with the appropriate desktop reader or a portable device.

Mobi

This is Amazon's format for e-books. You can read it on your computer with Kindle Reader for PC or Mac (available for download at www.amazon.com/gp/kindle/kcp). To read the book on a Kindle, copy the PRC file to your computer, and then transfer it to the DOCUMENTS folder on the Kindle via USB. The book should appear normally on your list of books. You can download a Kindle Reader app to many non-Kindle devices as well.

ePub

This format is accepted on most reading devices, including the Nook and the iPad. You can read it on your computer with Adobe Digital Editions (available for download at www.adobe.com/products/digitaleditions/). To read the book on your portable device, copy the EPUB file to your computer, and then transfer it to the appropriate folder on the device via USB. For an iPad, you will need to have iTunes installed on your computer to transfer the file.

ePDF

This is simply a PDF that is enabled for reading electronically. You can read it on your computer with Adobe Digital Editions or Adobe Reader, and nearly all portable devices can accommodate it, including the iPad, Nook, and Kindle. Copy the PDF file to your computer, and from there you can transfer it via USB to a device. For an iPad, you will need to have iTunes installed on your computer. Most readers come with basic PDF-reading apps already installed, but better ones are usually available for download at the appropriate app store.

PDF of Glossary of Terms

We have included an electronic version of the glossary in PDF format. You can view the electronic version of the glossary with Adobe Reader.

Adobe Reader

We've also included a copy of Adobe Reader so you can view PDF files that accompany the book's content. For more information on Adobe Reader or to check for a newer version, visit Adobe's website at www.adobe.com/products/reader/.

System Requirements

Make sure your computer meets the minimum system requirements shown in the following list. If your computer doesn't match up to most of these requirements, you may have problems using the software and files on the companion CD. For the latest and greatest information, please refer to the ReadMe file located at the root of the CD-ROM.

- A PC running Microsoft Windows 98, Windows 2000, Windows NT4 (with SP4 or later), Windows Me, Windows XP, Windows Vista, or Windows 7
- An Internet connection
- A CD-ROM drive

Using the CD

To install the items from the CD to your hard drive, follow these steps:

1. Insert the CD into your computer's CD-ROM drive. The license agreement appears.

   Windows users: The interface won't launch if you have Autorun disabled. In that case, click Start ➢ Run (for Windows Vista or Windows 7, Start ➢ All Programs ➢ Accessories ➢ Run). In the dialog box that appears, type **D:\Start.exe**. (Replace *D* with the proper letter if a different letter is used for your CD drive. If you don't know the letter, see how your CD drive is listed under My Computer.) Click OK.

2. Read the license agreement, and then click the Accept button if you want to use the CD.

The CD interface appears. The interface allows you to access the content with just one or two clicks.

Troubleshooting

Wiley has attempted to provide programs that work on most computers with the minimum system requirements. Alas, your computer may differ, and some programs may not work properly for some reason.

The two likeliest problems are that you don't have enough memory (RAM) for the programs you want to use or you have other programs running that are affecting installation or running of a program. If you get an error message such as "Not enough memory" or "Setup cannot continue," try one or more of the following suggestions and then try using the software again:

- **Turn off any antivirus software running on your computer.** Installation programs sometimes mimic virus activity and may make your computer incorrectly believe that it's being infected by a virus.

- **Close all running programs.** The more programs you have running, the less memory is available to other programs. Installation programs typically update files and programs, so if you keep other programs running, installation may not work properly.

- **Have your local computer store add more RAM to your computer.** This is, admittedly, a drastic and somewhat expensive step. However, adding more memory can really help the speed of your computer and allow more programs to run at the same time.

Customer Care

If you have trouble with the book's companion CD-ROM, please contact Wiley Product Technical Support at (800) 762-2974 or online at http://sybex.custhelp.com/.

Index

Note to the Reader: Throughout this index **boldfaced** page numbers indicate primary discussions of a topic. *Italicized* page numbers indicate illustrations.

X

Y

Z